WITHDRAWN

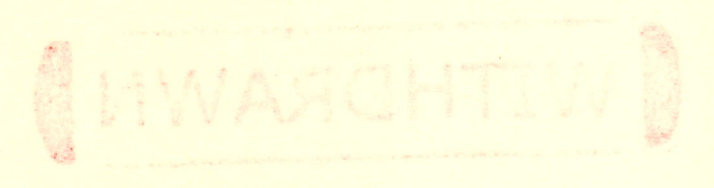

THOMAS ELYOT

DICTIONARY

1538

A Scolar Press Facsimile

THE SCOLAR PRESS LIMITED
MENSTON, ENGLAND
1970

THE SCOLAR PRESS LIMITED
20 Main Street, Menston, Yorkshire, England

Printed in Great Britain by
The Scolar Press Limited
Menston, Yorkshire, England

NOTE

Reproduced (original size) by permission of the Curators of the Bodleian Library. Shelf-mark: 4° △ 328.

Thomas Elyot's *Dictionary*, 1538, was the first Latin-English dictionary to be based on Renaissance humanist ideals of classical learning. Latin-English dictionaries were in existence before 1538 (e.g., *Catholicon Anglicanum*, 1483, *Medulla Grammatice* [ca. 1465], *Promptorium Parvulorum* [ca. 1440], and *Ortus Vocabulorum*, 1500), but they were based on mediaeval rather than classical Latin.

Elyot seems to have taken as his model the *Dictionarium* of Ambrosius Calepinus first published at Reggio in 1502. However, he was not entirely satisfied with the material taken from Calepine and in the Preface he blames himself for "to moche trust had in Calepine" (Aiii verso).

He also explains in the Preface how the dictionary acquired the Additions (Ffij recto – Llvi recto). The work was already at the printers, but Elyot was not confident that he had spent sufficient time on its compilation. Henry VIII heard of Elyot's worries and encouraged him to continue work and to make use of the royal library. Elyot immediately stopped the press and began to revise the entries after M – all before this had already been printed. He then went back to revise the first half of the alphabet, but now all additions and alterations had to be printed separately and therefore they appeared as an appendix.

Further editions appeared in 1542 and 1545 and it seems likely that Elyot was responsible for the revisions which they contain. From the second edition onwards the dictionary is known as *Bibliotheca Eliotae*. The Additions were now included in alphabetical sequence and the acknowledgement of authorities printed in the margins of the 1538 edition were reduced in number. The dictionary itself was enlarged, mainly from Robert Stephanus' *Dictionarium Latino-Gallicum*, 1538, but the influence of Suidas' *Lexicon* and Stephanus Doletus' *Commentariorum linguae Latinae* is also evident.

After Elyot's death in 1546 the dictionary came under the editorship of Thomas Cooper who produced editions in 1548, 1552 and 1559.

See further J. E. B. Mayor, "Latin-English and English-Latin lexicography" in *Journal of Classical and Sacred Philology*, Vol. IV, 1859, pp. 1–44; and De W. T. Starnes, *Renaissance Dictionaries*, 1954, pp. 45–84.

Reference: STC 7659.

DEVM TIME.
VIVT DEI

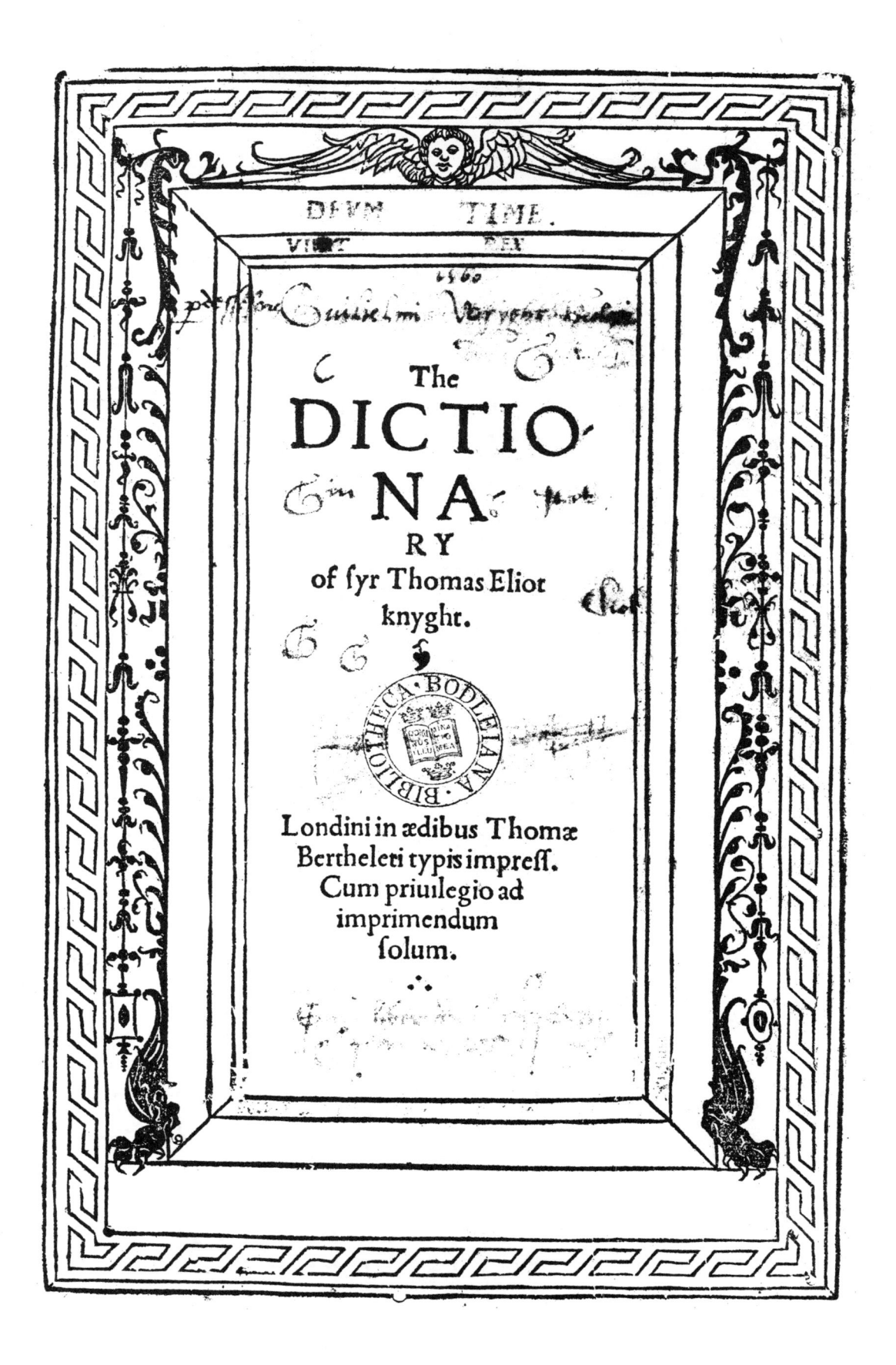

The
DICTIO
NA
RY
of syr Thomas Eliot
knyght.

Londini in ædibus Thomæ
Bertheleti typis impreff.
Cum priuilegio ad
imprimendum
solum.

THE COPIE OF THE KYNGES
GRACIOVS PRIVILEGE.

HENRY THE EYGHT, by the grace of God, Kynge of Englande and of Fraunce, Defendour of the faythe lorde of Irelande, and supreme heed in erthe immediately vnder God of the vniuersall Churche of Englande, To all prynters of bokes within this our realme, and to all other officers, mynysters and subiectes, these oure letters herynge or seinge, gretynge. we late you wyte, that we of our grace especiall, haue gyuen priuilege vnto our well beloued seruant Thomas Berthelet, that no maner person within this our realme, durynge the naturall lyfe of the sayde Thomas, shall printe any maner of bokes, what so euer our sayd seruant shal prynt fyrst or shall prynt agayne vpon other mens corrections the same within the space of syxe yeres nexte ensuynge the pryntynge of euery suche boke, so printed by our sayde seruant. wherfore we woll and commaunde you, that ye nor none of you, presume to prynte any of the sayde bokes, durynge the tyme of this oure priuilege, as ye intende to eschewe our displeasure.

TO THE MOSTE EXCELLENT PRINCE, AND OVR
moste redoubted soueraygne lorde kynge HENRY the. VIII. kynge of Eng=
lande, and Fraunce, defender of the faythe, lorde of Irelande, and supreme
heed in erthe immediately vnder Christe, of the Churche of En=
glande, his humble and faythefull seruaunt, Thomas
Elyot knyght desyreth persite felicitie.

TRVELY I am, and euer haue bene of this opynion, moste noble, moste puissaunt, and moste vertuouse Prynce, that the Royall astate of a kynge here in erth, next vnto god, is of men moste to be honoured, loued, and feared in an incomparable degree and facion. For no man hauynge the free vse of reason, beholdynge at his eien the disposition moste wonderfull sette by diuine proudence in thynges aboue vs, aboute vs, and vndernethe vs, with the sondry alternations of tyme, wyll denye, to be of those thynges one principall ruler and moderatour, by whose eternall sapience all thynges ben gouerned. Unto that office of gouernance is (as it were by the generall consent of al people) one name appropried, in the which although by diuersitie of langages, the letters and syllables are oftentymes chaunged, yet the worde spoken hath one signification, which implieth as moche as a KINGE in englyshe, as it may appere to them, which do rede holy scripture, and will marke howe often god is there callid kinge, and also the prophetes do so frequently name hym. More ouer the paynims beinge onely ladne with naturall affections, callyd Jupiter, to whome aboue other their goddis, they re Zevs serued the power vniuersall, kynge of goddis and of men: as who saythe, there may be no greatter name gyuen vnto hym, whome they supposed to be the gyuer of lyfe vnto creatures. To the whiche example, for the similitude of that diuine office men dyd attribute vnto their soueraygne gouernours that excellent denomination, calling them semblably kynges, and assigning to them the comune distribution of Justyce: wherby the people vnder their gouernaunce, shulde be kepte and preserued in quiete lyfe, not exercysed in bestiall appetite, but passed forth in all partes of honestie, they fynally shuld of god be rewarded with immortalitie. This wel consydred, it shall be to all men apparant, that they, whiche rebell agaynst kynges, be ennemies to god, and in wyll confounders of naturall order and prouidence. But aboue all thinges, I haue in mooste admiration, the maiestie of you, whiche be verye kynges raygnyng in Justice, whan I consyder, that therin semeth to be a thynge supernaturall, or (if it may be spoken without derogation vnto goddis honour) a diuine influence or sparke of diuinitie: whiche late appered to all them that behelde your grace syttyng in the Throne of your royal astate, as supreme heed of the churche of Englande nexte vnder CHRIST, about the descision and condemnation of the pernicious errours, of the moste detestable heretyke John Nicolson, callyd also Lambert, at the whyche tyme your hyghnesse, more excellently than my tunge or penne can expresse, declared to be in your royall persone the perfite image of kyngely maiestie, com
A ii pacte

THE PREFACE.

pacte of these excellent qualities, trewe Religion, Sapience, Justice, and Mercy, all men reioycinge at the manifeste and most honorable declaration of your euangelicall faythe: meruaylynge at the fulmination of the moste vehement argumentes procedyng from your hyghnes in the confutation of abhomynable heresyes: extollynge the iuste reprehencions of the peruerse opinions and interpretations of the arrogant masters of the said Lambert, in whose writynges, and his owne propre wytte, he more trusted (as your hyghnesse trewely alledged agaynste hym) than in the playne context of holy scripture, and the determinate sentence of holy and great lerned doctours: Inioyenge also as well at your gracis mooste wonderfull pacyence, in the longe sustayninge of the folyshe and tediouse obiections of the sayde Lambert, as also at your most christian charitie, in mouynge and exhortynge so stubborne an heretike, with the most gentyll and perswasible langage, to recant and forsake his myscheuouse heresies. This maiestie your true and louynge subiectes beholdynge, and than herynge the spirite of god speakyng in you, his enoynted kynge, and mynister elected: they were with ioy so replenyshed, that whan they despred to expresse eche to other the comforte, whiche they than receyued, the same comforte was of suche importaunce, that it mought none otherwyse be declared, but by abundance of teares, sent out of theyr eyen by vnspekable gladnes. More ouer the presence of you, whyche are kynges, do mynyster to them that be inferiours vnto you, an amplification of powers callyd naturall, contayned as well in the wytte and senses, as in the force or puissance of corporall membres, to the confirmation wherof, howe many men haue ben knowen, whyche er they haue attayned to the familyar acquayntaunce of kynges, haue bene demed to be, some but of a meane wytte and knowlege, some but of a base courage or prowesse, whiche afterwarde haue exceded in wytte or courage all mens expectations, and fynally bene of all men allowed for honourable and notable personages. Of this wonderfull maiestie in your royall person, most gracious souerayn lorde, I haue my selfe, in my selfe, late founde a meruaylous experience. For about a yere passed, I beganne a Dictionarie, declaryng latine by englishe, wherin I vsed lyttell study, beinge than occupied about my necessarye busynes, whiche letted me from the exacte labour and study requisyte to the makynge of a perfyte Dictionarie: But whyles it was in printyng, and vneth the half deale performed, your hyghnes being informed therof, by the reportes of gentyll maister Antony Denny, for his wysedome and diligence worthily callyd by your highnesse into your priuie Chamber, and of Wyllyam Tildisley, keper of your gracis Lybrarie, and after mooste specially by the recommendation of the most honourable lorde Crumwell, lorde priuie seale, fauourer of honestie, and next to your highnesse chiefe patron of vertue and cunnyng, conceyued of my labours a good expectation, and declaryng your moste noble and beneuolent nature, in fauouryng them that wyll be well occupied, your hyghnesse in the presence of dyuers your noble men, commendynge myne enterprise, affirmed, that if I wolde ernestely trauayle therin,

your

THE PREFACE.

your highnes, as well with your excellent counsaile, as with suche bokes as your grace had, and I lacked, wold therin ayde me: with the which wordes, I confesse, I receiued a newe spirite, as me semed: wherby I founde forthwith an augmentation of myn vnderstandynge, in so moche, as I iuged all that, whiche I had written, not worthy to come in your gracis presence, without an addition. Wherfore incontinent I caused the printer to cesse, and beginninge at the letter M, where I lefte, I passed forth to the last letter with a more diligent study. And that done, I eftesones returned to the fyrst letter, and with a semblable diligence performed the remenant. In the whiche my proceding, I well perceyued, that all though dictionaries had ben gathered one of an other, yet nethelesse in eche of them ar omitted some latin wordes, interpreted in the bokes, whiche in order preceded. For Festus hath manye, whiche are not in Varros Analogi: Nonius hath some, whiche Festus lacketh: Nestor toke nat all that he founde in them bothe. Tortellius is not so abundant as he is diligent: Laurentius Valla wrate only of wordes, which are called elegancies, wherin he is vndoubtedly excellent: Perottus in Cornucopie, dyd omitte almost none that before him were written, but in wordis compounde he is to compendiouse: Frypere Calepine (but where he is augmented by other) nothyng amended, but rather appaired that which Perottus had studiousely gathered: Nebressensis was both well lerned and diligent, as it appereth in some wordes, which he declareth in latin: but bicause in his dictionarie wordes are expounde in the spainyshe tunge, whiche I do nat vnderstand, I can nat of hym shewe myn opinion: Budeus in the exact triall of the natiue sence of wordes, aswell greke as latine, is assuredly right comendable, but he is moste occupied in the conference of phrasis of bothe the tunges, whiche in comparison are but in a fewe wordes: Dyuers other men haue written sondry annotations and commentaries on olde latine authors, among whom also is discorde in their expositions. Whan I consydred all this, I was attached with an horrible feare, remembryng my dangerous enterprise (I being of so smal reputation in lernyng in comparison of them, whom I haue rehersed) as well for the difficultie in the true expressynge the lyuely sence of the latine wordes, as also the importable labours in serching expending and discussing the sentences of ancient writers. This premeditation abated my courage, and desperation was euen at hand to rent al in pieces that I had written, had nat the beames of your royal maiestie entred into my harte, by remembraunce of the comforte, whiche I of your grace had lately receyued, wherwith my spirite was reuyued, and hath set vp the sayle of good courage, and vnder your graces gouernance, your highnesse being myn onely mayster, and styrer of the shyppe of all my good fortune, I am entred the goulfe of disdaynous enuie, hauynge fynished for this tyme this symple Dictionarie, wherin I dare affirme, may be founde a thousande mo latine wordes, than wer togither in any one Dictionarie publyshed in this royalme at the tyme whan I fyrste began to write this commentarie, which is almost two yeres passed. For beside the conference of phrases or fourmes

A iii   of spea-

THE PREFACE.

of speakynge latin and englishe, I haue also added proper termes belongynge to lawe and phisike, the names of diuers herbes knowen among vs: also a good number of fishes founden as wel in our occean, as in our riuers: Moreouer sondrie poysis, coyne, and measures, sometyme vsed among the aunctient Romaynes, Grekes, and Hebrues, whiche knowlege to the reders not only of histories and orations of Tullie, but also of holy scripture, and the bokes of auncient phisitions, shall be founde pleasant and also commodiouse. Nor I haue omitted prouerbes, callyd Adagia, or other quicke sentences, whiche I thought necessarie to be had in remembraunce. All be it for as moche as partely by negligence at the begynnynge, partly by vntrue information of them, whom I trusted, also by to moche trust had in Calepine, some fautes may be founden by dilygent redynge, I therfore most humbly beseche your excellent maiestie, that where your hyghnesse shall happen to doubte of any one worde in the fyrste parte of this warke, or perchance do lacke any worde, whiche your maiestie shall happen to rede in any good author, that it maye lyke your grace to repayre incontinente vnto the seconde parte, whiche is myn addition, sekyng there for the same worde in the letter, wherwith he begynneth, trustynge verply, that your highnes there shall be satisfied. And for as moche as by haste made in printyng, some letters may happen to lacke, some to be sette in wronge places, or the ortography nat to be truely obserued, I therfore haue put all those fautes in a table folowing this preface: wherby they may be easily corrected: and that done, I truste in god no manne shall fynde cause to reiect this boke, but rather thankefully to take my good wyll and labours, gyuynge to your maiestie mooste hartye thankes, as to the chiefe author therof, by whose gracious meanes menne beinge studious, may vnderstande better the latine tunge in syxe monethes, than they mought haue doone afore in thre yeres, withoute perfyte instructours, whyche are not many, and suche as be, are not easy to come by : the cause I nede not to reherse, sens I ones declared it in my booke called the Gouernour, whiche about .viii. yeres passed, I dydde dedicate vnto your hyghnesse. And for my parte, I render most humble thankes vnto your maiestie, for the good estimation that your grace retayneth of my poore lernyng and honestie, promysynge therfore to your highnes, that duryng my lyfe naturall, I shall faythfully employe all the powers of my wytte and body, to serue truely your maiestie in euery thynge, wherto your mooste excellent iudgement, shall thynke my seruyce conuenient & necessary, In the meane tyme and alway, as your bounden seruant, I shal hartily pray vnto god, to prospere your hyghenes in all your vertuouse procedynges, grauntynge also that your maiestie may longe raigne ouer vs, to the incomparable comforte and ioye of all your naturall and louynge subiectes.

AMEN.

THO. ELIOTA EQVES LEC-
TORIBVS VERE DOCTIS.

ETSI NIHIL DVBITO DE VESTRO candore, prudentia, ac benignitate (lectores candidissimi,) metus tamen liuoris alieni me uehementer cogit, ut in huius operis principio uos aggrediar præoccupatione quadam, non tamen artificiosa, sed perq̃ simplici ac uerecunda: qua solum erratula, perpauca nimirum deprecando, morsus inuidorum, qui nusquàm non sunt, facilius euitarem. Nostis optumi uiri q̃ periculoso certamine, lis adhuc pendeat inter huius ætatis medicos de re herbaria: qua, me hercle, ut nihil extet humanæ saluti conducibilius, si probe cognoscatur: ita nihil penè deterius, aut magis noxium, si quicq̃ in ea, male intelligendo, quod lectori futurum sit fraudi, perperam committatur: quod cum ipse cognorim, alioqui cupidus redigendi in hos cõmentarios quorumcunq; uerborum quę apud latinos authores reperiantur, sensus integros ac genuinos: cœpi cum quibusdam herbariis ac pharmacopolis agere, quos existimaueram ea in re perq̃ gnaros fuisse, ac perdiligentes, ut stirpium non solum nomina, uerumetiam figuras ipsas mihi scribenti suppeditarent. at homines uel improbe suam ignorantiam dissimulantes, uel ut mihi imponerent (quod magis existimo) turpiter mentiētes, alias figuras, aliaq; nomina mihi prębuerūt, quā earundē herbarū fuisse, quas ego nosse cupiebam, postea diligentius inuestigando per meipsum comperi: quo factum est, ut ab his delusus, uel potius proditus, aliquot herbas ac arbores aliena fide male deceptus, huic Dictionario sub falsis nominibus inseruerim: quod tandem cum ex solidioris doctrinæ uiris, sero propemodum consultis, tum ex inquisitione perdiligenti, tam in libris Dioscoridis et Galeni, q̃ in ipsis styrpibus a me iā uisis ac multo penitius consyderatis deprehendissem, adeo tantę negligentię me certe pœnituit, ut eo nomine tot mensiū labores (ut mihi uidebatur inaniter exhaustos) flammis consumpsissem: ni me potentissimi, ac longe sapientissimi Principis nostri Henrici octaui Regis Anglię numen, interpellasset: cui meam fidem in perficiundo hoc negotio paulo ante obstrinxeram: facturum igitur me satis existimabam uobis uestriq; similibus, uiris utiq; bonis æque atq; doctis, si in tabellam, appendicem huic epistolę, herbarum uocabula uel a me perperam interpretata, uel non satis cognita diligenter coegero, quo minore cum periculo lectores quicquid mihi deciderit imprudēti resarcire possint. Abest enim q̃ plurimum, ut huiusce rei me quicq pudeat, cum in manibus tractentur cottidie libri doctissimorum hominum, tertium aut quartum recogniti, nouisq; additionibus iterum atq; iterum in

lucem

lucem editi, quod hercle cur mihi tantum non liceat, neq; moribus ne dū legibus ullus quifquam prejudicauerit. Sed mihi obiicient æmuli, multa quidem uerba, quę apud Calepinum reperiantur, uel à me fponte prętermiſſa, uel mihi nimium feſtinanti ſtolide dilapſa. Neutrum confitebor hercle nam cum primum ſtatuiſſem Dictionarium latino anglicum (ita iam lubet rei nouę, nouum nomen effingere) pro quodam meo nepote cōficere: in animo tum erat neq; plureis grecas dictiones aggerere, q̄ quę uideri poſſent ualde neceſſariæ, ad eos authores intelligendum, qui latine ſcribentes clariſſimi reputantur. Igitur non alia greca uocabula defumpſi mihi, quā ea quę uel in ciuitatem receptę (ut dicere folent) locum quempiam apud probatum aliquem authorem adornaſſent, aut maiorem copiam, aut fenſum illuſtriorem prębuiſſent. cętera quæcunq; penes huiuſmodi authores uel nuſq̄ reperta, uel ab iis ipſis circumſcripta, ne meam operam in depingendis chartis nimium otioſis imprudenter luderem, libenter prętermiſi, quod ſcirem, grecas literas noſce cupientibus, aliorū librorum, quos Lexica uocant, haud minorem copiam extare, nec mihi duos parietes de una fidelia dealbare admodum uacabat: nam quid per deum immortalem arrogantius dici poſſit? quid equidem ſtultius? q̄ in latino Dictionario ex uerbis grecis, aceruos ingentes colligere, miſcellaneasq; cōfarſinare, cum ad rem literariam plæraq; nihil faciant, imo nonnunq̄ officiant cum inquirentem ſedulo latinam aliquam dictionem, diutius q̄ par ſit retineant. Deniq; prętermiſi nimia uetuſtate iam obſoleta uocabula, quę Terentii, Plautiq; uenerandam antiquitatem longe pręcedere, aut plebeiorum ſordes nimium olere uideantur. tum quod authores quibus uſui fuerunt eiuſmodi uoces nuſq̄ extent: tum quod nulla in re, latine loquentibus utiles, plurimum ſtylo, puritatiq; ſermonis officere uehementer poterint. Si quis obſcœna uocabula deſyderet, quibus iacentem uenerem inter legendum ſuſcitare queat: alios dictionarios conſulat, meūq; contemnat, hoc nomine (ſi lubet) quod eiuſcemodi uocibus careat. Noueram humani ſenſus quantum fuerint ſemper ad incendium prompti, ſi delitefcentem igniculum ex lafciuiuſculis uerbulis uel modicè delibauerint: ſciebam quam auidi ſint homines tam fœde, ac demū pœnitendę uoluptatis illecebris animos perluendi, quā pręcipites fuerit ad exequendū, quod libido ſuaſerit. Pręterea non ignorabā ipſam Venerem non tantopere ſolicitatam omnino quieſcere: leuioreſq; impreſſiones efficere. Malebam igitur (conſcius futurę rationis, quam apud Chriſtū iudicem initurus ſum) uideri quibuſdam gratum aliquid ſubtrahere, ob idq; male audire apud cinœdos q̄libet procaces: quam damno cum meo tum aliorum inexpiabili, facem ſæuienti Cupidini, laſciua uerboſitate
ſubmi-

LECTORIBVS VERE DOCTIS.

subministrare. Viculos quosdam, pariter atq; riuulos et monticulos admodum ignobiles, quos extra Cosmographorum tabulas, uel nusq̃ reperietis uel perq̃ raro, id tamen cum sui situs descriptione satis commoda non curarim tantopere, ut in his uellem tempus & chartam inaniter decoquere, contemptus idem accidit in otiosis nominibus, quę neque tropũ afferant, nec in quopiam authore fabulam illustrent. Ceterum pro tam inani farragine comparaui lectoribus suppellectilem longe commodiorem, ex his dictionibus, quæ in legendis authoribus, ob sensus diuersitatem, haud mediocrem difficultatem afferant. Adieci pręter herbarum ac piscium cognomina, quorum nullus dictionarius ante hunc meminit (ni fallor) mensuras ac pondera, tam ueterum gręcorum atq; latinorum q̃ etiam Hebreorum. hanc equidem operam, cunctis hominibus qui in literis tum sacris, tum prophanis studiosè uersentur, me pulchre nauasse iudicaueritis, quoties memineritis, quàm insigni uecordia ad lectionem iucundissimam rei tam uulgaris ignorantia perdocti homines cęcutire uideantur. Tandem ne nimis longa prefacione, uobis in rebus maioribus atq; grauioribus occupatis, potius fastidium q̃ benefitium afferam, id breuiter a uobis impetrare cupio, ut meam uoluntatem in hac re æqui boniq; consulatis. cogitetisq; apud uosipsos, id operis iam cœptum ab equite britanno, barbarissimo scilicet, utpote in paternis tantum ædibus educato, nec ab anno ætatis duodecimo ab altero quopiam preceptore literis instructo, sibi ipsi nimirum duce tam in scientiis liberalibus, q̃ in utraquè philosophia: quod procul abest, ut ostentando dicam uel arroganter: sed ut gratiis DEO OPT. MAX.
cum a me tum ab his, quibus hic meus liber fuerit
utilis, utrinq; redditis. alii musarum uberiori
benefitio freti, meo quidem exemplo, parem aut maiorem operam aggredi,
pro sua Republica non dubita-
rent. Vos ualete, memo-
res, primos conatus,
cuiquam scriben-
ti, uix un-
quam
feliciter cecidisse.

THE CORRECTIONS.

THE TABLE OF CORRECTIONS.

ACETABVLVM, rede a saulcer, wherin vyneger or other lyke sauce is put. put out the resydue, and reade it in the table of measures.
Acinicula, rede Acuncula.
Acus, rede it in the addition.
Aedilitas, litum, rede litium.
Agaranomus, rede Agoranomus.
Ambrosia, rede in the addition.
Antista, reade Antistita.
Apiastrum rede an herbe, whiche hath leaues lyke to blacke horehound, but greater, and more tender, and are nat so rough, and smelleth lyke a cytron, some do take it for Marche.
Appositus, iette to, rede sette to.
Archarius, rede in the Addition.
Assiptor, rede Ascriptor.
Assecia, rede Assecla.

Biothenatos, rede Biothanatos.
Biremes, adde to, also shippes, hauing ii. raunges of ores.
Boij, adde to, also the people of Beuar or Berne, and the Marches therof.
Brabenta, rede Brabeuta.
Buglossa, rede, is that herbe, whiche is cõmonly callyd Borage.

CAdus, rede in the Addition, and also in the table of measures.
Calix, rede in the addition.
Calydonia, rede, It is also a countrey in the northe parte of Scotlande.
Calta, rede in the addition.
Camerinam mouere, reade in the addition.
Carcritoma, rede Carcinoma.
Cardinum, rede Cardamus.
Carpatine, put out okers, and rede cokars.
Cerates, rede the foure score and sixtenthe parte of an ounce.
Chameleopardus, rede lyke a panther.
Censio, rede Censeo.
Chena, rede clena.
Chœnix, rede in the table of greke mesures.
Chus, rede in the table of greke measures.
Climacterius, rede climactericus.
Commeats, rede commeatus.
Consuersco, rede consuesco.
Coriarius, adde to, also a curriar.
Cura, carę, rede curę.
Cynomia, rede Cynomyia.
Congius, reade in the Table of Romayne measures.

DEcussis, rede in the addition.
Demeanoulum, rede demeaculum.
Demensum, rede in the addition.
Duellium, rede Duellum.
Hęmatices, rede hęmatites.
Increpo, pere, adde to, uel pare.

LApathos, rede in the addition.
Latico, rede latito.
Legacitius, rede Legatitius.
Leucantha, rede Leucacantha.
Latumę, rede Latumię.
Lonem radere, rede Leonem radere.
Lesbos, for Ageum, rede Aegeum.
Lingua bula, rede Lingua bubula.
Litem suam facere, there for oae, rede one.
Lucifigus, rede Lucifugus.

MAlo, marul, rede mauult.
Marconiani, rede Marcomanni.
Mastiche, adde to commonlye callyd Mastix.
Mater matrina, rede z hath a mother liuing.
Medimnus, rede in the table of measures.
Mediocris, dlcre, rede mediocre.
Medius, a, um, in the myddell.
Melamirus, rede Melanurus.
Membraneus, rede of parchmyn or velam.
Merdo, oreur, rede ordure.
Metreta, & metretes, rede the greke table of measures.
Mina, rede in the addicion and in the tables of poyse and money.
Modius, rede in the table of measure.
Muralis, adde to the end pelitory of the wal

NEdum, after, for fundere, rede funderem, Nihil cum fidibus graculo nihil cũ amacino sui, rede, cum amaracino sui.
Nucamenta, thynges on the bowghes of nutte trees or pitche trees hangyng down lyke frynges, and be nat leaues.
Numeris omnibus absolutus, on euery parte perfyte, put out ly.
Olus atrum, for persely rede Alysander.
Ozinum, rede ozimum.

PAralleli, for lon rede son.
Patrizo, for lyke a father, reade lyke his father.
Pectunculus, a lyttell fyshe, adde therto, I suppose it is a cockyll.
Pharmacentice, rede Pharmaceutice.
Pituita, for rowme rede rewme.
Puuia, rede pluuia.
Pollex, rede a fynger bredth, and the third parte of a fynger.
Polus, of extre, rede of an axe tree.

Pupu-

THE CORRECTIONS.

Pupugi, rede the pretertence of pungo.
Putitius, a foole, rede a foole.

Qui, reade after the latine, wherfore was Epicurus more happy that he lyued in his owne countray, than Metrodorus whiche lyued at Athenes.
Quinarius, rede at the ende, whiche is of our money.iiii.pens farthing, or therabout.

Remuncope, for dryuen rede drawen.
Renones, rede after wherin the ancient Almaynes.

Salillum, rede a lyttell saltsellar.
Salinum, rede a saltesellar.
Saxatilis, pisces saxatili, rede saxatiles.
Scytæ, Scythia, putte theym out there, and reade them after.
Scorpiuros, putte out all the description of the herbe, and rede a lyttell herbe callyd also Scorpioides, hauyng small leaues, and the sede therof is like the tayles of Scorpions.
Sestertius, & sestertiū, rede them afterwarde in the table of coyne.

Sextarius, rede in the table of measures.
Singillatim, for euery ouche rede eueriche.
Specimen edere, to shewe a profe. put oute the residue.
Sprarchus, rede spirarchus.
Spithama, reade after in the table of measures.
Squilla, rede at the laste ende, I suppose it a prane.
Sernunt se somno, rede sternunt.
Struma, for whiche is, rede wherin is.
Sulcus, sometyme it is put of a dyche, rede for a dyche.

Thyrsus, put out all, for as moche as it is afore declared in Thyrsus.
Trachelum, reade for tho sayle, the sayle.
Trulla, rede a treye.
Tucetum, reade at the ende. also a sausage.

Vafer, for flye, reade flye.
Vlex, for to ti, rede to hym.

In the addition.

Adarca, for grownyng, rede growynge.
Aggerre, rede aggerere.

¶ Here endeth the Corrections.

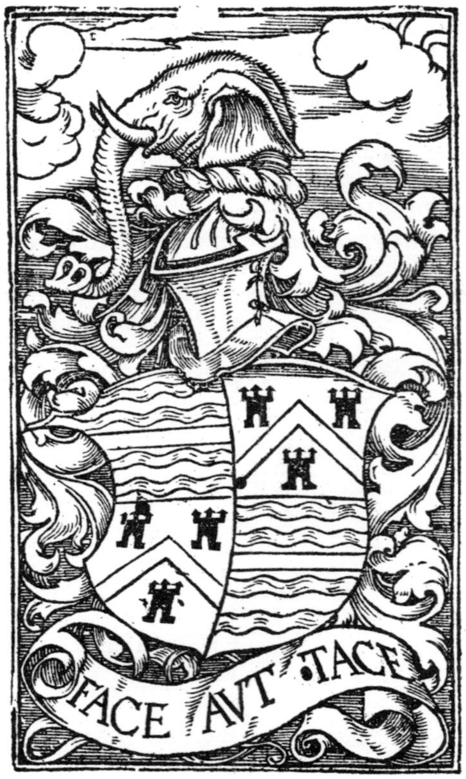
FACE AVT TACE

A ante B.

A Sygnifieth of, or from. Ab, and Abs, be of the same syngification, only A, goth before a worde, which begynneth with a cōsonāt: ab and abs goth before a word that doth begyn with a vowell.

A batis, two wordes made of the preposition, a, & the ablatiue case plurell of Batus, whiche in englysshe is a measure, signifieth an officer, that hath the orderyng of measures, as a clerke of the markette *Esdra.*

Ab accidentibus, an officer, vnto whome it belōgeth to write such thinges as do chance.

Abacti, officers deposed, or such as be constrayned to resygne their authoritie.

Abactores, theues that steale cattell.

Abacus, a countyng table, or cupborde.

Abaculus, of Plinie is taken for accompt.

Abalienatus, he whom a mā putteth frō him

Abalieno, aui, are, to put or tourne away.

Abana, a ryuer in the coūtrey of Damaske vnder the hyll called Libanus.

Abanec, a gyrdell that the priestes of Iewes ord weare. *Hieron.*

Abambulo, aui, are, to ascend or mount vp.

Abaphus, vndied or vncoloured.

Abauus, my great grandefathers father.

Abax, abacis, a cupboorde, or dresser, also an astronomers tables.

Abaci, the tables inbowed, wheron pylars doo stande.

Abbas, atis, an abbott

Abbatissa, an abbesse.

Abarimon, a countreye in Tartari, where men haue fete tourned backwarde, and be wonderfull swifte, and be wylde. *Plinius.*

Abaster, one of the horses of Pluto kyng of helle.

Abdera, a citie in the realme of Thracia.

Abderita, a citesyn of Abdera.

Abdias, the name of a prophete.

Abdico, aui, are, to expell or put out of fauour, or resygne an offyce, or to refuse his sonne, or kynsman.

Abdicauit filium, he refused hym for his sonne. Abdicauit se magistratu, he hath resygned his offyce or dignitie.

Abdico, ixi, cere, to denie or forsake.

Abdo, didi, dere, to hyde.

Abdomen, the fatte aboute the kydneyes. It is also the vdder and teates of a sowe, full of mylke, whiche is in Italy hadde for a delycate meate.

Abduco, xi, cere, to leade awaye, or leade out, or pull away, or take with.

Abelline, fylberdes of Abellino, a citie in Naples.

Abemo, emi, ere, to take or putte of a garment. Abemito uestem, put of thy cote. *Plau. cc.*

Abeo, iui, uel ii, ire, to departe, or go away.

Aberceo, to forbid. Eam abercet domo, he forbyddeth hir his howse.

Aberro, aui, are, to erre or wāder very moche, to depart ferre of, or a sonder.

Aberūco, aui, are, to wede out, or pluck out.

Abessa, the name of a Iuge in Israel.

Abfore, to be awaye.

Abgrego, aui, are, to seuer or take oute of the flocke, or to drawe sheepe.

Abhinc, before this tyme.

Abhorreo, ui, rēre, to abhorre, to hate.

Abhorresco, to feare to beholde.

Abiecto, aui, are, to caste often away.

Abies, ietis, a fyrre tree.

Abietarius, a carpentar.

Abigeatus, tus, felony in stealynge cattell.

Abigêus, a stealer of cattell.

Abigo, egi, gere, to dryue away any thinge, that is euyll or noyous. also to driue awaye cattell by thefte or deceyte.

Abiicio, ieci, iicere, to cast away, to renoūce to despise.

Abintegro, yet ageyne eftsones.

Abintestato, intestate or without testament.

Abiudico, aui, are, to recouer or take away by iudgement.

Abiugo, aui, are, to vnyoke, discharge, or putte asonder.

Abiungo, xi, ere, to seuer or sonder.

Abiurati, sworne brethern, or confederatis.

Abiuro, aui, are, to denye by an othe, or to kepe a thinge wrongfully.

Abiudicatum, adiudged, gyuen by iugemēt.

Ablacto, aui, are, to weane.

Ablaqueo, aui, are, to rydde the erthe from trees or vynes, and cutte awaye the vpper rotes, that they may beare the more fruite.

Ablego, aui, are, to sende away.

Abligurio, iui, ire, to consume in banketting or farynge delycately.

Abloco, aui, are, to sette or let to an other.

Abluo, ui, ere, to wasshe of.

Abnego, aui, are, to denye vtterly.

Abnepos, otis, a sonne in the fourthe degree in lyneall discent.

Abnuo, nui, ere, to deny or refuse with coūtenance or becke, to becke away.

Abnuto, signifieth to do the same oftētimes

Aboleo, eui, uel ui, ere, to put out, or rase out to anulle, or vndo for euer.

Abolesco, to brynge to naught.

Abolla, a Senatours habyte, or a souldiours cloke.

Abominor, atus sum, nari, to take for ylle lucke, or haue in detestation.

Aborigines, people, whyche fyrste helde

A the

the countrey aboute Rome, & lyued abrode hauynge no houses. They may also be taken for any other people, whose beginning is not knowen.

Aborior, abortus sum, aboriri, to be borne afore naturall tyme.

Aborsus, an vntymely byrthe, nygh to the conception: which may be called aborsion.

Abortus, an vntymely byrthe, nighe to the iuste tyme of delyueraunce, whereby the chylde dieth.

Abortio, onis, et Abortiuus, the byrthe dystroyed with some hurte, or other mysaduenture, or medycine.

Abortio, tiui, tire, to brynge forthe a chylde, or it be perfecte.

Abortium, idem quod abortus.

Abortiuus, a, um, that thynge, whiche procureth the sayd vntymely byrthe.

Abpatruus, My fathers great vncle.

Abrado, si, dere, to pare or scrape away.

Ab re, out of the matter, or out of the purpose, vnsemely, vnconuenient.

Abrenuncio, aui, are, to renouce, or forsake.

Ab re tua, agaynste thy profite.

Abripio, pui, ere, to take fro, or take by force.

Abrogati, they whiche beinge at lybertie, submitte them selfis to an other mans rule, by theyr consente

Abrogo, aui, are, to take awaye.

Abrogare legi, to dissolue or repell a lawe.

Abrotanū, an herbe called southern wode.

Abrumpo, rupi, rumpere, to breke of, plucke vp, or cutte of.

Abs, of or fro.

Absarus, a ryuer of Armeny, that incloseth the lasse Armenie.

Abscedo, cessi, dere, to go away.

Abscessus, et abscessio, a departyng.

Abscessus, is of phisytions taken for an impostume or botche, or for a course of euyll humours to some parte of the body, wherby matter is ingendred.

Abscido, di, dere, to cutte of.

Abscindo, signifieth the same.

Abscio, iui, ire, to go out of remembrance.

Abscondo, di, dere, to hyde.

Absens, tis, absent, or awaye.

Absentaneus, a, um, that whiche in absence is doone.

Absentia, absence.

Absentio, tire, to thinke contrary.

Absento, aui, are, to be absent.

Absimilis, moche vnlyke.

Absis, idos, the strake of a cart whele, wherin the spokes be sette.

Absito, tere, to departe from a place. sometyme it signifieth to absteine or leaue of.

Absoleo, ere, to be out of vse.

Absoletus locus, a place vnoccupied or neglected.

Absoluo, ui, ere, to loose that whyche was bounden. also to performe or accomplyshe. Also to spare or forgyue, to pardon, to spede, to assoyle.

Absono, absonaui, absonare, to discorde or sowne euylle.

Absonus, na, num, that whiche sowneth nat wel, or discordeth, or scantly may be herde.

Absorbeo, bui, uel absorpsi, ere, to swalowe, or suppe of all, to deuoure or consume.

Absq;, without.

Abstemius, he that drinketh no wyne.

Abstentus, accursed out of the churche.

Absterreo, ui, ere, to prohybyte or lette, or putte fro.

Abstinentia, abstinence, a vertue in forbearynge to take an other mans goodes.

Abstineo, ui, ere, to absteyne or forbeare, or tempre.

Absto, stiti, stare, to stande farre of.

Abstorqueo, torsi, quere, to gette by force or tourmentes.

Abstraho, xi, ere, to take by force or by craft

Abstrudo, si, dere, to hyde.

Abstulit, of Aufero, he hath birefte, taken away, or borne away.

Absum, fui, abesse, to be away, or ferre of, or to fayle, or to be distant or absent.

Absumo, psi, ere, to spende or consume.

Absurdus, surda, surdum, inconuenient, foolyshe, discordinge, dishoneste, abhorringe, or odious.

Absynthium, wormewoode.

Absyrtides, be ylandes in the Uenitian see.

Absyrtus, the brother of Medea, whome she dyd cutte into pieces, and threwe into the see, whan she fledde frome her father with Jason.

Abundantia, haboundance, more than sufficient rychesse.

Abunde, habūdantly, plentuously, inough, and more than inough.

Abundo, aui, are, to habunde, to haue out of measure more than inough.

Abuolo, aui, are, to flee away.

Abutor, abusus sum, abuti, to abuse, to vse a thynge: dishonestely, vncomely, contrarye to that, that it serueth for, oute of order, or in vayne.

Abusiue, improprely, agaynste Nature, or custome.

Abydena, trifles, thinges of smalle estimation, wanton toyes, thynges vnseemely for menne to vse.

Abydeni, a people in Asia, whyche hauynge their Cytie distressed with a longe Syege, felle into a furye, or madnesse, and
slewe

flewe all their wiues, their chylderne, and afterwarde them selues.

Abydos, the citie of the sayd people.

Abyla, a hylle in the occean See agaynste Spayne, whiche is called oone of Hercules pylars.

Augustinꝰ Ambrosiꝰ.

Abyssus, is a depenes without bottom.

A ante C.

AC, signifieth sometyme, and. as Doctus ac iustus es, Thou arte kunnyng and iuste. Sometyme it is taken for Than, as Haud secus ac iussi faciunt, They doo none otherwise than they be commanded. Sometyme it dothe signifie as, as Superbis perinde, ac si Rex esses, Thou arte as proude as if thou were a kynge.

Acacia, is the iuyce of a fruite called siliqua. It maye be called also in Englande veriuyse.

Academia, a vniuersitie, whiche toke that name of a place nighe to Athenes, where Plato the great phylosopher taught phylosophye.

Academici, were a secte of phylosophers, whyche folowed and taughte the opynyons of Plato.

Acanthis, idis, a byrde that feedeth on thystelles, and maketh her nest with claye, and is called in englyshe, a Tytmusse. It was also a boye, whiche the poetes doo fayne was transformed into a floure of his name. It is also a bushe, lyke a whyte thorne, with lasse leaues, mosy, and pryckynge.

Dioscorides sayth, that it is an herbe, that groweth in stony and moyste grounde, and hath leaues broder and longer than letyse, in forme lyke to rockette, somwhat blacke, and in bropsynge softe and fatty, hauynge a stalke of two cubytes high, of thyckenesse of a mans fynger, garnyshed vnder the top with lyttell longe leaues and pryckynge, wherevnto groweth a whyte floure.

Acapna, drye wodde that smoketh not.

Acara, a towne in the myddelle of Hungarye.

Acarnania, a parte of a royalme in Grece, named Epirus. It is also a lyttell countreye in Egypte: and it is a citie by Syracusis in the royalme of Sycile.

Acarpia, lacke of fruite.

Acatalectos, a verse, wherein one syllable lacketh.

Acatium, the greattest sayll in the shyppe.

Accalaurentia, the name of her, that nourished Romulus and Remus, the fyrst builders of Rome.

Accedo, accessi dere, to goo to, or approche. Sommetyme it sygnifyeth to gyue an eare or harken, to take hede, and to make moche of.

Accelero, aui, are, to make haste or spede.

Accendo, di, dere, to kendle, inflame, prouoke, or gyue boldnes.

Accensi, were sowldiours appoynted to be aboute great offycers for defence of their persones. Festus saythe, that it were they, whiche after the dethe of souldiours were put in their places. Uarro affirmeth, that they were ministers redy at the commaundementes of principall offycers.

Accentus, an accēt or tune, wherby a syllable is pronounced.

Accepso, in the stede of acceperim, I haue taken.

Acceptabula, all vessayle or other thynge, that may receyue and kepe what soo euer shall be putte into it.

Acceptilatio, an acceptaunce, a word of the lawe, whyche hapneth in this wyse. One sayth to an other, Art thou contented with that that I haue promysed the? or that by my bargain I owe to the? The other saith, ye I am contented. This is Acceptilatio. Also wherin soo euer I haue bounden my selfe by receyuynge of any thynge, it maye be called Acceptilatio.

Acceptum, thankfull, pleasant, allowable.

Acceptum fero, to knowledge my selfe to haue receyued, that is not yet payde, also to take thankfully.

Accerso, siui, sire, to call forth, or sende for.

Accerso, sere, tertię coniugationis, to goo to calle, or fetche.

Accidens, is an accident, whiche may be, or not be, without corruption of that, wherin it maye be.

Accido, di, dere, to falle downe in doing reuerence.

Accingo, cinxi, cingere, to gyrde, to prepare, to make redye to do some thyng.

Accinctus, gyrte, redye, quycke in his busynesse.

Accio, iui, ire, to calle to.

Accipio, cœpi, cipere, to take, to here, to suppose, to knowe, to vnderstande, to receiue, to intreate or entertayne.

Accipiter, a hawke.

Accliue, stepe bendynge.

Acclino, aui, are, to enclyne or bende to.

Accliuis, siue accliuius, rysynge vpwarde to a smalle toppe.

Accludo, to shutte to.

Accola, the nexte inhabytant.

Accola campi, He that dwelleth nexe to the fielde. Also he that commeth oute of one countreye, and dwelleth in an other.

Accolo, to dwell by or nyghe, specially hilles or waters.
Accōmodo, aui, are, to accommodate, appropre, to applye, make apte, set in order, gyue, or inclyne.
Accredo, didi, ere, to giue credēce, to assent.
Accresco, creui, crescere, to growe to.
Accubitum, a bedde or couche to lye on by daye tyme, as it was the maner of the olde Romaynes, to eate lyenge on their beddis.
Accubitus, the lyenge in the said maner.
Accubo, accubui, bare, to lye by, or to sytte, or lye downe to eate.
Accumbo, cubui, bere, to lye downe, to lye by, to lie or sytte downe at feastes and bankettes. Accūbere mensā, to syt at one table.
Accumulo, aui, are, to accumulate or gather in heapes, to increase.
Accuro, aui, are, to take good hede.
Accuratus, ta, tum, wherin is moche dylygence, curiouse.
Accurate, diligently, curiousely.
Accurro, ri, rere, to rūne to, to spede thither
Accusatorius, ria, rium, whiche conteyneth an accusation.
Accuso, aui, are, to accuse.
Acedia, slouthe, pensyfenes, heuynesse of harte, werynesse.
Acedior, diatus sum, to be wery, or to waxe slouthefull.
Acentra, et acentreta, thynges wherof the poynt in the myddes is not knowen.
Aceo, acui, acere, to be sowre or sharpe.
Acephalus, la, lum, without a heed.
Acer, et aceris, a tree, the wodde wherof is moste gentyll to worke in, and is named in englyshe Dowgeon.
Acer, cra, crum, et Acer acris, acre, sower as vineger. sommetyme it betokeneth stronge, sometyme sharpe, Acer inimicus, a sharpe ennemye. Also sore, as Acres animaduersores, soore punyshers.
Acredo, Acritudo, Acritas, sharpenesse, or sowernesse.
Acriter, sharpely, or sowrely.
Acer, aceris, chaffe of mylsede.
Acerosum frumentum, vnkleane wheate.
Acerbitas, byttcrnes of taste, sharpenes of tyme, crueltie in man.
Acerbo, baui, are, to trouble, to make bytter, or abhomynable.
Acerbus, ba, bum, vnrype, bytter, difficult, or peynefulle, as, Robustorum iuuenum acerba mors, The dethe of yonge menne is peynefulle, as who saythe, they dye with greatte difficultie.
Acersecomes, He that neuer cuttethe his heare.
Aceruatim, in heapes.

Aceruo, aui, are, to gather into heapes.
Aceruus, a heape or gatherynge togyther, specially of grayne.
Acesco, sci, scere, to waxe sowre or tarte, specially in lykour.
Acetabulum, a kynde of vessell, which may be called a charger, or a basyn, and was a vessell, wherin were thinges sacrified.
Acetare, to moue or styrre.
Acetarium, a salate of herbes. it is also a gardeyn, where salate herbes do growe.
Acetum, vynegre.
Achæi, people in Grecia. and somtyme they be taken for grekes generally.
Achæron, tis, is of poetes taken for a ryuer of helle.
Achaia, a region in Grecia.
Acharcon, the mayne sayle of a shyppe.
Achates, was the name of the companyon or mynion of Aeneas the Troiane. It is also the name of a precious stoone founde in Sicile, which is in colour browne, and hath cerkles blacke and whyte.
Achetæ, gresshoppers, which chirpe loude and pleasantly.
Achilleum, a sponge, whiche is verye softe, and hath smalle holes.
Aciæris, a hatchet of brasse, which amonge the paynyms was vsed in sacrifice.
Acicula, a pynne.
Acidula, peares that be sower.
Acidus, da, dum, sowre, or sharpe.
Acies, betokeneth the edge of a knyfe, or other weapon or toole. Also the front of an hoste, at the ioynynge of battayle. more ouer that parte of the eie, whyche is called the syghte.
Acinacis, a crooked sworde that the Persyans vsed.
Acini, be lyttell kernels, whiche be in grapis, raisons, pomegranates, & other beries.
Accipenser, or Aquipenser, a kynde of fyshe whiche hathe the scales tourned towarde the hedde.
Aclanes, he that neuer cryeth.
Aclytes, a weapon vsed in the olde tyme.
Aconitum, an herbe, wherin is mooste feruent poyson.
Acontiæ, certayne impressyons in the fyrmament lyke to fyrye dartes, whyche doo seeme to flie.
Acopa, medicines to remedy werynesse.
Acopis, a precious stone lyke a glasse, with smalle golden dropes, wherwith yf oyle be heate, and the body therwith anoynted, it dissolueth all werynesse.
Acor, ris, a tartenes lyke vnto vnripe wyne or pomegranates.
Acquiesco, eui, escere, to leane, as to sleane my

A ante C.

my heed or arme vppon any thynge. Also it signifieth to assent to other mens sayinges.

Acquiro, siui, rere, to attayne a thynge that is sought for.

Acraton, pure wyne, about a lay, or vnmixte.

Acredo, dinis, the sharpnes that is in fruites, whiche be not rype.

Acredula, the wodde larke.

Acrimonia, tartnes, which biteth the tūge, and perceth the heed, as in the taste of garlyke, oynions, and other lyke thynges. It signifieth sometyme sharpnes in speking or mynde: sometyme lyuelynes and quyckenesse of wytte.

Acrochordones, a kind of wertes, as great as beanes, so small at the rootes, that they do seme to hange by a synewe.

Acroma, a subtyll sentence or lesson, requiringe moche study and serche. it is also taken for all thynges to be recited or doone, to delyte the audience.

Acta, water bākis, or which mē do cal strōdes, wheron the see floweth. Also it is that which we cal acts, cōcerning mens lyues or priuate busynes put in writing. also such dedes as haue hapned out of iugement. Actitata be those, whiche haue hapned in iugement, properly they, which be in doyng.

Acteon, the name of a mā, whom Diana, bicause he did se her nakid, turnid ito an hart: & so was he torne & slain of his own houdis.

Actio, onis, betokenith somtime pronunciation, sometime an oration writen, sometime an action in the lawe, sometyme an hystorie, sometyme a defence, otherwhyle a recompence in wordes for benefite receiued, as gratiarum actio, for thankes. generally it is taken for act or dede in euery thyng.

Actiosus, busye.

Actito, aui, are, to practise, specially in ciuile causes.

Actor, whiche dothe the dede. Also in the lawe the plaintife, complaynant, or demandaunt. Also a player of enterludes. Also a mannes factour or baylyffe, that hathe the charge of his busynesse.

Actualia nomina, names, which do procede of acte, as Rex, a regendo, of gouernynge, Dux a ducendo, of leadynge.

Actuarius, ria, rium, actiue.

Actuarius, a substantiue, signifieth a notary or scribe, or any other that writeth spedily. Also it betokenith a kynde of shippes, whiche be callid barkis.

Actum est, it is loste.

Actuosus, full of actes.

Actus, ta, tū, performed, also arryued, thrust in, brought to, or feared.

Actus, tus, a dede, the partes of a comedie

A ante D.

or play, a dayes warke in tyllage.

Actutum, anon, without tarienge.

Aculeus, a prycke or stynge.

Acumen, the sharpnes of euery thing. it signifieth also clerencs of witte.

Acumino, aui, are, to sharpen.

Acinicula, a smalle nedell.

Acuo, ui, ere, to make sharpe, as a knyfe, or other thinge lyke. somtyme it betokenethe to teache, otherwhile to steere.

Acupictores, imbrowderers.

Acus, ci, a fishe called a banstikle or bāning.

Acus, aceris, chaffe.

Acus, acus, a nedell, also chaffe of corne, also an order in battayle.

Acutus, ta, tum, sharpe, but in voyce it betokeneth high and small, as a treble.

A, ante D.

AD, by hym selfe, or ioyned to an other word, signifieth to, or at, as Vado ad oppidum, I go to the towne. Erat ad ripam fluminis ingens arbor, There was at the ryuers syde a great tree. Some tyme it signifieth agaynst, as, Ad illum mihi pugna est, Against him is my warre. Som tyme it betokeneth in comparyson, sometime cause, as, Ad quid hoc fecisti? For what cause, or wherto diddest thou this? Sometime about, as Ad duo millia hominū occisa sunt, There be slayne aboute two thousand men. Also after, as, Ad hæc, After this.

Ad annum, durynge a hole yere.

Ad diem, at the day appoynted.

Ad tempus, for a whyle.

Ad exemplum, to the example or lykenes.

Ad extremum, fynally at the laste.

Ad pedes desilio, I light on my fete.

Ad rem facit, it maketh for the matter, or is conuenient.

Ad rem pertinet, it belongeth to the pourpose.

Ad uerbum, worde by worde.

Ad unum, vnto the laste.

Adæque, semblably, so moche: as, Adæque miser, so moche a wretche.

Adagia, an olde wife, whiche late hadde a chylde.

Adagium, a prouerbe, or as I mought say, an olde sayde sawe.

Adamas, adamantis, a precious stone, called a dyamant.

Adamo, aui, are, to loue very well.

Adamussim, by rule, streight as a lyne.

Adapto, aui, are, to ioyne to.

Adaquo, aui, are, to water horse or cattell.

Adarea, a frothe or fome growyng on reedes in the fennes.

A.iii.   Ad

Ad calendas grecas, signifieth Neuer. For the olde grekes had no calendes.
Addico, xi, dicere, to saye, to iudge, to appoynte, or depute.
Addictus, he that is iudged, appoynted, or deputed.
Addictus, ta, tum, openly solde. Also Addicere was whan the iuge in the old tyme delyuered the dettour to his credytours, to do with hym what they lysted.
Addisco, didici, discere, to lerne wel, or adde to in lernynge.
Additus, ta, tum, added or put to.
Addo, didi, dere, to adde, ioyne, or put to.
Addoceo, cui, cere, to lerne.
Addormio, miui, ire, to slepe.
Adduco, xi, cere, to bryng to, or bring forth, sometyme to drawe or plucke togither.
Adducta frons, a frownyng foreheed. somtyme adducere is to extende or thrust out.
Adedo, di, dere, to deuoure.
Adeo, so moch, moreouer, surely, without doubte. Somtyme it signifieth euen, as Ture iam adeo eius audies uerba, Thou thy self euen nowe shalte here his wordes.
Adeo, iui, ire, to go to, to demaunde, to attempte, to make assaulte.
Adeps, adipis, the fatte of all thynge.
Adeptus, opteyned gotten, or founden.
Adhabito, taui, tare, to dwelle by.
Ad hæc, moreouer.
Adhæreo, to cleaue faste, to sette sure, to ioyne to.
Adhalo, to blowe or to breathe on a thyng.
Adhamo, aui, are, to bynde to, or tye, or grappell.
Adhibeo, ui, bere, to put to, to haue by me.
Ad hoc, furthermore.
Ad horam, at tyme appoynted.
Adhuc, yet, hitherto.
Adiaceo, cui, cere, to lye by.
Adides, short battes of a cubyte longe and an halfe, hauynge pikes of yron in theym, and were tyed to a lyne, that whanne they were throwen, he that did cast the, mought plucke them agayn vnto him, hurlebattes.
Adigo, egi, adigere, to procure or styre, to bynd by othe, or promyse, to bryng or dryue to, to fasten or ioyne to.
Adiiciales, feastes that pryestes made in the olde tyme.
Adiicio, ieci, iicere, to caste to, to adde or putte to, or increase.
Adiicere oculum, to loke on, or consyder.
Adimo, emi, ere, to take away, or diminishe.
Adineo, iniui, ire, to put in.
Adinstar, lyke to.
Adipales, feastes that priestes were wonte to make.

Adipatus, ta, tum, larded, basted.
Adipiscor, adeptus sum, to gette or optain: ioynid with a pson it signifieth to ouertake.
Aditio, tionis, an accesse, or repaire.
Adito, taui, tare, to go to.
Aditus, tus, accesse, commyng to, or entrie.
Adiudico, aui, are, to adiuge.
Adiugo, aui, are, to yoke or ioyne to.
Adiungo, xi, ere, to ioyne to, to applye.
Adiuro, aui, are, to denye with an othe, to coniure.
Adiuto, aui, are, to helpe often.
Adiuuo, aui, are, to helpe.
Adiutorium, helpe.
Adiumentum, helpe.
Adlimina, a porter, whiche dothe kepe the vtter gate.
Ad liquidum, clerely, euidently, playnly.
Admando, aui, are, to sende to, to delyuer any thynge to one to bringe to an other.
Ad manus, at hande, redy.
Adminiculor, aris, et Adminiculo, are, to ayde, to succour.
Adminiculum, ayde, supportation.
Admiratio, a wonderynge.
Admiror, raris, ratus sum, rari, to wonder.
Admissarius equus, a stalyon horse.
Admissionales, vshers of the chambre.
Admissura, the acte or tyme whan beastes doth their kinde in generation. Seasoning.
Admitto, misi, mittere, to admitte, to put to, to brynge in, to suffre, to susteyne, or take.
Admodū, very moche, somwhat, resonably.
Ad modum, as it were.
Admolior, iris, molitus sum, liri, to putte or adde to.
Admoneo, nui, ere, to warne, to exhorte.
Admordeo, momordi, dere, to byte soore.
Admoueo, ui, ere, to moue to, or put to.
Adoleo, leui, lui, ere, adultum, to begynne to grow, to do sacrifice with incense, or other fumes, to burne swete thynges.
Adolescentia, is the aege betwene chyldehode and mannes age, whiche is betwene xiiii. and. xxi.
Adolescentior, aris, atus sum, to be wanton, or full of youthe.
Adolescenturio, iui, ire, to playe the boye.
Adonia, festiual dayes, which were kept in the honor of Adonis, the derling of Uen⁹.
Adonis, the name of a chylde, whiche was sonne of Cynare, kyng of Cypres, whome Uenus had for her derlynge, whiche was slayn with a bore, whom the poetes fained, that Uenus turned into a purple floure.
Adonidis horti, gardeyns for a lyttell tyme pleasant, whiche shortely decayen.
Adoptio, an election of an heyre out of the cours of inheritance, as by wyll or gyfte.
the

A ante D.

Adoptitius, he that is adopted or taken in the stede of a sonne.
Adoptiuus, the son of him that is adopted.
Adopto, aui, are, to elect or apoint an heire.
Adoratio, reuerence due to god, or saintes. also an inwarde deuotion and affection to hym that reuerence is doone vnto: and is an expresse mocyon or acte of reuerence done with the body.
Adorea, et adoreola, A prayse that is giuen to them that haue victorie. Also a cake of fyne wheate, whiche they vsed in sacrifice.
Adoreum, sede corne.
Adordior, iris, adorsus sum, riri, to speake to, to beginne.
Adorior, adortus sum, to sette on sodaynly, to begynne. Adorior hunc, I sette on him.
Adoro, raui, are, to honour with inclination of the body, to beseche.
Ad plenum, perfectly, fully.
Adprimus, chiefe of all.
Adpulsus, Adpulsio, the dryfte of sheepe to the water.
Adrepo, psi, ere, to crepe to.
Adrumo, maui, to grudge or make rumor.
Adruo, rui, ere, to turne the erth in tyllage.
Adscire, to ioyne or putte to.
Adsum, fui, esse, I am here, or presente, or at hande.
Ad summam, in conclusion, finally.
Ad tempus, for a tyme.
Adueho, uexi, uehere, to bring to or cary to.
Aduena, a straunger.
Aduenio, ni, uenire, to come to.
Aduentitia bona, goodes whiche doo come vnloked for.
Aduentitius morbus, syckenes that cometh without our defaute, and of some menne is called an vncome.
Aduentitius, he that commeth to a place by chaunce.
Aduentito, aui, are, to come often to.
Aduento, aui, are, to come nigh.

Plautus in Mustellaria.

Aduentores, commune resorters, or haunters to a place.
Aduersarius, an aduersarie.
Aduersitores, seruantes, whiche do fetche home their maisters after dynar or supper.
Aduersor, satus sum, sari, to repugne or be contrarye, or to refuse.
Aduersus, contrary, or agaynst.
Aduerto, ti, tere, to tourne to.
Aduiuo, uixi, uiuere, to lyue yet.
Adulor, atus sum, lari, to flatter.
Adulatio, flatterye.
Adulter, adultera, a man or woman auoutrer.
Adulterinæ claues, counterfaite keys.
Adulterinus, na, nū, counterfaite, or forged.
Adultero, raui, rare, to couterfaite or forge.

Ae ante D.

Adulterium, auoutry.
Adultus, ta, tum, full growen.
Adumbro, aui, are, tomake or giue shadow, to represente or expresse, as peynters dog, that do shadowe ymages in playne tables, to make them shewe imboced or rounde.
Adunco, aui, are, to make croked.
Aduncus, croked or hooked.
Ad unguem, to the perfection.
Aduno, aui, are, to gather togyther.
Ad unum, eueryche one.
Aduocatus, an aduocate.
Aduoco, caui, care, to call to, or cal to help.
Aduolo, laui, are, to flie to, or nygh a place.
Ad uotū, after myn, or thyn, or his appetite.
Adusq̃, vntyll.
Adytū, the chauncell or other secrete place of the temple, where none came but priestes, or persones sanctifyed.

Ae, ante E

AEdere spiritum, to yelde vp the gost, to dye. — *Cicero x Attic.*
Aedere facinus, to do an yll dede.
Aedere stragem, to make a slaughter of mē. — *Tit. Liuio.*
Aedere nomina, to telle the names to be wrytten.
Aedere librum, to sette forth such a boke. — *Cicero in Venē.*
Aedere scriptum, to shewe forth writing.
Aedere prælium, to make battayle.
Aedepol, an othe amonge gentyles, sygnyfyenge by Pollux house.
Aedes, a house, and if there be ioyned thervnto the name of god or of a saynt, it sygnifieth a churche, or temple. Aedes saluatoris, saynt Sauiours churche.
Aedicula, an oratorie, or place, where images were kepte.
Aedificiū, al the hole building of the hous.
Aedifico, caui, care, to buylde.
Aediles, officers, whose charge was to see to the kepynge vp and mayteynyng of tēples, and priuate houses, and to make prouision for solemne playes.
Aedilitas, litum, the office of the Aediles.
Aedilitius, he that hadde ben ones in that authorytie.
Aedituus the prelate of the temple.
Aediticius, a Iudge or arbitratour chosen of the one parte.
Aedituor, ari, to rule ouer the tēple or hous
Aeditus, ta, tum, hygh and stronge.
Aedituus, the prelate of the temple or churche, and may be nowe called the persone or paryshe prieste.
Aedo, ædidi, tum, to set forthe or publyshe. Also it signyfyeth to brynge forthe by generacyon.

Ae, ante G.

Aeger, gra, grum, sycke.
Aegipanes, beastes lyke to men, hauynge fete lyke to gotes.
Aegre, greuously, or heuily.
Aegrimonia, syckenes.
Aegroto, aui, are, to be sycke.
Aegrotatio, syckenesse.
Aegrotus, sa, tum, sycke.

Ae, ante M.

¶Aemulor, emulatus sum, æmulari, to enuie without malyce, or to folowe, or studye to be lyke to an other.
Aemulus, he that foloweth or enuieth another, onely for desyre of glorie.

Ae ante N.

¶Aenatores, blowers in trumpettes.
Aeneus, enea, æneum, brason.
Aenigma, tis, a derke question, harde to be vnderstanded.
Aenigmatistes, he that pourposeth harde questions.
Aenum, a cawdron.

Ae, ante Q.

¶Aequabilis, eqwall.
Aequabilitas uitæ, wherin is no varietie or trouble.
Aequeuus, of one age.
Aequalis, equall, playne, lyke, of lyke age.
Aequaliter, lyke wyse.
Aequamentum, indifferencie.
Aequanimis, he that is neyther extolled with psperitie, nor discōforted in aduersite.
Aequanimitas, takyng in good parte.
Aequanimiter, moderatly, paciētly, coldly.
Aeque, iustly, or as well.
Aequi bonique facio, I take in good parte, I recke not, or care not.
Aequidiale, the tyme whan the dayes and the nightes be of one length.
Aequilibrium, of euen weight or poyse.
Aequimanus he that vseth the one hand as well as the other.
Aequinoctium, the tyme of the yere, whan the day is as longe as the night, whyche is twise in the yere. In sprying time about the viii. Calendes of Aprile: And in Autumne aboute the. viii. calendes of October.
Aequinoctiale, the adiectiue of æquinoctiū.
Aequiparo, aui, are, to cōpare or make equal
Aequipolleo, ui, ere, to haue lyke power, or be of lyke estimation.
Aequitas, equitie, iustyce, or euennes.
Aequivaleo, ui, ere, to be equiualente, or of lyke valour.
Aequiuocum, one worde hauynge dyuers sygnifycations.
Aequo, aui, are, to make euen or playne.
Aequor, the see, somtyme other waters.
Aequus, euen or playne.

Ae, ante R.

¶Aer, the ayre sommetyme wynde, blaste, breathe, or sounde.
Aera, ræ, money numbred.
Aerarii milites, sowldiours waged.
Aerarium, a tresory, where tresure is kept.
Aere diruti milites, sowdiours, whiche for some defaute were put out of wages.
Aeripes, whiche is as swyfte as the wynd.
Aerius, of the ayre or lyke to the ayre.
Aeratus, myxte with copper.
Aerugo, ginis, rust or canker in mettal, specially in copper or syluer.
Aeruginosus, rustye, or cankred.
Aerumna, labour paynfull, care of minde, with heuynes, infelicitie.
Aeruscare, to gette money by falsehode.

Ae, ante S.

¶Aes, æris, is proprely copper or brasse. It is oftentymes taken for money, sometyme for trumpettes.
Aes nostrum, Moneye that other menne do owe vnto vs.
Aes alienum, money that we doo owe to other men.
Aes suum, money that other men doo owe vnto hym, whom we speake of.
Aes ductile, mettal that wol be sone moltē.
Aesculum, an oke that beareth maste.
Aestas, Sommer.
Aestimabile, that whiche may be valewed.
Aestimatio, a peyne sette.
Aestimo, aui, are, to esteme, to value.
Aestiua, places to be in for shadowe in the sommer tyme.
Aestiuo, aui, are, to dwelle or be in a sommer place.
Aestuaria, places whervnto the see floweth and ebbith, or meres, filled with salt water.
Aestuo, aui, are, to waxe hotte, to bourne, to flowe lyke the see.
Aestuosus, hote, or feruente.
Aestus, tus, tui, heate of the wether, or burnynge of the sunne. Also the vyolence or troublous motion of the see.

Ae, ante T.

¶Aeras, age.
Aetate, an aduerbe, signifieth long tyme.
Aeternus, euerlastynge.
Aether, the fyrmament.
Aethera, ræ, the ayre.

Aethra,

Aethra, sygnifieth the same.

Ae, ante V.

¶ Aeuum, longe or euerlastyng tyme.

A ante F.

AFer, or Apher, a man born in Affrike.
Affabilis, a mā easy to be spokē vnto.
Affabilitas, gentylnes in heryng.
Affabre, counnyngly, craftily.
Affabrum, counnyngly or craftily wrought
Affaniæ, tryfles.
Affatim, abundantly.
Affecto, aui, re, to seke affectualli, to trouble whan it is put with damno, or other lyke.
Affectata oratio, a curyouse fourme of speakynge.
Affectatio, curyositie.
Affectate, curyously.
Affectus, ta, tum, troubled or vexed.
Affectus, tus, tui, et affectio, affection or naturall motion, as gladnesse, desyre, and suche lyke.
Affero, fers, attuli, afferre, to brynge to.
Afficio, eci, ere, to moue affection or disposition, either to good or to yll.
Afficit me gaudio, It maketh me gladde.
Afficit me dolore, It maketh me sory.
Affecit eum lætali uulnere, he gaue to hym his deathes wounde.
Affigo, gere, to nayle to, or fasten.
Affines, in fieldes betokeneth adioynyng: In men it betokeneth alyance by mariage.
Affirmo, aui, are, to affirme.
Affirmatio, affyrmaunce.
Affligo, flixi, gere, to punyshe.
Afflictatio, punyshement of the body with syckenesse.
Afflare, to blowe wynde.
Affluo, fluxi, fluere, to ouerflow or abunde.
Affore, to be presente.
Affrica, The thyrde parte of the worlde, wherin is Carthage, Numidia, and all the countreys nowe called Barbarye.
Africanus, a man of Affrike. Also the most noble capitayne Scipio, was called Affricanus, bycause he subdewed that countrey to the Romaynes.
Affrico, cas, caui, uel affrixi, to rubbe.
A fronte atq; à tergo, A prouerbe signifieng the conferrynge of thynges passed, with the state of thinges present.

A ante G.

AGamēnon, was the generall Capytayne of the grekes, atte the syege of Troye.
Agamnestor, was kynge of Athenes.
Age, Go to

Agedum, go to yet.
Agellus, a lyttell fyelde.
Ager, agri, a fielde. Somtyme a territorie belongynge to a towne, wherin is includid fieldes, medowes, woddes, and waters. Sommetime a manour with the demeanes. sometyme the arable felde onely.
Agger, eris, a heape of stones or turfe. also a bulworke, or a countremure to a fortresse or campe in battayle. sometyme it sygnyfieth a caulsey.
Aggero, aui, are, to heape vppe.
Agglomero, to make vppe on heape, by addynge to.
Agglutino, naui, nare, to ioyne togyther.
Aggrauo, aui, are, to be bourdenouse or chargeable.
Aggredior, gredi, to goo to, or come to, to inuade, to begynne, to attempt.
Aggrego, aui, are, to gather to gyther.
Agilis, nymble, or lyght.
Agilitas, nymblenes, dexteritie.
Agina, wherin the beame of a payre of balance is hanged.
Aginator, he that is meuid with a litle gain.
Agiographa, bokes of holy scripture.
Agito, tare, to do often, to pryck, to cōpell, to trouble, to persecute, to vexe, to consyder, to reuolue, to solycite.
Agmen, an hooste of men.
Agnati, kynsmen of the fathers syde.
Agnatum, that whyche is in byrthe more than nede requireth.
Agnomen, the surname that I haue by my father.
Agnosco, noui, noscere, to knowe.
Agnus, a lambe.
Ago, egi, agere, to do, to leade, to dryue, to labour, to here, to speake, to pronounce, to fayne, to goo. Nudi agunt, They go naked. to extende or sprede. Radices agunt, They sprede their rootes. I treate of a thynge, I gyue. Ago gratias, I gyue thankes. I brynge forthe, also to expell. Venena membris agit, It expellethē poyson oute of the membres.   *Pom. Mel.*
Agolū, a staffe to dryue cattell with.
Agonia, fere & heuines, or vexatiō of mynd.
Agonisma, the rewarde of victorie.
Agonista, a champyon.
Agonizo, aui, are, I contende, or fyghte valyantlye.
Agonothera, he that makethe a commune game, and payethe the rewarde to theym that do wynne it.
Agaranomus, he that setteth the pryce of vyttayle, a tasker.
Agoræus, a markette manne, a haunter of markettes.

Agrarius

Agrarius a landed man. Also he that fauoreth the lawes, whiche be made for the orderynge of possessions.

Agrarius, ria, rium, pertaynynge to landes or possessions.

Agrestis, agreste, wylde growen, withoute culture. Also he that is rude and beastlye, without gentyll maners.

Agricola, a husbande manne.

Agricolator, the same.

Aggripetæ, they that do aske their portion in diuision of landes.

Agrippæ, they whiche be borne with their feete forewarde.

A ante H.

Ahenum, a potte to heate in drynke.

Ahenus, a vessele of whyte brasse or copper, whyche is bryghte bothe within and without.

A, ante I.

¶ Aio, ais, ait, I saye, thou sayest, he sayth.

A, ante L.

Ala, a wynge of a byrde, and a wyng of a battayle, whyche is proprelye of horsemenne.

Alacer, et alacris, alacre, quycke of spirite, or of wytte, lusty of courage, mery, and he that lyueth in hope: proprely he that is in a meane betwene glad and sorie. Somtime it betokeneth a man redy and willing, therof commeth Alacritas, redynes or promptnes of wyll. also feruentnes of mynde.

Alatus, ta, tum, wynged.

Alauda, a larke.

Albarium, the parget of a wall.

Albedo, albetudo, albor, whytenes.

Albeo, bui, bere, to be whyte.

Albeus, et albeolus, a chessebourde.

Albico, aui, are, to be whyte.

Albidus, a, um, somewhat whyte.

Albo, aui, are, to make whyte.

Albugo, ginis, a whyte spotte in the eyen. also the whyte of an egge.

Album, a table openly sette vp, wherin eyther the names of officers, or some publike decree is wrytten.

Albumen, albuminis, the whyte of an egge.

Alburnum, the fatte that is in some tree.

Albus, ba, bum, whyte.

Alcedines, et Alcyones, are byrdes of the see, whiche do hatche their yong chykens on the lande, and do lay their egges on the sandes, in myddes of the wynter, and whā the see is mooste troublous, if they do lay, it becommeth sodaynly calme, and the stormes and wyndes do ceasse, vntyl these birdes haue all hatched, and brought vp theyr chykens, and made them redy to flee: whiche is in the space of .xiiii. dayes. This birde is lyttell more than a sparowe, his fethers be purple of colour, myxt with whyte, and hath a longe necke and a smal, his byl somwhat grene, longe, and sclender, and this byrde is sene very seldome.

Alea, a dye, playinge at dyes. somtyme it signifieth chance. Alea fortunæ, The chance of fortune. somtyme peryll.

Aleator, a dysar.

Alecula, a sprotte.

Ales, alitis, a byrde, sometyme it signifyeth swyfte in fleing, or runnyng: as Alite planta, swyfte of foote.

Alexicacon, a remedy to putte away myschiefe, or any yll thyng.

Alexipharmacum, the generall name of medicines, whiche do expell syckenes.

Alga, reyte, or wedes of the see.

Algeo, alsi, algére, to be in peyne, proprely for colde, to chyll for colde.

Algor, grefe, sometime it signifieth colde.

Aliás, an aduerbe, sygnifieth, or els, elles where, an other tyme, sometyme.

Alias res agis, Thou takest no heede what is spoken.

Alibi, els where.

Alica, a drynke made of wheate brayed in a stone morter, the huskes of the wheate beinge taken cleane away.

Alicubi, somewhere, aliubi.

Alicunde, from some place.

Alienigena, a straunger borne.

Alienigenus, na, num, that whiche comethe out of an other countrey.

Alieno, naui, nare,: to alienate, to putte away, or putte of.

Abalieno, are, to separate, to put a sonder.

Alienus, na, nū, diuers, vnlyke, not agreable.

Aliger, any thynge that hath wynges.

Alimentum, alimonia, sustynaunce, fode, or lyuynge.

Alioqui, or els, excepte that.

Aliorsum, to some other place.

Alipedes, swyfte runnynge horses.

Aliptes, he that anoynteth a man, and a surgion that healeth woundes.

Aliqua, by some place.

Aliquando, sometyme.

Aliquantisper, a lyttell whyle.

Aliquantum, aliquantulum, somewhat.

Aliquatenus, in some parte, by some reason.

Aliquid, some thynge.

Aliquis, some man. Aliquis est, He is a man of no small estimation.

Aliquo, to some place.

Aliquorsum, towarde some place.

Aliquot, some, nor many, nor fewe.

Ali=

Aliquoties, at somtymes.
Aliter, or els, contrary wise.
Aliunde, from an other place.
Alius, alia, aliud, other, or an other.
Allabor, labi, to flow by, sayl by, or rowe by
Allatus, brought.
Allecto, aui, are, to allure or drawe to, by fayrenes, to allure.
Allectus, allured.
Allego, lexi, gere, to ascrybe, to cheese, to assygne.
Allego, aui, are, to sende, to allege, or bring forthe, to depute, or gyue auctoritie.
Allegoria, a figure or inuersion of wordes, where it is in wordes one, and an other in sentence or meanynge.
Alleluya, prayse ye our lorde.
Alleuo, aui, are, to lyfte vp.
Allex, & allux, the greatte toe, whanne he lyeth ouer the nexte toe.
Alliatum, a sauce made with garlyke.
Allicifacio, feci, re, to allure, to drawe to.
Allicio, exi, licere, to allure.
Allido, si, ere, to squatte or throw any thing agaynst the grounde or walles.
Alligo, aui, are, to bynde to.
Allium, garlyke.
Allophylos, a straunger.
Alloquor, to speake to.
Allubesco, to doo it gladdely, to obeye, to fauour, to consente.
Allucinatio, a blyndenes of mynde.
Allucinor, to be deceyued in opynyon, to fantasye.
Alludo, allusi, alludere, to doo a thynge in iape, to speake merily, or consent. somtyme it sygnifieth to speake some thynge, which secretly hath some other vnderstandyng.
Alludere ad hystoriam, to speke or do some thynge agreable with somme hystorie before wrytten.
Alluo, lui, ere, to flowe nigh to, to washe as the water dothe the grounde, whan it floweth ouer it.
Alluuium, a floode caused by rayne, or by ryuers whan they rise.
Alluuies is whan abundance of water mixt with claye, couereth the grounde.
Almus, ma, mum, al thinge that noryssheth vs, proprely the erth is so called, Alma tellus, bycause we haue therof our sustinance. Sometyme it signifieth quiete, Almus dies, A quiete day. in Virgile.
Alma, a virgin hydde, or secrete.
Alnus, an alder tree. Somtyme it signifyeth a shyppe or bote.
Alo, alui, alere, to nouryshe or fede.
Alonge, farre of.
Alopecia, a syckenes of the heed, whereby

the heares do falle of.
Alpes, the mountaynes, whiche do depart nowe Italy and Fraunce.
Altare, an altar.
Alter, rius, teri, an other, the other, one of the two.
Alius, an other, the other. Alter, the other, the seconde. Sometyme it sygnifieth both. Vnus aut alter, one or bothe. Vnus et alter, The one and the other.
Alter, teris, siue alteres, teris, poyses of lead, made to lyfte vp with bothe handes, to exercyse men, whyche may not otherwyse labour: wherof there be now many in England, specially in the chambres of studētes.
Altercor, caris, to contende with wordes one with an other on sondry partes.
Alternatim, by tourne, one at one tyme, an other at an other tyme.
Alternis, nowe one, nowe an other.
Alternis diebus, sondrye dayes, where one day is betwene.
Alternare, to do thynges by tourne, nowe one and than an other.
Alternatio, succession by tourne.
Altero, aui, are, to alter or chaunge.
Alteruter, bothe the one and the other. also or the tone or the tother.
Althæa, the great malowes.
Altilis, in plurali, altilia, all thynge that is franked to make fatte, be it beaste, fyshe, or foule. Altilis gallina, a henne franked or fed
Altisonus, he that maketh noyse frō aboue.
Altitonans, he that thoundereth, whiche name the paynyms gaue to their god Jupyter.
Altiuolans, all thyng that flyeth hygh.
Altrinsecus, to the tone or the tother, to the tone parte, betwene the one and the other, in the higher parte. *Apuleius.*
Altus, ta, tu, high, depe, proprely in the see. it sygnifieth also excellent, glorious, anciēt. *Vergilius.*
Aluearium, et Alueare, a place where hiues be sette. also a stocke of hyues.
Alueolum, et alueolus, a basket or mawnde, also a culuerhole, a chessebourde, or tables to playe on.
Alueus et aluus, a hyue for bees, a vessaile to washe in, the bealy of any thing that lacketh lyfe. sometyme it signifieth a shyppe.
Aluini, they whiche be moche vexed with freattynges in the bealy.
Alumen, alumme.
Alumnari, to nourse or brynge vp.
Alumnus, a sonne or scolar that is brought vp of a man, as of his owne father, eyther with sustinance, maners, or lernynge.
Aluta, lether proprely tawed. somtime it is put for a bagge or a pourse.

Alu-

Alutamen, any thynge made of lether.
Alutarius, a tawyer.
Aluus, the bealy, also a hyue.

A, ante M.

Amabilis, bile, amyable, worthye to be loued.
Amabo, of felowship, a good felowshyp, a familiar word vsed among frendes.
Amabundus, he that is a great louer, or amorous.
Amando, aui, are, to countremaunde.
Amans, amantis, a louer be it man or woman.
Amanter, louyngely.
Amanuensis, a clerke or secretarye, alway attendynge.
Amaracus, maioram.
Amo, aui, are, to loue hartily.
Amaresco, sci, scere, to waxe bytter, or to be bytter.
Amaritudo, dinis, bytternesse.
Amarulentus, vexed with malyce.
Amasius et Amasia, he or she that louethe, or is loued.
Amator, a louer, or he that is amorous.
Amatorculus, a small or symple louer.
Amatorie, lyke a louer.
Amatorium, a drynke charmed, to make a manne a louer.
Amatorius, ria, rium, that whyche pertayneth to loue.

Cæsar cōmen, li.6. Ambactus, a seruaunte.
Ambages, a cyrcuite of wordes, or a tale drawen in length.
Ambagiosus, sa, sum, that aboundeth in suche fourme of speakynge.
Ambidexter, he that vseth bothe handes lyke welle.
Ambigo, to compasse. also to doubte.
Ambigue, doubtefully.
Ambiguum, a doubte.
Ambio, iui, ire, to compasse, to seke for promotion, to desyre, to praye, or intreate.
Ambitio, nis, inordynate desyre of honour or auctoritte.
Ambitiosus, he that immoderately desyreth honour.
Ambitus, ambitus, a cyrcute: also the offence of ambition, made by the lawes.
Ambo, bothe.
Ambrosia, was called of the Paynyms the meate of goddis. Some do saye, that it is an herbe of the kynde of Mugworte.
Ambulacrum, a priuate place to walke in, a walke or galerie.
Ambulatio, walkyng, and a walking place.
Ambulator, a walker or styrer.
Ambulo, aui, are, to walke or styrre aboute.
Amburo, bussi, rere, to bourne all about.

Amens, madde.
Amentum, a thonge, or that which is bounden to the myddes of a darte, or iauelyne, to caste it.
Ames, amitis, a perche for a hawke.
Ametor, he that lacketh his mother.
Amice, frendely.
Amicinum, a canne or potte, wherout they powre wyne.
Amicio, ciui, cire, to clothe, to putte on a garmente.
Amicitia, amitie or frendshyppe.
Amictus, cta, ctum, cladde.
Amictus, ctus, ctui, a garment or apparayle.
Amicus et amica, a frende, a louer.
Amicus, ca, cum, ioyned to a thyng, lacking lyfe, signifieth profitable, or holsome.
Amita, my fathers syster, myne aunte.
Amitini, cosyn germayns by broder & sister.
Amitto, misi, tere, to suffre to depart, to lose to sende, to lette passe, to take fro.
Amnis, a ryuer, or brooke.
Amodo, from hensforthe.
Amæno, naui, nare, to make mery, or glad.
Amænus, na, num, pleasaunt or dilectable.
Locus amænus, A delectable place.
Amænum ingenium, a pleasant wytte.
Amænitas, tatis, pleasure, dilectablenesse, or myrthe.
Amolior, I remoue with great peyne.
Admolior, I put to, or sette vpon a thinge.
Amor, loue.
Amoueo, moui, mouere, to remoue, to put from a place or a thynge.
Amphora, a measure, whiche euery waye contayneth a foote. it may be vsed for euery potte that is caryed aboute.
Amphorarius, he that beareth the potte, a taukarde bearer.
Amplector, ti, to imbrace.
Amplio, aui, are, to make more, to draw to.
Ampliatus, a manne repried, or delayed in iugement, vpon some difficultie or consyderation.
Amplitudo, greatnesse of power or maiestie, sometyme it sygnifyeth largenes, Terræ amplitudo, The largenes of the coūtrey.
Ampliuagus, moche wandryng.
Amplius, more.
Amplus, pla, plum, large, wyde.
Amplustra, Amplustria, uel Aplustra, The takelynge of the shyppe.
Ampulla, an oyle potte. Also a bottelle or flagon, sometyme it signifyeth a thyng that is blowen or puffed. Suetonius vseth that worde for a drynkyng glasse. *Suetonius in Domitiano.*
Ampullor, I swelle for pryde.
Amputo, taui, tare, to cutte of.
Amula, a water pot, and it may be vsed for
a holy

holy water potte. See Calepine.
Amuletum, any thinge that is ordeyned agaynst poysonynge.
Amurca, the mother or rome of all oyles.
Amussis, the masons or carpenters rule.
Amigdalus, an almonde tree.
Amigdalum, an almonde.

A, ante N.

AN, whyther, or if.
Anas, natis, a ducke.
Anatinus, lyke a ducke.
Anatarius, ria, rium, of a ducke.
Anathema, in holy Scripture betokeneth separation, els where it signifyeth a thyng offered or sette vp in a temple or churche, as thynges offered and hanged vp.
Anathematizo, aui, are, to curse or gyue to the deuylle.
Anatomia, anotomie or cuttyng of men by phisytions, to consyder the inwarde partes and membres.
Anceps ancipitis, doubteful.
Anchora, an anchore.
Ancile, a shielde without corners, such one in the tyme that Numa was king of Rome, was sene falle out of the skye.
Ancilla, a mayden seruant it was propzely taken for a bondewoman.
Ancillor, to serue humbly and diligently.
Anclo, aui, are, to drawe wyne or other lykoure.
Anfractus, windinges and turnynges, specially in the grounde.
Angaria, a constraynt or compulsion.
Angelus, an aungelle.
Angina, a disease in the throote, called the Quynse.
Angiportus, a great hole in the erthe with many tournynges, or that whyche hathe none issue out, or a lane in a towne, whyche leadeth the nexte waye to a strete, or that whiche lyeth on an hauen, whereby marchandyse is caried from the water, or re caryed.
Ango, anxi, angere, to tourmente or vexe.
Angor, anguythe of body or mynde.
Anxietas, anxietudo, anguysshe or sorowe.
Anguilla, an ecle.
Anguis, a snake.
Angularis, lare, cornerde.
Angulatim, cornerwise.
Angulosus, full of corners.
Angulus, a corner.
Angustia, straytnes, or perplexitie of mind.
Angustus, ta, tum, strayte.
Anhelitus, brethe or wynde of a man.
Anhelo, aui, re, to fetch wind, or draw breth.
Anhelus, he that drawethe his breathe peynefullye.
Animaduerto, tere, to consyder, to take heede, to sette my mynde, to beholde, and to thynke.
Animaduersio, consyderacion, punisshment.
Animæquius, mequia, quium, pacyente, or sufferynge.
Animal, all thynge that hathe lyfe, and is sensyble, commonly it is taken for a beaste.
Animalis, le, that wherin is lyfe.
Animans, idem quod animal, sauynge that it is more larger. For it maye sygnyfye all thynge that hath spirite, as welle in heuen, as on erthe.
Anima, the sowle. sometyme lyfe.
Animatus, animata, matum, that hath sowle or lyfe.
Animo, aui, are, to gyue courage or boldenesse, to quycken.
Animositas, boldenesse.
Animosus, bolde.
Animus, the mynde, the wyl. somtime it is put for the soule: sometyme for affection or delectation, sometyme for wynde or blast, somtyme for wrathe, sometyme for a sowne.
Annitor, to resyste, or to helpe, to sette to my mynde.
Annales, Histories of actes yerely done.
Annalis, le, Annarius, ria, rium, that whiche is done yerely.
Annascor, to grow or to be borne by a place or manne.
Anniculus, la, lum, that whyche is of oone yere olde.
Annilis, le, aged.
Annilis fabula, an olde wyues tale, or a tale without fruite.
Annona, vyttayles, sustynance, or lyuynge. Somtyme it betokeneth fyndyng in borde and apparayle.
Annonariæ expensæ, expenses in vitayle.
Annosus, sa, sum, aged.
Annoto, aui, are, to note, to intitle.
Annotinæ naues, shyppes that cary corne.
Annuatim, yerely.
Annuus, a yere.
Annus, a, um, that duryth one yere.
Anquina, the corde wherwith the sayle is bounde to the maste.
Anquiro, to seke.
Ansa, the eare or handel of a potte or cup. And sometyme it sygnifieth occasion. somtyme a bouckle.
Anser, a goose.
Anserinus, na, num, lyke a goose.
Antæ, the postes on euerye syde of the doore.
Ante, antea, before.

Ante alios, aboue other, before other, more than other, or besyde other.
Antecapio, cœpi, capere, to preuent.
Antecedo, cessi, dere, to go before, to excel.
Antecello, cellui, lere, to excell or haue preemynence.
Antecessum, payde before hande.
Antecœnium, a colation or drynkynge betwene dynar and supper.
Anteeo, iui, ire, to precede or excell, or goo before.
Antefero, to putte before, or set more by.
Ante hac, before this tyme, or before that tyme.
Anteloquium, the fyrst tourne in speaking.
Antelucanus, na, num, that which is before daye lyghte.
Anteluco, aui, are, to wake before daye.
Anteluculo, before day lyght.
Antenna, the crossepiece wherto the sayle is fastened.
Antepagmentum, a portall.
Antepono, sui, nere, to preferre.
Anterius, longe before.
Antes, outwarde pyllars or postes, wherby the house or frame is susteyned.
Antesignani, they whiche be next the standarde, appoynted for to defende it.
Antesto, to excelle, or stande before.
Antestor, to make my iudge.
Anteuenio, ueni, nire, to preuente.
Anteuerto, to preuent.
Antiæ, the heare of a woman, that is layde ouer hir foreheed, nowe gentylwomen do call them their rolles.
Antica, all that is before vs.
Anticipo, aui, are, to preuente.
Antidotarius, a boke of medicines.
Antidotum, a medicine to expell poyson.
Antigraphum, an example.
Antilena, a peutrell.
Antiquarius, he that sercheth for antyquities, or redethe olde warkes, or vseth olde forme of speakynge or writinge.
Antiquo, aui, are, to make voyde, to reduce to the fyrste state, to repelle. Antiquare legem, to repell a lawe.
Antiquus, a, um, auncient or olde, sometime it signifieth noble or worshypfull.
Antiquitas, tatis, auncientie.
Antiquitus, of auncient or olde tyme.
Antistes, antistitis, a prelate.
Antista, an abbesse or priozesse.
Antistitium, prelacy, or preeminence.
Antistitor, he that hathe ouer other preemynence.
Antlia, a pumpe to drawe water.
Antrum, a denne.
Anularius, a ieweller that selleth rynges.

Anulus, a rynge.
Anus, nus, an olde wyfe.
Anus, ni, an arse.
Anxifer, he that causeth sorowe.
Anxius, anxia, carefull or heuye.
Anxietas, anxietudo, care or heuynesse.

A, ante P.

APage, remoue, putte away, or dryue away. Also it hath a signification of a more vehemency: as Apage hanc caniculã, Away with this bytche: or, hens away with this bytche.
Apage sis, lette be, gette the hens.
Apella, withoute a skynne. So be the Jewes called of Horacius, bycause they be cyrcuncyded.
Aper, apri, a bore.
Aperio, ui, ire, to open, to disclose, to expownde.
Apes uel apis, a bee.
Apex, apicis, the crowne of the heed, the toppe of euery thynge, it sometyme sygnifyeth a mytar.
Apexabo, the gutte whiche is ful of blode, mixte with grease.
Aphrica, one of the thre partis of the world wherof the inhabitantes be at this day called generallye Moores or Morynes, the countreyes be nowe called Tunyse, Fese, Marocke.
Apianus, na, num, that wherein bees doo delyte.
Apiarium, the place where as hyues be sette.
Apiarius, he that nourisheth bees.
Apiastra, a byrde whiche doothe deuowre Bees.
Apiastrum, smallage, an herbe.
Apicæones, shepe, hauynge smalle bodies, and lyttell wolle.
Apicula, a yonge bee.
Apinæ, nuttes without shales.
Apionia mala, rounde appulles, whyche I take to be they, that are called pomeroyall.
Apium, an herbe called ache, somtyme it is taken for our commune persely.
Apologia, a defence or aunswere to a rebuke.
Apologo, aui, are, to requyre or aske.
Apologus, a fable, wherin beastes or trees doo speake.
Apophoretum, a presente.
Apopthegma, matis, a shorte and quycke sentence.
Apoplexia, a sodeyne palsey.
Apostata, a Rebelle. It is nowe vsed for them,

them, whiche do forsake the relygion, that they haue ones receyued.

Apostema, an impostume, wherin corrupted humours haue recourse in any parte of the bodye.

Apostolus, an apostel. it properly signifieth a messanger.

Apotheca, a wyne seller, or shoppe, wherin thinges be sette to sale.

Appareo, rui, rêre, to appiere.

Apparitores, officers of iustice, attendyng on the great ministers, to somon or attache whom they wyll commaunde.

Apparitura, the offyce of a Sergeaunt or baylyffe.

Apparatus, tus, apparaylynge or deckyng.

Apparatus belli, preparation for warres, artyllerye.

Appellatio, a namynge, or appelynge to a hygher iuge.

Appello, aui, are, to name or calle familiarly to me. Also Ulpian the great lawyer wyl haue it to sygnyfye, to wowe a mayden to haue her virginitie. sometyme it sygnifieth to arryue : Sommetyme to appeale to a higher iudge.

Appello, appuli, appulsum, to aryue. sometyme to apply or sette my mynde, to direct.

Appulsus, appulsus, commynge of beastis to wateringe.

Appendeo, appendis, pendere, to hange by or nighe.

Appendix, that which hangeth at an other thynge.

Appendo, dis, dere, to hange vp, to waye in a balance or beame.

Appeto, tii, tere, to desyre moche, to go to. sometyme it signifieth to be at hande. Dies appatebat, The daye was come, or at hand. somtyme to wounde or stryke at, as, Leuâs se alis, os oculosq́ hostis, rostro et unguibus appetit, Rysynge with his wynges, his talons and beke, he wounded the face & eies of him that faught on the other parte.

Applaudere, to moue handes or feete for ioye, or to beate any thyng to the ground.

Applico, applicaui, applicare, uel applicui applicere, to ioyne to, to laye to, or sette to, or to applye.

Applodo, plosi, dere, supra applaudere.

Appluda, chaffe.

Apporto, aui, are, to brynge to.

Appositus, ta, tum, put to, or set to. somtime it signifieth conuenient, or to the purpose.

Apprime, chiefely, principally.

Approbus, very honeste.

Apricari, to sytte or go abrode in the ayre, or in the sonne.

Apricus, a place sette agaynste the sonne.

Aprilis, the moneth of Apryll.
Aprinus, bores fleshe.
Aprono in genua, to knele on my knees.
Aptitudo, aptenes.
Apto, aui, are, to ioyne, to agree two thinges togither.
Aptus, ta, tum, apte, agreable, mete, necessarye.
Apud, at, whan it is ioyned with a person, it signifieth with.

A ante Q.

Aqua, water.
Aquagium, a cundyte.
Aqualiculus, a lyttell trowgh.
Aqualicus, the panche.
Aqualis, A basyne to wasshe in mennes handes.
Aquaricola, a place, wherin water is caste.
Aquariolum, Aquarium, a wasshyng place.
Aquaticus, that whyche haunteth the water, or lyueth therin.
Aquatilis, the same.
Aquatus, ta, tum, that, wherinto water is putte. Vinum aquatum, Alayed wyne.
Aqueus, a, um, watrye.
Aquila, an egle.
Aquilex, he that sercheth for water, or conuayeth it.
Aquilifer, the standarde bearer of the Romaynes.
Aquilo, the northest wynde.
Aquilus color, russette.
Aquiminaria, all water pottes.
Aquitania, Guyen.
Aquo, aui, are, to fetche or beare water.
Aquosus, sa, sum, full of water.
Aquula, lyttell water.

A ante R.

Ara, an Aultare.
Aranea, a copwebbe. Sommetyme a spyder.
Araneus, a spyder.
Arator, a ploughmanne. and sommetyme a ploughe oxe.
Aratrum, a ploughe.
Arbiter, tri, an arbitratour.
Arbitrarium, arbitrable.
Arbitrium, arbytrement, wyll, an espyall.
Arbitror, to trowe, to iudge, or awarde.
Arbor, et arbos, a tree.
Arborator, a lopper of trees.
Arborescere, to waxe to a tree.
Arboreus, ea, reum, of a tree.
Arbustum, a place where trees be sette, properlye Elmes, wythye, or Salowe.

it may be taken for an orchard, or a hoppe-
yarde, or a vyneyarde, where vynes doo
growe vp by trees.
Arbustum, a vyne that runeth vp in height
by a tree or a pole.
Arbusto, aui, are, to sette vines by trees.
Arbutū, an appull called a wyldinge.
Arbutus, a wyldyng tree.
Arca, a coffer.
Arcanum, a thynge secrete, or of fewe
knowen.
Arcatus, bent lyke a bowe.
Arceo, cui, ere, to strayne, to putte of, to
dryue away.
Arcera, a horse lytter.
Arcesso, to accuse, to calle for.
Archarius, a stewarde of housholde.
Archetypus, the firste example or paterne.
Archiater, tri, a chiefe phisytion.
Archimagirus, chiefe Coke.
Architector, aris, ari, to make craftily.
Architectura, the cunnyng of diuysyng of
buyldynge.
Architector, et architectus, a diuiser of buil-
dyng, or a maister of the warkes.
Architriclinus, mayster of the feaste.
Archiuum, the treasorie of Monumentes
and euydences belongynge to a kynge or a
Cytie.
Arcto, aui, are, to strayne oftentymes.
Arctus, ta, tum, streyght.
Arcuatus, facioned lyke a bowe.
Arcubalista, a crossebowe.
Arcula, a lyttell coffer or caskette.
Arculus, a rolle that womenne doo weare
on their heedes, to beare water or mylke
easylye.
Arcus, a bowe, the vaut of a roufe.
Ardea, a byrde called an heron.
Ardelio, a besy manne medlynge with ma-
ny thynges.
Ardeo, arsi, dére, to burne, to loue ardent-
ly, or excedyngly, to make haste, to be cō-
sumed, to desyre.
Ardens, tis, hasty in doinge, quycke witted.
Ardesco, to be hasty.
Arduus, high and difficult, hard to com to.
Area, a large place in a Cytie kepte e-
uer cleane, where marchauntes do assem-
ble: as I haue sene in dyuers cyties in Al-
mayne. Also it is euerye place marked oute
to buyld or to set an house in. Also a floore,
where corne is thrashed.
Areator, a thresher.
Arefacio, to make drie.
Arena, sande.
Arenaceus, ea, eum, sandy.
Arenatus, arenata, natum, pargetted with
lyme and sande.

Arenosus, sandye.
Arenula, fyne sande.
Areo, rui, rere, to be made drie.
Areola, a bedde in a garden.
Aresco, scere, to waxe drye, or to be made
drye.
Arctalogus, a bragger or a vaunter of his
owne vertues, sometyme a forger of lyes,
to make men merye.
Argentariā facit, he maketh or occupieth a
banke for exchaunge.
Argentarius, a banker, with whom men doo
make their exchaunge of money.
Argenteus, a, um, of syluer.
Argentum, syluer. sommetyme it sygnifyeth plate.
Argilla, potters claye.
Argumentatio, the declaration of an argument.
Argumentor, mentaris, mentari, to argue
or raison.
Argumentosus, sa, um, that whiche is done
with great reason.
Argumentum, is a raison, makyng a profe,
wherby one thinge is gathered by an nother, and the whiche confirmeth that, whiche is doubtefulle, by that whiche is not
doubtefull. somtyme it signifyeth a mattier,
sommetyme coniecture, sometyme a shorte
exposition of that whiche foloweth, other
while sentence.
Arguo, gui, ere, to reproue, to impute, to
accuse, to shewe.
Argutiæ, sharpe wordes or shrewde.
Argutor, aris, ari, to speke sharply, shrewd-
ly, or pertely.
Argutulus, somewhat perte.
Argutus, ta, tum, reproued. sometyme it sygnyfyeth shrewde, and he that can in speakynge sharpely inserche a mans mynd. Also shryll of voyce.
Arguti homines, they that speake moche in
fewe wordes.
Argutum, sclender or smalle.
Ariditas, et aritudo, dryenesse.
Aridus, drye.
Aries, arietis, a Ramme. Also a piece of
ordynaunce or engyne, made lyke a ram-
mes heed, to beate downe a walle. It is al-
so oone of the xii. sygnes that the Sunne
passeth by.
Arietinus, of a ramme.
Arieto, taui, are, to hytte or throwe downe.
Arista, the berde of corne. sometyme it is
putte for wheate.
Arithmetica, aulgoryme, the scyence of
noumbrynge.
Arma, orum, harneyes and weapon. Also
the instrumentes of all maner of craftes.
Also

Also standardes and baners, sommetyme battayles.

Armamenta, tooles, instrumentes, all store for warres or shyppes.

Armamentarium, an armorie or storehouse for shyppes or ordinance.

Armarium, a study where bokes are laide, or a drye larder.

Armati, armed men.

Armatura, armure.

Armator, an armorer.

Armentarius, the keper of the armorie.

Armentum, store of horse or nete. somtyme it sygnifyeth cattell.

Armiger, geri, proprely an esquyer for the body, as he, whiche alwaye attendynge about a knyght, beareth his hedpiece, his speare, and his shielde, a custrell.

Armillæ, rynges that gentylmenne vsed to weare aboute their armes, as at this daye some men and women do vse, called bracelettes.

Armille neutri generis, a facyon of deceipt.

Armillum, a vessel wherin they vsid in their sacrifice to put wyne.

Armipotens, puissant in armes.

Armo, aui, are, to arme.

Armus, the shoulder of a beaste, or the pynion of a fowle.

Aro, aui, are, to eare or plowe lande.

Arquatus morbus, the syckenesse calleddé the iaundise.

Arreptitius, he that is obsessed with an yll spyrite.

Arrha et Arrhabo, ernest money.

Arrigo, rigi, ere, to water grounde.

Aripio, pui, ere, to take.

Arrogo, aui, are, to gyue to moche, to presume, to make myne heyre.

Arrogans, arrogant or presumptuous.

Arrogantia, arrogance, presumption.

Ars, artis, a crafte, subtyltie.

Arteria, a synewe lyke to a vayne, wherein the spirite of lyfe doth walke, as the blode dothe in vaynes.

Articulatim, from ioynte to ioynte.

Articulo, aui, are, to ioyne one ioynte to another.

Articulus, a ioynt. also a moment or parcel of tyme. also a colour of Rhetorike.

Artifex, a craftesman.

Artificium, the practise of a crafte.

Arto, aui, are, to strayne, to thraste togyther, to wrynge.

Artocopus, a baker.

Artoptitius panis, breadde made of wheat, whiche is harde and soore dryed, biskatte.

Artuo, aui, are, to cutte a sonder.

Artus, membres.

Aruina, talowe.

Arundinetum, a place where reedes doo growe.

Arundo, a rede, or cane.

Aruspex, he that telleth of thinges to come by lokynge in beastes bowelles.

Aruum, a falowe felde.

Arx, arcis, a fortresse or castelle, specyally standynge hyghe.

A ante S.

As, assis, a pounde weyghte. In the olde tyme in the partition of lande, or other lyke thynge inherytable, they called the hole, As, and the partes diuided, ounces.

Asarotum, peynted pament, whiche maye not be swepte.

Ascendo, di, ere, to clymme, to ascende, to goo vp.

Ascia, a chyppe axe.

Ascio, aui, to chyppe or cutte with an axe.

Ascio, is, to knowe surely.

Ascisco, sciui, scire, to presume, to take vpon me a thinge.

Ascisco, ascisci, asciscere, to admytte, to take to me.

Ascribo, psi, bere, to adde to, to attribute, to impute.

Asscriptitius, he that is added to the nombre of other.

Assciptor, oris, he that foloweth the example of an other, or he that writeth many copies of others exaumples.

Asella, the arme hole.

Asia, one of the thre partes of the worlde.

Asinarius, an asseherde.

Asinus, an asse.

Asotus, prodigall, wanton, incontynente.

Aspecto, aspectaui, aspectare, to beholde stedfastely.

Aspectus, syght, beholdynge.

Asper, vnpleasant, as well in sight and herynge, as in taste. also harde or greuous.

Aspergillus, a holy water stycke.

Aspergo, aspersi, gere, to sprynge or caste water.

Aspergo, ginis, a spryngynge of lycour.

Aspernabilis, he that is worthy to be dispysed, or refused.

Aspernor, aris, ari, to despyse, to refuse, to abhorre.

Aspero, asperaui, asperare, to make sharper or harde.

Asphaltum, the deed see. Also a certayne claye there founden, whiche ones burning, wyll neuer be quenched.

Aspicio, aspexi, aspicere, to beholde, to see.

B.iiii. Aspiro,

A ante S.

Aspiro, aui, are, to aspire, to loke to come to a thynge, to blowe, to fauoure, to gyue ayde, to gyue all my studye and wytte to optayne a thynge, to touche, to go to.
Aspis, an adder or serpent.
Asporto, aui, are, to carie away.
Asatura, roste meate.
Assecla, a page, and he that foloweth in all thynge the wylle of an other man.
Assector, aris, ari, to kepe company.
Assensor, oris, he that consenteth.
Assentio, si, tire, & assentior, to consente, or assente.
Assentor, aris, to flatter in commendyng an other mans actes that be yll.
Assequor, eris, qui, to folowe, to gette, to optayne.
Asseres, bourdes.
Assero, ris, to sowe, or plante by. Also to clayme, to affirme or approue, to manumise or make free.
Assertio, an affyrmaunce.
Assessor, oris, associate to a man in offyce or auctoritye.
Asseruo, to kepe diligentely, to take heede of one.
Asseuero, as, are, to affyrme.
Afsideo, I sytte with or by an other, or I am assocyate.
Afsido, is, dere, to reste me, to sytte downe, to sytte by.
Afsiduus, contynuall, or sufficient.
Afsidui fideiussores, Sufficient sureties.
Afsigno, aui, are, to assygne or appoint.
Afsilio, ui, ire, to leape forth also Afsilire, is to leape, as a horse leapeth a mare.
Afsis, is, a sawen bourde.
Afsisto, stiti, afsistere, to be here, to defende a mannes cause.
Asso, aui, are, to laye bourdes, to roste.
Assuefacio, wonte.
Assuetudo, wonte, or custome.
Assuetus, accustomed.
Assula, a chyppe.
Assulatim, in chyppes.
Assumo, assumpsi, mere, to take, propiely it sygnyfyeth to take to moche on me.
Assuo, ui, assuere, to sowe to, or piece.
Assurgo, rexi, gere, to ryse to an other better than my selfe, to gyue place, to growe vpwarde.
Assus, a, um, rosted.
Ast, but. also therfore, as well, moreouer.
Aster, a Sterre.
Astericus, a lyttell marke in wrytynge like a Sterre.
Asthmaticus, he that drawethe his wynde shorte.
Astipulor, to leane to, to fauour.

A ante T.

Asto, astiti, to stande by, to be present.
Astragalizo, to playe at dyse or tables.
Astragalus, the play at tables.
Astringo, to ioyne, or bynde togyther, to bynde by couenant or promyse.
Astrolabium, an Astrolabe or instrumente of astronomy.
Astronomia, the parte of astronomye that concerneth iudicials and practise.
Astrologia, the speculation and reasonyng cócernyng the celestial or heuenly motiōs.
Astrum, a celestial body compacte of many sterres, as a sygne.
Astruo, to buylde, to ioyne oone house to an other, to fortifie, to affirme.
Astus, crafte or subtiltie.
Astu, craftily, or subtylly.
Astutiæ, subtylties.
Astutus, ta, tum, subtyll or crafty.
Asylum, a saynctuarie.

A, ante T.

At, a voyce, whiche signifieth in the wordes that do folowe, wrath or indignation. Sommetyme it signifieth (but yet) whyche is a discrepaunce in the wordes that are spoken. Sommetyme it sygnifyeth Sed.
At contra, contrarye wyse.
Attamino, aui, are, to fowle or defyle.
At at, tusshe, or fye.
Attauus, a greatte graundefather
Atar, tra, trum, blacke or darke.
Athleta, a greatte wrastler, or a great runner at commune games.
Athletica, the craft of wrastlyng or runyng.
Athletheta, the iuge in games of wrastling or runnynge.
Atomus, a thynge so small, that it may not be deuyded or made smaller. Also Atomi, be motes of the sonne.
Atq;, and so, as it were.
Atqui, surely, all be it.
Atra bilis, Melancoly.
Attramentarium, an ynkehorne.
Attramentum, ynke, blacke, that showmakers do occupie.
Atratus, a mourner that gothe in blacke.
Atri dies, dysmall dayes.
Atricus, a porter that kepeth a gate.
Atriensis, an husher of the halle.
Atrium, an inner courte.
Atrox, atrocis, cruell, terrible, or sowre in countenaunce.
Attendo, di, dere, to take heede, to consyder, to intende.
Attente, intentifely, with a fyxed mynde.
Attentio, a mynde sette or fyxed.

At

Attento, to attempte.
Attenuo, to appeyre, to make weaker.
Atticismus, a peculyare eloquence vsed in Athenes.
Atticisso, to speake like a man of Athenes.
Atticus, ca, cum, of Athenes.
Attiguus, by or nigh ioynynge to.
Attineo, ui, ere, to pertayne. Attinet, it besemeth, it is conuenient.
Attingo, attigi, tingere, to touche almoste.
Attollo, to auaunce, to lyfte vp, to brynge to, to take away.
Attonitus, ta, tum, amased or abashed.
Attrecto, aui, are, to feele.
Attribuo, bui, ere, to attribute, to put vpon one by blamynge or accusynge, to assygne, to commytte.

A ante V.

Avceps, a fowler or byrder.
Auctio, onis, an increase, or an open sale of priuate goodes.
Auctio hastæ, portesale of the goodes of men attaynted for treason or felonye.
Auctionarius, the salesman.
Auctionor, to sell by porte sale.
Aucto, aui, are, to gayne, to wynne.
Autor, he that begynneth any act, or is the fyrste causer or procurer of any thynge.
Autoramentum, an indenture or obligation wherby a man is bounden to do seruice. Also ernest money.
Autorare, to bynde by erneste or wrytynge to serue.
Autoratus, he that is bounde to serue, specyally in warres.
Autoritas, tatis, autoritie. sometime it signifieth power.
Auctuarium, uel auctrarium, ouer measure or weyghte.
Aucupatorii, lyme twygges.
Aucupium, et aucupatio, byrding or fouling.
Aucupor, to go a byrdynge, or a foulyng, or hawkynge. Also it signifieth, to serche by craftye meanes.
Audacia, hardynesse.
Audacter et audaciter, boldly, aduēturously.
Audaculus, hardye, spoken in derisyon, or contempte.
Audax, audacis, bolde or hardy, or trustyng well in hym selfe.
Audeo, ausi, audêre, to dare, to presume.
Audio, diui, dire, to here, to consyder, to perceyue, to graunt that whiche is asked, to do the thynge that is cōmanded.
Auditio, herynge, or audience.
Auditorium, a place where menne do here lessons, or propositions.

Auditus, tus, herynge, one of the fiue wyttꝭ.
Aueho, to carye awaye.
Auellana, a fylberde nutte.
Auena, otes. Somtime it is put for an ote strawe, or a wheate strawe, or reede.
Aueo, uêre, to couaite.
Aue, be thou gladde or ioyfull, as the vulgar people sayth, Reste you mery.
Auersor, aris, to abhorre, to refuse.
Auersus, backewarde, or on the backehalf. also angrye.
Aduersus et auersus, forewarde and backewarde.
Auerto, ti, tere, to tourne away.
Auertor, teris, ti, to disdayne. sommetyme it signifyeth to tourne away, to tourne fro.
Auerunco, aui, are, to tourne away, or putte awaye.
Aufugio, gi, ere, to flee hense.
Augeo, auxi, gere, to increase.
Auctus, ta, tum, increased.
Augesco, sci, scere, to waxe greatte, or be great, to be growen.
Augmento, mentaui, mētare, to increase, or make more.
Augur, auguris, he that telletheby byrdes voyces, or by their flyeng or syttyng, what shall happen.
Auguro, as et auguror, aris, rari, to telle by suche crafte, what shall happen.
Augustus, noble, or full of maiestie. wherfore the emperours of Rome were and yet be called Augusti. Augustus is also the moneth nexte after July.
Auia, a grandame.
Auiarium, a thycke wodde without waye. Also a place where byrdes be kepte and nouryshed.
Auiarius, a keper of byrdes.
Auicula, a lyttell byrde.
Auidus, a, um, couetyse.
Auis, a byrde.
Auitus, ta, tum, that whiche is lefte by auncetours. Auitus ager, Olde inheritance.
Auius, a, um, without waye.
Aula, a haule. somtyme the palaice or court of a prince.
Auléa, tapesry, hangynges of noble mennes houses.
Auoco, caui, care, to calle away.
Auolo, aui, are, to flee away.
Aura, sometyme betokeneth a softe wynd, somtyme brightnes, somtime fauour.
Auramentum, gyltynge.
Auraria, a golde myne.
Aurarii, gylters.
Auratus, ta, tum, gylte.
Aureæ, the hedstall of a horse.
Auris, an eare.

Au

Aureus, a piece of golde in money.
Aureus, a, um, of golde.
Aurichalcum, latyn mettall.
Auricomus, he that hath heare as bryghte as golde.
Auricula, the eare lappe.
Auricularius, a secretarye or priuye councellour.
Auriferum, that beareth golde.
Aurifex, ficis, a goldesmyth.
Aurificina, a goldesmythes shoppe.
Aurifur, a thefe that stealeth golde.
Auriga, a carter or driuer of a cart.
Aurigor, aris, to driue a cart or some thing lyke. Also to gouerne.
Auriscalpium, an eare pyker.
Auritus, greate eared.
Auro, aui, are, to gylte.
Aurora, the mornyng, or sonne risynge.
Aurum, golde.
Ausculto, aui, are, to here diligently, or giue good eare.
Auspex, auspicis, idem quod augur. Also it signifieth the persone that maketh the maryage on the mannes parte. Also the chiefe capytayne in warres.
Auspicium, the sygne or token shewed by byrdes of thynges that shall folowe. Also it betokeneth fortune gouernance, or disposition of a capytayn. Also it is a token or signification of thynges to come.
Auspicor, aris, cari, to take lykelyhode. Also to begynne or entre into a busynesse.
Auster, tri, the southe wynde.
Austerus, sowre or sharpe. Also soore or without pitie.
Austro, aui, are, to make moyste.
Aut, or, either.
Autem, verily, but, or els.
Autographum, his owne hande wrytynge.
Autumo, to suppose, to affirme.
Autumnus, haruest.
Auunculus, the vncle of the mothers side.
Auus, the grandfather.
Auxilior, aris, ari, to ayde or helpe.
Auxiliarius, he that commethe in ayde of an nother.
Auxilium, ayde, or helpe.

A, ante X.

Axis mundi, is a lyne imagined to go streight from the north to the south, dyuydynge the worlde as it were in two partes: at the endes are supposed to be two poyntes in heuen, whiche are called the northe pole and the southe pole.
Axungia, swynes grease.

¶ B, ante A.

Bacca, a berye, as a baye bery, an hawe berye, an eglantine berie.
Baccatus, garnysshed with precious stones.
Bacchanal, lis, the place where the solemnitie of Bacchus was kepte.
Bacchanalia, feastes of the paynyms, whiche they dydde celebrate with all abhominations of lechery.
Bacchar, a wyne potte. It maye be called a quaffinge potte.
Bacchor, aris, ari, to celebrate the feaste of Bacchus, to runne vppe and downe lyke a madde man.
Bacchus, amonge the paynims the god of wyne or drunkennes.
Baculus, a staffe.
Balius, a horse of bay colour.
Baiæ, arum, a place in the royalme of Naples, where be naturalle bathes of warme water bothe plesant and holsome: And by translation some poetes do so call all other naturall hote bathes.
Baiulo, aui, are, to beare.
Baiulus, a porter or cariar of bourdens.
Balæna, a greatte fishe, whiche I suppose to be a thurlepoll.
Balanus a kynd of acornes. it is also a suppositorie to helpe them that be costife. Also a swete oyntmēt made of Mirabolanes.
Balo, aui, are, to blete lyke a shepe.
Balbucinor, aris, to maffle in the mouthe.
Balbus, he that can not pronounce well his wordes whan he speaketh.
Balbutio, iui, ire, to stamer or stutte.
Balinea, a bayne or a bathe.
Balius, balia, liū, baye colour.
Balista, a crossebowe, or a brake. It may be vsed for a gunne.
Balnearia, all thinges belongyng to a bain.
Balnearius, of a bayne, Balneatorius.
Balneator, the keper of a bayne, or he that serueth in a bayne.
Balneum, a priuate bayne.
Balnea pluraliter, a commune bayne.
Baltheus et baltheū, a belt, a sworde girdel.
Bambacium, cotton.
Baptisterium, a bathe or vessell to wasshe in the body. A dienge vate, a fonte.
Barathrum, a vnmeasurable depenes.
Baratro, an vnthrift that in lechery & glottony deuoureth his substance.
Barba, a berde.
Barbari, in the olde tyme were all people, excepte grekes. proprely it be they, which

do speake grossely, without obseruynge of congruite, or pronounce not perfectly, specially Greke or latyne. Also they that abhorre all elegancie. Moreouer it signifieth them, whyche be without letters, fiers or cruelle of maners or countenaunce, barbarouse.

Barbaria, the countreye where dwellythe people rude or beastly.

Barbaricarii, weauers of cloth of baudekin.

Barbaricus, barbarous.

Barbarismus, the corrupte fourme of speakynge or pronouncynge.

Barbatus, ta, tum, berded.

Barbitium, the berde.

Barbitos, an instrument of musyke, whiche I suppose is that, that men call doulsimers.

Bardiacus, a garment.

Bardocucullum, a thrummed hatte, or a shepardes cloke.

Bardus, a foole. Somtyme a mynstrel that syngeth iestes or fables.

Barrire, to braye lyke an olyphant.

Barritus, the brayinge of an oliphant.

Barrus, an olyphaunt.

Basia, honest kysses, swete kysses.

Basiator, a kysser.

Basiatio, a kyssynge.

Basilica, a place where people do assemble for suites in the lawe, and ciuile iugementis be exercised, and counsayles holden. Also it maye be taken for a halle, or other large place, where suiters do attende, or men do wayte on rulers, or great feastes be kepte. It also sygnifyeth a cathedral churche.

Plaut. in Epi. Basilica nux, a wall nutte.

Basilicon, a kynges robe.

Basilicus, ca, cum, royall.

Basilice, royally.

Basilicanus, he that kepeth the place called Basilica.

Basiliscus, a Cocatrice, whiche is a serpent in the desertes of Aphrica, with a whyte cyrkle aboute his heed, hauynge a sharpe heed, redde eyen, and is somewhat blacke of colour, and is so venymous, that he sleeth men and beastes with his breth, & with the syght of his eyen.

Basis, the foote of a pylar, or that whiche susteyneth any lyke thynge. Also it signifieth the foundation or grounde of a matter.

Batris, a vessell with a longe handell.

Batillus, a fyre panne.

Battiola, a wyne potte or flagone.

Batuo, i, ere, to beate with a rodde.

Batus, a measure for wyne or oyle.

Baubare, to barke lyke a dogge.

Baxiæ, slyppers, proprely of phylosophers, or suche other.

Beatus, is he, whiche hath abundaunce of all thynge that is good, and is perfecte in all thynges that be worthy prayse, or ought to be desyred of a good man. sometyme it is taken for noble or fortunate.

Beatitudo et beatitas, is a heape of good thynges gathered togyther, of it selfe sufficient without lacke, and a very perfection accordyng to vertue.

Bellaria, bankettynge dysshes, as tartes, marchepaynes, and other lyke.

Bellarius, ia, um, apte for the warre.

Bellator, a warryour.

Bellatrix, a woman warriour.

Bellatulus, bellatula, a wanton worde, whyche is as moche to say, as lyttell fayre one, well fauoured chylde, praty mayden.

Bellax, acis, vsed or haunted in warres.

Bellicosus, fiers or warlyke.

Bellipotens, puissant in battayle.

Bello, and Bellor, aris, ari, to make warre.

Bellus, la, lum, fayre, pleasant, good.

Bellulus, la, lum, somewhat fayre.

Bellum, signifieth al the tyme that the warres do contynue. also battayle or warre.

Bellua, a great cruell beast or a monster.

Beluata, tapesry, wherin is wrought or paynted the fygures of beastes.

Beluinus, na, num, beastely. Beluina rabies, a beastly furye.

Bene, well, honestly, or prosperously.

Bene de te mereo, I intreate the wel. Thou arte beholden vnto me.

Benedico, dixi, cere, to prayse, to saye welle of a manne.

Benedicus, a man wel tunged, or faire spoke

Beneficiarius, he that receyueth a benefitte or good tourne of an other.

Beneficus, he that is beneficiall or lyberall.

Bene uertere, to turne to good. Precor deū, ut hæc res bene uertat tibi, I pray god this thynge may tourne the to good, or maye be for thy profite.

Bene uolo tibi, I wolde the good.

Beneuolus, fauourable.

Beneuolentia, fauour or good wylle, an intente to do well.

Benignus, na, num, gentylle, benygne, and bounteouse.

Benignitas, bounteousenes.

Beo, aui, are, to comfort, to make happye.

Berillus, is that whiche is commonly called Crystalle.

Bes, bessis, a waight of .viii. ounces.

Bestia, a beaste.

Bestiarii, men whiche in olde tyme faughte with beastes in the syghte of the people.

Beto, to walke forthe. *Varro.*

Bibaculus, he that drinketh often. **Bibax**

Bibax, cis, bibosus, a great drynker.
Biblia, the wyfe of Duilius the Romayne, whiche was of so greate chastitie, that she was at that tyme an example, whan it was a thynge monstrous to here of vnchastitie.
Bibliopola, a stacyoner, or a boke sellar.
Bibliotheca, a lybrary.
Bibo, bibi, bere, to drynke.
Bibulus, la, lum, that souketh vp shortly.
Biceps, bicipitis, that which hath ii. heedes
Biclinium, a chambre with. ii. beddes.
Bicornium, that whiche hath two hornes.
Bicorpus, that whiche hath two bodies.
Bidental, a place where they vsed to sacryfyce shepe, whan any house was bourned with lyghtnynge.
Bidentes, shepe with. ii. teth, called in some place hogrelles, or hogattes.
Biduum, the space of two dayes.
Biennis, bienne, any thing of two yeres old.
Biennium, the space of two yeres.
Bifariam, in two partes, or two maner of wayes.
Bifarie, the same.
Bifera arbor, that beareth twyse in a yere.
Bifidus, clefte.
Bifores, that hath two doores.
Bifrons, he that hath two forcheedes.
Bifur, a double thefe, or he that hath stollen twyse.
Bifurcatus, ta, tum, double forked.
Biga, a carte drawen with two horses.
Bigamus, he that hath hadde two wyues.
Bigenera, beastes commen of two sondry kyndes.
Biiugi, cattaylle or beastes yoked two togyther.
Bilanx, lancis, a beame with two balances.
Bilbilis, a towne in Spayne.
Bilibris, Bilibre, waying two poundes.
Bilinguis, double tunged.
Bilis atra, the humour of Melancoly, proprely that whiche bryngeth a man to fransy or madnesse.
Biliosus, he that hath abundaunce of that humour.
Bimaritus, he that hath had two wiues.
Bimembris, of two partes, hauynge two membres.
Bimestris, two monthes olde, or two yere, accompted of the moone.
Bimulus, of two yeres age.
Bimus, of two yeres.
Binus, na, num, two, idem quod duo. Binæ litteræ, two letters. Bini tabellarii, two messangers, bina iuga boum, two yoke of oxen
Binarius numerus, the numbre of two.
Binominus et binominis, he that hath two names.

Bion, the name of a philosopher.
Biothenatus, he that is violently slayne.
Bipalium, a spade to dygge with.
Bipara, she that hath had two byrthes.
Bipatens, open on bothe sydes.
Bipennis, hauynge twoo wynges. Also a twyebyll, wherwith carpenters doo make theyr mortaises.
Bipertior, iris, tiri, to diuyde in two partes.
Bipes, pedis, hauynge two fete.
Bipedalis, et Bipedaneus, twoo foote longe or brode.
Biremes, shyppes with two toppes.
Bis, twyse.
Bisaltæ, a people in Scythia.
Bisellium, a seate or fourme, wheron two men onely may sytte.
Bisextus, one day added to, in foure yeres.
Bisextilis annus, the leape yere.
Bison, tis, a beeste hauyng oone horne, and a very longe mane.
Bistonis, a citie, and also a greate meare or poole in the countrey of Thrace.
Bisulcus, ca, cum, clouen footed.
Bythynia, a royalme in Asia, whiche nowe the turke hath.
Bithynium, a citie in Bithynia.
Bitumen, a kynde of naturall lyme, wherof the olde walles of the Cytie of Babylon were made.
Biuium, a way hauynge two pathes.
Bizen, a cytie of Thracia, of Plynie called Bizian. *Plin, li. 4.*

B ante L.

Blesus, he that stamereth, omittynge some letters in speakynge.
Blandicus, he that flattereth.
Blandidicus, a fayre speaker, or flatterer.
Blandior, iris, iri, to flatter, to speake fayre for aduauntage.
Blanditiæ, flatterynge, fayre speche.
Blasphemia, cursynge, reprochynge, commonly blasphemy, whiche is nowe onely referred to the despite of god.
Blasphemo, aui, are, to curse, to reproche, to speake in the derogation or despyte of an nother.
Blatero, aui, are, to bable in vayne, and from the pourpose.
Blatta, is proprely the longe flye that flyeth in the leame of a candell, and is of the kynde of mothes. It is also a sylke worme: and blatteus, beinge an adiectiue, is purple colour. Vestis blattea, a purple garment.
Blattaria, an herbe, also called Verbascon.
Blax, softe, delicate, wanton, that can not decerne thinges, and whiche vaynely bosteth hym selfe.

Blepharo

Blepharo, onis, he that hath great browes.
Bleptæ, a people in Aphrike, whiche haue their visages in their breastes.
Blittus, an herbe being of the kynde of betes, hauynge no sente. Blittea meretrix, an vnsauorie queane.

¶ B ante O.

Plin. lib. 8. capi. 14.

BOa, a serpent in Italy, so greatte and large, that on a tyme whan one was kylde, there was a chylde all hoole founde in his bealy, as Plinie writeth.
Boarium forum, the markette place, where oxen be solde.
Bocchyris, a mans name.
Bodellium, a kynde of sweete smellynge gumme.
Boemia, the royalme of Boeme.
Boeotia, a countrey in Grece, wherin was the cytie of Thebes.
Bætis, a ryuer in Spayne by the countrey of Granado.
Boiæ, gyues or fetters.
Boii, people of Germany.
Boletus, a mushcrom.
Bolis, idis, a darte with wylde fyre.
Bolus, a masse or lumpe of mettall, or other lyke thynge.
Bombitatio, the noyse that bees make.
Bombus, a great sowne or noyse, as it were of a trumpe, or gunne, a bownce.
Bombycinus, na, num, of sylke, Bombycina uestis, A garment of sylke.
Bombix, icis, a sylke worme.
Bonæ fidei possessor, a feffee of truste.
Bonaria, calmenes of the see.
Bona uenia, By your lycence, No displeasure to you.
Boni consulas, take it in good parte.
Bonitas, goodnesse, honestie and iustyce.
Bonum, good, whiche is contrary to yll.
Bonus, a good man: Also beneuolent, peasyble, lyberall, playne, easye to speake to, worshypfull, treatable, mercyfull.
Boo, oas, are, to belowe lyke a cowe.
Bootes, a sterre whiche foloweth Charles wayne.
Boreas, the northesterne wynd.
Boreus polus, the northe sterre, callyd the lode sterre.
Boristhenes, a great ryuer in the countreye of Scythia.
Borith, a herbe that fullers vse.
Bos, bouis, a rother beaste, be it bulle, oxe, or Cowe.
Bosphorus, the name of a parte of the see, whiche lyeth in two sondry costes: one by Constantinople, the other more northe.

Bostar, an oxe house.
Bostrychites, a precious stone lyke to womennes heare.
Botrys, a cluster of grapes.
Botrytes, a precious stone lyke to a blacke graape.
Botulus, a puddinge made of the inwarde of a rother beaste.
Bouatim, lyke an oxe.
Bouicida, a slauter man.
Bouile, an oxe stalle.
Bouillæ, larum, a town not far from Rome.
Bouinator, he that with great noyse crieth out on a nother man.
Bouinor, aris, to belowe out lyke a cowe.

¶ B ante R.

BRabenta, he that is ordeyned a iuge in any game of wrastlynge, runnynge, or leapynge.
Bracca, that kynde of mantell, whiche nowe commeth out of Irelande, or a longe garment made of rough frise.
Braccharii, the makers of suche clothe.
Brachiale, the wrestebone of the hande.
Brachialia, bracelettes, whiche some gentylmen and gentyll women doo vse aboute theyr armes.
Brachiatus, that whyche lyke an arme holdeth any thinge vp, a proppe, or shore.
Brachium, an arme.
Brachylogia, shortenes of speche.
Bracmane, philosophers of Inde.
Bractea, thynne plates of mettalle, horne, or wodde.
Bractearius, a worker of plates.
Bracteator, the same.
Bracteola, leaues of golde or syluer.
Bragada, a ryuer nere to Vtica.
Branchiæ, the gylles of a fyshe.
Branchos, the rewme or cattarre, whiche falleth downe by the chekes.
Brassica, Colewortes, proprely Cabeges.
Brauium, the rewarde for wrastlynge, runnynge, or leapynge, commonly called the chiefe game.
Breno, a capitayne or leader of the frenche men called Galli, whiche, buylded Verona a citie of Venece.
Brephotrophia, an hospitalle, where chyldren be kepte and nouryshed.
Breue, Shortly, et breuiter, et breui.
Breuiloquus, he that speaketh his mynd in a fewe wordes.
Breuiloquium, a short fourme of speakynge.
Breuiloquentia, the same.
Breuitas, shortenesse.
Breuis breue, Shorte.

Bre-

Breuiarium, a brigement.
Briareus, a gyant, whiche was of an excedynge greatnesse.
Britannia, Brytayne, whiche doth contein Englande, Scotlande, and wales.
Britannus, et Brito, a man of that countrey.
Bronchus, the inner parte of the throte.
Bronchi, they whyche haue their mouthe and tethe standyng farre out, tut mouthed.
Bruchus, a flye, whyche eateth corne, as it groweth.
Bruma, wynter.
Brundusiū, a citie in the royalme of Naples.
Bruseum, an herbour or hedge made with thornes and briers wounde togither.
Brutii, people in the royalme of Naples, ioynynge to Sycile.
Brutus, dul and grosse witted like to a beest.
Brionia, an herbe called withwynde.
Brisso, aui, are, to bruse oute.

B ante V.

Bvbalus, a beaste called a bugill.
Bubastis, a cytie of Aegipte.
Bubo, a shriche oule. also a botche.
Bubsequa, a coweherde.
Bubulcito, tas, to playe the herdeman.
Bubulcus, a herde man.
Bubile, an oxe house.
Bubulus, la, lum, that whiche longeth to an oxe or cowe, as Lac bubalum, cowe mylke.
Bucardia, a stone lyke to a bugles harte.
Bucca, the holownes of the cheke.
Buccea, a morsell.
Buccella, the same.
Buccellatum, breadde called byskat.
Buccina, a trumpette.
Buccino, aui, are, to blowe a trumpette.
Buccinum, the sowne of a trumpette.
Buccones, they whiche haue great chekes.
Bucculenti, idem.
Buccula, a lytell cheke. Also that parte of a helmet, wherby wynde is taken.
Bucentarius, a great shyppe or carrike.
Bucentes, styngynge gnattes.
Bucentrum, a goodde prycke.
Bucephalus, an oxe heed. and the horse of Alexander the great was so called.
Bucera armenta, herdes of nete. Bucolica, the same.
Bucula, a heckfar.
Buculus, a bullock, or steere.
Bufo, onis, a tode.
Buglossa, an herbe called langedebefe. Also a fyshe called a sole.
Bugones, bees.
Bulbito, aui, are, to caste durte on one: proprely it is of chyldren, whiche nourysshe

do name cackynge.
Bulbus, wyld garlyke hauynge a leafe lyke to a lylly. it is taken generally for all rotes that be rounde.
Bulga, a male of lether, wherin clothes be caried.
Bulimia, great famyne or hunger.
Bulis, a name of a citie.
Bulla, a tablette or other thynge hanged aboute ones necke, proprely whan it is holowe. A bobell of water, somtyme the heed of a nayle, otherwhyles studdes in girdels or other thinges.
Bullatus, he that is garnyshed with tablettes or studdes.
Bullio, iui, ire, to boyle, or sethe.
Bullare, to bubble, as water whan it boyleth.
Bumastos, a great teate.
Bumelia, a kynde of ashe.
Bupina, great thurste.
Bupodes, great feete.
Bura, or Buris, the hynder part of a plough whiche is croked.
Burcana, an ile in the occean of Germany.
Burdo, onis, a mulette.
Burgundia, Burgoyne.
Busyris, a tyraunt, whyche was kynge of Aegypte.
Bustum, a place where deade bodyes haue ben brente.
Buteo, a kynde of hawkes, whyche hathe thre stoones.
Buthysia, was called a great sacrifice, suche as Hecatombe is.
Butyrum, butter.
Buxentum, a towne that the grekes calle Pyxunta.
Buxeta, a place where boxe trees growe.
Buxus, or Bussus, boxe tree.

¶ B ante Y.

Byrsa, a hyde of a beaste.
Byssus, fyne sylke.
Byzantium, a citie of Thrace now called Constantinople, whiche was somtyme buylded by a kynge of Spartane, called Pausania, wherof the people and inhabitantes were called Byzantæ. Afterward it was augmented by Constantine the emperour, and was the chiefe and heed of all the empire orientall.
Byzari, fantasticall men, and of straunge inuentions.
Byrseus, a tanner, or cordynar.
Byssus, a maner of fyne flaxe or lynnen. I suppose it to be cotten.

C. ante

C ANTE A.

CABALLI, peple of Asia.
Caballus, an horse. yet in some partes of Englande, they doo calle an horse a cable.
Cabyle, a cite in Thracia
Cabyria, a cytie of the lower Asia, all thoughe Cabyrii, be people in India.
Cacabus, a pot or cauldron, wherin meate is sodden.
Cacus, a gyant, whome Hercules dyd slee.
Cacabo, as, are, to calle lyke a pertryche.
Cacodemon, an yll spirite.
Cachinnus, a scorne, or a lowde lawghter in derysyon.
Cachinnor, aris, ari, to laugh immoderately and with a loude voyce.
Caco, cacaui, care, to shyte.
Cacaturio, idem.
Cacoethes gen. neut. an yll maner.
Cacosyntheton, an yll or defourmed composytion.
Cacula, a page.
Cacumen, the toppe of a hylle.
Cado, cecidi, cadere, to falle, to dye.
Cadere, to happen.
Cadere causa, to be nonsuite in an action.
Cadere formula, idem.
Cadauer, eris, a dead body, or carrayn.
Caducus, ca, cum, fallynge, decayinge. Caducus morbus, the fallynge euyll.
Caducarii, men hauyng the fallyng euyll.
Caducor, ceris, duci, to be ouerthrowen.
Cadule gutte, dryppyng of rosted meate.
Cadiuus, ua, uum, that whiche falleth by it selfe, as Cadiua folia, leaues fallyn downe by them selfe. Cadiua poma, appulles fallen from the tree.
Cadꝰ, a wine vessel, it may be take for a pipe.
Caduceus, et Caduceum, a rodde, whiche poetes supposid that Mercury bare in his hande, as messanger of Jupiter.
Caduceator, an ambassatour or herault sent for peace, or to take a truse.
Cadurcum, a keucrlede of lynnen, mooste propzely a quilte.
Cadiscus, a vessell wherin lottes for election or consent of a multitude be put.
Cadmus, the name of a Prynce, whyche browghte oute of Phaenicia into Greece syxetene letters, and was the fyrste that wrate in prose, and founde out the fusynge and castynge of mettalles.
Caecias, the easte northest wynde.
Caecus, ca, cum, blynde, also darke.
Caeci morbi, syckenesses which be not ap-

parant: the causes wherof be hydde from phisitions.
Caecilia, a sloworme that is blynde.
Caecutio, tiui, tire, to se but lyttell, to be half blynde.
Caeculto, aui, are, to haue a dymme sight.
Caeco, caui, are, to make blynde.
Caedes, dethe, slaughter or murder.
Caedo, dis, cecidi, cedere, to beate, or whyp, to cutte, to stryke, to kylle, to breake. Caedere ianuam saxis, to breake the doore with stoones.
Cedo, to departe, to gyue place, to obeye.
Cedere bonis, to leaue the goodes.
Cedere iuri, to gyue ouer a ryght or tytle.
Cede manum, gyue me thy hande.
Cedere, to succede.
Cedo, say, Cedo cuium puerum, Tel or say, whose chylde or seruant.
Cedo, gyue, Quin tu mihi argentum cedo, But yet gyue thou me thy money.
Caedua sylua, woddes vsed to be cutte, Coppeyses.
Caesim, edgelinge. Also at one cutte or choppe.
Caelum, heuen or the firmament. also a grauynge yron.
Coelestis, celeste, heuenly, or of heuen.
Celicus, ca, cum, idem.
Celitus, heuenly.
Celites, heuenly creatures.
Celicola, he that inhabiteth heuen.
Celebs, a syngle man or woman. Also euery chaste persone.
Celibatus, a single lyfe without mariage.
Celsus, a, um, hygh.
Celius mons, a mountayne in Rome.
Celo, aui, are, to graue in mettall.
Cementum, morter, or any other grosse matter, wherwith walles be made.
Cementarii, daubers, pargetters, rowghe masons, whiche do make onely walles.
Cementitius, a, um, of morter.
Caene, a citie.
Cepe, an oynyon.
Cepula, a chybboll.
Cepi, the preter perfect tense of Capio, I haue taken.
Ceruleus, a blewe colour.
Cera, waxe. Also Cere were writynge tables couered with waxe.
Cero, aui, are, to laye waxe on any thinge.
Ceratura, the waxinge.
Cereus, cerea, cereum, of waxe. Also fatte or tydye.
Ceratum, a seared clothe.
Cerefolium, an herbe callyd cheruyll.
Caereus, a taper, or waxecandell.
Cereolus, a sixe candell.

Caerulus,

Cærulus, la, lum, et Cæruleus, lea, leū, blewe of coloure.
Cærosus, a, um, that whiche is myxte with water.
Cærium, a soore, whiche is lyke to a honye combe.
Cæroma, an oyntment made with oyle and netes dunge, wherwith men that wrastlyd vsed to anoynte their bodies. Also it sygnifyeth the place where wrastlers were anoynted.
Cerete, an ancient citie in Tuskay.
Cerinthe, thre leaued grasse, whiche bringeth furth whyte hony suckles, called clyuer grasse.
Cæsar, the emperour.
Cæsarea, a citie in the coūtrey of Palestina.
Cæsaraugustana, a citie in the realme of Aragon.
Cæsareus, ea, eum, pertaynynge to the emperoure.
Cæsaries, heare, or a bushe of heare.
Cesenna, a citie in Italy.
Cesa, a waipon, somtyme vsed in Fraunce. It is also a parte of an oration, not concludynge a sentence: as it were a pyece of a sentence.
Cesura, a piece as it were cut of from the remenaunt, proprely of a verse.
Cestrum, an instrumente, wherwith iuorye was bored. Also a weapon lyke a dagger.
Cesitium, a sheete.
Cæsius, gray of colour or blunket. Also he whiche hath grey eyen.
Cæsones, they whiche be cutte oute of the mothers or dames belyes.
Cæspes, cespitis, a turfe.
Cæspititius, a, um, made of turfes.
Cæspito, taui, tare, to stumble.
Cæstus, tus, a weapon hauyng great plummates hangyng at the ende of a clubbe.
Cæstus, cæsti, a gyrdell or corse, whiche the husbande dydde putte aboute his wyfe, whan he was maried, and at nyght dydde plucke it of.
Cæter, cætera, cæterum, the remenaunt or resydewe.
Cæterum, et cætera, be aduerbes sygnyfyenge, sometyme moreouer, somtyme from hensforthe, sometyme Cæterum, is a coniunction, and signifieth sed, but.
Caycus, the name of a ryuer in Phrigia.
Cain, in hebrewe signifieth enuie.
Caius, a propre name of a man.
Cala, a byllette.
Calabra, a conuocation place, where matters concernynge deuotion were treated.
Calabria, a countrey ioynynge to Naples.
Calaber, bra, brum, of Calaber.

Caladrius, a byrde.
Calæ, arum, a cytie in India.
Calagurium, a towne in Biskay.
Calamintha, an herb called calamēt or nep.
Calanus, a philosopher of Inde, whiche in the presence of the greate Alexander, beinge of the age of. lxxiii. yeres, felynge hym selfe sycke, made a bonefyre, and wente into the toppe therof, and bourned hym selfe.
Calaris, a citie in Sardina.
Calamus, a rede, or wheate strawe, Also a penne. It is also taken for a pype, or whystell. Also a fyshynge rodde, and a twigge, wheron birde lyme is put. Also small braunches of trees, also it is a pole to mete with, conteynynge syxe cubytes and a spanne, a mette polle.
Calamarium, a pennar.
Calamitas, generalle dystruction, or myserye.
Calamitosus, myserable or ful of aduersitie.
Calamistrum, a pynne of wodde or iuorye, wherwith men and womē do set or trimme vppe their heare.
Calantica, a tyre or burlette for a woman.
Calones, boyes and knaues, which do folowe hostes, and do either carye the weapons of souldiours, or serue them of wode or water.
Calathis, the name of a citie.
Calathus, a baskette or hamper.
Calx, hic, calcis, the heele. it sometyme signifieth the ende of a matter. sommetyme a stroke with the heele.
Calx, hæc, lyme made of burned stones.
Calcatus, cata, catum, pergetted or whyte lymed.
Calcaria fornax, a lyme pytte.
Calcarius, a lyme burner.
Calcaneus, et calcaneum, the heele.
Calceus, a showe.
Calcearium, a showmakers shoppe.
Calceolarius, a showmaker.
Calceo, aui, are, to putte on shoen.
Calceamen, et calciamentum, a showe, pynson, or socke.
Calcar, a spurre.
Calcitro, aui, are, to kycke or wynse.
Calcitro, tronis, a horse that dothe flynge or kycke.
Calcitrosus, a, um, that oftentimes flyngeth or kycketh.
Calculus, a peble stone. Also the stoone in the body. Also a chesse man. also accompt. also the leste weight or poyse that may be. Moreouer a knyfe made of a stone.
Calculosus, he that is moche diseased with the stone. Calculosus locus, a stonye place.

Calcu-

Calculo, aui, are, to caste accompte.
Calco, aui, are, to treade or presse downe.
Caliga, a hose, or legge harnaysse.
Caligatus, hosed.
Caligo, ginis, darkenes.
Caliginosus, darke.
Caligo, aui, are, to make darke, or be darke.
Calor, et caliditas, heate. Caldor idem.
Caleo, calui, calére, to be hotte or warme.
Calesco, to waxe hotte.
Calefacio, to make hotte.
Calefio, I am made hotte.
Calidus, da, dum, hotte.
Calorificus, ca, cum, that whiche makethe hotte or warme.
Callus, brawn, or hardnes of the fete made with goinge.
Callidus, slye, or craftye.
Calliditas, slyenesse.
Calleo, ui, ere, to be harde as brawne. Also to knowe perfectly.
Calendæ, the firste day of euery monthe.
Callis, a way moche vsed.
Callimachus, the name of a poete.
Calisthenes, the name of a philosopher.
Cales, a towne in Fraunce.
Calistho, the mother of Archias, whiche gaue the name to the countreye of Archadia, whom poetes fained to be transformed into a beare.
Calypsos, the name of an yle, also of a woman, whiche receyued Ulysses whanne he escapyd drownynge.
Calyptra, a womans cappe or bonette.
Calliope, oone of the vyrgines, whiche be named Musæ.
Calix, a cuppe to drynke wyne in. Also a potte, wherin potage is sodden.
Calyx, the parynge or skynne of an apple, or other lyke fruite. Also a keueryng made of clay. Also that parte, wherout spryngeth a floure, whiche is grene.
Calliblepharon, a medycyne to make the eyen fayre.
Callirohe, a fountayne in Grece.
Calydon, et Calydonia, a citie in Grece. also it was a great forest and wodde in Brytain, nowe called Englande.
Calypso, the doughter of Athlas, a Nimph or woman of the see.
Calopodium, a patyn, or slypper.
Calopus, a beaste in Syria, which with his hornes throweth downe great trees.
Calænu, a citie in the countrey of Naples.
Calpæ, a mountayne in the southwest part of Spayne.
Calua, the sculle.
Caluities, et caluitium, baldnesse.
Caluo, aui, are, to make balde.

Calueo, I am balde.
Caluesco, to waxe balde.
Caluaria, all the heed, whanne the fleshe is awaye.
Caluo, ui, ere, to deceyue or disapoynt.
Calumnia, a false or crafty accusation.
Calumniator, he that accusethe or seweth a man vniustly.
Calumnior, aris, ari, to accuse or sue a man vniustely.
Calumnarius porcus, a swyne fed with graines, and suche other vyle thynges.
Calastri pueri, syngynge boyes.
Calta, an herbe growynge amonge corne, hauynge a yelowe flowre.
Cambio, iui, ire, to chaunge. In the olde tyme it signified to fyght, to begyn a iournay, or to tourne in a iourney.
Campso, aui, are, to tourne an other way.
Cambyses, a kynge of Persia, grandfather of Cyrus. It is also the name of a ryuer in the countrey of Hyrcania.
Camera, the false roufe of a house, sollar, or chamber.
Camerare, to make a fauce roufe of a hous, or to make a solar, or to sylde.
Camerium, a towne of Italy in the countrey of Picenum.
Camertes, the inhabitauntes of Camerine, a towne in Sycile.
Camerina, an herbe, whiche beinge brused, prouoketh a man to vomite: wherof camme this prouerbe, Ne moueas camerinam, for, procure not harme to thy selfe.
Camillus et Camilla, was in old tyme a boy, or a wenche that seruyd the byshop, whan he dydde sacrifyce. Also the name of a man or womanne.
Chamamelum, et Camomilla, an herbe callyd Camomyll.
Caminus, a chymnay or fournayse.
Caminatus, ta, tum, made lyke a fournayse or chymney.
Camænæ, idem quod Musæ.
Campana, a belle.
Campania, the royalme of Naples.
Campus, a felde.
Campestria loca, playne countreys.
Camparius, the keper of the feldes.
Campsores, exchaungeours.
Campe, a worme which eateth herues, r is rough with many fete, r is callyd a palmer.
Camus, a bytte or snaffyll. also a rayne or corde, wherwith men beinge condempned were bounde.
Canabus, a wyne sellar.
Canna, a cane. also an oyle pot or canne.
Canales, pipes, wherby water doth runne into a cundyte.

Canalicula, a lyttell pipe.
Canaliculatus, facioned lyke a pipe.
Cannabis, hempe.
Cannabinus, na, num, made of hempe.
Cancelli, latteses, or any thynge made lattese wyse. Also secrete places to looke oute. Also windowes made with barres of wodde or yron with dyuers holes.
Cancello, aui, are, to rase or put out, to cut or teare any thyng that is written.
Cancer, cri, a kynd of fyshe called a crabbe, also a signe in heuen.
Cancer, eris, a disease called a canker.
Cancri, is the same that Cancelli be.
Cancris, a pylle in medicine.
Candax, acis, a quene of Aegypte.
Candifacio, to make whyte, to bleache, to make to glowe lyke a burnyng cole.
Candela, a candell.
Candelabrum, a candelstycke.
Candeo, ui, dere, to glowe lyke a burnynge cole. Also to be white.
Candico, aui, are, to be whyte, or to make whyte.
Candidatus, was he amonge the Romains whiche laboured for some of the great offyces in the publyke weale: and they were so named bycause they dydde weare in the tyme of their election white apparayle. It maye be taken by translation at this tyme, for them that in vniuersities be called inceptours, or regent maisters. Also for theym that be lately christened, or newely entred into some honorable or worshypfull state.
Candido, aui, are, to make whyte.
Candidus, da, dum, whyte. It is somtymes taken for gentyll or easye: as Candidus lector, a gentyll reder, whiche dothe not openly reproue that which he redeth. Candidus iudex, A gentyll or easy iuge.
Candide, gentylly or easily.
Candidus, sometyme sygnifyeth fortunate, and it sygnifyeth more than Albus, as oryente whyte.
Candifico, aui, care, to make whyte.
Candor, oris, bryghtnesse.
Canentæ, were of the olde Romaynes named the apparayle pertainyng to the heed.
Caneo, et canesco, scere, to be hore, or gray heared.
Canephora, a mayden, whiche bare on her heed a basket or cofer, wherin were iewels or images of the goddes.
Cangrena, a sore called a canker.
Cani, be taken for white heares for age.
Canicæ, branne, gurgeons.
Caniceps, a beaste, whiche hathe onely the face of a dogge.
Canicula, a lyttell dogge or bytche. Also a sterre, wherof canicular or dogge dayes be named Dies caniculares.
Caniculus, a whelpe.
Caninus, doggisshe, or of a dogge.
Caninum prandium, a dinar without wyne.
Canis, a dogge, a kynd of fyshe called dogfishe, a play at tables, a signe in heuē, wherof there be two sterres, oone called Canis maior, the other canis minor.
Canistrum, a baskette.
Canities, graynesse of heares.
Canna, a poete whiche was in the tyme of Martialis.
Canna, a cane or rede. also a canne or pot. also a village in the countrey of Galilee.
Cannæ, narū, a towne in the countrey of Apulia, where a greatte hooste of Romayns was slayne by Hanniball.
Cannetum, a place where kanes or reedes do growe.
Cannitie, thatched houses.
Cano, cecini, nere, to synge, to playe on the shalme or other instrument. Also to praise, to prophecye.
Canere receptui, to blowe the retraicte in battrayle.
Canon, a rule, also the inner parte of a targate, whiche keuereth the hande.
Canopus, a citie in Aegypte.
Canor, oris, melody, lowde.
Canorosus, a, um, full of melody.
Cantabri, people in Spayne.
Cantabria, a countrey in Spayne.
Cantharia, a stone whiche hath the prynte of a blacke flye called a byttell.
Cantharis, idis, uel Cantharida, cantharidæ a greene worme shynynge with a glosse of golde, whiche is bredde in the toppe of asshes, and laide to a mannes body, maketh it to blyster.
Cantharus, a pot or a iugge. Also a beaste, wherof there is founde noo female. Also a kynde of fysshe. also the blacke flye called the bytill.
Cantherium, a maner of a charyot or wagen. also a perche or a rayle.
Cantherius, a geldynge. Also a traunsome of timber.
Canthus, the yron wherwith the extremytie of wheeles be bounden, the straake of a carte.
Canthes, organ pipes.
Canticum, a pleasant or mery songe.
Cantilena, the melody of the songe.
Cantio, a songe.
Cantiuncula, a lyttell songe.
Cantito, aui, are, to synge often.
Canto, aui, are, to synge or to charme.
Cantus, tus, a songe.

Canus

Canus, an olde man.
Canus, na, num, graye or hore.
Canusium, a towne in the countreye of Apulia.
Capax, acis, that taketh or conteyneth any thynge, able to receiue.
Capedo, the greatnesse of a vessell, or lyke thynge that contayneth.
Capena, a towne by Rome.
Caper, a gelded gote. sometyme it is taken for the bucke gote. it also was the name of an olde grammarion.
Capero, aui, to frowne or lowre.
Capesso, si, sere, to take, or to goo aboute to take, to receyue. sommetyme it sygnifyeth to brynge in.

Plautus.

Capetus, the name of a kynge.
Caphareus, a mountayne in Grece.
Capharnaum, the chiefe citie in Galilee.
Capillamentum, the heare of a mans heed. somtyme the toppes of herbes, where the seedes do growe.
Capillo, are, to make heare.
Capillatus, a, um, that hath heare.
Capillitium, the heare of the heed.
Capillotenus, iuste to the heare.
Capillus, the heare.
Capillus ueneris, an herbe callyd Mayden heare.
Capio, cœpi, capere, to take wyllyngely, or vnwyllyngly. Sommetyme it sygnifieth to delyte, to mitigate, to deceyue, Capti dolis, deceyued with cautels. somtyme to cōteyne. Dii boni, quid turbæ? ædes nostræ uix capiunt, Good lorde, what a company? vneth our house woll conteyne theym. Also to make.
Capti oculis, blynde. also great louers be named capti.
Capis, dis, a cuppe.
Capistro, are, to halter, or putte on a rope, or corde.
Capistrum, a haltar.
Capitale, et capital, an offence punyshed by deathe.
Capitalis homo, a man that deserueth deth. Also that is prone and redy to murder.
Capitalis ira, mortall wrathe.
Capitalis locus, the place of execution.
Capitatus, ta, tum, that groweth greatte in the heade.
Capite censi, were amonge the Romaynes the poore sorte of the people, whiche were discharged of all exactions, and remayned in the citie onely for generation.
Capitellum, a lytell heed or top of a thing. Also the hyghest parte of a pyllar.
Capitiū, any thing that couereth the heed, commonly they do call it a hoode.

Capitis diminutio, a condemnatio, wherby a man loseth either libertie of his person, or is made bond: or is banished his countrey, or put out of the kynges protection, or renouncynge his owne familie, is adopted or take into an other, whiche is not now vsed.
Capitolinus, was the surname of hym, that found the heed, whan the Capitole shulde be buylded.
Capitoliū, the palaice of the citie of Rome.
Capito, tonis, he that hath a great heed. also heddy or obstinate in opinion.
Capitosus, he that hath a great heed, or a dull heed.
Capitulatum, any thynge that is growen to a heed.
Capitulū, a lytle heed, also a chapiter.
Cappa, the name of a greke letter, for whiche the latins vse C.
Cappadocia, a countrey in the lesse Asia.
Cappadox, docis, a man of that countrey.
Capparis, a frute called Capers, wherwith we do make salates & sauce for mutton, whiche catē before meles, be very good for the stomake, & ageinst diseases of the splene.
Capra, a goote.
Capella, a lyttell goote.
Capreolus, a kydde.
Capraria, an yle in the see called Ligusticū.
Caprarius, a goote herde.
Caprea, a beaste whiche doth see wonderfull quickly. It is also a kynde of vynes soo named. Moreouer an yle by Naples.
Capreolus, a beaste called a roo. It is also the tendrell of a vyne, whiche wyndeth diuers ways, called also Pampinus.
Capreus, a, um, that whiche is of a gote. Caprillus, a, um, idem.
Capricornus, a sygne in heuen, conteininge xx. sterres.
Caprificacio, the paryng away of the barke of a tree.
Caprificus, a wylde fygge tree, which runneth vp by walles.
Caprigenus, na, num, that whiche is of the kynde of a goote.
Caprile, a stable or pen, where gotes be kept.
Caprimulgi, birdes like to gulles, which appere not by day, but in the night they come into gote pennes, and do souke the gotes, wherby the vdders of them be mortified.
Caprinus, na, num, of a gote.
Capronæ, the toppe or lyttel mane, that is in the forheed of a horse, or other beast.
Caprunculum, a greatte vessell.
Capsa, a coffer or cheste.
Capsaces, a vessell wherin oyle is kept.
Capsariꝰ, he that kepith chestis, or apparel.
Capsus, a couered cart.

Captio,

Captio, nis, the acte of takynge or deceyuynge, or that wherby any thynge is taken.
Captiuncula, the diminutiue of Captio.
Captiosus, captious or deceytfull.
Captiuus, a pryfoner taken in warres, or a sclaue.
Captiuitas, captiuitie or bondage.
Capto, aui, are, to gette the fauour of oone with fayre wordes, pleasant dedes, or rewardes. Also to deceyue or take quyckely.
Captator, oris, he that vseth that crafte.
Captatio, the acte or crafte to gette fauor. also deceyte or subtyltie.
Captura, the apprehendynge or gettyng.
Captus, ta, tum, taken.
Captus, tus, chaunce. also deceyte, perceyuynge of a thinge, or capacitie. Captus hominum, Mens capacitie. sometyme dilectation, Non possum adduci et suscipere e pecunia captum, I may not be brought therto, and take dilectation of the money.
Capua, a citie in the royalme of Naples.
Capula, a cuppe with a handell.
Capularis senex, an olde manne redye to be layde in his beere.
Capulum, a rydynge knotte.
Capulus et Capulum, what so euer may receyue any thynge into it: propzelye it is a beere, wherin deed corpsis are borne: also the hyltes or handell of a sworde.
Capus, a capon.
Caput, a heed. Also the begynnynge of euery thynge. Also a chapiter of a boke.
Caput facere, to gather a sore to a heed.
Capys, a mans name that buylded Capua.
Carabus seu Caramus, a fysshe calledde a Crabbe.
Caraxus, was the brother of Sapphus.
Carbasus i plurali Carbasa, a kynd of lynnen cypres: also the saylle clothe of a shyppe. Moreouer it is a fyne garment of women of sylke or lynnen.
Carbo, a cole. It was also the name of a Romayne.
Carbunculare, to haue a Carbouncle or botche.
Carbunculus, a botche, whiche commeth of inflamation. it is also a kynde of precyouse stones, whiche do shyne lyke a bournynge cole. Moreouer a defaulte in a vyne, and other trees, wherby they ar burned, whiche happeneth about the canicular dayes. Also it signifyeth erthe, wherin is founde blacke flatte stones.
Carcer, ceris, a pryson. Also Carceres were stables, wherin horses were sette, whanne they shulde runne.
Carcerarius, ria, rium, of a pryson.
Carchesium, a standynge cuppe with handelles.
Carchoquios, a kynde of frogges, hauyng on their bealyes yelowe spottes.
Carcina, a cytie.
Carcritoma, atis, a sore called a canker.
Cardamomum, a kynde of spice.
Cardiacus morbus, a syckenes which happeth by weakenes of the body, with moch sweatte and feblenesse of the stomake.
Cardinalis, le, chiefe or principall.
Cardineus, the same.
Cardinum, an herbe, whiche some do suppose is Cressis.
Cardo, dinis, the poste, whereon the doore hangeth, and is moued. Also a mere or boudes, whiche passith through the felde from the southe to the northe.
Cardo rei, the effect of the matter or thing: the chiefe poynte of the matter.
Cardo causæ, the matter in lawe.
Carduelis, a byrde called a goldefinche.
Carectum, a place full of sedges.
Careo, rui, rere, to lack propzely those good thynges, which ones were had. Somtyme it sygnifieth to be without a thyng: as Careo culpa, I am without faute. Careo febre, I am without feuer.
Cares, the name of a caruer, the scholar of Lysyppus.
Carex, ricis, an herbe harde and prickinge.
Caria, a region in Asia the lasse.
Caries, a lyttel worme that eateth wodde: It is also putrifaction or fylthe growen by age or contynuance.
Carina, the keele or bottom of the shyppe.
Carinæ, narum, a strete in Rome, wherein Pompey dwelled.
Carino, aui, are, to make a thyng of the facion of a shyppes bottome. Also to speake to a mannes reproche.
Caritas, tatis, scarcitie, propzely of that whiche serueth for the sustinance of man.
Carius, the name of Jupiters sonne.
Carmania, a countrey of the lasse Asia.
Carmelus, the name of two sondry hylles in Judea.
Carmen, minis, a verse or metre. Also the hole warke whiche is made in versis. Som tyme it signifieth a charme.
Carmenta, the name of a lady, whiche had the spirite of prophecy, and gaue aunswere in verses.
Carminare, to carde wulle, or other lyke thynge.
Carminarii, they that do pike or make clene wulle, or carde.
Carmon, a place in Messenia, and the temple of Appollo in Laconia.
Carnarium, a larder, wherin hangeth salte fleshe.

fleſhe, ſometyme it ſygnifyeth a bowchers ſhambles.
Carnarius, a boucher.
Carnarius, a, um, that pertayneth to fleſſhe.
Carneus, a, um, that whiche is of fleſhe.
Carni, the name of certain people in Italy.
Carnifex, ficis, a boucher of men, or hangman, that cutteth theym in pieces.
Carnificina, the place where ſuche execution is doone. Alſo the offyce or acte of a hangemanne.
Carnificium, the ſame acte.
Carnificinus, na, num, pertaynynge to the ſayde acte.
Carnificor, aris, ari, to playe the hangmannes part.
Carniuorum, any thynge that deuoureth fleſhe.
Carnoſitas, abundance of fleſhe.
Carnoſus, fleſſhye.
Carnotum, the mydle region of al France.
Carnuntum, a towne in the border of Germanye.

Donatus. Caro, carnis, fleſhe, proprely of that whiche is deade.
Carpatine, plowghemens bootes, made of vntanned lether, they may be called okers.
Carpathos, an Ile agaynſte Aegypte, the myddes betwene Rhodes and Candy.
Carpentarius, a carte wright, or carpentar.
Carpentarius equus, a carte horſe, or charyotte horſe.
Carpentum, a chariot or wagen.
Carpinus, a kynde of trees.
Carpio, a fyſhe called a carpe.
Carpo, pſi, pere, to gather or plucke. Alſo to cheſe, to reproue, or taunt, to vſe. i. fruor. Alſo carpere uires, is to make feble.
Carpere uiam, to walke.
Carpere uitales auras, to lyue.
Carpere lanam, to toſe woll.
Carpere cibum, to eate.
Carprim, pykynge out here and there.
Carra, re, a citie of Arrabie.
Carruca, a carte.
Carrucarius, a, um, pertaynyuge to a carte.
Carrus, a charyotte.
Carteia, a towne in Spayne.
Carthaginenſis, pertaynynge to Cartage.
Carthago, thaginis, the cytie of Cartage in Affryke.
Caruncula, a lyttell fleſhe.
Carus, a, um, deere.
Carya, the name of a citie in Grece.
Caryatides, the images of women holding garlandes, or other lyke thynge ſette vp to garnyſhe howſes.
Caryca, a fygge, ſpecially drye.
Caryota, a date.

Caſa, a cotage.
Caſaria, the woman that kepeth the cotage.
Caſcus, a, cum, olde.
Caſeus, cheſe.
Caſeus muſteus, Rowen cheſe.
Caſius, a hyll, in the borders of Aegypte.
Caſia, a ſpice, whiche hathe the vertue of Cynamome, and is wonderfull ſoote in ſauoure.
Caſito, aui, are, to fal or droppe oftentimes.
Caſpiæ portæ, certain Mounntayns in Aſia.
Caſpium mare, the ſee whiche ioyneth to the ſayde hylles.
Caſſes, ſis, nettꝭ which may be called hays. Alſo an helmette, but than it hath Caſſidis in the genitiue caſe.
Caſſiculus, a lyttell haye.
Caſſida, æ, an helmette.
Caſſiope, a ſigne in heuen, that hathe xiii. ſterres, and is figured lyke to a woman, ſittynge in a chayre.
Caſſita, a larke.
Caſſitias, the gumme that droppeth out of a firre tree.
Caſſo, aui, are, to put oute, or make of none effecte.
Caſſius, a propre name of a man.
Caſſus, a, um, voyde and of none effecte.
Caſtalius, a fountayn in the fote of the hill of Pernaſſus, whiche was dedicate to the Muſis.
Caſta mola, was a kynde of ſacrifice, that the vyrgins Veſtales made.
Caſtaneum, a cheſten, or cheſte nutte.
Caſtellani, the inhabitauntes of a lyttelle walled towne.
Caſtellatim, one lyttelle walled towne after an other.
Caſtellum, a lyttell walled towne. It is alſo a cundyte, oute of the whyche water ronnethe.
Caſterium, a docke where ſhippꝭ be laid vp.
Caſtigo, aui, are, to chaſtiſe with wordis. alſo to correcte or amende.
Caſtitas, tatis, chaſtitie.
Caſtor, a Beuer, whiche hath the taile of a fyſhe, in the reſidue is like to an ottar.
Caſtor et Pollux, were bretherne both atte one byrth, which were honored for goddꝭ.
Caſtra, caſtrorū, an armie of men of warre, whan they lye or abyde in any place. Alſo the place where the hoſte lodgethe. Alſo the Pauilions beinge pyched.
Caſtrametor, to lay or lodge an army.
Caſtro, aui, are, to gelde. Sometyme to cut of generally.
Caſtrenſis, caſtrenſe, that which pertaineth to an hooſte or armye.
Caſtrum, a caſtell or fortreſſe.

Caſtu

Castula, lynnen clothe, wherwith maidens dyd gyrde them selfe vnder their pappes.
Castus, ta, tum, chaste, honeste, and contynent, or vncorrupted.
Casura, a falle a decay.
Casus, happe, ruyne, mysfortune, or myserie. also a case.
Catrabathmus, a towne in Aphrica.
Catechesis, instruction or informacyon to hym that begynneth any thynge.
Catechiso, aui, are, to instructe, to infourme or teache.
Cataclysmus, an vnyuersall fludde.
Catadromum, the place where horses be coursed.
Catalecticum metrum, a verse wherein one onely syllable lacketh.
Catalogus, speche or wrytyng where thinges be recyted in order and numbre, a rehersalle.
Cataphractus, armed at all pieces.
Cataphracti equites, horsemenne on barbyd horses.
Cataphractæ naues, kcuered shyppes.
Cataphrygæ, Certayne heretikes, whiche sayde that the holy goste was not in the apostels, but onely in them selfes.
Cataplasma, a playster made with herbes and sewet.
Cataporia, pylles in medicine.
Catapulta, an arowe.
Catarrhacta, a portculious. Also cloudes. somtyme caues in the erthe.
Catarrhactæ, gret courses of water, falling downe from highe places. Also the places from whens they do falle.
Catarrhus, a rewme or styllynge downe of water or fleme from the heed.
Catascopium, a shyppe that watcheth or espieth for other.
Catasta, a cage, wherin men be sette, whiche are to be solde. also wherin they were punyshed.
Catastroma, parte of a shyppe or pauement.
Catastrophe, a subuersion, or a volume.
Catechumenus, he that is newly instructid.
Categoria, accusation.
Catellus, catella, a lyttell hounde.
Catena, a chayne.
Cateno, aui, nare, to chayne togither.
Catenula, a lyttell chayne.
Caterua, a company of men of warre. some tyme a multitude of people.
Cateruarii, they that doo assemble in companyes.
Cateruatim, by companyes.
Catharctica, purgatiue medicines.
Cathedra, a benche or stoole.
Cathinea, a kynde of erthe, wherof latyne mettall is made.
Catholicus, vniuersalle. nowe it is vsed for hym that kepeth the faithe, as the vniuersall churche hath obseruyd it.
Catillatio, a great reproche layde to gentylmen, whiche had robbed the countreis, that were alied to the Romaynes, and had riottously consumed the goodes.
Catillones, lycke dyshes, glottons.
Catillus, the ouer stone of a mylle, callyd the runner.
Catina, a citie in Sicile.
Catinus, a potage dyshe.
Catillus, idem.
Cathortoma, the righte worke of vertue, a ryght dede.
Cathortosis, a right affection.
Catus, wyse, or wytty. Also the name of a noble and wyse familye in Rome.
Catularia, one of the gates of Rome.
Catulire, the desyre of female kynd, to company with the male kynde, proprely to goo assaute, to rudder, to horsynge, or to blysfonynge.
Catulitio, the goinge assaulte. &c.
Catullus, the name of a poete.
Catulus, a kytten or yonge catte. Also it is putte generally for the yonge kynde of all beastis. also for a dogge.
Catus, a catte.
Caua, a hole, wherin byrdes do brede.
Cauedium, is a place at large, hauyng many porches, whiche serueth to a commune, lyke a market place.
Caucasus, a very hygh mountayne in Inde.
Cauda, a tayle of a beaste. somtyme a mans priuye membre.
Caudacus, gentyll and pleasant.
Caudax, dacis, the lower part of a tree next the roote. Also a table, hauynge many leaues or tables.
Caudicariæ naues, a shyppe whyche caryeth vytayles.
Caudis, a towne of Samnie.
Cauea, a caue or darke place in the groūd. Also a cage or cowpe, wherein byrdes be kept. Morcouer a place where a comedy or enterlude is playde.
Caueo, caui, cauēre, to beware, to eschue: also to prouyde diligently, to take hede. Caue tibi, Take hede of thy selfe.
Cauerna, a caue or holowe place in the grounde.
Cauilla, uel Cauillum, a mocke or a ieste.
Cauillo, aui, are, uel cauillor, ari, to ieste to mocke, to bourde.
Caula, a shepe house, but proprely a folde.
Caulescere, to growe into stalke.
Cauliculus, a tender stalke.
Cau=

Caulis, a stalke or stem of an herbe or tree. Also it is an herbe called colewortes. It is somtyme taken for all pot herbes, the rupe of a beaste, and for a shafte or iauelyn.
Caulon, a towne, whiche of Plinie is situate in the fyrste region of Italy.
Cauma, atis, heate.
Caunus, an yle in the occean see.
Cauo, aui, are, to make holowe.
Caupo, onis, a howkster that selleth meate and drynke.
Caupona, a woman that selleth wyne. Also the tauerner.
Cauponaria, tauerners crafte.
Cauponius, ia, iu, ptaynyng to the tauerne.
Cauponor, to sell as howksters do.
Cauros, was an yle, whiche afterward was called Andros, and after that Antandros.
Caurus, a westerne wynde.
Causia, a hatte or cappe after the facion of Macedonye.
Causon, nis, a burnynge feuer.
Caussa, a cause or matter in suite.
Caussarii milites, souldiours, which for causes reasonable, were discharged oute of the armye.
Caussaria missio, a discharge of a souldiour for a reasonable cause.
Caussatio, an in warde syckenes.
Caussatiuus, tiua, tiuum, that is cause that a thynge is done.
Caussidicus, a man of lawe.
Caussificor, aris, to complayn me of a thing that dothe greue me.
Causso, aui, are, to cause.
Caussor, aris, to fynd the matter, or to bring for excuse.
Caustica medicamenta, medicines, whiche do burne the skynne or the fleshe.
Cautêres et cautéria, is a markynge yron, or an instrument, wherwith soores ar burned.
Cauteriatus, ta, tum, marked or burned with that instrument, or marked with an yron.
Cautes, a ragged rocke, or hylle fulle of greatte stoones.
Cautum est, It is ordeyned or prouided by an acte of parlyament or counsayle.
Cautio est, it is nede to prouide or beware.
Cautus, a man that is circumspecte.
Cauus, a, um, holowe.
Cauus, an holowe place.
Causter, a fludde of Lidie.
Cayſtrus, fœm. gen. a citie of Cilycie.

¶ C ante E.

Cecrops, pis, the fyrste kynge of Athenes.
Cecropius, a, um, of Cecrops.
Cecropidis, a man or womanne, commynge of hym.
Cecropide, men of Athenes.
Cecriphalea, a rocke in the see, or an yle.
Cedar, a region of Arabie.
Cedo, cessi, dere, to gyue place, to goo away, to voyde, to withdrawe, to graunte, to gyue.
Cedo bonis, I leue my goodes to an other.
Cedere intercessioni, to procede no further, to admytte the contrary.
Cedo iuri, I release my ryghte.
Cedunt mihi ea bona, those goodes ar com or happened vnto me.
Cedite manus, gyue me your handes.
Cessit, it hapned.
Cedo, in the imperatiue mode, Tell thou.
Cedit dies, amonge lawyers is, The tyme is come, that the dette is due to be payde.
Cedria, the first sweatyng of the pitche tre.
Cedrides, the fruite of the cedre tree.
Cedropolis, a towne in Caria.
Cedros, an yland in the costis of Germany.
Cedrosis, a whyte vyneyarde.
Cedrus, a kynde of trees, whiche is excellent for buyldinge, forasmoche as the tymbre therof is great, & very lyght: also it dureth longe, and is neuer eaten with wormes, and is soote in sauour, hauyng leaues lyke to a cypresse tree.
Celebresco, I am in greate fame, or am renoumed.
Celebris, bre, famous. Also swifte, honourable.
Celebritas, tatis, renoume. Also a great assemblye.
Celebriter, honourably.
Celebro, aui, are, to celebrate or brynge in renoume, to make good reporte. Also to haunte, to honour, or worship.
Celer, eris, swyfte, quycke.
Celero, aui, are, to doo a thynge quyckely, to make haste.
Celetes, runnynge horses.
Celeustes, he that calleth on the mariners, to rowe or labour.
Celeusma, the shoute or crye that shypmen or botemen do make, whan the master doth whystell or calle.
Cella, a cellar, wherin any thyng is kepte. Also where we be pryuily wasshed. Also a secrete place in the temple.
Cellaria, a wyne sellar.
Cellarium, a storehouse.
Cellarius, he that hathe the charge of a cellar or storehouse.
Celatim, priuily.
Celo, aui, are, to hyde, or wyll not knowe.
Celox, a swyfte shyppe, or barke.

Celsus

Celsus, hygh.

Celtæ, frenche men.

Celtiberi, a people in Spayne, of Celtis, frenche men, and Iberis Spayniardes associate togyther.

Celtis, a kynde of sweete trees growynge in Affryke.

Celydrus, a womannes apparayle.

Cemellio, a towne in Liguria.

Cenchris, a byrd lyke an hauke, which maketh a great sowne whan he crieth. Also it is the name of a town or coūtrey in Grece.

Cenina, a citie of Italy.

Cenomani, people in Lombardy.

Cenodoxia, vayne glorye.

Cenotaphium, a tombe, where no manne is buryedde.

Censio, sui, ere, to suppose, to shewe myne opinion or sentence, to determyne, to be discontent, to numbre people, to the intent to take them, whiche be apte for the warres, or to leuye or taxe a subsidie.

Censio, nis, a chastysement.

Censor, a iudge of mens maners. Also suche as was appoynted to valewe mennes goodes.

Censorius uir, he that hath bene a Censour, or is worthy for his grauitie to iuge and correcte other mens maners.

Censualis, he that dothe assiste or accompany the iuges of maners called censors.

Censui agri, were those fieldes, whiche by the lawe ciuile mought be boughte & solde.

Censura, the authoritie or iudgement of a censour. Also correction of maners, lawe, or decree, concernynge maners.

Census, sus, yerely reuenues. Also valuation of goodes. Also a subsidie, the numbring of the people.

Census, si, he that is assessed or taxed, capite censi, taxed by the polle, or he that payeth heed syluer.

Centaurea, a kynde of herbe called Cētory

Centauri, a people in the coūtrey of Thessaly, whom the poetes dyd fayne to be the one halfe lyke a man, the other halfe lyke a hors. Also they be certayne great shyppes.

Centaurus, a ryuer, whiche was fyrst called Euenus.

Centimanus, hauynge a hundred handes.

Centipeda, a worme called a Palmer, whiche is heary, and hath many feete.

Cento, a quylte, or a iakke, or other lyke thynge stuffed with linnen, floxe, or cotten, or a cushyn made of pieces of cloth of dyuers colours.

Centrum, the poynt, whiche is in the very myddes of a thynge.

Centum, a hundred.

Centies, a hundred tymes.

Centum uiri, certayne iudges in Rome, beinge of the numbre of a hundred and fiue. And their iugementes were called Centum uiralia iudicia.

Centunculus, a vyle garment.

Centuria, a parte of an hoste, conteynynge an hundred men. Also a portion of ground in the felde, contayning an hundred acres.

Centuriatim, by a hundred togyther. Also plentuousely, or in a great numbre.

Centurio, nis, a capitayn ouer one hundred of foote men.

Centurio, aui, are, to diuide men into a company, contaynyng an hundred persons: or feldes into a hundred acres of lande.

Centussis, a hundred pounde weyghte, or a hundred pieces of that money that were called Asses.

Cephale, or lis, sygnifieth the heed.

Cephalea, the heed ache, whan al the heed dothe ake.

Cephalus, the name of a man, and of a fishe.

Cepheus, the name of a kynge of Ethiope.

Cephisia, the region Attica.

Cephisis, a laake nere to the see Athlanticū

Cepites, a precious stoone, hauynge manye whyte strikes.

Ceporus, a gardyner.

Ceramicus, a place in Athenes, where men beinge slayne in battayle, were buryed. Also an nother place, where commune women dwellyd.

Cerastes, a serpente, whiche hathe hornes lyke a ramme.

Cerasus, a chery tree.

Cerasum, a cherye.

Cerates, a smalle weight or poyse, whyche is the fourth part of a scrippule, the .xlviii. parte of an vnce.

Ceratinæ, is of Quint. called a spece of reasonynge inexplycable.

Cerberus, the porter of hell. Also a dogge with thre heedes, which Hercules drewe out of Helle.

Cercopithecus, a beast called a Marmoset.

Cerdo, nis, a cobblar.

Cereale, pertaining to Ceres the goddesse.

Cerebrum, the brayne.

Cerebrosus, a mā being braynsycke, or wild brayned, trustynge onely to his owne wyl.

Ceres, the goddesse of corne. sometyme it is vsed of Poetes for the selfe corne, or breadde.

Ceretani, a people in Spayne.

Ceretum, a towne in Italye.

Cerinthe, es, an herbe called a honysuckle.

Cerinthus, a thynge which is founde in honycombes, wheron bees do feede.

Ceritus

C ante E.

Cice. Do-
lobelle. &
ad Attic.

Ceritus, madnes or frensy.
Cerno, creui, cernere, to see or perceyue, also to consyder: sometyme to iuge, or determine. somtyme to trie out. Also to fyght in battayle, to entre into lande, which is happened vnto me by inheritance or gifte.
Cernuus, stowpynge or lookynge downewarde.
Certamen, a conflycte or byckerynge.
Certatim, oone contendynge or stryuynge with an other.
Certisso, aui, are, to be certified or sure.
Certitudo, dinis, certaintie or suretie.
Certo, aui, are, to contende or stryue.
Certus, ta, tum, certayn, sure, without dout. sometyme it sygnifyeth euen as we wolde haue it.
Certè et certò, surely.
Ceruus, a harte, or a forke, wherwith cotages be propped vp.
Ceruinus, na, num, of a harte.
Ceruicale et ceruical, a bolstar.
Ceruisia, ale or beere.
Ceruix, uicis, the hynder part of the necke.
Cerumina, eare waxe.
Cerus, a kynde of oken trees.
Cerussa, Ceruse, or whyte leade, wherwith some women be paynted, and colde playsters be made of it.
Cerix, cis, a pursyuant or bedyll.
Cespes, cespitis, a tirfe. some do call theym sottes, grasse and erthe togither.
Cessim ire, to recule or go backe.
Cesim ferire, to stryke edgelynge.
Cesso, aui, are, to ceasse, to leaue warke, to abyde.
Cessator, he that is slowe in dooinge his dewtie.
Cestrum, an instrument, wherwith iuorie is made holow. also a dagger, or a wimbyl. also an herbe, whiche is called Betayne.
Cetariæ, places nyghe the see syde, where Tunye and other greatte fysshes be taken and saltyd.
Cetarius, a fysshemonger, or taker of great fysshes.
Cetra, a lyghte tergate.
Cetrati milites, Sowldyours with lyghte tergates.
Cetus, a great fyshe called a whale.

¶ C ante H.

Chabrias, the name of a noble philosopher & capitayne of Athenes, which vsed to say, that more terrible was an hoste of hartes, hauynge to their capitayn a lyon, than an hoste of lyons, hauyng an harte their capitayne.

C ante H.   XVIII

Chalar.., a citie of Perse, whiche nowe is called Aetisiphon.
Chalaza, a gatherynge vnder the skynne lyke the diseafe called Bubo.
Chalastra, a certayne apparayle.
Chalcedonia, a citie in Asie agaynste Constantynople.
Chalcis, dis, the name of a citie in Grece. alfo of an yle, and of a byrde.
Chalcites, a stone of the colour of brasse, but more blacke.
Chaldæa, a region in Asia, ioyning to Arabic, wherin was the great cite of Babylon.
Chaldei, be taken for greate astronomers of the contrey of Assiria.
Chalestra, a citie of Thessaly on the se cost.
Chalyx, a flynte stone, oute of the whiche fyre is stryken.
Chalybes, a people in the lasse Asia, in the countrey called Pontus, whiche people do dygge greatte plentie of yron naked. It is properly taken for steele. And alfo it is the name of a fludde in Spayne.
Chamæcissos, an herbe called grounde iuy.
Chamædaphne, an herbe whiche groweth in length wynding togither in dyuers partes, and hath leaues lyke to lawrel or bays, and hath a floure lyke to a vyolette, and is called of some men perwyncle.
Chamædreos, an herbe called Germander.
Chamæleon, ontis, a lyttell beaste, hauynge his skynne spotted lyke to a lybard, whych chaungeth into dyuers colours, accordyng to the thynge that he seeth. They be ingendred in Inde, and is of the quantitie and figure of a lysard, but that his legges be lenger, and goeth vpryght, and hath a snoute lyke a swyne, a longe tayle, and small at the ende, his eyen be neuer closed, he doth neuer eate or drynke, but is nourisshed onely by ayre. Chameleon is also an herbe.
Chamæmelon, an herbe called camomylle.
Chamæteræ, maydens whiche were wonte to sytte at their maystresses feete.
Chamelopardalis, a beaste whyche is as great as a camel, of skynne and colour lyke Panther, hauynge spottes of sondrye colours, and hath his forelegges and necke longe, and the heed lyke a camell, his fete and legges lyke an oxe.
Chamelus, a beaste called a camelle, comuncly knowen.
Chania, the countrey callyd Epirus, Chaones, men of that countrey.
Chaos, a confuse matter without fourme, made fyrst of nothyng, wherof poetes supposed all other thynges to procede.
Characote, a frame, aboute the whiche vynes be wounde and tourned.

Characias

Characias, an herbe callyd Spourge.
Character, a token, a note made with a pen, a fygure, a style or fourme of speakynge.
Characteres, letters.
Charadrius, a greatte deuowrynge byrde of the see.
Caraxes, the brother of Sapphus.
Charistrium, a grene marble stone.
Carrisius, the name of a grammarion.
Charistia, the plurell numbre, is as it were a Christmas feaste, or a wake, where kynnesfolke do resorte togither, bryngyng or sendynge presentes mutually.
Charitas, charitie or loue, proprely toward men, or a mans countrey.
Charites, the graces, whiche were supposed to be the doughters of Jupiter, which were thre in noumbre, whose names were Aglaia, Thalia, Euphrosyne: And where in speakynge or wrytinge appered to be a meruaylous dilectation or swetenes, it was said that therin was a grace, in latine, Charis.
Chariophilon, a kynde of soote spyce that groweth in India.
Charon, tis, was named of the Paynyms, the booteman, that caried sowles ouer the three ryuers of Helle, Acheron, Stix, and Cocytus.
Caropus, amyable, pleasant, gratious.
Charta, paper. Also a leafe of paper, or other lyke thyng, wherin we do write. also a mayden that had neuer chylde.
Chartaceus, of paper.
Chartilago, ginis, a gryftell.
Chartophylacium, a coffer, or other lyke thynge, wherin papers and rolles be kept.
Charundas, the name of a man, which gaue lawes to the Atheniens.
Charus, well beloued.
Charybdis, a gulf of the see by Sicyl, wher in is daungerous saylynge, by reasone of stremes flowynge contrarye eche agaynst other, wherby shippes be therin deuourid.
Chasma, a gapynge, or openyng of the firmament, or of the erthe.
Chele, the klees of a Crabbe, Crauaise, or Scorpyon.
Chelonophagi, eaters of snayles.
Cheledonia, an herbe callyd Selandine. also a westerne wynde.
Chelys, a snayle. somtyme it is taken for an harpe or lute.
Chelydros, a see snayle.
Chemites, a maner of tombe, like to yuorie.
Chemiscus, a parte of the foreshyp, wherby the ancre doth hange. sometyme it is taken for all the shyppe.
Chennis, is an yland, as Pompon. writeth.
Chenoboscion, a place where geese be fed.

Chenopus, a goose foote.
Cheospes, a kynge of Aegypte.
Cherronesus, the parte of Grece callydde nowe Morea. It is sometyme taken for the north part of the great Asia, it is also callid Chersonesus.
Chersina, a kynde of lande snayles.
Chersydros, a serpent, whiche abydeth as well in water, as on londe.
Cherubin, one of the holy orders of aungelles, wherein is the science dyuine and mystycalle.
Cherusci, a people of Germany.
Chibis, an herbe.
Chilorus, a ryuer of Macedonie.
Chiliarchus, a capitayne of a thousand men.
Chilias, adis, the numbre of a thousande.
Chilon, one of the. vii. wyse men of Grece.
Chilones, men hauynge great lyppes.
Chimera, a gote. Also a mountayne in Lycia. Also a monster, hauynge thre heedes. one lyke a lyon, an other lyke a goote, the thyrde lyke a dragon.
Chimerinos, a cerkle of heuen, into the whiche whan the sonne cometh, the days be at shortest.
Chymus, the iuyce procedynge of meate digested, whiche by the vaynes commeth into the membres, and restoreth that whiche is consumed by heate.
Chios, an yle in the see callyd Eous, whiche was somtyme called Aeolia, where mastix growith.
Chiragra, the goute in the fyngers.
Chiragricus, he that hath suche a disease.
Chiridota, a cote with longe sleues.
Chirographum, et chirographus, an obligation or lyke instrumente, wherby a man is bounden, and hath put to his hande.
Chiromantia, palmestry.
Chiron, nis, the name of a man, whom poetes doo fayne to be the one halfe of a man, the other halfe lyke a hors: who fyrst dyd fynde the vertues of herbes, and taughte Aesculapius phisike, and Apollo to harpe, and Astronomy to Hercules, and was master to Achylles, and excelled all other men of his tyme in vertue and iustyce.
Chironium, is a sore in the legges or fete, which is hote, & swelleth by the two sydes.
Chironia, wylde vyne.
Chironomia, a facyon of gesture with the handes vsed in daunsynge, or in keruynge of meate.
Chirotheca, a gloue.
Chirurgia, surgerye.
Chirurgus, a surgion.
Chena, a cloke.
Chlamis, idis, a cloke, whiche proprely is
worne

worne by men of warre.
Chlamidatus, cloked.
Chobar, signifieth all the greatte floodes, which be in the region of Caldee.
Chœnix, icis, a certayne measure, contaynynge foure tymes the measure callyd Sextarius.
Cholera, an humour callyd choler. Also a syckenes callyd the colyke.
Choliambi, a certayne kynde of verses.
Chondros, a grayne of frankensence.
Choragium, stuffe, proprely wherwith that place is adorned, where as shall be enterludes or disguysynges.
Choragus, he that kepethe suche stuffe or apparayle.
Chorannei, certayn men that lyue in woddes in Persia, whiche are soo swyfte, that they take hartes with runnynge.
Choraula, the crafte to blowe trumpettes, or to playe on shawlmes, or other lyke pypes.
Choraules, players on the sayde Instrumentes.
Chorda, a corde or rope.
Chorea, a daunse.
Choriambus, a fote in meetre, which hath the fyrste syllable, and the laste longe, and two in the myddell short.
Chorius, a fote in meter, whiche by an other name is called trochæus, & is but of .ii. syllables, the fyrst longe, the seconde short.
Chorobates, a measure to meete grounde with, or a masons rule.
Chortos, hay, or grasse mowen.
Chorus, the company of players or dauncers. also a quyar.
Chresis, is vse, & catachresis is abusyon.
Chreston, an herbe called cycorie.
Chytrapus podis, a treuytte.

Columella Chrestus, the name of a noble authour of Athenes.
Chria, a notable sentence spoken shortly, to exhorte to vertue, or disswade from vyce.
Chrisis, vnction.
Christus, annoynted.
Chromaticus, whose colour neuer chaungeth, but is alway one.
Chronica, corum, an historie of actes done, with the tymes expressed. Cronicles.
Chronicus, ca, cum, temporal, or pertaynyng to tyme.
Chrysia, a cytie in Phrigie, and an ylande in Indie.
Chrysendetū, any thing bouden with gold.
Chryses, the name of a Prophete amonge the gentiles. Also of a maiden giuen by the grekes to kinge Agamenon at the battayle of Troye.

Chrysippus, the name of a famous and noble phylosopher.
Chrysoaspides, knyghtes that hadde shyldes of golde.
Chrysocolla, a stone with the pouder wherof paynters do make a golden colour. also goldsmythes do vse it to sowder golde.
Chrysocoma, golden heare.
Chrysocomus, he that hath golden heare.
Chrysogonum, that bryngeth forth golde.
Chrysolampis, a stone of fyrye coloure by nyghte.
Chrysomela, apples of the colour of gold. by an other name callid apples of Armeny.
Chrysolitus, a precious stone of the colour of golde.
Chrysopastus, a stone with golden spottes.
Chrysothemis, the doughter of Agamemnon and Clytemnestre.
Chrysostomus, the name of a byshoppe of Constantinople, and also of an hystoryen, whiche were so called for their eloquence. for Chrysostomus is in englysshe a golden mowthe.
Chus, a certayne measure conteynynge syx tymes the measure called Sextarius.
Chytra, a pot with feete, or a tryuette.

C. Ante I.

Cibale, pertaynyng to meate.
Cibarium, meate. cibarius, a, um, vyle.
Cibarius homo, a vyle persone.
Cibarium uinum, yll wyne.
Cibo, aui, are, to feede.
Ciborium, a kynd of appuls of Alexandry.
Cibus, meate.
Cicada, a grassehopper.
Cicatricosus, he that hath many tokens of woundes.
Cicatrix, icis, a token or scarre, where a wounde hadde ben.
Cicer, eris, a grayne lyke to peason.
Cicercula, differeth frome Cicer oonely in coloure.
Cicero, onis, the name of the mooste noble Romayne, whyche was the father of latyne eloquence.
Cichorea, & Cichorium, an herbe callydde Succorye.
Cicina, a nyght crowe.
Cicindula, a fly whiche shineth by nyghte.
Cicinia, a lyttell leane serpent in Italy.
Cicones, a people of Thrace.
Ciconia, a byrde called a storke. also it is a certain rule or measure.
Ciconi°, the name of him that buildid Brixia
Cicorium, an herbe that groweth euery where.

Cicum, the thyn rynde of Pomegranates.
Cicur, uris, tame.
Cicuro, aui, are, to make tame.
Cicuta, a venomous herbe, which groweth two cubytes in height, with a grene stalke full of knottes, bushy in the toppe, hauing leaues smaller than Coriander, and seedes greatter than anyse sede, and is horrible in sauour: Some dothe nowe vse that name for Hemlocke.
Cidaris, a cappe, which the kynges of Persia dydde vse, and also the byshoppes in the olde lawe.
Cieo, & cio, ciui, to meue a thyng, or to cal. Bellum ciebant, They dydde sette forth to battaylle.
Cileo, lui, ere, to meue or stirre a thyng.
Cilicia, a countrey ioynynge to Syria.
Cilicium, any clothe or garmente made of heare.
Cilium, the ouer skynne wherwith the eye is closed.
Cilix, licis, an inhabytant of Cilicia.
Cillibe, & cilliba, a rounde table.
Cilones, men hauynge great rounde foreheedes.
Cima, the teder part of the stalk of herbis.
Cimatia, thinges that be foure square.
Cimbri, a people called Danes. In the old tyme they inhabyted not onely Denmarke, but also all the yles frome Selande to the northe see.
Cimerii, people of Scythia, they that doo dwell in the countreys, where as is continuall colde and moche darkenes.
Cimex, a stynkynge worme bredynge in wodde or paper.
Cimolia creta, fullers klaye.
Cinedie, stones founde in a fyshes heed.
Cinedus, a wanton boy without shamefastnes. Also a daunser of galyardes and wanton maskes. It is also taken for a tumblar.
Cincinni, heares that be trymmed. Cincinnati, men hauynge their heare trymmed.
Cincticulus, a short cote called a ierkyn.
Cinctus, tus, a shorte garment, whiche the Consulle dydde weare, whan he profered battaylle.
Cinis, neris, asshes.
Cineraceus, & Cinereus, a, um, of the colour of asshes.
Cinericius, a, ū, bakē or rosted vnder asshes.
Ciniflo, nis, he that maketh hote the instrumentes, wherwith men or womenne dydde trymme their heare.
Cingo, cinxi, cingere, to gyrde or compasse aboute.
Cingria, a shorte pype, hauynge a smalle sownde.

Cingula, a gyrthe for beastes.
Cingulum, a gyrdell for men.
Cinna, a citie of Thessaly. also the name of a Romayne, whiche exceded in crueltie.
Cinnabaris, a stone callyd a Sanguinary. it is also callyd in latyn Sanguis draconis, dragons bloudde. it is put into sondrye medycynes to staunche bloudde.
Cinnamomum, & Cinnamum, a spyce callyd Cynnamom.
Cinniligium, a gyrdell, whiche a bryde or newe wedded wyfe weareth, a corse.
Cinnus, a heare of a man or womans heed, or a medly of dyuers thinges togither.
Ciperum, a soote plante or herbe, whiche is good to breake and expulse the stone.
Cippus, a payre of stockes. Also a lyttelle hylle, whiche menne calle a barowe. Also a tombe, a pyllar.
Circa, aboute, nyghe.
Circe, the name of a woman, by whome a citie in the countrey of Campania, callyd Circium, was buylded. Also a wytche, whiche tourned the companye of Ulysses into beastes.
Circēses ludi, were certain games in Rome wherin horses ranne with chariottes.
Circerus, a greate shyppe, whiche they of Asia vsed.
Circino, aui, are, to compasse, to make a cerkle.
Circinus, an instrument called a compasse.
Circiter, about: and it is referred somtime to tyme, as Circiter calendas Iunias, About the fyrste day of June. sometyme it is referred to the place. Circiter in media arce, Aboute the myddes of the castell. somtime to the thynge. Circiter duo millia hominum cesa sunt, There were nygh two thousande men slayne.
Circites, hoopes of brasse or yron.
Circitores, officers in cities, whiche do go aboute to see that good rule be kepte.
Circius, a sowtherne wynd, which is wonderfulle vehement.
Circuitores, the serchers of watches. Also they whiche do go about the stretes to sell garmentes or lynnen clothe.
Circulo, aui, are, to compasse or close with a dyche, or other lyke.
Circulatim, by cerkles, or in the fourme of a cerkle.
Circulator, he that gothe aboute to shewe hym selfe, or what he can do, or to deceyue the people.
Circulatorius, ia, ium, pertaynyng to suche auaunters or deceyuers.
Circulatrix, she that gothe aboute to gette money with daunsynge or tumblynge.

Circu=

Circulus, a cercle or compasse.
Circum, aboute.
Circumago, egi, agere, to leade aboute, to tourne about.
Circumiaceo, ieci, iicere, to put about.
Circumlitio, onis, bournishinge, klensynge, or polishinge.
Circummitto, to sende about.
Circummunio, iui, ire, to inclose, walle in, or dyche in.
Circumnascor, to growe aboute.
Circumplector, to imbrace or close in.
Circumscribo, psi, bere, to wryte, or drawe aboute with a lyne. Also to deceyue one in bargaynynge with hym. Fratrē circumscripsit in diuisione hereditatis, He deceyued his brother in particion of the inheritaunce. Also to gather, comprehende, or descryue throughely. Cuius scientię summam breuiter circumscribo, The effecte of whose lernynge I wylle comprehende or descryue shortely.

Apuleius. Circumsecus, on bothe sydes.
Circumsedeo, cessi, sedere, to besiege.
Circumsido, sedi, sidere, to go aboute to besiege.
Circumsisto, stiti, sistere, to stande about one, to defende hym.
Circumspectus, Circumspect.
Circumspicio, exi, cere, to looke about.
Circumspicuus, a, um, that maye be beholden on all partes.
Circūsto, steti, stare, to stande about.
Circumuado, to inuade, or perce on al partꝭ.
Circumueho, uexi, uehere, to cary about oftentymes.
Circumuenio, to compasse a man, to deceiue hym, to close him i, as in warres, to oppsse. Fœnore circūuentus, Oppressed with vsury.
Circumuolito, aui, are, to flee about.
Circumcelliones, tauerne haunters, or raylers aboute.
Circūcido, cidi, cidere, to cut about a thing.
Circumcolo, colui, colere, to dwel now here nowe there.
Circumcolumnium, a place sette about with pillars.
Circundare, to go aboute as a rynge dothe about a mās finger, or a diche about a close.
Circumeo, iui, ire, to go about any thynge.
Circumfero, to cary or beare about. Also to clense. Idem ter socios pura circumtulit vnda, Also he clensed his company thre times with cleane water.

Vergil, 6. Circumflexus, bowed.
Circumfluo, to abounde.
Circumfluere, is also to flowe or rounne aboute, as water aboute a cytie or Countreye.

Circumfluus, a, um, that floweth aboute.
Circumforaneus, a, um, that maye be, or is often caryed aboute.
Circumforanei, malaperte guestes and tellars of tydynges in markettes.
Circuo, iui, ire, to go aboute.
Circus, a Cercle. Also a rounde place walled aboute, of the whiche there were thre in Rome, where there was made certayne games.
Circius, the name of an yle in Mysia.
Cirnea, a cuppe.
Cirri, heares curled, or fethers that doo growe on the toppe of abyrdes heed, as a larke or an heron.
Cirtacus, a kynde of baume.
Cis, a worme amonge corne, which I suppose to be called weuyls. Also it sygnifieth on this syde: as Cis Rhenum, on this side the Ryuer of Rhyne: Cis Alpes, on this syde the mountaynes callyd Alpes. Some tyme it sygnyfyeth lasse. Cis naturę leges, Lesse than the lawes of nature may suffre. Salust vseth it ones for beyonde. Cis Rhenū atq̄ intra mare nostrum et oceanum, Beyonde the ryuer of Rhine, and within our see, and the occean see.
Cisalpina Gallia, was somtyme that countreye, whyche is frome the mountaynes callydde Alpes, vnto the Ryuer of Rubycon.
Cicium, a carte.
Ciciarius, a cartar.
Cispius, a mountayne in Rome.
Cisseus, a kynge of Thrace, father of Hecuba, quene of Troy.
Cissybium, a cuppe or bolle made of iuy.
Cissites, a precious stone lyke an yuy leafe, bright of colour.
Cista, a cheste, coffer.
Cisterna, a cesterne.
Citatus, called, sommoned, or cited.
Cithara, a harpe.
Citharis, a byshopes myter.
Citharista, an angle of Fraunce by Marcile, lyinge out to the see.
Citharistria, a woman harper.
Citharizo, aui, are, to harpe.
Citharœdus, a harper.
Cytisus, an herbe called chickwede.
Citimus, ma, mum, the laste.
Cito, aui, are, to cite, to sommon, or call.
Citorus, a mountayne where groweth plētie of boxe trees.
Citra, on this syde, sometyme without. Citra adulationem, without flatterye.
Citreum, an orenge.
Citrus, a tree called a citron tree.
Citrum, a fruite callyd pome citron.

D.ii. Cittium

Cittium, a towne of Cyprus.
Citus, quycke, hasty, swyfte. Sommetyme deuided or parted.
*Cito, soone, shortly.
Ciuicus, ca, cum, is the same that ciuilis is.
Ciuica corona, a garlande of oken leaues, vsed to be gyuen to them that had saued a citesyn in battayle.
Ciuilis, le, that pertayneth to a cytesyn.
Ciuilis homo, a man experte in those thinges, that appertayne to the ministration of a common weale.
Ciuilitas, tatis, courteysy, ciuilitie.
Ciuis, a citesyn or denisen. Also Ciuis meus my countrey man.
Ciuitas, tatis, a citie, proprely it is the multitude of cytesens gathered togyther, to lyue accordyng to lawe and ryght.
Cius, a ryuer of Thrace.
Cizicus, a citie in Asie the lesse.

¶ C ante L.

Clades, dis, a discomfyture in battaile, a distruction of men.
Clam, priuilye, vnwares. Clam me profectus est, vnwaares to me, he wente his waye.
Clamo, aui, are, to crye, to calle.
Clamor, oris, a crye, a clamour, a noyse.
Clamosus, a, um, clamorous or ful of noyse.
Clanculum, secretely.
Clandestino, priuily, or secretly.
Clandestinus, a, um, priuie, or secrete.
Clango, xi, gere, to sowne a trumpette.
Clangor, oris, the sowne of a trumpet. somtyme the crie that geese or other lyke byrdes do make.
Clanius, a citie of Champayne, nere to the citie Acerras.
Clareo, ui, ere, to appere, to be wel knowen, and to be clere.
Clare, clerely, apparantly.
Clarifico, eci, cere, to make clere or apparāt
Clarigatio, a clerynge, a subsydie or taske graunted by a commune consent.
Clarigo, aui, are, to aske clerely.
Claritas, tatis, clerenes. sometyme nobylitie, or honourablenes.
Claro, aui, are, to make noble or honorable.
Claros, a citie in Grece.
Clarus, a riuer, whiche rounneth from the high mountaynes of Alpes, into the ryuer callyd Danubium.
Clarus, ra, ū, clere, noble, honorable, famous
Classiarius, diligent.
Classicus, an officer, which with a trūpette or tabore called people togither. sometime a man beinge in reputation.

Classicum, a peale or noyse of trumpettes, or belles to calle menne togither, or to goo to battaile.
Classicus, ca, um, pertaynynge to nauyes.
Classis, a nauie of shyppes. sometyme it is taken for one shyppe. somtyme companyes or sortes of people, ordered in a citie after the value of their substaunce. Also Classes be degrees or formes in scholes : as prima classis, the fyrste degree or fourme. zc.
Clatro, aui, are, to shutte a wyndowe, specially a lattyse wyndowe.
Clatrum et clatrus, a lattyse wyndowe, or any thynge made lyke a lattyse.
Claua, a clubbe.
Clauarius, an offycer appoynted to deale the emperours gyfte of money or corne amonge the souldiours.
Clauator, he that vseth a clubbe.
Clauatus, sette with nayles.
Claudeo, to halte. somtyme to erre.
Claudianus, the name of a poete.
Clauditas, haltynge, lamenesse.
Claudius, the name of an emperor of Rome
Claudo, si, dere, to shytte. somtyme to compasse : also to put of : also to halte.   Salustius.
Claudus, a, um, lame.
Clauicula, a lyttell kay or clubbe.
Clauicularius, he that beareth the kayes.
Clauiculus, the tendrelle of a vyne.
Clauiger, idem quod clauicularius.
Clauis, a kaye.
Claustrarius, a maker of kayes and lockes.
Claustrinus, a keper of the cloyster, or of any other place, wherin any lyuyng thyng is inclosed.
Claustrum, a cloister, or other place, where any lyuynge thinge is inclosed.
*Clausula, a lyttell sentence, or a parte of a sentence.
Clausura, a shuttynge in.
Clauus, a nayle. Also the sterne of a shippe. Also a corne on a mans toe or fingar. More ouer, Claui be lyttell swellynges of harde fleshe in the corner of mens eien. Also puffes growing in the stemmis of great trees. Also in harneys, that whiche is callyd the ryuet. Moreouer Clauus is a garment pirled or powdred with spangles, lyke nayles heedes. Wherfore the propre garmente of a Senatour was callyd latus clauus.
Clazomenæ, a citie of Jonie, whiche Paralus buylded.
Clazomenia, an ylande, whiche is called Marathusa.
Cleantes, the name of a philosopher, whiche succeded Zeno in his schole.
Clearch9, the name of a philosopher. There was a noble capytayne of the same name,

of

of whom Xenophon wryteth in thexpedition of Cyrus the lesse.
Clemens, tis, mercyfull.
Clemencia, mercy.
Clementer, mercyfully.
Cleobulus, the name of oone of the seuen wyse men of Grece.
Cleodamas, the name of a geometrician in the tyme of Plato.
Cleombrotus, the sonne of Pausanias, capitayne of the Lacedemons.
Cleopatra, the name of a lady quene of Egypte.
Clepo, psi, pere, to stele.
Clepsydra, a dyall, which dyuided the houres by the rounnynge of a certayne measure of water. It was also the name of a fountayne in Athenes.
Cleronoma, herytage.
Cleronomos, an heyre.
Clerus, chosen by lotte. Also a worme, whi the distroyeth and corrupteth hony cōbes.
Clibanarius, he that fyghtethe in iustynge harnayse.
Clibanus, an ouē, or the mouth of a furneis.
Cliens, tis, a clyent or seruant retayned.
Clientela, the nombre of clyentes or of seruantes retayned, also their offyce or dutie.
Clientularium, an yerely fee, for counsayle, or assystence.
Clima, tis, is a porcion of the worlde betwene south and north, wherin is variacyon of tyme in the lengthe of the daye, the space of halfe an houre, whiche is set oute in the tables and chartes of Cosmography
Climacterius, ca, cū, signifyeth the degrees of mans lyfe by seuen yeres, in the whyche he is in daunger of death or mysfortune.
Climactericum tempus, the sayde daungerouse tyme.
Climacterum, idem.
Climax, a ladder, and the fygure callydde gradation.
Clinicus, a phisition, that healeth with medicines. Also he that is so syck, that he can not aryse out of his bedde.
Clinopodion, an herbe.
Clinopale, wrastlynge in the bedde.
Clio, the name of one of the musis.
Clisis, declynation.
Clitelle, a packesaddell. Also the name of a place in Rome.
Clitellarii, packehorses or mules, that doo serue for caryage.
Clitomachus, the name of a phylosopher.
Clitorius, a fountayne in Grece.
Clitumnus, a ryuer in Italy.
Cloaca, a synke, whereby water passethe, or gutter.

Cloris, a mayden or nymphe, whiche was maryed to Zephyrus, vnto whome was assygned for her dower, to haue reule ouer flowers.
Clotho, one of the fatall ladyes, hauynge power ouer mannes lyfe, in dyssoluynge thereof.
Cludo, si, dere, to shytte.
Cluo, ui, ere, to contende or fyght.
Clumę, the huske of barley.
Clunaculum, a bowchers choppyng knife.
Clupea, a cyte of Affrike, next to Cartage.
Clunes, the buttockes or haunches.
Clymene, the moder of Promotheꝰ, daughter of Oceanus.
Clypeus, a shielde or targate of fotemen.
Clismus, a pourgation or washynge.
Clytemnestra, the wyfe of Agamemnon.
Clyster, eris, and Clysterium, a glyster.

¶C ante N.
¶Cneus, the name of a man.

¶C ante O.

Coacesco, coacesci, coacescere, to waxe all sowre.
Coætaneus, of one age.
Coagmento, taui, tare, to ioyne togyther, or make lyke.
Coagulo, aui, are, to gather into a kourde or creame.
Coagulum, curde or creame.
Coalesco, coalui, coalescere, to gather togither, to increase.
Coarcto, aui, are, to strayne or presse togyther.
Coasso, to planke or bourde.
Coaxare, to make a noyse lyke a frogge or tode.
Cocalus, a kynge of Sycile, to whom Dedalus fledde out of Creta, whome Minos kynge of Crete pursued.
Coccentum, a meate made of honye and popye sede.
Cocceus, a, um, et Coccineus, a, um, of scarlette colour.
Coccina, a scarlette vesture.
Coccinus, et Coccus, scarlette colour.
Coccum, grayne wherwith cloth and silke is grayned.
Cochlea, a snayle. somtyme the shelle, somtime cokles. Also a winding staire or vyse.
Cochleare, a spone.
Cochlium, a wyndynge stayre.
Cochlides, rounde ladders.
Coclites, a man, hauynge but one eye.
Coctie, a parte of the mountayns of Alpes.
Coctilis, hoc coctile, soden or baken.

D.iiii.   Coctis

Coctito, aui, are, to boyle.
Coctiuus, a, um, easy to be boyled.
Coctonum, cotten.
Coctus, ta, tum, sodden ynough.
Coculum, a potte to boyle in. sommetyme cocula doo sygnyfie styckes, whyche wyll soone be on fire.
Cocus, a Cooke.
Cocynthum, a mountayne in Italy, that diuideth two sees.
Cocytia, sacrifices that were doone in honour of Proserpine.
Cocytus, a ryuer of Helle.
Coccis, igis, a byrde called a cocowe.
Coda, a tayle.
Codatremula, a byrde callydde a waggetayle.
Codex, icis, the body of a tree, or a greate boke or volume.
Codicillus, a lybell.
Codiculus, a dyminutife of codex, whan it is put for a boke.
Codonia, an yland, that the almayns kepe.
Codrus, the propre name of a kynge of Athenes, which to saue his coūtrey, willingly loste his lyfe.
Cœliacus, he that is sycke of the colycke.
Cœmeterium, a churche yarde.
Cœna, a soupper.
Cœnacularia, the way or crafte to ordayne a supper.
Cœnaculariam facere, to lette a house in diuers partes to sondry persones, wherein are many parlers or drynkyuge houses.
Cœnacularius, he that doth lette such houses to hyre. Vlp. de pignor. act. l. Solutum.
Cœnaculum, a parler, or other place where men do soupe.
Cœnaticus, ca, cum, pertayning to suppers.
Apparatus cænaticus, ordinance for supper.
Sermo cænaticus, communication mete for suppers.
Cœnatio, a lowe parler for to soupe in, a sommer parler.
Cœnatorius, a, um, bilongynge to suppers.
Cœnaturio, ii, ire, to labour or endeuour my selfe to soupe.
Cœnipeta, a goer about to suppers vnbodē.
Cœno, aui, are, to soupe.
Cœnobium, a Monasterye or other place, where men lyue in commune.
Cœnula, a lyght soupper.
Cænum, myre.
Coëo, iui, ire, to come togither with other, to ioyne to, to drawe togyther, to gather togither, to do the acte of generation.
Coerceo, cui, cere, to restrayne, to bynde harde or straight, to compell or constrayn.
Cœtus, an assembly of people.

Cogitatim, aduysedly.
Cogito, aui, are, to thynke.
Cogitatio, onis, a thought.
Cognati, kynnesmen.
Cognitor, oris, he that pleadeth an nother mannes cause, his clyent beinge present.
Cognobilis, knowen.
Cognomen, a surname, whiche a man hath of his auncetours.
Cognomines, dyuers men of one surname.
Cognomino, aui, are, to gyue a surname.
Cognosco, noui, noscere, to knowe, to consyder, to vnderstande, to lye with a woman, to iuge a matter, or here a mattier to iudge it.
Cogo, coëgi, cogere, to constrayne, to gather to gyther, to mylke a beaste, to make lycour thycke or harde, to presse into, to set or brynge in order.
Cohibeo, ui, ere, to restrayne, to keepe of, to lette.
Cohors, tis, a company of men of warre, a courte wherin pultrie is kepte.
Cohortor, aris, ari, to exhorte.
Cohum, a thonge or lyngell, wherwith the oxe bowe & the yoke are bounden togider.
Coinquino, aui, are, to soyle, or make foule.
Cois, a garment of fyne sylke.
Colaphizo, aui, are, to buffette.
Colaphus et colaphum, a buffette.
Colasis, a kynde of punyshemente that is done for chastisemente.
Colax, a flatterer.
Colchis, an Ile in Asia, where Medea was borne.
Coleus, the codde of a man.
Coliculus, a tender stalke of an herbe.
Colidos, an Ilande in the occean of Inde.
Coliphium, a kynde of breadde.
Colis, the braunche of a vyne.
Colitia, a great furrowe for water to runne into, for sauynge of the corne.
Colla, a kynde of glewe.
Collabello, aui, are, to ioyne lyppes in kyssynge.
Collacrimo, aui, are, to wepe with other.
Collare, a coller for a hounde.
Collactaneus, he that souketh with me one norise, a foster brother.
Collatina porta, the name of a yate in Rome
Collatinus uenter, a great swollen bealye.
Collatio, onis, a conferrynge togither.
Collatis signis pugnare, to fyght in a fielde pyghte.
Collectanea, thynges writen, gathered out of many warkes.
Collectitius, a, um, that which is gathered.
Collega, a felowe or companyon in offyce.
Colliculus, a hyllocke.

Col-

Collido, si, ere, to beate togither.
Colligo rationem, I make accompt.
Colligo, legi, ligere, to gather togyther, to take a way, to bryng togither. Seipsum colligere, to brynge home agayne the partes of the mynde, that were dispersed. Also to prepare. Se colligit in arma, he made hym redy to fyght. *Ci. Tus. 4. Virgilius.*
Colligo, aui, are, to bynde togither.
Collimare, to wynke with one eye.
Collina porta, a yate at Rome.
Collino, to lyne, or lay by lyne.
Collis, a hylle. also colles the backe.
Colossus, an ymage as hygh and great as a towre.
Colluco, aui, are, to make a glade in a thycke wodde.
Collum, a necke.
Colluuiarium, a synke or gutter.
Colluuies, whan the erthe is couered with water by greatte floodes.
Collutilo, aui, are, to defyle.
Collyrida, a cake.
Collyrium, a medicine for soore eyes.
Colo, aui, are, to strayne out lycour.
Cola, a streynour.
Colo, ui, ere, to worshyp, to loue, or fauour, to haunte, to inhabyte or dwelle, to leade. Hanc uitam colo, I leade this lyfe. to tylle, or husbande grounde.
Colobium, a iacket or cote without sleues.
Colocasia, a beane of Egypte.
Colochynta, a frute whiche purgeth fleme.
Colon, a gutte, whiche goth from the left syde vnto the right, in the which the dunge taketh his fourme, and there is the disease called Colica, the colyke. It is also a membre or parte of a sentence.
Colonia, people sent to dwell in a place, whiche is not inhabyted. Also a house of husbandrye.
Colonicus, ca, cum, pertaynynge to housbandrye.
Colonus, a husbandemanne. also coloni be they, whiche are sent to inhabyte a countrey or towne. Also a hygh place in Athenes, where Neptune was worshypped.
Colophon, onis, the name of an yle: and also of a citie in Grece.
Colophonem addere, to make an ende, or fynishe a warke.
Color, oris, colour.
Coloriæ uestes, garmentes made of wolle vndyed.
Colorificus, he that maketh colour.
Coloro, aui, are, to gyue or make a colour.
Colos, the fundement.
Colostrum, creame of mylke.
Colotes, the name of a manne that was a peynter. Quint. li. 2.

Coluber, a serpent, which lyeth in the shadowe of woddes.
Colum, a strayner.
Columbar, aris, a pyllory.
Columbaris, et hoc columbare, of a doue.
Columbarium, uel columbaria, a douehouse or culuerhouse.
Columbatim, in the maner of doues.
Columbarius, he that taketh doues.
Columbaria, an ylande in the Tuskayn see.
Columbus, et columba, a culuer or doue.
Columbinus, a, um, of a culuer.
Columella, the name of oone that wrate of husbandry moste eloquently.
Columellares dentes, cheke tethe.
Columen, luminis, the succour or staye, the wynde beame of a house.
Columis et hoc colume, hole.
Columna, a royall citie in Bruce.
Columna, a pyllar.
Columnus, was in olde tyme that we calle nowe culmus.
Coluri, certayne cerkles in the celestialle Sphere.
Colus, a distaffe.
Colymbades, olyues, or oyle beries.
Collybus, an exchange of money.
Collybistes, an exchaunger.
Collybia, fygge tartes, tartes of Portyngall, or other lyke thinges.
Coma, al the heare togyther called a bushe
Comagena, a countrey in Syria.
Comare, to haue moche heare, or a greate busshe.
Comatus, ta, he or she that hathe a greatte bushe. By translation it is sayde of trees or herbes, that haue longe leaues or floures.
Comara, a shepardes name in Theocr.
Comata Gallia, all Fraunce, a this half the mountaynes.
Comatulus, a boye with a fayre busshe of heare.
Combino, aui, are, to combyne or confederate togyther.
Comburo, bussi, burere, to burne or cōsume with fyre.
Come, an herbe callyd gotes bearde.
Comedo, edi, edere, to eate.
Comedo, donis, he that consumeth his own goodes ryottously.
Comes, mitis, a companyon or felowe. Also a name of dignitie, which we cal an erle.
Comessatio, a bankette after soupper.
Comessari, to bankette.
Comessabundus, vsyng to bankette.
Cometes et cometa, a blasynge sterre.
Comis, gentyll, full of good humanitie.
Comiter, gentylly.
Comitatus, tus, a felowshyppe,

Co=

Comitialis dies, the daye whan people assembled at Rome, for the election of officers.
Comitialis morbus, the fallynge sycknes.
Comitium, a congregation or assemble of the people for election of officers. Also the place where the election is made.
Comitor, aris, to accompanye or goo with one, or kepe felowshyp with other.
Comma, a poynt ending a sentence, where many sentences be: as, Nihil tibi profuit nocturnum presidium palacii, nihil urbis uigilis, nihil timor populi, nihil concursus omnium bonorum: There is Comma foure tymes.
Commanducatus cibus, chewed meate.
Commanducare, to chewe meate.
Commeatus, tus, a saulfe conduct, or leaue to departe. sometyme vytailes for an army or multitude of menne. sommetyme for a passage of men.
Commemoro, aui, are, to remembre.
Commendaticius, a, um, that wherwith a man is remembred or recommended.
Commendo, aui, are, to commend or praise, sometyme to recommende.
Commentaculum, a marshals or huyshers rodde.
Commentor, taris, to thynke on, to make mencyon, to dispute, to write comentaries, or bokes for remembrance.
Commentarium, uel commentarius, a brigement or other boke, conteynynge thynges briefely writen. Also it signifieth a coment. Also a boke of remembrance or a Register or exposition.
Commenticius, a, um, fayned, or deuysed for the tyme.
Commentum, a comment or exposytion, a matter fayned.
Commeo, aui, are, to go hither and thider, or to go to, or with an other.
Commertium, an entercourse or lybertie to cary marchandyse from one place to an other. Also a commutation or forme of bieng and sellynge togither. Also a famylyarytie or custome.
Commereo, ui, ere, to commytte. Si senserit te timidum pater, arbitrabitur commeruisse culpam, If thy father doo perceyue the to be aferde, he woll suppose, that thou arte gyltie, or haste committed the offence. Also commerere, to deserue. *Terent.in Phor.*
Commessari, to feede more than ynough. *Q. Curtis*
Commigro, to go with one to a place.
Comilitones, felowes togyther in warres.
Commilitium, felowshyp in warres.
Comminiscor, sceris, to cal to remembrance.
Comminus, forthewith atte hande, hande to hande.
Commissura, a ioynt of any thynge that is closed and opened, as proprely of tables, whiche be ioyned.
Commitigo, gaui, gare, to knocke. Tibi uti comitigari uideam sandalio caput, That I may see the knocked on the heed with his slypper. *Terentius.*
Committo, misi, mittere, to commyt, or in ioyne, to offende, to ioyne togither. Also to do and begynne. Quibus dictis mox preliu commisere, That spoken, they began batayle. Also to delyuer, to compare, to bring in contencion, to put togither, to confiscate or sease for a forfayture. *Salustius.*
Commodata res, a thynge lende withoute aduauntage. *Ci.in Ver. act. 3.*
Commodatarius, he that taketh a thynge of lone, he that boroweth.
Commoditas, ratis, a commoditie.
Commodo, aui, are, to do for an other mannes commoditie. Also to lende.
Commodum, profite or commoditie. Also good, apte, or conueniente. sometyme it is an aduerbe, and than it sygnifieth the same tyme, in good tyme, scarsely. Commodum discesseras heri, cum Trebatius uenit, Thou were scasely departed, whanne Trebatius was come.
Commodus, a, um, profitable, or apte.
Commoereo, rui, rere, to be all heuy or sory.
Commonefacio, feci, facere, to warne.
Commoneo, nui, ere. Idem.
Commotria, a mayden that dothe araye or apparayle her maystresse.
Commoueo, ui, ere, to trouble, to turne or change a mans mynde. to hurt. somtyme to depart. Tu et cura, ut ualeas, et te istinc ne temere commoueas. Farwell, and take hede that thou departe nat hense to hastily. *Ci. Tyro.*
Communico, aui, are, to comunicate or departe some thynge with an nother, whyche I haue.
Communis, commune, common.
Commuto, aui, are, to chaunge one thynge for an other.
Commutare uerba, to chyde, or to grue a shrewde worde for a good.
Como, psi, ere, to apparayle gorgiously, to trymme, proprely it belongeth to wome.
Comoedia, an enterlude, wherin the common vices of men and womenne are apparantly declared in personages.
Comoedice, gentylly and pleasantly.
Comoedior, aris, to ieste, or scoffe.
Comoedus, a player in enterludes.
Comicus, a maker of enterludes.
Compactum, an agreement or appoyntmet
Compagino, aui, are, to put or ioyne togyther a thynge that is lowsed.
Compago, ginis, a ioining togither of thing.

Com

C ante O.

Compar, aris, equall, or euen lyke.
Comparatiuus, a, um, comparatiue, wherin begynneth excesse in comparyson.
Comparo, aui, are, to compare or make equall, or more, to ordeyne, to prepare, to ioyne, to deuyse, to bye.
Comparatio, comparyson, preparation, or brenge.
Compasco, to fede or kepe cattell.
Compascuus ager, a common fielde.
Compedes, gyues or fetters.
Compeditus, a, um, fettred or gyued.
Compello, puli, pellere, to compelle or constrayne, to ioyne or brynge togither.
Compello, aui, are, to speake to, to accuse.
Compendiarius, a, um, copendious or brefe.
Compendiosus, a, um, very profitable.
Compendium, a sauynge or sparyng, or aduauntage, a compendious or shorte fourme in wrytinge or other acte.
Compendifacio, to make compendious.
Compenso, aui, are, to make recompense, or amendes.
Compensatio, onis, a recompense, or satisfaction.
Coperendino, to deferre, or put of, or delay.
Comperendinatio, a delaye.
Comperendinaria dies, a daye ouer in matters of lawe.
Comperio, ii, ire, to knowe of an other man.
Comperior, iris, to fynde, or imagin in myn owne opinion.
Compertus furti, founden gyltie of felony.
Compertum habeo, I knowe or perceyue.
Compernis, he that hath his knees nyghe to gither, or longe fete.
Compesco, scui, scere, to assuage, to mitigate
Competo, tii, tere, to aske, or sue for an offyce, or other lyke thinge agaynst an other that dothe the semblable. Competit, It is mete or couenient. Hoc illi competit, That is mete or conuenient for hym. Also it is suffycyent.
Compilo, aui, are, to take by extorcyon or wronge, or as the vulgare speche is, Compilare is to polle and shaue.
Compilati, polled by extorcion.
Compingo, pegi, pingere, to thruste. Quid faciam nunc, si tres uiri me in carcerem compegerint? Howe shall I do nowe, if the offycers thruste me into prison. Sommetyme Compingere is to compact, or put togider.
Compita, many pathes goynge into oone waye.
Compitalia, feastes or drynkynges, made where as be many pathes.
Compitalicius, cia, um, belongynge to the sayde feastes.
Complector, eris, to imbrace or hold straite

C ante O.   XXIII

Complector te amore, I loue the hartilye.
Complector cogitatione, I beare in mynd.
Complector animo, I consyder.
Compleo, eui, ere, to fulfylle, or fyll to the toppe, to fynyshe, or perfome, to make vp, or supply that lacketh.
Complex, plicis, partener, copanyon in act.
Complexus, imbracynge or collynge. Also agrement in wordes or sentences.
Complico, aui, are, to folde or wrappe togyther.
Complodo, si, dere, to clappe togyther the handes for ioye.
Complura, ryght many.
Compluries, very often.
Compluuium, a gutter, wherin fallyth rain from many houses.
Compono, to put or ioyn togither, to make ordeine, or dispose. Also to compare, to adorne, to gather, to recreate, to appease, to conclude, to accorde or agree, to redeme, to dissemble or fayne.
Compos, potis, he that hath his purpose or desyre. also euer content.
Compos animi, of sownde remembraunce, not madde.
Compos uoti, he that hath his own desire or appetite.
Compositio, onis, a makynge, an ornament, a composition or agrement.
Compredes, sureties or pledges togither.
Coprimo, pressi, primere, to presse or thrust togither, to holde or refrayne. Also to defloure a woman.
Compressus, a defloration or rauyshement.
Comptus, tus, freshe apparayle.
Compulsus, a, um, compellyd or hytte with any thynge.
Compunctus, a, um, marked, or spotted.
Compungo, xi, gere, to punche, or prycke, or stryke.
Computo, aui, are, to deme, to accounte, to decerne, to impute.
Comum, a cytie of France on this syde the mountaynes, the inhabytantes wherof are called comenses.

¶C ante N.

Concateno, aui, are, to bynde togither with chaynes.
Concauus, a, um, holowe.
Concedo, cessi, dere, to graunt, to permitte, or suffre, to departe away, to go to a place, to consente.
Concentus, tus, a consente, many voyces in one tune, or accorde in musyke.
Conceptaculum, or conceptabulu, any thing holowe and apte to receyue or holde, as a vessell.

Con-

Concepta uerba, wordes expressed and pronounced.

Conceptus, ta, tum, conceyued.

Conceptus, tus, a conception of a chylde within a woman. And also a conceyte or thyng conceyued in thought.

Concernere, to concerne.

Concertatum, debated in reasonynge.

Concha, proprely a muskle. sometyme the shell of a muskle, oyster, or cockle. Also euery vessell that is holow, and open aboue, proprely a bolle, wherin lynnen clothes be washed. somtyme a wyne vessel Also a trumpet, as it semethe made of erthe, lyke to suche as the poore men do vse, which haue the fallyng sycknes, and do come from the place in Ducheland, called saint Cornelius.

Conchis, a meate made of beanes.

Conchon, is called a vessell of the grekes, or the holownes of the eies.

Conchus, a perle.

Conchile, & conchilium, a kynde of shelle fyshe, out of the whiche a lycour is taken, wherwith sylke is dyed purple. it is sometyme taken for the purple colour.

Conchiliata uestis, a purple garmente.

Concido, cidi, ere, cisum, to cutte in pieces, to die. Cæsar.

Lactātius. Concido, concidi, ere, concasum, to falle downe all togither. Et muri ciuitatum concident, And the walles of all cities shal fall all togither.

Conciliabulum, a counsell house.

Conciliabundus, he that is redye to gyue counsayle.

Consiliatrix, a woman that endeuoureth hir to make agreemente betwene menne and their wyues.

Concilio, aui, are, to accorde or make frendes togither.

Conciliare affinitatem, uel pacem, to make alyance or peace.

Conciliare odium, uel inimicitias, to get hatred or displeasure.

Concilium, counsayle, or the assemblye of counsaylours.

Concinnitudo, dinis, aptenes, or proprenes.

Concinno, aui, are, to make apte, or propre, or fytte.

Concinnus, a, um, apte, fytte, propre.

Concinere, to agre in one song, or one tune.

Concio, ciui, cire, to call togyther a multitude.

Concio, onis, a pulpet or stage, wherein he standeth that exhorteth people. Also an assembly or congregation of people, callyd togyther, to here the commaundement of the kynge, or other in authorytye in the weale publyque. Also it is the oration or proposition made vnto them, called a cōcion.

Concionalis, he that is wont to make orations or propositions to the people.

Concionatorius, ria, rium, pertayninge to a Concyon.

Concionor, aris, ari, to preache or purpose a matter to the people.

Concionator, oris, he that preachethe or purposeth an oration.

Concipio, cœpi, cipere, to conceyue or apprehende, to delyberate, or determyne in mynde.

Concipere iusiurandū, to swere in recyting the othe, as it is ministred.

Concito, aui, are, to steere.

Conclamatum est, it is at a poynte, or paste remedy.

Conclaue, a priuy or secrete chambre. sometyme a bankettynge chambre.

Concludo, clusi, dere, to conclude or make an ende.

Conclusio, onis, a conclusyon or ende of a matter.

Concordare, to be at a cōcorde or agremēt.

Concoquo, coxi, concoquere, to digest.

Concordia, concorde or agrement.

Concorporo, aui, are, to make one thynge of dyuers.

Concors, dis, of one wyll or mynde.

Concrepare, to make a greatte noyse, or to creke, as a doore dothe in the openyng.

Concretum, congeled or conglutinate.

Concubitor, oris, he that medlethe with a womanne.

Concubium, the fyrste slepe in the nyghte, or the depest of the nyght.

Concumbo, bui, concumbere, et concubo, aui, are, to lye togither, to accompany togither, in the acte of generation.

Concupisco, piui, piscere, to coueyte or desyre feruently.

Concupiscentia, a feruent desyre or appetite carnall.

Concutio, tii, tere, to shake.

Condecet, it well becommeth.

Condecenter, agreably.

Condecentia, a besemynge.

Condemno, aui, are, to condemne.

Condecoro, aui, are, to make cleanly, or honeste, to polyshe.

Condico, xi, cere, to appoynt, to ordeyn, to promise, to aske agayn, to denye, to assigne by mouthe, to denounce, or declare. **Titus. Li.**

Condictio, onis, an action in the law, or appoyntment to a day certayne.

Condictum, a promyse.

Condio, iui, uel dii, dire, to season meate, to pouder, or otherwise order it, to preserue it from corruption.

Condi-

Condimentum, that wherwith thynges be preserued from corruption, or elles made dilectable in tast.

Conditaneus, a, um, that whiche is to be preserued.

Conditio, onis, Condicion, fortune, estate, election, or choyse.

Conditionem accepit, He toke the bargain or promise, or he agreed.

Conditicia cibaria, powderid meate, or other wise preserued.

Conditiuus, a, um, that which may be powdered or kepte.

Conditor, oris, A maker.

Conditorium, a Sepulchre, a place wherin ordinaunce for warre is kepte.

Condo, didi, dere, to laye saulfe, or hyde. sometyme to make, or buylde.

Ci. Tus. lib. 5. Condocefaceo, feci, facere, to make to knowe.

Condris, an herbe, called false dittayn, by cause it is lyke dyttayne, but it hathe lesse leaues.

Conducibile, profitable.

Conduco, xi, cere, to brynge with me, to hyre, to take a house or lande. also to gather, to conuert.

Conducere, to profyte.

Conducit, it is profytable.

Conductitius, a, um, that whiche may be hyred or taken, or is vsed to be hyred.

Condalium, a rynge.

Condyloma, atis, a swellynge in the fundement, somtyme harde, somtyme softe.

Condylos, the knuckle of a fynger.

Confecta, thynges voyded or concluded by reason.

Confercio, to stuffe, or porre.

Confertus, ta, tum, gathered as people be gathered in a prease, thycke sette.

Confertissima turba, in the thyckest prease.

Plautus. Confero, tuli, ferre, to put togither, to sette forthe, to prepare, to put in. Ne posterius in me culpam conferas, Put not at the last the defaut in me. Consilia conferunt, They kepe their counsels togither. To lay to, or ioyne.

Terentius Nouissima conferam primis, I wyll lay to, or ioyne the laste to the fyrste. Conferre, to profyte. Conferre in pauca, To conclude shortly. Also conferre, to lay togither. Sitq́; utriq́; proximum horreum, quo conferatur *Columella* rusticum instrumentū, To bothe, next there muste be a barne, wherin maye be layde vp togyther instrumentes longyng to husbandry. Also Confero, I gyue. Multa contuli in Catonem, I haue gyuen or attribute moch to Cato, I haue fauored moche Cato. Contuli me domum, I went home. Contuli me ad Catonem, I went vnto Cato.

Conserua, an herbe whyche groweth in freshe waters lyke to a spunge.

Confessor, oris, a confessour.

Confestim, eftesoones.

Conficio, eci, ficere, to performe or finyshe, *Lactātius.* to perishe or be consumed, to distroy or sle, to explicate or declare. Honestatis pars confecta est, quā tibi cupio esse notissimam, The *Cic. offic.* part of honestie is declared, which I wold shulde be vnto the perfitely knowen. Also to bring to passe, Si me amas, cōfice, If thou louest me, bryng it to passe. Also to gather money. Permagnam dices ex illa re pecuniā confici posse, Thou wylt say, that a greate somme of money mought be made of that thynge. Conficere to breake. Nucem denti *Plinius.* bus conficere, To breake a nutte with his tethe. Also to cōsume or waste. Qui cum hic *Terentius* non uideant me, credant me conficere argentum suum, who bicause they se me not here they beleue I waste their money. Also Confici, to be made. Quomodo potest ex multorum deorum aceruo unus deus confici? By what meanes maye there be of a heape of goddes one only god made?

Cōfido, di, dere, to trust, to be sure, to dare.

Confidens, tis, he that regardeth no lawes, nor feareth any thynge. somtyme it sygnyfieth constant, assured.

Confidenter, constantly, assuredly, somtime hardily, boldly, aduenturously.

Confinis hoc confine, next to or adioyning.

Confinium, a border or marche of a countrey or lande.

Confit, it is made to gither.

Confiscare, to scase for a forfaiture.

Confiteor, eris, to confesse.

Conflages, places, wherinto many wyndes do blowe.

Conflare, to blowe togither, to blowe lyke as one bloweth the fyre.

Conflata pecunia, money coyned.

Conflare mendacium, to imagine a lye.

Conflare inuidiam, inimicitias, odium, to stire or procure enuy, hostilitie, hate.

Conflauit æs alienum, he is runne in dette. Also Conflare, to gather. Conflauit ex his omnibus populum, Of all those he gathered a great multitude. Also to make. Et cur *Vergilius.* uę rigidum falces conflantur in ensem, And the croked sithe into the harde sworde is made.

Conflatile, that which is apt to be wrought lyke mettall.

Conflicto, aui, are, to fight often.

Conflictor, aris, ari, to be vexed or troubled, to fyghte.

Confligo, fligi, gere, to fyght as men doo in battayle.

Con.

Confluere, to come or runne to gether, or flowe.

Confluges, places, in to the whiche many ryuers do flowe.

Conformis, hoc conforme, of a conformitie or lyke in facion, conueniente.

Conforto, aui, are, to comforte.

Confugio, fugi, gere, to flee with other.

Confundo, fudi, dere, to confounde, to medel together.

Confuto, aui, are, to reproue or vaynquyshe by wordes. Also to steere.

Congedus, a Ryuer in Spayne, nere to a towne called Bilbilis.

Congenulo, aui, are, to knele.

Congero, gessi, ere, to gather to gyther, or heape vppe.

Congiarium, An almes, or other lyberalle gyfte, giuen by the prince vnto his people, be it in money corne or vitayles.

Congius, a certayne measure, wherin Sextarius is syxe tymes, and the lycour therin conteyned wayeth tenne pounde.

Conglobare, to brynge or come rounde to gether.

Congratulor, aris, ari, to reioyce with a nother man of his good fortune.

Congredior, eris, gredi, to go with an other to fight, or dispute.

Congressus, us, A batayle.

Congrex, of the same flocke.

Congruo, grui, ere, to agree.

Congruum, Agreable.

Cōgrus, & Cōger, A fishe called a Conger.

Coniectarium, effectuall, or parfyte.

Coniecto, aui, are, to suppose, to iudge.

Coniector, oris, an interpretour of dremis, A Coniectour, that dothe coniecte what shall happen.

Coniectura, A coniecture.

Coniecturale, that whiche is coniectid, or gathered by coniecture.

Coniectus, us, a certayne direction of rayson vnto the trouthe.

Conifera arbor, a tree whiche beareth fruites beinge smaller at the one ende than at the other, lyke a pyne appull.

Conjicio, ieci, ijcere, to caste, to coniecte.

Coniecit se in fugam, He put him to flyghte.

Coniicere in uincula, To cast into prison, or to laye a man in the stockes or gyues.

Coniecit se intro, He went his way in.

Coniicit se in pedes, He toke hym to flight, he toke hym to his legges.

Coniicere tela, to cast dartes, or to shoote.

Coniicere in letitiam, to bringe to a gladnes.

Coniugalis thorus, the chamber where the husbande and wyfe do lye.

Cōiugo, aui, are, to yoke together, or mary.

Coniugium, mariage.

Coniungo, xi, ere, to ioyne together.

Coniunx, iugis, A wyfe.

Coniugus, a, um, that whiche ioyneth.

Coniuro, aui, are, to cōiure or conspire with other for an yll pourpose.

Coniuratio, a Conspiracye.

Conniueo, & Cōniuo, is, iui, uel xi, to winke, and is vsed to be spoken, when men wol let thynges passe, that ought to be loked on.

Connubium, matrimony.

Conoides, the female of the Cipresse tree.

Conon, nis, the name of a kyng of Athenes.

Conopœum, A Canapy, properly suche one as hangeth ouer beddes, and is wroughte lyke a net, to kepe out gnattes, whiche do stynge men in theyr beddes.

Cōquinisco, cōquexi, cōquiniscere, to ducke with the heed.

Consalutare, to salute one an other.

Consanguineus, Coseyne.

Consanguinitas, tatis, Kynred.

Conscendo, di, dere, to klyme.

Conscientia, Conscience.

Conscisco, sci, scere, to consent, determyne, or graunt to a mattier wyllynglye.

Consciscere mortem, To kill wylfully.

Conscius, conscia, that knowith of an other.

Conscius sceleris, partie or priuy to the offence, accessarye.

Conscribo, psi, bere, to wryte thynges together.

Conscripti, they whose names be written or registred to supply a numbre, whiche doo lacke: or suche as be newe chosen or added vnto the other.

Consecranei, suche as be dedycate to one secte or opinyon. *Tertullianus.*

Cōsecro, craui, are, to dedicate or cōsecrate.

Consectanei, they whiche be of one secte.

Consector, aris, to folowe all together.

Consensio, A Cōsent or accord of one mind or pourpose.

Consentio, tii, tire, to Consente.

Consentaneus, a, um, agreable.

Conseptum, An inclosure or place inclosed.

Conseptus, ta, tum, inclosed.

Consequentia, thynges whiche do folowe or insue.

Consequiæ, sequeles.

Consequor, to folow immediatly, to optain, or get, to expresse. Verbis consequi non possunt, They may not be expressed in wordes.

Conserere manus, to fyght hand to hande.

Consero, seui, serere, to sowe or sette herbes togither.

Consessus, sus, When syttynge togyther. It may be taken for a sessyons or syttynge of men, whiche be commissioners.

Conside

Confido, fidi, dere, to fytte or abyde togyther. It may be vsed to fytte at a feffyons.
Confiliarius, a counfellour.
Confilio, iui, uel lui, lire, to leape togyther.
Confilior, aris, to take counfayle.
Confilium, a counfayle. It may be taken for commyffioners or iudges affigned.

Cic. pro Rofc. Confifto, ftiti, fiftere, to ftande fafte or fure, to abyde boldly by a thynge.
Confiftorium, a counfell houfe, fpecially in a princis palays.
Confobrini, coufyns germains of two bretherne or two fyfters.
Confolabundus, he that comforteth a man.
Confolida, the name of an herbe, callyd Confery.
Confolor, aris, ari, to gyue comforte, or take comforte.
Confono, nui, are, to make one fowne togyther. Alfo to accorde or agree.
Confors, tis, a felowe or companyon. fome tyme it fygnifieth lyke.
Confortium, felowfhyp or company.
Confpicio, fpexi, cere, to fee or beholde.
Confpicilium, a lowpe to looke oute of a howfe, or walle.
Confpicilia, fpectakles.
Confpico, fpexi, ere, & Confpicor, aris, ari, to beholde.
Confpicuus, a, um, circumfpect, wytty, or of a fharpe and quycke witte. Alfo apparant or playne to perceyue.
Confpiro, aui, are, to confpire or confente. Alfo to blowe togyther.
Confpiratio, nis, a confpiracye.
Conftantinopolis, Conftantinople, a cytie in Thrace.
Confternium, a place where men, whanne they were baynd, layde their garmentes.
Confterno, aui, fternere, to throwe downe, to ouerthrowe.
Confternati, men ouerthrowen. fometyme abafhed.
Confternatio, tionis, an abafhement.
Confterno, ftraui, fternere, to ftraw, to paue.
Conftituo, ftitui, ftituere, to ordeyne, to gouerne, to prouyde, to couenant, to fourme.

Cicero. Corpus bene conftitutum, A body well cõplexioned.
Conftitutio corporis, the complexion, Conftitutio caufe, whiche our lawyers do calle the matter in lawe.
Conftitutus, ta, tum, ordeyned.
Confto, ftiti, ftare, to perfyfte or abyde in a thynge.
Conftat animo, He is of a ftedfafte mynde.
Conftat pedibus, He is fure of his fecte, or hoole.

Sifennia. Conftat, it cofteth, it is folde for.

Conftare, to ftande togyther, to be manyfefte or knowen, to agree.
Conftans, tis, conftant or ftedfafte.
Conftanter, conftantly.
Conftantia, conftance, or ftedfaftenes.
Conftruo, ftruxi, ftruere, to buylde, to ordayne.
Confuefco, fueui, fuefcere, to be wonte, fomtyme to vfe carnallye. Cum eius confueuit matre clanculum, He hadde company with his mother priuelye. Alfo to vfe for a cuftome. fometyme to lyue. Nec magis humo $\bar{q}$ ftagno confueuerunt, They lyue as welle on lande, as on water. *Terentius*
Columell.
Confuetudo, dinis, cuftome or vfage. Alfo carnall company.
Confuéfacio, to accuftome.
Conful, lis, a chiefe officer among the Romaynes.
Confularis, He that hadde ben confulle, or were mete to be confull.
Confulatus, tus, the offyce of Confull.
Confulo, lui, fulere, with a datyue cafe, to gyue counfayle: with an accufatiue cafe, to afke counfaylle. Alfo with a datiue cafe, it fygnificth to prouyde, to helpe to. Grauiter de fe confulere, To doo fomme hurte to hym felfe.
Confulto, taui, tare, to gyue or afke counfayle often, to delyberate or fhewe myne aduyfe often.
Confulto, delyberately, or aduyfedly.
Confultor, toris, he that gyueth counfayle, fomtyme he that afketh counfayle.
Confultus, ta, tum, a wyfe man.
Confultus, tus, & Confultum, the thing that is confulted. Sometyme an acte of counfaylle.
Confummo, aui, are, to fumme vp in a reckenynge, to fynifhe or performe, or make vp, or make perfite.
Confummatus, ta, tum, perfyte, at a pointe.
Confumo, fumpfi, fumere, to confume, or diftroye.
Confuo, ui, ere, to fowe togyther, or ioyne.
Confyderate, with a confyderation.
Confyderatus, he that dothe a thinge with confyderation.
Confydero, aui, are, to confyder.
Contabulari, to bourde, or to laye bourdes on a roufe or floure.
Contagium, & Contagio, Contagionis, & Contages, an infectiue fyckeneffe.
Contamino, taminaui, taminare, to vyolate, or defyle, with myxtynge thynges togyther, to difhonefte.
Contemno, contempfi, contemnere, to difpyfe, or contempne, whyche is laffe than defpyfynge.

E Con-

Contemptus, tus, despyte.
Contemplatio, onis, a beholdynge, specially in the mynde with deuocion to god.
Contemplo, aui, & contemplor, aris, to beholde intentifely with great affection.
Contemporanei, they which be at one time.
Contemptibilis, bile, he that is to be despysed, or not regarded.
Contemptor, aris, to sette lyttell by.
Contendo, di, dere, to contende, or resyste, or stryue, to caste or shote a darte or arow: to contynue, to make haste, to inforce.
Contentio, onis, resystence, stryfe, or debate. Also a sharpe oration apt to confirme or repreue, a continuance, an inforcement or settynge forth with vehemence.
Contentus, ta, tum, that whiche is contayned. also content or satisfied.
Contineo, nui, ere, to contayn, to withhold, to lette.
Conterraneus, countrey man.
Contestari, to aske togither wytnesse.
Conticeo, ticui, cere, to hold my peace with other. Conticesco, idem.
Conticinium, bedde tyme, or the fyrst part of nyght, whan men prepare to take theyr rest, and all thing is in silence.
Contigno, aui, are, to raufter a house.
Contignatio, onis, the raufterynge.
Continens, tis, firme lande, that is none ile. also contynuall.
Continenter, continually, contynentely, or fyrmely.
Continentia, continence, a vertue, refusing thinges that are pleasaunt. Also resistence of ylle.
Contineo, nui, ere, to refrain, to kepe back, to contayne, to kepe togither.
Contingo, tigi, tingere, to touche.
Contigit, It hath hapned.
Continuo, aui, are, to contynue.
Continuus, a, um, contynuall.
Continue, contynually.
Contor, aris, to abyde.
Contortę res, thinges wounden and twysted. Also suche matter, as oone parte can not agree with an other.
Contra, agayn a place, a person, or a thing on the other parte.
Contracto, aui, are, to attayne, or comprehende.
Contradico, dixi, dicere, to contrary in wordis, to saye contrary.
Contraeo, to goo contrarye or agaynste a thinge.
Contraho, traxi, trahere, to gather togither. Contrahere æs alienum, To be indetted, to commytte, to make a contracte or bargayne, to drawe togyther. Contrahere, to shrynke. Nerui contrahuntur, the synewes be shrunken.
Contrahere frontem, to lowre. Bona contracta, goodes gotten by conqueste.
Contrarius, a, um, contrarye.
Contrauenio, ire, to happen contrary, come contrarye.
Controuersia, a controuersie or variance.
Controuersiosus, lytigious, or full of controuersye.
Controuersor, aris, to contende or vary.
Controuersus, a, um, contrary, or in contrary wise. Res controuersa, mater in controuersye.
Contubernium, a felowshyp or a companie.
Contubernalis, a felowe or companyon, or of one company.
Contumax, macis, disobedient, or frowarde in opinyon, he that wyl not be perswaded.
Contumacia, dysobedyence, a selfe wylle, or frowardenes.
Contumelia, a reproche, a thynge done or spoken to a mans rebuke.
Contumeliosus, he that vseth to speake rebukefully.
Contundo, tudi, tundere, to breke to peces, or stryke downe.
Contuosi oculi, eien loking narowe.
Contus, a longe speare or morys pike. also a longe pole with yron at the ende, wherwith shypmen do gauge the water.
Conuallis, a valey hauynge hilles on bothe sydes.
Conuaso, aui, are, to gather by stelthe.
Conuenę, people assembled of diuers countreys, dwelling in one countrey or towne.
Conuenientia, a congruence. Also a cōming togither of people.
Conuenire, to come togither, or to assemble in one place. Also to agree, to sewe at the lawe, or bringe in iugement. Also to determine, to speake with one, to accorde. Conuenit inter me atq̃ hūc, it is agreed betwene him and me, De pretio conuenit, we are agreed of the price. In manū conuenit, She is my wyfe.
Conuentę, couenantes of mariage.
Conuenticulum, a congregation, most commonly for an yll purpose.
Conuentio, onis, & conuentū, a couenaunt.
Conuentus, an assembly of people, warned by the chiefe officers commaundement.
Conuentus maximus, may be taken for a parlyament. Minores conuentus, sessions of the peace.
Conuersor, aris, to be conuersaunt.
Cōuersatio, conuersation or familiaritie.
Conuerto, uerti, tere, to conuert, or tourne.
Conuexum, the outwarde part and roūdenes

C ante O.

nes of a thynge that is holowe.
Conuicinium, a neyborhode.
Conuicior, aris, ari, to speake in reproche.
Conuicium, a reproche or rebuke.
Conuictor, oris, a dayly companyon at table, or a dayly geste.
Conuiualis, le, pertaynynge to feastes.
Conuiuor, aris, ari, to feaste or bankette, or to take meales with other men.
Conuiuator, toris, a feaster or banketter.
Conuiua & conuictor, a beden gest, he that is inuited or beden to dyner or supper.
Conuiuium, a feaste or bankette.
Conuoluolus, a lyttell worme with manye feete and heary, that eateth the leaues of vynes. Also an herbe runnynge vppe by bushes, hauynge a floure lyke to a lyly, but it hath no sauoure. peraduenture that whiche is called withwynde.
Conuoti, sworne bretherne, or men making one auowe or promyse.
Conus, properly the pyneapple tre, by translation it is a figure in facion lyke to a pyne appull. Also the crest of an helmet or salet.
Coniscare, to bushe or streke heed to heed as rammes do.
Conoides, pyneappull trees female.
Coos, uel Cos, uel Co, uel Coum, the name of an yle nigh to the Rhodes.

Plautus Cous, a, um, of that yle.
Copis, plentuouse.
Copia, plentie, eloquence, power, leaue, or licence, multitude.
Copiæ cornu, is reherfed, whan we wylle sygnifie to be plentie of all thinges, in that whiche we speake of.
Copiosus, a, um, plentuouse.
Copula, a couplyng or ioynyng togyther, couples or fetters.
Copulatiuus, ua, uum, that coupleth, or may cowple.
Coquina, a kytchyn.
Coquinor, aris, ari, to do the office of a coke
Coquinaria, cokery.
Coquinarius, a, um, pertaynyng to cokery.
Coquo, coxi, coquere, to seethe or boyle, to make ripe, to make redy, to digest.
Coquus, a cooke.
Cor, cordis, the herte. somtyme it is taken for the mynde.

Eras. in Chilia. Cor ne edito, Do not tourment thy mynde with care or heuynesse.
Cora, a cytie that Dardanus buylded, of which the inhabitantes are called Corani.
Coracesius, a part of the hyll Taurus.
Corallium, a stone callyd corall.
Corallobachates, a stone with golden rays.
Coram, before, openly, in presence.
Corambla, an herbe that maketh the eies

C ante O. XXVI

dufke and weake of syght.
Corax, acis, a crowe.
Coraxicus, a parte of the hyll Taurus.
Coraxis, a mountayne in Asia, also a flood.
Corbis, a baskette.
Corbita, a great shippe, called a foyst.
Corbona, the treasure of the temple amonge the Iewes.
Corchorus, a vyle herbe.
Corculum, sweete harte. also wyse menne were so called amonge the Romayns.
Corcyra, an yle in Grece.
Cordatus homo, a wytty man, and of great memorie.
Cordi est, it is to my mind, it cotenteth me.
Cordolium, sorowe, grefe at the harte.
Corduba, a citie in Spayne.
Cordus, a, um, that thynge, whiche spryngeth or cometh late in the yere. Cordum fœnum, latewarde haye.
Cordi agni, latewarde lambes.
Coreaceus, a, um, of lether.
Coriago, aginis, the syckenesse of cattalle, whan they are clunge, that their skynnes do cleaue faste to their bodies.
Coriarius, a tanner.
Corinthiacus, a, um, of Corinthe.
Corinthia uasa, plate made of the mettal of Corinthe, whiche was myrt mettall.
Corinthus, a citie in Achaia, whiche was in that parte of Grecce, that is nowe callyd Morea: wherof came a prouerbe, Non est cuiuslibet Corinthum appellere, It is not in euery mans power to arue at Corinthus, whiche doth signifie, It pertayneth not to euery man to atttempt thingis dangerous, or harde to acheue. Vide originem in chiliadibus adagiorum Erasmi, uel in Aulo Gellio.
Corium, the skinne of a beaste. also lether, the pane of a wall made with lyme & sande.
Corna, e, the name of. ii. cities.
Cornelia, a noble woman of Rome.
Cornetum, a groue of hauthorne.
Corneus, a, um, of hawthornes.
Cornicen, a blower in a horne.
Cornicor, aris, ari, to make a chattryng like a choughe.
Cornicularius, a certayne offyce in armes, concernyng capitall sentences.

Eras. in Chilia. Cornicu oculos configere, to pricke out the crowes eien, is a prouerbe vsed, whan we wold signifie, that one with a newe deuise, had obscured the doctrine or estimation of them, which had ben afore him, & had made them to seeme, that they knewe or see nothing. It may be also saide, where one man wyll make all other men blynde, that haue ben before him: & reproue or dissolue that, whiche hath ben allowed by wyse men.

E.ii. Corni-

Corniculum, a garment pertaynyng to souldiours. Also somtyme a towne in Italy.

Cornigenus, a, um, of the kynde, whyche hath hornes.

Corniger, geris, al thing that bereth a horn.

Cornupes, pedis, euery beaste that hathe horne on his fecte.

Cornix, nicis, a byrde called a chowgh.

Cornu, a horne: by translation, the corners and wyndinges of ryuers. Also the twoo endes of a battayle be callid, Dextrum cornu, et sinistrum cornu.

Cornucopię, was a horne that Hercules plucked from Achelous, whiche horne the Nymphes or immortall ladyes fylled with swete flowres and fruites.

Cornupeta, a beaste that stryketh with his hornes.

Cornus, nus, a hawthorne tree.

Cornutus, a, um, that whiche hath hornes.

Corolla, a garlande.

Corollarium, that whiche is aboue the very measure. also a lytell crowne.

Corona, a crowne, a garlande, a chaplette, a company of people standyng rounde like a cerkle. Also the cerkle about the mone.

Coronamentum, a multitude of crounes, or garlandes.

Coronarius, ria, a maker of crownes, or garlandes.

Corone, a towne in Greece in the partes nowe named Morea.

Coronea, a cytie in the partes of Bœotia, in Greece.

Coronis, nidis, the nose of a shyppe. Also an ende, the extreme parte, the toppe, the horne, or other lyke.

Corono, aui, are, to crowne, or sette on a crowne or garlande.

Corporalis, le, corporall.

Corporatio, corporatura, the quātitie, state, or facyon of the body, corporature.

Corporeus, ea, um, that which is of a bodily substance.

Ennius. Corporo, aui, are, to kyll.

Corpulentus, corpulente or grosse in body, fleshy.

Corpus, corporis, a body. sometyme it signifieth but flesshe onely. also sometyme all maner of substance.

Corrado, rasi, dere, to shaue or scrape, to take away, spoyle, sell, or alienate.

Corrigo, rexi, rigere, to correcte, or amēde.

Corrector, toris, a correcter, or amender.

Corripio, pui, pere, to rebuke. proprely it is to take a thinge quyckely, and with haste.

Corripitur febre, he is taken with a feuer.

Corripitur somno, He is faste a slepe.

Corriuare, is proprely of beastes, to go together to watrynge.

Corrugi, furrowes made in hylles, to conuey water, to washe the owre of mettall.

Corrumpo, rupi, rumpere, to corrupte, to viciate, to distroy, to suborne, to tempte, or procure by gyftes.

Corruptela, corruption or defylynge.

Corsica, an Ile in the myddell see betwene Scan and the Ile of Sardinia.

Cortex, corticis, a rynde or barke.

Cortina, a dyers fatte. Also it is the table of Apollo, from the whiche he gaue aunswere. Cato taketh it for a vessell, oute of the whiche oyle is lette runne. Also that whiche is called a corteyne of lynnen cloth or sylke. Also places deuided with cortaynes be called Cortine.

Cortinale, the place where vesselles be set, wherin wyne and hony is sodden.

Cortinon, radyshe seede.

Cortona, a citie in Tuscane.

Cortyna, or gortyna, a cite i the ile of Cādy

Corus, the northwesterne wynde. Also a measure contaynynge xlv. bushels.

Corusco, aui, are, to brandyshe or glytter.

Coruus, a crowe.

Corybantes, the priestes of the idoll Cybeles, which as madde men waggyng their hedes and daunsynge, playinge on cymbales, ranne about the stretes, prouokyng other to do the semblable.

Coryces, curious persons, crafty inuestigatours or serchers of mattiers. Also a hylle in Crete, lyenge on the see syde.

Corycium, a gardeuiandes or walet, or other lyke thynge to put in vitayles.

Corycum, the name of a cytie and mountayne in Sycile.

Corydalus, a larke.

Coryletum, a groue of hasylles.

Corylus, an hasyll and a hasylle nutte, or fylberde.

Corymbi, bearies of an yuy.

Corymbites, a kynde of spurge.

Coripheus, the chiefe in euery order.

Corythus, a bowe case, or a quyuer for arowes.

Corythus, a town in Tuscan nere to Arerii

Coryza, the pose, or distillation out of the heed into the eyes and nose.

Cos, cotis, a whetstone.

Cosmeta, a chamberer, or woman, that apparayleth hir maistresse.

Cosmicus, ca, cum, worldly.

Cosmographia, the descriptiō of the world.

Cosmographꝰ, he that discribith the world.

Cosmus, a propre name.

Cossi, wormes bredde in trees, which the people of Phrigia, dyd eate for a delycate meate.

C ante O.

meate. Also men or women that haue their bodies riueled or full of wryncles.
Costa, a rybbe.
Costus, uel costum, a tree or herbe, whiche is very soote in sauour.
Cosyros, an Jle in Aphrike.
Coticula, a touche stone, wheron they trye golde and syluer.
Cotidie, dayly, day by day.
Coton, a hauen made with stoone. Also a towne in Syria, of the whiche a certayne kynde of smalle fygges, are called plurally, cotona, uel coctona.
Cotoneum, a quynse.
Cothurnus, a slipper, specially high corked. somtime it is taken for a hygh and arrogāt forme of speakynge or writynge.
Coturnix, nicis, a byrde named a quayle.
Cotyla, a vessell or cuppe to drynke of, suche as Diogenes vsed, before he lerned of a chylde to drinke out of his hande.
Cotyle, all the holownes of a cuppe: also a measure aboute the quantytie of halfe a pynte: also the ioynte of a mans thygh. also a weight of .ix. ounces.
Cotylum, a place in the mountayne of Jda, out of the whiche runneth thre great ryuers, Scamander, Granicus, & Aesopus.
Couinum, a maner of a chariot.
Couinarius eques, horsemen that faughte leapyng out of a chariot vnto horsebacke.
Coxa, ex coxendix, dicis, the thigh of a man. somtyme the hyppe or ioynt of the thigh.
Conuictus, tus, a lyuyng togither in house, or at one table.
Conuoco, caui, care, to call togyther.

¶ C, ante R.

Crabro, onis, a great waspe, callyd a hornette.
Cranaus, a kynge of Athenes.
Craneum, a place of exercyse atte Corynthe.
Cranium, the forcmooste parte of the schulle.
Crantor, oris, the name of a philosopher.
Crapula, an inflamation and heed ache, whiche commeth of excesse of drynkynge. It is also taken for drunkennes.
Cras, to morowe, in tyme commynge.
Crastino, is the same.
Crassamentum, thyckenesse. (Eras. in Chil.)
Crassa Minerua, a grosse witte, which doth nothynge exactely.
Crascesco, cessi, cessere, to make fatte, or ful of fleshe, or thycke.
Crassiore Musa, with a more playne or intelligible sense.

C ante R. XXVII

Crassus, a, um, fatte, fleshy, thycke, grosse, poysye.
Crassities, & crassitudo, fatnesse, thicknes, grossenes.
Crastino, aui, are, to deferre frome daye to daye.
Crastinus, na, num, pertaynynge to to morowe, or tyme to come.
Cratera, uel crater, teris, a greatte cuppe. Also a greatte hoole on the toppe of the meruaylouse hylle of Ethna in Sycyle, out of the whiche issueth flames of fyre.
Craterus, the propre name of a manne, of whom Persius speaketh in his .iii. Saty.
Crates, grates of yron or wodde. Also the name of a phylosopher, whyche to the intente he moughte the more quietely studye phylosophye, he beyng ryche, threwe all his goodes into the see, saying, hens with a myschiefe ye vngracyous appetytes, I hadde leauer drowne you, thanne ye shoulde drowne me. Supposynge, that he moughte not haue vertue and rychesse togyther.
Crathis, the name of two ryuers, the one in Grece, the other in Calaber.
Craticula, a gredyron, whereon meate is broyled.
Cratinas, a ryuer in Affrike.
Cratinus, a poete whiche wrate comedies.
Cratyles, the name of a philosopher, to whom Plato wrate a boke.
Cratio, iui, ire, to couer with grates.
Cratippus, the name of a philosopher.
Cratos, power, or dominion.
Creo, aui, are, to make of nothynge. Also to gette chyldren.
Creatura, a creature or thinge made of nothynge.
Creber, bra, brū, frequent, or accustomed.
Crebro, often.
Crebresco, crebrui, crebrescere, to be wont, to be commune.
Credibile, that whiche may be byleued.
Creditor, oris, he vnto whom a man oweth any thynge.
Creditum, that thinge that is owed.
Credo, didi, dere, to beleue, to truste, to cōmytte, or delyuer a thynge to be saufelye kepte, to publyshe.
Credulus, he that beleueth lyghtly.
Credulitas, tatis, lyght beleue.
Crementum, increase.
Cremera, a ryuer.
Cremium, fried meate burned to the pane.
Cremor, oris, the iuyce of barly steapyd in water, beaten and pressed.
Crene, the dentis about the leaf of an herbe or tree lyke to a sawe. Also it is the scores,

E.iii. whiche

whiche men vnlernyd do make on styckes for their remembrance. Also Crena, is the nocke of a bowe or arowe.

Creontes, the name of a king, whose daughter Jason maried, whā he had left Medea.

Creophilus, the name of a poete.

Creperus, a, um, doubtfull, ambiguous.

Crepida, & crepis, pidis, a shoe with lachettes, some take it for a corked shoe or slypper, bycause of the noyse, which it maketh whan a man goeth.

Crepidarius, rii, he that maketh showes or slyppers.

Crepido, inis, a creeke on the waters side, wheron the water beateth. Also the mouth of a well, & the extreme part of any place.

Crepitaculum, a tymbrell, or other instrument, which being touched with the hand, maketh a sownde.

Crepito, taui, are, to make a noyse or bounsynge.

Crepitulum, an ornament of the heed, whiche with meuynge of the heed yeldethe a sowne.

Crepitus, a bounse or great dynne or noyse.

Virgilius. Crepo, pui, pere, to make a greatte noyse or sowne. Crepere, to be broken.

Crepundia, tryfles or smal gyftes gyuen to lyttell chyldren, as napkyns, lyttell belles, tymbrelles, and suche lyke toyes. Also the fyrst apparayle of chyldren, as swathels, wastcotes, and such lyke. And by translation they say, A crepundiis erat uirtuti deditus, From his chyldhode he was euer giuen to vertue.

Crepusculum, the breake or fyrste sprynge of the daye, called the twie lyght.

Cresco, creui, crescere, to grow or increase.

Creuit hereditatem, He is increased in his lyuelode, or he hath taken possession.

Creta, an Jle called nowe Candy: also a stone called Chalke.

Cretatus, ta, tum, layde with chalke.

Cretęus, & Cretensis, a manne of Crete or Candye.

Creterra, a buckette to drawe vp water.

Eras. in Chil. Cretizare cum Cretensibus, a prouerbe vsed where a crafty man wyll deceyue hym that is crafty: a theefe steale from a thefe, or a lyer lye before them, whiche vse to make leasynges.

Creticus, ca, um, of Crete or Candy. Also a foote in metre, whiche hath the fyrst and thyrde syllable longe.

Cretosus, a, um, full of chalke.

Cribro, aui, are, to syfte or sarce.

Cribrum, a sieue or a sarce.

Crimen, minis, a faulte, an offence, blame, matter layd agaynst one by action or suite. sometyme a false suspicion.

Criminale, criminalle, wherin is an offence or faulte.

Criminor, aris, ari, to blame, to rebuke, to lay to ones charge, to accuse.

Criminosus, a, um, rebukeful, worthy blame

Crimissus, a ryuer of Grece.

Crines, heare of the heed.

Crinire, to laye forth the heare.

Crinitus, he that hath moch or long heare.

Crinita stella, a comete or blasynge sterre.

Crinon, a redde lylye.

Crisa, the name of a towne builded by Crisus, Phocus sonne.

Criticus, he that iudgeth the actes or warkes that men do write.

Critici dies, the dayes wherin physytions gyue iudgement of the contynuance of the syckenesse.

Crito, a philosophers name of Athenes.

Critobulus, was a phisition, of whom Plinie speaketh lib. vii.

Crobylon, a cawle to weare on ones heed.

Croco, crocito, to make a noyse like a rauē.

Crocinum et croceum, colored like saffron.

Crocodilus, a beaste in Aegypte, lyuynge somtyme in water, somtyme on lande: and is facioned in the body lyke a dragon, sauinge that he lacketh wynges.

Crocotirium, cakebreade.

Crocotulę, garmētis of the color of saffron.

Crocotularius, a dyar.

Crocus, saffron, a spice.

Crocuta, a beaste in Ethiope, whiche with his tethe breaketh all thynges in pieces, & deuoureth it, be it wodde or mettall.

Cronia, feastes dedicate to Saturne.

Crotalum, an instrument, whiche the Egiptians vsed in sacrifice made of. ii. plates, whiche beaten togither, made an harmony.

Crotalus, he that hath a sownynge voyce, and a shyll.

Crudaria, a vayne of syluer.

Crudelis, le, cruell.

Crudesco, crudui, crudescere, to be rawe.

Crudus, da, um, rawe, fresh, or newe made, not rype. Crudus homo, whose stomacke can not digest well.

Cruditas, tatis, rawnes, or lack of digestion.

Cruento, aui, are, to make blody.

Cruentus, a, um, blody, cruell.

Crumena, a purse.

Cruor, bloudde whiche commethe out of a wounde.

Crus, cruris, the parte of the legge, whyche is from the knee down vnto the ancle called the shanke.

Crusta, the vtter parte of euery thyng that is not eaten. Also the scurfe of a scabbe or
wounde

C ante T.   C ante V.   XXVIII

wounde. also playster of a walle.
Crusto, taui, are, to lay playster, or pargette.
Crustata, wheron is layde playster, or thyn shardes of stone.
Crustarius, a pargettour.
Crustulata, a meate made of crustes of bread
Crustulum, crustum, a crowst of bread, of a pasty, or of rosted, broyled, or fryed meate
Crustumina pira, peares redde on the one syde.
Crustuminum, a towne in Italy.
Crux, crucis, a crosse, galowhowse, or other lyke.
Cruciatus, tus, tourment.
Crypta, a secrete place within the erthe.
Crypticus, ca, cum, secrete or hydde vnder the erthe.
Cryptoporticus, a place vnder grounde, with wyndowes lyke to a parler, where men do dyne in the sommer tyme for heate.
Crystallus et chrystallũ, a stone callyd cristal.
Cristallina, vessell & cuppes of cristal stone.

C, Ante T.

Ctenes, certayne teethe.
Cteniatrus, he that healeth diseasis of horses and catell.
Ctesiphon, the name of a worke man, which builded the temple of Diana, at Ephesie, a worke wonderfull, and renoumed through the worlde: the whiche was after bourned of one Herostratus, onely bycause he wold for some dede be spoken of.

C, Ante V.

Cubatus, tus, a sittyng on broode, as a henne dothe.
Cubicularius, a seruant that awayteth in the chamber: a chamberlayne, or grome of the chamber.
Cubicularis, lare, that perteynethe to the Chaumber.
Cubiculum, a bedde chamber.
Cubile, a bedde, sometyme it is taken for a closet.
Cubito, aui, are, to lye often with one.
Cubitus, et Cubitum, an elbowe, sometyme a measure called a cubite, that is to say, one foote and an halfe: but a cubite in geometrie conteineth vi. of our common cubites.
Cubitale, a forsleue of a garmente, whiche keuereth the arme from the elbowe downwarde.
Cubo, cubui, cubare, to lye downe, properly it is of sicke men.
Cubatio, a lyinge.
Cubus, is a figure foure square on all partes like a dyce.
Cucubo, aui, are, to make a noyse lyke an oule.
Cuculio, onis, a keuerynge of the heddē, whiche men dydde vse when they walked in the nyght.
Cuculus, et Cucullus, a byrd called a cuckow.
Cucullus, a cloke to defend rayne & winde.
Cucuma, a chafar, wherin water is het.
Cucumer, eris, et Cucumis, a fruite callyd a cocumber.
Cucumerarius, a garden where cocumbres do growe or be kepte.
Cucurbita, a frute called a gourde. Also cucurbita, & Cucurbitula, is a cup, wherwith Surgyons do drawe out bloud with scaryfying of the skynne, called cuppynge.
Cucurbitarium, a place where gourdes be sowen.
Cucurbitarius, a louer of gourdes.
Cucurio, iui, iri, to make a noyse like a cock.
Cudo, cusi, cudere, to strike, as smythes do.
Cudere pecuniā, to make or coyne moneye, also cudere, to breake or broyse.
Cuias, cuiatis, of whense.
Cuius, cuia, cuium, whose. Cuium pæcus, whose catall.
Culcitra, a mattresse.
Culeus, a sacke, also a measure conteynyng xxx. bushels.
Culex, culicis, a gnatte.
Culigna, a bolle or dyshe to drynke of.
Culina, a kechyn, sometyme the meate that is dressed.
Culinor, aris, ari, to do the office of a cooke.
Culleolum, the vtter shale of a nut, whiche is grene.
Culullus, an erthen cup, suche as the galye cuppes be.
Culmen, culminis, the roufe of a house.
Culmus, the reede or strawe of corne, from the rote to the eare.
Culpa, is an offence done not weetinge, or not intendynge to do hurte.
Culter, et Cultrum, a knyfe.
Cultellum, a lyttel knife or a whittill.
Cultrarius, was he that kylled the beast, and diuided him in the sacrifice to Idolles. It maye nowe be taken for a slaughter man.
Cuitus, cultus, apparayle, somtyme it is taken for honour done to god.
Cum, with, whan, whiles, where, albeit, for asmoche, as well. Cum mihi tum illi, Aswel to me as to him. In cum is some thing lasse vnderstande, in Tum somme thynge more. Quod cum omnibus confitendum est, tū nobis præcipue, whiche thinge oughte to be confessed of all men, and of vs moste specially. The auncient wryters, whan it sygnified

nifyed whan, where, and forasmoche, they wrate it Quom.
Cum dicto, forthewith after that he hadde spoken.
Cum imperio est, he beareth a rule.
Cum maxime, excedyngly.
Cum potestate est, he is in authoritie, or in an high offyce.
Cum primis, very. Cum primis nobilis, very noble.
Cum stomacho, dysdaynfully.
Cum tempore, in a certayne space.
Cum uenia tua, with your lycence.
Cuma, a towne in Grece.
Cumæ, a citie in Campania.
Cumanus, a man of that citie.
Cumatilis, ule, a colour called blewe.
Cumera, a greatte vessele, wherin corne was kepte.
Cumerum, a vessell vsed at weddynges.
Cuminum, an herbe and sede called comyn.
Cumulo, aui, are, to make an heape, to fyll, to adde more.
Cumulatim, in an heape, or heaped vp.
Cumulus, an heape.
Cunę, et Cunabula, cradels, wherin chyldren be rocked. somtyme it is taken for the age of infancy.
Cunctator, oris, a tariar, a differrer.
Cuncti, alltogither.
Cunctor, et Contor, aris, to tary, to prologe tyme, to abyde, to doubte.
Cunctatio, onis, a tarienge, an abydyng, a prolongynge of tyme, a doutynge.
Cuneus, an axe to cutte woode, whiche is smalle and thyn before, and brode & thycke after, that the wodde may ryue the better, also a wedge to cleaue wodde with. By translation it is a company of fotemē in batayle, that goth in a lyke order, smal before, and brode behynde: there was a lyke forme in the Theatre or place, where men beheld playes, it is sometyme taken for a company of people.
Cuneatim, in the fourme afore declared.
Cuneatus, ta, tū, that whiche appereth to be in the sayde fourme of Cuneus.
Cuniculus, a beaste called a cony.
Cuniculum, an hole in the grounde.
Cunila, an herbe called sauery, wherof be dyuerse kyndes.
Cunire, to dunge as a childe dothe.
Cunnus, a womans wyket.
Cupa, a cuppe.
Cupedinarius, an hucster that selleth meate and drynke.
Cupes, Cupedia, et Cupedula, delicate meates, or desire of deynty meates.
Cupido, Cupidinis, the sonne of Venus, god of loue. Cupido in the feminine gender, vehement desyre or appetite.
Cupidus, da, dum, desyrouse. sometyme it signifieth a louer.
Cupiditas, tatis, couaytise.
Cupide, desirously.
Cuprum, metall called coper.
Cur, wherfore or why.
Cura, care, thought, study, diligence, warke or labour, also loue.
Curatio, cure.
Curator, gardeyn in socage, or he to whom the custodye of a man madde or folysshe is commytted. Also he to whom any thyng is commytted to suruey, or to prouyde thynges necessary for a weale publyke, or to order suche thinges as he hath in charge, cōcernynge as well priuate thynges as they that do belonge to a comminaltie: he maye be properly called a suruayour.
Curatorius, a, um, belonginge to surueinge.
Curcura, an ilande in the see Adriatike.
Curculio, onis, a littell worme in grayn called a myte or wyuell. It is also the wesyll of the throte of a man, wherby he draweth wynde.
Cures, a citie of the Sabines.
Curetes, a people of the Ile of Crete or Candy.
Curia, a courte, that is to say, where the senate is, or officers exercisynge suche thinges as they haue in charge. it is sometyme taken for the persons in the courte.
Curiales, they whiche be of that courte.
Curio, onis, a bedell or criar.
Curionem agnum, Plautus calleth a leane lambe.
Curio, also of Varro is taken for a place, where priestes consulted of thynges concernynge diuine ceremonies.
Curiosus, sa, sum, curiouse, taken sometyme on the yll parte, where more dylygence is vsed, than is necessary or expedient: sometyme on the better parte, where we be very carefull and busy about thynges, concernynge eyther our selfes or other men.
Curiositas tatis, curiosytie, or to moche dilygence.
Curius, the name of a noble Romayne, vnto whom whan the ambassadoure of Samnytes hadde brought a great somme of golde for a present from theyr people, desyrynge hym to take it, and vse it at his pleasure, he answered, that Marcus Curius hadde leuer haue dominion ouer ryche men, than to be ryche him selfe, and that he, which could not be vaynquisshed in battayl, mought not be corrupted with money.
Curo, aui, are, to care, to be doinge of a thynge.

thinge. somtyme to prepare, to heale one that is sycke, to take refection or comfort.
Curriculo, quyckely.
Curro, cucurri, currere, to runne.
Cursus, us, et cursura, a course.
Cursor, oris, he that runneth in poste.
Cursim, runnynge.
Cursito, aui, are, to runne often.
Curso, aui, are, to runne alway or often.
Cursorius, a, um, pertainyng to runnyng.
Curruca, a lyttell byrde, whiche hatchethe and bryngeth vp cuckowe byrdes.
Currus, a carre.
Curriculus, a lyttell carre.
Curriculum, a shorte space of tyme. Also a runnynge place.
Curtus, ta, tum, shorte.
Curuamen, minis, a crookednesse.
Curuesco, uesci, uescere, to be croked.
Curuipes, he that hath a croked fote.
Curulis & curule, were lyttelle carres, or drayes, hauyng in them chaires of yuorie, wherin they satte, whyche were heed officers in Rome. somtyme it is vsed of poetes for the same offycers.
Curuo, uaui, are, to bowe or make croked.
Curuus, a, um, croked.
Cuspis, idis, somtyme signifieth the poynte of any weapon, sometyme the stele, sometyme a speare heed.
Custodia, the custody, kepynge, or warde: somtyme he that kepeth, somtyme he that is kepte, somtyme the prison.
Custodio, diui, dire, to kepe, to obserue.
Custoditio, the kepynge.
Custoditus, ta, tum, kepte.
Custos, odis, a keper.
Cutis, the inner skynne.

C, Ante Y.

Cyamea, a stone, whiche beinge broken, is lyke to a beane.
Cyaneæ, or Cyanitæ, ylandes or rather rockes vnder Thrace Bosphore.
Cyaneus, a, um, & Cianus, a, um, a brighte blewe colour, or blunket.
Cyathus, a cuppe: it is also a measure, contaynynge as moche as a reasonable manne may drynke at one draught.
Cybele & cybeles, was the wyfe of Saturne, & was named of painims, the moder of the goddes, whiche hath dyuers other names, as it shall appere in their places.
Cyclades, yles in the greke see.
Cyclas, cladis, a womans kyrtell.
Cyclus, a rounde place in Athenes, where thynges were sold. Also a coyne or poyse.
Cyclops, clopis, an auncient people, inhabitynge the yle of Sycile, whiche were lyke gyauntes, hauynge but oone eye in theyr foreheed.
Cydnus, a ryuer of Sicile, the water wherof was meruaylous colde. and as Plinie sayth, auayleable for the goute in the fete.
Cydon, one of the notablest townes of Candy.
Cygnus, a swanne.
Cylindrus, an instrument, wherwith menne do beate floores, or doo ramme with. Also euery thinge that tourneth about quyckly. Also stones rounde and longe lyke beade stones, called langattes.
Cylindraceus, a, um, in the fourme of a langatte.
Cyllene, a hylle of Archadie, where they say Mercurius was nouryshed.
Cyllenius, one of the names of Mercury.
Cylydros, a serpent that rolleth hym selfe, as he gothe.
Cyma, yonge colewortes. Also the tender parte of the stalke of euery herbe.
Cymatilis, chamlette.
Cymba, a boote.
Cymbalum, an instrument of musike.
Cymbalistæ, they that play vpon cymbals.
Cymbium, a pece or cup to drynke wine in.
Cyminum, cummyne.
Cyminus, a laake in Italy.
Cynæthium, a citie of Archadie.
Cynanche, a syckenes called the squynce, whiche is in the throte and iawes.
Cynegetica, volumes wryten of huntynge.
Cynici, a sect of phylosophers, whych liued in pouerte without shame, like doggis.
Cyniphes, biting gnattis with long legges.
Cynocephalus, a beaste hauynge the bodye lyke to an ape, and the heed lyke a dogge. Also people vnder the greate cane, hauing heedes lyke dogges.
Cynoglossa, an herbe callid houndes tuge.
Cynomia, dogge flyes, whiche doo souke bloode from a beaste.
Cynorrhodos, the floure of Eglantyne.
Cynos, in latyne is canis, a dogge. Also a citie in Locris.
Cynosbatum, a thorne, the leafe wherof is lyke the steppe of a mans fote, and hathe blacke bearies like to grapes.
Cynosura, a figure of sterres in heuen, called Vrsa minor.
Cynozoon, a stynkynge herbe.
Cynthia, one of the names of the moone.
Cyparissus, a cypresse tree.
Cypirus & cyperis, an herbe, hauyng leaues lyke sedges. also a rote like to ginger.
Cyprium æs, copper, mettall.
Cyprus, an yle callyd cypers.

Cyrcerum,

Cyrcerum, a great shyppe, or carrike.
Cyrene, nes, a famouse cytie in Libia. Also a citie in the yle of cypers.
Cyreneus, a man of that citie.
Cyrnus, the yle whiche is callid Corsica, or Corse.
Cyrnea, a goblette to drynke wyne in.
Cyrrhea, a citie in the mountayne of Helycon.
Cyrrus, the name of .ii. ryuers, one in Armenia, the other in Media.
Cyrus, the name of diuers kinges in Persi.
Cyssius, a kynde of yuye, that groweth alone. also the name of a ryuer.
Cythera, plural. an yle agaynste Candy.
Cytheron, an hylle in Boeotia.
Cytisus, an herbe, whiche is good to gyue to cattell agaynst the rotte.
Cyzicus, the name of an Ile by Grece.

¶ D, Ante A.

DACIA, a countreye beyonde Hungry, on the northe parte of the ryuer of Dano, or Danubius.
Daci, & Dani, people of that countrey.
Dacicus, ca, cum, pertaynynge to that countrey.
Dacus, ca, cum, idem.
Dactylus, a fynger, a fote in metre, hauing one longe syllable, and .ii. shorte. it is also a date.
Dactylides, grapes beinge longe lyke a fynger.
Dedalus, the name of an excellent carpentar of Athenes, whiche fyrste founde the sawe, the twie bylle, and the awgor: and made the place in Crete callydde Laberynthus.
Demogorgon, onis, whome paynyms called the god of the erthe, fyrste creatoure of the erthe.
Demon, nis, a damned spiryte. sometyme it is taken for the sowle, beynge in the body of manne.
Demonicus, ca, cum, dyuellyshe.
Demonium, a spirite. sometime it is vsed for a godheed amonge the paynyms.
Demoniacus, & demoniosus, possessed with an yll spirite.
Dalmatia, a countrey on the ryuer of Dano, called nowe Slauony.
Dalmata, a man of that countrey.
Dalmaticus, ca, um, of that countrey.
Dalmaticatus, apparailed like a Slauanoise.
Dama, a falowe dere.

Damascus, a citie in Siria.
Damia, one of the names of the goddesse Cybele.
Damatris, the prieste of hir temple.
Damnas, condemned.
Damnifico, feci, facere, to do harme.
Damno, aui, are, to condemne, to disherite, to compell, to delyuer.
Damnum, harme, or hurte.
Damnosus, a, um, harmefull, or hurtfull, or hauynge moche harme.
Damoetas, a shepardes name in Virgill.
Damon, a philosophers name of Pythagoras secte.
Dan, a towne whiche is the boundes of Judea, on the northe parte.
Danaus, the kynge of Argyues, whiche hadde fyfty doughters, who all, sauynge one, slewe all their husbandes in one night.
Danaides, the doughters of Danaus.
Dani, a people nowe called Danes.
Danisma, vsury.
Danista, he that lendeth for vsury.
Danubius, a famous ryuer, now called Danowe, wherinto do flowe .lx. ryuers.
Danunt, Plautus dothe vse for dant, they gyue.
Dapalis cœna, a soupper, wherat be many and dyuers meates.
Dapatice, feastfully, plentuously.
Dapes, delycate and precious dysshes, or bankettes.
Daphne, the propre name of a lyttell maiden, and also of a wodde.
Daphnis, nidis, in latine is a laurell. also the sonne of Mercurie. It was also a delectable place without the citie of Antioche. Also it was the name of a porcion of Lycia by the see syde.
Daphnites, one of the names of Apollo.
Daphnoides, an herbe lyke to Laurell, now called Laureole, as I suppose.
Daphnon, a place, where laurell groweth.
Dapifer, he that bearith a dishe at a banket.
Dapino, to gyue, as it were a delicate dishe.
Dapsa, a sacrifice, which was made in winter, and in sprynge tyme.
Dapsile, abundantly.
Dapsilis, abundant, liberall, or large.
Dardanarii, forstallers of markettes, whyche do bye before hande, to selle dere afterwarde.
Dardaniæ artes, witchecrafte.
Dardanus, the name of a prince, reigning in that parte of Phrigia, where Troy stode, whiche was of him called Dardania.
Darius, the name of dyuers kynges of Persia.
Daricus, money of Persia.

Darideus, the name of a kynge of Perſia in the tyme of Tyberius, Caius, and Claudius themperours.

Datarius, a, u, giuen. alſo an officer in Rome whiche ſubſcribed the date of letters.

Datatim, one gyuyng to an other, as at the toſſynge of a balle.

Daunia, a parte of Italy, nowe called Appulia.

D Ante E.

DE, of, ioyned with a verbe, or nowne, it ſignifieth withdrawinge or taking away, as, Decorrico, I barke or take away the rynde: Depilo, I plucke away the heare. ſometyme it ſignifieth downeward, as Deorſum deſcendo, I go downewarde. Sometyme contrary, as, Dehortor, I giue contrary aduyſe: Dedoceo, I teache contrary. ſometyme it ſygnifieth for, as, *Quantum me amas de fidicina hac ? Howe well doſt thou loue me for this ſinging wenche?* — Terentius

Deambulatorium, an aley to walke in. it may be ſomtyme vſed for a galery.

Deambulo, aui, are, to walke vp and downe.

Deamo, aui, are, to loue hartily.

Deartuo, aui, are, to ioynte, or to cut of by the ioyntes.

Deauro, aui, are, to gylte, to laye ouer all with golde.

Debacchor, aris, ari, to rage, as it were in a drunkenneſſe, to be wodde angrie.

Debello, aui, are, to vanquyſhe, or take one in battayle.

Debeo, bui, ere, to owe, or ought.

Debilis, weake or feble.

Debitor, toris, he that oweth.

Debitio, onis, the acte of owinge.

Debitor, toris, a dettour.

Debitum, a dette or duetie.

Debiti iudicatus, condempned in an action of dette.

Debrior, aris, ari, to be drunke.

Decachinnor, aris, ari, to ſkorne.

Decachordum, an inſtrument with tenne ſtrynges.

Decacumino, aui, are, to ſtrike of the toppe.

Decalcatum, layde with lyme.

De calcaria in carbonariam, out of the lyme kyll into the cole pitte. A prouerbe, wherby is ſygnifyed frome oone myſchiefe to an nother. — Eraſ. in Chilia.

Decalogus, the boke of holy ſcripture, conteynynge the tenne commandementes.

Decapolis, a countrey in Iudea, beyonde the ryuer of flume Iordane, contaynynge tenne cyties.

Decapulo, aui, are, to empty pottis or cuppes.

Decedo, decedere, to depart from a place, to mynyſhe or appaire.

Decedere uia, to goo out of the waye, or to gyue the way to an other of courteiſye.

Decedere de ſuo iure, to remytte ſomewhat of his ryght.

December, the name of one of the twelue monethes.

Decemiugis, a teeme of tenne horſes.

Decempeda, a perche or poll ten fote longe.

Decempedator, he that meateth with ſuche a polle.

Decendium, the ſpace of tenne dayes.

Decerno, decreui, decernere, to decree, determyne, or diſcuſſe.

Decerpo, pſi, pere, to pull, or plucke of.

Decerto, aui, are, to contende or fyght togyther.

Decet, it beſemeth, it is conuenient.

Decens, tis, conuenient.

Dedecet, it is inconuenient, vnſyttynge.

Decido, di, dere, to cutte of. alſo to decide or diſcuſſe a matter in variance.

Décido, ere, to fall of, or away.

Decidua, are thoſe thinges that fall away, as leaues of trees.

Decima, a tenthe parte.

Decimanus, ſiue decumanus, na, num, great, as Decumana porta, The great yate or entrie into a campe of an armie.

Decumanus, a generall receyuer or collectour of taxes or ſubſydies, or other lyke exactions.

Decimo, aui, are, to take awaye the tenthe parte from the reſydue.

Decimari legiones, was whan the tenthe perſone of euery legion was put to dethe.

Decimus, ma, mum, the tenthe, the chiefe or principalle, as, Decimum quodq; ouum, Euery tenthe egge.

Decimus quiſq; fluctus, Euery tenth ryuer.

Decipio, decepi, decipere, to deceiue.

Decipula, a grynne or trap to take byrdes.

Decircino, aui, are, to vnbowe, or to bringe out of compaſſe, or roundeneſſe.

Decius, the name of a noble howſe of the Romaynes.

Declamo, aui, are, to declame, or to exerciſe in feyned orations.

Declamatorius, a, um, pertaynynge to ſuch exercyſe.

Declamatio, onis, an exerciſe in fained orations.

Declaro, aui, are, to declare, to open a thing whiche is darke.

Declino, aui, are, to eſchewe, to leaue, to tourne away, to leade away, to alienate.

Decollo, aui, are, to ſtryke of a heed by the necke. alſo to deceyue, or diſapoynte. *Vna eſt,* — Plautus

est, quę decollauit, One womanne there is, which hath deceyued hym.
Decolor, oris, ylle coloured.
Decoloro, aui, are, to stayne, to spylle the coloure.
Decoquo, decoxi, decoquere, to boyle, or to sethe very moche. somtyme to chaunge, or digest perfitely. Also to consume or wast a mans substance, or to brynge detrymente or losse.
Decoctor, toris, he that hath wasted all his substaunce, and is brought to extreme pouertie, speciallye by lecherye and dyse playenge.
Decor, decoris, a beautye.
Decoro, aui, are, to beautifie or make faire, or pleasaunt to the eyes or the eares, to honoure.
Decorum, a semelynesse, or that which becommeth the person, hauynge respecte to his nature, degree, study, offyce, or profession, be it in doinge or speakynge, a grace. sometyme it sygnifyeth honestie.
Decorus, ra, rum, honest, semely, fayre.
Dedecus, dishenestie in acte, reproche.
Decortico, aui, are, to barke.
Decotes, a bare or thredebare garment.
Decrepitus, a very olde man.
Decrepita senectus, extreme age.
Decresco, scere, to waxe lesse.
Decretorius, a, um, iudiciali. Also decreed, stablyshed.
Decretorium tempus, decretorium sydus, wherby iudgement is giuen of the increase that shall succede of any thinge.
Decretum, a decree, a thynge determined.
Decubo, aui, are, to lye downe.
Deculto, aui, are, to hyde vnder.
Decubo, cubui, cumbere, to lye downe, also to dye.
Decuplatus, ta, tum, tenne tymes dowbled, or tenne folde.
Decuplo, aui, are, to double tenne tymes. If it be an aduerbe, it sygnifyeth tenne times, or tenne folde. Decuplum, like wyse.
Decuppa, he or she that sellethe wyne by the potte.

Cicero in Pisonem.

Decurio, onis, an offyce or dignitie, hauyng authorite either ouer tenne men of armes, or the tenthe parte of a companye. Also it was taken for the lorde Chamberlayne to the Emperour. Also they were in other cities the same that Senators were at Rome.

Suetonius in Domit. Cicero.

Decuria, was the order, office, or company, whiche was vnder the office of Decurio. Also the company of iuges, as we haue of the kynges Benche, Commune place, and Escheker. And Decurio, he that is chiefe of theym.

Decurro, decucurri, rere, to runne downe. by translation it sygnifieth to runne from the one ende to the other.
Decursio, Iustes, as at the tylte or randon.
Decursionem indicere, to proclaime iustes.

Suetonius in Nerone.

Decurtatus, ta, tum, shortened, abbreuiated.
Decus, decoris, honour.
Dedecoro, aui, are, to disshonour, reproue, or defyle.
Decusso, aui, are, to cutte or drawe oute in lengthe, or to cut or deuyde in ten partes.
Decussatim, in tenne partis.
Decussis, the perfyte numbre of tenne.
Decutio, cussi, tere, to stryke of.
Dedico, aui, are, to dedicate, or tell a message.
Dedignor, aris, ari, to disdayne.
Dedisco, dedidici, dedicere, to vnlerne, or forgette.
Deditio, a renderynge vppe of a place besyeged.
Dedititius, a, um, gyuen, or subiecte to an other mans commandement.
Dedo, dedidi, dedere, to gyue vtterly, or for euer: or to become subiecte, to render vp, or yelde.
Dediditionem facere, sygnifieth the same.
Dedoceo, cui, cere, to teache a manne other wise, than he hath before lerned.
Dedoleo, lui, lere, to cease frome sorowe, or payne.
Dedolo, aui, are, to hewe or cutte, lyke a Carpenter.
Deduco, xi, cere, to bryng down, or to leade, or drawe, or brynge from one place, or one thynge to an other. somtime to moue from his purpose. sometyme to bryng home honorably from any place.
Deerro, aui, are, to go out of the right way, or reason.
Defalco, aui, are, to cutte of, take away, defalcate.
Defamo, aui, are, to defame.
Defæco, aui, are, to draw from the dregges, to clense or fyne.
Defectio, onis, rebellyon, decreasynge, defaulte, lacke.
Defectus, ta, tum, that whiche faylethe, or decayeth.
Defectus, tus, lacke.
Defectus solis & lunę, the Eclyps of the sonne and the mone.
Defectus animi, sownynge or lyenge in a traunce.
Defecta corpora, bodies consumed with syckenesse.
Defendo, di, dere, to defende, to putte of, to prohybyte.
Defensito, taui, tare, to defende often.

Defero

Defero, detuli, deferre, to brynge to, to dis=
close, to accuse, or appeale, to bestowe, to
giue office or dignitie, to attribute. Deferre
nomen, to complayne.
Deferueo, ferui, ere, to be cold, or pacyent.
Deferuesco, sci, scere, to waxe pacyente or
colde, to appease hym selfe, or withdrawe
his furye.
Deficio, feci, ficere, to fayle, not to suffyse,
to lacke, to leaue, to disagree, to rebelle,
or departe from hym, with whom he is re=
tayned, or goeth frome one Capytayne to
an nother.
Defectus, tus, lacke, rebellion, or departing
agaynste couenant or promyse.
Defector, oris, he that so departeth or re=
belleth, or goth from one to an other.
Defigo, fixi, figere, to sette or fyxe on, or to
perce or thrust through.
Definio, iui, re, to define, determie, or discuss.
Definitio, definitionis, a definition, whyche
expresseth in fewe wordes, what it is that
is spoken of, as, Homo est animal, ratio=
nale, mortale, A man is a thyng lyuely, re=
sonable, and mortalle.
Defioculus, he that lacketh sight in one eie.
Defit, there lacketh.

Cicero.
Deficio, defeci, deficere, to lack, or to be vn=
sufficient. Also to forsake or fayle. Pruden=
tia nunq̃ deficit oratorem, Prudence neuer

Cæsar.
fayleth an oratoure. Quem sanguis uiresq̃
deficiunt, whom bloode and strength fayl=
leth. Also to forsake his capitayne, and go
to his aduersary. Ab eo defecerat, He went
from him to his ennemye.
Deflacco, aui, are, to weare out.
Deflagro, aui, are, to bourne excedyngly.
Deflecto, xi, tere, to bowe downe.
Defloreo, & deflosco, ere, to fade, or to fal
away as flowres doo: or to lese beaultie.
sometyme it signifieth to burgen or floure.
Defluo, xi, ere, to flowe downeward, to fall
of or away, or come to nothynge.
Defluus, a, um, that whiche floweth or fal=
leth away from any thynge.
Defluuiũ, defluxus, the fallyng of the heare.
Defodio, di, dere, to burye or hyde a thinge
in the grounde, to dygge downe or into
the erthe.
Defœtus, ta, tum, destytute.
Deformis, me, foule, deformed.
Deformo, aui, are, to destroye, or waste, to
make in picture the fourme of a thing.
Defraudo, aui, are, to begyle, to minisshe or
take away the profyte from an other.
Defrico, caui, are, to rub moch, or to rub of.
Defrigo, xi, gere, to frie moche.
Defringo, xi, re, to breke downe, or cut down.
Defrugo, aui, are, to consume or weare out

the profite, specially of grounde, wherof
shulde come corne or frute.
Defrutare, to boyle newe wyne.
Defrutum, sodden wyne.
Defugeo, gi, ere, to refuse.
Defundo, fudi, dere, to poure downe.
Defungor, geris, to vse no lenger, to leaue
or resygne, to perfourme.
Degener, is, he that in his maners is vnlike
to his auncetours, or base of lynage.
Degenero, aui, are, to be vnlyke to his aun=
cetours in maners. It may be said of frui=
tes, whiche waxe wylde.
Deglabro, aui, are, to plucke of heares.

Plautus.
Dego, degi, degere, to leade, to lyue, to ex=
pelle, to pulle of. Degitur corium de tergo
meo, The skynne is pulled of my backe.
Degulo, aui, are, to consume in glotony.
Dehinc, from hensforth, moreouer.
Dehisco, sci, scere, to gape wyde open.
Dehonestamentum, a disfyguringe, or dys=
honestye.
Dehonesto, aui, are, to dishoneste.
Dehonestus, ta, tum, very honeste.
Deianira, the wyfe of Hercules.
Deidamia, the concubyne of Achilles, on
whom he begatte Pirrhus.
Deiero, aui, are, to take an othe, to sweare
deepely.
Deiicio, ieci, iicere, to throwe downe, to cast
downe to tourne away, to put out of office.
Dein, moreouer, furthermore.
Deinceps, one after an other in order, from
hensforth, or thensforth, afterwarde.
Deinsuper, vpwarde.
Deintegro, from the begynnyng to thende.
Deiphile, the mother of Diomedes.
Deiphobus, the name of a sonne of Pria=
mus and Hecuba.
Deiugo, aui, are, to vnyoke, to vnioyne,
to disseuer.
Deiurium, a great and solemne othe.
Deiurus, he that sweareth solemnely.
Delabor, delabi, to be let downe, or fal down
to be consumed or wasted.
Delachrimor, aris, ari, to wepe or sende out
droppes lyke tearcs.
Delanio, aui, are, to cutte in pieces.
Delapidata, pauementes.
Delasso, aui, are, to make wery.
Delator, toris, a secrete accuser, a coplainer
Delatio, an accusation secretely made, or a
secrete complaynt.
Delebile, that whyche maye be put oute, or
put awaye.
Delectatio, delectation in the seces of he=
ryng, seinge, taste, and smellyng.
Delecto, aui, are, to delyte, to leade, to al=
lure to a thynge.

Delector, aris, ari, to take delectation or pleasure.
Delectus rerum, choyse or election of thinges. Also of men.
Delectum habere, sommetyme signifieth to take musters for the warres.
Delego, aui, are, to assigne to som office message, or other necessary and great busynes, to commytte a cause or matter to be determyned, to sende in ambassade or message.
Deleo, leui, ere, to distroy, to putte out any thynge that is writen, to remoue or putte awaye.
Deleterion, venome.
Deletile, that distroyeth or putteth out.
Deliacus, ca, cum, of the yle of Delus.
Delibero, aui, are, to be aduised, to take aduyse, to determyne, to doubte, to consult.
Deliberatiua oratio, wherin any thynge is consulted.
Delibo, aui, are, to taste a thynge. somtyme to vyolate, to distroy, to sacrifice, to drain water by forowes.
Delibro, aui, are, to pul of the barke or rind of a tree.
Delibutus, ta, tum, oynted.
Delicatus, cata, catum, delycate, wantonlye broughte vppe.
Delicias facere, to be wanton, to be squaymyshe, to play the cockeney.
Delitium, & delitie, a wanton worde, which vneth may be expressed in englysshe, vsed betwene a man and a woman in wanton pastyme. Meum delitium, mee delitie, my swete harte, my darlynge, my ioye, and suche other lyke, expressed best by theym that be Venus secretaries.
Delico, aui, are, to explane.
Delictum, an offence whan a thinge is vndone, omission.
Deligo, legi, ligere, to chose or pyke out.
Delimo, aui, are, to fyle or shaue of frome any mettall.
Delinimentum, delectation, an allectyue, or swetenes in feelynge.
Delinio, iui, ire, to anoynte, to rubbe pleasantly, to towche.
Delinitus, touched swetely, anoynted, pacified, appeased.
Deliniare, to drawe, as a paynter dothe, er he do lay on colours.
Delitum, blotted.
Delinquo, deliqui, delinquere, to omytte to do well, to offende.
Deliquium, lacke. Deliquium animi, whan a man is in a swowne.
Deliquium solis, the eclyps of the sonne.
Deliro, aui, are, to go out of the ryght way, properly to go out of the forow, and make a balke, as ploughmen do. Also to dote.
Delirus, he that swarueth from reason, a dotarde or dotynge foole.
Deliteo, tui, ere, to hyde me.
Delitesco, I go to hyde me.
Delos, an yle nygh to Grece.
Delphi, a citie and people in Grece.
Delphicus, ca, cum, of that citie.
Delphin, inos, a greatte fysshe, called a Dolphyn.
Delphis, a temple of Apollo in Grece.
Delubrum, a place, wherin be dyuers images of god and sayntes.
Deludo, si, ere, to mocke.
Delumbis, be, weake, somtyme wanton.
Deluo, lui, ere, to wash cleane, or washe out.
Deluto, aui, are, to lay klaye on any thyng.
Demagis, moche more.
Demando, aui, are, to committe holy.
Demarathus, a kynge of Spartan.
Demarchus, a ruler of the people.
Demeanculum, a place to descende into a Cellar.
Demeare, to go downe, or go away.
Demens, tis, madde.
Dementia, madnesse.
Demensus, sa, sum, measured.
Demensum, wages gyuen euery month.
Dementio, tiui, ire, to be madde.
Demento, taui, tare, to be madde, to make madde, to make foolyshe.
Demereo, rui, ere, to wynne or gette.
Demereor, eris, reri, to bynde by frendship, to wynne ones fauoure, to make a frende, to deserue moche.
Demetior, to mette diligently, to esteme.
Demeto, tri, tere, to mette.
Demetrias, a towne of Thessalie.
Demetrius, a mans name.
Demiror, aris, ari, to meruayle moche. some tyme it signifieth to knowe not.
Demitto, misi, tere, to send downe, to humble my selfe, to laye downe.
Demissitia tunica, a longe cote.
Demissus, a, um, humble.
Demo, mere, to take away, or abate.
De capite demptum, appayred in substance or valewe.
Democratia, a fourme of a common welth, where the people haue authoritie. *Ti. Liuius*
Democraticus, he that fauoreth the common welth, where the people hath auctoritie.
Democritus, the name of a philosopher.
Demodocus, the name of a harper in Homer.
Demolior, iris, to throwe downe any thing that is buylded.
Demonstro, aui, are, to shewe openly.
Demonstratiuus, a, uum, that sheweth, or is shewed, or mete to be shewed.

Demon-

Demonstratio, onis, a shewynge.
Demonstratiuum genus, a fourme of speakynge, wherin oratours didde either commende or dispraise any man openly.
Demophon, the sonne of Theseus and Phedra kynge of Athenes.
Demorior, eris, to dye vtterly.
Demoror, aris, to tary longe, to kepe back, or cause to tarye.
Demosthenes, the name of a famous orator.
Demulceo, cere, to stryke gentilly and softly with the hande, as we do to chyldren or houndes, whan we make moche of them.
Demum, at the laste. sometyme it signifieth onely, or alway.
Demussata contumelia, displeasure done by dissimulation.
Denarius, a certayn coyne, after the diuersities of countreys, dyuers in weight. it is taken nowe for a peny.
Denarius, a, um, that whiche contayneth the numbre of tenne.
Denarro, aui, are, to tell in order.
Denaso, to cutte or pull of the nose.
Denato, aui, are, to swymme downe.
Denego, aui, are, not to gyue, or to denye to gyue.
Denigro, aui, are, to make blacke.
Deni, tenne togither. Cæsar lib. 5. Vxores habent deni duodeniq́ inter se communes, They haue wyues tenne and twelue men togither, commune amonge them.
Deniq́, in conclusyon.
Denomino, aui, are, to name.
Denoto, aui, are, to blame.
Dens, dentis, a toothe.
Denso, aui, are, to thycken or make thycke.
Densus, a, um, thycke, harde, closed togyther, compacte.
Densitas, tatis, & densitudo, dinis, thicknes.
Dentale, the share of a plough.
Dentatim, in order lyke tethe.
Denticulus, dentatus, ta, tum, dẽtosus, sa, sum, toothed.
Denticulare, to thruste in his teethe.
Dentifricium, a medycyne, wherewith the tethe be rubbed, to make them white.
Dentiloquus, he that speaketh betwene the tethe, or lyspeth.
Dentio, ire, to putte forthe tethe, or breede teethe.
Dentiscalpium, an instrumente, wherwith teethe be scraped.
Dentitio, onis, a puttyng forth or growinge of tethe.
Denubo, psi, bere, to mary or wedde.
Denudo, aui, are, to dispoile or make naked.
Denuncio, aui, are, to shewe or tell a thinge to an other man, or denounce. Also Denunciare testimonium, to brynge wytnesse into the courte of iugement, as they too in the Chauncerie, where wytnesses are compelled to come.
Denuo, agayne.
Deorsum, downewarde.
Depalmo, aui, are, to buffette.
Depango, xi, gere, to plant or sette.
Depeciscor, cisceris, to couenant or promise or agree, or patise. Depectus, a, um, couenanted or patised. Depectus est cum hostibus, he patised with the ennemies.
Depecto, xui, uel, xi, tere, to keme diligently.
Depexus, a, um, kempte, trymmed.
Depeculor, aris, ari, to robbe a commune weale, a prince, or a place halowed.
Depelli portenta, whã monstruous or strãge thinges do happen, betokenynge some yll auenture to happen, to repele it by prayers, auowes, or other goood dedes.
Depello, puli, pellere, to putte downe, putte away, or remoue.
Depulsus, putte downe.
Dependeo, ere, to hange downe of a thing, to depende.
Dependo, di, dere, to paye.
Dependere penas, to be punysshed, to suffre peynes.
Deperdo, ere, to lose.
Depereo, ii, ire, to perysshe, to dye, to loue inordynately.
Depesco, scui, ere, to dryue cattell.
Depessus, rente, torne.
Depilis, without heare.
Depilo, aui, are, to pull of heare.
Deplano, to make playne.
Deplanto, to sette.
Depleo, pleui, plere, to fylle.
Deploro, aui, are, to lament, to bewayle.
Deploratus, ta, tum, without hope of recouery or remedy.
Depono, posui, nere, to laye downe, to depriue or take away, to leaue a thynge in an other mans custody.
Depositus, ta, tum, layde downe, lefte in an other mans kepynge. also desperate.
Depopulor, ari, to distroye or waste a countreye.
Deporto, aui, are, to cary or brynge awaye, to banysshe.
Deportatus, banysshed.
Deposco, poposci, deposcere, to desyre moche, or requyre.
Depositorius, he that leaueth a thyng with an other man.
Depositum, that whyche is lefte in an nother mannes kepynge: or that is layde to pledge.
Depredor, ari, to robbe a countrey or toune.

Deprauo, aui, are, to make ylle, to depraue.
Deprecor, cari, to beseche. Deprecari ueniam, to aske forgyuenes. Also Deprecari, to refuse, to desyre the contrary, to put awaye, or denye that whiche we wolde not haue, to haue in detestation, to resyste, to delyuer a man by prayer.
Deprehendo, di, ere, to take a man vnwares. Deprehensus est in sermone, He was taken in his wordes. Deprehensus est in scelere, He was taken with the faulte. Also deprehendere to knowe, to perceyue.
Deprimo, re, to kepe down, to thrust down.
Depromo, to drawe out, to declare.
Depso, psi, psere, to warke a thynge with the handes, to the intent to make it soft.
Depuber, depuberis, a chyld or yonge beast, whiche are not come to ripe yeres.
Depudet, he hath layde asyde shame.
Depudico, caui, are, to dishoneste or vyolate a womanne.
Depugno, aui, are, to fyght valyantly.
Depurgo, aui, are, to clense any thing vnder
Depuro, to make cleane or pure. (fote.
Deputo, aui, are, to cutte of, to esteme, to iudge, to repute.
Depuuio, ere, to beate.
Derbn, the name of a people in Asia.
Derce, a well moste colde in sommer.
Derelinquo, dereliqui, derelinquere, to forsake vtterly.
De repente, sodaynly.
Derideo, risi, dere, to laugh, to scorn, to mock
Deripeo, ripui, pere, to take away, to dispoil.
Deriuo, aui, are, to deriue from one to an other, to lay to one, as to lay to a mans default, or charge, to take from one, and giue to an other.
Derogo, aui, are, to mynysshe, to derogate, to take awaye.
Dercæi, a people of Grece in the costes of Thrace.
Deruncinare, to cut or pull of that whyche is superfluous.
Deruo, ui, ere, to fall downe.
Desæuio, sæui, uire, to be wodde angry. somtyme to cease to be angry.
Descendo, di, ere, to go downe, to descende.
Descio, iui, ire, to knowe nat.
Descisco, iui, sciscere, to disagree, to leaue one and go to an other, to rebell.
Discobinatus, wounded or cutte.
Describo, psi, ere, to write out of a copy, to order or appoynt, to paynte or write aduysedly, to declare or describe.
Deseco, aui, are, to cutte in sonder.
Desido, sedi, ere, to sytte styll, or contynually, to syt on a thing, to sit on a chamber stole. it is also proprely whan the erth doth gape or chinke. Terra desedit, the grounde openeth or gapeth.
Desero, ui, ere, to leaue or forsake.
Deserto, taui, are, to forsake.
Desertus, forsaken, not inhabitable, where no man dwelleth, a desert or wyldernesse.
Deseruio, uiui, ire, to obey or serue humbly, somtyme to do yll seruyce.
Deses, desidis, vnoccupied.
Desiderium, a desyre.
Desidero, aui, are, to desyre.
Desiderati, deed or slayne.
Desidia, slouthfulnes.
Desidiosus, a man ful of idelnes, slouthfull.
Designo, aui, are, to assigne, to note or signifie, to do a thinge newely.
Designator, toris, a marshall, which setteth or appointeth euery man to his place, conuenient to his degree or office.
Designatus, assigned, ordeyned.
Desilio, lui, ere, to leape or lyght downe.
Desino, sii, nere, to leaue, to cease.
Desinere artem, to leaue the crafte.
Desipio, pui, ere, to do folishly, to war folish.
Desisto, destiti, desistere, to leaue of.
Desolo, aui, are, to make desolate.
Desolatus, a, u, that is made desolate or distroyed.
Desolor, ari, to comforte. (stroyed.
Despectio, onis, a despysynge.
Despecto, aui, are, to loke behynde.
Despectus, ta, tum, despised.
Desperatio, onis, despayre.
Despero, aui, are, to despaire.
Desperatus, a, um, desperate.
Despicabilis, to be despised.
Despicientia, despectus, despectio, dispite.
Despiceo, spexi, cere, to looke or beholde downe, to despise. Despicor, caris, to dispise.
Despicus, a watcheman, to se who cometh, as it is in Calyce.
Despolio, aui, are, to dispoyle or to robbe.
Despondeo, di, ere, to affyance or betrouth. also to promyse.
Despondere animum, to be in desperation, or wery of lyfe, to despaire of any thynge, that a man seketh for.
Despondere sapientiam, to despaire, to com to great wysedom.
Despumo, aui, are, to skymme or claryfye any lycour.
Despuo, ui, ere, to spet downe, or spette on a thynge.
Desquammo, aui, are, to skale a fyshe.
Destino, aui, are, to pourpose, to appoynte, to depute, to prepare, to chese, to tye to a thinge, to sette a pryce.
Destituo, ui, ere, to forsake, to leaue, to depriue or take fro, to lowse, or vnbynde, to sette downe a man. Destituit omnes seruos ad Cecilius.

ad mensam ante se, He dyd sette downe all his seruantes at the table before hym.

Destringo, xi, ere, to bynde harde or cutte.

Destructile, that whiche shall be distroyed.

Destruo, xi, ere, to distroy or throwe down that whiche is buylded.

Desubulo, aui, are, to perce, proprely with an awle or bodkyn.

Desudasco, to sweate.

Desudo, aui, are, to sweate moch or labour.

Desuesco, ueui, scere, to discusse or brynge out of custome.

Desuetudo, dinis, a disuse.

Desultor, toris, he that can vaunte a horse, and leape frome one horsbacke vnto an other. Also those men of warre, that in time of battaylle wolde leape downe of their horses quyckely, and fyghte on foote, and leape vppe agayne as quyckely, were Desultores.

Desultorii equi, horses whiche serued for that purpose.

Desum, defui, deesse, to lacke.

Desuper, from aboue. Desursum, the same.

Detego, tegi, tegere, to disclose or discouer

Deter, lackynge somwhat.

Detergeo, tersi, gere, to wype of, to make cleane.

Determino, aui, are, to determin, to discusse.

Detero, teri, terere, to bruse, to beate oute, as grayne is beaten oute of the eare with threshyng or treadynge.

Deterreo, ui, ere, to putte in feare, to lette by feare.

Detestabile, abhomynable.

Detestor, ari, to abhorre. Amonge Ciuilyons, detestari is to summon a manne with wytnesse.

Detestatio, abhorryng, execration, summonyng with wytnesse. Also Apuleius takith it for geldynge.

Detexo, xi, xere, to weaue, or to wynde.

Detineo, nui, ere, to withholde, to restrayne from lybertie.

Detondeo, detondi, dere, to sheare or clyp.

Detono, aui, are, to make a great sounde.

Detorqueo, si, quere, to bowe, to turne out of the ryght waye.

Detracto, aui, are, to eschue, to forbeare, to hynder by reporte or acte.

Detractores, detracters, backbyters.

Detraho, xi, here, to drawe of, to report yl.

Detrimentum, detriment or damage.

Detrimētosum, that which is cause of moche damage or hurte.

Detrudo, si, ere, to thruste downe. somtyme to constrayne or inforce.

Detrullo, aui, are, to put from one vessel into an other.

Detrunco, aui, are, to cutte of shorte.

Deturbo, aui, are, to beate downe.

Deturpo, aui, are, to make fowle, or defyle.

Deucalion, onis, the name of a kynge, who in fables is sayde dydde restore mankynde distroyed with a floode.

Deueho, xi, ere, to cary from a place.

Deuenio, ueni, nire, to comme downe frome highe to lowe, from rychesse to pouertie, from prosperitie to aduersitie.

Deuenusto, aui, are, to make fowle.

Deuerbero, aui, are, to beate moche.

Deuerro, ri, ere, to swepe cleane.

Deuestio, uestii, ire, to vnclothe.

Deuexo, aui, are, to vexe moche.

Deuexus, a, um, holowe or lyke to a valaye.

Deuincio, xi, cire, to bynde faste.

Deuinco, uici, uincere, to vanquyshe.

Deuio, aui, are, to go out of the waye.

Deuirgino, aui, are, to defloure a mayden.

Deuito, aui, are, to eschewe.

Deuius, a, um, out of the right waye.

Deunx, cis, a poyse, whyche is a pounde, lackynge an ounce.

Deuoco, aui, are, to call asyde, or awaye.

Deuolo, aui, are, to flee or rounne frome a hygher place to a lower.

Deuoluo, ui, uere, to tumble or roll downe. by translation it signifieth, it is falle, or com from one to an other, or hapned. Deuoluta est hereditas, The iheritāce is falle or com.

Deuoro, aui, are, to deuoure. sommetyme to beare. Hoc tędium mihi deuorandum est, This labour I must susteyne.

Deuotio, onis, a curse, a vowe to dye, or to make a man dye.

Deuoto, aui, are, to bynde by a vowe.

Deuotorius, a, ū, concerning a vow or curse.

Deuotus, ta, tum, vowed or cursed.

Deuoueo, ere, to vowe or curse, to consente to dye.

DEVS, god.

Dexter, dextri, of the right hande. somtyme it signifieth apt, conuenient, quicke and dyligent, prosperous, fauourable.

Dexteritas, tatis, aptnes and redynes in the thing that a man goth about.

Dexter, tra, trum, ryght, or apte.

Dextero, aui, are, to couple horses in a teme.

Dextrale, a bracelet to weare on the ryght arme. Dextrocherium the same.

Dextrarii, horses ioyned in a teeme.

Dextrorsum, towarde the right hand.

Dextimi, horsemenne beinge on the righte wynge in battayle.

¶D Ante I.

DIA, an addicion to womens names, whan theyr folyshe louers wyl make them equall to goddesses.

F.iii.   Diabo-

Diabolus, the dyuell, howe be it in greke it sygnifieth proprely a fals accuser.

Diaconus, a deacon.

Diadema, a cappe, whiche an emperour or kinge weareth vnder his crowne.

Diæta, a parler to suppe in. Also dyete in eatynge and drinkyng. Also a place where iugementes were gyuen.

Diætarii, seruauntes that do awayte on the table. Sometyme suche as do haunt dyners & suppers, to the intent to steale somwhat.

Dialectus, a maner of speche, as we wolde saye diuersities in englysshe, as Northerne speche, Southerne, Kentyshe, Deuenishe, and other lyke.

Dialexis, dysputation.

Dialectica, logyke.

Dialis, Jupyter. Also it sygnifyeth of one day, as Consul Dialis, a Consul of one daye.

Dialogus, a disputation betwene two.

Diameter, a lyne, whiche diuydeth any fygure into two equall partes.

Diana, the doughter of Jupyter, whyche ficinge the company of men, to the intente that she wolde not be meuyd with carnalle lustes, she contynually exercysed her selfe in huntynge wylde beastes: and for hyr chaste lyfe, she was honoured of the paynyms for a goddesse. She is also taken for the Moone.

Diapasma, a sprynkelynge of water, or other lyke.

Diapason, a concorde in musyke of fiue tunes, and two halfe tunes.

Diapente, of fyue.

Diaphanum, clere throughout, as chrystall.

Diaphonia, a discorde.

Diaphora, a difference.

Diaphoreticus, ca, cum, that whiche dothe dissolue and sende forth humoures or vapours.

Diaphragma, is a thynne skynne or caulle in the body, whyche separateth the harte and lunges from the splene and lyuer, and is called the Myddrese.

Diarium, prouysion for oone daye. Also a boke declarynge what is done day by day.

Diastole, a distinction or poynte, whereby one worde or sentence is distincte frome an nother.

Diatessaron, of eyghte.

Diatretum, a cuppe imboced, and cunningly wrought.

Dibapha, purple twyse dyed. Also a garment therof.

Dica, a cause, an accusation, a iudgemente.

Dicacitas, tatis, scoffynge or bourdynge.

Dicaculus, & dicacula, mery in talkyng.

Dicæarchus, a iuste Prince. Also the name of a phylosopher.

Dicax, cacis, a rayler, or reprocher.

Dico, caui, to vowe, to offre, to dedicate.

Dico, xi, cere, to saye, to telle, to bydde, to promyse, to affirme, to defende: as Cicero dixit causam Milonis, Cicero defended Miloes cause.

Dicere sententiam, to gyue sentence or iudgemente.

Dicere leges, to appoynte lawes, or condycions of peace, as by the vanquysher to hym that is vanquyshed.

Dicere diem, to sewe a man, or call him vp, (as we vse to say) by action, writte, or commandement, proprely to cause a man to be bounden to appere and make aunswere.

Dicere causam, to make aunswere to action or playnte.

Dicere mulctam, to sette or assesse a fyne or summe of money to be payde by hym, whiche hath commytted a trespace.

Dicere ius, to gyue commandement or sentence on a peyne. Sometyme it sygnifyeth to gouerne by lawes a towne or countrey.

Dicere sacramento, to take an oth, proprely as they do, whiche be retayned in warres.

Dictannus, an herbe called dittayne.

Dictator, the hyghest offyce in the publyke weale of the Romaynes, whiche was also called Magister populi, the mayster of the people: whiche for the space of syxe monethes, hadde the authoritie of a kynge. And therfore that dignitie was neuer giuē but onely whan the state of the citie was in any ieoperdie.

Dictatura, the office or dignitie of dictator.

Dicte, a citie in the yle of Crete or Candy.

Dicteria, tauntes, or quippies, or short and sharpe reasons.

Dictio, onis, a worde, a forme of speaking.

Dictito, aui, are, to speake ofte or in dyuers places.

Dicto, aui, are, to speake or declare that an other writeth, or beareth in remembrance. Also to inuestigate or expounde the sence of any authour. Also to brynge to remembraunce.

Dictata, Interpretations, exposytions, or declarations, made by maysters vnto their scholers.

Dictum, spoken, or sayde.

Dicta, sygnified mery sentences.

Dicturio, iui, ire, to goo aboute, or prepare to speake.

Dictynna, one of the names of Diana.

Dictynnus, a hylle, wherein the temple of Diana was sytuate.

Dictys, one of the Centaures, and an hystographier of Candy.

Didas-

Didascalus, a schole mayster.
Dido, the name of a lady that buylded Carthage.
Diduco, xi, cere, to brynge into sondry partes, or to diuide or pulle aparte.
Didymæ, arum, ylandes of Aphrike, that bounde on Aegypte.
Didynnis, the name of a man, and in latine it signifieth Geminus, in englyshe, a twinne or double.
Diecula, a lyttell while.

Plautus. Dierecta, in an yll tyme.
Dies, diei, a daye. Sometyme it sygnyfyeth tyme or seasōn.
Dies critici, the dayes in whyche phisitions do gyue a certayne iugement in syckenes.
Diescit, it is daye, it waxeth daye.
Dies legittimi, amonge lawyers be callyd ordinary dayes, or dayes in courte.
Diem dicere, an, dicere diem.
Diespiter, one of the names of Jupiter.
Dieteris, the space of two yeres.
Diffamo, aui, are, to sprede by fame.
Differo, distuli, differre, to spare or deferre. sometyme to brynge frome one place to another. somtime to reporte abrode, somtyme to deuide or cut asonder, somtyme to set in order. sometyme differ or be in difference. Cic. At vide quid differat inter meam opinionem & tuam, But se nowe what difference is betwene thyne opinion and myne.
Diffibulare, to vnbuckle, to open, to vngird.
Difficilis, difficile, harde, vneasye.
Diffido, dere, to mystruste.
Diffindo, di, ere, to cleaue in sunder.
Diffinio, niui, ire, to diffine or declare in few wordes playnely, the sygnyfycation of a thynge.
Diffinitio, onis, a diffinition, or declaration of the nature qualitie or propre sygnification of a thynge by generaltie, specialtie, and difference.
Diffiteor, fisus sum, diffiteri, to denye.
Diffluo, xi, ere, to flowe abrode.
Diffugio, gi, gere, to flye asonder, or on dyuers partes
Diffundo, di, dere, to powre oute, or scatter.
Diffundere diem, amonge lawyers, to contynue the matter vntyll an other daye.
Digamma, amonge latynes is the letter F.
Digamus, he that hath had two wiues, commonly called Bigamus.
Digama, a womanne that hathe hadde two husbandes.
Digeries, a disposition or order.
Digero, gessi, gerere, to dispose, to order, to interprete or make playne, to deuyde, to dygeste.
Digitalis, le, pertaynynge to the fynger.

Digitali crassitudine, The thyckenesse of a fynger.
Digitalia, thinges worne on the fyngers.
Digitus, a fynger.
Digitum transuersum, sygnyfyeth in a sentence, a lyttell or smalle distaunce. Digitum transuersum ab eo non discedebat, He went not from hym a fynger bredde.
Digladiari, to fight togither with swordes. by translation to contende or stryue.
Dignatio, fauour or familiaritie. *Liuius.*
Dignitas, tatis, honour gyuen or dewe to a man for his merites. sommetyme astate of nobilitie, or great authorytie. sommetyme beautie, proprely of a man, specially in gesture and communication.
Digno, aui, are, & dignor, ari, to iuge one to be worthy, or to be estemed worthy.
Dignosco, noui, scere, to discerne or knowe by dyuers meanes.
Dignoro, aui, are, to marke, as men marke beastes to knowe them.
Dignus, na, num, worthye.
Digne, worthyly.
Digredior, dieris, gredi, to departe or goo awaye.
Digressio, & digressus, a departynge.
Diiouis, Jupyter.
Diiudico, caui, care, to iudge betwyxte two thynges.
Dilabor, eris, labi, to slyppe or go awaye, to falle downe, as a howse doeth. sometyme it signyfieth to fayle.
Dilacero, aui, are, to teare or rent in pieces.
Dilapido, daui, are, to consume goodes, or spende ryottously or wastefully.
Dilato, aui, are, to stretche out in breadth.
Dilēma, tis, an argument, whiche on euery parte taunteth him, to whom it is spoken.
Diligens, tis, diligent, or louynge.
Diligentia, dilygence or loue.
Diligo, lexi, ligere, to fauour or loue meanly, somtyme to diuyde. *Plautus.*
Dilorico, aui, are, to vndo, or cutte a cote, or other thynge beinge sowed.
Dilucescit, the daye appereth.
Dilucidus, clere, bryghte.
Diluculo, an aduerbe, whiche signifieth betyme iu the mornynge.
Diluculo, laui, lare, to waxe daye, to appere to be daye.
Diluculum, that porcion of daye, whiche is before that the sonne ryseth.
Diludium, the leauyng of play, or the space betwene recreations or playes.
Diluo, ui, ere, to wasshe, to make cleane, to putte away, to release, to alaye, as wyne is alayde with water: or to tempre, to purge, or discharge a crime.

Dilutus,

Dilutus, ta, tum, alayed or tempred.
Dilutus color, a faynt colour, or unperfect coloure.
Dilutum, is wyne or other lycour, wherein any herbe or other thing is depid by a certayne space, whiche some phisytions calle infused.
Diluuium, is whan the erth is surrounded or drowned with moche rayne.
Dimano, aui, are, to flowe abrode, as diuers streames out of one springe.
Dimembro, aui, are, to deuyde.
Dimensum, & demensum, measured.
Dimico, aui, are, to fyght or contende with some thynge.
Dimidius, a, um, the halfe deale of that whiche is diuided.
Dimidium plus toto, is spoken where a manne intendeth to shewe that the meane is beste.
Dimidiatus, a, um, the halfe deale of that which is not seuered or diuided.
Diminuo, ui, ere, to minyshe, to cutte of.
Dimissoriæ literæ, letters sent from oone to an nother.
Dimitto, si, tere, to sende dyuers persones into dyuers places. Somtyme it sygnifieth to let to departe, to gyue leaue, to ceasse, to leaue, to lette passe, to suffre, to humble. Deiecit uultū & dimissa uoce locuta est, She dyd cast downe hir loke, and with an humble voyce sayde. Also to gyue, to let down.
Dimissus, a, um, is sommetyme taken for abiecte.
Dimulgo, aui, are, to publyshe abrode.
Dynastæ, potestates.
Dindymene, & Dindyme, one of the names of Cybele, called the mother of the goddꝭ
Dindymus, the rydge of the hylle of Ida in Phrigia.
Diobolares meretrices, harlottes, whyche be hyred for lyttell moneye.
Diolares, harlottes, whiche kepe abrode in the feldes and woddes.
Diœcesis, sios, a iurisdiction, a gouernance. Also the diocese of a byshop.
Diminutus capite, & diminutio capitis, Vide ante, capitis diminutio.

Ci. in Bruto & Tus. lib. 5.

Diodorus, a philosopher of Socrates sect, and Diodorus Siculus, a story writer. and an other Diodorus, a stoike phylosopher, of whom Cicero writeth.
Diogenes, a famous philosphers name.
Dione, a goddesse of the see, mother of Uenus.
Dioptra, a geometricall instrument, to discerne altitudes and distaunce. Uictruuius vseth it for wayinge or pluckynge vppe of water.

Dioscoron, an yle in the borders of Italy.
Diospolis, a cytie of Aegypte. There be foure other of the same name in Aegypte, but very small cities in comparyson of this.
Diotæ, vessels of erth with handels, wherin wyne was kepte.
Diphthera, a shepeherdes cote made with shepe skynnes.
Diphthongus, two vowels ioyned togither called a dipthonge, as æ, œ, au, ei.
Diploma, tis, a charter of a prince or cytie, or a wrytte.
Diplois, idis, any garmente lyned, but it is taken for a doublette.
Dipondium, a weight of two pounde.
Dipsacon, whyte brere.
Dipsas, a serpent, of whom if a man be bitten, he dyeth for thyrste.
Dyrrachiū, a citie in the realme of Naples.
Diræ, cursynges.
Dirce, a womans name, the wyfe of Lycus kynge of Thebans.
Diribitores, distrybuters of money, or paye maysters.
Dirigeo, gui, gére, to shrynke for colde, or for feare.
Dirigo, exi, gere, to make streight, or ryght.
Directus, a, um, ryght or streyght.
Directé, streight, or in a right fourme.
Dirimo, remi, ere, reptum, to breke or leaue of. Ea res consilium diremit, That thynge brake or dissolued the counsayle. also to put of, or deferre.
Diripio. Vide in deripio.
Diris, an hygh hylle of Maurytayne nowe callyd Atlas.
Dirus, ra, rum, vengeable.
Diritas, tatis, crueltie, vengeance.
Dirumpo, rupi, rumpere, to braste or breake a sonder.
Diruncio, iui, ire, to wede out, or purge that whiche is nought.
Dis, ditis, callyd the god of rychesse, sometyme it signifieth ryche.
Discapidino, aui, are, to vnclose or open.
Discedo, scessi, dere, to departe. sometyme it signifieth an exception: as, Quum discesserim a fratre, nemo est mihi te charior, Excepte my brother, no manne is to me more dere than thou arte. Also it sygnifieth dyuysion or openynge. as, Quum terra discessisset, magnis quibusdam imbribus, discendit in illum hiatum, whan the erthe by thoccasyon of moche rayne opened, he wente downe into the cleft or swalowe.
Discepto, aui, are, to dspute or contende.
Disceptatio, disputation or contencion.
Discerniculum, diuersytie.
Discerno, decreui, cernere, to depart or sunder

Ci.l. off.

dre one thyng from an other. Also to striue or varie, to knowe distinctly.

Discerpo, psi, ere, to pluck or teare in piecis.

Discinctus, dissolute, or neglygent, or vnable for the warres, cowarde.

Seruius. Discindo, scidi, scindere, to cutte of.

Disciplina, lerning as it is perceyued of the scholer. It is also a good forme of lyuing.

Disciplinosus, apte to lerne.

Discipulus, a scholer or disciple.

Discludo, si, dere, to shutte out.

Disco, didici, discere, to lerne.

Dedisco, ere, to forgette that whiche was ones lerned.

Discobolus, he that throweth a dyshe.

Disconuenio, ni, nire, to disagree or discord.

Discordia, discorde.

Discors, dis, he that agreeth not with an nother.

Discrepo, aui, are, to disagree or discorde.

Discretio, onis, a separation. somtyme election of good from yll, discretion.

Discretus, seuered or parted. Valla saythe, that it is he that discerneth the qualyties of men, and value of thinges.

Discrimen, minis, diuersite or difference. also the shedynge or partynge of the heare. Also it sygnifieth peryll.

Discriminale, an instrument, wherwith the heare is parted or shadde.

Discriminatim, asunder here and there.

Discrimino, aui, are, to deuyde.

Discrutior, ari, to be moche vexed or troubled in mynde.

Discumbo, cubui, cumbere, to syt at meales.

Discuneatus, opened with a wedge or other lyke thynge.

Discurro, rere, to runne hither and thither, or wander.

Discus, a dyshe. Also a rounde thynge of wodde or mettalle, whiche in playinge is throwen from one man to an nother. It is sometyme taken for the hole fygure of the sonne or the moone.

Discutio, ssi, tere, to caste or shake downe, to remoue, to examyne, or discusse.

Disertus, eloquent in wordes.

Disiicio, disieci, disiicere, to caste a sonder.

Disiungo, xi, ere, to vnioyne, to separate.

Dispalescere, to publyshe abrode.

Dispalo, aui, are, to wander.

Dispalati, scattered.

Dispello, dispuli, dispellere, to expelle or put from many places or many wayes.

Dispendiosus, sa, sum, harmful, vnprofitable.

Dispendium, losse by neclygence, or superfluous expenses. Also it signifieth harme.

Dispēdo, di, ere, to spede, also to stretch out.

Dispenno, ere, to stretche.

Dispensator, toris, a stewarde, or other offycer, layinge out money for howseholde: a disposer of thinges.

Dispenso, aui, are, to laye out money.

Dispereo, rii, rire, to be loste vtterly.

Disperdo, di, ere, to lose.

Dispergo, spersi, gere, to sowe abrode, or to scatter.

Dispertio, tiui, ire, to gyue parte to one, part to an nother.

Dispesco, cui, ere, to dryue beastes frome their pasture.

Dispesso, ssi, ere, to sprede abrode.

Dispicio, xi, cere, to discerne, to espye, to consyder.

Dispicientia, circumspection, aduysement, diligent consyderation.

Displodo, si, dere, to sprede.

Dispondæus, a fote in meter, that hath four syllables longe, as Oratores.

Dispono, sui, ere, to dispose, to order.

Dspungo, xi, gere, to take accompt, or examyne any maner of thinge writen.

Dispunctio, an examination.

Disputo, taui, tare, to dispute, to make plain to be vnderstande.

Disquiro, siui, rere, to inserche diligently, to inquyre.

Disquisitio, where euery mans opinyon is asked in a matter, whiche requyreth iugemente.

Disraro, raui, rare, to make thynne that whiche is thycke.

Dissuauior, ari, to kysse swetely, and with moche delectation.

Dissecatus, ta, tum, cutte as a bodye is in an anotomye.

Dissectio, onis, an Anotomie.

Disseco, caui, care, to cutte in pieces.

Dissentaneus, a, um, not accordinge.

Dissentio, tire, & dissentior, tiri, to think contrary, or to disagree.

Dissero, rui, rere, to sowe sedes, sometyme to dispute or declare.

Disserto idem.

Dissertio, a particion of landes.

Dissideo, ere, to be at variance or discorde.

Dissidium, variance or discorde.

Dissilio, liui, ire, to lepe down from a place, somtyme to braste.

Dissimulo, aui, are, to dissemble or fayne a thynge, whiche is not as it semeth to be.

Dissipo, aui, are, to scatter or sprede abrode or dispatche. also to bringe vnto noughte.

Dissitus, ta, tum, sette farre of, distant.

Dissoluo, ui, uere, to lose or vnbynd, to spede to paye seuerall dettes.

Dissolui, to be paide or discharged.

Dissoluere religionem, to do agaynst the religion,

lygion, to breake the relygion.

Dissonus, na, num, that whyche dothe not accorde.

Dissulto, taui, tare, to leape hither & thither.

Disto, aui, are, to differre, to be distant.

Distantia, distaunce.

Distendo, di, dere, to stratche out, or retche, to fyll, as a bottell is fylled.

Distentus, fulle.

Distero, terere, to breake smalle, to pounde or to braye fyne.

Distichon, two versis.

Distillo, aui, are, to distylle, or drop downe.

Distillatio, onis, a distyllyng, specyally from the heed, callid a reume or catarr, the pose.

Distineo, nui, ere, to lette or withholde with busynesse, or vrgente causes, to holde or putte backe.

Distinguo, xi, ere, to dyuide. Also to make dystinction.

Distito, aui, are, to stande aparte, or be dystant one from an other.

Distraho, xi, here, to plucke away, or to dyuide, or to withdrawe a thynge. sometyme by translation it is taken for to sell. Also to fynisshe or conclude matters in variaunce. Controuersias distrahere, to ende controuersies or suites.

Distribuo, ui, ere, to dystrybute, or gyue in sondry partes to dyuers persones.

Distringo, xi, gere, to bynd fast, or to strain harde, to rubbe of or clense the fylthe or soyle of the body, to thretten to stryke, or to drawe out a swerde. Gladium distrinxit, he drewe out his sworde. Sommetyme to gather, as, Sereno cælo manibus distringi oliuam oportet, In a fayre cleere daye the olyues must be gathered by hande. Districtus negotiis, lette with busynesse.

Columel.

Distorqueo, distorsi, quere, to drawe awrye, or asyde.

Disturbo, aui, are, to caste downe.

Disulcus, an hogge, which hath the briistils of his necke deuided.

Diteo, & ditesco, sci, scere, to make ryche, or be ryche.

Dithyrambus, a verse made in the honoure of Bacchus.

Ditio, onis, a domynion.

Dito, aui, are, to make ryche.

Ditrocheus, a fote of four sillables in verse, hauynge one longe, an other shorte, an nother longe, the fourthe shorte.

Diu, longe tyme. also the day tyme. wherof commeth Interdiu, in the day tyme.

Diutius, lengar. diutissime, lengest.

Diuagor, ari, to wader from place to place.

Diuarico, aui, are, to stryde, or to spred wide one from an other, as bowghes of a tree.

Diuello, li, ere, to pull away by violence.

Diuendo, didi, dere, to selle to dyuers persones, or in dyuers parcelles.

Diuerbia, the partes of a comedy or interlude, where many persons speke togither.

Diuersito, aui, are, to turne often to a thing, or to resorte.

Diuersor, ari, to resort, or repaire to a place.

Diuersorium, an inne, wherto men in iourney doo resorte to bayte or be lodged: a lodgynge.

Diuersorius, a, um, pertaynynge to an inne, or lodgynge.

Diuersus, a, um, dyuers or separate.

Diuerticulum, a bywaye, or syde way, oute of the high way.

Diuerto, ti, tere, to tourne from one thinge to an other, to take lodgynge, or to bayte.

Diuerto ad te & apud te, I come to lodge with the, or to tary for a tyme with the.

Diues, diuitis, ryche. ditior, rycher, diuissimus, rychest.

Diuexo, aui, are, to vexe or trouble.

Diuidia, tediousnes. somtime it betokeneth discorde.

Diuidiculum, an heed of a cundyte.

Diuidium, a particion or diuident.

Diuido, si, dere, to tiuide or parte in sonder.

Diuiduum, that whiche may be seuered or diuyded.

Diuinipotens, he that hath power in diuine thynges.

Diuinitus, godly, or of god.

Diuino, aui, are, to telle truthe, as well of thynges present, as of thinges passed. for the more parte it signifyeth to coniecte of thinges present, what shall happen.

Diuinatio, onis, a foreiugement or coniecture. Also where a matter cometh in iugement, without writinge or wytnesse on any of the partes, that iudgement may be called Diuinatio, a diuination.

Diuinus, na, num, that whiche pertayneth to god, diuine.

Diuisio, onis, wherby we declare what is in variance, or whereby we doo expresse of what thinges we wyll treate. Also a diuysyon into sondry partes.

Diuisor, oris, amonge the olde Romaynes was he, whiche at the election of greatte officers, diuidid or gaue money to the people, in the names of them whiche sued for the office, to thintent for to attayne it.

Diuitię, diuitiarum, diuitiis, diuitias, ryches.

Diuito, aui, are, to make ryche.

Dium, the day light vnder the fyrmament. whan we say, Sub dio aliquid fieri, it sygnifieth some thynge to be doone abroode, or out of the house.

Diunt,

D ante O. XXXVI

Diunt, old wryters vsed for dant, they gyue.
Diuortium, a dyuorse, or separation of a man and his wyfe. sometyme a departyng from any other thynge.
Diurno, aui, are, to lyue longe.
Diurnus, na, num, pertayninge to daye, as Diurni libri, bokes conteynynge the actis done euery day. sometime a dayes hyre.
Dius, dia, come of a gentyll stocke.
Diutulé, a lyttell whyle.
Diutinus, tina, num, longe contynuynge.
Diutissimé, very longe, or to longe.
Diuturnus, na, num, longe continuynge.
Diuus, ua, uum, worthy a diuine remembrace. Nowe they take Diuum, & diuam, for a man or woman saynct.

¶ D Ante O.

Terentius — DO, dedi, dare, to gyue. Also to offre, or proffre. Vt res dant sese, As thynges offre them selues. Also to brynge.
Vergilius. — Magnam dabit ille ruina arboribus, He shall brynge a great fall vnto trees. Also to say, Quamobrem has partes didicerim paucis dabo, For what cause I lerned that parte, I wyll telle the in fewe wordes. Also to o=
Terentius — beye, to conforme. Da te mihi, Conforme the to my wylle. Also to committe or doo. O Aeschine, pol haud paternum istuc dedisti, O Eschines, in good faith in this thou hast not done lyke a father.
Dare operam, to applye, to gyue or take hede, or to helpe.
Do manus, I reder me, or I am vanquished.
Dare pœnas, to suffre punyshement.
Dare ueniam, to forgyue.
Dare potestatem, to commytte authoritie or power, or remyt a thinge to an other mans pleasure or lybertie. Suarum ominum reru illi potestate dederat, He gaue hym the rule of all that he had.
Dare fidem, to promyse faithfully.
Dare facultatem, to gyue lybertie or power to do a thynge.
Dare manum, to putte into his hande pryuily, as they do to men of lawe, or priuy solyciters, or corrupt offycers.
Dare damnas, to pay damages, or to make satisfaction.
Salustius. — Dare auribus, to flatter, or speake to please.
Ci. Teren. Plaut. Eras. in Chilia. Vergilius. — Dare negotium, to assigne or appoynte busynesse, or a thynge to be done.
Dare in uiam, to take a iourney.
Dare in pedes, to flee or runne away.
Dare uerba, to deceyue by fayre promyses, or pleasant demonstration.
Datum est, It is predestinate.
Doceo, cui, cére, to teache or gyue knowe=

lege, or to informe, to aduyse.
Docibilis, apte to be taught.
Docilis, lyghtly taught or instructed.
Docilitas, aptenes to lerne.
Doctrina, æ, doctrine, whiche procedeth of the teacher. Disciplina, lernynge taken of the scholer.
Documentum, a lesson.
Doctus, ta, tum, lerned, that is to say, knowynge a thynge without experience. Vide peritus.
Dodona, a citie in Greece, whereby was a woode, in the whiche men thoughte that trees spake.
Dodone, the daughter of Iupiter and Europa.
Dodra, was a drinke made of nine thynges, herbes, iuyse, water, wyne, salt, oyle, bread, hony, and pepper.
Dodrans, antis, a poyse wayeng. ix. ounces.
Dogma, atis, a certayn determination, whiche in sectes of philosophers euery oone had, without the whiche the secte fayled. sometyme they be called placita.
Dolabra, a carpentars axe.
Dolabro, aui, are, to hewe as a carpentar.
Dolentia, griefe.
Doleo, ui, ére, to fele peyne or grefe.
Dolere caput, pedes, oculos, the heed, fete, or eyen to ake.
Doleo tuis rebus aduersis, I am sory for thy mysfortune or trouble.
Doleo tuam uicem, I am sorye on thy behalfe.
Dolium, any great vessel of wine, as a tune, pipe, butte, or hoggisheed.
Doliaris, great as a tunne. Doliaris heluo, a gorbelyed glutton.
Doliarium, a wyne sellar.
Dolichus, a space of grounde contaynyng xii. furlonges.
Dolo, aui, are, to cutte or hewe with an axe or sythe.
Dolio, iui, ire, to graue in mettall.
Dolobella, an hatchette.
Varro. — Dolon, the propre name of a man of Troy, that was very swifte of fote.
Dolones, a scourge, hauynge a dagger, or other lyke thyng closed within it. It is also a certayne taklynge of shyppes. Also a lyttell sayle called a trynkette. — *Seruius. Liuius.*
Dolopes, a people of Thessaly.
Dolor, is, griefe or paine of body or mynd, also sorowe.
Dolorificus, ca, cum, that whiche makethe griefe or sorowe.
Dolus, deceypte.
Dolus malus, euery crafty deceite to compasse a man, wherby he receiueth damage.
Dolo-

Dolosus, deceytefull, or crafty.
Doma, tis, a solar or flatte keuerynge of a howse. it is somtyme taken for the house.
Suetonius Domesticatim, by householdes.
Domesticus, ca, cum, pertainynge to housholde. sometyme it sygnifieth tame.
Domestici, housseholde seruantes.
Domicilium, a mansyon place.
Domicœnium, an home suppar.
Dominor, ari, to rule or haue souerayntie.
Domiporta, a pylar or other lyke thynge, that beareth vp an house.
Dominus, a lorde or maister, to whom other doo seruyce.
Dominium, a lordeshyp or rule ouer other.
Lucretius. Domis, was taken of olde wryters for dominus.
Domitalis, apte to be tamed or broken.
Domitura, the acte of tamynge or brekyng of any wylde beaste.
Domo, aui, are, to make tame, sommetyme to vaynquyshe, as Domare hostes, to vaynquyshe ennemyes.
Domitor, oris, a tamer or breaker of that, whyche is wylde.
Domitio, onis, a retournynge home.
Domus, mus, mui, a house generally.
Domus, domi, mo, a dwellyng house.
Domuncula, a lyttell or poore house.
Donum, a gyfte or rewarde.
Donarium, a howse, where suche thynges were kepte, that were gyuen to the goddes. It is sometyme taken for a gyft or rewarde.
Donatiuum, a gyfte in money or grayn, giuen by emperours vnto the people. also to sowldiours aboue their wages.
Donatiuus, he that is able to gyue.
Donatus, he to whom any thynge is giuen. rewarded.
Donax, cis, a reede or cane, whereof they made arowes.
Donec, vntyll. sometyme as longe. Donec uiuo, as longe as I lyue.
Dono, aui, are, to gyue lyberally and frely.
Donysa, an yle in the see Aegeum.
Dorcas, cadis, a bucke or a doo.
Doria, & Dorica, names of countreys ioynynge to Athenes.
Dorion, a towne of Achaie.
Dores, people in Grece nygh to Aetolia.
Doris, a Nimph of the see, and is interpretate bytternesse.
Dormio, miui, ire, to slepe.
Dormito, aui, are, to slepe soundely.
Dorsualia, panels, which horses do weare on their backes, whan they carie or drawe.
Dorsuarius, ia, um, that whiche beareth or carieth any thinge on the backe.

Dorsum, a backe of man or beaste.
Dorilaus, the name of a riuer in Phrigia.
Doryphorus, a yoman of the gard, or other lyke, whiche for gardyng of his maysters person, beareth alway a iauelyn or byll.
Dos, dotis, dowery, lande gyuen in maryage, to the husbande or wyfe, for cause of the mariage onely.
Dotes animi, indowmentes of the sowle, that is to say, vertues and good maners.
Dotes corporis, indowmentes of the body, that is to say, beautie, strength, helth. &c.
Dotalis, le, that pertayneth to dowerie, as bona dotalia.
Doto, aui, are, to indowe.

¶D ante R.

Drachma, æ, a poise or weyght, ponderynge. lx. whete cornes, taken out of the myddes of the eare. Also a coyne of Athenes, signed with a bullocke.
Draco, nis, a dragon.
Draconarius, a standerde bearer.
Dracones, of Plinie be taken for old branches of vynes. also it is an herbe, which is otherwise called Pyretum, it bourneth and byteth the tongue, as welle the leafe as the roote.
Draconites, a precious stone, taken out of the heed of a dragon, whyle he lyueth.
Dracontium, an herbe called dragons.
Dracunculus, a lyttell dragon.
Dragma, a grype or hande full.
Dracontia, an herbe called dragons.
Drama, matis, where in a comedy or interlude, dyuers personages be broughte in, some abydyng, some departynge.
Drangiana, a prouince in Asia the more.
Drepanum, the name of a citie.
Dromedarius, a beaste lyke to a camell, but of a wonderfull swiftenes.
Dromus, the place where men do rounne horses.
Drupe, a kynde of olyues.
Drusus, the name of a Romayne, of ryght noble lynage, and eloquence: but he was proude and ambicious.
Dryas, the propre name of a man of Thesfaly, frende of Nestor.
Dryades, were fairies of woddes.
Dryide, siue Druide, were in the olde tyme religious, or rather superstitious persones in Fraunce, whiche vsed arte magike.
Drylon, a ryuer of Dalmacie.
Drymodis, afterwarde Pelasgus, is nowe called Archadie.
Dryos, slyme growynge in okes.
Drypete, a kynde of olyues.

D ante

D, ante V.

Plaut. Dubio, aui, are, to be in doubte. Dubiat quid agat. He is in doubte, what he shulde do.
Dubito, aui, are, to be in doubte, or to tracte tyme.
Dubitatio, & dubietas, doubte.
Dubitanter, dubitatim, doubtfully.
Dubius, a, um, doubtfull, Dubius is he that hath two wayes, and woteth not whiche to take.
Ducatus, tus, the act of a capteyn, or guyde. Also a duchy. also Ducatus, ti, a coyne callid a ducat.
Ducenarius, a captayne of. CC. men.
Duco, xi, cere, to leade them that be wyllynge, to haue respecte to a thynge. some tyme it signifieth to allecte or styrre with some pleasaunt meane. also to reuolue: also to drawe, as a man draweth a sworde, also to gette. sometyme it signifieth doinge, as Ducere somnos, to slepe. Also to buylde or make vp. somtyme to tourne away. as Ducere uultus, to tourne awaye the visage. to delaye or prolonge. to go downe. Ego me duco ab arbore, I wente downe of the tree. Also to wedde, or do the act of mariage.
Varro. Duco, aui, are, to gouerne.
Ductarius funis, a corde that is drawen.
Ductilis, & ductile, easy to be drawen.
Ductim, with leysour.
Ductito, aui, are, to leade aboute often.
Ducto, aui, are, to leade aboute.
Dudum, but late.
Duella, a poyse, contaynynge. ii. drammes and ii scruples.
Duello, aui, are, to fyghte within lystes, or in battayle.
Duellator, he that dothe battayle.
Duellona, men in olde tyme called Bellona.
Duillus, a citesens name of Rome, whiche Duelium, battayle.
fyrst tryumphed for victorie on the see.
Duis, of the auncient writers was vsed for dederis.
Dulcadium, euery swete meate.
Dulcis, & dulce, swete.
Dulcedo, Dulcitas, Dulcitudo, & Dulcor, swetenesse.
Dulcesco, sci, scere, to become swete.
Dulciarius panis, a marchepayn made with almondes and sugar.
Dulciarius, a pastlar.
Dulcifluus, flowynge swetely.
Dulciloquus, he that speaketh swetely.
Dulcisonus, sownynge swetely.
Dulco, caui, dulcare, to make swete.
Dulia, the seruyce of a bondeman or slaue.

Dulichium, an ile in the see Maliake, or as some saye, Ionio.
Dum, sometyme signifieth whan, or whyles, as, Dum dormis, sures domū intrant, whyles thou slepest, theues entre in to the house. somtyme vntyll, somtyme as longe. Also it signifieth wherfore: also, so that. somtyme it doth but make vp a worde: as, Adesdū, paucis te uolo, Come hyther, I wolde a fewe thynges with the.
Dummodo, so that.
Dumtaxat, onely.
Dumetum, a thorny or busshy grounde.
Dumus, all kyndes of thornes or breres.
Duo, two.
Duo, dui, ere, to gyue. **Plautus.**
Duodeni, twelue togyther. Vide deni.
Duplaris numerus, a nombre doubled.
Duplares, knyghtes, or suche souldiours as had double alowaunce.
Duplex, duplicis, double, or two. **Cato de re**
Duplico, aui, are, to make double. **rustic.**
Dupli, double so moche.
Duplus, a, um, double.
Durabile, durable.
Dutacineuue, grapes with thicke skynnes.
Duram, some thinke to be the name of a ryuer, nere to whiche the grantes made the towre Babel: Some woll it to be a fielde, as in Daniel. **Daniel. 3.**
Duramen, & duramentū, the arme of a vyne.
Durateus, ea, um, wodden, or of wodde.
Dure, & duriter, hardly, or cruelly.
Dureo, rui, ere, to be harde or cruell.
Duresco, sci, scere, to waxe harde.
Dureta, the Spayniardes call a vessell, that they vse to washe and bayne them in.
Duria, or Turia, the name of a ryuer nere to Valentia.
Duricia, & duricies, hardnes.
Duro, aui, are, to indure, to sustaine or suffre.
Durus, ra, rum, harde, paynfull, or cruell.
Dux, ducis, a capitayne or leader.

D ante Y.

Dynastes, a lorde, a prince, a ruler.
Dynastia, myght, power.
Dyrrachium, a citie in Cicile, whiche fyrst was called Epidānus.
Dys, in composition, signifieth yuell, difficile, or impossible.
Dyscolia, difficultie.
Dyscolus, intractable.
Dysenteria, freatynge of the guttes.
Dyspnœa, difficultie in fetchynge breth.
Dysuria, a sycknes, whiche letteth a man that he can not pysse, called the strangurie.

ERE TVA, pertaynyng to thy profyte.

E Republica, concerning the common weale.

E ante A.

Eantes, the name of a story wryter, whiche was in that age, that Pygmalion reigned in the east parte.

Eatenus, vnto that, in that maner of wyse.

Ebenus, uel ebenum, a tree, which is blacke in colour, and is odoriferous, whanne it is bourned, it hath vertue to clense the eyen. This tree groweth in India, which beinge cutte, waxeth as harde as stone. Sola India nigrum fert ebenum, India alone bryngeth forth blacke Ebenus. Virg. 2. Geor.

Eboratus, a, um, of yuorie without.

Eboreus, ea, um, of yuorie.

Ebosus, an yle, betwene the Iles Ophiusa and Pythiusa, the erthe of whyche yle serpentes can not abyde.

Ebrio, aui, are, ebriulo, to make drunke.

Ebrius, ia, um, drunken. sometyme abūdant.

Ebrietas, tatis, drunkennes.

Ebriosus, a, um, often drunke.

Ebron, a mountayne in Palestina.

Ebudes, yles in the see aboute Englande, where the people do lyue by whyte meate and fysshe.

Ebuleus, the sonne of Jupyter and Proserpine.

Ebullo, aui, are, to braste out, or bubble vp, as water dothe whan it rayneth.

Ebulum, an herbe, of some called walwort.

Ebur, & ebor, oris, yuorie.

Eburneus, ea, um, eburnus, of yuorie.

Eburones, people of the countreye called Liege, or Luke, beyonde Brabant.

¶E Ante C.

Ecbasis, a fygure in speakynge, callyd digression, where a manne leaueth for the tyme the principall matter.

Ecbatana, the chiefe citie of the royalme of Mede. There is a citie in Syria of the same name, sommetyme called Ephiphania, and maye be writen Egbatana.

Ecce, an aduerbe demonstratiue, whiche sygnyfyeth, Lo, see, proprely where a thyng sodaynly happeneth. Ecce tibi, wylt thou see, take hede.

Ecclesia, an assembly, a counsayle. Amonge christen authours, it signifieth the congregation of people in the faythe of Christe.

Ecclesiastes, a preacher.

Eccubi, lo where.

Eccum, eccam, eccos, eccas, lo he is here: lo she is here, lo these men be here, loo these women be here.

Echemythia, taciturnitie, or stylnesse.

Echeneis, a lyttell fysshe, whyche retayneth a shyppe vnder saylle, that he canne not moue.

Echidna, a water serpent.

Echinades, bene Ilandes in the see Malyake.

Echinus, the vttermooste shaale of a cheston nutte. It is also an Hedgehogge. Also a fyshe lyke to the same beast, also a vessell of tynne, wherein cuppes be washed. Also the name of a citie.

Echion, a certayne medicyne.

Echioni, Thebans, so callyd of Echyon, oone of the fyue, that holpe Cadmus to buylde Thebes.

Echites, a stone specked lyke a Serpent.

Echo, a sounde, whyche rebowndeth to the noyse or voyce, that is made in a valay, or in great woddes.

Eclegma, atis, a medycyne, whyche muste not be eaten or chewed: but beinge in the mouthe, suffred to styll downe into the stomacke by lyttell and lyttell.

Eclipsis, a wanynge or faylynge.

Econa, an ymage.

Econcula, a lyttell ymage.

Econtrario, contrary wyse.

Ecphrasis, a playne interpretation of the letter.

Ecquando, at what tyme, or lo whan.

Ecquis, but who, see who.

Ecquid, but what, lo what.

Ecstasis, a stonye, a dampe, a traunse, whan a man forgetteth hym selfe.

Ectasis, a fygure, whereby a syllable naturally shorte, is produced.

Ecthlipsis, where, in, ioyned with a vowell, is not sowned.

Ectropium, whanne the nether lydde of the eye falleth, and canne not ioyne with the ouer lydde.

Hecyra, a mother in lawe.

¶E Ante D.

Edax, edacis, a greatte eater or consumer.

Edo, edonis, the same.

Edentatus, tootheles.

Edento, aui, are, to make tootheles.

Edentulus, toothelesse.

Edera, Iuye.

Edessa, a Cytie beyonde the ryuer of Euphrates.

Edico, xi, cere, to commaunde, to ordeyne, to declare.

Edicta,

Edicta, ordinaunces or commaundementes of them, whiche be in great authoritie.
Edo, es, edi, esum, uel estum, to eate or fede.
Ede nasturtium, is applied to a dull & grosse persone: and for as moche as Nasturtium, called Cressis, being eaten, dothe make the nose tynkell, and therby causeth the dulle spirites to wake, therfore by this prouerb is ment, Plucke vp thy spirites: or, awake dullarde or luske.
Edituus, a sexten of a churche.
Edilia, all thynges that appertayne to be eaten.

Pac. Edissero, edisseris, to explane, to declare. Edissere fabulam hanc, Declare this fable.
Edolo, aui, are, to hewe or cutte cleane and smothe.
Edom, Esau was soo called, and the countrey where he reigned.
Edomus, a hylle nere to Pangeum in the borders of Thessalye.
Edones, people of Thrace, nere to the see coaste.
Edonides, were women which sturred with a diuyne furoure, dydde celebrate the mysteryes of Bacchus.
Edonii, people of Thrace.
Edonus, a hyll, where the same people inhabyteth.

Cicero in Phil. Edormire crapulam, to slepe out a surfette.
Educo, xi, cere, to bryng forth, also to drawe out, as, Hoc dicens, eduxit corpore telum,

Virgilius. That sayenge, he drewe the weapon oute of his bodye. Sometyme to reyse vp.
Educo, aui, are, to nouryshe or brynge vppe from chyldehoode.
Educatio, nourishyng or bryngyng vppe of chyldren.
Edulco, aui, are, to make very swete.
Edulis, le, that may be eaten.
Edulium, is what so euer is set on the table at diner & supper to be eatē, saue the breed.
Edurum, not harde.

E ante E & F.

Eeton, Andromaches father, that reygned at Thebes in Cilicie.
Effartio, effarsi, ire, to stuffe or fil a thīg.
Effari, to speake.
Effaxillo, aui, are, to cut of by the arme pit.
Effero, extuli, efferre, to cary out or put out. sometyme to ouercome or subdue. also to cōmende: somtyme to holde vp, to set forth: somtyme to mynisshe or appayre.
Effero, aui, are, to make ymages of wylde beastes.
Efficax, acis, effectuell.
Efficatia, effect or vertue.
Efficio, eci, icere, to brynge to effect.
Effectus, effect.

Effigies, a signe made to the lyuely similitude of man or beast. *Plaut.*
Effigia, the same.
Effingo, xi, gere, to make lyke.
Efflagito, aui, are, to desyre or aske a thynge importunately.
Efflictim, excedyngly.
Efflo, aui, are, to blowe away, or blow forth.
Effloreo, & effloresco, to blo, as a flour doth at the first commynge out.
Effluo, uxi, ere, to flowe or rounne out, as water dothe out of a fountayne.
Effodio, ssi, & di, ere, to dygge oute.
Effœmino, aui, are, to effeminate or make delycate.
Effœminati, menne wanton and delicate, or tender, enduryng no hardnesse.
Effœta, she that hath lately brought forthe a chylde. Also a womanne paste teemynge. Terra effœta, land spent or worne with bearynge of moche grayne.
Effœtus, ta, tum, barayne, consumed, feble.
Effrenus, na, num, without a brydell.
Effugio, gi, ere, to escape.
Effundo, fudi, ere, to powre out. somtyme it signifyeth to consume, to put out.
Effusus, sa, um, discomfited, scattered, putte oute, or powred out.
Effugium, discomfiture, or flyght.
Effutio, iui, ire, to speake vnadnisedly, or folyshely, or hastily.

¶E ante G.

Egelaste, a towne in the hyther Spayn.
Egelidor, aris, to relent or dissolue, as yse that thawith.
Egenus, nedy, or lackynge somwhat.
Egeo, egui, ere, to nede or lacke.
Egens, lackynge.
Egesta, a citie in Sicile, whiche Aeneas bhylded.
Egestas, tatis, necessitie or lacke of thynges necessary, pouertie.
Egero, ssi, rere, to beare out.
Egestosus, a, um, very poore.
Egredior, eris, gredi, to go forth, or go out.
Egregius, a, um, excellent.
Egregie, excellently.
Egurgito, aui, are, to drawe out, as lycoure out of a place.

E ante H, & E ante I.

Eho, an Interiection of callynge. it signifieth howe. Eho dum ad me, Howe come hyther to me.
Eia, sommetyme it exhorteth, sommetyme it blameth.
Eiiceo, eieci, eiicere, to cast out, or put out.
Eiectitius, a, um, beinge caste out.
Eiulo, aui, are, to crie oute, to wayle.
Eiurare, to do besyde the lawe.

Eiusmodi, & eiuscemodi, the same.
Eiusdem farinæ, of the same sort or cōdiciō.
Eiusdē notæ, of the same estimatiō or state.

¶ E Ante L.

Elabor, eris, elabi, elapsum, to slyppe or slyde. sometyme to escape.
Elaboro, aui, are, to labour.
Elacatena, a sawce vsed in the olde tyme.
Elamitę, be called the prynces of Persyanes, of Elam the sonne of Sem, as Iosephus sayth.
Elatus, proude, hyghe.
Elea, a citie in the countrey of Lucania.
Eleates, a man of that citie.
Electio, onis, an election, an approbation.
Electo, aui, are, to chose.
Electrum, that whiche is in englishe called ambre, wherof beades be made. It is also taken for a mettalle, parte golde, parte syluer. Plin.
Eleemosina, almesse.
Elegans, tis, elegaunte, fresshe, gorgyous, cleane, polyte.
Elegantia, elegancy, gorgiousnes, clennes, beautie in wordes.
Elegia, a lamentable songe or verse.
Elegus, the same.
Elegiacus, ca, cum, pertaynynge therto.
Elegiographus, a writer of lamentable versis, or balades.
Elego, elegi, eligere, to chose.
Elei, people in Grece in the countrey some tyme called Peloponessus, nowe Morea.
Elementa, the fyrste or pryncipall matter, wherof al thinges do take their beginning: whiche be foure in numbre, fyre, ayre, water, and erthe. Also the letters, wherof syllables be made, are called elementa.
Elenchus, an argument, reprouynge subtilly an other argument. It is also a table in a boke, to shew the places by letter or other wise. It is moreouer a great perle, or other precious stone, whiche women were wont to hange at their eares.
Eleo, cui, ere, to spotte, or soyle.
Elephas, antis, uel elephantus, ti, a beast, callyd an olyphaunt. It is sometyme taken for yuory. sometyme a sycknes callyd lepry.
Elephantezographi, be called these peynters, whiche peynt with yuorie.
Elephantia, seu elephantiasis, a kynde of lepre, wherin the flesshe dothe swelle, and is full of spottes.
Elephantiacus, a lepre.
Elephantini libri, amonge the olde Romaynes were bokes, wherin their lawes were written, whiche concerned the nobilitie.
Elephantinus, pertaynynge to an olyphant.

Eleus, a ryuer, whiche watereth a greatte parte of Media.
Eleuies, a purgation.
Eleuo, aui, are, to lyfte vp. somtyme to take away, to mynyshe, to extenuate.
Elusa, an yle agaynst Cypers.
Elusis, & elusin, a Cytie in the prouynce of Attica, not farre from Athenes.
Eleusina sacra, ceremonies of Ceres the goddesse.
Elutherius, the name of a man, and is interpretate, free, gentyll.
Elutheria, freedome, gentylnesse.
Elices, forowes in the fieldes, to conueye water.
Elicio, cui, cere, to brynge out, to drawe out, to prouoke.
Elicito, to drawe often.
Elico, aui, are, to tourne vp so downe.
Elico, onis, he that tourneth thynges oute of order.
Elido, si, dere, to hytte agaynste a thynge, to breake, to presse out, to exclude, to strangle, to kylle.
Eligo, legi, eligere, to chose.
Elimino, aui, are, to putte or cast forth from a place ferre of.
Elimo, aui, are, to putte out.
Elinguis, without a tunge, specheles.
Elinguo, aui, are, to plucke out ones tunge.
Eliquo, aui, are, to melte.
Elis, a citie of Archadie.
Elissa, one of the names of Dido.
Elixo, aui, are, to sethe or boyle.
Elixus, a, um, sodden or boyled.
Elychnium, the matche, whiche is in a lāpe, and standeth in oyle.
Elogium, a testification or witnesse in wordes, of praise or dispraise, of honoure or reproche.
Elocutio, onis, a propre fourme of wordes and sentences.
Elongo, aui, are, to remoue fer of, to make longe, to deferre.
Eloquentia, eloquence.
Eloquium, speche in a pleasant maner.
Eloquor, eris, qui, to speke. pprely it is, whā I set a thynge forth in speking, that the herers may vnderstād it, as I conceyue it.
Elote, among the Lacedemonians was as moche to saye, as commune mynysters or seruauntes, as sergeauntes, or suche as in London they do call yomen.
Elpenor, a companion of Ulysses, whiche with other, Circe tourned into an hogge.
Elucesco, sci, cescere, to be very bright.
Elucifico, caui, care, to depriue of lyght.
Elucus, he that is sycke of the drynke of yesterday. Also a louer of trifles.

Elugeo,

Elugeo, gi, gere, to leaue mournynge.
Elucido, aui, are, to shyne or make bryghte outewarde.
Eludo, si, ere, to mocke or deceyue. Also to leaue playenge.
Elumbus & elumbis, he that hath feble loines, and can not stande vpright.
Eluo, lui, luere, to washe out.
Eluo, aui, are, to lyue in glotony, or to spend superfluousely.
Elusco, aui, are, to make one purblynde.
Eluto, aui, are, to soke out water.
Elutrio, aui, are, to powre out of one vessell into an other.
Eluuies, ordure or fylthe caused of aboundance of water, or other lycour.
Elysium, a place where poetes dyd suppose the sowles of good men to dwell.
Elysii campi, the same place.

E ante M.

Emacio, aui, are, to make leane.
Emancipo, aui, are, to infraunchyse or make free, or sette at lybertie. somme time it is vsed in the cōtrary sence, to bynd or make bonde. It is most cōmonly where a man dispossesseth him selfe, and doth alienate his lande to an other.
Emancipator, a feffour, or alienour.
Emaneo, emansi, emanere, to dwelle out of a place.
Emano, aui, are, to issue or flowe out.
Emansor, oris, he that wandreth longe, and at the laste retourneth home: a lurker.
Emargino, aui, are, to take awaye scurfe aboute the brymmes of woundes or soores.
Emasculo, aui, are, to gelde, or to take away the courage of a man, or to abuse a manne chylde in lechery.
Emath, a citie that is nowe called Antioch.
Emathia, a parte of the realme of Macedonia.
Emaus, a notable citie of Palestine, which nowe is called Nicopolis.
Emax, cis, he or she that is redye to bye any thynge.
Emacitas, tatis, redynes or custome to bye.
Embamma, matis, sawce.
Emblema, blematis, pictures made of wod, stone, or mettal, of one colour, set in wodde stone or mettall of an other coloure: as we see in chesse bourdes or tables, callid couters: it is moche vsed in Italy.
Embrio, onis, signifieth the childe conceyued before it receiueth perfecte shappe of a man or woman.
Emedullo, aui, are, to take out marowe.
Emendico, caui, care, to aske in fourme of beggynge.

Emendo, aui, are, to amende.
Emergo, emersi, gere, to issue or come oute of the place where a thinge is drowned.
Emereor, emereri, to deserue to the vttermooste.
Emeriti milites, old worne souldiours, whiche were pardoned of warres, & not withstandynge had pencyons, which were called Emerita stipendia.
Emineo, eminui, eminere, to shewe or excel aboue all other, to be higher than other.
Eminulus, a, um, a lyttell rysynge in height.
Eminus, ferre of.
Emissarium, a sluse, or place to lette water out of a ponde or ryuer.
Emissarius, sommetyme it signyfieth hym, whiche is sent before in battrayle to espie, or to skyrmyshe. sometyme a seruant, whiche is alway at hand, redy to be sent forth. Also it signifieth suche a persone, whyche is ordeyned of him that is in any great office or authoritie, to aduaunce his bribery. Also it sygnifyeth a horse stalyon, which serueth to gette coltes.
Emissisius, a spyall.
Emitto, misi, mittere, to sende forth, to publyshe, to manumise.
Emo, emi, emere, to bye.
Emodus, a hyll, whiche aboute the border of Indie, is diuided into two bowghtes.
Emolumentum, profyte gotten of labour.
Emortualis dies, the day of dethe.
Emorior, emori, to die vtterly.
Empedocles, the name of a Phylosopher, which supposed all thynges to haue theyr beinge of amitie, and variance.
Emphasis, an expresse signification of that, whiche is intended.
Emphyteosis, the making of a thynge better than it was, whan it was receyued or letten, as lande.
Emphyteota, he that taketh a thynge, and promyseth or couenaunteth to make it better than he receyued it.
Emphracta, shyppes or barges kouered.
Empiricus, a phisition that practiseth.
Emplastratio, is graffyng betwene the bark and the wodde.
Emplastrum, a playster.
Emporetica charta, paper, wherin marchantes or grossers do putte their wares.
Emporium, a place wherin is kept a marte or fayre.
Emporeuma, shepmanshyppe.
Emptitius, a, um, that whiche is or maye be boughte.
Emptito, aui, are, to vse to bye.
Emunctorium, an instrument, wherwith the snuffe of a candell is taken away, a snuffer.

Emungo, xi, gere, to snuffe a candelle. Also to make cleane a mans nose. somtyme it signifyeth to dispoyle a man of money, properly by crafte.

Terentius Horatius. Emunctus auro, spoyled of his treasure.
Emunctę naris, of a cleane and sure iudgemente.
Emusſicata, made or wrought by rule.

E ante N.

EN, loo, see.
Energia, a demonstration, whan a thing is so discryued, that it seemeth to the reder or herer, that he beholdeth it, as it were in doinge.
Encęnia, an innouation or renewynge. It was amonge Iewes the feaste of dedication of their temple.
Encanthis, a disease in the eies.
Encaustū, vernyshe, enamyll, or other pycture, wrought with fyre.
Enchiridion, a handell of a thyng. somtime a dagger, somtyme that part of an ore, that the waterman holdeth. It is vsurped for a boke in so lyttell a volume, that a man maye alway carye it with hym.
Enchiros, a beaste bredde in the oriente, as great as a bull.
Enchrista, thynne oyntementes.
Encimibomata, maydens kyrtelles, or pety cootes.
Encyclios, & Encyclia, the cyrkle or course of all doctrines.
Encyclopędia, that lernynge whiche comprehendeth all lyberall sciences & studies.
Endelechia, a consummate perfection, whiche Aristotle dyd put besides the foure elementes.
Endeploro, aui, are, to make intercessyon with teares.
Endoprocinctum, whan men wente oute of the campe vnto battayle.
Endromis, midis, a mantell suche as Irishe men and women do nowe weare.
Endymion, the name of a manne, whiche founde the course of the mone. wherfore the poetes fayned, that the moone loued hym, and descended downe to kysse hym, whyles he slepte.
Enérgia, an efficacie or operacion.
Energificus, effectuall.
Eneruo, aui, are, to debilitate or make feble.
Eneruis, & Eneruus, without synewes.
Engaddi, a citie in Iudea, from whens the precious balme cometh.
Enim, forsothe. sometyme it is expletiue, and dothe but fylle vp a sentence, to make it sounde well. sometyme it is a copulatiue:

Sed enim, but forasmoche.
Enipeus, a ryuer of Thessaly, nere to whiche the battayle was fought betwene Cesar and Pompey.
Eniteo, tui, tere, to indeuour, to inforce to do a thynge.
Enitor, teris, enixus sum, eniti, idem quod eniteo.
Enixe, & Enixum, dilygently with all force.
Enna, a cytie of Sycile, sytuate in a hyghe place.
Ennius, the name of an auncient poete.
Enoch, a mans name in holy scripture.
Enodis, enode, without a knotte.
Enodo, aui, are, to cutte away the knottes, or to vnknytte.
Enormis, enorme, great out of measure.
Enos, is interpretate a very man.
Ens, entis, the beinge of euery thynge.
Ensis, a sworde.
Enthymema, enthymematis, a shorte or imperfect syllogisme.
Enucleo, aui, are, to take out the kernell of a nutte. It is also to declare or make playne a sentence.
Enascor, sceris, sci, to growe or sprynge of a thynge.
Enarro, rare, to tell out at length.
Enarratio, a playn declaration or expositiō.
Enyalius, the sonne of Bellona.

¶ E ante O.

EO, is, iui, ire, to goo.
Eo uenum, ire uenum, to be solde.
Eon, the compas of the eie.
Eo, therfore, forasmoche, vnto that.
Eous, the easte.
Eo usqʒ, in so moche.

¶ E ante P.

EPaminondas, the name of a valiant capitayne of the Thebans.
Epanalepsis, a replication or repetitiō.
Ephabus, the sonne of Iupiter that builded Memphis in Aegipte.
Eparcus, the presydent of a prouince.
Epauxis, an increase.
Ephebia, the age wherin oone entreth into the state of a man. xv. or. xvi. yeres.
Ephebus, he that is of that age.
Ephemeris, a boke, wherin is written that, which is done daily, or a boke of reckning.
Ephemerinos, a feuer contynuyng one day.
Ephi, a measure conteynynge. iii. bushels.
Ephippium, the harneis of a horse or mule.
Ephori, greate officers amonge the Lacedemonians, by whome the kynges power was

was restrayned.

Ephira, re, or Ephire, res, a towne of Achaie, whiche nowe is called Corinthus.
Epialos, a feuer caused of fleume.
Epibata, a souldiour on the see.
Epibatra, the ladder that gothe vp to the toppe castell.
Epicharmus, the name of an excellent phylosopher of Syracuse.
Epicheremata, argumentes made in reasonynge.
Epicedium, verses in cōmēdacion of a deed man, a gay laude.
Epictetus, the name of a stoik philosopher.
Epicurus, the name of hym, which dyd put the principal goodnes in voluptuositie.
Epidamnus, a cytie in Sycile, but the Romaynes after they had subdued it, wolde haue it called Dyrrachium.
Epidaurus, a cytie in Grece.
Epidicticon, demonstratiue.
Epidromes, the armynge of a nette.
Epiglossis, a small thynge in the innermost parte of the tunge, lyke a littell tunge.
Epigramma, a superscription.
Epigrammatarius, he that wryteth verses, called Epigrammata.
Epigriphus, he that hath a croked nose.
Epilepsia, the fallynge syckenes.
Epilepticus, he that hath that disease.
Epilogus, a cōclusion in writing or spekyng.
Epimenides, the name of a philosopher.
Epinicia, verses contaynyng prayses.
Epinyctides, a wheale or pushe, whiche ryseth on the skynne by nyght.
Epiphanes, notable, or famous.
Epiphania, a manyfestation. It is also a solemne feaste in the churche.
Epiphonema, an exclamation.
Epirrhedium, a waggen, or carte.
Epirus, a countrey in Grece.
Episcopatus, a byshopryche.
Episcopium, a byshoppes palays or house, or a place to espie out of.
Episcopius, a, um, pertaynynge to espiall.
Episcopus, a byshoppe, sometyme an espie, sometyme a clerke of the markette.
Epistola, a letter sent from one to an other.
Epistolium, a lyttell epistle.
Epistomium, a spowte sendynge forth water from a cundite.
Epistylium, the chapiter of a pylar.
Epitaphium, a scripture written on a graue or sepulchre.
Epithalamium, a songe beinge songe atte a weddynge, or verses made in the praise of them that are maried.
Epithema, a medicine layde to the regyon of the harte or lyuer, to coole it.

Epithetes, a disceyuer.
Epitheton, an addition, proprelye applyed to a thyng for some notable qualitie, which it sygnifieth, as Seuū mare, The rough see. Garrula pica, The chatterynge pie. Crudelis Nero, The cruel Nero. Campi florigeri, The flouryshynge fieldes.
Epithymia, mis, concupiscence, desyre.
Epitogū, i, a garment worne vpon a gowne.
Epitome, mes, a brigement, or brcuiate.
Epitritus, a foote of foure sillables, of whiche one differeth euer from the other thre.
Epitrope, procuration, wardshyp.
Epityrum, a chese cake.
Epithyrum, a meane to conserue olyues.
Epos, epodos, a kynde of verse, or songe, which contayneth thynges concernyng as well god as manne. Also whiche hath the fyrst verse lengar than the seconde, as,
Beatus ille, qui procul negotiis
Vt prisca gens mortalium.
Epulę, meates.
Epulum, a greate feaste, wherunto all the people assembled, whiche amonge the olde Romayns was made either to the honour of some of their goddes, or at the burieng of some notable personage. It may be now taken for a churche feest, or feest of a brotherheed, or dyner made at a buriall or interment. It hath bene sometyme vsed for a uate bankette. *Cicero p L. Planco.*
Epularis, are, bilongynge to a feaste or banket, as Epularis sermo, cōmunication mete for a feaste or bankette.
Epulor, ari, to eate at feastes or bankettes.
Epulatorius, ia, ium, apt to be eaten at a feest or bankette.
Epulis, fleshe that groweth on the gumes about a mans tethe.
Epulo, nis, plurali epulones, men boden to a great feaste, or they which come vnboden, to eate the reuercion. Amonge the gentils they were called by the pristes, to eate that whiche was lefte of the sacrifice.

¶E ante Q.

EQuarius, ia, ium, pertainyng to horses. *Vale. Max.*
Equarius medicus, a horse leche.
Eques, a horseman, contrary to a fote man. sometime it is taken for a knight. But I suppose, that amonge the Romaynes, Equites, were taken for theym, whome we calle gentylmen.
Equester, equestris, equestre, pertaynynge to eques, as, Equestris ordo, the state or degree of gentylmen. Equestres copię, the numbre or company of horsemen.
Equestria, the places assigned to gentilmen, where

where they satte to beholde any solempne syghtes or playes.
Equidem, verily.
Equiferus, a wylde horse. *(Plinius. Varro.)*
Equila, a lyttell mare.
Equile, a stable for horses.
Equimentum, the hyre of a stallyon to season a mare.
Equinus, na, num, of a horse.
Equio, iui, ire, whan a mare desyreth to be seasoned.
Equiria, runnynge with horses: a playe dedicate to Mars.
Equisessor, a man on horsbacke.
Equisetum, an herbe called horsetayle.
Equiso, onis, a horsebreaker.
Equitabilis, bile, able to be ridē, also a place in whiche horses might casily walke.
Equitatus, an hoste of horsemen. also the acte of rydynge. sometyme the state or order of gentylmen.
Equitium, the esquirie or companye of the stable.
Equitius, the propre name of a manne, and surname of a familye in Rome.
Equito, aui, are, to ryde.
Equitatio, a rydynge.
Equuleus, a horsecolt. Also a maner of turment made of bournynge plates, lyke to a horse, wherin men were tourmented.
Equulus, a nagge or lyttell hors.
Equus, a horse.
Equa, a mare.
Equus citatus, a horse taken vp.
Equus carpentarius, a carte horse.

¶ E ante R.

Erado, asi, ere, to scrape of, or out of a thynge.
Erasinus, the name of a ryuer.
Erasistratus, the name of a famous physytion.
Erato, the name of one of the Musis.
Eratosthenes, the name of a philosopher.
Erciscere, to diuide, proprely landes.
Erciscundę familię, of householde to be deuided or parted amonge dyuers heires.
Ercinia, a wonderfull greatte wodde in Germany.
Ercius, one of the names of Jupiter.
Erebus, one of the ryuers of Hell.
E regione, on the other syde.
E re nata, by occasion wherof.
Erembi, people in Arabia, which go naked.
E re mea, uel tua, for my profite or thyne.
Eremodicium, a discontynuance of action, doone throughe absence or neglygence of the parties.

Eremus, a deserte or solytary place.
E republica, for the profyte of the publyke weale.
Eretum, a streate of the Sabynes.
Erga, towarde. Erga festum natalis Christi, Agayne Christmasse.
Ergasterium, a warkehouse.
Ergastes, siue ergasticus, a workeman.
Ergastulum, a house, where men were compelled to worke on stone or mettall. Nowe is it taken for a pryfone, and sometyme for the prisoners.
Ergastularius, the gayler or keper of the prysone.
Ergastulus, a gayler. sometyme it signifieth a labourer.
Ergasylus, the propre name of a man.
Erginus, was a tyranne, whiche Hercules subdued and slewe.
Ergo, therfore. somtyme it is spoken dysdaynously. Fac ergo quod libet, Than doo as the lyste. sometyme exhortynge. Ergo age, go to. sometyme it signifyeth bycause, Illius ergo, for his sake. Virtutis ergo, bycause of vertue.
Ergatum, an engyne to drawe vp thynges of great poise or weight, callid a crane.
Erguminus, a man possessed with an yl spirite
Eriboea, the stepmother of Mercury.
Erica, an herbe growynge in woddes, and is lyke to maioram.
Ericthonius, the fyrste kynge of Athenes, whiche inuented a chariotte.
Eridanus, a ryuer in Italy, now called Po.
Erimantus, a diuinour.
Erinaceus, an hedgehogge or vrchyn.
Erinnys, the name of oone of the furyes of helle.
Eriphyle, the wyfe of Amphiaraus, & systar of Adrastus, whiche betrayed hir husbande for a bracelette at the siege of Thebes.
Eripio, pui, pere, to take awaye, to delyuer.
Eripuisti mihi pecuniam, Thou haste taken my money from me. Eripuisti me a periculo, Thou haste delyuered me frome perylle.
Eripuisti a me librum, Thou haste taken my boke from me. sommetyme to make haste.
Eripe fugam, Flee away in haste.
Eris, an herbe growynge in Aegypte, and may be interpretate contention.
Erodius, a fowle, the greattest that fleeth, and ouercometh and catcth the Egle.
Erogo, aui, are, to distribute.
Errabundus, moche wanderynge, or vacabunde.
Erraticus, ca, cū, that crepeth here & there, as, Vitis erratica, a crepyng vine, that shoteth out in dyuers places.
Erratus, tus, erratum, ti, an errour or synne.

Erro-

Errones, startars asyde, vagabundes.
Error, errour, properly where falsehode is affirmed or taken for trouth : or trouth for falsehode.
Erro, aui, are, to erre, to wander.
Erubesco, bui, bescere, to be ashamed, or to blusshe.
Eruca, an herbe called Rokat. also a worme called the canker worme, whiche comonly is vpon kolewortes.
Eructo, taui, tare, to belke or breake wynde out of the stomacke.
Erudero, aui, are, to throwe out, or cary awaye rubbell, as morter, stones, and other lyke thynges of olde buyldynge decayed, or pulled downe.
Erudio, iui, ire, to teache any arte or science.
Eruditio, doctryne or teachynge.
Eruditus, lerned or taught.
Eruila, a grayne called tares.
Erunco, caui, care, to wede out.
Eruo, ui, ere, to drawe out with force.
Eruum, a kynde of pulse.
Erugo, an vnkindly moisture, wherby corne growynge is putrified.

Plin. lib. 4
Erymāthus, a mountayn in Archady, where Hercules ouercame a bore, that destroyed the fieldes. There are also a wodde and a ryuer of the same name.
Erythace, bees meate, whyle they labour.
Erythacus, a byrde called Robyn redbrest.
Erythea, an Ile, the countraye of Gerion, where the ayre is so benigne, that men well nere are there immortall.
Erytheus, was a kynge of Athenes.
Erythios, an herbe called redde betes, as I do suppose.
Erythræum, is called the redde see, this see is betwene the Indie & Aethiope occean.
Eryx, the name of a mountayn in Cicile, and of a citie theron buylded, wherin was edified a temple to Venus, wherof Venus is called Erycina.

Ouidius.
Quid geminas Erycina meos sine fine dolores? O Venus, why doest thou continually double my sorowes?

¶ E Ante S.

Esca, all maner of meate, as welle for men, as beastes.
Escarius, a, um, pertaynynge to meate.
Escaria mensa, a table, wherat men do eate meate.
Esculentus, ta, tum, any thynge to be eaten.
Esculus, an oke bearynge acornes.
Esito, aui, are, to eate.
Essei, certayn religious men of the Jewes.
Esseda, a wayne.

Essedones, a people, whiche doo eate theyr frendes, whan they be deed, and drynke in the sculles of their heedes.
Esto, be it.
Esuriales feriȩ, wake dayes.
Esuries, hunger.
Esurio, iui, ij, ire, to be a hungred.

E Ante T.

ET, and, as well. Te admirantur & ciues & hospites, As well thy countrey men as straungers do wonder at the. some tyme it signifieth but, by an interrogation, sometyme, That is to saye, Annos natus is sexaginta, & senex, Nowe thre score yeres olde, that is to say an olde man.
Etsi, all be it.
Etenim, for.
Etesiȩ, wyndes which do cōmonly blowe in sommer, about the canicular dayes.
Ethalia, the name of an yle in the see called mare ligusticum, whiche is by Geane.
Ethanion, the name of a certayne vessell.
Eteocles, the sunne of Oedipus and Iocasta his mother.
Ethicus, morall.
Ethmus, the myddell brydge of the nose.
Ethnicus, a gentyle.
Ethologos, he which with voyce, gesture, and countenance expresseth the maners of menne.
Etiam, also, moreouer, ye, ye forsothe.
Etiamnum, also.
Etymologia, true sayenge, or true exposytion, or reason.
Ethopeia, an imytation of other mennes maners.
Ethici pictores, paynters, whiche in pyctures doo lyuely sette out the maners and affections of men.

¶ E Ante V.

Euado, si, uadere, to escape, to passe with daunger, to appere, to clymme, to delyuer, to be, to come to.
Euadne, Mars daughter, of Thebes, the wyfe of Aesopus: and the wyfe of Capanei was soo called, whyche louyd her husbande so feruētly, that whan she harde he was take at Thebes, she fell nere deed in a swowne, and after whan his funerall was celebrate, she lepte into the fyre.
Euȩnetus, a kynge of the Lacedemoniās.
Eualeo, lui, ere, to waxe hole or stronge.
Eualesco, scere, to waxe very stronge.
Eualuo, aui, are, to putte or sette out of the doores.

Euan.

Euan, an exclamation to the praise of Bacchus, and is as moche to saye, as Bone puer, O good chylde.

Euander, the propre name of Carmentis sonne, and is interpretate a good man: he lefte his countrey Archadia, and came into Italy, and entryng into the mouth of Tyber, and expulsyng the inhabitantes, rested in the hylle Palatine, where he beganne to buylde the towne Palanteum.

Euaneo, et euanesco, scere, to vanishe away.

Euangelium, good tydynges.

Euanidus, a, um, vnfruitefull.

Euapelus, a foole or idcote.

Plautus. Euax, an interiection of reioycynge. Euax iurgio uxorem tandem abegi, Heida, I haue yet at the laste dryuen my wyfe away with chydynge.

Euboea, an yle in the greke see, & the name of a citie situate in the same.

Eubulus, the name of a storie writer, and is interpretate prudente.

Eucarpia, a citie of Phrigia, where growe great plentie of very fayre grapes.

Eucharistia, good grace, a renderynge of thanke. It is nowe taken for the sacrament of the aultar.

Euchila, meates of good iuyce.

Euclides, the name of a famous Geometrycian.

Eueho, euexi, euehere, to cary out. somtyme it sygnifyeth to extoll or lyfte vp.

Lactātius. Euemerus, the name of an old story writer.

Euenire, to happen by chaunce.

Euênus, a ryuer descendyng from Thrace, and deuydynge Calydonie.

Euentus, tus, happe. somtyme it is taken for the ende, or conclusion of a thynge.

Euenta, thynges whyche happen in conclusyon.

Euentum prestare, to waraunt al that, whiche shall happen.

Euerriator, he that hath goodes of the testatour with condicion, that if he performe not his laste wyll, or do distourbe it, he shal lese all that he hath.

Euerro, rri, rere, to swepe cleane.

Euerto, ti, tere, to tourne vp so downe.

Euestigio, by and by, at an instant.

Euganei, people of Venece.

Euganei montes, mountaynes in Italy by Padowe.

Euge, well done.

Euidens, entis, euident, apparant.

Euilla, a countrey in the orient, aboute the whiche the ryuer Phison, whiche we calle Ganges, that commeth out of Paradyse, dothe rounne.

Euiratus, of womanly or chyldyshe condicions, also he that lacketh his genitours.

Euiro, aui, are, to take away a mannes membres of generation.

Euiscero, aui, are, to bowel or drawe out the guttes of any thinge.

Euito, aui, are, to flee, to eschew, or beware.

Eulogium, a worde well spoken, a praise, a benediction.

Eumelus, the sonne of Admetus, kynge of Thessaly, gotten on Alcesta his wyfe.

Eumenides, furies of helle.

Eumolpus, a mās name of Athenes, whom Suidas writeth to be the sonne of Museus the poete.

Eumonides, a mans name of Thebes.

Eunucho, & eunuchiso, to gelde men.

Eunûchus, a man gelded.

Eunomia, a iuste constitution or ordynance of lawes.

Euoco, aui, are, to call out, to call forthe, or calle away. Euocare testes, to brynge forth wytnesse.

Euocati, souldyours, whiche for some necessitie be sodaynely called out of the fieldes vnto battayle.

Eupalia, a towne in Locris, whiche somme call Eupalion, and some Eupolyon.

Euphonia, a good sounde.

Euphorbium, an herbe.

Euphorion, a poetis name of Calcidonye, whom Gallus did translate.

Euphrasinū, an herbe called Buglosse.

Euphrates, one of the ryuers, that comme out of Paradyse, whiche passeth through the citie of Babylon.

Euphrosyna the propre name of a woman.

Eupilis, a laake in France Cisalpine.

Euryale, the daughter of kynge Minois, whiche brought forth to Neptune, Orion. ther was an other of that name, the daughter of Proetus, kyng of Argiue.

Euryalus, the name of one of the princis of Peloponnese. Girgil feineth a Troyane to be so callyd.

Euripides, the name of an excellente poete amonge the Grekes.

Euripus, a small cundyte rysynge of a great height. Also a diche made to inclose places to play in, in the stede of hedges. some do take it for a small ponde or stewe.

Euripus, an arme of the see, or a narrowe passage betwene two places.

Euronotus, a northeaste wynde.

Europa, that parte of the worlde, whyche we do inhabyte, so named and called of Europa, the daughter of Agenor, kynge of Phenice.

Eurotas, a ryuer that rounneth before the towne of Lacedemonia.

Eurus,

Eurus, the easte wynde.

Euricion, the name of a goldesmythe.

Euricratidas, a man of Lacedemonye.

Virgi. Euridamas, a man of Troye.
Plut. Euridame, was the wyfe of Leutichis,
Ouid. kynge of Spartans.
Herod. Eurydice, the wyfe of Orpheus.

Eurylochus, the kyng of Phlegia, whiche distroyd Thebes, before Cadmꝰ buildid it.

Eurypylus, one of the sonnes of Hercules that reigned in the yle Cous.

Euterpe, one of the Musis.

Eutheca, a storehouse.

Euthymia, quietenesse, suertie of mynde, or hartis ease.

¶E Ante X.

EX, sygnifyeth of, or fro.

Ex fide, fama. Cic. ad Atticum, Summa erit hęc, statues, ut ex fide fama, reꝙ mea uidebitur, This shall be the hoole effecte, that thou doo, as it shall seeme to be for myne honestie, accordynge to the trust that I putte in the, and for my profyte.

Ex dignitate tua, et ex repub. facis, Thou doest accordynge to thyne auctoritie, and for the weale of thy countrey.

Exactio, a pyllynge of the people.

Exactor, a demaunder of money. some englyshe it a Comtroller.

Exactus, ta, tum, passed, verye dylygente, exacte.

Exacerbesco, ere, to waxe sharpe.

Plautus. Exędifico, aui, are, to buylde perfectely. also to dryue out of the house.

Exaggeratio, a heapynge togyther.

Exagito, aui, are, to vexe, to angre.

Exalto, aui, are, to mounte or lyfte vp, some tyme to prayse very moche.

Examen, minis, a swarme of bees, Also the nedyll or tounge in balaunces and beames. Sommetyme it sygnyfyeth a iuste examynacyon.

Examino, aui, are, to examyne.

Examurco, aui, are, to drawe oyle cleane from the mother.

Examussim, iustely by rule.

Exanclo, aui, are, to drawe oute cleane, to emptye, sommetyme to suffre, to make. Non
Pac. potest hic sine tua opera exāclari clauꝰ, This nayle can not be made without thy helpe.

Exanguis, exangue, without bloode, tymorous, or fearefull.

Exanimalis, without sowle or lyfe.

Ex animo est, It is as nature requyreth.

Ex animo facio, I do it with my good wyll, or as my mynde gyueth me.

Ex animi sententia, accordynge to myn appetyte, or as I wolde desyre it.

Ex animo illi faueo, I fauour hym with all my harte.

Ex animo, aui, are, to kyll, somtyme to make *Plaut.* aferde. Priusꝙ intus redii exanimatus fui, Or *Q. Curti*. euer I came in agayn, I was made aferde. Multos exanimauit rigor insolitus niuis, The vnaccustomed chyllyng of the snowe depriued many of their lyues.

Exanimus, ma, mum, & exanimis, exanime, deed, put in feare.

Exanimatus, ta, tum, made aferde, or troubled in mynde: somtime it signifyeth deed.

Exanio, aui, are, to put cleane away. *Columel.*

Exanthema, a wheale or a pushe in a mannes skynne.

Exaresio, exarefieri, to be dried vp.

Exaresco, sci, scere, to drie.

Exarmo, aui, are, to make tame, proprelye to breake the tethe of wylde beastes.

Exarmare, to vnarme, or to take harneysse from a man.

Exarmare nauem, to take away the taklyng from a shyppe.

Exarmare actionem, to make the accyon faynte or feble.

Exaro, aui, are, to eare well, also to write.

Exasceare, to polyshe, or make playn, as carpentars doo after that they haue hewed.

Exaspero, aui, are, to make sharpe, Also to make very angrye.

Ex asse, of the hole. Hæredem fecit ex asse, He made hym heire of all the hole.

Exauctoro, aui, are, to putte out of wages, somtime to disgrade a knight, or other like.

Exauctorati, souldiours or seruantes putte out of wages, or dismissed of their seruice.

Exauctoratus, deposed, or put out of office.

Exaudio, iui, ire, to here beneuolentelye or perfectely.

Exbalisto, aui, are, to trumpe or deceyue. Ego hunc communem meum, atꝙ nostrum omnium hostem exbalistabo lepide, I wolle feately deceyue this mun enmy, and al ours in commune.

Excandescentia, vehement angre or wrath.

Excanto, aui, are, to charme. sommetyme to *Plaut.* shutte out.

Excandesco, sci, ere, to be very angry.

Excandefacio, feci, facere, to chaufe, or make angry, or to make very hote.

Excarnificatus, torne or rente with tourmentes.

Excarnifico, caui, care, to rente or cutte in pieces.

Excedo, cessi, dere, to departe or go forthe, to passe or excede.

Excello, li, ere, to excelle.

Excelsus, a, um, hyghe or great.

Excep-

E ante X.

Exceptio, an exception.
Excepto, aui, are, to take or drawe to.
Exceptor, oris, he that wryteth faste that whiche other men do speake.
Excerebro, aui, are, to beate out the braynes of any thynge.
Excetra, a serpent, of whom the heed being cutte of, thre came vp for it. It was also called Hydra.
Excerno, excreui, excernere, to shite. properly it is to trye out the yll from the good.
Excerpo, psi, pere, to gather here and there the chiefe of any thynge.
Excidium, the sackynge of a towne or citie, or the vtter destruction therof.
Excido, excidi, dere, to fall out of a thynge. excidere, to cutte out of a thynge.
Excidere animo, to be forgoten.
Excidere formula, to lose his action.
Excieo, exciui, ire, to moue or shake out.
Excio, ciui, ire, to moue vehemently, or to call out, to waken.
Excipio, excepi, excipere, to excepte, to take or receyue, to trye or inserche, to separate, to take by crafte, to gather, to hyde, to succede, to resyst without any busynesse.
Excipere notis, to wryte in cyfer, or other compendiouse fourme.
Excipula, a weele to take fysshe.
Excipuus, a, u, wherwith any thing is taken.
Exciso, aui, are, to crop, to teare, or to beate.
Excisus, a, um, gelded.
Excito, aui, are, to stire, procure, or incorage.
Exclamo, aui, are, to crye oute, to calle for alowde.
Excludo, to shytte out, to deliuer, to hatche egges, to make to appiere.
Excolo, excolere, to garnyshe or decke.
Excomposito, in order appoynted.
Excorio, aui, are, to plucke of the skynne or hyde of a beaste.
Excors, excordis, a foole, or a man hartles.
Excreo, aui, are, to spytte out.
Excrementum, thinges of dygestion expulsed moyste or drie, vrine, or siege.
Excresco, excreui, excrescere, to grow oute, or to growe moche.
Excretum, the refuse or offall of any thing.
Excubię, biarum, watche, as well by daye as by nyghte.
Excubitor, he that watcheth.
Excubitus, watche.

Erasmꝰ in Chiliad.

Ex diametro opposita, so contrarye the one to the other, that they may neuer agree.
Excubo, aui, are, to watche, as they whiche in battaylle, or in the garde of a pryncis personne doo.
Excudo, excusi, excudere, to beate or stryke out, sometyme to fynde out with study. Vt

E ante X.

primum filicis, scintillam excudit Achates, As soone as Achates had stryken fyre of the flynte. Also to hatche.

Vergilius.

Excurio, aui, are, to put out of court. Apolonium ideo excuriauit, quia nihil habebat, Therfore dyd he put Apolonius out of the courte, bycause he had nothyng.

Varro.

Exæquire, to be pacified, to be assuagid of ire

Cæsar.

Excursio, a digression in speakynge, a skyrmyshe in warres.
Excuso, aui, are, to excuse.
Excusatoria epistola, a letter of excuse.
Excussorium cribrum, a rengyng syue, also a bulter.
Excutio, ssi, tere, to shake, to choose.
Excussus, a, um, shaken.
Excussores equi, gambaldynge horses.
Exdecimo, aui, are, to tythe out.
Exdisposito, by an order, of a purpose.
Exdorsuo, aui, are, to breake the backbone.
Execo, aui, are, to cutte withoute.
Exectus, gelded.
Execro, aui, are, to abhorre, to curse.
Execratio, cursynge.
Exedo, di, dere, to eate, as a worme or soore dothe, to eate vp.
Exedra, a parlour, or other lyke place.
Exegematicus, a forme of spekyng, where the poete onely speaketh.
Exemplum, an example to folowe, eschewe, or beware.
Exemplar, a sample, wherby we attempt to make a thynge lyke to it. somtyme the one is vsed for the other. oftentymes they both do signifye an example, where one thynge is compared with an other.
Exemptus, exempt or priuileged.
Exemptus est rebus humanis, he is deed.
Exemptilis, exemptile, that whiche may be taken away, or taken out.
Exeo, exiui, exire, to go out, to exchewe, to braste oute. In memoriam exire, to be in remembraunce. Exit in fabellam, It is made a fable. Exit de potestate, He is not able to go uerne hym selfe: he is in warde, or vnder a gardayne.
Exentero, aui, are, to make a hole in a thing.
Exequię, funeralles, the whiche are doone in the buriall of any person.
Exequior, aris, ari, to execute the funerals.
Exequor, eris, qui, to do or execute. somtime to declare or expresse.
Exerceo, cui, cere, to exercyse. sometyme to driue out of the house, to sette on warke, to vse. Exercere discordias, et simultates, To haue variance or contencion. also to get or wynne. Exercere sumptus, To gette theyr expenses. Exercere tellurem, to tylle welle the grounde.

Exer-

Exercio, ciui, ire, to amende or repaire.
Exercitium, exercise or vse.
Exercito, taui, tare, to exercise.
Exercitatio, exercyse, vse, or custome.
Exercitus, ta, tum, exercised, vsed in labour, weried, hardned.
Exercitus, tus, an hoost of men of warre.

Statius. Exero, erui, erere, to go forth, to drawe out, as a man wyll drawe out a sworde. Fulgentég exerit ensem, And he drewe oute his bryght sworde. Also to lyfte vp.
Exertus, ta, tum, shewed forthe.
Exerto, aui, are, to shewe forth abrode.
Exfio, I pourge or clense.
Exhæredo, aui, are, to disherite.
Exhalo, aui, are, to puffe oute.
Exhaurio, iui, rire, to drawe oute cleane, to make empty.
Exherbare, to plucke vp herbes or wedes.

Columel. Exherbandus est locus, The place muste be weeded.
Exherbatio, weedynge.
Exhibeo, bui, bere, to proffre, to set abrode, for all men to beholde.
Exhibere negotium, to putte to busynesse, or trouble.
Exhomologesis, confession.
Exhorreo, rui, rere, to feare horryblye, or with tremblynge.
Exibilo, aui, are, to whistyll or hisse a manne out of the place. Exifilare, idem.
Exigo, exegi, exigere, to expell or shutt out. also to require, to inquyre, to do.
Exigere pecuniam, to demaunde money.
Exactus, ta, tum, expelled, demanded, perfectly done, or perfourmed.
Exilium, exyle.
Exilio, lii, iui, ire, to goo out hastilye, or to leape out.
Eximium, excellent, very great.
Eximo, exemi, mere, to take away, to except
Eximor ex reis, Eximor noxę, I am acquite or discharged of the offence or trespas.
Eximor ex ærariis, I am clerely discharged of all paymentes.
Eximere actionem, to barre the action.
Exin, from thensforthe.
Exinanio, niui, ire, to emptye, to brynge to nowghte.
Exinsperato, vnloked for, whiche no manne hooped.
Existimo, aui, are, to trowe or suppose, to decerne or iudge.
Existimatio, supposel. somtime reputation.
Existo, extiti, existere, to be, to appere, to be sette vp, or aduanced.
Exitiabilis, bile, deedly.
Exitialis, le, deadely, or that causeth dethe, or myschiefe.

Exitium, dethe, or mischiefe.
Ex iure manum conserere, to derayne batayle in the triall of ryght.
Exlex, he that lyueth without loue, or oute of loue.
Exodium, a songe at the ende of a comedy or interlude. also the ende of a matter.
Exolesco, exoleui, exolescere, to leaue growynge. sometyme to growe mightily.
Exoletus, he that is passed growynge. also olde, or out of vse, it signifieth also a manne childe abused agaynst nature.
Exoluo, ui, uere, to vnbynd, to pay al clerely, to recompence or gyue in rewarde, to delyuer. Suspitione exoluere, to deliuer frō suspicion. Exoluere religione, to discharge from vowe or conscience.
Exoculatus, he that hath his eien put out.
Exomida, a garmente without sleues, a taberde or chymere, or suche as hermytes do weare, or mūkes whan they do ride.
Exopolis, he that dwelleth in the subbarbes of a towne or citie.
Exorabulum, a crafty forme of desyryng or askynge a thynge.
Exorbito, aui, are, to go out of the track or carte lose, or to go out of the right way.
Exorcismus, an adiuration of coniuryng.
Exorcista, an adiurour or coniurour.
Exorciso, aui, are, to adiure or coniure.
Exordine, without ceassynge.
Exordior, iris, iri, to begynne.
Exordium, a begynnynge.
Exorior, iris, riri, to be borne, to appere out, to ryse, as the sunne dothe, to inuade.
Exorno, aui, are, to garnyshe or make faire, to apparayle rychely, to ordeyne. Somme tyme to make foule, or out of apparayle.
Exoro, aui, are, to induce or optayne by desyre, to desyre hartily.
Exors, exortis, out of felowshyppe.
Exos, without bones.
Exosso, aui, are, to bone, or plucke out boones. Also to pulle oute the strynge of a lamprey.
Exoticus, a, um, a stranger, that is come out of another countrey, and dwelleth here.
Expalpo, aui, are, to grope out.
Expando, di, ere, to sprede out.
Expapillo, aui, are, to make nakyd to the pappes.
Expato, aui, are, to come abrode, or into an open place.
Expecto, aui, are, to tarye or abyde, to obserue or take hede. Expecto quid uelis, I marke what thou wylt saye: or elles I desyre to knowe what thou woldest. Also to hope. Expectate uenis, Thou comest euen as I wolde haue the.

H   Expe-

Expectoro, aui, are, to put out of the breste or stomacke.

Expeculiatus, he that hathe nothynge of his owne.

Expedio, iui, ire, to delyuer, to spede, to carye out. Expedire manus, to holde vp the handes. Expedit, signifyeth also, It is expedient or necessary. it is come to passe.

Expeditus, ta, tum, delyuered.

Expediti milites, souldiors in light harneis.

Expeditio, a settyng forth toward battayle.

Expello, expuli, pellere, to expell or put out.

Expendo, di, ere, to ponder or weye, to examyne straytely, to paye truely, to spende moneye.

Expense, expenses, or dispenses.

Expensum ferre, to spend or lay out money.

Expergiscere, Expergefacere, Expergificare, to wake a man out of his slepe.

Expergiscor, eris, Expergisio, I am wakyd, or wake.

Experrectus, Expergefactus, ta, tum, wakened. Expergitus, slepte ynough.

Expergo, experrexi, expergere, to waken.

Experientia, experience.

Experior, iris, iri, to attempte, or assaye, or proue.

Expertus, ta, tum, attempted, taught.

Expertus, a man of experience.

Expers, tis, without any parte, lackyng experience. Expers doloris, withoute peyne. Expers mortis, neuer dyenge. Expers lucis, without lyght.

Expersus, persa, persum, spronge with licour or wette.

Expes, without hope.

Expeto, iui, tii, ere, to desyre moche, or coueyte, to happen, to wylle. sommetyme to take, to passe ouer.

Expilo, aui, are, to robbe, polle, or take by extorcion, or deceyte, to spoyle.

Expio, aui, are, to pacyfie god with satisfaction or prayer, whan we thynke that he is displeasyd.

Expiro, aui, are, to dye.

Expiscor, aris, ari, to seke for fysshe, to fishe out, or serche priuilye, to gette or wynne. Tandem nescio quid ab eo expiscatur, Fynally I can not telle what he wynneth or getteth by hym.

Explano, aui, are, to make playne.

Ter. Heau. Expleo, eui, ere, to fylle, fulfylle. also to sacyate, to comforte.

Ouidius. Explico, plicaui, plicare, to extende. Also to vnfolde, to declare. Explicat ensem, He draweth out his sworde. Explicat cae-

Martialis. nas unica mensa duas, He maketh two suppers at one table.

Explodo, osi, dere, to dryue oute with noise or rebukes, or clappynge of handes.

Explosus, sa, sum, conuicted, or reiected.

Exploro, aui, are, to bewayle with exclamation, to serch out diligently, to proue with serchynge, to be aduysed, to drye or exhauste.

Explorator, an espie, or priuye serchour.

Exploratus, a, um, well knowen.

Expono, sui, nere, to expowne or declare, to set or brynge a thyng out of that, wherin it is. sometyme to caste out a thynge, to thintent that it may perishe. Also to spend, to sette forthe.

Expositio, an exposytion or declaration, of anye thynge diffyculte or harde to be vnderstande.

Expositi, chyldern cast out, to be perished.

Expositiui, the same.

Exposco, exposcere, to aske or desyre instauntely.

Expostulo, aui, are, to complayne, to make a quarell. also to wyl. Expostulare iniuriam, To complayne of wronge or displeasure, to hym that dothe wronge.

Expostulatio, a quarell or complaynt.

Expostulator, he that complayneth of wrong done by his frende.

Exprimo, to presse or wring out, to expresse or declare playnely.

Exprobro, aui, are, to imbraide or twyte. also to lay in reproche.

Expromito, misi, mittere, to promyse or vndertake for an other.

Expromissor, he that promiseth, or is suretie for an other.

Expromo, prompsi, mere, to shewe forthe, or open.

Expugno, pugnaui, are, to wynne by assault or force.

Expulso, aui, are, to meue a thyng with moche thrustynge, or to put awaye.

Expulsor, & expultrix, a putter awaye, man or womanne.

Expungor, geris, expungi, to be cancelled or put out, or rased. it is also spoken of iuges, whan they be put out of comission. It is also to quyte, as, Munus munere expungitur, One good tourne is quyte with an other.

Expungo, punxi, pungere, to putte awaye, or remoue.

Expuncti, were souldioures discharged, or put out of wages.

Expuo, pui, puere, to spytte out.

Exputo, aui, are, to shrede or loppe a tree, to vnderstande perfytely.

Exquiliç, a mountayne in Rome, where watche was kepte.

Exquilinus mons, the same mountayne.

Exquiro, exquisiui, exquirere, to serche out.

Ex

E ante X.

Ex syngrapha agere, to do thinges extremly or rigorously: as it were that one sued a nother vpon an oblygation sealyd.

Exta, the inwarde: as the harte, the lyuer, the lunges or lightes, and the splene.

Extemplo, forthwith.

Extemporaneus, ea, eum, sodayne.

Ex tempore, sodaynly, without study, or for the tyme.

Extemporalis, & extemporanea oratio, an oration or matter spoken or wrytten without studye.

Extendo, di, dere, to extende.

Extenuo, aui, are, to mynyshe or make lytle.

Exter, tera, terum, straunge, comen farre of.

Exterus, tera, terum, idem.

Exterebro, aui, are, to perce through. Also to enserche curiously.

Extermino, aui, are, to dryue out, or pulle downe.

Pacuuius. Exterminatus, banyshed.

Externo, aui, are, to make madde.

Externus, na, num, whyche is not of that countrey, a straunger.

Extero, teri, terere, to beate out. also to whette or grynde.

Exterreo, ui, rere, to put in feare.

Extillo, aui, are, to droppe out.

Extimesco, extimui, extimescere, to dreade moche.

Extimus, a, um, the outwardemost, or laste.

Extinguo, xi, guere, to put out, properly as fyre, whiche may be eftesoones kendlyd: sometyme it signifieth to slee, or destroye: sometyme to make a distynction or dyuersitie betwene thynges.

Extispices, sothesayers by lookynge in the inwardes of beastes.

Extispicium, & extispicina, the crafte of soth sayenge.

Exto, extiti, extare, to be, to remayne, to be apparant.

Extollo, extuli, extollere, to aduaunt or praise.

Extorqueo, torsi, quere, to fynde oute the trouthe by tourmentes, to take awaye by force, or plucke away.

Extorris, is he that is made to voyde, or is dryuen out of his countrey: also a vagabud.

Extra, without.

Ex tripode, whan we speake of thynges, whiche are very true, and nat to be douted, as it were spoken of goddis own mouthe.

Extrarius, he that is not of the same house or kynredde.

Extrema linea, is spoken, where a man wold signifie a thing to be laste, & after all other.

Extremis digitis attingere, to towche with the fynger toppes, is spoken, where is sygnified, that a manne hath vnneth touched

F ante A.

or felte a thynge.

Extra telorum iactum, out of arowe shotte, out of gunne shotte, signifieth out of daunger, or in safegarde.

Extremus, a, um, sometyme it signifyeth the begynnynge, sommetyme the ende, sommetyme the warste.

Extrico, aui, are, to delyuer, to shake of any thynge that letteth.

Extrinsecus, outwarde.

Extro, aui, are, to goo out.

Extrorsum, from without.

Extrudo, si, dere, to thraste oute.

Extruo, si, truere, to ordeyne, to buylde or sette vppe.

Extubero, aui, are, to swelle moche.

Extundo, tudi, tundere, to fynde oute with moche labour.

Exturbo, aui, are, to put away, or to put oute or from a thynge by vyolence.

Exubero, aui, are, to abounde.

Exuccum, without iuyce.

Exudo, aui, are, to sende forth lycour.

Exugo, exugi, gere, & exugeo, to sucke out.

Exul, exulis, a banyshed man.

Exulo, aui, are, to be banyshed, to lyue in exyle.

Exultabundus, reioysynge very moche.

Exulto, aui, are, to reioyce excedyngely, to bragge, to leape oute.

Exundo, aui, are, to ouerflowe.

Exuo, ui, uere, to putte of, to dispoyle, or vnclothe.

Exupero, aui, are, to excede.

Exurdo, aui, are, to make deaffe.

Exuuię, clothynge. Also hydes or skynnes of beastes. Exuuię serpentis, an Adders skynne.

Exybaphon, a salate of herbes

¶ F Ante A.

FABA, a beane.

Faba cudetur in me, The beane shall be knockyd on me, sygnyfyeth the peine or blame shal light on me.

Fabacia, a beane cake.

Fabalia, the refuse or offall of beanes.

Fabarię Calendę, the Calendes of June.

Fabarius, fabaria, fabarium, pertaynynge to beanes.

Fabella, a shorte tale.

Faber, fabri, almoost euerye craftes manne that warketh with the hande. Faber lignarius, a carpenter: Faber ferrarius, a smith. Auri faber, a goldesmythe.

H.ii. Faber,

Faber, fabra, fabrum, pertaining to a smith.
Fabre, workemanly.
Faberrime, kunningly, very craftily, or wel.
Fabianus, the propre name of a man.
Fabitor, in the ancient tyme was taken for a maynteyner.
Fabius, the name of a noble Romayne.
Fabrefacio, fabrefeci, fabrefacere, to warke cunnyngly, to buylde.
Fabrica, a warkehouse, or forge. sometyme the frame or warke.
Fabritius, a noble Romayne, who beinge wonderful pore, not withstandyng refused a great some of money, sent to him by king Pirrhus, towchynge with his handes all his membres, and sayinge vnto the kynges messangers: As longe as he mought rule all that, whiche he touched, he coulde lacke nothynge.
Fabrico, caui, are, & Fabricor, cari, to make, to inuente.
Fabrilis, fabrile, bilonging to handy craftis.
Fabula, a fable or tale.
Fabula palliata, a comedy of Greke.
Fabula togata, a comedy of latyne.
Fabulator, a teller of fables.
Fabulor, aris, ari, to talke.
Fabulosus, moche talked of.
Facesso, cessi, cessere, to go aboute to doo a thynge: sommetyme to go awaye. Facesse hinc, Get the hens. Facessit tibi negotium, he putteth the to busynesse.
Facetie, mery wordes or deedes withoute dishonestie.
Facetus, ta, tum, mery, pleasant.
Faceté, meryly, pleasantly.
Facies, a face, sometyme the proporcion of all the body.
Facile, lyghtly, or easily, withoute lette or doubte.
Facilis, facile, lighte, easye, good to be entreated.
Facilitas, easynesse, gentylnesse.
Facinorosus, full of myschief, vngracious, harmefull.
Facinus, an acte or dede. sommetyme an ylle dede.
Facio, feci, facere, to doo, to be occupied, to make. Facio plurimi, I make moch of. Floccifacio, I sette not a strawe by it. Facere uerba, to speake. Facere lucrum, to wynne. Facere sumptum, to bestowe coste. Facere iter, to go or ryde. Facere terrorem, to put in feare. Facere copiam, to gyue leaue. Facere iacturam, damnum, naufragium, to lose, to take harme, to go to wrecke. Facere, is also to sacrifyce, to profyte. Faciam ut te plurimum amem, I woll loue the moche. Fac te esse qui sum, ymagin that thou were as I am. Facere conuicium, to rebuke, or putte to rebuke. Facere nomina, to gette dettours, as by lendyng: as they do nowe by exchaunge, and in shyftes, proprely called vsury: and in bargaynes of corne, cattell, and other lyke, or in letting of landes.
Factio, a diuisyon of people in sondry opynions. also an acte.
Factitius, a, um, made or counterfayte.
Factito, aui, are, to do often tymes.
Factor, oris, a maker, a factour.
Factum, a dede.
Factum atq; transactum, done and brought to good passe.
Factura, the warke.
Facturio, iui, ii, ire, to desyre to do.
Factus, tus, the dede.
Facula, a lynke, or lyttel torche.
Facularii, torche bearers.
Facultas, tatis, power to do or speake. some tyme rychesse. also facultie.
Facundus, a, um, eloquent, well spoken.
Facundia, eloquence, or sw ete and pleasant speche.
Fæcatum uinum, wyne that drynketh of the lyes.
Fæciniæ uuæ, grapes, whereof commethe wyne, hauynge moche lyes.
Fæculentum, full of lyes or dregges.
Fæcutinus, na, num, pertaining to dregges.
Fæx, fæcis, lyes, dregges, or groundes of any kynde of lycour.
Fagus, gi, a beche tree.
Fala, a tower made of tymber.
Falcarius, he that fyghteth with a byll.
Falcarius, ia, um, pertaynyng to a bylle.
Falcatus, ta, tum, hooked, also any thynge, wheron be hookes or other lyke thynge.
Falcicula, a lyttell hoke or byll.
Falcidia lex, wherby legacies were defalcate or cutte of, where the fourthe part of the goodis were not assignid to the heires.
Falcifer, he that beareth a byll or hooke.
Falcito, aui, are, to cut with a byll or hooke.
Falco, aui, are, to cutte of or mowe.
Falco, conis, a hawke.
Falernus, a countrey in Campania, now in the royalme of Naples, wherin grewe the beste wynes of Italy, callyd falernum.
Falisci, people in Italye. Also a kynde of puddynges.
Fallacie, deceytefull wordes.
Fallaciter, deceytefully.
Fallax, acis, a person deceytefull.
Fallo, fefelli, fallere, to deceyue, also to be hydde.
Falsarius, a forger of wrytynges.
Falsidicus, & falsiloquus, a lyer, or false reporter.

Falsi-

Falsifico, aui, are, to forge dedes, writinges, or seales.
Falsitas, tatis, falsehode.
Falso, aui, are, to forge.
Falsum habere, to deceyue.
Falx, falcis, a hooke or bylle.
Fama, fame or renome. somtyme opinion.
Famelicosus, often hungrye.
Famelicus, ca, cum, hungrye.
Famen, faminis, speche.
Fameo, famui, ere, to be hungry.
Fames, hungre.
Famiger, geris, a spreder of fame.
Famigerabilis, famous.
Famigerator, a teller of newes or tydynges, or a spreder of fame.
Famigerulus, the same.
Familia, a housholde, a family, or kynred.
Familiaria, were places of buryall for men and their seruantes.
Familiaris, are, pertaynyng to housholde, also familyar.
Familiariter, famylyarly.
Famosus, a, um, famous, as well in good, as in ylle.
Famulanter, humbly, seruysably.
Famularius, a, um, seruisable.
Famulatio, housholde, or meyny.
Famulatus, & famulitium, seruyce.
Famulus, & famula, a housholde seruant.
Famulor, ari, to serue.
Fanaticus, madde. In the olde tyme before that Christe expelled the dyuel, whan that dyuelles were honoured in ydols, certayne persones, aswell men as women, were possessed with dyuels, which lad them, where they lysted, agaynste their propre wylles, and caused them to speke wonderful thinges, some also sodaynely, and often tymes telle what shoulde happen: wherfore they were thought to be inspired with goddis: those persons were called Fanatici. Some tyme Fanaticus, is taken for the keper of the Temple or chappell, where the deuyll gaue answeres.
Fanesii, people in the northe partes of the worlde, whose eares be so great, that with them they keuer all their bodies.
Fanum, a Temple, where the dyuell gaue answeres out of an ydoll.
Far, farris, sometyme sygnyfyeth all maner of corne. All be it among aunciente phisytions it is taken for wheat meale.

Cælius lib. 15. Farraria, amonge the olde Romaines were the ceremonies of matrimonie.
Farcimen, minis, a puddynge.
Farcio, ciui, cire, to stuffe. Also to franke or fede, to be fatte, to cramme.
Farfarus, or Farfar, a ryuer of Syrie.

Faris, fatus sum, fari, to speake.
Farraca, meates made of meale.
Farrago, ginis, a myxture of sondrye kyndes of grayne and corne. Sometyme it is taken for a myxture of thynges good and badde.
Farreatio, a sacrifyce made with cakes.
Farreum, a wheaton cake.
Farrinus, na, num, & farrinaceus, a, um, pertaynynge to wheate.
Farrinariu, a place where wheate or meale is kepte.
Farcilis, le, any thynge stuffed.
Fartile, stuffynge, or that wherewith any foule is crammed or franked.
Fartim, full stuffed or crammed.
Fartores, & fartrices, puddynge makers.
Fartum, a puddynge.
Fartura, the crafte or maner of stuffynge or crammynge.
Fas, lefull before god.
Fascelis, a name of Diana.
Fascia, a swathell or swathynge bande, or other lyke thynge. sometyme any gridell.
Fascior, fasciari, to swathe a chylde.
Fasciculus, a grype, or thyng bounden togither. It is also a nosegay, or any thynge knytte togyther, whiche may be borne in a mannes hande.
Fascino, aui, are, to transforme by inchauntment, or to bewytche.
Fascinus, & fascinum, & fascinatio, an inchauntmente to transfourme or disfygure any thynge. whiche so inchanted, is of the comune people called, taken, or forspoken, or forlooked.
Fasciola, a lyttell bande.
Fascis, is a burdeyn or knytche of wodde, or any other thyng. Also Fascis sagittarum is taken for a sheffe of arrowes.
Fasces, roddes bounden togyther, and an axe in the myddell, whiche were borne before the chiefe offycers of Rome, in declarynge their authoritie, wherof some had syxe, and some mo.
Fasellus, a boote.
Fasti dies, were certayne days, wherin the offycer of Rome, called Prætor, mowghte speake onely these three wordes, Do, dico, addico. It maye be nowe vsed for holy dayes.
Fasti, were certayne bokes, wherin were conteyned certayne ceremonies and causes of sondrye thynges amonge the Romaynes, concerninge their feastes and solemnities, whyche were longe kepte from the knowlege of the common people, vntyll they at the laste were deuulgate by one Caius Flauius.

H.iii. Fastis

F ante A.

Fastidio, iui, ire, to contemne with disdayne, to abhorre or haue in abomination.
Fastidiosus, a, um, full of disdayne.
Fastiditus, ta, tum, hatred, abhorred, abhomyned.
Fastidium, hated, proprely where one abhorreth the sight or presence of any thing.
Fastigio, aui, are, to make or rayse vp in heyght.
Fastigium, an altitude, or the top or height of any thynge. Sometyme it signifieth the state of a persone in any dignitie, somtyme the ende of a thynge.
Fastigium imponere, is spoken whan a man wyll signifye a matter or thynge to be fynysshed and brought to a poynt.
Fastus, tus, hautenes of mynde, pryde.
Fatalis, le, pertaynynge to destenye, fatall. somtyme mortall.
Fateor, fassus sum, fateri, to affirme, to confesse.
Fathisco, scere, to gape wyde, as the erthe dothe in a great drythe.
Fatidicus, fatidica, a reder or teller of destenyes, or a southsayer.
Fatifer, fatifera, a brynger of deth or pestylence.
Fatiloqua, a witche.
Fatigo, aui, are, to make wery, to trouble moche, to stryke, to stere or prouoke, to restrayne or lette.
Fatiloquus, fatiloqua, a sothsayer.
Fatisco, fatiscere, to be wery.
Fator, aris, ari, to speake moche.
Fatuitas, atis, folyshnes.
Fatum, the ordinance and disposition of almyghty god. Desteny, goddis prouidence. somtyme deth.
Fatuus, an ydiote, that lacketh naturall knowlege.
Fauentia, a citie in Italye.
Faueo, ui, fauere, to fauour.
Fauere linguis, to kepe silence.
Fauilla, a sperke of fyre.
Fauni, goddis of the woodes.
Fauonius, one of the wyndes, called the southwest wynde.

Gel. Fauorabilis, fauoured of many.
Fauorinus, the name of a philosopher.
Faustulus, a shepeherde, whiche was the nourisher of Romulus and Remus.
Faustus, a, um, prosperous.

Plaut. Fauste, prosperousely.
Fauulus, a lyttell hony combe.
Fauus, a hony combe.
Faux, faucis, a cheke.
Fauces, strayght passages.
Fax, facis, a torche, a candell, or other lyke thynge, whiche brennynge grueth lyght.

Faxim, let me do.
Faxint, let them do.
Faxo, I wyll or shall do.

¶ F Ante E.

Febricito, aui, are, to be sycke in a feuer.
Febricula, a lyttell feuer.
Febriculosus, he that hath often the feuer.
Febrilis, le, pertaynyng to a feuer.
Febrio, iui, ire, to haue a feuer.
Febris, a feuer.
Februarius, the monthe of Februarie.
Februo, aui, are, to pourge sowles by sacrifyce or prayer.
Februa, sacrifices and ceremonies for purgynge of sowles.
Februatus, ta, tu, that which was so purged.
Februum, in the Sabines tounge is callyd purgynge or clensynge.
Fecialis, was a certayne offycer of armes, whiche denounced warre or peace, where as was hostilitie or cause of battayle: whiche may nowe be taken for an ambassadour, sent for suche a purpose, or for an Heralde.
Fel, fellis, the gaulle. sometyme it is taken for griefe of the mynde.
Felis, a Catte: sommetyme it sygnifyeth a weasyll.
Fello, aui, are, to soucke.
Femen, minis, plurali femina, the inner and backe parte of the thygh.
Feminalia, the keuerynge of the thighes.
Femur, femoris, the thygh. some englysshe it the hamme.
Femoralia, breeches.
Fenestella, the propre name of a story wryter, whiche flourished in the later dayes of Tyberius Cesar.
Fenestra, a wyndowe, sometyme an entrie into a thynge.
Fenestratus, ta, tum, open. Nulla est fenestratior domus, No howse is more open. Plaut.
Fenestrenula, a lyttell wyndowe.
Ferabites, wylde.
Feræ, ferarum, feras, wylde beastes.
Feralis, le, deedly or mortall, lamentable.
Feralia, & feralis dies, a day dedicate to the infernall goddis, to pacifie them towarde the soules departed.
Feralia, were also the sacryfyces doone for sowles.
Feralia amicula, wyndynge shetes, and suche lyke thynges, wherin deade bodyes were lappyd.
Feralia officia, solemnities about deed bodies
Feralis cultus, mournynge apparayle.
Feralis dies, the daye of buryenge.
Ferax, acis, fruiteful, or that bryngeth forth moche

moche fruite.

Ferbeo, bui, ere, to boyle or sethe.

Ferculum, a dysshe with meate. Also a pagent, caryed or borne to be loked on. some tyme it signifieth the stage or place, wherin the pagent is.

Fere, almoste, nygh, welnygh.

Ferentarii, men armed in lygyt harnes, redy to come quickly to socours: whiche fought with dartes, swordes, or slynges.

Ferentinum, a citie, whiche after Plini. standeth in the fyrst region of Italye.

Ferentum, a towne of the Sabins, or Samnites.

Feretrius, a name of Jupiter, gyuen by Romulus, the first kynge of Romanes.

Feretrum, a beere, wheron deed bodies are borne. somtyme a thinge, wheron ymages, relikes, or iewelles are borne.

Feretrus, a mountayne, of whiche the house of Pheretre was named, of which the duke of Urbyne is descended.

Feriæ, feriarum, ferias, holy dayes.

Ferinus, na, num, wylde as a beast.

Ferio, percussi, ferire, to stryke, to stablyshe, to knocke.

Ferire fœdus, to make a league or truse.

Ferire iugulum, to slee, to hit the marke.

Ferior, aris, ari, to cesse from labour.

Feriatus, vnoccupyed or ydell.

Feritas, tatis, a naturall wyldnes.

Fermé, almoste, welnygh.

Fermentescere, to increase or waxe.

Fermento, taui, are, to meddel or myxt well togyther, as leuen with dow. also to leuen.

Fero, fers, tuli, ferre, to beare, to suffre, to leade or brynge, to saye, to name, to desyre, to brynge forth, to haue, to boste. Ferre ad populu, to aske the people aduyse. To take away, to receyue, to optayne, to accustome.

Ferre fortunam, to vse fortune: Ferre in oculis, to fauour moche.

Ferre acceptum, to receyue, to wryte that whiche is receyued, to knowlege to haue receyued a benefyte or profyte.

Ferre expensum, to spende or laye out, to wryte expenses, to bestowe.

Ferocio, ciui, cij, cire, to be fierse.

Ferocitas, tatis, fiersnes.

Ferociter, fiersely.

Feronia, the goddesse of woodes. also a citie vnder the hyll Soractes.

Ferox, ferocis, fierse, hardy.

Ferramentarij, they whiche warke in yron.

Ferramentum, an instrumēt or tole of yron.

Ferraria, an yron myne.

Ferrarius, a, u, ptaynyng to yron, or of yron.

Ferre iudicem, to agree to the sentence or iudgement.

Ferreus, ea, eum, of yron.

Ferro, aui, are, to sette yron on.

Ferratus, ta, tum, hauyng yron on it, or closyd in yron.

Ferrugineus, a, um, grene coloure.

Ferrugo, ginis, ruste of yron, a murray colour, some calleth it a sadde blewe.

Ferrum, yron, sometyme weapon.

Ferrumen, minis, glewe, syse, sowder, or suche other byndynge or cleauynge matter.

Ferrumino aui, are, to ioyne or myxe togyther, proprely mettalles, to sowlder.

Fertilis, le, fertile, or fruitefull.

Fertum, a Cake made of sondry graynes and spyces.

Ferueo, es, is, iui, ere, to be chauffed or hette.

Feruefacio, to cause to boyle.

Feruidus, a, um, feruent, dilygent.

Ferula, a rodde or stycke, wherwith chyldrens handes be striken in schooles. also a cane or rede. also a potte stycke.

Ferulatius, a, um, lyke a cane or rede.

Feruor, oris, heate.

Ferus, a, um, wylde, cruell, terrible.

Feritas, tatis, wyldenes, crueltie.

Fescenini, versis sunge at weddinges.

Fessus, a, um, werye.

Festinanter, hastily, quyckely, or swyftly.

Festinato, spedily, in haste.

Festino, aui, are, to make hast, to be troublid.

Festinus, a, um, hasty, quycke.

Festina lente, spede the slowely, is spoken, where a man wyll sygnifye a thynge to be done, neither to hastyly nor to slowely, but in a conuenient temperance. See my booke of the Gouernour, in the chapiter of Maturytie.

Festinatio, haste or spede.

Festiuitas, tatis, myrthe.

Festiuo, aui, are, to kepe holy day.

Festiuus, a, um, mery, prouokynge myrthe, ioyous. also pertaynyng to holy dayes.

Festuca, the yonge tender spring of a tree, or herbe. Also a moote.

Festus, ta, tum, feastfull or solemne.

¶ F Ante I.

Fiber, a beaste called a beuer, whiche is also called Castor, whose stoones are vsed in medicine, and are called Castoreum. It is also a kynde of waspes.

Fibre, are the extreme partes of the liuer, the hart, or the lunges, or of other thinges wherin is any diuysyon, they maye be called lappes, brymmes. Also the spires of herbes or trees newe sprongen.

Fibula, a buckle of a girdell, or other thing lyke therto.

Fibus

Fibulo, aui, are, to buckle, to ioyne togither tymber, or bordes, or other lyke thinges.
Ficaria, a fygge tree.
Ficarius, an eater of fygges.
Ficedula, a byrde.
Ficetū, a place where figge trees do grow.
Ficetor, oris, he that loueth or gadereth fygges.
Ficolea, a staffe or stake of a fygge tree.
Ficosus, full of sores in the heed or berde.
Fictilis, fictile, erthen, or made of erthe.
Fictitius, tia, um, fayned, or dissembled, or counterfayte.
Fictor, oris, a counterfayter, a fayner.
Ficulnea, a fygge tree.
Ficulneus, a, um, & ficulnus, a, um, of a fygge tree.
Ficus, in the masculyne gender is a fygge: in the feminine gender, is a figge tree. it is also a soore or scabbe, growyng in the places of a mans body, where that heare is.
Fidei cōmissarius, a feoffe of trust.
Fide bona, without fraude or couyne.
Fideicommissum, a feoffement of truste.
Fidei cōmitto, misi, tere, to infeffe.
Fideiussor, oris, a suretie, or borowe.
Fidelia, a vessell seruynge to dyuers pourposes.
Fidelis, faithfull, loyall, trusty, or sure.
Fidelitas, tatis, faythefulnesse, loyaltie, or suretie.
Fidem astringere, to promyse faithfully.
Fidem fallere, to breake promyse.
Fidem labefactare, to lose credence.
Fides labefactata, credence loste.
Fide sua, mea, tua, iubere, to vndertake.
Fidena, a towne in Italy.
Fidentia, confidence.
Fides, fidei, belefe, truste, promyse. It is a stablenes and truthe in promyses and couenauntes. It is also a faythfull execution of thinges commytted or promysed.
Fidem habere, to beleue.
Fidem accipere, to be beleued.
Fidem liberare, to kepe promyse.
Fides, fidis, the strynge of any instrument. sometyme a harpe or lute.
Fides publica, the credence or promyse of all the people and rulers.
Fidicen, cinis, a harpe: it maye be called a fyddell. it is also he that playeth on the instrument.
Fidicina, a woman harper or luter.
Fidicula, a rebecke, or gytterne.
Fidiculę plurali, a tourment made with cordes or strynges, wherwith menne be tourmented, to make them to confesse treason or felonye.
Fido, fisus sum, fidere, to truste.

Fidutia, trust, confidence: somtyme hope: it is properly that truste, wherin any thyng is deliueryd by one man to an other, to the intent that he shall redelyuer it, whan he is required.
Fiduciaria possessio, a possession to an other mans vse, or vpon condicion.
Fiduciaria mancipatio, aut uenditio, a state in landes made vpon confidence of truste, or a morgage.
Fidus, a, um, trusty.
Figmentum, the warke or warkemanshyp: sometyme a lye, or a thing fayned.
Figo, xi, figere, to thruste in. sommetyme it sygnifyeth to driue or fasten in the erthe. Palum humi fixit, He droue the stake into the grounde, also to plant or sette. Ipse feraces Figat humo plantas, He wolle sette in the grounde the fruitefull plantes. Sometyme to stryke.

Columel. Virg. Ge. lib. 4.

Iuuenal.

Figlina, æ, a potters warkehowse, or potters crafte.
Figlina, plurali, vessell of erthe.
Figulus, a potter.
Figura, a fygure.
Figuro, aui, are, to make or fourme.
Filiaster, a sonne in lawe by an other wyfe, or an other husbande.
Filius terre, a newe begunne gentylman, or a gentrylman of the fyrste heed.
Filicula, ferne growynge on trees, callid in a greke name polypodion.
Filius, a sonne, filia, a doughter.
Filii, somtime dothe conteyne both sonnes and doughters.
Filistim, a countreye, that is nowe callyd Ascalon.
Filix, licis, ferne.
Filum, a threde. sometyme the proporcion of a thynge.
Filo, aui, are, to spynne or make a threde.
Fimbria, the skyrtes or hemme of a garmente.
Fimetum, a dunge hylle.
Fimum, a boxe, out of the whiche men doo caste vpse.
Fimus, dunge of cattell.
Finalis, le, fynall, or laste.
Findo, fidi, findere, to cutte, to cleue.
Fissilis, le, that whiche may be cutte.
Fissura, a cutte or clefte.
Fingo, xi, gere, to make, to forme, to fayn.
Finio, iui, ire, to fynyshe or ende.
Finis, the ende, the conclusyon. also intente or purpose, wherunto any other thing hath relation, or is made or done for.
Fines plurali, the borders or marches of a countrey, boundes.
Finitimus, ma, um, nygh ioynynge.

Fini-

Finitio, a definition.
Finitor, oris, a setter of boundes.
Fio, fieri, to be, to be estemed.
Firmamentum, a suertie or stabylitie. also that, whyche is called the grounde of a cause or matter. Also the firmament or heuen vysyble.
Firmo, aui, are, to make stable or sure.
Firmus, stable, constant, well fortified.
Firmitas, & firmitudo, stablenes, constãce, surenesse.
Fiscalis, le, pertaynynge to the kynges treasure.
Fiscella, a chiese fate. Also it is a thynge made with withes and halters, wherwith cattell were so moselled, that they mought not byte anye yonge sprynges or buddes of trees.
Fiscellus, a lyttell hyll in Italye, not farre from Tyber.
Fisci, fiscinæ, fiscelle, greate sachels, wherin were put great sommes of money.
Fiscus, the priuate treasure of princis.
Fiscum, the kynges escheker.
Fiscina, a greatte baskette.
Fiscibilis, le, that maye be cutte or slytte. fiscilis, the same.
Fistula, a pype, as well to conuey water, as an instrument of musyke. Also the wesell or throte bolle. also a tappe or faucette. also a disease or soore, whiche commeth of a putrified humour, and contynually runeth.
Fistulosus, full of holes lyke a spunge.
Fistuca, an instrumente, wherwith piles of wodde be dryuen into the ground, and stones in pauynge, called a rammer.
Fistucatio, pylinge, or pauynge.
Fitiges, be beastis of Aethiope, of a browne colour, hauynge two pappes in the breste, as man hath: nor they be not so wylde, but they may be tamed, nor so tame, but they woll hurte those, that greue them.
Fixus, a, um, fyrme, faste.

¶ F Ante L.

Flabellum, an instrument, wherwith in the heate of sommer wynde is fanned blowen into mẽs visages, to koole thẽ.
Flabrum, a blowynge or puffe of wynde.
Flacceo, & flaccesco, ere, to wydder, or waxe feble.
Flaccidus, a, um, wythered, feeble, weake, hangynge downewarde, lollynge, or flagynge.
Flaccum, bruysed.
Flaces, the ortes of olyues.
Flagella, the smalle braunches or twigges of trees or vynes. sometyme scourges or flayles, wherwith corne is threshed.
Flagello, aui, are, to scourge, to thresshe, to blame or rebuke.
Flagitiosus, an vngracious persone, full of myschiefe.
Flagitium, an yll or myscheuous dede, worthy rebuke and punyshement.
Flagito, aui, are, to aske importunately and with clamoure.
Flagratores, they whiche for moneye doo suffre them selfes to be beaten.
Flagrio, onis, a slaue.
Flagro, aui, are, to bourne with a flame of fyre. Sommetyme to loue or desyre inordynately.
Flamea, clothe or sylke of vyolette colour.
Flaminica, the priestes wyfe, or a wedding gowne of vyolet colour.
Flameum, a typpet of vyolet sylke, whiche the newe wedded wyfe dyd weare.
Flamen, hoc, the blaste in an instrument.
Flamen, the great prieste amonge the gentyles.
Flaminia, the house of the archeprieste.
Flamineum, a kerchiefe or typpette.
Flamma, a flame. sometyme peryll.
Flamescere, to be inflamed.
Flammeus, ea, eum, burnynge or flamynge.
Flammiuomus, sendyng out flames.
Flandria, a countrey called Flaunders.
Flaueo, & flauesco, aui, ere, to be lyke golde, or of yelowe colour.
Flauus, a, um, yelowe, or of the coloure of golde.
Flebilis, le, lamentable.
Flecto, & flexo, xi, tere, to bowe, to bende, to leade.
Flegma, fleume.
Fleo, eui, ere, to wepe.
Fletus, wepynge.
Flexanima oratio, an oration or spech, wherby a mans mynde is stirred to pitie, reioysynge, or other lyke affection.
Flexilis, le, any thynge that may be easlye bowed or bente.
Flexura, the bowynge.
Fligo, xi, ctum, to tourment or vexe.
Flo, aui, are, to blowe. also to make coyne of mettall.
Floces, lyes or draftes of wyne.
Flocci, flockes of the shearynge of wollen clothes.
Flocculi, fyne flockes.
Floccifacio, & floccipendo, I set nought by.
Floralia, florales ludi, plays made in the honour of Flora, an harlotte, whiche gaue a great treasure vnto the people of Rome.
Floreo, rui, ere, & florido, aui, are, to flourish or to haue floures. Also to excell. somtime

to prosper.
Flos, floris, a floure.
Floresco, sci, scere, to bourgen or to brynge forth floures.
Floreus, a, um, made of floures.
Floridus, da, dum, garnyshed with floures. sometyme freshe or lusty.
Floriger, eris, bearynge floures.
Florulentus, ta, tum, full of floures.
Fluctio, onis, the reume or pose.
Fluctiuagus, wandring in riuers or waters.
Fluctuo, aui, are, to be tossed as a shyppe is in the see. also to doubte.
Fluctuatim, troublously, doubtfully.
Fluctuosus, a, ū, troublous, vnquiete, stormy.
Fluctus, a floudde, a waue of water styred by tempeste.
Fluentum, a ryuer, or streame.
Fluescere, to be resolued or relented.
Fluidus, da, dum, flowynge, relentyd, resolued.
Fluito, aui, are, to flowe contynually, sometyme to flytte or swymme.
Flumen, inis, a great ryuer. sometyme the course of the water.
Flumineus, a, um, of the ryuer.
Fluminosus, a, um, full of ryuers.
Fluo, xi, ere, to rounne, as water dothe, to procede or come of a thynge, or to growe.
Fluor, fluxus, & fluxio, a flyxe.
Fluta, a fyshe, lyke to an eele, callyd a Lampreye.
Fluuialis, le, of the ryuer.
Fluuiatilis, le, that whiche is in the ryuer.
Fluuius, a floudde or ryuer.
Fluxura, lecherye.
Fluxus, a, um, vnstable, or that whyche dureth but a whyle, large, or wyde, relented, lecherous, and wanton.

F, Ante O.

Focale, a kerchiefe, whiche menne and womenne dydde weare aboute theyr cheekes.
Focaneus, a braunche of a vyne, whyche groweth out of a twyste or forked bough.
Focaria, a fyre panne.
Focatius, bread baken on the hote coles.
Focillo, aui, are, to nouryshe.
Focula, nourishynge meates.
Foculo, aui, are, to nouryshe or sustayne.
Foculus, a litle panne, wherin fyre is borne.
Focus, a panne or herthe, wherein fyre is. sometyme it sygnifieth fyre. somtyme priuate houses or tenementes.
Fodico, aui, are, to dygge.
Fodina, a place where a thyng is dygged.
Fodio, fodi, fodere, to delue.

Fœcundo, daui, are, to make fruitefulle, or plentuouse.
Fœcundus, a, um, plentuous, or fruitefull.
Fœcunditas, plentie.
Fœdo, aui, are, to polute or defyle, to destroye, to rent or teare, to consume.
Fœdero, aui, are, to confederate.
Fœderatus, a confederate.
Fœdifragus, a breaker of leage or truse, or entercourse.
Fœdus, da, dum, fowle, defourmed, cursed, or cruelle.
Fœdus, deris, a leage betwene princis, an entercourse, a truse after battayle: sometyme it signifyeth a lawe made in the tyme of warres.
Fœlicitas, tatis, felycitie, prosperitie, abundaunce of all thynges.
Fœlicito, aui, are, to make prosperous.
Fœlix, licis, hauing abūdance of al thinges, prosperous, commodious, or profytable.
Fœmina, a womanne. Also in beastes the female.
Fœnarius, ia, um, pertaynynge to haye, as Falces fœnariæ, hookes or sythes for to cutte haye.
Fœnebris, bre, pertaynyng to vsurye, or vnreasonable gayne.
Fœneratitius, a, um, the same.
Fœnerator, oris, an vsurer or lender for vnreasonable gayne.
Fœnero, aui, are, & fœneror, rari, cum datiuo, to lende for vsurie. Fœneror cum ablatiuo, To borowe, or make a shyfte, or to laye to morgage.
Fœniculum, fenell.
Fœnile, an hey howse.
Fœnisecium, haye haruest.
Fœnisex, secis, a mower of haye.
Fœnogræcum, fenegreke.
Fœnum, haye.
Fœnus, noris, vsurye, vnreasonable, or vnlefull gayne, commyng of that thyng, whiche is lente.
Fœteo, tere, to stynke.
Fœtidus, a, um, stynkynge.
Fœtifico, aui, are, to brynge forth, most cōmonly as a beast or a byrde dothe.
Fœto, taui, are, the same.
Fœtor, oris, stynche, or yll sauour. *Varro*
Fœtuosus, a, um, full of bredynge.
Fœtura, the tyme from the conception vnto the byrthe. Also the increase of cattell. sometyme it signifieth the increase or commynge forth of other thinges.
Fœtus, tus, all thynge that is brought forth by generation, somtyme the fruite of trees.
Fœtus, ta, tum, full, or great with yonge, as a woman with chylde or a beaste.

Folia-

Foliacius, a, um, full of leaues.
Foliatus, ta, tum, leaued, or hauyng leaues.
Folium, a leafe.
Follico, caui, care, to snuffe or fetche backe wynde with the nosethrylles.
Folliculus, the huske, wherein the eare of wheate or other corne is inclosed, whan it is grene, called the hose. Also for a sacke, wherin corne is putte.
Follis, a belowe, wherwith fyre is blowen. also a ball blowen full of wynde: semblably a bedde stuffed onely with wynde. it is also a bagge, wherin money is.
Fomentum, a nourishment of natural heate. It is also any thynge layde to the bodye in the fourme of a playster, to mytygate the peyne or griefe of any disease, callyd fomentation.
Fotus, the same.
Fomes, fomitis, any matter, wherwith fire is kendlyd and kepte burnynge. sometyme it sygnifieth that, whych feruently styrith vs to do any thynge.
Fons, fontis, a fountayne or well.
Fontanus, a, um, of a fountayne: as Aqua fontana, well water.
Fonticulus, a lyttell well or sprynge.
Foramen, minis, a hole.
Foras, without.
Foraria, a market woman, whyche selleth egges, chykens, and other lyke thynges at the markette.
Foratus, tus, a hole.
Forbea, a kynde of hotte meate.
Forcipes, a payre of tonges or other lyke instrument.
Forcus, a propre name of a man.
Forda, a mylche cowe that bryngeth forth caulfes.
Forem, res, ret, I shuld or had be, thou shuldest or had be, he shulde or had ben.
Fore, to be hereafter.
Forensia, habytes or robes, worne onely in places of iugement.
Forensis, se, pertaynyng to places of iugemente or courtes, where lawes be exercysed: also a furrour.
Fores, doores.
Forfices, sheares.
Forficuli, lyttell sheares.
Fori, the hatches of a shyp, or place where men beinge in the shyppe, do walke vp and down. Also stages or galeries, from whes the noble men of Rome beheld the playes callyd Circenses.
Foruli, huches, wherin bokes were kepte: nowe be they taken for keuerynges of bookes.
Foria, dunge that is lyquide or thynne.

Forica, commune draughtes or Jakes.
Foriculę, lyttell doores.
Forinsecus, without.
Forio, iui, ire, to discharge the bealy of ordure.
Foriolus, lose bealy, or he that hath a laske.
Forma, forme or shappe. somtyme beaultie.
Formię, a towne in Campania.
Formica, an Emote, or Ant, or pismere.
Formicatio, that whiche is commonly callyd a rynge worme.
Formidabilis, le, that whiche is to be drad.
Formido, dinis, drede or feare.
Formido, aui, are, to haue great feare.
Formidolosus, he that feareth other: also he that is feared of other.
Formo, aui, are, to forme, to make in facion.
Formosus, a, um, fayre.
Formucales, a peyre of tonges.
Formula, an instrument or dede in writing, a style in wrytynge, and a fourme in pleadynge.
Formula iniuriarum, an action of trespas.
Formulam intendere, to brynge an action.
Fornacalia, dayes whan the women dydde nought els but bake breadde.
Fornax, a chymney, or ouen.
Fornax calcaria, a lyme kylle.
Fornax lateraria, a brycke kyll.
Fornicarii, they which haue stalles or bouthes vnder the vaultes or arches of churches or palayces, where they sel theyr wares to them that passe by, as they do in west mynster halle.
Fornicarius, ia, um, pertaynyng to lechery.
Fornico, aui, are, to make an arch or a vault.
Fornicor, ari, to commytte fornication.
Fornix, nicis, an arche or a vaulte.
Foro, aui, are, to perce or boore a hole.
Forpices, cyssars to clyppe heare.
Forte, peraduenture, perchaunce.
Fortasse, fortasis, forsan, forsitan, the same.
Fortesco, sci, scere, to waxe stronge.
Forticulus, a lyttell stronge.
Fortifico, aui, are, to fortifie or make stroges.
Fortis, stronge, puissant, valyant of corage. also fayre, sometyme ryche.
Fortitudo, dinis, strength, valyant courage.
Fortuitus, ta, tum, that hapneth by chaunce.
Fortuna, fortune.
Fors fortuna, good fortune or chaunce.
Fortunatę insulę, the fortunate ilandes, be so callyd of the abundaunce of fruites, of whiche Strabo writeth. li. i.
Fortunatim, fortunately.
Fortunatus, ta, tum, fortunate.
Fortuno, naui, are, to make prosperous, to augment with good fortune.
Forum, a market, where thynges be solde.
Also

Also a place where iudgementes are practised, and matters in lawe pleaded. Forum whan it is taken for a market, hath comonly an other worde ioyned therwith, as Forum boarium, the markette where cattell is solde. Forum holitorium, the markette where herbes be solde. Forum piscarium, the fyshe markette.

Forum Iulium, a region or coutrey of Italy whiche somtyme was called Iapidia.

Forum Cornelii, a cytie of Italye, whyche nowe is callyd Imola.

Fossa, a dyche, or dyke, or a mote.

Fossilis, le, that whiche is dygged, or maye be dygged.

Fossio, dyggynge.

Fossitius, a, um, that is dygged.

Fossor, oris, a digger or dycher.

Fossula, a lyttell dyche.

Fossura, a dyggynge.

Fotus, ta, tum, nourished.

Fouea, a denne.

Foueo, ui, uere, to nouryshe, to sustayne, to mayntcyne, to weate or washe a thynge, to ordeyne or sette, to defende.

¶F Ante R.

Plautus in Amp.

Fracesco, sci, scere, to putrifie for age.
Fracidus, da, dum, more than rype, rotten as fruite is.
Fræno, aui, are, to brydell, to restrayne.
Frænum, a brydell.
Frænum mordere, to take the bytte in the teethe, syginifieth to set naught by.
Frætus, ta, tum, trustynge, ayded.
Freti uirtute & uiribus, ayded with strength and puissance.
Fraga, strawberies.
Fragesco, sci, scere, to braste.
Fragilis, le, brokell, soone broken.
Fragilitas, brotylnes, inconstancy.
Fragiliter, weakely, inconstantly.
Fragitides, the two great veynes, whyche do appere of eyther syde of the necke.
Fragmen & fragmentum, a pece or gobette of a thynge broken.
Fragor, oris, the noyse, whyche is made at the fallynge of any great thynge, rushyng.
Fragosus, a, um, uneasy to clymme.
Fragro, aui, are, to render a great sauour.
Fragrans, tis, hauyng great or sote sauour.
Framea, a speare, or iauelyn.
Frango, fregi, frangere, to breake.
Franosus, a deceyuer.
Frater, tris, a brother.
Fraterculus, a lyttell or yonge brother.
Fraterne, brotherly.
Fraternus, na, um, of a brother.

Frater patruelis, a brothers sonne.
Fratilli, the fringe of tapesry, that hangeth next the grounde.
Fratrare, proprely is sayde of chyldernes brestes, whan they do growe, to waxe imbocyd.
Fratria, a brothers wyfe.
Fraudo, aui, are, to begyle, to disappoynte.
Fraudare genium, not to satisfie the necessitte of nature, or carnall appetite.
Fradulenter, deceytefully.
Fraudulentus, full of deceyte.
Fraudulosus, a begyler.
Fraus, fraudis, deceyt. Also peryll, danger.
Fraxinus, an ashe.
Fraxo, aui, are, to go in watche.
Fregella, a lyttell towne in Italy.
Fremitus, a rorynge, proprelye of waters. sometyme a murmuryng, rumble, or noyse of people assemblyd togyther.
Fremo, mi, mere, to rore or make a noyse lyke great waters.
Frendeo, dui, dere, to grynde the tethe togyther for angre or payne. Also to grunte or grone for peyne.
Frequens, entis, acustomed, moche hanted, also assembled togither, abundant.
Frequens Senatus, al the Senatours assemblyd togyther.
Frequentia, greatte haunte, and companye of folke.
Frequento, taui, tare, to haunte, to goo togyther.
Frequentatio, an hauntynge, an assembly.
Fretum, a narowe parte of the see, where it is mourynge and troublous. Sometyme it is taken generally for the see.
Friabilis, le, soone broken in smalle pieces.
Fribolus, almoste worthe an halfepeny.
Frico, caui, cui, care, to rubbe.
Frictus, fricatio, & frictio, rubbyng.
Frigefacio, feci, facere, to coole.
Frigefio, frigefieri, to be colde.
Frigeo, gui, & frixi, to be colde or slowe.
Frigero, aui, are, to coole.
Frigesco, scere, to waxe colde.
Frigidulus, a, um, somewhat colde.
Frigidus, da, dum, colde, daungerouse, or noyfull.
Frigilla, a byrde, which syngeth in the cold wether, a ruddocke.
Frigo, xi, & frigui, gere, to frye.
Frictus, & frixus, a, um, fryed.
Frigorificus, ca, cum, made colde.
Frigus, goris, colde. sometyme feare.
Frigutio, tiui, tiri, to leape vp, or hoppe.
Frio, aui, are, to breake smalle, specially betwyxte the fyngers.
Frisii, people by Holande.

Frit.

F ante R.

Frit, the grayne in the toppe of the eare, whiche is lasse than a corne.

Fritilla, a froyse or pancake.

Fritillus, a boxe, out of the which dise were caste on the tables.

Friuolarius, he that selleth stuffe of lyttell valewe.

Friuolus, a, um, vayne, lyght, of none estymation or value.

Frixorium, a fryenge panne.

Frondarius, ia, ium, of leaues.

Frondatio, a slyppynge of of leaues. Also brousynge.

Frondator, oris, a brouser, a wodlopper.

Frondeo, & frondesco, descere, to beare or haue leaues.

Frondeus, ea, eum, that is of leaues.

Frondo, daui, are, to brynge forth leaues.

Frondosus, a, um, full of leaues.

Frons, tis, the foreheed, the frunt. Also it signifieth shamefastnes. also countenance.

Erasm⁹ in Chiliad. Frontem ferire, is spoken where a man sygnyfyeth, that one disdayneth extremely an nother.

Frons, frondis, the leafe of a tree, with the braunches.

Frondifer, bearynge leaues.

Frontale, the hedstall of an horse.

Fronto, tonis, he that hath a brode forhed.

Frontosus, hauynge a greatte forehed, or not abashed.

Fructifer, bearynge fruite.

Fructificus, & fructuosus, fruitefull.

Fructuarius, he that taketh the frute or profite of a thynge. Pernour of profytes.

Fructuarius, ria, rium, that whiche beareth fruite, or doth pertayne to fruite.

Fructus, tus, & ti, fruite. also al profite or reuenues that cometh of the grounde.

Fruges, aut frux, frugis, increase of all those thynges, whiche the erth bryngeth forth, moste proprely of grayne or corne. sometyme it signifieth rent or reuenues.

Frugi, moderate, profitable, necessary.

Frugi homo, a good man, a thryfty man, an honest man, temperate in expenses.

Frugalitas, ratis, moderation in liuing, specially in apparaylle and dyete, sobre rule, also suffycyencye.

Frugalior, frugalissimus, more temperate, moste temperate.

Fruiscor, sci, to vse at lybertie.

Frumen, the vppermost part of the throte, the gargyll.

Frumentaceus, of corne.

Frumentarius, ia, ium, pertaynyng to corne.

Frumentatio, takynge of corne.

Frumentator, toris, a taker or pourueyour of corne.

Frumentor, aris, to gather or puruey corne.

Frumentum, all corne, that hath berdes or eyles. it is moste vsed for wheate or rye.

Frunitus, wyse in vsynge of a thynge.

Fruor, fretus sum, frui, to vse with dilectation and profyte.

Frustatim, in piecis or gobettes.

Frustillatim, piece meale.

Frustra, in vayne.

Frustro, aui, are, & frustror, aris, ari, to deceyue. also to do a thyng in vayne, or vainly to employe.

Frustum, a piece or gobette.

Frustulum, & frustillum, a lyttell gobette.

Frusus, a kynde of brembyls, whose prycckes be not hooked.

Frutex, that which hath a great stalke, and yet it is no tree, as fenelle, caules, certayne malowes, and other lyke herbes. somtyme it is taken for the stemme or stalke.

Frutetosus, a, um, hauynge abundaunce of suche great herbes.

Frutetum, seu fruticetū, a place where groweth herbes with great stemes or stalkes.

Fruticescere, to be a stalke.

Frutico, aui, are, & fruticor, fruticaris, ari, to sprynge in stalke.

¶ F Ante V.

Fucilis, le, false, colouryd.

Fucinus, a lake in Italy.

Fuco, caui, care, to lay on a colour.

Fucatus, ta, tum, coloured or paynted, as some women be.

Fucus, a dorre or bee without stynge, whyche entreth into hyues, and eateth vp hony. Also payntynge, where oone colour is layde on an nother. It is also vsed for desceyte or falsehode.

Fuga, flyght.

Fugax, gacis, he that flyeth lyghtly. Also it signifieth swyfte.

Fugio, gi, gere, to flye, to runne awaye, to escape, to forgette.

Fugiens laboris, abhorring labour or peyn.

Fugitiuarius, a, um, startyng away, flyttyng.

Fugitiue aquæ, waters, which be taken out of a commune ryuer by stelthe.

Fugitiuus seruus, he that runneth frome his maister, wyllyng neuer to returne, or goth to a place, from whens he supposeth that his mayster can neuer recouer hym.

Fugito, taui, tare, to vse to runne away.

Fugo, aui, are, to dryue away.

Fulcio, si, cire, to supporte, to fortyfie.

Fulcra, beddestedes.

Fulgeo, si, gere, & fulgo, gi, ere, to shyne.

Fulgetrum, a leame of lyghtnynge.

Fulgi

Fulgidus, da, dum, bryghte.
Fulgor, bryghtnesse.
Fulgur, uris, uel oris, lyghtnynge.
Fulguratio, the lyghtnynge whenne it is in the clowdes.
Fulgurator, the sender of lyghtnynge.
Fulgurio, riui, rire, to caste lyghtnynge.
Fulguritas, lyghtnes or bryghtnes.
Fulguro, aui, are, to sende forth lyghtning.
Fulica, a se byrd, more thā a culuer, & black.
Fuligo, ginis, the soote of a chymney.
Fullo, onis, a fuller of clothe.
Fulmen, minis, lyghtnynge.
Fulmino, aui, are, to lyghten.
Fultura, a shore.
Fuluus, ua, um, a colour mixte of grene and redde, a darke yelowe.
Fumarium, a smoky place, where wine was layde, to the intent that it moughte the soner waxe olde. also the shanke or tonell of a chymneye.
Fumifico, aui, are, to make smoke, to incēse.
Fumigo, aui, are, to parfume.
Fumo, aui, are, to smoke.
Fumus, smoke.
Funale, a torche.
Funales equi, horses, whiche coupled with an halter, dyd go before the charyot.
Funambulus, he that walketh on a rope.
Funda, a slynge. Also a castinge nette, a sachell or purse lyke a nette. Also a cerkle of golde, or other mettalle, wherein stones be sette.
Fundamen, & fundamentum, a fundacion.
Fundibularii, slyngers of stones.
Funditores, the same.
Fundito, aui, are, to poure out often.
Funditus, from the foundation vtterly.
Fundo, aui, are, to founde, to make stable.
Fundo, fudi, fundere, to yette or cast mettall, to powre out, to sheede, to throwe downe, to scatter, to gyue aboundantlye, to speake moche, to lay downe.
Fundum, the bottome of a thynge.
Fundus, that whyche is vsed to be callyd lande or soyle.
Funebris, bre, funeralle.
Funepeus, a goer on a corde.
Funerale, pertaynynge to funeralles.
Funereus, rea, reum, pertaynynge to the deed bodye.
Funero, aui, are, to burye.
Funesto, aui, are, to vyolate a place with a deed bodye.
Funestus, ta, tum, vyolated with deade bodies. Also mortalle, blouddy. also pertaynynge to deed bodies or dethe.
Funetum, bowed or howped, as somme vynes be.

Fungor, functus sum, fungi, to exercyse an office. Fungi uita, to lyue. Functus uita, He that hath fynished his lyfe.
Fungus, a tadde stole, a mousherom.
Fungosus, lyke a musherom.
Funiculus, a small rope.
Funis, a rope.
Funus, funeris, funerall exequies, or solemnitie of buriēge. Sometyme it sygnyfieth the deed corps.
Fuo, fui, futum, to be.
Fur, furis, a these.
Furax, acis, theuyshe, a great picker.
Furca, furcula, an hey forke.
Furcifer, ciferis, a seruant, whiche for some lyghte offence, was compelled to beare a forke on his necke, hauynge both his handes bounden faste thereto, and so to goo through the towne, confessynge his defaut, and exhortynge other, that they shulde not in lyke case offende, whyche was a greate reproche.
Furcilis, a dungeforke.
Furcilla, an heyforke, also a galowes.
Furfur, uris, branne.
Furfureus, & furfuraceus, a, um, of branne.
Furiæ, the furyes of Helle, whyche were thre, Alecto, Tisiphone, Megera.
Furiatus, a, um, furyous.
Furibundus, a, um, woode or very madde.
Furio, aui, are, to make madde or woode.
Furiosus, a, um, madde, or wodde, frantyke.
Furnaceus, a, um, baken in an ouen.
Furnaria, bakers crafte. Also a womanne baker.
Furnus, an ouen.
Furo, furi, furere, to be woode for angre.
Furor, aris, ari, to steale.
Furor, roris, madnesse: Also furye, whyche is a vehement concytation or styrrynge of the mynde.
Furtim, by stelthe, priuilye.
Furtificus, a pycker or priuye stealer.
Furtiuus, a, um, that which is done by stelth, or very pryuyly.
Furtum, thefte. it is defyned to be a deceitfull handlynge or vsynge of any thynge, or the possession therof, to haue therby gayne or auauntage, whiche is by the lawe of nature prohibited to be suffred. It is somtime any act that is done priuily, or to the intent it shuld be secrete.
Furti teneri, aut obstringi, to be answerable to felonye.
Furuę hostiæ, sacrifice doone to Pluto and Proserpine.
Furunculus, a litle these, also a beest called a Stote, that killeth rabettis. It is also a sore callid a felon. also a sore callid a cattisheer.
Fuscina,

Fuscina, a speare with many teethe, wherwith fyshers do take troutes, or yeles, by throwynge of it, a troute speare, an yele speare.
Fuscinula, a fleshe hooke.
Fuscus, ca, cum, browne of colour, not fully blacke.
Fusile, that whiche may be molten.
Fusim, abrode, as it were molten.
Fuse, in lengthe, longe.
Fusores, melters.
Fusorius, a, um, pertaynynge to meltynge, As Ars fusoria, the crafte of meltyng. Vas fusorium, a meltynge potte.
Fusus, a, um, molten.
Fusus, si, a spyndell.
Fustigo, are, to beate with a staffe.
Futilis, le, that whiche wyll be soone powred out.
Futilis, he that speketh all that he knoweth shortely or vnaduisedly.

¶G Ante A.

GABALVS, a galowe tree or gybet, whereon men be hanged.
Gabata, a potagedyshe.
Gabinus, a garment with two lappes, wherof the one caste backward, dyd gyrde him that did were it, whych garment the consule ware, whan he denounced warres.
Gades, two yles by the further partes of Spayne, beyonde Granade.
Gætuli, people in Affrike.
Gætulia, a countrey in Affrike.
Gagates, a stone called Jeate.
Galactophagus, an eater of mylke.
Galactopota, a drynker of mylke.
Galatę, people that inhabyte Galatia.
Galbanus, a gumme of a certayn tree, whiche is moche vsed in playsters.
Galbinus, a, um, delycate, wanton.
Galbuli, thynges whiche do hange on cypresse trees, lyke small hearts.
Galea, an helmet or salette.
Galenus, the name of a noble phisition.
Galerita, a larke.
Galerus, & Galerum, a hat. also a pirwike.
Galla, a fruite called Gaulles.
Gallicanus, a, um, of Fraunce.
Gallia, Fraunce.
Gallicia, a royalme in Spayne, callydde Galyce.
Gallicinium, the tyme whanne the Cocke croweth.
Gallicus, ca, cum, frenche.

Gallina, a henne.
Gallinaceus pullus, a chyke.
Gallinaceus, a howse cocke.
Gallinarium, a place where pultry is kept.
Gallinarius, & gallinaria, he or she that kepeth pultrye.
Gallus, a, um, frenche.
Gallo, are, to be madde.
Gallogretia, a countreye in Asia, callyd also Galatia.
Gallus, a cocke, a Frencheman, a prieste of Cybeles, callyd the mother of the goddes.
Gamale, a towne in Judea.
Gammarus, a fyshe callyd a lopstar. *Salustius.*
Ganea, & ganeum, a brothell house, a house of baudry and ryotte. Also Ganea, is taken for gluttonye.
Ganeo, onis, a Ruffyan, a haunter of baudy houses, a ryotter. Also a rauyner of delycates, a frauncher.
Ganges, a greatte ryuer, whiche enuyronneth India, wherin is founde bothe golde and precyous stones.
Gangeticus, ca, cum, of that ryuer.
Gangręna, a sore callyd a cankre.
Ganymedes, a Troyane chylde, whyche was fayned to be rauyshed of Jupyter, and made his butlar.
Gannio, nire, to bark or houle lyke a dogge.
Gannitus, tus, barkynge, or howlynge.
Garamantes, people in Affrike.
Gargânus, a hylle in Apulia.
Gargara, a mountayn, & also a citie in Asia.
Gargarisso, are, to gargaryshe or washe the mouthe and throte of a man.
Garrio, ire, to bable.
Gariophylum, a spyce callyd cloues.
Garrulus, a babblar.
Garum, sawce made with fyshe.
Garumna, a ryuer in Fraunce.
Gaudeo, gauisus sum, gaudere, to reioyce, to be gladde.
Gaudere in sinu, to reioyse by hym selfe.
Gaudium, ioye, myrthe, an affection of the mynde, conceiued of an opinion of a thing good or pleasaunt.
Gaulus, a lyttell rounde bote.
Gausape, a mantell to caste on a bedde: also a carpette to lay on a table, some calle it a daggeswayne.
Gausapina, a certayne garment.
Gaza, the treasure of a kynge.
Gazophilaciū, a place where tresure is kept *Curtius.*

¶G, Ante E.

GEbenna, a hyll and towne in Sauoy, nowe called Geneura.
Gedeon, the name of a iuge in Israel.

Geenna, is taken in holy scripture for hell.
Gela, a ryuer in Sycile.
Gelabilis, le, that maye be frosen.
Gelasco, scere, to be frosen.
Gelasini, the foreteethe, whiche be shewed in laughynge.
Gelasinus, he that laugheth to make other men laughe.
Gelicidium, a froste.
Gelidus, a, um, colde as yse.
Gelo, aui, are, to freese.
Geloi, fyeldes in Sycile.
Geloni, a people nowe callyd Tartariens.
Gelu, yse, sommetyme colde.
Gemellus, lyttell or smalle twynnes.
Gemibundus, full of waylynge.
Geminus, a, um, the noumbre of two. Also geminus, is a twynne, where many chyldren are borne at one burdeyne, althoughe they be thre or mo. Also it is the name of a man, whiche in hebrewe is Thomas.
Gemino, aui, are, to double.
Gemma, the yonge budde of a vyne. Also a precious stone.
Gemmo, aui, are, to budde or sprynge, as a yonge graffe or vyne dothe.
Gemmascere, to begynne to budde.
Gemmatus, a, um, budded.
Gemo, mui, ere, to grone, or to wayle, or to make a lamentable noyse.
Gemoniæ scalæ, a place frome whense the bodyes of persounes condempned were throwen downe.
Gemonide, women great with chylde.
Gemursa, a corne, or lyke griefe vnder the lyttell too.
Gena, the eye lydde. It is sommetyme taken for the chekes.
Genauius, a, um, glouttonous.
Genealogia, a pedegrewe.
Gener, he that maryeth my doughter.
Generalis, le, generall.
Generatim, generally.
Genero, aui, are, to ingender.
Generosus, a, um, of a gentyl or noble kind.
Genesis, generation.
Genethliacus, an astronomer, or other lyke, whiche by the sterres set at a mannes natiuitie, telleth his fortune.
Genialis homo, a manne in his house verye lyberall and freshe.
Geniculatim, ioynted, as a wheate straw is.
Geniculum, the ioynt of a strawe, or stalke of an herbe.
Genista, broome.
Genitalis, le, pertaynyng to the byrthe of a man. genitale solum, the naturall countrey or place, where a manne is borne. genitalis dies, the daye of natiuitie. genitale semen, the sede of generation. genitalia, the membres of generation.
Genimen, generation.
Genitor, a father.
Genitrix, a mother.
Genitura, sometyme generation, sometyme the sede of generation.
Genitiuus, a, um, that hath power to ingender, or that whiche procedeth with generation. genitiuæ notæ, markes, wherewith a man is borne.
Genitus, ta, tum, begotten, ingendred.
Genius, an aungell. Amonge the Paynims some supposed it to be the spirite of a man. Some dydde put two gouernours of the sowle, a good and an euyll, Bonus genius, & malus genius, whyche neuer departed from vs. sometyme it is taken for nature it selfe, or dilectation meued by nature.
Genii, men, whiche do gyue all their studye to eatynge and drynkynge.
Geniæ, olde veckes full of vnhappynes.
Genio dare operam, to lyue voluptuousely.
Genium defraudare, to absteyne from all thynges pleasaunt.
Genocha, a beast lasse than a fox, of colour betwene blacke & yelow, medlid with black spottes, whiche wyll soone be made tame.
Gens, gentis, a people, sometyme a kinred.
Gentiana, an herbe callyd Gencyan.
Gentilis, a kynseman of the same name and stocke. sometyme it signyfyeth a gentyle or paynyme. somtyme a countrey man.
Gentilis, le, propre, or familyar to that people, or kynrede.
Gentilitas, tatis, gentilitie, the multitude of the people or famyly.
Gentilitium nomen, the surname or ancyent name of a mans aunectours.
Gentilitius, a, um, of the people or nation, gentilitia sacra, ceremonyes of that countrey or people.
Genu, a knee.
Genua, a great cite callid Geane.
Genuini, the innermoste cheke teethe.
Genuinus sermo, the natural speche or mother tunge.
Genus, generis, is the begynnynge of euerye thynge, eyther of the persone that ingendred it, or of the place, where it was ingendred. Orestes a Tantalo ducit genus, Orestes hathe begynnynge of Tantalus, or is of the bloudde of Tantalus. Plato genere Atheniensis est, Plato is of his bloudde or auncetrye an Athenyens. Also it sygnifieth kynde. genus uitæ, a kynd of lyfe. genus mortis, a kynd of deth. genus animalium, a kynde of beastes. Also it signifieth that, whiche conteineth many sondry kyndes

kyndes, as Animal comprehendeth a man, a byrde, a fyshe, and euery of them is genus to that, whiche in theym is comprehended. As a brute beast is genus to a horse, a lyon, a bulle, a dogge. &c. A byrde is genus to an egle, a crowe, a larke, a sparowe. &c. A fishe is genus to a whale, a porpese, a haddocke, a playce. &c.

Geographia, the description of the erth.

Geomancia, superstitious warkinge in sorcerye, by cerkles and prickes in the erthe.

Geometer, a geometritian.

Geometria, geometry, measuring and proporcionyng of fygures in the erthe.

Georgica, pertaynynge to husbandry.

Germani, Germaynes, or Almayns, They be also bretherne of one father and oone mother.

Germania, the countrey named Germany, or Almayne.

Germen, minis, a branche of a tree or herbe.

Germino, aui, are, to branche out.

Gero, gessi, gerere, to beare. sometyme it signifieth to haue.

Gerere magistratum, to exercise an offyce.

Gesta, & gestures, actes, thynges practised or doone.

Gerrę siculę, tryfles.

Gerres, fyshe of the kynde of herrynges, it may be called pylchardes.

Gerrones, talkers of tryfelyng thinges, or lyght matters.

Gerulus, a porter, or a man hyred to carye bourdeynes.

Gerula, a mayde that kepeth a chylde.

Gerusia, a place where the Senate dyd assemble, a parlyament house.

Geryon, onis, the name of a king of Spain, whiche was slayne by Hercules.

Gesa, a haulberde.

Gessoriacum, as some men do suppose, was the towne, whiche is now named Caleys.

Gestamen, minis, what soo euer is borne, a burden or caryage.

Gestatorium, that wherin any thyng is caried or borne, a flagon, a horse lytter.

Gestatio, the exercise, where a man is borne or caried on any thinge.

Gesticularius, a, um, pertaynyng to sygnes or tokens of myrthe, with meuyng the body or handes.

Gesticulator, he that playith with puppettꝭ.

Gesticulor, aris, to make suche sygnes or tokens of myrthe, as in daunsynge.

Gestio, iui, ire, to shewe the affections of the mynde by meuyng of the body, or any part therof. somtyme it signifieth to delite.

Gestito, taui, are, to beare or were ofttimes

Gesto, aui, are, to beare longe. Gestat ventrē, she is with chylde.

Gestuosus, full of tokens of myrthe.

Gestus, ta, tum, borne, or done.

Gestus, tus, gesture, or coūtenance with meuynge of the body.

Getuli, a people in Affrike.

¶ G, ante I.

Giarus, a littell ile in the see called Gonium, wher vnto menne condempned were exyled.

Gibber, & gibbosus, ꝯ gibberosus, he which hath a croked backe, or a great bunche on any parte of the body.

Gibbus, & gibba, a great bunche.

Gigantomachia, a battayle of geantes.

Gigas, gigantis, a gyaunt.

Gigno, genui, gignere, to ingender or gette.

Giluus, ua, um, yelowe colour.

Gingeria, uel gigeria, a mete made of sondry kindes of fleshe, or of garbage of foule.

Gingiuæ, the iawes, wherin the teth be set.

Gingiuerim, siue gingiberim, gynger.

Gingrio, gingrii, ire, to cry like a goose.

Gion, a greate ryuer in Egypte, otherwise callyd Nylus.

Girgillus, a rele, wheron threde is wouden

Gith, a sede, whiche is nowe callyd Nigella Romana: it is blacke lyke to onyon sede, and is very soote, and the sauoure thereof exhausteth reumes of the heed.

¶ G ante L.

Glaber, bra, brū, smothe, without hear.

Glabella, the space betwen ye browes.

Glabresco, scere, to be without heer, or smothe.

Glabreta, a place, hauynge nothynge growynge in it.

Glabriones, they which lacke heare.

Glacialis, le, where yse is.

Glacior, aris, ari, to be frosen.

Glacies, yse.

Glacitare, to make a noise like a gander.

Gladiatores, were men, whiche faught vnarmed with swordes.

Gladiatorius, ria, rium, pertainynge to that maner of fyghtynge.

Gladiatura, the arte or feate to fyghte with a sworde.

Gladiolus, a lytel sworde or wodknyfe, also the name of an herbe lyke to sedge.

Gladius, a sword. also a kind of fishe, which hath a bone in his forheed like to a sworde.

Glandario, fedynge of swyne with maste, callyd paunage.

Glandium, glandionica, the parte of a bore next the necke, the shelde or gammonde.

Glans, glādis, mast growing on okes, bech, chestons, and other lyke, it is also a pellette

G ante L.

of leade. Also a kernell growyng betwene the skynne and the fleshe, it is more ouer the foreparte or nutte of a mans yerde.
Glandifer, fera, diferum, that whiche beareth maste.
Glaphirus, a, um, iocunde, plesant, ingraued, polyte, holow, famous, subtyll.
Glarea, sande, proprely sandy grauel.
Glareosus, a, um, sandy.

Cæsar. Glastum, an herbe lyke to plantayne, whiche maketh a blewe colour, wherwith the auncient Britons dyed their vysages. some men englyshe it woadde.
Glaucinum, oyle, whiche dothe come from the olyues before they be pressed.
Glauciolus, a horse with a wall eye.
Glaucium, an herbe, which crepeth on the erthe nygh to salt waters.
Glaucoma, matis, & glaucomatum, ti, & glaucoma, mę, an humour in the eien, lyke cristall, whiche letteth the syght.
Glaucopis, pidis, a man or womanne with graye eyes.
Glaucus, ca, cum, gray colour.
Glaucus substantiuum, a god of the see. also many men were called by that name. also the name of a fyshe.
Gleba, a turfe or piece of erthe.
Glessum, crystall, or beryll.
Glycyrrhiza, lykoresse.
Glis, iris, a fielde mous, whiche slepeth all the wynter.
Glis, glissis, potters claye.
Glis, glitis, a thystell.
Glisco, sci, scere, to growe, to waxe fatte, to couette or desyre feruently.
Globo, aui, are, to gather rounde.
Globus, & globum, a boule, or other thing very rounde. Also a multitude of menne or beastes gathered rounde togither.
Globosus, a, um, rounde as a boule.
Glocido, aui, are, to cackle as a henne doth.
Glocio, cire, idem.
Glomero, aui, are, to wynde in rounde. also to gather togither in an heape.

Quint. Gloria, the consent of good men in the praise of a man or woman, callid renome, glory.
Glorior, aris, to auaunt, to thintent to haue praises, to extolle with bostynge.
Gloriosus, a, um, renomed, somtyme in the yll part, vaynglorious, or bosting hym selfe.
Glos, gloris, the systers husbande, or brothers wyfe.
Glossa, a glose, or exposition of dark spech.
Glossemata, wordes not moche vsed.
Glossematicus, he that maketh a commente on a boke.
Glubo, bi, bere, to pulle of the barke or rynde of a tree.

G ante N.

Gluma, the huske of wheate.
Gluo, glui, ere, to streyne or wringe harde.
Gluten, & glutinum, glewe.
Glutinamentum, al glewyshe matter.
Glutino, aui, are, to glewe or ioyne.
Glutio, tiui, tire, to swalowe.
Gluto, tonis, a glutton.
Glyciamerides, a kynde of meate.

¶ G, ante N.

Gnasalon, a certayne floxe.
Gnarus, a, um, skylfull.
Gnare, skylfully.
Gnaritas, tatis, skylfulnes.
Gnomones, the teethe, wherby the age of an horse is knowen. They be sommetyme taken for that, whiche sheweth the houres in a clocke or diall.

¶ G, ante O.

Gobius, a fyshe, callyd a gogeon.
Goetia, a spice of wytchecrafte.
Gomor, a measure among the iewes.
Gomorrha & gomorrhum, a citie in Judea whyche was consumed for horryble synne agaynst nature.
Gonorrha, a disease, wherby a mans seede gothe from hym vnwyttyngly.
Gorgia, the name of a great rhetorician.
Gorgones, monstruous womenne, whyche were vanquyshed by Perseus.
Gortys, a citie of Candy.
Gossampinus, a tree, which beareth cotten.
Gossipium, cotten.

¶ G, ante R.

Grabatus, a cowche.
Graculus, a byrde callyd a Jaye.
Graculo cum fidibus nihil, The Jaye hath nought to do with the harpe. whyche is spoken of theym, whyche lackynge eloquence or good letters, doo scorne theym that haue it.
Gracus, & graculus, a chough or cadese.
Gracchus, the name of a noble famylye or house in Rome.
Gracilis, le, gracilentus, ta, tū, leane, or slender, sometyme softe.
Gracile, sclenderly.
Gracilitas, cilitatis, leannesse, sclendernes, or softenesse.
Gradus, a greese or steppe, a degree in consanguinitie.
De gradu deiici, to be caste downe from his place: wherby is sygnifyed to be abasshed or moued from constancy of mynde.

De-

Deturbari gradu, hath the same significatiō.
Gradior, to go by steppes, or steppe.
Gradator, a great goer.
Gradarii equi, amblynge horses.
Gradatio, a fourme of speakynge, whan of the fyrst sentence sprin geth the seconde, of the seconde the thyrde, and so forthe.
Gradatim, in order, or by course.
Gradiuus, one of the names of Mars.
Gradior, eris, gressus sum, to go.
Grecus, a man borne in Grece, a Greeke.
Grecus, a, um, of Grece.
Grecia, Grece.
Grecanicus, ca, cum, come out of Grece.
Grecostasis, a place where Ambassadours abode, vntylle they were sente for into the Senate.
Graiugenę, Grekes.
Grecor, caris, ari, to ryotte in bankettynge and rybaudrye.
Gralę, crouches, or styltes.
Grallatores, they whiche do go on styltes.
Grammatica, grammer.
Grammaticus, he that teacheth grammer, or expoundeth authours, a profounde grammaryan.
Grammatista, a smatterer in grammer, a meane grammarian.
Grāmaticus, ca, cū, pertaynynge to grāmer.
Grammatice loqui, to speake congruely.
Grammatocyphon, he that wrytethe on his knee.
Grammatophylatium, the place where the recordes, or commune writinges be kepte.
Grammateus, a chauncellour.
Gramme, a length without breadth.
Grammia, the fleume in the eyen.
Gramen, grasse: sometyme all herbes togyther, the swarthe.
Graminosus, a, um, growen with grasse or herbes.
Grando, dinis, hayle. Also a pushe lyke to a boyle in the fleshe, whiche greueth a man whan it is touched.
Grandinosus, a, um, full of hayle.
Grandinatus, ta, tum, hurt or wounded with haylle.
Grandebalę, heares in the arme holes.
Grandis, grande, auncient, or great.
Grandiusculus, la, lum, somwhat great, or of good age, well stryken in yeres.
Granditas, tatis, the aboundaunce of lyeres, aunctentie.
Grandeuus, very olde.
Grandiloquus, eloquente, he that speaketh as it were with a greatte magnyfycence in wordes.
Grandiloquentia, stately eloquence.
Grandio, diui, ire, to make great.

Grandesco, ere, to waxe great.
Granum, grayne or corne.
Granarium, a graynarde, wherein corne is kepte.
Graphis, phidis, the arte of portraiture.
Graphium, a pensyll, wherwith menne doo write in tables.
Graphicus, ca, cum, kunnyngly, or perfectly wrought.
Graphicus homo, a propre man.
Graphice, proprely well, and kunnyngly.
Graphiarium, a case, wherin pensiles were kepte, it may be called a pennar.
Grassator, he that by highe wayes, lyeth in awayt to robbe or slee men, an extorcioner.
Grassor, aris, ari, to robbe or slee men passynge by the hyghe wayes. Also to goo or come on one with a violent rage. Therfore in a sodayn and violent pestilence, it is said, morbus grassatur, The sycknes kylleth me sodaynely.
Gratia, grace, somtyme it significth thanke, sometyme a benefyte, sometyme rewarde: also peace or loue, sometyme cause or respect, also prayse.
Gratus, ta, tum, thankfull, pleasant, acceptable.
Gratiosus, very thankfull. Also in fauour, with the people, or well estemed.
Gratis, an aduerbe, betokenynge withoute rewarde: sometyme without deserte.
Gratuitus, ta, tum, without rewarde or vnhyred.
Gratuito, an aduerbe sygnifienge, of good wyll, without benefite.
Grates, thankes.
Gratificor, ari, to gratifie, or doo a thynge thankfull, or to conferre a benefite, or doo a good tourne.
Grator, ari, to giue thankes to god with offrynges, also to reioyce of good fortune.
Gratulor, ari, with a datiue case, to be ioyous for hym selfe or an other for any good thynge that hath hapned. Tibi de hac tua foelicitate gratulor, I am ioyous with the, or as gladde as thou arte, of this prosperitie that thou arte in. Sometyme it sygnifyeth to gyue thankes vnto god: but with an accusatiue case it signifieth to take thankfully any acte. *Liuius.*
Grauis, graue, heuy, greuouse, sommetyme substancial, graue, or hauyng grauitie, contrary to lyghtnes or wantonnes, also great or puissant, sometime olde or aged, somtime sure or constant, sommetyme plentuous or full. Terra grauis, lande laded with corne.
Grauiter, et graue, greuousely, heuily, substancially, moche, wisely, sadly.
Grauatus, greued.

Graue-

Grauedo, dinis, heuynesse, griefe, disease. Somtyme the murre or reume of the heed.
Grauedinosus, he that hath a heuye heed.
Grauedinosus, a, um, that whiche maketh a heuy heed.
Graueolentia, stenche or stynke.
Grauo, aui, are, to greue, to burden, or lade.
Grauor, ari, to be grieued, or to take grieuouslye.
Grauate, & grauatim, greuously, or displesantly, or paynfully.
Grauesco, scere, to be laded.
Grauida mulier, a woman great with child.
Grauido, are, to gette a woman with chyld.
Grauastellus, aged.
Grex, gregis, a flocke, as well of menne, as of cattelle.
Gregarius miles, a souldiour taken at aduenture, not chosen.
Gregarius pastor, the chiefe shepard, whiche hath the charge of the hole flocke.
Gregarius canis, a curre dogge.
Gregalis, le, cattell, whiche is in the flocke.
Gregatim, in sondry flockes.
Gremiale, an apron.
Gressus, a steppe, or goinge.
Gressibile, apte to goo.
Gressutus, ta, tum, idem.
Grossus, a, um, greatte.
Grossi, greene fygges.
Grossuli, yonge fygges.
Grossipion, seu grossapinus, a tree, wherof commeth cotton.
Grossapina, cotton.
Grus, gruis, a Crane.
Gruo, gruere, to crye lyke a Crane.
Grumus, a barowe, or hyllocke.
Grumma, a thynge, wherwith grounde is measured.
Grumia, a mydde place, from whense goth foure wayes.
Grunnio, ire, to grunt lyke a swyne.
Grundio, idem.
Gryllus, a beaste, more than a grasshoppe, whiche destroyeth corne.
Gryphus, a grype or gryffon. also a captious, an insoluble, or diffuse argumente, a ryddyll.
Grypus, a nose rysynge in the myddell.

G, ante V.

Gula, the throte, sometyme glottony.
Gulosus, a glutton.
Gulioce, the grene shale of the walle nutte.
Gummi, gume, whiche droppeth frō trees.
Gummatus, ta, tum, dressed with gumme or rased.
Gummate arbores, Trees that bryngethe forthe gumme.
Gumminum, oyle made of gumme.
Gurges, gurgitis, a swallowe or depe pyll in a water, or a goulfe.
Gurgito, aui, are, to swolowe or deuoure.
Gurgulio, gulionis, the gully or gargylle of the throote, or throote bolle. It is also a worme that bredeth in barnes, and eateth vppe corne.
Gurgustium, a darke and vyle habitation, a cabban or cotage.
Gustus, tus, taste.
Gustatus, tus, idem.
Gusto, aui, are, to taste.
Guttus, a cruet, or other lyke thynge, oute of the whiche lycour is poured dropping.
Gutta, a droppe.
Guttatim, by droppes.
Gutturnium, a lauer, or yewer.
Guttur, gutturis, the throte.
Gutturosus, he that hath a swollen throte.

¶G, ante Y.

Gygeus, a laake of Lydie.
Gygemorus, a lyttell hylle, not farre from Thessalye.
Gyges, the name of a kynge of Lydia, also a ryuer of Lydia was callydde by the same name.
Gymnastes, he that teacheth chylderne to exercyse them in wrastlynge, or other like.
Gymnasium, a place, where is commune exercyse of the bodye. Sommetyme a schoolehouse.
Gymnasticum, the arte of exercyse.
Gymnasiarches, the chiefe mayster of the schole or place of exercyse.
Gymnosophiste, phylosophers of Inde, whiche went alway naked.
Gymnici ludi, playes exercysed naked.
Gymnus, a beaste, whyche commethe of a horse and an asse mare.
Gynœcium, a nourcerye.
Gyneconitis, that parte of the house, whyche serueth onely for women.
Gynephilus, a great louer of women.
Gypsus, playster.
Gypso, aui, are, to playster.
Gyrus, a cyrcute or compasse.
Gyro, gyraui, gyrare, to compasse or goo in cyrcuite.
Gyttheum, a towne, whiche Hercules and Apollo, layenge there asyde theyr stryfe and debate, buylded togyther, and the inhabytauntes of the same towne are called Gytthetes.

H ante

HABEO, HABVI, HAbere, to haue, to hold, to possede or occupie, to esteeme or suppose, to call, to dwelle. Pensi habere, to take hede. Frustra habere, to deceyue. Habere bene seu male, to doo or prosper well or yll. Bene habet, it is wel. Res ita se habet, the thinge is at this point. In custodiis haberi, to be kepte in pryfone. Fortunas suas uenales habuit, he hath solde all his goodes. Habeo tibi fidem, I put my truste in the. Habeo rationem, I haue busynes, or I haue to do. Habere rem, to medle with a woman. Habere rem cum aduersario, to contend. Habere gratiam, to thanke. Habeo audire, I can here. Habeo polliceri, I canne promyse. Habet frustra, he is dysappoynted.

Habitus, habitus, the fourme or state of the body, sometyme of other thynges, Also apparayle. Also it sygnyfyethe a qualytie or proprietie, whiche a manne hath conceiued by education, longe exercyse, or custome, habyte.

Habitudo, dinis, the same.
Habitior, oris, more corporate.
Habilis, le, hable.
Habena, the rayne of a brydell.
Habito, taui, are, to dwelle.
Habitaculum & habitatio, a dwellyng place or habitation.
Hactenus, hytherto, so moche.
Hadrianopolis, a citie in Thracia.
Hadrobalum, a kynde of swete smellynge gumme, that groweth in Media.

¶ H, ante Ae.

Haedui, people in Fraunce, whiche be nowe callid Burgonyons, and Burbonoyses.
Hedus, a kydde.
Hedina caro, kyddes fleshe.
Hedile, a stable, wherin kyddes be kepte.
Hedera, Iuye tree.
Hederatius, ia, ium, of Iuye.
Hematices, the sanguinarie or blode stone.
Hemonia, the countrey callid Thessaly.
Hemorrhois, a disease in the fundemēt lyke teates or wartes, out of the whiche issueth bloudde, callyd emorrodes or pyles. Also a serpent, of whom if a man be stryken, he bledeth to dethe.
Hereo, hesi, herere, to cleaue or stycke to a thynge. sometyme to doubte.
Heret in te omnis culpa, In the is putte all the blame.

Heresco, scere, to sticke fast, or be thrusty in.
Hesito, aui, are, idem quod hereo.
Haeres, heredis, an heyre, or he, which succedeth an other in his landes or goodes.
Hereditas, tatis, inheritance or succession.
Hereditarius, ia, ium, pertaynynge to inheritance. Bona hæreditaria, goodes whiche do come by inheritaunce.
Heredipeta, crauers of goodes, flatteryng men to be their heires.
Heredium, lande, wherin a man hath a state of inheritaunce.
Heredidum, a lyttel inheritance.
Hæresis, heresios, a secte, an heresy, an obstynate opynion.
Hæresiarches, an arche heretike.
Hæreticus, an heretike.
Hagnus, a lambe.
Hagnellus, a lyttell lambe.
Hagninus, a, um, of a lambe.
Halec, lecis, a fysshe callyd herryng. Also a sawce made of fysshe.
Halesius, a ryuer nat farre from Aetna.
Halialmon, a ryuer of Macidon.
Halietus, an Egle, that haunteth aboute the see.
Halieutica, bokes contayninge the properties of fysshes.
Halimon, a thorne lyke to a whyte thorne, growynge by the see syde, and hath leaues lyke to an olyue tree, but they be broder.
Halo, aui, are, to sende forthe sauour.
Halitus, breathe or vapour.
Halo, the cirkle or garlande aboute the Moone.
Halicarnasus, a citie in the lasse Asia.
Halophanta, a great lyer.
Halosis, the captiuitie.
Halito, aui, are, to vapour out.
Halizones, people of Paphlagonie, so called bycause they ar inuironned about with the See.
Hallucinor, ari, to be in a dreame, to be deceyued, to erre, or to take a matter wrong.
Hamadriades, Nymphes or fayries of the woddes.
Hamus, a hooke. sometyme a chayne.
Hamo, aui, are, to crooke.
Hamatus, mata, tum, to be furnysshed with hookes.
Hamiota, uel hamota, an angler or fysshcr with an angle or hoke.
Hamatilis, le, pertaynynge to a hoke. piscatus hamatilis, fysshynge with a hooke, or anglynge.
Hamonus, a, um, a colour somwhat redde.
Haphe, a colour on the body, lyke to them that be leperous.
Hammon, onis, Iupiter in the egiptian tūge

Hare

Harena, uide ante in arena.
Hariolus, a sothesayer.
Harmonia, harmonie or melody.
Harpasa, a towne of Asia.
Harpe, a sworde lyke to a sythe.
Harpago, aui, are, to take by violence.
Harpago, ginis, a grapull of a shyppe. also a coupers instrument, wherwith he dryueth on howpes, an addysse.
Harpa, & harpax, acis, a grapelyng yron, for to close shyppes togyther: also a poll with a hoke on the ende, that shypmen vse.
Harpocrates, the god of sylence.
Harpocratem reddere, to put one to silence.
Harpalice, a womans name, the doughter of Harpalus kynge of Thrace.
Harpyie, monstruous byrdes, hauyng maydens vysages, and talons of a meruaylous rapacitie. wherfore men that be rauenous, and great gatherers of goodes, be named sometyme Harpyie.
Haruspex, spicis, a dyuynatour, or tellar of thynges to come by the lokynge in the bowelles of beastes. Also he, whiche obserneth tymes in doinge of thynges.
Haruspicina, the arte of hym, whyche is a dyuinatour.
Haruspicium, the diuynation or tellynge of thynges to comme, by the lokynge in beastis bowelles.
Haspis, pidis, the bowyng made lyke a cerkle in roufes of houses, or of a whele.
Hasta, a speare.
Hastæ puræ, were without yron: and in the olde tyme were gyuen for a price to theym that vanquished firste in battayle.
Hastati, speare men.
Hastile, a speare staffe.
Hastarium, sellynge vnder the standerde.
Hastam abiicere, sygnifieth to leaue sute, to dispayre of the matter in variance.
Hasticus ludus, rounnynge at the tylte with speares.
Haud, in no wyse.

Vergilius. Haurio, siui, iui, rii, ire, to drawe or take out, to here, to see, to take a thyng gredylye, to wounde, to fatigate or make wery, to make empty, to consume. Haurire supplicia, to suffre punyshement or peynes
Haustus, tus, a draught in drynkynge.
Haustum facere, to drynke.
Haustrum, a bucket to drawe water.

¶ H, Ante E.

Heautontimorumenon, the name of one of the comedyes of Terentius, whiche is as moche to saye, as tourmentynge hym selfe.

Hebdomas, madis, & hebdomada, e, a wike. Also the numbre of seuen in dayes, yeres, or other tyme.
Hebenus, a tree, wherof the wod is blacke lyke geate, and it beareth neyther leaues, nor fruite.
Hebes, hebetis, dulle.
Hebeo, & hebesco, ere, to be dull.
Hebeto, aui, are, to be duske or made darke.
Hebetudo, dinis, dulnesse, or duskyshenes.
Hebiones, of men in olde tyme were callid poore folkes.
Hebraicus, Hebrician or of Hebrewe.
Hebron, a vyllage by Jerusalem.
Hebrus, a ryuer in Thracia.
Hecameda, the daughter of Arsinoi, whiche was gyuen to Nestor for a gyfte.
Hecatombe, a sacrifice, wherein were kylled a hundred beastes.
Hecatompolis, a countrey hauyng an hundred cities therin.
Hecatompus, he that hath an hundred fete.
Hecate, a name of the mone.
Hecta, the yerynge of a man. also a lyttelle puffe, whiche riseth in breadde whanne it is baken.
Hectica febris, the feuer that consumeth.
Hector, the sonne of Priamus.
Hecyra, a mother in lawe.
Hedonius, expenses in voluptuous thingis.
Heiulo, aui, are, to wayle, crienge out.
Heliocaminus, a place whiche is hette with the sonne.
Helcium, the harneys of carthorses, wherby they drawe.
Helenium, an herbe commonly called Enula campana, in englyshe Helycampane.
Heliopolis, a cytie in Grecia called also Corinthus.
Heliochrisos, an herbe hauynge a yclowe floure, A marygolde.
Helioscopium, a lyttell tree lyke to a fygge tree, and hath leaues lyke a plane, but greatter and blacker.
Helioselinum, an herbe lyke to Smallage, whyche groweth in watery groundes, and hath but one leafe.
Heliotropium, a flowre whiche in the sonne rysynge dothe open, and at the sonne sette closeth. Some supposeth it to be Marygoldes or ruddes.
Helix, icis, of some men is taken for a kynde of wyllowe tree, of some men for yuie.
Hellas, ladis, the countrey of Grece.
Helleborus, an herbe, the rote wherof purgeth melancoly.
Hellenes, the sonne of Deucalion, of whom the Grekes were named Hellenes.
Hellespontus, an arme of the see, whyche ocur-

deuideth Grece and Asie.
Heloi, in hebrewe signifieth god almighty.
Helorus, a ryuer in Sycile.
Heluatia, a garment which was vsed in Lidia, and was of the color of a cowes hyde.
Heluela, small wortes.
Heluetii, people called Suycers, or Suyches, by desyre of warres, ennemyes to all mankynd: subiectes neither to god nor to Prynce.
Heluo, onis, he whiche in catyng and drinkyng spendeth al his substance, a reueller. somtyme a glutton onely.
Heluo libroru, an insaciable reder of bokes.
Heluatio, reuell, or spendynge in ryot.
Heluor, aris, ari, to spende in ryot.
Heluolum, a colour betwene redde & white lyke the coloure of clothe, called frenche tawnye.
Helxine, an herbe, which hath stalkes som what redde, and smal burres on the toppe, whiche do cleaue faste vnto clothes.
Hem, an interiection of blamynge, disdaynynge, meruaylynge, or shewynge.
Hemeridion, whiche dureth but one day.
Hemerodromus, a currour, which runneth many myles in one day.
Hemicranea, a peyne in halfe the heed, callyd the mygrim.
Hemicyclum, a compasse chayre.
Hemicyclus, an halfe cerkle.
Hemina, a measure of licour or corne, whiche may nowe be taken for a pottell.
Hemiola, gayne of all, and halfe as moche, as if of .iiii.s. be goten .vi.s.
Hemiolus, a proportion in Arithmetike, contaynynge the hole noumbre, and halfe that nombre: as one to thre .xv to ten.
Hemiomu, an herbe good agaynst all yexis.
Hemis, halfe.
Hemispherium, half the compasse of the visyble heuen or firmament.
Hemistichium, halfe a verse.
Hemitogium, halfe a gowne.
Hemitritæus, an halfe tercian feuer, whose course is in euery .xxxvi. houres, or whych hath the course of a tercyan.
Hemodes, certayne iles in the douche see.
Hemerobius, one dayes sustynaunce. also a worme, whiche lyueth but one day.
Hemichorium, halfe a daunce.
Hemus, a mountayne in Grece in the realm of Thrace, which is syxe myles in height.
Hendecasyllabus, a verse of a .xi. syllables.
Henula, a lyttell chappell.
Hepiolus, a flye lyke a butterflye, whyche flyeth at nyght into the leame of a candell.
Hepsema, muste boiled to the thyrd part.
Heptapolis, was sommetyme the name of Egypte, by reason of seuen cities, whyche fyrste were in it.
Hepthemimeris, where a syllable naturally short, is made longe in a verse, which doth happe in the begynnynge of the fyrst fote.
Hera, the name of Juno.
Heraclea, a town in the cofines of Europa.
Heraclee, a towne very nere to Naples.
Heracleon, an herbe lyke to Organum, it groweth in watry places, and hath a floure lyke a lyllye: and whan the floure is fallen, it hath a heed lyke popie. It is also another herbe growynge in plasshes, hauynge a lyttell stalke, whiche excedeth not foure fyngers hygh, hauynge a redde floure, and leaues lyke Coriander: this herbe healeth all woundes, if it be layde vnto them. It is called Heraclion syderion.
Heracleotica nux, a walle nutte.
Heraclides, the name of a philosopher.
Heraclitus, a philosopher, whiche alwayes wepte, whan he behelde the people: his warkes of a purpose were obscure & harde to be vnderstande.
Heraclius, the name of an Emperour, it is also a touche stone.
Herba, an herbe. Also generally all thynge that groweth on the erthe, not being wod. somtyme a wede.
Herbam dare aut porrigere, where a manne yeldeth hym, or confesseth hym selfe to be vanquyshed.
Herbula, a lyttell herbe.
Herbosus, a, um, full of herbes or grasse.
Herbaceus, a, um, of herbes or grasse.
Herbidus, a, um, idem.
Herbarius, he whiche knoweth the propreties of herbes, and maketh medycynes of therm.
Herbarius, ia, ium, pertaynynge to herbes.
Herbare, to brynge forthe herbes.
Herbesco, ere, to make herbes or wedes.
Herceus, one of the surnames of Jupiter.
Hercinia, a great wodde in Germany, whiche is in breadth .ix. dayes iourney.
Herculanus, na, num, of Hercules.
Hercules, the sonne of Jupiter & Alcumena.
Hercle & Hercule, an affirmatiue othe.
Herculeius, a Romayne, whiche fauoured the parte of Marius.
Herculeus, ea, eum, puissant or mighty.
Herebus, the depest place in hell.
Heri, yesterday.
Hericius, an yrchin or hedgehogge.
Herillus, a philosopher of Calcidonie.
Herma, an ymage of Mercurius. It is also an image, the heed wherof may be chagid.
Hermæ, be also Jmages sette or layde on Sepulchres.

Her-

Hermathena, an ymage contaynyng the figures of Mercury and Pallas.
Hermaphroditus, the sonne of Mercurye & Venus. Also he that is both man & woman.
Hermerotes, small images, propzely of lytell chyldren with whynges.
Hermes, is, & hermetis, Mercurye.
Hermodocus, a philosopher of Ephesie.
Hermogenes, a propre name.
Hermoglyphus, a grauer of ymages.
Hermon, a lyttelle hylle that standethe on Jordane.
Hermopolis, the name of a citie that Hermes buylded.
Hermupoa, an herbe callyd Mercury.
Hermus, a ryuer, which in the middes, parteth the fyldes of Smyrnee: and fallynge from the hylle Dozylao, dyuideth Phrigia from Caria.
Hernia, the disease, wherof men be called brosten: for that their bowels, or other matter, is fallen into their coddes.
Hernici, people in Campania.
Herniosus, he that is brosten.
Herodius, a byrde named a faucon.
Herodes, the sonne of Antipater, whyche in the.r.yere of Augustus, was of the Romaynes declared kynge of Jewes, and he reigned.xxxvii.yeres.
Heroida, a noble woman.
Heroicus, ca, cum, noble, or pertaynynge to noblenesse.
Herpeta, a tetter.
Hersilia, the name of Romulus wyfe.
Herus, a lorde or master.
Hesperia, Italy. Hesperia ultima, Spayne.
Hesperus, the weste sterre.
Hesperides, the thre daughters of Atlas, whiche kepte the gardens, wherin grewe the golden appuls, that were taken awaye by Hercules.
Hesperidum horti, the gardeynes, wherein were the golden appulles, nowe callyd Orenges.
Hesternus,na,num, of yesterdayes.
Hestica, is a parte of Thessaly sayth Strabo, and Ptol. and in Homerus, it is a town in Euboea. Stephanus sayth, it is a Cytie in Acarnania.
Heterogenus,na,um, of an other kynde.
Hetruria, the countrey of Thuscan wherin the citie of Florence is.
Heu, alas.
Heus, howe.
Hexaclinum, a parlour, wherein syxe persones may soupe.
Hexagonum, syxe cornerde.
Hexameron, of syxe dayes.
Hexametrum, a verse of syxe fete.

¶H ante I.
Hiarbas, the sonne of Jupiter, whiche was kynge of the Getulians.
Hiacynthus, an herbe with a pourple floure, and hath a rounde roote.
Hiacynthine uestes, garmentes of pourple colour.
Hiato, aui, are, to gape often.
Hiatus, tus, a gapynge.
Hibiscus, an herbe lyke to malowes, hauing a gretter lefe, and a heary stalke, holyhok.
Hic, this man. also here or in this place.
Hiera, an yle betwene Sicile and Liparis. Also the name of a way, of a womanne, the wyfe of Thelaphus kynge of Misic.
Hicranthemis, the floure of the herbe Camamele.
Hierapicra, a medycyne to pourge flewme and cholere.
Herapolis, a citie in Asia.
Hierarchia, the holy gouernaunce, or principalytie.
Hieri, people beyonde Sauromatas.
Hierobotane, an herbe callyd holy herbe.
Hieroceps, an yle in Cyprus, nere to Paphᵒ.
Hierocomion, a laserhouse.
Hieroduli, ministers in temples & churches.
Hierogliplice, mystical letters or cyphers.
Hieron, uel hiereon, a chappell.
Hierophanta, the declarer of mysteries or holy scripture.
Hierosolyma, Jerusalem.
Hierotheus, the propre name of a man.
Hila, a small gutte or ars gutte.
Hilaresco, scere, to be mery.
Hilaria plurali, the.viii.calendes of Aprile, whan the day & nyght haue equall houres.
Hilaris,re, & hilarus, mery, or ioyous.
Hilaritas, tatis, myrthe.
Hilarius, the propre name of a man.
Hilaro, aui, are, to make one mery or ioyous.
Hilarodus, a synger of a wanton and delycate songe.
Hilum, the lyttell blacke, whyche is in the ende of a beane. It is sometyme taken for nothynge or nought.
Himera, a ryuer in Sycile, deuided into two partes, the oone freshe water, the other salte.
Hin, a measure of the Jewes, whiche contayned of wyne or water, the weyghte of xviii.pounde.
Hinnio, iui, ire, to neygh lyke a hors.
Hinnulus, a fawne or hynde calfe.
Hio, aui, are, to gape.
Hippacen, chese made of mares mylke.
Hippaco, aui, are, to fetche breth quyckely.
Hippagium, cariage on horsebacke.
Hippago, ginis, a ferybote.

Hippar

Hipparchus, the maister of the horses.
Hippeas, a kynde of crabbefyshe.
Hippiades, ymages of womenne on horsebacke.
Hippias, a philosopher, whiche was expert in all sciences and craftes.
Hippiatrus, an horse leche.
Hippo, mascul. gen. the name of .ii. cities.
Hippocampi, fyshes lyke horses.
Hippocentaurus, a beaste beynge halfe a man, halfe an horse.
Hippocomus, an horseskorcer.
Hippocrates, the name of a phisytion moste excellente.
Hippocrene, a fountayne in Bœotia.
Hippodame, mes, & hippodamia, miæ, the name of a woman.
Hippodamus, a breaker of horses.
Hippodromus, a brode way, wherin many horses may runne togither.
Hippoglotios, an herbe called Alexander.
Hyppolytus, the sonne of Theseus, who at the complaynte of Phedra his stepmother, was pursewed by his father, and he in a charyot fleynge, was outerthrowen amonge the sharpe stones, and rente all to pieces. Afterwarde Aesculapius reuyued hym, and restored hym to helthe. wherefore he wolde be called Virbius, that is to saye, twyse a manne, forasmoche as he had twise lyued.
Hippomachia, tournayenge on horsebacke and iustynge.
Hippomanes, an herbe, wherof yf horses done eate, they forthewith rounne madde. It is also a venomous humour, rounnynge out of the shappe of a mare, whiche yf a man happe to receyue inwarde, he shall be madde. Plinius saythe, that it is a lyttelle fleshe in the forheed of a colte, whan he is newe foled, blacke, and as moche as a date, whiche the mare plucketh awaye with hyr tethe, as soone as she hath foled: and if any man do take it away before her, she neuer after wyll loue hir fole.
Hippomarathron, an herbe lyke fenell, but hauynge greatter leaues.
Hipponomus, a herde or keper of horses.
Hippopera, a maale or bougette.
Hippopodes, people in the Scythik occean whiche haue fete lyke horses.
Hippopotamus, a beast lyuyng in the ryuer of Nyle, hauyng fete lyke an oxe, his back and mane lyke a hors, & neyeth like a hors, a wyndyng tayle, and tusked lyke a boore.
Hipposelinum, an herbe lyke parcely, and groweth in drye groundes, whereof horses do gladly eate.
Hippotela, a fole of an asse.

Hippotoxata, an archer on horsebacke.
Hippuris, an herbe called in latine Equisetū, or cauda equina, in englyshe, horsetayle.
Hir, Hiris, the palme of the hande.
Hira, the gutte, which e is called Ieiunum.
Hircipilus, a man that is hearie.
Hircosus, a, um, that stynketh lyke a gote.
Hirquitalus, a chylde, whiche passethe the age of .xiiii. yeres, and begynneth to be styrred with lecherye.
Hirquitallire, to enter into that age, or aptnes to lecherye.
Hircquus, the corner of the eie. also he that is gogle eyed.
Hirculus, a kynde of spikenarde.
Hircus, a gote bucke. it is also the ranke sauour, which issueth out of the arme holes.
Hircinus, a, um, gotyshe.
Hirrio, iui, ire, to narre lyke a madde dogge.
Hirsutus, ta, tum, rough.
Hirtus, ta, tum, idem.
Hirudo, inis, a horseleche, or blode sucker.
Hirundo, inis, a swalowe.
Hisciacus, he that gapeth moche.
Hisco, sci, scere, to gape as one doth for slugishenes, after slepe, or for lacke of slepe. Also it is to proffre to speake, or open the mouthe to speake.
Hismaëlita, a sarasyn.
Hispalis, a citie in Spayne, nowe callydde Sibyle.
Hispania, a countreye in the weste parte of Europa callyd Spayne, and was sometyme callid Iberia, and Hesperia, & is inuyronned on the southe part with the see, callid Mare mediterraneum, whiche dyuydeth Europa from Affrica: on the northe parte with the see called Mare Cantabricum, on the weste with the great occian see with the mountaynes called Pyrenei, and the royalme of Fraunce. And this countrey is diuided by Ptholome into thre regiōs, Bethica, wherin is Granado, Siuyle, Corduba. &c. Lusytania, wherin is Portugal, Galicia. &c. Tarraconensem, wherin is Castyl, Lyons, and Arragon. At this tyme it conteyneth fyue relmes, Granado on the south part toward Affrike, Portugall on the west, Galicia and Biscay on the north, Arragon on the easte part, Castyl and Lions in the myddell.
Hispidus, a, um, bristled or rough heared.
Historia, a storye.
Historicus, a writer of stories.
Histrio, onis, a player in enterludes and stage players.
Histrionicus, ca, cum, pertaining to players.
Histrix, icis, a beaste hauyng sharpe prickes on his backe, called a porkpine.
Hiulco, aui, are, to make to gape or chinke.

Hiulcus, ca, cum, gapynge, or chynked, as the grounde is in a great drythe.

¶ H Ante O.

Hoc, this or that.
Hodie, to daye.
Hododocus, a robber by the hyghe waye.
Hodœporicum, a boke to carie in iourney, whiche may be called a iournall.
Hodœporus, a trauayler by the waye.
Holocaustum, proprely the beaste, whiche hauynge his bewelles taken out, is layde hole on the aulter and bourned.
Holographum, a testament all writen with the hande of the testatour.
Holor, oris, a swanne.
Holoserica uestis, a garment all of sylke.
Holus, alias Homolus, a hylle of Thessaly.
Homeromastix, ticis, the reprocher of Homere, generally Homeromastices, be taken for all reprochers, and false correctours of lerned menne.
Homerus, the poete of all other moste famous and excellent, who wrate the battaile betwene the Grekes and Troyanes wonderfull eloquently: but howe truely, wyse men may coniect. Also he wrote the trauayle of the prudent Ulysses. Finally both workes are worthy to be radde, for the meruailous inuention, and profytable sentences in them contayned.
Homicida, a murderer, a mankyller.
Homicidium, mourder, or manslaughter.
Homilia, a Sermone.
Homo, a lyuynge creature, hauynge capacitie of reason, subiecte to death, a manne, woman, or chylde.
Homocapnus, a man, whiche sitteth alway in the smoke, or by the fyre.
Homœosis, a simylitude.
Homogalactos, a foster brother.
Homogenes, of one kynde.
Homoglossus, of the same tonge or language.
Homoleum, a cappe of the olde facion.
Homologia, a confession, consent or couenant
Homomeria, lykenes in partis or membres
Homonœa, the propre name of a woman, wherby is signified concorde.
Homonymon, of like name.
Homo triū literarū, signified somtime in mokage a man of a noble linage, bicause noble men wrate their forenames, their names & surnames with thre letters, as. P. Cor. Scipio, C. I. Cæs. It is sommetyme taken for a thefe, bycause in Fur are but thre letters. [Erasm⁹ in Chiliad.]
Homousios, of lyke substaunce.
Homosipyi, they whyche sleepe together vnder one ruffe.
Honestas, tatis, honestie.
Honesto, aui, are, to rewarde with honour.
Honestus, ta, tum, honeste.
Honor, oris, honos, noris, honour, dignitie, sometyme beautie, also reuerence, honesty.
Honorarium, a present giue to ambassadors, great officers, and iustices at their first comyng, or executing of their autorities.
Honorem præfari, to speake with reuerēce, as whan a thinge shall be spoken, which is vyle or dishoneste.
Honoraria, playes made at Rome, to the honour of Bacchus.
Honorarius, ia, um, pertaining to honour.
Honorificens, honorificentior, honorificentissimus, a, um, vsynge or doinge thynges honourablye.
Honorifico, aui, are, to do honor, or to honor
Honorificus, ca, cum, that bringeth honour.
Honoro, aui, are, to honour.
Honorus, a, um, that is with honour.
Hopistographi, rolles writen on both sides.
Hora, an howre.
Horæum, sommer honye. It is also a sauce made of fyshe.
Horarium, the space of an howre.
Horda, a cowe great with calfe.
Hordearius, ia, um, pertaynyng to barley.
Hordeum, barley.
Horestes, the sonne of kyng Agamemnon, whiche slewe his mother, bycause she conspired with Ægisthus her aduouterer, to slee his father.
Horia, a fyshers bote.
Horizon, tis, a cerkle dyuidynge the halfe sphere, or ouer part of the firmament, from the other halfe, where, to our syght, it seemeth that the heuen toucheth the erthe.
Hormesion, a precious stone of the colour of fyre.
Horminode, a grene stone, compassed with a cerkle of the colour of golde.
Hornus, na, um, of this yeres, Hagnus hornus, this yeres lambe. Hornę fruges, This yeres grayne.
Hornotinus, a, um, of one yeres growynge.
Horologium, a dyall or a clocke.
Horomasdes, among the Caldees was named the good god.
Horoscopos, the diligent markynge of the tyme of the byrthe of a chylde.
Horoscopo, are, to marke the howre.
Horoscopus, that part of the firmamēt, whiche euery houre riseth from the east, astronomers do call it the ascendent.
Horoscopus, pa, um, euery thynge, wherein howres be marked.
Horrearius, the keper of the barne.

Horreo,

Horreo, rui, ere, whan a man thynketh that his heare doth ryse, also to quake for cold or feare, somtime to feare moche.

Horresco, scere, whan a man feleth within hym great colde or tremblynge to begyn, as in a feuer, or in a greatte feare: Somme tyme to quake.

Horreum, a barne, wherin corne is layde. Sometyme a store house, wherin any other thynge is kepte.

Horribilis, le, horrible or terrible.

Horrificus, idem.

Horridulus, tymorous.

Horridus, da, um, rough, also terrible.

Horrifico, aui, are, to make aferde.

Horripilo, aui, are, to be rough.

Horrisonus, na, sonum, hauynge a terryble sowne or voyce.

Horror, oris, tremblyng for colde or feare, also horryblenes.

Hortatus, tus, exhortacyon.

Hortensia, the daughter of Hortensius, a woman moste eloquent.

Hortensius, an excellent oratour of Rome, of a wonderfull memorie.

Hortor, aris, ari, to exhorte.

Hortus, a knotte gardeyne, or a gardeyne for pleasure, or an orcharde.

Horula, a lyttell howre.

Hostomaticus, syckely.

Hospes, hospitis, a geste, or mutual frendes dwellyng in sondry countrays. also a stranger or a man, inhabiting out of the coūtrey.

Hospita terra, a countrey, wherby a manne maye peasibly passe.

Hospitalis, le, vsynge a gentyll entertaynement, or gladly receyuynge a straunger.

Hospitor, aris, ari, to receyue frendely into his howse.

Hossimi, they that be borne without nose thryles.

Hostia, an hooste or sacrifice offered to attayne vyctorie of ennemies.

Hosticus, ca, um, hostyle, or ennemye.

Hostilis, le, pertaynynge to an ennemy.

Hostimentum, recōpence, one for an other.

Hostio, iui, ire, to recompence, to asswage, or abate, to offende.

Hostis, an ennemye.

Hostium, a measure of a hundred and forty bushels. Also a doore.

Hostorium, the staffe, wherwith all measures be made euen, a stryke.

¶H Ante V.

Huber, bera, berum, fruitefull, or plentuouse.

Huber, eris, a pappe or vdder.

Hubertas, tatis, plentye.

Hubertim, plentuousely.

Huberrime, very plentuousely.

Hubero, raui, rare, to make plentuouse or fruitefulle.

Hubertus, ta, tum, aboundant or plentuous.

Huc, hyther.

Huic, to that place. Also to him or her.

Hui, an interiection of scornynge.

Huiusmodi, & huiuscemodi, suche.

Hulula, a shriche owle.

Hululo, aui, are, to howle.

Humanitas, humanitie or nature of man. also doctrine, pertainynge to man.

Humanitus, of men.

Humaniter, gentylly.

Humanus, na, um, gentyll, tractable, courteyse, mercyfull and frendely.

Humecto, aui, are, to make moyste.

Humeo, mui, ere, to be moyste or wette.

Humesco, scere, idem.

Humerus, the shoulder.

Humidus, moyste.

Humigatus, wette.

Humilis, le, base, lowe. also simple or pore, abiecte, vyle.

Humilio, aui, are, to make lowe, poore, or abiecte.

Humilitas, tatis, basenes, or lowenesse, humilitie, whiche as Speusippus defyneth, is a gentylnesse of the mynde, lackyng wrath or angre.

Humo, aui, are, to burye, or hyde.

Humor, oris, humour or moysture.

Humus, erthe beynge moyste.

Humi, a lowe on the grounde.

Hunni, people which came out of Scithia, and inhabyted Hungarye.

¶H Ante Y.

Hyacinthus, is a precious stone, of the colour of fyne golde, whiche beinge worne in suche wise, that it toucheth the fleshe agaynst the hart, or the vain, whiche comith from the hart into the left hād, preserueth one frome the pestilence. It is also a purple floure, whiche hath a rounde roote, some do suppose it to be callyd in englyshe, flowre gentyll.

Hyacinthina, were solempne ceremonyes done in the nyght. *Hieronimus cōtra Iouinianū*

Hyapes, seuen sterres, in whose rysynge & goinge downe it alway rayneth.

Hybrides, halfe wylde.

Hyalargus, a glasyer.

Hyalus, glasse.

Hyalinus, glasye.

Hyberia, a region in Asia, ioynyng to Armenie, enuyronned with the mountaynes, callid Caucasi. It is also the olde name of Spayn.

Hyberna, places where men of warre doo reste them in wynter.

K.ii. Hyber

Hybernacula, places prepared to winter in.
Hybernia, Irelande.
Hyberno, aui, are, to make abode in wynter.
Hybernus, na, um, pertayninge to wynter.
Hyberus, a greatte ryuer in Spayne, nygh to Tarrhacon.
Hyble, uel hybles, a cytie in Sycile, and a mountayne nygh to it, whiche doth growe full of tyme: And therfore the hony, whiche is there, is of all other moste pleasant.
Hybrida, is a dogge, ingendred betwyxte a hounde and a mastyue, called a lymmar, or mongrell.
Hybris, idis, a kynde of hawkes, whyche seldome is sene in the daye, but seeketh his pray in the night.
Hydaspes, a great ryuer in Indie.
Hyderon, a disease, whan the skynne is fylled with water.
Hydraulis, an organ player.
Hydra, a water serpent. It was also a monster, with whom Hercules faught: and as soone as he had stryken of one heed of the monster, immediately sprange vp an other.
Hydram secare, to medle with an endelesse matter, or where after one myschiefe happeneth an nother.
Hydria, a water potte.
Hydrolapathon, water dockes.
Hydromantia, diuination in callyng of spirites to appere in water.
Hydromel, water & hony sodden togither.
Hydropota, he that drinketh alway water.
Hydrops, hydropis, the droppesy.
Hydrus, a water serpent.
Hydruntes, a citie in Calabria.
Hyemo, aui, are, to rest in the wynter time.
Hyems, wynter.

Arist. de Animal. Hyena, a beaste lyke a wolfe, whiche hath a mane ouer all his backe and neck, but the heares be longer and harder.
Hymber, a showre of rayne or hayle.
Hymen, a skynne in the secrete place of a mayden, whiche whanne she is defloured, is broken.
Hymenæus, was called the God of maryage.
Hymera, the name of a ryuer.
Hymettus, a hyll by Athenes, where was hony of all other moste precyous.
Hymnus, a prayse in a songe.
Hyoscyamos, an herbe called henbane.
Hypœpa, a citie, where were meruayllous fayre women.
Hypætra, an aley in a gardayne, or galerye without any couerynge.
Hypagogeus, an Instrumente, wherewith stones are polyshed.
Hypanis, a ryuer in Scythia.

Hypata, a citie of Thessaly.
Hyperaspistes, a protectour, a great shield.
Hyperbaton, a longe dependynge, or superfluous sentence.
Hyperbole, excesse in aduauncynge, or depressynge: As higher than heuen, whyter than snowe, swyfter than lyghtnynge, slower than a snayle, warse than the dyuell.
Hyperbolicus, ca, um, excedyng credence.
Hyperborei, people in the northeaste parte of the worlde.
Hyperthyrum, that whyche is nexte ouer the browe of a manne. Also somme saye
Hyperthyron, is a transumpte or haunce.
Hypercatalecticum metrum, where aboundeth one syllable or two.
Hyperion, the sonne.
Hyphen, where diuers wordes be pronounced vnder one accent, as quādoquidem, utcunq̨. &c.
Hypnales, adders, which styngyng a man, he dyeth slepynge.
Hypocaustum, a hote howse or stewe.
Hypocrisis, false dissimulation, fayned holynesse.
Hypocrita, an hypocrite.
Hypocondrium, the inwarde parte of the body aboue the nauil, & vnder the stomake.
Hypodidascalus, an vsher or substytute in teachynge.
Hypogeum, a place vnder grounde.
Hypomnema, matis, an expositiō or cōment.
Hypopodion, a foote stoole.
Hypostasis, substaunce. it is also that, whiche dothe ryse in vryne, where there is good digestion; if the residence be white, lyght, and rysynge in facion lyke a peare, the smalle ende vpwarde.
Hypothicos, a lynnen rochette.
Hypothyron, a groundsyll or thresholde.
Hypothyra, seu hypothyrides, the doore, or rather the place open, where the doore is.
Hypozigia, all drawynge cattell.
Hypsicratea, the wyfe of kynge Mythridates, whiche folowed hym in al his warres, beinge armed lyke a knyght.
Hypsipile, a ladye, whyche loued Jason, and whanne he retourned not at the tyme, whiche he promysed, she threwe her selfe into the see.
Hypethra, an alaye to walke in.
Hyrcania, a countrey in Asie.
Hysginum, a colour lyke scarlette.
Hysopus, & hysopum, an herbe callydde Isope.
Hysterologia, & hysteron proteron, a maner of speakynge, where the laste is sette before the fyrste, and as it is sayd, the cart before the horses.

I Ante

IACCHVS, one of the names of Bacchus, called god of wynes.

Saluſtius.

Iaceo, cui, cēre, to ly. ſomtyme to be. In medio cãpus iacet, In the middel is a feld. alſo to be deed.

Lucanus. Cic. de finibus.

Ille iacet, he is deed. ſomtyme to be contēned or nought ſet by. Maximas uero uirtutes iacere neceſſe eſt, uoluptate dominãte, Carnal dilectation ruling, nedes muſt excellent vertues be nothyng ſet by.

Iacio, ieci, iacere, to throwe, caſte, or ſhoote, ſometyme to ſette or lay. Iacere fundamenta, to laye the foundation.

Iacobus, a propre name.

Iactanter, boſtyngely.

Iactantia, booſte. Iactatio, idem.

Iactito, raui, tare, to boſte often.

Iacto, aui, are, to throwe, to reuolue, or toſſe in the mynde, to vexe, to throwe downe & beate, to auaunt or glorie, to ſpeake vaynly, to ſette forth, to toſſe, to caſte out.

Iactuoſe, braggyngly.

Iactura, damage or loſſe, proprely as whan a man hath moche goodes in a ſhyppe, and by force of tēpeſt, is conſtraynced to throw it into the ſee, leſte the ſhyp ſhuld periſhe.

Iaculatio, iaculamen, & iaculamētum, a ſhot, or caſt with a darte, or iauelyn.

Iaculo, aui, are, to ſhoote or caſte farre.

Iaculor, aris, idem.

Iaculum, any thynge that maye be ſhotte or caſte farre, moſte cōmonly a dart or light iauelyn.

Iaculus, a ſerpent, that lyeth vnder trees, and ſodaynly with a meruaylous vyolence perceth any beaſte, whiche happeneth to paſſe by hym.

Iam, nowe.

Iambus, a fote in meter, whiche hathe the fyrſt ſyllable ſhort, the other longe.

Iam diu, longe agone.

Iamdudum, now late, but a whyle ſens.

Iamiam, euen nowe.

Iam olim, nowe late.

Iampridem, a lyttell whyle paſte, but late. ſometyme forthewith.

Iam tum, fro that tyme.

Ianiculum, a towne not farre from Rome.

Ianira, the daughter of Ocean & Tethis.

Ianitor, toris, a porter.

Ianthina, violet colour, or purple.

Ianua, a doore or yate.

Ianuarius, the moneth of Ianyuer.

Ianus, ſome ſuppoſe to be Saturne, ſome to be Iaphet, one of the ſonnes of Noe. Cicero calleth hym the ſuperiour worlde, or heuen, he was made hauynge two viſages, either bycauſe the heuen tournynge, the yere retourneth, where it beganne: orels bycauſe it knoweth what is paſſed, and aforeſeeth what ſhall happen. This god, or rather ydoll, had a temple in Rome, which in the time of warres was alway open, and in the tyme of peace was ſhutte. And therfore whan in ſtories mencion is made, that the temple of Ianus was ſhutte, than is it to be vnderſtande, that the Romaynes had peace vniuerſally.

Iapetus, the father of Prometheus.

Iapigia, a coūtrey in the realme of Naples.

Iapix, gis, a wynde, which commeth out of the partes of Apulia, & is a weſtern winde.

Iaſon, onis, he whiche firſte conquered the Flecce of golde.

Iaſpis, pidis, a ſtone callyd Iaſper.

Iatraleptes, a phiſition or ſurgion, whiche cureth with oyntmentes.

Iatralepticé, curynge by oyntmentes.

¶ I Ante B.

IBerus, a ryuer in Spayne.

Iberia, the auncient name of Spayn, alſo an other countrey nye to Armeny.

Iberi, & Iberes, Spanyardes.

Ibi, there.

Ibis, a foule or byrde of Egypte, whych is high, and hath ſtiffe legges, and a long byl. They profyte moche to the countreye in kyllyng and eating ſerpentes, whiche oute of Libia be caried into Egypt, with a ſowtherne wynde. Alſo it is taken for an enuyous perſon.

¶ I Ante C.

ICaria, an yle in the ſee Icario, whiche is alſo called Icaros.

Icarus, the father of the chaſt Penelope. There was alſo an other Icarus, whiche was the ſonne of Dedalus, who hauinge winges, with his father flewe out of the yle of Crete: but whan he flewe higher than his father commanded him, the waxe, wherwith the fethers of his winges were glued, being molten with the heate of the ſunne, and the fethers fallynge of, Icarus was conſtrayned to fall into the ſee, whych was afterward callid Mare Icariū. Alſo Icarus is a mountain in the regiō of Athenes.

Ichneumon, a beaſt in Egipte, of the greatnes of a catte, and is factioned like a mous, who crepeth into the body of a Cocodryl, whan he gapeth, & eatinge his bowels, ſleeth hym. It is alſo a kynde of waſpes.

Ichnographia, an inſtrumente lyke a compaſſe, wherewith are made the deſcripcyons of the ſonne.

Ichnusa, the yle nowe called Sardinia.
Ichthiocolla, fyshe glewe.
Icthybolus, a fysher.
Icthyophagi, people whiche doo lyue by eatynge of fyshe.
Icthyopola, a fishmonger, or seller of fishe.
Icthyopolion, a fyshe markette.
Icthyotrophia, a ponde or stewe, wherein fyshes be fedde.
Ico, ici, icere, ictum, to stryke.
Icona, uel Icon, an ymage.
Iconicus, ca, cū, so paynted or fourmed, that in euery membre the very similitude is expressed.
Iconismus, a description.
Iconium, a towne in the countreye of Capadocia, an other in Asie the lasse. it is also a mans owne image like him selfe.
Icteros, a sycknes called the Jaundise.
Icterus, a byrde called a yelowe hamer.
Ictericus, he that is disesed with the Jādis.
Ictis, idis, a white wesyll, whiche destroyeth bee stalles, and eateth the hony.

¶ I Ante D.

ID, that. Id quod res est, which is trouth.
Id ætatis, of that age.
Ida, a mountayn, which lieth nigh Troy.
Idei dactili, people called also Corybantes.
Ideus, a, um, of the mountayne of Ida.
Idalium, a cytie in the yle of Cypres.
Idalus, a mountayne & a wodde in Cypres.
Idaspes, a famous ryuer, whiche passeth by Parthia and Inde, wherin is golden grauell, and precious stones.
Idcirco, therfore.
Idea, a fygure conceyued in ymagynation, as it were a substance perpetuall: and lyke as of one seale procedeth manye pryntes, so of one Idea of a manne procedeth many thousandes of men, and semblably of other Ideas procedeth thynges innumerable. So that Ideæ, be as it were eternal examples, wherby all other thynges be created: and this is Idea, wherof Plato speaketh.
Idiopathia, the propre passion of a disease.
Idem, the same thynge, or the same man.
Identidem, eftesones, in the same wyse.
Ideo, for that cause.
Idicus, ca, cum, of the mountayne of Ida.
Idiographum, a priuate wrytynge.
Idiographę literę, a priuate letter.
Idioma, matis, a propre forme of speche.
Idiota, Idiotes, a man or woman vnlerned.
Idolatra, a worshypper of idolles.
Idololatria, ydolatrie.
Idolium, a lyttell ydoll.
Idolothysia, offrynges to ydols.

Idolothytum, that which is offred to idols.
Idolum, an ydoll.
Idoneus, ea, eum, apte.
Idula, a shepe that was offred euery Idus to Jupyter.
Idumęa, a regyon in Syria, ioynynge to Egypte, and bordereth vpon Palestina.
Idus, Ides of monethes, whiche do diuide Nonas from Calendes.

¶ I Ante E.

IEcur, coris, & iecinoris, the lyuer of a mā, or other thynge lyuynge.
Iecusculum, a lyttell lyuer.
Ieiunium, fastynge.
Ieiuno, aui, are, to faste or absteyne.
Ieiunum, the gutte, whiche goth downe to the fundement.
Ieiunus, he that is fastynge.
Ientaculum, a breakefaste.
Iento, aui, are, to eate meate afore dyner.

¶ I Ante G.

IGitur, therfore, from hensforth, afterwarde.
Ignauia, cowardenesse.
Ignauus, a, um, cowarde.
Ignifacio, eci, facere, to sette on fyre.
Ignesco, scere, to be sette on fyre, or to be made fyre.
Ignarium, any thynge, oute of the whyche fyre may be beaten.
Ignia, certayne fautes, whiche erthen pottes haue in the inealynge.
Igniculi, are certayne prouocations, naturally gyuen to imbrace vertue.
Igniculus, a sperke of fyre.
Ignio, iui, ire, to inflame.
Ignipotens, one of the surnames of Vulcanus.
Ignis, the fyre. Sometyme it is taken for an harlotte.
Ignis sacer, a sore, wherin is an excedynge inflamation and burninge.
Ignitabulum, a fyre panne.
Igniuomus, he that spytteth fyre: the sonne is sometyme so called.
Ignobilis, le, vnnoble, vnknowen, foolyshe, of none estimation.
Ignominis, without renoume.
Ignominia, reproche, infamye.
Ignorabilis, le, vnknowen.
Ignoro, aui, are, to knowe not.
Ignarus, ignorant, without knowlege.
Ignorantia, ignorance, lacke of knowlege, and is referred to the wyt of the persone.
Ignoratio, lacke to be knowen, and pertaineth to the thynge or acte.

Ignos

Ignosco, noui, noscere, to lerne and knowe perfectly. Also to forgiue, to haue excused to knowe not, or be ignoraunt.
Ignotus, vnknowen, also ignorant.

¶ I Ante L.

Ila, the leeste porcyon of a thynge, that may be imagined. Also the stuffynge of a puddynge, or other lyke thynge.
Ila, or Ilua, an ylande in the Tuscayne see.
Ile, is that whiche is set in the highest part of a man.
Ileosus, the colycke, and he that hathe the colycke.
Ileos, the colycke.
Ilex, licis, a tree callyd holy, or holme.
Ilia, the guttes.
Iliacus dolor, the frettynge of the guttes.
Ilias, adis, the warke of Homerus, of the syege of Troye.
Iliberis, a citie in the prouince of Narbone.
Iliceus, a, um, of holy or holme.
Iligneus, a, um, idem.
Ilione, the propre name of a daughter of Priamus.
Ilioneus, the propre name of a Troyane.
Ilissus, the name of a ryuer in the prouynce of Athenes.
Ilium, the palais of Priamus.
Illætabilis, le, without myrthe, or lackynge myrthe or pleasure.
Illatebro, aui, are, to hyde in corners.
Illaudatus, not worthy to be named.
Ille, he.
Illecebræ, thynges dilectable, whiche draweth and allurethe the mynde to imbrace them, flyckerynge intycementes.
Illecto, aui, are, to drawe pleasantly.
Illex, illegis, lawlesse, also wanton. Illex oculus, a wanton eie.
Illibatus, ta, tum, vntouched, vntasted.
Illiberaliter, vngentillye, excedyngely ylle, myscheuously.
Illicet, nowe go to, incontinent.
Illiceo, illicui, cere, to prouoke or styre pleasauntlye.
Illectus, ta, tū, plesantly stired or prouoked.
Illicium, a prouocation.
Illico, anon, in the same place.
Illido, lisi, dere, to driue or beate to a thyng.
Illisus, a, um, dryuen or beaten to.
Illineo, iui, ire, to anoynte on.
Illino, iui, ire, to annoynte harde, to spotte or soyle.
Illix, licis, a prouocation or styringe.
Illuceo, xi, cere, & illucesco, scere, to be light or cleere.
Illudo, si, ere, to mocke, to hurte in iapyng, or playenge.

Illuminus, a, um, without lyghte.
Illunis, dark, whan the mone doth not shine
Illustris, famous, clere, noble in renoume.
Illustro, aui, are, to make lyght or cleere, to make famous or well knowen.
Illuuies, vncleannesse, fylthynesse in manne or garment.
Illiria, a countrey nowe called Slauonye, whiche hath on one parte Italy, on an nother part Germany, on the east side Grece, on the weste the Uenyce see.
Illiricus, ca, cum, of Illiria.
Ilus, the kynge of Troyanes sonne, that buylded Ilium.

¶ I Ante M.

Imaginarii, baner bearers, wherin be ye mages paynted.
Imaginatus, ta, tum, fygured or fourmed into an ymage.
Imagino, naui, nare, to make ymages, or to counterfayte.
Imaginor, aris, ari, to imagyne.
Imago, imaginis, an ymage, a symylitude, a shethe, or case. *Vergilius.*
Imaguncula, a lyttell ymage.
Imaus, a mountayne in Judea.
Imbecillis, le, & imbecillus, a, um, feble.
Imbecillitas, tatis, feblenesse.
Imbellia, cowardyse.
Imbellis, le, vnapte to warres, cowarde, or weake.
Imber, a showre.
Imberbis, be, beardelesse.
Imbibo, bi, bere, to drynke in.
Imbrex, bricis, a spowte or gutter, oute of the whiche rayne is conuayed frome the house. It is sometyme taken for the tyle or slatte, that lyeth on the house.
Imbricium, the coueryng or eueisynge of the howse.
Imbrico, to couer with tyle, or other lyke thynge.
Imbricosus, a, um, full of gutters.
Imbrus, an Ilande of Thrace, and a towne in the same is so called.
Imbrifer, bryngyng showres.
Imbubino, aui, are, to defyle with menstruous flyxe.
Imbulbito, taui, tare, to defyle with chyldes dryte.
Imbuo, bui, buere, to dye clothe or sylke, to teache.
Imitor, aris, ari, to folowe the exaumple of an nother.
Immanis, ne, cruell, great, horryble.
Immanitas, tatis, crueltie, greattenes.
Immineo, nui, nere, to procure, to endeuour
Imminuo, nuere, to cutte of.

Imminu-

I ante M.

Salusti⁹ in tō. Catil. Imminuere ius, to defalcate or mynyshe the auctoritie or state of a person.
Immissum, layde in to abyde, as a beame of a house, or other lyke thynge.
Immitto, misi, immittere, to sende in. Sometyme it sygnifieth to lette growe in length.
Lucilius lib. 30. Neque barbam immiseris istam, Neither let this berde growe in length. Respicimus dira illuuies, immissaq; barba, we behelde, O what an horryble fylthynesse and a bearde growen in lengthe. Also to bryng or sende on the contrary parte.
Virg. æne. lib. 3.
Lact. li. 4. Hoc futurum esse dixerunt; ut post breue tempus immitteret deus regem, qui expugnaret Iudæos, It shoulde come to passe sayde they, that god shulde sende to the contrary parte a kynge, whiche shulde vanquyshe the Iewes. Alij Tarquinium, a Cicerone immissum aiebant, ne Crassus, suscepto malorum patrocynio rempub. turbaret, Some sayde, that Tarquine was brought in craftily by Cicero, lest that Crassus, in takynge on hym the defence of mysdoers, shulde therby brynge sedicyon into the weale publyke.
Salusti⁹ in tō. Catil.
Immo, but rather, ye rather.
Immolo, aui, are, to offre in sacrifyce.
Immunis, exempt, without office or charge.
Imminutas, tatis, fraunches or libertie.
Immunitus, ta, tum, not defended.
Impago, ginis, a tenon, whiche is put into the mortais, also a pynne, whiche is driuen into tymber, to make it ioyne and abyde.
Impeccabilis, he that neuer offendeth.
Impedimentum, lette, impediment in warres. Impedimenta, is the caryage and trafyke, that goth with the hooste.
Colum. 5. Plautus in Amphitr. Impedio, diui, dire, to lette, to staye, or supporte, to defyle.
Impeditus, is proprelye he, that hathe his fete so bounde, that he can not goo.
Impedo, aui, are, to vndersette.
Impello, puli, pellere, to perswade instantly, to inforce, to plucke downe, or infeble.
Impulso, aui, are, to perswade often.
Impulsus, perswaded, prouoked, inforced.
Impendeo, di, dere, to hange ouer.
Impendio, very moche, or more.
Impendium, expense, or coste.
Impendo, di, dere, to spende or lay out money, to bestowe, to lay out.
Impensa, benefytes.
Impensa, æ, expenses.
Impense, pro valde. Est impense improbus, he is a very yll man.
Impensius, excedynge, more greuouse, or displeasunt.
Impensibilis, without consyderation.
Imperator, the chiefe capitayne in warres, nowe, the emperour.

Imperiosus, a maisterly manne, rigorous, or cruell in gouernaunce.
Imperiose, stately, rigorously.
Imperitabundus, ful of rule, or ruling moch.
Imperitia, lacke of knowlege.
Imperitus, not expert, easy to be deceiued.
Imperito, aui, are, to rule or gouerne.
Imperium, a solemne commaundemente, a preeminence in gouernāce, autoritie royal.
Impero, aui, are, to commaunde.
Imperatum, commaunded.
Impetus, tus, & impes, petis, violence.
Impetigo, ginis, a rynge worme.
Impeto, tiui, tere, to inuade.
Impetrabilis, le, that may be gotē by desire.
Impetrasso, petrassi, ere, to gette by desyre or instaunce.
Impetritus, infyxed, mortaysed, as it were in a stone.
Impetro, traui, trare, to obtayne by desyre, or requeste.
Impiatus, not purged of synne.
Impiger, diligent, not slowe, valyant.
Plautus in capt. Terent. in Phor. Impingo, pēgi, impingere, to hytte oone in throwynge some thynge at hym. Impingere compedes, to putte on gyues. Dicam tibi, impingam grandem, I wyll laye a waighty matter vnto the.
Impinguo, aui, are, to make fatte.
Impius, cruell, hatynge god & good men.
Impietas, pietatis, hatrede of god, crueltie, wyckednesse.
Impiè, wyckedly, cruelly.
Implano, aui, are, to deceyue.
Impleo, eui, ere, to fylle.
Implexus, wounde in.
Plautus. Implico, caui, are, to wrappe in, to tye faste, to detayne. Implicat ad speculum caput, she bounde vp her heed at a glasse.
Implicitus, ta, tum, wrapped or tied fast togyther. Implicitus morbo, attached or detained with syckenes.
Imploro, aui, are, to desyre lamentably.
Impluuia, a cloke to weare in the rayne.
Impluuiū, a place in the house, where they vsed to receyue rayne water. It maye be englyshed a lowuer.
Impolitia, negligēce about the wele publike.
Impono, sui, nere, to put one thyng on another. also to gyue, to inioyne, to laye to ones charge.
Imporco, aui, are, to make a balke in earing of lande.
Importunus, na, ū, out of seson, importunate.
Importunitas, tatis, which hath no commoditie of tyme nor of place.
Impos, poris, vnable, without power.
Impostor, oris, he that deceyueth with promises, or selleth false ware for good.

Impo=

I ante M.

Imposturam facere, to deceyue in maner aforesayde.
Impotens,tentis, he that can not resyste his appetite or affections. sometyme it is vsurped for puissaunt.
Impotentia, debilitie. sometyme immoderate power. also vnabilitie to resyste.
Impresentia, & impresentiarum, at this time, or for this present tyme.
Imprecor, aris, ari, to desyre, to wyshe.
Impressio, ionis, a violent assaulte.
Imprimo, impressi, imprimere, to prynte, to seale.
Improbus, an yll man, dishonest, obstinate, wanton, malaperte, wyly, vnsacyable.
Improbitas, bitatis, dishonesty, vnthriftines, wantonnesse, obstynacy, malapertenes, rauecny, wylynesse.
Improperium, imbraydynge of a defaulte.
Impropero, aui, are, to imbrayde a manne with some defaute.
Vergilius. Imprudens, imprudentis, vnware. Also not circumspecte. sometyme very circumspect.
Impubes, & impuber, a man chylde before the age of. xiiii. yeres, a mayden before. xii.
Impudens, shameles.
Impudenter, shamefully, dishonestly, vnaduysedly, wantonly.
Impudicus, vnchaste, vncleane in lyuynge.
Impudicitia, vncleannes of lyuynge.
Impune, without damage, without punyshment or griefe, in vayne.
Impunitas, tatis, lacke of punyshement, libertie withoute punysshemente, pardon of punyshement.
Impurus, impura, purum, dishonest, vile, reprocheable.
Imputo, taui, tare, to repute or ascribe, to lay the blame or defaute.
Imputatus, ta, tum, vncutte, or neuer cutte.
Imus, ma, mum, the lowest or most lowe.

¶ I Ante N.

IN, sygnifieth in. Also In rempub. toward the publyke weale. In meam partem, on or for my part.
In parricidam, agaynst a murderer.
Vergilius. In nauem ingreditur, he went into the shyp. also it sygnifieth space of tyme. In noctem, vnto nyght. In lucem, vntyll day. also for.
In magno munere, for a great rewarde.
In diem addicere, to sel vpon condicon, that a thynge be done by a day.
In dies singulos, daye by daye.
In horam, for oone houre. In horas, frome houre to houre.
In manu vel manibus est, It is in his power, at hande, or easy, or in hande.

I ante N.

In manum dari, to be gyuen a parte or seuerally.
In medium afferre, to bryng forthe to a common vse or commoditie.
In mentem uenire, to come to mynde, or remembraunce, to be consydered.
In numerum, in order.
In ordinem ducere vel cogere, to brynge downe from authoritie, to mynyshe estymation or power.
In posterum, finally, in conclusyon.
In re tua, for thy profyte.
In rem presentem uenire, where the landes in debate cometh in viewe, by the assignement of Iuges, vnto them whiche be called viewers, whiche shall see the boundes and quantitie of the lande in variance. *Budeus.*
In spem uenire, to begynne to hope.
In rem presentem producere, to brynge the matter to lyght, to expresse the thing perfectelye. *Plinius in epist.*
In re presenti, in a playn and euident matter. *Quintil.*
In tempore, in season, oportunately.
Inaccessa, an ylande of Egypte, to the whiche is no commynge.
Inachus, the fyrste kynge of Argiues.
Inanescere, to be vayne, and of none estymation.
Inaniloquus, a bablar.
Inanimus, ma, um, without sowle.
Inanio, iui, ire, to make emptye.
Inanis, inane, empty, vacaunt, ydell, lyght in estimation.
Inanitas, & inanitio, emptynes, voydenes.
Inaresco, scere, to drye vp.
Inarime, an yle in the Tuscayne see. Also a mountayne.
Inaudio, diui, dire, to here.
Inauditus, ta, tum, neuer harde of, straunge to here.
Inauris, a rynge, or other lyke thynge, hangynge at the eare.
Inauro, aui, are, to make ryche.
Inauspicato, vnluckyly.
Inceduus, a, um, vnused to be cutte.
Incero, aui, are, to keuer with waxe.
Incalesco, lui, scere, to be or waxe very hot.
Incallidus, symple, without crafte or subtyltie.
Incandesco, dui, descere, to be verye hotte angrye.
Incanto, taui, tare, to charme.
Incantatio, & incantamentum, a charme.
Incapistro, aui, strare, to halter, or to bynde with a halter.
Incassum, in vayne.
Incautus, vnware.
Incedo, cessi, cedere, to go or walke, to goo stately, to enter.

Incendo,

Incendo, di, dere, to inflame, to sette fyre on a thynge.
Incentio, onis, the sowning of instrumentes.
Incepto, aui, are, to begynne often.
Incerniculum, a rayinge syue, wherin corne is clensed, or it be ground. also a sarcer.
Incerno, ni, nere, to syfte in.
Incerto, taui, tare, to make doubtefulle, or vncertayne.
Incertus, ta, tum, vncertayne or doubtfull.
Incesso, ssi, ssere, to make angry, to do displesure to one, to accuse.
Incesto, aui, are, to pollute.
Incestuosus, he that dothe often pollute.
Incestus, ta, tum, polluted.
Incestus, tus, is lechery cōmitted with one, whiche is nygh of kynne or aliance to him that commytteth it. Also it sygnyfyeth all maner of pollucion. *Seruius.*
Inchoo, aui, are, to begyn, also to performe.
Incido, di, ere, to cutte, to graue.
Incisa, loste. Spe incisa prius quam prædicta dies adesset. Hope beinge lost, er euer the sayd day was commen. *Liuius.*
Incido, di, ere, to happen, to fall sodaynely, to come by chaunce.
Incile, a gappe or trenche.
Inciles, trenches, to conuay water from a ryuer, into a medow, or other low ground.
Incilo, aui, are, to blame or reproue.
Incino, ni, nere, to synge, properly to fayne a small breste.
Incipio, cœpi, cipere, to begynne.
Incisim, pece meale, gobet meale.
Incisio, onis, incision, or cuttynge.
Incisura, a cutte or garse. Also Incisure, be the lynes in the palme of the hande.
Incitabulum, incitamen, & incitamentum, a prouocation.
Incitas, pouertie, necessitie.
Incitega, a thynge wheron great vesselles of wyne are couched.
Incito, taui, tare, to prouoke.
Inclamo, aui, are, to call for one, to cry oute on one, rebukefully to call in.
Inclementer, withoute mercye, cruellye, sharpely.
Inclementia, crueltie, lacke of mercy.
Inclino, aui, are, to inclyne or bowe downe.
Includo, si, ere, to include or shutte in.
Inclytus, ta, tum, glorious, famous.
Incoctile, a potte, wherin meate is sodden.
Incœnatus, not hauyng souped. It incœnatus cubitum. He goth to bed supperlesse. *Plautus in Pseud.*
Incœnis, without supper.
Incogitabilis, forgetfull, not consyderynge what he dothe.
Incogitans, vnaduysed.
Incognitus, ta, tum, vnknowen.

Incolatus, dwellyng in a straunge coūtrey.
Incolo, ui, ere, to dwell in a place.
Incola, he that dwelleth in an other countrey, than where he was borne.
Incolumis, hole without syckenes.
Incolumitas, tatis, helthynes.
Incomitatus, being without company alone
Incommodo, aui, are, to hurte.
In commune, equally.
Incompactum, vnioyned, or yll ioyned.
Incomprehensus, not comprehended.
Inconsiliari, to be callyd before the coūsell.
Inconcinnus, a, um, vninete, il proporcionid.
Inconcussus, stable, that can not be shaken.
Inconditus, ta, tum, out of order or facyon. rude. Also weryshe.
Inconditus, ta, tum, vnmade, vnbuylded.
Incongelabilis, le, that can not be frosen.
Inconsultus, lackynge aduyse, or consyderation, he that wyll not aske counsayle. In consultu meo, without my counsayle.
Inconsutilis, without any seame.
Inconsutus, ta, tum, vnsowed.
Inconsyderatus, he that nothing cōsiderith.
Inconsyderate, vnaduysedly.
Incoxo, aui, are, to sytte as women or taylours done without a stoole.
Increatus, neuer created.
Incredibilis, le, incredible, not to be beleued, meruaylous.
Incrementum, increase.
Increpito, aui, are, to blame or rebuke oftē.
Increpo, pui, pere, to sounde or make noyse. also to rebuke, to prouoke.
Incresco, eui, scere, to growe moch or more.
Incubus, a spyrite, whiche assumynge the fourme of a man, medleth with womenne. Also that whiche is called the mare, wherwith men be oppressed in their slepe.
Incubo, aui, are, to lye in or vpon, to cleaue to, to sytte ouer a thynge, to syt on egges, as a henne dothe, to occupie, to possede, to imbrace, to nouryshe, to dwell in, to care.
Incubatio, & incubitus, lyenge in, syttynge to hatche egges.
Incudo, donis, he that warketh on an anuil.
Inculco, aui, are, to porre in.
Incultus, a place vnhusbanded or vntilled.
Incumbo, bere, to indeuour, to take in hād, to happe, to leane vppon, or fall on a thing.
Incumbo ad studia, I gyue my mynde to a thynge, I applye me.
Incunabulum, a cradell.
Incuria, neglygence, yll husbandrye.
Incurro, rere, to rounne agaynste oone, to rounne in.
Incursus, & incursio, inuasion of enemies.
Incuruesco, scere to bow down, or be crokid
Incuruo, aui, are, to make croked.

In

Intutuus, a, um, croked.
Incus, udis, an andeuyle.
Incuso, aui, are, to accuse.
Incutio, cussi, cutere, to throwe in.
Indago, aui, are, to seke or serche.
Indago, ginis, serche.
Inde, from thens, there, from thensforthe.
Indecor, coris, not regarded.
Indecorum, vnhoneste.
Indefensus, without defence.
Indefinitus, ta, tum, not determyned or discussed.

Salusti⁹ in Iugurth. Indemnatus, he that is condempned without makynge aunswere.
Indemnis, without hurt or harme, defendid.
Indeprecabilis, he that wol not be intreatid or wyll not forgyue. Pæna indeprecabilis, punyshement without remission.
Index, dicis, he that accuseth or appeacheth an other man. Also he that for to escape punyshement, or for some rewarde, disclosith the conspiracie, whereunto he was made priuie. It is also the forefinger, and a touch stone to trie golde, also the table of a boke, whereby certayne chapyters or notes be founden.
India, the countrey called Indie.
Indicatio, estimation or valuation.
Indicatura, idem.
Indicatus, idem.
Indicium, & indicina, a detection or accusation.
Indico, caui, care, to disclose, to manyfeste, & make openly knowen, to demonstrate, to accuse, to sette or tell the price, to delyuer in possession that whiche is bought.
Indico, indixi, indicere, to denounce or declare solemnely, and for a greate cause. As battayle, fastynges, funeralles, counsayls, triumphes, and other great thinges. Also to sette a tribute or taxe, and to appoynte.
Indictio, the space of xv. yeres.
Indictiuus, ua, um, that whiche is declared or appoynted.
Indictus, dicta, tum, declared or denounced solempnely.
Indicta causa, the cause or matter not knowen, declared or defended.
Indidem, from thens, forthwith, the same.

Ti. Liuius Indies, dayly, from daye to daye. Crescente indies multitudine, The multitude or noumbre dayly increasynge.
Indigena, of the same countreye or towne borne and bredde.
Indigeo, gui, gere, to lacke.
Indigentia, nede or necessitie.
Indigeste, inordinately.
Indigestio, yll digestion.
Indigetes, goddis made of mortall menne, some take them for priuate goddis, pertaynyng to particular places.
Indigitamenta, bokes contaynyng the names of goddis, and the mistycal sygnification of them.
Indigito, taui, tare, to name, or cal by name.
Indignor, aris, ari, to disdayne.
Indignus, vnworthy, myserable.
Indigus, nedy, or lackynge.
Indipisco, sci, scere, & indipiscor, sceris, sci, to optayne, to vsurpe.
Indiscriminatim, indifferently, withoute diuersytie.
Indisertus, without eloquence.
Indiuidium, that maye not be dyuyded or separate.
Indo, indidi, indere, to sette, or name. Also to prynte.
Indocilis, a dullarde, that can not be taught.
Indoctus, vnlerned.
Indolentia, lacke of peyne. Indoloria, idem.
Indoles, towardenes, & disposition to vertue, in chylderne, In men, token of vertue. Also very nobilitie, or honour, aptenesse to good or euyll.
Indomabilis, le, that may not be made tame.
Indomitus, wylde, vnbroken.
Indubitatus, ta, tum, vndoubted.
Indutię, truce, or peace for a certayn tyme.
Induco, xi, cere, to induce, to bryng in, to persuade, to allure, to incline, to deceiue, to cancelle, to defete, to put on, proprely hosen or shoen, to infix or stablish. Ita induxi in animū, I haue infyxed or stablyshed in my mynde.
Inductio, a fourme of argument, proceding from the particulars vnto the vniuersalles. Also an argument, whyche by gettyng the assent in thinges not doubtfull, proueth the thynge, whiche is intended.
Indulco, caui, care, & indulcoro, aui, are, to make swete.
Indulgeo, dulsi, gere, to graunte lyghtly, to consent to a request, to pardon. Indulge ua- *Cf. Tyr.* letudini tuę, Take hede to thy helth. Nimiū *Ter. Heau.* illi indulges, Thou carist to moche for him. Also it is to gyue respite, to be gentyll and mercyfull.
Indulgentia, & indulgitas, gentylnes in sufferance, also mercy.
Indumentum, a garment.
Induo, dui, ere, to put on a garment, or other lyke thynge, to transfourme, or translate, to caste on, to annoynte.
Induperator, oris, an emperour.
Indus, a great ryuer in Inde.
Indusium, a petycote.
Indusiarius, a maker of petycotes.
Indusiatus, cladde in a petycote.
Industria, a vertue comprehendynge bothe study

study and diligence, industrie.
Industrius, he that is wytty and actyue.
Induuiæ, apparayle.
Inebrior, briaris, ari, to make dronke, or be dronken.
Inedia, hunger.
Ineffigiatus, ta, tum, vnfacyoned, withoute good proporcyon.
Ineo, iui, ire, to begyn, to go in, to deserue, to gette, to wynne, to optayne, to treate.
Inire fœdus, to make a leage or treatie of peace.
Inire pacem, to make peace. Inire bellum, to make warre. Inire uiam, to fynde the way. Also Inire, is to leape, as a horse doth on a mare. Inire fugam, to flee, as men do in batayle, to consyder, to vnderstande.
Initor, oris, a stalyon.
Ineptio, iui, ire, to tryfle.
Ineptus, ta, tum, vnapte.
Ineptus, a tryflar, vsyng nothyng in order, vnapte to the purpose.
Inermis, vnarmed, a man yolden.
Iners, inertis, without any science or craft, an ydell persone, also vnprofitable.
Inertia, lacke of crafte, ydelnes.
Inerticula, a vyne, wherof the wyne is soo good, that none euyll procedeth therof.
Inesco, sci, scere, to cramme or feede. Also to deceyue.
Ineuitabilis, le, that can not be eschewed.
Inexercitus, ta, tum, not exercysed, vnoccupyed.
Inexplorato, without serche.
Inexputabilis, le, that may not be numbred.
Inextricabilis, le, that can not be shaken of, or dissolued.
Infabre, vnkūningly, vncraftily, yl fauored.
Infamia, infamye.
Infamis, me, infamed. Infamis digitus, the myddel fynger.
Infamo, aui, are, to infame, or yll report.
Infandum, that may not be spoken.
Infans, a chylde that can not yet speake. it is also euery thyng that is very yong. Also it signifieth not eloquent, somtime an ideot that can not speake.
Infantia, chyldehode, also folyshenes.
Infantilis, le, pertaynynge to chyldehode.
Infarcio, cii, & ciui, cire, to infarce or stuffe, or fylle.
Infatuo, aui, are, to make foolyshe.
Infector, ctoris, a dyar, that dyeth clothe, wolle, or sylke.
Infectus, ta, tum, infected, dyed, stayned, poysoned. Also vndoone, or not doone, not made.
Infectus, tus, dyenge, or staynynge.
Infensus, displeased, moued with angre or hate towarde an other. Also he that beareth malyce.
Inferiæ, sacrifice done to infernall goddis.
Infernalis, le, infernall.
Infernus, helle.
Infernus, na, num, lowe.
Infernas, atis, the lowe.
Inferne, alowe, or benethe.
Infero, intuli, inferre, to brynge in, to throw in, to adde to, to cast in, to conclude. Inferre arma, to make warre. Stuprū inferre, to cōmytte aduoutry or fornication with a kynswomanne.
Inferus, ra, rum, where nothynge is lower.
Infesta signa, standerdes or baners displayd in battayle on bothe partes.
Infestiuus, ua, um, vnmete for disporte.
Infesto, aui, are, to do displeasure with sondry incursions or rodes.
Infestum mare, the see occupied with pyrates and robbers.
Infestus, a mortall ennemye.
Infestus, ta, tum, that standethe agaynste a man, to the intent to indamage hym.
Infibulo, aui, are, to claspe to gyther.
Inficias ire, to denye.
Inficiator, oris, he that denyeth.
Infici, feci, ficere, to dye clothe, to stayne or infecte.
Inficior, aris, ari, to denie, or disafferme.
Infidus, da, dum, vnfaythefulle.
Infimates, the base people.
Infimo, aui, are, to brynge lowe.
Infimus, a, um, the lowest or moste base.
Infirmo, aui, are, to make weake.
Infirmus, ma, um, vnstable, sycke, feble.
Infirmitas, tatis, vnstablenes, weaknesse, syckenes.
Inflammo, aui, are, to inflame or set on fire.
Infligo, xi, gere, pœnam aut opprobrium, to punyshe or rebuke.
Informo, aui, are, to shape or fourme, to enforme or teache good maners.
Inforo, aui, are, to declare at the barre in a place of iugement, to pleade, also to perforate or make a hole.
Infortunium, yll chaunce.
Infra, within, bynethe: In numbre it signifieth lasse or fewer.
Infractio, slowthfulnesse.
Infractus, ta, tum, vnbroken, sure, Infractus animi, styffe of courage. somctyme it signifieth discouraged.
Infrendo, di, dere, to crasshe the teethe for angre.
Infrendes, chylderne lackynge teethe.
Infringo, infregi, gere, to breake to pieces.
Infrunitus, a foole, that knoweth not howe to vse a thynge.

Infu-

Infulæ, be the labelles, whiche do hang on euery syde of a mytar. It was in the olde tyme the attyre that priestes dyd weare on their heedes. They were also tapettes of linen, wherwith temples were hanged.
Infumibulũ, the shank or tonel of a chimney.
Infumo, aui, are, to drye in the smoke.
Infundibulum, a tounnell, whereinto licour is poured, whan vessels are fylled.
Infundo, infudi, infundere, to poure in.
Infurnibulum, a piele, wherwith breadde is put into the ouen.
Ingemo, gemui, ere, to lament or bewayle moche.
Ingeniculor, aris, ari, to bowe the knee, or make courtesye.
Ingenium, the propre nature of a thynge. Also wytte.
Ingeniosus, wyttye.
Ingens, tis, wonderfull great.
Ingenuatus, comme of an honeste stocke or kynrede.
Ingenuus, a free man borne, or a gentylmã.
Ingenuitas, tatis, freedome.
Ingenuus, a, um, naturall.
Ingenuè, freely, frankely.
Ingero, gessi, gerere, to bryng in, to myxt.
Ingitas, tatis, pouertie.
Inglorius, ria, um, of no renome or fame.
Ingluuies, gluttonie. Also the cray or gorge in byrdes.
Ingrandesco, sci, scere, to waxe greate.
Ingratis, agaynst my wyll, or our wylle.
Ingrauesco, sci, scere, to ouercharge.
Ingredior, eris, gredi, to entre.
Ingruo, ui, ere, to inuade, to be imminẽt, proprely spoken of battayle or tempest.
Inguina, the pryuie membres of menne and womenne.
Inguinaria, an herbe which cureth the diseases in pryuie membres.
Ingurgito, aui, are, to deuoure gluttonously.
Inhæreo, to cleaue or stycke to.
Inhæresco, sci, scere, to stycke faste.
Inhalo, aui, are, to drawe in brethe.
Inhibeo, bui, bére, to forbydde.
Inhio, aui, are, to gape. also to couete moch.
Inhonor, withoute honour.
Inhorreo, rui, rere, Inhorresco, scere, to abhorre, to quake for feare.
Inhumanus, cruell, vncourteyse.
Inibi, euen there, anon, amonge them.
Iniicio, inieci, iniicere, to caste or throwe in, to cast at some thynge, to throwe with violence, to putte on.
Iniicere manum, to sease or take possessyon of a thynge. Manus iniectio, a seaser of lande.
Inimicitia, hostilitie, contrarye to amytie.

Inimico, caui, care, to make enemies.
Inimicor, caris, cari, to practise hostilitie.
Inimicus, an ennemye.
Ininde, from thens.
Iniquus, a, um, not euen or playne. Also not indifferent or iuste, sometyme great, strait, or narrowe.
Iniquitas, tatis, parcialite, cõtrary to iustice.
Initio, aui, are, to instructe in thynges concernynge relygion. Initiatus, instructed or entred in rules concerning religion. also to begyn to do a thynge.
Initior, aris, ari, to begynne: also to be weaned, as chylderne be.
Initium, a beginnyng, a sacrifice to Ceres.
Inito, aui, are, to walke in.
Iniuges, catell neuer yoked or broken, whiche were sometyme sacrificed.
Iniungo, xi, gere, to inioyne, to appoynt, to lay on, as a mã wil adde to a great burdein.
Iniuria, wronge, iniurie, reproche, damage. Taken like an aduerbe, it signifyeth, without cause, without deserte.
Iniuriosus, a wronge doer.
Iniurius, a, um, wrongfull, he that doth any thynge agaynst the lawe.
Innitor, teris, inniti, to assaye, to indeuour.
Innato, aui, are, to swymme in a place.
Innocuus, a, um, vnharmefull, he that doth none harme.
Innotesco, sci, scere, to be knowen.
Innoxius, a, um, wherin is no damage, that whiche can do none harme.
Innumerato, in a redynesse.
Innuo, nui, ere, to graunt or assent with noddynge of the heed.
Ino, the name of Cadmus daughter, the wyfe of Athamas kynge of Thebans.
Inocco, aui, are, to harowe in.
Inoculo, aui, are, to greffe.
Inodorus, without sauoure.
Inolesco, sci, scere, to waxe greate.
Inopiosus, a, um, needye.
Inops, pis, poore, lackynge helpe. Also vnburyed.
Inora, beastes without mouthes.
In posterum, at the laste, in conclusyon.
Inprimis, specially, principally, chiefly.
Inquies, quietis, & inquietus, ta, tum, vnrestefull, vnquyete.
Inquieto, aui, are, to vnquyete or trouble.
Inquilino, inquilinaui, quilinare, to dwell in a straunge place.
Inquilinus, he that dwelleth in a place, where neither he, nor his auncetoures were borne.
Inquino, aui, are, to defyle or polute.
Inquio, I saye.
Inquiro, siui, quirere, to inquyre.

L   Inqui-

Inquisitius, more intentifely, more inwardly
Insanio, iui, ire, to be madde or peuysshe, to dote, to do vnaduisedly.
Insanus, madde, peuysshe, regardyng no counsell, frowarde, vntractable.
Insania, madnes, peuysshenes, dotage, frowardenesse.
Inscitia, ignoraunce.
Inscius, a, um, ignoraunt.
Inscienter, ignorauntly.
Inscribo, scripsi, scribere, to write in or vpon, to name or intitle.
Inscriptus, a, um, vnwritten, written vpon, named, or intitled.
Insecta, be all flyes and wormes, that be diuided in their bodies, the heed and breaste from the bealy and tayle, as bees, waspes, emotes, or pismeres, and suche lyke.
Insequor, eris, sequi, to folowe or pursue.
Insero, serui, rere, insertum, to set in, to ioyn. whan it hath inseui, insitu, it sygnyfyeth to
Inserto, aui, are, to sette to.   (greffe.
Insertorium, the bond or thonge, wherwith a terget or buckeler is hanged on a mans
Inseruio, uiui, ire, to serue.   (arme.
Insideo, es, sedi, sidere, to sytte on, to sytte in, or be in, to besiege, to abyde in a place.
Insidiæ, wiles to vntrap a man, er he be ware.
Insidior, aris, ari, to practyse wyles, to intrappe or betray a man.
Insidiosus, a, um, full of wyles.
Insidiose, wylyly, craftily.
Insido, is, sidi, re, to entre to thintet to abide.
Insignia, signes or tokens of honour, wherby euery astate or great auctoritie is knowen, as robes, maces, swordes borne vpright, cappes of mayntenaunce, and other lyke thynges. Also somtyme tokens of doctrine and vertue: as staues typped with syluer, which bedels bere before doctors, hodes furred, crownes of laurell. &c.
Insignio, iui, ire, to note with somme sygne. Also to doubbe knyghtes.
Insignis, ne, notable, excellent, marked with some speciall token to be knowen.
Insigne, a notable signe or token.
Insignite, & insigniter, notably.
Insilio, luii, ire, to leape in or vp.
Insimul, togyther.
Insimulo, aui, are, to accuse or appeale, also to fayne or dissemble.
Insimulatio, an accusation or appeale.
Insinuatus, a, um, wounde togither.
Insinuo, aui, are, to bringe into, to conioyne, to put in a mans mynd couertly & craftily.
Insinuatio, a colourable & crafty beginning of an oration, dissembling som thing, where the matter may not be fauorably herde.
Insipidus, a, um, vnsauerye.

Insipiens, entis, without discretion.
Insisto, institi, insistere, to set fast and fyrmely, to indeuour, to prouoke or solicite. som
Insitio, onis, greffyng.   (time to assyst.
Insiritium, the stocke.
Insitium, the greffe. Also a iegot or other lyke meate stuffed with fleshe and egges chopped or mynced.
Insitiuus, ua, uum, infarcyd or stuffed.
Insolens, not wont or accustomed, haut, arrogant, presumptuous.
Insolentia, seldomnes of vse in any thynge, vnhauntynge of a place. Also presumption
Insolitus, not wont.   (wanton pride.
Insolo, aui, are, to drie in the sonne, to blech.
Insolatus, a, um, sunned. Insolatio, a sonnyng.
Insomnia, æ, lacke of powar to slepe.
Insomnium, a vayne dreame.
Insomnes noctes, nyghtes without slepe.
Insomniosus, slepy, or he that slepith moch.
Insons, insontis, innocent, or not gyltie.
Insonus, a, um, without noyse.
Inspectius, more aduysedly.
Inspecto, taui, tare, to beholde attentiuely, to wayte on.
Inspicio, spexi, cere, to beholde, to ouersee, to controll, to consyder a thing throughly.
Inspectio, a beholdynge, an ouersyghte, a controllemente.
Inspector, an ouerseer, a controller.
Inspico, aui, are, to make a thyng smalle, like to a wheate reede.
Inspiro, aui, are, to inspire, to blowe in.
Instans, tis, an instant, the least part of time.
Instantia, thinges that be present.
Instanter, instantly.   Instantia, diligence.
Instar, as it were or lyke.
Instatio, the instant tyme.
Instauro, aui, are, to new make, or begin any thig. somtime to renue or reform, to reedify
Instat, it is nigh, it is com, it is at hand. Cæsar ubi se diutius duci intellexit, et die instare, qua die frumentum militibus metiri oportebat, whan Cesar pceiued that he was delayed, & the day was nigh come, whan he muste nedes delyuer corne to his men of warre.
Insterno, straui, sternere, to couer, to sprede.
Instrara, trappers of horses.
Instratū, a counterpoynt. also it signifieth all tapisry, which serueth to couer any thing.
Instigo, inxi, gere, to meue inwardely.
Instinctus, inwardly meued.
Instigo, aui, are, to stere or pricke forwarde.
Instita, a purfyll.
Instito, aui, are, to repugne, or withstande.
Institor, oris, a chapman, a mercer, also he that selleth apparayle and fyne stuffe, goinge about therwith.
Institorius, ia, ium, pertaynyng to chapman.
Insti=

Cicero.
Ti. Liui%.

Instituo, tui, tuere, to institute, to begynne, to instructe or teache, to ordayne.
Institutiones, instructions in doctrine.
Instituta, ancient maners & customs, also ordinaces. Pro meo instituto, for my purpose.
Insto, as, institi, instare, to require instantely, to solicite, to stycke to, to resiste, to persist, to prease on, to come on, or immediatly folowe. Instat, it is nowe.
Instratum, the trappier or apparayle of an horse, a horseclothe.
Instrumentum, an instrument or toole. Also ordinance of warre, vessell and all necessaries of housholde and husbandry. sometyme it signifieth a dede or charter, cōcernyng lande dettes or couenantes.
Instruo, xi, struere, to sette in order or aray, to instructe, to fournyshe, to prepare.
Insubres, lumbardes, proprely menne of the duchy of Melayne.
Insucco, aui, are, to soke in lycour.
Insuesco, sueui, scere, to be wonte.
Insuetus, ta, tum, not vsed.
Insula, an yle inuirōned with water. It is also a hous in a town, hauig none other hous ioyned to it, but stretes on euery syde of it.
Insularis, re, belongyng to an yle.
Insularius, a, um, mooste vyle, proprely men banyshed into Iles to tygge mettall.
Insulatus, ta, tum, made an yle.
Insulto, taui, tare, to leape vppe, to scorne or speake in the reproche of a man.
Insultura, a leapynge vp or into a thyng.
Insum, inesse, to be in some thynge.
In summa, vniuersally, alway, fynally.

Augustinᵒ Insummo, are, to fynyshe.
Insumo, psi, ere, to spende or lay out money.
Insuper, furthermore, moreouer.
Insusurro, aui, are, to whisper in ones eare.
Integer, gra, grum, yf it be spoken of age, it signifieth yong & lusty: if it be spoke of a mā it signifieth honest in al poyntes & qualites, in a thynge it sygnyfyeth entier or hoole.
Integer æui, lustye of age.
Integrasco, sci, scere, to be renewed.
Integro, aui, are, to begyn agayn, to renewe.
Integrum mihi est, It is in my power, or at my pleasure, at myne arbiterment.
Intellectus, vnderstandynge.
Intellectualis, of vnderstandynge.
Intelligibile, that maye be vnderstande.
Intelligo, lexi, ligere, to vnderstande.
Intelligentia, the perceyuyng of the minde.
Intemerata, perfecte sacryfyces, all thynges obserued.
Intemperiæ, goddesses, hauynge power to doo harme.
Intemperies, & intēperātia, vntemperatnes.
Intempesta nox, mydnyght, whan all thing is in sylence.
Intempestas, tatis, the caulme of the water, whan there is no tempeste.
Intempestiuus, ua, um, thinge out of tyme or season. Intempestiué, vntymely.
Intendo, di, dere, to bende or stretche. Also to loke diligently on a thynge, to knytte or tie, to inforce with myght.
Intendere animū, to set or fixe the mynde.
In tenebris saltare, signifieth to do a thynge vnaduisedly, and without any iugement.
Intentatus, not assayed.
Intentio, signifyeth not intente or purpose, but for the act that is apointed or executid.
Intento, aui, are, to menace.
Intentus, ta, tum, sette or fyxed.
Inter, betwene, amonge.
Inter sacrum et saxum, in the poynte to peryshe and be vtterly loste.
Interamna, a citie in Italye.
Interaneus, a, um, that whiche is within.
Interanea, the inwardes of man or beast.
Interaresco, sci, scere, to be dried vp.
Interbibo, bi, bere, to drynke all out.
Intercalaris, re, & intercalarius, a, um, put or set betwene. Intercalaris dies, the daye of the leape yere.
Intercalo, aui, are, to set or put betwene.
Intercalaris mensis, the moneth, in the whiche certayne dayes were sette, that lacked to make the yere complete, whych moneth is Februarye.
Intercalaris uersus, a syngular verse, often repeted amonge other verses. Some doo call it, in englyshe balades and songes, the foote or refrette of a ditie.
Intercapedo, dinis, a space or pawse.
Intercedo, cessi, cedere, to make intercessiō. also to go betwene, or be betwene.
Intercedit mihi tecum amicitia, There is amite betwene the and me. Tribuni intercesserunt, The tribunes dyd let or prohibite.
Intercessio Tribunorum, a let or prohibition of the Tribunes agaynst the auctoritie of other offycers.
Intercido, cidi, re, to cut asōder in ȝ middis.
Intercisa & porrecta, cut of & made longer.
Intercido, cidi, ere, to decaye or perisshe betwene this and that.
Intercino, nere, to synge betwene or in the myddell of a thynge.
Intercipio, cæpi, ere, to preuent or apprehēd one vnware, to take in the middes, or in the meane while, sometyme to take all.
Intercisi dies, were dayes diuided, part holy day, parte warkedaye.
Intercludo, si, ere, to shut in, to stoppe, to let.
Intercolumnium, the space betwene pilars.
Intercus, cutis, a disease betwene the skinne

Salustiᵒ in Iugurth.

Vide Calepinum.

L.ii.   and

and the fleshe: whan it is an adiectiue, it signifieth inwarde. Intercutibus uitiis madens res, ouerwette with inwarde vices.

Intercutaneus, ea, eū, that is within the skin.

Interdico, xi, cere, to prohibite greuously: also to resyste or lette.

Interdictum, a prohibition.

Interdiu, in the day tyme.

Interdum, sometyme.

Interea, in the meane while. also neuer the lesse. Interea loci, in the meane space.

Intereo, rii, ire, to dye vtterly.

Interitus, deathe.

Interequito, aui, are, to ryde betwene.

Interest mea, tua, sua, nostra, uestra, it behoueth me, the, hym, vs, you, or it prineth to me, the, hym. &c. also it maketh matter, or is a diuersitie. Nihil interest tui, It is no matter to the. Si nihil interest regis, peto ut dum dico, uinculis liberer, If it be noo matter to the kyng, I pray you, whiles I do speake, lette me be without gyues. Sometime it signifieth to be in the myddes.

Interfœmineū, a womans priuy tokē, wherby she is knowen from a man.

Interficio, feci, to slee.

Interfluo, xi, ere, to flowe betwene.

Interfundo, fudi, fundere, to poure betwene.

Intergerimus, a wall added to an olde foundation or walle, to sustayne it.

Interhæc, in this meane tyme.

Interi, they that be within.

Interiaceo, cui, cere, to put betwene, to cast betwene.

Interibi, in the myddell of that place.

Interiectum tempus, the meane tyme.

Interiicio, ieci, iicere, to laye or put betwene.

Interim, in the mean space or time, in the mean season. also sometime, sodainly, otherwhile.

Interimo, emi, imere, to kylle.

Interior, & interius, the inner.

Interiungo, ere, to tarie.

Interlino, inere, to enterline.

Interloquor, eris, qui, to speke in a māns tale.

Interluceo, lucere, to shyne betwene, or in the myddes.

Interluco, care, to make a glade in the myddell of a wodde.

Interluniū, the space of tyme, in the whiche neither the old mone doth appere, nor the newe moone is seene.

Interluo, ere, to flowe betwene, to wasshe betwene meales, or other actes.

Intermedius, a, um, in the myddell. *Ci. de ora.*

Intermestris luna, the newe mone at the very chaunge.

Intermestrum, the tyme whan the moone is at the poynt to chaunge.

Intermico, to shyne in the myddes.

Interminor, aris, ari, to threten sore.

Intermitto, tere, to leaue or put of for a time.

Intermorior, to dye vtterly.

Intermortuus, a, um, deed for a season.

Interneco, are, to slee all at ones.

Internectiuum bellū, warre to vtter distruction or dethe.

Internecio, a vniuersall slaughter.

Internicinū bellum, warre to the vtterance.

Internodium, a ioynt in a mans fynger. also a ioynt in a strawe or rede.

Internosco, noscere, to knowe a thynge amonge other thynges.

Internuncius, a messager, or meane betwene two persons being at variance.

Internus, a, nū, that whiche is within, or inward. Inter opus, euen in the doinge.

Interordiniū, a space betwene that which is in order. Interordo, dinis, idem.

Interpello, are, to interrupt or lette one that speaketh or dothe any thynge, also to require, to aske or demaunde.

Interpensiua, certayne pieces of tymber, whiche are sette frome the corners of the walle, to the endes of the rafters, to conuaye rayne water into the spoutes.

Interpensiui parietes, walles, which rise vppon an other walle, and haue no fundacion in the grounde.

Interpola, newe inuentions, or deuyses.

Interpolo, are, to putte or sette betwene, to renewe or refreshe any thynge.

Interpolator, oris, & interpolatrix, tricis, he or she that refresheth olde thynges, and do make them seme newe.

Interpolis, le, interpolus, la, um, renewed, refreshed.

Interpono, sui, nere, to put betwene.

Interponere fidem publicā, to promise vpon the credence & consent of all the people. *Salustius in Iugurth.*

Interpremo, to stoppe or close in.

Interpres, pretis, an interpretour or translatour. Also a styckler betwene two, whiche are at varyaunce.

Interpretamentum, & interpretatio, an interpretation or translation.

Interpretor, aris, ari, to interprete, expoune, or translate.

Interputo, are, to cutte betwene.

Interrasile, that whiche is playne betwyxte two partes grauen or imbosed.

Interrex, regis, he that ruleth in the meane tyme, betwene the cessynge of the auctoritie of one principall gouernour, by deth or otherwise, vntylle an other be elected into the same offyce.

Interregnum, the saide meane tyme of gouernaunce or rule.

Interrogo, are, to demaunde a question.

Inter-

Salusti⁹ in Catalinar. Cic. in Prę tura urba.

Interrogati legibus, to be tried by examinatiō, that they had offēded agaīnst the lawis.
Interrūpo, rupi, pere, to breke in the middes.
Interscalmia, the spaces betwene thē oores in a bote or galey.
Interscapilium, the space betwene the shulders vnder the necke.
Interscindo, di, scindere, to cut in the middis.
Intersepio, sepsi, pire, to diuide in the middel with some inclosure.
Intersepta, the gristell, which maketh particion betwene the nosethrilles.
Intersero, seui, serere, to sowe or set betwene or in the myddes.
Intersono, are, to make noyse in the middes or betwene.
Interspiro, are, to spring vp in the middes.
Intersterno, to strawe betwene, or throwe thynges betwene.
Interstitium, a distance or space betwene.
Intersum, interesse, to be present. also to differ, to be diuers. Stulto intelligēs quid interest? what diuersitie is there betwene a fole and a wise man?
Intertextus, a, ū, woue or wrought betwene. or tinselde, as cloth of tinsyl, or bawdekyn.
Intertrigo, ginis, gallynge, whiche hapneth by the occasion of sweate betwene the legges, the toes, or fyngers.
Intertrimentum, & intertritura, the losse of bothe partes, or on bothe sydes.
Interturbo, are, to trouble excedyngly.
Interuaco, are, to be vacant or void betwene
Interuallum, a space betwene.
Interuello, ere, to plucke vp here & there.
Interuenio, ire, to come in the meane while, to be present amonge other.
Interuenium, the space betwene the vaines.
Interuerto, re, to take away craftily or falsly.
Interuiso, ere, to visite among, or now & thā.
Interula, a shyrte or smocke.
Intestabilis, he whiche by the law can make no testamēt. somtime it signifieth detestable.
Intestatus, he that dyeth without makynge any testament, intestate. Also he that dieth makyng none heyre by testament. also a mā out of credence, whome no manne wylle take for a wytnesse.
Intestina, the bowelles, or inwarde parte of man, or other thynge lyuynge.
Intestinum bellum, where people do warre within their owne realme.
Intestinum odium, hate with hart & mynde, mortall hatrede.
Intestinum opus, the inwarde buyldynge of tymber and pargette.
Intingo, xi, gere, to depe, as one dothe his fynger into lycour.
Intorqueo, si, quēre, to thrust in by throwing

of a darte, or other lyke thynge. Also to tourne or wynde in.
Intra, within. Intra modum, lesse thanne a meane, shorte of a meane.
Intra famā, les thā the opiniō that mē haue.
Interius, more inwarde.
Intimus, moste inwarde, moste secrete.
Intrarius, idem.
Internus, na, num, whiche is within.
Intrico, are, to wrappe.
Intrimentum, damage eyther to the gyuer, or to the receyuour.
Intrinsecus, within.
Intritus, brayed in a morter.
Intro, into a place.
Intro, are, to entre or goo in.
Introcludo, si, dere, to shutte in.
Introduco, xi, cere, to brynge or leade in.
Introéo, iui, ire, to goo in.
Introgredior, eris, gredi, to comme in.
Intromitto, misi, mittere, to lette in.
Introrsus, into, within.
Introrumpo, rupi, rumpere, to breake in.
Introspicio, spexi, spicere, to loke in.
Introuoco, are, to calle in.
Intueor, eris, eri, to beholde in.
Intus, in a place.
Intusium, a shyrte or smocke.
Intutus, ta, tum, vnsure.
Intybum erraticum, cicorie or white endiue.
Inuado, si, re, to inuade, to entre, to apphēd.
Inualesco, lui, scere, to waxe stronge, to be confyrmed or stablyshed.
Inualidus, da, dum, feeble, weake.
Inualetudo, dinis, feblenesse.
Inuectiue orationes, orations made ageynst one in reprouyng his maners and lyuynge.
Inueho, uexi, uehere, to carye in a thinge, to carye a thynge into a place.
Inuehor, eris, uehi, to rebuke one vehemently, and with violent and soore wordes.
Inuenio, ire, to fynde a thing, whiche a man seeketh for.
In uerba iurare, to be sworne as princis coūsaylours and seruantes be sworne vnto thē. Also to do feaultie.
In uersum, in numbre and order.
Inuerto, tere, to tourne in, to tourne vppe so downe, to turne in and out after the vulgar speche, properly to turne euery thyng contrary to the ryght fourme or facion.
Inuestes, yonge children without heare on their bodies.
Inuestigo, are, to seke out, to finde in sekīg.
Inuestigabilis, le, that maye not be founde with sekynge.
Inuestio, iui, ire, to adorn or garnishe a thing.
Inueterati, olde shrewes or vnthriftes, men in lyuynge vnthriftily waxed olde.

Galenus. Plinius. Columel.

L.iii. Inue-

I ante N.

Inueteresco, raui, scere, to were out for age, to be oute of vse, to be aged or olde. Also worne out, almoste consumed.

Inuicem, togither, one the other. Inuicem diligunt, they do loue one an other. also it signifieth for thy parte. Habes res urbanas, inuicem rusticas scribe, Howe thou knowest the affaires of the citie, for thy parte write what is done in the countrey.

Inuidentia, enuy, griefe to beholde or here that an other man prospereth.

Inuideo, uidi, dere, to haue enuy at an others prosperitie. Inuideo tibi doctrinam, I haue enuy at thy lernynge. Also to see inwardly or through a thynge.

Inuisus, uisa, uisum, hated.

Inuidia, enuy, hatred, yll wyll.

Salusti⁹ in Iugurth. Inuidia facti sui, the displeasure of his acte, or attemptate, or the dede wherfore he was enuied and hated.

Inuidiosa res, a thynge, whiche bredeth enuye or hatred.

Inuidiose, enuyousely.

Inuidiosus, an enuyous persone. sometyme he, whiche is enuied.

Inuidus, he that hath enuye.

Inuigilo, are, to haue watche of a thynge, or to lay watche, to care.

Inuinius, he that neuer drynketh wyne.

Inuisus, a, ū, neuer sene. also hatid or odious.

Inuitatus, boden, as to a feaste or bankette.

Inuito, are, to bydde. also to delyte, to fylle the bealy.

Inuitus, ta, tum, vnwyllynge, or agaynste a mannes wylle.

In uniuersum, vnyuersally.

Inuius, a, um, lackynge a way, or where nothynge can passe.

Inumbro, are, to make shadowe: somtyme it signifieth to defende.

Inunco, uncare, to catche, as it were with an hooke.

Inundo, to ouerflowe, or surrounde.

Inundatio, a floudde.

In unguem, to the poynte, perfectly.

Inuoco, care, to calle in, to call for helpe, also not to calle.

Inuolo, are, to steale, to lay violent handes on one, to flee out.

Inuolucris, a byrde not redy to flee.

Inuolucrum, that whiche is wrapped.

Inuolucre, as a thinge whiche is wrappped togither.

Inuoluo, uere, to wrappe.

Inuolutus, ta, tum, wrapped.

Inuoluolus, & inuoluola, a worme lyke a canker, whyche is on vynes, and whan he is taken of, he wrappeth hym selfe rounde togither.

¶ I Ante O.

IO, an interiection, signifieng sometyme grefe, as in Tibullo. Vror io, O I burne. Sometyme excessiue gladnesse, as in Ouidio. Dicite io pæan.

Iochabella, the name of Moyses mother. *Iosephus*

Iocus, plurali ioca, a mery worde, disporte.

Iocor, aris, ari, to speke merily, or in disport.

Iocosus, a, um, & iocularis, lare, mery, sportfull, prouokynge myrthe.

Ioculus, a lyttell sport or myrthe.

Iolaus, the sonne of Iphiclus, of whom the people of Sardinia, were named Iolenses.

Iole, the daughter of Euritus, kynge of Aetolia, whom Herculus loued.

Ionia, a region of the lasse Asia, wherein were the citie of Ephesus, Miletum, & Clazomenæ.

Ion, a stone of a vyolet colour.

Ionia, a citie of the Athenienses.

Ionicus, ca, cum, & Ionius, a, um, of Ionia.

Ioppe, a citie of the countrey of Palestina, not farre from Ierusalem, standyng by the see, whiche some men do suppose to be the hauyn, callyd Port Iaffe.

Iordanis, a ryuer of Iudea, commonly callyd flume Iordane.

Ios, an yle where Homerus was buried.

Iotapata, a citie in Syria.

Iouiniani, were men of armes, so called of Maximian the emperoure, whiche dydde valyantly in the countrey of Illiria.

Iouis, the genitiue case of Iupiter.

¶ I Ante P.

IPhianassa, the wyfe of Melāpos, whom for her beautie Iuno tourned into furye or madnesse.

Iphigenia, the daughter of kyng Agamemnon, with whom he dydde sacrifice going to Troye.

Ips, ipos, a lyttell worme, bredynge in hornes and vynes.

Ipse, ipsa, ipsum, he, she, that same, by demonstratynge or shewynge the persone or thynge spoken of.

Ipsemet, he hym selfe.

Ipsippe, to hym and none other.

Ipsulces, plates embosed like to fygures or images of men or women.

Iphitus, the sonne of Praxonidis, whiche fyrste ordayned the solempne playes callyd Olympiada.

¶ I Ante R.

IR, the holownesse of the hande. somme tyme it sygnifieth the hole hande.

Ira, wrathe, an appetite to punyshe him, of whom

of whom we be offended.

Iracundia, angre, displeasure agaynst one, a desyre to be reuenged.

Iracundus, shortly or soone angrie, hastie.

Irascor, eris, irasci, to be angrye.

Iratè, angrely.

Iratus, angrye.

Irceus, a kynde of pud dynges.

Ircipes, an harowe.

Ire inficias, to denye.

Ire pedibus in sententiam, to consente to the sentence or raison of an other, which hath spoken, or to be of the same opinyon.

Irenarches, & irenarcha, he whiche is in auctoritie to see peace kepte in a countreye or citie, which amonge vs may be callyd a Iustice of the peace.

Iris, iris, uel iridis, the rayne bowe. it is also a floure deluce, the roote wherof is verye soote, and is commonly called Yreos.

Irnium, oyle of Ireos.

Ironia, is a fygure in speakynge, whanne a man dissemblyth in speche that whyche he thynketh not: as in scoffyng or bourdyng, callynge that fayre, whyche is fowle in dede, that good, whiche is yl, that eloquét, which is barbarous. Semblably reasoning contrary to that I thinke, to the intente to mocke hym, with whome I doo dyspute or reason.

Ironice, mockyshly, scoffyngly.

Ironicus, he that vsethe that fasshyon in speakynge.

Irrasus, vnshauen.

Irraucio, raucui, cere, to be hoorse.

Irrenumerabile, that may not be rewarded or recompensed.

Irreparabile, that maye not be repaired or restored to the fyrste astate.

Irrepo, psi, pere, to crepe in.

Irreprehensus, a, ū, that can not be reprouid.

Irretio, iui, ire, to be taken or holden in, as it were in a nette.

Irretitus, taken, lapt in with crafte, or faire promyses.

Irrigo, to water grounde, to brynge water into the fieldes out of a ryuer.

Irriguus, gua, guum, the grounde or fielde that may be casyly watered. sometyme the water, whyche may be casyly diryuted into the fieldes.

Irripio, pere, to plucke in.

Irrito, are, to make voyde & of none effecte.

Irritus, ta, tum, voide, of none effect or force.

Irrito, hauynge the laste syllable sauynge one, longe, to prouoke, to kendyl wrathe, to styrre vppe.

Irrogare mulctam, to sette a payne.

Irructo, are, to blowe in by belkynge.

Irrugio, gere, to braye oute.

Irrumo, are, to sucke in.

Irrumpo, rupi, irrumpere, to breake in, or enter with force. somtyme to breake asonder.

Irruo, to rounne hastilye or furiously into battayle, or vppon any thynge. sometyme to falle in, or cast in.

¶ I Ante S.

Is, a pronowne, whiche signifieth he.

Iseus, a famouse rhetorician, whiche inuētid to make euery matter cōpendious.

Isagoge, an introduction.

Isagogicon, a waye to introduce, or begyn to teache.

Isapis, a ryuer nygh to Cecenna.

Isara, a ryuer commynge oute of the Rone, where the hylle callyd Cemenus is ioyned to the Rone: and so runneth by Druentia into the goulfe of Uenyse.

Isacia, an yle ageynste Uelia, callydde also Oenotris.

Isauria, a region of the lasse Asia.

Isaurum, a cite in the countrey of Paphilia.

Ischia, the houckle bone. it is somtyme taken for the ache in the sayde bone, whiche vulgare physicions do call Sciatica.

Ischiadicus, uel Ischiacus, he that hathe the ache in the hyppe, cōmonly callid Sciatica.

Isiaci, the priestes of the goddesse Isis.

Isis, called also Io, one of the harlottes of Iupiter, whom he tourned into a cowe for feare of Iuno his wyfe.

Isitium, a certeyne puddynge. some calle it an Isynge.

Ismarus, a mountayne in Thracia.

Ismenias, the name of an excellent minstrel, whiche played on the shalmes.

Ismenus, a ryuer in the cuntrey of Boeotia.

Isocolon, where two sentences are in lyke lengthe.

Isocrates, the name of a famous oratoure, of wonderfulle eloquence, oute of whose schole proceded the moste excellente oratours of Grece.

Isodomon, a fourme of buyldynge, where euery thynge is equally strayght.

Isonomia, equalite of lawes, as where they be indifferent & like to al maner of persons.

Isopleurus, thre edged.

Israel, sygnifieth a man seinge god.

Issa, an yle in the Uenician see ioynynge to Slauonie.

Issus, a citie in Sicile, and a ryuer of Siria.

Ister, istri, the great ryuer callyd Danubius, in duche Danowe.

Ister, the greattest ryuer of Europa, called also Danubius, Danowe.

Istic, there, where thou arte.

Isthmus,

Isthmus, a narowe parte of the countreye, where two sees are but a small distaunce asonder. There be dyuers suche places in Grecia, and of them were certayn playes called Isthmia.

Istria, a parte of Italye, marchynge on Illiria, callyd nowe Slauonye.

¶ I ANTE T.

ITA, so, so moche, therfore.
Ita sane, ye truely.
Italia, Italye.
Italus, an Italyan.
Italica, a citie in Italia, whiche by an nother name is called Confinium. There is an other in Spayn, where Silius Italicus was borne.
Italicus, ca, cum, of Italye.
Italicensis, a citesen of Italica.
Item, in lyke wyse.
Iter, eris, itiner, itineris, a iourneye. also a way. Iter habeo ad Cæsarem, I take my iorney to the emperour.
Itero, are, to do a thynge eftesoones, to goo backe agayne.
Iterum, eftesoones, or agayne.
Ithaca, the countrey of Vlysses.
Ithome, a towne in Peloponeso, an nother in Thessaly.
Ithonia, a countrey in Grece.
Ithyra, a towne on the mountain of Taurus.
Ithyphallus, the name of Priapus the most dishonest and abhominable ydoll. Also the secrete membre being in prosperite.
Iridem, semblably, also.
Itinerarium, a commentarye or boke of remembraunce, contaynynge thynges commytted in iourneyes. Also it is a kalender of myles in the distance of places, with the tyme of abode in euerye place, lyke to iestes of princis.
Iteneror, aris, ari, to goo in iourneye.
Ito, taui, tare, to go moche.

Cicero. Ituria, a region in Arabia, or Siria, of whiche the people are callyd Ituræi.
Itus, & itio, a goinge. Quid noster itus & reditus, what our goinge and commyng.
Itys, the sonne of Tereus and Prognes, who, as poetes doo fayne, was tourned into a fesaunt.

¶ I, Ante V.

IVBA, the mane of a beaste. Also the name of a kynge of Barbarye.
Iubar, a sterre, whiche is also callid Lucyfer and Hesperus. it is somtyme taken for bryghtenesse.
Iubeo, iussi, iubere, to commande, to desire, to wyshe, to exhorte, to decree.
Iubilo, are, to declare in the voyce, the ioye and gladnesse of the harte, whiche maye not be expressed with wordes.
Iubilum, ioye and gladnes in voyce, not expressed in wordes.
Iucundor, aris, ari, to be ioyous and mery.
Iucundus, a, um, he or that, whiche is the cause that an nother reioyseth, dylectable, pleasaunt to see or here.
Iudæa, Iewry, or the countrey of Iewes.
Iudæus, a Iewe.
Iudex, iudicis, a iudge.
Iudex ordinarius, he that hath auctoritie of his propre iurysdiction, to sytte in iugement without commission. As the chiefe Iustice of Englande, the Mayre of a cytie incorporate, and a Coroner.
Iudex delegatus, he that sytteth by commission, as all other iudges and iustices.
Iudicialis, le, of a Iudge.
Iudiciarius, a, um, pertaynynge to a iuge, or that whiche is to be iuged.
Iuditium, iudgement.
Iuditium habere, to gyue iugement.

Lau. Valla in Barpt.fa ciū.lib.2.

Iudico, are, to iudge or deeme, to suppose, to gyue sentence, to condemne.
Iugale uinculum, the bonde of matrimonye.
Iugalis, he that is yoked.
Iugantinus deus, was amonge paynyms the god, whom they supposed to haue auctoritie ouer the rydges of hylles.
Iugarius, a streete in Rome, where was an aultar of Iuno, whyche men supposed dyd ioyne matrimonie surely.
Iugeratim, by sondry furlonges.
Iugere, to crye lyke a kyte.
Iugerum, & iugus, geris, as moche grounde as one yoke of oxen wyll eare in a day. som suppose it to contayne in length 240. feete, in bredth halfe so moche. some saye, that it is more. Leonardus Portius saythe, by the auctoritie of Columella, that Iugerum containeth .xxviii. thousand v.viii. hudred fete.
Iuges, oxen lyke in greatnes, callid yokes, or payres.
Iugis, contynuynge in one thynge.
Iugiter, contynually.
Iuglans, andis, a wall nutte.
Iugo, are, to yoke or couple togither.
Iugosus, rydged.
Iugula, a celestyalle Sygne, contaynynge thre sterres.
Iugulo, are, to slee, not onely with weapon, but also with syckenes. Quartana neminem iugulat, The feuer quartayn sleeth no man.
Iugulus, the foreparte of the necke, whyche is dyuided in two great synewes, Dexter, & sinister.

Celf.li.4.

Iugulum ferire, to slee proprely in the neck.
Iugulum petere, whan an oratour or man of lawe, toucheth vehemently the poynte of the

the matter, and with manyfeſt and ſore argumentes and reaſons, ſeemeth to aſſaulte and oppreſſe the contrarie parte, as it were with ſharpe weapons.

Iugum, a yoke. alſo the rydge of an hyll or banke, alſo the beame, wheron weauers do tourne their webbe. Alſo a thynge lyke to a galowes, vnder the whiche in ſygne of reproche, they whiche were vanquiſhed, were conſtrayned to creepe, whiche was made with two ſpeares ſtandynge, and one ſpeare ouerthwarte. Alſo a frame, wheron vynes are ioyned. Alſo a beame, whereon balaces do hange. Alſo the ſyde beames in a ſhyppe, in the whyche the traunſomes are faſtened.

Iulis, a citie in the yle of Cæa, the countrey of Simonides the poete.

Iulia, a kynred, whiche proceded from Aſcanius, ſonne of Aeneas, callyd Iulus. alſo a towne in Cales, in the coūtrey of Spain.

Iulius, the moneth of July, which toke his name of Iulius Ceſar.

Iulus, otherwiſe namid Aſcanius, the ſonne of Aeneas. Iulus, is alſo a litle worme with many fete, bredynge in vynes & okes, whiche is alſo callyd Conuoluolus, Inuoluolus, & Voluola. It is alſo the moſyneſſe of the outwarde parte of fruites. Alſo the yonge fruite immediately after that the flowres be fallen.

Iuli, be alſo the moſyneſſe or ſofte heares, whiche do growe on the beardes & viſages of yong men, before that they be ſhaue: and ſomtyme it ſignifieth the ſame yonge men.

Iulus, is alſo a fyſhe, whiche is guyde vnto whales: whiche alſo is called Hegeter. it is moreouer a ſonge dedicate to Diana.

Iumentum, euerye beaſte that drawethe or beareth burdeyns. alſo a lyttel carre.

Iunctim, ioyntely.

Iunculi, meate callid iunkettes: alſo a freſhe cheſe made on ruſhes, callid a iackeman.

Iuncus, a bullē ruſhe.

Iuncus odoratus, a ſpyce that is medicinable, ſpecially to make the brethe ſwete.

Iungami, people in the coūtrey of Liguria.

Iungo, xi, gere, to ioyne.

Iunix, icis, a yonge cowe or hefar.

Iuniculi, ſmall vynes ioyned togyther.

Iuniperus, a ſwete buſhe, called Ieoneper.

Iunis, ne, yonge, whereof commeth Iunior, yonger.

Iunius, the monethe callyd June. alſo a mannes name.

Iuno, the wyfe of Iupyter. it is ſometyme taken for the ayre.

Iunonia maior, & minor, be two of the fortunate Iles.

Iupiter, iouis, the name of a greate prynce, whiche for his wyſedom and prowes was honoured of the gentyles for chiefe of all goddes. It is alſo the name of a planette, whiche is alwaye beneuolent in his influence and courſe.

Iuramentum, an othe.

Iuratus, ſworne.

Iurgioſus, a, um, braulyng, full of contētion.

Iurgium, a braulynge, or a ſmall contention.

Iurgo, are, to braule or chyde.

Iuridicus, ca, cum, accordynge to the lawe, or belongynge to the lawe.

Iuriſdictio, iuriſdiction, power, or auctoritie to miniſtre and execute lawes.

Iuro, iurare, to ſweare.

Iurulentus, ta, tum, full of iuice, or lycoure.

Ius, iuris, lawe, auctoritie, lybertie, power, ryght. ſomtyme the place, where the lawe is miniſtred. Alſo lycour or iuyce. De iure meo, tuo, ſuo decedere, to omytte ſome part of the rygour or extremitie of the lawe. Pro ſuo iure agere, & ſummo iure agere, to take the extremite of the lawe. Summū ius, the rygour of the lawe.

Iuſcum, & iuſculum, brothe, wherein meate hath ben ſodden.

Iusiurandum, a ſolempne othe or promyſe made to GOD.

Iuſſa, commaundementes.

Iuſſus, a, um, commaunded.

Iuſta, ſacrifices done for deed men: now it may be vſed for funerall exequies.

Iuſta ſoluere, is propzely in funeralle obſequies, to do and performe al thinges thervnto neceſſarie. *Cicer pro Roſcio.*

Iuſtitia, iuſtice, rygtuouſneſſe.

Iuſtitium, a ceſſynge for a tyme from miniſtration of lawes in places iudiciall.

Iuſtus, a iuſte or rightuous man, an vpright and true meanynge manne. It is taken ofte tymes in holy ſcripture for a vertuouſe mā or good man.

Iuſtus, ta, tum, equall, meane betwene twoo extremities. Iuſta magnitudo, neither more nor leſſe, the iuſte quantitie. ſomtyme it ſygnifyeth greatneſſe. Iuſta pars, the greatte parte. Iuſto labore, with great labour. Iuſtas inimicitias, great hoſtilitie. ſometyme it ſignifieth amonge lawyers, true or very. Iuſtus filius, his very ſonne.

Iuturna, the ſyſter of Turnus.

Iuuamen, iuuatio, & iuuamentum, helpe.

Iuuenalia, playes vowed for the helthe of yonge menne.

Iuuenalis, le, pertaynyng to youthe.

Iuuenalis dies, a day celebrate to youth.

Iuuenalis, is alſo the name of a poete, whiche wrate Satyres.

Iuuen-

Iuuencus, & iuuenca, yonge, not onely men but also beastes. Iuuenculus, idem.
Iuuenesco, scere, to waxe, or be yonge.
Iuuenilis, le, yonge.
Iuueniliter, yongely.
Iuuenis, a yonge man.
Iunior, oris, yonger.
Iuuentus, tutis, youthe. sometyme a multitude of yonge men.
Iuuo, uas, iuui, are, to helpe, to delyte.
Iuxta, nighe, ioyntly or togither, euen like, accordynge. *Nunc uero quo in loco res nostræ sint, iuxta mecum oēs intelligitis*, Howe howe the matter standeth, ye all knowe as well as I: or els, in what case our busynes is, ye vnderstande all as moche as I do. [*Salustiꝰ in Catalinar.*]
Iuxtim, nygh to.
Ixon, a greate whyte byrde, of the kynde of Rauens.

¶ L ANTE A.

LABASCO, labascere, & labascor, sceris, to fayle or decaye.
Labefacio, labefacere, to breake or destroye.
Labefacto, ctare, to make feble, to appaire.
Labellum, a lyppe.
Labeo, onis, a manne or womanne hauynge greatte lyppes.
Labes, a spotte, whiche sodeynely hapneth to thynges that are smothe, a blemyshe.
Labecula, a lyttell spotte.
Labia, & labra, lyppes. Also Labrum is the brymme or brynke of a ryuer or fountayne. Also a fatte or lyke vessell necessarie to be bayned in. somtyme a fatte for wyne after that it is pressed. It may be vsed for a keele vate, wherinto ale or beere is putte.
Labicanum, a towne in Italy.
Labici, the inhabitantes of that towne.
Labicus, was the name of the sonne of Minos, who was named also Glaucus.
Labilis, bile, vnstable, whyche wylle soone falle, slypper.
Labina, slypperness.
Labo, are, to falle downe sodaynly.
Labor, eris, lapsus sum, labi, to slyde, to dye, to fayle, to fall downe by lyttell and lyttell.
Labor, labour, trauayle.
Laboriæ the name of a countrey in Italye, vulgarly called Terra laboris, the lande of laboure.
Laborinus, a felde in Campania, where the stubbyll of corne is so great, that the people do burne it in stede of wodde.
Laboriosus homo, a paynefull man.
Laboro, rare, to laboure, to be in heuynesse or griefe.
Labrusca, wylde vyne.
Labyrinthus, a maase, or any buildyng made like a maase, out of the which it were hard to gette forthe.
Lac, lactis, mylke.
Lacena, a kynde of apparayle. also a woman of Lacedemonia.
Lacedemon, uel Lacedemonia, a citie in the parte of Grece, which is nowe called Morea, wherof Menelaus was kynge.
Lacer, & lacerus, a, um, torne or rent.
Lacerna, a shorte cloke, whiche menne of warre be wont to weare.
Lacernatus, cloked, or cladde in a cloke.
Lacero, are, to teare in pieces, or to gyue many woundes.
Lacertus, & lacerta, a Lyzerde, an Euet: also the parte of a mannes arme, from the elbowe to the wreste of the hande, properly the brawne and synewes of the arme.
Lacertosus, hauynge greatte brawnes and synewes.
Lacesso, siui, & cessi, ssere, to rent, or goo aboute to rent the good renoume of a man. Also to prouoke a man to wrathe or displesure, with wordes, writynge, or acte: to rayle on a man, to prycke a man with some yll language or acte.
Lachana, all kynde of herbes.
Lachanopoles, a syller of herbes.
Lachanopolium, the herbe markette.
Lachesis, one of the thre ladies called Parce, whiche poetes dyd fayne, to haue the rule and contynuance of mans lyfe.
Lachrima, a teare in weepynge.
Lachrimo, are, to weepe.
Laciniæ, gardinges of a garment, properly where the skirtes be cutte in sondry facion. In lacinias, in peces. Lacinia, is also a redde musheron, whiche spryngeth at the rote of a chesten tree.
Laciniosus, a, um, cutte in sondrye facions, wyndyng and tournynge dyuers wayes.
Lacinium, an elbowe of lande, lyenge betwene the see, called Hadriaticum, and the see callyd Ionium.
Lacon, onis, a man of Lacedemonia.
Laconia, the countreye, where Lacedemonia standeth.
Laconicus, nica, nicum, of the countraye of Laconia.
Laconicum, a hotehowse or dric bayne.
Laconismus, a shorte fourme of speakinge.
Lactarius, ia, um, meate made of mylke, all herbes, whiche haue iuyce lyke mylke.
Lactarius, rij, he that maketh sondry meates of mylke.

Lacteo.

Lacteo, ere, to sucke mylke.

Lactes, places within the rybbes of a man, benethe the nauyll, soo tender, that it maye not suffre any wounde or stroke, as Probus sayth. Some say that they be caules, wher in the small bowelles do lye.

Lactesco, scere, to be tourned into mylke, or to be fylled with mylke.

Lacteus, a, um, of mylke or lyke milke, also that whiche is nourished with mylke.

Lacticinia, white meates made of mylke.

Lactidiaci, stryken aboute the nauyll.

Lacto, are, to fede with milk, also to deceiue with faire wordes.

Lactuca, an herbe callyd letuse.

Lacuna, a dyche, wherin water standeth, also a trenche, wherby fieldes are drayned. Some englyshe it, a synke.

Lacunar, a beame of tymber. Also suche a thynge as doth yet hange in marchauntes houses, ouerthwart their halles, wheron be set a great numbre of candelles.

Lacus, cus, a depe place alway full of water whiche is deriued into brokes and riuers, also the vessele, whyche receyueth wyne, whanne the grapes are pressed. Also the pryncipalle beame that gothe ouerthwarte the howse.

Lacuturres, greatte cabages.

Ladanum, a swete gumme, whiche goth into the makynge of pommanders.

Ladon, a ryuer in Arcadia.

¶ L ANTE AE.

Laedere maiestatem, to derogate anye thynge of the kynges auctorytie or prerogatiue.

Lædo, læsi, dere, to hurte or do displeasure.

Læsę religionis culpa, heresye, or lollardy, contempt of religion or ceremonies. *Cf. in Ver.*

Lęmargia, gluttonye.

Lęmargus, a glutton.

Lęmuschaton, the rewarde gyuen to hym that vanquyshed at playenge or fyghtynge with weapons.

Læna, a garment lyned, whiche the druynours callyd augures, dyd weare.

Laerte, a citie in Cilicia.

Laertes, the father of Ulysses.

Laertius, the name of one, whiche wrate the lyues of Phylosophers.

Lætabilis, gladde, or reioycefull.

Lætamen, compasse or mucke layde in the fieldes, to make corne and grasse to growe plentuously.

Lætifico, are, to make gladde.

Lætisco, scere, to be gladde.

Lætitia, gladnesse, reioyrynge of the mind,

whiche doth also appere outwardly.

Lætitudo, inis, idem.

Læto, are, to make gladde.

Lætor, aris, ari, to be gladde, or to reioyce with outwarde sygnes.

Lætus homo, a gladde man.

Læta ouis, a good shepe. Læta seges, & letū legumen, plentyfull corne and grayne. All other thynges, not hauynge lyfe, beinge called Læta, do sygnifye dilectable to beholde, or that do please the eye of the beholder.

Læuigo, are, to plane, or make playne, or to polyshe.

Læuis, læue, smothe or playne.

Læuitas, tatis, playnnesse or smothenesse.

Læuo, are, to make smothe.

Læuor, oris, smothenesse.

Lagari uersus, verses, whiche do halt in the myddes of the foote.

Lageos, a kynde of grapes.

Lagana, be thynne cakes made with floure and water, wherto was putte satte brothe, pepper, saffron, and cynnamom.

Lagonon, the frettynge of the guttes.

Lagœna, a pytchar potte.

Lagia, one of the names of the ile of Delos.

Lagois, a kynde of fyshe, whiche maye be called the hare fyshe.

Lagophthalmos, he that hathe eien lyke a hare, or in whom the ouerlyds of the eien do not meue downewarde.

Lagotrophia, a warren or parke of hares.

Laguncula, a lyttell pytchar.

Lagygies, people in Sarmacia.

Laicus, a lay man.

Lais, the name of a famouse harlotte, vnto whom for her beautie repaired the richest men of Grece.

Laletania, a countrey in Spayne.

Lalisiones, coltes of wylde asses.

Lallare, to speake lyke a baby: in the whiche worde the greke doth approche nerer to the englishe than to the latine, as baba-zin, whiche made a latine worde, is baba-re, it maye be transferred to the mother or norice, that babeleth with hir childe whan she giueth to it the dugge. *βαβαζειν*

Lamæ, the raggydnesse of rockes.

Lambo, bere, to lycke with the tounge. also to touche, to flowe, or runne softly.

Lambrus, a ryuer in Italy, whiche meteth with the ryuer of Po, called Padus.

Lambrani, people dwellyng about the sayd ryuer of Lambrus.

Lamentabilis, le, lamentable.

Lamentarius, a, um, that causeth lamētation.

Lamentor, aris, ari, to lament or bewayle.

Lamentatio, onis, lamenting or waylyng.

Lamiæ,

Lamiæ, be women, whyche beholdynge chyldren, or gyuyng to theym gyftes, doo alter the fourme of them, whiche children be afterwarde called elfes, or taken with the fayrye. And some suche women wylle sucke the bloudde from chyldern. They be also those, whyche be called ladyes of the fayry, whiche do allure yong men to company carnally with them, & after that they be consumed in the acte of lecherye, they couette to deuoure them.

Lamia, is also a beaste, whiche hath a womans face, and the fete of a horse. It was also the surname of a noble Romayne, and also of a famous harlot.

Lamina, a plate of mettall.

Lamirus, one of the sonnes of Hercules.

Lampas, a leame of fyre, or bryghtenes of the sonne, moste vsed for a lampe.

Lampetra, a fyshe called a lamprey.

Lampsacus, a citie on the border of Asia, vpon the ryuer called Hellespontus.

Lampsacenus, a, um, of that citie.

Lampyris, a glooworme, or a worme callid a globerde.

Lana, woulle.

Lanaris, re, that beareth or hath wolle.

Laneus, a, um, woullen.

Laneus, a fyshe.

Lanitium, the occupienge of woll.

Lanitius, a, um, wollen or of wolle.

Lanare pecus, beastes hauyng woll.

Lanarius, a wulle man, or he that occupieth or selleth wolle.

Lanatus, a, um, cladde or wrapped in wolle.

Lanatus lup[9], a fishe so called for his whitenes and softenes.

Lancia, a spanish iauelin with a brode heed.

Lancearius, he that beareth a Iauelyn.

Lanceatus, armed with a iauelyn. also wouded with a iauelyn.

Lanx, cis, a dyshe, whiche of some is callid a potenger. also a balance.

Lancino, are, to strike, to rent with the teth.

Lanerum, a garment made of vndied woll.

Langa, a beast, whiche is found aboute the ryuer of Po.

Langueo, & languesco, ere, to languyshe, to be sycke, to be faynt, to be aferd, to be idell.

Languidus, da, dum, faynt, sick, aferde, idell.

Langurium, langettes of aumbre, lyke to longe beadestones.

Languor, oris, languour, faylyng of stregth and naturall moysture.

Laniena, the flesh shambles, or shop where fleshe is solde. Sommetyme it sygnyfyethe dismembrynge.

Lanificium, cardinge and spinning of woll.

Lanificus, he that dothe worke woulle, to make it mete for the clothyar. It maye be called also a woll wynder.

Lanio, are, to cutte lyke a boucher.

Lanifex, ficis, idem qui lanificus.

Lanionius, a, ü, ptaynyng to bouchers craft.

Lanista, he that had the reule ouer sworde players, and caused them to be taught, and after solde them. Also that ordayned byrdes to fyghte.

Lanium carnarium, a slaughter house.

Lanius, & lanio, onis, a boucher.

Lano, are, to put in woll, or to dresse ẅ woll.

Lanugo, the soft heares or mosynes in the vysages of chylderne and women. Also on fruites called peaches, and some herbes as longe wort, clary, and suche other.

Laodicea, a citie in Asia.

Laodomia, the wyfe of Prothesilaus.

Laomedon, ontis, the father of Priamus.

Lapa, & lapathes, an herbe called Clote, whiche beareth bourres, that cleauen to clothes and cattell.

Lapathos, seu lapathiū, an herbe called sorel.

Lapicida, a mason.

Lapidarius, a, um, pertainyng to stones.

Lapidesco, ere, to be made or tourned into a stoone.

Lapidicina, a quarre of stones.

Lapldo, are, to strike with stoones. also to strike somtyme without stones.

Lapillus, a lytle stone, also a precious stone.

Lapio, iui, ire, to make harde as a stone.

Lapis, pidis, a stone but lasse than that, whiche is called Saxum.

Lapis, is sommetyme taken for a myle. Ad tertium aut quartum lapidem, at the thirde or the fourthe myle. De lapide empti, were slaues or bondmen solde.

Lapithe, people of Thessalie, of whom Perithous was kynge.

Lapsana, wylde colewortes.

Lapsio, a falle.

Lapso, are, to falle often.

Lapsus, us, a falle. Also a small offence done by neglygence, an ouersight.

Lapythos, a citie in the yle of Cypres.

Laqueare, laquear, & laquearium, the roufe of a chaumber, which is imbowed or fretted. also a playne beame in a rouffe.

Laqueatus, a, um, haltered, snarled, tyed or bounde faste. sommetyme it sygnyfieth holowe or bowynge.

Laqueus, an halter.

Lares, goddes, whiche the paynyms didde suppose euery person had belongyng vnto hym: which were also called Penates, both the whiche wordes be also taken for pryuate dwellynges or houses. Mei lares, mei penates, my house or dwellynge place.

Laran-

Laranda, a cytie of Lycaonia.
Lararium, a priuate chappell or closette in a mannes house.
Lardum, larde, or the fat of an hogge, sometyme swynes fleshe salted.
Larentia, a famous harlotte, which bycause she made the people of Rome her heyre, they named her a goddesse, and callydde hyr Flora.
Largior, iris, iri, to gyue lyberally.
Largitas, tatis, largenes, or lyberalitie.
Largitio, lyberalle expenses, to wynne a mannes pourpose.
Largus, a, um, large, or free of expenses.
Largé, abundauntly.
Larine, a fountayne in Attica.
Larissa, the name of one citie in Thessalia, an other in Asia, the thyrde in Italy.
Larius, a brooke by the citie of Comum.
Larix, icis, a tree of the kynde of firre, out of the whiche issueth a soote gumme.
Larodij, people in Scithia.
Larua, a spyrite, which apperethe in the nyght tyme. Some do call it a hegge, some a goblyn. Also a masker, or he that weareth a visour. it is sometyme taken for the same visour.
Laruatus, he that is feared with a spirite, & is becomme madde. It sommetime signyfieth a masker.
Laruale, an ymage defourmed, pale, leane, and horrible to beholde.
Larum, a lyttell blacke waterfowle.
Lasanum, a chaumber potte, or vrynall.
Lasciuio, ire, to be wanton.
Lasciuus, a, um, wanton.
Lasciuia, wantonnesse.
Laser, the iuyce of an herbe called Laserpitium, commendable in sondry medicines.
Lasibus, olde writers vsed for Laribus.
Lasseo, & lassesco, lassus sum, sere, to be wery.
Lascea, an yle in the see called Egeü. It was also called Andros.
Lasso, are, to be weery.
Lassus, a, um, weery.
Lassitudo, werynesse.
Lastaurus, a greatte lechour.
Latebra, & latebre, brarum, a priuye place, where men do hyde them. Sommetyme it sygnifieth an excuse.
Latebro, are, to hyde.
Latebrosus locus, where as be many priuye places.
Lateo, tui, tere, to be hydde.
Later, a tyle.
Laterani, yeman of the garde.
Lateranus, the name of a cõful of Rome, of whose hous was made a church of sainte Iohn, whiche is nowe callid Lateranensis.

Laterculus, a lyttell tyle.
Laterem lauas, thou losest thy labour.
Lateritius, a, um, made of tyles.
Laterna, a lanterne.
Lato, latescere, to be brode.
Latex, ticis, all maner of lycour: but it is moste commonly taken for water.
Latomia, a dungeon in the prison at Rome.
Latomus, a mason.
Latialis, le, & latiaris, re, of latin, of that part of Italy, whiche was called Latium.
Latibulo, are, to be hydde.
Latibulum, a denne or bury, where beastis do hyde them. somtime it is vsed for a secrete place or caue, wherin men be hidde.
Laticlauius, a Senatour.
Latifolium, that whiche hath brode leaues.
Latifundium, a greatte or large felde, great and large possessions.
Latiing, narum, sacrifyces to Iupiter named of the latins, who fyrst dyd ordayne them.
Latiné, in the fourme of laryne.
Latinitas, tatis, latyne speche.
Latinus, na, um, latin, or of the people callyd latines.
Latinus, the propre name of Aeneas father in lawe.
Latico, are, to lurke.
Latium, a parte of Italy.
Latius, a, um, of that countrey.
Latmius, a mountayne in Ionia, where poetes say the mone kyssed Endymion.
Latomiæ, was a strayte prison in the citie of Syracusis in Sicilia, an other in Spartha. It is also a quarry, out of the whiche stones are dygged.
Latona, was mother of Apollo and Diana.
Latonia, called also Diana, and is also taken for the moone.
Latria, the honour and seruyce, wherewith god onely is worshypped.
Latres, a seruaunt.
Latrina, a syege or iakes.
Latro, are, to barke as a dogge dothe.
Latrocinium, thefte, robberie.
Latrocinor, trocinari, to robe, also to serue in warres.
Latrones, robbers by the high waye. Also souldyours retayned. Amonge the Romaynes it were those, whyche were alwaye aboute the kynges or Emperoures persone, as the garde is aboute the king. Also Latrones, seu Latrunculi, be chessemenne, with whiche menne doo playe at the chesse.
Latrunculator, a iustyce of gayle delyuery, or any Iustyce, whyche dothe gyue sentence on theues.
Latus, lata, latum, brode.

L ante A.

Laté, abrode, in many places.
Latitudo, dinis, bredthe.
Latunię, quarres where stones are digged.
Latus, lateris, a syde.
Latus clauus, a senatours robe or garment. it is put somtyme for the dignitie of a Senatour. semblably Laticlauium.
Lauacrum, a bathe or bayne.
Lauatrina, a synke, wherinto fowle water is caste or swepte, wherby pauementes are made cleane.
Lauce, an yle in the see called Pontus.
Laudabilis, le, laudable, commendable.
Laudatio, a prayse or commendation.
Laudo, are, to prayse. Laudo testem, I take to wytnesse.
Lauerna, a goddesse, vnder whose protection theues were in Rome.
Lauinium, a citie in Italye, called also Laurentum.
Lauo, uaui, are, & lauo, ui, ere, to wasshe.
Lautus, & lotus, ta, tum, wasshed.
Laurea, a leafe of a laurell or bay tree, some tyme a garlande made of Laurell.
Laurens, tis, a manne of the towne callyd Laurentum.
Laurentū, a citie in Italy callid also Lauiniū.
Laureo, are, to put on a garlande of laurell.
Laureola, a crowne or garlande that victours ware in theyr triumphe.
Laureus, a, um, of laurell.
Lauretum, a place, wherin doo growe laurelles or baye trees.
Laurifer, & lauriger, is, he that wearethe a garlande of laurell.
Laurinum, oyle of laurell or bayes.
Laurion, a place in Attica, where syluer was dygged.
Laurus, a laurelle or baye tree.
Laus, laudis, prayse.
Lautia, were presentes, which the Romās did send to ambassadors of other realmes.
Lautitia, magnifycence and neteneffe in dyners and bankettes.
Lautrices, the wyfes of two bretherne.
Lautulę, weate baynes.
Lautus, ta, tum, wasshed. also nete or cleane, or elegant, ryche.
Laxitas, tatis, & laxamentum, releafe, pardon, lowsenes, lybertie.
Laxo, are, to lowse or sette at lybertie, to releafe.
Laxus, a, um, lowse, large, wide, soft, weke.
Laxum, an aduerbe, signifieth wyde.

Cęsar. Laxare manipulos, was in batayle, whan the sondry bendes or companyes of fote men were set in a ray, one man a conuenient distance from an nother, that they mought fyght the more at their lybertie.

L ante E.

Lex, an Ilande by Cyrenaica, a regyon of Affrike.
Leæna, a lyonesse.
Leander, the name of a man.
Lebes, lebetis, a caudron to boyle in.
Lebadia, a cytie in Bœotia.
Lectica, a thynge lyke to bed, wherin riche men, and noble men were borne by six seruantes. It may be taken for a lyghter.
Lecanomantia, a diuination or prophecy by the noyse of basons.
Lecticarij, they whiche bare Lecticam.
Lectio, onis, reedynge.
Lectipes, an herbe.
Lectisterniator, oris, a chaumberlayne, or he that maketh the beddes.
Lectisternium, a solemnitie among the paynims whan in the honour of their goddis Iupiter, Iuno, and Minerua, beddes were spradde in the temples, in the which fyrst the idolles were layde, in the resydue as many as mought lye and eate.
Lectito, are, to rede often.
Lectrum, a part of Asia, lyenge into the see.
Lecturio, ire, to desyre to rede.
Lectus, a bedde. Lectulus, a lyttell bedde.
Lecythus, a potte of erthe, whiche serued onely for oyle.
Legatarius, ia, to whome any thynge is bequethed.
Legacitius, pertaynynge to legacies.
Legator, oris, he that bequetheth any thing, the testatour.
Legatum, a legacye or bequeste.
Legatus, an ambassadour, that hathe commissyon to treate of mattiers. He that is sente oonely to salute or congratulate, is callyd Orator.
Legerda, a citie in greate Armeny.
Legirupio, onis, a breaker of lawes.
Legio, onis, a company of men of warre, contaynyng comonly, syxe thousand fote men, seuen hundred thyrty and two horsemen.
Legionarius, a, um, pertaynyng to a legion.
Legirupa, a breaker of lawes.
Legislator, a maker or gyuer of lawes.
Legifer, idem.
Legittimus, a, um, accordynge to the lawe.
Legittimi dies, dayes in banke, whanne the partie shulde appere or pleade.
Legittima iuditia, iugementes confirmed by lawes written, or auncient custome.
Legiuncula, a small legion.
Lego, are, to sende as an ambassadour, or as a legate, or deputie, to commytte, or appoynte, to bequeathe.
Lego, gi, gere, to gather, to rede, to passe by (to stryke.
Legula, a fyllet.
Leguleius, a lawyer.
Legulus,

Legulus, a gatherer of small thynges.
Legumen, minis, all maner of pulse, as beanes, peason, vetches, tares. &c.
Legumentum, & legarium, the same.
Leleges, seu lelege, people, whiche were alway wandrynge, and dwelled sommetyme in Thessalia.
Lema, a teare.
Lemanus, a ryuer whiche runneth into the ryuer of Rone.
Lembus, a swyfte lyttelle shyppe, whyche may be callyd a barke.
Lemnisci, labelles hangynge downe frome garlandes.
Lemnos, an yle in the see called Aegeum.
Lemnia terra, that whyche is nowe callyd Terra sigillata.
Lemosi, they that weepe lyghtly.
Lemonici, a people in Guyan, Lemonoise.
Lemures, spyrites, whyche doo walke by nyght with horrible fygures.
Lenæus, one of the names of Bacchus.
Lenas, a bawde.
Lendiginosus, a, um, full of nyttes.
Lenio, iui, ire, to pacifie, to appease, to treate gentilly, to make plain, or smoth, to cōforte.
Lenis, lene, that whiche hath no roughnes, meke, tractable, softe of condicions.
Lenitas, & lenitudo, mekenesse, gentilnesse, easynesse to please, softenes, smothenes.
Leniter, softely, swetely, moderately.
Leno, a baude, a marchant of hoores.
Lenobates, a treader of grapes.
Lenocinium, the practyse of bawdry. some tyme immoderate and exquisyte clenlynes or elegancye, to styrre a manne to vyce.
Lenocinor, ari, to practise baudrye. Also to speake fayre, or allure oone with wordes, and other pleasaunt thynges.
Lenonius, a, um, pertaynyng to bawdes.
Lens, lendis, a nytte.
Lens, tis, a kynde of poulse called fatches.
Lentesco, scere, to be smothe, or tender.
Lenticula, a poulse called chittes.
Lenticula, a maner of vessel, out of the whiche kynges and princes were annoynted, a Chrismatorie.
Lenticularis, re, lyke a chytte or fatche.
Lentigo, ginis, a thynge lyke a lyttell warte in the face redde or blacke.
Lentiscus, a lyttell tree, out of the whyche cometh Mastix, a swete gumme.
Lente, easily, softely.
Lento, lentare, to doo a thynge softely or easyly, slowely.
Lentus, ta, tum, softe, gentylle, easye, slowe, remysse, ydell, cleauynge, or clammy.
Lenulus, a lyttell or yonge bawde.
Lenunculus, idem. Also a lytel fishers bote.

Leo, onis, a Lyon.
Leo risit, a prouerbe touching thē, which be sowre of countenance, fierce, & vncurteyse.
Lonem radere, spoken where one attēpteth a thynge dangerous, and almost impossible.
Leocrates, the name of an excellent grauer.
Leodamas, the ppre name of a philosopher.
Leon, a philosopher.
Leonides, was kynge of the Lacedemonians, whiche dyd feates of warre agaynste Xerxes kynge of Persia incredible, and finally was slayne in defendyng Grece, with foure thousande and eight hundrid grekes onely, against. xvii. hundred thousande of the hooste of Xerxes. There was also an other Leonides, which was tutour to king Alexander, whan he was a chylde.
Leonina, an herbe, whiche groweth on hilles, whose floures are like to a lions mouth whan he gapeth.
Leontopetalon, an herbe, hauynge leaues lyke to colewortes, the stalke halfe a foote high, the sede in huskes as great as smalle peason, the rote lyke a rape rote, great and blacke, whiche helpeth ageynste the styngyng and bytynge of all maner of serpētis.
Leontophon, a lyttell worme, whiche if the lyon do byte, he dyeth incontinent.
Leontophona, a lyttell beaste, whose heed is tourned into asshes, wherwith men doo myxte fleshe, and cast it in the ways, wherby lyons do passe, wherof if they doo eate, they dye incontinent.
Leontopodion, an herbe callid Pee de lyon whiche hath floures lyke roses vnspradde.
Leopardus, a Lybarde.
Lepadusa, the yle of Sicile.
Lepidiū, an herbe lyke to a wyld parsnippe.
Lepidus, a, um, nete, polyte, and pleasaunte, as well in speeche, as in gesture.
Lepor, oris, & lepos, oris, purenesse or netenesse in speeche. Also the good grace and dilectablenesse in speche and gesture.
Leporarium, an inclosure, or place inclosed, wherin are kepte any beastes for pleasure or huntynge. *Varro. 3. de re rust.*
Leporinus, rina, rinum, of an haare.
Lepra, leprye.
Leprium, a cytie in Achaia.
Lepus, poris, an hare.
Læptoludię, blacke frygges.
Lepusculus, a leuret or yonge hare.
Lerna, a place, wherein the citie of Argon layde all their ordure and fylthe.
Lernæus, a, um, of Lerna. Lerna malorum, the dunge heape of mischiefes.
Leros, an Jlande in the see Jcarie.
Lesbos, an ile in the see called Aggum.
Lesbius, a, um, of the yle of Lesbos.

M.ii. Lessus.

Lessus, us, a lamentable voyce, vsed in the burieng of men, as we do saye, Alas.

Lestorum, a region of Indie.

Lestrygones, a people in the extreme parte of Italye, whiche dyd eate the companyons of Ulysses, rostynge them on broches.

Letalis, le, mortalle.

Letania, uel litania, a supplycation or commune prayer.

Lethargus, a syckenes, whiche causeth one to slepe continually, and to forget al thing.

Lethargicus, he that hath the slepynge or forgettynge syckenesse.

Lethe, a ryuer of hel, the water wherof as soone as it is drunke, causeth a man to forgette all thynge that is passed.

Letificus, ca, cum, causynge deathe.

Leto, tare, to flee. Letatus, stayne.

Letum, deathe.

Leua manus, the lefte hande.

Leuca, a promontorie or elbowe of lande, nygh to Corinthus.

Leucantha, white bryer.

Leucanthemis, an herbe, which phisytions of late dayes calle Camomylle.

Leucates, a mountaine in Epiro. also an yle.

Leuce, a littell towne not far from Smirna.

Leucola, an yle by Cypers.

Leuconium, whyte cotton.

Leucopheus, a browne or a russette coloure.

Leucopheatus, he that dothe weare a russet garment.

Leucopum, & leucopus, white of naturalle coloure.

Leucophlegmantia, a white dropsye.

Leucosyria, a countrey, whiche is now called Cappadocia.

Leucosia, an yle agaynste Pestanum, in the the see Thyrrhenum.

Leucothea, the goddesse, whiche was called Matuta, & Aurora.

Leuctrum & leuctra, a towne in Bœotia.

Leuis, leue, lyght. Leuitas, tatis, lyghtnes.

Leui, one of the sonnes of Iacob, the patriarch.

Leuiathan, a dragon of the see: it is taken in holy scripture for the dyuell.

Leuiculus, a, um, somwhat light. also waton.

Leuidensis, se, thynne wrought, and of small substance.

Leuifidus, da, um, of light credence or trust.

Leuir, ri, the husbandes brother.

Leuo, are, to lyfte vp, somtime to take away, to abate.

Leuus, a, um, lyght. Also whan it is spoken of worldly thynges, it sygnifieth lefte, vnhappy, contrary: whan it is referred to celestiall thynges, it betokeneth ryghte, fortunate, prosperous. For that whiche to vs is the lefte hande, to them, whiche are aboue vs, and do looke towarde vs, is the ryghte hande.

Lex, legis, lawe.

Lex municipalis, the peculyar lawe, whyche euery citie hath.

Lex orchia, a lawe, whyche assigned howe many persones shulde be boden to souper, and that men shulde soupe at their doores, to the intent that it moughte appere, howe the lawe was obeyed.

Lex plagiaria, wherby men were whipped.

Lexipyreti, medycines, whyche doo heale menne of feuers.

Lexouii, people in hyghe Fraunce aboute Burbon.

¶L ANTE I.

Lis, be holes in the toppe of a maste, whiche doo receyue the cabulles, or roopes.

Liba, an yle in the Indian see.

Libamen, minis, libamētum, & libatio, a taste or say taken, proprely in sacrifice.

Libanius, the name of a great Rhetorician.

Libanotis, tidis, an herbe callyd Rosemary.

Libanotus, a wynde, whyche dothe blowe out of the northweste.

Libanus, a mountayne betwene Araby and Phenicia. It is also a tree, whyche bryngeth forthe incense.

Libellio, a writer of bokes.

Libellorum præfecti, maysters of the requestes, whiche do receyue billes of supplication, being put in, to the kyng or prince. *Hieron.*

Libellulus, a very lyttell boke.

Libellus, a lyttell boke. also sometyme an epistell, a supplication, a lybell or declaration in the lawe, of dette, trespasse, couenant, and other lyke.

Libens, wyllynge.

Libentiæ, dylectations, pleasures.

Libenter, wyllyngely, gladly.

Libentina, one of the names of Uenus.

Liber, beri, the fynder of wyne, called also Bacchus & Dionysius.

Liber, ra, rum, free, at lybertie, not bounden, large, or greatte.

Liber, libri, a boke or warke writen, the inner rynde of a tree.

Liberalis, le, lyberall. Liberales artes, the lyberall sciences, or sciences belongynge to a free manne.

Liberale iudirium, & liberalis causa, where a man contendeth for his lybertie.

Liberalia, orum, the festiual days of Bacch⁹.

Liberaliter, lyberallye.

Libe-

Liberalitas, tatis, lyberalytie.

Liberi, chyldren, as well women as men.

Plinius. Liberides, conies.

Libero, are, to delyuer, to sette at lybertie.

Liberare creditorem, to content, or satisfie hym, of whom money is borowed.

Libertas, tatis, lybertie taken alwaye in the good parte.

Libertinus, & libertus, he that of a bondeman is manumised or infranchised.

Libet, it lyketh or contenteth.

Libethra, a caue, wherin was a well, callyd Libethros, where the Muses beinge conuersant, were therfore called Libethrides.

Libethrides, the Muses, or ladies of scieces.

Libethrus, a moūtain in Macedonia, where the Muses dyd dwelle.

Libidinarius, a haunter of lecherie.

Libidinosus, lecherous, wylfull.

Libido, dinis, sensualitie, vnlefull appetite or luste. Sometyme it sygnifieth onely appetite or wylle.

Libitina, a goddesse, in whose temple were solde all thynges pertaynyng to sepulture or funeralles. sometyme for buriēge. Also for dethe, or the beere, wheron deade bodyes are caryed.

Libitinarius, he that hath the suruayeng and charge aboute burienges.

Libo, are, to tast any thing : somtime to touche, somtyme to sacrifice, somtyme to take.

Libra, a pound, weight: somtyme a payre of balaunces. it is also one of the .xii. sygnes.

Libra Attica, conteined a hūdred dragmas, and was called Mna, or Mina.

Libra Romana, contayned .xii. ounces, that is to say foure score & syxtene dragmas.

Libralis, le, a pounde weight.

Libramentum, poyse or weyght.

Libraria, a lybrary.

Librarius, a, um, pertaynynge to bokes, or of a pounde weyght.

Librarius, a scriuener, a boke bynder.

Librile, the hanging equally of the balance.

Librilla, a cogell or stone, to throwe at one.

Libripens, dis, a weyer. It was also amonge the Romaynes he, whiche bought a bondman or slaue, takynge a pounde weighte of brasse in his hande, and sayeng: This man, whiche with this money and brason pound is boughte to my vse, by the lawes of the Romayns, I say, is myn owne.

Libro, are, to way, to poyse, to make weightye, to houer.

Libs, a wynde, the whiche bloweth out of the southe.

Libum, a chiese caake.

Liburni, people of the countrey called Liburnia, also commune messangers.

Liburnia, a part of Dalmatia, or Slauony.

Liburnum, liburna, liburnas, & liburnica, a lyght shyppe, as a barke or galias.

Libya, & libye, a royalme in Affrike.

Libycis, cidis, a citie in Iudea, on the easte parte of the ryuer of Iordane.

Libycontes, stones, which ar not very clere.

Libycus, ca, cum, of Libia.

Libys, & Libyssa, a man & woman of Libya.

Libyophœnices, people in Affrica.

Liceo, cere, to cheapen.

Liceor, ceris, ceri, to sette the price.

Licenter, rashely.

Licentia, licence, vnlefull libertie.

Licentiosus, rashe, vsynge vnlefull libertie.

Licet, it is lefull. sommetyme it is vsed for maye. Mihi licet, I maye. Tibi licet, thou mayste. sometyme be it so, admytte it.

Lichas, a measure, whiche excedethe not foure fyngers.

Lichenes, ryngewormes or tetters.

Lichenis, a foule breakyng out, whyche begynneth aboute the chynne. Some do take it for the frenche pockes.

Licia, be thredes, whiche sylke women do weaue in lyncelles or stooles.

Liciatoriū, a weauers shyttel, or a sylke womans tauell, wheron sylke or threde beinge wounden, is shot through the web or lome.

Licinia, a kynde of olyue trees.

Licitator, toris, a chepener, a chapman. sometyme it signifieth a broker.

Licite, lefully.

Licitor, aris, ari, to bye and selle for gaynes, or to bargayn by exchaunge or cheuisance, to fyght, to deceyue a manne by a craftye bargayne.

Lictor, a sergeant, or other lyke minister to execute corporall punyshement. A Consul of Rome had .xii. other heed officers: syx which bare euery one in their handis, roddes and axes bounden togither, to do with them execution, as they were cōmaunded.

Lictorius, a, um, pertaynyng to sergeantes and other lyke officers.

Lictus, ta, tum, lycked.

Lidoron, a tyle in lengthe one foote and an halfe, in bredth one foote.

Lien, nis, the splene.

Ligamen, minis, ligamentum, a bonde.

Ligellum, a cotage.

Liger, eris, a ryuer in France called Loire.

Lignor, aris, ari, to go to carie wodde.

Lignarius faber, a carpentar.

Lignator, a carier of wodde.

Lignile, fuell, or a wodde stacke.

Lignosus, a, um, as harde as wodde.

Lignum, wodde.

Ligo, are, to bynde,

Ligo, onis, a spade.
Ligula, a lyttell tongue.
Liguria, the countrey in Italye, where the citie of Geane is sette.
Ligurio, ire, to eate lycorously, or to deuoure sweete or dayntye meates. Also to eate daintily or curiously.
Liguritor, toris, a daintie feder, an eater of delicate meates.
Ligus, guris, of the countrey of Liguria, a Ianuens of Ianeway.
Ligusticum mare, the see that is by Ieane.
Ligusticus, ca, cum, of Liguria.
Ligustrum, a tree, which dothe beare white floures, and soote: wherof is made an oyle called oleum cyprinum: and this tree doth growe in watrye places, as wyllowes and salowes do. It is also an herbe, which some men do cal Maior, and groweth by hedges.
Ligyes, are people of Asye, whyche with Xerxes warred agaynste the Grekes.
Lilibeum, an hyll in Sicile on the see banke. Also a towne.
Lilietu, a place where do grow many lilyes.
Lilinum, oyle of lylyes.
Lilium, a lylye.
Lima, a fyle.
Limatulus, a lyttell fyled.
Limatura, pouder, whiche cometh of filing.
Limax, cis, a snayle. Also a man, which prieth or seketh for some thynge to consume.
Limborarius, a maker of gardes or purfils.
Limbus, a purfyll of a womans garment, or a garde of a mans garment.
Limen, minis, signifyeth not only the thrasholde of a doore, but also the haunse, somtyme it signifieth the entre of the dore. som tyme frendeshyppe, after the exposytion of Seruius.
Limenarcha, the wardeyn of the portes.
Limes, mitis, sygnifieth a bounde or butting in fieldes.
Limetanei agri, feldes lyeng in the extreme marches of a countrey.
Limetanei milites, souldiours appoynted to kepe the borders of a countrey.
Limito, are, to bounde or lymitte how ferre a thynge doethe extende.
Limitatus, ta, tum, bounded, lymytted.
Limo, are, to fyle, to polyshe.
Limus, a vesture from the bely downward. Also mudde or slime, which is in the water.
Limus, a, um, croked, a wrie, askewe.
Limis oculis spectare, to looke wantonly on the one syde, to caste a wanton eie, to loke askewe.
Linamentum, lynnen.
Linarius, a warker of lynnen.
Linea, a carpenters lyne or corde. it sygni-

fieth also euery line generally, either made or ymagined to be.
Lineamentum, the facyon of a body.
Linearis, are, pertaynynge to a lyne.
Lingo, xi, gere, to lycke with the tunge. also to sucke downe by lyttell and lyttell.
Linctus, tus, lyckynge or suckynge downe.
Lingones, people in France, called Langres.
Lingua, a tongue. also a language. Also an instrument, wherwith men do take medycines or salues out of a boxe.
Lingula, a lyttell tunge. Also a lachet or lingell. Also Lingua & lingula, do sommetyme signifie a spoone.
Lingua bula, an herbe called Langdebefe.
Linguax, acis, a great speker, ful of wordes.
Lingulaca, a woman full of wordes. Also a fyshe called a soole.
Linio, iui, ire, to annoynte.
Lino, ni, ere, to annoynte or laye on somme thynge, that is thycke. also to lyne.
Linostrophron, an herbe, whyche is also callyd Marubium.
Linozostis, an herbe callyd Mercurie.
Linquo, liqui, linquere, to leaue.
Lintearius, a mercer of lynnen.
Linteolum, a piece of lynnen clothe.
Linteo, onis, a lynnen weauer.
Linternus, a ryuer and towne in Campania.
Linteum, a shete. It is taken for all lynnen clothes. sometyme for syles.
Lintres, lytell botes made of holowe trees.
Linum, lynnen.
Linus, he that brought fyrst letters out of Phenicia into Grece, and was mayster to Hercules.
Lynx, a beaste, whiche hathe the face of a lyon, the body spotted lyke a panther, and is of the greatnesse of a doo, whose vryne is sodaynly tourned into a precyous stone.
Lipara, an yle by Greece. It is also a softe playster.
Liparis, a ryuer in Cilicia.
Lipopsichia, a soundyng, where one semeth to be deade.
Lipopthymia, a traunse.
Lippio, iui, ire, to be porreblynde, or sande blynde, or dymme of syght.
Lippus, bleare eyed.
Lippitudo, the blearenesse of eyen.
Lipsana, scrappes, or leauynges of vitayle, or other thynges.
Liquamen & liquatu, greace, or talow molten, sewet.
Liquefacio, cere, to melte.
Liquentia, a ryuer in Lombardy.
Liqueo, iui, ire, to be liquide or soft, as oyle.
Liquesco, scere, to relente.
Liquet, it appereth, it is sure.

Liqui-

L ante I.

Liquido, are, to discouer, or make to appere.
Liquidus, da, um, lyquide runnynge & softe. sometyme pure, also prosperous.
Liquido, playnely, apparantly, purely.
Liquo, are, to melte.
Liquo, ere, to runne out, as lycour dothe.
Lira, a rydge of lande, whiche is ouer the furrowe. sometyme it sygnifyeth an harpe.
Liræ be trifles or iapes.
Liratim, in ridges.
Liris, a ryuer in Campania.
Liro, are, to make rydges.
Litem æstimare, to assesse damages and costes for the playntyfe in an action.
Lis, litis, debate, variance, controuersie.
Litem suam facere, where one medleth in an other mans matter, as it were his owne.
Litera, a letter. Literæ, a letter or letters that be sent. sometyme it signifieth sciences.
Litera salutaris, was in the olde tyme, A, as betokenynge absoluynge, Litera tristis, B, as sygnifyenge condemnynge.
Literæ fugientes, blynde letters, whyche eyther in defaulte of the ynke, or of the parchemente, or for auncientie, maye not be radde.
Literarius, a, um, pertaynynge to letters or sciences.
Litterator, oris, a grammarian, or a mayster of grammer.
Litteratura, grammer.
Literosus, lettred. Litteratus, idem.
Liticen, a blower of a smalle trumpette.
Lythargyrium, lytarge, or white leed.
Lithargyrus, a stone of syluer.
Lithiasis, the griefe of the stone.
Lithocolla, a cement, wherwith stones are ioyned togyther.
Lithoglyphus, a grauour in stones.
Lithologema, a heape of stones.

Theophrastus.

Lithospermon, an herbe, which hath sedes lyke stoones, and groweth amonge corne: whyche herbe curethe the stoone of the bladder.
Lithostratus, a place paued with square stoones.
Lithotomia, a masons warkhouse, or quarre
Litigator, oris, a stryuer.
Litigiosus, a, um, full of stryfe.
Litigium, a debate, or variance.
Litigo, are, to varie, to stryue, to sewe one an nother.
Lito, tare, to please god with sacrifyce, and to optayne my desyre.
Littus, toris, the bankes, as well of the see, as of a great ryuer. sometyme lande butting on the see callyd the see syde.
Littoreus, rea, um, & littoralis, littorale, of the see syde.

L ante O.

Litura, a blottynge or stryke through that, whiche is writen, cancellynge.
Lituro, are, to blotte or stryke throughe, or cancelle.
Litus, ta, tum, enoynted.
Lituus, a croked staffe, which the diuinours called Augures, helde in their handes, whā they appoynted places in their diuination. Also a scepter, and a trumpette.
Liueo, ere, to be blacke, to enuye.
Liuesco, scere, to enuy.
Liuidus, a, um, he that hath his skyn blacke with beatynge, also enuious.
Liuius, the prince of latyn historiens.
Liuor, the coloure, whiche is lefte on the skynne, after beatynge or whippynge. somtyme it is taken for enuye. Liuor edax tibi cuncta negat, The gnawyng enuie denayeth the all thynges. Rabiem liuoris acerbi Nulla potest placare quies, No quiete canne content the ragynge of bytter enuy. *Lucanus.* *Claudius lib. 3.*
Lix, asshes.
Lixa, a skullyon, whiche carieth wodde or water in an hoste, or to the kychen.
Lixabundus, he that for a smalle rewarde dothe moste vyle seruyce.
Lixinium, lye made of ashes to wasshe clothes cleane.
Lixo, are, to whette.
Lixos, a towne in Affrica.

¶ L ANTE O.

Lobus, the lappe of the eare.
Loba, a braunche of the grayn callyd Millium.
Locarium, the hyre of a house or lodgyng.
Locatarius, he that letteth house or lande, a lessour.
Locellus, a lyttell place.
Locito, are, to lette.
Loco, care, to set or lay, as a howse is set in a place, a foundation is layde. Also to laye vp, as a thing is to be kepte. Sometyme to gyue in mariage. Also to lette a thynge to hyre: or to rent, to make a lease.
Locator, toris, the lessour.
Locrus, a citie in the vttermoste parte of Italy, whiche was named Magna grecia.
Locrenses & locri, people of Locrus. there were also people so named in Grece.
Loculamenta, places made with bourdes, wherin tame culuers, and other byrdes or conyes are kepte to brede.
Loculatus, ta, latum, dyuyded into sondrye places.
Loculus, a lyttell place. Also a purse, an almorie, a lyttell coffer, a bierc, wheron decd bodies are borne to be buried.
Locuples, pletis, ryche, abundāt, sufficient,

Locu-

Locuples fideiussor, a sufficient suretie.
Locupleto, tare, to make ryche of yerelye reuenewes.
Locus, a place. somtime a family or kinred. also stede, as Loco patris te habeo, I take the in stede of my father.
Loci, plurali numer. the secrete partes of a womanne.
Locusta, a flye with longe hynder legges, whiche bourneth corne with touchynge of it, and deuoureth the resyduc. In India be of them thre foote in lengthe, whiche the people of that countrey do eate. It is also a see fishe, like to a creuys, called a lopster.
Locutor, cutoris, & loculeius, a prater or a iangler.
Lodex, uel lodix, icis, a sheete.
Loedoria, a taunt or reproche in scoffyng.

Aristo. Metheor. 2. Loelaps, a blaste of wynde tourned frome the erthe vpwarde.
Logica, logike, one of the lyberall sciences, the crafte of reasonyng or arguinge.
Logion, a place where iuges gyue sentēce: also a gatherynge of rent, or other reuenues.
Logodædalus, he that speaketh craftily to deceiue: or in eloquente wordes induceth sentences vayne, or of lyttell purpose.
Logomachia, a contencion with wordes, or an vndiscrete altercation.
Logos, vsed for a latyn worde, is taken for triflynge wordes, or vayne language.
Loligo, ginis, a fyshe, which hath his heed betwene his fete and his bealy: and hathe also two bones, one lyke a knyfe, the other lyke a penne.
Lolium, a wiede growynge in corne, callyd Cockyll.
Longobardia, a regyon of Italye, callyd Lunibardye.
Lombricus, a lampraye.
Lomentum, beane meale.
Longa Alba, a citie in Italye.
Longeuus, longe lyued.
Longanimis, he that suffreth longe.
Longanon, a gutte, out of the whyche ordure issueth.
Longe, an aduerbe, signifieth longe, farre, excedynge.
Longinquus, a, um, far of, farre, straunge.
Longisco, scere, to be longe.
Longitudo, dinis, lengthe.
Longobardi, Lumbardes.
Longurius, a longe pole.
Longus, a, um, longe.
Longum, a longe tyme.
Lopades, a shelle fyshe.
Loquacitas, tatis, babblynge.
Loquacito, are, to babble or speake moche.
Loquax, cis, a babler or greatte speaker.

Loquela, speeche.
Loquor, eris, qui, to speake.
Loquitor, tari, to speake moche.
Lora, siue lorea, a drynke made of grapes, after that they be pressed, callyd Seconde.
Lorarii, seruantes whiche serued to bynde men, or to beate them, whan they were by their maisters commaunded.
Lorica, an haberion, a place made vppon walles lyke an open galery, with grates of tymber or hurdels, to kepe men frome fallyng. It is also the walle plate, before that morter is layde on it.
Loricatus, armed with an haberion.
Loricatio, wallynge with morter.
Lorico, care, to put on an haberion.
Loricion, a mantell.
Loricula, in warfare is a munymēt or fortification, that the besigers of cites do make.
Loripes, edis, whose fete ar, as if they were bounden or grite.
Lorum, a thonge of lether, or a colar, or other lyke thynge, wherewith beastes are bounden or tyed. sometyme a whip, wherwith a man or beaste is whypped.
Lotaringia, a countrey betwene Pycardye and Normandy.
Lotophagi, people in Affrike, whyche doo lyue by eating only of a frute, callid Lotos.
Lotium, vryne or pysse.
Lotos, & lotis, lotidis, is a notable tree in Affrike, or herbe, of whose fruite if a stranger do eate, he dothe incontinently forget his owne countrey.
Loxias, one of the names of Apollo.

¶ L ANTE V.

Lvbentia, & libentia, myrthe, pleasantnes, moste proprely in wordes.
Lubido pro libido, sensuall appetite.
Lubrico, care, to make slypper.
Lubricus, ca, cum, slypper, waueryng. some tyme redy to slyppe or slyde.
Luca, a citie in Italye, of whiche the inhabytantes are called Lucenses.
Lucæ boues, were taken of the olde latines for Elephantes.
Lucania, a countray belongyng to the royalme of Naples.
Lucani, people of the countrey of Lucania.
Lucanica, a pouddynge made of porke, & sawsage.
Lucanus, a famous poete, which wrate the battayle betwene Cesar and Pompeye.
Lucar, money bestowid in woddes, dedicate to goddis, called Luci.
Lucaria festa, feastes, whiche the Romains made in holy woddes.
Lucellum, a lyttell gayne, a small markette.

Lux,

Lux, lucis, light, sometyme it signifieth day.
Luci, by daye.
Lucens, that whiche hath his lyghte of another thynge.
Luceo, luxi, lucere, to shyne.
Luceres, the thirde parte of the people of Rome, distributed by Tatius & Romulus.
Luceria, a citie of Apulia.
Lucerius, a kynge of Ardea, whiche holpe Romulus agaynst Tatius.
Lucerna, a lanterne.
Lucernarius, the lanterne bearer.
Lucernula, a sconse.
Lucesco, scere, to be bryght or clere, as day.
Lucetius, a name of Jupiter.
Lucetia, one of the names of Juno.
Lucibile, that whiche is light of it selfe.
Lucido, are, to make clere, or to gyue lyght.
Lucifico, care, idem.
Lucidus, da, dum, cleere.
Lucifer, the daye sterre.
Lucifugus, ga, whyche fleeth frome lyghte, and delyteth in darkenesse.
Lucilius, the name of an olde poete.
Lucina, one of the names of the mone, called also the goddesse of byrthe.
Lucini, they whiche haue lyttell eyen, and smalle syghte.
Lucius, a mans name.
Lucretilis, an hylle in the countreye of the Sabynes.
Lucrifuga, he that fleeth frō lucre or gaines
Lucrinus, a mere or great water in Capania.
Lucrio, onis, a couetous manne, an inordynate gayner.
Lucror, aris, ari, to gayne, or to wynne.
Lucrum, lucre or gayne.
Lucta, wrastelynge.
Luctarius Catulus, a cytesyn of Rome.
Luctiferum, cause of waylynge.
Luctificus, ca, cum, idem.
Luctitor, tari, to wrastell ofte.
Luctor, aris, ari, & lucto, are, to wrastle.
Luctuosus, a, um, lamentable.
Luctus, tus, weepynge and waylynge, the habyte of mournynge.
Lucubro, are, to make any thynge by candelle lyghte.
Luculentus, ta, tum, full of lyght, cleere.
Lucullus, the name of a noble Romayne.
Lucus, a hygh and thycke wodde. somtime it signifieth lyght, whan it is of the fourth declination. It is also a citie in Spayne by Compostella, which is now callid Lucensis.
Ludia, a daunsynge wenche.
Ludibrium, a mocke, or any thynge that is mocked.
Ludibundus, a, um, playing, or full of playe.
Ludicrū, any play or pastime, or an enterlude

Ludicrus, cra, crum, pertaynynge to playe or myrthe.
Ludifico, are, to mocke.
Ludii, & ludiones, players in enterludes or stage playes.
Ludius, & ludio, onis, a player.
Ludo, si, dere, to playe, to mocke or deceiue in game. Opera luditur, The warke or labour is loste.
Ludus, play in actes, myrth in wordes: also a schoole or place of exercyse.
Lusus, us, idem.
Lues, pestilence in men, murrayn in beastis.
Lugdunum, a citie in Fraunce, callid Lions.
Lugeo, luxi, lugere, to mourne, to lamente.
Lugubris, bre, pertaynynge to mournynge.
Vestis lugubris, a mournynge garment.
Luma, a brembyll.
Lumbago, ginis, feblenes of the loynes.
Lumbare, breeches of hosen.
Lumbrici, wormes callyd easis.
Lumbi, the loynes.
Lumen, luminis, lyghte.
Luminare, that whiche gyueth lyght.
Luna, the Moone.
Lunaris, re, pertaynynge to the moone.
Lunaticus, he that is madde or sycke at a certayne tyme of the moone.
Lunatus, ta, tum, lyke the moone.
Luo, ere, to suffre punyshement or dethe.
Luere capite, to haue the heed stryken of.
Lupa, a female wolfe. also an harlotte.
Lupanar, a brothell howse.
Lupanaris, re, pertaining to a brothel hous.
Lupanarium, a brothell howse.
Lupari, to meddell with cōmon harlottes.
Luparius, a hunter of wolfes.
Lupatum, a harde bytte.
Lupercal, a place dedicate to Pan, the god of shepeherdes.
Lupercalia, sacrifices & plays made to Pan.
Luperci, minysters of that solemnitie.
Lupinus, na, num, of a wolfe.
Lupinus, a kynde of poulse.
Lupus, a wolfe. Also a bytte for a hors. also a hoke to drawe vp thinges out of a pyt. Also a kynde of spyders.
Lupus est in fabula, a prouerbe, whan he cometh, whiche is spoken of.
Lupum auribus tenere, a prouerbe in thynges that be daungerous, eyther to retaine, or to lette goo.
Lura, the mouthe of a bottelle.
Luridus, da, dum, pale of colour.
Lurco, are, to eate rauenously.
Lurco, onis, a deuourer of his own substāce
Luscinia, a nyghtyngale.
Lusciosus, poreblynd. Luscio is the disease.
Luscitus, he that seeth playnely by nyghte.
Luscus

Luscus, porblynde. sommetyme a man hauynge but one eye.
Lusitania, the realme called Portugall.
Lusito, tare, to playe often.
Lusorius, a, um, pertaynynge to playe.
Lustralis, le, pertayning to riot and lechery. sometyme a thynge done euery fyfte yere.
Lustrici dies, the day whan a chylde is fyrst named, whiche in men chylderne was the nynth day, in womenne children it was the viii. day. It may nowe be vsed for the daye of christenynge of chylderne.
Lustro, are, to go aboute in circute, to make satisfaction by sacrifice, to consyder in the mynde, to shadowe, to beholde aboute.
Lustror, aris, ari, to serche out.
Lustrum, a denne or caue of wylde beastes in woddes, an hidde place and vyle, a hous where gluttonye and lecherie is haunted, also the hauntynge of the same vices: some tyme it sygnifyeth the space of fiue yeres, Also the generall purgation of the citie by sacrifice euery fyfte yere.
Luter, eris, a cuppe, wherin wine is delayde with water.
Lutesco, scere, to be claye.
Luteus color, the colour of yelowe, approchinge towarde redde, of the colour of the yolke of an egge, or of waxe newe made.
Luteola, a lytell floure of the colour of yelowe, in greatnes and sauour, not moch vnlyke a vyolette.
Luteum oui, the yolke of an egge.
Luto, are, to claye.
Lutra, siue lytra, a beuar, or a beast moche lyke to it, whiche gnaweth trees asonder, and dothe haunte greatte waters, and lyueth lyke an Ottar.
Lutum, claye.
Lux, lucis, lyght.
Luxo, are, to lowse or make loose.
Luxatus, whose bones are out of ioynte.
Luxurio, ire, to excede, to abunde more than is necessarie in the body or personage.
Luxurior, aris, ari, to abounde excessiuely in thynges concernynge the mynde or goodes: Also to be wanton with to moch welth or prosperitie.
Luxuriose, to prosperouse, or lyuynge in to moche pleasure.
Luxuriosus, a, um, excedynge in abundance.
Luxus, luxuria, & luxuries, all superfluitie or excesse, as well in carnalle pleasure, as in sumptuous fare, apparayle, or buyldyng.

¶ L ANTE Y.

Lyæus, one of the names of Bacchus, called god of wynes.
Lyceum, was the schole of Aristotell in Athenes.
Lycæus, a mountayne in the countreye of Archadia.
Lycaon, the kyng of Archadia, whom Jupiter tourned into a wolfe.
Lycaonia, a countrey in Asia: after somme writers, it is a parte of Archadia.
Lycaones, people in Asia the lesse, nere to Lycia, as writeth Ptolome. *Ptho, li. 3.*
Lycastus, a citie of Candy.
Lychnis, an herbe whose floure shyneth by nyght, and fyrste spryngeth, and longest dureth: whiche in drynke helpeth them that are stongen with the Scorpion.
Lychnites, whyte marbyll.
Lychnobij, they whiche do tourne the daye into nyght, and the nyght into daye.
Lychnus, a matche of a candelle, sometyme the selfe candell.
Lycia, a countrey in the lasse Asia.
Lycidas, the name of a Centaure, and of a shepeherde in Vergile.
Lycion, a thyng made with the iuyce of an herbe, wherwith soore eis be cured.
Lycisca, a dogge commen of a wolfe and a dogge.
Lycius, one of the names of Apollo.
Lycurgus, a kynge of the Lacedemoniens, whiche gaue to them their fyrste lawes.
Lycus, a ryuer in the countreye of Cæsaria.
Lydia, a royalme in Asia the more.
Lydus, a, um, of the countrey of Lydia.
Lyenteria, the flyxe or continuall lowsenes of the bealye.
Lympha, water.
Lymphaticus, a madde man, which lyke to a wodde dogge, runneth hither and thither.
Lympidus, a, um, cleere, smothe.
Lynceus, was a manne, who (as Varro writeth) coulde see shyppes on the see. Lxxx. myles from hym, & dyd nombre them. And some wrate, that he coulde see throughe a walle. And therfore they, whiche haue very sharpe syghtes, be sayde to haue
Lynceos oculos, the eien of Lynceus.
Lyndus, a citie atte the Rodes, where they dyd sacrifice to Hercules with reproches and curses.
Lynter, eris, a cockebote.
Lynx, cis, a beaste lyke to a wolfe, hauynge many spottes, whose syght dothe perce all thynges. It is also a bryde, whyche hath a tongue lyke a serpente.
Lyra, an harpe.
Lyricen, cinis, an harper.
Lysander, a Capitayne of the Lacedemonyans, a man contentious, whiche dydde sette all Grece in the Lacedemonians top, and was slayne of the Thebans.

Lysa-

M ante A.

Lysanias, an oratour of Grece.
Lysias, an oratour moste pleasant, of whom Quint. speaketh.
Lysimachus, a noble man of Macedony, the scholar of Callisthenes.
Lysippus, an excellent caruer.
Lysius, a ryuer of Archadie.
Lytta, a worme in a dogges tongue.

¶ M ANTE A.

MACARIUS, the name of a manne. In latyn it sygnifieth blessed.
Maccabeus, the name of certayne noble menne, whiche were capitains of the Iewes.
Macedonia, a realme ioynyng to Grece, whereof the great Alexander was kynge.
Macedo, onis, a man or woman of Macedony.
Macedonicus, ca, cum, of Macedonie.
Macellarius, a vittayllour or seller of all maner of vittayle.
Macellum, a place where all maner of vytayle is solde. Macellus is somtyme taken for a leane man.
Maceo, & macesco, scere, to be leane.
Macer, cra, crum, leane.
Maceresco, scere, to make softe with lyeng longe in lycour.
Maceries, & maceria, a wall of stone without morter, made in the stede of an hedge. also leannesse.
Macero, are, spoken of the body, signifieth to make leane, or thynne, or softe by steapynge in lycour: referred to the mynde, it sygnifieth to vexe or inquiete.
Machera, a sworde.
Macherophorus, a sworde bearer.
Macheropios, a Cutlar, or a bladesmythe.
Machaon, the sonne of Aesculapius, an excellent surgeon.
Machina, a thynge craftilye inuented, or a crafty inuention, an engyne.
Machinor, aris, ari, to inuent craftily, to deuyse, to ymagine.
Macies, & macritudo, leannesse.
Macidatus, ta, rum, wette. *Apuleius.*
Macilentus, leane.
Macio, aui, are, to make leane.
Macra, a ryuer, whiche ronneth betwene the mountaynes of Liguria.
Macresco, scere, to waxe leane.
Macreo, ere, to be leane.
Macrobij, people of Aethiopia, whiche do lyue very longe.

M ante A.

Macrobius, the name of a great lerned man.
Macrochie, he that hath longe handes.
Macrochera, a garmente with longe sleues.
Macteæ, precious meates.
Macticus, he, whiche hath greatte chekes, and a gapynge mouth.
Macto, are, to slee or kylle: also to beate, sometyme to honour.
Mactra, an hutche, wherin breade is putte: some doo calle it a brake, wherwith dowe is wroughte.
Macte uirtutis & uirtute, procede in vertue.
Macte animi, be of good courage.
Macti ingenio, men of excellent wyttes.
Macula, a spotte, a blemyshe: Also infamye or reproche. Sometyme the masshe of a nette or hole betwene the thredes: also a nette, images wroughte in marble. *Varro.*
Maculo, are, to spotte or make fowle.
Maculosus, spotty, vncleane, or foule.
Madaura, a citie set in the boundes of Getulia and Numidia.
Madefacio, cere, to weate, to washe, to bain.
Madefio, fieri, to be washed.
Madeo, ere, to be wette or washed.
Madesco, scere, to sweat, or be through wet.
Madian, a citie beyond Arabia on the south part in the desert of the Sarasyns, ageinst the easte parte of the redde see.
Madido, dare, to make wette.
Madidus, dida, didum, wete or washed with lycoure.
Madifico, facere, to make weate.
Mador, oris, moysture. sometyme sweate.
Mados, a certayne kynde of white vynes.
Madulsa, dronken.
Meander, a ryuer of the countray of Phrigia, whiche hathe many tournynges and wyndynges: and of that all crooked and subtyll tournynge wayes, meanes, and deuyses, be called Meandri. There is also of that name a mountayne in India.
Media, a citie in the realme of Thracia.
Mæe, a kynde of great crabbes of the see.
Memacterion, the moneth of Septembre.
Menala, uel Menalus, a hygh mountayne in Archadia.
Menas, adis, a fyshe, whiche I suppose we do calle a Menowe.
Menades, women, whiche dyd alwaye folowe Bacchus, with their heare scatterid like mad women, running hither & thither.
Menoles, one of the names of Bacchus.
Meonia, is a countrey in Asia the lasse, callyd also Lidia.
Meonius, a, um, of Meonia. Homere the excellent poete was named Meonius, eyther bicause that he was borne in that coūtrey, or els that his fathers name was Meon.
Meotis,

Mæotis, a greatte mere in the countrey of Scithia, whiche is alway frosen.
Mereo, es, loke after in Mereo et Mereor.
Mæro, are, to make heuy.
Mæror, heuinesse with wepynge.
Mæstitia, et mæstitudo, heuynesse.
Mæsto, et Mæstifico, care, to make heuy.
Magalia, villagis.
Magia, Magike, whiche is in two sortes, one is the secrete knowlege of the naturall qualyties and hydde operations and causes of thynges, and that is called Magia naturalis, naturall magike: Another is superstitiouse & deuillishe, called witche crafte, sorcery, or other lyke detestable names, whiche is vnlefull by the lawes of god and man.
Magicus, ca, cum, perteynyng to magike.
Magidæ, kychen bourdes, or instrumentes perteynynge to the kechyn.
Magida, a kynde of breade.
Maginor, aris, ari, to trifle.
Magis, more.
Magisteriū, the dignite or office of a master.
Magistratus, tus, a great offycer, a man hauynge autoritie in gouernance of people. all be it that some haue more authoritie by the lawes, and some haue lesse.
Magister populi, the chefe ruler of the people, by the whiche name the Dictatour amonge the Romaynes was called.
Magister, tri, a master or teacher of scieces.
Magistro, are, to rule.
Magister scriniorum, an offycer lyke to the mayster of the rolls.
Magmata, confections made of dyuerse sweete spices in paste only for the sauour, as pomaundres and wasshing balles. somtyme it is taken for the dreggis of sweete oyles.
Magna Grętia, that parte of Italy from Larentum to Cumas.
Magnalia, gret thinges to be wondered at.
Magnarius, a greate marchaunt.
Magnanimitas, tatis, valiantnesse of courage or harte, magnanimity.
Magnas, atis, et Magnatus, a noble man, a mā of great estimation.
Magnes, etis, an Adamant stone.
Magnesia, a parte of Macedonia.
Magnifico, are, to extoll.
Magnificus, he that doth great thynges.
Magna, at a great price.
Magnificentia, a disposition and administration in doinge or makynge of great thynges and sumptuous.
Magnus, a, um, great.
Magog, the sonne of Japheth.
Maguderis, a kynde of Caules called also Laserpitium.

Magus, signifieth in the Persiane tongue a wyse man, expert also in the misteries of theyr ceremonyes, sometyme it signifieth a witche.
Maia, the mother of Mercurius.
Maiestatem constituere, to confirme the astate of princes dignitie.
Maiales, barowe hogges.
Maiestatem soluere, to lese the preeminence of princes dignitie.
Maiestas, tatis, maiestic.
Maiestatis crimen, mysprision.
Maiores, auncetours, progenitours.
Maior, oris, greatter.
Maius, the monthe of Maye.
Malæ, the chekes.
Malaca, a citie in Spayne.
Malatia, calme of the See, also the griefe of the stomacke not susteynyng meate, abhorrynge all thinges, as a womanne with chylde, some do cal it the abhomination of the stomake.
Malachites, a stone of a dark grene colour.
Malacisso, are, to knede or make softe.
Malaces, ces, a kynde of malowes. *Plaut. in Epi.*
Malacostracha, soft as fishe without shelles.
Malacus, ca, cum, softe.
Malagma, tis, a mollifienge playster, wherby hard impostumes be made soft or ripe.
Malasso, are, to make softe or rype. Also to exercyse.
Male, ylle, vnhappily, vncommodyousely, myscheuousely
Malea, a promontorie or hylle lienge into the see by Laconia, which is daungerous for shyppes to passe by.
Male audire, to be yll reported of, to haue an yll name.
Male cogitare de aliquo, to haue yll opynion of one.
Male accepti, yll handled, yll intreated. *Ci. in Ver.*
Maledicentia, yll reporte. *Brutus in*
Maledico, xi, cere, to curse. *Cice.*
Maledicus, yll tonged.
Malefica, a wytche, whiche with sorcerye dothe hurte to her neyghbours.
Maleficus, a harme doer.
Maleficium, & maleficentia, damage, wrong displeasure, hurt, a myscheuous dede.
Malefice, myscheuousely, harmefully.
Male meritus est de me, he hathe ylle intreated me.
Male optare, to curse.
Male accipere, to intreate one ylle.
Male accipere uerbis, to gyue ylle language to one.
Male acceptus, yll intreated, yll handelyd, shrewdely welcome.

Male

M ante A.

Male cadere, to chaunce ylle.
Male conciliatus, coste lost, he on whome a man hath lost al that he hath bestowid. Fugitiue prodi, male conciliate, Come forthe mycher, on whome I haue loste all that thou costest me.

Plautus in Amph.
Male formido, I am yll or sore aferde.

Plautus in Asinar.
Male me habet hæc res, I am sorie or yll apayde for that mattier: or that mattier greueth me sore.

Plaut. in Castel.
Maleloqui, & maledicere, to curse.
Male maceror, I am yl vexed, I am il at ese.
Male mereri, to doo displeasure.
Male metuo, I am yll aferde.
Male moratus, yll manerde.

Terent. in Adelph.
Male morigerus, disobedient, or frowarde.
Male odi, I hate deedly.
Male precari, to aske a vengeaunce.
Male uertat illi, God sende hym yuell lucke therof, yll maye he brooke it.
Male suada, she that giueth shrewed councel.
Maleuolentia, malyce, yll wylle.
Maleuolus, malyciouse.
Malicorium, the rynde of a pomegranade.
Maligne, enuiously, disdainfully, maliciously
Malignor, & maligno, to beare malyce, to be hatefulle.

Vergilius. Plinius.
Malignus, a, um, wycked, cruell, enuyous, & couetous. maligna uia, an yll way.
Malignus ager, grounde that is ylle to be broughte to tylthe.
Maligna lux, a dymme lyghte.
Malignitas, tatis, wickednes, malignitie, enuye, malyce, vnprofytablenesse, the vyce contrarye to lyberalitie.
Malitia, contrary to vertue & goodnes. somtyme it signifieth subtiltie with deceyte.
Malitiose, malyciousely.
Malleatus, a, um, hammered.
Malleo, are, to warke with an hammer.
Malleolus, a lyttelle hammer. It is also a smalle boughe or twygge of a vyne. Also Malleoli be sommetyme taken generallye for smalle stickes.
Malleus, an hammer.
Malluuium, & malluuie, arum, a basyn, wher in menne do washe their handes.
Malobathrum, a swete oyntment, wherwith men were wont to washe their heare.
Malo, I had leauer, or rather: mauis, mauul.
Malobathron, whiche in latyn is callyd foliū, is a swete herbe growing in India, vpon waters without any roote.
Malta, a clay, whyche touchynge anye other mattier or substaunce, settethe it on fyre.
Malua, an herbe callyd Mallowes.
Malus, an appull tree of the femynyne gender.

M ante E.

Malus assyria, uel medica, an orenge tree.
Malus, in the masculyne gender, a maste of a shyppe.

Terent. in Phorm.
Malum, beinge an aduerbe, sygnifieth with a myschiefe, or like thyng. Quid uos malum ergo me sic ludificaminis? Than wherfore with a myschiefe do you thus mocke me. Quid tua (malum) id refert? what with a myschiefe reckest thou therfore, or hast thou therwith to do?

Malus, a, um, yll, contrary to good: somtime labour, vexation, sycknesse, grefe, malice.
Mamertini, people in Campania.
Mamilla, a lyttell dugge, or pappe.
Mamma, a dugge or pappe.
Mammare, to gyue the dugge or breste to a chylde.
Mammeata, a womanne with greatte dugges or breastes.
Mammillare, a kerchefe, wherwith women do couer theyr pappes.
Māmona, in the language of Syria, worldly substaunce, rychesse.

Plaut.
Mammosus, sa, & mammeatus, ta, tum, hauynge great dugges.
Mammothreptus, the chylde that souceketh longe.
Mamphula, a certayne bread vsed in Syria, whiche ere it be throughe baken, fallyth into coles.
Mano, are, to droppe or stylle out, or runne out softly. also to descende, to procede.
Mana, in the olde tyme, was taken for Bona, good.
Manapia, an Ilande in the northe parte of Britannia.
Manceps, cipis, he that byeth or hyreth any thynge of the people.
Mancinati, persones condemned.
Manciole, lyttell handes.
Mancipium, that whiche is solenely bought before wytnesses. Also a mannes propre goodes or catell. sometyme a bondeman.
Mancupi, the solempne fourme or maner of byenge any thynge before wytnes, by lyuerye and seyson, or possessyon takynge, with other thynges executed, requysyte for the assuraunce of any bargayne & sale.
Mancipatio, the assuraunce by lyuerye and possessyon.
Mancupes, the principall takers of lande, or other thynge, wherof groweth yerely reuenues. Also they, whiche doo take on them to perfourme any worke in greatte.
Mancupio dare, to gyue or selle a thynge with warrantie.
Mancupio accipere, to take a thynge with warantie of hym, the whyche grueth or selleth it.

N   Man.

M ante A.

Mancipi, the interest or right of a thinge.
Mancipo, are, to delyuer in bondage, to delyuer possession, to make lyuery & sayson.
Mancipij sui esse, to be his owne manne, and none other mans subiect or seruant.
Mancipio dare, to delyuer possession, reseruynge a rente.

Vitruuius. Mancipio accipere, to take possession or lyuerye and saison.

Mancus, lackynge one hand. also generally that, whiche lacketh any thyng necessary.
Mandatarius, he to whome commaundemente is gyuen.
Mandatum, a commyssion. Also a commandement, a charge.
Mandatus, ta, tum, giuen in charge.
Mandibula, a iawebone, wherin the teethe be sette.
Mando, are, to comitte. memoriæ mandare, to remembre, to put in remembraunce, to leaue in memorie, or for a memoriall.
Mandare æternitati, to wryte a thing, to the intent to be in perpetuall remembraunce.
Mandare literis, to put in memorie.
Mandare fidei alicuius, to put a man in truste with a thynge. Mandare terræ semina, to putte sede into the grounde.
Mando, di, dere, to chewe meate, or grynde it with the tethe.
Mando, onis, a great eater, or he that is alway eatynge.
Mandra, a cabin, a shepehouse, or oxehous.
Mandragora, an herbe callyd Mandrag, whiche beareth a lyttell apple: the iuyce whereof dronken or smellyd to, causeth a manne to slepe.
Manduces, imagis caried about in pageantis with great chekes and wide mouthes.
Manduco, are, to chewe meate.
Manduco, conis, a gret eater.
Manducus, idem.
Mane, earely, also the mornynge.
Maneo, mansi, manere, to abyde, to tary, to persiste, to happen hereafter.
Manere promissis, to kepe promyse.
Mane dum, tarye a whyle
Mansio, onis, a place to abide in, also a poste place, for conuayinge of letters or other thynges spedyly.
Manes, the good and badde aungell. Some tyme they be taken for deuylles, somtyme for spyrytes or sowles, not pourged of synne, sommetyme for the peynes, whiche soules do suffre.
Mango, onis, was taken for a seller of childerne to abhominable vses. It is also taken for suche one as polysheth or paynteth a thynge with a fals colour, to selle it the deerer.

M ante A.

Mangonicus, a, ū, pertainynge to that craft.
Mangonium, the crafte to make thynges saleable:
Mangonizo, nizare, to polysshe, paynte, or trymme a thynge, to make it more vendible, or to be better solde.
Mania, madnesse.
Maniacus, a madde manne.
Maniæ, arum, ymages defourmed.
Manibus, pedibusq̄, with all might & mayne.
Manibus pedibusq̄ ire in sententia, is where in a parlyament, greatte counsayle, or other great assembly, to haue the consente of many men, the greatter parte consentyng to one mannes opinyon or sentence, to goo towarde hym, holdynge vp theyr handes, in token that they be therevnto agreed.
Manicæ, sleues of a garmente. Also manacles to tie the hādes togither. Also gantlettes and splyntes, and myttaynes, or longe gloues.
Manichei, a secte of heritikes, so callyd of an Archeherytyque called Manychen.
Manicula, a lyttell hande.
Manifestarius, a, um, notoryous.
Manifesto, tare, to manyfeste or make apparaunt.
Manifestum, manyfeste or clere.
Manifestum habere, to knowe surely.
Manifestus mendatij, proued a lyer.
Manifesto, an aduerbe, sygnyfyeth clerelye, playnely.
Manifestarius, a, um, clere, euydente, openly knowen.
Manimoria, thynges, whiche doo abyde in remembraunce.
Maniolæ, yles agaynst India, beyonde the ryuer of Ganges, where as be rockes of Adamant stones, which do drawe to them shyppes that haue yron nayles.
Manipulus, an handefull, a grype, a bende of men, proprely of tenne souldiours.
Manipularis, & maniplaris, a standerd bearer, or baner bearer.
Manipulatim, by bendes.
Manliana imperia, cruelle gouernaunce or rule, without any mercy.
Manlius, a noble Romayne.
Manna, a delycate meate, whiche god sent to the Iewes beinge in the deserte. also a sweete dewe, whyche falleth in the mornynges, and lyethe on leaues congelyd lyke whyte hony, whyche phisicions do vse for a medycine to purge coler easily.
Manna thuris, the pouder or duste that cometh of frankincense.
Mannus, an amblynge hackeney.
Mannor, aris, ari, to steale.

Man-

M ante A.

Mart.li.12

Mannobarbulus, a balle of leade to throw, also the caster therof.
Mannulus, a nagge, a lyttell hors.
Mansisterna, a pytcher potte.
Mano, are, to runne oute, as lycour dothe: also to droppe out, to appere out, as sweat out of the pores.
Mansio, one dayes iourney.
Manstus, stollen.
Mansito, tare, to abyde longe.
Mansuesco, scere, to waxe tame or gentyll.
Mansues, for mansuetus.
Mansuetudo, dinis, mekenes, gentylnesse, a moderate temperance betwixte pride and symplicitie.
Mansuetus, ta, tum, meke, gentyll, tame.
Mansuete, mekely, gentylly.
Mansum, meate, whiche the nourices doo chewe, and after giue it to the chyld, puttynge it into his mouthe.

Festus.

Mansutius, a great eater: also ripe and apt to be eaten.
Mansus, a, um, chewed.
Mantelum, & mantelium, & mantile, a towel wherwith menne do wype their handes, whan they haue washed. Also a cloke.
Manteum, a place where dyuels in ydolles gaue aunsweres.
Manthicora, a beast which is in India, in body like to a lion, but more rough, hauynge a face like to a man, & in his mouth iii. rewes or set of teeth, the taile of a scorpion, & the voyce of a smalle trumpette: and is of colour redde, and wyll neuer be made tame.
Mantica, a bagge, sometyme a cloke.
Manticula, a purse.
Manticularius, a stealer of napry, also a pike pours, or cutte pourse.
Manticularia, towels or other lyke thyngis wherwith men do wype their handes.
Manticulor, aris, ari, to do a thynge slyly, as to pike a purse.
Manticulatio, slyenesse, deceite.
Mantinea, a cytie in Grece.
Mantis, a prophete.
Mantiscinor, aris, ari, to stele or pike craftuly.
Mantissa, the addition in weight.
Manto, tare, amōg the old wryters to abide.
Mantua, a noble citie in Italy, where Vergile the excellent poete was borne.
Mantuanus, a, um, of Mantua.
Mantuariæ tunicæ, sleuyd iackettes.
Manuarius, a, um, manuall.
Manubię, the pray taken of ennemies: also money, for the whiche the pray was solde.
Manubinarius, the partner of a proye.
Manubrium, the hylte or handle of a weapon or instrument.
Manuleatus, ta, tum, hauinge longe sleeues.

M ante E.

Manum de tabula, a prouerbe, sygnifienge, Leaue whiles it is wel.
Manum conserere, to ioyne in battayle, to ioyne in issue, whan one sueth a nother.
Manum ferulæ subducere, to lerne as scholers do in the scholes.
Manumitto, to manumyse or infraunchise a bonde man.
Manuconsertum ex iure vocare, to chalenge right or proprietie in a thynge, it maye be taken for derayning of battayle in a wryte of ryght, after the lawes of Englande.
Manus, a hande, a grapul to fasten shippes togither, somtime it signifieth a multitude of men in the ayde of one, sometyme power, sometyme wrytynge, also the nose or snoute of an olyphant.
Manus iniectio, attachement, also saisen or saisure of a thing, wherunto we make title.
Mapalia, cotages builded rounde like oues.
Mappa, a table clothe.
Marathon, a felde in the countrey of Athenes, and also a towne there.
Marathron, et Maratrum, an herbe, whiche is called fenell or fenkill.
Marathusa, an yle wherin is abundaunce of fenell, and it is also called Clazomenia.
Marceo, cui, cere, to corrupte, to putrifie
Marcellus, a propre name.
Marchia, a countrey in base Germany.
Marcor, oris, corruption, or putrifaction.
Marconianni, people in Germany, whiche are nowe supposed to be either of Boeme or of Morauia.
Mardi, people adioyninge to Persia.
Mare, the Sec.
Mare cœlo miscere, to trouble al the world.———
Marcipor, oris, the seruant of Marcus.
Mareotis, otidis, a Ryuer in Egipte, also a parte of Libia, a parte of Epirus.
Mariotides, grapes of that countrey.
Margaride, smalle dates, rounde and white.
Margarita, margaritum, margarites, margaris, garidis, a perle, a Margarite: sometime generally all preciouse stones are called Margaritæ.

Plinius.

Margaritarius, a seller of perles.
Margariteferus, ra, rum, that which beareth Margarites.
Margina, a region in Asia.
Margo, ginis, the brymme or edge of euery thynge, the margent.
Margus, a riuer in Asia.
Maria, a propre name.
Mariaba, the chiefe citie in Saba.
Marinus, na, um, of the sec.
Mariscę, vnsauery frygges, wylde frygges, frygges which do open, that the sedes do appere, also great piles in the fundement.

Mariscus.

M ante A.

Mariscus, a bull rushe.
Marita, a wedded woman, a wyfe.
Maritigenus, a, ū, com of the kynd of Mars
Maritimus, of the see syde, or of the see.
Maritus, a wedded man, a husbande.
Marito, are, to wedde.
Marius, a propre name of a man.
Marmarica, a countrey of Affrike.
Marmor, oris, marble stone.
Marmoratus, ta, tum, wrought with marble.
Marmoratio, buyldynge with marble.
Marmoreus, a, um, of marble.
Marpesus, an hyll in the yle callyd Parus.
Marpesius, of the same hylle.
Marplacidę, shyps or barges vsed in Media.
Marra, a mattocke.
Marrubium, an herbe called horehounde.
Marrucini, people in Italye.
Mars, martis, callyd god of battayle. some tyme it is taken for battayle.
Martia, a countrey in Italye.
Marte suo, of his owne propre wytte, without any counsayle.
Marspiter, the father of Mars.
Marsupium, a powche or pourse.
Martiacus, ca, cum, belongynge to warres.
Martiaca, wages gyuen to souldyours.
Martialis, borne vnder the planet of Mars.
Martius, a, um, pertaynyng to Mars.
Martius campus, a fyelde at Rome, dedycate to Mars.
Martius mensis, the moneth callid March.
Martyr, in greke, a wytnesse.
Martyrium, martyrdome.
Mas, maris, a man, or mankynde.
Masculus, a, um, manly, great, wyse.
Masculesco, sci, scere, to be manly, great, or wyse, to be come of the male kynde.
Masculo, are, to make manly, or stronge.
Masdoranus, a mountayne, whiche diuydeth Parthia from Aria.
Massagetę, a people in Asia, whiche rounnynge on horsebacke throughe desertes, doo drynke their horses bloudde myxte with mylke, they also doo eate theyr parentes, if they die for age: but if they be sycke, they caste theym to wylde beastes to be deuoured.
Massinissa, kynge of Numidia, and greate frende to the Romaynes.
Massica, a countrey in the southe parte of Spayne.
Massicus, a mountayne in Campania.
Massilia, a cite in hygh France, callid Marsiles.
Massiliensis, se, of Marsiles.
Massylia, cum y, a countreye in Affrike, amonge the westerne Moores.
Masticeos, reuerende, honourable.
Mastiche, a soote gumme.

M ante A.

Mastigia, & mastigeus, a knaue worthye to be beaten.
Mastigophorus, a felow worthy to be whipped. Also certayne ministers, which with whyppes remoued the people, where there was moche prease.
Mastos, a teate. also a cisterne, whereinto water doth runne, and eftesones runneth out by a cocke or spoute.
Mastruca, a garment, whiche men of Sardinia vsed to weare.
Mastix, cis, a whyppe.
Mastrupari, to touche dishonestly the priuy membres of a man.
Masurius, the name of a famous lawyer, whiche wrate on the lawes ciuyle.
Matella, an vrinall, or other vessell, seruyng to that pourpose.
Matellio, onis, idem.
Mataeotechina, the vanitie, whiche is in a science or crafte.
Mater, tris, a mother.
Materfamilias, æ, an houswife, goodwyfe of the house, she that hath gouernaunce of other women, be she maried or vnmaried.
Mater matrina, she that is a mother, & hath mother lyuynge.
Materia, & materies, matter, wheerof any thyng is made, be it mettal, wodde, stone, erthe, or any thynge elles.
Materialis, le, that which is of som matter.
Materiarius, a carpenter.
Materior, aris, ari, to warke in tymber.
Materis, a frenche speare, or a iauelyn.
Matertera, an aunte or mothers syster.
Mathematicus, he that is cunnynge in aulgryme, musyke, geometry, and astronomy.
Mathesis, & mathema, lernyng by a demonstracyon.
Matralia, the solemne feastes of Matuta, called the mother of goddes.
Matresco, scere, to be lyke a mother.
Matricida, he that kylleth his mother.
Matrimonium, wedlocke, matrimonie.
Matrix, cis, the mother or matrice in a woman, in the whyche the chylde is conceiued. also matrix is any female kynde that conceiueth and beareth. Also the citie in a countrey, where as is the archbishops see is callyd matrix vrbs, whiche in greke is callid Metropolis.
Matrona, a wyfe. also the name of a ryuer in Burbon.
Matronalis, pertaynynge to a wyfe.
Matruelis, the sonne or doughter of my mothers syster.
Matta, a matte.
Mattiacę pilę, sope balles.
Mattiacum, a towne in Germanye.

Plautus in truculen. Plaut.

Matura,

Plaut. in Milite.

Matura ætas, full or perfyte age.
Maturate, quickely. Iube maturate illam exire huc, Byd her come forthe quickely.
Mature, tymely, nor to soone, nor to late.
Maturesco, scere, to be rype.
Maturitas, tatis, rypenes in all thynge, and as it were perfection.
Maturo, are, to make rype or perfyte, to do a thynge perfectly in due tyme & measure: sometyme to do a thyng spedily or quickly.
Maturus, a, um, rype, perfite, somtime it signifieth aged. Maturus homo, an aged man.
Matuta, the mornynge, or morowe.
Matutinus, a, um, of the morowe.
Mauors, ortis, Mars.
Mauortius, a, um, pertayninge to Mars.
Mauritania, Moriske, or the countreye of Moores.
Mauri, people called Moores.
Mausolus, the king of a realme callid Caria
Mausoleum, a sepulchre or tombe, whiche Arthemisia made for her husbād Mausolꝰ, which for the excellent warkmanship was accoūtid to be one of the meruailes of the worlde, & for the famousnes therof, euery gret & notable sepulchre is callid Mausoleū
Maxilla, the cheke bone.
Maximus, a, ū, greatest, or most in estimatiō.
Maximates, the greattest men in auctoritie.
Maximitas, tatis, auncient wryters vsed for greatnesse.
Maza, a cake made of floure and mylke.
Mazaca, a cytie in Cappadocia vnder the hyll callid Argeus, nowe called Cesaria.
Mazeras, a ryuer in the mouthe of the see, called mare Hircanum.
Mazononiū, a platter wherin meat is caried

¶ M, ANTE E.

Meapte, myne owne.
Meatus, tus, a passage, a waye.
Mecastor, a fourme of swearynge, as who sayth, so Castor helpe me.
Mechanicus, a craftes manne.
Mechanica ars, a handy crafte.
Mecœnas, atis, minion to Augustus the emperour, and bicause he was the supporter of great lerned men, all fauourers and succourers of lerned men be so called.
Meconis, a kynde of letuse, which causeth a man to slepe.
Mecon, in greke, is popye in englyshe.
Mecū, with me. Mecū facit, it maketh for my purpose. Mecū sentit, he is of min opinion.
Medea, wyfe vnto Jason, a witche and cruelle womanne.
Medela, remedy by medicine.
Mederga, for erga, towarde me.

Medeor, eris, eri, to heale or cure.
Media, a region in Asia.
Media vocabula, wordes whiche maye be taken in a good or ylle parte, as tempestas whiche signifieth tempest and tyme, facinus, a notable dede good or ylle, ualitudo, helth, or syckenes, and other lyke.
Medianus, na, nū, that which is in the midle.
Mediastinus, a drudge or lubber, which doth in the howse all maner of vyle seruice, as swepe or clense the house, carie wodde to the kytchen, and other like drudgery. *Budeus.*
Mediastimus, a, um, the myddelmoste.
Mediastrinus, the seruant, whiche hath the rule of the hous vnder his maister.
Medica, an herbe, whiche specially nouryssheth horses, and ones beinge sowen, efte sones springeth ten yeres continually, and commonly it is called Sylla.
Medibile, in state to be healed, curable.
Medicabilis, le, curable.
Medicamentarius, a phisycion.
Medicamentarius, a, um, pertaynyng to medicyne.
Medicina, medicamen, medicamētum, a medicine. sometyme it sygnifieth poyson.
Medicinalis, le, medicynable.
Medico, & medicor, aris, ari, to hele or cure.
Medicus, a phisycion.
Medicus, ca, cum, pertaining to phisike.
Medimnus, a certayn measure of corne, contaynynge syxe tymes the measure callyd modius. Vide modium.
Mediocris, diocre, measurable, in a meane, moderate.
Mediocritas, tatis, a meane.
Mediolanum, the chiefe citie of Lombardy, callyd Myllayne.
Medioximus, a, um, meane, or in the middes
Medipontus, an instrumente, wherwith ropes are made.
Meditabundus, cerefull, studiouse.
Meditari se, to exercise hym selfe.
Meditate, studiously, perfectelye on the fyngers endes. *Plautus in Stich. in Bacch.*
Meditatio, a thynkynge or drymsynge in thought. also an exercise, aswell of minde, as of bodye.
Meditatorius, a, um, whyche belongethe to medytation.
Mediterraneus, in the myddel of the lande, and furthest from the see.
Meditor, aris, ari, to thynke deepely, and in thynkynge to fynde out, to purpose, to lay snares, to synge or playe swetely.
Meditrina, the goddesse of phisyke.
Meditrinalia, ceremonyes vsed by theym, whyche dranke muste or newe wyne.
Meditullium, the myddell.

N iii.   Medius,

Medius, a, um, the myddes equally distant from the extremytes, sometyme meane.

Medium commune, amonge all.

Medius, a meane or mediatour betwene .ii. menne.

Medius fidius, an othe, whiche althoughe somtyme it had a nother signification, yet may it nowe in a commune fourme of spekynge be vsed in this wise, by the faythe of my body: sens Dius for Jupiter, and fidius for filius, be nowe out of vse.

Meduacus, a Ryuer aboute Uenyce, called nowe Brent.

Medulla, marowe, whiche is in bones.

Plaut. Medullo, are, to take out marowe, somtime to expresse vtterly. Narra iam rem nobis omnem, atq́ emedulla, Tell and expresse vtterly to vs all the hole matter.

Medullitus, innerly into the marowe.

Medusa, a lady, of whom fables do report, that her heares by Minerua were tourned in to adders, and they which behelde her were tourned into stones: whom Perseus afterward slewe. she is somtyme taken for one of the furies of hell.

Mesansilium, a certayne weapon to throwe.

Mægabizi, priestes of Diana, whiche alway were gelded.

Megera, a furie or turmentour of hel, whiche the Paynyms supposed dyd prouoke and stere men to woodnes.

Megalesia, the festiual day, dedicate to Cybele, called the mother of goddes among Paynyms.

Megalenses, & megalesia, playes to the honour of Cybele.

Megalium, a swete oyntement.

Megaloprepeia, an honourable facyon in gyuynge or imployeng of great thynges, whych besemeth a man of great courage.

Megaloprepes, he that doth great thinges accordynge to his dignitie.

Megara, a Cytie belongynge to Athenes. It was also the name of oone of Hercules wyues.

Megaris, idis, a countrey in Achaia.

Megistanes, whome we doo calle nobles or peres of the realme.

Me hercle, an othe sworne by Hercules.

Meio, iere, to pysse.

Mel, mellis, hony.

Mellene, a citie in Arcadia.

Melampus, a mannes name.

Melamphyllon, an herbe.

Melancholia, melancolye.

Melancoryphus, a byrde called a fynche.

Melanthia, an herbe called also Nigella.

Melanurus, a fysshe hauynge a blacke taile.

Plini. Melandria, the leane partes of the fisshe called Tunny.

Melculum, a wanton worde spoken by louers vnto their paramours, my litel hony.

Meleagrides, byrdes, whiche we doo calle hennes of Genny.

Melegina, an yle in the Uenecian see.

Melenetus, a kynde of faukons very lytell of body, black and puissant, which haunteth mountaynes, and feedeth her byrdes alone, a merlyon as J suppose.

Mælibeus, a shepardes name.

Melibœa, a citie in Thessaly.

Meliceris, idis, a soore or skalle in the hed lyke a hony combe, out of the whiche cometh an humour lyke hony.

Melicraton, wyne & hony sodden togither.

Melicerta, whome the gentyls dyd honour for one of the goddes of the see.

Melicus, a musycyin:

Melilotos, an herbe called melilote.

Melimela, swete appulles.

Melina, a swete shalme.

Melinus, na, num, whyte russette, or a gynger coloure.

Melioresco, scere, to be better.

Melipecta, meates made with honye.

Melis, seu melius, a beaste called a graye, a brocke, or a badger.

Melisphillon, smallache.

Melissa, a woman, who with her syster Amalthea, nouryshhed Jupyter. It is also an herbe, commonly called baume.

Melite, siue melita, an Jle lyeng betwene Jtaly and Epirus. Also a citie made by the Carthaginensis.

Melitites, a drynke made of hony and must, or newe wyne.

Mellitones, places where bees be norished.

Melitæi canes, & melitenses, were praty litel houndes, in the whiche ladies toke plesure and delyte, whiche were brought out of the sayde yle of Melite.

Melites, a precyous stone of the colour of an orenge.

Melissus, the name of hym, whiche dydde fyrst sacrifice vnto ydolles. also the name of an auuncient philosopher.

Mellium, a dogges coler.

Mellarius, a hony man, or sellar of hony.

Mellarius, a, um, of honye.

Mellatio, the tyme of druynge of hyues, whan hony is taken out.

Mellatiu, new must, wherin hony is sodden.

Mellifico, care, to make hony.

Mellificatio, makynge of honye.

Mellificum, idem.

Mellifluus, a, um, swete as honye.

Melligo, ginis, a mell dewe, whiche falleth on leaues of trees, and somtime on corne.

Mellilo-

Melliloquus, a sweete speaker.
Melilla, my hony, my sweetynge, a worde of wanton dalyers.
Mellisones, they which doo practyse dressynge of honye.
Melliturgus, a warker or maker of hony.
Mellitus, a, um, myxte with honye.
Melitus, the name of hym, whiche accused Socrates.
Melizonum, a confection made with honye clarifyed.

Apitius. Melleus, a, um, of hony. also swete, as Vox mellea, a swete voyce.
Mellica, a kynde of poulse, of the coloure of redde, of the fourme of Mylle.
Melo, a ryuer callyd also Geon.
Melodia, melodye.
Melodes, he that syngeth cunnyngely, and swetely.
Meloessa, an yle by Sicile, in the whyche was great plenty of shepe.
Melomeli, whan apples, very rype & fayre, be conserued in hony.
Mellonia, uel Melona, callyd the goddesse of honye.
Melos, odis, melodye, armonye.
Melota, & melote, a shepes felle or skynne.
Melpomene, one of the nyne Musis.
Membrana, parchement or velume, wherin men do write, also the euermoste skynne of any thynge.
Membrosus, a, um, hauyng a great membre.
Membraneus, a, um, the parchemente or velume.
Membranulum, a small membre.
Membrare, to fourme membres.
Membratim, by euery membre.
Mēbratura, the setting or order of mēbres.
Membrum, a membre.
Memet, my selfe.
Memini, I remembre.
Memerylus, a lyttel tree lyke a citron tree.
Mēnon, the sonne of Thiton, whiche came to the ayde of the Troyans.
Mēnonis aues, byrdes, which were supposed to growe of the ashes of Mēnon.
Memor, oris, he that remembreth.
Memorabilis, le, worthy remembraunce.
Memoratus, tus, et Memoratio, a remembrynge.
Memoria, memory, remembraunce.
Memoriale, a thynge, which shulde be remembred.
Memoriosus, he that hath a good memory.
Memoriter, parfitely by hart, or with good remembraunce.
Memoro, are, to remembre, somtyme to tel, or expounde, to recite or reherse.
Memphis, a great citie in Egipt.

Memphiticus, of that citie.
Memphe, idem.
Mena, a lyttell fyshe, blacke in somer, and white in wynter.
Menechmi, the name of a comedy of Plaut.
Menalippa, quene of Amazon, whom Hercules vaynquished.
Menapii, people of the coūtrey called Gelarlande, or Gylderlande.
Menander, a famouse poete, a wryter of comedies.
Menaria, an Ile in the see betwene Carthage and Sicile.
Menceps, he or she, whiche is oute of her wytte.
Menda, et Mendum, a faulte or vice in wrytynge.
Mendatium, a lye.
Mendaculum, a lyttell fault or lye.
Mendax, acis, a lyar.
Mendicabulum, beggynge.
Mendaciloquus, a teller of lyes.
Mendicitas, tatis, et Mēdicimoniū, beggery.
Mendico, are, to begge.
Mendicula, a certayne vesture.
Mendicus, a beggar.
Mendix, an offyce amonge the olde Italyans called Osci.
Meneletus, a byrde lyke to a small egle.
Memana ædificia, buyldynge outewarde in prospectes or galeries.
Menix, an Ile agaynst the lasse Affrica.
Mens, tis, the hyghest and chiefe parte of the mynde.
Mensa, a table or bourd to eate on. somtime dyner or soupper.
Mensarius, the banker or exchaungeour, of whom men do borow money vpon gayne, called exchaunge.
Mensio, a measure.
Mensis, a moneth.
Menstrualis, & menstruus, a, um, pertaynyng to a monethe.
Menstruatus, ta, tum, that which hath floures lyke to women
Menstruum, a womans naturall purgation called floures.
Menstruus, a, um, that whiche hapneth euery moneth.
Mensura, a measure.
Mensurnus, a, um, monthly.
Menta, et Mentula, the preuye membre of a manne.
Mentagra, a dyseafe, whiche couereth all the face with a skurfe.
Mente captus, a madde manne.
Mentha, an herbe called mynte.
Menthastrum, wylde mynte.
Mentibor, for mentiar, I shall make a lye. Plaut.

Mens

Mentigo, a dysease, whiche infectith beastes with scabbes aboute theyr mouthes and lyppes.
Mentior, iris, iri, to lye.
Mentoas, the famous ryuer, whiche is now called Danubius.
Mentor, an excellent grauour of vessel.
Mentum, a chynne.
Menus, a riuer in Germany.
Meo, are, to go, to flowe.

Sidonius. Meo nomine, for my cause, on my behalfe.
Mephiticus, ca, cum, stynkynge.
Meatus, condutes or wayes, wherby any humour floweth.
Mephitis, a stenche or yl fauour, which procedeth of corrupt water or licour, mixt with erthe.
Meopte ingenio, by myn owne wytte.
Meracus, ca, cum, et Merax, racis, pure without any mixture.
Vinum meracum, wyne without any water.
Mercalis, le, Uendible, or that, which maye be bought.
Mercator, oris, euery byar, a marchaunt.
Mercatura, the feate of marchaundyse.
Mercatus, tus, the act of byinge.
Mercatus, ti, a market, or fayre.
Mercatus, ta, tum, bought.
Mercenarius, an hyred seruaunt.
Mercenarius, a, um, that whiche maye be hyred.
Merces, cis, marchaundise, ware, chaffer.
Merces, cedis, wages, the reward of labour or seruice.
Mercimonium, that whiche is tourned in brynge and sellynge.
Mercor, aris, ari, to bye for to sel for gaynes. sometymes to bie generally.
Mercurialis, an herbe called mercury.
Mercurius, was of the paynimes called god of Eloquence, and messager of Jupiter, it is the name of one of the seuen planettes.
Merda, the excrement or ordure of a man or beaste.
Merdo, are, to expell ordure.
Merenda, meate eaten at after noone, a collation, a none mele.
Mereo, ere, et Mereor, eri, to take wages, to deserue, to exercise a vile occupation. Mereor bene de te, I do somewhat for the, I deserue to haue the my frende, or to haue thy fauour. Male mereor de te, I doo the displeasure, I do yll deserue thy fauour. Also Merere, to serue in warres. Merere stipendia, to take wagis as a souldyour, or to be a souldiour.

Plautus in milite. Meretricie, hoorishely.
Meretricius, hooredome, or brothelry.
Meretricium, a, ū, perteyning to brothelry.

Meretricor, aris, ari, to lyue in brothelry, to playe the harlote.
Mere, purely.
Meretrix, icis, an harlot, or brothell.
Merge, pitcheforkes for to take vp sheues.
Mergites, gripes of corne.
Mergi, vines, or other small trees, whiche ar bowed and haue the toppes bowe wise tourned and set into the erthe.
Mergo, si, gere, to drowne in the water.
Mergulus, an instrument where the matche of a lampe is conteyned.
Mergus, goris, a bukket to drawe vp water.
Mergus, gi, a waterfoule called a dyue doppar, some do call it a foule of the see lyke to a gull, whiche dyueth vnder the water to take fishe.
Meribibulus, he that drynketh moch wyne without water.
Meridies, noonetyde.
Meridianus, a, um, perteynyng to none.
Meridio, are, et Meridior, ari, to dyne, to eate meate at noone, to slepe at none.
Meridiatio, noone reste.
Merismos, a fygure called also dystributio, wherby the oration is distributed into sondry sentences.
Merito, worthily, with good cause.
Merito, are, to be worthye, also to serue in warres.
Meritorius, a, um, that whiche is let or sette for aduantage.
Meritoria taberna, a house wherinto a man is receyued for his money.
Meritoria, howses or shoppes let to hyre.
Meritum, a benefite, a deserte good or ylle.
Meritus, ta, tum, deserued, conuenient.
Meritus, a mountayne in the thirde part of Europa beyonde Grece.
Meroe, an yle on the great ryuer of Nilus in Egipte.
Mero, was in scorne the name of Nero, bicause he was so great a drynker of wyne.
Merobiba, she that drynkethe wyne without water.
Merops, a bryde which doth eate bees.
Meroctes, a lyttell stone of the coloure of leekes, whiche sweateth a lyckour lyke to mylke.
Meropes, men of dyuers languages.
Meropus, a moūtain in Grece by Thessaly.
Meros, a hylle of Inde, at the foote wherof is the citie callyd Nisa.
Merso, are, to drowne often.
Merto, idem.
Merula, a bryde.
Merum, wyne vnlayde, without water.
Merus, a, um, soole, mere, pure.
Merx, cis, one kynd of marchandyse.

Mesa, a ryuer whiche runneth by Braband and the lande of Luke and Gellar, called the Mase.

Mesapia, a countrey called also Apulia.

Mesauli, entrees betwene the haule and the parlour.

Mesia, a Countrey ioynynge to Hungrye, Wyse.

Mesochorus, he that plaieth on a flute or other pype in the myddes of the daunsers.

Budeus. Mesonauta, a drudge in a shyppe, or a shyp page, whiche dothe all vyle seruice in the shyppe.

Mesoleucos, a precious stone, blacke, hauynge a whyte strake in the myddes.

Mesomelas, a whyte stone, hauyng a blacke lyne in the myddes.

Mesonyxion, midnyght.

Mesopotamia, a countreye lyinge betwene the two greatte ryuers Euphrates, and Tigris.

Mespilus a medlar tree.

Mespilum, a fruite called a medlar.

Messala, a noble oratour of Rome.

Messalina, wyfe to the emperour Claudius a woman of vnsaciable lechery.

Messana, a citie in Sicile.

Messene, a citie in Grece.

Messias, Christe.

Messis, haruest, sometyme it sygnifieth the corne or the grapes newe mowen or gathered.

Messio, onis, a reapynge

Messor, oris, a reaper.

Messorius, messoria, rium, perteynynge to reapynge.

Meta, a but, or pricke to shote at, somtyme a marke or gowle in the felde, where vnto men or horses do runne, somtyme a boūde in landes. Also a reyke of corne or heye, also the lower part of a myll.

Meta lactis, a Chese.

Metabasis, a passage.

Metabole, chaunge.

Metagonium, a promontory or mountayne lyinge into the see, whiche diuideth Affrica fro Numidia.

Metalepsis, a fygure, whereby a worde is put from his commune signification.

Mettalli, hyred souldiours.

Metallici, they which do dygge and warke mettall out of the mynes, wherin mettall is founde.

Metallum, mettalle.

Metamorphosis, eos, a transformation or chaungynge of fygure.

Metaphora, a translation of wordes frome their propre sygnyfycation.

Metaplasmus, a fygure callyd transformation. It is a translatyng of wordes being in prose into a fourme of meter, eyther for necessitie, or to augmente the elegancye.

Metapontū, a citie in the realme of Naples.

Metempsychosis, the transposyng of soules after the opinion of the Pythagoriens, out of one body into an other body.

Metathesis, where one letter is transposed from one place in a worde into an nother as Tymber Tymbre.

Metaurus, et metaurum, a ryuer of Umbria, whiche runneth into Flaminia.

Metellus, the propre name of dyuers noble Romaynes.

Meteoria, speculation in high thynges.

Meteorologus, he that is studious in suche speculation.

Meteora, are bokes of Aristotle, wherin he treateth of sterres, and suche other celestiall thynges.

Meteoroscopus, a beholder of high thingis

Methodus, a compendious or redy way, or a rule certayne to lerne by any science.

Metonymia, a fygure called denomination, as Bacchus for wyne, Venus for lechery, Cupido for loue.

Methymna, a citie in the yle of Lesboe.

Meticulosus, temerouse or fearefull.

Metior, tiris, tiri, to mete or measure, to giue by measure, to passe ouer.

Meto, messui, metere, to reape.

Metona, a towne in Grece called Modon.

Metor, aris, ari, to sette boundes, to measure lande, to dispose.

Metopion, oyle of almondes, also a tree in Affrica, whiche destylleth downe gumme lyke to rosyn.

Metoposcopus, he that consydereth a māns face, and therby iudgeth his condycions or affectes.

Metreta, a measure for lyckour, whiche is also called Amphora, and contayned euery way square one foote.

Metropolis, the chiefe citie.

Metropolitanus, a man of that citie.

Metropolites, the bishop of the chiefe citie.

Metrum, a verse.

Metuo, tui, tuere, to feare or dreade with tremblynge.

Metus, tus, feare, drede.

Metys, the refuse of waxe.

Meu, an herbe.

Meuania, a citie in the part of Italy, callyd Umbria, wherein Propertius the poete was borne.

Meneuia, a citie in wales called saint Dauid.

Meus, a, meum, myne.

Meum est, it is my duetie or my parte.

¶ M, ANTE L

Mi, to me.
Mica, a crumme of breade.
Mico, care, to glisten, or shyne. Dignus qui cū in tenebris mices, is applied to one, whiche is reputed to be an honeste man, and a trusty, whiche wyll kepe touch and deceyue no man. It may be this wise translated, in a commune fourme of speakynge, He is one, with whom thou mayst assuredly bargayne. also to holde vp now one fynger, nowe two, as men do whanne they trete or bargain togyther by signes.
Miconium, an herbe called Popy.
Microcosmas, a lyttell worlde.
Micrologia, curiositie aboute thynges of no valour.
Micrologus, a lyttell communication.
Micropsichia, feble courage, faynt harted.
Micropsichi, they which haue faint hartis.
Micturio, ire, to pysse.
Mictyris, poore folkes potage.
Mida, a worme bredynge in beanes.
Midas, a kynge of Phrigie, who excellyd all other in rychesse.
Miesa, a towne in Maccdonia.
Migro, are, to remoue frome one place, to dwell in an other.
Miles, militis, a man of warre, a souldiour.
Mihipte, Lato vsed for mihi ipsi.
Miletus, a citie in Grece.
Milesius, a, um, of that citie.
Militaris uia, the hygh way.
Militariter, warrely.
Militia, warre. sommetyme the exercise of warre.
Milito, tare, to goo on warfare, or to be in warres.
Milium, a smalle grayne callyd Myll.
Mille & millia, a thousande.
Millepeda, a worme hauynge a great numbre of feete.
Millearium, a myle, alfo a cawdron, also a pyller in Rome, wherein was grauen all the wayes of Italye.
Milliarius, a, um, of a thousande weight.
Millies, a thousande tymes.
Millus, a mastyues colar, made of lether with nayles.
Milo, onis, the name of one, whiche at the game of Olimpus, with his bare hande, slewe a bulle, and after caried hym a furlonge, and the same daye eate hym euery morsel. It was also a noble Romayne, for whom Tullie made an oration, conteining incomparable eloquence.
Miluina tibia, a cornette, or smalle shaulme.
Miluus, & miluius, a kyte. There is also a fyshe and a sterre of the same name.
Miluinus, na, num, of a kyte, or lyke a kyte.
Mimallones, women dedicate to the folishe ceremonies of Bacchus.
Mimas, a mountayne of Thracia.
Mimus, a bourder or rayler, which in mockynge other men in gesture and countenaunce, dothe folowe them, faynynge to be the same persones, whome they do reproue. Mimi, be verses counterfaytynge moche wantonnes without any reuerēce, hauynge not withstandynge somme wyse sentences myngled therwith.
Mimicus, ca, cum, of suche wanton facion.
Mimographus, a wryter of suche wanton matters.
Mina, & mna, was the pounde of Athenes, which in weight cōtained. lxxv. dragmas: in money it contcined a hundred dragmas or olde poyse grotes, wherof. viii. wente to one ounce.
Minæ, arum, thretenynges. also battylmentes of walles.
Minax, acis, full of thretnynges.
Minaciter, thretnyngly.
Mincius, a ryuer of the Uenecians.
Minei, people in Arabia, nigh to the red see
Minera, & mineralia, are of somme vsed for mynes, out of the which mettal is digged.
Minerua, called goddesse of doctryne and wysedom, which was also named Pallas.
Minerual, & mineruale, a rewarde gyuen somtime by scholers vnto their maysters, in meate or drynke.
Mingo, gere, to make water, to pysse.
Miniacius, a, um, redde, of sinople colour.
Minime, & minimum, leste. minime gentiū, leste in all mens opinions. sometyme minime significth no, in no wise. minime doctus vnlerned. minime sapiens, vnwyse. minime mirum, lyttell meruayle.
Minio, are, to dye redde.
Miniati libri, limned bokes, hauyng letters of dyuers colours.
Minister, tri, a seruant.
Ministerium, seruice, sometyme generallye all warke. somtyme ministeria be seruātis.
Ministro, are, to serue, to gyue a thynge in doinge seruyce.
Minor, aris, ari, to thrette.
Minitor, aris, ari, to thrette soore.
Minium, Synople or redde leade.
Minius, a ryuer in Spayne.
Minoa, the name of a citie in Sycile, of an other in the ile called Amorgos, by Sicile
Minos, was the kynge of Crete, and gaue to theym lawes, whome paynyms for his excellente iustice, supposed to be chyefe Judge of helle.

Minthos,

Minthos, dunge or ordure.
Minotaurus, was a monster kepte in Crete, halfe a man, halfe a bulle.
Minturnę, a citie in Campania.
Minuo, ere, to mynishe.
Minurizo, are, to synge smalle, or to feyne in syngynge.
Minus, lesse.
Minutal, a meate made with chopped herbes, a iussell.
Minutarius, a seller of tryfles or smalle haberdashe ware.
Minutatim, pece mele, in gobettes.
Minutim, idem.
Minutia, the smallest thing that may be sene.
Minutus, a, um, minished.
Minyæ, a towne in Thessalia.
Miniariæ, mines, they be also vaynes of metall, out of the whiche is taken synope.
Mira, wonders or meruayles.
Mirabilis, le, meruaylous, wonderfull.
Miraculum, a miracle, a thynge excedynge nature, or commune reason.
Mirifico, care, to make wonderfull.
Mirificus, ca, cum, wonderfully done, mervaylouse.
Mirmeciæ, wertes in the priuie partes.
Mirmillones, chalengers at fightynge with swordes.
Miror, aris, ari, to meruayle, to like a thing.
Mirum in modum, in a meruaylouse facion.
Misanthropos, he that hateth the company of men.
Miscellanea, a myxture of dyuers thynges.

Vide compos.

Misceo, cui, scere, to myxe or meddyll together, to confounde together, to trouble or to do a thynge out of order or reason, sometyme it sygnyfyeth to serue one with drynke.
Misellus, a lyttell wretche.
Miser, eri, a wretche, sometyme innocent.
Miserabilis, le, myserable, wretched, lamentable.
Miserabiliter, miserably, lamentably.
Miserandus, to be pitied.
Miserator, he that dothe an acte of charytie on hym whom he pytieth.
Misericors, dis, mercifull.
Miseré, miserably, pitiousely, vnhappyly.
Miseré amat, he loueth excedyngely.
Miserior, eris, misereri, to haue pitie.
Miseresco, scere, to be moued with pitie.
Miseret me, I haue pitie.
Miseretur, I am moued with pitie.
Miseria, misery, infelicitie.
Miseritudo, idem.
Misericordia, pitie.
Misericorditer, pitiefully.
Miseriter, miserably.

Miseror, aris, ari, to haue pitie.
Misogynia, an hater of women.
Missenus, an hyll in Campania.
Missiculo, are, to sende often.
Missile, all thynge that is throwen.
Missilia, thynges whiche the auncient emperours were wonte to caste amonge the people, as breade, cakes, swete oyntement, and suche lyke thynges, whiche was done in the Theatre, in the feastes, called Saturnalia.
Missio, a message, also leaue to departe.
Missito, tare, to sende often.
Missus, a, um, sente.
Missus, us, a course, whan one thynge commeth in a distance after a nother, a turne.
Missum facere, to omit or passe ouer a thing, also to gyue leaue to departe.
Mitellum, a lyttel miter.
Mitis, mite, micke, symple, quiete.
Mitesco, scere, to waxe tame or quiet, somtyme to waxe rype.
Mithra, the Persians do call the sonne, and also the chiefe priest of the sonne.
Mithrax, a stone of the colour of a rose, but agaynst the sonne he is chaungeable.
Mithriaca sacra, ceremonies of the sonne.
Mithridates, a puissaunt kynge of Ponthus in Asia.
Mithridaticum, a medicine lyke to tryakle, called Mitridate.
Mithylenæ, arū, a citie in the ile of Lesbos.
Mitigo, are, to mitigate, to swage.
Mitifico, to pacifye or make quyete.
Mitra, a myter. It was also a tyre of womennes heedes.
Mitto, misi, mittere, to sende, to leaue or lay aparte, to gyue. Mittere sanguinem, to let bloudde. Mittesanguis, a bloudde lettyng, or a bloudshede.
Mitterin, an Iyle syxe dayes saylynge oute of Englande, wherein is greatte plentie of tynne.
Mittas frenum affectibus, Brydelle thyne affections.
Mitte hunc ire, Lette hym goo.
Mitte hanc noxiam, Forgyue me that faute.
Mittere in consilium, to lette the iuges departe to gyue sentence, after that the oratour hath finished his oration, or the lawyer his plee.

Cice. pro Cluencio. Asc. Ped.

Mixtarius, a cuppe, wherin wyne is alayde with water.

M, ANTE N.

Mna, idem quod mina.
Mnemosyne, memory.
Mnesteræ, wowars.
Mnestheus, the name of a Troyane.

M ante

¶ M, ANTE O.

Moab, a citie of Araby, also the name of oone of the sonnes of Loth, of whom the peple are called Moabite
Mobilis, le, mouable, sone moued.
Moderatus, ta, tum, moderate, temperate.
Moderator, oris, a gouernoure.
Moderor, aris, ari, et Modero, are, to gouerne, to rule, to sette a measure in thynges, to moderate.
Moderatio, moderation, temperaunce.
Modestia, modestie, temperaunce.
Modeste, temperately, sobrely, aduisedly.
Modestus, temperate, well aduised.
Modialis, le, that which conteineth a bushel
Modicus, ca, cū, which exceedeth not, measurable, sometyme lyttell or fewe.
Modice, meanely.
Modificor, caris, cari, to take the measure of a thynge.
Modiolus, a buckette, where with water is drawen out of a well: or a pot fastned to a whele, whiche bryngeth vp water, & poureth it out.
Modiparatores, men ordeyned to see measure kepte.
Modius, a bushell: it was proprelye a measure of drye thynges, whiche conteyned xvi. Sextarios, vide postea in sextario.
Modo, nowe, nowe late, sometyme it signyfieth so that. Non refert, modo id faciat, It maketh no matter, soo that he doo it, also onely.
Modo nostro, after our facion.
Modulor, aris, ari, to make or doo a thynge by numbre and measure, also to synge.
Modulus, et Modulamen, a songe, a modulation, the tyme in syngynge.

Cf. ad At. Columel. — Modus, maner, measure, furme, facion, way, quantite, ende. Etsi nihil scripsit, nisi de modo agri, although he wrote nothyng but of the quantitie of the felde.

Plautus in Castel. — Mœchor, aris, ari, to committe auoutry.
Mœchus, an auoutrer, or lechour.
Mœchisso, are, to committe auoutry.
Mœnia, walles of a towne or castell.

Plautus in Bacch. — Mœnitus, ta, tum, walled.
Mœreo, ere, to be sorowfull.
Mœro, are, to make one sadde and heuy.
Mœror, oris, sorowe.
Mœstitia, idem.
Mœsia, a prouince in Asia nygh to Pontus.
Mœstiter, heuyly, sorowfully.
Mœro, are, to make one sorye.
Mœstus, a, um, sory or sorowfull.
Mœsto, are, Mœstifico, care, to make sorowfull.
Moga, a countreye in Asia, called nowe Cesaria.

Moguntia, a noble Citie in Germany, called Mense.
Mola, a myl, it is also a great pece of fleshe without shape, growen in a woman, whiche causeth them somtyme to thynke, that they be with chylde, it is also a cake made of mele and salte.
Molaris, a cheke tothe.
Molaris, re, et Molarius, ia, um, perteynīg to a myll.
Molendinarius, ia, um, idem.
Molarius equus, an horse, whiche dryueth about a malte myll.
Molendinarius, a myllar.
Moles, a thynge that is verye greatte and weightye: sommetyme it is taken for difficultie.
Molestia, griefe.
Molesta tunica, a garment which was myxt with some mater, whiche gathered fyre, putte on some persones that shulde suffre deathe.
Moleste, greuously.
Molesto, are, to greue, to offende, to do displeasure to one.
Molestus, a, um, that whiche greueth, offendeth, or discontenteth.
Moletrina, a morter or querne, wherin any thynge maye be grounde with the hande.
Molimen, et molimentum, that whiche we go about and endeuour vs to do.
Molior, iris, iri, to moue, to be moued, or styred to doo a thynge. moliri classem, to prepare a nauy. moliri iter, to perfourme a iourneye. moliri habenas, to rule. moliri insidias, to laye snares, to laye in awayte. Moliri arcem, to buylde a fortresse. Moliri bellum, to make warre. Moliri is somtime to deuyse or inuent, also to go about to do a thynge, to make, to be taryed or lette.
Moliri moram, to tary.
Molitor, oris, a myllar.
Mollesco, scere, to waxe softe, to be pacified from wrathe.
Molestra, a shepes fell.
Mollicies, et mollicia, softnesse, tendernes, delicatenesse, womanlynesse.
Mollicina, fyne clothe or silke.
Molliculus, la, tender delycate.
Mollifico, to make softe or tender.
Mollio, ire, to make softe or tender, to pacific or appayse, to make wanton or teder.
Mollis, softe, tender. molle ingenium, a wit whiche lyghtely taketh. mollis homo, a man effemynate, or womanly, not hardye or constant of wytte, inuolued in wanton pleasures and sensuall appetite, somtyme mollis sygnificth rype, also remisse, sometyme

tyme pleasaunt, also easy to be pleased.
Molliter, gentylly with good wylle, easily, delycately.
Mollitudo, inis, softnes and gentylnes.
Mollusca, a nutte with a softe shale, a fylberde.
Molluscum, the wenne of a tree.
Molo, molui, lire, to grynde.
Molochinus color, a colour like to the floures of mallowes.
Molorthus, a plumrule, suche as masons and carpenters doo occupie in squarynge of stone and tymber.
Molossa gens, people in the parte of Grece called Epirus.
Molossus, a mastiue dogge. it is also a fote in meter.
Molothros, a kynde of white vynes.
Molucrum, a square piece of tymber, wheron the paynyms dyd sacrifyce. It is also the trendyll of a myll. Also the swellynge of a womans bealy, whiche dothe happen as well to maidens, as to wyues.
Molybdena, an herbe called also Plūbago, it is also the ooze of leade or syluer.
Molybditis, the spume or fome of leade.
Momentaneus, a, um, that whyche durethe but a lyttell whyles, or shortly altereth.
Momentarius, a, um, that whiche is done in a lyttell space.
Momentum, the leste parte of tyme, which can not be assigned, a moment.
Momus, called the god of reprehencion.
Momo satisfacere, to contente hym, whom almoste nothynge may please.
Momo iudice decertare, to contende afore a rigorous and extreme iudge.
Monachus, a solytarie person, all be it that it is vsed for a monke.
Monachris, a mountayne in Archadia.
Monarcha, a prynce, whiche reuleth alone without piere or companyon, monarche.
Monarchia, the rule of one monarchie.
Monas, monadis, the numbre of one, vnitie.
Monasterium, a place solytarie.
Monedula, a byrde callydde a Choughe or Cadesse.
Moneo, monere, to warne, to putte in remembraunce.
Monitor, toris, he that warneth a man, or putteth hym in remembraunce.
Moneta, money. also the name of Juno.
Monetalis, le, pertaynynge to money.
Monetarius, a maker of money, a coyner.
Monile, a colar or bee, whiche women vse to weare aboute their neckes. It is also a poytrell of a horse.
Monitio, warnynge.
Monitus, tus, idem.

Monitorius, a, um, that whiche doth warne, or exhorte.
Monna, an Ile pertaynynge to Englande, whiche some do suppose to be Anglesey, somme Manne, betwene Lancaster and Irelande.
Monobeli, they whiche haue a longe thing lyke to spyttes. Also they that be verayd hyghe in personnage and aboue other. Lampridius in uita Alex.
Monochordium, an Instrumente, hauynge manye strynges of oone sowne, sauynge that with smalle pieces of cloth, the sounes be distincte, as Clauycordes be.
Monœchus, a hauen of Liguria.
Monoceros, otis, an Vnycorne.
Monoculus, a man hauynge but one eye.
Monodia, a lamentable or mournyng song, suche as is songen in funeralles.
Monodos, was a manne, whyche in stede of teethe, hadde but oone boone, lyke as kynge Pirrhus hadde.
Monogamus, he that neuer hadde but one wyfe.
Monogammi, menne leane and yuelle coloured.
Monologium, a longe tale of one mattier.
Monomachia, a battayle, wherein oonely two menne doo fyghte.
Monomachus, he that fyghteth alone.
Monophagia, a meale of one onely meate or dyshe.
Monopodium, a table sette on one footeor trestylle.
Monopolium, where one manne ingrosseth thynges, to haue all in his owne hande, that no manne maye gayne, but he onely. It maye be also one countrey or market, that taketh away the gaynes from other countreyes or markettes.
Monoptoton, a worde hauyng but one case.
Monosceli, men in India, whiche haue but one legge, so greate, that therwith they couer them selfes from the sonne.
Monostelon, where as is but one pyller.
Monotropos, solitarie, of one facion alway.
Monoxylon, a bote made in oone piece of tymber.
Mons, tis, a mountayne or hylle.
Mons feratus, a countrey in Italye.
Monstrificus, a, um, monstruous.
Monstro, are, to shewe.
Monstrum, a monster, that which excedeth or lacketh in naturall fourme or order.
Monstruosus, monstruosa, struosum, monstruous.
Montanus, a, um, of a mountayne.
Monticulus, a lyttell hylle.
Montigena, borne on a hylle.

M ante O.

Montiuagus, wandringe by hilles.
Montosus, a, um, full of hilles.
Monumentum, a remembrance of some notable acte, as sepulchres, images, pylars, grete stones, inscriptions, bookes, and other lyke: whereby any thinge excellent, concernynge grete wittes, kunnynge, entreprise in armes, puyssaunce, or rychesse is remembred.
Monycha, che, the name of saynct Austens mother.
Monychus, a gyant, one of the Centaures.
Monyma, the wyfe of kynge Mithridate, whiche after that her husbande was vainquisshed, killed her selfe.
Mopsopia, the contray of Athenes.
Mopsus, the name of a Poete.
Mora, taryenge, leysar.
Moralis, le, pertayninge to maners.
Moramentum, taryenge, or abode.
Moratus, instructed in good maners.
Morbidus, a, um, sycke or scabbed.
Morbificus, ca, cum, that which causeth disease or sickenesse.
Morbus, sickencsse, disease, a sore.
Morbus animæ, a vice inueterate and harde to be cured, as ambition, auarice.
Morbus regius, the yelow iaundyse.
Mordax, acis, he that doeth byte, be it with the teeth, or with langage.
Mordeo, momordi, dere, to byte, to detract, or rebuke vehemently.

Erasm. in Chil. Mordere frenum, to gnawe on the brydell, which is spoken where it signifieth one to repugne against seruitude or bondage.
Mordicibus, with bytinges.
Mordico, care, to hurt with bytinge.
Mordicus, bytinge harde and faste, as a man holdeth a thinge.
Mordicus tenere, to holde fast, to persist obstinately in an opinion or sentence.
Moribundus, dyenge.
Moriger, geri, obedient.
Morigeror, aris, ari, to obaye, to do as a man bedeth, to conforme one mannes maners to anothers.
Morini, people in fraunce, dwellynge about Turwan.
Morio, onis, a foole.
Morior, iris, & eri, moriri, & mori, to dye.
Morologus, he that speketh treatably, sometyme wordes treatably spoken: sometyme it signifieth him, that speketh foolyshely.
Moror, aris, ari, to tary or abyde, to let, or cause to tary.
Moros, a foole.
Morosus, waywarde, dyuerse in condicions, whome no man can please, more curiouse than nedeth.

Morotis, & Morosis, a madnesse or frenesy, where a man loseth his memory.
Mors, tis, deth.
Morsicatim, bytynge one another.
Morsiuncula, a lytle bitte or snacke.
Morsus, us, a bytt with the teeth, a taunt in spekinge.
Morsus, a, um, bitten. *Plinius.*
Mortalis, le, mortall.
Mortarium, a mortar, wherin thinges are, brayed or grounden.
Morticina caro, moren fleshe, whiche dyeth by it selfe, carrayne.
Morticini, cornes which be on mennes fete.
Morticinum, corrupt.
Mortiferus, a, um, which causeth any thinge to dye.
Mortuale, pertayninge to deed men.
Mortuū mare, a grete mere in Syria, where in no heuy thinge may synke.
Morula, a lytel taryenge.
Morus, a Mulbery tree, and a brembyl that beareth blacke beryes.
Morum, a Mulbery, or blacke bery.
Mos, moris, a maner, a cōdiciō, also custome.
Morem gerere, to obey.
Moscatulæ, pearis, whiche do sauoure lyke muske.
Mosculus, a calfe, also an herbe.
Moschum, Muske.
Moscus, a Region in Asia nyghe to the ryuer of Phasis, deuyded into thre partis, in the one doo dwell people called Colchi, in the second Hiberes, in the third Armenii.
Moses, sis, si, the great captayn of the iewes which lad them out of Egipte.
Mosini, people in Asia towarde the north.
Motabilis, alwaye mouinge.
Motacilla, a byrd called a wagtayle.
Motiuus, a, um, mouynge, not abydynge.
Moto, are, to moue often.
Motus, ta, tum, moued. Motus, tus, mouing.
Moueo, ere, to moue, to remoue or put away
Mouere animū, to styre or allure the minde.
Mouere tragœdias, to do thynges to be lamented.
Mouere camerinam, to stere thinges, which shall be to his owne displeasure, that begynneth it.
Mox, anon, forthwith.
Muceo, cui, to be fylthy or vinewed.
Mucidus, a, dum, fylthy, vinewed.
Mucor, oris, fylth, vinue, suche as is on bred or meate longe kept.
Mucro, onis, the point of a sworde or knife. sometyme it is taken for a sworde.
Mucronatus, ta, tum, poynted.
Mucus, the fylthe, whyche commeth oute of the nose.

Mugil,

M ante V.

Lucilius. Mugil, lis, a fishe called a codde.
Muginor, ari, to murmure.
Mugio, gire, to bellowe lyke a cowe or bull: somtyme it signifyeth the noyse of thunder, or grete wyndes.
Mugonia, a gate at Rome, whereby catell dyd entre into the citie.
Mugitus, tus, bellowynge of kyne, or other noyse lyke.
Mularis, re, pertayninge to a mule.
Mulceo, si, cere, to pacyfye, to appease, to mitigate, to make sweete, to anoynte, to polyshe.
Mulciber, eris, one of the names of Vulcane, called god of fyre.
Mulctor, ctaris, ctari, to punysshe, or be punysshed.
Mulcta, a penaltie, a condemnation, a fyne sessed.
Mulctam dicere, to gyue an iniunction.
Mulctam committere, to forfayte, to runne in the peyne.
Mulctam remittere, to pardone.
Mulctra, the mylkyng, the payle, wherinto it is milked, whiche is also called Mulctrale.
Mulctrum, the acte of mylkynge.
Mulei, certayne shooes of purple coloure, whiche the kynges of Alba ware, and afterwarde the noble men of Rome.
Mulgeo, mulsi, mulgere, to mylke or stroke.
Mulgo, are, to publishe.
Muli mariani, forkes, wheron fardels were trussed and borne by men.
Muli mariani, a prouerbe referred vnto thē, whiche be obedient to euery commaundment, be it neuer so greuouse. It may also be applied vnto thē, which be inuolued in perpetuall and intollerable laboures and businesse.
Muli mutuum scabunt, mules do gnappe one an other, a prouerbe applied to persones ylle and defamed, whan one of them commendeth the other.
Mulier, eris, a woman, proprely she that is no virgine.
Muliebre folliculum, dicebant vuluam.
Muliebria, naturall euacuations, which women haue, called their floures.
Muliebris, bre, perteynynge to women.
Muliebritas, delicatenesse, tendernesse.
Muliebriter, womanly, delicately, tenderly.
Mulierarius, a folower, or dotar on women.
Muliero, are, to effeminate, or make lyke a woman.
Mulierosus, a great louer of women.
Mulio, onis, & Mulius, a dryuer of Mules, a muletour.
Mullus, a fish called a Mullet.
Mulsum, wyne and hony soden togither.

M ante V.

Mulsus, a, um, any licour mixt with hony.
Multa, idem quod mulcta.
Multatitius, pertayning to a forfait, or payne assessyd.
Multesima, a part representinge an infinite quantitye. Quàm paruula pars, quam multesima constat, so lytle a porcion, se of how wonderfull gretnesse it is.
Multibarbus, he that hath moche heare on his bearde.
Multibibus, he that drinketh moche.
Multicolorius, a, um, of many colours.
Multifacio, ere, to make moche of, to esteme moche. — Apuleius.
Multifariam, many wayes, in many facions.
Multifarius, dyuers in maners or condiciōs.
Multigeneris, re, of dyuers kyndes. — Plautus.
Multiforatilis, le, with many holes. — Lucilius.
Multi iugus, a, um, dyuerse, many dyuerse, manyfolde.
Multiloquus, full of speche.
Multipes, hauynge many feete.
Multiplex, plicis, manyfolde, dyuers.
Multiscius, a, um, knowinge moche.
Multitia, garmentes made of fyne thredes or sylke.
Multiuidus, he that seeth moche.
Multiuolus, desyringe dyuerse thinges.
Multo, & Mulcto, are, to punysshe, to condemne, to put fro, to intreate yl, or disorder.
Multare matrimonio, to deuorse, or dissolue matrimony.
Multus, ta, tum, moche, many.
Mulus, a Mule.
Mundanus, na, um, worldly.
Mundities, & Munditia, clenlynesse.
Mundifico, are, to klense.
Mundo, are, to wype, to make clene.
Mundus, the worlde, a womans attyre.
Mundus, da, dum, clene, nete.
Muneralis, le, pertayning to gyftes.
Munerarius, he that maketh a cōmune game or playe at his propre charges.
Muneror, aris, ari, & munero, are, to rewarde
Mungo, xi, ere, to make clene, proprely ones nose.
Municipalis, le, priuately or particulerly, belonginge to one citie.
Municipale ius, the priuate lawe of euery particuler citie.
Municipalia magisteria, ciuile offices in euery citie or towne.
Municipatim, towne by towne.
Municipium, a citie or towne incorporate, hauynge their propre officers and lawes.
Municeps, a citezen, or burgeyse, enioyinge the liberties of the towne.
Munificus, liberall, Munificentior, more liberall, Munificentissimus, most liberall. in the olde

olde tyme Munifici, were taken for them, whyche consented to that, whiche theyr frendes dyd or spake.

Munimen, & munimentum, a fortifycation of a towne or castelle.

Munio, iui, & ij, nire, to fortifye, to prepare, to repayre.

Munia, commune dueties, offices.

Munis, he that beareth the charges, whiche the people shulde do.

Munus, neris a gyft, a charge, a duetie or offyce. Munera, commune playes and gaye sightes for the peple to behold, to reioice them, prepared by officers of cities. As in Rome, sondry playes, sworde players, called Gladiatores, huntyng of wyld beastes. Also now in the citie of London, the watches & syghtes on midsomer nightes.

Munychia, orum, the solemnities of Pallas.

Murena, a lampraye.

Mnrenule, smalle chaynes, whiche women do weare.

Muralis corona, a garlande gyuen to hym, whiche in the siege of a citie fyrste skalyd the walles, and entred.

Muralis herba, an herbe callyd perytorye, or pelytorie.

Murani, were the kynges of Alba.

Muratus, ta, tum, walled.

Murcia, goddesse of slouthe.

Murcus, a slouthfull or luskyshe person.

Murex, icis, a shelle fyshe, of whome commeth the lycour, whyche maketh purple colour. Sometyme it sygnifyeth the same coloure. Also an herbe, whiche groweth in a pyt, where no sonne shyneth.

Murginor, ari, to tary, to be slouthfulle.

Murgitana regio, a countrey in the southe partes of Spayne.

Murgizo, murgizonis, an ydell or slouthesfull persone.

Muria, water, wherin salt is sodden, brine.

Muricatus, salted in bryne.

Murices, caltrappes, lyke thre yron pryckes so ioyned, that beinge throwen, one standeth vpryghte, vsed in battayle for horsemenne.

Fulgenti9. Muricati gressus, where oone gothe fearefully, as if he went on caltraps or thornes.

Plaut. Muricidus, a mousekiller, a sole, a rat killer.

Muries, a bryne made with salte sodden in water.

Murmilonica scuta, targettes, wherewith men faught vpon walles.

Murmur, the noyse of rounnynge water.

Murmurillum, idem.

Murmurabundus, & murmurator, he that murmureth.

Murmuro, to murmour, or make noyse lyke to water.

Murmurillo, idem.

Murmurillum, a murmurynge. *Plautus.*

Murrha, a stone of dyuers colours, clere as cristall, hauynge spottes purple & whyte.

Murrheus, & murrhinus, a, um, of that stone called murrha, wherof cuppes, pottes, tables, and other vessels were made: there be of them dyuers sent from Venyce.

Murrhina, seu murrhynia, was wyne made with dyuers spices, as that whicè is callyd ypocras.

Murtius, a hylle atte Rome, callyd also Auentinius.

Murtia, one of the names of Venus.

Murus, a walle.

Mus, muris, a mouse or ratte.

Musa, a swete songe.

Muse, Musee, were maydens, whome poetes fayned to be the doughters of Jupiter and Memorie, and that they were ladyes and gouernours of poetrie & musyke, whiche were in numbre nyne. Some call them gyuers of eloquence, and doo name them goddesses.

Musea, Musaica, & Musiua, be warkes cunnyngely paynted, that they seme to be in some place imbocid out, in som place grauen, although it be all playne.

Museus, an auncient poete, whiche was in the tyme of Orpheus, & was one of them whiche went with Jason to the wynninge of the fliece of golde.

Museum, a house, whervnto lerned men in all sciences vsed to repayre, and dispute: it is also a house dedicate to the musis.

Musca, a flye.

Muscula, a smalle flye. *Boetius.*

Muscari, to be couered with mosse.

Muscarium, & muscaria, a flappe to dryue away flyes. It is also the toppe of fenelle, dylle, and suche other like herbes, wherin be the seedes.

Muscarius, a, um, pertaynynge to flyes.

Muscenton, a certayne Rose, that springeth of a stalke with many smal braunches, and hath leaues lyke to an olyue tree.

Muscerda, mouse dunge.

Muschus, a beaste, whiche beareth muske, a muske catte.

Muscinus, a, um, of a flye.

Muscio, onis, a catte.

Muscipula, a trappe, wherwith myse or rattes are taken.

Musculus, a lyttell mouse. Sommetyme an engyne of warre, whereby they are defended, whiche doo approche the walles of a place besyeged, to fylle the dyches. It is also a lyttell fyshe, whiche guydeth the

the whale that he do not runne on rockis.
Musculi, be certayne pieces of harde fleshe compacte with synewes in the body, whiche do inclose the spirituall membres.
Muscus, mosse, whiche groweth in welles and moyste placces, sommetyme on trees, specially in colde countreyes.
Musica, & musice, musyke.
Musice, hole, that nothynge lacketh.
Musicus, a musycion.
Musmones, shepe with hearye wolle.
Mussitabundus, a manne speakynge to hym selfe priuily.
Mussito, tare, to speake or talke alone.
Musso, are, to talke softely and secretely, to kepe sylence.
Mustace, a tree hauynge leaues lyke to laurell, but greatter and weaker.
Mustacula, a lyttell instrumente made with two rules, betwene whiche the showe is put, whyles the sole is in sowynge.
Mustaceus, & mustaceum, a caake or paste made to comforte the stomacke.
Mustela, a beaste called a wesell. also a fishe lyke a lampraye.
Mustelinus, a, um, of a wesyll.
Musteus, a, um, swete as muste, or mustye.
Mustum, newe wyne, newe ale, newe beere.
Mustus, ta, tum, newe, yonge, late made.
Mutabilis, le, chaungeable, mutable.
Muteo, mutui, tere, & mutesco, scere, to be muete, or dumme.
Mutili, horned beastes, of nature lackynge hornes, as oxen, gotes. &c.
Mutilus, la, lum, lackynge somme principalle part, mutilate.
Mutilo, are, to cutte of, to mynyshe, to take awaye.
Mutinensis color, a naturall colour, as wull or clothe neuer dyed.
Mutio, tiui, tire, to speake softely, or with an vnperfyt voyce, to muttre.
Mutito, tare, to feaste one an other.
Mutuli, scaffolde holes, or places made on the walles for culuers to brede in.
Muto, tare, to chaunge, to translate, to barter one thinge for an other.
Muto, tonis, the priuie membre of a man.
Mutuatitius, a, um, borowed.
Mutunus, who was also called Priapus.
Mutuó, togither, or one an other, Mutuó diligebant, They loued one an other.
Mutuare, sygnyfieth bothe to borowe and to lende.
Mutuor, aris, ari, to borowe.
Mutus, he that can not speake.
Muté, dumme.
Mutuum, a lone, that whiche is borowed.
Mutuus, a, um, one for an nother, mutualle.

Mutuus amor, mutuall loue, where one loueth an nother equally.

¶ M ANTE Y.

Mya, a shel fishe in the see called Bosphorus, whiche bryngeth forth lytell redde stones, and rounde.
Myagrus, the god of flyes.
Mycæne, & Mycæna, a citie in the parte of Grecia, called Peloponesus, and a lyttell region, where Agamemnon raigned, the chiefe capitayne of the grekes agaynste Troy, called nowe Morea.
Mycon, the name of a famous paynter.
Mycone, nes, a lyttell yle.
Mydia, an yle, named also Delos.
Mydriasis, a syckenesse of the eyes, where no colour of the eies ar changed, but maketh them moche broder: all be it it taketh away the syght, or maketh a man to se the lasse, and the thynges, whiche be sene, to seme lasse than they are.
Mygale, a ratte.
Mygdonia, a part of Macedonia on the see syde, where Niobe was tourned in to a stoone. Aristotle saythe, that it is a parte of Phrigia, ioynynge to Lidia. Solynus sayth, that it was called Bebrycia, and after Bythinia.
Mylochos, a butterfly, whiche is in mylles.
Myoparo, onis, a kynde of shyppes vsed in the see called Mare Tirrhenum.
Myophnos, a kyller of myse.
Mymphur, a tourners pynne or spyndelle, wheron he turneth or warketh any thing.
Myra, a citie in Licia, wherof saynte Nycholas was byshoppe.
Myriarches, a captayn of ten thousand mē.
Myriades, many tymes tenne thousande.
Myrias, adis, the numbre of ten thousande.
Myrica, a lyttell bushe called in Italye Tamarico.
Myrinus, the male kynde of a lampray, whiche hath a tothe out of his mouthe.
Myrmus, the propre name of Apollo.
Myriophillum, an herbe called myllfoyle.
Myristica nux, a nuttemygge.
Myrlea, a towne in Bythinia.
Myrmecia, a lyttell warte.
Myrmecites, a stone, wherin is the fygure of an emotte.
Myrmetiū, a kynd of spiders, lyke an emote hauyng a black bealy with white spottes.
Mirmillones, were sworde players, where the one prouoked the other to battayle.
Myrsenium, a kynd of fenell, hauyng gretter leaues, and a sharper taste.
Myrsum, a towne in the part of Grece, callyd Peloponesus.

Myrmicoleo, a lytell beaste, which deuoureth emotes.
Myrobalanum, a fruite growinge in India, lyke vnto plummes or damsyns, whereof be dyuers kyndes, which easily do purge al superfluous humours, and also comforteth nature, in so moche as a manne, whiche eateth them, beinge condite, shall not loke oldely.
Myrobrecharij, they whiche do make swete oyntmentes.
Myron, onis, the name of an excellent caruer. also olde oyle.
Myropola, a seller of oyntmentes.
Myropolium, a place where oyntmentes were solde.
Myrothetium, a boxe of swete oyntmētes.
Myrrha, a swete gumme, callyd myrre.
Myrrheus, & myrrhinus, a, um, of myrre.
Myrtetum, a place, where Myrtelle trees be sette.
Myrteus, & myrtinus, a, um, of myrtelles.
Myrtopetalum, an herbe called blodewort.
Myrtoum, a porcyon of the see, whiche is betwene the sees called Aegeum & Ioniū.
Myrtus, a lyttell tree, bearynge bearyes of swete odour.
Mys, mios, the name of a cunnyng grauer. also a shelle fyshe of the see.
Mysia, a countrey beyonde Hungarye, toward Grece. Ptholomeus writeth of two countreys called Mysia, the more and the lasse, and both in Asia, beyonde Bythinia, not farre from Ida.
Mysteria, mysteries, thynges secrete or hid in wordes or ceremonies.
Mysticus, ca, cum, mysticall.
Mystris, a fyshe called a see mouse.
Mythologia, a declaration or exposytion of fables.
Mythos, a fable.
Myxa, the fylthe whiche commeth oute of a mannes nose.
Myxus, a snuffe of a candell.

¶ N, ANTE A.

NABATHA, the name of a certayne citie.
Nabathea, a countreye betwene the redde see and the see callyd Persicum, contayning within it Arabie.
Nabatheus, a, um, of that countreye.
Nabis, in the langage of Ethiope, is a beest hauyng a heed lyke a camell, a necke lyke a hors, legges and fete lyke an oxe.
Nablum, & nablium, an instrument of musyke, called a psaltrie.
Naccæ, & neæ, fullers.
Nactus, the participle of Nanciscor, Nactus sum, I haue gotten, nactus es, nactus est, thou, he hath gotten.
Næ, syngnifieth valde, or nimis. Næ tu homo facetus es, thou arte a very mery felowe. somtyme it signifieth Certè, profectò, ita. Næ illi vehementer errant, surelye they be farre out of the waye. Næ ego multo libentius emerim diuorsoriū Tarracinę, In good faythe I had leauer haue bought a howse at Tarracine.
Nęera, a womans name.
Nęnia, a mournynge songe, wont to be songen at burielles, somtyme it signifieth the sōge that the mother or nource doth singe dandyllynge of her chylde.
Neuia, a womans name.
Neuus, a mole or lyke marke in the body or face, from the tyme of the byrthe.
Naiades, fayries, of the ryuers and fountaynes.
Nain, a citie of Galyle.
Nais, a riuer, whiche cometh out of the hil called Taurus, and runneth in to the see called Pontus.
Nam, for, therfore.
Nanciscor, sceris, nactus sum, nancisci, to get or opteyne. sometyme to fynde.
Nancisci hospitium, to fynde a lodgynge. Pom. Fest.
Nancitor, for nactus erit.
Nanq, verily, truely : if it be sette afore other wordes : if it be putte after, it sygnifyeth for.
Nanum, a lyttell vessell and brode. Plaut.
Nanium, a lyttell woman.
Nanus, a lyttell person, a dwarfe.
Napatęi, people in Ethiopia.
Napeę, called goddesses of flowres and woddes.
Napęi, people in the yle called Lesbos.
Naphtha, a kynd of pitche, also lyme, wherwith fyre is nourished.
Napina, a place where Nauewes be sowen.
Napitę, people in Scithia.
Napus, a Nauew.
Nar, the name of a riuer.
Narane, a riuer in Dalmatia.
Narbasis, a citie in Spayne.
Narbonēsis gallia, the south part of Fraūce wherin is Dolphinay, Prouance, Langedok. &c.
Narciscus, a flowre in facion lyke a lyllye, and whyte, sauing that the chalese, wherin the floure is closed, is purple: some haue purple floures, leaues narower than leke blades.

blades, a stalke halfe a foote hygh, plaine without leaues, a rounde rote and white. Also the name of a yonge man of excellēt beautie, who for the loue of a maidē died, and after the fables of poetes, was transfourmed into the same lylly.

Narcoticum, a qualytie or vertue in thynges to make a manne to slepe. also to make a membre insensible. Physytions vse medycines, whyche haue this vertue, where the griefe or ache is otherwise incurable, or where they wylle cutte any parte of a mannes bodye.

Nardinum, the name of a swete oyntment.

Nardus, the herbe and rote, whiche is called Spikenarde.

Virg. Geor. Nare, to swymme. sometyme to flee.

Nares, nosethrylles.

Narica, the name of a lyttell fyshe, whiche dothe swymme very swyftely.

Naris, a ryuer in Umbria.

Naritia, an yle in the see called Aegeum.

Naritium, a citie of the people named Locri in Grece.

Narnia, a towne in Italy.

Narnienses, men of that towne.

Narratio, a narration or report of thynges that are doone.

Narratiuncla, a lyttell narration.

Narro, are, to telle.

Nartheticium, a place, wherein medycines are kepte.

Nasamones, people in Affrike about Libia.

Nasamonites, a stone of coloure sanguyne, hauynge blacke vaynes.

Nascor, sceris, sci, to be borne.

Nasica, the surname of one of the Scipions a noble Romayne.

Nasiterna, a water vessell, wyde aboue, hauynge handelles.

Naso suspendere, to mocke couertely, or craftely.

Nassa, a fyshers weele or bow nette, wherin if a fyshe be ones, he can not gette out.

Nasturtium, an herbe callyd Cresses.

Nasus, a nose: somtime sharpenes in speche, and tauntynge wytte. also iudgement in letters.

Nasuti, taunters, checkers, skorners, somtyme wytty personnes, whiche do quikly perceyue a thynge. also men, which haue their priuie membres very great.

Nasute, wyttyly, skornefully, tauntyngely.

Nasutula, a tauntynge wenche, or a shrewe.

Natalis, le, et natalitius, tia, tium, the daye of birthe or natiuitie.

Natales, is taken for progeny or dyscente, or bloude. Generosi natales, gentyl bloud. Obscuri natales, a poore dyscente or lowe byrthe, somtyme it is vsed for yeres.

Natalibus restitui, where a man hath armes and tytle of nobylitie, gyuen vnto hym by the kynge. *Budeus.*

Natatilis, that whiche can swimme.

Natatitius, a, um, that which doth swimme.

Natator, toris, a swymmer.

Natatorium, natabulum, et natatio, a place wherin men do swymme.

Natatus, tus, the acte of swymmynge.

Nates, buttockes.

Natinatores, trauaylours, or they whiche haue moche businesse.

Natio, a nation.

Natiuitas, tatis, byrthe.

Natiuus, where a thyng is borne or begon.

Natiuus color, the naturall colour.

Nato, are, to swymme, sometyme to go, to tremble, to sayle, or rowe.

Natrix, a water serpēt. also an herbe, whose rote smelleth lyke a gote.

Natura, nature, membres of generacyon. Sometyme facion or maner.

Naturalis, le, naturall.

Naturalia, the priuy membres.

Natus, ta, tum, borne.

Natus, nata, sonne and doughter.

Natus grandis, aged or olde.

Naualis, le, pertaynynge to shyppes.

Nauale, the docke where shyps be laid vp.

Nauale, a docke or place where shyppes are made.

Nauarchis, the admyralles shyppe.

Nauarchus, an admyrall.

Nauaria, a countrey in Spayne called Nauarre.

Nauci, a nutte shale, a thynge of naughte.

Nauci esse, to be naught worthe.

Naucifacere, to set naught by one.

Naucleriacus, et nauclerius, a, um, perteynynge to a shyppe mayster.

Nauclerus, & nauiclarius, a shyppe maister.

Naucrates, a citie in Egypte.

Naufragium, a shypwrecke.

Naufragor, aris, ari, to peryshe on the see.

Naufragus, whose goodes are peryshed.

Nauia, a holowe tree lyke a shyppe, whiche is occupied whan grapes be gathered.

Nauicularius, a capitayne of a shyppe.

Nauiculor, aris, ari, to rowe or be rowed in a bote for solace.

Nauigabilis, le, where a shyppe maye passe. Nauigable.

Nauigatio, a iourneye or goinge by water in a shyppe.

Nauiger, the pilate of a shyppe, whych ruleth the sterne.

Nauigium, the leadynge or settynge forth of the shyppe. It is also all kynde of vessels ſelles to ſayle or rowe in.

Nauigo, are, to ſayle or rowe, that is to ſay, to be caried on water in a ſhippe or any other thynge lyke.

Nauis pompatica, a ſhyppe whiche ſerueth onely for pleaſure, hauynge chaumbers and bankettynge tables for greate men to ſolace in.

Nauis, a ſhyppe.

Nauiter, diligently, valyauntly.

Naulium, a citie in Liguria.

Naulum, the fraite or fare paied for paſſage

Naumachia, battayle on the ſee, alſo the place where the batayle is.

Naumachiarij, they which do fyght on the ſee or water in ſhyppes or botes.

Nauo, are, to accomplyſhe dylygently, to gyue, to applye with effect, to be in ayde. Iam mihi videor nauaſſe operam q̃ huc venerim, nowe me ſeemeth I haue well applyed my labour, that I am come hyther.

Nauare beneuolentiam, to conferre or declare beneuolence.

Naupegus, a ſhyppe wrighte.

Naupontus, a ryuer, whiche paſſeth out of Slauony.

Nauſea, the abhorrynge of thynges ſeene, wherby a man is prouoked to vomyte.

Nauſeoſus, a, um, dyſpoſinge to vomyte.

Nauſiabundus, dyſpoſed to vomyte.

Nauſeo, eare, et nauſeor, to be dyſpoſed to vomyte, ſomtyme to vomyte.

Nauſicaa, was doughter to Alcinous, kyng of Pheaces, whiche founde Ulyſſes, whan he eſcaped from drounynge, and brought hym to her father.

Nauſio, ere, to open or gape as a beane doth whan he ſpryngeth.

Nauſithous, the ſonne of Neptunus, and father of Alcinous.

Nauſtibulum, an hiue made of the facion of a ſhyppe.

Nauta, et nauita, a ſhyppeman.

Nautea, curriers bleche or lycour, alſo the ſtynkynge water, which iſſueth out of the pumpe of a ſhyppe.

Nauticus, a ſhyppe mayſter.

Nauticus, ca, cum, perteynyng to ſhipmen.

Nautulus, a ſhypman, alſo a fyſhe, which is in ſimilitude lyke to ſome that ſayled.

Nautilia, the craft of ſhypmen.

Nauus, quicke, actife.

Naxos, an yle in the ſee called Aegeum.

Nazareus, a man conſecrate or dedycate to god. Nazarei were men, which had made vowes vntyll a certayne tyme.

Nazaret, a lytle towne in Galilea.

Nazara, a citie in Cappadotia, afterwarde called Cæſaria.

NE, an aduerbe, ſignifieng forbeading or diſſuading. Tu ne cede malis, giue thou not place to aduerſitie or myſaduentures. ſometyme it is a coniunction copulatiue, and ſignifieth nor or neyther. ſomtime rational, and ſignifieth wherfore. ſomtyme cauſal, & ſignifieth not. ſomtyme leſte, alſo or not, whither. ſomtyme it is an interrogatiue. Ego ne? I troweſt thou?

Nea, an ile betwene Lemnos & Helleſpont.

Necunde, nor from any place.

Ne plura, ne multa, but to be ſhort, what nedeth any longer tale, to make a ſhort tale. *Cice. pro Cluencio. & in Ver. Ci. p Clu.*

Ne multis, in fewe wordes. Ne multis Diogenes emitur, In fewe wordes Diogenes is bought.

Ne dicam, I wyll not ſaye.

Nectere moras, to make delayes. *Cor. Tacitus li. 13.*

Nec, nor. neque, nor. nequaquam, no.

Necnon, and, or alſo.

Nequicquam, in vayne, no or not.

Ne viuã, I wold I lyued not. Ne viuã ſi tibi concedo, I wolde I lyued not, or I wold I ſhulde not liue, if I graunt that to the. *Cicero.*

Neutiquam, in no wyſe.

Nequaquam, no.

Necubi, in no place.

Nedum, not onely. ſomtyme nor yet, where the thynge of leaſt eſtimation is put laſte.

Nedum, ſygnifieth not onely, as Fundere pro te ſanguinem, nedũ pecuniam, I wolde ſpende for the not only my money, but alſo my bloode. where the thinge of mooſt eſtimation is laſt put, it ſignifieth nor yet. Ne crederem tibi obulum, nedum vitã meam, I wyll not committe my lyfe vnto thy credēce, nor yet lende the one halfepeny.

Nec dum, nor yet.

Neapolis, a citie called Naples.

Neapolitanus, na, num, of Naples.

Nebrides, feaſtes in the honour of Bacch., alſo ſkinnes of dere wherwith they were clad which kept the ceremonies of Bacch.

Nebrodes, an hyl in Sicile, where there is great plentie of falowe dere.

Nebrundes, the ſtones of beaſtes.

Nebula, a vapour or myſt ryſynge from the water, whiche eyther tourneth forthwith into a cloude, or ſhortly vanyſheth.

Nebularium, a houſe where corne is threſhed, or wynnowed in tyme of rayne.

Nebulo, onis, a thefe, a knaue, a lewde perſon, or vacabunde.

Nebuloſus, a, um, myſty.

Neceſſarius, a kynneſman.

Neceſſarius, a, ũ, neceſſary, nedefull.

Neceſſe vel neceſſũ, of force, it muſt nedes be.

Neceſſitas, tatis, nede, neceſſitie. ſometime a bonde of frendſhip or kynrede.

Neceſ

N ante E

Necessitudo, dinis, idem. also amitie.
Necim, the olde writers vsed for nec cum, nor with.

Perottus. Necunquam, for necunquam aliquem.
Necne, or not.
Necum, in the olde Spanyshe tungue was the image of Mars, garnyshed with beames lyke the sonne, it also signyfied in latyne mas, the male kynde.
Necydalus, a sylke worme, whan he is yonge sprounge out of the sede.
Neco, caui, care, vel necui, to flee.
Neci datus, slayne without weapon, as with poyson, famyne, prisonement.
Necromantes, a Necromancer, or caller vp of yll spirites.
Necromantia, necromancy.
Necromanticus, a necromancer.
Nectar taris, the drinke of goddes, somtime it signifieth immortalitie.
Nectareus, a, um, immortall, deuyne.
Necto, nexui, nectere, to wynde or plat togither.
Necubi, in no place.
Necunde, from no place.
Nefandus, da, dum, horrible, not to be spoken or named.
Nefarius, a, um, cursed not worthy to lyue.
Nefas, a cursed dede, a wycked thynge, execrable, detestable.
Nefasti dies, dayes whan it is not lefull.
Nefrendes, pygges weaned, called shotes.
Negabundus, he that denyeth.
Negabundus, for negans, denyenge.
Negatio, a denyer, a nay.
Negatiuus, a, um, that whiche denyeth.

Plautus in mercatore Negito, tare, to denye.
Negligo, glexi, gligere, to neglect, to haue lyttel regarde.
Neglectus, tus, contempte.
Neglectus, ta, tu, contemned not regarded.
Negligentia, negligence.
Negligens, tis, negligent.
Negligenter, negligently, contemtuously, dysdeynously.
Nego, aui, are, to deny, to refuse, to say not.
Negocialis, le, perteynynge to denyenge.

Plautus in Bacch. Negato esse ituram, say that she wyl not go.
Negotior, aris, ari, to practyse marchaundyse, to be occupied in busynesse.
Negotiosus, he that is moch occupied with busynesse.
Negociator, toris, a marchaunte, he that is busied in an other mans affaires.
Negotialis, ale, perteynyng to busynesse, occupation, or trouble.
Negotium, remedye. Omnis res palam est, neq vllum pol de hac re negotium est, quin male occidam, All the matter is knowen:

therfore in this case in faith there is no remedy, but that I wyll kyll hym.
Negotiosus, a, um, full of businesse, care, or trouble of mynde.
Negotium dare, to gyue in charge.
Negotium, busynesse, occupation, somtyme trouble, care, or labour of mynde.
Negotiorum curator, a factour or sollicitor in a mannes busynesse.
Neleus, the father of duke Nestor, whiche was at the siege of Troye.
Nem, was vsed of old writers for somtime, also for but, or excepte.
Nemea, a greate wodde, where Hercules slewe an horrible lyon.
Nemeeus, of the wodde callyd Nemes, whiche is in Grecia, not farre frome the citie of Argos.
Nemesis, a goddesse, whiche was supposed to take vengeance on malefactours. some tyme it sygnificth fortune, also iustyce, also reproche.
Nemartes, nymphes or maydens of the see.
Ne my quidem, is applied to hym that dare not speke. Ne my quidem facere audet, he dare not ones mutte, or make coutenance to speake.
Nemo, no man, or none.
Nemo non, some man.
Nempe, is an aduerbe confyrming a thing, for bycause, surely, verily, sometyme for.
Nemus, nemoris, a wod for pleasure, wherin deere or other beastes may fede.
Nemoralis, et nemorensis, perteynynge to a woode.
Neo, neui, nere, to spynne.
Neogamus, newe maried.
Neomenia, the fyrst day of the newe mone.
Neophitus, a newe man, or a plante newely sproungen.
Neoptholemus, is in englishe a new knight, It was also the name of Pirrh° the sonne of Achilles.
Neotericus, he that is nowe, or was of late tyme.
Nepa, vel nepes, a scorpion.
Nepenthes, a drynke or an herbe, whiche causeth a man to forgete heuynesse. Also the herbe called borage.
Nepeta, a citie of the countrey of Thuscane in Italy.
Nephalia, feastes wherin no wyne was sacryfysed or drunke, but onely mede, and they were called the feastes of sobre men.
Nephele, a cloude. also the name of a womanne, whiche was mother of Helles, who gaue the name to the see callydde Hellespontus.
Nephritis, peyn in the raynes of the backe.

Nepita,

Nepita, an herbe called nepe, or calament.
Nenum, was somtyme put for non.
Nepos, otis, the sonne or doughters sonne, sometyme a waster of goodes, a riottouse person. Nepotes, do sometyme signify all the discent, whiche commeth after a mans sonnes or daughters.
Nepotor, ari, to liue prodigally, or riotously.
Nepotulus, a dimynutiue of Nepos. Meus Nepotulus, my lyttell sonne, or yonge son, from the fyrst discent.
Nepotatus, tus, ryot, superfluous expenses.
Neptis, the doughter of a mans sonne or doughter.
Neptunus, callyd god of the see.
Nepus, vncleane.
Nequa, no where.
Nequalia, detrimentes or harmes.
Nequam, a noughty felowe, a manne to be nothinge estemed.
Nequando, at no tyme.
Nequaquam, in no wyse, not a whitte.
Nequior, oris, Nequissimus, warse, warste of all.
Nequiquam, in vayne, Nequicquam, not.
Ne quid nimis, nothyng to to, that is to say, moche excedynge, or moche lackynge.
Nequino, are, to be wanton, also to denie.
Nequinū, a citie in Italy, now callid Narnia.
Nequinunt, in the olde tyme they vsed for nequeunt, they may not.
Ne quis, that no man.
Nequitia, vnthriftynesse, lecherous, wantonnes, vicious dalyaunce.
Nequitus, & nequiter, vnthriftily.
Nereides, nymphes or maidens of the see.
Nereus, was called oone of the goddis of the see, and somtime it is put for the see.
Nerio, enis, the wife of Mars, called god of battayle.
Neritæ, a certayne kynde of shelle fysshe. see Plinie.
Neritos, vel Neritum, an yle or citie nyghe to Epirus, a countrey of Grece.
Nerium promontorium, Compostella, where saint James the apostelle lyeth. It is also a lyttell tree, hauyng leaues lyke to an almonde tree, but greatter and fatter.
Nero, the name of an emperour, of a monstruous and cruell nature.
Neruiæ, harpe strynges, or lute stringes.
Neruiceus, a, um, of synewes.
Neruicus, he that hath pein in his sinewes.
Neruij, people aboute Tournay.
Nerulani, people by Rome.
Nerulonenses, people in Campania.
Nerulum, a towne in the countreye callyd Lucania.
Neruosus, a, um, that whiche hath many sinewes. It is somtyme taken for stronge.
Neruus, a synewe, it signifieth sommetyme strength. Also stockes, wherin offenders be put. Nerui be also stringes of an instrument. Sometyme it sygnifieth the priuye membre of a manne.
Nesa, a countrey in Sicile, ioynynge to the hyll of Ethna, which alway sendeth forth flames of fyre or smoke.
Nescio, sciui, scire, to not know, to be ignorant of a thynge.
Nescius, he that dothe not knowe, or is not knowen.
Nesium, uel Nesis, an yle by Campania.
Nesia, a nymphe or mayden of the see.
Nessus, & Nesius, sonnes of Ixion the Centaure.
Nessotrophion, a place, where duckes are kepte to be made fatte.
Nestor, oris, a Capytayne of the Grekes, which were at Troy, who lyued the ages of thre olde men, and in gyuynge counsell was excellent.
Neu, for ne ue, nor yet.
Neuceria, a citie of Vmbria, whyche is a parte of Italy.
Ne ue, or not, or no.
Ne unquam, in no wyse.
Neuolo, I wyll not.
Neuri, people of Scithia.
Neurobate, goers on cordes.
Neuter, tra, trum, neutrius, none of them.
Neutiquam, in no maner of wyse, in no condicion.
Neutralis, le, neutre, of no parte.
Neutro, neyther on the one parte, nor the other.
Neuus, a marke in the vysage or body of a manne or womanne, as a mole, a redde or blacke warte.
Nex, necis, deathe by force.
Nexilis, nexile, any thynge that may be knit.
Nexo, as, & is, nexui, nexere, to knitte often.
Nexus, a, um, knytte, bounden.
Nexus, nexus, uel nexi, a bond, an obligation
Nexi, free men, that do bynde theym selues to labour or seruyce, to be acquited of the dettes, whiche they owe. *Varro.*
Nexus inire, to be bounde by oblygation or couenaunt. also to be wrapped in bondes, as is the commune sayenge.

¶ N, ANTE I.

NI, but if, except, leste that.
Nicander, the propre name of a man.
Nicanor, a mans name.
Nicator, a great vanquysher.
Nicea, & Nicia, a citie in Asia.

Niceteria, thynges gyuen for vyctorie, as rynges, colers of golde, and crownes or garlandes.

Nicopolis, a citie in Egipte, where the emperour Octauian vanquysshed Antonie & Cleopatra.

Nicomedia, a citie in the countrey of Bithinia, in the lasse Asia.

Nicostrata, the mother of Euander the old kynge of latynes.

Nicto, tere, to vent as the hound doth, whiche foloweth the dere or hare, or other game.

Nicto, are, to wynke.

Nictus, tus, a wynkynge, as whan one doth sygnifie his mynde to an other by lokinge.

Nidifico, are, to make a neste.

Nidere, somtime to sauor, somtime to shine.

Nidor, oris, a sauour or smell of some thing burned or rosted: sometyme it signifyeth grennynge. also brightnes.

Nidulor, aris, to brede as a byrde dothe, to make a neste, or eyre.

Nidulus, a lyttell neste.

Nidus, a neste, sommetyme it signifieth the byrde that bredeth. Also a vesselle lyke to a neste. Also Nidi be coffyns, wherin marchantes do lay their sondry wares.

Nigella, a wiede growinge in corne, callyd also Lolium, cockle. Also a blacke seede, good to smelle vnto agaynste rewmes or distillations.

Nigellus, a, um, somewhat blacke, browne.

Niger, gra, grum, blacke, fowle. Also it is sometyme vsed for deed.

Nigidius, a noble philosopher of Rome.

Nigredo, nigrities, & nigritia, black colour.

Nigrefacio, & nigrefio, to make blacke.

Nigreo, & nigresco, to be blacke.

Nigrico, care, to be somewhat blacke.

Nigris, a fountayne in Ethiopia, whiche is of somme men supposed to be the heed of the greatte ryuer Nilus.

Nigro, are, to make blacke, also to be black.

Nigror, oris, blackenesse.

Nihildum, not yet.

Nihilifacio, cere, to sette naught by.

Nihili pendo, ere, to esteme nothynge.

Nihilominus, netheleffe.

Nihil, & nihilum, nothynge, nought.

Plautus in Bacch. Nihil cum fidibus graculo, Nihil cum amacino sui, The dawe hathe nothynge to doo with the lute: nor the sowe with maioran: A prouerbe applyed to them, whiche presumynge to moche of their owne wyttes, do meddel malapertly with thinges, wherof they can no skylle.

Nil, nothynge, none, nought.

Nilion, a stone lyke a Topace, but that it is more duskyshe.

Nilus, a great ryuer in Egipte, callyd also Geon, and is one of the greattest ryuers of the worlde.

Niliacus, & niloticus, ca, cum, of Nile.

Nimbifer, the bringer of stormes or showres.

Nimblis, an yle in the see called Ionium.

Nimbus, a sodayne great showre or storme of rayne or hayle. Also a cloude or a great wynde, also a vessell, oute of the whyche wyne is drawen or powred.

Nimbosus, stormy, or showrynge.

Nimirum, vndoubtedly, surely. somtyme it signifieth but yet, no meruayle.

Nimis, & nimium, an aduerbe, signifyenge abundance.

Nimis bonus, to good. Nimis malus, to ylle.

Nimietas, superfluousnes.

Nimius, a, u, wherof is to moch, or excesse.

Ningo, ninxi, ningere, to snowe.

Ninguidus, da, guidum, where there is moche snowe.

Niniue, a great cite in Assyria, also an other greatte citie in the corner of Judea, towarde Arabia.

Ningulum, none, nor any.

Ninus, a great kynge of Assiria, & Babilon.

Niobe, a woman, who hauynge a greatte numbre of chyldren, and they beyng deed all at ones, so moche lamented and sorowed, that she loste hir speche: wherfore the paynyms fayned, that she was turned to a stone.

Niphates, a ryuer in the coutrey of Scithia.

Niptrum, a lauer.

Nis, was of olde tyme vsed for nobis.

Nisse, a ladye of the fayrye.

Niseus, a place in Media, where fayre horses were bredde.

Nissa, a citie in Lydia.

Nisi, but if, excepte.

Nisus, a kynges name, of whome it is fayned, that he had one golden heare. It is also a kynde of haukes.

Nisus, sa, um, the participle of Nitor, teris.

Nisyros, a lyttell yle by Grece.

Nitedula, a feld mouse. Also a glow worme that shineth by nighte.

Nitella, a toothe pike. sometyme it signifyeth elegancy in speche.

Niteo, tui, tere, to be cleane, nete, gaye.

Nitesco, idem.

Nitide, clenlye.

Nitido, are, to make cleane or bryght.

Nitidus, da, dum, cleane, brighte.

Nitor, teris, niti, to be styffe, or to resyste agaynste a burdeyn, to indeuour, to leane on a thynge, to flee, to be sustayned, to inforce hym selfe, or take pein, to trauayle.

Nitere, to lyue a pleasaunt lyfe.

Nitor, oris, clennesse, brightnesse, gaynesse.
Nitrea, a region or Contray in Egypte, also the name of two cities in Egypte, aboue the citie of Memphis.
Nitrum, Salte peter.
Niualis, le, of snowe.
Niuatus, ta, tum, made colde as snowe.
Niueus, a, um, of snowe, snowy.
Niuosus, full of snowe, or where it snoweth often.
Nixurio, I will endeuour me, I will assay to do a thinge.
Nixus, a, um, borne as a childe is.
Nixus, us, ui, birth of a childe.
Nix, niuis, snow.

¶ N. ANTE. O.

No, are, to swymme.
Nobilis, noble, notable.
Nobilitas, nobilytie, noblenesse.
Nobilito, tare, to make noble, or to adde to dignitie, or estimation, to cause to be knowen.
Noceo, cui, cere, to hurt, to indamage.
Noctesco, cere, to be darke.
Noctes atticæ, a booke that Aulus Gellius made, which was so called, bycause it was writen in the wynter nyghtes at Athenes.
Nocticorax, a night crowe.
Noctifuga, he that fleeth or exchuith the night.
Noctiluca, is a name, whereby the Moone is called bycause that she doeth shyne by night, also a lytle beest, which shyneth by nyght.
Noctiuagus, a wanderar or goar by nyghte.
Noctu, at night, or in the nyght, by nyght.
Noctua, an owle.
Noctuæ Athenis, oules to Athenes, a prouerbe, whereby is signified any thinge to be abundant, and more than ynoughe.
Nocturnus, na, um, of the night.
Nocuus, a harme doar.
Nodo, are, to knytte.
Nodus, a knot.
Nodosus, a, um, knotty, or full of knottis.
Nodus herculis, where there can be founde nor begynnynge nor endinge, that whiche may neuer be losed.
Nodus is also in an host in batayle, a throng of men, so thicke, that it can not be perced.
Nodum in scyrpo quæris, Thou sekest for a knot in a ruihe, it is applyed to him, which is scrupulouse in a thing that is not doubtfull, but playne.
Noëgeum, a whyte napkyn.
Noëma, maye be called euery sentence.
Noënon, for non.

Noeolæ, the wertes, which be in the chekis of a gote or swyne.
Noes, a ryuer in Thracia, whiche runneth into the ryuer of Ister, or Danow.
Nolani, people in Italy.
Nolito, for Noli, do not.
Nolo, non vis, nolui, nolle, to not will.
Nolo, I will not.
Nomarcha, a mayre, bayliffe, or prouoste.
Nomades, people in Scithia, called nowe Tartary.
Nomæ, sores, which be greuous.
Nomen, minis, a name, or nowne, sometyme it signifieth worshyp, auctoritie, noblenesse of bloode, kynred. Also cause. Eo nomine, for that cause. Meo nomine, for my sake.
Nomenclator, oris, an officer, which called euery man by his name.
Nomenclatura, a namynge of men.
Nomentum, a towne in Italy by Rome.
Nomina, besyde the commune signification, doeth also signifie dettours or dettes, also articles writen.
Nomina facere, to lende to many men.
Nomina exigere, to demaunde or calle for dettes.
Nominatim, by name.
Nominibus honestis, for an honest pretence or consyderation.
Nomino, are, to name.
Nomisma, coyne.
Nomissis, nyne pounde weyght of brasse.
Nomophilax, acis, a kepar of lawes.
Nomus, a iurisdiction, as a mayraltie, a baylywyke, or prouostshyp of a towne.
Non, no, not.
Nonaginta, fourescore and ten.
Nongenti, nyne hundred.
Nonus, a, um, the nynthe.
Non ita pridem, not longe agone.
Non modo, not onely.
Nonnullus, some man.
Nonnunquam, sometyme.
Non sobrius, drunke.
Non tacenda, praysworthy.
Nonacris, a place in the countray of Arcadia.
Nonæ, nyne dayes in euery moneth before the Idus.
Noricum, a contray in Germany, wherein is the duchy of Bauaria, or Beuar, also the towne of Aurenbergh.
Norma, a rule.
Normandia, a contraye in Fraunce called Normandy.
Normatus, a, um, ruled.
Noruegia, a royaulme called Norwaye.
Noscito, tare, to knowe moche.
Nosco, noui, noscere, to knowe, to fauoure tender-

tenderly.

Noscomion, an hospytalle or place, where sycke folke are kepte.

Notabilis, le, notable.

Notæ, notes, cyfers, markes, made for remembraunce of some thynge.

Notarius, a clerke, whiche wryteth instrumentes or plees.

Notesco, notui, scere, to be knowen or made knowen.

Nothus, a bastarde.

Nothia, that whiche by some lawes is appoynted to a mans bastarde.

Notifico, are, to make knowen.

Notio, knowlege. Notitia, idem.

Noto, are, to note or marke, to make a mark or token, to write after an example.

Notus, ta, tum, knowen: also a frende, or of acquayntaunce.

Notus, noti, the southwynde.

Nouacula, a barbers knyfe or raser.

Noualis, lande sowen euery other yere.

Nouelletum, a newe growen vyne.

Nouello, are, to tylle newe grounde, or set newe vynes.

Nouellus, a, um, newe.

Nouem, nyne. Nouenus, the nynthe.

Nouenarius numerus, the numbre of nyne.

Nouendium, the space of nyne dayes.

Nouendiale sacrum, ceremonies the nynth day after the burienge.

Nouenniæ, a citie in Thracia.

Nouerca, a stepmother, or stepdame.

Nouercari, to do lyke a stepdame.

Nouitius, a, um, newe or late begonne.

Nouo, are, to make newe.

Nouocomenses, a people in Italy.

Nouum Comum, a towne in Italy.

Nouuncium, of nyne ounces or ynches.

Nouus, ua, um, newe, fresshe, late commen vp or begonne.

Noui homines, men of late commen vppe, whiche are not gentylmenne of an auncyent stocke.

Nouissimus, ma, mum, the laste.

Nouiter, newely, or lately.

Nouissime, laste of all.

Nox, noctis, nyght.

Notesco, scere, to be nyght.

Noxa, peyne, offence, or trespace. somtyme it significeth hurte or harme.

Noxia, a faulte.

Noxius, noxia, noxium, harmefull.

¶ N, ANTE V.

Nvbecula, a lyttell clowde.
Nubes, a clowde.
Nubilarium, a howse, wherinto corne is caryed for feare of rayne.

Nubilis, maryable, of ful age to be wedded.

Nubilo, are, to make clowdy or darke.

Nubilosus, a, um, full of clowdes.

Nubilus, a, um, clowdy, darke.

Nubo, nupsi, nubere, to be wedded, or to wedde, proprely of the womans part.

Nucamenta, thynges hangynge downe from the boughes of trees or pitchtrees, and are no leaues.

Nuceria, a towne in Campania.

Nuceus, ea, eum, of a nutte.

Nuci frangibula, a nutte cracke.

Nucleus, the kernell of any thynge.

Nucula, & nucella, a lyttell nutte.

Nudipedalia, ceremonies done bare foted.

Nuditas, nuditatis, nakednesse, symplenesse, playnnesse.

Nudius tertius, the day before yesterdaye: Nudius quartus, Nudius quintus, Fowre dayes passed, fyue dayes sens.

Nudare, to make naked, to discouer, or opē.

Nudus, da, dum, naked, vncouered.

Nugę, nugarum, tryflynge tales, fables, mery matters.

Nugalis, le, tryflynge.

Nugamenta, tryfles.

Nugatorius, a, um, tryflynge.

Nugax, acis, a tryfler or fabler.

Nugigerulus, & nugigerus, a teller of lyes.

Nugiuendus, a seller of tryfles.

Nugor, aris, ari, to tryfle, or go about vayne thynges.

Nugator, toris, a tryfler or mocker.

Nullatenus, in no wyse.

Nullibi, no where.

Nullo negotio, withoute peyne or laboure, without any difficultie.

Nullus, a, um, none.

Nullus sum, I am vndone.

Nullus dum, no man yet, none to this day.

Num, for an, or vtrum, whiche hapneth in a demaunde or question. Num ego te spoliaui? Dyd I robbe the?

Num nam, for num.

Numa, was the seconde kynge of Romaynes.

Numario, hauynge great store of money.

Numellę, a tumbrelle, wherein menne be punysshed, hauyng their heedes and fete put into it.

Numen, proprelye is the wylle of God. Sommetyme the power of god, somme tyme it sygnyfyeth god, sommetyme apparayle.

Numerabilis, rabile, that may be numbryd.

Numeralis, rale, pertaynynge to numbre.

Numerarius, seu numerator, he that casteth accompt, or reckneth a thyng in numbres.

N ante V.

Numerarius, ia, um, wherin is numbre.
Numeratim, in numbre, or by numbres.
Numerato, promptely, redily, sometyme in accompt or reckenynge. De Actore facile dicente ex tempore dictum est ingenium eū in numerato habere, of the plaintyfe, whā he speaketh quyckely and without study, it is sayde, that he hath a quycke wytte and a redy. Claudius Isidorus testamento suo dixit, quamuis multa Ciuili bello perdidisset, tamen relinquere seruorum quatuor millia, iuga boum tria millia sexcenta, reliqui pecoris ducenta quinquaginta millia, In numerato pōdo sexcenta millia, Claude Isidore sayde, that not withstandynge that he hadde loste moche in the Ciuyle warres: yet hadde he lefte in his testament foure thousande slaues, thre thousande and syxe hundred yoke of oxen, of other cattel two hundred and fyfty thousande, In money redy tolde syx hundred thousande pounde. *Fab. Quin. vi.* *Plin. li. 31.*
Numero, are, to numbre or counte, to telle money, to reken catell.
Numerosus, greate in nombre.
Numerus, nombre, sometyme quantitie, as of grayne. it is also a precise order in harmony, in lengthe and shorteneffe of syllables. And therfore sommetyme verses be called Numeri. Also it signifyeth company or felowshyp. It is also taken for the warste sorte of the people. *Erasm. in Chil.*
Numeris omnibus absolutus, on euery part perfytely.
Numidia, a royalme in Affrike.
Numida, a man of Numidia.
Numitius, a ryuer in Italy by Lauinium.
Nummarius, nummaria, rium, pertaynynge to money.
Nummarius, a keper and louer of money.
Nummatus, moneyed, ryche in money.
Numitor, toris, the grandfather of Romulus and Remus on the mothers syde.
Nummularius, he with whome exchaunge of money is made.
Nummulus, a lytle coine or piece of money
Nummus, & numisma, moneye. It was a coyne, whiche was the tenthe parte of a golden peny.
Nummus adulterinus, counterfayt money.
Numella, a payre of shakelles, or fetters for a horse.
Nunc, nowe, at the laste.
Nunquando for num aliquando.
Nuntiatio, reporte, relation. *Valla in Rauden.*
Nuntio, are, to tell or sygnifye.
Nuntius, a messanger, sometyme a message.
Nuntium, idem.
Nuncupo, are, to name.

Nuncupare uota, to make a solemne auowe. *Cæsar.*
Nuncupare testamentum, to declare a wylle or testament by mouthe.
Nuncupatio, a namynge, a declaration of a wylle.
Nundinæ, the market dayes, whiche in olde time was the nynthe daye: and than dyd the husbande men come to the citie to bie and selle, and also to here their lawes declared, whiche were newe made.
Nūdinalis le, & nūdinarius, a, um, pertaining to a market or fayre.
Nundinatio, marchaundyse exercysed in fayres.
Nundinator, toris, a market man.
Nundinor, naris, to selle openly: sometyme to bye often. *Ci. in vet.*
Nunquam, neuer.
Nunquam non, euer.
Nunquid, a demaunde. Nunquid ego sum? Is it not I?
Nunquis, que, quid? Is there any.
Nunquid vis? wylle ye anye thynge with me? or, Is there any thynge that I maye do for you?
Nuper, late, awhyle agoone. Sommetyme longe ago.
Nuper admodum, a lyttell whyle ago.
Nuperrimus, the laste of all.
Nuperus, a, um, signifieth late done, or happened, or newe begonne. *Plautus in capt.*
Nuptialis, le, pertaynyng to mariage.
Nuptie, mariage or weddynge.
Nupturio, ire, to desyre to marye.
Nuptus, ta, tum, maryed.
Nuptus, & nupta, the husbonde and wyfe.
Nuptus, tus, mariage.
Nursia, an olde citie in Italy.
Nurus, a daughter in law, the sonnes wyfe.
Nusquam, no where.
Nusquam gentium, no where, neuer.
Nusquam non, for vbiq;, euery where. *Valla in Rauden.*
Nutrico, are, & nutrio, ire, to nouryshe.
Nutricatus, tus, norture.
Nutritius, the foster father.
Nutritius, nutritia, nutritium, that nouryssheth.
Nutrix, cis, a nourse.
Nutricula, idem.
Nutus, tus, a becke, or countenaunce with mouynge the eye or hande.
Nuto, tare, to becken or wynke.
Nutu, ac renutu, with a becke and rebecke, with a calle and a becke.
Nux, nucis, a nutte.
Nux auelana, a fylberde.
Nux iuglans, a walle nutte.
Nux pinea, a pyneappull.
Nux greca, an almonde.

¶ N, ANTE Y.

Nycteris, a reremous or backe, with litel fete, that they seme to haue none.
Nicticorax, racis, a nyghte crowe, or shryche crowe.
Nictileia, sacrifices by night vnto Bacchus.
Nyctilopes, he that dothe see nothynge by nyght, and lyttell in the euenynge.
Nictimene, the daughter of Nictes, which lay with her father, and afterwarde was tourned into an owle, who wolde not be seene but at nyght.
Nymphæ, goddesses of the waters, or spirites, beinge conuersaunt aboute waters, elfes, women of the fayrie. sometyme the Muses be so called. also yonge bees, as sone as they haue receyued their fourme.
Nymphea, naturall bathes.
Nymphus, he that is wedded, the brydegroome.
Nysa, a mane name. also a citie in Arabia.
Nysia, a kynd of Iuie, hauyng black beries.
Nyserus, an yle by Grecia.
Nysus, the name of a manne.

¶ O, ANTE A.

Oatarica, the spaune of fisshe salted.
Oaxis, a ryuer in the yle of Crete or Candy.
Oaxus, a cytie in Crete or Candye.

¶ O ANTE B.

Plaut. Ob, for at, ob rem, for my profyte, ob oculos, before myn eyes.
Obæratus, bounden by ernest money.
Obacero, are, to lette a man that he can not telle out his tale.
Obambulo, are, to walke a gaynst an other. also to walke togither, or with an other.
Obacerbo, are, to make one angrie.
Obaresco, scere, to drye all aboute.
Obaudio, ire, to here hardly, or vnwillyngly. sometyme to obey.
Obba, a bottelle.
Obceco, care, to blynde.
Obdo, dere, to thruste agayne, or put to.
Obdormio, ire, to slepe fast or soundly.
Obduco, xi, ere, to lay ouer, or couer a thing somtyme to vncouer or open. also to bring agaynst or ouerthwart a place.
Obdulcesco, scere, to be swete aboute.
Obdureo, rui, ere, & obduresco, scere, to be harde. Obduro, are, to make harde.
Obedio, dire, to obeye.

Obedo, dere, to consume or eate al aboute.
Obeliscus, a great stone, square like a butte, waxing smaller & smaller, vntyl the toppe, of a great height, made plaine by a warkman: there were of them diuers in Rome.
Obelus, a spyt or broche, also a longe strike in writing like a spit, for a note or diuersite.
Obeo, iui, ire, to go to, to go aboute, to be at hande, to mete with one.
Obesus, a, um, fatte, grosse of body.
Obire mortem, obire diem, to dye.
Obire vadimonium, to go to be suretie. *Liuius.*
Obire legationem, to go in ambassade.
Obire prouinciam, to exercise auctoritie.
Obire bellum, to go to battayle.
Obire hereditatem, to take possession of landes, wherein a manne hath a state of inheryteunce.
Obedibo, was in the old time vsed for obediam, I shall obey.
Obequito, tare, to ryde aboute.
Oberro, are, to wander aboute.
Obesco, care, to fede fatte.
Obesus, a man that is very fatte.
Obesitas, fattenesse.
Obesus, a, um, in Virgil is fatte, in Neuio it sygnifieth leane or lyttell. it is most commonly taken for fatte in the bodye. *Vergilius. Suetonius*
Obex, bicis, an obiecte or lette.
Obgannio, & oggannio, ire, to whisper in ons eare. Also to tell a thynge often.
Obherbesco, scere, to growe vppe as herbes doone.
Obiaceo, cui, cere, to lye aboute.
Obiecto, tare, to obiect, or often impute, or lay to ones charge, also to caste out.
Obiectum, any thynge that is before a mannes eyen, and may be sene.
Obiectus, ta, tu, throwen or layde agaynste.
Obiectus, tus, the layenge or settynge of a thynge before ones eyes.
Obiicio, ieci, iicere, to lay or throwe agaynst, or to lay before one.
Obigitare, to stere or moue before.
Obinunt, they dye. *Sex. Pom.*
Obiter, by the waye, incidently, besyde the purpose, in the meane tyme, precisely.
Obitus, ta, tum, the acte or conclusion.
Obitus, tus, the dieng or decesse of a mā. somtime the cōming of one. The ancient writers toke obitum for the accesse of one.
Obiurgo, are, to chide or rebuke.
Obiurgatio, chydynge, rebukynge.
Obiuro, rare, to bynde by an othe.
Obiurgator, & obiurgatrix, he or she that chydeth or rebuketh.
Oblatio, offryng. Oblatus, ta, tum, offred.
Oblecto, ari, & oblector, ari, to delite. Oblectatio oblectamē & oblectamentū, recreatiō

P.ij. Obli-

O ante B.

Oblicio, to take recreation or pleasure.
Obligo, are, to bynde.
Obligatio, an obligation or bonde.
Obligurio, ire, to eate delicate meates gredily or rauenousely, and to consume goodes in feastynge and bankettynge. to Egott.
Obliquus, a, um, contrary to straight.

Cor. Tacitus lib. 2. Oblique perstringere, to taunte or checke.
Oblimo, are, to couer with mudde or softe claye. sometyme to stoppe or daube.
Oblino, ere, to imbrue or make foule.
Obliteratus, ta, tum, scraped out, or blotted.
Oblitero, are, to scrape out, or putte out of remembraunce.
Obliteratio, a scrapynge or blottynge oute of a worde.
Oblitus, ta, tum, forgotten.
Oblitus, imbrued, defyled.
Obliuiosus, a, um, forgettefull.
Obliuiscor, sceri, sci, to forgette.
Obliuium, forgetfulnesse.
Oblocutio, yll reporte.

Plautus in Curgul. Obloquor, eris, qui, to speake agaynste or contrarie, to reporte ylle, to curse.
Obloquutor, an yll reporter, or detracter.

Plautus. Oblucinio, are, to erre.
Sex. Pom. Oblucinasse, to haue erred.
Sex. Pom. Obmanens, abydynge longe.
Sex. Pom. Obmoueto, moue or putte to.
Obmordeo, ere, to byte.
Obmutesco, as we communely say, I holde my peace, I speake not, I hold my tonge.
Obnato, tare, to swymme agaynste.
Obnecto, to knytte faste.
Obnexus, a, um, faste knytte.
Obnexio, a faste knyttynge.
Obnitor, teris, ti, to resyste.
Obnoxius, a, um, bounden, subiecte, apt, in daunger. sometyme it sygnifyeth gyltie or fautie. Sum tibi obnoxius, I am bounden vnto the. obnoxius morbis, subiect to sickenesse. Periculis obnoxius, subiecte to perylles. &c. Minari interdu ferro, nisi sibi obnoxia foret, And thretned hir sommetyme with his weapon, yf she wold not be obediente to his requestes. Obnoxium feris,

Salustius. Colum. 5. caste out to wylde beastes.
Ci. ad At. Obnoxie, fearefully, lyke a subiecte.
Obnubo, bere, to hyde.
Obnubilo, are, to make darke.
Obnuere, to couer the heed or body.
Obnuntiare, to denie, to resyste agaynste a thynge purposed.
Obolus, a poyse wayinge halfe a scruple. it was also a coyne of syluer, whiche varied in poyse after the countrey, as obolus Atticus, obolus Romanus, obolus Hebraicus.

Salu. in orati. Memmii. Oborior, ri, to begin to spring or come forth
Obrado, rasi, dere, to shaue against the heer.

Obortus, a, um, begonne or spronge, as rumor obortus, tydynges spronge.
Ob rem, for the purpose.
Obrepo, pere, to come priuily or steale in, to come vnwares or vnloked for.

Ci. in Pis. Obrepere ad honores, to come or attayne to honour by crafty dissimulation.
Obreptio, the gettynge or obteynynge of a thynge in fourme aforesayde.
Obrepticie litere, letters opteyned by the sayde meanes.
Obrideo, dere, to laugh agaynst one.
Obrideo, si, dere, to laugh at one, or to mock one. Obsio, a mocke.
Obrigeo, gui, gere, & obrigesco, scere, to be or waxe styffe for colde.
Obrion, one of the yles called fortunate.
Obryzum, pure or fyne golde.
Obripio, ripui, ripere, is in hydynge somme thyng, whiche shuld be spoken, to atteyne the thynge that we desyre.
Obrodo, rosi, dere, to gnawe aboute.
Obrogo, are, to checke or interrupte a man in his speeche. Obrogare legem, to derogate one lawe by an other.
Obruo, ere, to ouerthrow, to couer a thing in castynge an other thynge ouer it.
Obrutania fulmina, lyghtnynges, which sodaynely happen, throwynge downe and burnynge thynges, before they be procured or loked for.
Obsaturo, rare, to be fylled to moche with a thynge.
Obsaluto, are, to offre my selfe to salute one.
Obsatum, olde writers vsed for halowed.

Plautus in Epid. Obsæuio, ire, to be wode angry against one.
Obscœno, are, to brynge or cause yll lucke.
Obscœnus, na, num, abhomynable, all thyng whiche is to be eschewed, dyshonest, vncleane, pernicious, Also brynging yl lucke.
Obscœnitas, villany in actes, rybauldrie.
Obscurus, a, um, darke, hydde, dyffuse, vnknowen, of no gentyll bloode.
Obscuritas, darkenesse, difficultie, vngentylnesse of bloudde.
Obscuro, are, to make darke, to shadow, to hide, to kepe in silence or from the knowlege of other, to make of no reputation.

No. Mar. Obsecratio, a speciall desyre.
Obsecro, are, to besech or hartily pray, Obsecrare ab aliquo, to desyre of one.

Terent. in Eunucho. Obsecro, is somtyme an aduerbe. Hem, obsecro an is est? Howe, I pray the is that he?
Obsecundo, are, to make prosperouse, also to obey or do all thing at an other mans wil, to make a thing better than it semeth to be.
Obsecundanter, obediently.
Obsepio, iui, ire, to inclose about with an hedge
Obsequela, diligence, indeuour.

Obse-

Obsequia, thynges done to the pleasure or appetite of hym, that they be done for.
Obsequens, obedient.
Obsequentissime, with great obedience.
Obsequere animo, Take thy plesure, make good chere
Obsequibilis, diligent, redy to do that, whiche is commaunded.
Obsequiosus, idem.
Obsequium, redynes to do all that is commaunded. sometyme it sygnifieth flattery.
Obsequor, eris, qui, to folow an other mannes pleasure.
Obsero, seri, rere, to sowe or sette aboute, to plante.
Obsero, are, to locke or shutte a doore.
Obseruabilis, le, mete to be obserued, worthy to be had in reuerence.
Obseruantia, reuerence, obseruaunce.
Obseruatio, idem.

Plautus in Asinar. Obseruo, are, to awayte diligently with the eyes, and also the mynde, to honoure, to take good hede, to haue in reuerence.
Obseruare ianuam, to kepe the doore.
Obses, idis, an hostage, or pledge in warres
Obsessi, they whiche ar besieged, that they may not issu out of the place where they ar.
Obsessor, oris, he that layeth siege.
Obsidiæ, arum, lyenge in awayte, to take away any thynge craftily.
Obsidianum nitrum, a glasse whiche is pure blacke.
Obsidionalis corona, a garlande gyuen to them, whyche delyuered a towne or fortresse besyeged with ennemyes, whyche was of grasse.
Obsidior, aris, ari, to ly in await to take one.
Obsidium, obsidio, obsessio, a syege about a towne or fortresse.
Obsido, & obsideo, sessi, dere, to lay siege.
Obsigno, are, to close letters & seale them. Also to sygne them.
Obsignator, toris, he that putteth to his seale or sygne to a dede or instrument.
Obsipo, are, to throwe or caste, as whanne men of the countrey do say,
Obsipa pullis escam, Caste meate to the chyckens.
Obsisto, stiti, sistere, to resyste.
Obsitus, ta, tum, wrapped, sette about with herbes or trees.
Obsolesco, scere, to decaye, to waxe olde, to be out of vse.
Obsoletus, ta, tum, decayed, olde, oute of vse, worne, as a garment, whan it is bare.

Valla in Rauden. Obsonium, all meates, excepte bread and potage.
Obsonus, sona, num, that whiche hathe an yll sowne.

Obsono, & obsonor, nari, to feest or banket.
Obsonito, tare, idem.
Obsonatio, feastynge or bankettynge.
Obsonator, & obsonatrix, he or she that maketh feastes or bankettes.
Obsono, are, to sowne yll.
Obsorbeo, bui, bere, & obsorbo, psi, bere, to suppe vp all.
Obsordeo, dui, sordere, to be fylthye or vncleane, or sluttyshe. Nonius declaryth it to waxe olde.
Obstaculum, an obstacle or impediment.
Obstetrico, care, to do the offyce of a mydwyfe.
Obstetrix, tricis, a mydwyfe.
Obstinate, obstinately, or fyrmely.
Obstinatus, ta, tum, obstinate, firme, or stable
Obstinatio, obstynacie, styffenes in opinion.
Obstino, are, to be obstinate, or persist firme in one sentence or purpose.
Obstipo, pare, to stoppe.
Obstipus, crouped shouldred.
Obstitum, croked, sometyme vyolated.
Obsto, stiti, stare, to withstande, to lette.
Obstrepo, pere, to crye out on one, or make a noyse.
Obstrigillo, are, to resist or repugne against, to speake in detraction of one.
Obstringo, xi, gere, to bynde or tye.
Obstrictus, bounden.
Obstringere fidem, to make a faythefulle promyse.

Obstrudo, si, dere, to hyde, to stoppe a mans throte, that he cannot eate meate. *Plautus in Stich. Pom. Fest.*
Obstrudulentum, a stoppynge.
Obstruo, xi, struere, to shutte, to stoppe.
Obstructus, stopped or shutte.
Obstruere luminibus, to lette that a manne canne not loke out of his wyndowes, or to stoppe his lyghtes. *Cice. pro domo sua.*
Obstupidus, a, um, astonyed.
Obstupefacio, facere, to abasshe, or make abashed. *Plautus in Milite.*
Obstupesco, scere, to be abasshed.
Obsum, obfui, obesse, to hurte or hynder, or indamage.
Obsurdesco, obsurdescere, to be or waxe deaffe.
Obtempero, perare, to obey, or be at commaundement.
Obtendo, to laye an excuse.
Obtendiculum, a colourable answere.
Obtentus, tus, a pretence.
Obtero, triui, obterere, to treade or thruste downe, to suffocate, to bruyse.
Obtego, obtegere, to couer aboute.
Obtestatio, an humble desyre, proprely not to do a thyng. Also to take god or some other thynge to wytnesse.

O ante B.

Obtestor, aris, ari, humbly to beseche, to desyre for goddes sake, or for the remembraunce of some thinge, whyche to hym that is desyred, is thankfully herde.

Obtexo, ere, to wayue aboute.

Obticeo, cui, cere, to keepe sylence, not to speake.

Obturo, are, to shutte.

Obtueor, eri, to beholde, to loke on.

Obturatio, shuttynge.

Obtineo, nere, to opteyne, to holde, to retayne styll, to gete, sometyme to haue. Si istam animi firmitudinē obtines, salui sumꝰ, If thou haste that firmenesse of courage, we be saulfe.

Obtingere, to happe.

Obtigit, it happened.

Obtorpesco, obtorpui, pescere, to be verye slow or dull.

Obtorqueo, obtorsi, obtorquere, to wringe or wrythe aboute.

Obtrecto, tare, to ylle reporte, to depraue, to haue in despyte.

Obtrectator, toris, an yl reporter, or backbyter.

Obtrectatio, ylle reporte.

Obtrigo, are, to bynde by an othe.

Obtrudo, si, dere, to thruste downe, to putte to with force. Obtrudit fores, He pullid to the doore. Also to set forth. Aliquid prius obtrudamus, Lette vs fyrste sette forthe sommewhat.

Plautus in Curgul.

Terent. in Andria. & Hecyra.

Obtrudere vxorem, to gyue to a man a wyfe against his will or appetite.

Obtrunco, uncare, to slee, also to stryke of a mans heed.

Obtundo, dere, to stryke, to breake, to make dull, to hurte a man with speking, to make werye.

Obturbo, are, to trouble all.

Obtusus, a, um, dulle.

Obtuitus, tus, & obtuitus, a looke or regard.

Obuagio, gire, to crye oute, as a childe.

Obuallo, are, to enuyronne or compasse aboute with a dyche or walle.

Obuaricator, toris, he that tourneth one out of the ryght waye, or letteth hym that he maye not passe.

Obuaro, are, to peruerte.

Obuarico, care, to stoppe or lette oone of his passage.

Obuenio, nire, to comme agaynste, to mete with. also to happen.

Obuersor, aris, ari, to be presente, to come in remembraunce.

Cicer. pro Sextio.

Obuerto, & obuerso, tere, to tourne agayne, or backe. Sed mihi ante oculos obuersabatur reipub. dignitas, quę me ad se rapit. But before myne eyes camme the estate of the

O ante C.

publyque weale, whiche plucketh me vnto hyr.

Obuiam, an aduerbe, which signifieth before in the waye, against one. Obuiam ire, to go against one, to preuent.

Obuio, are, to meete with one.

Obuius, a, um, that which meteth with one.

Obumbro, brare, to make darke with a shadowe: sometyme to defende.

Obuolo, are, to flie againste.

Obuos sacro, the auncient Romayns vsed for obsecro, I beseche you.

¶ O, ANTE C.

Occa, an harowe or dragge, whyche hath yron teeth, wherwith cloddes are broken.

Occatio, a breakynge of cloddes, or harrowynge.

Occęco, care, to make blynde.

Occalleo, ere, to waxe or be harde fleshhed, or brauned, lyke as a bore is.

Occano, & occino, occanui, & occini, occanere, & occinere, to synge agaynst one, to laye in rebuke.

Occaso, sere, to be loste, or vndone.

Plautus in Casi.

Occasio, occasyon.

Occasiuncula, a smalle occasyon.

Occasus, us, dethe of manne or beaste. Also the goynge downe of the sonne, or sonneglade.

Occatorium, an harrowynge.

Columel. li. 2. Pom. Fest.

Occedo, pro accedo.

Occentassint for conuitia fecerint, They shal gyue rebukes or wordes of reproche.

Occento, tare, to crye oute against one with rebukefull wordes.

Occentus, tus, where one syngeth against another. It maye be also taken for a countretretenor.

Occepso, pro incepero, I shall begynne.

Plautus.

Occidens, tis, the west, or ponent.

Occidio, onis, a slaughter.

Occido, di, dere, to slee or wounde to deth, to fall greuously.

Occisa res est, the matter is dasshed.

Occitantur, for frequenter occiduntur, they be slayne here and there, or in dyuers places.

Occido, dere, to fall downe, to perysshe vtterly, to dye, to goo downe, as the sunne doeth, and other sterres.

Occidit spes nostra, oure hope is lost.

Plautus in Pseudolo.

Occisa est hæc res, this thinge is lost or in despayre.

Occiduum, the place where the sunne goeth downe.

Occino, nere, to synge to another.

Oc-

O ante C.

Plaut. in Casina.
Occilare, to beate or buffat.
Occissimus, of all other mooste lost or desperate.
Occisio, onis, a slaughter or deth of men or catell.
Occidi, I am deed, I am lost.
Occipio, pere, to begynne.
Occiput, & occipitium, the hynder parte of the heed.
Occlamito, tare, to crye oute.
Occludo, dere, to shytte faste.
Occludere linguam, to stoppe a man frome speakynge.
Occlusus, occlusior, occlusissimus, fast shut.
Occo, occare, to harrowe and breake cloddes and balkes in the corne fieldes. Also to couer with erthe.
Occulo, lere, to hyde.
Occulto, tare, idem.
Occultus, ta, tum, hyd, whiche is not knowen.
Occulte, pryuyly, vnknowen.
Occumbo, cubui, cumbere, to be slayne, to be deedly wounded.
Occupatitius ager, the fielde, whiche is neglected of the owner, & labored by other.
Occupo, are, to occupie, to get or take before an other man, to vse in commune, to take or holde a thynge with force, to lette or empeche, to possede, somtyme to lende for auauntage.
Occupans, tis, he that dothe occupie or vse a thynge, the occupier.

Ci. in Ver. act. 2.
Occupatus, let, in busynesse, occupyed.
Occupatio, a colour in rhetorike, where the playntyfe in preuentynge the wordes of the defendaunt, rehercheth that whiche he will laye for excuse, and disproueth it.

Plautus in Menech.
Occupare consilium, to fynde aduyse or counsayle.

Liui. li. 33.
Occupare locum, to take or kepe a place with force.
Occurro, ri, rere, to meete with, to come to remembraunce, to offre hym selfe. Also to resiste, to runne, to come to mynde, or remembrance, also to be proffred.
Occurso, are, the frequentatiue of occurro, to come often to remembraunce, to mete ofte, or runne agaynste one.
Occursus, us, a runnynge agaynste one.
Oceanus, the see, whiche gothe aboute all the worlde. Alsoo a great poole made in Rome, for many persones to swymme in.
Oceanius, a, um, of the occean see.
Ocellatus, ta, tum, that whiche hath eyen, or holes lyke to eyen.
Ocha, a goose.
Ocquinisco, scere, to inclyne or bow to.
Ochus, a ryuer which passeth throughe Acarnania, a countray in grece.

O ante D.

Ochra, oker, whiche paynters do vse.
Otior, aris, ari, to be vnoccupyed, or without busynesse.
Otiosus, ydell, vnoccupied, quyete.
Otium, vacation from labour, leyser, quietnes, ydelnes, lacke of busynes.
Ocreæ, legge harneyse, bootes.
Ocreatus, boted or harneised on the leggis.
Octangulus, a, um, eight cornerd.
Octo, eight.
Octies, eight tymes.
Octonus, a, um, the numbre of eight, in sondry partis.
Octobris, the moneth of Octobre.
Octopes, hauynge eight feete.

Sueton. in Cali. Quint.
Octophorum, a carre with eight wheles.
Oculatus, full of eyen, also quick sigted, circumspect, espyenge a thinge shortly.
Oculatus testis, a witnesse whiche sawe the thinge.
Oculeus, full of eyen, wyly.
Oculis captus, blynde.
Oculitus eam amat, he loueth her as well as his owne eyen.
Oculus, an eye, alsoo a yonge budde of a tree.
Oculū adijcere, to be in loue with the thing, which is sene.
Ocymum, an herbe.
Ocyor, swifter, ocyus idem.
Ocyssimus, a, um, most swift.
Ocyus, sooner, quicklyer.

¶ O, ANTE D.

Odea, places, wherin syngynge is exercysed.
Ode, a songe.
Odfacio, for olfacio, cere, to smelle.
Odi, I hate, or haue hated: Odisse, to hate, or haue hated.
Odiosus, he that is hated, displesant, troublous, tediouse.
Odiose, with hate, displeasantly.
Odit eum cane peius, & angue, He hatethe him wars than a dogge or a serpente: as who sayth, mortally without hope of reconcylynge.
Odites, oone of the sonnes of Ixion the Centaure.
Odium, hate, displeasure, tediousenes.
Odœporicon, an Itenerary, wherin is writen the distance of one place from another, or a lyke thyng, as the iestes of princis are, assignynge their iourneys.
Odor, oris, & odos, sauour, sente.
Odoramentum, euery thynge that sauoureth well. also sauour.
Odorarius, a maker or seller of thinges that
smelle

O ante E.

smelle swete.

Odoratus, ta, tum, that which is perfumed, sometyme that whiche doth sauour, odoriferous, or smellynge swete.

Odorator, a hounde made to the sute.

Odoriferus, a, um, idem.

Odorisecus, a hounde or spanell, which hunteth by sent.

Odoro, & odoror, ari, to smell.

Odorus, a, um, that whiche sendeth furthe sauour, or hath a good sauour.

¶ O, ANTE E.

Oeagrus, a ryuer in the countraye of Thracia.

Oeanthe, a citie, alsoo the floure of a vyne.

Oebades, kynge Darius horsekepar, by whose polycye he atteyned to the kyngedome of Persia.

Oebalia, the countraye in Grece, called also Laconia.

Oebalus, a mannes name.

Oechalia, a citie in Laconia.

Oeconomia, the orderinge and prouydinge of thinges concernyng housholde, alsoo an order in writinge, whereby every thinge is set in his propre place.

Oeconomica, pertaynynge to husbandry.

Oeconomus, a stewarde of housholde.

Oeci, placis, where women do sitte & worke with woull or sylke.

Oecumenicus, vniuersall, pertaynynge to all the worlde.

Oecumenicum consilium, a general counsail, wherein thinges are vniuersally treated concerninge all countreys.

Oedipus, a man, which dissolued subtyll and darke questions.

Oedipodionius, nia, um, belongynge to Oedipus.

Oenanthe, the bery of a wylde vyne.

Oenanthinum, an oynemente made of the sayde bery.

Oeneus, the father of Deianira, the last wife of Hercules.

Oenophorus, a seruaunte, whyche bringeth wyne to the table.

Oenophorum, a potte wherein wyne is caryed.

Oenopola, a vyntenar, or tauernour.

Oenopolium, a wyne tauerne.

Oenotria, Italy.

Oenotrides, two Iles nyghe to Calabria.

Oesipum, the fylthy oyle, which is in wull, that is in the flankes of a shepe, or aboute his necke, which oyle is soden oute, & vsed for medicyne.

O ante F.

Oestrum, woodnesse, or madde fury: alsoo a fly, which maketh a great noyse, whan he flyeth, some do suppose it to be, a dor, lyke to a bee, but that he is blacke & grettar.

Oeta, a mountayne in Thessaly.

Oeteus, the father of Medea, wyfe of Iason.

¶ O, ANTE F.

Offa, a poodinge, also a dish made with fatt broth, harde chese, peper, and cynamom, or other lyke iunkat. somtyme it is taken for a morsell.

Offarius, & offaria, a maker of suche iunckettes.

Offatim, in morselles.

Offector, toris, a dyar.

Offella, a lytell morsell, as of fleshe mynced, also a potage made with pieces of fleshe, as stuyd brothe or forced gruell.

Offendo, dere, to meete with, to fall into, to fynde by chaunce, to stryke or hytte any thinge vnware, to offende. Offendere apud aliquem, to do a thinge, whyche lyketh not theym that do see it done.

Offendiculum, an impediment or let, an obstacle.

Offendimentum, & offendix, the knotte of a ribon or lase, wherewith a bonet or hatte is knytte fast to the heed.

Offensa, offensio, & offensus, us, an offence.

Offensatio, a metynge.

Offensaculum, that which is layd in a mans waye, whereat he stumbleth.

Offensator, satoris, he that stackereth in redinge, as yf he were not perfyte in reding, or redeth otherwyse than it is wryten. *Quint.*

Offensans, tis, that which hurteth or letteth.

Offenso, are, to hytte ofte, or to lette.

Offensiuncula, a small offence.

Offercio, to stuffe or fill.

Offero, obtuli, offerre, to offre, or present, to gyue willyngly, to promyse.

Offerumentæ, strypes. Ne offerumentas habebis plureis in tergo tuo, q̄ vlla nauis lōga clauos, tum ego ero mendacissimus, and yf thou haue not moo strypes on the skyn of thy backe, than a galy hath nayles, J shall be the falsyst lyar that euer was. *Plau in Ruden.*

Offerumenta, offryngs, thynges offred to God.

Offerre auxilium, to promyse ayde.

Offerre crimen, to put a complaynte against one. *Iustin.*

Offerre incendium, Cice. ad Pont. Domus ardebat in Palatio non fortuito, sed oblato incēdio, My house in the Palaice dyd burne not by any chaunce, but by fyre thrast in *Cicero in Lælio.*

by

O ante G.

Plautus in Ruden.
by some man.
Offerre mendicitatem, to bringe one vnto pouertie.
Offerre moram, to let.
Cic. off. 3. Terent. in Adelph.
Offerre se obuiam, to mete with one.
Offerre stuprum, to commit aduoutry.
Offerre vitium virgini, to defloure a virgyn.
Officere luminibus, to stoppe the lyghtes.
Officina, a werkhouse, a shoppe.
Officialis, ale, pertayninge to offices or dueties.
Quintilia.
Officialis, an officer.
Officio, ficere, to hurte, sometyme to do, also to dy cloth.
Officiosus, a seruysable man, or he that is glad to please, or doeth well his duetye.
Officiosus dolor, a grief which procedeth of a good cause or raison.
Officium, office, duetye, or a thinge, whiche ought to be done. It is sometyme taken for honour done to one, and it may be vsed for that, whyche we do calle homage, done in suche fourme as our lawe doeth appoynt it, it is also taken for benefyte.
Cic. de amicitia.
Officium vsurpare, to do his duetye.
Officiose, diligentiy, seruisably.
Offirmo, are, to abyde in one purpose or opinion, to be obstinate.
Offlecto, xi, tere, to tourne a thinge contrary or aboute.
Offoco, are, to powre water into the mouth of a man or beast.
Offriti, crafty or deceytfull taches.
Offringo, ere, to breake with a plough, lande eared before.
Offucie, cawtellis, crafty wayes to deceyue.
Offula, a lytell morsell.
Offundo, fusi, dere, to powre aboute, to make darke or blynde, to stayne, to cast in, or bringe in.
Offuco, care, to put water or other lycour into a mannes mouthe, to sowke downe, as they vse to do to syke men, which for feoblenesse canne not by them selfes take any sustenaunce.
Offusco, are, to make blacke, or darke.

¶ O, ANTE G.

OGdous, a kynge of Egypte, whyche first buylded the citie of Memphis.
Ogdoas, adis, the numbre of eyght.
Ogdolapis, a ryuer which commeth oute of the hilles called Alpes, and runneth to Rome.
Oggannio, ire, to prate, to braule, to speake with chydinge.
Oggero, ssi, gerere, to cast in, or set.
Oculos oggerere, to caste or set the eyes

O ante L.

on one.
Oggrassari, to go.
Plaut. in Trucu.
Ogyges, he which first buylded the citie of Thebes.
Ogygeus, a, um, made or foude by Ogyges.
Ogygea, an Ile betwene Phenicea and Syria.
Ogyris, an Ile in Syria.

¶ O. ANTE. H.

OHe, an exclamation, signiffenge that he, which speketh that worde, is saciate or wery of that, which he seeth or heereth.

¶ O, ANTE I.

¶ Oinomeli, wyne and hony soden togither

¶ O, ANTE L.

OLea, is moost properly the frute of an olyue: yet sometyme it is vsed for an olyue tree.
Oleaceus, a, um, oyly.
Oleacu, a colour, which is mixt with grene, blacke, yelowe, and whyte.
Oleaginus, a, um, of an olyue tree.
Oleagineus, idem.
Olearis, re, & olearius, a, um, pertayninge to oyle.
Olearius, a maker of oyle.
Olearus, one of the Iles called Ciclades.
Oleaster, a wylde olyue.
Oleastellus, a diminutif of Oleaster.
Oleastrinum, oyle of wylde olyues.
Oleatus, a, um, of oyle.
Oleitas, the tyme of gatheringe of olyues.
Olenus, a citie in Grece.
Olenius, a, um, of that citie.
Olentica, thinges which haue an yll sauour.
Oleo, eui, & olui, olere, to sauour, or haue sauour.
Oleosus, a, um, ful of oyle.
Olesco, lescere, to growe.
Oletum, a place where olyues do growe, also the dung or ordure of a man, properly it is a draught or iakes.
Oleum, oyle.
Olfacio, feci, facere, to smell.
Olfacto, are, to smell moche or often.
Olfactus, tus, the sence of smellyng.
Olibantum, a measure of wyne.
Olidus, da, dum, that which hath a great sauour, eyther good or badde, mooste comunely stinkinge.
Oligarchici, they whiche doo aduaunce the state of noble men and ryche men, aboue the

O ante E.

the popular astate.

Olim, sometyme, as well in the tyme passed as in the tyme to come, nowe late, longe tyme passed.

Olitor, a gardynar, or seller of herbes and rootes.

Olitorius, a, um, pertayning to a pot garden.

Oliua, an olyue tree.

Oliueta, the tyme of gatherynge of olyue beryes.

Oliuetum, a place where doo growe olyue trees.

Oliuina, plenty of olyues, alsoo reuenues, which do come of olyues.

Oliuitas, & oleitas, the qualytie of olyues, the gatheringe tyme of olyues.

Oliuo, are, to gather olyues.

Plautus in Pseudolo. Oliuum, oyle olyue.

Olla, a pot.

Ollares, grapes conseruyd in pottes.

Varro. Olli, for illi.

Ollula, a lytell pot.

Ololygones, crokynge frogges.

Olor, oris, a wylde swanne.

Olus, leris, herbes which serue for potage, pot herbes.

Oluscula, small herbes.

Olus atrum, an herbe called persely.

Olympia, a citie betwene the hilles of Ossa and Olympus.

Olympia, orum, playes and greate games, on the hyll of Olympus, made to the honour of Jupiter.

Olympiacus, ca, cum, pertaynynge to that playes or hyll.

Olympias, piadis, the space of fyue yeres, wherby the olde grekes dyd account, as we do now by the yeres of oure lorde: as the first Olympias, the seconde, the third, and so forth.

Olympicus, ca, cum, of Olympus.

Olypionices, he that hath had victory in the games at Olympus.

Olympius, a, um, heuenly.

Olympus, a mountayne or hyll in Grece, aboue the which appereth no clowde: and therfore amonge the Poetes it is vsurped for heuen.

Olynthus, a citie in Thracia.

Olyras, a ryuer in Grece by the place called Thermopylas.

Olysippum, a citie in portugall, nowe called Ulysbona, in englysh Lusseborn.

¶ O. ANTE M.

Omasum, a fat gut, or chitterling.

Omen, minis, lucke, also a worde or sentence sodaynly spoken, after the which some thing hapneth to folowe according therunto, aboue the expectation of them which herde it.

Omentum, the call or sewet, wherein all the bowelles are lapped, also the thynne skyn in the heed, wherein the brayne is contayned: of some called the ryme of the brayne, and of surgeons Pia mater.

Omentatus, ta, tum, mixt with sewet.

Ominor, aris, ari, & omino, aui, are, to gesse what shall happen or folowe.

Ominator, oris, he that telleth a mans lucke or fortune.

Ominosus, a, um, lucky.

Omissus, a, um, left, not medled with. Omisso animo, Vbi te vidi animo esse omisso, whā I sawe that thou caryddest for nothinge. *Teren. in Heaut.*

Omitto, omisi, omittere, to forbeare, to leue, to neglect. *Teren. Phorm.*

Omitte hunc, let hym alone, pardon hym.

Omitte me, let me go.

Omne tulit punctū, he touched euery point, A prouerb. applyed to hym, whiche omitteth nothinge expedient or necessary, and is therfore of all men commendyd.

Omnibus numeris, in all poyntes. Res est omnibus numeris absoluta, it is a thing perfyte in all poyntes.

Omnifariam, all maner of wayes, of euery kynde.

Omnifarius, a, um, sondrye, dyuerse.

Omnigenus, a, um, of euery kynde.

Omnimodus, da, dum, all maner.

Omnino, holy, throughly, allwaye, finally.

Omnipotens, tis, allmyghty.

Omnis, ne, all.

Omophagi, they which doe eate raw fleshe.

Omphax, acis, a grape not fully rype.

Omphacium, licour made of frute that is not ripe, as of grapes, and than is it called veriuyse.

Omphacium vinum, a grene wyne not pleasaunt or swete.

Omphacinum oleum, oyle made of olyues, not beinge rype.

Omutesco, tescere, to be dombe, and can not speke.

¶ O. ANTE N.

Onæ, swete fygges.

Onager, onagri, a wylde Asse.

Onerarius, a, um, that which serueth for bourdon.

Onero, are, to charge, bourdon, or lade.

Onerare populum, to put impositions or taxes on the people.

Oneratus, ta, tum, bourdayned, ladyd.

Onerarius, raria, rarium, that whercon bourdayne

bourdayne is layde.

Onerosus, a, um, bourdeinous.

Onixes, a kynde, of marble.

Oniscus, a worme, which bendeth him selfe lyke a bow whan he goeth, which is reed, and founde vnder trees, which haue lyen longe on the grounde.

Onoba, a citie.

Onocentaurus, a beast halfe a man, halfe an asse.

Onocrotalus, a byrde lyke to a swanne, whiche putting his heed into the water, brayeth lyke an asse.

Onomatopeia, a worde made of sowne or pronouncinge, as bletinge of a shepe, lowinge of a cow, hissinge of an adder.

Ononium, a blynde nettyll.

Onus, oneris, a bourdon, a lode.

Onustus, ta, tum, lodyd.

Onyx, ychis, a whyte stone, lyke to a mannes nayle, also some be founde in Inde, which are of dyuerse colours, hauynge whyte spottes lyke vnto eyen.

Onychinus, na, um, made of the stone called Onyx.

¶ O, ANTE P.

Opaco, care, to shadowe.

Opacus, ca, cum, shadowed, or in the shadowe.

Opera, æ, wark, labour.

Operæ, plurali tantum, warkmen, labourers.

Opera, warkes, buyldinges, priuate or commune.

Operam do, operam impendo, operam nauo, I do myne yndeuour, I put to my diligēce I spend my labour.

Operarius, a laborar.

Operarius, a, um, that whiche is done with labour.

Operculo, are, to keuer a vessell.

Operculum, a keucringe or lede.

Operæprecium, profytable, necessary, a ioyfull thinge, moche to be estemed.

Operimentum, any thinge that keuerith.

Operio, rui, to keuer, or hyde.

Operior, iris, iri, to tary, to abyde.

Operor, aris, ari, to wark.

Operatio, the wark, or that wheraboute a man laboureth.

Operosus, a, um, busy, diligent in labouringe laboriouse, paynefull.

Opertorium, a coueringe.

Ophiaca, pertaynynge to serpentes, they were bookes, which Nicander, and Petridius wrate, of the nature of serpentes.

Ophiophagi, people in Ethiope, whiche do eate serpentes.

Ophincus

Ophiucus, the name of Esculapius, bycause that he is ymagyned to holde a serpent in his hande.

Ophites, a stone hauynge spottes lyke a serpente.

Opicus, pica, picum, vnclene, dishonest, shameles.

Opici, they whyche vsed abhominable rybauldry.

Opifex, ficis, a warkman, a craftys man.

Opificium, the wark.

Opigena, Juno. Juno was so called of women, bycause they supposed, that she holpe them when they trauayled.

Opilio, onis, a shepeherde.

Opima spolia, the spoyle, which by one chief Capytayne is taken frome another in batayle, as his cote armure or harneys.

Opimé, aboundauntly, richely.

Opimo, are, to make fat.

Opimus, ma, mum, fat, also riche.

Opimium, seu opimianum vinum, wyne whiche moughe endure good, two hundred yeres.

Opinabilis, le, that maye be conceyned in opinion.

Opinio, onis, opinion, sometyme hope, also fame.

Opino, for opinor, I suppose.

Opinor, pinaris, nari, to suppose, to haue opinion. *Plautus in Bacch.*

Opinatus, ta, tum, supposed.

Opinator, toris, a supposar.

Opiparé, plentuously.

Opiparus, a, um, aboundaunt, freshe, or gaye. Cœna opipara, a delicate souper.

Opis, opis, a lady, companyon to Diana, she was also wyfe to Saturnus, and by her is signified the erth amonge the Poetes.

Opistographus, a booke wryten on the back syde.

Opisthotonicus, he that can not tourne his necke.

Opisthotonos, the cricke, or diseases, whiche letteth a man to tourne his necke.

Opiter, itris, he whose father deyed before his grandfather.

Opitulor, aris, ari, to helpe.

Opitulator, oris, a helpar.

Opitulus, Jupiter, Jupiter the helpar at neede.

Opium, the iuyce of an herbe called blacke Popye, alsoo Opius, is he that fighteth in armure.

Opobalsamum, balme naturall, whyche in a part of Judea, called Jerocinthe, stilleth oute of a lytle thorne.

Opoponax, acis, the iuyce of an herbe, called Panax.

Opo-

O ante P.

Oporice, a medicine made of fruytes.
Oporæ, all fruites whiche do growe in the last ende of somer.
Oporotheca, a place, wherein frute is kept.
Oportet, it behoueth, it is expedient or necessary.
Oppedo, dere, to fart against one.
Oppeto, tere, to dye: also to be slayne.
Oppetere febrem, to fall into the feuer.
Oppidanus, a cytezen or townes man.
Oppidicus, idem.
Oppidatim, towne by towne.
Oppidò, an aduerbe, signifienge very moch, sometyme it signifieth furthwith, veryly.
Oppidulum, a lytell towne.
Oppidum, a walled towne, or citie.
Oppignero, are, to laye in pledge.
Oppilo, are, to stoppe or shit.
Oppleo, ere, to fill full.
Opploro, are, to lament.
Oppono, ere, to lay or put against.
Opportunus, na, num, that whiche is in due tyme, and as it ought to be.
Opportunus iniuriæ, fete or apte to take wronge. *(Salustius in Iugur.)*
Opportunitas, tatis, oportunitie, conuenient tyme.
Opportunè, opportunatly conueniencely, as it ought to be.
Opprimo, ere, to oppresse, to kepe or shit in, to take sodaynely, to rauyshe a woman, to grieue, to thrust harde.
Opprobrium, & opprobramentū, a reproche
Opprobro, are, to object against one, to reproche.
Oppugno, are, to assault.
Ops, opis, the suster and wyfe of Saturne: also it signifieth ayde or helpe.
Opes, richesse.
Opsonator, atoris, a puruayour of vytayles, or Catar.
Opsonatus, tus, & opsonatio, preparation for dyner, or souper.
Opsonito, tare, to prepare often for dyner or souper.
Opsonium, al thinge belonginge to a meale, except bred and drynke.
Opsono, nare, & obsonor, onari, to prepare thynges necessarye for dyner, souper, or banket.
Optabilis, le, that which is desyred.
Optato, with desire.
Opticus, ca, cum, perspectife, pertaynynge to sight.
Optice, the science whereby the raison of sight is knowen.
Optimates, the heed men of a citie, also they whiche defende the parte of nobilitie and riche men.

O ante P.

Optimatus, tus, the state or condiciō of heed men of a towne or contraye.
Optimus, best.
Optio, the choyse, the request or desyre. It was also to a captayne in warres, a ministre to do his commaundement, and be assistent vnto hym.
Opto, tare, to desyre, to chouse, to require. Adopto, coopto, exopto, vide suis locis.
Opulento, tare, to make riche or plenteouse.
Opulentus, ta, tum, ryche abundant.
Opulentia, & opulentitas, rychesse.
Opuncalo, he that syngethe lyke to a sheparde.
Opulesco, scere, to be ryche.
Opus, operis, a warke, a laboure. Eius opere by his meane or diligence.
Opus est, it is necessary, or nede. Si opus sit, yf nede be.
Opus, opuntis, a citie in Locris.
Opus intestinum, that which most commun- ly is called implemētes of housholde, proprely of tymber, as fourmes, stooles, cupbordes, and other lyke thinges
Opus est conuento. Ita res subita est, celeriter mihi hoc homine opus est, The chaunce is so sodayne, or the mater requireth suche hast, that I must nedes speke with the man shortly or quickely.
Opus est facto, it must nedes be done, or executed.
Opus est remissam. Vosmet videte iā Laches & tu Pamphile, remissam opus sit nobis an reductam domum, Now Laches and Pāphile aduyse your selfes wel, whither it be necessary, that she be sent home, or fetched home. *(Terent in Hecyra.)*
Opus sunt tibi, thou hast nede of them. Vt cū desponderim, des qui aurum ac vestem, atq̃ alia quæ opus sunt, That whan I haue affiauncyd her, thou delyuer money and aparayle, and all other thinges nedefull. *(Plautus in Capt. Terent. in Heau.)*
Opere maxumo, with all meanes possible, in most harty wyse. Rex Seleucus me opere orauit maxumo, vt sibi latrones cogerem, Kynge Seleucus desyred me, as moche as he possibly mought, that I wolde geate him souldiours to be aboute his persone. Thais maxumo te orabat, opere vt cras redires, Thais desyred the as hartyly as she can, that thou woldeste come agayne to morowe. *(Plautus in Milite. Terent. in Eunucho.)*

¶ O, ANTE R.

Ora, the extreme part of euery thing, as the edge, the brym, the skirtes, the hem, the border, the cabull that tyeth the shyppe.

Cra,

Ora marittima, the see fyde.
Oraculum, where aunfweres were gyuen by ydolles: fometyme the aunfwere, fomtyme the fayinge of fome wife man.
Orarium, the veftement, wherin the prieft dothe faye maffe.
Orata, a fyfhe called a gylte heed.
Oratio, an oration, a prayer.
Orator, toris, an oratour.
Oratoria, Rhetorike.
Oratoriæ, lyke an oratour, or in fourme of Rhetorike.
Oratorius, a, um, pertaynynge to an orator.
Oratus, tus, prayer.
Orbiculatus, ta, tum, made rounde.
Orbiculus, a lyttell cerkle.
Orbicus, ca, cum, rounde.
Orbis, a cerkle. Alfo the worlde.
Orbes, dyfhes, the holes of the eien. fome tyme the eyen.
Orbem facere, where people doo gather them rounde togyther in battayle.
Orbita, a whele. fometyme the tracke that wheeles do make in the grounde.
Orbo, are, to depryue.
Orbus, propreley blynde.
Orbi, they whyche haue lofte their chylderne. Alfo orphanes.
Orbitas, the lacke of chylderne: fometyme the lacke of a father.
Orbitus, ta, tum, rounde as a cerkle.
Orca, a great monfter of the fee: alfo a great veffell, as a butte or vate, wherein Rennyfhe wyne is putte. Alfo a boxe, wherin dyce be fhaken, and after throwen on the tables. fometyme a coffer, wherin womēs payntynge is kepte.
Orchades, thyrty Iles in the fee by Scotlande.
Orcheftra, a place, wherin the Senatours & honourable perfons fat to behold plays
Orchomenus, a mountayne in Theffaly. alfo a citie in Euboea.
Orcomana, a beere, wheron deade corfes doo lye.
Orcus, a ryuer of helle: alfoo an nother in Theffalye. it is fometyme taken for helle.
Ordinarius, a, um, wherin order is obferued ordinarye. fometyme a fcoffer or gefter.
Ordinare, to order or difpofe.
Ordior, iris, orfus, iri, to begynne to fpeake.
Ordo, dinis, order, the dewe place, the a ftate of menne.
In ordinem redigere, to keepe oone within his boundes, that he doo not excede his degree.

Saluftius in Iug.

Ordines, is in battayle that, whyche is callyd the raye.
Ordines feruare, to kepe the raye.

Ordinatim, in order.
Ordines conturbare, to breake or fcatter the raye.
Orea, the bytte for a horfe.
Oreus, a name of Bacchus.
Oreftes, the fonne of Agamemnon.
Ore tenus, to the mouthe.
Orexis, is mofte taken for vomyte, all be it fygnifieth appetite.
Organa, all inftrumentes of mufyke.
Organum, an inftrumente pertaynynge to buyldynge, alfo an ordinance of warres.
Organarij, makers of inftrumentes.
Orgia, ceremonies or fonges, pertaynyng to infernall goddes, or to Bacchus.
Orgyia, a meafure contaynynge vi. foote. Suidas dothe write, that it is thē fpace, whiche is conteyned betweene the handes ftretched abrode, whyche I fuppofe is a fpanne.
Oria, a fyfhers boote
Orichalcum, a mettal, whiche as I fuppofe is lattyn.
Oriculum, for auricula, a lytell eare.
Oricos, a citie of Epire.
Oriens, orientis, the Eafte.
Orificium, the mouthe of any thynge.
Origanum, an herbe, callyd organny.
Origo, ginis, a begynnynge, kynde.
Orion, a fygne in the fyrmament.
Orior, eris, & oriris, riri, to be borne, to ryfe, to appiere.
Oriundus, commen by auncetours oute of fome countrey or citie. fommetyme borne, Nati Carthagine, fed orundi a Syracufis, Borne at Carthage, but by auncetoures defcended frome Syracufe in Sicile.
Oriza, a grayne callyd Ryfe, which is moft commonly eaten in Lente, with Almonde mylke.
Orminium, an herbe lyke to horehounde.
Ornamentum, apparayle, alfo honour.
Ornithobofcion, a howfe where poultry is fedde, a cowpe.
Ornithon, thonis, a place wherein byrdes are kepte.
Orno, nare, to garnifh, to decke or trymme, to make faire, to prepare, to make meete, to honoure with fome auctoritie or dignitie.
Ornatus, ta, tum, apparayled, trimmed, garnyfhed, inftructed, fournyfhed.
Ornatus, tus, apparayl, trymming, deckyng.
Oro, orare, to praye, to demaunde, to fpeke openly and eloquently, as Oratours do, to pleade.
Orobia, a kynde of Frankynfence in lytell graynes.
Orontes, a ryuer by the cytie of Antyoche.
Orphanus, he whyche lacketh his father

and

and fatherly succour.
Orpheus, a poete, sonne of Apollo, and Calliopes.
Orpheus, a, um, of Orpheus.
Orsus, he beganne.
Orsus, he that begynneth to do a thynge.
Orsus, a, um, begonne.
Orthodoxia, the right opinion or faith.
Orthodoxus, a man of the ryghte opynyon or faythe.
Orthogonius, a ryght corner.
Orthographia, the ryght forme of writing.
Orthopnœa, a disease, whan a manne can not fetche his breathe, but holdynge his necke vpryghte.
Orthopnœci, they which haue that sicknes.
Orthostadios, a garmente, whiche was alwaye worne vngyrte.
Ortus, ti, vide Hortus.
Orti pensiles, gardeynes made on howses, or pyllours.
Ortus, ta, tum, borne.
Ortus, tus, the byrthe or natiuitie, Also the rysynge of the sonne.
Ortygia, the name of an Ile.
Ortix, tigis, a byrde callyd a quayle.
Oryx, gis, a beaste of the kynde of gotes.

¶ O, ANTE S.

Os, oris, the mouthe, also the vysage: sometyme the proporcion of all the body, sometyme countenance, also presence, and language.

Salustius in iugur.

Os distorquere, to make a mowe.
Os durum, a shamelesse knaue.
Os sublinire, to mocke or deceyue craftily, with faire wordes or promyses.
Os, ossis, a bone. Ossum, idem.

Plin. de vi. illust.

Osæ, lawes concernynge deuotion.
Osanna, I pray the saue vs.
Osasum, for Odi, I hate.
Oscedo, dinis, yanynge or gapyng. sommetyme stenche.
Osci, people in Italye.
Oscillo, are, to bowe downe.
Ocilla, lytle images of waxe to be offred.
Oscillum, a lyttell mouthe. sometyme a lyttell ymage or poppette.
Oscines, byrdes, whiche by theyr voyces do sygnifie somewhat to come or happen.
Ocinum, a generall name of byrdes, whyche do synge, a syngynge byrde.
Oscis, the abhomynable vse of carnalle synne.
Oscito, tare, to gape, as menne do for lacke of sleepe.
Oscitatio, gapynge, Also quyetenesse from laboure.

Oscitanter, softely, aduysedly, sobrely.
Oscitabundè, idem.
Osculana pugna, battaylle, wherein they, whyche were before vaynquysshed, haue the vyctorie.
Osculum, a lyttell mouthe, also a kysse.
Osculor, aris, ari, to kysse.
Osiris, osiridis, the sonne of Jupiter begot on Ncobe, the daughter of Phoroneus, which succeded Phoroneus in the kingdome of the Argiues, and afterward was kyng of Egypt, who after his death was honoured for a god.
Ossa, a bighe mountayne in Thessalye.
Osseus, a, um, bonye, or of a bone.
Osiculatim, one boone from an nother in pieces.
Ossifragus, fraga, gum, that whyche breaketh boones.
Ossilegium, a gatherynge of bones.
Ossiculum, a lyttell bone.
Ossuaria, a shryne or lyke thyng, where the bones of deed men are put.
Ostendo, di, dere, to shewe.
Ostento, ostentare, to shewe often. Alsoo to booste.
Ostentum, a thynge, whiche happeneth seldome, and betokeneth, that some strange thynge shall happen. As a blasyng sterre, thunder on a fayre daye. Sometyme it significth a thynge monstruous.
Ostento, tare, to boste.
Ostentatio, boostynge.
Ostentus, tus, a skorne.
Ostia, ostiorum, the entrees of greatte ryuers, sometyme hauens.
Ostia, a towne nyghe to Rome.
Ostiarius, a porter.
Ostiatim, from doore to doore.
Ostiensis, a lyttell hauyn at Rome.
Ostium, a doore or gate.
Ostracismus, a maner of exylynge of men atte Athenes, whyche excellyd other in power or authoritie: whyche exyle was doone by delyuerynge of oyster shelles, wherin the name of hym, whiche should be exyled, was wryten.
Ostracum, a shelle.
Ostrea, an oyster.
Ostrearius panis, Browne breadde, the whyche menne are wonte to eate with oysters.
Ostreatus, ostreata, ostreatum, harde as an oyster.
Ostrinæ uestes, garmētes of purple coloure.
Ostrum, purple or other lyke colour.
Osus, osurus, participles of Odi.
Osus sum, osus es, osus est, I hate, thou hatest, he hateth.

O, ante

¶ O, ANTE T.

Otior, swyfter.
Otior, ari, to be ydell or at reste.
Otiosus, a, um, ydell, sure.
Oriose, idelly, at leiser, surely, without care.
Otium, idelnes, vacation from labour, also leyser, reste, quietnes.
Othryades, a mans name of Lacedemonia.
Othrys, a hylle in Thessaly.
Otides, byrdes lyke to partriches.
Otus, a shryche owle.

¶ O, ANTE V.

Ovalis corona, a garlande of myrtels, gyuen to hym, whiche had vyctory without effusion of bloudde.
Ouatio, a small triumph of a prince or captayne, whiche had victorie of his enmies without slaughter of men, or where bataylc was not denounced: in the whyche tryumph the capitayne went on foote, or onely dyd ryde on a horse, with a garland of myrtelles on his heed, and his souldyours syngynge aboute hym.
Ouatus, ta, tum, whiche is in symylitude of an egge.
Ouans, ouantis, reioysynge, being ioyfull.
Ouiaria, a flocke of shepe.
Ouicula, a lyttell sheepe.
Ouifera gallina, a broude henne.
Ouile, a folde or sheepchowse.
Ouillus, a, um, of a sheepe. Ouinus, idem.
Ouis, a sheepe.
Ouo, are, to reioyce with noyse or voyce in a multitude.
Ouum, an egge.
Ouum ouo simile, one egge lyke an nother, applyed vnto theym, whiche be lyke of condicions or persone.
Ouo prognatus eodem, of oone father and mother, or brought vp vnder one maister, or in one schoole.

¶ O, ANTE X.

Oxygala, sower mylke.
Oxygarum, sharpe sawce.
Oxylapathon, sorrell.
Oxymeli, honye and vynegre sodden togyther.
Oxyporon, sharpe sawce.
Oxyporopola, he that selleth meat in sharp sauce, or sowce.
Oxysaccharum, suger and vynegre sodden togither, of somme menne called Syrupus acetosus symplex.
Oxytoca, medicines to make a womanne to brynge forth hyr byrthe quyckely.

¶ O, ANTE Z.

Ozena, soores aboute the nose, which haue an yll sauour.
Ose, stynche of the mouthe.
Ozinum, an herbe callyd basyll.

¶ P, ANTE A.

Pabularis, pabulare, pertaynynge to fourrage or meate for beastis.
Pabulatio, fourragynge.
Pabulator, a forragiour.
Pabulor, aris, ati, to goo in forragynge, somtime to fede, as a beast dothe.
Pabulum, forrage or meate for beastes.
Pacare, peasybly.
Pace tua, pace uestra, by thy lycence, by your leaue, or lycence.
Pachiri, hylles in the lasse Asia.
Pachisos, a ryuer of Sicile.
Pachynus, a mountayne in Sicile on the see syde, or an elbowe of the lande there.
Pacifer, feri, a brynger of peace.
Pacificatorius, a, um, that whiche dothe pacyfie.
Pacifico, care, to pacifie.
Pacificor, sceris, sci, to make couenaunte, to bargayne, *Plinius.*
Paco, are, to mitigate, to apease, to accorde.
Pactilis, le. platted, Pactilis corona, a platted garlande.
Pactio, an accorde, agreement. *Erasm. in Chiliad.*
Pactoliopes, excedynge rychesse.
Pactolus, a ryuer in Lydia, hauynge golden grauelle.
Pactum, sometyme a participle sygnifienge couenanted, promysed, somtime a nowne, signifienge a couenant.
Pactum transitionis, a safe conduite, to passe from one countrey to an other, a pasport. *Ti. Liuius.*
Pacuuius, the name of a noble poete.
Padua, & Patauium, a Cytie in Italye, by Uenyce.
Padus, a ryuer in Italye callyd the Po.
Padusa, a ryuer, whyche somme saye is an arme of the Po.
Pæan, an hymne in the prayse of Apollo, sommetyme the same Apollo. It is nowe taken for any hymne, made to the laude of God, or our Ladye.
Pædagium, lodgynge for seruauntes and chylderne.

Q. ij. Pæda-

Pædagogium, a bonde seruaunt.
Pædagogus, he that is appoynted to awaite on chyldern to see them well ordred.
Pædaretus, a mans name.
Pæderastes, a louer of chylderne in vnhonestie wyse.
Pæderastia, a vicious loue of chylderne.
Pædia, erudition and institution in good artes, as Gellius teacheth.
Pædico, pedicaui, pedicare, to commytte buggerye.
Pædor, pædoris, sluttysshenesse, vncleannesse, fylthe.
Pædotribes, & pedotriba, a schoolemayster.
Pæon, a foote in metre, whiche is of oone longe syllable and thre shorte.
Pæonia, an herbe callydde Pyonye. Also a countreye in Europa, and is a parte of Macedonye.
Pæsum, a citie in Lucania, where there is abundance of Roses.
Pæstanus, na, num, of that citie.
Pætus, he that loketh a squynte vpward.
Paganalia, ploughmens holyday, as wakes be nowe adayes.
Paganus, a man of the countreye, or of the vyllage: sommetyme it is taken for hym that goth not to battayle.
Pagasa, a towne of Thessaly, whiche after was called Demetrias.
Pagatim, vyllage by vyllage.
Pagina, the syde of a leafe in a boke.
Paginula, a lyttell syde of a leafe in a boke.
Pago, gis, pepigi, gere, pactus, to make couenaunt.
Pagus, a vyllage.
Pagyris, the name of a ryuer and of a citie, of whiche the people are called Pagyrite.
Pala, a spade, also a piele to put in breadde into the ouen. Also a fanne to make wind. Also the brodest parte of a rynge.
Palæ, wedges or pieces, or gaddes of mettall whan it is fyned.
Palaca, pieces of fyne golde.
Palæmon, onis, was callid a god of the see.
Palæstina, a countrey in Syrie, ioynynge to Arabie, called in holy scripture Philistiim.

Ci. de oratare primo
Palæstra, a wrastlyng place: also the exercyse of wrastlynge. It is also the comelynesse of mouynge and gesture, according to the state or degree of the person, which sheweth it.
Palæstricum, idem.
Palæstricus, a wrasteler.
Palæstricus, ca, cum, pertaynyng to wrastelynge.
Palæstrita, he that vseth wrastlynge.
Palam, openly, before men, that all menne may see it.

Palamedes, a noble greke, whyche founde certayne letters of greeke, Also to sette an arraye in an hooste, and the fourme of watches, with the watche worde.
Palange, leauers or porters, wherewith they left and beare tymbre, and suche like thynges of greatte weight.
Palango, palangare, to beare on leyuars or porters.
Palangarii, men, whyche do beare on leyuers or porters, thynges of great poyse or weyghte.
Palatiar, & palatual, a Sacrifyce doone at Rome on the hylle callyd Palatinum.

Vitruuius, li. 2.
Palatio, onis, a foundacyon made in a maryse grounde with pyles of tymber.
Palantes, they that wander about, and wote not whither to go.
Palanteum, a citie buylded on the hyll callyd Palatinus.
Palantia, a citie in Arragonia.
Palatha, a pressed frygge.
Palatim, an aduerbe sygnifienge scattered and wandrynge here and there.
Palatina officia, offices within a princes palayce or courte.
Palatinus mons, an hylle at Rome.
Palatium, a palaise of an emperour or great kynge.
Palatus, seu palatū, the roufe of the mouth.
Palea, chaffe of corne, also a gristell, whyche fallethe downe frome the necke of a cocke or capon.
Palearium, the Dewelappe of a Rudder beastie. Also a place, wherein chaffe is kepte.
Paleatus, made or myxte with chaffe.
Pales, called goddesse of shepeherdes and of pasture.
Palene, a cytie, soo called of Pallena, the daughter of Sython, and wife of Cletus.
Palepaphos, a cytie of Cypres.
Palescamander, a ryuer in Troye.
Palicenus, a fountayne in Sicilia.
Palilia, shepcherdes holydayes kept in the honour of Pales.
Palimpsestus, parchemente rased.
Palingenesia, a regeneration or second natruitie.
Palinodia, a contrarye songe, or retractynge of that, whiche oone hathe spoken or wryten: Nowe of somme menne called a recantynge.
Palinodiam canere, to retracte that, whyche one hath spoken or writen.
Palinurus, was the Mayster of the shyppe, wherin Aeneas camme into Italye. Alsoo an Elbowe, of the lande of Sycile into the See.

Paliurus, a bryer, whiche beareth a codde, wherin are thre or foure blacke sedes.
Palla, a womans gowne.
Pallace, a concubyne.
Palladium, the ymage of Pallas.
Palladius, a mans name, whyche wrote of husbandrye.
Pallancana, a sharpe oynyon, whyche causeth the eyen to water.
Palladius, a, um, that longeth to Pallas.
Pallas, antis, the sonne of Euander, somme tyme kynge of Latynes. Also a Gyant.
Pallas, adis, called goddesse of battaile, and also of wysedome.
Pallax, acis, a concubyne, suche as one kepeth in stede of his wyfe.
Palleo, lui, lere, to be pale.
Pallescere, idem.
Palliastrium, a course mantell.
Palliate fabulæ, Comedyes or enterludes made in Grecia, and the personages ther in were Grekes, as Togatæ fabulę, were enterludes in Rome, and the personages Romaynes, soo called bycause the ouermoste habyte of Grekes was called Pallium, of the Romaynes Toga.
Palliatus, cladde in a mantell.
Pallio, are, to concele or hyde.
Palliolatim amictus, cladde in a palle.
Palliolatus, idem.
Palliolum, a shorte mantelle.
Pallium, a mantelle, suche as knyghtes of the garter do weare.
Pallor, oris, a palenesse of colour.
Paluster, ris, tre, & tra, trum, of the fenne.
Palma, the palme of the hande. Also a mesure called a handbrede, sometyme an ore to rowe with. Also a palme tree or date tree. sometyme it sygnifyeth vyctorie.
Palmam prȩripere, to take the praise or honour from an other.
Palmare facinus, an acte worthy the palme or sygne of vyctorie.
Palmarium, worthye the sygne or token of vyctorie.
Palmaria spacia, a handbrede space.
Palmata, & palmaris uestis, a garmente of bawdckyn, whiche the consule dyd weare in tyme of peace, and the vyctour in tyme of warre.
Palmes, itis, the small and tender branches, moste proprely of a vyne.
Palmetum, the place, wherein date trees do growe.
Palmeus, a, um, of a palme tree.
Palmifer, & palmiger, that beareth palme, or date trees.
Palmipedalis, a measure, of a foote and a handebrede.

Palmipedes aues, all byrdes, whyche haue hole fete, as comonly al water foules haue.
Palmipes, splay footed.
Palmyra, a great castelle or fortresse in the myddell of Syria.
Palmyrena, a countrey in Syrie.
Palmo, are, to bynde togyther: Also to do any thynge with the palme of the hande.
Palmosus, full of palme trees.
Palmula, a lyttell oore or sculle. also a date.
Palmus, & palmeum, a mesure. If it be palmus maior, it is of fyue fyngers, or a hāde bredth If it be minor, it is but four fingers
Palo, are, to hedge or pale in: also to wader.
Palor, palaris, to go asonder here and there scattered.
Palpebræ, the heares whiche do growe on the cheekes.
Palpito, tare, to quake or tremble.
Palpator, toris, & palpo, ponis, a flatterer.
Palpo, & palpor, ari, to fele, also to flatter.
Paludamentum, a cote armure.
Paludatus, cladde in a cote armure.
Palumba, & palumbus, a stocke douue, or rynge douue.
Palumbarius, a certayne hawke, whiche is longe and blacke, and flieth the most part by nyghte.
Palumbes, wodde culuers.
Palus, li, a stake or pooste.
Palus, paludis, a fenne or maryse.
Pamphagi, people in Ethiopia, whiche do eate of all maner of thynges.
Pamphilia, a region in the lasse Asia.
Pampillum, a charyotte.
Pampilona, a cite in the royalme of Nauer.
Pampinarium, a heape of grene braunches. It is also the tender braunche, whyche groweth out of the harde tree.
Pampinarius, a, um, & pampineus, a, um, of grene braunches.
Pampino, are, to cutte of the small branches of a vyne.
Pampinus, a vyne leafe, or grene braunche.
Panagron, a greatte sweepe nette, whyche taketh all maner of fyshe.
Pan, panis, callyd the god of shepardes.
Panax, acis, an herbe, whiche hath a leafe lyke to the leaues of a fygge tree. Also a longe stalke mosy, and on the top a knap, wherein are sweete seedes, with a sharpe sent: and a hath a yelowe floure, and groweth in dyuers partes of Grecia.
Panarium, a pantry, where bread is kepte.
Panchaia, a region in Arabie.
Pancarpia, a garlande made of dyuers floures, or of all floures that maye be founde.
Pancraciastes, a man experte and excellente in all feates of actiuitie.

Pancra

Pancratium, exercise in all feates, as wrastlynge, rounnynge, leapynge, castynge of the barre, and other lyke exercyses of strengthe.
Pancratius, he that dothe exercyse the said feates.
Pandana porta, a gate of the citie of Rome, whiche was fyrste and laste opened, for all thynges to be brought into the citie.
Pandecta, comprehendynge all thynges: it is also the volume of the lawe ciuile, called also the digestes.
Pandiculatio, gapynge.
Pandiculor, aris, to gape as they do, which come from slepe.
Pando, didi, dere, passum, & pansum, to open
Pando, aui, are, to bowe downe.
Pandocheus, an inholder.
Pandochium, an inne, or commune lodging.
Pandus, a, um, open.
Panegyris, a mart or fayre, or great assembly.
Panegyricus, an open and solemne commendation of princis.
Pangeus, an elbowe of Thracia.
Pango, pepegi, & panxi, pangere, to set, to plante, to ioyne one thyng to an other, to fasten, to dryue in, to wryte, to singe, to tel.
Panhormus, a citie in Sicile.
Panicum, a sodayne feare, wherby somme tyme men be distraught, or oute of theyr wyttes.
Panicula, that whiche on somme herbes or trees do hange downe lyke heares, longe and rounde.
Panicum, a grayne.
Panifex, ficis, a baker.
Panificium, the crafte of bakynge.
Panis, breadde.
Panis nauticus, byskette.
Panis secundarius, raunged bread, or chete breadde, or crybell breade.
Paniscus, a god of the woddes.
Pantacratiasta, he that fyghteth with handes and feete.

Suidas. Pantathlus, he that contendeth in all maner of games.
Panneus, a, um, woullen.
Pannstularia, thynges of smalle valure.
Pannicularius, a draper that selleth clothe.
Pannonia, the royalme of Hungary.
Pannonij, Hungariens.
Pannosus, he that weareth pore apparell.
Pannuelium, a handekercher.
Pannus, clothe.
Panompheus, a name of Jupiter, sygnyfyenge that he hereth all mens voyces.
Pansa, playne footed.
Panselmos, the full moone.
Pantagia, a ryuer in Sicyle.

Pantasilea, a quene of Amazon.
Pantheon, a temple of all the goddes.
Panthera, a beaste callyd a Panter, whiche hath spottes of sondry colours.
Pantheron, a nette, wherwith all maner of foule is taken.
Pantices, a greatte bealye, also the fluxe.
Pantomimus, a dyssarde, whyche can fayn and countrefeyte euerye mannes gesture.
Panurgia, subtylitie.
Panus, panula, & panulla, a kyrnell in the share or gryne of a manne, or behynde the eare. It is also a weauers rolle, whereon the webbe of cloth is rolled or wounden.
Papare, to calle dad as a chylde dothe.
Papas, a father, as chylderne doo calle Dadde.
Papauerata uestis, a garment not pure white, but of the colour of popye.
Papauer, eris, an herbe callyd Popie.
Pape, an interiection of wondrynge, wylle ye see, a wonderfull thynge.
Papeus, in the tongue of Scithia, sygnyfieth Jupyter.
Paphlagonia, a regyon in Asia.
Paphos, & Paphia, a cytie in the ylande of Cypres.
Papia, a cytie in Lumbardy, callyd Pauia.
Papilio, onis, a butterflye.
Papilla, a lyttell wheale or pousshe in the skynne of a man. Also a cocke in a cundyte, whereout water commeth. More ouer the nyppell or teate of a womannes breaste.
Pappa, pappe made with mylke and floure.
Pappo, pappare, to eate.
Pappus, a grandesyre or grandfather. It is also an herbe called groundswell.
Papula, a whelke.
Papyrus, seu papyrum, is a great rushe, whiche groweth in the fennes & marys groundes in Aegypt and Syria, tenne cubytes hygh: wherof the fyrst paper was made, wheron men dyd write. we haue growing in our fenny groundes lyke russhes with blacke knoppes, longe and rounde, whiche are called   Nowe Papyrus is callyd paper, wherin menne doo vse to wryte or prynte bokes.
Papyratius, of paper, or of the sayd rushe.
Papyrius, the surname of a noble Romayn.
Par, ris, lyke, equalle, meete, euen, reasonable.
Pares, two lyke one to the other in fourme or degree.
Parem esse, to be sufficient, to do or sustayne a thinge.
Paria, payres, two togither of any thinge.
Paria facere, to requyte, to do one thinge for

another, lyke for lyke.

Par referre, idem.

Par pari, to recompence one thinge with another of equall estimacion.

Par impar, a game that children vsed, called euen or odde.

Parabilis, le, that which may be sone goten, or will be sone redy.

Parabola, a comparison, or resemblaunce.

Paracletus, an exhortar, a comfortar, an aduocate.

Paraclytus, a man infamed, yll reported of.

Paradiastole, a dilatinge of a mater by an interpretation.

Paradigma, an example.

Paradisus, Paradise.

Paradoxa, a sentence, contrary to the opinyon of dyuerse.

Paradromis, a galery, or walke.

Paraenesis, a precepte contaynynge an exhortation.

Paraeneticus, ca, cum, contaynynge such precepte or instruction.

Paragoge, is a figure, whan a letter or syllable, is added to a worde, as Dicier for dici.

Paragraphe, a thynge wryten before a sentence.

Paragraphus, & paragraphum, a paragrafe.

Paralipomenon, left oute, vnspoken, or vnwriten, which ought to haue bene spoken or wryten.

Paralleli, lynes in the sphere of the worlde equally distaunt, whereby the son, whan he passeth, causeth variacion in houres of the daye.

Paralysis, a sickenesse called the Palsy.

Paralyticus, he that is take with the Palsey.

Paranymphus, he that is the mediatour in matrymony betwene the man and the woman: she whiche is on the womans part is called Pronuba.

Varro. de lin. lat. Parapechium, a lyght cloke.

Parapherna, that whiche is added vnto the womannes dower, called the ioynture.

Paraphrasis, an imitation of wordes, setting oute the sence or meanynge of the autour more playnely.

Paraphrastes, he that doeth not translate worde by worde, but expresseth the sentence of the autour more openly.

Pararium aes, was double wages, gyuen to horsmen for hauinge two horsis.

Parasanga, a myle in Persya, contaynynge fifty furlonges.

Parasceue, a preparacion, also good fryday.

Parasiopesis, a figure in spekinge, whan we fayne that we will not speke, and yet couertly it is declared what we do meane.

Parasitus, a haunter of other mennes tables vncalled for, also he which to fill his bely with meate and drinke, speaketh allway to the appetyte of hym, with whome he dyneth or soupeth.

Parasitaster, he that countrefayteth him that is called Parasitus.

Parastate, certayne stones in pylars. Parastata also one of the bones in the shanke of the legge.

Parastates, stones, which do sustayne bothe sydes of a doore, called Jambes.

Paratragoedio, are, to bragge or crake, to speke grete or hyghe wordes.

Parcae, ladyes of desteny, also it signifieth the selfe destyny, or disposicion in prolonging or shortnynge lyfe.

Parco, peperci, parcere, to spare, to forgyue, or pardone, to let or prohibite, to leue, to forbeare or absteyne.

Parcere pretio, to spare for cost.

Parcere metu, to put awaye feare. *Vergilius.*

Parce, scarcely, nyggardly, nyghly, fayre and softly.

Parciter, idem. *No. Mar.*

Parcitas, frugalytie, or moderacyon in lyuynge.

Parcus, a nygarde.

Parcus, ca, cum, nighe, or nygarde, scarce in expences, sometyme it signifieth seeld.

Parcus comitatu, he that hath a smal trayne.

Parcus opera, an easy warkeman, he that is more ydell than occupyed.

Pardus, a catte of the mountayne, some take it for a Panthere.

Pardalus, a byrde of dunne colour, whyche fleyth in flockes.

Parectata, & Parectatus, he that is newly issued out of a childes yeres, and beginneth to haue the tokens of a man. *No. Mar.*

Parectonia, the mother of Plato, the moost noble philosopher.

Parens, father, mother, or any other auncetour.

Parentela, auncetry.

Parentalia, festes made at the buryenge of auncetours.

Parenthesis, is a sentence comprehendyd within another sentence, without any detriment therunto, beinge marked with one halfe circle at the begynnynge, and another at the ende, as in thiswyse. Nihil adeo principem decet, (quod omnes quidem fatentur) quantū iustitia, prudentiç, atq̃ liberalitati æqualiter coniuncta, Nothinge so well becometh a prince (which all men do confesse) as Justice equally ioyned with wisdome and bountyousnes.

Parento, tare, to celebrate the funeralles of auncetours or frendes.

Para-

Pappi, the floures of thistels, whiche be lyke fethers.
Pappous, a, um, pertaynynge to my grandfather.
Paranomasia, a figure in spekinge, where one worde is lyke to another, but of dyuers sygnifications. Nam inceptio est amentium, non amantium, this begynnynge is of madde men, not of louers.
Paratus, ta, tum, redy.
Parate, redyly.
Pareo, rui, rere, to appiere, to be seene, to obeye.
Parergon, some thinge added to, beinge no part of the matter, as whan a payntour doeth make an ymage, he doeth adde to trees, or townes.
Parethonium, a whyte colour that peynters do laye, whiche is fonde in Egypte.
Paribit, for pariet, she shall brynge forth a childe.
Parici, iuges assigned for capitall causes, as murdre or felony that requireth deth.
Paries, etis, a wall of a house.
Parieti loqueris, thou speakest to the walle, which maye be sayde of him, that will not eftsones reherce that, whyche he heryth spoken.
Parietaria, an herbe called Pelitory.
Parietinæ, olde walles.
Parilia, festiuall dayes, which the Romains kept for preseruation of their cattell.
Parilis, le, equall.
Parilitas, equalytie, symilitude in quantitie or qualitie.
Pario, peperi, parere, to bringe forth children, the lyke thinge in beastes, sometyme to bringe forth generally.
Parius, a, um, of the yle called Parus, frome whens is brought marbelle stone, called Parium marmor.
Parito, tare, to prepare.
Pariter, in lykewyse, equally, semblably.
Parma, a Targat, which foote men dyd vse.
Parmula, a bucklar.
Parnasides, the nyne muses, or ladyes of sciences.
Parnassidæ vestes, apparayle belongynge to maydens.
Parnassus, a mountayne in Grece, hauynge two toppes, vnder the whyche the nyne musis dydde inhabyte or dwell.
Paro, are, to prepare, to geate, to apparell.
Paro, onis, a lytell shyppe or hulke.
Parochus, an officer, whiche prouyded for wood and salt, for ambassadours, also it is now vsed for a preest, which is a curate, or parish preest.
Parœcia, a paryshe.

Parodus, a passage.
Parœmia, a prouerbe accommodate to the mater and tyme.
Parœci, paryshonars, or they, whiche do dwell within one parishe.
Paropsis, idis, a potage dishe, or potynger.
Paros, an yle.
Parotides, kernelles behynde the eares.
Paroxismus, the fitte in a feuer.
Parrhasia, a countrey in Grecia, called also Archadia.
Parrhasius, an excellent payntour.
Parricida, murderars of their parentes, betrayours of their countray, somtyme murdre generally.
Parricidium, murdre of kynsfolke, or traison to the propre countraye.
Patricidium, Matricidium, murdre of father and mother.
Pars, partis, part.
Partes primas agere, to playe the first part.
Partes primæ, the chiefe parte.
Parsimonia, moderate expenses.
Parsi, the pretertence of parco, I haue spared.
Parthenis, an herbe called Motherwort. *Dioscorid.*
Parthenium, is an herbe whiche hath small leues lyke to Corian der, & a floure whyte somewhat yelowe within, and hath a greuouse sauour. Some poticaryes do take it for the lasse mugwort, but I fynde not, that it is taken for feuerfue. Celsus wryteth, that it groweth on walles.
Parthenope, the olde name of the citye of Naples.
Parthia, a countraye in Asia.
Parthi, people of that countraye.
Parthicus, a, um, of the countray of Parthia.
Partiarius, a partinge felowe, or copartner.
Particeps, cipis, he that taketh part.
Participo, are, to gyue part, or take part, to make another man partner, or of counsayl.
Particula, a portion.
Particularis, re, particuler.
Particulariter, particulerly.
Particulatim, particularly.
Particulones, coheyres, or comperceners, which haue inheritaunce togither.
Partim, partly, in part, some tyme part. Partim hominum venerunt, part of the men dyd come.
Partio, onis, a byrth. *Plaut. Aul.*
Partior, iris, iri, partitum, & partio, ire, to part to deuyde.
Parthissus, a ryuer on the north part of Germania.
Partitio, a particion, or diuision.
Partitudo, for partus, the byrth of a childe.
Partus, ta, tum, goten with labour.

Partus

Parturio, iui, & rij, to labour as women do in trauayle with childe.
Partus, tus, & parti, & partuis, the byrth of a childe, sometyme the childe selfe.
Parulis, a swellynge of the goomes.
Paruifacio, cere, to set lytle by.
Parui æstimo, idem.
Paruipendo, idem.
Paruitas, the lytelnesse.
Parum, a lytle.
Parumper, a lytle whyle, or tyme, also very lytle: sometyme quickely.
Paruus, a, um, lytle.

Salustius

Paruulus, a lytell one.
Parum habere, to set lytle by.
Pasalli, pomaunders.
Pascales, shepe or pultry, whych do fede at large.
Pascha, Easter.
Paschalis, le, pertayninge to Easter.
Pasceolus, a letherbagge.
Pascito, tare, to fede.

Varro. de re rust.

Pasco, paui, pascere, & Pascito, are, to feede, to gyue meate to another, to noryshe or brynge vp, to augmente.
Pascere oculos, to content or playse the eye with the beholdinge of a thinge.
Pascor, sceris, pasci, to fede as beastes done.
Pascua & Pascuum, pasture.
Pascuus, a, um, that whych serueth to feede catell.
Pasiphae, the wyfe of Minos the kynge of Crete, who hauinge company with a bull, brought forth the monstre, called Minotaurus, whyche was halfe a man and halfe a bulle.
Passales, be as well shepe as pultry, whiche fede abrode.
Passer, eris, a sparowe, also a fisshe, called a playce.
Passerculus, a lytle sparowe.
Passili, a lytell grayne called vatches or fitches.
Passim, here and there, sometyme it signifieth frome all places, sometyme indifferently, also ouer all.
Passio, a passion, grief.
Passiuus, a, um, that which signifieth passion, or causeth passion or grief.
Passiui amatores, they whyche doo loue all women indifferently.
Passum, licour made of raysons.
Passus, a, um, spred abrode, or open.
Passus, us, a pace, which doth contayne fyue feete.
Pastillus, vel pastillum, a pasty.
Pastinaca, an herbe called parsnyps, allso a fisshe.
Pastino, are, to delue in the garden: repastino,

vide in R.
Pastinatus, tus, deluinge.
Pastinum, a debill, or settynge sticke.
Pastio, onis, pasturinge, or fedinge of catell.
Pastomis, an instrument, which is set on the nosethrilles of horsis, that will not be ruled, and is called of horsebreakers, Barnacles.
Pastophori, certayne preestis in Egypte.
Pastophorium, the chamber of the Sexten, or him which kepeth the Temple.
Pastor, oris, a sheparde or herdman.
Pastoralis, le, pertayninge to the shepharde or herdman.
Pastorius, a, um, idem.
Pastoricius, a, um, of fedynge or grasinge of catell.
Pastus, a, um, he that hath eaten.
Pastus, tus, meate, fedynge.
Patagium, a cloke of cloth of golde, vsed to be worne on riche garmentes.
Patagiati, they whyche doo weare ryche clokes.
Patagiarij, the craftysmen that maketh such clokes.
Patara, a citie in the countraye of Licia.
Patauium, a citie in Italy called Padua, nigh vnto Uenice.
Patauini, men of that citie.
Patefacio, cere, to make open, to declare, to disclose.
Patefio, fieri, to be disclosed or discouered.
Patella, a lytle panne or a skillet.
Pateo, tui, tere, to be open.
Pater, tris, a father.
Patera, a brode piece or bolle of golde or syluer.
Paterfamilias, the good man of the house.
Paterpatratus, to whome it pertaynyd, whā trues shulde be take, to receyue the othes and appoyntement of bothe partes, and was there in, chief and principall ambassadour.
Pater patrimus, he that is a father, and hath his father lyuynge.
Paternus, a, um, pertaynynge to a father.
Patesco, scere, to be open.
Pathe, troubles or vexacions of mynde, passions.
Pathetica oratio, an oration mouing the hearer to indignation or pitie.
Pathmos, an Ile in the se called Aegeum.
Patibulum, a woden lock of a dore, or a barre wherewith the doore is made fast, alsoo a place of tourment, a gybbet, galowes, or crosse.
Patientia, patience.
Patillum, a paire of tongues or other lyke instrument, wherewith coles are taken vp.

Patina

¶ ante A.

Patina, a dyſh wherein meate is caryed.
Patinarium, meate, which is ſtewed vppon a chaffynge dyſſhe.

Plautus in Aſinar.
Patior, pateris, pati, to ſuffre.
Patitor, ſuffre thou.
Patræ, rarum, a citie in Achaia.
Patrator, oris, he that doeth a thinge.
Patres conſcripti, ſenatours.
Patria, a countraye.
Patriarcha, a prince or chief man of the fathers. It was alſo the name of dignytie, of fyue chief Archebyſhoppes, as of Rome, Antioche, Alexandry, Jeruſalem, and Conſtantinople.
Patriarchatus, the dignitie of a patriarcke.
Patricida, he that killeth his father.

Plautus in Caſi.
Patricidium, the murdre of a mans father.
Patricé, nobly, or lyke a noble man.
Patricius, a ſenatours ſonne, or commen of Senatours.
Patrimonium, goodes commen by inheritaunce, patrimony.
Patrinus & Patrimis, he whiche hath his father lyuinge.
Patrinus, a, um, of the father, or pertayning to the father.
Patritus, ta, tum, that which happeneth to one by his father.
Patrius, a, um, of the countreye.
Patrizo, & Patriſſo, are, to be lyke a father.
Patro, are, to perfourme.
Patrocynor, aris, ari, to defende them, which be poure, or be falſely accuſed.
Patroclus, a noble greke, companyon to Achilles.
Patrocinium, defence of men beinge in trouble or ſuyte.
Patronymicum nomen, a name taken of an auncetour, as Priamides the children of Priamus.
Patronus, he that is aduocate on the defendauntes part.
Patrueles, coſyn germayns, or right coſyns on the fathers ſyde.
Patruus, the fathers brother.
Patruus magnus, my fathers vncle.
Patruus maximus, my grandfathers vncle.
Pattagia, a ryuer in Sicile.
Patulico, care, to be open.
Patulus, a, um, wydeopen.
Patulus bos, an oxe or cowe, whoſe hornes do ſtande wyde open.
Paucis, in fewe wordes.
Paucus, ca, cum, fewe.
Paucitas, tatis, fewneſſe.
Pauculus, a, um, very fewe.

No. Mar. Pom. Feſt.
Paucies, ſeldome.
Pauciens, idem.
Pauens, tis, he that feareth for a tyme.

¶ ante A.

Paueo, ere, to feare.
Pauera, wheate, whyche ſpringeth not well out of the hoſe whan it groweth in care.
Paueſco, ſcere, to be aferde.

Cato de re ruſt.
Pauicula, a pauynge bytell, wherewith ſtones be dryuen into the grounde in the makinge of a pauement.
Pauidus, he that allwaye feareth.
Pauidé, fearefully.
Pauimento, are, to make a pauement.
Pauimentum, a pauement, or place paued, a floore.
Pauio, ire, to ſtryke.
Pauito, tare, to be ſore aferde.
Pauliſper, a very lytle whyle.
Paulum, & Paulo, a lytle.
Paulatim, lytle and lytle.
Paulominus, lytle laſſe.

Plautus in Menech.
Paulo mox, by and by.
Paulo prius, a lytle erſt.
Paululum, very lytle.
Paululum modo, neuer ſo lytle.

Terent. in Heau.
Paululo tum erat contenta, ſhe was than content with a very lytle.
Pauo, onis, & Pauus, a pecoke.
Pauor, oris, extreme feare.
Pauper, pauperis, a poure man.
Pauper, peris, an adiectif poure.
Pauperies, & Paupertas, tatis, pouertie.
Pauper, ra, rum, poore.
Pauperculus, & paupercula, a poore man, or poore woman.
Paupero, are, to make poure.
Paupertinus, na, num, poure.
Pauſa, a pauſe, leyſour.
Pauſias, a noble payntour.
Pauſo, are, to pawſe.
Pauxillatim, by lytle and lytle.
Pauxilliſper, idem.
Pax, pacis, peace, a quiete lybertie.
Paxillus, a lytle ſtake.
Pax ſequeſtra, a truce betwene two hoſtis.

¶ P. ANTE E.

Peccatum, a ſynne, an offence.
Pecco, care, to offende or ſynne.
Pecorarius, a herdeman, alſo he that doeth hyar catell.
Pecorarius, a, um, pertayninge to catell.
Pecorinus, a, um, of rother beaſtis.
Pecten, inis, a wayuers lowme, alſo a combe. it is alſo the place aboute the pryuy membres, where heare doeth growe, it is alſo the ſtickes, wherwith a mā ſtryketh doulcemers whan he doeth playe on them, alſo a fiſhe, ſometyme a harowe.
Pectinatim, in the facion of a combe.
Pectino, to kembe, or to harowe.

Pecti=

Pectitus,ra,tum, kembyd, or harowyd.
Pecto,xui,tere, to kembe, or trymme heare, to carde woulle, to sette a harpe or other lyke instrument.
Pectoralis,le, pertaynynge to the brest. Fascia pectoralis, a brest kerchef.
Pectorium, a certayne carte sometyme vsed in Fraunce.
Pectorosus,a,um, grete brestyd.
Pectunculus, a lytell fisshe.
Pectus,toris, the brest.
Pectusculum, a lytle brest.
Pecuaria, store of catell: alsoo places where they be kept, also multitude of catell, alsoo reuenues that commeth of catell.
Pecuariam rem facere, to brede catel.
Pecuarius, a breedar of catell.
Pecuarius,a,um, belongynge to catell.
Pecu,indeclinabile. Pecua, in the plurell numbre, catell, beastes.
Peculator, & Peculatrix, he and she that stealeth a commune treasor.
Peculatus, robbery of the comune treasour, or of a prince.
Peculiaris,re, propre, or speciall.
Peculiariter, proprely, specially.
Peculio,are, to punysshe by the purse.
Peculiosus, riche, of grete substaunce.
Peculium, substaunce, that rychesse, which is onely in money and catell.
Peculor, aris, ari, to steale a commune treasour, or any thinge frome a prince.
Pecunia, money, it is taken of the olde Ciuilions, for all thynges, whyche we calle catell.
Pecuniosus, ryche.
Pecus, cudis, seu Pecus, pecoris, all maner of catell: sometyme the multitude or flocke of catell, sometyme it is taken onely for shepe or gotes.
Peda, & Pedatura, the steppe or token of a mannes foote.
Pedalis, of a foote.
Pedamen, & Pedamentum, a stake or forke, whereby a vyne, hoppes, or other lyke thinge is sustayned, or borne vppe.
Pedaneum, idem.
Pedaneus,a,um, of the quantitie of a foote, in length, or distaunce.
Pedanei iudices, inferior iuges, which went on foote.
Pedarij, were Senatours, whiche dyd not shewe their opynions in wordes, but onely meuynge them selfes towardes those personnes, whiche had raysonned, whose sentences they dyd approue, lyke as they do in the parliament house.
Pedatim, where one fote goeth with the other, foote by foote.

Pedatio, the settynge vp of vynes.
Pedato, sodaynly. *Cato.*
Pedatus, footed.
Pedem struere, to take him to his feete, to runne awaye.
Pedem referre, to retreate or go backe. *Cæsar.*
Pedem conferre, to come to a point of a mater in controuersy. *Cicer.pro Plan.*
Pedepressim, a foote pase, softly.
Pes,pedis, a foote, somtyme it is taken for al the legge, frome the thyghe to the sole of the foote.
Pedes ire, to go on foote.
Pedes, feete in metre, sometyme lyse.
Pedes, ditis, a foote man in batayle.
Pedester, he that goeth on foote, or is on foote.
Pedetentim, softely and fayre, by lytle and lytle.
Pedecosus, lousy, or full of lyse.
Pedem ponere, to begynne a mater.
Pedare, to set proppes, or to prop vp a vyne or tree, that it shal not fall or bowe downe.
Pedem reuocare, to retrayte or recule back.
Pedestris oratio, a numerouse speakynge or wrytinge in the fourme of a verse, or metre allthoughe it be not a verse.
Pedicillus, a lytle worme, whyche bredeth betwene the skynne and the flesshe.
Pediculatus,ta,tum, any thinge whiche hath a stalke, as the moost part of frute.
Pedicularis morbus, the lousy sickenesse.
Pedio,dire, to stampe with the foote.
Pediolus, a lytle foote.
Pedica, any thinge, wherewith the foote is tyed, as a fettar, a payre of gyues, or stockes.
Pedicosus, & Pediculosus, lousy.
Pediculus, a fisshe, the stalke of an apple or peare, or other frute: also a louse.
Pedissequus, & Pedissequa, a seruaunte, who foloweth allwaye the master, or mastres.
Peditatus, an hoste of footemen.
Pedo,pepedi,pedere, to farte.
Pedum, a shepecroke.
Peganon, the herbe called Rue, or herbe grace.
Pegasides, the Musis.
Pegasus, a horse, which was fayned to haue wynges: it is also a signe or numbre of sterres in heuen.
Pegma,matis, a stage, whereon pageantes be set: or whereon plate z iewels do stand to be loked on.
Peieratio, periury, a forsweringe.
Peiero,are, to swere falsely.
Peior,peius, warse.
Pelagus, the see.
Pelagicus,ca,cum, of the see.

Pela

Pelamis,midis, fisshe called Tuny.
Pelargos, a byrde called a storke.
Pelasgis, a countraye in Grece called Arcadia.
Pelasgi, people whiche came out of Grece, & inhabited Italy: they be also Arcadiens.
Pelasgicus,ca,cum, of Arcadia.
Pelias, a kynge of Thessalia, vncle to Iason.
Pelicus, a prince, of whom the people called Peligni toke their name.
Pelides, the surname of Achilles.
Peligni, people in Italy, which came out of Illiria.
Pelion, a hill in Thessalia.
Pella, a citie in Macedonia. alsoo a payle, whereinto kyne are mylked.
Pellax, acis, he that deceyueth with fayre wordes.
Pellacia, fayre speche to deceyue.
Pellex, she that is a wedded mannes harlot.
Pellicator, a deceyuer with fayre wordes.
Pellicatus,tus, the acte or lyfe of her, which companieth with a weddyd man, aduoutry on her part.
Pellicio, pellexi, cere, to deceyue with fayre wordes, to moue a man pleasauntly to do a thynge.
Pellectus, meuyd, tempted.
Pelliceus,cea,ceum, of a skynne or hyde.
Pellicula, the skynne.
Pelliculo,are, to couer with a skynne.
Pellio,onis, a skynnar.
Pellis, a skynne.
Pellitus, cladde in skynnes.
Pello, pepuli, pellere, pulsum, to put oute or expell.
Pelluceo, cere, to shyne bryght, to shyne through.
Pellucidus,a,um, very cleere.
Pellucide, clerely.
Pelluo, luere, to wasshe cleane.
Pelluuium, a bason, wherein mens fete are wasshed.
Peloponnesus, a countraye in Grece, called nowe Morea: and lyeth betwene the see called Ionium, and the see called Aegeum.
Pelops, pelopidis, whiche vaynquysshed on horsbacke in runnynge Oenomaus, father of Hippodamia, and wedded her.
Peloris, a kynde of shelfisshe.
Pelorus, a hill in Sicile on the see syde.
Pelta, a Targat or buckler, lyke an halfe moone.
Peltati, they whyche do weare suche bucklars.
Peluis, a bason.
Pelusium, a citie in Egypte.

Pom.Fest. Peminosus,a,um, stinkinge.
Penates, the gentyles called goddis of mans lyfe: they be somtyme taken for the mooste secrete partes of the house.
Penarius; & Penarium, a cellar or store house.
Pendeo, es, pependi, pendére, pensum, to hange, or be hanged, to depende, somtyme to be in payne.
Pendere animi, to be troubled in mynde, to doubte what to do, to cesse frome all other thinges, and to attende to one thynge, to be in suspence.
Pendere pœnas, to be punyshed.
Pendo,is,pependi, dere, to ponder or waye, to consyder, to esteme or value, to paye, to sustayne or suffre, looke for dependo, suspēdo, expendo, in their first lettres.
Pendulus,la,lum, that hangeth.
Pene, allmoost.
Penelope, the wyfe of Ulyxes.
Penelopes telam retexere, signifieth to do & vndo, to take moche labour in vayne.
Penes, with, or at.
Penes hunc, with him.
Penetrabilis, trabile, that maye perce, or be perced.
Penetrale, the inner part of the house.
Penetro,are, to perce.
Peneus, a ryuer in Grecia, which dyuydeth the countrayes of Elis and Achaia.
Penicella, a paynters pencell, wherewith he paynteth.
Penicillus, peniculum, & penicillum, a paynters pensell.
Peniculamentum, the hemme of a garment, the skirtes.
Peniculus, siue peniculum, any thinge whyche serueth to brusshe or wype cleane any thynge.
Penis, a tayle: also the secrete membre of a man.
Penitus,ta,tum, tayled, hauynge a tayle, also pénitus inwarde.
Penitus, an aduerbe, vtterly, to the vttermoost, farre of.
Penna, a penne, or quyll.
Pennarium, a pennar.
Penniculum, a fether.
Penniger, pennigera, gerum, that which beareth fethars.
Pennula, a lytle fether.
Pensa, that whyche is payed for a thynge bought, the payement. Pensa, in the plurell numbre, thredes of flax or woull, whan it is spunne, whyche maye be called yarne.
Pensiculaté, wayghtely.
Pensiculo,are, to ponder a thynge.
Pensilis,le, that whych hangeth, or stondeth on hyghe.
Pēsile horreū, a garnard, where corn is kept

Pen-

Pensilis homo, a man hanged.

Val.in po. Pensi nihil habere, to ponder or consyder no thynge, not to ponder or consyder any thynge.

Pensio, a pencion or yerely rent.

Pensito, tare, to ponder welle a mattier, to pay money, to make recompence.

Pensitor, a ponderer or wayer. Verborum pensitatores subtilissimi, The mooste subtyll ponderers of wordes. Gellius.

Penso, are, to ponder or way a thynge.

Pensor, oris, a wayer.

Pensus, a, um, wayed, examyned, somtyme it sygnifieth good and wyse.

Ci. de ora. Pensum, the flaxe, whyche is bounden on the distaffe, out of the whiche the threde is drawen. sommetyme it sygnifieth the threde that is spunne. It is also the execution or mynystration of an offyce. Also regarde that one hath to a thynge.

Plautus in truculen. Pensilis hortus, a gardeyne made vpon the roufe of a house, or vpon pyllars.

Pensilis vrbs, a citie standynge on vaultes.

Pentaphillon, seu pentepatalon, an herbe called cinkefoyle, whiche hath fyue leaues.

Pentapolis, a countray betwene Palestina and Arabia, wherin were the cities of Sodom and Gomor, bourned by the vengeance of god for synne agaynst nature.

Pentacontarchus, a captayne of fyfty men.

Pentarchus, he that is captayn of fyue men.

Pentateuchus, the volume of the fyue bookes of Moyses, that is to saye, Genesis, Exodi, Numeri, Leuiticum, Deuteronomium.

Pentathlus, he that exercyseth any of these fyue games, castynge of the ball, or tryndell, runnynge, leapynge, wrastlyng, and throwynge the darte.

Pentecoste, whytsontyde.

Pentesilea, a queene of Amazon, whyche was slayne at the syege of Troye.

Pentimimeris, is a parte of a verse, where a sentence is fynyshed in the fyrste syllable of the thyrde foote.

Pentorbon, an herbe callyd also peony.

Penula, a Cloke, worne whanne hit raynethe.

Penularium, a cloke bagge.

Penulatus, cloked.

Penuria, extreme necessitie, penurie.

Penus, penoris, & penum, & penu, & penuarium, a storehouse. Sometyme store or prouysion of vytayles.

Plautus in Aulularia. Penussime, vtterly.

Peonia, an herbe callyd pronie, whyche beareth a redde floure, and great rounde sede, wherin is meruailous vertue against the fallyng euylle.

Peplus, uel peplum, a kerchiefe or other lyke couerynge of the heed.

Peperci, I haue spared, or forborne, or pardoned.

Pepigi, & pupugi, the preter tence of pungo. Also pepigi is the preter tence of pango. Pepigit foedus, He made a league or alyaunce.

Pepo, onis, a Melon.

Per, sygnyfyeth by, ioyned with an nother worde it sygnyfyeth perfection. Perpulchrum, Uerye fayre. Pergraue, Uerye greuouse. Per ætatem, for or by reasone of his age.

Peptica, medycines, whiche do make good concoction in a man, that the meate eaten, maye digeste welle. Also salues and oyntementes, whyche doo make impostumes rype.

Pera, a scryppe or bagge.

Perago, egi, agere, to perfourme, to make perfyte, to consyder, to drawe or cause to be drawen with force.

Peragere reum, to accuse one, and to sewe hym to a condemnation.

Peragro, are, to walke or go about a place.

Peramo, are, to loue well.

Peranno, annare, to contynewe or lyue ouer yere.

Perardeo, dere, to bourne out or throughe.

Perareo, ere, to drie vp, to be very drye.

Peraro, rare, to tylle all through.

Perbelle, very well, ryght well.

Perbibo, bibere, to quaffe or drynke all out.

Perbitere, for præire, to go before. Plautus in Pom. Fest. Cicer. ibi.

Per causam, for a cause.

Percedere, to departe.

Percello, li, ere, to stryke and ouerthrowe.

Percino, nere, to synge stylle, to contynewe syngynge.

Perclam, verye pryuyly.

Perduaxo, for perdo.

Peredia, a meale, where men eate hugrely.

Percipio, cæpi, cipere, to perceyue, to take, or receyue.

Percitus, styrred.

Percoarcto, are, to bryng into a lytel roume.

Percolo, ui, ere, to worshyp moche.

Percontor, aris, ari, to serche.

Percudo, di, dere, to breake.

Percussus, & percussus, stryken.

Percunctor, aris, ari, to inquire, to demande.

Percuro, are, to heale perfytely.

Percurro, rere, to runne apace, to runne by.

Percutio, cussi, tere, to stryke, or smyte.

Perdite, extremely.

Perditus, ta, tum, loste, peryshed, withoute recouerie, out of hope.

Perdius, abydynge all the day, or watching

all the day, or he whiche doth any thynge in the daye tyme.

Perdix, dicis, a partryche.

Perdo, didi, dere, to lose, to flee.

Perduco, duxi, ducere, to brynge to an ende, to brynge or leade by force.

Perduellio, onis, treason agaynst the king, or the countrey. Also a traytour.

Perduellis, an ennemye.

Peredo, edi, edere, to eate moche.

Peregre, out of a mannes propre countrey. Peregre uado, I go out of the countreye, or on pylgremage. Peregre uenio, I come out of straunge countrayes, or from pylgremage.

Peregrinor, aris, ari, to go into strange countreys, or on pylgremage.

Peregrinus, a straunger or alyen.

Perendie, the daye nexte after to morowe.

Perendinus dies, idem.

Perennis fluuius, a course of water that cometh with rayne, or a brooke that is only made with rayne.

Perenniter, contynually.

Perennis, ne, perpetuall, euer durynge.

Perennitas, tatis, contynuaunce, longe abydynge.

Perenno, are, to dure or contynue.

Pereo, iui, uel ii, ire, to be loste or consumed, also to dye.

Pererro, are, to go or ryde al aboute.

Perfacul, the auncient wryters vsed for facile, lyghtly.

Per fas & nefas, by ryght or wronge, by one waye and other.

Perfecté, perfitely.

Perfectus, a, um, perfytte, accomplysshed, optayned.

Terent. in Eunucho. Perfector, toris, he that bryngeth a thynge to passe, or to a poynte.

Perfero, tuli, ferre, to brynge in conclusion. Also to brynge or telle tidinges, somtime to suffre or endure.

Perficio, cere, to accomplyshe, to brynge to a poynte, to optayne.

Perfidiosus, a, um, full of disloyaltie.

Perfidiosé, disloyally, trayterously.

Perfido, dere, to truste moche.

Perfidus, false of promyse, he that dothe any thynge against the trust that is put in him, disloyall.

Perfidia, falsehode against promyse or trust, disloyaltie.

Perfidus, very trustye.

Perfines, for perstringas, strayne thou hard.

Pom. Fest. Perflatus, a great blaste of wynde.

Perflo, are, to blow vehemently or strongly.

Perfluo, xi, fluere, to rune out as water doth out of a broken vessell.

Perfodio, dere, to bore or perce through, to stryke through, to dygge through, or to the bottome or depest of any thynge.

Perfore, to come well to passe.

Perforare, to perce, or to make an hoole throughe.

Perfortiter, myghtily.

Perfossus, a, um, perced through, stryken or dygged through.

Perfracté, obstynately.

Ci. offic. 3i Perfrigefacio, perfrigefacere, to make very colde.

Perfrico, care, to rubbe moche.

Perfricuit faciem, aut frontem, aut os, Is in a prouerbe as moche to saye, as he hath layde aparte shame, or he is shamcles, or without abashement.

Perfricté frontis, withoute shaame or honestye.

Perfructus est, he hathe taken the fruite or pleasure of a thynge, he hath vsed or exercysed a thynge, or hathe lefte the vse or exercise therof.

Perfruor, perfructus, perfretus, aut perfruitus, perfrui, to take all the profyte or commoditie, to take pleasure or recreation in any thynge.

Perfuga, he that fleeth to the contrary part in battayle, or forsaketh his capitayne.

Perfugio, gere, to rounne vnto oone for succour.

Perfugium, a place, wherevnto a manne runneth to haue succoure, or to be kept frome daunger: It is also taken for anye thynge, whereby a manne maye be succoured.

Perfunctorié, passynge ouer lyghtely.

Perfunctorius, a, um, that whyche passethe lyghtly away, or tarieth not longe.

Perfunctus, he that hath doone diligently his offyce or duetie.

Perfundo, perfudi, fundere, to poure out, or droppe out, or fylle oute. Perfunditq; ge- Ouidius. nas lachrimis, The teares dropped downe on his chekes.

Perga, a towne in Pamphilia, wherof Diana was called Pergea.

Pergama, orum, the towers of Troy.

Pergamena charta, parchement.

Pergamum, siue Pergamus, a Cytie in Asya, the countrey of Galene, the famous Phisycion.

Perge, go to, passe forthe.

Perge in virum, playe the man, goo to lyke a man, go to hardily.

Pergin? wylte thou not leaue? wylte thou not be gone.

Pergrandis, de, very great.

Pergo, perrexi, pergere, to go, to procede,

to endeuour to do a thyng, to continue, to make haaste, to assaye. Ire perrexi, I endeuoured to go. Suspenso gradu placide ire perrexi, I assayed with a lyght pase to go softely. *Terent. in Phorm.*

Pergræcor, aris, ari, to be ryottous, in eatynge, drynkynge, and hauntynge harlottes.

Pergraue, very greuousely.

Pergula, a galerye, propicly where it is open on bothe sydes. It is also the place in a shyppe, wherein menne doo walke. Also a vyne raysed in the fourme of an herber. Sommetyme the companye of warkemenne, obeyenge to the chyefe warkeman.

Perhibeo, ere, to say, to gyue, to set a price. Prætium perhibere.

Perhibere testimonium, to beare wytnesse.

Perhibere uerba, to saye.

Perhorreo, rere, to be sore aferde.

Perhorresco, idem.

Perhumane, & perhumaniter, right gentilly.

Periander, oone of the seuen wyse menne of Grecia.

Periclimenon, an herbe callyd woodbynde.

Pericles, a noble man of Athenes, in whom was a naturall eloquence incomparable.

Periclitor, aris, ari, to be in peryl, also to experyence or proue a thynge.

Periculosus, a, um, daungerous.

Periculum, peryll or daunger. somtyme experience or profe.

Periculum facere, to proue.

Perhiodus, a clause, a circute in wordes, or contynuance in speakynge.

Perhiodicę febres, feuers, whyche come by courses or fyttes.

Perillus, was an artifycer, which made a bul of brasse wherinto (being glowing hotte) men shuld be put, that in tourmentynge of them, by theyr crienge, a noyse shulde issue out lyke the mowynge or belowynge of a bulle, the whiche engine whanne Perillus hadde gyuen to Phalaris, the crucll tyraunt, he caused the craftes manne to be fyrste putte into it, to proue his owne experience.

Perimo, emi, imere, to kylle.

Peremptus, ta, tum, kylled.

Peridoneus, a, um, very meete.

Periegesis, a compasse or cyrcuyte.

Perii, I am loste or distroyed.

Perii animo, my harte or courage is gone.

Perire mulierem, to loue a womanne feruentely.

Perinde, soo, in lyke wise, euen lyke, verye moche, euen as, in this facion.

Perinthus, a cytie of Thrace, whiche nowe is called Heraclia.

Periodicus, ca, cum, that goethe and commeth by courses.

Periodica febris, a feuer, whiche commeth by courses, as tercians and quartanes.

Periœci, companions or dwellers togyther in one house.

Peripatasma, the hangyng of a house, with tapisrye or other lyke thynge.

Peripateticus, a philosopher of Aristotels secte or opinion.

Peripheria, a cyrcumference.

Periphrasis, circumlocution, one word expressed by many.

Periplorema, a fygure, whanne a part of a sentence nothynge necessary, is added vnto a verse.

Peripneumonia, syckenesse of the lounges with the coughe.

Peripneumonicus, he whyche hathe that disease.

Peripsema, matis, the powder or dust that commeth of fylynge or shauynge of mettalle or wodde.

Periscelis, idis, sloppes, whyche womenne were wont to weare.

Perissologia, a superfluous speakynge.

Peristeræ, house culuers or doues.

Peristereon, a culuerhouse.

Peristerotrophium, idem.

Peristroma, tapesry, or couerlyds of Aras or Verdure.

Peristylium, a place set about with pyllers.

Perito, tare, to peryshe or be loste.

Perithous, the companyon of Theseus.

Peritia, cunnynge in any science.

Peritus, cunnynge, perfyte in a science.

Periuro, rare, to sweare vntrewely, to be periured. *Plautus in Bacch. Plautus in truculen.*

Periuriosus, a manne whiche is often forsworne.

Periurus, forsworne, periurid.

Periurium, periurie.

Perizoma, matis, a breeche.

Perizonium, a corse or brode gyrth, wherwith maydens were wont to be gyrte vnder their pappes.

Perlego, legere, to rede ouer all.

Perlecebra, a thynge whiche pleasauntlye draweth a man to fauoure it.

Perlepidus, perlepida, perlepidum, veray fayre.

Perliberalis, very lyberall.

Perlibro, to waye diligentely.

Perligo, gare, to bynde harde or faste. *Colum. 4.*

Perlitus, ta, tum, anoynted harde.

Perloquor, qui, to speake out all to an ende, to speake perfytely.

Perlucidum, & pellucidum, cleere, that a man

P ante E.

manne may see through, as water, glasse, horne.
Perluo, luere, to washe ouer or all.
Perlustro, strare, to beholde all aboute.
Permadesco, to be moche wette, or to be made very moyste.
Permadefacio, cere, to make verye moyste, or to wette moche.
Permagnus, a, um, verye greatte.
Permano, & permanesco, are, & nescere, to be disclosed, knowen, or diuulgate.

Plautus. Permaneo, mansi, nere, to abyde.
Permano, are, to runne all ouer, or to fall in to, to be declared openly.

Ti. Liuius. Per manus traditum, that whyche is lefte from one to an other, or is taught by one to an other: As the father telleth or leaueth to his sonne, and he to his sonne, and so contynually by lyne.
Permaturesco, scere, to be through rype.
Permerdo, to defyle ouer all.
Per me, aut re, aut illum, aut aliquid aliud stare, whanne we, or anye other thynge is the cause, that a thynge is not doone.

Plinius. Omnia iam parata erant, nisi per eum stetisset, Nowe al thynges were redy, if by his occasyon it had not be lette.
Permessus, aut permessis, ssidos, a Ryuer in Grece, dedicate to the Muses.
Permisceo, permiscui, miscere, to myxte all togyther.
Permissio, a suffraunce.
Permitto, misi, mittere, to suffre, to yelde, or delyuer, to thraste in, to throwe downe, to committe, to sende forthe, to let downe, as to lette downe one by a rope, or other lyke thynge.
Permulceo, cere, to appease, addoulce, or mytigate a mans displeasure.
Permulti, very many.
Permuto, mutare, to chaunge oone thynge for an nother.
Permutatio, an exchaunge.
Permutator, he that exchaungeth.
Perna, the pestyll and also the gammonde of bakon.
Perniciabilis, pernicialis, & perniciosus, causynge deathe, mortall.
Pernicies, deathe.
Pernicitas, swyftenesse.
Pernitior, tius, wars, more dangerous, more full of myschiefe.
Pernicissimus, cissima, mum, warste, mooste daungerouse.
Perniciter, dangerously, myscheuously.
Pernio, onis, a kybe on the heele.
Perniunculus, a lyttell kybe.
Pernix, cis, swyfte, flyghty, sometyme stubborne, also deedly.

Pernocto, noctare, to tarye all the nyghte, to watche, to praye, to reste, to walke, to stande, to dwelle, to slepe, to lye oute of his owne house.
Pernosco, scere, to knowe perfectly.
Pernumero, are, to telle oute money.
Pernox, all nyghte.
Pero, onis, a showe of rawe lether, Also a sacke.
Perogiganus, perogita, he that putteth a stalyon to the mare, to season her.
Peroleo, to fauour or stynke moche.
Peronatus, he that weareth rawe lether shoen, boteux or cokers lyke a plough man.
Perorior, iris, re, to begyn, spryng, or growe by the occasion of some thynge.
Peroro, are, to speake or raison to an ende, to reason perfectly, somtyme to moue the herers to indignation.
Peroratio, the last part of an oration, wherin the affectes of the herers are chiefelye styrred.
Perrori, a people of Aethiopia.
Perosus, sa, sum, extremely hated.
Perpaco, care, to sette all thynge in peace.
Perparum, very lyttell.
Perparce, very scarsely, verye nyghely, or nygardely.
Perpasco, perpaui, perpascere, to feede to the vttermooste.
Perparuus, a, um, a very lyttell one.
Perpaucus, ca, cum, very fewe.
Perpauxillus, a, um, idem.
Perpauefacio, pauefeci, facere, to make sore affrayde.
Perpello, perpuli, perpellere, to constrayne, to moue or induce one to do a thynge.
Perpendicularis, are, that is directly downe ryghte.
Perpendiculum, a plumlyne, such as masons and carpenters haue, with leadde at the ende, whereby they doo proue the euennesse of their squares.
Perpendo, dere, to examin, also to confyder.
Perpensé, aduisedly, with a consideration.
Perperam, amysse, ouerthwartely, vnhappily, wrongefully.
Perperi, fooles, idiotes, shrewes, lyers.
Perperitudo, shrewdenes, foolyshenes.
Perpero, are, to marre a thynge.
Perpes, perperis, perpetuall
Perpessus, he that suffreth with moch peyn.
Perpetim, perpetually.
Perpetro, trare, proprely to doo or to committe an acte good or ylle.
Perpetuo, are, to continue without ceassing.
Perpetuus, petua, petuum, perpetuall euerlastynge, contynualle, holl, not in porcyons or dyuyded.

Quint.

Perpes

P ante E.

Perpetior, perpeti, to suffre pacientely, to endure.

Perpeto, perpetere, to aske importunately without ceassynge, to perfourme.

Perpetratio, an acte good or badde.

Perpetuitas, eternitie, an euerlastyng contynuaunce.

Perpetuum, & perpetuó, aduerbes, sygnifienge continually, alway, for euer.

Perplaceo, perplacui, perplacere, to content very moche.

Perplector, perplecteris, plecti, to bynde or twyste harde or faste, to meddle so togyther, that a manne can not know what the thynge meaneth.

Perplexé loqui, to speake nowe one thyng, nowe an other, that a manne wotteth not what he meaneth.

Perplexim, idem.

Perplexor, aris, ari, to speake doubtefullye, as wordes, wherin are two intendementes. At scio, quo vos pacto soleatis, perplexarier, pactum, non pactum est, Non pactum, pactum, est, quod vobis lubet, well, I knowe wel ynough, in what facion you are wonte to speake, that a manne canne not telle howe to take you: It was promysed, It was not promysed, It was not promysed, It was promysed, euen as hit lysteth you. *(Plautus in Aulularia.)*

Perplexabile, a worde spoken, whych hath twoo dyuers vnderstandynges, or that whyche is one thynge in herynge, an nother in vnderstandynge.

Perplexabiliter, doubtefullye.

Perplexus, plexa, plexum, perplexed, twysted togyther, or harde to be lowsed, intrycate, doubtefull.

Perpluit, perpluere, to rayne in the myddell of a howse.

Perplus, moche more.

Perpol, an othe, sygnyfyenge by Pollux. Sommetyme the worde Per, dothe pertayne to the wordes folowynge. Perpol quam paucos reperias meretricibus fideles euenire amatores, By God thou fyndeste verye fewe trewe louers happen to commune womenne. where per belongethe to quam paucos, and not to Pol. *(Terent. in Hecyra.)*

Perpoto, perpotare, to drynke all day, or to drynke stylle, or contynually, or vntyl one be drunke.

Perpotatio, a contynuaunce in drynkynge, drunkerye.

Perpulcher, perpulchra, perpulchrum, verye fayre.

Perpulchre, verye well done. *(Plautus in Stich.)*

Perprurisco, perpruriscere, to haue a greate ytche, or desyre to clawe or scratche.

Perpurgo, gare, to make all thynge cleane, or nette.

Perputo, perputare, to declare al. Nunc operam date, ut ego argumentum hoc uobis plane perputem, Nowe take ye hede, that I maye playnly declare al this matter vnto you. *(Plautus in Cistel.)*

Perquàm, added to any nowne adiectiue, augmentethe his power. Perquàm doctus, Verye well lerned. Perquàm stolidus, very foolyshe.

Perquiro, quisiui, quirere, to make dilygente serche, to examyne.

Perraro, very selde.

Perrepto, tare, to goo softely, or with moche peyne.

Perrideo, perrisi, perridere, to lawgh hartlye.

Perrisio, sere, to scorne, to laugh at one, or to make an nother to laugh. *(Perottus.)*

Perrogo, gare, to desyre hartily.

Perrumpo, rupi, rumpere, to breake on sonder, or in the myddes.

Persa, a manne or woman of the countrey of Persia.

Persæpe, verye often.

Persancté, veraye deuoutelye, or solempnely.

Perscribo, perscribere, to wryte a thynge throughe, or to an ende, to regyster or inrolle a thynge.

Perscriptio, a deede of a mans owne wrytynge.

Perscrutor, scrutari, to serche or inquyre dilygentely.

Persefacul, the olde and auncyente writers vsyd for perfacile, verye lyghtely, or verye casyly. *(Pom. Fest.)*

Persenex, persenis, verye olde.

Persentisco, scere, to perceyue well.

Persephone, the Surname of Proserpina, and sygnyfyeth the vertue of seedes in spryngynge.

Persepolis, a Cytie in the countreye of Persya.

Persequor, eris, qui, to pursewe, to contynue in that, whiche is begonne, to persecute, to be auenged.

Persero, perseui, perserere, to sowe aboute, or abrode.

Perseuerantia, a stable abyding in any thing reasonable.

Perseueranter, constantely.

Perseuéro, rare, to contynewe with a stedfaste mynde.

Perseus, a noble knyghte, whyche delyuered a fayre lady callyd Andromeda frō a whale, and also slewe Medusa, whyche

R.iij. tour-

tourned men into stones. Also it is a signe amonge the sterres.

Persia, a countreye in the easte parte of the worlde, where nowe Sophy reigneth.

Persica poma, a fruite callyd peaches.

Persicus, ca, cum, of Persia.

Persideo, dere, to sytte by.

Persisto, stere, to abyde.

Persoluo, uere, to pay truely, to paye all, to accomplyshe.

Persoluere grates, to gyue thankes.

Persolus, alone, without companye.

Persona, a vysour lyke to a mans face. also person or personage, amonge dyuynes and late philosophers: somtyme the qualitie of a man.

Personatus, a masker, or he that weareth a visour.

Seneca Personata fœlicitas, a counterfayte felicitie.

Personata uulnera, hydden woundes.

Personata, an herbe, whyche groweth by the water syde, hauynge great brode leaues lyke gourdes, but that they be greater & harder: I suppose it to be the herbe, which in some countrey is called Donye.

Personatus, tus, a maske.

Persono, personare, to sowne oute, or sowne perfectely.

Plautus in Milite. Perspecto, tare, to loke well aboute.

Perspicacitas, tatis, quyckenesse of syghte, consyderation.

Perspicace, aduysedly, with good consyderation.

Perspicaciter, idem.

Cl. de of. l. Perspicientia, persyte knowlege.

Perspicue, cleerely, openly.

Perspicax, acis, he that seeth quyckely, and doth all thynges with consyderation.

Perspiceo, spexi, spicere, to se or vnderstand playnely.

Perspicuitas, tatis, clerenesse, propzelye in wordes or sentences, easynesse.

Perspicuus, a, um, clere, playne, easye.

Perspisso, an aduerbe, very late.

Plautus. Perstino, are, to sette a pryce on a thynge.

Persto, as, stiti, stare, to abyde fyrmely.

Perstrepo, pui, ere, to make a great noyse.

Perstrictores, iugglers.

Perstringo, perstringere, to wrynge harde, to towche a thynge shortely in speakynge or wrytynge, to dull or darke with to moche lyght. Perstringere aures, to fylle the eares with noyse. Perstringere nomen aut famam, to gyue a man an ylle name.

Horatius. Persuadeo, persuasi, persuadere, to induce one to beleue or truste, to aduyse, to styre vehemently.

Persuasibile, & persuasibiliter, in suche wyse as it may perswade.

Persuasor, oris, a perswader or inducer to do a thynge.

Persuastrix, a woman, whiche inducethe or moueth one to do an acte. *Plautus in Bacch.*

Persuo, ere, to sowe vp all.

Pertedeo, dere, & pertedescere, to be verye weerye.

Pertego, tegere, to couer all.

Per tempus, in tyme conuenyent, in season.

Pertendo, dere, to extende.

Pertento, tare, to tempte, to assay or proue moche.

Pertero, triui, terere, to rubbe or frotte a thynge.

Perterreo, rui, perterrere, to make aferde.

Perterrefacio, cere, idem.

Pertesus, displeased, annoyed. Sermonis pertesus, werye of the communication. Pertesus ignauiam suam, displeased for his slouthefulnesse. *Plaut. in Mostell. Suetonius in Cæsar.*

Pertexo, texi, texere, to make an ende, to conclude, propzely to wayue out, or to weaue perfectely.

Pertica, a staffe, a cogell, a perche or polle, wherwith grounde is mette.

Pertimeo, & pertimesco, pertimescere, to feare moche.

Pertinatia, obstinacye, perseuerance.

Pertinaciter, obstynately.

Pertinatius, more obstynatelye.

Pertinax, acis, obstinate, he that holdith fast.

Pertinatior, pertinacissimus, more and moste obstynate.

Pertingo, tingere, to touche moche, to ioyn harde vnto a thynge.

Pertisum, olde writers vsed for pertesum.

Pertolero, rare, to indure to the ende, to sustayne valyantely.

Pertondeo, dere, to clyppe or sheare all.

Pertraho, xi, here, to drawe to with force.

Pertranseo, siui, & sii, ire, to passe throughe.

Per transennam inspicere, to loke on a thing ferre of, or on parte, and not all.

Pertundo, tudi, tundere, to stryke harde, or breake a thynge in strykynge.

Pertundo, pertusi, pertundere, to beate with hammers.

Pertineo, nui, nere, to pertayne or belonge, to be ioyned to.

Perturbo, are, to trouble moche.

Perturbatio, a trouble of mynde.

Perturbate, with trouble of mynde.

Pertusa uasa, vesselles cracked or broken in somme parte.

Peruade,

Peruado, peruasi, uadere, to go ouer all.

Peruagor, ari, to wander aboute.

Peruello, elli, ellere, to plucke, sometyme to pricke.

Perue-

P ante E.

Peruenor, ari, to hunt ouer all.
Peruenio, uenire, to come to a place or to an ende.
Peruersus, a, um, frowarde.
Peruerse, maliciousely, myschieuously, ouerthwartly.

Plautus in Merca. Peruerse vides, thou seest naughtyly.
Peruerto, to make yll, to peruerte, or depraue.
Peruestigo, gare, to fynde in sekynge.
Peruestigator, oris, he that seketh or loketh for a thinge.
Peruicax, cacis, harde ouerthwart, yll to intreate, stubbourne, obstinate, sometyme constaunt.

Noni. Peruicacia, obstinacy: but sometyme it is vsed in a good part, and taken for a perseueraunce and constancy in a good act. Pertinacia allwaye in an yll part.
Peruicatior, oris, more obstynate, more stubbourne: sometyme more constaunt.
Peruicaciter, obstinatly, stubbournly, constauntly.

Actius in No.Mar. Peruico, for Peruicaci.
Peruigil, lis, he that watcheth. alsoo diligent and industriouse.
Peruigilium, moche watche: alsoo watchinges, or vigiles before solemne dayes.
Peruigilo, are, to watche all nyght.

Pacuuius in No.Mar. Peruinco, uici, uincere, to surmounte.
Peruitere, the olde wrytars vsed, for perire, to be lost, to peryshe.

Plautus in Cap. Peruiuo, uixi, uiuere, to lyue longe, or vntyll the vttermoste. Et si peruiuo vsq; ad summam ætatem, tamen breue spacium est perferundi, quæ minitas mihi: Althoughe I lyue yet to the vttermooste age, yet is the tyme lytle to suffre all: wherewith thou thretteste me.
Peruius, uia, uium, that maye be gone in, penetrable.
Peruolo, are, to flee oute, or to the ende.
Peruoco, care, to call them all.
Peruro, ussi, urere, to burne all, or euery where.
Peruolo, peruelle, to desyre.
Perula, a lytell bagge or scrippe.
Perusia, a citie in Italy.
Peruulgatus, ta, tum, commonly vsed or knowen.
Pes, pedis, a foote, whiche now contayneth xii. ynches, the olde foote contayned. xvi. fyngres bredeth.
Pessinus, nuntis, a towne in Phrigia.

Qu. Curti. Pedes, & Pedibus, put for an aduerbe, signifieth on foote. Pedes agmen circuibat, the hoste went about on foote. In agmine non nunquam equo, sæpius pedibus anteibat,
Suetonius in Cæs. In the hoste, he wente allwaye afore,

P ante E.

sometyme on horsebacke, but moore often on foote.
Pedibus stipendia facere, to be a foote man in warres.
Pes, a louse: allsoo a corde, wherewith the sayle in a shyp is bent.
Pesnas, olde wrytars vsed for pennas. *Pom.Fest.*
Pesestas, in olde tyme vsyd for Pestis, Pestilence. *Pom.Fest.*
Pessum eo, ire, to go backewarde, to be lost or destroyed, to be nowght set by.
Pestifer, & Pestiferus, a, um, that which bringeth in Pestilence.
Pestilens, tis, pestilent, vnholsome.
Pessulus, a barre or bolt, wherewith doores or gates be made fast.
Pessum, an aduerbe, which signifieth backewarde, downewarde, vnder foote.
Pessundo, dedi, dare, to cast vnder foote, to put to the warse.
Pestis, Pestilentia, & Pestilitas, a pestilence, a mortalitie of men.
Petalum, a leafe.
Petasatus, he that weareth a hatte.
Petaso, onis, a flitche of bakon.
Petasus, a hatte, a rounde kouerynge of a house.
Petaurista, a propre daunser.
Petaurum, a corde, or a staffe, or a bourde, or other lyke thinge, whereon lyghte personages do daunce and proue maistryes. it is also a rouste, where pultry doeth syt in the nyght. *Iul.pol.*
Petesso, sere, to aske or require.
Petigo, tiginis, a tettar that runneth ouer all a mannes face.
Petilansura, the howse of a whyte horse.
Petilara, thinges that are drye. *Pom.Fest.*
Petilus, la, lum, smalle.
Petilius, a floure whyche groweth amonge brembilles, in the later ende of somer, and is lyke a wylde rose in coloure, and hath fyue small leues, the budde of dyuerse colours, hauynge within it yelowe sedes. *Plinius.*
Petimen, a sore in the shoulders of beastes, which I suppose is a fassion. *Pom.Fest.*
Petitia, a certayne kynde of appulles.
Petisso, sere, olde wrytars vsed for Peto, to aske or demaunde. *Peto.*
Petitor, toris, he that asketh or demaundeth: amonge lawyers he is called the demaundaunt: also it is a beggar, which asketh almes from doore to doore.
Petoritum, a chariot or wagon.
Petiolus, a lytle foote: also a perche wheron frutes or onyons be hanged.
Petitio, onis, a petition.
Peto, petij, petere, to aske, to gette or attayn, to desyre, to laye awayt, to abide, to strike,
to go

P ante E.

to go to a place, to seke. Petere gladio, to stryke with a sworde. Petere veneno, to poyson. Petere blandicijs, to flater. Petere tactu, to feele. Petere mutuum, to borowe: also to remembre. Petere iugulum, to kill, to folowe. Petere auribus, to heere. Petere naribus, to smelle. Petere oculis, to behold. Petere osculis, to kisse. Petere vi, to inforce. Petere, is also to assayle or make assault on one.

Pom. Fest. Petra, a stone.
Petrones, Carles of the countraye: also a wether shepe.
Petroselinum, an herbe called Persely.
Petulans, tis, wanton dishonest, reprocheful, prowde, viciouse, redy to do wronge.
Valla in Rauden. Petulantia, wantonnesse, viciousnesse, pryde.
Petreus, a, um, of a stone.
Petrileon, an oyle, which naturally runneth out of a stone.
Petrosus, a, um, stony or full of stones.
Petulanter, wantonly, proudly.
Petus, he that hath one eye lasse than the other.
Petulcus, wanton.
Pexo, are, to kembe.
Pexæ vestes, Some men in expoundynge Pliny, do suppose Pexas vestes, to be of suche thynge, as is shorne, as fyne woullen clothe, or veluet.
Pexati, they which do weare suche maner of cloth, or sylke.
Pezitæ, mousherons, growynge at the rootes of trees.

¶ P, ANTE H.

Phæaces, people of the Ile of Corcira.
Phæcasius, a shoo.
Phædra, the wyfe of Theseus, & stepmother to Hypolytus.
Phaeton, the sunne.
Phagedæna a, runnyng cancre or pock, whiche shortly eateth the flesh vnto the bones.
Phagones, greate eaters.
Phalacron, bolde.
Phalacrocorax, acis, a water crowe, it maye signifie a coote.
Affranius. Phalango, gare, to moue or dryue a thynge vppon rollers.
Phalaris, a cruell tyraunt, which raigned in the citie of Agrigentum.
Phagus, a beeche tree.
Phagineus, a, um, of beeche.
Phalangæ, staues, whereon men doo carye packes, playne staues, also leauars, to lifte thinges that be heuy.
Phalangarij, portars, whyche doo carye packes.

P ante H.

Phalangium, a spyder.
Phalanx, angis, an hooste of footemen, sette in suche order, that they maye incountre with their ennemyes, foote to foote, man to man, shylde to shylde. It is also the beame of a balaunce.
Phalanges, are the ioyntes or spaces in the fyngars: they be also rollers, whereon shippes or greate pieces of tymber be remoued.
Phalarica, an instrument of warre, wherein wylde fyre is inclosed, that whan it is by shot fastened to tymber, it burneth all shortly.
Phaleræ, a traper or bardes for a horse.
Phaleratus, trapyd, or bardyd.
Donat. in Teren. Phorm. Phalerata dicta, gaye wordes, pleasaunte speche.
Phalerij, a citie in Tuscane.
Phalisti, people in Italy.
Phanaticus, frenetyke, he that hath vayne vysions.
Orpheus. Phaneta, one of the names of Bacchus.
Phanni, fantasyes, which happen to men in dremes.
Phantasia, fantasy.
Phantasma, matis, a visyon.
Phanum, a temple.
Pharetra, a quyuar for arowes.
Pharetratus, he that beareth a quyuar.
Phariseus, a Pharyze, whych was of a secte of Jewes, which lyued in a more strayghter fourme than the commun people dyd.
Pharias, phariæ, a serpent, whiche maketh a furrowe in the grounde with his tayle, as he creapeth, and so lyfteth hym self vppe.
Pharmacentice, that part of physike, which healeth with medicynes.
Pharmacopola, a potycary.
Pharmacum, a medycyne: sometyme it significth poyson.
Pharos, an Ile in Egypte.
Pharsalia, a countraye in Thessalya, where the batayle was betwene Julius Cæsar and Pompey.
Phasæ, a worde of Hebrue, which signifieth a departynge.
Phaseolus, a kynde of poulse corne, I suppose it be that, which is called Tares.
Phasianus, a fesaunt.
Phasis, a greate ryuer in the countraye of Colchos.
Phasma, atis, an horrible vision or sight.
Pherecydes, a famouse Phylosopher and wrytar of Tragœdies, which dyed of the lousy sickenesse.
Pheretra, thinges borne at great feastis or triumphes, as pageantes or iewels of gold or siluer, images, and suche lyke thinges.

Phe-

Pheretrius, Jupiter.
Pheretrum, a thinge, wheron pageantes are borne: also deed corpsis.
Phia, the generall name to all plate, whiche serueth for wyne.
Phiala, a potte or cuppe of golde or siluer, which serueth for wyne.
Phidias, an excellent warkman, in makinge great images of golde or yuory.
Phidiacus, ca, cum, of Phidias.
Phiditia, the soupers, whiche the Lacedemonians vsed, whyche were openly kepte with a meruaylouse temperaunce, euery man bringynge his measurable porcion of meate and wyne.
Philadelphia, a citie in Asia.
Philagathus, he that loueth goodnesse.
Philanthropos, a louer of mankynde: also gentyll and kynde.
Philargyria, couaytousnesse, auaryce.
Philargyrus, couaytouse.
Philema, a kisse.
Philetes, a kissar.
Philodolus, he that loueth his seruauntes.
Philenus, he that loueth wyne.
Philippei, a certayne coyne of golde.
Philippi, a citie in Thracia.
Philippenses, men of that citie.
Philocalus, a good man, a clenly man, or elegaunt.
Philomela, a nightingale: also a fayre mayden, whyche was defloured by Thercus, husbonde to her sister, whome poetes do fayne was transfourmed to a nightingale.
Philologus, a louer of wordes.
Philonicus, a brawler: sometyme a louer of victory.
Philosophia, philosophy, the loue or fauorynge of wysedome.
Philoginos, he that doteth on women.
Philopæs, he that loueth children.
Philoponus, laboriouse, paynefull.
Philosophaster, he that wolde be lyke a philosopher.
Philosophice, lyke a phylosopher.
Philothesia, a solemne feaste amonge the Grekes.
Philosophicus, ca, cum, philosophicall.
Philosophor, aris, ari, to study wysedome.
Philosophus, a philosopher.
Philoxenia, hospitalitie.
Philoxenus, he that kepeth good hospitalytye.
Philtrum, a drinke charmed, whiche causeth a man to be madde for loue.
Philura, seu Philyra, smalle thynges hangynge downe of trees or herbes, like vnto heares.
Phyma, matis, a sore on the fynger, whyche maye be called a whytblowe.
Phlebes, veynes.
Phlebotomia, bloodeletinge.
Phlebotomum, the instrument, wherewith bloode is leten, a fleme.
Phlegethon, ontis, a ryuer of hell, which allwaye burneth.
Phlegias, the son of Mars, a kynge in Thessaly, and father of Ixion.
Phlegrę, a people in Thessaly.
Phlius, a place in Grecia.
Phlox, a yelowe floure lyke a violet.
Phlegma, matis, flewme.
Phlegmon, onis, & Phlegmone, nes, an inflammacion of bloode, which groweth into an impostume.
Phoca, a se calf, it maye be supposed to be a Seale, whych is fisshe, and breedith on the lande.
Phocensis, of the countraye called Phocis.
Phocion, a noble counsaylour of Athenes, whose lyfe is a myrroure to all counsayllours, which let theym rede in the warke of Plutarchus, intytled the lyues of noble men.
Phocis, cidis, a countraye in Grece.
Phœbus, the Sunne.
Phœnices, people in Syria.
Phœniceus, a, um, right Crymson.
Phœnicia, a regyon in Syria.
Phœnicopterus, a great byrde, hauing redde fethers.
Phœnissa, a woman of Phenicia.
Phœnix, nicis, a byrde, whiche lyueth aboue syx hundred yeres, and finally caryenge swete spices vppe to a hyghe mountayne, by the heate of the sunne, and labour of hir wyngis, kyndleth fyre, whereby she being all burned, of her axen ryseth another like byrde: it is also a date tree, or palme, also a lytell ryuer in Grecia: it was also the brother of Cadmus, which raygned in Phœnicia.
Pholoe, a mountayne in Archadia, full of woode.
Phonastus, he that techeth one to pronouce and moderate his voyce.
Phorbas, a shepeharde that founde Oedipum, after that he was hanged vpp by the feete.
Phorcus, one of the sonnes of Neptunus, whyche was taken for a god of the see.
Phoroneus, the mooste auncient kynge of Grecia.
Phosphorus, the daye sterre.
Phrasis, The propre fourme, or maner of speache, which in one countraye is oftentymes dyuerse: as Southerne, Northerne, Deuenysshe, Kentyshe, Frenche, Picard, Gas-

Gascoyne, walon: some do set the negatife before the affirmatife, some contrary, some speache is quicke, some graue, some flouryshynge, some temperate.

Phrene, the mydryfe, whyche dyuideth the rmbles of a man or beaste, frome the bowelles.

Phreneticus, he that is vexed with a frenesy.

Phrenitis, seu Phrenisis, a sycknesse called frenesy.

Phrine, a famouse harlotte at Athenes.

Phrigia, a countraye in Asia the lasse.

Phrygio, onis, a brawdrour.

Phrynos, a lyzarde.

Phryx, gis, a man of Phrigia.

Phthia, a citie in Thessalia.

Phthiriasis, a syckencsse, in the which lyse do growe in suche multitudes, that they deuoure the body.

Phthirophagi, people dwelling nyghe to the greke see, which lyued onely by fisshe.

Phthisicos, he that hath the consumpcion of the lunges.

Physeter, a great fysshe in the Frenche Occean see, whyche ryseth lyke to a pylar aboue shippes.

Phthisis, a consumption of the body by a distillation frome the heed into the lunges, whereby the lunges are exulcerate.

Phu, a plante or herbe, which some call Valeriane.

Phygeton, a lytle swellyng or botche, harde and redde, burnynge and prickinge.

Phylira, a tree called also Tylia.

Phyllis, a woman, doughter of Lycurgus, kynge of Thrace, which hynge her selfe, despayringe of the commyng of Demoophon, whome she loued, whome poetes fayne to be turned into an Almonde tree.

Physica, warkes treatynge of the nature of thinges, or the operacion of nature.

Phisicus, a naturall philosopher.

Physiologus, idem.

Physionomia, seu Phisiognomia, a rule to knowe a mannes naturall affections by his vysage or fourme of his membres.

Phyton, one of the names of Apollo.

Phitonicus, & Phitonica, he or she, whyche hath a spirite within theym, that grueth aunswere of thinges to come.

¶ P, ANTE I.

Piabile, for the whych satisfaction maye be made, and god pleased.

Piacularis, re, that whiche is gyuen or offred to god for satisfaction.

Piabilis, that which maye be pourged or satisfyed.

Piacularia auspicia, tokens in sacrifice of some heuy chaunce to come.

Piaculum, any thinge done for satisfactiō of some greuouse synne; sometyme a greate & haynouse offence.

Piamen, seu Piamentum, that which was gyuen or occupyed aboute satisfaction.

Pica, a byrde called a pye.

Picatus, cata, catum, pytched or rasyd with pitche.

Picea, a piche tree.

Picenum, a countraye in Italy.

Picens, tis, a man of that countraye.

Picentus, ta, tum, of the countraye of Picenum.

Piceus, a, um, of pyche.

Pico, care, to dresse with pyche.

Pictatium, a table, pertaynynge to Iuges or bysshoppes: it is sometyme a playster for the stomake or heed.

Pictes, a wrastler.

Pictor, toris, a peyntar.

Pictura, an image peynted.

Picturatæ vestes, imbroudred apparayle, or rather of bawdekyn.

Picturo, are, to make sondry pictures.

Picus, a lytle byrde, which maketh a hole in trees, wherein he breedeth: it was also the name of an olde kynge of Latines.

Picunnus, a pye.   No. Mar.

Pieria, a mountayne in Grece, dedicate to the Musis.

Pie, & Pienter, mercyfully, deuoutely, louyngly.

Piens, tis, mercyfull, &c.

Pientior, Pientissimus, more and moost mercyfull, most louynge towarde his parētes or countraye.

Pierides, the Muses.

Pietas, etatis, the reuerend loue towarde a mannes propre countraye and parentes, of dyuines it is taken for the loue and honour due vnto god. Lactantius calleth it iustice, and deuoute worshyppynge and knowlege of god.   Lact. lib. 5.

Piger, gri, slowe.

Pigere, to be sory.

Pigritia, Pigrities, Pigredo, Pigritas, Pigritudo, slownesse, ydelnesse.

Piget, piguit, pigere, it greueth, it dulleth, it lyketh or contenteth not. Facti piget, he is sory for that, that he hath done: sometyme, I am sory.

Pigmentum, payntinge: also false colour in speakynge, disseytefull wordes, pleasaunt lyes.

Pigmentarius, a maker or sellar of payntynge.

Pigne, slouth.   No. Mar.

Pigneratio, a pledgynge or gagynge.
Pigneratitius, a, um, that which is layde in pledge.
Pignora capere, to take a distresse. *Ci. de ora.*
Pignora, is sometyme taken for children.
Pignero, Pignerare, & Pigneror, pignerari, to laye to pledge or gage, sometyme to take pledge.
Pignus, noris, a pledge or gage, or pawne.
Pigresco, scere, to be or waxe slowe.
Pigré, slowly.
Pigredo, slouthfulnesse.
Pigresio, fieri, to be made slowe.
Pigritia, slownesse.
Pigritudo, idem.
Pigror, idem.
Pigro, are, to holde backe, or tary one.
Pila, a mortar, wherein any thinge is beten with a pestill: also a pilar, a ball, or any thinge rounde as a ball.
Pilani, they which fyght with dartes.
Pilates, a certayne stone that is whyte.
Pilatim, one pilar by another.
Pilatus, armed with dartes.
Pileatus seruus, a slaue that is solde with his cap on his heed.
Pilentum, a wagan.
Pileolus, a lytle bonet.
Pileus, a cappe, sometyme lybertie, for asmoche as bondmen, whan they were infraunchysed, ware copped cappes.
Pilo, are, to begynne to be heary, or growe in heare.
Pilosus, a, um, heary.
Pilula, a lytell ball: also pilles made for purgations.
Pilum, a barbours knyfe or rasour, also a dart of fyue foote longe and a halfe.
Pilumnus, a man which founde the maner to dunge lande, and to grynde corne.
Pilus, a heare.
Pilus, idem quod Pilum: it is also a pestell to braye or breke any thynge withall in a mortar.
Pinaster, a wylde pyne tree.
Pina, a fysshe that hath twoo grete shelles.
Pinachidia, tables made in bookes.
Pinachtheca, a case or place wherein tables are put or set.
Pinarij, an aunciente house or famyly in Italy, of the which were the preestes that sacrifised to Hercules.
Pindo, dis, si, sere: to braye or grynde.
Pindus, a mountayne in Thessalia: also a cytye there.
Pinea nux, a pyne apull.
Pinetum, a woode of pynetrees.
Pineus, a, um, of a pyne tree.
Pingo, xi, pingere, to paynte.

Pinguedo, & Pinguitudo, inis, fatte or fattenesse.
Pingue, inconuenient, sometyme frutefull, commodiouse. *Vergilius.*
Pingues horti, gardens that brynge forth good herbes.
Pinguefacio, cere, to make fatte.
Pinguesco, scere, to be fatte.
Pinguiarius, he that loueth that thinge, whiche is fatte.
Pinguitudo, fatnesse.
Pinguis, gue, fatte, he that is fatte, corsy, vnweldy.
Pingue, grease.
Pinna, a quyll, or penne, the harder part of a fether.
Pinnæ, imbatelmentes of a walle, a muskle, which is founden in muddy waters.
Pinnæ, the fynnes of a fysshe.
Pinnaculum, a pynnacle of a tower.
Pinnula, the ouer part of the eare, a lytle quyll.
Pinsito, tare, to braye in a mortar.
Pinso, sui, sere, to braye or grynde.
Pinso, are, idem.
Pinsor, he that gryndeth in a qwerne: also a baker.
Pinus, pinus, a pyneappull.
Pio, ij, ere, to honour god. *Plautus.*
Pipatio, a clockinge of a henne.
Pinus, seu Pinea, a pyne tree.
Pipare, to clocke lyke a henne.
Piper, eris, peper.
Pipio, iui, ire, to peepe lyke a chicke.
Pipio, onis, a pigeon.
Pipleides, the musis.
Pipleus, an hill in Grecia.
Pipulum, a rebuke. *Plaut.*
Pirum, a peare.
Pirata, a rouer or robber on the se, a pyrate.
Piratica, the practise of pirates or robbers on the see.
Pirrhica, a daunsynge in harneys.
Pisa, a citie in Grece betwene the two mountaynes of Olympus and Ossa: also a citie in Arcadia.
Pisæ, arum, a citie in Italy, called Pise.
Pisani, people of the citie of Pise.
Pisarurus, a ryuer in Italy.
Pisaurum, a citie in Italy.
Piscor, caris, ari, to fisshe.
Piscaria, the fysshe markat.
Piscarius, a, um, pertayninge to fysshynge.
Piscarius, a fysshe mongar.
Piscatorius, a, um, pertayninge to a fysher.
Piscator, toris, a fisshar.
Piscatus, tus, & Piscatio, the acte of fisshinge.
Piscina, a fysshe ponde: it is also generally euery ponde, allthoughe therin be no fish.

¶ P ante I.

Piscinalis, le, pertayninge to fisshe.
Piscinarius, he that nourysheth fysshe.
Pisis, a fysshe.
Pisces, also one of the .xii. sygnes.
Piscosus, a, um, that may be fysshed, or is full of fysshe.
Pisculentus, idem.
Pisciculus, a lytell fysshe.
Pisei, people of the citie Pisa in Gretia.
Pisidæ, people in Asia.
Pistacia, a certayne kynde of nuttes.
Pisistratus, a noble man of Athenes, whiche chaunged the commune weale of that cytie from the rule of the people, to the rule of one gouernour: and therfore he was called a tyraunt, notwithstandinge that (as he wrate vnto Solon, which mayntayned the populer astate) he rulyd by their owne lawes, and was rightwyse and gentyll vnto the people.

Varro. Piso, sere, is proprely to braye, for in the old tyme men vsed to braye or breake corne in mortars: but after that they had quernes to grynde with the hande, they vsed Pisere to grynde, and Pisor for a gryndar.
Piso, sonis, the name of a noble famyly or house in Rome.
Pistillum, a pestell.
Pistor, oris, a baker.
Pistoria, a citie in Italy.
Pistoricus, ca, cum, & Pistorius, a, um, pertaynynge to bakynge.
Pistrilla, a mille.
Pistrinum, & Pistrina, a bakehouse, or gryndinge house: somtyme it signifieth for payn full seruice.
Pistris, a shyppe.
Pistrix, cis, a woman baker: also a monstruouse fysshe in the Indiane see.
Pistura, the craft of bakynge.
Pistus, ta, tum, grounden or brayed.
Pisum, a pease.
Pithacusæ, Iles in the se agaynst Campania.
Pythacua, a certayne tyle, sometyme made in Spayne, which beinge cast into the water, wolde not synke.
Pithagoras, he which first brought vppe the name of a phylosopher: who was borne in Samia, and was a beautyfull man, and of excellent wytte, and therewith of a pure and cleane lyuynge, absteyninge from the eatynge of any thinge that lyued: whose Phylosophy was mysticall and secrete, & declared by numbres and proporcions.
Pitheta, a Comete or impression in the firmament, which is lyke a tunne, and doeth appiere as it were through a myste.

Plautus in Milite. Pithecium, a defourmed or yll fauoured woman.

¶ P ante L.

Pithonoscomes, a place in Asia, where after the Idus of August, great flockes of Storkes do assemble togither.
Pitpit, in the olde tunge of Oskes sygnified quicquid, whatsoeuer.
Pittacus, one of the seuen sages of Grecia, and was of the cytie of Mytelene.
Pityocampe, a worme which is in a pyneappull tree, whose bytinge is venymouse.
Pitysma, spettyll.
Pitho, the lady and presydent of eloquence to persuade.
Pitisso, are, to syppe, or drynke lytle.
Pituita, flewme, or rowme, descending from the heed: alsoo the pyppe, whiche chykens haue.
Pituitosus, flewmatike.
Pitylisma, matis, an exercise, where a man goeth fast on his toes, and moueth his armes forewarde and backwarde.
Pitylisso, are, to exercyse in that fourme.
Pityusa, an Ile, called also Myletus.
Pius, a, um, religiouse, deuoute, pitiouse, gentyll, chaste: he that loueth his parentes or countraye.
Pix, picis, Pytche.
Pix liquida, Tarre.

¶ P, ANTE L.

Placabilis, easy to be pleased.
Placabiliter, thankefully, contentfully.
Placator, toris, a pacyfyer of debate.
Placæ, plates of golde or siluer.
Placendus, da, dum, that whyche ought to content.
Placenta, a tarte.
Placentia, a citie in Liguria.
Placentini, people of the citie of Placentia.
Placeo, cui, cere, to please, to lyke, to glory.
Placide, quietly, paciently, peasybly.
Placidus, da, dum, gentyll, meeke, pacient.
Cor. Tac. lib. 14. Placita, studyes or exercises. Ipse placita maiorum colebat habitu seuæro: He in a sage garment, haunted the studyes of the auncient fathers.
Placitum, a firme consent in an opinyon, an ordinaunce.
Placitus, ta, tum, that whyche lyketh or contenteth.
Placo, care, to pacyfye, to appease.
Pladarotes, a disease, whereby the eye lyddes waxe feble, and wyll vneth be pluckked vppe.
Plaga, a wounde, also a nett to take beastis, sometyme the armyng cordes: also a great space in the erthe, called a Cooste: alsoo a shete for a bedde: moreouer a great space on the erthe, called also Clima.

Pla-

Plagæ, & plagulæ, blankettes.
Plagiaria lex, a lawe made agaynst theym, whiche were called Plagiarij, whyche for theyr offence were whypped.
Plagiarius, he that whyppeth men. Alsoo he that byeth a man for a slaue, knowinge hym to be free. Alsoo he that intyseth a mans seruant to go from his master: also a stealer of bokes.
Plagiger, he that is borne to be whypped.
Plagiosus, a schoole mayster, whyche is a greatte beater.
Plagium, the offence, for the whiche oone is whypped.
Plagosus, fulle of strypes, or he that beateth moche.
Planaratrum, the culter of a ploughe.
Plancæ, plankes.
Planci, they whyche be splaye footed.
Planctus, tus, waylynge, sorowynge.
Plancus, a noble man of Rome.
Planè, truely.
Planeta, a planette.
Plango, xi, gere, to wepe or wayle, to strike or hytte.

Catullus. Plangor, plangoris, a noyse made with the mouthe, as in lawghynge, or weepynge.
Planidus, playne.
Planidior, more playne.
Planities, a playne or leuell grounde.
Planior, playner, euenner.

Diomedes Planipes, he that gothe withoute showes. Also a player in an enterlude.
Planta, the foote with the toes. Sommetyme onely the soole of the foote. Alsoo a plant or tre newely sette: sometyme an herbe that groweth lowe.
Plantago, ginis, an herbe callyd Plantayne.
Plantaria, settes or plantes, or the places, where plantes be sette.
Plantaris, re, pertaynynge to the foote.
Plantarius, a, um, mete or redy to sette.
Plantigeræ arbores, trees whyche brynge forthe settes.
Planto, tare, to sette or plante.
Planula, a playne, a ioyners instrument.
Planum facere, to declare or expounde.

Plaut. in milite & in persa. Planus, na, num, playne, euen, cleare, apparaunt.
Planus, ni, a deceyuour or mocker. Also a Jugglar, whyche makethe thynges to seeme in apparaunce, where in deede noo suche thynge is: As water to come into the howse, or trees to growe, or money of leaues or stones.
Plasma, plasmatis, the warke of a potter, or of hym, whyche worketh in erthe. Also a playster.

Plasmo, are, to make pottes, or any other thynge of erthe.
Plastes, a warker of ymages or other lyke thynge in erthe.
Plastice, the crafte of warkynge in erthe.
Platanus, a plane tree.
Platanetum, a place where plane trees doo growe.
Platanodes, a promontory or hyll in Italy.
Platanonis, ne, of plane tree.
Platea, a high waye or strete. Also a court in great places. Moreouer a see gull.
Plateæ, a cytie in Bœotia, not farre from Thebes.
Plateenses, people of the citie of Platee in Greece.
Plato, tonis, the Prynce and chiefe of all philosophers, as welle in wysedome and counnynge, as in good lyuynge and eloquence.
Plaudi, they whyche haue great hangynge eares.
Plaudo, plausi, plaudere, to reioyce with countenaunce
Plausibilis, plausibile, that whiche the people doeth receyue with ioye, and clapping of their handes.
Plautus, a wryter of comedies.
Plaustrum, seu plostrum, a carte.
Plausus, sus, a reioycynge with voyce and gesture, clapping of hades togither for ioy
Plebecula, the poore people.
Plebeius, a, um, of the people.

Plautus in penulo. Plebeius, plebeius, one of the comminaltie, not beinge a gentylman.
Plebeus, idem.
Plebicola, a fauourer of the comminaltie.
Plebiscitum, a lawe, whiche sometyme was made by the onely consent of the common people of Rome, without the autoritie of the Senate.
Plebs, bis, seu plebes, plebei, the commune people.
Plecto, plexi, plectere, to punishe, to stryke.
Plectrum, an instrument, wherwith menne played on the harpe or doulcymers, for hurtynge of their fyngers. Also a spurre sette on a fyghtynge cocke, whan he lacked naturall spurres.
Pleiades, the seuen sterres, whyche marynours do vse in tryenge of costes.
Plemmyrium, a citie in Sicilia.
Plenè, largely, abundantly.
Plenilunium, full moone.
Plenitudo, dinis, fulnesse.
Plenus, na, num, fulle.

Pom. Fest. Plerus, plera, plerum, of old tyme was vsd for more. Plera pars, the more parte.
Pleriq,, pleræq,, pleraq,, many, a great sorte.

P ante L.

Terent. in Hecyra. in Andria.
Plerusq̃, pleraq̃, plerunq̃, the more parte of any thynge.
Pleriq̃, sygnifyeth some.
Pleriq̃ omnes, for the more parte.
Plerunq̃, oftentymes, sometyme.
Pleonasmos, a fygure, wherin is superfluitie of wordes.
Plethrum, a measure of lande, contaynyng a hundred fete.
Pleuritis, tidis, & pleuresis, a sycknes in the syde, callyd the Pleurisye.
Pleuriticus, euritica, he or she, whiche hath the Pleuresy.

Cato in No. Mar.
Pleuitas, vnnobilitie, basenesse of bloudde.
Plexus, a, um, wounden or bounden.
Plico, caui, uel plicui, care, to folde.
Plicatilis, le, that whiche may be folden.
Plinius, the name of two noble lerned men, the one wrate the moost excellent warke, callyd the hystorie of Nature, the other wrate eloquente Epistles, and an oration to Traiane in his commendation, whiche oration is called Panegyricus. There is also a warke of the practise of phisyke in the name of Plinius, but whither it were of the fyrste Plinie or no, it is not verye certayne.
Plocum, a smalle reede.
Plodo, si, dere, to make noyse with handes or feete.
Ploro, are, to weepe.
Ploratus, tus, weepynge.

Cato.
Plorabundus, he that weepeth moche.
Plostrum, for plaustrum, a wayne or carte.
Plostrarius, a, um, that whiche belongeth to a wayne or carte.
Plostellum, a lyttell wayne.
Plota, a lampray.
Ploti, they whiche haue playne feete withoute holownes in the soles of the feete.
Ploxinum, a coffer or cheste.

Vopiscus.
Plumo, mare, to be in fethers. Also to enbrowder.
Pluma, a fether.
Plumarius, ria, rium, of fethers, a warker with fethers.
Plumatilis, le, made of fethers.
Plumbago, aginis, a vayne of mettalle or oore, wherin is bothe syluer and leade, it is also an herbe, whiche hath leaues lyke sorrell, and a great rote and rough.

Plautus in Penulo.
Plumbea ira, wrathe whyche longe contyneweth.
Plumbatura, sowlder.
Plumbata, a pellette of leadde.
Plumbario, sowlderynge.
Plumbarius, a plummer or worker in leade.
Plumbatę, balles or clubbes of leade, wherwith men faught.

Plumbeus, plumbea, beum, of the colour of leadde, leedye.
Plumbeus homo, a lumpyshe man withoute courage or spirite.
Plumbo, are, to leadde, to sowlder or ioyn mettalle.
Plumbum, leadde.
Plumesco, scere, to be or waxe penned.
Plumeus, a, um, of fethers.
Plumiger, that beareth fethers.
Plumo, are, to be fetherid, or haue fethers.
Plumula, a lyttell fether or plume.
Pluo, plui, pluere, to rayne.
Plura, many. Pluria, idem.
Plurifarius, a, um, of dyuers facions.
Plurifariam, many wayes, in many places.
Plurimifacio, cere, to sette moche by.
Plurimum, very moche. **Ci. in Ver.**
Plurimus, very moche, many, longe.
Plurisfacio, cere, to make more of.
Plus, more. Pluris uendo, I selle for more or deerer.
Plusculus, a, um, a lyttell more.
Plutealis, le, that whiche is sette in a table or case.
Plutealia sigilla, smalle Images in tables or cases.
Pluteum, a space or distaunce, whereby the lower pyllers were dyuided frome the higher in the fronte or foreparte.
Pluteus, an engyne of warre, to conuaye men to the scalynge of walles, kepynge theym frome ordynaunce. Also hutches or greatte coffers, or other lyke places, wherin bokes, tables, or suche thynges are kepte.
Pluto, tonis, callyd god of helle.
Puuia, rayne.
Pluuialis, pluuiatilis, & pluuius, a, um, rayny, or of rayne.
Pluuia aqua, rayne water.
Pluuiosus, full of rayne.
Plyssima, auncient writers vsed for plurima, very many.

¶ P. ANTE, N.

Pneuma, atis, spirite or wynd or breth.
Pneumaticus, ca, cum, wherein wynde or breathe is vsed.
Pneumonici, they whiche be sycke of the longes.

¶ P ANTE O.

Pocillator, pocillatoris, he that bryngeth cuppes to the table, or a cuppe bearer.
Pocillum, a lyttell cuppe.

Poculum,

Poculum, a cuppe. sometyme a draught.
Podagricus, & podagrosus, sa, sum, fulle of goute.
Podagra, the goute, peyne in the feete.
Podalirius, one of the sonnes of Esculapius a greatte surgeon.
Podaris, a longe gowne to the feete.
Poderis, a straite garment of lynnen cloth: It maye nowe be callyd the Albe, whiche priestes doo weare whan they saye masse.
Podex, dicis, the arse.
Podia, the corde, wherwith the sayle is spredde.
Podium, a place made without a walle, for men to stande and beholde thynges, Also a stage, wheron is set candelles or bokes.
Poëma, matis, & poësis, a poetes warke.
Poena, peyne, tourment, execution.
Poenalis, le, penall, peynefull.
Poenam pendere, to suffre punyshement.
Poenas petere, to be aduenged, to punishe.
Salustius in Iugurt. Poenas reddere, to be punyshed.
Poenas luere, idem.
Poenio, auncient writers vsed for punio.
Poenitens, tis, penitent, repentant.
Poenitendus, da, dum, to be ashamed of, to be lyttell estemed.
Poenitentia, repentance, penaunce.
Perottus. Poeniteor, I am in payne, I am greued.
Poenitudo, repentaunce.
Poeniturus, to be sorye.
Poenula, a cloke.
Paeon, a man, whom Homer calleth excellently lerned in phisike.
Paeonia, an herbe callid Pyonie. Also a region or countrey in Macedonia.
Poenicus, poenica, cum, of Affrike.
Poeninsula, a place, whyche for the more parte is inclosed with water.
Poenitet, tuit, tére, to repent, to forthynke, to be sorie for a thynge.
Poenus, a manne of the cytie of Carthage
Poëta, a poete.
Poeticé, ces, poetrie.
Poeticus, ca, cum, poeticall.
Poetor, aris, ari, to exercyse poetrie.
Poetria, & poetris, idis, a woman poete.
Pogonia, a blasing sterre, with a long beam afore lyke a berde.
Pol, an aduerbe of swearynge, as it were by Pollux.
Polenta, was barley ordered in this forme. They stepyd barley in water one night, and dryed it, and the next day they fried it, and than grounde it. And soo kepte it longe, whyche theyr slaues and pultrye dydde eate.
Polentarius, a, um, pertaynynge to barleye grounde, as is aforesayde.

Polite, freshely, gayly, klenly.
Politia, ciuilitie, politike gouernance.
Politicus, politica, liticum, ciuile or pertaynynge to a citie.
Politiones, they whyche are dylygente in husbandrye.
Politius, more cleane or trymme.
Pollen, linis, wheate floure.
Pollens, tis, puissaunt.
Polliceor, polliceri, & polliceo, pollicere, to promyse.
Pollicitatio, a promesse.
Pollinaria cribra, a rangynge syue, wherewith the floure is syfted from the branne, it may be called also a boulter.
Pollinarius, pollinaria, narium, pertaynyng to flowre.
Pollit for pila ludit.
Polimenta, the stones of boore pigges.
Polio, poliui, polire, to polyshe, to garnyshe or decke.
Politus, polita, politum, polysshed, decked, trymmed.
Polities, cleanlynesse.
Pollentia, power, also a citie.
Polleo, ére, to may, to haue power, to shine.
Pollex, licis, a thumbe of the hande, It is also an ynche, whiche is a fynger bredthe and a halfe.
Pollicaris, re, of a thumbe.
Pollincere, to minister aboute funerals, also to bpulte meale.
Pollinctor, toris, the administratour or officer in ordaynyng of funeralles.
Pollinctura, the ministration of funeralles.
Pollintor, toris, a baker that syfteth meale.
Pollis, linis, & pollen, inis, meale.
Pollubrum, a bason.
Polluceo, cere, to mynyster sacrifyce, specially to Hercules.
Pollucibilis coena, a costely supper.
Pollucibiliter, costely, gorgiously.
Polluctum, a costely supper.
Polluo, luere, to pollute or defyle.
Pollutus, ta, tum, polluted, defyled. Pom.Fest.
Polus, the pole. There be imagyned to be twoo certayne poyntes in heuen, as hit were the endes of Extree, where aboute heuen is meuyd, the oone is in the Northe, and is callydde Polus arcticus. The other in the Southe, callydde Polus antarcticus.
Pollux, lucis, was brother to Castor, bothe being borne at one bour deyn, whych Poetes doo fayne to come of one egge, layd or brought forthe by a woman, called Leda, with whom Jupiter companied in likenes of a swanne.
Polyarna, he that hath many lambes.

S.ii.   Poly-

Polybotes, a graunte, whome Neptunus slewe.

Polycarpus, he that hath many flowres.

Polycrates, a tyraunt, whyche was soo fortunate, that he neuer suffered any aduersytie, or griefe. wherfore he at the laste dredynge the chaunge of the fauoure of fortune, hauynge a rynge with a stone of an excellent valewe, dydde caste the same rynge into the see, to the intente that he wolde suffre somme displeasure, and soo satisfie fortune: but a fysshe deuourynge the rynge, was the same daye taken of a fysher, and gyuen to the kynge, for the greatnesse of the fysshe, whyche beynge opened, there was the sayde ryng founde and brought to the kynge: wherat as wel he, as all other aboute hym meruayled. Sone after the same kyng was oppressed by his people, and hanged.

Polydamas, a Troyane, oone of theym, whyche betrayed the cytie with Eneas and Anthenor.

Polygonum, an herbe, whyche is also callyd Sanguinaria, and hath leaues lyke to Rewe, but it runneth on the grounde as grasse, the iuyce therof put into the nose, stoppeth bledynge. It is supposed to be swynes grasse, or knotte grasse.

Polyhistor, oris, he that knoweth moche, or of many thynges done.

Polilogus, he that hath many wordes.

Polymitus, mita, tum, of twyne or twysted thredes.

Polymita, a garmēt made of twisted threde or sylke.

Polymnia, one of the Muses, which word syngnifieth moche memorie.

Polymorphus, of many formes or facions.

Polymyxos, a candelstycke, whiche bereth many lyghtes.

Polyphagus, a greatte eater.

Polyphemus, was a graunt, that had oone eye in his forehead, whiche was put oute by Ulyxes.

Polypodium, an herbe lyke to ferne, growynge on trees.

Polyposus, he that hath a soore in the nose.

Polypus, a fysshe, hauyng many feete, whyche chaungeth his coloure often: Also a piece of fleshe, growyng in the ouermost parte of the nose, whiche causeth a stynkynge ayre out of the nose.

Polyrizon, that whiche hath many rootes.

Polysyntheton, a fygure, where manye artycles comme into a sentence, as Ille trahebat, Hic vociferabatur, He drewe, and he cried out.

Polytes, one of kynge Priamus sonnes.

Polytrichon, an herbe callyd Maydenheer.

Polyxena, the daughter of kynge Priamus whom cruell Pirrhus slewe on the tombe of Achilles.

Pomarium, an orcharde, sometyme a place wherin fruites be kepte.

Pomeridianus, & postmeridianus, a, um, any thynge done after noone.

Pomiferus, a, um, bearynge appuls.

Pomilius, & pumilio, onis, a lyttelle personage, a dwarfe.

Pomœrium, the grounde without the walles of the citie, whiche moughte neyther be ploughed, nor inhabyted, the territory.

Pompa, a pompe, or solemne syght.

Pompeius, the name of a noble Romayne.

Pompeianus, of Pompeius parte, or a fauourer of Pompeius.

Pomum, the generall name of all fruites. It is moste vsed for an appull.

Ponderitas, hefte, poyse.

Pondero, raui, rare, to waye, to ponder, to consyder, to esteme.

Pondo, a pounde weight, sommetyme. xii. pounde. It was amonge the Romaynes the pounde of moneye, as Mina, & mna, was in Athenes, whyche was of the value of a hundred old poyse grotes, wherof. viii. went to an ounce: so that in those grotes after our rate, it contayned a poūd and a marke of newe grotes tenne to the ounce. ii. pounde and fyue grotes.

Pondus, deris, weight. sometyme it signifieth numbre, also auctoritie. *Varro.*

Ponderosus, a, um, wayghty.

Ponere spem, to hope.

Pone, after, or behynde. *Plautus in capt.*

Pone eum esse victum, Putte the case that he be vanquyshed.

Pono, posui, ponere, to putte, to set, to cesse, to buylde, to laye a parte.

Pons, pontis, a brydge.

Pontica nux, a kynde of sylberdes, whiche came from the countreye called Pontus in Asia.

Ponticum, is a taste, whiche hath no sente to be discerned.

Ponticulus, a lyttell brydge.

Pontifex, ficis, an archebysshoppe.

Pontificatus, tus, the dignitie of a bysshop.

Pontificius, a, um, of a bysshoppe.

Pontones, whyry botes.

Pontus, the see, whyche is from the great fenne, callydde Mæotis, vnto Tenedum. It is somnetyme vsyd for all the see. It is also a prouynce in Asie the lesse.

Popa, fatte, greace.

Popana, fatte oyntementes.

Popanum, a cake of breadde.

Popellus,

Popellus, the lyttell or poore people.
Popina, a tauerne or vyttaylynge howse, where meate is eaten out of due tyme.
Popinatio, ryotte.
Popinalis, le, pertaynynge to ryot, or places of ryotte.
Popinor, aris, ari, to eate oute of due tyme, to be ryottous.
Popiniones, haunters of tauernes.
Poples, poplitis, the hamme of a mans legge behynde the knee.
Poppisma, matis, the noyse made with the mouthe and the hande, in ryding, or wanton dalyaunce.
Populabundus, wastynge the countreye, or he that gothe in forragynge or robbynge of countreyes.
Popularis, re, pertayning to the people, accepted or fauoured of the people. Also it sygnifyeth a familiar frende, or as we vse to call countrey man.
Populariter, & populare, homely, lyke the people.
Populatus, ta, tum, wasted, distroyd.
Populeus, a, um, of a popler tre.
Populnus, & populneus, idem.
Popularitas, the coniunction or amytie of people of one countrey. also affabilitie, humanitie, towarde the people.

Libetius I
No.Mar.
Popularia, boyes playes.
Popularim, of al the peple. also euerich one.
Populatio, a wastynge of the countreye, a fourragynge.
Populator, a forrageour or waster of countreyes.
Populifugia, was a daye in the moneth of June, at the whiche daye by reason of a rumour, the people fledde.
Populor, aris, to wast or distroy a coūtrey.
Populosus, a, um, full of people, populous.
Populus, people. Also a poplar tree.
Porca, a sowe, a rydge of lande, a balke.
Porcarius, a, um, of a swyne.
Porcarius, a swyneherde.

Pom.Fest.
Porceo, cere, to prohibyte.
Porcetra, a yonge sowe, or yelte.
Porcinus, na, num, of a hogge.
Porculatio, bryngynge vppe of swyne.
Porculator, a fatter of swyne.
Porcus, a hogge.
Porcellus, a pygge.
Porculus, a shoote, a porcatte.
Porcus troianus, a hogge roosted with manye other beastes and fowles within his bealye.
Porgam, vsed of the auncyent wryters for porrigam, I wyll delyuer or take to one.
Pori, poores in the bodye, out of the whiche issueth sweate.

Porphyretes, a redde marble.
Porphyreticus, ca, cum, of redde marble.
Porphyriacus, ca, cum, of purple colour.
Porphyrio, a byrde, whiche drinketh as yf he dyd byte the water, he hath longe red legges and bylle.
Porraceus, a, um, of the coloure of leeke blades.
Porrectus, ta, tum, stretched.
Porrecte, streyght out.
Porriginosus, a, um, lyke to lekes.
Porrigo, porrexi, rigere, to sprede oute, to offre, to ouerthrowe.
Porrigo, ginis, skales whiche do falle from a mannes heed or berde, lyke branne.
Porro, surely. also longe before, farre of, after, in tyme commynge, beyonde, forsoth.
Porrum, porri, in the pluꝛell numbꝛe lecke.
Porraceus, a, um, of a leeke.
Porsena, the name of a kynge, that besyeged Rome.
Porta, a yate.
Portendo, dere, to sygnifie before a thynge happeneth.
Portentiferus, a, um, that whiche signifieth strange or monstruous thinges comming.
Portentificus, ca, cum, idem.
Portentosus, a, um, monstruouse, sygnifieng some thynge to come.
Portentum, a thynge monstruous or verye seldome sene, whiche may sygnifie somme what to come.
Porticus, cus, a porche.
Portio, a porcion. portiuncula, a litle porciō.
Portiusculus, the pylate of a shyppe, whyche ruleth the maryners.
Portitor, oris, the customer of a hauen. Also a porter, that dothe beare thynges that be bought, whither as the byer wyll haue hym. Also he that beareth men fro the hauen to the shyppe.
Porto, tare, to beare, to brynge.
Portorium, the frayte payde for passage or caryage of merchaundyse.
Portulaca, an herbe callyd purselan. *Salustius in iugur.*
Portuosus, full of hauens.
Portus, tus, an hauen.
Posca, a sawce made with vyneygre and water.
Poscinumius, mia, um, that whiche requyreth money.
Posco, poposci, poscere, to aske, to requyre, to prouoke, to assayle.
Pos, a brydge.
Positio, a settyng of a thyng. *Varro.*
Positura, idem.
Positus, ta, tum, putte or sette.
Positura, & positus, tus, a setting or putting.
Possessio, onis, possession.

S.iij. Posses

P ANTE O.

Possessor, oris, he that hath the possession, the owner.
Possideo, sedi, sidêre, to possede.
Possum, potui, posse, to maye.

Cæsar.
Post, after, afterwarde, behynde.
Postea, afterwarde.
Postergo, are, to leaue behynd, to cast back.
Posteritas, tatis, the worlde to come.
Posterius, later, slower, vyler.
Posterus, ra, rum, that whiche commeth after. Postera dies, the day after. Posteri pedes, the hynder fete.
Post fero, to sette after or behynde, to set lesse by. Post habere, idem.
Posthac, from hensforthe.
Posthumus, ma, a chylde borne after that the father is deade.
Posthumus, ma, mum, folowing, or to come.
Posticum, & posticus, a backe doore.
Postica, all that is behynde vs, lyke as Antica is all that is before vs. It is also a line whiche diuideth the feldes from the easte to the weste.
Postilena, a crouper.
Postis, a poste.
Postliminium redire, is whan any man happeth to go from vs to oure enemies, and after retourneth home.
Postmitto, tere, to leaue behinde, to forget.
Postmodum, afterwarde.
Postquam, after. Postremo, at the laste.
Postridie, the day after to morowe, the day folowyng the day before expressed.
Postomis, a braake, wherewith a horses mouthe is broken, and is made to beare his heed easyly.
Postulo, are, to require, to demande a thing whiche is dewe to the asker. Also to accuse or sewe oone in the lawe, or to complayne on one. Sometyme to desyre.

Pli. in epist.
Postulatio, a supplication made to a prince.
Potens, tis, myghty, puissant, hable.
Potentia, power, puissace, habilite, gret rule.
Potenter, myghtily, puissantly.

Cæf. lib. I. belli galli.
Potentatus, tus, power.
Potestas, tatis, power, auctoritie, counsayle, and reason.
Potestatem sui facere, to suffre men to come to hym, or to speake with hym.
Potiono, are, to gyue a medicyne.
Potior, potius, better.
Potior, potitus sum, potiri, to haue in possesyon, to optayne, to take pleasure of.
Potestur, for potest, he maye.
Potis sum, I maye, potis est, it is possyble.
Potitius, Hercules prieste.
Potito, tare, to vse to drynke.
Poto, tare, to drynke: Also to gyue drinke to one.

P ANTE R.

Potorium, a cuppe.
Potus, ta, tum, that which hath drunke, and that whiche is dronken.
Potus, tus, drynke.

¶ P, ANTE, R.

PRæ, before, in regarde, or in comparyson, for. Præ amore, for loue. Also of. Præ studio, of study. Præut, sygnyfieth than. Modestior nunc quidem est de uerbis, præut dudum fuit, He is more softe or gentyll of wordes, than he was wonte to be, or than he was late.
Præbitere, to passe by, or passe forthe in iorney. sometyme perire, to lese, to cast away. *Plautus. Pom. Fest.*
Præbeo, bui, bere, to gyue, to shewe.
Præbia, orum, thynges gyuen to sicke men.
Præcaluus, balde before.
Præcarus, ra, rum, very deere.
Præcedo, cessi, dere, to goo before.
Præcello, lui, lere, to excelle.
Præcentio, that whiche is songen or playde at the beginning of a songe or balade.
Præcentor, toris, he that first singeth. it may be taken for the chaunter in a quyre.
Præsultor, toris, he that leadeth the daunse.
Præceps, pitis, a high place stepe downe.
Præceps homo, he that is to hastye in his busynesse, and doth thynges vnaduisedly.
Præceps, heedlynge.
Præceptum, a precepte, a rule gyuen, a cōmaundement.
Præcidanea porca, a swine, which the Paynims dydde sacrifice before they dyd cut downe their corne.
Præcidaneus, a, ü, that which is fyrst kylled. *Cice. in Achad. quest*
Præcido, dere, to speake or tell precisely, or certainly, to strike, to cut of, to beate, to denye styffely. Plane sine ulla exceptione præcidit, Truely he styffly denied it without exception. *Ci. ad At. lib. 8.*
Præcino, nui, nere, to synge before or fyrst, also to tell a thynge before it hapneth.
Præcipio, cœpi, cipere, to preuent or take first, to forsee : also to commaunde.
Præcipitium, a downe right place or steppe, whiche maye not be gone on.
Præcipito, tare, to throwe downe heedling.
Præcipitanter, heedlynge, vnaduysedly.
Præcipuus, a, ü, chiefe, speciall, principall.
Præcipuè, chiefly, specially, principally.
Præcise, precisely, determinately.
Præcisum, harde, intractable, cutted, verye shorte, Qui præcisis conclusionibus obscuri, Salustium atq Thucydidē superant, The whyche beinge harde to be vnderstand in their cutted sentences, doo excede bothe Saluste and Thucydides. *Quintilia. lib. 9.*
Præclas

P ante R.

Preclamo, are, to crye before.
Preclare, very excellently, very nobly.
Preclarus, very noble: sometyme it signifieth goode.
Precognitus, ta, tum, knowen before.
Præco, conis, a cryar, a publysshar of thynges.
Preconium, a solemne cry: sometyme it signifieth prayse or glory.
Precoquor, queris, qui, to be sone rype.
Precordia, the skynne, whiche dyuideth the ouer part of the body from the nether: it is also taken for the place vnder the rybbes: sometyme al the numbles, as the hart, the splene, the lunges, and lyuer.
Precox, cocis, & Precoquus, a, um, sone rype or tymely rype.
Preda, a proye, a thynge goten or taken in warres.

Qu. Curti. Predabundus, goynge on foragynge in the tyme of warre.
Prædaceus, a, um, of a proye.
Prædatiuus, idem.

Saluſtius Predator, a seekar for a proye.
Predator ex socijs, a robber of his company.
Predensus, a, um, very thicke.
Prædestino, are, to purpose before.
Prædiator, toris, a man of lawe expert in actions reall, or maters concerning landes.
Prædiatorius, a, um, pertayninge to landes.
Prædicatio, a publysshynge, or open declaration.
Prædico, care, to publysshe, to tell a thynge openly, to prayse.
Prædico, xi, dicere, to tell before.
Prædiolum, a lytle manour.
Prædisco, didici, discere, to vnderstande before.
Præditus, ta, um, adourned: also Preditus mœrore, replenyshed with heuynesse: Preditus lachrymis, wasshed with teares, or full of teares.
Prædium, a manour.
Prædonulus, a lytle robber.

Cato. Prædo, donis, a robber of countrayes.
Prædor, aris, ari, to robbe a countraye, or to take prayes.

Pom. Feſt. Predotiunt, they chiefly desyre.
Præduro, are, to be harder than it was wōt.
Præeo, iui, ire, to go before.
Præfacio, feci, facere, to set more by.
Præfanda, not honeste to be spoken or reherced.
Præfari, to speake or saye before.
Præfatio, onis, a preface.
Præfectus pretorij, was with Emperours the principall officer in his court: as nowe in Fraunce the great maſter.
Præfero, tuli, ferre, to preferre.

P ante R.

Præfericulum, a great bason, which was caryed before hym that dyd sacrifice. Pom. Feſt.
Præfestino, are, to make to moche haste.
Præfica, a woman, which is hyred to lamēt at the buryenge of men or women.
Præficio, feci, ficere, to put in auctoritie, or to gyue rule.
Præfectura, an auctoritie or rule.
Præfectus, a rular.
Præfigo, xi, gere, to shut afore
Præfinio, niui, ire, to determyne before, to assigne or appoynte.
Præfinitus, ta, tum, prefixed.
Præfoco, care, to strangle, or choke.
Præfractus, cta, ctum, harde and vnflexible, whyche wyll rather breke than bowe: also that which was before broken.
Præfracte, obstinately.
Præfrigidus, da, dum, very colde.
Præfulcio, cire, to fortifye. Plautus in
Præfulgeo, fulsi, gere, to shyne moche. Pseudolo.
Præfurnium, the mouth of an ouen or fournayse.
Prægelidus, da, dum, excedynge colde.
Prægigno, nere, to begyn, to brynge in first. Nolebam ex me morem pregigni malum, I wolde not that an yll custome shoulde be brought vp by me.
Prægestio, ire, to reioyce moche.
Prægnans, tis, a woman with childe.
Prægrandis, de, very greate.
Prægrauatio, a great griefe.
Prægredior, gredi, to go before.
Prægrauo, are, to greue moche.
Prehendo, di, dere, to take. Manum prehen Cic. in P ſo
dere, to take by the hande. & ad Atti.
Prehensatio, a solicitinge or laboringe for Ti. Liuius.
the attayninge of some greate office.
Prehenso, are, to imbrace or set honde on one, to solicite.
Præiacio, præieci, præiacere, to cast before a thinge. Colum. 9.
Præiacio, cui, cere, to lye before.
Præire iuramentum, to ministre or gyue an othe.
Præiuditium, a thinge which being ones decyded and determyned, maketh a rule or example to men that do folowe, to discusse semblably in a lyke mater. As those which we do cal rulyd cases or maters in the law, which be as examples to iuges.
Præiudico, to iuge before: sometyme to condemne, also to let.
Præiuro, rare, to sweare before other.
Præiuratio, the othe that is taken by hym that first sweareth.
Præiurator, toris: he whiche firste taketh an othe, as the fore man of a iury, or the first witnesse, or any other, after whome other men

men do sweare, accordynge to the othe gyuen vnto him.
Prælabor, beris, bi, to fall firste.
Præliaris, are, pertaynynge to batayle.
Præliator, toris, a warriour.
Prælicenter, very wantonly.
Prælior, aris, ari, to fyght in batayle.

Cato

Præliganeum vinum, a præligando, which I suppose to be so called, eyther bycause it is fyrste tunned or put into vessels, or els bycause it is put into a sacke, which is fast knytte afore.
Præligo, gare, to bynde afore.
Prælium, batayle also the fyght in batayle: sometyme the acte of generation.
Prælongus, a, um, very longe.
Præloquium, the begynnynge of a communication, or thinge spoken, as that which in rhetorike is named exordium.
Præloquor, queris, qui, to speake or telle before.
Præluceo, cere, to beare lyght before one, as a torche or candel: also to gyue more light than another.
Prælucere alijs virtute, to shyne in vertues before other.
Præludium, a proheme, or that which Musicians and Mynstrelles doo playe at the begynnynge, er they come to the songe, which they purpose to playe.
Præludo, si, dere, to playe before.
Prælum, a presse.
Prælumbo, are, to breake ones loynes.
Præluo, luere, to pourge or wasshe cleane afore.
Præmando, daui, to sende before.
Præmanibus, redy at hande.

Plaut in Mostell.

Præmature, to soone, or before the iust tyme.
Præmature vita careo, I dye afore my tyme.
Præmeditor, taris, tari, to aduyse before a man do a thinge.
Præ me fero, præ me tuli, præ me ferre, to declare by deede, worde, or gesture. Præ te fers iracundiam, thou shewyste thy selfe to be angry: also to confesse: also to haue before him a thynge (as it were) in remembraunce.
Præmercor, caris, cari, to bye aforehande.
Præmessum, a sacrifyce or offrynge to Ceres, of the eares of corne that was fyrste repyd.
Præmetium, the fyrst croppe.
Præmiatores, theues which steale by nyght, as we mought saye, whyche commytte burglary.
Præmiator, is a rewarder.
Præmineo, nui, ere, to be better than another or excel aboue another in astate or vertue.

Præmior, aris, ari, to gyue rewardes.
Præmiosus, ryche of money.
Præmissio, a sendinge afore.
Præmitto, misi, tere, to sende afore.
Præmium, a rewarde, gyuen to hym which hath done any notable and laudable thing.

Gellius.

Præmoderor, aris, ari, to playe before on an instrument.
Præmodum, aboue measure.
Præmolestia, feare of a thinge to come.

Ci. Tus.

Præmollis, le, very tender or delicate.
Præmoneo, nui, nere, to forewarne.
Præmonstrator, toris, he that telleth or sheweth a thynge before that it happeneth.

Terent. in heau.

Præmonstro, are, to shewe before.
Præmordeo, dere, to byte or rebuke before.
Præmorior, riris, ri, to dye er the tyme come.
Præmunio, iui, ire, to prepare.
Prænarro, rare, to tell before.
Prænato, tare, to swymme afore.
Præneste, a citie in Italy.
Prænestini, people of the citie of Præneste in Italy.
Prænestinus, a, um, of Præneste.
Prænomen, the firste name: as Marcus, Quintus, Lucius: and as we now haue the name at baptysme.
Prænosco, noui, noscere, to knowe afore.
Prænoto, tare, to make annotations or inscriptions.
Prænuncio, are, to shewe afore.
Prænuncius, the first messenger, he that fyrst bryngeth rydinges.
Præoccupatio, a fygure in Rhetorike, whan we will saye that we will not tell a thinge, and yet therby couertly we wil declare the matter, or make it suspected.
Præoccupo, pare, to take or possede a thinge by preuencion.
Præopto, tare, rather to desire.
Præordinatio, the fyrst ordinaunce.
Præordinator, he that made the fyrst ordynaunce.
Præordino, are, to ordayne afore.
Præparcus, ca, cum, very scarce or nygarde.
Præparo, are, to prepare, to make redy.
Præpedimentum, a let before.
Præpedio, diui, to let moche.
Præpendo, dere, to hange afore.
Præpes, præpetis, swyft.
Præpetes aues, were the byrdes, which shewed them selfes first to the diuinours called Augures, whereby they supposed to knowe what shulde ensue.
Præpeto, tere, to begynne first.
Præpilatus, ta, tum, hedded with yron, as a Iauelyn or dart: also sharp afore lyke the heed of a dart, thoughe it hath none yron: as the hornes of a lopster, wherewith he swym-

swymmeth.
Præpinguis, very fat.
Præpondero, are, to waye more, to be more worth.
Præpolleo, lere, to excede other.
Præpono, sui ponere, to put or set before.
Præpositus, ta, tum, set or aduaunced aboue other, set in autoritie.
Præpositus, ti, he that is in autoritie, or chief in any office.
Præpotens, very puissant or mighty.
Præpoto, tare, to drynke afore, to brynge good lucke in drinkinge.
Præposterus, ra, rum, ouerthwart, oute of ordre.

Saluftius in Iug. Præposteri homines, they that do that thing last, whiche they shulde haue done first.
Præpostere fieri, to be done against all good ordre. As whan the seruaunt commaundeth his master, the peple their rulars, or a foole a wyse man.
Præproperus, ra, rum, very quicke or hasty.
Præputium, the skynne which couereth the heed of a mans priuey membre.
Præripio, pui, pere, to preuent, to catche.
Prærideo, dere, to lawghe before.
Prærisor, oris, he that laugheth afore one.
Prærodo, si, dere, to gnawe or eate very moche.
Prærogata beneficia, benefytes afore employed.
Prærogo, gare, to employe or gyue afore.
Prærogatiua, & prærogatiuum, a prerogatife, where one is preferred afore another.
Prærumpo, pere, to breake asonder.
Præruptus, ta, tum, all to broken. it is sometyme taken, where a hyll is broken by the sydes, and harde to go on.
Prærupta loca, places broken here & there, that no man maye passe.
Præsagio, gire, & presagior, to perceyue or knowe a thinge before that it happen.
Præsagus, a pronosticatour, or perceyuer of thinges er they happe.
Præsagium, & presagatio, amonge the auncient writars, a perceyuing of a thinge before that it happeneth, sometyme a coniecture.
Præscientia, an vnderstandinge and perfyte knowlege of all that shall happen.
Præscius, he that knoweth perfytely thinges er they happen.
Præscio, scire, to knowe afore.
Præscribo, psi, bere, to assigne, to note or intitle, to put, to laye before, to telle before, to appoint or determyne.
Præscriptio, & præscriptum, a rule, a lawe, an ordre, a fourme.
Præscriptum, a precepte, a fourme, a rule.

Præseco, care, to cut before, sometyme to cut on sonder.
Præsegmina, the parynges of a mannes nayles.
Præsens, tis, present. In presentia, & in presentiarum, at this present tyme.
Præsentius, better.
Præsentissimus, a, um, the best, the surest.
Præsentissimum venenum, the greatest and moost feruent poyson: also stronge.
Presens animus, a stronge or good courage, also fauorable. Deum præsentem habet, he hath god fauorable vnto hym.
Præsentaneum remedium, a short or sodayne remedy.
Præsentia, presence.
Præsentio, & presentisco, cere, to fele or perceyue before.
Præsento, tare, to haue redy.
Præsepe, & presepium, & presepes, a stable, a stall, a shepehouse.
Præsepio, pire, to hedge afore a thinge.
Præsertim, specially.
Præseruatio, a preseruation.
Præseruare, to preserue.
Præses, sidis, he that hath autoritie in a prouince next vnder the prince: sometyme it signifieth a defendour, alsoo sure. Locum presidem, a sure place. *Plautus in Casina.*
Præsideo, dere, to be in more autoritye, or of a more dignitie: also to haue authoritye or rule.
Præsideratio, tempest, whiche commeth at the begynnynge of wynter, sooner than it is loked for, or is accustomed to happen.
Præsidero, are, where tempest commeth very soone, and before the tyme accustomed.
Præsicco, care, to drye afore.
Præsidiarius, a, um, that which is ordayned to be ayde to another thinge.
Præsidium, a garyson of men with a capytayne, set by the chief capitayne, to defend a fortresse: sometyme it is taken generally for all maner of ayde or defence: also for a fortification of a thinge.
Præsilio, silire, to lepe before, to sterte oute.
Præsisto, tere, to stande or be set afore.
Præspeculor, ari, to loke afore.
Præspicio, spexi, spicere, to see afore.
Præstabilis, le, excellent.
Prestabilius, bettar.
Præstantia, excellency.
Præstat, it is bettar.
Prestans, tis, excellent.
Prestanter, excellently.
Prestare culpam, to take the blame on hym.
Prestare officium, to do his deuoyre. *Cicer. Tu.*
Prestare iusiurandum, to take an othe.
Prestega, a place open afore, and keuered behynde

behynde lyke a porche, where men do syt for recreacion after their busynesse.

Præster, a venymouse serpent, of whome he that is stryken, dyeth for thurst.

Præstigiator, toris, a iuggler.

Pom. Fest. Præstes, titis, of the auncient wrytars called a prelate.

Præstigium, a iugglynge caste, an inchauntment, a delusyon.

Præstino, are, to prepare in byenge a thinge.

Præstituo, ere, to determine before, to prescribe or appoynt before, what shal be done.

Cl. de ora. Istam enim culpam, quam vereris, ego præstabo, for the blame, which thou fearest, I will take vppon me.

Præsto, stiti, stare, to be better than another thinge, wherewith it is comparyd, to excell: also to vndertake, to waraunt, sometyme to graunte, also to do, to be beneficiall, to beware, to exchue, to feare, to do or **Cl. ad Q.** perfourme, to gyue, to exhibite, to represent or shewe, to lende, to assigne or ap- **fratrem** poynt, to do a thinge.

Præsto, an aduerbe, redy, at hande. Presto sis, helpe me. Presto esse, to appiere, as men do in places of iugementes.

Præstolor, aris, ari, to tary, to be at hande, or redy to do seruice.

Præstringo, xi, gere, to bynde fast, to shut, to dasell the eyen, to touche quickly, or shortly, to shaue, to greue somewhat.

Præstruo, struxi, struere, to ordayne firste, to buylde.

Præsul, lis, a prelate.

Præsulatus, tus, the dignitie of a prelate.

Præsulto, are, to leape or daunse afore.

Præsultor, præsultoris, he that leadeth a daunse.

Præsum, fui, preesse, to be afore or aboue an other, to be of more dignitye, to be in autoritye.

Præesse negotio, to be chief in the busynesse.

Præsumere animo, to coniecte.

Præsumo, sumpsi, sumere, to take fyrste, to preuente.

Præsumptio, a takinge or receyuynge before: it is also that, which is called preoccupation, whan we declare first what our aduersary will saye, or what is the iuges opynyon: and against that we do argue, to dissolue it with reason.

Præsuo, ere, to sowe afore.

Præsurgo, gere, to ryse afore or first.

Prætego, gere, to hyde or couer chiefly.

Prætendo, ere, to laye for a thing er it come: also to cary or beare afore, also to shew or pretende, to allege, to set a thinge aboute for an inclosure. Prætendere sepem, to make a hedge aboute.

Prætento, tare, to tempte or assaye afore.

Prætenue, very sklenderly.

Prætrduco, cere, to leade afore, to leade forth.

Prætergredior, di, to passe by, to go beyond.

Præteritus, ta, tum, passyd.

Præteriti, deed, departed, decessyd: also they which in suynge for an office, dyd suffre repulse, or were put backe.

Præter propter, for an other cause than that which is rehersed.

Præter, except, also besyde, ouer and aboue, before. Præter oculos, before the eyen, Against or contrary. Præter morem, againste the custome or facion. Præter spem, vnloked for. Præter opinionem, otherwyse than I thought. Præter cætera, more than the other. Præter æquum, against raison.

Præterbito, tare, to go by.

Prætera, moreouer, besyde, none els. Mihi credis præterea nemini, Thou beleuest me, and none els. also it signifieth afterwarde.

Prætereo, iui, ire, to go ouer or passe, to leue oute a thynge, which shulde be spoken of.

Prætermitto, misi, tere, to leue vntouched, to forgete, to leue oute.

Prætermissio, forgetynge, or leuinge out of a thynge.

Præterquàm, but onely, otherwyse than, moreouer.

Præterq̃ quod, but.

Præterueho, here, to carye throughe.

Præteruolo, are, to passe throughe quickly.

Prætexo, ui, ere, to make or ordayne firste, to couer or hyde.

Prætexta, a longe garment myxte with purple silke, whiche was the vesture of noble mennes sonnes, vntyll they came vnto .xvii. yeres of age: and therfore suche children were called Prætextati, but they had alsoo aboute their neckes, a lytell round iewell of golde, facyoned like a hart, wherin was inclosed some thinge of great vertue.

Prætexta, was also the robe of estate, whiche the kynge of Romaynes, or the other chief officers dyd weare, whan they sate in their maiestie.

Prætexta comœdia, an enterlude, wherin are personages of highe dignitie.

Prætextatus, ta, tum, dishonest, or vnclene in **Suetonius** speche or actes. Festus taketh it in the con- **Gellius.** trary sence. **Macro.**

Prætextum, a pretence or coloure.

Prætiamitatores, officers which went before the prelates called Flamines, proclayming openly, that all men shulde ceasse of theyr warke, bycause it was not lefull to those prelates to beholde any man warkynge.

Prætimeo, ere, to be sore aferde.

Præ

P ante R.

Prætingo, gere, to touche afore.
Prætondeo, to sheere or klyppe, or rounde before.
Prætoritius, a, um, for Prætorius.
Prætorium ius, lawe made by the Prætor.
Prætor, toris, a chief capitayne in warres, in a citie or contraye.
Prætor is he, whiche hath autoritye to sit in iugemente, and to gyue sentence in causis.
Prætorianus, he that is attendant to him that is Prætor.
Prætorium, the house or pauylyon of hym that is Prætor. it is alsoo a princes palayce or manoure: it is somtyme the place, where iugementes are gyuen, sometyme the counsayle, wherevnto Prætores are assembled.
Prætorius, he that hath bene Prætor.
Prætorius, a, um, belonginge to the office of Prætor.
Prætura, the dignitie and ministration, of him that is Prætor.
Præualeo, lere, to preuayle, to be better or of more value.
Præualidus, a, dum, very stronge or myghty, sometyme very greate.
Præuaricatio, is a collusion: alsoo it is where one toucheth a thing lytely, which ought to be inculked with a more playn declaracyon, or els repeted, as makynge moche to the purpose.
Præuaricor, aris, ari, to swarue from truthe, to go out of the right waye, to leue vnsayd that, which shulde be spoken, to touche a thinge shortely in spekynge, to warke by collusion, in suffringe his aduersary to optayne, to hurte another person.
Præuaricator, toris, he that leueth the ryght waye, or speketh not that whych ought to be spoken: also he that in spekinge for him selfe aydeth the cause of his aduersary, or doeth any thinge by collusion.
Præueho, here, to brynge first.
Prælo, are, to couer or hyde afore.
Præuello, lere, to pull or plucke afore.
Præuenio, nire, to come before or preuent.

Ti. Liuius. de bell. pu.
Ci. de Di.

Præuentio, a preuention.
Præuideo, dere, to foresee, to beware.
Præuius, he that leadeth the waye.
Præuerto, uertere, to set more by, or to care more for. Nec me vxorem præuortisse dicant, præ repub. Nor let them not saye, that I set more by my wyfe, than by the weale publyke. Also to tourne or set a syde. Neq̃ præripio pulpamentum; neq̃ præuorto poculum, Nor I take awaye thy meate, nor set or tourne asyde thy drynke.

Plautus in Amphi.
Plautus in milite.

Præuertor, deponens, idem quod præuerto: also to go afore. Inde illico præuertor domum, from thense I went home afore. Al-

Plautus in capt.

P ante R.

so to be tourned furth. Foreis enim clausit, ne præuorteretur foras, he hath shyt fast the doore, leest he shulde be turned forth. Also to do any thinge firste or before any other thinge. Præuorti hoc certum est rebus alijs omnibus, Surely this shall be done before any other thinge.

Plautus in Amph.

Præuertere serio, to turne it to ernest. Si quid dictum est per iocum, non equum est id te serio præuortier. If any thinge be spoken in iape, it is not rayson to tourne it to ernest.

Plautus in amph.

Præuerti pigritiæ, to be taken with slouth. Caue pigritiæ præuortier, beware that thou be not taken with slouthe.

Plautus in Merc.

Præuersus, a, um, that which is done or sped first, or before any other.
Præuersum fulgur, lyghtenynge whyche is not knowen, whyther it be by daye or by nyghte.

Pom. Fest.

Præuolo, are, to flee before.
Pragmaticus, a practiser in the lawe.
Pragma in greke, is in latyne negociatio, an acte or busynesse: alsoo an exercise of marchaundyse.
Pragmatica sanctio, a determination of practisians of the lawe.
Prandeo, prandi, & pransus sum, prandere, to dyne.
Prandiculum, a brekefast.
Prandiolum, a lyter dynar.
Prandium, a dynar.
Pransito, tare, to dyne or eate often.
Pransor, oris, he that is at dynar, or he that is boden to dynar.
Prasinus, na, num, greene lyke leekis.
Prasius, a greene stone.
Prasoides, a stone of the coloure of leekes.
Pratensis, se, of the medowes.
Pratense fœnum, medowe haye.
Pratulum, a lytle medowe.
Praué, shrewedly, noughtyly, vnhappely, or vérthwartly.
Prauitas, shrewdenesse, vnhappynesse, ouerthwartnesse.
Pratum, medowe.
Prauus, a, um, croked.
Praxiteles, an excellent caruar in stone.
Precarius, a, um, that whiche is borowed, at the wyll of the lender, that which is occupyed, at another mans pleasure.
Precario, by desyre at another mans will.
Preces, prayer.
Precium, pryce, value.
Preciosus, a, um, deere, preciouse.
Precor, aris, ari, to praye.
Prehendo, prehendi, dere, to take. Et manum prehendi, & osculum detuli tibi, I toke you by the hande, and also gaue you a kysse.

Pre-

P ante R.

Premo, pressi, premere, to presse: sometyme to vexe, to vygge, to prese on, to thruste, to destroye, to thrust downe, to constrayne, to restrayne.

Vergilius. Premere dolorem, to hyde heuynesse or sorowe. Premit alto corde dolorem, he hyd his sorowe in the secrete parte of his harte.

Varro. Premere, to dryue or put oute.

Verg. Premere, to shyt or close. Pressiq; oculos, ac vulnera laui, I closed his eyes, and washed his woundes.

Ver. geo. 1 Premere, to cut awaye. Et ruris opaci, falce premes vmbram, and with a sythe thou shalt cut awaye the shadowe of the darke feldes.

Vergili. 2. Premere, to trede doune. Veluti qui sentibus anguem, pressit humi retens, lyke as he, which thrastyng his fote to the grounde, tredeth doune the snake, that lyeth in the brembles.

Premere testimonio, to conuicte a man by witnesse.

Presa porca, a swyne which was offred in sacrifice to Ceres, in satisfaction for a hole bousholde, for as moche as a part of that sacrifice was made in the presence of the corps, which than was to be buryed.

Pressatus, ta, tum, oppressed, charged troden downe.

Cor Nep.
As. pedian. Pres, predis, he that vndertaketh, if any incommoditie do happen, that he shall make sufficient recompence: it is also he that is bounden for suche money as is borowyd of a commune treasure or stocke.

Presbiter, biteri, an auncient, or father in yeres or dygnytye. It is vsed for a preest.

Presso, are, to presse or thrust togither.

Pressus, ssa, ssum, subtyll, compacte, heuy, pressed.

Pressus, ssus, & pressura, pressinge, also oppression.

Pretiosus, a, um, preciouse, dere, of grete estimacion.

Pretiosior, pretiosius, more preciouse or dere.

Terent. in
prol. Hec. Pretium, the pryce or value: alsoo the rewarde: sometyme peryll or daunger. Pretio emptas meo, bought with my peryll or daunger.

Pri, of olde tyme was vsed for Præ.

Priamus, the noble kynge of Troye, whose history is to no man vnknowen.

Priapismus, a sickenesse, wherein the pryuy membre of a man allway standeth, without hauinge any appetite to lechery.

Priapus, an ydolle, vnto whome the Paynymes, commytted their gardynes to kepe.

Pridem, late.

Pridianus, a, um, that which is done the daye before.

Pridie, the daye before.

Primas tenere, to haue the preeminence, to be chief, to holde the bettar part.

Primas dare, to esteme aboue other.

Primæuus, a, um, the elder.

Primarius, a, um, chief.

Primas, atis, in chief autoritie.

Primanus Tribunus, he that assigned tribute to the first legion.

Prima lux, the sprynge of daye.

Prima vespera, the euenynge.

Ci. de ora. Primæ, the chief prayses. Cui primæ sine cō trouersia deferebantur, to whome the chief prayses were gyuen withoute any controuersye.

Primitus, first.

Primetium, sacrifice of the eares of corne, which were first gathered after that they were repyd.

Plautus. Primores, the toppes of any thynge.

Digitulis primorib*, with the fingar toppes.

Labriis primoribus, with the fore part of the lyppes.

Primoribus labris gustare, to touche a thing skantely, to smater of a thinge, and not to knowe it substancially or perfitely.

Primicerius, chiefruler.

Primigenus, gena, genum, fyrste borne or growen.

Primigenius, a, um, that commeth naturally of it selfe, and is vnmixt.

Primigenia, the tytle of the eldest childe in inheritaunce.

Primipara, she that hath her fyrst childe.

Primipes, he that in batayle fyghteth fyrste with a sworde, and after chaungynge his fourme of fyghtynge, vseth a Iauelyne or darte.

Primipilaris, is he that fyghteth nexte to the standarde. It is mooste proprely the Capytayne of a companye in the fowewarde.

Primitium, the principall or chief.

Veget. l. 2. Primipilus, a capytayne of a company in the forewarde or vauntgarde, whiche hadde vnder hym fower hundred Souldiours.

Primiter, & Primitus, first.

Primitiæ, the first frutes.

Primitius, a, um, the fyrst or foremoost.

Primitiuus, a, um, that whiche hath none other begynnynge.

Primesius, a stake, whereto a cabell or rope of a shyppe is tyed.

Primò, an aduerbe, signifyeth fyrst.

Primodum, for Primo.

Primogenia verba, wordes whyche be not diry-

ued from any other.
Primogenitus, ta, tum, fyrste begotten.
Primordium, the fyrst begynnynge.
Primores, the fyrste, the chiefe. Primores uiri aut feminæ, Noble men or womenne, or gentyll men and gentyll women.
Primulus, the diminutiue of Primus.
Primum, an aduerbe, whyche sygnifyeth fyrste, er euer.
Primus, a, um, fyrste, beste, the chiefe. Primo quóque tempore, atte the fyrste tyme. Prima quaq; occasione, at the fyrste occasyon that shall happen.
Princeps, cipis, a prince, the fyrste or chief.
Principalis, le, principall, also, pertaynynge to a prynce.
Principaliter, pryncipallye.
Principio, an aduerbe, fyrste, or at the begynnynge.

Liuius
Terent.
Suetonius

Principia, the place in a Campe, where as are pyghte the pauilions of the heed capitaynes: but the more propre significatyon therof is, that it is the seconde warde in battayle, where in olde tyme were the princis and noble men. Also it was taken for the order of ray of noble men.
Principior, piari, to begynne.
Principor, pari, to rule.
Principium, the begynnynge.
Prior, the fyrste.
Priora tempora, the olde tyme.
Priscus, a, um, auncient, or of the old tyme.
Pristinus, na, num, that whyche was many yeres passed. Sometyme it sygnifyeth the fyrste, auncient.
Pristis, a fysh, of wonderful length, & slender, whyche cuttethe the wawes, as he swymmeth.
Priuatus, he that is in none auctorytie or dygnitie.
Priuatus, ta, tum, that is proprely a mannes owne, that whyche pertayneth to oone man or fewe, also particular. Sometyme it signifieth depriued.
Priuatim, & priuate, priuyly, aparte.
Priuernum, a towne in Campania.
Priuignus, na, the chylde by an nother husbande, or other wyfe, whyche is decd, son or doughter in law to the husband or wife.
Priuilegium, a lawe concernynge pryuate persones. also a priuate or speciall lawe.
Priuo, are, to take awaye, to depriue.
Prius, an aduerbe, sygnifyeth before.
Priusquam, before that.
Priuus, ua, uum, pryuate, synguler, euerye mans owne or propre.
Pro, for, before. Pro rostris, at the barre or place of pleding. Pro tribunali, in the place of iugement. also after or accordyng. Pro Platonis sententia, accordynge to the sentence of Plato. Pro opere, in the warke. Pro merito, accordynge to his deseruing. Pro curia, before the courte. Pro uirili, to my power.

Salust. in Iugurt.

Prô sancte Iupiter, O blessed Iupiter.
Prô deum atq; hominum fidem, O the faith of god and man.

Vide com.

Proauus, my greatte grandfather.
Proauia, my great grandame.
Probabile, that whiche may be proued.
Probatica piscina, a ponde, where sheepe are washed.
Probatio, a proufe.
Probatus, ta, tum, proued.
Probè, honestely, well, wysely.
Probiter, idem.

Vide com.

Probus, a vertuous man, a good man.
Probitas, goodnes.
Problema, tis, a sentence purposed, hauing a demaunde therto annexed.
Probo, are, to proue, to prayse, to approue.
Proboscis, dis, a longe snowte, as an Olyphant or swyne hath.
Probro, are, to reproche or rebuke.
Probrosus, a, um, reprochefull.
Probrum, a reprocheful act. Also a reproch or rebuke, an infamie.
Procax, procacis, malaperte in askynge, or desyrynge, shameles, wanton in crauing, yll tounged.
Procacitas, malapertnes, or wantonnesse in askynge or crauynge.
Procare, to wowe, to craue, to be ymportunate.
Procapis, a progenie, whyche commeth of one heade.
Procaciter, malapertely, wantonly, without shame.
Procalo, are, to calle one to.
Procatum, & prociū, void, or of none effect.
Procedo, cessi, cedere, to go forthe, to procede, to prosper.
Procella, a storme.
Proceleumaticus, a foote in meter of foure feete shorte.
Procello, ere, to streeke, to turn vp so downe
Procellosus, a, um, stormye.
Procensu, the company or felowshyppe of yonge men in the cytie, as we beholde in London the Bachelers togyther, whan the Mayre taketh his othe.
Proceres, the heed men of a towne.
Procêrus, a, um, longe, talle.
Proceritas, lengthe, talnesse.
Proceriter, an aduerbe, whyche sygnifyeth longe, or of lengthe.
Proceritus, rita, tum, incensed or prouoked with an yll spiryte, madde or woode.

T Pro-

P ante R.

Plautus in Penulo. Proceriti lapides, vengeable.
Procerto, surely.
Procet, for prouocet, let hym prouoke, let hym appeale.
Processus, us, processe or successe.
Processrium, a galerye to goo frome oone chambre to an other. Also the ouermoste parte of the walles within the imbattylmentes, where men maye go: some doo calle it a trenche before the campe, in defence therof from artyllery.
Prochyta, an jle in the see, in the gulfe or rode of Puteolis, a citie in Campania.
Procidentia ani, whan the bone of the fundement appereth oute.
Procido, dere, to fall downe prostrate.
Perottus. Procico, ere, to prouoke or cal from far of.
Procincta classis, a nauy pparid redy to fight
Procinctus, tus, the prouysyon before that any thynge is done.
Procingo, xi, gere, to prepare, to make redy.
Procinctus, ta, tum, redy, prepared.
Procino, cinui, nere, to pronouce in singing, to synge out.
Procio, ciui, ire, to afke.
Procito, tare, to prouoke.
Proclamo, are, to crie out, to proclayme.
Procliué, redily, easily in doinge.
Procliuis, ue, redy to falle, inclyned. Also redy or easy to be done.
Procliuitas, tatis, inclynation to euyll.
Proclus, a noble phylosopher of the secte of Plato.
Proco, & procor, ari, to afke malapertely. Also to dalye with wanton language, to eye or beholde a woman wantonly.
Proconsul, lis, he that was sent with an extra ordinarie power of Consul into a prouynce of the Romayns.
Procrastinatio, a delaye.
Procrastino, nare, to prolonge the tyme, to deferre.
Procreo, are, to bygette chylderne.
Procreatus, ta, tum, begotten.
Procubitor, toris, he that kepethe watche and warde without the campe.
Procubo, bare, to watche.
Procudo, dere, to stryke or beate a thynge, to make it lesse or thynner.
Qu. Curtl. Ti. Liuius. Procul, farre of, from farre.
Procul urbem, farre from the cytie.
Procul muros, farre from the walles.
Proculco, care, to treade downe.
Proculdubio, out of doubte, doubtlesse.
Perottus. Proculeio, ere, to extende, to promyse.
Proculiunt, old writers vsed for promittunt,
Pom. Fest. they promyse.
Proculus, he that is borne whan his father is farre out of the countrey.

P ante R.

Procumbo, cubui, cumbere, to lye flatte or prostrate, to come narowe togyther.
Procuro, rare, to do or solicite an other mannes busynesse, to inserche dylygentely, to helpe or sustayne, or succour.
Procuratorius, ia, um, pertaynyng to a proctour or factour.
Procurator, toris, a proctour, a factour.
Procuratio, mynystration of thynges concernynge an other man.
Procurro, rere, to runne farre, or beyonde.
Procuruus, ua, um, very croked.
Procus, a wower, to haue a womanne in mariage, but moste proprely where there be two, whyche woweth euery oone for hym selfe.
Procyon, a sterre called the Doggesterre, whyche appereth in the canycular days.
Prodeo, diui, uel drj, to goo forthe or oute of a house, to come before one.
Prodigium, a thynge seldome seene, whiche sygnifyeth, that somme thynge shall happen veraye good or veraye ylle, as blasynge sterres, fyres, or fygures in the fyrmamente, thynges monstruouse or agaynste nature.
Prodigo, digere, to lasshe oute moneye in vayne, or in thynges not necessary. somtyme to signifye somme straunge thynge to happen.
Prodigus, prodigall, wastefull, an outragious expender.
Prodo, didi, dere, to forsake, to differre, or putte of, to caste forthe, to putte oute or farre of, to shewe or disclose, also to differ, to spreade, to betraye.
Prodere memorie, to leue in remembrance. Also to wryte.
Prodire obuiam, to go agaynst one, or to go to mete with one, whiche is commynge.
Prodire in publicum, to goo abrode, to go in the stretes.
Prodico, dixi, dicere, to speke more or prate. Quamobrem excuriemus omnes istorum delitias, omnes ineptias, si prodixerint, wherfore we wyll set forthe al these mennes pleasures and fantasyes, if they wylle prate any more. **Cicer. pro Cælio.**
Prodigalitas, prodygalytie, or outragyouse expenses.
Prodigé, excessyuely, outragiously, prodigally, wastefully.
Prodigialis, digiale, that whyche pertayneth to the procuryng of strange tokens or sygnes.
Prodigiator, he that by straunge tokens or sygnes, tellethe before what shall afterwarde happen.
Prodigiosus, sa, sum, that whyche makethe strange

straunge signes or tokens.
Prodigitas, prodygalitie.
Prodimentum, a treason or betrayenge.
Prodinunt, for prodiunt, vsed of Ennius, to issue or come forthe.
Prodius, further in.
Proditio, treason.
Proditor, toris, a traytour.

Terent. in Heaut. Prodere uitam, to put his lyfe in daunger.
Prodromus, he that runneth before, as a lackey, or he that bryngethe tydynges of ones commynge. Prodromi, be also sterres in heuen, the whyche doo ryse in the Northe easte. viii. dayes afore the canicular dayes.

Vergilius. Produco, duxi, ducere, to prolonge, to bryng forthe, to consume or spende. Producere aliquem falsa spe, to holde or kepe one in a fooles paradyse, to put forewarde: also to folowe.
Productilis, le, that whiche is made out at length with beatynge.

Plautus in Asinar. Producere, to sette forthe to hyre. Audientem dicto mater produxisti filiam, Thou beinge hir mother, and she being obedient vnto the, thou haste sette hyr to hyre.
Producere filios, to begette chyldrene.
Productio, the makynge of a thynge longe.
Producte, an aduerbe, signifieth longe.
Productus, ta, tum, made longe or sette out at lengthe. also brought or put out.
Proedifico, care, to buylde.
Proedificatum, that whiche being a priuate place, is made commune or publyke.
Profanatum templum, the churche suspendyd, where any horrible cryme is therin commytted.
Profano, are, to conuerte thynges beynge halowed to a temporall vse.

Varro. Profanus, na, num, that whiche is not halowed, temporall, men vnlerned, and that do hate lerned men. Also that whiche is ioyned or annexed vnto the temple.
Profari, to pronounce, to speake abrode.

Ci. de bello ciuili. Profectio, a passage or settynge forthe towarde a vyage, a departynge frome the place, where a man is.
Profecto, in very dede, for sothe.

Pli. in epis. Profectum facere, to profyte or goo forthe, proprely in study and lernynge.
Profectus sum, the pretertence of proficiscor, I wente.
Profectus, tus, profyte.
Profero, tuli, ferre, to bryng forthe, to shew forthe, to pronounce, to inlarge, or dylate, or make greatter, to prolonge.

Plautus in Casina. Profere dolum, to put a disceit in experiece.
Profere gradum, to make hast in going.
Profesti dies, warkedayes.

Proficio, ficere, to profyte, to precede.
Proficiscor, cisci, to go and to come.
Profiteor, to promyse openly, to tell frankly or boldly. Also to tell or declare, howe moche a man hath of money, cattal, corne, or any other thynge. Also to speake or auaunt. Also to discouer or confesse a thing. Also to rede openly a lesson. **Ci. de senectute, & de amicitia.** **Plautus in capt.** **Ci. de ami.**
Professio, an open confession, an open redynge or lecture.
Professor, oris, a reder in open scholes.
Profligo, gare, to ouerthrowe, to dryue awaye, to brynge to distruction, to putte to flyghte.
Profligatus, ta, tum, ouerthrowen, dryuen away, put to flyght, distroyed. somtyme it signifieth finished, brought to a poynte.
Profligo, gis, gere, to stryue moche.
Proflubeo, ui, ere, to runne out.
Profluens, tis, a ryuer: being a participle, it signifieth flowynge.
Profluo, xi, ere, to runne out of a thynge, to runne from farre.
Profluuium, a fyxe or laske.
Profluus, a, um, that whiche floweth.
Profore, to profite. Quę nocuere sequar, fugiam quę profore credam, That whyche hath done harme wyl I folowe: & eschew wyll I those thynges, whyche I beleue shulde profyte me. **Horatius.**
Profugio, gere, to flye farre.
Profugium, a place, whereto a man flyethe for succour.
Profugus, he that gothe farre oute of his owne countrey.
Profunda auaritia, insaciable auaryce. Profunda cupido, insaciable couetyse. Profunda libido, insacyable lecherye. **Salust. in Iugurt.**
Profunditas, depenesse.
Profundo, fudi, fundere, to poore out largely, to spende excedyngely.
Profundus, da, dum, depe, sometyme hyghe.
Profusus, excedynge lyberall.
Progener, ri, the husbande of my dowghters dowghter, or sonnes dowghter.
Progenies, progenie, succession in bloode.
Progigno, nere, to gette a chylde.
Prognare, openly.
Prognariter, hardyly. **Festus**
Prognatus, ta, tum, begotten.
Prognosis, prescience, or knowledge afore that a thynge happeneth. **Plautus in Penulo.**
Prognosticon, a pronostication.
Progredior, grederis, gressus sum, gredi, to go forthe.
Progressus, sa, sum, passed ouer.
Progressus, us, a marchynge forthe, or passynge forthe.
Progressio, the same.

Progymnasma, an assay or profe in exercise.
Prohibeo, bui, bēre, to prohibite, to forbyd, to tourne awaye.
Proiecta, the ouer partes of a howse, which do leane outwarde from the neither part, as they be nowe in some townes toward the stretes: some men do cal thē garrettis.
Proiecta audatia, foole hardynesse.
Proiectare aliquem probris, to rebuke one.
Proiectitius, a, um, a chylde caste forthe and nouryshed of a straunger.
Proiectura, a penthowse to conuaye rayne from the walles.
Proiectus puer, a chylde whiche is layde abrode in the strete, no man knowyng who is the father or mother.
Proiectus, proiecta, iectum, throwen or cast out afarre.
Proiectus ad audendum, foolehardy.
Proijcio, ieci, ncere, to throwe or cast, to set forth, to leaue, to extende or holde oute a thynge at length.
Proin, therfore.

Salustius in Iugurt. Proinde, therfore, wherfore, lyke as.
Prolabor, beris, bi, to slyde or slyppe forth.
Prolambo, bere, to lycke.
Prolatio, an extendynge forthe. Also pronouncyng, or pronunciation, sommetyme brihgynge forthe or shewyng of a thynge.
Prolatare, to deferre or putte of, vntylle a longer tyme.
Prolatus, ta, tum, set forthe, brought forthe.
Prolectibilis, le, that which tickleth or plesantly moueth one.
Prolepsis, a fygure in speakyng, where we doo preuente, to dissolue by reason that, whyche we thynke to be in the opinion of our aduersary, or of the iudge.
Proles, issue or fruite of a mannes bodye. Also of a beaste.
Proletarii, amonge the Romains were they whiche for pouertie were not able to goo to the warres: and therfore they were lefte at home to gette chylderne.
Prolibo, are, to tast, or to sacrifice afore.
Prolicio, prolexi, olicere, to induce or drawe.

Plautus in Curcul. Eius amor cupidā huc me per tenebras prolicit, The loue of hym hathe drawen me hyther in the darke, beynge desyrous of his company.
Prolixe, lyberally, abundantly, at length.

Colum. 5. Prolixo, lixare, to make a thynge sharpe in lengthe. Quare magnopere mouendus putator est, ut prolixet aciē ferramenti, & quātum possit, nouaculæ similem reddat, wherfore the cuttīg of the vyne oughte to be warned, that he make sharpe in lengthe the pointe of the instrument, and as moch as he may, that he make it lyke to a raser.

Prolixus, a, um, longe, large, sometyme superfluous.
Prolixitas, & prolixitudo, length, largenes.
Prolocutio, the fyrste speche or fyrst entree into communication. *Plautus.*
Prologium, idem.
Prologus, a prologue.
Prolongo, are, to prolonge, to deferre. *Festus.*
Proloquium, the begynnynge of an oration or sentence.
Proloquor, queris, qui, to speake at length, to telle a longe tale. Also to speke before, to speake that whyche we thynke, to declare our opynyon.
Proludo, dere, to flourysshe, as musytians doo, before they come to the principalle mattier: and as fence men doo with the sworde or the two handstaffe.
Prolugeo, xi, gēre, to mourne longer than hath bēn accustomed.
Proluo, ere, to wasshe moche, to drowne or surrounde.
Proluuies, the fylthe or ordure, whyche is washed of any thynge.
Proluuium, idem. Also prodigalitie.
Promellere, to promote or sette forth suite in the lawe.
Promercalia, thynges set forth to be solde, specially that whiche is solde by retaylle.
Promercale aurum, golde solde in suche wyse, that besydes the iuste value, so moche golde remayneth to the seller, as may serue to his propre vse, as our nobles and royalles solde beyonde the see at a greater price than they be valewed at here in this royalme.
Promercor, caris, cari, to bie thynges good cheape, to the intent to sell them deere, to bye at the fyrst hand, to sel them at retail.
Promereo, rui, rere, to deserue.
Promereor, reri, idem, Also to bynde oone by his actes to do for hym. Also to helpe, to profytte.
Promereri de aliquo, to doo a man a good tourne.
Promerens, tis, he that dothe pleasure or seruyce. Promerenti optime hoccine pretij redditur? He that hathe done verye good seruyce, shall he haue this rewarde for his laboure? *Plautus in Asinar.*
Promeritum, deserte.
Promeneruat, olde writers vsed for monet, he exhorteth or warneth. *Festus.*
Prometheus, he that fyrst found and taught astronomie in Assiria, and also the craft to make ymages of erthe.
Promico, are, to extend or set out at length.
Prominenter, at legathe.
Prominentia, the extendynge or settynge
out at

out at lengthe.

Promineo, nui, nere, to appiere farre of. *Festus.*

Promiscam, olde wryters dyd vse for promiscue.

Promisceo, cui, scere, to mengle togyther.

Promiscue, one with an other, myxte.

Promiscuus, scua, scuum, confused, myngled one with an nother.

Promissa barba, a longe berde.

Promisse, longe, in lengthe.

Promissio, a promyse.

Promissor, he that promyseth.

Promissum, a promyse.

Promitto, misi, mittere, to promyse, to lette growe in lengthe. Also to thretten. *Vide cōp.*

Promo, prompsi, mere, to speake out, to tel, to take out of a coffer or other lyke thyng.

Promontorium, a mountayne or high place of a lande or countrey, whyche lyeth as it were an elbowe into the see warde.

Promptaria cella, a prison from whens men be brought to be whipped or hanged.

Promptarius, a, um, that frome whens any thynge is brought or taken.

Promptarium, & promptuarium, a storehowse.

Prompte, promptly, redylye.

Promptior, more prompte or redy.

Promptitudo, promptnesse.

Prompto, tare, to brynge often forthe. *Plautus in Bacch. & in Pseudolo.*

Promptus, ta, tum, prompte, redye to doo a thyng without tarieng. also redy. Promptum ingenium, A redye wytte. Res est in promptu, The thynge is redy. also manyfeste. In promptu res est, The thynge is manyfeste.

Promulco nauis agitur, the shyppe is drawen with a bote.

Promulgator, & promulgatrix, he or she that dothe publyshe a thynge.

Promulgo, gare, to publyshe.

Promulgatio, a publycation.

Promulsis, idis, a bede, made with water and hony.

Promurale, a countermure, one wall without an nother.

Promus, he that hath the kepynge of the storehouse or drie larder.

Pronepos, potis, & proneptis, my sonnes or daughters sonne or daughter.

Prone, redyly.

Pronis, olde writers vsed for prona, prostrate or on the grounde.

Pronomen, a pronowne.

Pronuba, she that attendeth on the bryde, and is housewyfe durynge the feaste.

Pronubo, nupsi, pronubere, to haue a rule in weddinges or ioynynge of couples.

Pronubus, he that leadeth the bryde home to her husbandes house, and hath the surueyenge of the house, durynge the tyme of the solemnisation.

Pronubus, he that dothe celebrate the solemnitie in mariage. it may be nowe taken for the prieste, whiche dothe mynister the solemne wordes of matrimonye.

Pronunciatio, a pronunciation or vtterance of speeche.

Pronuntiatum, a statute. *Plautus in Trin.*

Pronuntio, are, to pronounce, to declare openly, to gyue sentence, to saye.

Pronuper, longe agone.

Pronurus, the wyfe of my sonnes sonne, or daughters sonne.

Pronus, redy, inclyned, stowpinge downe, nygh hande.

Prooemium, a proheme or begynnynge of a mattier.

Propago, gare, to sprede as a tree dothe on the toppe, to make to spreade, to sende farre of.

Propagatio, a spreadynge.

Propages, a longe rewe.

Propago, ginis, an olde vyne spred in many braunches. Sometyme it sygnifyeth kynde or generation.

Propalam, openly, clerely in the syghte of all menne.

Propalo, lare, to telle abroode, to growe in lengthe.

Propatruus, my gret grandfathers brother.

Propatulum, wyde open.

Prope, nygh, almooste.

Propediem, nowe euery day, shortly.

Propello, propuli, pellere, to dryue or putte awaye, farre of.

Propemodum, almoste.

Propendere, to hange vp. Propendere, to examyne or consyder farre of.

Propensus, inclyned.

Propere, quyckely, hastily.

Properatim, quyckely.

Properanter, & properiter, idem.

Properantia, & properatio, an approchyng. *Catullus.*

Properitas, the same amonge olde writers.

Properus, a, um, quycke, sodayne.

Propero, rare, to go quyckely or hastely, to say or do any thynge quyckely or hastely.

Propetro, trare, to commande that a thyng be doone. *Festus.*

Prophasis, an excuse.

Prophetis, & prophetissa, a womanne prophete.

Propheto, tare, to prophesye, to syng prayses to god: somtyme it signifieth to preache or interprete.

Propheta, a prophete, he that telleth thynges, whiche shall happen.

Prophetia, a prophecye.

Propilo, are, to make sharpe byfore.

Propina, a place by the commune baynes, where after baynynge menne toke theyr refection.

Propino, propinare, to drynke to an nother manne, to quaffe, to brynge to. Sommetyme to gyue. Propino tibi salutem, I salute the.

Propinator, a cuppe bearer.

Propinquus, a neyghbour. Also a kynnesman, of alyaunce.

Propinquitas, affynitie, alyaunce.

Propinqué, nyghe.

Propinquior, quius, nerer.

Propitiabilis, le, that whiche is sone bowed or inclyned to desyres.

Propitialis, idem.

Propitiatio, sacrifyce to appease or pacyfye goddis displeasure.

Propitium, sommetyme sygnyfyeth veray deuoute or louynge.

No. Mar. Propitij, peasyble men, or men soone appeased or satisfied.

Propius, nerrer, or nerre.

Proplastice, ces, the crafte to make mouldes, in the whiche any thynge is caste or fourmed.

Propingeon, the place in a bayne or hotte house, in the whyche fyre inclosed, sendeth forth heate.

Propitiatorium, a table sette on the arke of the olde testament.

Propitio, & propitior, ari, to appease, or to make mercyfull, or fauourable.

Propitius, pitia, tium, appeased, fauourable, mercyfulle.

Propior, nerer.

Propola, he that sellyth any thynge at retayle, specyally vyttayle, a hukster.

Propolis, a subburbes of a towne. It is also that whyche bees doo make at the entrie of the hyue, wherby colde and other annoyaunce is defended.

Propono, proposui, ponere, to purpose, to be aduysed, to promyse a pryce or reward for any notable acte, to sette oute to the shewe.

Propontis, a see betwene Grece and Asie.

Proportio, a proporcyon.

Propositio, a matter pourposed to be dysputed or reasoned. It is also that, wherby we shewe generallye, whereof we wyll speake.

Propositum, a purpose.

Propretor, toris, he that was in the steede of Prætor, or Mayre.

Proprié, properly.

Lucretius. Propritim, idem.

Proprietarius, a, um, wherunto the proprietie of a thynge belongeth.

Proprietas, propretie.

Proprius, propria, prium, propre.

Propter, for. Sommetyme nyghe. Alsoo at or in.

Propterea, therfore.

Proptosis, a dysease, where the eyen meuyd with inflammation, too falle oute of their places.

Propudium, shame, dishonestie. Alsoo the moste abomynable vse of lecherye, in an inconuenient fourme.

Propugnaculum, a fortresse, a strong hold.

Propugnator, toris, a defendour.

Propugno, are, to fyght farre of, to fyghte valyauntly, to defende.

Propulsator, he that resysteth a thynge, or dryueth any thynge away.

Propulso, are, to put of, to dryue away.

Propyleum, a porche.

Proquestor, toris, he that exercyseth the offyce of Questor in his absence.

Prora, the foreparte of a shyppe.

Prorepo, prorepsi, prorepere, to creepe further.

Proreta, he that hath the rule of the foreshyppe or decke.

Porideo, ridere, to laugh afarre of.

Proripio, pui, pere, to withdrawe or depart. ioyned with me or se, Domum se ex curia proripuit, He departed or withdrew hym homewarde from the courte.

Prorito, tare, to prouoke.

Prorogatio, a prolongynge or delayenge.

Prorogo, gare, to prolonge.

Prorsus, & prorsum, vtterly, alway, in any wyse, strayght towarde a place, surely.

Prorsi, lymyttes in boundynge of landes directed into the easte.

Prorumpo, rupi, rumpere, to breake forthe, to sende forthe with vyolence, to leape or go out of a place with violéce, to brast out

Proruo, ruere, to dryue downe, or beate downe.

Prosa, prose, that whiche is not meter.

Prosapia, a progenye, a dyscente of blode, a petygree.

Proscenia, the place, wherein enterludes were played by the personages.

Proscindo, proscidi, proscindere, to cutte out or vnder, to infame, to rebuke shamefullye.

Proscribo, scripsi, scribere, to sell openly, to proclayme any thynge to be solde, to banysshe, to condemne.

Proscriptio, a condemnation, an attayndre.

Proscriptus, condemned, attaynted.

Proseco, care, to cut a sonder.

Prosecta, bowelles cut in sacrifice.
Proseda, a strumpette or commune harlot.
Prosedanum, a disease, which happeneth to Rammes at blysomynge tyme.
Proselytus, a straunger borne.
Prosemino, are, to sowe furth.
Prosequium, an affection.
Prosequor, qui, to folowe after, to pursue. Prosequor amore, I loue. Prosequor odio, I hate. Prosequor honore, I honoure. Prosequor verbis, I chafe him with wordes. Prosequor officijs, I shewe to hym great kyndnesse, I do him many pleasures. Prosequi præmio, to rewarde.
Proserpere, to creape or slyde furth lyke a serpent.
Proserpina, the wyfe of Pluto.
Proseuche, a prayer to God: alsoo a beggynge. *Iuuen.*
Proseucha, a beggar. *No. Mar.*
Prosferari, to be optayned.
Proficium, that whiche is cut of frome any thinge, and cast awaye.
Prosilio, lij, lire, to leape furth.
Prosocer, ceri, the father of my wyfes father. *Plì. in epiſ. lio.*
Prositum, olde wrytars vsed for propositum purposed.
Prosodia, the craft of accentinge.
Prosonomasia, the lykenesse of one worde or name to another: as locus and lucus, orator, and arator.
Prosopopœia, where as personages are supposed or fayned to speke, as one man to an other: a man to a beaste: one beaste to an other &c.
Prospectus, ctus, a syght farre of, a prospecte.
Prospecte, aduysedly.
Prospecto, spectare, to beholde, proprely farre of.
Prospere, prosperously.
Prosperiter, idem.
Prosperitas, prosperitie.
Prospica, & Prospicus, he that beholdeth a thinge farre of.
Prospices, for prospice, beholde. *Festus.*
Prospiro, are, to fetche breth or wynde.
Prosper, & prosperus, prosperi, prospero, that which geueth felycitye. Felix, he that receyueth it.
Prospicientia, proudence, circumspection.
Prospicio, spexi, spicere, to see farre, to foresee, to prouyde, to beware.
Prospicuus, circumspect.
Prostasis, preeminence.
Prosthesis, an addicion of a lettre: as gnatus, for natus.
Prosterno, straui, sternere, to ouerthrowe, or to vaynquysshe in batayle.

Prostibulum, a commune brothelhouse: also a commune harlot.
Prostibula, idem.
Prostituo, tuere, to be a commune harlot. Prostituere pudicitiam, to be commune to al men or women in the acte of lechery.
Prosto, tare, to stande ferre of, or afore: also to stande to be solde or hyred.
Prosubigo, gere, to dygge deepe.
Prosum, fui, desse, to be profitable.
Prosumia, a lytle barke.
Prosumirium, a place withoute the walles of Rome, where the bysshoppes of the gentyles made their diuinations, or toke their significations of thinges to come.
Prosupero, are, to excede, or haue more than ynoughe.
Protasis, a proposicion. *Donatus.*
Protego, texi, tegere, to defende.
Protectio, a defence.
Protector, toris, a defendour.
Protentus, ta, tum, stretched oute.
Protela, lare, to differre, or tracte the tyme, to put oute, to dryue awaye, to vere.
Protendo, dere, to set forth, or put forth, to stretche forthe.
Protermino, to incroche.
Protero, triui, terere, to trede downe.
Proterreo, rere, to make aferde farre of.
Proteruia, wantonnesse: it was also a sacrifice, wherein the maner was, that as moch as was left vneaten, shulde be consumed with fyre.
Proteruiam fecit, he hath consumed all that is lefte.
Proteruio, ire, to playe the wanton.
Proterue, proudely, immoderatly, shamefully. Quis est, qui tam proterue, foribus facit iniuriam: who is he, that so proudely rappeth at the doore? Ecce autem tu quoq; pro terue iracundus es, Lo and thou also arte shamefully angry. *Plautus in Ruden.*
Proteruiter, idem.
Proteruitas, tatis, pryde, foly.
Proteus, the sonne of Occanus, a iugglar, whyche coulde shewe hym selfe in sondry fourmes.
Protestor, staris, stari, to declare manyfestly, what shulde be exchued and not done.
Protestator, he that manifestly declareth, what is to be exchued and not done.
Protestatio, a protestation.
Protina, for protinus, furthwith.
Proteruus, a, um, wanton, malaperte, shamelesse, and (as I mought saye) knauysshe, or lewde.
Protinus, afarre of. Also forthewith, without taryenge.

Pro-

Plautus in Styc. Prothymia, promptitude: also gentyll enter taynement. Proh Di immortales quot ego voluptates fero, quot risiones, quot iocos, quot suauia, saltationes, blanditias, prothymias? O lorde god, howe many pleasures haue I, what lawghingis, what pastymes, what bassinges, daunsinges, daliaunces, & swete entertaynementes?

Prothyrum, a porche at the vtter doore of a house.

Protipon opus, an image or fourme, wherof mouldes are made, in the whiche thynges be cast of metall or erthe.

Protogenes, of the first kynred or famyly: it was also the name of an excellent paynter.

Protocollum, that whiche is firste made or writen, which requireth correction.

Protogenus, the first childe.

Protogenia, the daughter of Deucalion and Pirrha.

Protologia, a preface.

Protollo, lere, to prolonge.

Protomartyr, the first martyr.

Protomedicus, the chief phisicion aboute a Prince.

Protomysta, the chief preest, or deane.

Protonotarius, a protonotary, or chief scribe or Secretary.

Protopages, & Protopagus, firste made or wrought, or late made.

Protoplastes, & Protoplastus, first fourmed so was Adam called.

Protos, Proton, first.

Prototocos, a woman late bringynge forth her first childe.

Prototomus, the stalke which is first cut.

Prototypus, & prototypon, the first exemple, or paterne.

Protraho, traxi, trahere, to differre or prolonge.

Protrepticus, a boke to instructe one, a doctrinall.

Protrimenta, meate mynced small.

Proueho, uexi, uehere, to brynge or cary further.

Prouectus etate, aged.

Prouectum ingenium, a longe proued wytte: also to promote, aduaunce.

Prouectus ad dignitatem, promoted or aduaunced to honour.

Prouectus etate, runne farre in yeres.

Prouectus, ta, tum, promoted.

Prouectus, aged.

Plautus in Menech. Prouenio, ire, to come forth: alsoo to growe or increase, to happen or chaunce. Nimis prouentum est nequiter, It is vngraciously chaunced.

Prouentus, tus, reuenues, yerely profytes.

Prouerbe, diligently.

Prouerbium, a prouerbe.

Prouide, circumspectely.

Prouideo, dere, to prouyde, to foresee, to beware.

Cice. & Quint. Prouidentia, prouidence, foresight: somtyme it is vsed for god.

Prouidus, prouident, circumspect.

Prouincie, were countrayes, which the Romans gate farre frome Rome, where only their officers did rule. Prouincia is somtyme taken for the rule or autoritye of an officer: also an office, alsoo for a countraye or royaulme.

Prouincialis, he that dwelleth in a prouince.

Prouinciatim, frome countray to countray, or one countraye with another.

Prouiso, prouisere, to see or beholde, to goo to see.

Prouidens, uidentis, foreseynge, prouident.

Prouidentior, dentissimus, more prouident, moost prouident or circumspect.

Prouocator, he that prouoketh one, or he that appeleth, the appellant.

Prouoco, care, to call from a farre, to stere, to inuite, to prouoke, to exhorte, also to apele to an hygher iuge.

Prouocatio, an appele to an hygher court.

Prouolo, are, to flye awaye, or beyonde, also to runne frome aferre.

Prouoluo, uere, to rolle or tumble a greate stone or other lyke thinge: sometyme to lye downe prostrate.

Prout, for Sicut, as.

Festus Proxeneta, a brokar.

Prox, of olde wrytars was taken for Proba vox, a good voyce or noyse.

Proximo, proximare, to approche or drawe nyghe.

Proximurium, a place withoute the walles, ioyninge to the cytie, where bysshoppes dyd assemble in their conuocations.

Cato. Proxime, next.

Proximi, for proximo: die proximi, the next daye.

Proximitas, nyghenesse, neyghbourhede.

Proximior, more nere.

Proximus, a, um, nexte.

Prouulgo, aui, are, to publysshe, or declare openly to the people.

Prudenter, wysely.

Prudens, prudentis, wyse, prudente, knowynge.

Prudentia, wysedome in desiringe and exchynge of thynges.

Prugnum, olde wrytars vsed for Pronum, prone or apte.

Pruina, frost.

Pruna, a burnynge cole.

Prunioli, smalle musherons.

Pru-

P ante S.

Pruinosus, a, um, frosty.
Prunetum, an orcharde sette with damsyne trees, or plumme trees.
Prunus, a damsyne tree or plumme tree.
Prunum, a damsyne, prune, plumme, slo, or bullase.
Prurio, rii, rire, to yche.
Pruritus, tus, ychinge.
Prurigo, ginis, ychinge with a delectation, as in the steryng of lechery.
Prusias, a kynge of Bythinia, vnto whome Hanniball fledde after that he was banyshed frome Carthage.
Prymnesius, a post or stake, where vnto the cabull of a shyp is tyed.
Prymnos, a nymphe or mayden of the see, one of the dawghters of Oceanus.
Prytaneium, a counsayle house.
Prytaneia, a counsayle assembled of great officers and iuges.
Prytanis, the president or chief of the counsayle.

¶ P, ANTE S.

Psallo, li, lere, to synge.
Psalmodia, a dyuerse or mixt songe.
Psalmus, a songe propelly to god, or of God.
Psalterium, an instrument lyke to a harp, also the Psalmes called the Psalter.
Psaltes, a syngynge man.
Psaltrix, tricis, & Psaltria, a syngynge woman.
Psecas, adis, a drop.
Psegma, the pouldre or dust, which cometh of the frylynge of brasse.
Psellus, the name of an olde writar, whiche wrote of diete.
Psephisma, atis, a decree.
Psephopecta, an auditour or caster of accompte.
Pseudoadelphus, a counterfayt brother.
Pseudoangelus, a false messager.
Pseudolus, a false seruaunt.
Pseudo martyr, a false wytnesse.
Pseudopropheta, a false prophete.
Pseudothyrum, a faulse posterne.
Pseudo, false or countrefait: and euery other nowne ioyned therewith, is thereby made false or countrefayt: as Pseudopropheta, a false or countrefayt prophete.
Psilotrum, an oynement to take awaye heares.
Psimmithium, that which we do call Ceruse or whyte ledde.
Psitta, a fysshe, whyche we call a playce.
Psittacus, a popynjay.
Psycolutres, he that delyteth to bathe in colde

P ante T.

colde water.
Psycomantium, a place where Nigromancers do call vp spirites.
Psora, scabbydnesse.
Psylli, people in Libia, whose bodyes are venyme to serpentes: and they also do cure the styngynge and poysonynge of serpentes by soukynge the place, whyche is venymed.

¶ P, ANTE T.

PTe, a syllable ioyned oftentymes to the ablatyue case, as meapte, tuapte, suapte, myne owne, thyne owne, his owne.
Pteris, ferne.
Pteromata, greate arches ouer the roofes made lyke wynges.
Pterigium, a lytle skynne, whyche groweth frome the corner of the eye, and keucreth the syght: it is also a grief vnder the fore part of the nayle, whan the flesh goeth fro the nayle with payne.
Pterna, the lower part of a sayle.
Ptisana, the water, wherin barly is soden, also barly husked, or excorticat, also frumety made of barly.
Ptyas, adis, an adder hauynge the coloure greene, drawynge towarde the colour of golde.
Ptynge, a rauenouse byrde, whyche taketh his praye by nyghte: and sometyme syghteth with the Egle so valiantly, that in crabynge togither, they fall both doune to the grounde, and are taken by Shepchardes.
Ptysis, is spettyll: it is alsoo an exulceration or soore in the lunges, with a consumpcyon of all the bodye, and spettynge of bloode.
Ptisanarium, a morter, wherein barley is brayed.
Ptochotrophia, an hospitall for beggars, a spyttell house.
Ptolomeus, the name of kynges of Egypte.
Ptosis, ruyne, also the case of a nowne.
Ptolemais, maidis, the name of a citie.

¶ P, ANTE V.

PVbens, he that is betwene a yonge man and a boye, of the age of xiiii yeres.
Puberesco, scere, to growe as a childe doeth towarde mannes state.
Pubeo, es, & Pubesco, ere, to begyn to haue a bearde benethe: sometyme to sprynge, as herbes done.
Puber, beris, & Pubes, beris, a yonge mosy bearde

bearde, whyche spryngeth in the nether partes of a man at .xiiii. yeres of age: of a woman at yonger yeres, wherfore a man or woman at those yeres is called Pubes: sometyme youth, or a multitude of yonge men: also the priuy partes of the body: also beynge an adiectif, it signifieth yonge or tender.

Pubertas, the yonge age of men and womē, whan they begynne to be apte vnto gene= racion: it is also the first commynge forthe of heares aboute the priuey membres.

Publicani, were they whyche toke in ferme of the people of Rome the rentes and re= uenues due to the cytie at a rent certayne.

Publica sacra, sacrifice done for the people. Publica fides, a saulfe condute, a generall lycence.

Publicanus, a fermour.

Publice, & Publicitus, openly in the face of the worlde. Sumptus publice dati, his ex= penses borne of the citie or towne.

Publicola, a fauorar of the people: the whi= che name was gyuen to Ualerius, whiche was one of the first consules of Rome.

Publico, care, to publysshe, to manifeste, to make openly knowen.

Publicum consilium, the commune coun= sayle.

Publicus, ca, cum, commune, but more pro= prely, publike, that is to saye, pertaynynge to euery state of the people ioyntly and se= uerally: See the true definicion therof in my booke called the Gouernour.

Publipor, poris, Publius boye, or seruaunt.

Publius, the name of a Romane.

Pucinum vinum, wyne growynge nyghe to the gulfe of Uenice.

Pudefio, fis, fieri, to be asshamed.

Pudenda, the priuy membres.

Pudens, tis, shamefast.

Pudenter, with shamefastnesse, basshefully.

Pudeo, dui, dere, to be asshamed.

Pudet, pudebat, puduit, puditum est, to be as= shamed.

Pudibunde, shamefastly.

Pudibundus, da, dum, shamefast.

Pudice, chastly, honestly.

Salustius in Cat. Pudicitia, chastytye, clennesse of lyuynge.

Pudicitiā habere, to be violated in the acte of lechery.

Cicer. pro Flac. Puditum, asshamed. Nonne esset puditum, si hanc causam agerent seuere? had it not bene a shame, yf that they had pursuyd that ma= ter rigorously?

Pudicus, ca, cum, chaste.

Pudor, doris, a moderacion that letteth the mynde, that it do not any thinge wantonly, or dishonestly, shamefastnesse, to saye or do any thinge dishonest.

Puella, a wenche, in Cambrige shyre they cal her a modder.

Puellaris, re, childisshe.

Puellascere, to waxe yonge agayne, to be maydenly.

Puellus, a lytle childe, a babe.

Puer, a chylde, a boye: also a seruaunt.

Puerilis, puerile, of a chylde, chyldysshe, or boyisshe.

Puerilitas, a chyldes acte, chyldysshenesse, boyishenesse.

Pueritia, chyldchode.

Puerpera, a woman that lyeth in of chylde.

Puerperium, the tyme of a womanne to tra= uayle of chylde, sometyme the chylde, also the byrth.

Pugil, a champyon.

Pugillaris, & Pugillare, pluraliter Pugillares, a payre of tables to wryte in.

Pugillatorius follis, a ball fylled onely with wynde, which is stryken with a mans fiste, and not with the palme.

Pugiunculus, a short daggar.

Pugillatus, wrastlynge with colars.

Pugillus, a handfull, in gatherynge of herbes or other lyke thynge.

Pugio, onis, a daggar.

Pugna, batayle, the acte of lechery: also an assault, a disceyte.

Pugnaciter, valyauntly in batayle.

Pugnator toris, a fightar.

Pugnax, nacis, a great fightar.

Pugnatior, & Pugnacissimus, more or moost fightinge.

Pugnicula, a skyrmysshe.

Pugnitariola, idem. **Festus. No Mar.**

Pugnitus, in batayle.

Pugno, are, to fyght. **Vide ⊂Sp**

Pugnus, a fyst.

Pulcher, chra, chrum, fayre, stronge, good, talle.

Pulcherrime, moost beautyfully.

Pulcherrimus, a, um, fayrest.

Pulchralis, le, fayre.

Pulchre, an aduerbe, signifyeth fayre, beau= **Ennius** tyfully, well fauoredly: somtyme valiaunt= ly, also wysely: sometyme it is put for val= de. Ac dum accubabam, quam videbar mihi **Terent. in** esse pulchre sobrius, And whan I layde me **Eunucho.** downe, I thoughte my selfe to be very sobre.

Pulchellus, a fayre lytle one. **Cl. ad At.**

Pulchellus puer, a fayre lytle boye.

Pulchrior, oris, & Pulchrius, fayrer.

Pulchritas, beautye.

Pulchresco, scere, to be fayre.

Pulchritudo, dinis, beaultye, talnesse of per= sonage.

Pus

Pulegium, an herbe callyd Peny royall.
Pulex, licis, a flee.
Pulicinus, a, um, of a flee.
Pulicosus, a, um, full of flees.
Pullarius, the keper of chykens.
Pullarus, a wesyll or Stote, whiche kylleth chyckens.
Pullaster, a yonge chycken.
Pullatio, hatchynge of chyckens.
Pullatus, a mourner. Somtyme a manne in poore apparayle, somtyme rude, vnlernid.
Pullesco, scere, to sprynge or burgen.
Pullicenus, a newe hatched chycken.
Pullicies, a bryngynge forthe or hatchynge of chyckens. also the folynge of coltes.
Pulligo, ginis, blackenesse.
Pullinus, na, num, of a colte. Pullini dentes, coltes tethe, whiche be fyrste caste.
Pullulatio, a spryngynge forthe of a thinge in growynge.
Pullulasco, scere, to bourgen.
Pullulo, lare, to sprynge, to come vp yonge.
Pullus, yonge, tender, in all kynde lyuinge. also a colte or fole, also a chycken.
Pullus, a, um, russette, sometyme blacke, but rather puke color, betwene russet & black.
Pulmentarium, potage made with fleshe or fyshe, as forced gruell, or coleyse.
Pulmentum, gruelle.
Pulmo, the lunges or lyghtes.
Pulmonarius, he that is disesid in the lunges.
Pulmonaria, an herbe callyd Lungworte.
Pulmonia, be certayne apples, whyche be called in some place a hundred shyllingis.
Pulpa, a lyttell synewe lyke to a vayne.
Pulpamentum, a delycate dyshe or meate.
Pulpitum, a hault pace or pulpyte.
Puls, a meate made of meale, water, hony, cheese, and egges. It maye be taken for potage.
Pulsatiles uenę, the poulses of a manne or womanne.
Pulsatus, ta, tum, striken as a harpe or other instrument is, whyche hath strynges.
Pulsim, as a thynge were stryken.
Pulso, are, to beate, to stryke, to hurte, to play on a harpe, or other lyke instrument. Pulsare hostium, to knocke at the doore.
Pulsus, the wreste of the arme, wherto the had is ioyned: but it is more properly the poulse or stroke that the arteries or beatyng vaines do make, wherby the strėgth or debilitie of the sycknes is knowen in touchynge them.
Pultarius, a potage dyshe.
Pulto, tare, to beate at a doore.
Pulticula, a lyttell potage.
Pultiphagi, & pultiphagonides, greatte eaters of potage.

Puluero, rare, to lay with doust, to be dusty.
Pululeresco, scere, to be tourned in to poulder or duste.
Puluerius, a, um, of poulder or duste.
Puluerulentus, ta, tum, full of duste.
Pulueratio, a layenge of fyne erthe aboute vynes. — *Seruius.*
Puluinar, a bolstar of a bedde. also a bedde whyche was wont to be made in temples, as it were for the goddis. It is taken som tyme for a temple. also a tabernacle, wherin an ymage standeth.
Puluinatus, ta, tum, softe as a pyllowe.
Puluinus, a pyllowe, somtyme a fetherbed, also a cusshyn, also a bedde of herbes in a gardeyne, also grauelle, also an engyne, wherewith shyppes are broughte into the docke.
Puluis, ueris, powlder, duste.
Puluisculus, fyne pouder or duste.
Pumex, micis, a pomeyse to make parchemente smoothe, also to take cleane oute spottes or letters.
Pumico, care, to pomeyse.
Pumicosus, a, um, lyke a pomeyse.
Pumigatio, pomeysynge or polyshynge.
Pumigatus, ta, tum, pomaysed, or polysshed.
Pumilis, lyttell in stature.
Pumilio, onis, & pumillus, a dwarfe, or any thynge lyttell in stature.
Punctim, foynynge.
Punctus, seu punctum, a poynte or tytle.
Punctus temporis, a moment, the leest part of tyme.
Pungo, pupugi, pungere, to prycke. — *Vide cõp.*
Punicus, a, um, of Affrica.
Punicus, aut puniceus color, redde.
Punicum malum, a pomegranate.
Punio, iui, ire, to punyshe.
Punitio, punyshement.
Pupa, a yonge wenche, a gyrle, a modder. it is also a poppette, lyke a gyrle.
Pupilla, the balle or apple of the eye.
Pupillaris ætas, the noneage of hym that is in warde.
Pupillus, he that is in warde, or within age not able in yeres to occupye his propre lande. Also he that hath no father alyue.
Puppes, & puppis, the foreparte or decke of the shyppe.
Pupus, a yonge chylde, a baby. also a poppette or ymage lyke a chylde.
Pupugi, the pretertence of purgo, I haue prycked or pounched.
Pure, purely. Puriter, idem.
Purgamen, seu purgamentum, fylthe, whyche cometh of any thyng that is clensed.
Purgatio, a purgation or purgyng.
Purgo, gare, to make cleane, to purge. also

P ante Y.

Vide cōp.   to excuse.
Purifico, to puryfye, or make pure.
Purificatio, a purifyenge.
Purimē, old wrytars vsed for purissime, most purely.
Puritas, tatis, purenes, cleannesse.
Puro, rare, to make pure.
Purpura, a Purple, whiche is a shell fysshe, wherof purple colour commeth. somtime it signifieth a garment of purple.
Purpurarius, a, um, pertaynynge to purple colour.
Purpurasco, scere, to be of purple colour.
Purpurissum, idem quod purpurissa.
Purpureus, a, um, of purple colour.
Purpuratus, apparayled in purple.
Purpurati, be the noble men of a Royalme, callyd peeres.
Purpurissa, redde paintynge, wherewith harlottes doo paynt their vysages.
Purpurisso, are, to paynte the visage ruddy.
Purulentus, lenta, lentum, full of matter, or corruption.
Purus, ra, rum, cleane, pure, fyne.
Pus, puris, matter, whyche commeth oute of a soore.
Pusillanimis, faynt harted, feble couraged.
Pusillanimitas, faynt courage, cowardyse.
Pusillanimiter, cowardly.
Pusillus, a, um, lyttell.
Pusio, a boye.
Pustula, a pusshe or lyttell wheale.
Pusule, blystars, which do ryse on bred whā it is baken.
Pusum & Pusam, olde wrytars vsed for Puerum & Puellam, a boye and a gyrle.
Pustulatum argentum, roughe sylver whan it is newe molten.
Putamen, minis, the shale of a nutte, or parynge of an apple or peare.
Puteal, the seate of a great offycer, also the couerynge of a welle.
Putealis, & puteanus, a, um, of a welle.
Puteanus, a, um, of a pytte or well.
Puteana aqua, well water.
Putearius, he that diggeth a pytte or well.
Puteo, tui, tere, to stynke.
Puteoli, a cytie in Campania.
Puteus, a welle.

Plautus.   Puticuli, places where the commune people was buryed.
Putidus, da, dum, stynkynge, vnsauery, vnpleasaunt.
Putilatum aurum, pure or fyne golde.
Putisco, scere, to stynke.
Putitius, a foole.

Vide cōp.   Puto, taui, tare, to cutte of or plucke awaye, that, which is superfluous, proprely from trees. Also to suppose, to consyder, to discusse, to gather, or conferre, to esteme, to iuge. Putare rationem, to make accompt.
Putor, toris, stenche.
Putrefacio, to make to stynke.
Putreo, truii, trere, to waxe leane, to be resolued into stynkynge matter.   Vide cōp.
Putresco, scere, to putrifye.
Putris, tre, corrupte, rotten.
Putridus, da, dum, idem.
Putredo, dinis, corruption.
Putulentum, stynkynge.
Putus, ta, tum, pure, tryed, fyne.
Purum putum, fyned.

¶ P, ANTE Y.

Pycnostylon, a house or place buylded, where pylars stande thicke togither.
Pycta & Pyctes, a wrastler with a coler
Pyctatium, a table, wherein the names of Iuges were wryten.
Pygargus, a beaste lyke to a falowe deere: it is also a byrde lyke to a hawke, hauynge a whyte tayle, I suppose hym to be that, which we call a ryngetayle.
Pygmachia, wrastlynge with colars.
Pygmachus, a wrastler.
Pygmæi, people betweene Inde and Cathay, which are but one cubyte longe.
Pympleides, the musis.
Pyr, fyre.
Pyra, a bonfyre, wherin deed bodyes were burned.
Pyralis, a fly, which commeth of the fyre, & as longe as he is therin, he lyueth: & whā he is farre frome it, he dyeth incontinent.
Pyragmon, one of the names of Vulcanus.
Pyrama, a certayne rosen.
Pyramus, a yonge man, whyche slewe hym self for the loue of a maydē called Thisbe: it is also a ryuer in Cilicia.
Pyramis, midis, a great thynge of stone or other matter, whiche is brode beneth, and vpwarde is smalle and sharpe on the top.
Pyratium, a kynde of Sydar, callyd Pery.
Pyrausta, a worme lyuynge in the fyre, It is also a kynde of spyders, whiche hurteth hony combes.
Pyrenei montes, Mountaynes, whiche do dyuyde Fraunce from Spayne.
Pyretrū, & pyretra, an herbe callid Pelitory.
Pyretus, a burnynge feuer.
Pyræus, an hauen at Athenes.
Pyrgobaris, a howse buylded lyke a towar.
Pyrgoteles, was a cūnyng grauer in stones.
Pyrgus, in latyne a towar: also a boxe, oute of the which men do cast dyse, whan they playe: it is also a certayn company of horsmen in batayle.

Pyr-

Q ante V.

fourmes or facyons.
Quadriga, a carte drawen with foure horses, somtyme a carte horse.
Quadrigarius, a carter.
Quadriiugi, foure beastes yoked togyther.
Quadrilaterus, ra, rum, with foure sydes.
Quadrimembris, of foure partes.
Quadrimus, & quadrimulus, a child of four yere olde.
Quadringenta, & quadringenti, foure hundred.
Quadrinoctium, foure nyghtes.
Quadripartitor, tiri, to diuyde in foure.
Quadriremis, a shyppe with foure rewes of oores, or with foure toppes.
Quadrisyllabum, of foure syllables.
Quadriuium, where as foure wayes doo meete.
Quadro, are, to brynge in square, to consente or agree.
Quadrum, a fygure foure square.
Quadrupedantia, & quadrupedia, foure foted beastes.
Quadrupedo, dare, to go on foure fete.
Quadrupliciter, foure maner of wayes.
Quadruplico, care, to double foure tymes, or to make a thynge foure tymes as moche as it was.

Festus — Quadrurbs, a cytie, vnto the whyche doo come, or are broughte all the people, beinge lefte in foure cities, by the whyche name the citie of Athenes was callyd of Actius the poete.
Quadrus, a, um, square.
Quadrupes, quadrupedis, a beaste hauynge foure feete.
Quadruplatores, were they, whiche for acusynge of other, hadde the fourth parte of the goodes of theym, that were condempned.
Quadruplex, fowre double.
Quadruplo, & quadruplor, ari, to appeache a man for to haue parte of his goodes.
Quadruplum, foure tymes as moche.

Plautus in capt. — Quæ, the whyche woman or other female kynde.
Ci. in Ver. — Quæ malum, what a myschiefe.
T i. Liuius — Quæcunq̃, all that, what soo euer.
Quærceus, a, um, of oke.
Quercicus, ca, cum, idem.
Quercus, cus, an oke.
Quercerus, ra, rum, colde, with a shakynge, as in a feuer.
Quæritabundus, studyous or diligente in seekynge.
Quærere liberos, to gette chylderne.
Quærneus, & quernus, querna, num, of an oke.

Vide com. — Quæro, quesiui, querere, to demaunde, to aske, to get, to serche, to examyne.
Quærquetum, & quercetũ, a groue of okes.
Quærito, ritare, to seeke, serche, or inquyre dylygently.
Quæsitor, a iustyce or commyssyoner to inquire of crymes, defaultes, or abuses agaynste the lawe. — As. pedian.
Quæsitio, an inquirie, an exaiation, a serch.
Quæso, siui, sere, to beseche.
Quæsticulus, a lyttell gayne.
Quæstio, a questyon.
Questiuncula, a smalle or lyght question.
Quæstionarius, an examynour.
Quæstor, toris, the treasourer of the commune Treasourye, a Treasourer of the warres, a Lyeuctenaunt to the chyef capytayne in warres. Alsoo a Justyce by Commyssyon of Oyer and Determyner.
Quæstores Parricidij, Justyces to inquere, of treason, or murder. we maye calle the coroners by that name.
Quæstores urbani, were as the chaumberlaynes of London be nowe.
Quæstores ærarij, Offycers of the Receypte, as the Chaumberers and tellers be nowe.
Quæstorius, quæstoria, storium, pertaynyng to the receypte.
Quæstorium, was suche a place as the eschequer is.
Quæstor ærarij, a generall receyuour: but it seemethe to be suche an offycer, as the eschetour is nowe in Englande.
Quæstorius, torij, he that hadde bene in the offyce of Questor.
Quæstorius, a, um, that pertayneth to the offyce of Questor. Vir quæstorius, a man, whiche hath ben in that offyce.
Quæstuariæ artes, craftes, wherby men do gayne money.
Quæstuosus, a, um, of moche gayne, studyous of greatte lucre.
Quæstura, the offyce of Quæstor.
Quæstus, tus, gayne, wynnynge.
Qualibet, where it lyketh the.
Qualisqualis, what so euer.
Qualiscunq̃, suche as it was.
Qualiter, in the facyon or fourme.
Qualis, le, what, of what qualitie.
Qualitates, qualytyes, as fowle, fayre, wyse, foolysshe, stronge, weake, dylygente, slowe, &c.
Quallus, a baskette, oute of the whyche wyne runneth, whan it is pressed: Alsoo a baskette or hamper, in the whyche womenne doo putte their spyndelles, their bottomes of threede, and suche lyke thynges.

Quam,

Quam, thanne, Sommetyme after that. Sommetyme byfore that. Pridie quam occideretur, The day before that he was slayne. Quam bene, howe well? Quam fortiter, howe valyauntly. Also it is often ioyned with the superlatiue degree, to make it more vehemente: as, Quam paucissimi, As few as may be. Quam doctissimus, excellentely lerned. Somtyme it importeth as moche as verye. Cum quo quam familiarissime uixerat, with whom he lyued very familyarly. Alsoo it sygnifyeth as. Duplo accepit quam perdiderat, He receyued dowble as moche as he loste.

Quamlibet, quantumuis, quantulibet, what soo euer.

Quammox, as soone, sodaynely.

Quamobrem? wherfore? for what cause? what to doo?

Quam pene, almooste, hit lackydde but a lyttelle.

Quamplures, howe manye, verye manye, a greatte sorte.

Quamplurimus, quamplurima, quamplurimum, very moche.

Quampridem, longe before.

Quamprimum, very shortely or soone.

Quamuis, & quanquam, althoughe. sometyme for Quantumuis.

Quandiu, as longe, durynge the tyme.

Quando, whan. also sens that.

Plautus in Amphi. Quandogentium, whan.

Quandudum, howe late sens, howe longe agoo?

Quanquam, all be it, all though.

Quandoque, sometyme.

Quandoquidem, for as moche as.

Quanti, for howe moche, of what pryce or valewe.

Quantillus, & quantulus, a, um, howe lyttell or smalle.

Quantillum, howe lyttell.

Quantitas, quantitie.

Quanto, howe moche.

Quantisper, how longe.

Quantus, quanta, quantum, howe moche, whyche is referred to noumbre, weight, and measure.

Quantum, howe moche, as to, as concernynge. Quantum intelligo, as farre as I vnderstande. Quantum suspicor, as farre as I suppose. Also, accordynge as. Id de imperatore Romano, quantum euentus postea predictum patuit Iudæi ad se trahentes, rebellarunt, The Jewes gatherynge that of the Emperoure, accordynge as the thynge, whyche was afore shewed of that whyche shoulde happen, appered afterwarde, made rebellyon.

Quantū potes, in al spede that thou mayste.

Quantuscunq̄, howe moche, or howe many soo euer it be.

Quantuslibet, idem.

Quantusquantus, idem.

Quanuis, all be it, all though.

Quanuis, for ualde.

Quapropter, wherfore.

Quaquauersus, & quaquauersum, on euerye syde.

Quaqua, on euery syde.

Quare, wherfore.

Plautus in Epid. Quarto, & quartum, the fowrthe tyme. All be hit proprelye Quarto sygnifyethe the fourthe in order, as Quarto Consul, he that hadde three in the office afore hym. Quartum Consul, he that hath ben the fourthe tyme Consul.

Quartana, a feuer quartayne.

Quartanarius, he that hathe a quartayne feeuer.

Quartarius, a Mulettour or keper of mules, whiche taketh but the fourthe parte of the wages or gayne.

Quartusdecimus, the fourtemthe.

Quartus, ta, tum, the fourthe.

Quasi, Lyke as. Amas me quasi filium, Thou louest me, as yf I were thy sonne. Alsoo, as who faythe, as thowghe. Tu obiicis, quod uxorem repudiauerim, quasi tu idem non feceris, Thou imbraydest me, that I haue forsaken my wife, as who saythe, thou haste not doone soo to.

Quasillum, a lyttell hamper.

Plautus Quassabundus, he that shaketh or moueth his heade.

Quasso, are, to shake moche or often, alsoo to breake.

Quassus, & quassatus, quassata, satum, shaken, braste.

Quatefacio, cere, to make or cause to shake or moue.

Quatenus, howe moche, to the intent. also for as moche, also howe.

Quater, foure tymes.

Quaterdecies, fouretene tymes.

Quatergemini, foure chyldern atte oone bourdeyne.

Quaternarius numerus, the nūbre of foure.

Quaternio, quaternionis, a quayre as in a booke, a leafe beynge folded into fowre partes.

Quaterni, foure.

Quaternus, a, um, the fourthe.

Quaternum denum, the foure tenthe.

Quarinus, a coniunction, whyche sygnifyeth for, for as moche.

Vide com Quatio, quassi, quatere, to shaake a thynge. Also

Q ante V.

also to vexe, to caste out.

Quatriduum, fowre dayes, the spaace of foure dayes.

Quatuor, foure.

Quartus, ta, tum, the fourthe.

Quadruplus, quadrupla, quadruplum, foure dowble.

Quæ, for &, sygnyfyeth and. Also that is to saye.

Quearah, a measure of the Jewes, contaynyng two ounces and .ii. drammes.

Quentia, olde wryters vsyd for potentia, puissaunce, power.

Queis, for quibus.

Queiscum, for cum quibus, with whome.

Quemadmodum, lyke as.

Queo quis, quiui, quire, I maye.

Quercus, cus, vel ci, an oke.

Querceus, a, um, of an oke.

Suetonius in caligula Gelli. ult. Quercicus, ca, cum, idem quod quernus.

Quercerus, ra, rum, quyuerynge or shakyng for colde. somtyme it was taken for great and greuous, as Festus sayth.

Quercetum, a groue of okes.

Querela, & querimonia, a complaynt.

Queribundus, a, um, lamentable.

Quærimoniarius, a complaynant.

Quernus, na, num, of an oke.

Querna folia, oken leaues.

Vide com. Queror, quæstus sum, quæri, to lamente or complayne.

Querquedula, a waterfowle callyd a teale.

Querulus, la, lum, that which complaineth, or is full of complayntes. It is put some tyme of the Poetes for shrylle or lowde in syngynge. Cicadę querulę, grassehoppers, whyche doo synge lowde, or with a shrylle voyce. *Vergiliꝰ in georgic.*

Quesitah, amonge the Jewes dydde sygnifye a coyne, sometyme a lambe, somme tyme a sheepe.

Quæstus, quæstus, a complaynte, a lamentation.

¶ QVI, the whyche. Also sometyme it sygnyfyeth howe. Efficite, qui detur tibi, Doo what ye canne, howe or by whatte meanes thou mayste haue hyr. Qui uocāre, Howe arte thou callyd? Also yt sygnyfyeth why. Dauo istuc dedam negoti. S. Non potest. P. Qui? S. Quia habet aliud magis ex sese. I wyll commytte this mattier to Dauy. S. That may not be. P. why? S. For he hath an nother greatter mattier to doo for hym selfe. Also it sygnyfyeth frome whense. Qui istæc tibi incidit suspectio? From whens is this suspycion happened vnto the? Also it sygnyfyeth wolde to God. Qui illum Di omnes perdiunt, I pray god that *Plautus in Amph.* *Ter. in An.* *Ter. in An.* *Terent. in Phorm.*

a vengeaunce lyghte on hym. Also yt sygnyfyethe bycause. Nam in prologis scribundis operam abutitur, non qui argumentum narret, sed qui maleuoli ueteris Poetæ maledictis respondeat, for he spendethe his laboure in wrytynge of Prologues, not bycause he wyll telle the argumente, but for as moche as he wolde make aunswere to the yuell reportes of the olde enuyouse Poete. *Terent. in prolo. An.*

Also it sygnyfyeth wherefore. Qui enim beatior Epicurus, quod in patria uiuebat, quam Metrodorus, quod Athenis? wherefore was Epycure moore happye, that he dydde dye in his countreye, than Metrodorus that he dyed at Athenes. *Cice. Tus.*

Quia, for. Also hit sygnyfyeth that. Sed tamen recordatione nostræ amicitiæ sic fruor, ut beatę uixisse uidear, quia cum Scipione uixerim, All be it I take this pleasure in remembrynge oure frendeshyp, that I maye seeme to haue lyued moste fortunatelye, that I lyued in Scyppiones companye. Also it sygnyfyeth for as moch. Sed quia multis & magnis tempestatibus vos cognoui fortes, fidosque mihi, eo animus ausus est maximum atque pulcherrimum facinus incipere, But for as moch as in many great stormes or daungiers I haue proued you to be valyaunt, and faythefull vnto me, therfore my hart is bolde to begynne an excellent and commendable enterprise. *Cl. de ami.* *Salustius in Catil.*

Quia nam, wherfore.

Quia ne, in dede.

Quias, quiatis, for cuius, cuiatis.

Quias, a, um, for cuius, a, um.

Quibus in extremis, for quorum in extremo. Literę dantur mihi a te, quibus in extremis scriptum est? I receyued letters frome you, in the laste ende of the whyche hit is wrytten.

Quicquid est, all that is, what so euer it be, what so euer.

Quicquid pauxillum, neuer so lyttell. *Plautus in truculen.*

Qui cum, for cum quo. Qui cum loquitur filius? with whome dothe my sonne talke?

Quicunque, who soo euer.

Quicquam, any thynge.

Quid, what. Quid causæ est? what is the cause? Quid ætatis? howe olde? of what aege? Quid animi? what mynde? Quid animi est? what mynde is he of? Quid captiuorum? Howe manye pryfoners? Tum Captiuorum quid ducunt secum? Thanne howe many pryfoners doo they bryng with them. Quid id sit hominis, cui Lyco *Plautus in mercatore* *Plautus in Epidico.*

Q ante V.

Plautus in pænulo.
Terent. in Heau.

Lyco nomen fiet, what man is he, whose name maye be Lyco? Quid mulieris uxorem habes, what maner of woman haste thou to thy wyfe? Quid rei est? what is the mattier. Ibo intro ut quid huius sit rei sciam: I wyll goo in, that I may knowe what the mattier is. Quid rei est tibi cum illa, what haste thou to doo with hyr?

Terent. in Eunucho.

Quid sententie? what is his or thyn opinyon? Quid istuc uerbi est? what meanest thou therby? Also quid is taken for Aliquid, somewhat. Also ob quid for what, or wherfore. Quid? senem quoad expectas uestrum. But nowe? howlonge wyll ye tary for your maister? Note here that after the dayly forme of speakynge, quid is rehersed, whā we passe from one matter to an other. Quid mecum est tibi, what haue I to do with thee? Quid faceret aliud? what shoulde he doo els? Quid eo, what to doo? Propere curre ad Pamphilum. P. Quid eo? D. Dic me orare ut ueniat. Rūne quyckely to Pamphilus. P. what to do? D. Say that I prayed hym to come. Quid uerbis opus est? what nede manye wordes? Quid multa uerba, idem. Quid multis moror? what shall I longe tarie? Quid mea refert, what care I? Also quid signifyeth wherin. Quid enim indigens Affricanus mei? wherin had Scipio any nede of me? Quid istic? Si certum est facere, facias: uerum ne post conferas culpam in me, what woldeste thou I shoulde doo? If thou be determyned to doo it, goo to on goddis name: but afterward put not the fault in me.

Terent. in Phorm.
Plautus in Pseudolo.

Terent. in phormi.

Donatus.

Plautus.

Cicero de amicitia.

Terent. in Eunucho.

Terent. in phorm.

Quidnam, what is hit, or wherfore is it? Quidnam ille commotus uenit? what is it that he commeth soo chaufed? Also it sygnifieth what. Reuiso quidnam Cherea hic rerum gerat, I come to se what Cherea doth here.

Terent. in Eunucho.

Terent. in Heaut.

Quid ni, why not? Quo ore appellabo patrem tenes, quid dicam? S. quidni, with what countenaunce shall I speake to my father? wotest thou what I wyll say? S. wherfore shuldest thou not do so? Also it signifyeth ye. Archimedem nosti? P. quid ni? knowest thou Archimedes? P. ye mary doo I.

Terent. in Eunucho.

Quidam, one, any man. in the plurell numbre it sygnifieth some.

Quid agimus, what shall we do?

Quidem, an aduerbe, affirmyng that, which ys spoken. Sommetyme yt sygnyfyeth verylye. Sommetyme it hathe no sygnyfycacyon, but ys oonely a dystinction of thynges: as, Ego quidem scribo, tu uero legis, ille autem dormit, I doo wryte, thou reedyst, he alsoo slepethe.

Quid ita, for Cur, wherfore.

Quidpiam, any thynge, or any wyse.

Quid quæris, what wylt thou more? what nedeth any more wordes?

Quid tum deniq, Quid ergo, quid tum postea, Quid itaq, quid interea, quid demum, all these doo sygnifye, whereto speakest thou this? what than, or what meanest thou hereby?

Quiescas, uel quiesce, holde thy peace, Leane.

Plautus in milite.

Quiescas cætera, care not for the reste.

Quies, & quietudo, reste, ease, slepe.

Quiesco, quieui, quiescere, To take reste, to ceasse.

Vide com.

Quietalis, was a name of Pluto, callydde god of Helle.

Quietus, quieta, quietum, quyete, peasible, in reste.

Quietus esto, care not.

Quilibet, cuiuslibet, cuilibet, who thou wilt. also it sometyme signifieth vyle or base in estymacyon.

Quidlibet, what I, thou, or he wyll.

Quin, but, why not. Quin uenis, why commest thou not?

Quin pergis, why goste thou not?

Ter. in An.

Quin dic quid est, go to, tell me what it is.

Quin, for etiam, alsoo. Pudet me. S. Credo, neque id iniuria: quin mihi molestum, I am asshamed. S. I beleue, and not without a cause: And I am alsoo sorye therfore. Quin taces? wylte not thou holde thy peace. Also it sygnyfyethe but yet, or but for all that. C. Perij. S. Quin tu animo bono es. C. I am vndoone. S. But for all that be thou of good cheere. Also therfore. Quin tu uno uerbo dic, quid est quod me uelis, Therfore telle me atte oone worde, whatte thou woldest haue me doo. Also more ouer, or that moore is. Quin, ipsi pridem tonsor ungues dempserat, collegit, omnia abstulit præsegmina, And that more is, the other daye, the barbour paryd his nayles, he gathered the parynges togyther, and caryed them all away with hym.

Terent. in Heauton.

Terent. in Andria.

Terent. in Adelph.

Plautus in Aulularia.

Quincunx, quincuncis, of fyue ounces. Also the gayne of fyue in oone hundrede by exchaunge amongeste Marchauntes. It was alsoo an order of settynge of trees in a gardeyne or orchard veraye exactelye, that whyche waye soo euer that a manne dydde looke, the trees stoode dyrectely oone agaynste an nother.

Quinarius, a, um, the nombre of fiue. quinarius lapis, a stone of fyue pounde weyght.
Quinarius, narij, was amonge the olde Romains their halfe peny, whiche was fyue pounde weight of brasse, callyd As, It is two soulces of frenche money, whyche is of our money.
Quincentum, of olde wryters was vsed for quingentum, fyue hundred.
Quincuntialis, le, of fyue ynches.
Quincuplex, cuplicis, fyue double, or fyue folde.
Quincuplus, a, um, fyue tymes so moche.
Quindecies, fyftene tymes.
Quindecim, fyuetene.
Quindeceremis, a barge with fyftene ores.
Quindecuplex, fyuetene double or folde.
Quindecuplus, a, um, fyuetene tymes so moche.
Quindenus, a, um, the fyuetenthe.
Quin ergo, wherfore then. Quin ergo quod iuuat, quod charu æstimant, id semper faciant, wherfore than, what so euer lyketh them, that whiche semeth pleasant vnto them, let them doo it as longe as it pleaseth them. *Salustius in Iugurt.*
Quingeni & quingenti, fyue hundred.
Quingentarius numerus, the noumbre of fyue hundred.
Quingentenus, & quingentesimus, the fyue hundrethe.
Quingenties, fyue hundred tymes.
Quingentuplus, a, um, fyue hunderde tymes so moche.
Quinimo, but rather.
Quinquagenarius, genaria, rium, of fyftie yeres olde.
Quinquaginta, fyftye.
Quinquagenus, a, um, of fyftie.
Quinquagesimus, a, um, the fiftieth.
Quinquagies, fyftye tymes.
Quinquagesies, idem.
Quinquangulus, a, um, fyue cornerde.
Quinquatria, trioru, a feast dedicate to Pallas, whiche duryd fyue dayes.
Quinquatrus dies, a feast so called, bycause it was after the fyfth Idus of Marche.
Quinque folium, an herbe callid cynkfoyle, or fyue leauyd grasse.
Quinque, fyue.
Quinquies, fyue tymes.
Quinquemestris, tre, of fyue monethes.
Quinquenalis, le, that whiche hapneth or is done euery fyfthe yere.
Quinquennis, ne, of fyue yeres.
Quinquennium, the space of fyue yeres.
Quinquepartior, tiris, tiri, to dyuyde in fyue partes.
Quincupertitus, in fiue partes diuided.

Quinquertium, the exercyse of fyue sondrye craftes.
Quinquertiones, they whiche exercised fiue sondry craftes.
Quinqueremis, a barge with fyue oores, it may be nowe taken for a shyppe with fiue toppes, or with fyue sayles.
Quinqueuiratus, an office or auctorite, wherin fyue men were associate.
Quinqueuir, oone whiche is in the sayde authoritie.
Quintana porta, was a gate in the Campe, where the armye was lodged, whyche was the chiefe gate next to that whiche was called Prætoria, where the market was wont to be kepte.
Quintus, ta, tum, the fifthe.
Quintia porta, & quintia prata, was a gaate and medowes at Rome, whyche tooke their names of one Quintius, a noble consule of Rome.
Quintilis mensis, the moneth of July.
Quintipor, tiporis, the boye or seruaunt of Quintus.
Quintius, & Quintus, the names of dyuers Romaynes.
Quintius, a, um, pertainyng to Quintius.
Quinus, a, um, fyue: quini denarij, fiue pens.
Quipote, howe is it possible?
Quippe, surely, forasmoche.
Quippini, why not.
Quire, for posse, to maye. *Plautus in Mene.*
Quirinalis collis, an hylle at Rome, where the temple of Romulus was sette.
Quirinalis porta, the gate next to that hyll.
Quirinalia, orum, dayes, in the whyche men dydde sacryfyce to Romulus, callydde Quirinus.
Quirinus, a, um, of Romulus.
Quiris, quiritis, a Romayne.
Quirites, was a name, wherby the Romans were callyd of their fyrste kynge Romulus, called Quirinus, as hit were Quirinus people.
Quiritatus, ritatus, a crye of Romayne chylderne.
Quirinus, was the name of Romulus, after that he was taken for a god.
Quiritare, to crye out, to styrre vp the Romayns with a crye.
Quisnam homo est, what man is that?
Quisputas, idem.
Quisquam, any manne. It is somtyme vsyd in the femynyne gender for any woman.
Quisquam gentium, idem.
Quisque, euery manne. Doctissimus quisq, Euery welle lerned man. Decimus quisq, Euery tenthe.
Quisquiliç, arum pluraliter, be those thynges whiche

Ci. ad At. 1 whyche in makynge cleane of a garden or orcharde, be caryed oute, as stickes, leues, and weedes: it is vsed of Cicero for noughty men, the refuse of all other.

Quisquilium, a lytle braunche of a kynde of holy, whyche beareth grayne, wherewith scarlet and crymsyn colours be made.

Quiuis, in the genitiue case cuius cuius, who so euer.

Quiuis, in the genitiue case cuiusuis, any man: one of them.

Quis, quæ, quod, vel quid, who or what.

Quis, is sometyme taken for some man.

Quispiam, some man.

Quisquis, who so euer.

Terent. in Adelph. Quó, whyther. Quó abis, whyther goest thou?

Quo non, Perreptaui vsque omne oppidum, ad portam, ad locum, quo non? I went all the towne aboute, to the gate, to the lake, there is no place but that I was in it. Also it signifieth frome whense and where. *Terent. in Adelph.* Illuc quæso redi, quo cœpisti, I beseche the tourne backe agayne, where thou begannest: also, bycause. *Terent. in Eunucho.* Non pol quó quenquam plus amem, aut plus diligam, eo feci, In good fayth I dyd it not bycause I more louyd or *Ter. in An.* fauored any man: also, wherfore. Forma bona memini videre, quo equior sum Pamphilo, I remembre she is well fauored, wherfore I am the lesse displeased with Pamphilus.

Quo gentium, whyther: also Quo, signifyeth, that. *Plinius.* Neque enim id feci, quo tibi molestus essem, For I dyd it not, that I wolde displease you: also, to what purpose or vse. Quo mihi fortunam, si non conceditur vti, For what purpose shall fortune serue, if I may not haue commoditie by it?

Quoaxo, are, to crye lyke a frogge.

Quoad, vntyl, as longe.

Quoad eius, as moche as he maye.

Ci. pro lege Agraria Quoad quenque peruenit, aut peruenerit ex preda, ex manubijs, ex auro coronario? Howe moche of the praye or spoyle, garlandes or crownes of victours is come, or shall come to any of your handes?

Ci. de ora. Quoad eius facere possum, as moche as I may do.

Quoadusque, vntyll.

Quocirca, wherfore.

Quod, that, wherein. Sed si quid sit, quod *Terenti.* mea opera opus sit, aut tu plus vides quám ego, manebo, But yf there be any thynge, wherein ye shall haue nede of my seruice, or that ye perceyue more than I do, I will tary: also it is put for Quem. *Plautus in Asinar.* Alienum hominem intromittat neminem, quod illa aut amicum, aut patronum nominet: She maye

let in no man, whome she will call derlyng, or master. Nube grauida candicante, quod *Plinius.* vocant tempestatem albam, grando imminebit: whan there doeth appiere a greate clowde, that waxeth whyte, whiche they call a whyte tempeste, ye shall haue hayle shortly after: also it sygnifyeth for as moch or bycause. Senatusconsulta duo facta sunt *Cice. Atti.* odiosa, quod in consulem facta putantur, Catone & Domitio postulante: Two actes of counsayle were made very displeasant, for as moche as they were supposed to be made, at the desire of Domicius and Cato: also it signifyeth but. Quod si quiescem, ni *Ter. in An.* hil euenisset mali, But if I had let it alone, there hadde none yll happened, or it had bene well ynoughe: also, as moche. Tu ve *Cice. Ter.* lim, quod cum commodo valetudinis tuæ fiat quàm longissime poteris, obuia nobis properes: I wolde that ye, as moche as maye be with the helthe of your persone, make speede to meete with vs, as farre from home as ye can. Also it signifyeth why. Si *Vergilius* ad vitulam spectes, nihil est quod pocula *in Buc.* laudes, If thou consyderest the caulf wel, there is no cause why thou shuldest prayse so thy pottes. In viam quod redes hoc tem *Cice. Ter.* pore, nihil est, There is no cause why thou shuldest take thy iournay at this tyme: Also it signifyeth wherfore. Quod te per ge *Nor. in ep.* nium, dextramq, Deosq, penates obsecro & obtestor, vitæ me redde priori: wherfore I beseche and praye the, for thy good aungelles sake, and for the loue betwene the and me, and for the sainctes which be thyn auouryes, restore me eftsones, to my fyrst lyfe, or to the state that I was in erst. Also *Ter. in Eu.* it signifyeth, as to that. Sane quod tibi vir videatur esse, hic nebulo magnus est. As to that, that thou thynkest hym a man, surely he is a stourdy vagabunde.

Quod absq; molestia fiat, so that it be no dis *Cice. Sulp.* pleasure vnto you. Quare pergratum mihi feceris, si eum in amicitiam receperis, atque eum (quod absque molestia fiat) si qua in re opus ei fuerit: wherfore ye shall do me singuler pleasure, if ye take hym into your fauour, and (so that it be no displeasure vnto you) whan neede requyrethe, be good lorde or master vnto hym.

Quod quidem, no that. Non nouisti me? P. *Plautus in* quod quidem veniat in mentem. Doeste *Epidico.* thou not know me? P. No that I remembre me.

Quodammodo, somewhat. Quamobrem vt *Ci. de ami.* hi, qui superiores sunt, summittere se debent in amicitia, sic quodammodo inferiores extollere, wherfore lykewyse as they, which are superior in state or degree, shuld humble

Q ante V.

ble them selfes in frendshyp, so they whiche are inferior shulde aduaunce and sette them selfes forewarde.

Quodcunq, what so euer.

Cice. atti. Quodcunq militum, for quotcunque milites. Vos hortor, vt quodcūque militum contrahere poteritis, contrahatis, I aduyse you, that as many souldiours as ye can gete, ye gather vnto you.

Terent. in andria. Quominus, for Vt non. Si poterit fieri, vt ne pater per me stetisse credat, quo minus he fierent nuptiis, volo: If it may be brought to passe, that my father maye beleue, that it is not in my fault, that this mariage is not concluded, I am content.

Plautus in Aulul. Quomodo, howe, by what reason, in what maner, by what meane. Quomodo tibi res **Plautus in** se habet? Howe is the matter with the? Sed **milite.** quomodo dissimulabat? But in what maner dyd he dissemble? Primulo diliculo ab-**Plautus in** iisti ad legiones, By tyme in the mornynge **amph.** thou wentest to the armye. Amph. Quomodo? In what maner or facion? also it signifieth wherfore. Illa quidem nullū sacri-**Plautus in** ficabit. G. Quomodo? quid igitur me volt? **Stich.** She will doo no sacrifyce. H. wherfore what thynge wolde she than with me?

Plautus in Quomodocunque, howe so euer it be. Sed **penulo.** tamen quomodocunq, quamquàm sumus pauperculi, est domi quod edimus: Yet how so euer it be, thoughe we be poure folkes, we haue at home somewhat to eate.

Quomodolibet, idem.

Quondam, Sometyme, ones: signifyenge the tyme past, or tyme to come. Quondam **Verg.** tua dicere facta Tempus erit: The tyme shal be ones, whan thyne actes shall be declared. Also it is put in the tyme present.

Vergill. Quondam etiam victis redit in precordia virtus, Ye, and in them that are vaynquyshed, sometyme good courage eftsones imbracith their stomakes. Sometyme it signyfyeth allwaye. Vt quondam in stipulis magnus sine viribus ignis, Lyke as in stubbyll or holme fyre is allwaye greate without any puyssaunce.

Plautus in Quonam, whyther. Eamus intrò, sequere. S. **Trin.** Quo tute agis? C. quonam, nisi domum. Let vs go in, folowe me. S. whyther wylt thou go? whyther shulde I goo but home to my house?

Quoniam, for as moche as.

Quo officio es? what is thyne office?

Quopiam, any whyther. Iturane Thais quopiam es? Thais, wylte thou goo any whyther?

Quoquam, any whyther.

Quoque, also.

Quoquo, wheresoeuer.

Q ante V.

Quoquo pacto, In any maner of wyse. Tum **Ter. in Ad.** si maxime fateatur, cum amet aliam, non est vtile hanc illi dari: qua propter quoquo pacto celato est opus, Than yf he vtterly cōfesse it, for as moch as he loueth another, it were not conuenient, that he were maryed to this woman, therfore in any maner of wyse, this thinge must be kept secrete.

Quoquo modo, idem.

Quo quouersum, seu quoquouersum, euery waye, on euerye parte. Eius imperio **Cæs. in cō.** classem quo quouersum dimittunt, By his commaundement they dyspeched the nauy in euery part. Rates duplices quoquouersum pedibus triginta è regione solis collocabat: he sette shyppes double agaynste the sonne, thirty feete euery waye.

Quorsum, seu quorsus, apud Plinium, whyther, to what place, or thinge.

Quorsum istuc? to what purpose.

Quot, how many.

Quota pars, how small a porcion.

Quotannis, yere by yere, euery yere.

Quotennis? of what age? howe olde?

Quot annos natus, idem.

Quotenus, a, um, how many.

Quotidianæ formæ, a commune beautye or **Ter. in Eu.** facion, euery daye sene.

Quotidiani sumptus, dayly expenses.

Quotidianus, quotidiana, quotidianum, a thynge that is or happeneth dayly or daye by daye.

Quotidie, dayly, euery daye.

Quoties, howe oftentymes.

Quotiescunq, as often.

Quotquot, as many.

Quotuplex, how many sortes.

Quotuplus, howe moche in measure or wayght.

Quotus, ta, tum, of what numbre, howe many, Hora quota est, what is it a clocke? Dic **Horatius.** quotus es? Telle howe many be of you. Quotas ædes dixerit, id ego admodum incerto scio: How many houses he spake of, I am not well assertayned, or I remembre not well.

Quotusquisque, how many.

Quouis, whyther, or to what place ye wyll.

Quouis gentium, idem.

Quousque, how longe, how farre.

Quousque tandem, how longe yet.

Qur, & Quor, wherfore.

Quum, seu qum, whan, in the whiche.

Quum primum, as soone.

R, ante

Rabia, olde wrytars vsed for Rabies.

Rabidus, da, dum, madde or woode, as a madde dogge.

Rabies, madnesse of a dogge.

Rabiosus, a, um, madde or very angry, woode angry.

Varro. Rabio, bire, to be madde or woode as a dogge.

Rabiosulus, a, um, somewhat madde.

Rabula, one which is hasty or wilfull, in any cause, ianglynge, or full of wordes.

Racemarius, a twygge of a vyne, out of the which the grapes do sprynge.

Racematio, the gatheringe of grapes after that the greate clusters be gathered to make wyne, the glenynge of grapes.

Racematus, ta, tum, that hath grapes.

Racemosus, full of grapes.

Racemus, a grape or a cluster of grapes.

Racha, a reprochefull worde of Hebrewe, which signifyeth, thriftlesse, braynlesse, fynally it is a rebukefull worde sygnifyenge the extreme ire of the personne that speaketh it.

Radicitus, frome the roote, or vppe by the roote, Radicitus euellere, to plucke vppe by the roote.

Radico, care, to roote or take roote.

Radicula, an herbe, the iuyce whereof is good to wasshe woulle: also a lytle roote.

Radio, are, to sende forth beames lyke the sunne.

Radius, a beame of the sun, or other bright sterre, sometyme of the eyes: also a rodde or yerde, that Geometricians haue to describe lynes: also a wayuers shyttell, wherwith he throweth the yern in to the webbe also the spoke of a wheele, alsoo an instrument, wherwith measures be shauen: alsoo longe olyues or oyle beryes.

Radix, dicis, a roote.

Rado, si, dere, to shaue, or make smoothe, to cut or pull vp, to hurte, to rent, to offende, to fatigate. Aures delicatas radere, to offende or fatigate delicate eares.

Radula, an instrument to shaue with.

Radulanus, a, um, that whiche is shauen of, frome any thynge.

Ragadia, & Ragades, cleftes or choppes in the fundament.

Raia, a see fysshe called Raye or skete.

Ralla, a thynne garment.

Rallum, the staffe, wherewith plowghmen in tyllynge do put the erthe frome their share.

Ramalis, le, a bowghe.

Ramale, a seryd or deed bowghe.

Ramentum, a lytle piece of any thynge.

Rameus, a, um, that whyche is of a bowgh.

Ramex, micis, a kynde of rupture, whan the bowels do fal downe into a mans coddes: also a rayle or barre, whiche goeth ouerthwart a pale or a gate.

Ramicosus, he that is broken.

Ramnus, a whyte thorne.

Ramulus, & Ramusculus, a lytell bowghe.

Ramus, a bowghe.

Rana, a frogge: also a sickenesse which doth anoy cattell.

Rana Seriphia, is a prouerbe applyed to thē that canne not speake in tyme conuenient.

Ranceo, cere, to be mouldy or putrifyed.

Rancidus, da, dum, rankled, mouldy, or putrifyed: also vnsauery, or vnpleasaunt.

Rancidulus, la, lum, a lytle mouldy or putryfyed.

Rancor, oris, rancour, fylth.

Randus, in olde tyme was taken for æs, brasse.

Randuscula porta, the brason gate.

Rantum, in the olde tyme was a quarterne of a pounde.

Ranunculus, a lytell frogge, or frosshe.

Rapa, a plant and roote called Rape.

Rapacia, rape leaues.

Rapatior, more rauenous or catchinge.

Rapacissimus, a, um, moost rauenous.

Rapacitas, raueny.

Rapaciter, rauenousely.

Rapax, acis, rauenouse.

Raphanus, a plante, and roote called Radysshe.

Rapere aliquem in ius, to arrest one, or cause him to be arrested to appere before iuges.

Rapide, quickly.

Rapidus, a, um, very swift.

Rapina, robbery.

Rapinator, a robbar. *Varro.*

Rapio, pui, pere, to take by violence, hast, or fury: also to rauysshe a woman.

Rapo, Raponis, for Rapax.

Raptim, hastily.

Raptio, violent takynge of a persone.

Raptus, rauysshynge or deflourynge of a woman.

Raptito, tare, to take often violently.

Rapto, to take or drawe violently.

Raptor, toris, a rauysshour or vyolente taker.

Rapulum, a lytle rape roote.

Rapunculus, a lytle roote, whyche is eaten in salates.

Rara auis, a byrde seldome seene: wherby is signifyed any thynge that seldome happeneth.

Rare.

Rarefacio, cere, to make thynne or slender.
Rarefio, fieri, to be thynne or slender.
Rarenter, seldome.
Raresco, scere, to waxe thynne, or not thicke growen, to be or happen seldome.
Rari, a sonder, here and there one or a few.
Raripilus, la, lum, thynne heared.
Rarior, rarius, more selde.
Rarissimus, a, um, seldest.
Rarissime, moost selde.
Raritas, seldomnesse.
Raro, selde, rare.
Raro, aui, are, to make scant or selde.
Rarus, ra, rum, selde or not ofte, thynne, not thicke growen or set.
Rasamentum, shauinge or shredes.
Rasilis, file, that maye be shauen or made smoothe.
Rasito, tare, to shaue ofte.
Rasor, soris, a barbour, or shauour, alsoo a fydler.
Rasorius, a, um, pertaynynge to shauynge.
Rasta, a duche myle.
Rastellus, a lytle rake.
Rastrum, & Raster, a rake.
Rasura, the shauynge.

Cęs, in cō.

Ratariæ naues, lyghters, or woode barges.
Rates, tis, are pieces of tymber pynned to gither, wheron haye or other lyke thinge beinge layde, they are drawen on ryuers, as on the great streames of Germany and France is now sene: but they be communly vsed and taken for shyppes, or the syde beames of a shyppe.
Ratiarius, the master of a shyppe.
Ratifico, care, to ratyfye, or confirme.
Ratificatio, a ratification or confyrmation.
Ratio, rayson, counsayle, purpose, care, respecte, cause, the maner, the waye, the fourme, proportion.
Ratiocinatio, raysonynge.
Ratiocinator, oris, a caster of accompt.
Ratiocinor, aris, to rayson, to gather in argument, to accompte.
Rationabilis, le, raysonable.
Rationale, that whiche hath the vse of raison: alsoo that whiche a preest weareth at masse on his heed, & after putteth it backe lyke a hoode.
Rationes referre, to yelde accompt.
Rationem dare, idem.
Rationem dictare, to accompte.

Plautus in amph.
Terent. in Heau.
Ter. in Ad.

Ratio de integro ineunda est mihi, I muste fynde another meane.
Rationem subducere, Nunquàm ita quisquam bene subducta ratione ad vitã fuit: quin res, ætas, vsus semper aliquid apportet noui, There was neuer man in the ordre of his lyfe so well aduysed: but that mater, age &
experience bringeth to hym somwhat that is straunge.
Ratio constat, the matter appiereth, or is shewed.
Rationarius, a boke of accompt: also a boke belongynge to the counsayle of Princes, wherin actes done and to be done are writen: also an auditour.
Ratiuncula, a lytle accompt or rekenynge.
Rationes putari, whan accomptes be examyned and tryed.

No. Mar.

Ratare, olde wrytars vsed for Ratificare, to ratify, to confyrme.
Ratum habere, idem.
Ratus, ta, tum, stablysshed, confyrmed, supposed.
Ratus, a participle signyfyenge, Supposynge.
Ratus sum, I supposed.
Raua vox, a voyce that maye not be well harde.

Festus.

Raucæ, wormes, beinge in the rootes of trees, and cateth them.
Rauce, horsely.
Rauceo, Raucio, cere, to be horse.
Raucesco, scere, idem.
Raucus, ca, cum, horse.
Raucedo, & Raucitas, horsenesse.
Raudus, a thynge vnwrought, and vnpolysshed: it was also taken for æs, brasse.
Rauenna, a citie in Italy.
Rauilia, purblynde or dull sighted.
Rauio, are, to be horse.

Festus.

Rauus, horsenesse.
Rauiscellus, a, um, lytell broune of colour.

Plautus.

Rauus, a, um, horse: also Rauus color, a dull or sadde colour, or broune.

¶ R, ANTE E.

Realis actio, an action concernyng the goodes.
Reapse, in the selfe or very thinge.
Reate, a citie in Italy.
Reatus, a fault or offence.
Rebellare, to rebell.
Rebellis, a rebell.
Rebellio, rebellion.
Rebito, tare, to retourne. At vnum hoc te queso, si huc rebitet è Philocrate, vt eius mihi facias conueniendi copiã, But one thinge I praye the, if he retourne frome Philocrates, finde the meanes, that I may speke with him.
Reboo, are, to sowne agayne.
Recalcitro, trare, to stryke with the heele, to kicke.
Recalesco, scere, to waxe warme.
Recaluaster, tri, he that is balde before.

Recal-

Recaluus, idem.
Recalueo, ere, to be balde agayne.
Recanto, tare, to charme awaye or charme out a thynge, which was brought in by inchauntement, as the witches called wyse women are wont to do.
Recapitulatio, a rehercynge of thynges in chapiters.
Recedo, recessi, recedere, to departe or goo awaye.

Cic. de off.
Recedere a conditione, a persona, a statu, is to chaunge or alter the condicion, person, or state. Quanquàm id nomen durius efficit iam vetustas, à peregrino enim iam recessit, All thoughe auncienty maketh that name diffuse, yet is it now altered from beinge a straunge worde.
Recello, cellere, to plucke backe, or withdrawe.
Recens, tis, newe late.
Recentior, newer.
Recentissimus, newest, or latest.

Plautus in Trin.
Recēti pede recurrere, to runne eftsones after that he hath rested him, to make a fresh course. Postquam thermopotasti gutturem, recipe te, & recurre pede recenti: After that thou haste warmed thy throte with good drynke, take thy harte to the, and make a fresshe course.
Recenter, newly, fresshely.
Recentius, more newly.
Recento, tare, to renewe.
Recentor, taris, tari, to be renewed.
Recenseo, ere, to numbre or tell, to reken.
Recensus, us, & Recensio, a tale or rekenynge.
Recensitus, ta, tum, tolde, or rekenyd.
Receptaculum, the place, which receyueth thinges: also a place of suerty or comfort.
Recepti in ciuitatem, they whiche of straungers be made Citezens.
Recepto, tare, to receyue often.
Receptitius, a, um, that whiche is reserued from other.
Receptum, taken in custome.
Receptus, tus, a retrayt in batayle.

Erasm. in Chiliad.
Receptui canere, to blowe the retrayte: also it is a prouerbe, which signifyeth to fynyshe or ende the contention.
Recessim, an aduerbe, whyche signifyeth, goynge backe.

Plautus in Menech.
Recessus, us, a goynge awaye or backe.
Recident in te hæ contumeliæ, those rebukes shall lyght on the.

Terent. in prolo. He.
Recidit ad paucos, it is come to a fewe personnes.
Recidipna, a garment to soupe in.
Recidiuus, a, um, eftsones restored: somtyme eftsones decayed or fallen.

Recido, dere, to fall eftsones: or to fal backwarde.
Recido, di, dere, to cut agayne, to cut behynde.
Recinium, a square garmente, whiche they that dyd weare them, dydde caste the one part thereof ouer their shoulders at their backe, lyke to frenche clokes.
Reciniati, they that dydde weare suche clokes.
Recino, ere, to synge agayne.
Recipere se, to retourne or come agayne.

Terent. in Phorm.
Percunctatum ibo ad portum, quoad se recipiat frater, I wyll go seeke at the hauyn, vntyll my brother come agayne.

Plautus in Capt.
Recipere se ad cœnam, to come to souper. Hic homo ad cœnam recipit se ad me, This man will come to me to souper.

Plautus in Per.
Recipe te ad me, come hyther to me.
Recipere se ex opere, to retourne frome his busynesse.
Recipere se domum, to go home.

Plautus in cist.
Recipere in aures, to heare: Nō ædepol istæc tua dicta nūc in aures recipio, In good soth I do not heare now what thou sayest.
Recipere se in portum, to arryue at an hauyn.

Plinius in panegyr.
Recipere se in Principem, to take on hym as a Prince.

Plautus in mercatore
Recipere anhelitum, to fetche brethe or wynde. Priusquam recipias anhelitum, vno verbo eloquere, vbi ego sum, Or euer thou fetchest breth, tell me at a worde, in what case I do stande.
Recipe animum, take breth.

Terent. in Adelph. Cicero in Cato. Cato speaketh here of Fabius the wyse Captayne
Recipere, to recouer. Cum quidem me audiente Salinatori, qui amisso oppido fugerat in arcem, glorianti atque dicenti, mea opera Quint. Fab. Tarentum recepisti: Certe, inquit ridens, nam nisi tu amisisses, nunquàm recepissem: For in my hearynge, to Salinator, which (the towne of Tarentum being lost) fledde into the castell, sayenge vnto hym, Thou hast recouered Tarentum Q. Fab. by my meanes: That is true sayde he, laughinge: for if thou haddest not lost it: I had not recouered it. also to reserue to a mans owne vse.
Recipie, Cato vseth for Recipiam.
Receptus, ta, tum, receyued.

Plautus in Asinar.
Receptio, a retourne backe, drawynge or bryngynge agayne. Quid tibi huc receptio ad te est meum virum? why draweste thou my housbande eftsones backe vnto thy house.
Reciprocatio, a goynge backe, or retournynge to the place that he came fro.
Recipio, cœpi, cipere, to receyue or take, to admitte, to call agayne, to brynge in saulfgarde

gardt, to delyuer, to vndertake, to promyse: also Recipere, is to rescrue to hym selfe, or to exceptе a thinge in gyuynge or bargaynynge.

Reciproco, care, to turne backe, to repete, to go backe.

Reciprocus, ca, cum, that whiche is repeted or eftsones rcherced.

Recisamentum, a lytle piece, a gobat.

Recisus, a, um, new cut.

Recito, tare, to reade that other maye here and vnderstande: to recite or telle eftsones.

Reclamo, are, to denye with a lowde voyce or crye.

Festus. Val. in po. Verg. Recliuia, & Recliuium, is whan the skynne of the fyngar is loose frome the nayle.

Recludo, si, dere, to open. Infernas reserat sedes & regna recludat pallida, Undo he the lockes of places infernall, and let hym set wyde open the pale regions of deth. Justinus putteth Reclusus for clausus, shut.

Recocta, seconde or course cheese.

Recogito, tare, to remembre.

Recognitio, a knowlege.

Recognosco, noui, noscere, to recognise, to knowe perfectly, to ouerloke.

Recolligo, legi, ligere, to assemble or gather togither: also to reconcile. Quod scribis, etiam si cuius animus esset in te offensior, a me recolligi oportere, quid dicas? where thou wrytest, that moreouer yf any man be displeased with the, that he shoulde be reconcyled by my meanes, whatte sayeste thou?

Recolo, lere, to repute, to repete, to calle to remembraunce.

Recomminiscor, sceris, recomminisci, to remembre, or call to remembraunce.

Reconcilio, are, to reconcyle, to restore vnto fauour.

Reconcilior, aris, reconciliari, to be reconcyled.

Plautus in cap. Reconciliare in libertatem, to sette at lybertye.

Reconciliatio, a reconcylynge.

Reclusus, a, um, opened.

Reconcinno, nare, to newe make, to make meete, properly a garment.

Recondo, dere, to hyde, to laye vppe.

Recordor, aris, ari, to remembre.

Recoquo, coxi, coquere, to boyle or seeth eftsones, to amende with study.

Recordatio, remembraunce.

Recreatio, a recreation, a restoringe.

Recreo, aui, are, to recreate, to refresshe, to restore.

Recresco, scere, to growe agayne.

Recrudesco, scere, to renewe a fault made

by Princes to their familiars.

Recta, a souper, where they sate all in a rewe.

Rectangulus, is where lynes are soo ioyned, that no part is longar or shortar than another.

Recta, an aduerbe signifyenge strayghte. Cur non recta introibas? why wentest thou not strayght, or the strayght waye in. *Terent. in Eunucho.*

Recté, well ynoughe. Quid tu igitur lachrymas? aut quid es tam tristis? Pamp. Recté mater. S. Quid fuit tumulti? Than wherefore doest thou mourne? or why arte thou so heuy? Pamph. It is well ynoughe mother. S. what was all this noyse? *Terent. in Hecy.*

Recté parere, to brynge forth no monster.

Recté, of good right, with good raison.

Recté dicis, thou sayest truely.

Recté est, it is ynoughe, or I haue ynough. Tum quod dem ei, recté est, I haue also ynough to gyue hym. *Terent. in Heauton.*

Recté facere alicui, to do good to a man. Stultus & sine gratia es, tibi recté facere: quando quod facias perit, Thou art a foole and without thanke, to do hym any good, whan all is lost that thou doest. *Plautus in Aulularia.*

Recté ferre, to take paciently. Si sapis, neq́ preterquam quas ipse amor molestias habet, addas: & illas quas habet, recté feras, If thou be wyse, adde to no more griefe than loue bringeth with hym, and them that he bringeth, suffre paciently. *Terent. in Eunucho.*

Recté, signifyeth sometyme nothynge, as Donate sayth. Rogo, nunquid velit. recté, inquit: abeo, I asked if he wold any thyng, Nothinge, he sayde: I went than my way. also ye, straight waye. S. Tu rus hinc abis? D. recté, goest thou now into the contray? D. ye strayght waye. *Ter. in Ad.*

Recté valet, he or she is in good helth.

Rectius, better.

Rectitas, & Rectitudo, Justice or rightwysnesse.

Rector, toris, a rular.

Rectus, the nominatife case.

Rectum intestinum, the gutte frome whense the ordure passeth.

Rectus, ta, tum, straight, which is not crooked, vpright, iust.

Recubitus, a lyenge at reste.

Recubo, are, to lye and rest.

Recudo, cudi, dere, to newe hamer, or newe worke, as it were on an anduylde: also it is taken for, to make newe, or newe prynte.

Recuperatores, iuges assigned, or commissionars, for a pryuate mater.

Recumbo, to sytte at a table, or at meales: sometyme to leane on one. Recumbebat mecum vir egregius Fidius Rufinus, super cum eum municeps ipsius, There satte with me that worshypfull man Fidius Rufinus, and aboue hym his neyghbour.

Recuperatio, & reciperatio, & reciperantia, was of olde wryters sayde, where there was a lawe made betwene the people of Rome, and other nations & cities, wherin they accordyd, that pryuate thynges taken, shoulde be redelyuered, whyche is nowe vsyd in our leagues and entercourses with straunge countrayes and prynces.

Recupero, rare, to recouer.

Recupio, cupiui, cupere, to desyre moche. Quin ita faciam, ut recupias facere sumptum, & si ego uetem: And yet wylle I sou handle it, that thou shalte moche desyre to spende, although I wolde forbyd the.

Recurro, rere, to rounne agayne, to goo or come agayne quyckely.

Recursus, us, a runnyng backe, a recourse.

Recurso, are, to runne often back or agayn.

Recurué, an aduerbe, signifieng bowid bakwarde, crokydly.

Recuruitas, tatis, a bowynge backe.

Recuruo, are, to bowe backe.

Recuruor, ari, to be bowed backe.

Recuruus, a, um, bowed backe, or crooked

Recusabile, that whyche is worthye to be refusyd.

Recusatio, a refusall.

Recusator, a refuser.

Recuso, are, to refuse, also to defende.

Recuritus, he that is circuncysed, somtyme exulcerate.

Redabsoluo, uere, to discharge or dispeche. Sequere hac, te redabsoluam, qua aduenisti gratia, Folowe me thyther, I wylle dyspatche thy mattier, for the whyche thou camest hyther.

Redactus, ta, tum, brought.

Plautus, in Curcul. Redambulo, are, to retourne. Cura q̄ optime potes. Er. bene ambula, & redambula, Do the beste that thou canste. Er. wel get the hens, and come agayne quyckely.

Redandruo, are, idem.

Redamo, aui, are, to loue mutually.

Redarguo, guere, to reproue.

Reddo, di, dere, to render or yelde, to delyuer, to restore, to gyue, to make.

Reddere certiorem, to assertayne.

Reddere rationem, to make accompte, or rekenynge.

Reddere, to putte in other. Tempestas uenit, confringit tegulas imbricesq̃, ibi dominus indiligens reddere alias ne uult, The tempeste camme, and brake the Tyles, and the Eueyses, where as the neglygente owner wolde not putte other in theyr places.

Reddere commotum, to cause one to make haste, to haste hym forwarde. *Ter. in An.*

Reddere dictum ac factum. Videre egisse iā nescio quid cum sene. S. De illo quod dudū dictum ac factum reddidi, It seemeth thou haste done late, I wote not what with the olde man. S. Meanest thou that, the other daye? thou haddest not so soone spoken, but it was doone.

Reddidi impetratum, I brought it to passe. *Plautus in Epid.*

Reddere operam, to requyte a good turne or an ylle.

Reddere aliquem, to resemble or be lyke to oone.

Redemptio, redemption.

Redemptito, demptitare, to redeeme or bye agayne often.

Redempto, tare, to redeme.

Redemptor, toris, a redemer.

Redeo, diui, diī, redire, to retourne.

Redhibeo, hibui, bere, to cause the seller to haue agayne that whiche he solde.

Redhibitio, restitution.

Redigo, degi, digere, to brynge by force or cunnynge. sometyme to restore.

Redigere in ordinem, to compelle menne to lyue accordyng to their astate or professiō

Redis ad ingenium, thou doest after thyne olde facion, or as thou arte wonte to do. *Terent. in Hecy.*

Redire ad se. Sed paululum sine ad me ut redeam, But lette me take breathe a lyttelle. Tandem reprime iracundiam, atque ad te redi: Nowe leaue thy fume, and remember thy selfe. *Ter. in An.*

Redeam ad pauca, Vt ad pauca redeam, ac mittam illius ineptias, To the intente that I wyll be shorte, and passe ouer his foly. *Terent. in phorm.*

Redi ad rem, goo to the pourpose, or to the mattier. *Terent. in Heaut.*

Redijt ad restim res, Opera tua ad restim mihi quidem res redijt, By thy meanes I am brought to the poynte to hange my selfe. *Terent. in phormi.*

Redijt ad rastros. Nam si illi pergam suppeditare sumptibus Menedeme, mihi illæc uere ad rastros res redijt, Surely if I shuld mayntayne his expenses Menedemus, it wolde brynge me to rake corne or grasse for my lyuynge.

Redit res in eum locum, the thynge is come so to passe. In eum iam res redijt locum, ut sit necesse, The matter is come so to passe, that there is no remedy.

Redit mihi animus, my courage is comme vnto me. *Terent. in Hecyra.*

Redit animo, it commeth to my mynde.

Redire in concordiam, to be agreed.

Redire in gratiam, idem, Also to be eftesones in fauour.

X Redi-

R ante E.

Redimicula, the ornamentes or apparaylle of a womans heed: as a veluette bonette or frenche hode.
Redimio, iui, ire, to adorne or apparayle, or trymme.
Plautus in Ruden. Reditur, is retourned.
Redhibitum, restored.
Redico, cere, to tell or saye agayne.
Rediculi, a temple at Rome withoute the gate callyd Capena, where Hannyball beynge aferde, retyred backe.
Redimitus, ta, apparayled on the heed.
Redimere, to take in charge.
Redinunt, for redeunt, they retourne or comme agayne.
Redintegro, a renewynge, a fortification.
Redipiscor, sceris, sci, to recouer or gette agayne.
Redimo, demi, dimere, to redeme, to bye, to recouer, to recompence, to take in bargayne.
Redemptores, they that hyre lande, or taketh any thyng in great or taske.
Ti. Liuius Cst. in co. Redintegrare, to begynne a freshe.
Redintegrato animo, with courage reuyued, with a freshe courage.
Redito, tare, to retourne by and by.
Reditus, tus, a retourne.
Reduuia, whan the skynne commeth withoute the nayles of the fyngers. alsoo an adders skynne.
Rediuiuum, that whiche retourneth eftsones to lyfe. Also that whiche of an old thynge is made newe or yonge.
Rediuias, a worme callyd a tycke, whyche souketh bloode from a man or beaste.
Redoleo, ere, to smelle or sauour.
Redonatio, a gyuynge agayne of the thing that is taken.
Redono, are, to gyue agayne.
Redorior, riris, riri, to begynne agayne.
Redormio, to awake.
Redormitio, an awakynge out of slepe.
Festus. Redostio, tire, of olde wryters was taken for to gyue thanke.
Reducem, & reduces, they do cal such whiche are brought out of exile or captiuitie.
Reducere, to brynge saulfe. Méque oppido in arcem reduco, And I conueyed my self quyckely into the Castell. Alsoo to pacyfye or appease. Numenq; reducant, Lette theym appease the wrathe or dyspleasure of god.
Apuleius.
Vergilius
Reduco, duxi, ducere, to brynge backe, or plucke backe, to delyuer or set out of peryll, to reconcyle.
Reductus, a, um, brought backe or safe.
Redundo, are, to ouerflowe, to reflowe or retourne backe, to redounde.

R ante E.

Reduro, are, to stoppe or close. *No. Mar.*
Reduplico, care, to double eftsones.
Redulcero, rare, to impostume or make an impostume in some parte of the body.
Refello, to proue fals, to repreue of falsehode, to denye that whiche is obiected.
Referio, rire, to stryke agayne.
Referre ad aliquem, to aske one counsayle in any matter.
Referre de re aliqua ad Senatum, was whan the Consuls purposed a matter in the Senate, desyrynge the Senatours to reason and consulte therof.
Referre pedem, to set forthe a foote, or goo. Eutyche hãc nolo rem prius agi, quam meũ intro refero pedem, I wyll that this thyng Eutyche be doone, or I go oone foote in. *Plautus in mercatore*
Retulit ad me pedem, He came toward me. *Plautus in Epidico.*
Referunt hæc ad rem, these thinges pertain to the matter.
Refero acceptum, Omnia quæ uidimus, si recte rationabimus, uni accepta referemus Antonio. All that we see, yf we recken well, we may impute it onely to Antonie. *Cicero.*
Quod uiuit, mihi acceptum refert: He confesseth to be longe of me, that he nowe lyueth. Verum omnem tranquillitatem & quietem senectutis refert acceptam clementiæ tuę, But all the tranquyllytie and quyetenesse of his age, he confesseth to procede or haue receyued of your mercy and goodnesse. *Cicer. pro Cluen.*
Referre gratiam, to gyue thanke. Nunquam ego illi possum gratiam referre, ut meritus est de me, I canne neuer gyue hym thanke suffycyent for that he hathe doone for me. Spero ego mihi quoque tempus tale euenturum, ut tibi gratiam referam parem, I trust the tyme shal come, that I shall doo you as moche pleasure. Non enim sperasti mutuam tibi gratiam relaturum, ut uicissim tuos compellarem, Thou dyddest not thynke, that I wolde in this wyse haue requyted the, in remembrynge thyne auncetours, as thou haste doone myne. *Plautus in Mostell.*
Plautus in merca.
Ci. in Sal.
Referri in acceptum, to be brought in a reckenyng. Posteaquam reus factus est, primo negabat opus in acceptum referri posse, after that he was accused, fyrste he denyed, that the warke mought be brought vnto a reckenynge.
Referre in melius, to turne it to a better vse.
Referre mores, to expresse the condicyons or maners of an other.
Referre oculos, to caste the loke vpon one.
Referre par, to requyte. Ille quem beneficio adiungas, ex animo facit, studet par referre, whom thou gettest with benefytte, he dothe *Plin. epist. 156.*

he dothe all thynges with a good harte, and studieth to requyte the.

Referre pedem, uel gradum, to steppe back, to retreate.

Referre, to shewe or tel. At illa retulit, quæsiuitq; quidnam mihi uideretur, She tolde me all, and asked what I thought therin.

Cicer. pro Seruilio. Refert. Cuius consilii magni referebat te interesse. At the whiche counsayle, it hadde bene very necessarye, that ye shulde haue bene. *Terent. in phorm.* Parui retulit non suscepisse, It made lyttell matter, that he tooke hir not. Mea quid refert? what care I? Mea nihil refert? I haue noughte to doo with it. Tua refert, It is for thy profyte. Quid refert me fecisse regibus, ut mihi obedirent, si me hodie hic umbraticus deriserit? what auayleth it, that I haue made kynges to obeye me, yf nowe this lewde knaue shall laughe me to scorne? *Ver. geor.* Refert, It is expedient or necessarye. Neque enim numero comprehendere refert: It is not necessarye, to reherce them in numbre.

Refercio, cire, to fylle.

Refero, tuli, ferre, to brynge agayne, to resemble, to reporte, to referre, to reuoke. Referebam me, I retourned. To adde to, or ascribe, to turne, to renew, to brynge, to declare or expresse.

Ci. in Pis. Refero impensum, I make accompt of that whiche is bestowed.

Referre rationem, to yelde or make accompte.

Refectus, ta, tum, restored, renewed, amended, made eftesoones.

Reficio, ficere, to recreate, or restore, to amende, to make agayne.

Reficior, ceris, ci, to be restored, recouered from sicknes, Also renewed or new made.

Refigo, fixi, figere, to make faste or sure, to thruste in harde. Sometyme it signifyeth the contrarye, to drawe out that whyche is fastned.

Ci. Phi. 13. Refigere tabulas & leges, to undoo or destroye lawes. Acta Antonij rescidistis, leges refixistis: Ye haue cancelled the actes of Antony, and undoone or dissolued his lawes. *Ver. æneî.* Fixit leges, pretioque refixit, He stablyshed lawes, and for money eftesoones dissolued them.

Refirmo, are, to fasten or stablyshe agayne.

Terent. in Adelph. Reflatio, a contrary wynde.

Reflatus, tus, idem.

Reflecto, xi, tere, to bowe backe, to tourne back or agayn. Quē neque fides, neq; iusiurandū, neq; illum misericordia repressit, neq; reflexit, whom neither promyse, nor othe, nor yet pitie, withdrewe or pulled backe.

Reflo, are, to blowe agayne or contrarye.

Refluo, xi, fluere, to flowe.

Refluxus, us, the tyde, whanne the water floweth.

Refocillatio, a comfortynge or refreshyng, or recreation.

Refocillo, are, to recomforte, to refresshe, to recreate, to fortifye.

Reformo, mare, to reforme.

Reformator, a reformatour. *Plinius in panegyr. Plin. in epistol. 156. Plinius in panegyri.*

Refoueo, foui, fotum, fouere, to nouryshe or comforte eftesoones, to restore or set in his fyrste state.

Refractarius, obstynate, in a wylfulle oppinion.

Refragor, aris, ari, to resyste with wordes, or clamour.

Refrango, fregi, refrangere, aut refringere, to braste open.

Refreno, refrenare, to pull backe one from a purpose.

Refrico, care, to renewe a sore or grief, whiche was out of remembraunce.

Refrigeratorius, a, um, that whiche cooleth or maketh colde.

Refrigeratio, a koolynge. *Suetonius in Claudi.*

Refrigeratus, ta, tum, kooled: also refreshed or comforted.

Refrigerium, a recreation or aduauncynge of the mynde.

Refrigesco, scere, to make colde.

Refrigero, are, to coole, or make colde, to refresshe or recomforte.

Refrina, a beane, whiche the olde Romans were wont to bring home out of the felde, to doo sacrifyce for the good lucke of their corne. *Festus.*

Refuga, an unrulye persone, whiche wylle not be ordered.

Refugio, gere, to flee or run away or backe, also to refuse. *Colum. 4.*

Refugium, refuge, succour, or place where one may be succoured.

Refugus, a, um, that whiche gothe away, or is layde aparte. *Sidonius.*

Refulgeo, gere, to shyne.

Refundo, fudi, fundere, to restore that whyche lacketh. Quicquid deerit, ex meo refundam, whatte soo euer dothe lacke, I wylle make it uppe of myne owne. Also to paye home agayne, or to yelde. *Seneca.*

Id erat non tam accipere beneficium, quàm refundere, That was not soo moche, to receyue a good tourne, as to doo a good tourne. Also to caste uppe by vomyte. *Seneca de benefic.*

Quod hesterna crapula ingurgitauerat, palam refudit, That whyche in his yesterdayes ryotte he ingourged or deuoured, he openly dydde parbrake or vomyte hit uppe. *Plinius.*

V ij   Refu-

Refutatio, a denyenge, a replycation, an argument to the contrary.

Refuto, tare, to denie, to replye.

Regaliolus, a byrde, betwene whome and the egle is contynual hostilitie, and is yelowe of colour.

Regaliter, royally.

Regalis, le, royalle.

Regelo, are, to thawe, or resolue that, whiche is frosen.

Regenero, rare, to regenerate or eftesones ingender.

Regero, gessi, gerere, to putte in wrytynge, to brynge backe, to vomyte vp.

Regestum, erthe caste vp.

Regia, a kynges howse.

Regiesco, scere, olde writers vsed for crescere, to growe.

Regificus, ca, cum, that whereby a kynge is made.

Regilla, a kynges robe.

Regillus, a lyttell kynge. Also the name of a ryuer in Italy.

Regimen, minis, a rule or gouernaunce.

Regina, a queene.

Regionatim, place by place, by euery region or coste.

Regio, a region or countrey, also a coste, as easte, weste, northe, and southe.

Regium, a cytie beyonde the mountaynes towarde Italye.

Regius, a, um, of a kynge.

Regius morbus, the iaundyse.

Regno, are, to reigne.

Regnum, a realme, and the gouernance.

Rego, xi, regere, to rule, to gouerne.

Regor, geris, to be ruled or gouerned.

Regrador, deri, di, to goo backe.

No. Mar. Regredo, dere, to reuoke, or call agayne.

Regredior, regredi, to go backe.

Regressio, & regressus, us, a returne backe, a resorte backe.

Regula, a rule.

Regularis, regulare, that whyche is vnder a rule.

Regulo, are, to rule or dyrecte.

Regulus, a Prynce or lorde of a lyttelle countreye, properly Reguli, be the chylderne of kynges. Also Regulus is a lyttell byrde, callyd a wrenne, and a serpent callyd a Cockatryce, whiche sleeth a man with his syghte. It was alsoo the name of a Consule, whiche for kepynge of his promyse, was putte to cruelle deathe by the Carthaginensis. Also a great Rhetorician in the tyme of Plynie.

Reieculæ, uel reijculæ oues, sheepe drawen out of the folde for aege or syckenesse, kebbers, crones, or cullyars.

Reiectanea, of phylosophers be taken for thynges to be abhorrid, as sycknesse, pouertie, and sorowe. *Vergil. in Bucolic.*

Reiectio, parbrakynge.

Reiectio sanguinis, the yssuynge oute of bloudde atte the mouthe, the noose, or the vaynes.

Reiectus, ta, tum, caste out, caste awaye, or put forthe.

Reicio, ieci, ijcere, to caste awaye, to dryue backe. Tityre pascentes a flumine reiice capellas, Tityre dryue thy gotes, that doo fede, awaye from the ryuer. Also to refuse, to put away. Me uero tanquam inutilem reiecerunt, As for me they refused, as a person vnprofytable. Si altera illa magis instabit, forsitá nos reiiciat: If the other wil be importunate, perchaunce they wyll put me away. *Apuleius. Terent. in Phorm.*

Reiicere iudices aut testes, to refuse iudges or wytnesses.

Reiicere, to parbrake or vomyte. Senos sextantes non excessit: aut si excessisset, reiiciebantur, He exceded not twelue ounces, yf he passed that, they were caste vp agayne. *Seutonius in August.*

Relatio, a reporte, a respecte: Amonge Logycians, it is the effecte of the Relatyue, as the father, the sonne, the mayster, the seruaunt, the husbande, the wife. For withoute the oone, the other canne not retayne his name, for a sonne may not be withoute a father: nor a wyfe withoute a husbande, nor a seruaunt withoute a mayster.

Relati in ærarios, were they, whiche for some defaute were by the maysters of maners, called Censores, put out of the numbre of Citisens, and dyd only pay tribute, or heedsyluer, as straungers.

Relatiue, hauynge relacion to a thynge.

Relatiuum, a relatife, whiche hath relation to some thynge.

Relaxo, are, to lowse.

Relegatus, banyshed.

Relegatio, a banyshemente oute of his countreye.

Relego, relegare, to banyshe, to remoue, to seuer oone frome an nother, to sende awaye.

Religatus, ta, tum, faste bounde.

Relego, legi, legere, to rede agayne.

Relicinus, he that hathe a good busshe of heare, well trymmed behynde.

Relicina frons, a fayre large and hygh forheed, without heare.

Relictus, ta, tum, forsaken or lefte.

Relictus sum mihi, I am lefte alone.

Religio, onis, relygion, a reuerende drede, doubte

R ante E.

Plautus in Curgul. doubte leste he shall offende. Also conscience, or as a man mought say, a scruple of conscience.

Religiose, fearefully, doubtefully, daungerously, scrupulously.

Religiosus, sa, sum, relygious, dredefulle, doubtefull.

Liuius. 6. In religionem uertere, to feare leeste god were displeased.

Religionem inducere, to brynge in feare of goddis displeasure.

Suetonius in August. Religio est, it is not lefull. Huc introire, nisi necessario, & caste, religio est, To enter in there, but for necessitie, and chastely, it is not lefull.

Religiosus, sa, sum, religious. also superstitious.

Terent. in Heauton. Plautus in Styc. Religiose, auysedly, circumspectly, curiously.

Relino, releui, relinere, to open that whiche is stopped. Releui omnia dolia, I haue broched all the vesselles. Nolo ego nos pro summo bibere: nulli relerimus postea, I wolde not that we dranke all out: for I wyll for no manne sette any a broche afterwarde.

Religioni obstringere, whiche is commonly sayde to haue conscyence in a thynge.

Religioni obstringi, to be bound in cosciece.

Religioni exoluere, to discharge a mannes conscyence.

Religo, are, to loose or vnbynde.

Relimino, to gyue lyght.

Relinquo, liqui, relinquere, to leaue. Relinquere animam, to dye. Relinquit eum animus, his harte fayleth hym.

Reliquatores, they whyche bene in arrerage on theyr accompte. Also any other, whiche haue in their handes some part of that, whiche they ought to haue payde.

Reliquie, that whyche is lefte.

Reliquium facere, to leaue, to omytte.

Reliquus, a, um, the remenaunt, that which remayneth.

Reliquum est, the reste is.

Pli. in epi. Reluceo, luxi, cere, to shyne or be bryght.

Reluctor, tari, to contende or striue agayne.

Reluo, luere, to paye agayne that which is borowed, to fetch home a gage or pledge. Also to wasshe eftesoones.

Remandere, to chewe the cudde.

Remaneo, si, nere, to abyde stylle.

Remano, are, to tourne backe to a place.

Remansio, an abydynge.

Remeculi, lyttell shyppes, whiche men of Lemnos vsed.

Remedium, remedye.

Remeligo, a fysshe, whyche cleauynge to the keale of a shyppe, causeth hym to tary.

Remendo, are, to amende or correct a faut.

Remeo, are, to retourne or go back ageyn.

Remigatio, a rowynge or saylynge.

Remiges, they whyche doo rowe in a galaye or boote.

Remigium, the rowynge of a shyp or bote.

Remigo, are, to rowe.

Remigro, are, to go backe, to returne.

Remilium, a thynge croked and brode.

Reminiscor, sceris, sci, to calle agayne to remembraunce.

Reminiscentia, the remembraunce of that, whiche was ones in the mynde.

Remisse, fayntly, without courage, humbly: Somtyme meryly.

Remissio, remyssion, forgyuenesse, a recreatyng of mynde after study or labour.

Remissus, a, um, gladde, remytted or forgiuen, sente agayne.

Remitto, misi, remittere, to sende, to sende agayne, to sende backe, to release or forgyue, to graunt, to lette downe, to commytte, or remytte, to relinquishe or leaue.

Remittere animum, to putte awaye care, to vnbende or louse.

Remittere, to cesse. Remittere aliquid adolescentiæ, pardon him somwhat for his youth.

Plautus in cap. Remittere nuncium. Gratiam habeo tibi, qum copiam istam mihi & potestatem facis, ut ego ad parentes remittam nuntiu: I thanke the, that thou gyuest me this leaue, and also authoritie, that I maye sende to thy frendes, to prouyde for the els where.

Remissio, a release, a losynge, a withdrawyng. Oculorum remissio, a withdrawing of the looke.

Ci. de ora. Remora, a lyttell fysshe, whyche retayneth a great shyppe vnder sayle.

Remorbesco, to fall eftesones into sicknes.

Remordeo, dere, to tourment the mynde, or make one heuy.

Remores, byrdes, whyche by their flyght or voyce sygnyfyed, that the thyng purposed was not to be folowed.

Remoria, a place on the toppe of the hyl callyd Auentinus, where Remus stoode, and by the flyght of byrdes, aduysed the buyldynge of Rome.

Remona, the dwellynge house of Remus.

Remoueo, ere, to remoue, to take awaye.

Remouete moram, make ye hast, spede you.

Remoror, aris, ari, to tary or make to abide.

Remugio, giui, gire, to belowe or lowe agayne, to render a great sowne.

Remulco, care, & remulculo, is proprely to drawe a greatte shyp or barge with a lasse vessell, by translation it signifieth to drawe a thynge easyly.

Remulcus, a lyttell bote or barke.

Remulinus ager, Remus felde.

R ante E.

Perottus. Remuncope, instrumentes, wherwith shippes be dryuen on lande.
Remunero, are, & remuneror, ari, to reward to recompense a good tourne.
Remuneratio, recompense.
Remus, the brother of Romulus, whyche buylded Rome.
Renanciscor, sceris, sci, to gette agayne.
Renarro, are, to telle, to repete.
Renato, tare, to swym back, or swym agayn.
Renes, the kydneyes.
Renideo, dere, to shyne, to sauour or smell.
Renodo, dare, to vnknytte, or vndo a knot.
Renoues, garmentes made of skynnes of wolfes or other beastes, wherin the ancie Almayns were wont to lye in the warres.
Renouo, are, to renewe.
Renouello, lare, to make newe agayne.
Rentifolia, a kynde of wylde roses, whyche haue neither good sauour nor facion.
Renumero, rare, to paye agayne moneye, whiche is receyued.
Renuntiata, an Ile by Ethiope, soo ryche, that the inhabytantes doo giue for a hors by exchaunge, a talent of golde.
Renuntio, are, to report, to signify, to shew openly, to renounce, to refuse, to resigne, sometyme to restore.
Renuntiare uitæ, to refuse to lyue.
Renuntiatur Consul, he is declared consule.
Renuntiatio, a report, also a resignation of an offyce. also a summons by an offycer.
Plautus in Trin. Renuntij, they whyche do carye tydynges from one to an other.
Renuo, nuere, to refuse, to despyse.
Renutus, nutus, a refusalle or denyar with countenance.
Reor, reris, ratus sum, I suppose.
Repagulum, a doore or wyndowe or other thynge that shutteth or closeth.
Repages, idem.
Repandus, a, um, bent or bowed, and brode backwarde, as ores were in the old tyme.
Repando, dere, to bende backe.
Reparo, rare, to repayre, to restore to the fyrste astate.
Reparamen, & reparatio, a repayrynge or reparation.
Reparco, parsi, sere, to spare.
Repastinatio, a newe dyggynge aboute vynes. Also a bryngyng of grounde to temper with moche labour and dyggynge.
Repastinatus, ta, tum, newe digged or brought in temper.
Repastino, are, to dygge agayne about vynes, to alter lande or grounde, with ofte dyggynge or labourynge.
Repastinor, nari, to be eftesones dygged, or brought into temper.

R ante E.

Repauso, are, to take reste.
Repedo, are, to go awaye, to go backe.
Repello, puli, pellere, to put backe, to repel.
Rependo, di, dere, to recompence.
Repenso, are, to ponder, to ouersee, to iuge.
Repente, sodaynely.
Repentinus, a, um, sodayne.
Reperibitur, it shall be founde.
Repertor, he that fyndeth.
Repercutio, cussi, cutere, to stryke agayn, to reuerberate.
Repercussus, sus, a reuerberation or strykynge often.
Reperio, reperi, reperire, to fynde by auenture. sometyme otherwise.
Repetere, to calle agayne. Hem repudiatus repetor, Howe nowe, beinge ones refused, I am callyd agayne. Alta repetita, rehersed from the begynnyng, farre sought, or farre fette. *Plautus.* *Ter. in An.*
Repetere poenas, ab aliquo, to be auengyd on one.
Repeto, I remembre. Me quidem adolescentulo, repeto quendam principem nomine alternis diebus declamare, alternis disputare, I remembre me, whan I was a boye, that one, whyche was a prynce of name, dydde one daye declame, an nother daye dispute.
Repetenti memoria, to cal to remembrance.
Repeto, tij, tere, to aske again, to aske often, or eftesoones, to reherce agayne, or repete, to reuolue.
Repetundarum accusari, is proprely where a man sometyme beinge in great auctoritie and hauyng the rule of a countrey, is accused and callyd to a reckenynge, for all that he hath receyued, being in his office, aboue that whiche is his ordynarye allowaunce, also for all thynge that he tooke wrongefully from any persone or towne: whyche was the mooste necessarie action for a publyke weale, that mought be deuised, to be nowe put in execution.
Repignerator, he that redemeth or quiteth his gage or pledge.
Repignero, are, to quite or redeme a pledge or gage. It may be taken sometyme with vs, that whyche in our lawe is callyd to repleuy: and repignoratio, a repleuy: and repignoratitia actio, for a replegiare.
Replaudo, dere, to make noise with the handes beaten togither.
Replicatio, a replycation or vnfoldynge of a thynge.
Replico, care, to vnfolde. also to reply.
Replumbo, are, to vnsowlder.
Repo, repsi, pere, to crepe, to runne as rootes do in the grounde. *Iure 6. ff. de auro & argento.*

Repo=

Repoleo, liui, lire, to polyshe agayne.

Repolleo, lere, to be moche able, to be of power to doo.

Colum. 5. Repollesco, scere, to be eftesoones stronge or in force.

Reponere fidem, to truste.

Horatius. Reponere, is also to put in by wrytinge. Scriptor honoratum si forte reponis Achillem, Thou that writest, if peraduenture thou puttest in Achylles.

Repono, sui, nere, to putte or sette agayne in his place, to laye vp, to recite agayne, to hyde, to redelyuer or restore, to reuoke, to represse, to lay to more, or exaggerate, to heape one on another, to make to grow agayne, to brynge agayne.

Vergeo. 2. Et quantum longis carpent armenta diebus, Exigua tantum gelidus ros nocte reponet: Loke howe moche the sheepe in the longe dayes shall byte. The colde dewe in oone nyghte with growynge shall requyte.

Reporto, are, to brynge backe, or agayne.

Reposco, poposci, scere, to aske agayne that whyche is myne owne, or is as it were dewe to me.

Repositorium, a storehowse.

Repositus, & repostus, ta, tum, layd vppe, to hyde. Manet alta mente repostum, Iudicium Paridis, Depe in his minde, remayned the iudgement, that Parys gaue betwene the goddesses, of the whiche sprange the occasyon of the destruction of Troye.

Repotium, whan the day after the mariage frendes do come & drinke with the bride.

Reprehendo, dere, to plucke backe, to reproue. Reprehensi, caught.

Represento, tare, to represent, to render, to brynge in presence, or present a thynge, to laye before one.

Reprimo, mere, to refrayne, to lette.

Reprobo, are, to reproue.

Reprobus, a man reproued.

Reproces, sharpe.

Reptile, all thynge that crepeth.

Repto, tare, to crepe moch : also to go softly lyke a snayle.

Repudio, are, to forsake, as a man forsaketh his wife, also to refuse, to abandon, or leue.

Ter. in An. Repudio consilium, quod primum intenderam, I wyll nowe leaue the counsayle that I fyrste intended to folowe.

Repudium, a deuorce.

Repudium remittere, to be deuorced.

Repudium renuntiare, to declare a deuorce.

Plautus in Aulul. Is me nunc repudium renuntiare iussit tibi, He wylled me to declare to the, that he hath forsaken the.

Repudiosę nuptię, mariage, after the which foloweth sone after a deuorce, Necessitate me mala ut fiam facis, uerum uideto, me vbi uoles nuptum dare, ne hac fama faciat, repudiosas nuptias, Thou compellest me to be nought, but take hede, that where thou wylte mary me, by that reporte he shall make suche a weddynge as shall soone after be dissolued or broken. *Plautus in Persa.*

Repuerasco, scere, to be eftesones a chylde.

Repugno, are, to repugne or say contrary, to resyste.

Repugnanter, an aduerbe, whiche signyfyeth contrariously, displesantly. Vt igitur monere & moneri, proprium est verę amicitię, & alterum libere facere, non asperę : alterum pacienter accipere non repugnanter, sic habendū est nullam in amicitus pestem esse maiorem, quam adulationē, blanditias, assentationem, Lyke therfore as to giue counsayle, and to be counsailed, properly belongeth to very frendeshyp, also the tone to do euery thyng frankely, the tother to take all thynge pacientely, not displesantly : So it is to be considered, that in frendshyp there is no more pestilence, than flatterye, fayre wordes, and consentynge to all thynges. *Cicero de amicitia.*

Repugnantia, repugnācy, where one thing agreeth not with an nother.

Repungo, gere, to prycke agayne, or mutually displease or offende.

Repulsa, a puttynge backe of hym, whiche eyther demaundeth or looketh for authoritie or offyce.

Repulsor, oris, he that putteth an nother man backe.

Repulsus, he that is put backe.

Reputo, tare, to thynke often, to consyder moche, to reuolue in the mynde, to cōpt. Also to cut of eftesoones.

Requies, reste.

Requiesco, scere, to reste or take reste.

Requietus, ta, tum, that whiche resteth.

Requiro, requisiui, requirere, to seke eftesones or often, to requyre.

Res, occasion. Ere nata melius fieri haud potuit, q̄ factum est, Of the occasion begon it coulde not better haue ben doone, than it is. Also it sygnifieth meane. Iam repperi rem, quo pacto nec fur, nec socius sies : I haue nowe founde the meane, howe thou shalt be neyther a thefe, nor a companion with hym. *Terent. in Adelph.* *Plautus in Ruden.*

Rem facere, to gayne or wynne. Nunquam rem facies : abi, nescis inescare homines, Thou shalte neuer gayne penye : Gette the hense, thou canneste noo skylle to angle menne. *Terent. in Adelph.*

Rem habere cum aliquo, to haue to do with one,

Ter. in Eu. one, to meddell with one.
Res gerere, to haue or make warres. Scipione Aemiliano res in Affrica gerente, Polybius annalium conditor, ab eo accepta classe scrutandi orbis illius gratia circunuectus est: **Plinius. lib. 5.** Scipion Emilianus making warres in Affrike, Polybius the wrytar of Histories, with a certayne numbre of shyppes, was conuayed aboute that coste, to inserche that parte of the worlde.

Plautus in Epidico. Re iuuare, to helpe with deedes & not with wordes onely. Is amicus, qui in re dubia re iuuat, vbi re est opus, He is a frende, which in a case that is doubteful, helpeth me with his deedes, where deedes are required.

Terent. in Eunucho. Quid isti credam? res ipsa indicat: what shal I trust hym? the deede selfe declareth.
Verba ad rem conferre, to doo as he sayth.

Terent. in Eunucho. Vsque adeo ego illius ferre possum ineptias, & magnifica verba, verba dum sint, verū enim, si ad rem conferentur, vapulabit: Hitherto I can suffre his lewdenesse, and bragges, as longe as they are but wordes: but yf he do as he sayth, he shall smart therfore.

Re vera, in deede, in very trouthe, matter in dede.
Resalutatio, a courtayse speakynge to hym that speaketh to you, a resalutinge.
Resaluto, salutare, to salute hym that saluteth you.
Resarcio, si, cire, to amende, to refourme.
Resarrio, iui, ire, to weede eftsones corne.
Res, a thinge, the thinge, the matter: sometyme astate, condicion, busynesse, contention, cause, rychesse or substance, profyte, weale, experience.
Res est, it is matter in dede.
Res ad manticam rediit, it is all come to a bagge and a staffe, or a staffe and a walet.
Res comperendinata, a mater adiourned or deferred vntyll the thirde daye.
Res iudicata, the matter or cause finally determyned and adiuged.
Res controuersa, the mater in sute.
Res forensis, a mater in lawe.
Respublica, a publike weale.
Rescindo, scidi, scindere, to cut or breake in sunder, to take awaye, to destroye, to make **Vergil. Geor. li.1.** voyde or repell an acte or lawe, to breake vp. Cœlum rescindere fratres, Ter sunt conati: Thries the brethern assayed to breke vp heuen, for to enter.
Rescio, sciui, scire, to knowe a thinge, which is hydde and kepte secrete: also to knowe a thinge after that it is done, whiche was not knowen before.
Rescisco, scere, idem quod Rescio.
Rescribo, psi, bere, to wryte agayne, to redelyuer, to repay money.

Reseco, are, to cut awaye that which is superfluouse.
Resecare ad viuum, to pare to the quicke, to touche the quicke in a mater.
Resecro, crare, to praye or desire eftsones: also to assoyle one of his auowe.
Resegmen, the paringe of a mans nayles.
Resero, are, to open a thinge that is closed.
Resero, rere, to sow or set agayne.
Reseruatio, a reseruation, a kepyng of some thynge.
Reseruo, uare, to kepe a part frome other thinges, to reserue.
Reses, idis, ydell frome accustumed labour or occupacion.
Resex, secis, that which is cut and springeth **Col. lib. 3.** agayne, and beareth more fruyte than it dyd before.
Resideo, resedi, residere, to rest, to sytte, to stande fast.
Resido, sedi, sidere, to syt downe, also to abide. Nam Viennensium vitia inter ipsos residunt, nostra late vagantur, For the faultes **Plinius in Epistol.** of men of Uienne, doo abyde with theym, oures runne abrode, and be euery where knowen.
Resider in vultu, there doeth rest or appiere in the vysage. Quorum non in sententia so- **Cic. de Se** lum, sed etiam in nutu residebat autoritas, In whose sentence not onely, but also countenaunce, autoritie rested.
Residuus, a, um, the rest or remnaunt.
Resigno, are, to open that which is sealed: sometyme to seale fast, also to shyt, sometyme to restore agayne, also to resigne or surrendre.
Resignatum æs, wages stopped for negligent seruice in warres.
Resilio, lii, lire, to lepe backe, or steppe away quickely.
Resimus, he that hath a camoysenose, that is to saye, tourned vpwarde.
Resina, rosyn, all lyke gumme whyche runneth out of trees.
Resinatus, sinata, tum, rased, or dressed with rosyn.
Resipio, pui, pere, idem quod Resipisco.
Resipisco, resipui, resipiscere, to retourne to perfect vnderstāding, to be eftsones wise, where before he erred.
Resisto, restiti, resistere, to resyste or withstande.
Resoluo, uere, to resolue, to destroye, to pay detres, to remoue, to vndo or vnlowse.
Resolutio neruorum, the palsey.
Resono, nare, to sowne agayne, to make an Eccho.
Resorbeo, bui, & psi, bere, to poure out or disgorge the licour that was receyued.

Re-

R ante E.

Respecto, are, to see often, to loue, to helpe.
Respectus, tus, a looke: also, respect or regarde. *Plini.* Neq eo respectu commotus discesserat: Hauynge no regarde thereunto he departed.
Respergo, si, gere, to cast water or other licour about, to sprynkle.
Respergimen, a sprynklynge or castynge about of licour.
Respicere, to helpe or socour. *Ter. in An.* Age, me in tuis secundis rebus respice: Let se, nowe in thy prosperitie, socoure me.
Respicit nos deus, god hath pytie on vs.
Plautus in Bacch. Tace modo, deꝰ respiciet nos aliquis, peace now, some god wyll haue pitie on vs.
Respicere se, to take hede or haue regarde of hym self. *Plautus in Pseudolo.* Non soles respicere te, cum dicas iniuste alteri? Art thou not wont to take hede of thy selfe, whan thou sayest wrong of another man? *Terent. in Heaut.* Non tu te cohibes? non te respicis? non tibi exempli satis sum? wilte thou not beware? wilt thou not take hede of thy self? am not I a good example vnto the?
Respicio, exi, spicere, to loke backe, to haue regarde, to prouyde, to remedy, to kepe, to reserue, to loue.
Respiro, are, to take brethe, also to take coforte, to retourne to the fyrst state. *Cice. Aul. Torquato.* Si armis aut conditione positis, aut fatigatione abiectis, aut victoria detractis, ciuitas respirauerit: & dignitate tua tibi, & fortuna vti licebit: If that harneyse, eyther by condicions of peace beinge layde away, or by werynesse of both partes beinge throwen awaye, or pulled awaye by victory, the citie shall recouer her fyrst estimation, thou than shalt enioye thy possessions and dignitie.
Resplendeo, dere, to shyne.
Respondeo, di, dere, to aunswere, to appiere whan one is called, to agree, to consent or be lyke or equall, to be agaynst, as one thing set or lyenge agaynste another.
Responsio, an aunswere.
Responsito, tare, to make or gyue aunswere: it pertayned proprely to lawiars: and them whyche hadde the interpretation of ceremonyes.
Responso are, to aunswere. *Cicer. pro Cluen.*
Responsum, an aunswere.
Responsus, sus, sui, where one thinge doeth agree with another, a consent, a conueniencye.
Respuo, ere, to refuse, or reiect.
Restagno, restagnare, to contayne or holde water.
Restat, Restare, to be or remayne of that thinge, that is lefte, to stande backe, to resyste. Hoc me restat, that remayneth or abydeth for me.

R ante E.

Restauro, Restaurare, to restore, or make agayne.
Restibilis, that which is renewed, or sowen agayne.
Restibilis ager, a feelde which is sowen two yeres togither.
Restinguo, xi, guere, to stint or put oute, or cesse, as fyre, lyght, and thurst.
Restio, onis, a roper: also he that hangeth hym selfe.
Restipulatio, a puttynge in of pledges, put in gage or pledge, for to make aunswere to an action. *Plautus.*
Restipulor, aris, ari, to make aunswere in the lawe.
Restire, to be redy to be sowen, ploughed, or dygged.
Restis, a halter or corde, a rope or bunche of of garlyke or onyons.
Restem ducere, whan maydens and childrē daunse togither hande in hande, or with napkens, leadynge one another. Ad restim res redijt, the mater is in despayre, or desperate.
Restito, tare, to abyde or tary.
Restituo, ere, to restore, to yelde agayne.
Restitutio, restitution.
Resto, tare, to remayne, to tary. *Ter. in An.* Hic nunc me credit aliquam sibi fallaciam portare, & ea me hic restitisse gratia: He weeneth, that I warke hym some falshede, and that I tary styll therfore. *Cicero de finibus.* Nullam querentes voluptatem Stoici restant, The Stoike Philosophers do resist or sticke to their opynion, sekinge for no pleasure.
Restat mihi, it taryeth for me: it shal happen vnto me.
Restricte & Restrictim, straytely, or strayte.
Restringo, xi, stringere, to bynde or strayne backwarde, to bynde agayne, to restrayne: sometyme it signifyeth to lowse. Apulei. Iumentum restrinxit, abireq stabulō liberum sinit: he lowsed his horse, and let hym out of the stable at libertye.
Resulto, tare, to lepe agaynste a thinge, to rebounde, to rebelle, to leape or steppe backe.
Resumo, psi, sumere, to take agayne, to resume.
Resuo, ere, to sowe agayne, or make a double styche: also to ryppe or vndo that whiche is sowen, to vnstytche: *Suet. in au.* Sumenti virilē togam, tunica laticlaui resuta ex vtraq parte, ad pedes decidit: whan he came fyrste to mannes age, his Senatours cote beynge rypte on bothe sydes, fell downe to his feete.

Resu-

Resupinus, na, num, vpryght, the bely vpwarde.
Resurgo, rexi, gere, to aryse vppe.
Resurrectio, resurrection.
Resupino, nare, to tourne vpwarde, or vpright, to reuoke or callebacke, to differ, to peruerte.
Retæ, trees growyng on the bankes of ryuers, or in the ryuers.
Retardatio, a taryenge.
Retardo, dare, to make to tary.
Rete, tis, a nette.
Retego, Retexi, tegere, to discouer or disclose.
Retento, entare, to retayne often, to tempte eftsones.
Retexo, ere, to vntwyste or vntwyne, or vnwynde: sometyme to twist or wynde eftsones, to dissolue.
Retiaculum, a lytle net.
Retiarius, he that casteth a nette, properly in fyghtynge to apprehende his aduersarye.
Retia, nettes, sometyme it signifyeth one nette.
Reticeo, cui, ticere, to holde ones peace, to speake no worde, to kepe secrete, to saye nothynge.
Reticentia, silence, whan one holdeth his peace.
Reticula, a lytle net, wherin a mans heare or womens is trussed.
Reticulatus, Reticulata, culatum, made lyke a nette.
Reticulum, a cawle or coyfe: also a bagge, wherin meate is caryed.
Retinaculum, what so euer holdeth any other thynge, a staye.
Retinere, to holde vppe, that a man fall not.

Terent. in Heauton. Ah retine me obsecro. B. obsecro quid tibi est? An. Disperij. B. perij misera, quid stupes Antiphila? Oh holde me vppe I praye the. B. alak what ayleth the? A. I am vndone. B. alas that euer I was borne, why doth thy hart fayle the Antiphila?

Retineo, nui, nere, to holde agayne, to retayne, to kepe in remembraunce.

Terent. in Adelph. Retinere, to restrayne or let one frome doinge that, that he wolde. Pudore & liberalitate liberos retinere satius esse credo, quàm metu: I thinke it better to restrayne children frome their wanton willes, by shame and liberalitie, than with feare.

Retinens, he that kepeth still.
Retiolum, a Cawle, or coyfe.
Retondeo, dere, to klyppe all ouer.
Retorqueo, torsi, quere, to cast backewarde, to throwe or shute agayne.
Retorresco, retorrescere, to be burnedde with the sunne.
Retorridus, da, dum, burned or seryd.
Retracto, ctare, to calle backe, or reuoke a thinge that is done, to drawe backe, to excuse, to laye to another man, to drawe vp.
Retrahe, traxi, trahere, to pull or drawe back, or to drawe to.
Retribuo, buere, to recompence.
Retrica, old writars called the water, wherwith gardens are watered.
Retrimētum, the dragges of a thynge: somtyme ordure or dung.
Retro, behynde.
Retrocedo, cessi, cedere, to go backe.
Retrorsum, bacwarde.
Retrorsus, a, um, turned backewarde.
Retrudo, si, dere, to put backe.
Retundo, dere, to make blunt or dull, that whyche is sharpe: also to beate often on a thynge.
Retusus, a, um, dull, blunt, contrary to sharp. Aliæ agrorum partes, quæ acuta ingenia gignant, aliæ quæ retusa: Some partes of contrayes there be, whyche do brynge forth sharpe wyttes, some brynge forth dull. *Cic. de Di.*
Reualesco, scere, to be recouered frome sickenesse.
Reueho, uexi, here, to brynge or cary backe, or agayne.
Reuelatio, a reuelynge or a disclosynge of a thinge.
Reuello, reuellere, to plucke backe, to pull agayne.
Reuelo, are, to discouer.
Reuenio, nire, to come agayne.
Reuerendus, worthy reuerence.
Reuerens, rentior, rentissimus, he that doeth reuerence.
Reuerenter, reuerently.
Reuerentia, reuerence or honour doone to one.
Reuereor, reris, reri, to haue in reuerence. *Budeus.*
Reuersio, a retourne.
Reuertor, teris, ti, to retourne.
Reuerto, idem.
Reuincio, uinxi, uincere, to bynde backe or behynde, as to bynde ones handes behynde hym. *Vergil. Gell.*
Reuincere paratus est, whyche the lawyars do saye, Paratus est verificare, He is redy to auerr.
Reuiso, sere, to retourne to see.
Reuiuisco, scere, to be reuyued.
Reuoco, uocare, to calle backe, to reuoke, to brynge agayne, to drawe backe, to rayse frome deth.
Reuocare pedem, to turne backe, to recule.
Reuocare, to restore or renewe. Item circa omnium ordinum statum domi, forisq́;, aut
corre-

correxit, aut exoleta reuocauit, aut etiam noua instituit: Moreouer concernynge the state of al degrees, as wel within his house as withoute, eyther he dyd amende them, or renewed those thynges that were oute of vse, or els ordayned newe.

Reuocatio, a reuocation or callynge backe.

Budeus. Reuocare testes, to reherce the deposicions of witnesses, publication.

Reuolo, are, to flee backe.

Reuoluo, ui, uere, to turne uppe and downe, to reuolue, to tourne backe, to remoue.

Reuolutus, ta, tum, to be tourned backe, to be remoued.

Reuolutio, a tournynge backe to the firste place or poynt: a reuolucion or tournynge of celestiall bodyes or spheres.

Reuorto, tere, olde wrytars vsed for Reuertor, to retourne.

Reus, he that is sued or accused, sometyme he that is gyltye.

Reus facti, gylty of an offence.

Reus agitur, he is sued or accused.

Reus peragitur, he that is condemned.

Reus stipulando, he that bargayneth.

Reus uoti, he that hath auowed.

Reum subdere, to accuse one of gret offence

Rex regis, a kynge.

Rex sacrificulus, was a chief minister of sacrifices amonge the Romayns onely.

¶ R, ANTE H.

Rhabarbarum, Rubarbe, a precious roote, medicinable to pourge coler, also to corroborate the stomake and lyuer.

Rachinon, a spyder, hauynge a lytle blacke heed, and is somewhat whyte, and hath short feete, whose bytynge is as venymous as the styngynge of a Scorpion.

Rhadamanthus, was kynge of Licia, which was a strayghte executour of iustice: and therfore was supposed of the Paynyms to be afterwarde one of the iuges in hell.

Rhagades, & Rhagadiæ, certayne kleftes or as it were Scrachis aboute the siege or fundament.

Pli. li. 24. cap. 14. Rhamnus, a kynde of brembles, whyche is whyte, and beareth more frute than other do, and also hath floures, & sendeth forth braches with strayght prickes, not croked as other are, and hath brode leues.

Rhamnusia, was called goddesse of vengeaunce.

Rhamnusius, a man of a town called Rhamnus, by Athenes.

Rhampsinithus, the propre name of a kynge of Egypte.

Rhaphanus, an herbe called Radysshe.

Rhebanus, a ryuer in the mouth of Bosphorus, a countraye in Thracia.

Rhea, was called the mother of goddes, called also Cibele.

Rhea Syluia, the mother of Romulus and Rhemus.

Rheda, a chariot.

Rhedarius, a chariotman.

Rhegiam, a citie on the bordure of Italy towarde Sicile: also an other citye not ferre frome Parma.

Rheginus, a man of the citie of Rhegium in Calabre.

Rhemi, people in Fraunce, called also Rhemenses.

Rhenones, cotes made of the skynnes of beastes.

Rhenus, a noble ryuer in Germania, called the Rheyne.

Rhenense vinum, Rheynisshe wyne.

Rhenenses, people dwellynge on the ryuer of Rheyne.

Rheon, Reubarbe.

Rhesus, kynge of Thracia, whiche came to the ayde of the Troianes, and was slayne of Diomedes: of whome a ryuer aboute Troye was called Rhesus.

Rheti, a people in Italy.

Rhetia, a countraye in Germany, whyche some men doo suppose to be Bauaria, or Beuer, called in Duche, Berue.

Rhetor, oris, he that teacheth Rhetorike.

Rhetorica, Rhetorike, or the crafte of eloquence.

Rhetoricor, cari, to speake Rhetorike.

Rhetoricè, lyke a Rhetorician.

Rhetus, a gyaunt, whome Dionyse, beinge tourned into a lyon, slewe.

Rhetoricus, an oratour, or a man cunnyng in the craft of eloquence.

Rhetorisso, are, to speake in the fourme of Rhetorike.

Rheuma, a rewme or distillation of humours.

Rheumatismus, the disease of rheume.

Rhibis, a bremble called Raspys.

Rhinoceron, ontis, a best that hath an horne in his nose, whyche naturally is enemy to the Olyphant: it is also an oyle vessell, out of the which oyle is dropped.

Rhinocerotis nasum habere, is sayd of them that be witty. Iuuenesq̃, senesq̃, Et pueri nasum, Rhinocerotis habent, Yong men, olde men, And children, and all be witty. *Horatius.*

Rhodanus, a ryuer in Fraunce, called the Rone.

Rhodia, a kynde of vynes.

Rhodites, a certayne precyouse stone, of the

the colour of a rose.
Rhodope, a mountayne in Thracia.
Rhodos, an Ile called Rodes.
Rhodius, of the Rodes.

Plini. Rhododaphne, & Rhododendros, a tree, hauynge leaues lyke to an almonde tree, but greatter and fatter sedes, open lyke a horne, which hath in them wulle lyke purple silke, a longe roote, salte in tast, it groweth in watry places.
Rhodonia, a gardyn of roses.
Rhodophone, that part of Syria, that goeth ouer the mountayne of Taurus.
Rhodopeius, a, um, pertaynynge to the mountayne of Rhodope.
Rhombus, a fygure foure square, hauynge the sydes equall, the corners crooked. it is also a fysh called a Birt: also a spynnynge wheele or tourne.
Rhœas, whan the corners of the eyen are open, so that there doo still frome theym continuall dropes.
Rhomphea, a sworde.
Rhœtus, a mountayne of Troye, where Aiax Thelamonius was buryed.
Rhœton, wyne made of pomegranettes.
Rhopalon, a water lyly, called communely Nenuphar.
Rhoxia, a countraye by Polonia.
Rhoxalani, people on the north part, of the ryuer of Danubius, or Danowe.
Rhuteni, a people in Fraunce called Rhodes.
Rhymnus, a ryuer.
Rhyndacus, a ryuer, which runneth in to the see called Pontus.
Rhyparographus, a paynter of tryfles, a Stayner.
Rhytion, a vessell lyke to a moone.
Rhythmus, numbre or armeny in speakinge.

¶ R. ANTE I.

RIca, a garment of purple, hemmed or purfled. also a kerchief, whiche women do weare.
Ricinus, & Ricinum, euery garment that is foure square. also it is a kynde of Lucumbres. also an herbe lyke a fygge tree, but lesse, hauynge leues lyke to a plane tree.
Ricinium, & Ricinum, a cloke, whereof part was cast ouer a mannes sholder.
Ricula, a handekerchief.
Rictus, & Rictum, a grynnynge or scorneful openynge of the mouthe: also the fourme of the vysage, whan a man grenneth, or a dogge brawleth.
Rideo, risi, ridére, to laughe: also to skorne or mocke.

Ridibundus, da, dum, that lawgheth moche.
Ridica, a proppe, wherwith a vyne, or other lyke thinge is holden vp.
Ridiculare, a thinge to laughe at.
Ridiculum, idem. also a mocke.
Ridiculus, a man whome men doo mocke or lawghe at.
Ridicularius, a, um, idem quod Ridiculum.
Ridiculé, folyshly.
Ridiculosus, a, um, idem quod Ridiculus.
Ridiculosé, folyshly to be lawghed at.
Rigeo, gui, gere, to be feruently colde, alsoo to be harde or styffe.
Rigesco, scere, idem quod Rigeo.
Rigidé, styffely, sharpely, cruelly.
Rigidus, da, dum, colde, harde, styffe, sharpe or cruell.
Rigo, are, to make weate, or to water a garden or felde.
Rigor, Rigoris, colde, hardenesse, styfenesse.
Riguus, a, um, that maye be easyly weate or watered.
Rima, a chynke, or kleft in woode or stone, where it is not close ioyned.
Rimula, a lytell chynke or cleft.
Rimas agere, to be clouyn or chynked, as tymber or bourdes are with lyenge in the wynde.
Rimã inuenire, to fynde an excuse, or meane to escape. *Plautus in Cur. & in Casina.*
Rimor, aris, ari, to serche diligently, also to kleue as tymber doeth.
Rimosus, a, um, full of kleftes or chynkes.
Ringo, xi, gere, to grynne or shew the teeth, as a dogge doeth whan he will barke or byte. also to be angry, to brawle, to barke.
Ripa, a water banke.
Riparia, a byrde whyche breedeth in water bankes.
Ripæ, seu Ripei, mountaynes in Arcadia.
Riphei, mountaynes in Scythia.
Riscus, a cofer couered with lether: also a lytle wyndowe.
Risibilis, le, that which can lawghe.
Risus, laughter.
Risus sardonius, a lawghter without myrth, as of them that be madde or cruell, such as Irish men vse whan they be angry.
Rité, dyrectely, truely, euen as it shulde be.
Rituales, bookes, wherin the fourme of ceremonyes, and old maners and customes are wryten.
Ritus, tus, an approued custome.
Riuales, they whiche equally doo loue one womanne, or be woars togither. also they, whose landes be deuyded by a ryuer or brooke: also they which dwel vpõ ryuers.
Riualitas, tatis, enuy or obseruaunce betwixt the

R ante O.

Plautus in Aunar.
the louers of one woman.
Riuinus, a wower, idem quod riualis.
Riuus, a ryuer or broke.
Riuulus, a lyttell broke.
Riuo, are, is to go to watryng, as bestis do.
Rixa, a braulynge contention.
Rixose, brawlynge.

No. Mar.
Rixosus, a stryuer or brawler.
Rixor, aris, ari, & rixo, to contende with brawlynge.

¶ R. ANTE O.

Robigalia, the Ceremonyes pertaynynge to Robigus, the preseruatour of corne.
Robiginosus, a, um, moche blasted.
Robigo, was honored of the Romains for a goddesse, whom they supposed mought preserue their corne from blastinge. it is also that vice in corne called blasting.
Robigus, whome the olde Romaynes named the god, that preserued corne from blastynge.
Roboraria, places, whiche ar paled about.
Roboreus, ea, eum, of oken tymber.
Roboro, are, to fortifie.
Roboses, the old wryters vsed for robore, an oke.
Robur, roboris, hard oke. It is also stregth and hardenes of the body. sommetyme the strength or hardnes of any thing generally
Robus, olde wryters called redde of colour. Also al maner of matter, which had many redde vaynes, was called Robus. It is also a kynde of wheate, that yeldeth fayre meale, whiche we nowe calle redde wheate.
Robustus, ta, tum, stronge and harde.
Rodo, si, dere, to gnawe as a mouse or other lyke beaste dothe. sometyme to detracte or backbyte.

Festus
Rodus, da, dum, a thyng vnperfect or rude, vnpolyshed, vnwrought.
Rogamen, minis, a desyre.
Rogatarii, Notaryes, whyche requyred the partyes, that eche of theym shoulde promyse.

Plautus.
Rogator, rogatoris, a begger frome doore to doore.
Rogito, tare, to intreate or demande, to inquyre often, to aske for a thynge.
Rogo, are, to requyre, to pray, to inquyre, to aske of one, to inacte.

Quintilia.
Rogare populum, to treat with the people.
Rogare sacramento, to sweare oone, or to grue to hym an othe.
Rogatio, was amonge the Romaynes, whanne the Tribunes, whyche were the heed officers of the people, were content that any acte shoulde passe, whyche was made by the senate, or by the same Tribunes deuysed.
Rogus, a great fyre, wherein deed bodies were bourned.
Roma, the citie of Rome.
Romanensis, he that commeth from an nother countrey, and dwelleth at Rome.
Romania, is a countrey called Thracia.
Romanus, a Romayne.
Romanus, na, num, of Rome.
Romandui, Normandes.
Romula, a tree, vnder the whiche Romulus and Remus were founde.
Romuleus, a, um, & Romulidus, da, dum, of Romulus.
Romulus, the fyrste kynge of Romaines.
Ronchisso, are, to route or snorte.
Ronchus, a routynge. sometyme a scorne.
Ronchisonus, he that routeth or snorteth.
Rorarii milites, men in the vauntgarde, or forwarde of a battayle.
Roratio, is a disease in vynes, by the occasyon wherof the chiefe grapes doo falle away.
Roresco, scere, to be washed with dewe.
Rorifacio, cere, to spryncle.
Rores, dewes.
Roro, are, to dewe, or droppe downe lyke dewe.
Rorulentus, ta, tum, full of dewe.
Ros, roris, dewe.
Rosa, a Rose.
Rosaceus, a, um, of roses. Aqua Rosacea, Rosewater.
Rosalia, garlandes of Roses.
Rosarium, a gardeyn or bedde of Roses.
Rosetum, a gardeyne of Roses.
Roseus, a, um, of a rose.
Rosidus, da, dum, wette with dewe.
Rosmarinum, Rosemary, or a lyttel shonte.
Rostellum, a lyttell beake or bylle of a byrd.
Rostra, rorum, rostris, was a place in Rome afore the court callid Hostilia, wherin was a pulpite, in which the oratours of Rome were wonte to stande, whan they preched to the people, or declared any matter, of the whiche proceded this worde Pro rostris, in the pulpit, or at the barre.
Rostrum, a beake of a byrde, a snowte of a beaste or fyshe, also the stemme of a ship or boote.
Rota, a wheele.
Roto, tare, to turne a thynge lyke a whele.
Rotula, a lyttell whele. Rotella, idem.
Rotunde, roundly, aptely, elegantly, handsomly, properly in wordes.
Rotundus, tunda, dum, rounde, sommetyme welle

well compacte or facioned. Ore rotundo loqui, to expresse moche in fewe wordes.

¶ R, ANTE V.

Rubefacio, cere, to make redde.
Rubefio, fieri, to be made redde.
Rubellę, redde grapes.
Rubellum vinum, clarette wyne.
Rubeo, ere, to be redde.
Ruber, bra, brum, redde.
Rubesco, scere, to be redde.
Rubeta, a tode.
Rubetum, a busshy close.
Rubeus, ea, eum, redde.
Rubens, idem.
Rubi, borum, a towne in Campania.
Rubia, mader, wherwith clothe is dyed.
Rubicon, conis, a ryuer in Italye, whyche dyuideth Italy from Lombardy.
Rubicundus, da, dum, ruddy.
Rubidus, da, dum, a swarte redde. Alsoo rowghe or course, as bredde, hauynge moche branne.
Rubigino, are, to ruste.
Rubiginosus, a, um, rustye.
Rubigo, ginis, ruste.
Rubor, oris, rednesse.
Rubrica, red chalke, or ruddell, wherwith shepe are marked.
Rubriceta, rosette colour.
Rubrus, a, um, redde.
Rubricatus, ta, tum, coloured with redde, or ruddelyd, as shepe are.
Rubus, a bremble.
Ructo, are, to belke or breake wynde vppewarde.
Ructito, tare, to breake wynde often.
Ructuatio, idem quod ructus.
Ructus, belkyng or brekyng wynd vpward.
Rude donari, to be discharged of attendāce propzely in warres.
Rudē accipere, hath the same signification.
Rudens, tis, a cabell of a shyppe.
Ruderarium, a rangynge syeue.
Rudero, rare, to laye on olde stoones and rubbell.
Rudero, are, to daube or lay on morter.
Ruderatus, ta, tum, where moche rubbyshe lyeth.
Rudetum, a place, where lyeth moche rubbyshe or rubbell. Also lande, whiche hath lyen ley, and is newly put in tylthe.
Rudiarij, they whyche are dyscharged of fyghtynge with swordes, as they whiche were calledde Gladiatores, that openlye faught, one with an other, to animate the Romaynes, with shedyng of their blode. They be also bodgers or amēders of old garmentes, also seuiars, or makers of sieues.
Rudicula, a potte stycke.
Rudię, arum, a citie in the further parte of Italy, ioynynge to Apulia.
Rudimentum, the fyrst techyng of children.
Rudio, dire, to teche one, which is vnlernid.
Rudis, a rodde or yerde, whiche was gyuen to sworde players, whan they came to .lx. yeres olde, in token that they were sette at libertie. sometyme lybertie frome labour.
Rudis, de, rude, vnperfect, new, vnwrought
Rudus, ruderis, shardes or pieces of stones broken and scattered, rubbell or rubbyshe of olde houses.
Ruditas, rudenes, lacke of lernyng or wit.
Rudo, rudi, rudere, to braye lyke an asse. It is sometyme spoken of a man. sometyme of a woman.
Rufeo, & rufesco, scere, to be sommewhat redde.
Rufo, fare, to make redde.
Rufuli, certayne Captaynes made by the consul, who afterward were called Rutuli.
Rufus, a, um, somwhat redde.
Ruga, a wrynkle, or playte.
Rugio, giui, gire, to rore.
Rugo, gare, to be playted or wrynkled.
Rugo, xi, gere, to belke.
Ruina, ruyne, extreme decay.
Ruinosus, a, um, ruinous, in decaye.
Rulla, the staffe, wherwith the ploughman clenseth his culter.
Ruma, was of the olde writers callydde a teate, also it is the throte bolle.
Rumen, the dewlappe of a beaste. alsoo a place in the bely, a panche.
Rumentum, a brastynge oute, an aposteme that brasteth out of the fleshe.
Ruma, a goddesse, whom the paynyms did suppose to be beneficiall to womens brestes, and to suckynge chylderne.
Rumigare, to chewe the cudde.
Rumigero, rare, to carie tydynges.
Ruminatio, a chewynge of the cudde, as a beaste dothe.
Ruminalis ficus, a figge tree, vnder the whiche it is supposed that a wolfe gaue sucke to Romulus and Remus.
Rumino, minare, & Ruminor, ari, to chewe the cudde. Also to calle eftesones to remembraunce.
Rumex, icis, wylde sorell. also a weapon like to a speare.
Rumifero, are, & rumigero, rare, to beare or brynge tydynges.
Rumis, a teate.
Rumito, to beare tydynges.

Rumigerulus, a teller of tydynges.
Rumo, are, to gyue the teate to a chylde.
Rumor, rumoris, tydynges, a rumoure, a bruyte.
Rumpo, rupi, rumpere, to breake, to make werye. Rumpere moras, to make haste.
Rumpotinus, a busshe, whiche groweth in Fraunce, of whom Columella writeth, that no corne shulde be sowen within twentye foote therof.
Rumpotinetum, the place where suche busshes doo growe.
Rumusculus, a lyttell rumour or brute.
Rumula, a lyttell teate.
Runa, a weapon, sommetyme vsed in Fraunce.
Runca, a sawe, wherwith tymber is sawen.
Runcatio, weedynge.
Runcina, a whypsawe, wherwith tymber is sawen, it is also a bushesythe, or bylle, to cutte busshes.
Runcino, are, to sawe tymber.
Runco, care, to wede or pull vp.
Runsor, oris, oone of the names of Pluto, callyd god of Helle.

Vergil. Ruere, is also to ouerthrowe, to rune forth heedlynge. Quo moriture ruis, maioraque uiribus audes? Whyther runnest thou hedlynge to be slayne, and attemptest thinges aboue thy puissannces. Also to lyfte vp. Et
Ver. geor. ruit atram, ad cœlū picea crassus caligine nubem, And beinge thycke, it lyfted vp to heuen a cloude, as blacke as pytche. Some tyme it sygnyfieth to make a great noyse.
Ruit arduus æther, The highe firmamente rumbled, or made a great noyse.
Ruo, rui, ruere, to falle, to poure out, to be deceyued, to subuerte, to make playne, to plucke vppe, to breake a sonder, to throwe downe.
Rupes, be hylles, bankes, or rockes: soo stepe downe, as noo manne maye clymme theym.

In leg. xii. Rupicapra, a wylde goote.
tabularum Rupicias, for damnum dederis, thou shalte paye or yelde damages.
Ruptus, rupta, ruptum, broken or braste, weryed, torne or rent.
Ruralis, le, rusticall, or of the vyllage.
Rurestris, re, of the countreye, not of the citie or towne.
Ruricola, a husbande man.
Rurigena, borne in the countrey, oute of a citie or great towne.
Ruro, rare, to do after the countrey facion.
Ruror, raris, rari, to dwelle in the countrey, or out of the citie.
Rursus, & Rursum, eftesones or bakwarde, on the other parte.

Rus, ruris, the countreye, oute of the Citie, where as housbandrye is vsed and exercysed.
Ruscum, a wande.
Ruspor, ari, to serche dilygently. It is properly to shrape, as an henne dothe, whan she seketh for meate.
Russus, & russeus, a, um, redde.
Rustica, a byrde lyke a partryche, but he hath a longer byll.
Rusticanus, na, num, rustycall, of the countrey or vyllage.
Rustice, rustycally, vncourteysly, rudely.
Rusticane, idem.
Rusticarius, caria, carium, perraynynge to husbandrye.
Rusticatim, for rustice, an Aduerbe, churlysshelye.
Rusticitas, tatis, carlysshenes, sommetyme fearcfulnesse. Et si rusticitas non verat, ipsa rogat, And yf that foolysshe basshefulnesse lette her nat, she makethe requeste. *Ouidius.*
Rusticor, caris, cari, to dwelle in the countrey, or exercyse husbandrye.
Rusticus, ca, rusticum, rustycall, vplandyshe, homely, without curteysye.
Rusticus, is also the propre name of a man.
Ruta, Rewe, callydde alsoo herbe Grace. It is amonge the lawyers all that is dygged oute of the grounde, as stone, cole, leadde, and other mettalle.
Ruta & cæsa, All be it Mutius doth saye, that in Rutis & cæsis are those thynges, that be not faste in the grounde, nor are any parte of the buyldynge or the couerynge of a hous. Perchance we mought name theym heyre lomes.
Rutabulum, a coole rake, to make cleane an ouen.
Rutaceus, a, um, of rewe. *Plinius.*
Rutatus, ta, tum, made of rewe.
Rutatio, & rutus, for ructatio, belkynge.
Rutellum, a lyttell mattocke.
Rutilo, lare, te shyne.
Ruto, tare, for ructo, to belke or breke wind vpwarde. *Flac.*
Rutor, idem. *Cicero.*
Rutrum, a mattocke.
Rutum, idem.
Rutuba, trouble. Id postea uiderimus, nunc sumus in rutuba, we wyll afterwarde see, nowe be we in trouble. *Varro.*
Rutubatri, men that dygge with mattockes.
Rutulus, la, lum, a brighte redde lyke to coles that be kyndled.
Rutupinum promontorium, a goore or elbowe of lande in Englande, lyenge into the see, whiche I suppose is in Norfolke.

SABA, a citie in Ethiope.

Sabæi, people in Araby.

Sabbatarius, he that kepeth the sabbath daye.

Sabbatū, the day of reste from labour.

Sabaoth, in the plurelle numbre, in the hebrewe tunge, signifyeth of hostes, or armyes, or powers.

Sabath, a propre name, wherof cometh Sabatheni, the name of a people.

Sabbatismus, a vacation after labours.

Sabbatizare, to kepe sabbat daye.

Sabe, in the tunge of Siria, is the moneth of February.

Sabelli, people, whiche dwell in the mountaynes betwene the Sabines and Marsi, in Italye.

Sabim, amonge the Arrabians doth signifye god.

Sabina, a weapon lyke a bore speare.

Sabini, people in Italy.

Sabiusa, a gate at Rome, out of the whiche men went to the Sabines.

Sabora, a citie of Araby.

Sabucus, an elder tree.

Sabuletum, a grauell pytte.

Sabulum, greatte grauell.

Sabulosus, a, um, grauelly.

Saburra, lastage, or balese, wherwith shippes are euen poysed, to go vpryght, whiche is commonly of grauell.

Saburii, a kynde of sacrifice.

Saburro, rare, to balese a shyppe.

Sacal, a kynde of ambre founde in Egypte.

Saccarius, he that beareth a sacke.

Saccarum, sugar.

Saccellare, to apparelle or amende wynes putte into sackes.

Sacciperium, a powche.

Sacconia, a clothe to wype a thynge with, a napkyn, also a territorie.

Sacculus, & saccellus, a lyttell sacke.

Sacer mons, an hylle by Rome, an other by Galatia, wherin golde is founde.

Sacerdotalis, le, pertaynynge to a prieste.

Sacon, amonge the Indians, sygnifieth a bryght purple colour.

Sacondion, a precious stoone of a bryghte purple colour.

Saccularius, a crafty deceyuour, whiche in sellynge of grayne out of sackes, wylle conuey away parte.

Saccus, a sacke. Sacculus, a bagge.

Sacellum, a chapelle.

Sacer, cra, crum, holy: sommetyme cursed, detestable.

Sacer ignis, a sycknes, wherin is vehement inflamation and burnyng of the body.

Sacer locus, a place consecrate or dedicate.

Sacer morbus, the fallynge syckencsse.

Sacerdos, dotis, a prieste.

Sacerdotium, priesthode: sometime a benefyce or spirituall promotion.

Sacra uia, a streete in Rome, where peace was made betwene Romulus and Tacius, and through the whiche the vanquyshers passed with their triūph vnto the capitol.

Sacramenta, is taken for men of warre. *Iuuenalis.*

Sacramentum, an othe amonge vs christen men, it signifyeth a sygne, wherin is contayned a diuyne mysterie, and is callyd a sacrament.

Sacramento contendere, to sweare.

Sacramento teneri, to be sworne.

Sacrarium, a sextrie or vestrie, wherein are kepte thynges halowed, and relykes.

Sacratę leges, lawes, in the whiche it is enacted, that who so dothe offende agaynst theym, is accursed.

Sacratio, a consecration.

Sacratius, more holy.

Sacrator, he that dothe consecrate.

Sacrificium, sacrifyce.

Sacrifico, care, to do sacrifice, to consecrate to aske forgyuenes of god.

Sacrificulus, a prieste.

Sacrilegium, theft, or takinge away of thynges halowed, callyd Sacrilege.

Sacrilegissimus, an errant thefe in stelynge of thynges halowed.

Sacrilegus, he that violently taketh awaye or stealeth thynges halowed, or thynges vnhalowed out of a holy place.

Sacrimum, muste or newe wyne.

Sacriscrinius, he that keepeth the kynges letters or Recordes, concernynge the Crowne, or bokes of great affaires.

Sacrium, a kynde of aumbre, whiche commeth out of Scithia.

Sacro, crare, to dedicate or halowe.

Sacrosanctus, ta, tum, consecrate or halowid with a solemne othe taken.

Sacrum, any thynge dedicate to god. Also sacrifice. sometyme a temple or churche Paulus Iureconsultus. Sunt autem sacrilegi, qui publica sacra compilarint. Also sacra do signifye holy wordes. also charmes.

Sacrum Promontorium, a great mountayne or rocke in the southwest part of Spayne, lyenge on the see, callyd nowe, Cape sainct Uincent.

Sadducei, men of a speciall secte among the Iewes, that beleued not of any resurrectiō, or that there be any angels or spiritis.

Sæculū, is proprely the space of a hundred yeres: it is commonly taken for a space

of

of tyme, wherin one facion of the worlde hath contynued.

Sæpe, oftentymes. Sæpenumero, sæpiuscule, sæpicule, idem.

Sæpius, more often. Sepissime, very often.

Sæuio, uiui, ire, to be very angrye, to do vaylauntly, to be cruell, or exercyse tyranny.

Sæue, cruelly.

Sæuiter, rudely. Magis cogito, sæuiter, blanditer ue alloquar, I thynke more, where I may speake to hym rudely, or gentylly.

Sæuitia, & sæuitudo, crueltie.

Sæuus, ua, um, cruelle, horrible. sometyme angry, valyant, myghty.

Saga, a wyse or subtil woman, also a witch.

Sagaperium, a gumme or rosyn, which runneth out of a kyxe or tree, callyd Ferula.

Sagaris, a ryuer.

Sagaria, the craft to make clokes to weare on harneyse.

Sagarius, a seller of suche clokes.

Sagatus, apparayled in a souldiours cloke.

Sagax, acis, wyttye.

Sagaces canes, yernynge houndes.

Sagacitas, wyttynesse or sharpenes of wyt.

Sagaciter, wyttyly.

Sagda, a grene stone, whyche the Caldees haue made fast to their handes.

Sagena, a greatte nette.

Sagimen, & saginatio, nouryshynge.

Saginarius, a, um, that whiche is franked or made fatte.

Sagina, meate, wherwith all thynge is fatted. sometyme superfluous fatte.

Saginarium, a place wherein any thynge is franked or made fatte.

Sagino, are, to make fatte.

Sagio, ui, ire, to perceyue quickly or sharply.

Sagitta, an arow, also the top of a twygge or rodde.

Sagittarius, an archer. It is also one of the xii. sygnes amonge the sterres.

Sagitto, tare, to shoote.

Sagma, a packe saddell, or sumpter saddell. also an heape.

Sagmen, minis, grasse, plucked vp with the erthe, whiche in the olde time the ambassadours of the Romanes dyd, whan they denounced warres to other people.

Sagum, a souldiours clooke.

Sagulum, idem.

Saguntus, a citie in Spayn, whiche for the constant fydelitie, kepte to the Romains, was distroyed by Hanniball.

Saguntina fames, extreme famyne, a prouerbe made of the famyne, whyche was in the cytie of Saguntus, whan Hanniball besyeged it.

Sais, a citie of Egypte, where is one of the entries into the ryuer of Nilus, the entry or porte is callyd Saiticum.

Sal, salis, salt. somtime it is put for wisdom, myrth. Sales, quycke or sharpe sentences, iestynges. sometyme it sygnifieth the see.

Sala, a ryuer in Germanye.

Salaces, water that ryseth out of a quycke sprynge. *Vergilius.*

Salacia, was called goddesse of water.

Salaconia, pryde.

Salacones, they whiche are proude.

Salamandra, a beaste in fygure lyke to a lysarde, full of spottes, which beinge in the fyre, dothe extincte it, and is not burned.

Salamin, Salamis, mina, an Ile by Athenes.

Salaminius, a, um, of that yle.

Sal amoniacus, a kynd of salt founde vnder sand, which is lyke to alume, & is medicynable, in dissoluynge & purgyng of fleume.

Salanga, a very hygh hylle betwene great Brytayne and Irelande, nowe callid our ladyes hylle.

Salapusius, may be callid a mery iesting boy. It was a name giuen to Caluus an orator, which being of a childes personage, vsed moche iestynge and tauntynge meryly.

Salaria uia, an hygh way, by the whiche salt was caried to Rome.

Salarium, wages gyuen to seruauntes.

Salarius, a salter.

Salarius, a, um, pertaynyng to salte.

Salax, acis, lecherouse.

Salebræ, places whiche are not playne.

Salebrosus, a, um, vnplayne, where a manne can not goo, excepte he do leape.

Salentinum, a countrey in Italy.

Salentini, a people in Italye.

Salgama, thynges condite or conserued, as peares, figges, grapes, and other lyke.

Sali, a kynde of byrdes, whiche be greatte breders: as partriches or hennes, I suppose them to be hethecockes.

Saliares cœna, a banket or supper made by the priestes of Mars.

Saliares uirgines, maydens, whyche were with the priestes of Mars, and did sacrifyce with the byshops, wearyng on them cote armures, and byshoppes myters on theyr heedes.

Saliaris, re, ptaining to the pristis of Mars.

Salicastrum, a kynde of wylde vyne, rounnynge vpon wyllowe trees.

Salicetum, & salictum, a place where wyllowes growe.

Salientes, the cockes or pipes of cundites, oute of the whiche water spouteth.

Salignus, na, num, of wyllowe or wythy.

Salii, the priestes of Mars.

alillum, a lyttell salte seller.

Salina, a place, where salte is made.
Salinæ, narum, a citie in Sicile.
Salinator, the name of a noble mā of Rome.
Salinacidus, & salnacidus, a, um, that whiche is salte in taste.
Salinum, a salte seller.
Salio, iui, ire, to salte or powder.
Salio, iui, ij, ire, to leape.
Salitura, powdrynge or saltynge.
Salitus, ta, tum, salted.
Saliuo, are, to laye salue.
Saliua, & saliuum, spettell.
Saliunca, a plant, hauynge long leaues, som what yelowe, and a yelowe flowre, & groweth shorte, and hath many rootes. It is taken for the Spikenarde, that groweth in Fraunce, and is commonly vsed.
Salisi, people in the mountaynes of Alpes, confynes to the Swycers, and the people called Boii.
Saliuarius, he that layeth salue.
Salix, icis, a wyllowe or wythye.
Salmaris, a fountayne in Caria.
Salmacia, a praye gotten without labour.
Salmacidus, da, dum, that whyche sauoureth of salte.
Salmo, onis, a fyshe called Samond.
Salmonius, the kynge of Elides, which takynge foolyshely vppon hym, to haue diuine honours doone vnto hym, and wolde seme to caste lyghtnynges, lyke vnto Jupiter, being ouerthrowen with lyghtning, was caste into helle.
Sal nitrum, salte peter, whiche is putte into gunne powder.
Sallo, lere, to powder with salte.
Salo, a ryuer callyd also Bibilis, wherwith yron is tempred, and made stronger.
Salomon, & Solomon, monis, is interpreted peasible, the name of a kynge of Jewes, the sonne of kynge Dauid, who exceded all men in wisedome and knowlege, and neuer the lesse was by dotage on women brought to ydolatrie.
Salomonius, a, um, of Salomon.
Salon, a countrey of Bithinia, very cōmodious for the feedynge of cattell.
Salone, a cytie in Liburnia betwene Dalmatiam and Jlliriam.
Salpa, a fyshe whiche wylle not be sodden, excepte it be beaten, as stockefyshe is.
Salpyga, a kynde of emotes or pysmeres.
Salsamentarius, he that selleth sawce.
Salsamentarius, a, um, pertaynyng to sauce. Vas salsamentarium, a vessele, whereinto sawce is putte.
Salsamentum, sauce.
Salsedo, saltenesse.
Salsicortex, a tree, that bereth maste, which nothyng wyll eate, excepte onely swyne.
Salsilago, & salsugo, ginis, a salte lycour.
Salsura, meresawce or bryne.
Salsus, a, um, salte in taste.
Saltabundus, da, dum, that whyche leapeth or daunseth.
Saltatio, daunsynge.
Saltator, & saltatrix, a daunser.
Saltatorius, a, um, pertaynyng to daunsyng. Ludus saltatorius, a scoole of daunsynge.
Saltatrix, & saltatricula, a daunsynge wench.
Saltatus, tus, daunsynge.
Saltem, at the leste waye.
Saltiæ, people ioynynge to the see callyd Pontus Euxinus.
Saltim, uel saltuatim, by leapes.
Saltito, tare, to daunse, to leape often.
Salto, tare, to daunse.
Saltuarius, a keper of a wod, a wodwarde.
Saltuosus, a, um, full of woddes.
Saltus, a thycke wodde, also a leape.
Saluator, toris, a sauyour, he that kepeth or saueth a thynge from distruction or losse
Saluber, bris, bre, holsome, hole.
Salubrior, ius, Saluberrimus, a, um, more holsome, moste holsome.
Salubriter, holsomely.
Salubritas, helthe.
Salue, & Salueto, & saluete, god spede you, ye be welcome, sometyme contrary, farewell, God be with you.
Salueo, ere, to be saufe, or spede well, to be well at ease.
Salue. S. satis est mihi tuæ salutis, nihil moror non salueo, God spede. S. Jt suffyseth me that thou arte in helthe: but in fewe wordes J am not well at ease. [Plautus in truculen.]
Saluia, an herbe callyd sauge.
Saluiatū, a drench for a horse or other beest.
Saluifico, care, to make safe, or to saue.
Saluo, are, to saue.
Saluebis à meo Cicerone, my sonne Cicero commendeth hym vnto you. [Ci. ad Att.]
Salua res est, the matter gothe well.
Salum, the see.
Salus, lutis, helthe.
Salutarius, the forefynger.
Salutatio, a salutation.
Salutator, toris, a saluter.
Salutatorium cubiculum, a chamber, where men do stande and abyde to salute a prince or noble man in auctoritie, callyd nowe a chamber of presence.
Salutem, in the old tyme was vsed for saltē.
Salutem dicere, to salute or to haue recommendation to any man.
Salutifer, ra, rum, holsome.
Salutaris, re, holsome.
Salutaris digitus, the forefynger.

Salus

Salutariter, in helth.
Salutiger, he that bryngeth recommendacione from another person.
Saluto,tare, to salute, aswell at commyng as at departinge: also to honour.
Saluus,a,um, saulfe, hole, sounde, withoute damage or harme.

Ennius Sam, for Eam, her.
Samara, an hyl in the east Oceā se, at the further ende of the mōtayne called Caucasus.
Samarobrinæ, people in Fraunce, aboute Cambry.
Samaria, a countraye in Judea.
Sambuca, an instrument of musyke, now called doulcymers, an engyne of warre, wherwith fortresses were assaulted.
Sambucina, a woman whyche playeth on doulcymers.
Sambuceus,a,um, of Elder or Alder tree.
Sambucus, an Elder or alder tree.
Sambucistria, idem quod Sambucina.
Samia, vesselles made in the Jle of Samos.
Samius,a,um, of the Jle of Samos: the olde wrytars dyd vse it for sharpe, and Samiare, to whette or make sharpe.
Samites, people of Samnium a contraye in Italy called nowe Aprutium.

No.Mar. Samium, a shell.
Plautus. Samiolum, a lytle shell.
Samos, the name of an Jle in the see, called Icarium.
Samothracia, an Jle by Thracia in Grece.
Sampsuchus, & Sampsuchum, an herbe called Maioram.
Sanates, people dwellynge aboute Rome.
Sancio,xi,cire, to consecrate, to make firme.
Sancire leges, is to constitute lawes.

Festus Sancus, one of the names of Hercules.
Sanctè, firmely.
Sanctificatio, halowynge.
Sanctifico,care, to halowe.
Sanctitas, holynesse.
Sanctitudo, idem.
Sanctio, a lawe, a thynge decreed and stablysshed.
Sanctus, ta, tum, holy, inuiolable by a lawe, pure and cleane, vncorrupted. Vir sanctus, a blessed man.
Sanctimoniales, Nunnes.
Sanctimonium, the profession of religious personnes.
Sanctimonia, & Sanctitas, holynesse, perfection.
Sanctuarium, a place consecrate or halowed.
Sandalium, a slyppar.
Sandala, a spice called saunders.
Sandaraca, a colour founde in mynes of siluer, or golde, yelow ocker.

Sandaliotis, an Jle called now Sardinia.
Sandaracinus, colour made with yelowe Ocker.
Sandastros, & Sandaphorion, & Sandarison, & Sandassites, a preciouse stone, hauynge in a bright colour yelowe speckes, and is called also, Garamandita.
Sandyx,dicis, an herbe of a delicate odour, hauynge a short stalke, in the residue lyke to fenell. it is also a colour called a bryght yelowe.
Sandicinus color, idem.
Sanè, an aduerbe, whiche signifyeth, ye, or certaynely, on goddes name. Bellum sanè difficile gessit, he fought a very daungerouse bataile.
Sanè vt vis, be it as thou wilt.
Sanè quàm vtile, suerly very profytable. *Gelli.*
Sanè quidem, ye hardely. Nempe ergo aperté uis, quæ restant me loqui? D. Sanè qui- *Ter.in Ad.*
dem. But wilte thou than that I shall telle playnely all the rest? D. ye hardely.
Sanesco,scere, to be or waxe hole.
Sanga, a ryuer in Portugall.
Sangaris, a ryuer of Galatia, whyche runnynge through Phrygia, falleth into Propontis, the see.
Sanguen,guinis, & Sanguis, guinis, bloode. alsoo a tree, the barke whereof is of the coloure of bloode.
Sanguineus,a,um, full of bloode. also cruell. sometyme of sanguyne or bloody colour.
Sanguinolentus, idem.
Sanguiculum, the bloode of a kyd or swyne, wherwith pouddynges are made.
Sanguino,are, to bleede.
Sanguinaria, & Sanguinalis, an herbe that stoppeth bloode.
Sanguinarius, cruell, blody.
Sanguinolentus, idem.
Sanguis, guinis, bloode.
Sanguisuga, a worme, which is in standinge waters, and doeth sowke the bloode of men or beastes that come in to it. it is alsoo called Hirudo.
Sanies, mater, corrupted bloode.
Sanna, a scorne or mocke.
Sannio, onis, a dysarde in a playe or disguysynge: also he which in countenaunce, gesture, and maners is a foole.
Sanitas,tatis, helth.
Saniter, lyke a hole man.
Sannaus, a ryuer in Asia.
Sano,are, to heale.
Sansa, the stone of an olyue.
Sansucus, Maioram.
Sansucinus,a,um, of Maioram.
Sancæ, the stones of Olyues.
Sāterna, souldre, wherwith gold is soudred.

San-

S ante A.

Santones, people in Fraunce.
Sanus, na, num, hole, holsome.
Sanitas, tatis, helthe.
Sapa, muste or newe wyne sodden to the halfe deale.
Saperda, a dunge hylle.
Sapidé, sauourely.
Sapidius, more sauourely.
Sapidus, da, dum, sauoury, well seasoned.
Sapiens, tis, wyse.
Sapientia, the kunnynge of thynges diuine and humayne, wysedome.
Sapio, sapui, sapere, to tast or sauour, to fele, to be wise, to haue a right opinion.

Plautus in Pseudolo. Sapio rem, I knowe what I haue to doo.
Sapiunt male, they be yll aduysed.
Plautus in Epidico. Sapit hic pleno pectore, he is meruaylouse wyse.
Plautus in Trin. Sapit plus, he hath more wytte.
Sapit satis, he is wyse ynough.
Plautus in Persa. Sapis multum ad geniū, thou knowest howe to make good chere.
Sapor, oris, a sauour, a taste.
Sapphiratus, a Saphyr full of spottes.
Sapphirinus, na, num, of a Saphire.
Sapphirus, a stone called a saphyre.
Sappho, a woman poete.
Sappinus, the lower parte of a fyrre tree, whiche is without knottes.
Saprum, a drynke, made with salte and the fruite callyd Sorba, whiche helpeth men that haue the colyke.
Sapros, vynewed.
Sapsa, of olde writers was vsed for ipsa.
Sarcasmos, a maner of iestynge or scoffing bytyngely.
Sarcimen, a seame.
Sarcina, a trusse or packe, or fardell, sometime it is taken for an vnprofitable burden.
Sarcinas colligere, is properly of menne of warre, whanne they remoue or departe from their campe.

Plautus in Mostell. Sarcinas, atis, for sarcina.
Sarcinator, a taylour.
Sarcinatrix, tricis, a shepster, or seamester.
Sarcine, all stuffe that is closed or shutte vp in coffers.
Sarcino, are, to lade, sometyme to sowe.
Sarcio, ciui, cire, to make hole agayne, to amende a thynge decayed or appaired, to make amendes.
Sarcion, a stone of carnacion colour.
Ser. Sulp. Sarcito, pay the damages or costes.
Sarcté, hole.
Sarcophagus, a sepulchre.
Sarculo, are, to rake.
Sarculum, a rake.
Sarda, a red stone, wherin scales ar graue.
Sardanapalus, a kynge of Assiria, monstruouse in all kyndes of lechery, and therfore was slayne of one of his lordes as he satte spynnynge amonge harlottes.
Sardinia, an Ile in the see callyd Ligusticum, by Geane.
Sardis, a citie in Lidia.
Sardo, for intelligo, I vnderstande. *Neuius.*
Sardoa, an herbe lyke to smallage, whiche groweth in Sardinia, wherof if a manne eate, he shall grenne and make countenance of laughynge, and so dye.
Sardonius risus, a grennynge or laughyng without cause, a longe laughter.
Sardonychatus, hauynge apparayle garnished with the stone called Sardonix.
Sardonychus, idem quod Sardonyx.
Sardus, & Sardinensis, & Sardous, a, um, of Sardinia.
Sardonyx, onychis, a stone of the colour of a mannes nayle.
Sarepta, a towne in Siria, where Hely the prophete was borne.
Sargace, people in the northe parte of the worlde, ioynynge to the greatte mere of Meotis.
Sargus, a fyshe beinge in the see of Egipt.
Sari, an herbe, growynge in waters, hauing an harde roote, and wounden, necessarie for smythes.
Sarissa, a longe speare.
Saronicus, a bosome of the see agaynste Isthmus.
Sarmatia, all that great countrey, wherein is contayned Russia, Liuonia, z Tartaria.
Sarmata, a man of that countrey.
Sarmenta, twiggs or shroude of trees cut of.
Sarmentitius, tia, um, made of twygges or smalle boughes.
Sarnus, a ryuer in Campania.
Sarpa, a vyne cutte of, shradde.
Sarpedon, the kyng of Lisia, whiche came to the ayde of the Troyanes agaynste the Grekes.
Sarpo, pere, to clense or make cleane.
Sarra, an Ile callyd sometyme Tyrus: also the wyfe of Abraham.
Sarra, a citie in Epire.
Sarranus, na, num, of that citie.
Sarraballa, plurali numero, a worde of Caldey, signifienge breches.
Sarraca, the name of two cities, whereof the tone is in Media, the rother in Felici Arrabia, or the ryche Arrabie.
Sarracum, a certayne carre, wherin wodde or stones be caried.
Sarranæ uestes, garmentes of purple.
Sarrastes, people in Campania.
Sarrio, rire, to wede corne.
Sarritor, & sartor, toris, a weder of corne.

Sar-

Sarritura, & sartura, weedyng of corne.

Sarsina, an olde citie in Italy, where Plautus the writer of comedies was borne.

Sarta tecta, houses letten to certayne persones to kepe them alway repaired suffyciently, for a certayne somme of money.

Sarta tecta locare, to sette oute houses at a price certayne to be repaired.

Ci. in Ver. Sarta tecta exigere, to charge a man with reparations.

Sartago, ginis, a fryenge panne.

Sarte, hole.

Sarticum, an entrie in to the ryuer of Nilo.

Sartor, & sarritor, an harower or weder of corne.

Sartum tectum habere, to keepe hoole and sounde, or vncorrupted or hurte.

Sartutillus, the bealye of a swyne stuffed with meale.

Sas, olde writers vsed for suas.

Saso, an yle fyue myles frome the citie of Brundusium in the realme of Naples.

Sason, a ryuer.

Sat, for satis, inough. Quantum sat est, a moche as is sufficient. Sat habet, it is sufficient. Sat scio, I knowe well inough.

Satagiræ, people in the countrey nowe called Tartarie.

Satago, gi, gere, to be dylygent, to do with spede, to be busy about a thynge.

Satanas, is interpreted an aduersary, by the whiche name the diuel was called, bicause that he was aduersarye to Christe. Also what so euer is contrary to peace, is callyd Satanas.

Satarchæ, people in Scythia, which excluded from them the vse of golde & syluer.

Satelles, litis, one retayned to garde a mãs persone. Also a catchepoll or baylyff, that dothe attache men.

Satellitium, a garde, the offyce of suche a person or offycer.

Saterona, a beaste, whiche doth lyue sometyme in water, sometyme on lande.

Satias, sacietie, fulnes or werynesse in moche vsynge of a thynge, sometyme it sygnifieth abundaunce. Hi, saltibus occupatis,
Salustius. externorum agros inuasêre, frumentiq; ex inopia graui, satias facta, After that they had gotten the woddes or forestes, they inuaded the landes of them that were borderers, and from scarsitie of corne, they happened to haue their fylle or haboundaunce.

Satiabilis, le, that whiche may be easyly satisfyed.

Satietas, tatis, a sacietie or fulnesse.

Terentius. Satin, for satisne, Satin sana es? Arte thou not well at ease?

Satin saluæ? Be all thinges well?

Satio, rionis, the acte of sowinge of corne.

Satio, tiare, to satiate or fylle, whyche hath relation not only to the body and sences, but also to the mynde.

Satis, ynough, as moche as dothe nede.

Satis acceptio, a couenaunt, wherby a man is bounden, and sureties with hym.

Satisaccipere, to take ioynt suertyes.

Satisdatio, & satisdatum, dati, the suertie or bonde, wherby menne are bounden for another, for perfourmance of couenaunte, or the couenantour and suerties with him.

Satisdator, he that is bounden for perfourmaunce of couenant.

Satisdo, dare, to put in sureties for perfourmance of couenantes. also to be bounden with suerties for the performynge of couenauntes.

Satisfacio, cere, to satiffye.

Satisfactio, satisfaction.

Satispræstatio, idem.

Satis præsto, tare, idem quod satis dare, to fynde suretie.

Satis, superq;, ynough and to moche.

Satius, the comparatiue degree of satis, it sygnifyeth better.

Satiuus, a, ū, that may be sowen, or is sowen.

Satnois, a ryuer of Frigia.

Sator, toris, he that soweth corne.

Satrapa, amonge the Persians were as dukes and Erles be here.

Satrapia, a prouince, Duchie, or Countie.

Satullo, are, idem quod saturare, to saciate or fyll superfluousely.

Satur, turis, full fedde, sometyme aboundant or plentuouse.

Satureia, an herbe callyd Sauery.

Saturio, onis, he that hathe eaten ynoughe, and to moche. Plautus in Persa.

Saturitas, fertilitie, or plentuousnes. Also abundance in excesse.

Saturnalia, fyue dayes assigned to Saturne in December, wherin men vsed to feaste one an other, & to sende mutual presentes.

Saturnalitium, pertaynynge to the ceremonies of Saturnus.

Saturnia, was the name of a towne. Also high places were called Saturnia.

Saturnius, a, um, of Saturnus.

Saturniniani, were heretikes, whyche affyrmed, that onely seuen aungelles made the worlde agaynst the conscience of god the father.

Saturninus, a mountayne at Rome, whiche was afterwarde called Tarpeius.

Saturnus, one of the seuen planettes: also a god of the paynyms.

Saturo, are, to saturate or fyl with any thing super-

S ante A.

superfluously, moste commonly in eating.
Saturum, & Satyrum, a citie of Calabria, not farre from Tarentum.
Satus, ra, tum, sowen or begotten.
Satus, tus, the sowynge, also sede.
Satyra, a matter or poesye made in the rebuke of some astate or persone. *Florus.*
Satyria, a crowe.
Satyricus, & satyrus, a maker of suche matters.
Satyriacum, an ymage of Priapus.
Satyriasis, a sycknes, wherby the membre of a man standeth alway without appetite or dilectation.
Satyrica, was a comedye, wherin Satyres were brought in.
Satyrice, an aduerbe, whyche sygnyfyeth sharpely and with reproche.
Satyrus, a beast hauyng the heed of a man, and the bodye of a gote.
Satyrion, an herbe, hauynge leaues lyke a lylye, but smaller, a knappe with manye smalle purple floures, and a roote lyke the genytours of a man.
Saucio, are, to wounde.
Saucius, a, um, wounded, sometyme werye.
Sauior, aris, ari, to kysse swetely.
Saura, a lysarde, whiche lyeth in hedges.
Saurites, a stoone, whiche is founde in the bealye of a grene lysarde.
Sauromatæ, peple called also Sarmatæ, Russes, Tartariens, Moscouites.
Saxatilis, le, stonye. Pisces saxatilis, fysshes bredde amonge stones.
Saxeus, a, um, stonye, or of a stone.
Saxifragium, & Saxiphagos, an herbe called Saxiphrage.
Saxonia, Saxonie. Saxones, the people.
Saxosus, a, ü, full of great stones or rockes.
Saxulum, a lyttell rocke.
Saxum, a rocke. sometyme a stone.
Saxumferratum, a citie in Italy.
Saxum uolucre, to tourne the stone. A prouerbe applyed to theym that be fatygate or weryed with contynuall and vnprofytable labours.

¶ S, ANTE C.

Scabellum, a fote stoole, or lowe settle.
Scaber, bra, brum, rusty, rough, sometyme fylthye.
Scabies, scabiei, a scabbe.
Scabiosus, a, um, scabbed.
Scabo, bi, bere, to rubbe or scratche.
Scabredo, dinis, a roughnesse of the skynne, as whan it dothe wrynkle.
Scabre, roughely, not playne, or smothe.
Scabrities, & scabriua, rustynesse, filthines,

S ante A.

rowghnes.
Scabro, onis, a worme, which is ingendred of the carrayne of a deed horse.
Scea, an hauen at Troye.
Scei, people in Thracia.
Scæna, a place, whyche seruyth onely for enterludes or comedyes to be playde in, whiche was in the fourme of halfe a cerkle. It is also where trees or busshes, are cutte and layde ouer the heed, in suche fourme, so men may vnder them walke or sytte in the shadowe. It is also where a vyce or offence is openly detected, in suche wise as me do cry out or wonder at it.
Scenaticus, uel scenatilis, for a player in comedies or enterludes.
Scænicula, a diminutiue of scæna.
Scænicus, ca, cum, pertaining to enterludes.
Scænicus, a player in enterludes.
Scænitæ, people of Arabie, whiche dwelle alway in tentes, couered with the heares of gotes, amonge whome yf a swyne or hogge be brought, it dieth.
Scænoma, a tente, also a bagge.
Scænopegia, the feaste of the tabernacles, wherin the Jewes did set vp tabernacles or tétes in similitude of them, wherin they dwelled whan they came out of Egipte.
Scænos, in greke, is a tent or shadowe.
Sceua, the lefte hande, also he that vseth the lefte hande for the ryghte.
Sceuus, a, um, ylle, sometyme it sygnyfyeth good, as Scæuü omen, good lucke or chãce. *Festus.*
Scala, & scalæ, scalarum, a ladder. Alsoo a payre of stayres.
Scalmus, a lyttell piece of wodde, wherunto shyppemen doo bynde their oores, to rowe the more easyly.
Scalpo, psi, pere, to scratche, also to graue in mettalle.
Scalprum, & scalpellũ, an instrument, wherwith any thyng is scraped or rubbed, also a surgeons instrument, wherewith he taketh corrupte flesshe from the bones. It is also a grauynge yron.
Scalptor, scalptôris, a grauer.
Scalptura, grauynge in mettall.
Scalpturatum, pauement made with stones, of dyuers coloures, ioyned togither.
Scalpturio, riui, rire, to scrape as a Cocke dothe, or other fowles.
Scalpurio, rire, to scrape as a henne dothe.
Scamander, dri, a ryuer, whiche dyuydeth Europa from Asia.
Scamandria, a towne by the hauen of Iliũ, not farre from Troye.
Scamnum, a benche or fourme. Also a step or grise, wherby a manne gothe vp vnto a high bedde. Also a balke vntilled betwene

two

two forowes.

Scamonea, an herbe, the iuyce whereof is vsed in medicine to purge coler vehemētly. All be it that it is venemous, leaueth wars matter behynd, than it doth expell.

Scandalides, a kynde of dates.

Scandalum, occasyon to synne, gyuen by an nother to hym that synneth.

Scandinauia, an yle in the north occean see, the quantitie wherof was neuer founde.

Scandix, dicis, an herbe lyke to cheruyll, but it is sweter, and hath a whyte floure, and a lyttell roote.

Scando, di, dere, to clymme.

Scandulaca, an herbe, whiche runneth vppon corne, as iuye dothe on trees.

Scandulę, shyngle, whiche be tyles of wod, wherwith dyuers churches be couered.

Scandulum cōtectum, a house couered with shyngle, or wooden tyles.

Scansile, that whiche maye be clymmed or gone vppon.

Scansio, a clymmynge vp.

Scapha, a boote.

Scaphiarius, a boteman.

Scaphium, a bason or vesselle to receyue vryne or ordure.

Scapilium, the space betwene the shulders.

Scaprum, a knyfe, wherwith vynes and other lyke thynges are cutte.

Scaptensula, a place in Macedonia, where syluer was dygged.

Scaptia, an olde citie in Italy, wherof came Scaptia tribus.

Scapulæ, the hynder parte of the shulders.

Scapularis, a boye or wenche, whiche is oft beaten aboute the shulders.

Scapularis uestis, a garment, whiche couereth onely the shoulders.

Scapus, the heade of popie or other lyke herbes, wherin be the sedes, lykewise the huske of grapes, wherin the graynes be contayned.

Scarabęus, a fly with a blacke shell or huske called a bytell: whiche breedeth in cowe shardes, and is black. Also there is a kind of thē, which hath hornes like to an hart.

Scarabęus aquilam, a prouerbe applyed to suche as endeuour them self to do displesure to those that be more puissant thanne they are.

Scarifico, care, to launce or open a sore, that the matter corrupted may issue.

Scarificatio, launcynge.

Scarus, a fyshe, whiche dothe chewe lyke a beaste. some menne doo suppose it to be a Gylte heed.

Scatebræ, the bollynge or rysynge vppe of water out of a spryng or sourges of water.

Scateo, tere, to runne or brast out, as water dothe out of a narowe or strayte place.

Scaturigo, ginis, & scaturies, brastynge oute of water or other thynge in lyke maner.

Scaturio, ire, to runne out or abrode. also to springe or growe abroode, as somme herbes done.

Scaturitio, a runnynge as water dothe.

Scauri, they whiche haue their toes swollen, or their ankley croked, that they may not goo faste, it was alsoo an honourable house of the Romaynes.

Scazon, tis, a kynde of meter.

Scelerate, myscheuously.

Scelerator, ris, he that polluteth or defileth.

Sceleratus, he vnto whome a myscheuouse dede is done. sometyme it signifieth hym that dothe an yll dede. *Donatus. Vergil.*

Sceleratus campus, a felde at Rome, where the nunnes of Vesta were buryed quicke, if they were founde to lyue incontinently.

Scelerose, vngraciously. Sceleste idem.

Scelerosus, a, um, he that hath done an vngracious or myscheuous dede.

Scelestus, ta, tum, vngracious, ful of vnhappynesse, myscheuous, vengeable.

Scelerosus, full of vngraciousnes.

Scelero, rare, to pollute.

Scelus, sceleris, a myscheuous dede. also an vngracious person.

Scenoma, a pauyllyon, a sacke.

Scena, a pauyllyon or halle. Also a scaffold.

Sceparnon, a coverynge.

Scepsis, a citie in Phrigia.

Sceptici, were a secte of Phylosophers, whiche affirmed nothynge: the chiefe of that secte was Pirrhus and Berillus.

Sceptrum, a princis septre.

Scheda, a leafe of paper, a scrowe.

Schedia, a thynge lyke to a brydge with trees pynned togither, wheron thynges are caried in the water, in the steede of a barge, as it may be sene on dyuers greate ryuers in hygh Germany.

Schedion, any thynge sodaynly made, and without moche labour.

Schedula, a lyttel scrowe or leafe of paper.

Schema, atis, & schematū, a figure. also an ornamēt, specially in spech. somtime a garmēt.

Schesis, where a multitude of wordes are brought in togyther vnioyned, as, Nubila, nix, grando, procellæ, flumina, venti, Cloudes, snowe, hayle, showres, flouddes, wyndes.

Schilschi, amonge the Iewes was a weight of foure ounces.

Schisma, matis, a diuisyon, specially in the churche.

Schiston, the mylke that remayneth after that

that the mylke is sodden, whiche is callyd well courdes.

Schœnobates, he that gothe on a corde.

Scœniculæ, harlottes, whiche dresse theym selfes with strynkynge oynementes.

Schœnitę, people, whiche do dwelle in pauyllyons.

Schœnoplocos, a roper.

Schœnus, nuntis, a ryuer by Athenes, also an other in Archadia, and also a tree callid Lentiscus.

Schœnus, a space of grounde contaynynge thre score furlonges.

Schola, a schoole. Also a place in a bayne, where men dyd abyde, whiles other were bained, lykewise in a porche, wherin men taried for answeres. Scholę, are taken for dysputations betweene the mayster and his scholers.

Scholaris, lare, perraynynge to schooles.

Scholasticus, a scholer.

Scholasticus, ca, cum, scholasticall.

Terent. in Heaut.
Scibilis, le, that which may be easily knowē.

Terent. in Eunucho.
Scibo, for sciam, I shall knowe.

Scire fidibus, to be perfytte in playenge on instrumentes.

Sciens feci, I dyd it wittingly.

Scienter feci, I dyd it cunnyngly.

Scientia, counnynge.

Scilicet, as who sayth. It is moche, surely, moreouer. Sommetyme it implyeth a negatyue.

Scilla, an herbe, whiche hath a rote lyke an oynyon. some call it Squilla.

Scincus, a kynde of small cockodryls in the ryuer of Nilus.

Scindo, scidi, scindere, to cutte.

Scinpodium, a lyttell cowche or benche.

Scintilla, a spurke.

Scintillo, are, to sparkle.

Scio, sciui, scire, to knowe.

Scire sciscereq̨, to ordeyne and inacte, as it is in our parlyament.

Sciolus, he that knoweth somwhat.

Scio vti foro, I knowe what I haue to do, also I can accommodate my selfe to other mens maners, & to the condycions of the tyme and place present.

Sciomantia, a part of nygromancy wrought by shadowes.

Sciopodes, people, whiche lyenge vpryght do shadowe them selfes with their feete: all be it euery one man hath but one legge: and yet be they wonderfull swifte.

Sciotericon, a dyalle sette vppon a walle, to knowe by the sonne what is a clocke.

Scipiadæ, & Scipionidę, they whyche were of the progenye of Scipyons, the noble captaynes of Romaynes.

Scipio, the surname of a noble howse in Rome.

Scironia saxa, rockis in the see by Athenes.

Scirpea, a dunge potte, or colne made with roddes.

Scirpicula, a lyttell hooke, wherwith russhes, or any thynge is cutte of in byndinge of thynges.

Scirpita, howped vesselles.

Scirpo, are, to bynde.

Scirpus, a rushe, or an osyar. Nodum in scirpo querere, To seke for a knotte in a rushe is a prouerbe, wherby is signified, to seke to diligently for a thyng that maye not be found, or to make doubt of a thing, whyche is playne.

Scirpeus, a, um, of rushes.

Scirpiculum, a baskette.

Scirron, a thynge growen in a man or womans bealy, specially in them, which haue the dropsy, & causeth the bely to be great.

Scirophorion, the moneth of May.

Scirrhosis, a disease in the eyes, commynge of a longe inflammation, fleshe growyng in them somwhat blue.

Scirta, is a kynde of oynyous, growyng in wynter, callyd scalyons.

Sciscitor, taris, tari, & Scisco, sciscere, to demaunde. Alsoo sciscere, is to ordeyne or inacte.

Sciscito, gyue thou sentence or iudgement, gyue thy voyce or consent in election.

Scisco, sciui, sciscere, to knowe. Also to decerne or gyue sentence.

Scissilis, le, that whiche may be cutte.

Scissio, scissura, & scissus, us, a cutte.

Scita, ordynaunces made by the people.

Scitamenta, pleasant meates.

Scite, cunnyngly, craftily.

Scitor, aris, ari, to demaunde or inquire.

Scitum, a decree, or statute.

Plautus in Amph.
Scitus, ta, tum, wyse or wyttie, alsoo propre or feate.

Scytæ, people in the northe parte of Asia, whiche were cruell, and harde to be vanquished, they be nowe callyd Russyans, Moscouites, and Tartariens.

Sciurus, a squyrell.

Scius, he that knoweth a thyng.

Scythia, the name of all the countrayes togyther.

Scleriasis, a swellynge of the eye lyddes, with payne and rednesse.

Sclerophthalmia, where the eye lyddes ben harde, and waxe heuy with ache.

Sclopus, a sowne, which is made with puffynge of the chekes.

Scobina, an instrumēt, wherwith any thing is shauen. sometyme the shauyng selfe.

Sco-

Scobino, are, to wounde, to shaue of.
Scobs, scobis, that which comith of the shauyng or boryng of wodde or mettall: also grit of stones, wherwith metal is scoured.
Scoletia, a kynde of ruste or canker.
Scolopendra, a worme with many fecte and tough, callyd a palmer.
Scolymos, the floure of a thystell.
Scombrus, a fyshe.
Scomma, matis, a scoffe, or sentence spoken in myrthe, whiche sowneth otherwyse thā is ment of hym that speaketh.
Scopa, a brome or besome to swepe houses.
Scoparius, & scoparia, he or she that dothe swepe.
Scopei, men of lyttell stature.

Cicero ad Attic. Ci. de oratore perfecto. *Scopę, dyssolute men without wyt or cosicll.
Scopas dissipare, to say or do a thyng without any purpose or reason.
Scopo, pare, to swepe.
Scopelon, an hygh place, where men stande to beholde or espie.
Scopulosus, a, um, rocky, or full of rockes.
Scopula, a brushe, suche as payntours and pargettours doo vse.
Scopus, & scopulus, an high rocke, also it is a marke, wherat men do shote. sometyme it sygnifieth any thynge, wherevnto that whiche is spoken, hath a principal respect.
Scopi, be grapes, after that the wyne is pressyd oute.
Scoria, the refuse of metal tried out by fyre. Somtyme it signyfyeth care or grefe.

Ambrose. *Scorodon*, Garlyke.
Scorpena, a fyshe, whyche kepeth hyr selfe to one make.
Scorpionarii, they whyche doo shoote in crossebowes.
Scorpites, a stone of the colour of a scorpiō.
Scorpiuros, an herbe and floure called ruddes or marygoldes. It is also a worme like to that whiche is callyd Locusta.
Scorpius, & scorpio, onis, a venimous worm called a Scorpyon, whiche stryketh with his taylle, and neuer ceasseth to serche, where he maye haue occasyon to stryke. Also a sygne in the fyrmament. It is also a crossebowe. Som men take it to be an arkbushe. Also a whyppe, hauing plummettis of leade at the endes of the cordes. It is also an herbe, whyche hathe seedes lyke to Scorpyons.
Scortea, that which is of lether: as Scortei numi, lether money.
Scortes, the codde of a man or beaste.
Scorteus, tea, eum, that whyche is made of skynnes.
Scortor, aris, ari, to haunt or company with harlottes.

Scortum, an harlote or strumpette: it is also the hyde of a beaste.
Scotia, Scotlande.
Scoti, Scottes, or Scottyshmen, of whom saynct Hierom writeth in this wise. Quid loquar de cæteris nationibus, quū ipse adulescentulus, in Gallia uiderim Scotos, gentem Britannicam, humanis uesci carnibus: & quum per spluas porcorum greges & armentorum, pecudumq̃ reperiant, pastorum nates, & fœminarum papillas solere abscindere, & has solas ciborum delitias arbitrari? whatte shall I speake of other Nacyons, sens that whanne I was a boye, I sawe in Fraunce, Scottes, a people of Britayn, eate mennes fleshe: and whanne they founde in the forestes herdes of swyne, beastes, and cattayle, they wolde cutte of the buttockes of the boyes, whyche kepte theym, and alsoo the womens pappes, and toke that to be the moste deyntie and delycate meate.
Scotos, in Greke, darknes: It is more aptly callyd in the northerne tunge, myrke.
Scotoma, & scotomia, dymnesse of syghte.
Scranteum, a skynne, wherin arrowes are putte: it may be callyd a sheafe.
Scraptia, a worme, whyche is founden in leaues. Also a vyle and stynkyng harlotte, a driuelynge queane.
Screabile, that whiche may be spette or retched out of the lunges or stomake.
Screator, he that retcheth or spitteth.
Screatus, tus, spettynge or rechyng to spyt.
Screo, are, to reache in spettynge.
Scriba, a Secretarye, a Notarie, a Scribe, a Clerke.
Scribello, lare, the olde wryters vsed for Scribo.
Scriblita, a delycate meate made of paste stuffed and wounden lyke a rope. I thynk it to be suche as fartes of Portyngal are.
Scribo, scripsi, scribere, to write, also to make sometyme to paynte.
Scribligo, ginis, an vntrue fourme of speakynge or wrytyng, callyd also solœcismus.
Scrinarius, the keper of secrete letters.
Scriniolum, a caskette or forsar.
Scrinium, a coffer, or other like place, wherin iewelles or secrete thinges ar kepte, as euydences and recordes of iudgementes or inrollementes.
Scriptio, an inscription, or any other writing
Scriptor toris, a wryter.
Scriptorius, a, um, apt for writyng.
Scriptum, that whiche is writen.
Scriptura, writynge. sometyme style. Alsoo reckenynge of a baylyffe, whiche byeth and selleth cattell.

Budeus.

Scripturarius, he that writeth thynges whiche be commonly done, or bokes of reckenynge for baylyffes and reues.
Scrobs, scrobis, a dyche or furrowe.
Scrobulus, a lyttell dyche or furrowe.
Scropha, a sowe that hath pygges.
Scrotum, the codde or skynne, wherein be the stones of a man. Scrota, be also lyttel ymages made of paste, whyche are wont to be gyuen to chyldren.
Scrupulosa res, a thynge wherin there seemeth to be some difficultie.
Scrupulosus, a, um, scrupulous or doubtfull in lyghte thynges. sometyme it signifieth dyffuse or difficulte.
Scrupulatim, by small pieces.
Scrupulū iniicere, to bring into a mans mind, doubte, carefulnesse, or thought.
Scrupulū eximere, to put away dout or care.
Scrupulus, a lyttell sharpe stoone, whiche sometyme hapneth to falle into a mannes showe, and hurte his heele. It is also taken for moche sollicitude, also for dyfficultie, or spiced conscience. Also a poise, whiche is the thyrde parte of a dramme: and than is it also writen with y, as Scrypulus.
Scrupus a lyttell stone or piece of a stone.
Scrupeus, a, um, stonye.
Scruta, old garmentes, horseshoen, and such other baggage, solde for necessite. also litle ymages made in paste, sold to the people.
Scrutarius, he that selleth olde stuffe, or maketh suche ymages.
Scrutinium, a serche.
Scrutor, aris, ari, to serche.
Scrutellꝰ, the bely of a swine farcid or stuffid
Sculna, olde wryters vsed for sequester, an arbytrour.
Sculpo, psi, pere, to carue ymages in stoone. sometyme to graue in mettall.
Sculponeæ, wollen sockes.
Sculponeatus, he that dothe weare woullen sockes.
Sculptile, that whiche is carued or grauen.
Sculptor, a grauer, a caruer.
Sculptrix, a woman of that occupation.
Sculptura, Ingrauynge or caruynge.
Scurra, a railer, a scoffer. Scurrilitas, raylyng.
Scurrilis, le, pertaynyng to raylynge.
Scurriliter, in raylynge or scoffyng facion.
Scutarius, a buckeler maker, or a maker of tergates.
Scutarius, ria, um, pertaynynge to shyeldes or tergates.
Scutatus, armyd with a shielde or tergate.
Scutella, a sawcer.
Scutuca, a skourge.
Scutula, a rounde fygure, suche as spynners or spiders do warke. also a vessell, whyche contayneth. viii. ounces. also a staffe, wherwith flaxe is beaten.
Scutulatus, ta, tum, rounde and wroughte in the fourme of a copwebbe.
Scutigerulus, a custrell or page, which beareth his maisters shielde or bucklar.
Scutriscum, a diminutiue of scutra, or scutula.
Scutulata uestis, a garment of sylk, wherinbe wroughte fygures lyke to roūd copwebbes.
Scutulatus, is a colour, I suppose a wachet.
Scutulum, a lyttell shielde.
Scutum, a tergat or shielde, a buckelar. *Palladius.*
Sylace, a cytie in Grecia.
Scylla, a daungerouse Rocke in the see by Sycile. Also a ladye, daughter of Nisus, kynge of Megarensis, whyche for loue of Minois, hyr fathers ennemye, stale a pourple heare frome her fathers heed, whiche caused hym to be vanquyshed: But she being forsaken of Minois, threwe her selfe into the See, and was transfourmed into a byrde of hir name. It is also a kynde of fyshe in the ryuer of Liris in Campania.
Scyllaceum, a towne in the furthermooste parte of Italy, fryste buylded and inhabyted by men of Athenes.
Scylleta, places wherein is taken the fysshe callyd Scilla.
Scylleum, a promontorie or hyl in the part of Grecia, nowe callyd Morea.
Scyllis, the name of a Greke, whych swimmynge vnder water, dyd cutin sonder the Cables of the shyppes of the Persyans.
Scyllus, luntis, a towne in Achaia.
Scylurus, the name of a manne, whyche hauynge foure score sonnes, whanne he dyed, he callydde theym afore hym, and delyueryd to eueryche of theym a sheafe of arrowes, commaundynge theym to breake the sheafes incontynente: whyche whanne they moughte not doo, he toke out of the sheafes oone arowe after an nother, and brake theym all lyghtely, declarynge therby vnto his sonnes, that yf they contynued and agreed well togither, they shoulde be puyssaunt: and yf they varyed and were dysseuered, they shulde be feble and shortly distroyed.
Scymnus, the whelpe of a lyon.
Scynifes, bytynge gnattes.
Scyphus, a great cruse or iugge.
Scyricum, a blonket colour or light wachet.
Scyros, an ile in the see callid Ægeū, where Achilles was hid in a maidens garment.
Scytala, a lytel beaste callyd a shyrewe.
Scyritæ, people in India, whiche haue noo noses, but in the stede of a nose they haue two holes in their vysage.

Scy-

Scythia, is a great countreye, which stretcheth into the east from the ryuer of Tanais, & hath on the south part Sacos and Sogdianos, people vnder the kynge of Persia, and on the southe parte be countreyes vnknowen and deserte, and is nowe vnder the dominion of the greatte Cane of Cataye.

Scitha, a man or woman of Scithia.

Scythicus, ca, cum, of Scithia.

Scython, a countraye nowe called Thracia in Grece.

¶ S ANTE E.

SE, is a pronowne, and sygnyfyeth hym or hyr.

Sebasta, uel Sebastapolis, a citie in Siria.

Sebemytum, a cytie in Egipte.

Sebethos, a fountayn at Naples, which serueth the citie, running throughout the cite.

Secale, a certayne grayne, whyche serueth onely to putte away hunger.

Secedo, secessi, secedere, to goo backe, or to go out of company, to go away, to goo to play or sporte from labour.

Secerno, secreui, secernere, to diuide, or laye oone frome an nother, to laye or putte by it selfe.

Secespita, a cuttynge knyfe, wherewith the paynyms diuided their sacrifice.

Secessus, us, & secessio, a departyng, a vacation from busynesse, a secrete place.

Secinium, a cake of breadde cut in sacrifice.

Secius, later. Nec eo secius, neuer the later.

Secludo, si, dere, to shutte out.

Seclum, for seculum, the space of one hundred yeres.

Seclusa sacra, ceremonies, that be secretely vsed, to be hadde in the more reuerence.

Seco, cas, cui, care, to cutte. Viam secare, to leade the waye.

Secare, is also to folowe.

Secors, & socors, dis, hartelesse, apte to no purpose, profytable neyther to hym selfe nor to any other.

Seccordes agni, lambes late enyd or fallen.

Secordia, & socordia, sluggardnesse, vnaptnesse, luskysshenesse.

Secreta, thynges secrete. A secretis, of the pryuie councyll.

Secrete, & secreto, priuyly.

Secta, a dyuers consent in sondrye wylfulle opinions, a secte of philosophers, a sect of heretikes.

Sectacula, the sequele.

Sectarius ueruex, the bell wether, that goth before the flocke.

Sectilis, le, that which maye be cutte.

Sectio, onis, a cuttynge, a diuision, the partynge of a praye in takynge of a towne.

Sectio, all that is taken in pray at the wynnynge and sackynge of a towne. *Cæs. in co.*

Sectiuus, ua, um, that is often cut.

Sector, aris, ari, to folowe, to rounne after one. Also to folowe in maners or fourme of speakynge, or lyuynge. Also to hunte or chase a beaste.

Sectores, byers of forfayted goodes. Also they that do take profyte by the condemnation of other.

Sectura, a cuttig, caues vnder erth, or mines

Secubo, bare, to lye aparte.

Secula, a sythe, wherwith hey is mowen.

Seculum, some do suppose it to be the space of one hundred yeres, some of one thousande yeres, other of .xxx. yere. sometyme it is taken for tyme. Seculum sterile, a barrayne tyme. *Plini.*

Secunda mensa, the laste course, wherein commeth fruite and conserues.

Secundæ, darum, the after byrthe.

Secundarius, a, um, of the seconde sorte.

Secundo, the seconde tyme or place, alsoo eftesoones.

Secundo, are, to prosper or make prosperous.

Secundo lumine, the nexte daye. Cæsaris interdicta, si te secundo lumine hic offendero, respuentur, If I find the here the next day, I wyll set litle by Cesars cōmandementis.

Secundus panis, browne bread. Pasti siliquis, & pane secundo, Fed with beane huskes, and browne breadde. *Horatius.*

Secundum, an aduerbe, signifieth nye, or by. Secundum aurem, by the eare. Also nexte after. Secundum patrem, nexte after my father. sometyme for. Secundum te litem do, I iudge the matter for the. also in. Secundū quietem, in rest. also vppon. Secundum ea, therupon. Secundum Platonem, After the sayng of Plato. Secūdum Pythagorā uiuo, I lyue lyke to Pythagoras. Secundum flumen, Alonge by the ryuers syde. *Cæs. in cō.*

Secundus, da, dum, seconde or nexte to the fyrste. Also prosperouse. Secunda fortuna, Good or prosperous fortune. Res secundæ, that whiche dothe folowe our desire or appetite, good fortune. Secundo flumine nauigat, he gothe, or sayleth, or roweth with the streme. Secundus uentus, A good wynd. Secundum presentem, as if he were present. Et post edictum secundū presentē iudicabitur, And after the decre, iugement shall be gyuen, as if he were present. *Vlpianus.*

Securis, an axe. sommetyme it is taken for an offycer, whiche hath auctoritie to commytte men to thexecution of dethe.

Secure, quietcly, surely, in saufegarde.

S ante E.

Securus, ra, rum, sure, quiete, without care.
Securitas, quietenes, lacke of care, suretie.
Secus, by, or nighe to.
Secus flumen, feruntur salices, nyghe to the ryuer, wyllowes are sette. Also it sygnyfyeth otherwyse, or other, Non dixi secus ac sentiebam, I sayde none otherwyse thā I thought. Quid diximus tibi secus, quelles? what sayde we vnto the, other thanne thou woldest haue vs to say?
Sed, but. Sed autem, ye but.
Sedenim, all be it.
Sedentarius, ria, rium, that whiche is doone syttynge.
Sedeo, sedi, sedére, to sytte, to be ydelle, to content, to tarye or abide, to take council.
Sedes, a seate or place to sytte on. Also a mansion house. sometyme a sepulchre.
Sedicula, a setle. Sedile, idem.
Seditio, a sedition or discorde amonge the people.
Seditionarius, a seditious person.
Sedo, are, to mitigate, to pacifie, to asswage, to restrayne, to extincte.
Sedatio, a mitigation.
Seduco, xi, cere, to leade asyde, or leade away, sometyme to deceyue.

Cicer. pro Flacco. Seducere arrogantiam, to lay aparte pryde.
Seductilis, he whyche maye be deceyued.
Sedulo, in deede, dylygentely, withoute faynynge.
Sedulitas, dylygence, with moche care.
Sedulus, dylygente, he that playnely without crafte dothe a thynge diligently.
Sedum, an herbe callydde Syngreene or howfeleke.
Seges, segetis, corne, whan it standeth. sometyme the grounde falowed, and redye to receyue corne.
Segesta, a towne in Italye.
Segestria, was the strawe that was layde in a lyghter, wherin greate men were borne by their seruantes.
Segmenta, be certayne lynes ymagyned, by the whiche Cosmographers doo deuyde the worlde into porcions, whiche be callid also Paralleli, wherby the distance of places are founden.
Segmenta, the cuttynges of, of any thynge, sometyme the partes of the worlde diuyded by the sonne. also gardis, or other like thynges sowed to garmentes.
Segmentarius, he that maketh cloth of gold
Segmentum, a piece cutte of frome any thinge, be it mettall or stone. It is alsoo a bee or colar, whiche is aboute womennes neckes. Some doo take it for the purfyll of a womannes gowne. It maye as welle be taken for a garde or border aboute any

S ante E.

garmente.
Segmentatus, ta, tum, may be sayde of anye thinge, whyche hathe borders or trayles fynely wroughte, with small peces fastned theron, be it of mettall or tymber.
Segmentariæ uestes, garded or pourfylled garmentes.
Segnis, slowe and dulle wytted, barayne.
Segnitas pro segnitia, slouthfulnesse.
Segniter, slowely.
Segnities, slownesse, dulnesse, baraynnes.
Segrego, are, to seuer or separate.
Segobriga, a towne in the parte of Spaine, whiche is nowe called Byskay.
Segregare suspitiones, to put away suspition *Plautus in Trin. & in Asinar.*
Segregare sermonem, to speake no wordes. Si quis ibi est odiosus, abeo domum, sermonem segrego: If any man be there, whom I loue not, I gette me home, and speake neuer a worde. Segrega sermonem, tædet, Holde thy peace, I am weary, or it irketh me to here the. *Plautus in milite.*
Plautus in pænulo.
Segullum, is a vayne of erth in mynes, whiche declareth, that therein golde maye be founde. *Plin.li.33. cap.4.*
Segor, a cytie, whyche was preseruyd by the prayer of Loth, whan Sodoma was dystroyed by the vengeance of god.
Seir, a mountayne in the countrey of Edon, where Esau the brother of Iacob the patriarche dwellyd.
Seiugi & seiuges, a teme of syxe horses.
Seiungo, xi, gere, to separate.
Selectio, a chesynge out.
Selectus, ta tum, chosen amonge other. also chiefe amonge other.
Selecti Iudices, amonge the Romans were iudges appoynted of the state of gentylmen, callyd ordo equestris. *Cicero.*
Selenetes, a stone, wherin is a whyte, whiche decreaseth and increasethe, as the mone dothe.
Seleucia, the principall cytie of Siria, whiche is xxx. furlonges from Babylonia.
Seleucus, kyng of Siria, next after Alexāder the greatte.
Selibra, halfe a pounde.
Seligo, legi, seligere, to gather a part, or the chiefe thynges amonge many.
Selinus, a ryuer.
Selinon, an herbe called also Apium, wherof be dyuers kyndes, as Hipposelinon, Petroselinon. Seke for them in their places.
Seliquastra, a stole to sytte on.
Sella curulis, a Chayre, whereon the chiefe officers of Rome sate in a charyotte, and were soo caried, whanne they came from their houses. some do suppose that it was callid curulis, bicause the fete were crokid
the

the iugement therof, I remit to the reders.
Sellaria, places, wherin were fourmes and ſtooles for men to ſytte on.
Sellularii, artificers, which wroght ſittyng.
Semel, ones, alſo at one time, ſhortly, briefely, ſummaryly.
Semele, the daughter of Cadmus.
Semen, ſeminis, ſede, ſommetyme ſettes of yonge trees, or nurſgardeynes, ſommetime the kynde.
Sementicus, ca, cum, that may be ſowen.
Sementis, the acte of ſowynge, ſometyme ſede, ſede tyme.
Sementa facere, to ſowe corne.
Sementinæ feriæ, holye dayes ordeyned to praye, that corne beinge ſowen, moughte come forthe and increaſe.
Semento, tare, to brynge forthe ſede.
Semeſtris, tre, of ſyxe monethes.
Semeſus, a, um, halfe eaten.
Semet, hym ſelfe.
Semet, halfe a meaſure.
Semianimis, halfe deade.
Semianimus, halfe quycke.
Semicadium, halfe a barelle.
Semicęcus, halfe blynde.
Semicinctum, a ierkyn or ſhorte iackette.
Semicirculus, halfe a cyrkle.
Semicoctus, ta, tum, halfe ſodden.
Semicommeſtus, ta, tum, halfe eaten.
Semiconſumptus, ta, tum, halfe conſumyd or waſted.
Semideus, halfe a god.
Semidoctus, meanely lerned.
Semifera animalia, beaſtes ingendred betwene a wyld beaſt and a tame, as betwene a wolfe and a dogge, or betwene a wylde boore, and a tame ſwyne.
Semiferus, ſomewhat wylde.
Semigro, grare, to goo to dwelle in an nother place.
Semihomo, halfe a man.

Cicer. pro Rabi.
Semihora, an halfe howre.
Semiliſſula, & ſemilixula, a lyttell cake made with meale, cheſe, and water.
Semimadidus, da, dum, halfe wette.
Semimares, they whyche are not perfytte men, as thoſe, whiche are gelded.
Semimortuus, a, um, halfe deed.
Seminatio, ſowynge.
Seminarium, a place frome whenſe ſettes and plantes be tranſlated or remoued. alſo a tree of the whiche ſettes are taken.
Seminex, necis, halfe ſlayne.
Seminium, ſede, alſo the gayne of ſede.
Semino, are, to ſowe.
Seminudus, da, dum, halfe naked.
Semiobolus, the xii. part of a greke drame.
Semipes, pedis, halfe a foote.

Semipaganus, halfe an huſbandeman, halfe a carle of the countrey.
Semipedalis, le, halfe a foote in quantitie or heyghte.
Semipedaneus, a, um, idem.
Semiplagium, a lyttell nette.
Semiplenus, not full.
Semiplotia, were ſhowes, whyche couered but halfe the fote: whiche the Romaines did weare on, whan they went in hunting.
Semiquinarius, a, um, that whyche is halfe ſyue in numbre.
Semiramis, midis, the wyfe of kyng Ninus, and queene of Babylon, a woman of incomparable power.
Semirutus, partly decayed.
Semi, halfe.
Semiſenex, uel ſemiſeneus, halfe olde.
Semiſomnis, & ſemiſomnus, halfe a ſlepe.
Semiſopitus, he that is halfe ſlepynge, halfe wakynge.
Semiſoporatus, idem.
Semiſpathium, a ſhorte ſworde.
Semiſsis, half a cubite. It was alſo a certain coyne or money, that was halfe a piece of golde, as the halfe noble or halfe crowne.
Semiſsis homo, a vyle perſone.
Semiſsis vſura, the gayn of ſyx in a hūdred.
Semita, a pathe, alſo a footeway.
Semitatus, ta, tum, dyuided in pathes.
Semitogium, a ſhorte gowne.
Semitogatus, & ſemitogatulus, he that weareth a ſhorte gowne.
Semitritæon, uel hemitritæon, a feuer, whiche is a tercian and a halfe, and of fourty and eighte houres, and vexeth one xxxvi. houres.
Semiuir, an vnperfecte man.
Semiuiuus, halfe a lyue.
Semiuncia, halfe an ounce.
Semuncialis, le, of halfe an ounce.
Semiuſtus, a, um, halfe burned.
Semimodius, halfe a buſſhell.
Semoueo, uere, to moue or go awaye.
Semper, euer, alway.
Semperlenitas, the accuſtomed gentylneſſe or myldeneſſe.

Terent. in Andria. Donatus.
Semperuiuum, an herbe callyd Singrene.
Sempiterne, euerlaſtyngly.
Sempiternitas, the tyme euerlaſtynge.
Sempiternus, a, um, euerlaſtynge.
Senaculum, a councylle howſe. Alſo a lyttell Senate.
Senarius, a, um, that whyche is of the nūber of ſyxe. Senarij uerſus, & ſenarioli, verſes hauynge ſixe fete.
Senator, toris, a Senatour.
Senatorius, a, um, pertaining to Senatours.
Senatus, us, a ſenate or councyll.

Z iij   Senatus

Senatusconsultum, an acte of councill, or an ordinaunce made by the senate.
Senecio, onis, an herbe, which groweth on walles, and tyles, and is hore in sommer, and hath redde stalkes, called groūdswel.
Senectus, senecta, senium, age.
Seneo, & senesco, senescere, to be olde.
Senex, senis, an olde man or woman.
Senio, onis, a syce, or numbre of syxe marked in the dyse.
Seni, ng, na, syxe.
Sennaar, the fielde, where the towre of Babylon was buylded.
Senogallia, a cytie in Italy.
Senones, people in Fraunce.
Sensa, the senses, or those thynges, whiche we do meane.
Sensibilis, bile, that whiche may be felte.
Sensiculi, the diminutiue of sensa.
Sensificus, ca, cū, that which causeth feling.
Sensilis, le, that maye be felte.
Sensim, lyttell and lyttell.
Sensus, us, sense, or feelyng, or perceiuyng.
Senta, was called Fauna, or Bona dea, the good goddesse.
Sententia, sentence, iudgement, opinion, or councill spoken or writen concernynge the lyfe of man.
Sententiola, a lyttell or shorte sentence.
Sententiam dicere, to shewe his opinion.
Sententiā ferre, to giue sentence or iugemēt.
Senticetum, a place full of bryers.
Sentina, the pumpe of a shyp, a place where all frithe is receyued.
Sentinatia, a countrey in Italy.
Sentino, are, to auoyde peryl: also to pumpe vp water out of a shyppe.
Sentio, sensi, sentire, to perceyue, to vnderstande, to fele, to iuge, to suppose, to know.
Sentio tecum, I am of thyn opinion.

Ter. in An. Sentis, a bryar or bremble.
Senticosus, a, um, sharpe as a bryer.
Sentus, hearye, roughe.
Senum, the syxte.
Senumdenum, the syxtenthe.
Seorsum, a parte. also namely, or specially. Omnibus gratiam habeo, & seorsum tibi

Terent. in Adelph.
præterea Demea, I thank you al, but namely the Demea.

Plautus in cap.
Seorsum a te sentio, I am of an nother opinion than thou arte.
Seorsus, idem.
Separatio, separation.

Plautus in Ruden.
Separatus, ta, tum, separate or diuided from an other thynge.
Separo, rare, to putte aparte, or departe one from an nother.
Separatim, aparte.
Sepedes, emotes.

Sepelio, sepeliui, lire, to burye.
Sepes, sepis, an hedge.
Sepia, a fyshe callyd a Cuttell.
Sepimentum, an inclosure.
Sepio, sepiui, sepire, to hedge or inclose.
Sepius, piuntis, & Sipus, puntis, & Sipontum, a citie in the royalme of Naples.
Seplasiarius, a maker of soote oynementes.
Seplasium, uel seplasia, a shop, where swete oynementes are solde. It was a strete in the citie of Capua, wherin were dyuers delicate oynementes.
Sepono, posui, ponere, to putte or lay apart.
Seps, a venymous worme, of whose stroke or bytynge the fleshe rotteth.
Septa, the generalle name of all places inclosyd.
Septangulus, a figure, hauing four corners.
Septem, the numbre of seuen.
September, bris, the .viii. moneth.
Septemdecim, seuentene.
Septempedalis, le, of seuen feete.
Septimus, ma, mum, the seuenth.
Septenus, na, num, idem.
Septemuir, an officer, hauynge equall auctoritie with seuen other.
Septennis, of seuen yeres.
Septentrio, the northe coste.
Septentriones, the seuen sterres, which are sene by Charles wayne, or Vrsa maior.
Septemuiratus, the offyce, wherin be seuen ioyntely.
Septennium, the space of seuen yeres.
Septicollis, by that name Rome was called, bycause of the seuen hylles, whiche were in it, Palatinum, Quirinalis, Auentinus, Cœlius, Viminalis, Exquilium, & Ianiculum.
Septies, seuen tymes.
Septifariam, seuen maner of facions or wais
Septifarius, a, um, seuen dyuers.
Septimatrus, was a holyday kepte the daye folowynge the sixt Idus of euery month.
Septimana, a wieke,
Septimontium, a place hauyng seuen hilles.
Septingeni, & septingenti, seuen hundred.
Septingenties, seuen hundred tymes.
Septingentenus, & septingentesimus, the seuenth hundred.
Septingentuplus, seuen hundred folde.
Septuagies, thre score and ten tymes.
Septuaginta, thre score and ten.
Septuose, darkely.

Septum transuersum, the mydrefe, whyche dyuydeth the stomacke frome the lower bowelles. No. Mar.
Septunx, uncis, a poyse of seuen ounces.
Septus, ta, tum, inclosed.
Sepulchrum, a sepulchre or tombe.
Sepultura, sepulture or burienge.

Sepul-

Sepultus, ta, tum, buried or hydde. also lyke as it were deade.
Sepum, talowe.
Sepatius, a, um, as it were of talowe.
Sequana, a ryuer in Fraunce called Sein.
Sequani, Burgonions of high Burgoyne.
Sequanq̃, for seorsum quanq̃, euerye woman aparte.
Sequax, acis, that whiche foloweth.
Sequela, the acte of folowynge, sequele.
Sequester, tris, tre, indifferent to both partis.
Sequester, an arbitrer. Also he, with whom money is lefte.
Sequestro, are, to lay or sette a thynge indifferently, or in the kepynge of an indifferent person.

Terent. in Adelph. Sequi lites, to sue at the lawe.

Sequor, eris, sequi, to folowe.
Sera, a locke.
Serapis, idis, a god of the Egiptians.
Serenitas, fayrenesse of wether, dryth.
Serenissimus, is a terme appropried now adayes to kinges onely, and is vsurped for moste famous, or moste renoumed.
Sereno, are, to make fayre and clere.
Serenus, a, um, faire, clere, without cloudes.
Seres, a people in Asia, hauyng great plentie of sylke.
Sericæ vestes, sylken garmentes.
Seresco, scere, to be fayre and drie. also to be tourned into whay.
Seria, ernest wordes, and graue or sadde.
Seria, an erthen vessell, whiche is longe.
Sericarius, a weauer of sylke.
Sericatus, apparayled in sylke, or he that weareth a garment of sylke.
Sericeus, a, um, of sylke.
Sericum, sylke.
Sericus, ca, cum, of sylke.
Series, order.

Festus. Serilla, botes or shyppes calked with towe.

Seriola, a diminutiue of seria.
Serio, in erneste.
Seriphus, an Ile by Grecia in the see called Aegeum.
Serius, a, um, erneste, graue, of importance.
Sermo, monis, a speche, a fourme of speakynge: sommetyme an oration, also communication.
Sermocinor, aris, ari, to talke, to commyn.
Sero, are, to shutte or locke.
Sero, seui, serere, satum, to sowe, to plant, to ingender.
Sero, an aduerbe, signifyeth late, to late, after the tyme that it ought to be. Alsoo in the euenynge.
Seropta, a citie in Phœnicia.
Serotinus, a, um, that whiche is in the euenynge. sometyme late or latewarde. Sero-

tini fructus, latewarde fruites.
Serpens, pentis, a serpente.
Serperasta, a swathynge or swadlyng band.
Serpillum, an herbe, whiche growethe on olde walles aboute welles or pondes, and in some places it smelleth lyke tyme, and in some places lyke to saucry.
Serpo, psi, pere, to crepe.
Serpula, of olde wryters was vsed for serpens, a serpent.
Serra, a sawe.
Serra prœliari, is to fyght in battayle, sometyme marchynge forwarde, sometyme reculinge, as a sawe goth, whã it is drawen.
Serrata, & serratula, an herbe, which is callyd Germander.
Seruilis, le, of seruyle or bonde condycion or propertie.
Serratus, ta, tum, lyke a sawe. also sawed.
Serro, are, to sawe.
Serrula, a lyttell sawe.
Sertor, he that soweth seedes, or settethe herbes.
Sertum, a garlande of floures.
Sertus, ta, tum, sette with flowres, as in a garlande.
Sertula campana, an herbe callid Melylote.

Vergil. Seruo, are, to kepe, to preserue, to possede, or dwelle in a place.

Seruare fidem, to kepe touch, to be faithful.
Seruare de cœlo, to obserue tokẽs or signes in the heuen or firmament.

Plautus, in Amph. Seruaueris, take good hede what thou dost.

Seruator, toris, he that præserueth or delyuereth one from harme.
Seruiliter, lyke a bondman or slaue.
Seruire auribus, to flatter.

Cæs. in co. Seruio, uiui, uire, to serue.

Seruitium, seruyce.
Seruitia, bondmenne.
Seruitus, bondage.
Serum, the laste parte of the daye, the euen tyde. It is also whay of mylke.
Serus, a, um, late, sometyme great.
Serum bellum, great warre.
Seruus, a seruant, proprely whiche is compellyd to serue, as bondemen or apprentyses doone.
Seruum pœcus, is a prouerbe applied to him whiche in speakynge or wrytyng, dare not digresse from an other mannes steppes or fourme of writynge.
Sesama, & sesamum, a whyte grayne, whyche growith in Inde, wherof oile is made whiche is called oleum Sesaminum.
Sescunx, cuncis, an ounce and a halfe.
Sescuplum, the hole and the halfe parte.
Seselis, an herbe called also Siler.
Sesqui, as moche and halfas moche. ioyned to an

S ante E.

to an nother worde, sygnyfyeth halfe as moche more.
Sesquialtera, so moche and halfe so moche, a proportion in musyke.
Sesquihora, an houre and an halfe.
Sesquilibra, a pounde and a halfe.
Sesquimensis, a moneth and a halfe.
Sesquimodus, a busshell and a halfe.
Sesquiopera, one iourneye in tyllage and a halfe.
Sesquipes, a foote and a halfe.
Sesquipedalia uerba, great and stoute wordes, as some noble men do speake to their inferiours, whan they are displeased.
Sessio, a syttynge.
Sestans, et sexstans, that whiche is also callyd obolus, the syxt parte of a dramme.
Sestertius, was two pounde weighte and a halfe of copper, whiche amonge the auncient Romayns was alway estemed to the value of the fourthe parte of their syluer coyn called Denarius and Dragma, of the whiche .viii. went to an ounce.
Sestertium, contained .ii. li. and a half weight of syluer, estemed to two hundred & fyfty grotes, wherof .viii. went to an ounce, that is to say .iiii. li. iii. s. iiii. d.
Sestertius nummus, the fourthe parte of the syluer coyne of the auncient Romaynes, called Denarius and Dragma, amonge vs it may be named a sterlynge peny.
Sete, brystell heares.
Setia, a citie in Campania.
Setigerum, a beaste whiche hath brystelles.
Setinum uinum, wyne made aboute the cytie of Setia.
Setim, a tree, lyke to whytethorne, whyche doth neuer rotte: wherof moch of the tymber in the temple of Salomon was.
Setosus, sa, sum, full of brystels.
Setuosus, a, um, olde wryters vsed for obscurus, darke.
Setuose, darkely.
Seu, for siue, eyther, or.
Seuere, sharpely, cruelly.
Seueriter, idem.
Seueritas, tatis, grauitie, constantnesse, proprelye in mynystrynge Iustyce.
Seueritudo, idem.
Seuerus, ra, rum, graue, constaunt, cruelle, sharpe, daungerous to meddle with.
Seuoco, care, to calle aparte or away, to call asyde from other.
Seuosus, a, um, lyke to talowe.
Seuo, are, to make candels of talowe.
Seuum, talowe of beastes.
Sex, syxe in numbre.
Sexcenti, syxe hundred.
Sexcentoplagus, he that receyueth a hun-

Plautus in cap.

S ante I.

dred strypes.
Sexcuplus, a, um, syxe double, or syxe tymes so moche.
Sexennis, of syxe yeres olde.
Sexies, syxe tymes.
Sextans, tis, the syxte parte of a pounde.
Sextarius, a vessell amonge the olde Romanes, whiche contayned .xx. ounces of water or wyne.
Sextilis, is the monthe nowe callid August.
Sextula, the syxte parte of an ounce.
Sextus, ra, tum, the syxte.
Sexus, us, a kind. sexus uirilis, the male kind, sexus muliebris, the woman kynde.

¶ S ANTE I.

SI, yf, although, I wolde god.
Si diis placet, If god wyl, or on goddis name: a worde spoken eyther in dysdayne, or in mockage, for any thynge not well doone. Etiam latini, si diis placet, hoc biennio, magistri dicendi extiterunr, Ye and also the latines, on goddis name, haue ben these two yeres maisters of eloquence. Quinetiam, si diis placet, nephas aiunt, consulem plebeiũ fieri, They say also, on goddis name, that it is vnleful for a communer to be made Consul.
Si sapis, yf thou be wyse.
Siambis, an Ile in the brytysshe occean see, on the northe parte.
Sibaris, an old towne .xii. miles from Rome. Also a citie in Calabria. sometyme it is taken for delycate and wanton lyuynge.
Sibariticus, ca, cum, wanton or delycate.
Sibi, to hym.
Sibilo, are, to whystell.
Sibilus, a whystlynge.
Sibilla, a woman prophete, of the whyche were eyght, as Varro wryteth.
Sic, so, in lykewyse, accordyngly, so lightly. Mirabar hoc, si sic abiret, I wolde haue meruayled, if that it shoulde haue passed soo lyghtly.
Sibus, a sharpe wytted felowe.
Sic ago, so am I wont to do.
Sic sum, suche a one am I.
Sica, a shorte sworde.
Sicambri, the people of Nasson, and Hessen in Germanye.
Sicani, a people in Spayne.
Sicania, a countrey in the Ile of Sicile.
Sicarius, a murdrer.
Sicaneus, a, um, drye of nature.
Siccesco, scere, to drye.
Siccine, of that facion, in suche facion.
Siccine tu illam? Siccine nos habes ludibrio omnes? wylte thou handelle her of that fashion

Ci. in oratore.

Ti. Liuius.

Terent. in Andria.

Plautus.

faſſhyon? wylte thou in ſuche faſſhyon mocke vs all.

Siccitas & Siccitudo, drythe.

Sicco, care, to drye or be dryed.

Siccus, ca, cum, drye, wythered.

Sicera, all maner of drynke made of corne or frutes.

Sicileo, cilui, cilire, to cut agayne that whiche was not wel cut afore, proprely graſſe in a medowe.

Sicilia, the Jle of Sicile.

Siciliences, people dwellyng in Sicile, whiche were borne els where.

Sicilis, lidis, of Sicile.

Sicilides Muſæ, the Muſis of Sicile.

Siciliſſo, are, to ſpeake the language of Sicile.

Siciliqua, vel Sicilicus, a poyſe or wayght, wayinge two drammes: and is the fourth parte of an vnce.

Sicilites, the heed of a Jauelyn.

Siclus, the ounce of the iewes, which is the fourth part of our ounce.

Sicinnium, a kynde of daunſynge, wherein they that daunſed dyd ſynge, as they doo in Chriſtmaſſe, whan they ſynge Carolles: and as maydens do nowe vſe to doo in the ſtreates.

Sicubi, whereſoeuer.

Siculi, men of Sicile.

Siculum mare, the ſe by Sicile.

Sicunde, of any place.

Sicut & Sicuti, as, lyke as.

Sicyonia, an Jle in the ſe of Aegeum.

Sideratio, a ſickeneſſe, which in ſuche wyſe taketh ſome part of a mannes body, that it ſodaynly becometh drye, ſo that he felith it not, women do cal it takynge, or benummynge.

Sideratus, he that is ſo taken in any membre or part of his body, that he can not feele it or ſtere it, the homely people calleth benummed.

Siderites, an herbe, which groweth on tyles and olde walles.

Sidereus, a, um, of the ſterres.

Sideror, ari, to be blaſted, or taken, that a man maye not ſtere or moue his membres.

Sido, dis, ſedi, ſidere, to ſettyll.

Sidon, a citie in Phenicia.

Sidonius, a, um, of that citie.

Sidus, a numbre of ſterres gathered, which do make a ſygne or celeſtiall figure: ſometyme it is taken for one ſterre.

Sifilare, to whyſtell.

Sifilator, oris, a whyſtler.

Sigæum, a great mountaygne in the ſee by Troye.

Sigillaria opera, warkes wherein were ſet ſmall ymages.

Sigillatim, one after another.

Sigillo, are, to ſcale, ſometyme to cloſe or ſhut.

Sigillum, a lytle ymage.

Sigma, tis, a lytle table.

Signaculum, a ſcale.

Signatorius anulus, a ſignet.

Signatus, ta, tum, notable.

Signa infeſta, Standardes and baners aduaunced in batayle, in marchinge againſte enemyes.

Signia, a citie in Campania.

Signa cœleſtia, the twelue ſignes, by the whiche the ſonne and other planettes doo paſſe.

Signifer, he that beareth ſtandard or baner in a felde.

Significo, ficare, to ſignifye or gyue knowledge.

Signinum opus, a warke made with ſhelles and mortar, or tyles and mortar.

Signo, are, to make a ſigne, to ſigne or ſeale, to ſignifie or ſhewe by a ſigne or token, to wryte.

Signum, a ſigne, token, or marke, a miracle.

Signa, be alſoo ymages of metall, ſtone, or woode.

Silanius, an hyghe hill in Jrlande.

Silatum, brekefaſt.

Sila, an helmet.

Silenta loca, quiete places, wherein is no noyſe.

Silentium, ſylence, quietneſſe.

Silenus, the foſter father of Bacchus.

Sileo, lui, lere, to kepe ſylence, to ſpeake nothinge.

Siler, a kynde of wythy growing in water: it is alſo a ryuer in the royaulme of Naples.

Sileſco, ſcere, to be in ſilence, or quyete.

Silex, ſilicis, a flynt ſtone.

Silicatus, ta, tum, made with flynt ſtones.

Silicernius, & Silicernium, a certayne puddynge, eaten onely at the tyme of funeralles, ſome doo take it for a feaſte or dyner made at the funeralles or termēt of a man or woman.

Senem ſilicernium, is named of Terence for an olde Cryppel, redy to haue ſuche a dyner made for him.

Siliceus, a, um, of a flynt ſtone.

Silicia, ſiue Silicula, an herbe called Fenugreke.

Siligo, ginis, a grayne called Rye.

Siligineus, a, um, of Rye.

Siliqua, the huſke or codde of any thinge, alſo a certayne fruyt in Jtaly, which is in length of a mannes fynger, and brode, & ſomewhat hooked, the wayght of ſixe of theym them made a poyse called Scrupulus, a scruple: wherof thre do make a dramme. It is now called a Characte, and is vsed among fyners of golde and syluer, and also coyners in the fynynge and alayinge therof.

Siliquastrum, an herbe.

Siliquor, quaris, quari, to growe in huske or codde.

Silura, a countraye in the more Britayne.

Silo, onis, he which hath great browes.

Silosontis chlamis, is spoken in a prouerbe of hym, whiche bostith hym selfe of ryche garmentes.

Silus, a camoysed nose, or a nose whiche is tourned vpwarde.

Silphion, an herbe.

Silurus, a fissh called a Stourgeon.

Simia, & Simius, an Ape.

Simila, fyne mele of corne.

Similago, ginis, idem.

Simillimus, a, um, moste lyke.

Similitas, lykenesse.

Similiter, lykewyse, also.

Similis, le, lyke.

Similes habent labra lactucas, a prouerbe applyed to theym, whiche beinge of lyke yll condicions, be matched togither, as a lewde seruaunt with an yll master, an vnruly people to a negligent gouernour, a shrewde wife to a frowarde husbonde &c. Lyke master lyke man. Lyke will to lyke.

Similitudo, dinis, lykenesse.

Similo, are, to be lyke.

Simitu, pro simul, togither.

Simiolus, a lytle ape.

Simois, oentos, a ryuer by Troye.

Simonia, Symony, that is to saye, ambitio in spirituall thinges.

Simplariæ, symple thinges or of lytle value.

Simplares, they which doo weare hostinge harneyse.

Simplex, plicis, that is not double, syncere or playne, without deceipt.

Simplicitas, playnesse.

Simpliciter, playnly.

Simplicitus for simpliciter.

Simplus, a, um, sengle in numbre, one only.

Simpulum, a chalice or cup of erth, wherwith they sacrifyced in the olde tyme before that golde and siluer were in great estimacion. It is of Uarro taken for a cruet with a Pipe, out of the which wyne came droppynge by lytle and lytle.

Simpuuium, a vessell of tree.

Simul, togyther with other, moreouer also.

Simul ac, simul atq, as soone as, incontinent as.

Simulachrum, an ymage of a manne or woman.

Simulo, are, to indeuour, to be lyke to one, also to fayne.

Simultas, atis, pryuy displeasure or hatered, with dissemblynge countenaunce.

Simulatio, fantasye, also dissimulation.

Simulator, he that dissembleth.

Simulter, for Similiter.

Simulto, tare, to be at varyance with one, to hate one pryuyly.

Simus, a, um, flat.

Sin, or els, if not.

Sinapi, & Sinapis, Senuy sede, wherof mustarde is made.

Sinapium, mustarde.

Sinapodes, people in Affrike, whiche do go as they crept.

Sinarum Regio, a countraye beyonde the lyne equinoctiall.

Sinciput, the forepart of the hedde.

Sindo, donis, a fyne lynen cloth.

Sine, withoute. *T. Liuius.*

Sine vt veniat, let him come.

Sine fraude mea, my right saued.

Singillatim, to euery one, or of euery ouche, one after another.

Singularis, re, synguler, excellent, one without any mo.

Singulariter, singulerly, onely.

Singulatim, euery thinge by it selfe.

Singultio, tire, to yexe.

Singultiens, he that hath the yexe.

Singultiens gallina, a clockinge hen.

Singultus, tus, yexinge.

Singulus, a, um, euerych.

Sinistra, the lefthande, sometyme it sygnifieth, contrary to prosperouse.

Sino, sini, sinere, to suffre.

Sinope, pes, a cite in the contray of Pontus.

Sinopis, pidis, a redde stone, communely called Sinoper.

Sinistre, vnhappely, vnfortunatly.

Sinistrorsum, on the lefthande.

Sinuessa, a citie in Campania.

Sinuo, are, to tourne or winde in the fourme of a serpent, makinge holowe bosomes or furrowes: it is also applyed to garmentes that are pleyghted or gathered vp: also to streames of Ryuers, which do in runnyng make dyuerse tournynges. also to bankes which haue holow creekes or bosomes.

Sinuosas, a, um, that which hath many turnynges and wyndynges.

Sinus, us, a bosome. also the tournynges or holownesse of water bankes: somtyme the holownesse of eyen: sometyme a sayle. also a cuppe for wyne: also nettes. sometyme a sayle, whan the wynde fylleth it.

Siparium, a courtayne.

Siphones, the pypes of a Cundyt.

Siqua

S ante I.

Siqua, for si aliqua, if any.
Sipontum, a citie in Apulia.
Sipontinus, a, um, of that citie.
Siquide, for bycause. also if.
Siremps, for similis res ipsa.
Siren, & Sirena, a meremayden.
Siri, pittes, wherin corne was layde to be preseruyd.
Sirius, a Sterre, whiche ryseth the viii. Calendis of June.
Sirpea, mattes, or other thinges made of russhes.
Sirpices, were instrumētes made with teeth lyke to a sawe, which beinge drawen with oxen, plucked vppe by the rootes flagges and greate weedes, which grewe in medowes.
Sirpiculæ falces, hookes, wherewith vynes are cut.
Sirpo, are, to bynde, or wynde with russhes or osyars, or other lyke thinge.
Sirpus, a russhe. Nodū in Sirpo quæris, thou fyndest difficultie or doubt, where there is none. Sirpi, be also warkes or verses, which be very harde to be vnderstande.
Sirpiculum, a lytell basket.
Sisamum, a maner of poulce or corne.
Siser, a delicate roote to be eaten, whiche some men do suppose to be redde Carettes.
Sisara, & Sisarum, an herbe growynge in Eubœa, the flower wherof is moost pleasaunt to bees. it is also called Erica.
Sisto, ere, to make to tarye or stande styll, to retayne or kepe backe, to appere, as a mā doeth beinge sued in the lawe.
Sistas te, appiere thou.

Plautus in Cap. Ore sistere. Eminor, interminorq̄, ne quis mihi obstiterit obuiam, nam qui obstiterit, ore sistet. I threten, and I menace, that no man let me of my way, for whosoeuer letteth me, shall kisse the grounde.
Sistere uadimonium, to bringe in suerty.
Sistrum, an instrument lyke a horne, whiche was vsed in battayle, in the stede of a trumpet.
Sisyphus, was a great thefe, whiche was slayne by Theseus, of whom it is fayned, that in hell he tourneth a stone vppe to a great hill, but whan it is at the toppe, it falleth downe agayne, and remeueth his labour.
Sitanius panis, bred of newe wheate.
Sitarchia, a bagge, or gardeuiandes, wherin meat is put.
Sithonia, a countraye in Macedonia vppon the se syde.
Siticen, he that dyd blowe in a trumpet whā men were buryed.
Sitio, tire, to thyrst or be a thirst.

S ante O.

Sitiens, he that is a thirst.
Situlus barbatus, a lytle skyllet.
Sitella, a lytle potte, wherinto lottes were putte.
Sitibundus, a, um, very thursty.
Siticulosus, he that is allwaye a thirst.
Sitis, thirst, or desire to drinke.
Situla, & Sitella, a lytle cofer, wherin lottes were put, at the chesinge of officers: also a buckat to drawe water.
Situs, ta, tum, put or set.
Situs, tus, fylthynesse gathered of moysture, by lacke of klensinge. also of sluttisshnesse. also the settynge or standinge of a place, which is now called the syte or situatiō of a maner or countraye.

¶ S, ANTE M.

Smaragdus, a precious stone called an Emeraude.
Smigma, Sope, & all other thinge that doth put awaye spottis or vnclennesse.
Smigticus, ca, cum, the efficacy of klensing.
Smilax, acis, a tree, whiche hath leues lyke an yuy, with beryes, and a whyte floure, and smelleth lyke a lyly.
Smyntheus, one of the names of Apollo.
Smyrna, a citie in Asia.

S ANTE O.

Soana, a ryuer of Asia.
Soanes, people of Asia, dwelling about the extreme part of the mountayne, called Caucasus.
Soboles, issue or succession of children.
Sobrie, sobrely, aduisedly, prudently.
Sobrini, susters childerne.
Sobrius, a, um, sobre, well aduysed.
Soccus, & Socculus, a socke, which women and players in Comedies onely ware.
Socer, cri, the wyfes father.
Socrus, the mother.
Sociale bellum, that warre, whiche is made with confederates.
Sociare sermonem, to haue familiar cōmunication with one. *Qu. Curt. lib. 7.*
Socienus, a companion, or felowe.
Societas, tatis, felowshyp.
Socio, are, to ioyne or confederate. *Plautus.*
Socius, a felowe or companyon. also Socij, be confederates, they whiche in all counsayles and actes doo participate one with another. Loke for Comites and Sodales, in their places.
Socors, for Secors, luskysshe, apte to no goodnesse.
Socordia, for Secordia, luskisshenesse, somtyme

tyme it signifyeth ydelnes.
Socrus, my wyfes mother.
Socraticus, he that foloweth the doctrine of Socrates.
Sodales, they that kepe company togither, at meales or passetyme. they be also they, whiche be of one fraternitie or company, or gylde.
Sodalitas, tatis, a fraternite or brotherhode. Also a company incorporate of any misterie or crafte, generally al felowshyps pryuately assemblynge amonge the people.
Sodalitium, idem.
Sodes, yf thou dare.
Sodoma, orum, & Sodomum, a citie in Judea, whiche for synne, done agaynste nature, was by almyghty god consumed by celestiall fyre.
Sodomito, tare, to commytte or vse the syn of Sodoma, agaynste nature.
Sogdiana, a countrey in Asia, extendyng to the northe parte of Scithia.
Sol, solis, the sonne.
Soles, sygnifyeth sometyme the day, sometyme the beames of the sonne.
Solamen, minis, solace.
Solanum, an herbe callyd nyghtshade.
Solanum soporiferum, an herbe callid dwale.
Solaris, re, of the sunne.
Solarium, a place where by the sunne, houres are knowen. Also a soler of a house. Also a pencion payde to the prince, to liue out of commune busynesse.
Solari, they whych be dyseased or sycke by the heate of the sonne.
Solatium, solace or comforte.
Solea, a showe, callydde a galage or paten, whiche hath nothyng on the fete, but only lachettes. Also a fishe, called a sole also a groundsoyl, wheron standeth the wall of a house. It is also a shoe, wherwith horses and oxen be shodde.
Solearius, a paten maker.
Soleatus, ta, tum, shodde.

Suetonius in Auguft. Solemne, accustomed.
Plautus in castel. Solemnia, feastes or holydayes.
Solemniter, solemnely.
Solennis, ne, annuall or yerely, that whiche is done euery yere.
Soleo, solitus sum, uel solui, solere, to be wōt.
Solere, to kepe companye.
Solet, it was wont, or the vse hath ben.

Plautus in epidico. Solens, for ut soleo, Ego abcessi solens paulum ab illis, I went a lyttell from them, as I was wont.
Solers, tis, wytty, cunnyng.
Solertia, sharpenes or quyckenes of wytte, craftynesse or subtiltie in practysynge, or wyttynesse.

Solicito, tare, to shewe both hope and feare. Also to inquiete, or make sorye, to solicite or procure by meanes: sommetyme to labour the erthe.
Solicitudo, dinis, care.
Solicitus, ta, tum, carefull.
Solido, dare, to make fyrme, to consolidate.
Solidesco, scere, to close togither, as a woūd dothe, whan it healeth.
Solide, hole, perfytely.
Solidarij, they whiche do selle in grosse.
Solidipes, that hath fete hole without toes.
Solidus, da, dum, hole, contynuall, not holowe, not broken or cutte.
Solifuga, he that keepeth hym oute of the sonne, or fleeth from the heate of the son.
Solipunga, a flye, whiche in the heat of the sonne prycketh moste sharply.
Soliloquus, he that talketh beinge alone.
Soliloquium, communication, which a man beinge alone, hathe with god in contemplation.
Solinunt, for solent, they are wonte.
Solitarius, solitarie, alone without company
Solitas, solytarynesse.
Solitaurilia, an offryng of thre thynges of sondrye kyndes, as a bulle, a ramme, and a boore.
Solito, tare, to be wonte often.
Solitudo, deserte, where no man dwelleth.
Solitus sum, I was wonte.
Soliuagus, he that wandreth alone.
Solium, a place of astate, where a kyng sytteth: it is also a great vessell, whiche serueth to dyuers vses, as to translate lycour from one to an other, to washe linnen clothes, and for men and women to be bathed in. It sygnyfyeth also a coffin, where deed bodies are put.
Solœcismus, a vyce in speakynge, wherein the trewe congruitie and ryght speche is peruerted.
Solo, all in the ofke tunge.
Solon, lonis, one of the seuen wysemen of Grecia, which made lawes for the Athenienses.
Solor, aris, ari, to recreate.
Solox, course woulle, or lockes.
Solstitialis herba, an herbe, whyche dothe beare floures onely at the tyme, whan the sonne is at the hyghest, or as some menne suppose but one daye.
Solstitium, the stay of the sonne, whan he can not be eyther hygher or lower, which is twyse in the yere, that is in wynter, the eyght calendes of Januarie, and is callyd Solstitium hyemale, and in sommer, the viii. calendis of Julye, z is callid Solstitium æstiuale.

Solsti

S ante O.

Plautus. Solstitialis uita, a lyfe whyche dureth but a lyttell space.
Solstitialis morbus, a sycknesse whiche kylleth men shortly.
Solstitialis ægritudo, is of somme men taken for the burnyng feuer, whiche happeneth aboute the canicular dayes, of excedynge heate of the ayre.
Soluendo non est, he is not able to pay.
Solum, the soyle or grounde, generally it signifieth all thynge, whiche doth susteyne or beare any other thynge on it. It is also the sole of the fote. also the sole of a shoe.
Natale solum, a mannes naturall countrey.
Soluo, ui, uere, to lowse, to paye, to recompense, to put away, to delyuer, to resolue or melte. Soluere fidem, to breake promise.
Soluere uenas, to open the veynes.
Soluere uotum, to performe an auowe.
Soluere uita, to slee one.
Solummodo, onely.
Solute, wantonly, incontynently.
Solutus risus, a great laughter.
Solus, alone, one onely, solytarie.
Solutilis, le, that whiche wyll be soone lowsed or vndone.
Solutus, ta, tum, loused or louse, also payde.
Somniator, a dreamer.
Somnorinum, a dreame.
Somniculosus, slepy, a sluggarde.
Somniculosus, a, um, that whyche causeth one to sleepe.
Somnifer, feri, that which induceth or bryngeth slepe.
Somnificus, idem.
Somnio, somniare, to dreame.
Somnolentus, disposed to slepe.
No. Mar. Somnus, slepe.
Sonere, to sounde or make a sounde.
Sonito, to sounde often.
Sonipes, pedis, a lyght or swyfte horse.
Sonitus, tus, a sounde.
Soniuit, for sonuit.
Sono, sonare, to sounde or make a noyse.
Sonor, noris, a great sound or noyse.
Sonore, shyll or lowde.
Sonoritas, a shyllenesse, or lowdenesse.
Sonorus, ra, rorum, lowde, or makynge a great sounde.
Erasmꝰ in Chil. Sons, tis, gyltye.
Sontica causa, a great cause.
Sonticus, ca, cum, noysull.
Sonticus morbus, a contynuall syckenesse, or wherwith all the body is greued.
Sonus, all that may be harde.
Sophaci, people of Affrica.
Sophistice, ces, the parte of logyke, whyche is capciouse and subtylle.
Sophia, wysedome.

Sophisma, sophismatis, a craftye and deceytefull sentence, an oracyon or inuention, whiche seemeth to be trewe, whan it is false.
Sophista, & sophistes, a dissembler of wysedome, a deceyuer vnder an eloquente or crafty speakynge.
Sophocles, a wryter of tragedies.
Sophron, in Greke, is Temperance in englyshe, wherby carnall appetites and lustes be refrayned.
Sophos, aut sophus, a wyse man.
Sopio, piui, pire, & sopior, to sette at rest, to brynge aslepe.
Sopitus, brought aslepe, or to reste, or into a sowne with a sodayne stroke.
Sopor, oris, deed slepe.
Soporifer, soporiferi, & soporiferum, that bryngeth slepe.
Soporo, rare, to brynge or induce slepe.
Soporatus, faste aslepe.
Sora, an hyll in Italy.
Sorbeo, bui, bere, & sorbo, psi, bere, to suppe, as one suppeth potage.
Sorbiciuncula, a thynne brothe.
Sorbitio, onis, suppynge.
Sorbities, idem.
Sorbillo, lare, to syppe.
Sorbillum, a cawdell.
Sorbum, an harryshe pere.
Sordeo, & sordesco, dui, dere, to be fowle, or vnkleanly. **Plautus in Penulo.**
Sordes, fylthe, or vncleannesse.
Sordesco, sordescere, to be vncleane or sluttyshe.
Sordide, vncleanly, sluttyshely.
Sordidior, dius, vnclenlyer.
Sordidissime, moste vnkleanly.
Sordidissimus, ma, mum, vnclenlyest.
Sorditudo, fylthynes, sluttyshenes.
Sordido, dare, to make fowle.
Sordidus, da, dum, fylthy, vnclenly, sluttishe.
Sorex, ricis, a ratte, or a fielde mous.
Sorech, the Iewes do calle vynes, whiche contynually do brynge forthe moste pleasant and dilectable fruyte.
Soriantes, sworne bretherne.
Soriceus, a, um, of a ratte.
Soricinus, of a mouse.
Soriculata uestis, a garmente of chaungeable sylke. **Plaut.**
Sorita, a subtil & captious forme of arguing.
Soritæ, people whyche are diuyded frome Inde by the ryuer callyd Arabis.
Sorilla, shyppes whiche are calked or stopped with hempe or flaxe.
Sororiari, is properly of maydens brestes, whan they begyn to be imbosed.

Aa Soror

S ante O.

Soror, ris, a syster.
Sororiæ, maydens pappes.
Sororius, my systers husbande.
Sorracus, a cofer or baskette wherein are caried the instrumentes or apparayle seruynge for comedies or interludes.
Sors, fortis, chaunce, lotte, portion in enherytaunce: the hole somme in a commune banke or stocke, wherin many haue parte. It is also destyny, iudgement.
Sortes, were also the aunsweres of Idols.
Sorticula, the scrowe, wherein the lotte is wrytten.
Sortilegium, dyuynation by lottes.
Sortilegi, ben they, whiche do tell mennes destenies by takynge of lottes or verses of holy scripture.
Sortior, tiris, tiri, & sortio, tire, to make lottes, to take or haue any thynge by lotte or chaunce. Also to dispose or order.
Sortiri prouinciam, to receyue the rule of a countray by lottes. It is vsurped to haue auctoritie by election.
Sortito, an aduerbe, sygnyfyenge by lotte or chaunce.
Sortitus, ta, tum, taken by lotte. also chaungynge to haue a thynge.
Sospes, hole or saulfe. also he that gyueth helthe.
Sospitalis, le, cause of helthe.
Sospito, tare, to kepe in helthe.
Sos, olde wryters vsyd for eos.
Sosia, a mannes name.
Sostratus, a mannes name.
Soradicum carmen, metre hauyng. vii. fete.
Soticena, one of the names of Juno.
Soter, a saluyour.

¶ S ANTE P.

Spadicus, ca, cum, of scarlette colour.
Spadix, dicis, a date with the braunche plucked from the palme tree. It is also scarlette colour.
Spado, donis, a geldyng, be it man or beest.
Spadonia, a kynde of laurell.
Spargo, si, gere, to scatter or caste abrode. **Cor. Tacitus lib. 3.**
Spargere bellum, to make warre in sondrye partes of a countrey.
Spartam nactus es, hanc orna, a prouerbe sygnifienge the astate or office, whiche thou haste, order or applye it welle.
Sparganon, the roote of an herbe called cynquefoyle.
Spargapises, the sonne of Thomiris the quene of Massagetes.
Sparta, the chiefe citie of Lacedemonia.
Spartacus, was a famouse sworde player, whiche gathered an host of slaues, & made battayle agaynste the Romayns, and was vanquyshed by Crassus.
Sparteum, a money bagge.
Spartiata, & Spartanus, na, num, of Sparta.
Spartum, & Spartus, an herbe called brome.
Spara, be callyd caltroppes, sowen in tyme of batayl, to woūd the fete of men & horsis.
Sparus, a clubbe.
Sparum, a lyttell darte.
Spastici, out of the whyche any thynge is plucked.
Spatha, a two handed or bastarde sworde. it is alsoo an instrumente of the kytchen, to tourne meate that is fryed.
Spathalion, an ornamente, pertaynynge to women.
Spaticus, vexed with an yll spirite.
Spatiator, a wanderer.
Spatiosus, a, um, large, spacious.
Spatiosé, & spatiosius, largely, more large.
Spatior, aris, ari, to walke.
Spatium, a space as wel in tyme, as in place.
Specere, among olde wryters was taken for Inspicere, to looke in.
Specialis, le, speciall, peculiar, propre.
Speciatim, specially, peculyarly, propzely. **Cicero de reditu suo**
Species, ei, a fygure or image, a forme, kind, beautie, fauour. It is defyned by Logicyens, to be that, whiche is sayde of many thynges varienge in noumbre: as Homo, whiche is spoken of Plato, Socrates, Cicero, whyche doo not varye in fygure but in noumbre. Sommetyme species, doo sygnyfye spyces. Alsoo it is apparaunce. alsoo a syghte or thynge sene, spices.
Per speciem legationis in Asiam ablegatus est, Under the coloure of ambassade, he was banyshed into Asia. **Plin. de uiris illustr.**
In Speciem esse, to be to the honour. **Plautus.**
Specificus, ca, cum, partycular.
Specificé, particularly.
Specillum, a smalle Instrumente, wherewith Sourgeons doo serche the deepenesse of woundes and sores. Alsoo to annoynt sore eyes. It is also a Spectakle to loke with, also an eare pycker.
Specimen, speciminis, an example, a profe. also beautie.
Specimen ædere, to shew a proufe of a mannes counnynge.
Speciosus, a, um, beautyfull.
Spectabilis, le, worthy to be sene.
Spectaculum, a thynge to be sene or looked on. Sometyme the selfe beholdynge. alsoo the place from whens menne doo beholde thynges. **Budeus.**
Spectamen, a Sygne or token. Spectamen bono seruo, id est qui rem herilem procurat, uidet, collocat, It is a token of a good seruant **Plautus in Mene.**

seruant, that is to saye, whiche attendeth aboute his maisters busynesse, and dothe suruey all thynge, and sette it in order.
Spectatores, beholders, triers of money.
Spectatus, ta, tum, approued.
Specto, tare, to behold, to approue, to tende to some conclusion, to compare.
Spectatio, a tryall or proufe of money.
Spectrum, an ymage or fygure in a mannes ymagynation.
Specula, an hygh hylle or towre, whereon thynges be espyed far of, also lyttel hope, a diminutiue of spes.
Specularia, spectakles.
Specularis, re, any thynge, wherby a manne may see the better.
Speculatio, a beholdynge.
Speculator, an espyall in warres.
Speculor, aris, ari, to see farre, to consyder, to espye, to serche out.
Speculum, a lookynge glasse.
Specus, cus, & specoris, a denne.
Speluncha, idem.
Spelæum, idem.
Spepondi, for spopondi, I haue promysed.
Sperchius, a ryuer of Thessalia.
Speres, olde wryters vsed for spes, hope.
Sperma, spermatis, seede, mooste commonly vsed for the naturall humoure, whereof all lyuynge thynges be ingendred and fourmed.
Sperno, spreui, spernere, to despise.
Spero, rare, to hope.
Sperata uirgo, a mayden asked in mariage.
Spes, spei, hope.
Speutici panes, looues of breadde made in haaste.
Speusippus, a noble phylosopher cousyne to Plato.
Sphæca, a waspe.
Sphæra, a fygure in al partes equally round a speere.
Sphæristerium, a rounde place in a bayne, where men are exercysed, a tenyse play.
Spheromachia, playenge at tenyse.
Sphennida, a balle made of lether or cloth, greatter than a tenyse balle.
Sphragide, a stone whiche printeth perfitly.
Sphinx, gis, a monster, whiche had the heed and handes of a mayden, the bodye of a dogge, wynges lyke a byrde, nayles lyke a lyon, a tayle lyke a dragon, the voyce of a man, which purposed to men subtyl questions. It is also a beaste lyke an ape, but more rough, & with a longer tayle, I suppose it to be a munkay or babyon.
Sphondilium, a ioynt or knotte of the backe bone. xii. of them do make the chyne, and the v. resydue do make the loynes.

Spica, & spicus, the eare of corn. also a spice called Spikenarde.
Spica mantica, an eare of corne, hauynge no berde.
Spicatus, ta, tū, eared, or in eare, as corne is.
Spiceus, ea, eum, that whyche hathe eares lyke to corne.
Spicifera, the surname of Ceres callid goddesse of corne.
Spicilegium, glemynge of corne.
Spicilegium facere, to gleme.
Spicio, cire, to shute out in eare.
Spiculatores, they whiche be called of the kynges garde. Some men do take Spiculator, to be a hangeman, or other persone, whiche putteth men to deth by execution of the lawes.
Spiculo, culare, to make any thynge sharpe atte the poynte.
Spiculum, a darte, also an arrowe.
Spilumenes, a sluttyshe drabbe.
Spina, a thorne, also the backebone.
Spineus, a, um, of thorne.
Spineoli, a wylde fruite callyd Sloes.
Spinosus, a, um, full of thornes.
Spinther, a pynne, also a tacke, sometyme a braselette.
Spinturnix, a byrde whyche was wonte to comme to the aulters, and carye awayea burnynge cole, whyche was taken for an vnlucky byrde.
Spinus, a plumme tree or damsyn tree.
Spio, onis, idem quod Nimpha.
Spirabilis, le, luely, or that wherby we liue.
Spiritabile, idem.
Spiraculum, & spiramentum, out of whyche the ayre or brethe passeth. *Cicero*
Sprarchus, a capitayne in the fore warde.
Spiræ, thynges whyche doo tourne and wynde in dyuers cerkles lyke a trendell, or an adder lyeng rounde. Also spira, is an ornament of a womans heed. also the turning of cables or ropis, whā they be woūd vp. also the band or lace, wherwith a cappe or hat is made fast vnder a mans chyn. also the base of a pyllar. Also a cake made like a trendell. also a multitude of people. *Ennius*
Spirillum, a gotes berde.
Spiritus, spirite, brethe, wynde.
Spirituale, & spiritale, idem quod spiritus.
Spiro, spirare, to blowe as wynde dothe, to sende forthe odoure.
Spisse, an aduerbe, signifienge thicke.
Spissigradior, gradi, to go thycke, or make many feete.
Spissigradus, he that gothe thycke.
Spissitas, thyckenesse.
Spisso, are, to make thycke.
Spissus, a, um, thycke, slowe.

Spissi-

Spissitudo, thyckenesse.
Spithama, a measure of .xii. fyngers brode.
Splen, splenis, the splene.
Splendeo, dui, dere, to shyne.
Splendesco, scere, to shyne ofte.
Splendidé, an aduerbe sygnifienge clere or bryghte. also rychely.
Splendidus, da, dum, bryght, clere. Also he whyche vseth to haue his house rychelye decked with abundaunce of all thynges, is called Splendidus, contrarye to Sordidus & auarus.
Splendor, oris, lyght, bryghtnesse, somtyme honour or noblenesse in lyuynge.
Spleneticus, he that is sycke in the splene.
Splenium, a plaister of cloth or lether made to lay to the body of him, whiche is sicke.
Spoletium, a citie in Italy.
Spoletini, people of the citie Spoletium.
Spolio, are, to robbe or dispoyle.
Spolior, ari, to be robbed.
Spoliarius, ria, um, that whiche receyueth spoyle or thynges taken by robberie.
Sponda, the syde of a bedde.
Spondeo, spopondi, spondére, to promyse.
Spondeus, a foote in meeter of two longe syllables.
Spondilus, a wherue, whyche is a rounde thynge of stone, or wodde, or leadde, put on a spyndell to make it runne rounde. It is also o whyte harde thynge in an oyster, whyche is couered with the fyshe.
Spondium, that whiche cometh of lead like to soote, whiche is about vessels of brasse, that do hange ouer the fyre.
Spongia, a spounge, or that wherwith any thynge is wyped.
Spongiare, to wype cleane a sponge.
Spongioli, mousherons.
Spongiosus, a, um, lyghte, and full of holes lyke a spounge.
Spongites, a stone lyke a spunge.
Sponsa, a woman despoused or affianced.
Sponsalis, le, pertaynyng to spousage.
Sponsalia, the spousage, or betrouthyng of a man and womanne, before that they be wedded.
Sponsio, onis, a promyse, a bargayne.
Sponsus, us, idem.
Sponso, sare, to affyance or betrouthe.
Sponsor, oris, he that promyseth or bargaineth. Sometyme a suretie, whiche vndertaketh an other mans acte.
Sponsus, sa, sum, promysed.
Sponté, naturally, willingly, of his free wyl.
Spontalis, le, voluntaryly.
Spontaneus, ea, eum, that whiche dothe, or is done wyllyngly, naturally, without constraynt or helpe.

Spopondi, I haue promysed.
Sporade, yles nygh to Crete or Candy.
Sporta, & sportula, a basket or maunde, some tyme money or meate distributed by pryncis vnto the people.
Sportula, & sportella, a littell gyft or almes, also lyuerey of courte, callydde bowge of courte, was callyd Sportula.
Spretus, refused.
Spuma, the fome or frothe of any thynge lyquyde.
Spumeus, a, um, fomy or frothye.
Spumo, are, to fome or gather vnto fome.
Spumosus, a, ū, that wherof cometh a fome.
Spuo, spui, spuére, to spytte.
Spurce, vnkleanly, fylthyly.
Spurcidicus, ca, cum, that whiche speaketh dishonestly or vnclenly.
Spurcificus, ca, cum, that maketh thynges vncleane or fylthy.
Spurcitia, & spurcities, vncleannesse.
Spurco, care, to defyle or make vncleane.
Spurcum uinum, wyne myngled with water.
Spurcus, ca, cum, vncleane, fylthye, vnpure, stynkynge, blouddy.
Spurij versus, verses fayned, the authour beinge false named or vnknowen.
Spurius, a bastarde. also it was the surname of dyuers Romaynes.
Sputo, tare, to spytte.
Sputor, tari, to be spytte on.
Sputum, spyttell.

¶ S ANTE Q.

SQualla, olde wryters vsed for squalida.
Squalleo, lui, lére, to be filthy, shuttishe, soiled or stainid with som vnclene thing
Squallidus, da, dum, sluttishe, filthy, causing one to abhorre the sight therof. Somtime it signyfieth spotted. also carrayne leane.
Squallidus ager, grounde out of tylthe. also shynynge.
Squalor, loris, sluttyshenes, fylthynes.
Squalido, dinis, & squalliditas, the same.
Squalus, a fyshe.
Squama, the scale of a fyshe.
Squammosus, skaly.
Squatina, a sole fyshe with a rough skynne, wherwith fletchers doo make theyr arrowes smothe.
Squarosus, a, um, rough and sharpe, lyke to a thynge whiche is skalye.
Squilla, a certayne herbe, growynge in the see, also a fyshe.
Squinitij, people in Italy callydde Sabelli and Samnites.

¶ S ANTE T.

ST, a voyce of him that commandeth silence, as we say in englishe, husht, whā we wold haue one to holde his peace.

Stabilimentum, that whiche kepeth a thing stedfaste.
Stabilio, liui, lire, to make stedfaste or stable.
Stabilis, le, stable or stedfaste.
Stabularæ mulieres, women whiche keepe vyttaylynge houses, for to refresshe wayfarynge men.
Stabularius, an inholder. Also he that hath the charge of the howse, where cattayle is kepte.

Budeus. Stabulari damas aut ceruos, falowe deere or redde dere to be lodged or harborowed.
Stabulo, bulare, to stande as cattayle dothe in a stable.
Stabulatio, standynge or lyenge of cattelle, also harborowynge or lodgynge of dere.
Stabulum, an inne, where men do lodge or bayte. Also it is the generalle name of the place, where cattelle doo abyde, whanne they come from their pasture. also a stable wherin horses or mules are kepte.
Stactis, & stacte, the floure of myrre, or fatnesse, whiche fyrste distilleth out of it.
Stadium, a place, wherin runnynge is exercysed, as welle of men as of horses. It is also a furlonge or the eight part of a mile.
Stacteus, a, um, gummye.
Stadiodromos, the place ordeined to run in.
Stadiodromas, he that rounneth in a cours of rounnynge.
Stagma, an oyntement.
Stagno, are, proprely of water is to stande and not to flowe.
Stagnum, a standynge water, a poole. alsoo a certayne mettall called tynne.
Staloginum, a thyng to hange at ones eare, as Egyptians haue.
Stamen, clothe, whanne it is in the lome or frame. Also flaxe or woulle, whan it is on the dystaffe. also stamyne or worstede.
Stanneus, a, um, of tynne.
Stannum, mettall callyd tynne.
Stapedes, styroppes.
Staphyle, a vyne.
Staphylus, he that dyd fyrste myngle water with wyne.
Staphis, a kynde of vynes, whiche hathe a blacke stemme and strayt, and hath a fruite more lyke to a lyttelle bladder, than to a grape, which be grene, within the which is a kernelle thre cornerde.
Staphilinus, wylde parsnyppe.
Staphis agria, Stafesagre.
Stata sacrificia, sacrifyce custumably doone at certayne days of an olde ordynance.
Staræ matris simulachrum, an ymage, whyche was sette vp by the people in euerye strete at Rome.
Stare, somctyme sygnyfieth to abyde.

Stat mihi, I am determyned.
Status, ta, tum, fyrme, or stable, alsoo ordeyned or decreed.
Statarius, a, um, ordynarie.
Strater, teris, a certayne coyne, whiche was in value foure drammes.
Stratera, a beam to way without the balacis.
Staticulum, a certayne wanton meuynge in daunsynge. somtyme a lyttell cart.
Stati dies, dayes ordynarie, dayes in banke, for apparance, or for the parties to plede.
Statilinus, was callyd a priuate god, whiche men supposed to be alway with them.
Statina, an Ile.
Staticulum, a lyttell ymage.
Statuncula, idem, or a lyttell restyng place.
Statius, a noble poete.
Statim, anon, constantly, contynually.
Statio, onis, a place, where eyther menne of warre or shyppes doo abyde or reste for a certayne tyme.
Stationalis, le, that whyche standeth faste or abydeth.
Stationarij milites, souldiours, whiche are assigned to abyde stylle in one place, or to kepe a towne or fortresse, or the marches of a countrey.
Statiua, & statiuum, a certayne place fortyfyed, where men of warre lay at the siege of a fortresse.
Stator, toris, a seruaunt, whyche is alwayes redye attendynge aboute an offycer, to be at commandement. wherfore in that word be included pursyuantes, postes, sergeantes, baylyffes, and catchepolles. Also Jupiter, was called Jupiter stator of Romulus, bycause he supposed that he made the Romaynes to tarye whan they fledde, the Samnites pursuynge them.
Statua, an ymage of mettalle, yuorie, stone, or tymber.
Statuaria, the crafte of caruynge or yettyng of ymages.
Statuarius, he that carueth or yetteth imagℨ.
Statuarius, a, um, pertaynynge to ymages.
Statuere ex æquo & bono, to iudge or determyne, accordynge to equitie, lasse than the rygour of the lawe wolde requyre.
Statuere pretium, to sette a price on thynges vendible.
Statumen, minis, that whiche is sette vp to sustayne or beare a thynge, a proppe.
Statumino, nare, to proppe vp, to vnderset, to make sure.
Statuo, tui, tuere, to ordayne, to determyne, to set faste, to stable a thinge, to dedicate, to beate one thynge to an nother. Sublimē illum arriperem, & caput primum in terram statuerem, ut cerebro dispergam uiam,

I wolde lyfte hym on highe, and beate his heed to the grounde, that I mought scatter his brayne abrode in the hygh waye.

Statura, the stature of a man.

Staturus, a, um, the particyple future of sto, stas, stare, to stande.

Status, tus, state, it is amonge oratours and lawyers the case, whiche rysethe in contention, wherin the matter resteth, whiche muste be replyed vnto, and eyther be denyed, confessed, or trauersed: of Tullie it is callyd Constitutio causæ.

Status, stata, statum, firme. Stati dies, dayes appointed.

Steatoma, a gatherynge of greace or fatte in some place agaynste nature.

Stechades, thre lyttell yles by Marsiles.

Stega, a cabyn of a shyppe. alsoo a cote or cotage.

Stegnæ febres, feuers in the whiche a man maye haue neyther syege, nor vryne, nor sweate, nor none other euacuation.

Stelæ, lyttell pyllars.

Stella, a sterre. also a sterrefysshe, also the name of a poete.

Stella crinita, a blasynge sterre.

Stellatus, ta, tum, full of sterres.

Stellatura, was an extorcion of capytaynes in takynge from the souldiours the porcions of vyttayle appoynted vnto them by the Emperour.

Stellio, a beaste lyke a lysarde, hauynge on his backe spottes lyke sterres.

Stellionatus crimen, a dysceyte in dyssemblynge a thynge, to take profyte of an other iniustely.

Stellis, a kynd of byrdlyme made in Euboea.

Stello, are, to shyne or glysten lyke sterres, or be made lyke sterres.

Stemma, matis, a garlande of floures, alsoo the stocke or bloudde of a gentylle house. sometyme the degrees in kynrede. Alsoo an inscription grauen in a stone.

Stemo, was syster to Medusa.

Stenobœa, the wyfe of Pretus kynge of Ephyri, whiche loued Bellorophon, that vanquysshed the monster callyd Chimera.

Stentor, toris, was a man, whiche hadde a voyce as lowde as xx. men.

Stephanoma, euery herbe that seruethe for garlandes.

Stephanoplocus, a maker of garlandes.

Stephanus, in greke is a crowne.

Stercoratio, dungynge.

Stercorarius, ria, rium, pertaynyng to dunge or mucke.

Stercoratus, ta, tum, dunged or mucked, or compassed.

Stercoro, are, to dunge or compasse.

Stercus, stercoris, dunge, mucke, compasse.

Stercutius, the surname of Saturnus, bicause he fyrste founde and vsed doungynge of grounde.

Steresis, priuation.

Sterila, olde wryters vsed for sterilis.

Sterilesco, rilescere, to be barrayne or waxe barrayne.

Sterilia for sterilitas.

Sterilis, le, barrayne.

Sterilis amator, a louer, whyche lackethe money.

Sterilitas, barraynes, sterilytie.

Steriliter, barrayncly.

Sternax, nacis, a steerynge or ploungynge horse.

Sterno, straui, sternere, to throwe downe, to spreade, to couer, to lay the table, to make playne or smothe, to lye downe to reste.

Sternere lectum, to make a bedde.

Sernunt se somno, They layde them downe to slepe. *Vergilius*

Sternuto, tare, to snese often.

Sternuo, nuere, to snese.

Sternutamentum, sneesynge.

Sternutatio, idem.

Sterquilinium, a dungehylle or myxen.

Sterogonia, a kynde of frankincense callyd cōmonly olibanū, or in latin thus masculus.

Sterto, tui, tere, to route whan one slepeth.

Stesichorites, is the numbre of eight in dyse, so called of the sepulchre of Stesichorus the poete, whiche was made in figure like to eyght dyse.

Stesichorus, a famouse poete, of whome it is writen, that whanne he was an infant in his cradelle, a Nyghtyngale satte on his mouthe, and dyd synge, sygnyfienge that he shulde be the sweetest poete, that euer was afore hym. Also he founde fyrste syngynge of songes in a daunse.

Stibadium, a chaire or couche made of herbes wounde togyther: somme doo calle it an herber or sommer parler.

Stibium, a whyte stone founde in syluer mines, which stoppeth the runnyng of eies, and dothe make them seme very fayre.

Stichos, a verse or an order in a thynge.

Stigo, are, to pricke forthe.

Stigma, matis, a marke made with fyre, or with a hotte yron. Sometyme it sygnyfieth infamy and reproche obiected openly.

Stigmatici, persones infamed.

Stilla, a droppe.

Stilbo, was a philosopher. Vide stilpo.

Stilbon, the sterre of Mercury.

Stillicidium, the droppynge of a house.

Stillo, are, to droppe.

Stilpo, a phylosopher borne in the cytie of Me-

Megara in Grece, whiche his countreye beinge burned, and his wyfe and childern loste in the fyre, escaped, and departynge alone, whan the kynge Demetrius asked of hym, yf he had loste any thynge, he answered, I haue loste nothyng: for all that is myne, I carie with me, meanynge therby, that vertue, whiche is onely the propre goodes of a wyse mā, and may not be taken from hym, he toke away with hym.

Stilpones, dwarfes.

Stimulo, are, to prycke.

Stimulatio, a pryckynge or feruent mouing to doo a thynge.

Stimulator, he that prycketh.

Stimuleus, a, um, that whyche is done with pryckynge.

Stimulus, a gode, wherwith oxen ar driuen.

Stingo, & stinguo, guere, to put out lyght.

Stipa, for stupa, towe.

Stiparius, ia, ium, pertaynynge to stoppyng or beatynge harde togyther.

Stipatores, they whiche do frayte the shyp, or lay in suche fardelles or burdeynes as are to be caryed. Also they whiche be of the kynges gard, alway about his person.

Stipatus, enuyronned with men, to be defended, as princis are with their garde.

Stipendialis, le, pertaynynge to wages.

Stipendiarius, a, um, whiche payeth tribute, of some callyd contributarie, to the fyndyng of an army, or defence of a contray.

Stipendiatus, he that taketh wages.

Stipendiosus, he that hath bene oftentymes hyred or retayned in warres.

Stipendior, diari, to be hyred or retayned in warres.

Stipendium, wages proprely gyuen to souldiours. Also subsidie payde to princis.

Stipes, pitis, a stake, also a stycke.

Stipo, are, to stop chynkes or clyftes, proprely in shyppes or botes, with towe and pytche. also to enuyronne to the intent to defende one.

Ti.Liuius. lib. 34. Stipendia facere, to serue in warres, as a souldiour.

Stips, uel stipis, pis, wages to men hyred: also money gyuen to beggars.

Stiptica medicamenta, medycines that doo bynde or restrayne.

Stipula, holme, crige, or straw, apt to thatch houses. it is of some taken for the huske that closeth in the strawe.

Stipulatus, tus, & stipulatio, a bargayne or promyse, or obligation to pay money, or to perfourme a thynge, whiche is requyred.

Stipulor, aris, ari, to make a bargayn, to promyse effectually that whiche he is requyred to do. It hath both the actiue and passiue signification. Stipulor abs te, I require of the, or I am requyred of the.

Stiria, an ysykle or droppe of yse.

Stiricidiū, & stillicidiū, the droppig of a hous

Stirpices, wieders in gardeynes.

Stirpitus, vp by the rote.

Stirpo, are, to pull vp by the rote.

Stirps, stiripis, in the fēmynyne gender sygnyfyeth a stocke in kynrede, beinge the masculyne gender it sygnifieth the stemme of a tree or herbe.

Stitisse vadimonium, to haue brought forth suretie or pledges. *Gell. li. 2.*

Stiua, is that in a plough, whiche the ploughman holdeth, whan he dothe eare.

Stlata, a brode shyp or bote, callid an hulke.

Stlembus, slowe and heuye.

Stlatariū, any thyng that is borne on the see.

Stlatarius, a maker of hulkes or botes.

Stlitem, old wryters vsed for litem, variance.

Stlitibus iudicandis, for litibus iudicandis.

Stlopus, a sowne made with the mouth, whā the chekes are blowen.

Stlotium, for lotum.

Sto, steti, stare, to stande, to indure or abide. Stare promisso, to abyde by his promyse. To be full. Stat ager sentibus, the felde is full of brembles. Iam puluere coelum stare uident, Nowe sawe they the skye fulle of duste. To bose oute. Hic corpus solidum inuenies, hic stare papillas Pictor marmoreo, Here in this marble stone shalt thou fynde paynted, the body sounde, and the pappes imbosed. Also to be immouable, or alway certayne. Sic stat sententia, so the sentence abydeth immouable, or is determyned. Also Stat, my mynde is. Stat conferre manum Aeneae, my mynd is to fight with Aeneas. Stat, is sette. Omnis in Ascanio chari stat cura parentis, All the care of the tender louynge father was sette on Ascanius. Also stare, to coste, Neque ipse hoc periculum ignoro, expertus non leui documento, quanti steterit mihi, quod semel imperata non feci, Nor I am ignorant of that daunger, hauyng experience of no lyght warnyng, howe moch it cost me, that I dyd not those thynges, that I was commannded. *Cecilius. Vergil. Lucilius. Vergilius. Vergilius.*

Stare firmum, to stande faste.

Stat per me, per te, per illum, whanne I, or anye other is the cause, that a thynge is not done. Si poterit fieri, ut ne pater per me stetisse credat, quo minus he fierent nuptiae, uolo. I wolde if it may be, that my father shulde thynke, that it was not long of me, that this mariage toke none effecte.

Stat a me, he is of myne opinion.

Stat apud te fides parum, Thou arte of a swalle *Plautus in pseudo. Ter. in Eu.*

small credence.
Statur, I stande here.
Stoecades, foure yles in the frenche see agaynste Languedocke.
Stoici, a secte of philosophers, which affirmed, that no griefe moughte happen to a wyse man: and that felicitie was onely in vertue.
Stola, a womans gowne, It was also a long garment, whiche the pryncis of Persia dyd vse, and was the only garment of honour, as we do cal suche apparell a robe.
Stolatus, he that weareth suche a robe, also it may be callyd honourable.
Stolide, foolyshely, lewdely.
Stoliditas, foolyshenes, lewdenes.
Stolidius, more foolyshely.
Stolidus, da, dum, foolyshe, lewde of condicions, odyouse.
Stolones, braunches whiche do spryng out of the stemmes or rootes of trees.
Stomachicus, he that is sick in his stomake.
Stomachor, aris, ari, to haue indignation, to be vexed in mynde.
Stomachose, angerly, hatefully, disdainously.
Stomachosus, dysdaynous.
Stomachus, is the pipe, wherby meate goth downe. It is also that which is called Ventriculus, whereunto we haue none other name but the stomacke. sometyme it signifyeth indignation, vehemente wrathe, hatrede, and abhorrynge of a thynge that lyketh not vs, Sommetyme facylytie or gentylnesse.

Plinius.

Storax, racis, a swete incense or gumme, whiche is also called styrax, whereof be two kyndes, the one is callyd Storax calamita, the other is callyd Storax liquida.
Storea, any thynge that is spredde on the grounde. It is also a matte.
Strabo, he that looketh a squynte, or gogle eyed.
Strages, a slaughter of men, or a discomfiture.
Stragulum, euery ouermoste garment. Also a counterpoynte or couerlyd.
Stramen, minis, strawe, lytter.
Stramentum, idem.
Stramentitius, a, um, that whyche is made of strawe.
Stramineus, a, um, of strawe.
Strangulo, are, to strangle.
Stranguria, dyffycultie to pysse.
Stratagema, a polycie or wyse counsylle in warres.
Strategus, a generall captayne of an armye.
Stratia, an hoste or armye.
Stratiotes, a man of warre.
Stratiotes, an herbe, whiche groweth on waters without any roote.
Stratioticus, ca, cum, warlyke, pertainynge to warres.
Stratius, idem. Also the name of one of the sonnes of Nestor.
Stratumino, are, to paue.
Strator, toris, he that helpeth his mayster to horsebacke, yeman of the styrope.
Stratum, any thynge that is strawed, Also a bedde. Strata, all that is layde on the bed.
Stratum, a horse harneyse, a streate or caulsey, paued with stone.
Strebula, in the olde tunge of Umbri was a piece of the fleshe that was offered in sacrifyce.
Strena, a newe yeres gyfte, or present.
Strenue, valyantly, quyckely, boldly.
Strenuitas, tatis, actiuitie.
Strenuus, a, um, valiant, prompt, actife, bold.
Strepito, tare, to make a noyse often.
Strepitus, tus, a noyse made with the handes or fete.
Strepo, pui, pere, to make a greatte noyse, properly in goinge or clappynge of handes, sometyme generally.
Strepsiceroti, certayne beastes in Affryke, hauynge croked hornes.
Stria, a rabat or smal furrowe made in stone or tymber.
Striata, be also creuyses or small lines, whiche are sene in herbes.
Stribligo, ginis, a viciouse fourme in speking where the wordes agree not, and the partes of speche be out of order.
Striblita, breade made lyke to ropes or cordes wounden.
Stricte, straightly.
Strictim, shortly touched one after an other
Strictim referre, to reporte moche in fewe wordes.
Strictim attondere, to clyppe all at ones.
Strictior, tius, more strayte.
Strictissimus, a, um, moste strayte.
Strictiuella, a foule yll fauoured hoore.
Strictiuæ, olyues gathered with mans hand.
Stricture, sparkes whiche doo issue frome mettall whan it is taken oute of the fyre, and beaten with hammers.
Strideo, dui, dere, & strido, dis, dere, to crashe or make a noyse lyke to cordes, whan they be drawen.
Stridon, a towne in Dalmacia, where saynct Hierome was borne.
Striga, a rewe of thynges whanne they be layde in lengthe. Also a ridge of lande, wherof commeth strigatus ager.
Striges, shrycheoules, also women whyche are supposed to come by nyghte into houses, and sucke the bloudde of chylderne, some calle them hegges.

Strigia,

Strigia, wyde garmentes made of lether vsed in warres.

Strigil, gilis, an horsecombe, alsoo a thynge wherewith wrastelers bounde theyr bodyes, whan they had wrastled. Also a certayne vessell.

Strigiles, were rubbynge combes made of swete wodde, wherwith in India the men were rubbed for an exercise. Also kerchifes, wherewith wrastelers after their labours wyped their bodyes. also certayne vessels. also pieces of fyne golde founde in mynes, vnmyxt with any other matter. also lyttell fyshes moste commonly taken in wynter tyme. *Budeus.*

Strigilecula, a diminutiue of strigil.

Strigillo, are, to strayne harde.

Strigium, a spanyshe garment.

Strigmenta, fylthynesse, whiche commethe from a mans bodye, whan he is wasshed. also the corruption of oyle.

Strigo, gonis, a well pightman, or well compacte or stronge.

Strigosus, a, um, carrayn leane, it is properly spoken of horses or routher beastes.

Strimon, onis, a ryuer in Thracia.

Stringo, xi, gere, to strayne or wrynge. Also to stryke, to make thynne in cuttynge, to gather, to shaue, to wounde. Stringere ensem, to drawe a sworde.

Strio, striare, to make rabattes in stoone or tymber. Alsoo to make furrowes. It is properly whanne beastes in earynge atte the ende of a furrowe tournethe to make a newe furrowe. Somme doo calle hit, to wende.

Striare, is also to plane or to polyshe.

Stritare, to abyde or tarye with an yll wyll, or with moche payn.

Stritauum, olde writers vsed for Tritauo, my grandfathers grandfather.

Stritomellus, a sparowe, whiche hauntethe the see costes.

Strix, strigis, a shryche oule, a wytche that chaungeth the fauour of chylderne.

Striges, grosse herbes or wortes.

Strobilus, a pyne apple tree. sometyme the kernels, or fruite.

Strobus, a tree, wherof pfumes were made, myxte with the wyne of dates, whyche perfume was swete, but it made the heed heuy, all be it without any peyne.

Stroma, tis, tapisry.

Strombon, a kynde of Labdanum.

Strombus, a shelle fyshe of the see, whyche hath a kynge, whom they folowe. It was thought sommetyme that he whyche had seene that fysshe, shulde haue good lucke in his affaires.

Strongyle, & Strongylos, an Ile in the see called Aegeum, nowe callyd Axos, sometyme it was callyd Dia.

Stropha, subtyltie in arguynge.

Strophas, a whirlynge or sodayne turnyng.

Srrophades, two Iles in the grekysshe see.

Strophia, garlandes whiche priestes were wonte to weare.

Strophiolum, a lyttell garlande.

Strophos, frettynge in the bowelles.

Strophium, a maydens neckerchefe or lynnen partlette.

Structiles columnæ, pyllars made of diuers pieces.

Structilis, le, made of many pieces, or of diuers thynges.

Structor, toris, a caruer of meate at a table.

Structura, buylding, settynge of thinges in good order.

Strues, a pyle of wodde, also a cake.

Struices, an ordynaunce of many thynges togyther.

Strufectarij, they whyche dyd carye cakes to the temple to be offred, as they do now carie the holy lofe on the sondaye.

Struferarii, they which dyd sacrifyce at the trees that were burned with lyghtninge.

Strufetani, they whiche broughte meale to be offered.

Struma, a swellynge within the throte, whiche is gathered matter and bloode. some thynke it to be that, whyche is callyd the kynges euyll.

Strumosus, he that hath the kynges euylle.

Struo, struxi, struere, to sette in order.

Strumum, a medycyne or playster for the kynges euyll.

Strupearia, holydayes amonge the people callyd falisci, at the whyche daye, the people do go with garlandes on their heedis.

Struppum, is a lyke holydaye amonge the people cally d Tusculani.

Struppi, were lyttell wrethes made of leaues putte on the heedes of ymages in the temples, as nowe superstitious fooles do sette on images heedes in the churches.

Strutheus, the priuye membre of a man.

Struthia, a certayne kynde of quynces.

Struthiocamelus, an ostryche.

Struthio, idem.

Struthopus, a rounde foote lyke a sparowe.

Struthopedes, they whyche haue lyttelle rounde feete.

Strychius, an herbe, whiche maketh hym madde that eateth of it.

Strychium bibit, a prouerbe sygnyfyenge the man is madde.

Studeo, dui, dere, to studye, or to applye the mynde, or care for a thynge, to endeuour. *Studiose.*

Studiosus, studious, dylygent, constant, addicte or feruently disposed.

Studiose, studiousely.

Studium, studye, sometyme exercyse, wylle, or appetite, desyre.

Stultitia, foly, it is knowen by foure thynges, or if he hath not in remembrance that he shulde haue, or if he hath, he dothe not retayn it, or doth not folow good council, or dothe approue yll councill or affections.

Stultior moricho, he that neglecteth his owne busynesse at home, and applyeth other mens abrode. It is alsoo a prouerbe touchynge them, whiche do thynges, that cause them to be laughed to scorne.

Stultior Chorœbo, a prouerbe applyed to fooles, whiche wyll assaye to do a thynge that is aboue their wytte or lernynge: for Chorœbus, was a felowe, that assayed to number the wawes of the see, whā he him selfe coude not tell any number aboue fiue.

Stulte, folyshely.

Stultiloquentia, & stultiloquium, a foolysshe babblynge.

Stultiloquus, he that talketh or speaketh foolyshely.

Stultior, stultius, more foolyshe.

Stultissimus, ma, mum, moste folyshely.

Stultius, more folyshely.

Stultorum feriæ, was a tyme in the monethe of February, that fooles kepte holy, fooles holy daye.

Stultus, he that dothe a thynge vnaduisedly or without discretion.

Stupa, towe, the cours part of flaxe.

Stuparius malleus, the hammer, wherewith calkers do beate towe into shyps or botes

Stupefactus, astonyed.

Stupefio, I am astonyed or abashed.

Stupeo, & stupesco, pui, pere, to be astonyed or dismayde. somtyme to meruayle at.

Stupefacio, cere, to make astonid, or to cause to meruayle or be abashed.

Stupentia, uel stupida membra, the membres whiche haue loste all their sence or feling.

Stupiditas, an abashement.

Stupidus, dysmayed, abasshed, also he that feleth nothynge, or lacketh his sences.

Stupor, poris, abashement, the sodayne priuation of sence or felynge.

Stupre, dishonestly, shamefully.

Stupro, prare, to committe auoultrie or rape or to defloure a virgin.

Stuprum, auoutrie, or defloration of a virgin

Stura, an yle agayne the mouthe of Tyber.

Styga, a fenne in Egypte not farre from the citie of Memphis.

Stygeus, ea, um, pertaynynge to Styx, the greate fenne, whiche is fayned of poetes to be by the ficlde callyd Elysius, whiche the paynyms dydde suppose to be a place of pleasure, wherein rested the soules of good men.

Stylobata, a trowgh of tymber, wherein water rounneth, or is conuayed into a cesterne.

Stylus, a style, whyche qualitie of wordes in speakynge, sometyme harde, sometyme easy, sometyme in a meane, also an elegant fourme or order in writynge or speakinge.

Stymphalus, a ryuer in Arcadia.

Stymphalide, a coppe of fethers, whyche standeth on the heed of a byrde, as of a larke, an heron, a pecocke, and other.

Stipticus, ca, cum, that whiche stoppeth or bindeth, or straincth, if it be eaten or dronken. Also that whiche in tastynge seemeth to strayne the tunge, as a quynce or redde wyne.

Styrax, racis, a soote gumme callyd storax, wherof be two kyndes, the one is callyd storax calamita, the other storax liquida.

Styx, sygnifieth sorowe or heuynesse, poetes doo fayne, that it is a fenne, whyche is in helle.

S ANTE V.

Suada, callyd in greke Pitho, was callid the goddesse of eloquence or dylectable speche.

Suadela, persuasion, fayre speche.

Suadeo, si, dére, to speake fayre, to intreate with fayre wordes, to indeuour, to induce a man into our opinyon, or to beleue vs.

Suadibilis, le, that which may be persuaded.

Suasibilis, idem.

Sualternicum, a kynde of ambre, whiche is yelowe, wherof beades be made, and is callyd Laumbre.

Suapte, of his owne nature.

Suarius, a swyne herde.

Suasibiliter, an aduerbe signifyenge, in maner to perswade.

Suasio, an exhortation, a mocyon or persuasyon.

Suasor, soris, he that dothe exhorte.

Suasum, euery colour that may tourne into an nother colour.

Suauiatio, a swete kyssynge.

Suauiator, he that kysseth swetely.

Suauiloquium, a swete speche.

Suauiloquus, he that speaketh swetely.

Suasorius, a, um, that wherwith a man is or may be perswaded.

Suatim, lyke a sowe.

Suauior, aris, ari, & suauio, to kysse sweetely or for ioye.

Suauis.

S ante V.

Suauis, suaue, sweete in taste, soote in odour or smelle.
Suauitas, & suauitudo, swetenesse.
Suauiter, sweetely.
Suauium sumere, to kysse.
Suauium facere, idem.
Suauium, & sauium, swete harte.
Sub, vnder, by, or aboute. Sub lucem, by daye lyght. Sub idem tempus, In the same tyme, or aboute the same tyme. Sub horam pugnę, About the time of the battayl. Sub eas autem redditæ sunt, for they were deliuered after theym. Sub sarcinis, with the trussis or cariage.

Cicer. pro Planco. Sub uesperum, in the twye lyghte. Subuesperum Cæsar portas claudi, militesque ex oppido exire iussit, In the twie lyghte Cesar commaunded the gates to be shutte, and the men of warre to depart out of the citie.

Cæs. in cō.

Subacidus, cida, cidum, somewhat eygre, or sowre.
Subacidulus, a, um, a lyttell sowre.
Subactus, ta, tum, constrayned, subdewed, dryuen vnder, kneaded or wrought with handes, as dowe is, laboured, exercised.
Subæratus, ta, tum, that which is brasse with in, and other mettall without.
Subæro, rare, to myngle with brasse.

Plautus in cistell.

Subagito, tare, to solycite. Subagito blandis, & benedicis uerbis, I solicited with fayre and well spoken wordes. It is also to company with a woman carnally.
Subalaris, subalare, that whyche is vnder the wynges.
Subalpini, people vnder the Mountaynes called Alpes, called Peemountaynes.
Subalternatio, a succession by tourne.
Subalterno, nare, to succede by tourne.
Subaquaneus, a, um, & subaqueus, a, um, that whiche lyeth vnder the water.
Subaquilus, la, lum, broune of colour.
Subare, is spoken of women, whyche are as sylthye as swyne in the acte of lechery.
Subire, idem.
Subareo, & subaresco, rescere, to be or waxe somewhat drye.
Subasper, somewhat sharpe.
Subaudio, dire, to here or perceyue a lyttel.
Subausculto, tare, to harken a lyttell.
Subbasilicanus, he that walketh vnder the place, where iugementes are practysed.
Subbibo, bibere, to drynke a lyttell.
Subblandior, diri, to flatter.
Subcalidus, da, dum, somwhat hote, warme.
Subcernicula, a fyne bulter, wherwith the floure is seuered from the branne.
Subcerniculum, a rangynge sieue.
Subcingulum, a bracynge gyrdell.
Subcineritius, a, um, rosted or baken vnder the asshes, or axen.

Subcisiua tempora, tymes borowed or spared from seryous busynesse.
Subcisiua opera, warkes tone at tymes stolē frō ordinarie busines or labours necessary.
Subcollo, lare, to lay a thyng on ones necke.
Subcrispus, he that hath a curlyd heed.
Subcustos, an vnder keeper.

Plautus in milite.

Subcutaneus, a, um, that which is within the skynne, betwene the skinne and the flesshe.
Subdelego, gare, to commytte to an nother any matter, whiche is committed vnto vs by the kynge or prynce.
Subdialia, thynges whiche doo stande or be sette abrode out of the houre.
Subdialis, ale, abrode in the ayre withoute the house.
Sub dio, that is not in a howse, or vnder a couerynge.
Subdititius, ia, ium, whiche is not proprelye his or hirs, whose it is fained to be. Partus subdititius, a byrthe fayned of an nother mannes chylde. Libri subdititij, bokes with fals titles or counterfaite auctours.
Subditiuus, a counterfayte chylde.
Subditus, a subiecte.
Subditus, ta, tum, idem quod subdititius. also put in the place of an other.
Subditus iudex, a iudge which is sette in the place of a iudge departed.
Sub diu, in the day tyme.

Plautus in mostell. Plautus in epistol. & Plin. in epi.

Subdo, dere, to putte vnder, to adde to, to putte in the place of an nother, to putte in daunger or ieoperdie.
Subdolus, he that deceyueth craftely, cauteloufe.
Subdole, craftily cauteloufly.
Subdubie, somewhat doubtefully.
Subdubitanter, idem.
Subdubito, tare, I doubte somewhat.
Subdubius, somewhat in doubte.
Subdubitatio, a lyttell doubte.

Terent. in Andria.

Subducere, to deceyue. Etiam nunc me subducere istis dictis postulas? And yet nowe wylte thou goo aboute with these wordes to deccyue me?

Plautus in Curcu.

Subducere, to steale. Proximo magnum poculum ille bibit, caput ponit, cùm dormiscit, ei subduco anulum, At the laste he dranke a great draught, & layd downe his heed, whiles he slepte, I stale his rynge from hym.
Subduco, xi, cere, to take aways, to remoue, to lyfte vp, or drawe vp.
Subducere rationes, to make acccompt, to go or steale away priuily.
Subductum omnibus uentis ædificiū, a house in the daunger of euery wynde.
Subeo, iui, ire, to go vnder or in, to take.
Subire mortem, to receyue dethe.

Sub-

Subductio, a drawynge vp of a shyppe oute of the water.
Subdulcis, ce, somewhat swete.
Subduro, rare, to make somewhat harde.
Subduror, rari, to be made somewhat hard.
Suber, corke.
Subiaceo, cere, to lie vnder, also to be subiect
Subiacto, tare, & subiecto, to cast vppe, as corne whan it is fanned.
Subices, subiectes.
Subiecto, tare, to caste vnder often.
Subiector, toris, a forger of testamentes, or he that bryngeth forthe one testament for an nother.
Subicito, tare, to cōpany often with a womā.

Plautus in persa. Subiculum flagri, a beatynge stocke.

Subigo, egi, igere, to constrayne, to subdue, to dryue vnder, to whet, to beate or stāpe, sometyme to eare or tylle truely, to digge, to meddyll with a womanne, sommetyme to lyfte vp.

Vergil.

Subijcio, ieci, ijcere, to put vnder, to make subiecte. somtyme to cast vp, to reherse. Si meministi quod olim dictum est, subijce, If thou doest remembre, what was ones spoken, reherse it.
Subinde, more ouer, forthwith or anon, often tymes. Subin, idem.

Festus. Subingere arietem, to delyuer a shepe to be kylled for hym that doth sacrifyce.

Ci. Att. 2. Subinnanis, ne, somewhat vayneglorious.
Subire aleam, to be in daunger or peryll, to entre into peryll.
Subire periculum, to entre into peryll.
Subijt mihi, it cometh to my remembrance. also to succede, to resiste, to clymme.

Plinius in panegyri. Subire, to take charge of any thynge. Quis enim curæ tuæ molem sponte subeat? who wolde wyllyngly take on hym the greate weight of thy charge.

Cicer. off. Subire, to suffre or susteyne. Qui retinendi officij causa, cruciatus subierit vltro, He that wyll for the accomplyshement of his duetie suffre tourmentes wyllyngly. Alsoo to growe or sprynge vp. Also to come to re-

Vergil. membrance. Sera pœnitentia subijt regem, Late repentance came to the kynges remembrance. Cogitationi nostre nunq̄ subijt, It came neuer to our thought.
Subit recordatio, I or he remembred.

Vergi. Aeneid. X. Subire, to put vnder. Aeneas subijt mucronem, ipsumq̄ morando sustinuit, Æneas put vnder his sword, & tarieng, lyfted him vp.
Subire, to succede or come in place. In quarum locū subierunt inquilinæ, impietas, perfidia impudicitia, In whose place succeded newe inhabytauntes, contempt of vertue, disloyaltie, lechery.

Cic. in diuinatione. Subire, to aunswere or resyste. Poteris ne orationem eius subire? Oughtest not thou make answere to his oration?

Subire, to clymme or mount vp. Hemi excelcitas, sex millibus passuū subitur, the height of the mountayne of Hemus is clymmed or mounted in syxe thousande paces.
Subhasto, tare, to sell any thynge in tyme of warres that was praysed. Hasta, a yerde, whiche was delyuered to hym that was appoynted to selle anye thynge taken in warres.
Subfibulum, was a whyte ornamente, foure square and long, which the nunnes, callid Uestales, ware on their hedes, whan they dyd sacrifyce.
Subito, sodaynly.
Subitaneus, & subitarius, a, um, & subitus, ta, tum, sodayne.
Subiugalis, le, vsed to the yoke.
Subiugo, gare, to make subiecte.
Sub iugum mittere, to brynge in subiection.
Subiungo, gere, to adde or ioyne to.
Sublabor, beris, lapsus sum, labi, to slyppe awaye.
Sublabro, brare, to put into the mouthe.
Sublatior, tius, hygher.
Sublatus, ta, tū, lifted vp, mounted, aduāced.

Sublegere sermonem, Clam nostrum hūc illæ sublegerunt sermonem, Priuily they harkned, and bare away all that we cōmuned. *Plautus in milite.*

Sublego, are, to substitute.
Sublego, legi, legere, to steale. also to chese an other into the place of him that is deed.
Sublestus, ta, tum, feble, faynt, lyght, of noo force or value.
Subleuo, are, to helpe, or ayde, to defende, to lyfte vp, to sustayne.
Sublica, a proppe, a shore, a poste, or other lyke thynge, to sustayn or kepe a thing vp.
Sublicius, a briege at Rome.
Subligaculum, a nether coyfe or brieche.
Subligar, garis, idem.
Subligo, gare, to vnderbynde.
Sublimis, me, high, that which is aboue vs.
Sublimitas, heyght.
Sublimiter, highly, on height.
Sublimo, mare, to sette on high.
Sublino, liniui, nire, to annoynt or touche, to paynt or stayne.
Sublinitio, the fyrste colour that is layde or dyed. also staynynge with colours.
Sublitio, onis, the grounde colour, wheron the perfyte colour is layde, in cloth dyed, it is callyd grasynge.
Subluceo, cere, to shyne sommewhat, or to gyue a lyttell lyght.
Sublucide, somewhat lyght.
Sublucidus, da, dum, somewhat lyght.
Subluco, care, to vndershrede boughes, that the

that the lyght may come vnder the tree.
Subdialia, places without the house to walk in without couerynges.
Subducere, to go away by stelthe, that noo man do perceyue.
Sub iugum mitti, to be subdued, it was propzely whan a battayle was vanquished, the vanquishers caused thre speares to be set vp lyke a galowes, and constrayned them that were vanquyshed to go vnderneth it, in token that they were subdued, whyche was the greattest reproche that moughte be deuysed.

Cæsar de bell. gall. lib. 2. Subluere, to vnderwashe, as water, whyche runneth lowe vnder a banke or hylle, and washeth the foote thereof. Also to washe somewhat cleane.

Sublustris, tre, that hath some lyght.
Subluuies, a disease of cattell, whiche is betwixte the cleys of their fete.

Cice. pro Planco. Sub manu habere, to haue at hande.
Sub manu esse, to be at hande or redy.
Sub manu, after hande, forthewith.

Plautus in milite. Sub manus, easily, handsomly. Bono animo es, negotium omne iam succedit submanus. Be of good chere, all the matter is come to passe handsomly. Lepide hoc succedit sub manus negotium, This matter commeth well and easily to passe.

Sub merum, almoste pure.
Subminia, a womans garment.
Subministro, are, to do seruice vnder one, to gyue or delyuer any thing that is asked for.
Subministrator, he that serueth vnder another man, he that delyuereth any thynge that is callyd for.
Submissim, & submisse, softely, propzely in speakynge. also humbly.
Submissus, a, um, humble.

Cę. de bel. gall. lib. 5. Submitto, tere, to sende priuily or by stelth.
Submittere, to sende or brynge in the mean tyme. Also to put or set vnder propzely, as a calfe, a lambe, or a fole, is sette vnder the damme to sucke.
Submittere se, to humble hym selfe.
Submittere capillum, to let heare to growe.
Submoneo, nere, to warne one priuyly.
Submordeo, dere, to bite softely, or priuily.

Colum. 5. Plin. Submoueo, uere, to remoue or carie a thing farre of. also to dryue out of a place. also to discharge a man of his offyce.
Subnecto, tere, to bynde to, or hange to, also to subscribe.
Subnego, gare, to denye somewhat.
Subneruo, are, to cut synewes.
Subnexio, a byndynge or hangyng to.
Subniger, gra, grum, somewhat blacke.
Subnitor, nixus, niti, to leane agaynst a thing to be sustayned vp.

Subnodo, are, to make a knot vnder a thing.
Subnoto, tare, to note or marke.
Subo, are, to brymme as a bore dothe whan he getteth pygges.

Cic. ad Q. fratrem. Suboffendo, dere, to offende sommewhat, or a lyttelle.
Suboleo, lere, to sauour or smelle a lyttell.
Subopto, tare, to desyre a lyttell.
Subordior, dire, to begynne.
Suborno, nare, to prayse or honour, also to suborne or brynge in a false wytnesse, or messanger, or fayne one persone for another, to deceyue with.
Suborior, riris, riri, to begynne to sprynge or aryse, as the sonne dothe. to prayse or honour one with wordes. also to deceyue priuylye.
Suppudeo, dere, to be somewhat ashamed.
Subremigo, are, to rowe vnder.
Subrepo, psi, pere, to steale away or runne a waye priuyly.
Subrepere animo, to entre sodaynly or priuyly into the mynde.
Subreptio, theft, or a fals suggestion.
Subreptitiæ literæ, letters stollen oute by a fals suggestion.
Subreptitius, a, um, stollen or falsly come by.
Subrideo, risi, dere, to smyle or laugh priuily
Subripeo, to steale, to take away secretely, sometyme to lyfte vp hastily.
Subrisio, & subrisus, a smylyng.
Subrogo, gare, to substitute or subrogate, to make a deputie in an office, to put in an nother mans roume.
Subrufus, a, um, & subrubeus, a, um, somwhat redde. Subrumi, lambes that do sucke.
Subrumor, ari, to be souckeled, or putte to sucke as calfes, lambes. ⁊c.
Subruo, ere, to enter with force, or priuily by litle and lytle. also to dygge the erthe.
Subsanno, are, to scorne or mocke.
Subsannatio, a mocke with bendynge the browes, and snuffynge vp of the nose.
Subsannator, a mocker.
Subsarcinis, with trusses or burdeyns.

Cl. In Ver. Asco. F.d. Subscribo, scripsi, scribere, to write vnder, to subscribe, to fauour a matter, to assygne a cause why, to affirme.
Subscriptores, they whiche in causes iudyciall do fauour the parte of the accuser or playntyfe.
Subscudes, the vtter table, wheruunto other tables are fastned.
Subseco, care, to cutte vnder or cut a lyttell.
Subsellia, bēches, which were vnder hygher seates, they were also benches, on the whiche Judges dyd sytte.
Subsentio, sensi, sentire, to perceiue somwhat
Subsequor, queris, sequi, to folow forthwith.

Bb   Subs

Subsero, serere, to sowe or set vnder a thing
Subseuio, seuire, to serue, to accord, or agre.
Subsessæ, scoutwatches, wherby hostes of men are intrapped as they passe.
Subsideo, sedi, subsedére, to sytte vnder, to laye in awayte for one.
Subsidium, ayde.
Subsido, dere, to fall downe, to auale.
Subsigno, nare, to subscribe or write vnder.
Subsilio, liui, lire, & subsulto, sultare, to leape a lyttelle.
Subsilles, lytle plates belonging to sacrifice.
Subsimus, he that hath a campse nose.
Subsipere, to sauour somwhat.
Subsisiuum, that which foloweth or is next.
Subsisto, stiti, sistere, to resyste, to abyde, to be by hym selfe.
Subsolanus, the easte wynde.
Subsono, are, to sowne a lyttell, to make a lyttell noyse.
Subsortitio, a deputation, whan one maketh an other his deputie.
Subsortitus, a substytute.
Substantia, substance. also matter. somtyme goodes, whyche is also commonly callyd substaunce.
Substerno, straui, sternere, to strawe or laye vnder any thynge, as russhes, carpettes, and flowres.
Substillum, a ryme or fallynge myste, or a droppynge before and after rayne, It ys also a sicknes, whā a man may not pisse wel
Substituo, tui, tuere, to substitute in the place of an nother.
Substo, stiti, are, to sustain or abide constātly.
Substratus, a, ū, strawed vnder, or lay'd vnder
Substrepo, pere, to make a lyttell noyse.
Substringo, xi, gere, to shrinke vnderneth.
Substruo, truere, to vnderpynne a house.
Substructio, vnderpynnynge or groundyng of a house.
Substupeo, & substupesco, scere, to be some what dismayde.
Substupidus, somwhat dismayde or abashed.
Subsulto, tare, to ioumpe.
Subsultim, by iumpes.
Subsuo, suere, to sowe vnderneth.
Subsum, subesse, to be vnder, or within.
Subtal, the holownes of the fote. also the paulme of the hande.
Subtegmen, minis, the threede, whyche in weauynge is callyd the woufe.
Subtegulanea, places vnder the eueyse of howses.
Subtendo, dere, to purpose or diuyse anye thynge, to deceyue an nother manne, or to laye any thynge in a mannes waye for the same purpose.
Subtento, tare, to espye.

Subtepeo, pere, to be somwhat warme.
Subtepidus, da, dum, somewhat warme.
Subter, vnder.
Subterraneus, ea, eum, that whiche is vnder the grounde.
Subtercludo, dere, to shutte vnder.
Subterduco, cere, to withdrawe, to scape away.
Subterfluo, xi, fluere, to runne or flowe vnder a thynge, as water vnder a brydge.
Subterfugio, gere, to escape.
Subtergredior, di, to go vndernethe.
Subtero, riui, terere, to broyse, or weare. *Plaut*
Subticeo, cui, cére, to aunswere nothynge to that which is spoken. Subticesco, scere, idē
Subtondeo, dere, to clyppe vnder.
Subtraho, xi, trahere, to take away, to steale, *Plin.*
Subtrahere se, to draw vnto quietnes. Subtrahere famæ, to withdrawe from bruyte.
Subtrahere inuidiæ, to eschewe enuy.
Subtristis, te, somewhat heuy or sorye.
Subturpis, pe, somewhat foule, in part foule or dishoneste, the matter or thinge dishoneste, couered with cleane wordes.
Subucula, a shyrte. also a cake.
Subueho, uexi, uehere, to beare.
Subuecto, tare, to beare or cary often.
Subuenio, ueni, uenire, to helpe. *Festus*
Subuerbusta, meate burned on the spytte.
Subuerto, tere, to tourne vp so downe. alsoo to distroy, to subuerte.
Subuerso, sare, to subuerte often.
Subueteribus, was a place in Rome.
Subula, an aulle, that cordyners doo vse for a bodkyn.
Subulcus, a swyneherde.
Subulo, an harte hauynge hornes without tynes, callyd as I suppose, a spyttarde.
Subuolo, lare, to flee away.
Suburbanum, a maner or ferme without the walles of the citie.
Suburbia, the suburbes of a citie or towne.
Suburrana regio, the strete in Rome where the brothell houses were.
Subuulturius, a, um, that whiche apprehendeth men lyke as raupnes do carrayne.
Succedaneus, a, um, that whiche succedeth.
Succedere, to entre. Et nostris succede penatibus hospes, And enter thou my frende into my howse.
Succedere, to go vnder a thyng. Succedere, to spede wel, to be at a good poynt. Hāc nō succesit, alia aggrediamur uia, This way it spedeth not, let vs go to an other way.
Succedo, cessi, cedere, to succede.
Succendo, dere, to inflame to burne.
Succēseo, ui, ere, to be āgry for a good cause.
Succento, tonis, was a certayne garmente, whiche onely hoores dyd weare.
Succento, tare, to synge a base.

Succens

Succentor, toris, he that syngeth a base.
Succenturiatus, he that made vp the number of the bende of men that lacked.
Succenturio, are, to make vp the number of a hundred souldiours, or of that company that was callyd Centuria.
Succerda, swynes dunge.
Succerno, creui, cernere, to raunge meale in a syeue.
Successio, successyon.
Successor, soris, a successour.
Successorē dare, to depose a mā of his office.
Successus, a, um, that whyche prosperouslye happeneth, or spedeth well.
Successus, us, successe, be it good or yll.
Succida, woulle vnwashed.
Succidaneę hostiæ, beastes for sacrifice, whiche were kylled in the seconde place, or nexte to the fyrste.
Succidaneus, a, um, that whyche folowethe the fyrste.
Succidia, a piece or flyche of bakon salted. also larde.
Succido, cidi, cidere, to felle or cutte downe. also to falle vnder.

Plautus in Curcu. Succiduus, a, um, that whiche dothe succede or folowe. also lowe, redy to falle downe.
Succidusda, dum, moyst, or full of iuyse.
Succingo, xi, gere, to gyrde. Also to enuyron or compasse. Fruſtra ſe terrore succinxerit, qui ſeptus charitate non fuerit, armis.n. arma irritantur, In vayne shall he enuyron hym selfe with terriblenesse, which is not wallyd aboute with the loue of his countreye. For with vyolence, vyolence is styred.
Succingulum, a swordegyrdell.
Succino, cinere, to make a soft noise, to singe a base or tenour.
Succincta oratio, a compendiouse or shorte oracyon.
Succinctè, compendiousely.
Succinctorium, a shorte iackette or ierkyn.
Succinctus, ta, tum, gyrte.
Succinum, aumbre, whereof somme beade stones are made.
Succinus, na, num, of aumbre.
Succisiuum tempus, tyme of leysure, vacant from busynesse.
Succlamo, are, to crye softely.
Succollo, are, to putte vnder the necke or shulders, to beare a thynge.
Succortrila, a small voyce and a shryll.
Succresco, scere, to growe vnder, or lowe, or a lyttell and lyttell.
Succubo, bare, to lye vnder.
Succubonium, idem quod succuba, she that lyeth vnder.
Succubi, deuylles, whiche in the fourme of women, do company with men.

Succulentus, ta, tum, full of iuyse.
Succiplenus, idem.
Succumbo, cubui, cumbere, to be subdued, to be ioyned to, to falle downe vnder an heuy burdeyn, to fayle for feblenesse.
Succurro, ere, to help, to com to remēbrāce.
Suctus, tus, suckynge.
Succus, cus, cui, the suckynge of mylke.
Succus, iuyce or humour, whiche the body receyueth of meate and drynke, also generally all maner of iuyse.
Succussarius, & succussor, a trottyng horse.
Succuso, nis, idem.
Succusso, are, to shake as a horse doth whan he trotteth. also to trotte.
Succussatio, succussura, & succussatura, the trottynge or shakynge of a horse.
Succutio, cussi, tere, to shake a thynge.
Succula, a sowe pygge, also a certayn inner garment. also a certayne company of sterres, callyd the .vii. sterres, whiche do appiere the .xii. Calendes of June, and be callyd succulæ & Hiades.
Sudarium, a napkynne.
Sudes, a certayne speare, whiche is burned at the ende.
Sudo, dare, to sweate, to laboure soore, to haue moche to do.
Sudor, doris, sweate.
Sudum, the clere parte of the firmamente betwene cloudes. Also the clere fyrmamēt without cloudes.
Suefacio, & suefio, fieri, to be wont.
Suere aliquid capiti, to get a shrewde turne. Metuo lenonem, ne quid suo suat capiti, I am aferde of the bawde, leste he gette a shrewde tourne.
Suesco, sueui, suescere, to be wonte.
Sueui, a people in high Germany.
Sueuia, a countrey in Germanye.
Suffarcinatus, nata, natum, laded, truffed.
Suffarcino, nare, to lade or bourdeyne, to truffe vppe.
Suffarraneus, he that carieth meale or floure to any place to selle in lyttell quantytie.
Suffectus, is he, whyche an officer beynge deed, or remoued, is sette in his place.
Suffes, was amonge the Carthaginensis, as the Consul was at Rome.
Suffibulum, was an attyre, whiche the nunnes of Vesta dydde weare on theyr heedes, whan they dydde sacrifice, and was lyke to the tyres, whiche wyues of London dydde weare, and becamme theym moche better than bonettes of veluette doo nowe, wherwith they mocke ladyes and gentyllwomenne, and therby oncly doo gette the name to be callydde Maskynge ladyes.

Suffero, sufferre, to sustayne, to put vnder, to suffre.
Sufficio, feci, sufficere, to suffyse, to indure, to minister, to substitute, to stayne.
Sufficit, it suffyseth.
Suffimentum, perfume, or fumigation.
Suffio, fiui, fire, to perfume.
Suffiscus, the codde of a ramme, which was made for a purse, to conteyne money.
Suffitio, & suffitus, tus, a perfume or fumigacyon.
Suffitor, toris, he that bloweth the fyre.
Suffitus, ta, tum, perfumed.
Sufflamen, that wherwith a whiele is retained or stopped of his course.
Sufflatio, a blowynge.
Sufflator, toris, he that bloweth.
Sufflatus, ta, tum, blowen.
Sufflo, are, to blowe.
Suffocatio, a stranglynge.
Suffocator, he that strangleth.
Suffoco, care, to stop the breth, to strangle.
Suffodio, fossi, dere, to dygge vnder.
Suffossus equus, a stumblynge horse.
Suffragator, toris, a supporter or maintener.
Suffragium, the voyce of people assemblyd in gyuyng their consent. also helpe or succour. also a wrecke in the see.
Suffragines, the iointes of the hinder legge of a beaste, callyd the howx, sometyme it doth signifie the pasternes, they be alsoo the yonge sprynges of vynes.
Suffraginosi equi, horses, whyche haue the paynes or scratches.
Suffragor, garis, gari, to beare fauour.
Suffulcio, cij, cire, to proppe vp.
Suffulcior, cire, to be proppid vp or vnderset.
Suffundatum, vnderlayde.
Suffundo, dere, to caste downe or poure lycour on a thynge, to caste abrode.
Suffundo, dare, to buylde or sette vppon a foundation.
Suffuror, rari, to steale priuily.
Suffusio, a webbe in the eye.
Suffusus, a, um, sprynkled, indewed.
Suggero, gessi, gerere, to mynyster or gyue a thynge, to sende for the thynges, wherof are plentie.
Suggerere sumptus, to alowe expenses.
Suggestus, uel suggestum, a pulpitte or high place, oute of the whyche Oratours or Capytaynes made proposytions vnto the people.
Suggrundia, the euyse of a house, whyche defendeth the walles from rayne.
Suggrundaria, buryals of yonge infantes.
Suggrundatio, the eueysynge of a house.
Suggillo, lare, to make a blacke spotte in the skynne with beatynge. It is alsoo to scorne, to detracte, or infame, to reproue, to condempne.
Suggillatus, spotted, mocked, detracted, infamed, condemned.
Suggillatio, is a a marke in the visage black or blue, made by some stroke, a mocke, a detraction, an infamation behynde one, a condemnation.
Sugo, & sugeo, suxi, sugere, to souke.
Suinus, a, um, & suillus, a, um, of a sowe.
Sulcatim, in furrowes.
Sulco, care, to falowe.
Sulcus, cus, a furrowe. Serere tertio quarto quinto sulco, To sowe in the thyrde, the fourthe, the fyfthe falowe.
Sometyme it is put of a dyche. Also any maner of cuttynge of the erthe. proprely it signifyeth any thynge that is longe and sharpe edged. Bisulcum animal, A beaste that hath the fete clouen with two talons.
Sulla, was a cruell tyrant of the Romayns callyd also Sylla.
Sulmo, monis, a towne in the countraye of Peligna, where Ouidius the poete was borne.
Sulmonensis, a manne or woman of the citie of Sulmo.
Sulphuraria, a place where brymstone is boyled.
Sulphur, phuris, brymstone.
Sulphureus, ea, eum, of brymstone.
Sulphuratus, ta, tum, dressed with brimstone.
Sultanus, a sowdane, whiche was the name of the kynge of Egipte and Siria.
Sum, I am, es, thou arte, est, he is.
Sumanus, he that alway taketh.
Sũ Amphitrionis, I am Amphitrions seruãt. *Plaut.*
Sunt mihi bis septem prestanti corpore nymphæ, I haue fourctene maydens of excellent beautie. *Terentius*
Sum in mora illi, I make hym to tarie.
Sum in metu, I am aferde.
Sum in noxia, I am put in the blame.
Sum, olde wryters vsed for eum, hym. *No. Mar.*
Sit uestra benignitas ad audiendum? Pleasith you to here? *Plautus in milite.*
Sunt septem dies, It is seuen dayes agone. Howe this verbe Sum, shulde be sette and construed, rede Calepines vocabuler, also loke for Est, fuit, and such other partes of sum, in their letters before.
Sumanalia, a great cake made lyke a whele, suche as is made at brydales and churche goinges.
Summam facere, to summe a booke of accompte.
Sumen, minis, is made of the pappes of a sowe, cutte from hir the day after that she hath varowed, ad is powdred with salt.
Sume-

S ante V.

Cicero. Sumere, to hyre. Quoad enim peruentum, quo sumpta nauis est, non domini nauis est, sed nauigantium. Untylle they come to the place whither the shyppe was hyred, the shyppe is not the owners but theyrs, whiche are passagers.

Terent. in phormi. Sumere, to borowe.

Sumere, to spende or bestowe on one. In mala vxore, atq inimico, si quid sumas, sumptus est. On a shrewd wyfe, and an ennemy, what so euer thou bestowest, is waste.

Plautus in milite. Sumere aquam e puteo, to drawe water out of the welle.

Plautus in cap. Sumere confidentiã, to trust, to take corage.

Sumere mutuum, to borowe.

Plautus in Bacch. Sumere obsequium animo, to reioyce, to take comforte.

Terentius Sumere operam frustra, to labour in vayne.

Sumere optionem, to chuse.

Sumere personam, to counterfaite an other.

Sumere supplicium, to punyshe.

Summa, is a collection of thinges or wordes. also the principall poynte of a matter.

Sumates, the chief psons of a realme or citie.

Summatim, & summate, compendiously by euery parte of the matter, summarily. Ad summum duo, two at the moste.

Summe, excellently, chiefly.

Summenianæ uxores, hoores kepte in the stede of wyues.

Summenium, a place where bawdrye was kepte without the walles of a towne.

Summissi, murmurers.

Summissim, & summisse, softly, not lowde.

Summissus, a, um, base, lowe.

Summitas, heyght, or hygheneffe.

Summitudo, dinis, the height of a thynge.

Summitto, misi, mittere, to conuay in priuily, also to suffre to growe.

Summittere barbam, to lette the berde growe, to let to departe.

Summoenius, nia, um, that whyche is vnder the walles.

Summo, are, to make hyghest.

Cice. pro A. Cæsina. Summo iure agere, to take the rigour or extremitie of the lawe in suite.

Summum fastigiũ imponere, to finishe a thyng perfitely, to brynge a mattier to a poynt.

Summam manum addere, idem significat.

Summus, a, um, hyghest, extreme, greattest, or very commendable.

Summum, at the moste.

Varro de re rust. Sumo, sumpsi, sumere, to take vppon one, to take generally, to hyre, to consume.

Sumptifacio, cere, to spende.

Sumpti, for sumptus, plurali numero.

Sumptuariæ leges, lawes made for restraynynge of outragious expenses.

Sumptuarius, a, um, that whyche dothe pertayne to expenses.

Sumptuose, sumptuously, chargeably.

Sumptuosus, a, um, sumptuouse.

Sumptus, ta, tum, taken, or chosen.

Sumptus, tus, expense.

Sunium, a promontorie or elbowe of the countrey of Attica.

Suo, sui, suere, to sowe, to ioyne or make fast togyther.

Suopte ingenio, of his owne propre wytte.

Sup, for super, aboue.

Supellectilis, le, & supellex, household stuffe, all thynges mouable within the house.

Supellecticarius, a bondman or slaue, whyche is accompted for chatell.

Super, & supra, vppon aboue.

Super Garamantas & Indos proferet imperium, He shal aduance his empyre beyond the Garamantians and Indianes. **Vergil.**

Super Euclionis filiã, of Eucliones daughter

Super cœnam, at supper.

Super hęc, more ouer than this. **Plautus in Aulularia**

Super Priamus, super Hectore, of Priam, of Hector. Hac supre scribã ad te Rhegio, Of that mater I wil write vnto you fre Regiũ. **Plinius e pist. 87. Epist. 91. Vergilius.**

Super for propter. Nec super ipse sua molitur laude laborem, Nor he taketh the peyne for his prayse.

Super, for valde, His accensa sup, with those wordes she beinge kendlyd or styred. **Vergilius.**

Superaddo, dere, to putte or adde to.

Superbe, proudely. Superbiter, idem.

Superbia, pryde. Superbio, ire, to be proude.

Superbiloquens, & superbiloquus, he that speaketh proudely, or hautely.

Superbiloquentia, proude or haute wordes.

Superbos, olde wryters vsed for mortuos, deed, bycause of the pompe, whiche was at their burienge. Faciam ego hodie te superbum, nisi hinc abis, I wil kyl the, if thou gette the not hens. **Plautus in Amphi.**

Superbum bellum, vniust or vnhappy warre. **Vergil.**

Superbus, proude, sometyme magnifyke or noble, also hyghe, ornate, or garnysshed, ryche, wycked.

Supercido, dere, to falle on.

Superciliosus, soure in countenance.

Supercilium, the ouerbrowe. sommetyme it sygnifyeth pride, grauitie. It is alsoo the haunce, whiche is ouer the doore.

Superciliũ attollere, to be stately or proude.

Supercilium ponere, to laye aparte pryde or stately countenance.

Supercresco, scere, to ouergrowe.

Supercubo, bare, to lye ouer.

Superduco, cere, to put or lay on.

Superedo, dere, to eate after a thynge.

Superessit, for supererit, shall lyue, or be left on lyue. Supcrest, he lyueth, or is on lyue.

Bb iiij Supera

S ante V.

Terent. in phorm. Superest, there is plentie or more thanne ynough. Aliis quia defit, quod amant, ægre est: tibi quia superest, dolet, Some bicause they lacke the thynge that they loue, be discontent: and thou arte sorye that thou haste more than thou nedest.

Terent. in Heaut. Superesse, to be the reste or resydue. Porro ausculta quod superest fallatiæ, But yet here what was the resydue of that craft or deceyte. To defende or pleade for one. Cūctari se, ne si superesset, eriperet legibus reū, He wolde tary, leste yf he came and spake for hym, he shulde delyuer an offender.

Superexto, rare, to remayne ouer.
Superficiariæ ædes, houses buylded on the lande of an nother man than buylded them.
Superficiarius, he that hathe a house of his owne buylded on an other mans grounde, and payeth therfore a quyte rent.
Superficies, the ouermost part of any thing.
Superfœtatio, oone conception of a chylde after an other.
Superfluo, fluxi, fluere, to abounde, or be superfluouse.
Superflue, superfluousely. Superfluo, idem.
Superfluus, a, um, superfluous.

Sidonius. Superforaneus, a, um, idem.
Superfundo, dere, to poure vppon.
Supergredior, gredi, to go aboue.
Supera, for supra.
Superiacio, ieci, iacere, to caste on or lay on.
Superiiceo, superieci, iicere, to cast vpon, to laye vppon.
Superi, they whiche ben in heuen.
Superincido, dere, to falle on.
Superior, hygher.
Superior ætas, the tyme or age passed.
Superlachrimo, to wepe or droppe vpon.
Supermeo, are, to go ouer, or slyppe ouer.
Supernato, natare, to swymme ouer.
Supernati, they which haue the hinder part of the thighes next the buttockes cut away
Superne, a hygh, aboue.
Supernia, the inwarde part and hindermost parte of the thyghes nexte the buttockes cutte of.
Supernus, na, num, high, or ouer. Superna regio, the high countrey.
Supernumerarius, that whiche is in surplusage, aboue the true number.
Supero, rare, to go ouer. Also to vanquishe or ouercome. also to ouerlyue. somtyme to kylle. Quod superat, whiche is more, or is lefte in a surplusage.
Superpondium, ouerweight, that whiche is added to the iuste weight.
Supersedeo, dere, to omytte or leaue to doo a thynge.

Ci. Seruio Supersedeas hoc labore itineris, take not the peyne to come nowe, or forbeare the peyn takyng in this iourney.
Supersede istis rebus, let these thinges alone
Supersede istis uerbis, let these wordis passe, holde thy tunge.

Plautus in Epidico. Plautus in persa. Plin. epist. 102.

Supersedi scribere, I forbare to wryte, I left vnwriten.
Superstes, stitis, he that ouerliueth or remaineth alyue afterthat other be deed, also alyue. sometyme present, olde writers callyd Superstites, wytnesses.
Superstes, he that is saulfe. Deos quæso, ut sis superstes, I beseche god saue you, longe mought you lyue. also present. Superstitem utrunque monui, ne inuisi abeant, I aduysed them both, that they shoulde not departe with dyspleasure.
Superstitio, a superfluous or vayne religion or deuotion, an honouryng of that which ought not to be honored, a vaine reuerēce or feare towarde that thing, wherin is no efficacye or power, but by the illusyon of the dyuelle: as diuination by the cryenge or fleinge of byrdes, obseruation of times, and dreames, and other lyke vanites.
Superstitiosi, they which be tymorous without cause, fearinge that god is displeased, where there is none offence done: They were at the fyrste soo callyd, bycause they contynually prayid and offred to the goddis, to preserue theyr chyldern, that they mought ouerlyue them. Finally euery vndiscrete or vnreasonable deuocion or religion, may be callyd Superstition.
Superstito, stitare, to make hoole or recouer frome deathe.
Supersto, stare, to stande vppon.
Superstruo, struxi, struere, to buylde on.
Supersum, Superesse, to abounde, to remain, to vanquishe, to be superfluous, to indure.
Superuacaneus, a, um, superfluous.
Superuacuus, a, um, not necessarie.
Superuaganea auis, was of the diuinours or sothsayers callyd that byrde, which cried from the toppe of any thynge.
Superuenio, nire, to com vnloked for, to com vpon or after an other thynge.
Superuiuo, uixi, uiuere, to recouer from peryll of dethe, or whan a man semeth to be deade.
Superus, a, um, the highest or ouermost.
Superum mare, the see, which is callid Mare Hadriaticum, wherin standeth the Citie of Uenyce.
Supinus, na, num, vpryghte, the bealye vp vpwarde. somtyme it sygnifieth on an hyll or hygh place.

Horatius.

Suppar, almoste euen.
Supparasitor, taris, tari, to folowe and flatter for

for a mans dyner.

Supparium, a clothe or curtayne hanged vp where interludes were playde.

Supparus, uel supparum, a smocke. it is also a topsayle of a shyppe.

Suppedaneum, a foote stoole.

Suppedito, tare, to subdue, to minyster sufficiently, also to oppresse.

Plautus in Asinar. Suppedito, tare, to endure. Ac stomacho nō queo labori suppeditare, My stomake wyll not lette me indure the laboure. Alsoo to furnyshe expenses, to gyue as moche as a man wolde haue. Nam si illi pergam, suppeditare sumptibus Menedeme, mihi illæc

Terent. in Heautont. uero ad rastros res redit, Surely Menedemus, yf I wold gyue hym as moche as he wolde spende, that thynge wolde brynge me to the poynt to rake for my lyuynge.

Suppeditare, to subdewe or treade vnder. Nunc, uideo, in iudicio mecum contendere non uis, ubi suppeditari turpissimum, superare pulcherrimum est, Nowe I perceyue thou wylte not contende with me before iudges, where it were a great shame to be subdued, and very moche honestie to haue the better.

Suppetiæ, & suppetias, ayde or succours.

Suppeto, tii, tere, to aske priuily or craftily.

Suppetit, it is in a redynesse.

Plautus in Asinar. Suppetior, ari, to succour or ayde.

Suppetunt dictis data, aut facta. Non suppetunt dictis data, He perfourmeth not that, that he promysed. Vtinam quæ dicis dictis facta suppetant, wold god thou woldest do as thou sayest, or wolde god thy dedes did agree with thy wordes.

Plautus in Ruden. Suppetit lucrum, there is gayne sufficiente.
Res ita suppetit, the matter so requireth.

Plautus in Amphit. Suppetias mihi, Brynge to me succoures, ayde me.

Suppetias adueni, come and helpe me.

Suppetias ferre, to ayde or succour.

Suppilo, are, to steale vnderhand or craftily.

Supplanto, tare, to putte vnder the foote, to ouerthrowe, to supplant or deceyue, in preuentynge one to his hynderance or damage, to vnderplante or set a tree or vyne.

Supplaudo, si, dere, to reioyse priuely.

Supplementum, that whiche supplyethe or maketh vp that whiche lacketh in quantitie or numbre.

Suppleo, plere, to make vp that whiche lacketh, to make euyn.

Supplex, plicis, he that desyreth any thynge knelynge or prostrate.

Supplicatio, a prayer, a requeste.

Supplicassis pro supplicaueris.

Supplicans, tis, he that desyreth a thynge.

Suppliciter, humbly knelynge.

Supplicium, payne, tourmente, or execution of dethe. sometyme supplicia, are prayers. Salust. in bell. cat. Iugurt.

Supplitia pendere, to be put to execution.

Supplico, care, to beseche humbly.

Supplimentum, a makynge vp of a number, whiche lacketh or is minished.

Supplodo, plosi, ere, to stampe or make noyse with the fete. also to reiecte or caste away. Cor. Tacitus lib. 13.

Supplosio, a stampynge or noyse made with the fete.

Suppono, sui, nere, to put vnder, to put into the place of an other, to sette a false or fayned thynge in the place of that whiche is the very true thynge.

Supportare, to brynge or carie priuily. Cæsar de bell. Gall. lib. 7.

Suppositio, the puttinge or settyng of a fayned or fals thyng in the place of the thing selfe, as one chylde for an nother.

Suppostrix, she that cōmytteth that falshod.

Suppositus partus, whan the chylde of one woman is layde with an nother womanne, whiche is not the very mother, as though she had borne it.

Subprædes, counterfureties, they whyche are bounden to the sureties, to saue them harmelesse.

Suppressus, sa, sum, drowned, beaten vnder. Iustinus. Victi Persi in naues confugerunt, ex quibus multę suppressæ, multæ captę, The Persians fledde vnto their shyppes, whereof many were drowned, and many taken. Also hyd or concyled.

Supprimo, pressi, supprimere, to kepe downe to kepe secrete, to kepe in sylence.

Supprimere iter, to stay or omitte a iourney. Cæf. in cō. de bello ciuili li. 1. Plautus in milite.

Suppromo, psi, mere, to drawe out drynke.

Suppromus, a butlar. Bono cellà suppromo credita, The cellar or buttrie was cōmytted to a good butlar.

Suppudet, I am halfe ashamed, thou art half ashamed, or he is halfe ashamed.

Suppurantia, & suppuratio, matterynge of a sore.

Suppuratorius, ria, um, that whyche pertaynethe to impostumes, or to make a sore to matter.

Suppuro, are, to matter or be an impostume.

Suppuratio, an impostume or sore that hath matter.

Supra, aboue, or ouer.

Supra q̃, for supra id quod.

Supreme, hyghest of all, or aboue all.

Supremus, ma, mum, the highest or greatest of all other.

Supus, olde wryters vsed for supinus.

Sura, the cause of the legge. sometyme the hole shanke or legge from the kne downe.

Surculaceus, & surcularis, re, that which bringeth forth yonge settes or springes of trees

Sur

Surculus, a yonge set or slyppe, a nursegarden, also a slyppe of a tree or yong gresse.
Surcus, a stake.
Surculosus, a, um, full of slyppes.
Surdaster, he that is somwhat deafe and can not here.
Surdè, deafely.
Surdeo, dui, dére, to be deafe.
Surdesco, scere, to waxe deafe or be deafe.
Surditas, deafenesse.
Surdo, dare, to make deafe.
Surdus, da, dum, deafe, also that which hath no sauour.
Surrentum, a towne in Campania.
Surrentinus, na, num, of that towne.
Surregit, olde writers vsed for surgit, wherof commeth surrectio, a rysynge.
Surrepo, pere, to crepe vnder.
Surreptitius, a, um, that whiche is doone by stelthe that none other man knoweth it.
Surgo, surrexi, surgere, to ryse, also to growe or sprynge. *Vergil.*
Surrigo, surrexi, surrigere, to lyfte vp.
Surrigere aures, to laye his eare to a thyng, to harken. *Plautus in Amphit.*
Surripere operam, Clanculum abij a legione, operam hanc surripui tibi, I departed pryuyly from the hoste, this tyme haue I borowed to do you pleasure. *Plautus in Mene.*
Surripere se, to steale his away. Vt surripuisti te mihi dudū de foro? O, how diddest thou steale away frō me late out of the market?
Surripio, ripui, pere, to steale or take awaye priuily. also to lyft vp on hygh, to preuent.
Surpiculus, a baskette or hamper.
Surrogo, gare, to substitute, or put in an nother mannes place.
Surrogatio, a substitution. *Ci. in partitiōibus oratorijs.*
Sursum, aboue. Sursum uersum, vpwarde.
Sursum deorsum, vp and downe.
Sus, for sursum.
Suscio, scire, for scio, scire, to knowe.
Suscipere fidem, to promyse. Quas partes impleturum te, secundum susceptam fidem confido, whyche parte I truste thou wilt perfourme, accordyng to the promyse that thou madest.
Suscito, tare, to awake one out of his slepe, to call one to his warke. *Plautus in milite. in Ruden.*
Sus, suis, a sowe.
Sus Mineruam, a prouerbe applyed vnto hym, whyche presumeth to teache or correcte one, of whome he rather oughte to be taught or corrected.
Suillus, la, lum, of a sowe.
Susq; deq; fero, & susq; deq; habeo, I force not, I recke not, I care not.
Susa, a great citie in Persia.
Suscipio, scepi, scipere, to take. Suscipere liberos, to gette chyldrene.
Suscitabulum, a prouocation or sterynge.
Suscito, tare, to styre or prouoke.
Suspecto, tare, to beholde aboue. sometyme to see benethe, or to loke downe. *Mart.*
Suspendeo, dere, to be hanged ouer or an high, also to appere a lyttell. *Columel. Cicero.*
Suspendiosus, he that is hanged.
Suspensus, a, um, hanged vp.
Suspensus, he that douteth to speake or do.
Suspensa manu, timorously, doubtefully. *Plin. epist. 98. li. 6. Terent. in phorm.*
Suspenso gradu, Hæc ubi ego audiui, ad fores superiso gradu, placide ire perrexi, whan I harde those wordes, I went to the doore fayre and softly.
Suspendium, hangynge. suspensio idem.
Suspendo, dere, to hange vp, to be doubteful or sorowefull. Suspensus animo, hauynge doubte, or beinge adradde.
Suspenso gradu incedere, to go softely without makynge noyse.
Suspicio, spexi, spicere, to loke vp, also to honour, to answere.
Suspicans, he that hath suspicion, suspecting
Suspicor, cari, to haue suspicion, to suspecte. also to suppose.
Suspectus, ta, tum, suspected.
Suspicio, onis, suspicyon.
Suspiciosus, suspecyouse.
Suspiratus, tus, a syghe.
Suspiriosus, shorte wynded, or he whyche fetcheth his brethe paynfully.
Suspirium, a syghe.
Suspiro, are, to sygh. also to desyre feruētly.
Sussilio, lire, for subsilio.
Sustendere insidias, to lay watche.
Sustentaculum, that whiche sustayneth or beareth vp a thynge.
Sustento, tare, to sustayne or beare vp.
Sustineo, nui, nere, to holde vp, to suffre, to forbeare, to fede, to refrayne.
Sustollo, tuli, tollere, to lyfte vp.
Sustollere animos, to be proude, or to haue an hygh courage.
Sustollere æs alienum, to pay dettes. *Plin. de uiris illust.*
Sustollere puerum, to brynge vp a chylde.
Sustulit, is proprely of the father, as peperit, is of the mother.
Sustuli, I haue had, I haue broughte vp, I haue lyfte vp.
Susurratio, a whysterynge.
Susurro, are, to whyster.
Susurro, ronis, a whysterer. also he whyche with fals and secrete reporte maketh dissencyon betwene men.
Susurrus, & susurrium, a whystrynge, or softe murmurynge, or suche noyse as trees doo make with the wynde, or a ryuer whan it runneth, or byrdes whan they chatter.
Suta

Sutatis, a seamster or shepster.
Sutela, a subtyltie or craftie warkynge.
Suterna, showemakers crafte.
Sutilis, le, that whyche is sowen.
Sutor, toris, a showemaker.
Sutorium attramentum, soutars bleche.
Sutorius, a, um, pertaining to a showmaker.
Sutrina, a showemakers shoppe.
Sutura, a seame.
Suturnium, an ewer or lauour.
Suum, his owne, his propre goodes.
Suus, a, um, his or hirs. But how this word shall be most aptely and conuenictly vsyd, rede Ualla or Calepines vocabularie. For it is more abundantly and propycly declared of thē, than can be expressid in english.

¶ S ANTE Y.

SYades, sterres callid also Hyades, seuen in number.
Syagros, a wylde bore.
Sybaris, a citie in Grecia.
Sybarita, a man of that citie.
Sybaritica mensa, a prouerbe applied to feastes and bankettes, whyche doo excede in delycatenesse.
Sybaritici libelli, wanton bokes.
Sybaritici ludi, playes whyche are wanton and costly.
Sybariticum carmen, a verse or poeme contaynynge wanton matter.
Syboti, peple in the north part of the world.
Sychæus, a mans name.
Sycion, he that fyrste founde garlandes.
Sycomorus, a great tree lyke a fygge tree, whiche hath abundance of mylke, whose fruite commeth not oute of the toppes of the bowghes, as fygges doo, but oute of the same boughes, and swete like to a wild fygge: the graynes therof be les than the graines of figgis, & they be neuer ripe, except they be scrapid with an instrumēt of yron.
Sycophanta, he that falsly accuseth an innocent. Also a bearer of tales, or a cōplayner.
Sycophantia, a fals accusation, deceite.
Sycophantias struere, to deuyse, or inuente falsehoode.
Sycophantor, tari, idem.
Sycophantisso, are, idem.
Sycophantiose, deceytefully by crafte.
Sycon, olde wryters callyd a fygge.
Sycosis, a dyseafe in the fundement, which maketh a warte lyke to a fygge.
Sycosis, where within the eie lyd groweth a lyttell wart or other lyke thynge.
Sydera, the plurell number of sydus.
Syderatio, a spyce of the fallynge euyll in men, but in trees it is taken for blastynge.

Sydus, syderis, a sterre.
Syene, a citie in the confynes of Egypte and Ethiope.
Sygeum, a promontorie of Troye.
Syla, a mountayne in Lucania, & a wod in it.
Sylla, a great tyrant of Rome, whiche was of an vnsaciable crueltie.
Syllaba, a syllable.
Syllabatim, by syllables.
Syllabicus, ca, cum, pertaynyng to fillables.
Syllanion, a famous maker of images, whiche was neuer taught.
Syllepsis, a fygure, where the plurell number and the synguler are ioyned togyther, as sociis & rege recepto.
Syllogismus, a perfyte argumente, whyche hath a necessarye conclusion.
Sylua, a wodde or place ouergrowen with wedes. also any matter hastily written withoute studye.
Syluanus, was callyd the god of woddes.
Syluaticus, ca, cum, pertaynyng to woddes.
Syluecula, & syluula, a lyttell forest or wod.
Syluesco, scere, to waxe or growe into wodes or bushes.
Syluester, syluestris, tre, of a wodde or forest, woddy, wylde.
Syluicola, he that dwelleth in a foreste or wodde.
Syluius, a mannes name, whiche was borne in a foreste.
Syma, a cytie in Asia.
Symbolum, a collation. also a token gyuen by one to an other vpon certayn appointmentes, generally a signe or mark to know a thynge by.
Symbolus, a signet or sele, or a signe manuel.
Symbulus, a wyse and good counsailour.
Symmachia, ayde in battaile, or league made amonge men of sondry countreys, to fight agaynst the other parte.
Symmachus, a mannes name.
Symmetria, a concorde in measure, where sondry thynges be of equall proporcion.
Sympathia, a mutuall combination of thynges naturall in the operation of theyr powers and qualities, as water in coldenesse dothe participate with erthe, in moysture with the ayre, the ayre with the fyre in heate, with water in moysture.
Symphitum petreium, an herbe callyd bugle
Symphitum magnum, comfrey.
Symphonia, a consent in tune, alfo harmony.
Symphoniacus, a syngynge boye.
Symphonio, are, to agree or accord in one.
Symphonesis, colysion of vowelles.
Sympinatice, women addicte to ceremonies or deuocion.
Sympiniū, a cup seruīg for wyne in sacrifice.

Sym=

Symplator, a frende of hym that is maried, whiche accompanieth hym to feastes.
Symplega, warkes, in the which wrastlers, and they whyche contende in fyghtynge, are beholden.
Symplegades, two yles in the grekyshe see.
Symplegma, an imbracynge togyther.
Symposiastes, he that makith a fest or baket
Symposium, a bankette.
Sympotria, a woman whyche kepeth company at drynkynge.
Symnista, a secretary, or one of the pryuye councylle.
Sympsalma, a concorde in syngynge.
Sympudearia, funerals or playes, wherein playes were made.
Synada, a cytie in Asya.
Synæresis, a contraction of two wordes, as Bigæ, for biiugæ.
Synagoga, a cōgregatiō, specially of iewes.
Synalephe, a collision of vowels.
Synanche, a syckenesse in the throte, callyd the squynce.
Syncere, purely, vncorruptly.
Syncerus, ra, rum, sincere, pure, vncorrupted symple without dissimulation.
Synchronos, of one tyme.
Synciput, syncipitis, the forepart of the heed Also a swynes heed sowcyd.
Syncopa, a fygure, where a letter or syllable is taken away, as cōpostus, for cōpositus.
Synecdoche, a fygure, where parte is vsyd for the hole, or the hole for part.
Syndicus, an aduocate.
Syndipnium, a soupynge togyther.
Synechon, contynent.
Synephites, a stone, whyche is callyd alsoo Leucongra.
Syngrapha, syngraphus, & syngraphum, the wrytinge or dede, made or signed with the hande of hym that maketh a bargayne or couenaunte.
Synochitides, a stone, wherwith nygromancers do call vp dyuels.
Synodus, an assebly of mē, or general coūcil.
Synonimum, whiche in dyuers wordes sygnifieth one thyng, as Ensis, Gladius, both do sygnifie a sworde. Occidit, interfecit, necauit, do signifie, he kylled.
Synopis, synoper or redde leade.
Synstratiotes, companiōs togither in warre.
Syntagma, a treatie, an ordinaunce.
Syntaxis, order in construction.
Syntexis, lacke, or weakenes, whiche happeneth by longe syckenes.
Synteresis, the pure parte of conscience.
Synthema, a token gyuen to souldiours.
Synthesis, a short cote or ierkyn, also a vessell made of many vessels.

Syntomon, for circūcisum.
Sypharium, a curtayne hanged before minstrels whan they synge.
Syphax, was the kynge of Numidia.
Syracusæ, a famouse citie in Sycile.
Syracusius, & Syracusanus, of that citie.
Syria, a great realme in Asia, whiche hathe on the east the ryuer of Euphrates, on the weste the myddell see, and the realme of Egipte, on the northe Cilicia and Cappadocia, on the south Arabia.
Syriacum, a kynde of swete radyshe.
Syriacus, ca, cum, of Syria.
Syrictę, people whiche receyue their meat in oten redes.
Syricum, a color mixt with sinoper & ruddel
Syrium, wyne boyled to the thyrde part.
Syrinx, a pype or recorder.
Syris, corne kepte in holes in the grounde, and couered with chaffe.
Syrisca, a woman of Syria.
Syrissus, a, um, of Syria.
Syrma, tis, the traine of a womans gowne.
Syrnia, a shryche oule.
Syrophœnix, the see coste of Syria.
Syrtes, quycke sandes or shelpes in the water made by the dryfte of sande or grauel.
Syrtites, a lyttell stoone founde in the bladder of a wolfe.
Syrupus, a syrupe.
Syrus, a man of Siria, also an Iland belongynge to Grece.
Sysitia, feastes, and companyes assembled at feastes.
Sysymbrium, an herbe callid winter sauery.
Syzigiæ, synewes, whyche do come frome the brayne to the eyes, so that he, whiche cometh from the lefte syde, gothe to the right eye, and that whiche commeth from the right syde, goth to the left eye, so that the synewes do crosse eche other.

⁋ T ANTE A.

TABANVS, a flie, whiche hath foure wingis, & byteth a man or beest.
Tabefacio, ere, to corrupt
Tabella, a lyttell table.
Tabellarius, a caryer of letters, an auditour.
Tabellio, lionis, a scriuener that writeth commune instrumentes and dedes.
Taberna, euery vyle habytation, also a shop or tauerne, where wares be solde, and all thynge that is vendible, as wyne, oyle, or any other thynge.
Taberna meritoria, an ynne.

Taberna

Tabernaria fabula, a comedie or Interlude, wherin are base personages, and no persones of dignitie or state.
Tabernaculum, a pauyllyon or halle.
Tabernarius, he that selleth any maner of wares. also a tauerner.
Tabes, bis, corruption in the body. also extreme leannesse, by a longe consumynge syckenesse. It is also matter and corrupte blode myxte togither. Also the impostume of the lunges, procedynge of humoures descendynge frome the heed into the stomake, and so woundynge and corruptyng the lounges.
Tabesco, bui, scere, to languishe or consume, to be extremely leane, to be corruptid.
Tabidus, da, dum, corrupted, consumed.
Tabificabilis, le, that whiche may be corrupted, or falle into a consumption.
Tabificus, ca, cum, that whyche maketh one corrupted, or consumeth the body.
Tablinum, was a wynter parlour, wherein were painted tables and bokes of stories.
Tabo, a consumption, wastynge, or putrifaction of thinges.
Tabor, a mountayne in the countrey of Galilea, where Christe was transfigurate.
Tabula, a table. In the plurell numbre tabulæ, dothe signifie a testament, or any commune instrument or writynge. Also tabula is a table to play on with dise or chesse mē.
Tabulæ nouæ, were whan detters were not constrayned to pay their dettes, that they dyd owe, and the olde obligations were dissolued, and newe were to be made for that whiche shulde newely be borowed.
Tabularia, ar places, where euidences and writynges be layde.
Tabularium, a cheste, in the whiche euidences and recordes are put.
Tabulata, walles made of square stones, as if they were bourded. They be also the boughes of trees and bushes, whyche do growe streyght forth and not vpwarde.
Tabulatus, ta, tum, made of bourdes. Also tabulata, are walles sylded with bourdes, or made of stone playne lyke to bourdes. They be also the boughes of trees, whyche do leane playne outwarde, and do not growe vpwarde.
Tabulo, are, to make a thing with bourdes, or to ioyne bourdes togyther.
Tabulatio, a ioynynge or closynge of bourdes togyther.
Taburnus, an hyll in Campania, wherin do growe many olyue trees.
Tace, egomet conueniam iam ipsum, Lette aloone, I my selfe wylle commune nowe with hym.

Tacenda, those thynges whiche are not to be spoken.
Taceo, tacui, tacêre, to kepe sylence, to be in reste, to be quyete, to be sure.
Tacito pede, softely, by stelthe.
Tacitum est, not a worde is spoken of it. *Terent. in Adelph.*
Taciturnitas, tatis, sylence.
Tacitus, he that holdethe his peace, and is secrete.
Tacitus, citius audies, be styl, thou shalt here the sooner.
Tacitè, without speakynge one worde.
Tactus fulmine, somwhat burned or blasted with lyghtnynge.
Tactus, tus, feelynge.
Tædet, it weryeth me, it yrketh me, I am werye of it.
Tædium, werynes, or heuynes of mynde.
Tædulus, an olde dotarde, of whom al men are wearye.
Tænarus, a darke place at the fote of the hil callyd Malea, by the citie of Sparta, whiche was supposed to be an entry into hell.
Tænia, the edge of a fyllette. also a womās fyllette, or that whyche nowe they calle rolles: proprely it is a kerchiefe, whyche maydens do weare on their heedes. Also a whyte stoone, whyche in the water sheweth longe lyke a kerchiefe. It is alsoo a vyllage betwene Mirenas & Corinthum.
Tænon, a cite in Laconia, an other i Arcadia
Tagasta, a citie in Affrike.
Tagax, acis, a felon, whiche happeneth on a mannes fynger.
Tages, was he, whyche taughte fyrste the Thuscanes the crafte of diuynation, callyd Aruspicium.
Tago, gere, olde wryters vsed for tango.
Tagrus, an hylle in Portyngale, where, as it is wryten, that mares doo conceyue of the wynde.
Tagus, a ryuer in Spayne, wherin hath ben founde grauell of golde.
Taigete, is the name of oone of the seuen sterres, whiche soo appiereth, as it maye scantly be perceyued, which sterre is also called Maia, & Electra.
Talaria, were showes, whyche Mercurius dyd weare, wheron were set whynges.
Talaris, re, that whiche commeth downe to the ancley, as Toga talaris, a longe gowne to the ancley.
Talarius, ria, rium, pertaynynge to dyse, as Lex talaria, a lawe agaynst dyse playenge.
Talassio, was a songe contayned in certayn verses, sungen at weddynges. It was also a certayne exclamation or crie vsed at mariages, the begynnynge whereof beganne, whan Romulus and the Romaynes rauys-
whom

shed the maydens of the Sabines, amonge whom was one of excellent beautie, whom whan many of the Sabines wold haue reskued, they whyche caried her toward Romulus, to thintent that she shulde not be taken from them, cryed Talassio, whiche was the name of a noble prynce of the Sabines, as if they wolde haue broughte hyr to hym, and by that meane they escaped, & broughte hir to Romulus. And afterwarde they vsed at mariages to crie Talassio.

Talea, a stocke sette in the erthe, whereon men doo graffe. Also a truncheon, a staffe, a byllette.

Talentum, was a poyse, whyche after the countreye, wherein it was, it was dyuers. One was callyd talentum Atticum, whyche contayned .lx. poundes of Athenes, callyd Minas, or Mnas, and, lxxii. poūdes of Rome callyd libras: and this was also called talentum minus, the other was callyd Talentum maius, & Euboicum, which contayned .lxxx. poundes of Athenes, callid Minas, & lxxxiii. poundes & foure ounces of Rome weight. Loke before in Libra, et Pondo. Talentū Atticum, uel minus, was in value after the rate of olde poyse grotes. CLxvi. li. xiii. s. iiii. d. after .lx. to the pounde, after the newe grotes, tenne to the once. CCviii. li. vi. s. viii. d. Talentum maius, of olde grotes. CLxxxx. li. xiii. s. iiii. d. of newe grotes. CCLxvii. li. x. s.

Talgæ, an Ile in the see callyd Hircanum, where groweth plentie of corne and frutes without culture.

Talia, the blade of an onyon or chybol.

Talio, onis, an equall peyne in recompence of a hurte, as for the cuttynge of a mans hande, to lose a hande, or for puttinge out of an eye, to lose an eye.

Talior, ari, to be cutte: it is proprely spoken of wodde, whiche we nowe calle tallynge of wodde.

Talipedo, dare, to go on the pasternes.

Talis, tale, suche.

Taliter, in suche wyse.

Talitrum, a fyllyppe gyuen with ones fynger or nayle.

Talpa, a molle or want.

Talpa cæcior, blynder than a molle, a prouerbe applyed to them, whiche lacke iugement in thinges that are playne.

Talum reponere, to refourme that, whiche was negligently done, with more diligēce.

Talus, the ankle aboue the foote. It is also the pasterne bone of a beaste. Also a dye, or dyce.

Tam, as well. alfo, as, soo. Tam bonus, as good. Tā sum amicus republicæ, q̄ qui maxime, I am so frendely, or as moche frende to the publyke weale, as he that is moste.

Tama, whan with moche trauaile the blode commeth downe to the legge, and causeth it to swelle.

Tam magis, for tanto magis. Vergil.

Tamarindi, a fruite growynge in India, the tree wherof is like to a palme or date tree, the fruite sower, lyke grene damsins, whiche is medicinable in asswagyng the heate of cholere.

Tamarite, people in Asia, not farre frome the see callyd Caspium.

Tamarix, ricis, an herbe, whyche bearethe floures twyse in one yere.

Tamen, not withstandyng. also yet. Tamen á malicia non discedis, Yet wylte thou not departe from thy malyce. Sommetyme it signifieth forthewith, at the laste, soo that. Quod potero, faciam, tamē ut pietatem colam, I wyll doo that I maye: soo that not withstandynge I omytte not my duetie to my father.

Tametsi, all be it, alwaye.

Taminia, a wild grape, growing in woddes.

Tam ne, olde wryters vsed for eousq̄, vntyll that.

Tanager, a riuer in Lucania, betwene Campania and Calabria.

Tanagra, a towne in Perside.

Tanais, a great ryuer in the northe parte of the worlde, whyche dyuydeth Europa from Asia.

Tanaquil, was wife to Tarquinius Priscus, the kynge of Romaynes.

Tanaus, was kynge of Siria.

Tandem, at the laste, sometyme at the leste waye, also vneth, not withstandynge.

Tandiu, so longe.

Tango, tetigi, tangere, to touche, to meue, to vnderstande, or perceyue, to come to.

Tangere ulcus, to rubbe on the galde place, to speake to one of a thynge, whiche greueth hym to here it. Tarpsilus.

Tangere, to deceyue.

Tetigit aures meas, It came to myn eares. Plautus in Rudē.

Tanis, the principall citie of Egypte, where Moyses dyd shewe meruayles.

Tanos, a stone of the kynde of Emeralde, grene and blacke.

Tanquam, as it were, lyke.

Tantalides, the progenie of Tantalus.

Tantali horti, a prouerbe sygnifienge good thynges to be at hande, whiche not withstandynge a man may not vse.

Tantalus, a kynge, whom poetes do faine to be tormented in hell with hunger & thyrste.

Tanti, for so moche. This worde doth pertayne to byenge and sellynge. Tantidem, at that pryce, Tandidem idem.

Tanti

Tanti æstimo, tantifacio, tanti pendo, I sette so moche by, or I so moche esteme it.

Tantillus, la, lum, & tantulus, a, um, the diminutiue of tantus.

Tantisper, so longe.

Tantopere, so moche, so vehemently.

Tantum, onely.

Tantum non, almooste.

Terent. in Heautont. Tantum sat habes? arte thou content?

Tantummodo, all onely.

Tantundem periculum, so great dangier.

Tanuina, a wylde vyne callyd also Labrusca.

Tanto, an aduerbe, sygnyfienge so moche, as tanto magis, so moche more, tanto peior, so moche worse.

Tantum abest, it is soo farre frome, or soo moche vnlyke.

Plautus in pænulo. Tantundem, euen so moche.

Tantumnum, also, ye also.

Tantus, ta, tum, suche, sometyme so moche, or so greatte.

Taos, a stone of the colour of a pecoke.

Tapetia, hangynges of houses, or clothes wherwith pauementes are couered.

Tapetum, tapes, petis, tapisrye, or clothes, wherin are wrought diuers pictures with thredes of sondry colours.

Taphiæ, & taphus, an Ile by Grecia, where dwelled the people called Telebois.

Taphius, a citie in Egipt, the people wherof were callyd Taphnu.

Taphos, in greke, is a sepulchre or tumbe.

Tapinosis, a fygure, wherby a great thyng is basely described.

Taposiris, a citie in Egipte.

Taprobana, a noble Ile in the Indiane see, whiche yle is dyrectly agaynste this parte of the worlde, and there is abundance of all maner of spyces. And the people there lyueth aboue an hundred yeres.

Tapsus, an Ile by Sycile not farre frome Syracuse.

Tapulla, a lawe made for feastes.

Fest. pom. Tapyri, people in Parthia, whyche vse to gyue theyr wyues in mariage to other men, after that they haue hadde foure or fyue chyldren by them.

Taracina, a towne in Campania.

Taraconia, a countraye callydde nowe Aragon.

Taracon, the chiefe citie therof.

Tarandrus, a beaste in body lyke to a great oxe, hauynge a heed lyke to a harte, and hornes full of branches, the heare rough, of the colour of a beare, I suppose it to be a rayne dere.

Tarantula, a kynde of the beastes callydde Stelliones, lyke to a lysarde, of whose byrynge no man dieth, oncly it stonteth hym that is bytten.

Taras, the sonne of Neptunus, who buylded Tarentum.

Taraxis, whan the eyen do bolne out moch, and be redde.

Tarchesius, was a myschenous kyng of the people callyd Albani.

Tarchon, a duke in Hethruria, whiche was also a greate diuinour or soothsayer.

Tardatio, a tarienge.

Tardigradus, that whiche hath a slow pase, or gothe slowely.

Tardatio, a tarienge. Tarde, slowe, late.

Tardiloquentia, a slowe speche.

Tardiloquus, he that draweth his speeche in lengthe.

Tardior, slower.

Tardissimus, moste slowe, or slowest.

Tarditas, & tarditudo, & tardicies, slownesse.

Tardius, more slowely.

Tardiuscule, somewhat slowely.

Tardiusculus, somewhat slowe.

Tardo, dare, to tary, to be slowe.

Tardus, slowe, rude, somtyme well during, also thycke or grosse.

Tarentinus, a, um, of the citie of Tarent in Calabria.

Tarentum, a noble citie in Calabria.

Tarentū, a citie within the realm of Naples.

Tarmes, a wourme, whiche eateth flesshe, a magotte.

Tarpeius, an hylle at Rome.

Tarquinus superbus, was the laste kynge of Romaynes, whiche was expellyd oute of Rome for his pride and crueltie.

Tarracina, a towne in Campania callydde also Anxur.

Tarsus, the chiefe citie of Cilicia, where saynt Paule was borne.

Tarsis, a region in Judea.

Tartaria, a greate countray in the northeste parte of the worlde.

Tartarus, a place in hel, also a mā of Tartarie.

Tartarum, the lyes of wyne.

Tartareus, ea, eum, of helle.

Tartarinus, rina, num, olde wryters vsed for horrible or terrible.

Tartesii, a people in Iberia, amonge whom be cattes of excedynge greatnesse.

Tartessus, a citie in the vttermoste parte of Spayne, on the see syde by Gades, nowe callyd Cales, where Columella the moste eloquent and perfyte husband, was borne.

Tascaneum, a whyte claye or marle.

Tasimenes, seu tasmenes, one of the sonnes of duke Nestor.

Tata, dady, which chyldrē call their father.

Tatæ, a wanton worde, wherwith one aunswereth to an nother.

Cc Tateus

T ANTE A.

Tateus, a kynde of salt whyche cometh out of Phrigia, & is medicinable for the eies.
Taura, a barrayne cowe.
Tarianus, a mans name. Tatius, a mās name.
Taurarij, people in Scythia.
Tauria, a scourge made of neates lether.
Taurica Chersonesus, a contray in the north parte of Europa.
Taurici, people of cruell maners that offered strangers in sacrifyce.
Taurilia, were playes made in the honoure of infernall goddis.
Taurinus, na, num, of a bulle.
Taurius, one of the goddes of the see.
Taurominium, a mountayne in Sicile, soo callyd for the plentie of neate, whiche fed theron. Also there was by it a citie of the same name.
Taurominitanus, na, num, of the citie of Taurominium.
Tauroscythæ, people of Scithia, dwellyng by the mountayne callyd Taurus.
Taurus, a bulle, sometyme a stronge oxe. It is also one of the .xii. celestiall sygnes, also a great mountayne towarde India.
Tautologia, a fygure, where one thynge is twyse spoken.

Plautus in persa. Tax, a stroke.
Taxa, a kynde of bayes or laurell, wherewith herbars are made.
Taxatio, a settynge of a taxe or subsidie.
Taxatores, they whiche doo rebuke oone an nother.
Taxim, softely, scantly touched.
Taxis, olde wryters vsed for tetigeris, thou shalte touche.
Taxilli, small dyse.
Taxo, nis, a gray or brocke, or badger.
Taxo, are, to touche often. alsoo to taxe, or cesse a thynge at a certayne value. also to reproue one an other.
Taxus, a tree lyke to fyrre, whiche beareth bearyes, wherin is mortalle poyson. It is also callyd ewe, wherof bowes be made.
Taygetus, a hylle, vnder the whiche is sette the citie of Sparta and Amycle.

¶ T ANTE E.

Tearus, a riuer of Thracia, at the heed wherof Darius kynge of Persia, whā he went into Scithia, pighte his pauyllyons, and there abode thre dayes. And delytynge at the mooste pleasaunt water of that ryuer, be sette in the same place a piller graue with letters of greke, declaryng his being there, with cōmendatiō of the water.
Techna, a craft, also a wyle, or subtryl meane
Techines, were they, whiche also were callyd Corybantes, and were feined to be the sonnes of Minerua and Sol.

T ANTE E.

Technicus, ca, cum, artificiall, inuentiue.
Technides, a craftes man.
Technophyon, a settynge forthe of crafte.
Tectorius, a, um, pertaynyng to coueryinge.
Tecum, with the.
Tector, toris, a periettour.
Tectorium, the playstrynge or pariettynge of a house.
Tectoriū opus, perietting or plastring wark
Tectum, the roufe of a house. sommetyme all the house.
Tecum oro & quæso, I pray & byseche the.   *Plaut. in milite.*
Tecum sentio, I am of thyn opinyon.
Teda, a tree, out of the whiche sweateth a lycour, whan it is hette.
Tædulus, of whom al men be wery. somtime it signifieth him, whiche is wery of som thig.   *Fest. pom.*
Tegeum, a citie in Arcadia.
Tegeates, men of that citie.
Teges, gitis, a course blanket or couerlyd, whiche lyeth on poore mens beddes. It is alsoo a matte.   *Varro.*
Tegeticula, the diminutiue of teges.
Tegillum, a lyttell coueryinge.
Tegmen, & tegimen, & tegmentum, a coueryinge or couer.
Tego, texi, tegere, to couer, to hyde, to defende or kepe.
Tegula, a tyle. Tegulum, a coueryinge.
Teium, a citie in Paphlagonia, where Anacreon the poete was borne.
Tela, the clothe, whiche is spoken as welle of sylke as of lynnen clothe or wollen.
Tellane, a certayne kynde of fygges.
Telamones, ymages, whiche do beare vppe pyllers or postes.
Telemachus, the son of Ulisses & Penelope.
Teleboæ, people in Grece.
Telephium, an herbe callyd Orpyn.
Telephus, the sonne, whiche was nourished with an hynde. Telina, a certain garment.
Telonarius, & telo, lonis, a collectour or gatherer of tributes.   Telonium, the place where taskes or tributes are payde.
Telos, in greke is an end, honour, a legion, a tribute or pēcion, it is also the name of an ile, where the ointment callid telina is made
Telpussa, a citie in Arcadia.
Tellus, li, a māns name whom the wise Solon iuged to be more fortunate thā the rich king Tellus, luris, the erthe.   (Cresus.
Telum, al thynge whiche maye be throwen or cast with the hand, be it stone, wod, or irō it is also the generall name of al that, wherwith a man doth fyght, callyd weapon. sometyme it is taken for a sworde.
Temerarius, a, um, more hardy than nede, or wysedome requyreth, folehardy. somtime dredefull, or to be dradde.

Teme-

Temeritas, atis, & temeritudo, foolehardines.
Temere, vnaduysedly, foolyshely, aduenturously. sometyme it sygnifieth almoste. also without cause.
Temerius, more folyshe, or vnaduysedly.
Temero, rare, to vyolate.
Temetum, wyne.
Temulentus, ta, tum, drunke of wyne.
Temulentia, drunkennes.
Temno, tempsi, temnere, to sette lyttell by.
Temo, monis, the beame, whiche contayneth the yoke.
Tempe, a place in Thessalia wonderful plesaunt, hauynge trees and medowes meruaylous delectable, wherin brydes of dyuers kyndes, doo synge contynually with excellent melody. Therof al plesant woddes haue the name of Tempe.
Temperamentum, a moderacion.
Temperanter, temperately.
Temperantia, temperance, which is a firme and moderate gouernance of reson agaynst sensualitie and other vycyouse affections of the mynde.
Temperantior, teperantius, more temperate.
Temperatura, a temperance or moderation, in the mynglynge of thynges togyther.
Temperies, temperatenes, propryly in heate or colde. sometyme it is vsurped for temperamentum, and for temperantia.
Temperior, oris, more tymely.
Tempero, are, to temper or moderate in order or measure. Temperamus stylum, calamum, appetitum, whan we kepe in cure wrytynge a meane fourme, or do eate noo more than is nedefull.
Tempsa, a cytie in the countrey called now Calabria.
Tempestas, tatis, sygnifyeth sometyme the same tyme, somtyme tempest, sommetyme wether, sometyme a fayre wether.
Tempestiuus, ua, um, that whyche is done in conuenyent tyme.
Tempestiuitas, tatis, season or tyme conuenient, oportunitie.
Tempestiue, in season or tyme conuenient.
Tempestiu, olde wryters vsed for tempestiuu.
Tempestuosum, tempestuous or stormy.
Templum, a temple or churche. sometyme it sygnifyeth heuen. Alsoo the principall beame of a house. also a sepulchre.
Temporalis, le, that whiche duryth vntyll a certayne tyme.
Temporaneus, a, um, that whyche is doone sodaynly, and at a tyme.
Temporarie, temporanie, & temporaliter, vntylle a tyme.
Temporarius, ria, rium, that whiche dureth or contynueth for a tyme. also that whiche pertayneth to tyme.

Temporius, an aduerbe sygnifieth in tyme, or by tyme.
Tempus, poris, tyme, also the state of tyme. sometyme the temples of the heed.
Tenacia, & tenacitas, hardenes in sparynge of expenses, nygardshyp, perseueraunce, retaynynge, or kepynge.
Tenatior, & tenacissimus, the comparatiue and superlatiue degree of tenax.
Tenacissimæ memoriæ, of mooste sure remembraunce. Tenaciter, fastly, surely.

Colum. x.

Tenasmus & tenesmus, a desyre to go often to the stoole, and may do nothynge, with a burnynge and sometyme a bloody siege.
Tenax, nacis, that whiche holdeth faste, as glue. somtime sparyng or nygarde, to moche constant, hard to be moued.
Tendere, to assay, to holde vp. Paruumque patri tendebat Iulum, he helde vp lyttell Iulus vnto his father. Also to prepare, to go towarde a place.
Tendicula, a nette or snare to take byrdes or beastes.
Tendo, tetendi, tendere, to extende or stretche, to lay a snare, to dwelle, to go. Tendere insidias, to lay in wayte.
Tendures, olde wryters callyd them, whych had great teethe.
Tenebræ, the lacke of lyght, darkenes.
Tenebresco, scere, to be darke.
Tenebricor, caris, cari, to make darke.
Tenebricosus, a, um, that maketh darke.
Tenebriones, lyere and crafty knaues. Also they whiche wyll not be sene abrode by day tyme.
Tenebrosus, a, um, darke.
Tenedos, an yle in the see callyd Ægeum, betwene Mitelene and Hellespontum, not farre from Troye.
Tenedia bipēnis aut securis, a quick or sharp axe: a prouerbe applyed to iudges, which be hasty and cruell in their sentences.
Tenellus, a, um, tender.
Teneo, nui, nuere, to holde, to apprehende, to possede, to holde or kepe in, to couer, to vnderstande, to kepe backe, to performe.
Teneor, neris, neri, to be bounden, to be beholden to one.
Tener, ra, rum, tender, mercyful. Also a geldyd manne.
Teneritas, & teneritudo, tendernes.
Tenerasco, scere, to be tender or mercyfull.
Tenere consilium, to do by councill Precipe, ut teneat consilia nostra, Gyue hym aduyse that he may do by our counsayle.

Plautus in milite.

Tene, tene, tary, tary. Redi, quo fugis nunc? tene, tene, Tourne agayne, whither runnest thou nowe; tary, tary.

Cc ij   Tenere

Plinius in panegyri. Tenere consensum, to agree or consent vnto other.
Terent. in Hecyra. Tenet me amor, loue meueth me moche.
Plautus in cap. Tenere insaniam. Sed hoc primum expurgare tibi uolo, me insaniā neq̢ terere, neque mi esse ullum morbum, nisi quod seruio, But fyrste I wyll declare my self vnto the, that I am neyther out of my wyt, nor haue any syckenes, but that I am bonde.
Plautus in Amphit. & Epidico. Tenere ius, to knowe the lawe,
Tenere legem, to be vnder a lawe.
Terent. in Adelph. Tenere memoria, to remembre.
Tenere medium, to kepe a meane.
Plautus in mercatore Tenere modum, to kepe a measure.
Plautus in truculen. Tenere se, to take hede of hym selfe.
In Menec. Tenere aliquem mendatij, to take oone with a lye.
Sueton. in domitiano Tene tibi, take it as thyne owne.
Tenere causam, to vanquysshe or recouer agaynste one in a matter.
Plin. epist. 83. Teneri desyderio, to desyre moch or feruētly
Teneri ludo, to take pleasure in game.
Teneri furti, to be giltie of felonye.
Tenera ætas, youthe.
Teneris annis, in yonge yeres.
Tenere, & teneriter, tenderly, louyngly.
Tenni, olde writers vsed for tenui.
Tenitæ, were callyd goddesses of lottes.
Tenontes, the greate and stronge synewes, whiche do kepe the necke vpryght. Also a broode synewe, whyche gothe frome the hamme downe to the heele.
Tenor, noris, an order, a contynuaunce of a thynge.
Tenos, an yle in the greke see, one of them, whyche is callyd Cyclades.
Lucretius. Tenta, stretched.
Tentamentum, temptation.
Tentigo, tiginis, a styffenesse.
Tentipellium, a showe with an yron soole, wheron the ouer lether is stretched.
Tento, tare, to attempte, to assay or proue, to tempte one to do euyll.
Tentorium, a tent or pauylyon.
Tentum, a mans priuye membre.
Tentyra, a citie in Egypte.
Tentyri, uel tynterite, a venymous beaste in an Ile on the ryuer of Nilus, whose voice the cokodryll doth feare.
Tenuy, & tenuiter, poorely, symply.
Tenunculus, la, lum, very symple, or lyttelle in estimation.
Tenui filo, with a small threde, applyed to style in wrytynge, whyche is not elegant, but playne.
Tenuis, nue, lyttell or symple in estimation, smalle in quantitie, poore.
Tenuitas, tatis, smallenesse, pouertie.
Tenuo, are, to make smalle, to make leane, or feeble.

Tenus, ni, a snare. Beinge an aduerbe, hit sygnyfyeth vnto. Tenus urbem tendit, It extendeth vnto the cytie, or noo further than the cytie.
Tenus, a preposition, sygnifieth nyghnesse, or vntyll a thynge.
Tepifacio, cere, to make warme.
Tepefio, fieri, to be warme.
Tepeo, & tepesco, tepui, pescere, to be warm or hotte.
Tepidarium, a vesselle, wherein water is made temperate, also a chaumber, wherein to men do go out of a bayne.
Tepidus, tepida, tepidum, meane betwene hotte and colde, warme. Also kolyd from heate Somtyme noyfull or vnprofytable.
Tephrites, a stoone, whyche hathe the fygure of a newe moone, in colour blacke, or asshe colour.
Tepidior, colder.
Tepidissimus, a, um, moste warme.
Tepidulus, tepidula, tepidulum, a dymynutyue of tepidus.
Tepocon, a forme of wrytyng downwarde.
Tepor, oris, & tepiditas, tatis, warmthe, or warmenesse.
Ter, thryse.
Terapne, a contray in Lacedemonia, where the fayre Helene was borne. also an Iland nowe callyd Corsica.
Terebinthus, a tree, the wodde wherof is blacke and harde lyke boxe, oute of this tree rounneth a gumme, callyd commonly Turpentyne. All be it the common turpentyne is not it, but an nother, whyche is as cleere as glasse, and is a soueraygne medycyne to clense the stomake of putryfyed humours.
Ternarius, & ternus, terna, num, the thyrde in number.
Tertius, tia, um, the thyrd. Tertio, & tertium, the thyrde tyme.
Terdenus, na, num, the thyrdtenth.
Terebellum, a wymble or percer.
Terebratio, a borynge with a wymble.
Terebræ, siue terebrum, an awgour, wherewith holes are boored.
Terebro, brare, to bore or make an hole.
Teredo, dinis, a lytel worm that eteth wod.
Terentius, the mooste eloquente wryter of comedyes. Terentianus, of Terence.
Terentum, a place in the fyelde by Rome, callyd Campus Martius, wherein was an aultar of Pluto and Proserpyne.
Teres, teretis, longe and rounde, lyke a tree or a pyller. Teretrum, an instrument, wherwith a thynge is made rounde.
Terga dare, to run away, proprely in batalle.

Ter-

T ante E.

Tergemini, thre chylderne borne at oone bourdeyne. Tergestes, a citie in Italye.
Terginus, na, num, that whiche is made of a beastes hyde.
Tergiuersatio, a nonsuite in the lawe, whan the pleintife gyueth ouer his suite.
Tergiuersor, aris, ari, to turne back, to deny, in the lawe it sygnifieth to be nonsuite.
Tergo, & tergeo, tersi, tergere, to wype or make cleane.
Tergum, the backe of man or beare, or of any other thynge. sommetyme it sygnifyeth a hyde.
Tergus, tergoris, a hyde of a beaste.
Terma, matis, the extremitie, the ende of a thinge, also the sole of the fote.
Termentarium, a lynnen clothe, wherewith the body is couered.

Plaut. Termentum, for detrimentum.
Fest. Pom. Termes, a braunche plucked of a tree with the fruite on it. also a worme, whyche eateth the fleshe.
Termile, a mountayne in Lycia, callyd also Chimera.
Ter milies, thre thousande tymes.
Termillum, a potte for wyne, whyche was alway sette on the table, that euery manne mought take as moche wine as he wolde.
Terminalia, was a certayne holy day, at the latter ende of the yere.
Terminalis lapis, a mere stone, laid or pight at the ende of sondry mens landes.
Termino, nare, to ende or fynyshe.
Terminus, a sygne whiche declareth oone mans lande from an other, or one contrey or territorie from an other. also it signifyeth the buttynge.
Terminus deus, was an ydoll, whiche was supposed to haue preemynence ouer the boundes of lande, whose temple had euer an hole in the roufe, for as moche as they thought it to be vnlefulle that boundes of lande shulde be couered or hydde.
Termo, onis, old wryters vsed for terminus.
Ternarius numerus, the number of thre.
Ternus, na, num, the thyrde.
Ternundenum, the thyrtenthe.

Vide com. Tero, triui, rere, to rubbe, to breke or brosse. Terere iter, to go his way. Terere tempus, to cosume tyme. Terere otiu, to lyue idelly.
Terpander, dri, an olde musytian, whyche added .vii. stryngcs to the harpe.
Terpsichore, one of the nyne musis.
Terra, erthe: sometyme all the worlde, also a prouynce, a territorie, a countrey, land.
Terraceus, a, um, of erthe.
Terraneola, a byrde lyke to a larke, whiche we calle a buntynge.
Terrefacio, facere, to make aferde.

T ante E.

Terræ filius, he that is come vp of nought, and no man knoweth his kynrede.
Terremotus, erthequake.
Terrenum, a felde.
Terrenus, na, num, of erthe, or lyuynge on erthe, erthely.
Terreo, rui, rere, to make aferde. *Vide com.*
Terrestris, tre, erthely.
Terreus, rea, reum, of erthe. Vas terreum, an erthen vessele.
Terribilis, bile, terryble, that whyche is to be feared.
Terricola, he that dwelleth in the lande.
Terricrepus, he that rebuketh one terribly.
Terriculamentū, a feare, or a fearfull thyng.
Terrificus, ca, cum, terryble, or that whiche induceth feare.
Terrigena, begotten on the erthe. *Varro de*
Terriones, ploughmenne. *ling. latin.*
Terripauium, & terripudium, for tripudium, daunsynge.
Territo, tare, to make aferde.
Territorium, the fyeldes or countraye lyenge within the iurisdiction and boundes of a citie, a territorie.
Terror, roris, feare.
Tersus, sa, sum, cleane, pure.
Tersus dies, of olde wryters was taken for a fayre daye.
Tertiata uerba, wordes not perfytely pronounced: as whan one is in feare or drede of hym, to whome he speaketh, he tremblynge in speche, vnethe pronounceth the thyrde worde that he wolde saye.
Tertiarum, is a mixt mettall, wherin are two partes of leade, and one of tynne.
Tertio, are, to do a thynge the thyrde tyme, or to make the thyrde tylth in earynge.
Tertio Consul, where two haue bene Consules before hym. Tertium Consul, he that hath ben thryse Consul. So that Tertio signifieth the third in order, and place, two goynge afore. Tertiū sygnifieth the tyme, where t wyse gothe afore. The lyke is of Secundo, quarto, and other numbres.
Tertio pedato, at the thyrde retourne or *Cato.* comynge agayne. Tertius, a, ū, the third.
Tertius decimus, the thyrtenthe.
Tertullianus, a famous and eloquent autor, whyche for dyspleasure and malyce felle into heresye.
Teruncium, a poyse or coyn of thre ounces.
Tesca, a place where misticalle ceremonies *Varro.* were exercysed.
Tesqua, places harde or difficile to come vp to, where the Romaynes dyd practise their diuinatiōs by fleing of birdis, callid auguria
Tessellatus, ta, tum, that whiche is wrought with smal pieces of stone, wodde, or bone.

Cc iij

as in playenge tables or counterbourdes.
Tessella, a grosse.
Tessera, that whiche is in euery part square as a dye. also it is a dye. moreouer a watchworde or priuie token gyuen to souldiours. Also a token of warre and peace, a token gyuen to people to receyue corne of the kinges almes. Also a taile, wheron is scored or marked the numbre of thynges receyued, whiche is also called Tesserula.
Tesseradecas, fouretene.
Tesserarius, he that giueth the watcheword
Tesserulę, lyttell pauynge tyles.
Tesso, tessi, tessere, to dispoyle or pulle of a garment or harneis by vyolence.
Testa, a sharde of a potte or tyle. also an erthen pot. also all maner of shellfyshe.
Testaceus, a, um, that whiche hath a shelle.
Testeus, idem.
Testaceum flagellum, a prouerbe applyed to sodayn alteration of thinges, or of banishment vnlooked for.
Testamentarius, a forger of testamentes.
Testamentarius, ria, ium, pertaynynge to testamentes.
Testamentum, a testament.
Testatim, in pieces or shardes.
Testatio, & testimonium, wytnesse.
Testator, toris, he that maketh a testament.
Testatus, he that is deed, and hathe made a wyll. also openly knowen of all men.
Testiculor, cularis, lari, to putte the male to the female. Testillor, idem.
Testiculus, of a knowen sygnification.
Testificatio, a wytnesse bearynge.
Testificator, & testificatrix, he or she that bereth wytnesse.
Testificor, caris, cari, to beare wytnesse.
Testimonium, & testatio, wytnesse borne of a thynge done.
Testis, he that beareth wytnes.
Testes, be also a mannes genitours.
Testor, aris, ari, to beare wytnes, to calle to wytnes, to pray god. *Coteftor. Proteftor Varro.*
Testu, olde wryters vsed for testa.
Testuaceum, that whiche is boyled in an erthen potte.
Testudinatum tectum, a roufe, which is holowe in foure partes.
Testudo, dinis, a snayle. Also an engyne of warre to beate downe walles, whiche was made of bourdes, and couerid with lether or other thinges, which wold not bourne. within it was a piece of tymber, that had a great hoke of yron at the ende, whyche piece mought be plucked backe, and putte forthe with the strength of men, and therwith plucke stoones oute of the walles of townes besyeged. It is alsoo the roufe or vaulte of a howse.
Testus, tus, is a panne, wherin tartes, and other lyke thynges of paste are baken.
Tetanicus morbus, idem quod Tetanos.
Tetanothra, a medycine, wherwith the face of a man or woman is made smothe without wrynkles.
Tetanos, whan the synues are styffe, so that a man can nat bowe some part of his body
Tetarmorion, the fourth part of the zodiake cirkle, wherin are the .xii. signes. It is also that, whiche astronomers do calle the quadrate aspecte of planettes.
Te te, thy selfe.
Teter, tetra, tetrum, foule, stynkyng, cruell.
Teterrimus, a, um, moste foule or stynkyng, or cruelle.
Teterrimé, moste abhomynably. *Feft. Pom.*
Tethys, the wife of Neptunus, callid goddesse of the see.
Tetinierit, for tenuerit. *Feft. Pom.*
Tetinus, for tenus.
Tettigoniæ, lyttell grasschoppes.
Tettigometræ, the mother of grasshoppes.
Tetracinus, a coyne, whyche was in value foure dragmas, or olde poyse grootes, of viii. to an ounce.
Tetracolon, a sentence hauyng .iiii. mēbres.
Tetradoron, of foure handdbreth.
Tetragonus, a, um, a thynge hauynge foure corners.
Tetragrammaton, the name of god, whych the Iewes do call Ineffabile, that is to say, vnspeakable.
Tetragrammaton, in grecke, sygnifyeth of foure letters.
Tetrametrum, a kynde of metre, hauynge but foure fete.
Tetrarcha, the rule of the fourthe parte of a royalme.
Tetrasyllabum, of foure syllables, as, Im pe ra tor.
Tetré, sharpely, cruelly, wyckedly.
Tetrices, water, wherwith gardeynes are wateryd.
Tetricus, a sowre felowe, z alway vnplesant.
Tetrinno, are, to swymme lyke a ducke.
Tetritudo, crueltie or sharpenes.
Tetrius, more sharpe or cruell.
Tetro, trare, to make fowle, to pollute, to make bytter.
Tetulit, for tulit.
Teucer, & Teucrus, the name of a kynge of Troianes. also of the sonne of Telamone the valyant Greke.
Teucer, Teucra, crum, idem quod Troianus. of Troye.
Teumesus, a lyttell hylle in Bœotia.
Teumesus leo, a Lyon, whyche Hercules dyd

T ante H.

dydde flee, whan he was a chylde, and of his skynne made hym a cote.

Teurion, the herbe whiche is also callydde Tripolium.

Teuta, a quene of Illiria, which lyued euer chaste, and vanquyshed many noble capitaynes, and diuers hostes of the Romains

Teutates, was in olde tyme amẽg the french men taken for Mercurius.

Teuthania, a piece of the coūtrey of Troy.

Teutones, people nowe callyd Almayns.

Texo, texui, texere, to weaue or wind threde, Also to make to builde, to write, to gather, to ornate. *Vide com.*

Texta, an hearelace, wherwith the heare is bounden vppe.

Textilis, le, that which is weaued or woundē.

Textim, an aduerbe, sygnifieng in weauing or wyndynge vp.

Textor, toris, & textrix, tricis, he or she that weaueth or wyndeth.

Textrina, & textrinum, the place where thinges be weaued or wounden. also the craft of weauynge.

Textrix, & textricula, a woman, whiche warketh in a frame or stole.

Textura, the weauynge.

Textus, & textum, the texte.

¶ T ANTE H.

Thalamus, a chamber where the husbande and the wyfe do lye togither.

Thalassicus, chamblette.

Thalassio, uide Talassio.

Thassus bonorum, a prouerbe applyed to them that promyse great thynges, as a mā wolde say, a worlde, a countray of welthe.

Thalassomeli, is a lycour made of honye, salte water, and rayne water, and is put into a vessell rased with pytche.

Thales, a philosopher, whiche was one of the seuen wyse men of Grecia.

Thalestris, was a quene of Amasones, whiche came to kynge Alexander with thre hunderde womenne with her, to the intente to haue issue by hym and his menne: and whanne she perceyued, that she and her ladyes were spedde, they departed home agayne.

Thali, are in lyekes, garlyke, and oynyons, whan they do growe, the myddell stalke betwene the blade and the heed or rote.

Thalia, one of the graces, whiche the auncent poetes dyd suppose to be one of the doughters of Jupiter, and gyuers of dilectable speche, and plesant pronunciatiō.

Thamaras, was he, whiche fyrste playd on a harpe, without syngynge therto.

T ante H.

Thamnos, in latine arbustum.

Thanatos, mors in latyne.

Thapsus, an yle by Sicile.

Thapsia, an herbe lyke to fenell, and hathe a yelowe flowre, and a flatte rounde sede.

Tharia, pyckelle, wherein fysshe is salted, and kepte.

Tharsos, a citie in Cilicia.

Thasia, an almonde.

Thasia nux, callyd also græca.

Thasij, menne of the Jle callyd Thasus in Egypte.

Thasium, a certayn wine, which is in Egipt.

Thauma, in greke is a meruaile or myracle.

Theatralis, le, & theatricus, ca, cum, that whiche pertayneth to theatrum.

Theatridium, a diminutiue of theatrum.

Theatrum, a place made halfe round, wherin the people assembled to beholde playes and sondrye sbatementes, sometyme it sygnifieth the multitude that beholdeth.

Thebœ, arum, Theba, be, & Thebe, bes, the name of cities, wherof one was in Egipte, buildid by Busirides, an other in Bœotia, buylded by Cadmus: an nother in Cilicia, where Andromaches, the wyfe of Hector was borne.

Thebaicæ, & thebaides, dates of the beste sorte.

Thebais, idis, & idos, a countraye of Egipt, it is also the name of a boke made by Statius the poete.

Thebanus, na, num, a man of Thebes.

Theca, a case, a shethe or scaberde, a boxe.

Thelebox, people of an yle callid Capreæ, whiche lyeth agaynst Naples.

Thelebon, people of the Jle Capreas.

Thelephus, a kynge, whyche camme in the ayde of the Troyanes, and was slayne by Achylles.

Theligonium, an herbe, whyche hathe beries lyke to an olyue.

Thelphusa, a citie in Arcadia.

Thelphussiū, uel thelphossion, a cite in Bœotia, where Pyndarus praysed Bacchus.

Thelypteris, sheferne, or the female ferne.

Thema, matis, a thynge purposed to be disputed or resoned. it is also a figure, wherin astronomers doo write the state of heuen, in placinge or settyng the planettes in suche signes and degrees, as they be in at the tyme of a mans natiuitie, or whan any thynge shall happen that they serche for.

Thembinacha, a contrey called also Nemia.

Themes, an olde towne in the ile of Cipres where brasse was fyrste founde.

Themis, one of the systers of Jupyter, she was callid the goddesse, whiche cōmanded men to aske that whiche was leful. There

was

was an other woman callyd Themis, whiche was called also Carmentis, it was somtyme taken for fas, lefull.

Themiscyra, a cite in Capadocia, afterward callyd Cæsaria.

Themisones, people by Licia.

Themistius, a philosopher which wrate commentaries on Aristotels warkes.

Themistocles, a noble capitain of the Atheniensis, whiche beinge expelled out of his countrey, and commen to Xerxes king of Persia, was sent by hym with a great armye agaynste the Athenienses, but whan he perceyued his countrey in peryll to be distroyed, he dranke poyson, and chase rather to dye, than eyther to be vnfeythfull to Xerxes, or els to distroy his countrey, although it were vnkynde towarde hym.

Thensa, a halowed carte or chariot.

Theocritus, a poete of Grecia, which wrate Bucolica, or the contention of herd men.

Theologia, diuynitie.

Theomenia, the wrathe of god.

Theonino dente rodere, to rebuke a manne shamefullye.

Theophrastus, a noble phylosopher, and of excellent eloquence.

Theos, in greke is god.

Theotochos, the mother of god.

Theorema, speculation.

Theoria, speculation, vnderstandyng.

Theopolis, the chiefe citie of Syria, callyd also Antiochia.

Thera, a cytie by Athenes.

Theramnum, a citie in Thessalia.

Theriace, ces, seu theriaca, tryacle.

Thereotrophion, a place where wylde beastes are kepte, as a forest, or parke.

Therioma, a soore of the priuye members, wherby all the partes therabout, are corrupted, and therof issueth blacke and stinkynge humour.

Theristrum, a thynne vayle, which the women of Palestina dyd weare.

Thermæ, are bathes of hote water.

Thermefacio, cere, to chaufe or make oone hotte with outragious eatynge and drynkynge of hote thynges.

Thermopolium, a place where meates and drynkes were solde, wherwith men were made hote or warme in cold wether.

Thermodoon, a ryuer in Cappadocia.

Thermodontiacus, ca, cum, pertaynynge to that ryuer.

Thermopoto, tare, to drynke hotte or warm drynke.

Thermopylæ, a mountayne in Greece, hauynge a narowe entrie or passage, where two thousand Lacedemoniens, with their capytayne Leonidas, faught agaynst fyue hundred and .xxviii. thousande Persyans, and resysted them two dayes, vntylle the sayd Lacedemoniens were all slayne.

Thersites, was a prynce that came with the grekes to the syege of Troye, whyche in persone and condicyons was of all other moste defourmed.

Thesaurizo, are, to gather treasure.

Thesaurus, & thesaurum, treasure.

Theseus, a noble and valyant kyng of Athenes, companyon to Hercules.

Thesis, a clause in writyng or spekyng, whiche contayneth a sentence.

Thesmophoria, the ceremonyes of Ceres, the goddesse of grayne.

Thesmophoros, was a name of Ceres.

Thespia, a free towne in Bœotia.

Thessalia, a region in Grece.

Thessalicus, ca, cum, of Thessalia.

Thessalonica, a citie in Macedonia.

Thetis, tidis, the mother of Achilles.

Theucinis, a rushe growynge in Nabachia, whiche hath the taste of sharpe wyne.

Theositas, for sodalitas. *Fest. Pom.*

Theutones, & theutonici, people in Germanye, callyd Duchemen.

Thirromachus, one of the sonnes of Hercules by Megara.

Thiasias, he that is burste or broken in his stoones.

Thideus, was the name of the father of Diomedes.

Thieum, for succinum, aumbre.

Thita præfigere, for condemnare.

Thymelici, mynstrelles retayned with noble menne.

Thoa, one of the nymphes.

Thoas, the name of two kynges, oone of Taurica, the other of Lemnos.

Thoes, be wolfes in Ethiope, Arrianus doth calle them tygres in India.

Tholos, a scochen or small tergate. also the the syldynge of a house, or a round house.

Thomices, lyches of hempe, wherwith halters are made, they be also lyttel bolsters, whiche men do weare whanne they carye burdeynes, for frettynge of theyr neckes and shulders with cordes or ropes.

Thon, nis, he that fyrste brought phisyke in the fourme of a scyence, amonge the Egyptians.

Thoora, the daughter of Phorcus, on whom Neptunus gate Polyphemus.

Thoracatus, he that wearethe curettys or breste plates.

Thorax, racis, is propreleye the hole boulke of a man from the necke to the myddelle, it is also curettes or breste plates.

Thous,

T ante H.

sometyme it signifieth a towre.
Thous, a duke of Troye.
Thracia, a region of Europa, wherin is the citie of Constantinople.
Thraceas, uel Thrassias, a northwest wynd.
Thrasimedes, the sonne of Nestor.
Thrasomenus, a ryuer in Italye nyghe to Perusia.
Thrax, acis, a man of Thracia.
Threces, idem quod gladiatores.
Threnodia, a mournyng songe.
Threnos, a lamentacyon, whyche was vsyd at buryenge.
Thressa, a woman of Thracia.
Throni, be one of the .ix. orders of angels.
Thronus, the seate or chayre of an Emperour or kynge.
Thrulla, a trewell, whyche masons, tylers, and pargettours doo vse for layenge of morter.
Thrullisso, are, to laye on morter.
Thryallis, an herbe callyd in Italye Strella & Bipinella.
Thryps, a mowthe.
Thule, an Ile beyonde Scotlande.
Thunnus, a fyshe, callyd Tuny.
Thuribulum, a sensar.
Thuringia, Thuryn in Fraunce.
Thurini, a people in Italye.
Thuriferus, ra, rum, that whyche bearethe frankynsence.
Thurifico, to make a perfume, or to sence.
Thurius, ria, rium, of incense.
Thus, thuris, frankyncense.
Thuscana, a cytie in Italye.
Tusculani, a people by Rome.
Thusculum, a diminutiue of thus. Also a cite in Latium.
Thyas, a sacrifyce made to Bacchus.
Thyasus, a daunce dedycate to Bacchus.
Thiella, a storme.
Thyestes, whome his owne brother Atreus causyd to eate his propre chylderne.
Thymbra, an herbe callyd sauerye.
Thymele, es, a woman, whyche fyrst taught daunsynge in open places.
Thymelici, maye be callydde daunsers of Morysdaunces.
Thymiama, matis, a swete perfume.
Thymus, an herbe called tyme.
Thymū, a wart, which is as great as a bean.
Thynnus, a fyshe callyd Tuny.
Thyridion, a wycket or lyttell doore.
Thyrsus, the stalke of letyse and of other herbes, whiche may be eaten. Some doo take it for a speare with a sharpe heade, whyche hadde boughes and leaues of yuy wrapped aboute them: suche speares dyd Bacchus and his flocke of drunken har-

T ante I.

lottes, beare in theyr handes. Lucretius the poete taketh thyrsum, for furye or an ardent mocyon.
Thysus, the stalke of euery herbe, specially of letyse. It is also a staffe wounde about with yuy, whiche was borne of them that dyd sacrifyce to Bacchus.

¶ T ANTE I.

Tiara, an ornament, which the women of Persia dyd weare on their heedes, whiche was rounde, and couered onely the hynder parte of theyr heedes. Princis & pristis vsed also to weare it.
Tiatura, a cytie in the countray of Misia.
Tibareni, people in Scithia, being in Asia.
Tibia, the leg, proprely the shanke or shinne bone, it is also an instrumēt callid a shalme.
Tibialis, le, pertaynyng to shaulmes.
Tibiale, lis, pluraliter tibialia, geiues or legge harneys.
Tibicen, & tibicina, he or she that blowethe a trumpette or shalme.
Tibicen, is alsoo any thynge, whereby any thynge in buyldynge is susteyned, as a shore or proppe.
Tibi, to the.
Tibicis, a ryuer in Scythia.
Tibin, a baskette or coffyn made of wickers or bulle rushes, or barke of a tree: suche one was Moyses put into by the daughter of Pharao. *Origenes super Ex.*
Tibilustria, were dayes whan menne wente with trumpettes, as it were in processyon aboute their lambes. *Fest. Pom.*
Tibini, tunes made with shalmes. *Fest. Pom.*
Tiburtes, people in Italy nigh to Rome.
Ticinum, a citye in Lumbardye nowe callyd Pauia.
Tigillus, a rafter.
Tignarius, faber, a Carpentar that maketh a house of tymber.
Tignus, & tignum, a rafter of a house, whiche bearethe the roufe. It is also generally all the tymber, which serueth to a hous.
Tigrane, a riuer in the countray of Media.
Tigranes, the propre name of a kynge of Media, of the greatter Armeny.
Tigris, a beaste of a wonderfull swyftenes, it is also one of the foure ryuers, whiche commeth out of Paradyse.
Tigurini, people of Germanye, whiche do inhabyte the fourthe parte of Heluctia, or Swyzerlande.
Tile, an Ile beyonde Scotlande, callydde also Thule.
Tilia, a tree, whyche some do thinke is callyd quyckebeame.

Tilium

Tilium, a citie in the weste parte of Sardinia, on the see syde.

Tilos, an yle in the Indian see, wherein is plentie of perle, and trees of dyuers fruites, and the leaues of trees there growynge do neuer falle. also wolle groweth on trees there, whiche do beare gourdes of the greatnes of quynces, and beynge rype do open, in the whyche doo appiere the wolle, wherof are made fyne and precious clothes. About that place dothe begynne the mountain of Caucasus, whiche dothe passe through a greate parte of the worlde.

Timalos, an herbe and flower growyng in waters, callyd commonly of potycaries Nenufer.

Timæus, a noble phylosopher of Pythagoras secte.

Timauus, a ryuer in Italy besides Aquileia.

Timens, he that feareth for a tyme.

Timidus, he that alway feareth, callyd tymorouse.

Timeo, mui, mere, to feare or dreade.

Timeo te, I feare the as myn ennemy, leste thou shallt do me harme.

Timeo tibi, I am aferd of the as my frende, leste thou shuldest haue any harme.

Timeo mihi abs te, I am frayde that thou wylte do me harme.

Iuuenalis. **Timeo furem pomis**, I am afrayde that one wyll steale myn appulles.

Timeo moriatur, I am aferd that he wyl die

Timide, fearefully.

Timiditas, feare.

Timiopilæ, ingrossers or regraters of markettes, whiche doo bye moch corne or vitayle togyther, to make it scarse and dere.

Timor, moris, & timos, feare of some euyll commynge.

Timotheus, was the name of a noble capytayn of the Atheneses, who for the good fortune that he had in battayle, was paynted lyenge aslepe, and hauynge by hym a nette pytched, wherin fortune was taken. Also a cunnynge musitian, whiche vsyd to take of his scholers, which had lerned before, double salarie, that he toke of other, whiche neuer lerned, sayeng, that he toke with them double laboure, that is to saye, to make them to forgette that which they hadde lernyd afore, and thanne to teache them perfytely.

Tin, olde wryters vsyd for Eum.

Tina, & Tinia, a greatte bolle, whiche being ful of wine, euery man mought drynke therof as moche as he lysted.

Tinctor, ctoris, a dyer.

Tinctilis, le, that whiche is dyed.

Tinctura, dyenge.

Tinea, a mothe, they be also wormes in the bealye, also wormes bredinge in bee hiues.

Tineosus, a, um, full of mothes

Tinge, a promontorie or elbowe of Affrica.

Tingitana, a parte of Mauritania or Barbaria agaynste Spayne.

Tingo, xi, gere, to deepe a thynge into lycour, to dye colours.

Tinnio, nire, to rynge or make a sounde as mettall dothe, sometyme as in a mans eare.

Tinnimentū, a ryngyng in the eare of a mā. *Plaut. in rudent.*

Tinnunculus, a byrd, which maketh a sharp ryngynge noyse, and is of the kynde of haukes, and in some place dothe brede in houses, whiche with his voyce dryueth away other hawkes, and therfore the brydes of hym are kepte in erthen pottes couered with claye, and hanged vp in douehouses, whyche causeth culuers meruaylously to loue their house.

Tinnulus, la, lum, sharpe in sounde, as that which is made by beatinge on metall.

Tintinaculus, he that beateth with roddes, a transgressour of a lawe.

Tintinabulum, a lytle bell.

Tintino, nare, to ringe lyke a bell.

Tiphernum, a towne in Italy.

Tiphis, an excellent carpentar, the whiche founde first the meane to gouerne a shyp, a rether.

Tipula, a wurme, whyche runneth on the water as other wurmes doo on the lande, and hath sixe fete.

Tiresias, was kynge of Thebes, who had the knowlege of thinges whyche shoulde happen, and was blynde.

Tirius, a ryuer in Grecia: also the contray where Hercules was borne in Peloponesso, now called Morea.

Tirinthius, was a surname of Hercules.

Tirinthis, a famouse olde citie in Grecia.

Tis, for tui, the genitiue case of Tu.

Tisiphone, one of the furies of helle, which was supposed to tourment homycydes, or sleers of men.

Titan, & Titanus, was the brother of Saturne, and is taken for the sonne, and Titanis, for the moone.

Tithimallus, an herbe callyd werte worte, wherof the mylke woll take away wartes.

Tithymalus, an herbe whyche is commonly callyd Spurge.

Titillo, are, to tyckle, to prouoke or meeue pleasantly.

Titio, onis, a frebrande or wodde, whiche hath ben in the fyre.

Tiriuillitium, sygnifyeth nothynge.

Titubantia, stammmerynge.

Titube,

T ante M.

Titubo, are, to stacker in speking or going, as a man beinge drunke or sycke.
Titulotenus, no further than his title.
Titulus, the title or inscription of a warke or acte. sometyme dignitie; also a monumēt or other remembrance.
Titus, the name of a man.
Titus Liuius, the moste excellent hystorien or writer of stories, in whom was the foūtayne of the mylke of pure eloquence.
Tlepolemus, was the kyng of the Rhodes, whiche camme to the battayle of Troye, with nyne shyppes.
Tityus, the sonne of Jupiter, whom poetes fayned to be slayne by Apollo, bycause he wolde haue rauysshed Latona his syster. And therfore lyeth in helle, hauyng an egle alwaye eatynge his lyuer. And it is alsoo sayde, that his bodye was in lengthe nyne furlonge. wytnesse Tibulle, whiche was a poete, and also a greate louer, and therfore coulde not lye.

¶ T. ANTE M.

TMolus, a mountayne in Lidia, wheron dyd growe great plentie of saffron and vynes. It is also a lyttell busshe, whiche beareth floures of saffron coloure.

¶ T ANTE O.

TOdi, lytell brides, I suppose it be the bride, whyche is callyd a tytmous.
Toga, the common garmente of men and women, callyd a gowne. And bycause the Romaynes specially dydde weare that garment in the tyme of peace, toga was taken for peace, as arma was for warre.
Toga prætexta, a garment whiche the Romains dyd weare afore that they were of the age of. xvi. yeres. Afterwarde it was worne of them, whiche were in auctoritie.
Toga polymita, a garment made with thredes of sondrye coloures, as motleye or bauldekyn.
Togata Comœdia, a comedye or enterlude, wherein the maners of the Romaynes, were expressed.
Togata Gallia, the countrey nowe callydde Lumbardy.
Toga candida, was a garment, whiche they dyd weare, that sued for any great office in the citie of Rome.
Togati, apparayled in gownes.
Togatus, he that weareth a gowne.
Tolerantia, sufferance.
Toleranter, paciently.
Tolles, a waxynge kernell.
Tolleno, nonis, that wherein any thynge is

Ti. Lulus.

T ante O.

put or layde to be drawen vp. sometyme a buckette wherwith water is drawen vp. — Vegetius. Budeus.
Tollenon, an engyne to drawe vppe water, whiche hath a great poise at the one ende
Tolero, rare, to suffre, to endure, to beare, to lyue poorely, or nyghly.
Tolerare uitam, to lyue, or to mayntyene his lyfe.
Tolerabilis, rabile, that whiche maye suffre or beare.
Tollo, sustuli, seu tetuli, tollere, to lyfte vppe, or sette vppe.
Tollere clamorem, to crie oute.
Tollere cristas, to sette vp the crest, applyed to them that be proude or arrogante, & do stretche vp their browes with a dysdaynfull countenaunce.
Tolle digitum, hold vp thy fynger, confesse thy selfe vanquysshed.
Tollere gradum, to sette forthe, or to marche forthe.
Tollere, to take away. Tolle hanc patinam, take away this dyshe. — Plautus in milite.
Tollere, to haue a chylde by a woman.
Tollere, to nouryshe. Verum quod erit natū, tollito, what soo euer is borne, putte it to nouryshynge. — Plautus in Amphit.
Tollere, to deferre or prolonge, Omnes tollo ex hoc die in alium diem, I put them all of from one day to an other. — Plautus.
Tollere minas, to thretten or menace.
Tolutarius, & tolutaris equus, an aumblynge horse.
Tolutiloquentia, a swyfte or faste speche.
Tolutim, an amblynge pace.
Tolutim loqui, to speake faste oone worde after an nother.
Tomaculę, Tomacula, & tomacla, a certayn sorte of pouddynges, proprelye swynes pouddynges.
Tomentum, flore, which is shorne of wollen cloth, alio lockes clypped of white wolle.
Tomices, hempen cordes, also colers, whiche are put on carthorses, for hurtynge of their neckes.
Tomos, a pece of a boke, or a warke vnperperfyte. Alsoo a citie in the countraye of Ponthus.
Tomyris, was a noble queene of Massagetis in Scithia, agaynste whom whan Cirus the great kynge of Persia came, and hadde slayne her sonne, she pytchynge a fylde agaynste hym, and of purpose hauing great plentie of vytayles in her pauyllyons, after a lyttell skyrmysshe she and her host fled. And whan Cirus had a whyle folowed the chace, and blowen to the retraicte, he came to her campe, and fyndynge greate plentie of vytayle, he and his people dyd so moche
fylle

fyll theym selfe therwith, that fallynge a slepe, they were all taken by the quene, and slayne, and she causynge a great vessell to be fylled with the bloudde of Cirus, and the Persyans, dyd caste his heed therinto, sayinge, Bloode thou haste thyrsted, and nowe drynke therof thy fylle.

Tonarion, a certayne shaulme with a softe sounde, on the whiche in the old time some oratours vsed to haue, to playe by theym, whan they pleaded, that by the tunes of the shalme, the oratour mought moderate and order his pronunciation.

Tondeo, totondi, tondere, to clyp or sheare.

Tonesco, tonui, tonescere, to thunder.

Tonimus, for tonamus. *Ennius.*

Tonitrus, & tonitru, & tonitruum, thunder.

Tonitruo, are, to thunder.

Tonitus, thunder.

Tono, nare, to thunder, to make a greatte sounde or noyse, to speake loude.

Tonsæ, shepe, which be shorne or clypped. also ores of botes or shyppes.

Tonsilis, le, that which is shorne or clipped.

Tonsilla, a poste, hauynge the one ende armed with yron, whiche is pitched into the erth, to thende that shippes or botes may be tyed therat.

Tonsillæ plurali, a dysese within the chekes and mouthe lyke to great kernels.

Tonsi montes, hilles without woddes.

Tonsor, et tonstrix, tricis, he or she whyche clyppeth or sheareth.

Tonsorius, ria, rium, pertaynynge to clyppynge.

Tonstrix, tricis, a woman barbar.

Tonstricula, idem.

Tonstrina, a place where they do vse to clip or a barbers shoppe.

Tonsus, a, um, shorne or clypped.

Tonus, a tune or accent. also the space or distance, whiche is betwene the erthe and the moone.

Toparcha, he that hathe the gouernaunce and charge of one onely countrey.

Toparchia, the rule of one countray.

Topazion, & topazius, a preciouse stone of the colour of golde.

Tophus, a kynde of stone, whiche is soone resolued into sande.

Topiarium, a warke made of trees, bushes, bryers, or herbes, for pleasure, and contayned places to sytte or walke in, as it is vsed nowe with boxe, eglantine, iacymine, and other lyke trees or thornes, that be flexible, or wyll be wounden.

Topiarius, he that maketh suche warkes.

Topiaria, the warke.

Topica, warkes in that part of logike, whiche declareth the places, out of the whiche argumentes maye be inuented, that moste proprely pertayneth to oratours.

Topographia, the description of a place, as of a countrey or citie.

Topper, the olde wryters vsed for soone, shortly, or quyckely. *Festus.*

Toral, & toralium, in plurali numero, toralia, euery thynge that lyeth on a bed, as shetis blankettes and couerlyds. In the old time it were certaine floures and swete herbes wounden togyther in ropes, and hanged before the place, where men dyd lye. Like as nowe they vse in London at Mydsommer to hange afore their doores.

Torcular, aris, & torculare, & torculū, a presse for wyne, syder, or vertiuyce.

Torcularius, a, um, bylongynge to a presse.

Toreuma, matis, & tereumatum, grauen or polyshed warke.

Toreutis, a grauer.

Toreutice, ces, the crafte of grauynge.

Tormen, minis, frettynge or tourmente in the bealy and guttes.

Tormina, idem.

Tormentum, tourment, or an engyn to turment men, generally all ordinance pertaynynge to warre.

Torminosus, he that hathe tourmentes or frettynge in his guttes.

Tornacum, a towne callyd Tornay.

Tornatilis, le, that whiche is tourned with a whele.

Torniamen, may be nowe taken for a tournayment or iustes.

Torno, are, to torne or warke with a whele, as tourners done.

Tornus, the instrument or whele.

Torpedo, dinis, slouthefulnes. also a fysshe, whiche in the takynge maketh the handes of theym that doo drawe, to be stonyed or deed for the tyme.

Torpeo, & torpesco, pui, torpere, uel torpescere, to be astonyed, or slowe.

Torpor, poris, a debilitation or feblynge of mynde, an vnaptnes to do any thynge.

Torporo, rare, to astonye, or make astonied.

Torquatus, a rynge doue, or stocke doue. it is he also that weareth a colar or chayne.

Torqueo, torsi, quére, to wynde in, to whirle aboute lyke a whiele, to sustayne or beare vp, to tourment. *Vide cō.*

Torquere telum, to throwe a darte or iauelyn, that he runne rounde. *Vergilius.*

Torquére saxa, to tourne great stones. *Vergilius.*

Torquere, to spynne.

Torques, a colar, chayne, or bye of gold or syluer, suche as is worne by knyghtes or esquiers about their neckes.

Torre

T ante O.

Torrefacio, cere, to broyle or rost at the fire, or by the heate of the sonne.
Torrens, tis, a streame, that cometh downe of hylles, whiche is caused by moche rayne or snowe. Torrens, a partityple, sygnifieth flowynge with a great swepe. Torrentior, more flowing, with a greatter violence.
Torreo, rui, rere, idem quod torrefacio.
Torresco, re, to be broilid or rosted, or dryed.
Torridę zonæ, are two girdels imagined in the firmament on euery side of the equinoctial line, vnder whiche gyrdels the people whiche inhabyte there, are burned with the feruent heat of the sonne, bicause the sonne abideth longest in those .ii places & ar also named Tropicus cancri, & tropicus Capricorni.
Torridus, da, dum, dryed or burned.
Tortilis, le, that whiche is bent or bowed.
Torris, a stycke of fyre.
Tortiuum vinum, wyne of the laste presse.
Torto, tare, to tourment vehemently.
Tortor, toris, a tourmentour, or he that casteth a stone with a slynge.
Tortū, an engin, to throw great stones with.
Tortuosus, a, ū, woūde or turned many wais.
Tortus, ta, tum, crooked.
Torue, toruū, torua, toruiter, pprely in beholdyng sowerly or grymly.
Toruinus, an apparell of a womans heed.
Torus, a bedde, it was somtyme made with herbes wounden togyther.
Tori, the brawnes of the armes and leggis, or the fleshe myxte with synewes.
Torosus, a, um, myghty or stronge in brawnes of the legges and armes.
Torsio, sionis, Theodorus, Gaza, & Longolius supposed to be a sturgion. Paulus Iouius is of a contrary opinion.
Torulus, a lyttell bedde.
Torué, sturdyly in looke.
Toruitas, tatis, sturdynes.
Toruus, ua, uum, cruel and sturdy in loking.
Tostus, a, um, tosted or rosted.
Totidem, verily so many, euen as many.
Tot, as many. Toties, so many tymes.
Totus, ta, tum, all, the hole, euery whyt.
Toxicum, venym or poyson.

¶ T ANTE R.

Trabales, a certayne tourment.
Trabalis, le, pertayning to a beame.
Trabalis clauus, a yron pin or gret naill wherwith bemis ar made fast to the rafters
Trabea, a cerklet or kyrtell worn by kynges vnder theyr mantell.
Trabica nauis, a shyp made with gret bemes
Trabs, & trabes, a beame of a house.
Trachale, the ouer part of a fishe callid Murex, of whom purple colour is made.
Trachea, the weson or pype of the lunges.

T ante R.

Trachelū, the midle part of tho sail of a ship
Trachelus, the chine of a man or beast, from the heed to the haunche.
Trachida, Trachina, & Trachurus, I suppose is a banstykle.
Trachinia, a kynde of roses, not perfytely red, lyke to them, that we call french roses.
Traconia, a roughnes within the eie liddes.
Traconitidis, a parte of Judea.
Tractabilis, treatable, that may be intreatid.
Tractare, to handell.
Tractim, on length, a longe tyme or space.
Tracto, tare, to intreate. Hęc arte tractabat uirum, She handlid the man craftely, or of that sorte. alsoo to vse or exercise, to order or gouerne.
Tractoriū, a windlas to draw vp heuy thigis
Tractus, us, a space, a countrey.
Trado, didi, dere, to delyuer, also to teache, to commytte in trust to an other man.
Traditio, a tradition.
Traduco, duxi, ducere, to brynge from oone place to an other, to brynge ouer, to translate oute of one language into an nother.
Traducere tempus, to passe the tyme, to brynge vp or nouryshe.
Traduces, vynes or trees tranflated frome place to place.
Tragelaphus, a beaste in parte lyke a harte, in parte lyke a gote.
Tragemata, that whyche are commonlye callyd bankettynge dyshes.
Tragite, cruelly, in the maner of a tragedy.
Tragicum tueri, to loke grymly.
Tragicus, a wryter of tragedyes.
Tragœdia, a tragedye, whyche is an enterlude, wherin the personages do represent somme hystorie or fable lamentable, for the crueltie and myserye therin expressed.
Tragœdus, he that exercyseth some part in a tragedye.   Plin. 38. cap. 13.
Tragonis, siue Tragion, a tree growynge in Candy, lyke to Junyper, the iuyce wherof is lyke to mylke, and waxethe thycke lyke gumme.
Tragum, is lyke a tysan made of wheate, it is also a fyshers nette callyd a dragge.
Tragonia, an herbe nowe callid Taragon, late sene in this realme, whiche hath a tast lyke gynger: whiche herbe layde to the lefte syde, consumeth the splene.
Tragopa, a byrde in Ethiopia, greatter thā an egle, & hath on his hed horns like a gote.
Tragopogus, a fyshe callyd a barbyll.
Tragoriganon, an herbe whiche I suppose, is callyd Peny royalle, growyng wylde.
Tragula, a iauelyn with a barbyd heed.
Traguriū, an ile in the see callyd Hadriaticū.
Trigon, is a fyshe callyd a thornebacke.

Dd   Tra-

Tragulam inijcere, to practise deceyte.
Traha, a dray or flyd drawen about wheles.
Trahax, acis, a couetous persone, the whiche draweth all thynge vnto hym.

Vergilius. Trahere diem, noctem, tempus, to passe the day, the nyghte, or the tyme.

Plautus in trinummo Trahere, to tary. Atq̃ egomet me adeo cum illis una ibidem traho, And I my selfe taryed as longe with them. Trahere, to liue.

Cic. anteq̃ iret in exilium. Et uosut tutã tranquillãq̃ fortunã traheretis, mea perfeci uigilantiã. And by my vygilancy I brought to passe, that ye shulde lyue in a sure and quiete prosperitie.

Traho, xi, here, to draw, to leade, to deferre, or delay, to extend, to remoue, to prolong.
Traijcio, ieci, ijcere, to leade ouer, to carye ouer, to brynge ouer, to stryke through.
Traiectitia pecunia, money caried ouer ꝑ see
Traiectus, tus, a passage. Traiectio, idem.
Trallis, a citie in Lidia, an other in Phrigia.
Trallianus, a man of that citie.
Tralucidus, da, dum, clere, that a man maye loke through.
Trama, an vnder garment.
Trames, mitis, a crosse waye.
Trano, nare, to swymme ouer.
Tranato, tare, to swymme ouer.
Tranquille, softely without noyse.
Tranquillitas, tranquillitie, rest, quyetenes.
Tranquillo, lare, to make quiete.
Tranquillus, la, lum, quiete, in rest, peasible.

Plautus in casina. Tranquillum est, it is fayre wether.
Tranquillus locus, a good place to reste in, a place of quietenes.

Trans, ouer, from one place to an other.
Transactio, an agrement vpon cõmunicatiõ.
Transactus, a, ũ, passed, lõge agone, achiued.
Transalpina Gallia, Fraunce on this syde the mountaynes.
Trãsalpinus, a, ũ, ouer the moũtains of alpes
Transcendo, dere, to go ouer, to excede.
Transcindo, scidi, scindere, to cut on sonder.

Vergilius. Transcribere, is to giue or deliuer. Turne tot incassum fusos patiere labores, Et tua Dardaneis trãscribi sceptra colonis? wilt thou Turnus suffre thy labours to be lost, z thy realm to be giuen to the inhabytantes of Troy?

Agretius. Transcribere, the transposition of a possession from one to an other.

Transcribo, psi, bere, to write out of a copie, sometyme to translate.
Transcurro, rere, to runne forthe.
Transcurrit æstas, the sommer is passed.
Transcursus, us, a course. In transcursu, In passynge forthe.
Transenna, a loupe to loke out at. also a windowe, or casement. alsoo a rope stretched out, a snare or trappe.
Transeo, siui, & sii, sire, to go forthe, to passe ouer, to passe: Transire domum, to go home.

Transeunter, passynge by or ouer.
Transfero, tuli, ferre, to cary or bryng from one place to an other, to translate from one langage to an other, or from ones possessiõ to an others. Translatus, a, ũ, the participle.
Transfigo, xi, gere, to thruste through.
Transfuga, he that departeth from his own people or capytayne vnto the parte of the ennemies, or of theym that are suspected in tyme of truce.
Transfodio, dere, to dygge through.
Transfossus, a, ũ, digged or striken through.
Transfiguro, rare, to transfourme, to turne into an nother fygure.
Transfretatio, a passage ouer the see.
Transfreto, tare, to passe ouer the see.
Transfugere ad hostes, is to goo and yelde hym to the contrary parte.
Transfugium, an yeldynge to ennemies.
Transfulgeo, re, to shyne through.

Transfundere, to translate frome one to an other. Libentius omnes meas laudes (si modo sint aliquę meę laudes) ad te transfuderim, *Ci. Dolo.* I haue more wyllyngly tourned my prayse, (yf I haue any prayse) vnto you.

Transfugio, gere, to fle from place to place.
Transfundo, fudi, fundere, to poure oute of one vessell into an nother.
Transgredior, deris, di, to passe or go ouer or beyonde, to excede, to transgresse a law or commaundemente.
Transgressio, is a figure of retorike, where a mã leaueth the principal matter, z entreth into an other thing, z after returneth to his matter. we cõmonly call it, a digression.
Transgressus, us, a passing ouer the see.
Transigere uitam, to passe his or their lyfe. *Salust.*
Transigere, is also to perfourme.

Transigo, egi, igere, to dryue furth, to treate *Plaut. in Amphit.*
a mater, to agree or condescende, or come *Terent. in Andria.*
to a point: as hapneth betwene men, which do contend for somwhat.

Transilio, siliui, & silii, ire, to leape ouer.
Transitio, situs, a passing ouer, a going forth.
Transitorius, a, ũ, that which shortly passeth.
Translatio, a trãslation, or bryngīg frõ one place to another. Trãslego, ere, to rede ouer
Transluceo, cere, to shyne through.
Transmarinus, na, um, that whiche cõmeth from beyonde the se.
Transmigratio, a departinge or goynge frõ one place to dwell in another.
Transmigro, grare, to go further, to dwell further of, to transpose my dwellynge.
Trãsmissio, a going or sēding further or ouer
Transmittere mare, to passe ouer the see. *Plin. epist.*
Transmittere tempus, to passe the tyme. *173.*
Transmittere discrimen, to escape a danger. *Epist. 183.*
Transmitto, misi, mittere, to sende from one *Epist. 164.*
place

place to an other, to go or runne quickly, to send shortly or quickly to passe ouer a water

Transmoueo, ere, to remoue frō one place to an other. Transnato, are, to swym ouer.

Sueton. de claris grā maticis.

Transnomino, nare, to chaunge his name.

Transpareo, rēre, to be sene thrugh a thinge.

Transpicio, spexi, spicere, to loke through.

Plautus in mercator.

Trāsquietus, a, ū, in quiet or rest frō hēsforth

Transtra, transomes which do go ouerwhart a house, also the seates, wheron they do syt, whiche do rowe in a shyppe or bote.

Transtyberinus, rina, num, that whiche is or dwelleth beyonde the ryuer of Tyber.

Transuado, are, & trausuador, ari, to waade ouer a shalowe place of a ryuer.

Transueho, uexi, uehere, to carye ouer.

Transuerbero, are, to stryke through.

Transuersum agere, to tourne hastily away from the purpose which a man went about.

Transuersum unguem non discedere, not to go a nayle bredth from it. A prouerbe signifieng a litle distance. Trāsuersū digitū, idē.

Transuersus, a, um, ouerthwart, not straight or direct. Transuerto, tere, to turne awry, or out of the right facion or way.

Plautus in capt.

Transuideo, dere, to se through a clere thig.

Transulto, tare, to leape ouer.

Transumptū, that which is writē out of a record, and approued vnder the kinges seale, or the sygnynge of the iudge. In the common lawe they calle it an exemplifycation. Some do also call it a Transumpte.

Transumptio, a figure callid also Metalepsis, wherby one signification is gathered of an other: as of Nox atra, a blacke nyghte, is gathered Nox tenebricosa, a darke nyght.

Transuolo, are, to flye ouer, or leape ouer, or to go or runne beyonde a place.

Transumo, umpsi, sumere, to take of or from an nother, to remeue from one to an other

Transuo, ere, to sowe through.

Trapetes, petum, a myl wherin oyle is made

Trapeza, a table, wheron an exchāger doth tel moncy. Trapezita, an exchāger or bāker

Trapezus, zuntis, a citie in the countrey of Pontus. Trapezuntius, a man of that citie.

Festus

Trapit, olde writers vsed for vertit.

Traston, a certain rosine or gumme, the best of that which is callyd gummihamoniacum.

Traulius, he that spekith with gret difficulti

Trebellicū vinum, seu Trebulanū uinum, wine growing about the riuer of Trebia, in Lūbardye, the Italions do call it Trebiana.

Trebula, an olde towne nygh to Rome.

Trebulani, men of that towne.

Trecceni, thre hūdred. Trecēti, & trecentū, idē

Trecentenus, na, num, the thre hundreth.

Trecentesimus, ma, mum, idem.

Trecenties, three hundred tymes.

Tredecim, thyrtene.

Tremebundus, he that trembleth moche.

Tremefacio, feci, cere, to make to tremble or quake. Tremisco, scere, to tremble.

Tremo, ere, to quake as one doth in a feuer, also to feare. Tremulus, he that quaketh for feare. Tremor, oris, quakyng, also feare.

Trepidatio, tremblyng, feare.

Trepidanter, fearefully, tremblyng.

Trepido, dare, to feare, to make haste.

Trepidus, da, dum, fearful, also he that doth a thing hastily. Trepōdo, thre poūd weight.

Tres, thre. Tresis, thre pounde.

Treueris, a citie in Germany callid Tryre.

Treueri, people callyd Treues.

Triambi, were thre which spake togither in a tragedy. Triangularis, re, hauig. iiii. corners

Triangulus, la, lum, thre cornerde.

Triarchus, a master of a shyp with. iii. tops.

Triarij, souldiors that be set alway in the rere warde, which were the strongest men, they faught stādinge, bowing their knies, as they wold rather dy thā remeue frō their places

Triatrus, a festiuall day kept after the third Idus of euery moneth.

Tribaces, they which be worne with stripes

Tribrachus, a fote in meter of. iii. short sillables. Tribula, & tribulum, a flayle or other lyke thing, wherwith corne is threshed.

Tribulis, a kynnesman that commeth of the same stocke that I do.

Tribulor, aris, ari, to be troubled with heuynes of mynde. Tribulus, a bremble.

Tribunal, the place where a Iudge sytteth in iudgement.

Tribunatus, the office or dignite of a tribune

Tribunus, was an offycer amonge the Romaines, hauinge chiefe iurisdiction amonge the communes, also a capytaine in warres, hauynge auctoritie ouer soudiours, to view and see that they were welle armed and exercysed. Tribunitius, a, um, pertaynynge to the Tribunes.

Tribuo, buere, to gyue, sommetyme to sette moche by. Also to fauour.

Tribus, bus, a part of the people, somtime diuided into thre partis. It semeth that it was somtime taken for a family or particular iurisdiction among the people, and therof cometh tribulis. And therfore the partition of the people of Israel were into. xii. Tribus. hereof be sondry opinions. rede Calepine.

Tributarius, he that payeth tribute.

Tributim, by sondrye families or partes of the people. Tributum, tribute.

Trice, fethers in the fete of chykens & pygeons, whiche do let them to go, and therfore all thinges which do let a man ar callid Trice. Vide extrico, & intrico.

Dd. ij.　　　Tri

Tricaptum, a garment, whiche was so fyne, that it semed to be made of smalle heares.
Tricenus, na, num, cometh of triginta, thirtie. it is sometyme taken for tricentenum.
Tricentuplus, a, um, thre hundred folde.
Triceps, cipitis, hauynge thre heedes.
Tricerberus, a great hell hounde.
Trichiæ, be fysshes callyd Sardynes.
Trichila, a vessell hauynge thre lauers, oute of the whiche water is poured.
Trichomanes, an herbe callid Maidenhear.
Triclinium, a parlor to sup in, wherin were thre tables and thre beddes. For in the old tyme they vsed to lye, whan they dyd eate.
Triclinarius, the seruaunt, which doth serue in the parlour.
Triclinarius, a, um, pertaynynge to the parlour or dynynge chaumber.
Triclinarium, idem quod triclinium.
Tricolon, hauynge thre membres.
Tricones, men hauynge soure couuntenances, and that be neuer or seldome sene to laugh. Also pykers of quarels.
Tricongius, was oone whiche dranke or he rested, thre mesures of wine, callid congii, whiche as I suppose, was thre galons and a pynt of our wyne mesure. Wherfore Tiberius the Emperoure promoted hym to honour, and at the last made hym Consul of Rome.
Tricornium, that whiche hath thre hornes.
Tricubitalis, le, of thre cubytes in measure.
Tricubitus, ta, tum, idem.
Tricus, a stone, which although it be black yet sheweth he at the roote blacke, in the myddell sanguyne, at the toppe whyte.
Tridacna, an oyster so greate, that a manne must make of hym thre morsels.
Tridens, tis, euery instrument, toole, or wepon, hauynge thre tethe.
Triduanus, a, um, of thre days continuance.
Triduum, the space of thre dayes.
Triennalis, le, of thre yeres.
Triennium, the space of thre yeres.
Triennis, ne, thre yeres olde.
Triens, tis, a coyne whiche is the third part of a pounde, it is also a cuppe cuntaynyng that poyse.
Trientalis herba, an herbe, whiche hath leues as great as the coyne callyd triens.
Triental, a vessel contayning the thirde part of that mesure, whiche was named Sextariu.
Trierarchus, the capytain of a shyppe, whiche is callyd trieris.
Trieris, a greate shyppe, whiche hathe in it thre orders of seates for the rowers.
Trietericus, ca, cum, for triennalis, that whiche hapneth to be done euery thirde yere.
Trieteris, the space of thre yeres.

Trifariã, in. iii. partes, or thre maner of wais.
Trifarius, a, um, of the same signification.
Trifaux, faucis, hauynge thre chekes.
Trifax, & triforum, a weapon of thre cubytes longe.
Trifer, fera, rum, that which bryngeth frute thryse. Triferus, a, um, idem.
Trifera, is a medycyne and other delycate spyces, to expulse easily corrupt humours
Trifidus, da, dum, dyuided into thre partes.
Trifinium, the buttyng of thre feldes, whiche ioyne togyther.
Trifolium, maye be taken for the generalle name of all herbes hauynge thre leues. Albe it there is one herbe callid so proprely.
Trifur, furis, more than a thefe, thre tymes wars than a thefe. Semblably tri, ioyned with any thyng, signifieth more.
Triga, a carte drawen with thre horses.
Trigarium, a certain course with such cartis
Trigamus, he whiche hathe or hath hadde thre wyues.
Trigarius, a place by campũ Martiũ, at Rome
Trigemini, thre chyldern at one byrthe.
Trigeminus, na, num, idem quod tres, thre.
Trigemmis, a plant or slyppe hauynge thre ioyntes and thre buddes.

Columel. 3. cap. 19.

Trigesimus, ma, mum, the thirtieth.
Trigesies, thryty tymes. Triginta, thirty.
Trigla, a fyshe, I suppose it to be a sore mullette, suche as are taken in Deuonshyre and in Cornewall.
Trigles, a stone whiche is of the colour of a soore Mullet.
Trigo, gare, to brynde or to drawe a thynge close togyther.
Trigon, gonis, a balle. also a turtyll.
Trigonia, the thirde age.
Trigonalis, le, that whiche is thre cornerde, hauyng thre lynes.
Trigonus, na, num, thre cornerde.
Trilinguis, he that speaketh thre langages.
Trilix, licis, a gar̃met of thre diuers thredis.
Trimatus, tus, the tyme of thre yeres.
Trimembris, bre, hauyng thre members.
Trimestris, tre, of thre monethes.
Trimetrum, a verse of thre fete.
Trimma, a wyne made with spices, as that whiche is callyd ypocras.
Trimorion, is named of. iii. signes in heuen, whiche contayne. lxxx. degrees or porcions. Wherfore Timorion, is in calculation of natiuities from the time of the birth or coception, the. lxxx. & tenth part or degree.
Trimus, ma, mum, of thre yeres.
Trimulus, the diminutiue of Trimus.
Trimyxos, a lampe or candellstycke, bearynge thre lyghtes.
Trinacris, & trinacria, the contrey of Sicile.
Trine-

T ante R.

Trinepos, potis, he which is thre discentes lyneall from my chyldes chylde.
Trineptis, a woman in lyke degree of blode as trinepos is.
Trinitas, trinitie, the number of thre.
Trinoxius, a, um, thre nyghtes.
Trinundinum, the thirde faire or markette, whiche was wont to be proclaimed, to the intent that it shuld be the better remēbrid.
Trinus, na, num, thre.
Trioboli homo, & triobolaris, a man worthe thre halfe pens, of lyttell value.
Triobolus, thre halfe pens, or worthe three halfe pens.
Triones, plough oxen. Alsoo they be seuen sterres beinge in the northe.
Triophthalmus, a lyttell stone, hauynge in hym the fygure of thre eyen.
Triorchis, a kynde of hawkes, hauynge thre stoones.
Triparcus, a greatte nygarde.
Tripartior, tiri, to dyuide into thre partes.
Tripartito, an Aduerbe, sygnyfyenge in three partis.
Tripartitus, ta, tum, dyuided in thre partis.
Tripedaneus, a, um, hauyng thre fete.
Tripes, pedis, with thre feete.
Trifoliū, thre leaued grasse. Triphillon, idē.
Triplaris, thryse as moche.
Triplex, plicis, thre folde, treble, a table with thre leaues.
Triplicitas, treble.
Tripliciter, thre folde.
Triplico, are, to do or fold a thing .iii. times.
Triplium, a vessell lyke a baskette.
Triplus, a, um, treble.
Tripolis, a countray in Affrica, an other in Syria, the thyrde in Phenicia.
Tripolium, an herbe.
Tripondium, thre pounde weight.
Tripontium, a towne in Umbria in Italy, so callyd bycause it hath thre brydges.
Triptolemus, a man whiche founde the vse of grayne in the countray of Athenes.
Tripudium, daunsynge.
Tripus, podis, euery thynge that hath thre feete. Tripodes, were alsoo tables in the temple of Apollo, of golde.
Triquetra, a fygure thre cornerde. It was also a name of the Ile of Sicile.
Triquetrus, tra, trum, hauynge thre corners.
Triremis, a galeye.
Tris, thre or thryse.
Trismegistus, the name of Mercurius, in latyn Ter maximus.
Tristegum, a chamber in the third storye or floore of a house.

Hirtius in cōmentar.
Tristimonia, heuynesse or sorowe.
Trissis, thre pounde weight.

T ante R.

Tristis, is also taken for doctus, Iudex tristis & integer, A iudge welle lerned and of a good conscience.
Tristis, agaynste his wyll, not well content.
Tristitia, sorowe, or heuynes.

Terent. in Eunucho.
Tristis, sorowfull, heuy, also cruelle, of moche grauitie, bytter, more difficile or hard, sometyme angry.
Tristo, tare, to make heuy or sorowfull.
Trisulcus, ca, cum, hauynge thre edges.
Trisulcū telū, a weapon hauyng thre edges.
Trisyllabus, ba, bum, hauyng thre sillables.
Tritauia, my great grandfathers mother.
Tritauus, my great grandfathers father.
Tritheles, an herbe whiche hathe thryse in the yere flowres.
Triticeus, a, um, of wheate.
Triticum, wheate.
Trito, tare, to breake or beate smalle.
Triton, one callyd god of the see.
Tritonia, the name of Minerua.
Trituro, rare, to threshe corne.
Tritura, threshynge. Trituratio, idem.
Tritus, ta, tum, worne.
Triuenefica, a great sorceresse.
Triuia, a name of Diana.
Triuialis, le, commune or of smalle estimation vsed or taught in hyghe wayes, alsoo rude, not elegant.
Triuialis lingua, a homely forme of speche.
Triuium, where wayes do mete, also a place where commune recourse of people is.
Triuialiter, communely, in the vulgare or homely facyon.
Trium literarum homo, was spoken in scorn of hym, that wolde seeme to be a gentylle man, where he was none, whyche worde was made by this occasyon, that amonge the olde Romaynes gentylle men vsyd to wryte theyr names with thre letters, as Q, F, M, for Quintus Fabius Maximus. Also this prouerbe was spoken of them, whiche were theues, bycause that Fur, contayned but thre letters.
Triumphalis, le, belongyyng to triumphes.
Triumphator, he that tryumpheth or hathe triumphed for vaynquishyng his enmyes.
Triumphalis uir, he that hath triumphed.
Triumphatus, ta, tum, of the whiche one hath tryumphed.
Triumphatus, tus, a triumph. Triūphatio, idē.
Triūpho, are, to triūph, to reioice excedigly
Triumphus, a triumph, whiche is a solemne pompe or ceremonie, where a prince, a cōsul or principal capitayn of an armye, hath had vyctorie of the ennemies of his countray, & therfore is brought home & receyued with al reioycing & honor that may be deuised of the people. The order & forme therof

Dd iij

therof ye may se in Titus Liuius, Apianus, and Julius Capitolinus.

Triumuir, one of theym whyche is in anye office, wherof be thre in like auctorite.

Trium uiralis, le, pertaynynge to an office or auctoritie, wherin be thre persones.

Triumuiratus, is an offyce in the publyque weale, wherin thre men haue equall iurisdiction togyther. Triumuiratus, the office or auctoritie of triumuir.

Triuncis, & triuncium, thre ounce weight.

Trixalis, a worme lyke to that which is callyd Locusta, but he hath no wynges.

Troas, adis, the citie of Troy, and the coūtrey aboute it callyd the lasse Phrigia.

Trochæus, a foote in meter, whiche is of two longe syllables, and one shorte.

Trochilos, a lyttell byrde, whiche is callyd kynge of byrdes.

Trochiscus, a lyttell whele. Alsoo trochisci, be of phisitians callyd, lyttell balles flatte at bothe endes, whiche be made of sondry poulders.

Trochum, a certayne stoole or chaire, whiche wyll be tourned aboute.

Trochus, a top, wherwith childern do play.

Troclea, & trochalea, a poley wherin þ cord runeth, wherby any thynge is drawen vp. it is also the gyn, whiche is callid a crane.

Troezene, a citie in the parte of Grece, callyd Peloponesus. It is also a countraye in the lasse Asia.

Troglotidæ, people in Ethiopia.

Troia, the citie of Troy. also the countrey wherin Troye stode.

Troianus, na, num, of Troye.

Troianus ludus, was a playe of chylderne on horsebacke.

Troicus, ca, cum, for troianus.

Troiugena, idem.

Troius, a, um, of Troye.

Tropeus, he that dothe a shrewde tourne, and runneth away whan he hath done.

Trophæum, was a marke or token of tymber or stone, sette in the place where enemyes were vanquyshed or put to flyghte, sometyme it is taken for vyctorie.

Tropice, fyguratiuely.

Tropice, ces, a kynde of bulle russhes, the sede wherof wyll make one to slepe.

Tropicus, ca, cum, fyguratiue.

Tropei uenti, wyndes, whyche doo comme from the sec.

Tropologia, a figuratiue speakynge.

Tropus, a fygure, a maner or facion, an alteracion of a worde or sentence from his propre signification.

Tros, troos aut trois, a Troyane. alsoo the name of a kynge of Troianes.

Trossulum, a citie in Italye.

Trossulus, in the olde tyme was taken for a horsman or man of armes. It is also a person delycate, well fedde or fleshy.

Troximi, grapes to be eaten.

Trua, idem quod trulla.

Trucido, dare, to slee cruelly.

Trucidatrix, she that kylleth one.

Truciter, cruelly.

Truculente, idem.

Trucitas, crueltie.

Truculentia, crueltie.

Truculentius, more cruelly.

Truculentissime, moste cruelly.

Truculentitas, idem quod truculentia.

Truculentus, cruelle in countenaunces or menaces.

Trudo, trusi, trudere, to thruste oute with vyolence.

Truella, a vessel wherwith water is throwē into the synke.

Trulla, wherin meate is put whan it is roste or sodden. It is alsoo a pyssepotte, of somme it is taken for a great cuppe, brode and deepe, suche as greatte masers were wonte to be.

Trulla, a trewell, wherwith masons, tylers, and pariettours do lay morter.

Trulleum, a bolle.

Truncatio, a cuttynge in pieces.

Truncatus, ta, tum, cut in pieces.

Truncator, & truncatrix, he or she that cuts teth in pieces.

Trunco, are, to cutte of.

Truncus, a piece cutte of from the resydue specially of a tree.

Truncus, a, um, cutte of.

Truo, onis, a byrde callyd also Onacratalus, and is lyke to a swanne.

Trusatilis, le, that whiche maye be tourned and dryuen about with a mans hande.

Trusatiles molę, a querne, suche as malte is grounde in, or mustarde is made in, and is tourned with ones hande.

Trutina, a wayenge balance. sometyme it is taken for iudgement.

Trutino, nare, to waye or examyne.

Trux, trucis, cruell, horryble.

¶T ANTE V.

TV, tui, tis, tibi, thou, of the, to the.

Tuatim, after thy facyon or custome.

Tuba ductilis, a brason trumpette.

Tuba, a trumpette.

Tuber, beris, a puffe growyng on the groūd lyke a musheron or spunge. It is alsoo generally euery swellynge in a mans bodye or vysage. It is alsoo in a tree lyke to a

greate

greatte knotte.
Tubercula, a lyttell swellynge or pushe.
Tubero, are, to swelle.
Tubicen, cinis, a trumpettour.
Tubulus, a lyttell pype, wherin water runneth from a sprynge. it is also a riede.
Tubus, a pype, wherin water is conuayed to a cundyte.
Tuburcinor, aris, ari, to eate hastily.
Tubus, & tubulus, the pype of a cundyte. it was also a thynge, wherewith they made walles hote, before there were chymneis.
Tucetum, a meate made with choppid fleshe lyke to a gigot or alowe.
Tudertum, a citie in Italye.
Tudicula, a ladell, a pryntynge yron, wherwith vessell is marked.
Tudiculo, are, to steere, to prynte a marke.
Tuditantes, they that trauayle in busynesse.
Tuditanus, the name of a man, so callyd bycause he had a heed as bygge as a betyll.
Tuditis, a mallette.
Tudito, tare, to labour for aduantage.
Tuor, eris, eri, to defende. alsoo Tueor, tueris, to see.
Tugurium, a house of husbandry.
Tuguriolum, a cotage.

Fest. pom. Tu ipse, thou thy selfe.
Tulit, he broughte.

Festus. Tullii, some suppose them to be ryuers, som flowinges of bloudde out of sondry membres or ioyntes.

Salust. Tullianum, a dungeon within the common pryson of Rome.
Tum, than, whan he gothe before cum, it sygnifieth as welle.
Tumba, a holowe place in the grounde, a sepulchre.
Tumdemum, fynally.
Tumefacio, feci, to make to swelle.
Tumeo, & tumesco, scere, to swelle.
Tumet, thou thy selfe.
Tumidus, da, dum, swollen.
Tumor, ris, swellynge.
Tumulo, are, to make the grounde holowe, to burye.
Tumulor, ari, to be buryed.
Tumultuare, in haste, withoute moche aduysemente.
Tumultuarius, a, um, that whyche is doone without aduysement, or in haste.
Tumultuo, are, to make rumour.
Tumultuose, troublously, or without study.
Tumultuosus, a, um, troublous, or makynge rumoure.
Tumultus, tus, a rumour.
Tumulus, a lyttell hylle or barowe, sommetyme a tombe.
Tunc, thanne.

Tunc temporis, at that tyme.
Tundo, tutudi, tundere, to smyte, to braye or beate as in a mortar.
Tunnetu, a citie in Affrica callid now Tunise.
Tungo, gere, olde wryters vsed for Nosco, nosce, to knowe.
Tunica, a iackette.
Tunica pallia propior, my iackette is nerer than my gown. a prouerbe applyed where we wyll signifie that all frendes are not to be lyke estemed or made of.
Tunico, care, to put on a iackette.
Tunicatus, he that weareth a iackette.
Tuopte ingenio, of thyne owne wytte.
Tuor, eri, to beholde, all be hit that worde is not in vse.
Turarius, a strete at Rome.
Turbatio, trouble.
Turba, a multitude or assemblye of people. Quid illec turba est? nunam ego perij? what a multitude is yonder? am not I vndoone for euer? Also it signifieth trouble. Propter eam hæc turba atq; abitio euenit, For hyr sake is all this trouble or dissension. *Terent. in Eunucho. Terent. in Heautont.*
Turbasis, sterche.
Turbella, a lyttell trouble.
Turbide, troublousely.
Turbidus, troublous, not clere.
Turbinatus, ta, tum, rounde and sharpe, lyke a toppe.
Turbino, nare, to make sharpe at the ende.
Turbistum, is a thynge myxte with the lycour, wherwith woulle is dyed, which maketh the dye to synke into the woull, wher by the colour is made perfyte.
Turbo, bare, to trouble, to stere. *Vide com.*
Turbo, binis, a boystouse wynde, whyche dothe blowe downe trees and houses, also a toppe, wherwith chyldern do play. It is generally all thynge, whiche is round and brode aboue, and sharpe benethe.
Turbulentia, trouble.
Turbulentus, troublous, angry, full of contention.
Turdetania, a contray now callid Granado.
Turdetani, & turduli, peple of that contray.
Turdus, a byrde, whiche is delycate in eatynge, a thrustell or blacke byrde, alsoo a fyshe callyd an hadocke.
Turgeo, ere, & turgesco, scere, to be swollen.
Turgidilus, la, lum, sommewhat swollen or bollyd oute.
Turgidus, da, dum, swollen.
Turiones, the tendrelles of trees.
Turma, a companye of souldiours, contaynynge xxxii. horsemen.
Turmatim, in order of battayle.
Turpis, pe, fowle, dishoneste, cruelle. Alsoo greatte. *Vergilius.*

Tur-

T ante V.

Turpiter, shamefully, dishonestly.
Turpissimè, most shamefully or dishonestly.
Turpitudo, dishonestie, vyllany, deformitie, sometyme rebuke.
Turpo, pare, to defyle, dyshonest, or brynge out of good facyon.
Turreus, rea, reum, lyke a towre.
Turrifico, care, to cense.
Turris, a toure or any thing made like to it.
Turricula, a lyttell towne. also a boxe, oute of the whiche dyse are throwen.
Turriger, that whiche beareth a towre, as an Elyphaunt.
Turritus, ta, tum, high, also towred, or fulle of towres. also the name of the ydol, whiche was callyd mother of goddes.
Turtur, turis, a byrde callyd a turtelle. It is also a fyshe.
Turundæ, pellettes of bread or past, wherwith capone or other foules ar crammed. Also a tente whiche surgeons doo put into a wounde.
Tus, turis, frankyncense, it is alsoo wrytten whith h, as thus.
Tuscia, a countrey in Italye, wherin be the cities of Florence, Sene, Luca, and Pise.
Tusculum, a lyttelle piece of frankincense. also a citie by Rome.
Tusculanus, na, num, of that citie.
Tuscus, ca, cum, of the countrey of Tuscia.
Tussedo, dinis, the cowghe.
Tussicula, a lyttell coughe.
Tussilago, ginis, an herbe, whiche puttethe away the cough. some men suppose it to be coltes foote.
Tussio, siui, sire, to cough.
Tussis, the coughe.
Tutanus, was supposed to be a god, whiche had the custody of men.
Tute, thou thy selfe.
Tutela, the wardshyp or custody of infātes.
Tutelaris diuus, the saint whom we do take for our speciall aduocate to god.
Tutelina, was callydde a Goddesse, vnder whose custodye was corne, whyche was in barnes or rykes.
Tutissime, mooste sure.
Tutius, more sure.
Tuto, withoute perylle.
Tuto, tare, to defend. Tutor, taris, tari, idem.
Tutor, a gardẽ, he that hath the warde of an infante.
Tutorius, a, um, pertaynynge to a gardeyn.
Tutulus, a top of the heare wounden with a purple lace on the crowne of a womans heed, whiche was only worne of her that was wife to the great priest at Rome, callyd Flamen Dialis.
Tutus, ta, tum, sure, defended from peryll,

out of daunger.
Tuus, a, um, thyne.

¶ T, ANTE Y.

Tyber, a gret riuer, which is by Rome.
Tyberinus, of Tyber.
Tyberius, the name of an emperoure of Rome.
Tybur & tyburtum, a citie by Rome.
Tyburtinus, na, num, of the cite of Tyburtũ.
Tyburs, burris, & tyburtis, hoc tyburte, of Tyber.
Tydeus, the father of Diomedes the noble capytayne, whome Uenus dyd wounde at the battayle of Troy.
Tyle, callyd also Thule, an ile within one dayes iourney of the frosen see.
Tylus, a worme, whyche lyeth vnder stones and tyles, whiche haue lyen longe on the grounde, and is somewhat blacke and scalyd, and hath many legges, whych beinge touched, closeth hym selfe rounde as a pease, and is moste commonlye callyd a cheselyppe.
Tymbra, a great felde in the countreye of Troy, through which the ryuer of Tymber runneth into the riuer of Scamander.
Tymœtes, one of the sons of king Priamꝰ.
Tymolus, idem quod Tmolus.
Tympanista, he ꝶat playeth on a drumslade or tymbrell.
Tympanistria, a woman that playeth on a tymbrell.
Tympanites, a kynde of dropsy, wherin the bealy swelleth great, a tympany, whereof wynde is the chiefe occasyon.
Tympanizo, to play on a tymbrell, tabour, or drumslade.
Tympanotriba, idem quod tympanista.
Tympanũ, a tymbrel, a tabour, or drumslade. Seruius calleth it a couered charyotte or carte, other doo suppose it to be the strake of a carte whele. I suppose that it may be taken for that, whyche is callyd the corse of a charyotte or horselytter, made with bayles or bourdes ioyned, whiche is not moche from the opynyon of Seruius.
Tympanum, is also a great whele, wherein men do goo and drawe vp water. It is also a platter, whiche serueth for meate.
Tymphei, people in Etholia, whyche is in Grecia.
Tyndarus, the father of the fayre Helene, for whom Troy was destroyed, and alsoo of Castor and Pollux.
Typhon, & Typhos, was a great gyant, the sonne of Tytan. It is also a greate pursaunt wynde.

Typho

Typhonæ, be certayne impressyons in the ayre lyke globes of fyre or dartes.
Typhis, was a carpentar, whiche fyrst dyd fynde the way to gouerne a shyppe.
Typus, a fygure, an example, or a fourme, a lykenes or shadowe of a thyng.
Tyrannice, cruelly, tyrannously.
Tyrannicus, ca, cum, of a tyrant.
Tyrannis, nidis, a cruelle or violente rule or gouernance for a priuate commoditie, and not for a publyke weale.
Tyrannicida, he that sleeth a tyrant.
Tyrannicidium, the kyllynge of a tyrant.
Tyrannus, a tyraunt.
Tyranthina, a garment of purple colour.
Tyranthinus color, purple colour.
Tyrius, a, um, of the ple callyd Tyrus. Also vyolette or purple colour.
Tyro, ronis, a yonge souldiour or manne of armes. Also he that fyrst entreth into the experience of any science, art, or exercise.
Tyroniacus, ca, cum, of a younge souldiour or lerner.
Tyrocinium, the fyrst exercise in any thing.
Tyros, a cite in Phenicia. also an yle, where the colour of purple was fyrste founden.
Tyrunculus, a veraye younge sowldiour or yonge lerner.
Tyrotarichus, a sawce made with chese.
Tyrrheni, the people of Thuscane.
Tyrsis, the circuite without the walles of a town, wherin men may walk for their solace.

¶ V ANTE A.

Salusti. in Iugurt.

VACCA, a cowe. Also a citie in Numidia.
Vaccinus, vaccina, cinum, of a cowe.
Vacerra, madde, without wytte, percloses or railes, made of tymber, within the whych some thynge is inclosyd.
Vacillo, are, to moue inconstantly, to wagge or waue, to be vnstable, or vnsure.
Vacinium, the flowre, whiche is also callyd Hyacinthus, and hath longe leaues, a roud roote, a stalke of a spanne longe and more, hauynge on it many purple floures, wherwith in some places they do dye pourple. I doubte whither it be the flowre whiche is callyd Hartis ease, or Swete wyllyam.
Vacillatio, a waggynge or waueryng and inconstant meuynge.

Ci. Tyro.

Vacillantes literæ, letters wrytten crokedly or out of order.
Vacillans testis, a wytnesse, whiche inconstantly dothe varye in report or deposition.
Vacat, it serueth to no purpose, it is superfluous. Also it sygnyfyeth, I am at good leysure, or withoute busynes. sometyme it sygnifyeth to care or force. Et cui esse deserto vacat, And who careth to be wel spoken or eloquent.
Vacatio, vacation, or tyme whan a man is out of his common busynes.
Vaco, care, to applye wytte or studye. Vaco sapientię, I applye my study to wisedome. Vaco rei diuine, I apply my wytte to goddes seruyce. Also to be emptye or voyde. Fac uacent ædes, cause the house to be voided. Vacat occupatione, He is without occupation or ydell. Somtime it signifieth to be superfluous, or vnprofitable.
Vacuæ aures, Date mihi vacuas aures, dum eloquor, Gyue your eares oonely to me, whyle I speake, or here nothyng els.
Vacuefacio, cere, to empty or auoyde.
Vacuo, are, idem.
Vacuus, a, um, voyde, emptye, or withoute a thynge.
Vacuus animus, a mynde withoute care or solycitude.
Vacuna, was callyd a goddesse, vnto whom husbandmen after that harueſt was cleane done, dyd sacrifyce, as to the goddesse of quyetenes after labour.
Vacuitas, emptynesse.
Vadimonium, suretie to appiere at a daye assygned.
Vadis, & uas, uadis, he that vndertaketh for an nother.
Vadium, suretie.
Vado, dere, to go forth. also to fynd suretie.
Vado, dare, to wade.
Vador, aris, ari, to fynde sureties.
Vadimonio obstrictus, let to bayle or mainprise, whan a man is bounden to appere at a day assigned by a iustyce.
Vadimonium obire, to appiere at the daye assygned.
Vadimonium deserere, to make defaute at the day, and not to appiere.
Vadimoniū missum facere, to discharge the recognisance or sureties that were bouden.
Vadimonium differre, to gyue a longer day of apparaunce.
Vadosus, a, ū, ful of fordes or shalow places.
Vadum, & vadus, a fourde or shalow place in a water, where menne and beastes may goo ouer.
Veh, an interiection, wherwith we do curs.
Vafellus, he that is somewhat crafty.
Vafer, fra, frum, subtyll, crafty, slye.
Vaframentum, subtyltie or crafte, slynesse.
Vafre, craftily, fynely in deceyuyng.

Vaga-

V ante A.

Vagabundus, a wanderer aboute.
Vadigabar, an hebrewe worde, whyche in latyne is Numeri, one of the fyue bookes of Moyses.
Vageni, a people dwellynge amonge the mountaynes callyd Alpes.
Vagina, a shethe or scaberde.
Vaginula, a lyttell shethe.
Vagio, gire, to crye as a chylde.
Vagitus, tus, the crienge of a chylde.

Plaut. in milite. Vago, gare, for vagor, to wander.
Vagor, aris, ari, idem.
Vagus, ga, gum, wandrynge and abydynge in noo place.
Vah, an interiection, wherwith we wonder at a thynge, also of reioysynge.

Plautus in casina. Vaha, an Interiection of reioysynge or lawghynge.
Valacchia, a countrey beyonde Hungarie.
Valde, very moche.
Valdius, for validius.
Vale, farewelle.
Valens, puissaunt, hole, stronge.
Valentia, puissance, habilitie.
Valentior, ualentius, more puissant or strong.
Valentissimus, moste puissant, or stronge.

Plautus in casina. Valentulus, somewhat stronge.
Valeo, lui, lére, to be able, to be hoole. Male ualeo, I fare yll, I am yll at ease.
Valere, to be stronge or puyssant, to may do, or be of force or power. Neque tam imperita, ut quid amor ualeat, ne sciam, I am not suche a foole, but I knowe what loue may do, or of what power loue is.
Valere à morbo, to be recouerid fro sicknes.
Valere, also signifieth to be worthe.

Terent. in Andria. Valeat, farewel he, I care not for hym. Imo habeat, ualeat, uiuat cum illa, well lette him wedde her, I care not for him, moch good do it hym with her: or let hym haue her, god be with hym, lette hym make merye with her.

Cicero. Si deus talis est, ut nulla gratia, nulla hominum charitate teneatur ualeat, If god be suche oone, that he hathe neyther fauour nor loue to mankynde, I care not for hym. Valeant, qui inter nos dissidium

Terent. in Andria. uolunt, They that wyl haue vs at variance let them get them hense.
Valesco, scere, idem quod ualeo.
Valeria, the sister of Messala, wyfe to a noble man callyd Seruius, who beinge deed, whan she was asked, why she dyd not marye agayne, she answered, that she alwaye lyued by Seruius her husbande.
Valerius, a mans name.
Valesius, for Valerius.
Valetudinarium, a place where men do lye, whan they be sycke, as the fermerye in a monasterye.

Valgiu, an instrument to make flores smoth. *Plinius.*
Valgulatio, a question in rebuke of one.
Valgustus, a croked staffe. *Fest. Pom.*
Valgus, he that hathe his legges or feete bowed inwarde.
Valetudinarius, a, um, nowe and than sycke, oftentymes sycke.
Valitudo, & valetudo, dinis, sometyme signifieth sickenes, sometyme helthe.
Valide, valyantly, myghtyly.
Validus, da, dum, valyant, myghty.
Validior, validius, more myghty.
Validissimus, mooste myghty.
Validitas, tatis, myghte.
Vallecula, a lyttell valey.
Vallaris, re, pertaining to a trench in a feld.
Vallaris corona, a garlande gyuen to hym, whyche fyrste entred into the trenche of the enemyes campe.
Vallescit, olde writers vsed for perierit, he is loste or peryshed.
Vallis, a valey or dale.
Vallo, are, to inclose, to fortifye.
Valonia, was callyd the goddesse of valeis.
Vallum, & vallus, a trenche, which is made in a felde to defende an hooste, within the whiche pauilions are pytched. Also a post wher vnto vynes are bounde.
Valor, oris, value or price.
Valuæ, dores whiche be shut on two partis.
Valuulus, the codde of a beane or pease, or other lyke thynge.
Vanans, olde wryters vsed for fallens, deceyuynge. *No. Mar.*
Vandalia, a countray in the northe parte of the worlde.
Vanè, vaynely, foolyshely, lyengly.
Vanesco, scere, to vanyshe, to be broughte vnto noughte.
Vanidicus, a lyer or teller of folyshe tales.
Vaniloquus, idem.
Vaniloquidorus, idem.
Vaniloquentia, vayne speeche. *Plautus in Persa.*
Vanitas, tatis, vanitie, lyghtnes, lesyng, foly.
Vanitudo, vanitie.
Vanno, are, to vanne corne.
Vannus, a vanne.
Vanus, a, um, voyde or empty. Also folisshe or enuyous, a maker of lyes.
Vapor, oris, & vapos, a vapour, or hot breth issuynge out of a thynge.
Vaporarium, a place made hotte to sytte in in the wynter tyme.
Vaporo, rare, to hete or make warm a place.
Vappa, wyne, whyche hathe loste his verdure. It is sometyme taken for a manne, in whome is no wytte or perfyte reason.
Vapo, onis, a beast that fleeth.
Vapularis, he that is beaten.

Vapu

V ante A.

Vapulo, lare, to be beaten.
Variabilis, le, variable.
Variantia, varietas, & variatio, varietie, dyuersitie in thynges.
Varices, & varicae, variculae, ar vaynes whiche do swelle excedyngly.
Varicosus, he that hath such vaynes swollē.
Varico, aut varico, to transgresse, to passe ouer a thynge neglygently.
Varicus, an aduerbe, whyche sygnyfyethe strydynge.
Varae manus, croked handes.
Vari, spottes in the face.
Varie, dyuersely.
Variae, for Pantherę, bestes of diuers colors.
Variegatus, a, um, painted or garnished with sondrye colours.
Varius, a fyshe callyd a troute.
Vario, are, to make dyuerse.
Variolę, measylles.
Varius, a, um, dyuers, vnlyke, inconstaunt, varyable.
Varolus, a deuourer, also a pycker.
Varro, ronis, was a noble Romayne, of all other moste excellently lerned.
Varus, whose legges are croked inwarde.
Varus, a ryuer, whiche dryydeth that part of Fraunce, that is callydde Narbonensis, frō Italy. Also it was the name of a poete
Vas, vadis, a suretie, he that vndertakethe for an other man, also a pledge.
Vas, vasis, a vessele.
Vascones, Gascoynes.
Vascularius, a potter.
Vascularius, a goldsmythe, the whiche maketh plaate.
Vasa conclamare, to crye to trusse vp caryage and baggage, as whanne an armye dothe remoue.
Vasculum, & vascillum, a small vessell.
Vastatio, destruction.
Vasterna, a horselytter, or any thynge borne by two horses.
Vastescant, old writers vsid for inhorrescant.
Vasto, are, to waste or distroye.
Vastus, a, um, great, huge, somtime desolate.
Vastitas, tatis, vastitudo, & vastities, greattenes, also destruction.
Vasum, a vesselle.
Vates, a prophete, a poete.
Vatesco, scere, to be distroyed, to be dryed vppe, to be forsaken.
Vaticanus collis, a hylle by Rome.
Vaticinor, aris, ari, to prophecie, or tel what shall happen, to coniecte.
Vaticinium, a prophecye, a coniecture.
Vaticinatio, idem.
Vatidicum, for propheticum, that whiche is spoken in a prophecye.

V ante B.

Vatius, idem quod valgus, he that hath croked legges outwarde.
Vatrax, & vatricosus, he that hath ylle legges from the knee downewarde.

¶ V, ANTE B.

Vber, & huber, a womannes breaste. Vide Huber.
Vbi, where, in what place. somtyme whan, after. Vbiloci, idem.
Vbiq̃ gentium, in all countrayes.
Vbiq̃, in all places, euery where, in all.
Vbiq̃ loci, in euery place.
Vbilibet, where ye wylle.
Vbicunq̃, in euery place. Vbicubi, idem.

¶ V ANTE D.

Vdus, da, dum, moyste.
Vuidus, da, dum, moyste inwarde.

¶ V ANTE E.

VE, idem quod Vaeh, Alsoo it is putte for uel, or q̃.
Vecors, dis, madde.
Vecordia, madnesse.
Vectabulum, wherin any thynge is caryed.
Vecticularia uita, to haue moche to day, and nothynge to morowe, sodaynly ryche, and as sodaynely poore.
Vectigal, a tribute, a pencion, a rent, a yerely reuenewe.
Vectigalis, le, he that payeth trybute, pencyon, or rente.
Vectis, a barre, also a leauer, wherwith thinges be lyfte, or borne by men.
Vecto, are, to carye. Vectito, idem.
Vectatio, caryage.
Vector, toris, he that is caryed, sometyme he that caryeth.
Vectorius, a, um, apte to carye.
Vectura, caryage, also the hyre or moneye gyuen for caryage.
Vegeo, gere, to be in helthe.
Veget, for uegetat.
Vegerius, a noble man that wrate of marciall doctryne.
Vegeto, uegetare, to recreate, to quycken, to conserue.
Vegetus, ta, tū, hole, stronge in helth, quick.
Vegrandis, lyttell.
Vehea, for via.
Vediouis, & veiouis, was callid a god which had no power to do good, but onely harme.
Veheare, olde wryters vsed for vehere.
Vehemens, tis, vehemente, greate, vrgente, fyers, sharpe.
Vehementia, vehemency, myght.

Vehe-

Vehementer, vehemently, sharply, mightily.
Vehementior, tius, more vehement or sharp.
Vehementissimus, ma, mum, mooste vehemente or sharpe.
Vehes, a carte or wayne.
Vehia, in the old Tuscane tonge was a cart.
Vehiatura, for vectura, caryage.
Vehicularius, a carter.
Vehicularis equus, a carte horse.
Vehiculum, a generall name to all thynges, whyche serueth for caryage.
Veho, uexi, uehere, to carye.
Veios, a cytie in Hetruria.
Veientes, people, with whom the Romayns had longe tyme warres.
Veientanus, na, num, of the citie of Veios.
Veii, the people of Veios.
Veiouis, uide ante Vediouis.
Vel, or, sommetyme also, chiefely, namely, at the leste.
Velabrum, a place in Rome. It may be also callyd a tent, whiche craftes men do sette vp, where they haue noo howses, to be in stede of their shoppes.
Velamen, minis, a couerynge.
Velaria, clothes, wherwith tentis ar made. also the same tentes.
Velatura, a frayte.
Velatus, ta, tum, apparayled.
Veles, velitis, a souldiour that weareth light harneyse.
Velia, a fenne in Italy, in the countreye of Calabria.
Velifico, care, to sayle.
Velina, a strete in Rome, by the hyll callyd Mons Palatinus.
Velis equisq̃, by see and by lande.
Velitaris pugna, battayle done by them that are lyght harneysed.
Velitatim, by leapes or skyppes.
Velitor, aris, ari, & uelito, uelitare, to stryue, to brawle.
Velitatio, brawlynge.
Velitræ, plurali numero, a cytie in Italy.
Veliuolus, a, um, that whiche gothe with a sayle, or is occupied with sayles.
Vella, olde wryters vsed for villa.
Vellaturam facere, to lyue by cariage frome one towne to an nother.
Vellicatim, by pluckes.
Vellico, care, to pynche, somtime to rebuke, to byte, to rente.
Vello, lere, to plucke vp, or pull a thynge.
Vellus, velleris, a flyse.
Velo, lare, to couer or hyde, to bynde, to apparayle.
Velocitas, swyftenesse.
Velocior, velocius, swyfter.
Velocissimus, ma, mum, swyftest.

Velocissimè, mooste swyftelye.
Velociter, swyftely.
Velox, locis, swyfte.
Velum, a sayle, a curtayne.
Velut, veluti, as, lyke as.
Vena, a vayne.
Venabulum, a huntynge staffe.
Venalitiarius, he that selleth slaues.
Venalis, le, that whiche is sette to sale.
Venalitium, a place where any thing is sold.
Venalitius, he that selleth.
Venaphrum, a citie in Campania.
Venaria, an Ile, wherein be many vaynes of mettalle.
Venaticus, ca, cum, pertaynyng to huntyng.
Venatorius, a, um, idem.
Venaticus canis, a hounde.
Venator, a hunter.
Venatrix, a woman hunter.
Venatura, idem quod venatio.
Venatus, tus, huntynge. Venatio, idem.
Vendax, acis, he that gladly selleth.
Vendibilis, le, easy or redy to be solde.
Vendicatio, a clayme.
Vendico, care, to vendicate, to clayme.
Venditarius, a, um, redy to be solde.
Venditatio, an auaunt.
Venditio, a saale.
Vendito, tare, to selle often, to auaunt.
Vendo, didi, dere, to selle.
Veneficium, the act and craft of poysoning.
Veneficus, & venefica, a maker of poyson, a vser of sorcerie.
Venenariæ mulieres, womē that do sel poison
Venenatus, ta, tum, poysoned.
Veneno, nare, to poyson.
Venenosus, a, um, that hath poyson,
Venenum, poyson, it is the general name of all that dothe alter the nature or colour of that thinge, wherwith it is myxte.
Veneo, niui, nire, to be solde.
Venerabilis, worthy to be honoured.
Venerabundus, he that dothe wourshyppe any thynge. Venerandus, idem.
Veneranter, reuerentely.
Veneratus, ta, tum, humblye prayed vnto, Sometyme reuerende.
Veneror, aris, ari, to honour.
Veneratio, honour, reuerence.
Venereus, a man disposed to lecherie.
Venetiæ, arum, the citie of Venyce.
Veneti, values in Brytayne. Also the people of Venyce.
Venetus, ta, tum, of Venyce. Alsoo the colour of lyght blewe or blunkat.
Venia, pardon, forgyuenesse. Tua venia, by your lycence.
Venibo, auncient wryters vsed for veniam.
Venio, nire, to come, to sprynge.

Venire

Venire in mentem, to come to remembrance.
Venit in mentem, it cometh to my mynde.
Venitur ad me, they came to me.
Venila, for vnda, water in a ryuer.
Venor, aris, ari, to hunte, to gette a thynge craftylye.
Ventanea, thynges that seme to be daungerous, and yet therin is no daunger.
Venter, tris, the bealy or panche. sometyme it is taken for the stomake.
Ventilabrum, a fanne or flabelle, wherewith wynde is made.
Ventilatio, a fannynge or wynnowynge.
Ventilator, a vanner or wynnower of corne.
Ventilo, are, to gather wynde, to vanne or wynowe corne, to tourne out of one hande into an nother.
Ventito, tare, to come often.
Ventosus, a, um, wyndy, also lyght.
Ventositas, wyndynesse.
Vento uiuere, to lyue by the wynde. A prouerbe applyed to theym, whiche haue noo substance to lyue on.
Ventus, wynde.
Ventulus, a lyttell wynde.
Ventus operam dat, the wynde bloweth a good coole.
Ventus popularis, vayneglorie.
Ventrale, a stomacher.
Ventricosus, a gorbealy.
Ventriculus, the stomacke.
Venum ire, to be solde.
Venundo, dare, to selle.
Venundatio, byenge and sellynge.
Venus, veneris, callyd goddesse of loue, som tyme lechery, also carnall appetite, alsoo beautie, by whiche a man is styred to loue.
Venustas, tatis, beautie, proprely of women. somtime a dilectable pronuciatio or speche
Venuste, proprely, pleasantly, amyably.
Venustulus, a, um, somewhat fayre.
Venustus, ta, tum, fayre, dylectable.
Venusto, are, to ornate or make beautifull.
Veprecula, a lyttell bramble. Vepres, bryars.
Vepretum, a place full of bryers.
Ver, ueris, the spryng of the yere.
Veratrū, an herbe callyd also Helleborus.
Verax, racis, he or she that sayth truthe.
Veracitas, tatis, truthe in speche.
Verba dare, to deceyue.
Verba mortuo dare, to speake to a deed mā, a prouerbe whan a man loseth his labour.
Verbascū, an herbe wherof be. ii. kindes: of which one is supposed to be Molin or long wort, the other is supposed to be that whiche is callyd primerose, not withstandynge other menne redynge the description, lette theym iudge at theyr lybertie.
Verbena, & uerbenaca, an herbe callyd veruyn. sometyme Verbenæ, are all leaues sodeinly plucked vp, to garnyshe howses or churches, or to make garlandes.
Verber, a small longe stycke or yarde.
Verberalis, worthy to be beaten.
Verberatio, Verberatus, tus, a beatynge.
Verbereus, ea, eum, worthy to be beaten.
Verbero, rare, to beate, to punyshe.
Verbero, ronis, a persone worthy punyshement, the reproche of all seruantes.
Verberito, tare, to beate ofte.
Verbigero, rare, for verba facere, to talke.
Verbenarius, was one of the ambassadors sēt fro the Romans vnto their enimies, whiche ware on his heed a garland of veruyn.
Verbose, an aduerbe, signifienge with many wordis. Verbositas, moch talking or speking.
Verbis meis salutem dicito, salute him in my name
Verbosus, full of wordes.
Verbulum, a lyttell worde.
Verbi causa, as by example. Verbi gratia, idē.
Verbum, a worde, also a sentence compised in one worde, a prouerbe.
Vercellæ, was a citie in Liguria, nigh to the mountayns called Alpes. Vere, truely.
Verecundanter, & verecunditer, shamefastly.
Verecundia, shamefastnesse.
Verecunde, shamefastly.
Verecundor, aris, ari, to be ashamed.
Verecundus, da, dum, shamefaste.
Veredarius, a messanger that rideth by post.
Veredus, a lyght horse, a huntynge nagge, or swyfte geldynge.
Verenda, places in a man and woman, which without shame may not be named.
Verendus, da, dum, to be feared or dradde.
Vereor, reris, reri, to feare as the child doth the father. Timere, to feare, as the slaue or boye dothe his mayster.
Vereor dicere, I dart not tell.
Vereor abs te, I am aferde of the, leste thou wylt doo me dyspleasure.
Vergiliæ, the. vii. sterres, callid also Pleiades
Vergo, uersi, aut uerxi, gere, to declyne or bowe downe.
Veridicentia, truthe in speakinge a true tale.
Veridicus, ca, ū, he or she that telleth truthe.
Verifico, are, to verifie as lawyers do say, to auerre
Veriloquētia, idē quod ueridicētia.
Veriloquꝰ, & ueriloquax, he ꝑ speketh truth.
Verisimile, likely. Verisimiliter, idem.
Verisimilis, le, lyke to be true.
Verisimilitudo, lykelyhode.
Veritanus ager, a felde diuided amonge the people, so that euery mā may haue a porcio.
Veritas, trouth.
Vermiculatim, an aduerbe, sygnyfyenge in smalle pieces.
Vermiculus, a lyttell worme.

V ante **E.**

Versuerbium, a true tale.
Vermiculor, aris, ari, to be fulle of vermyne or wourmes.
Vermiculata opera, workes whyche are of small pieces of dyuers colours, wherin ar sette out sondrye pyctures, lyke as we see in spruse tables or counters.
Vermina, pryckinges in the body, that it semeth wormes were cutte asonder.
Vermino, nare, to haue wormes.
Verminatio, the dysease of the wourmes, proprely in cattell.
Verminosus, a, um, full of wormes, or that wherin wormes are.
Vermis, a worme. Also it is a fishe in the riuer of Ganges, whiche is in length .lx. cubytes, and is blue in coloure, whiche hath suche strength, that whan oliphantes com to the water and do drynke, he wylle take one of them by the nose, and plucke hym into hym.
Verna, a bondeman or bondewoman, borne in the house of the lorde, or in his owne countreye.
Vernaculus, la, lum, al that taketh beginning in our owne contrey, as Vernacula lingua, the countrey language, the comon speche, peculyar or propre to countrey or howse. Vernaculi, be also men of ylle maners and language, whych vse to flatter or to speake in rebuke.
Vernacula putatio, cuttynge of vynes in the sprynge of the yere.
Vernalis, le, pertaynynge to the sprynge of the yere. also seruyle.
Vernaliter, lewdely, flatteryngly.
Vernatio, the olde skynne of an adder. It is sometyme taken for age.
Vernilis, le, seruyle.
Cæcilius. Vernilitas, flatterye.
Vernilitus, olde wryters vsed for a flatterer.
Verniliter, flatterye.
Verno, are, to sprynge, as herbes done, also to synge as byrdes done.
Vernula, a dyminutiue of verna.
Vernus, a, u, lusty, freshe, as the spring time.
Vero, truely, verily. somtime it doth affirme that which foloweth. also but yet.
Vero, is also a ryuer in Byskay.
Vero, are, to saye truthe.
Verona, a citie in Italy.
Verones, people dwellynge nyghe to the ryuer of Vero.
Veronensis, & Veronius, a man of Verona.
Verpus, pa, pum, that whiche hath no skyn. It is also the myddell fynger.
Verpi, be alsoo Iewes.
Verra, an altar at Rome, wherat they prayid that children shulde not be wronge borne.

V ante **E.**

Verres, a hogge vngelded, a tame bore, as aper may be called a wylde bore.
Verricula, olde wryters vsed for articulus.
Verriculum, a nette callyd a dragge.
Verrineo, care, to tourne or chaunge a thing vnto better.
Verrinus, a, um of a bore.
Verruca, an hyllocke or knappe on a hylle. also a warte.
Verrucaria herba, warteworte.
Verrucosus, he that hath wartes.
Verrucula, a lyttell warte.
Verrunca, old wryters toke for a hye place.
Versatilia, thingis that ar tourned or wounden one about the other, as two cordes or two styckes wouden togyther. also pillers made of the same facion.
Versatilis, le, that whiche tourneth or maye be tourned.
Versicolor, oris, chaungeable, or that which changeth colour. also of sondry colours.
Versicolorius, a, um, any thyng tourned out of his naturall colour. also that whiche is of dyuers colours mixt togither.
Versiculus, a lyttell verse.
Versipellis, a crafty person that wyll tourne often as he lysteth.
Verso, are, to tourne.
Versoria, the needell in a shyppe, to knowe the costes. Versor, aris, ari, to be occupied in a thynge or matter.
Versura, a tournynge. it is also whan a man boroweth of oone to pay his dettes to another. and to borow in suche wyse is Versuram facere.
Versuram soluere, is to chaunge creditours, as to borowe of one man to pay an other.
Versus, sa, sum, tourned.
Versus, us, a verse. sometyme an order. also a songe. Versus, towarde.
Versute, craftyly.
Versutus, mutable, ofte tournynge, wylye, experte.
Versutia, wylynesse.
Versutiloquus, a crafty speaker.
Vertagus, a hounde whyche wylle hunte by hym selfe.
Vertat tibi bene, God gyue the therof good lucke. Di bene uertant, I pray god tourne it to good.
Vertebræ, places in the bodye, where the boones doo not meete: but are knytte togyther in suche wyse with synewes, that they may tourne the more lyghtly.
Vertere terga, to rounne awaye, or flye in battayle.
Vertere solum, to goo and dwelle oute of a mans propre countrey.
Vertere, for versuram facere.

Vers

V ante E.

Vertere stultitie, to repute foly in a thyng.

Plautus in Epidic. Vertere uitio, to put the blame in one. Quis erit, uitio qui id non uertat tibi? who is it, that wyll not put the blame in the?

Vertere, to translate or interprete oute of one tunge into an nother.

Vertex, & vortex, ticis, a whyrlewynde. also a whyrlepoole in a water. also the crowne or toppe of the heed. also the toppe of euery thynge.

Vertibulum, idem quod vertebra.

Vertibula, a fyshe callyd also vrtica.

Verticulum, a wherue, whyche is a rounde thyng set on a spyndel, to cause it to turne.

Verticillum, a lyttell wherue.

Vertigo, ginis, a sicknes of the heed, wherin it semeth to a man, that he seeth thynges tournynge.

Vertigus, a whyrlynge aboute.

Vertius, a man of great strength.

Verto, ti, tere, to tourne, to drawe, to translate, to consyder.

Vertunalia, the solemnitie of Vertunus, whiche was kept in Octobre.

Vertunus, was callyd the god of bieng and sellyng. it is somtime taken for the yere.

Veru, a spytte or broche.

Veruetius, a, um, lyke a shepe.

Festus. Veruecinus, a, um, of a wether.

Veruat, for circundat, it compasseth.

Verutum, a castynge darte with a strynge.

Veruactum, the sommer tylthe.

Veruculum, an instrument of goldesmithes lyke a lyttell broche.

Veruex, uecis, a wether shepe.

Verus, ra, rum, true, substanciall, vncorrupted, good, iuste, profytable.

Veritas, tatis, truthe.

Verum, an aduerbe, signifieth truly. also but.

Verumtamen, yet not withstandynge.

Vesanus, a, um, cruell, furious, woode.

Vesania, furye, woodnesse.

Vescor, sceris, vesci, to eate, to vse. Actius vsed it to see.

Vescus, ca, cum, euery thynge that may be eaten, also lyttell or leane.

Vesca, browse, leaues, wheron beastes doo feede in wynter.

Vesculus, a, um, very leane.

Vesicaria, an herbe, whiche potycaries do calle Alkakengi.

Vesica, a bladder.

Vesuuius, & veseuus, a mountayn by Naples which sendeth out continually smoke & fire.

Vespe, they whyche do burye deed corsis.

Vespa, a waspe.

Vesper, the euenynge, or euentyde, also the euenynge sterre.

Vesper, ra, rum, of the euenynge.

V ante E.

Vesperi, an aduerbe, signifienge late, at the ende of the daye.

Vespero, rare, to be euenynge.

Vesperasco, scere, idem.

Vesperna, old wryters vsed for cœna, supp.

Vespertilio, onis, a reremous or backe.

Vespertinus, na, num, that whyche is doone in the euenynge.

Vesperugo, ginis, idem quod vesper.

Vespices, places thycke of bushes.

Vespillo, onis, he that burieth menne in the nyghte tyme.

Vesta, the doughter of Saturnus, whiche for her chastitie was honoured for a goddesse. sometyme it is taken for pure fyre.

Vestales, were virgyns, whyche mynistred to Vesta.

Vester, tra, trum, your.

Vestiarium, a warderobe, wherein garmentes are layde.

Vestiarius, the yoman of the robes, or he that kepeth the warderobe.

Vestibulum, a voide place without the dore, where men do tary whyles they do knock and vntyll the doore be opened.

Vesticeps, cipis, a yonge man, which beginneth to haue a berde.

Vestigabundus, he that seeketh moche.

Vestigator, he that seketh for a thinge.

Vestigium, the prynt of a mans foote in the ground. It is taken also for a sygne or token of any thynge that is doone.

Vestigo, gare, to seke. *Vide com.*

Vestimenta, a vesture or garment.

Vestini, people in Italye.

Vestio, iui, ire, to apparel, to adorne, to keuer

Vestiplica, a mayden whiche layeth vp her maystresse garmentes.

Vestis, a vesture, a garment, sometyme it is put for a bearde.

Vestispicus, & vestispica, he or she which kepeth their maister or maistres apparayle.

Vestissimus, a, um, best apparailed, best clad.

Vestitus, ta, tum, apparayled.

Vestitus, tus, apparayle.

Vestrapte, & uestropte, of your owne.

Vestras, stratis, yours.

Vesulus, a mountayne in Liguria by Alpes, at the rote wherof the riuer callyd Padus or Po, spryngeth out.

Veter, olde. Veterior, ueterius, elder.

Veterrimus, ma, mum, eldest.

Veteramentarius, a coblar or botcher.

Veteraneus, a, um, auncient.

Veteranus, sometyme signifyeth olde. Also he that had serued a hole yere in the citie. sometyme he that hath longe continued in warres, an olde soudiour.

Veterator, oris, ueteratrix, a crafty begyler.

Ee ij Veteres,

V ante E.   V ante I.

Veteres, men of olde tyme passed.
Veterina, beastes whiche do serue for burdeyne, as horses, mulettes, and asses.
Ve, vide in Veh. Ve uobis, oute vppon you, sorowe come to you.
Veterinarius, he that letteth to hyre horses or mules.
Veterinarius medicus, a horseleche, or ferrer
Veterinarius, a, ū, belōging to horsis & mules
Veternus, slepe without waking, also slouth or sluggyshnes. also to moche slepe.

Cato. Veternosus, he that slepeth to moch, sluggish, slouthful. also he that hath the dropsy.
Veteresco, & veterasco, scere, to be olde.
Vetero, rare, to make olde.
Veto, rare, Veto, tere, to prohibite.
Vetulonia, a place in Tuscia.
Vetulus, la, lum, a diminutiue of vetus.
Vetus, teris, olde, auncient.
Vetustas, age. Vetuste, agedly.
Vetustesco, scere, to be olde, to be the wars for age. Veteresco, scere, to be the better for age.
Vetustus, ta, tum, olde.

Festus. Veuina, a longe darte.
Vexillarius, & vexillifer, the baner bearer.
Vexillum, a baner.
Vexo, are, to vexe or trouble.
Vexabundus, he that troubleth or vexith other.
Vexatio, vexation.
Vexator, & vexatrix, he or she that vexethe.

V ANTE I.

Via, a waye, a iourneye, the maner, or meane, custome.
Viam munire, to make or repair a way
Viatica coena, a banket gyuen to a man atte his departynge.
Viaticor, aris, ari, to prepare vytayles necessarie for iourneye.
Viaticū, necessaries for iourney, be it in vitaile, or other thing, preparation for iorney.
Viator, toris, a trauayler by the way, a way farynge man, whiche warneth men to assemble to counsayle, and serueth offycers, to calle men vnto them.
Viatorius, a, um, pertaynyng to the way.
Viatoria vasa, vessels whiche doo serue for iourneye.
Vibex, bicis, a spotte remayninge in the skin after beatynge.
Vibratio, a brandyshynge.
Vibrisse, heares in a mans nose.
Vibrisso, are, to quauer in syngynge.
Vibro, brare, to shake a thynge, or to make a thynge to shake or quauer.
Viburnum, the sprynge whyche commethe out of the roote of a tree.

Vicani, men of the vyllage.
Vicarius, a, um, that whiche is in the steede or place of an other. Also the seruaunte of hym, whiche is a seruant.
Vicatim, in vyllages or stretes. also streete by strete, or vyllage by vyllage.
Vice, vice, plurali, uices, uicibus, time & times. p'multas uices, multis uicibus, many tymes. Vnica uice, ones. Somtyme it sygnyfyeth paynes. Also perylle. sommetyme place or stede, Fungar uice cotis, I wyl vse it in the stede of a whetstone.   *Horatius.*
Vicenarius, a, um, the twentieth.   *Vergilius.*
Vicenus, a, um, twenty.   *Horatius.*
Vicia, a certayne grayne, whiche lyke to a vyne, runneth vpon the stalkes of herbes. whiche do growe hye.
Viciarium, the sowynge of suche grayne.
Vicies, twenty tymes.
Vicinia, the neyghbourheed, whiche coruptely we calle vicinetum.
Vicinitas, tatis, nyghnesse. somtime the multitude of neyghbours.
Vicinus, a neyghbour.
Vicissatim, by tymes, by tournes.
Vicissim, by tourne, nowe one, nowe an nother, sometyme it sygnifyeth, on the other parte. sometyme semblably.
Vicissitas, idem quod vicissitudo.
Vicissitudo, dinis, the tourne, nowe oone, nowe an nother.
Victima, the beast that is kylled in sacrifice.
Victimarius, the mynister, whiche serueth to the sacrifice. Also he whyche boughte the sacrifice to selle it.
Victito, tare, to lyue by eating certain meat.
Victor, toris, he that vanquysheth.
Victoria, vyctorie.
Victoriatus, a certayne coyne, wherin was the image of vyctorie.
Victoriosus, accustomed to haue vyctorye.
Victricus, a fader in law, my moders husbād
Victrix, plurali victricia, ptaining to victory.
Victrix, a woman that vanquysheth.
Victurus, the participle of the future tense, as well of Viuo, as of Vinco.
Victus, tus, & victuis, sustinance or fedynge. Also a kynde or fourme of lyuynge.
Victus, ta, tum, vanquyshed.
Vicus, a strete in a towne. also a vyllage.
Viculus, a lyttell strete or vyllage.
Videlicet, as who sayth. sometyme it signyfieth surely.
Video, di, dere, to see. It is sometyme applyed to other sences, as, Vide qualis est sonus, here what a noise it is. Vide quid oleat, Smell wherof it sauoureth. Vide q̄ durum sit, Fele howe harde it is. Also it signyfieth to take hede or cōsider, to prouide. Vide tibi

prouyde

prouide for thy selfe. Tu uideris, loke therto wel, take good hede, for I care not for it.
Videro, I wyll prouyde.
Videor, I remember me well.
Videre uideor, me thynketh I see.
Videtur mihi, me semeth.
Viden, for Vides ne? doest thou not see?
Vidua, a wydowe.
Viduertas, calamytie or myserye.
Viduitas, widowhed, lack of thigs necessary
Vidulum, wherin any thing is kepte.
Viduo, duare, to dyuide or take awaye, to leaue alone.
Viduus, a, um, dyuyded, alone.
Viēna, a cite in Austria, an other i Dolpheni
Vieo, ere, to bende, to bynde.
Vietor, toris, a couper, whiche with howpes byndeth vessels.
Vietus, ta, tum, softe, weake, bendynge.
Vietus, a howpe, or strake of a carte.
Vigeo, gui, gēre, to lyue, to be stronge, to thryue in growynge.

Lusus. Vigesimæ, as decimæ, Vigesimariū aurū, idē.
Vigesimus, ma, mum, the twentieth.
Vigil, lis, watchful, vigilant. also a watchmā.
Vigilans, tis, vigilant, watchefull, dylygent, circumspecte.
Vigilanter, watchefully, dylygently, vygilantely, cyrcumspectly.
Vigilantia, vygilancy, dylygence.
Vigiliæ, watches, aswel by day as by night. somtyme the men whyche doo watche.

Vide com. Vigilo, lare, to wake, or watche, to be vigylant, or very dilygente. Also to here dilligently. Also to take peyne. Vigilare decet *Iuuenalis.* hominem, qui uult sua tempori conficere *Plautus in* officia, a man muste take payne, that wylle *Ruden.* finyshe his busynes in tyme conuenient.
Vigisonus, a broke by the citie of Padua.
Viginti, twenty.
Vigor, goris, strength, force.
Vigorosus, a, um, stronge, firme.
Vilis, le, vile, of no value. also good cheape, of lyttell price.
Vileo, & vilesco, scere, to be vyle, or of small or none estimation or price.
Vilitas, good chepe, contrary to derthe.
Viliter, an aduerbe, sygnyfienge cheape.
Vilito, tare, to make cheape.
Villa, a manour out of a citie or towne. also a vyllage.
Villanus, a man of the vyllage.
Villaris, re, & Villaticus, ca, cum, pertayning to the vyllage.
Villico, & villicor, aris, ari, to be occupied about husbādry, to haue the rule of husbādry
Villicatio, occupation about husbandry. also the rule of husbandry vnder the owner.
Villicus, & villico, a baylyffe of husbandry.

Villula, a lyttell vyllage.
Villum, smalle wyne.
Villus, heare.
Vimen, minis, roddes, whiche wyll wynde lyghtly, wherof baskettes are made.
Vimineus, a, um, wyckers, wyndynge roddes, or osyars.
Viminalis, le, apte to wynde.
Viminalis collis, a lyttell hylle at Rome.
Vinacea, kernels of grapes.
Vinaceus, a, um, of wyne.
Vinago, ginis, a kynde of stockedoues.
Vinale, the vyntage.
Vinarius, a vyntener.
Vinarius, a, um, pertaynynge to wyne.
Vinca, an herbe, whiche wyndeth about euery thynge. some do call it Perwynke.
Vincia, olde wryters vsed for Continens.
Vincibilis, le, easy to be vanquyshed.
Vincio, vinxi, vincire, to bynde. *Vide com.*
Vinco, vinxi, cere, to vanquyshe. *Vide com.*
Vinctus, ta, tum, bounden. sometyme it signifyeth a prysoner.
Vinculum, & uinclum, a bonde. also vincula pluraliter, is taken for a pryson.
Vindelicia, a countray in Germany, wherin is the citie of Augusta, callyd Ausburgh.
Vindemia, the tyme of gatherynge grapes to make wyne. it sommetyme sygnyfyeth the gatheringe of other thinges, as hony and syder.
Vindemialis, le, & vindemiatorius, a, ū, pertaynyng to gatherynge of grapes or fruite.
Vindemiatio, a gatherynge of grapes, to make wyne, also a makynge of hony.
Vindemiator, toris, he that doth gather grapes to make wyne.
Vin demio, are, to gather grapes or ripe frute *Salust. in*
Vindex rerum capitaliū, the mynister of execution, cōmonly callyd the hangeman. *Catal.*
Vindex, dicis, a reuenger of wronges. some tyme it sygnyfyeth a proctour or attourney, whyche prosecuteth an nother mans cause. Also he that delyuereth hym selfe out of bondage.
Vindiciæ, assercyon of lybertie or fredome.
Vindicias secundum libertatem dare, to put *Ti. Lusus*
in pledges to proue hym or hir to be free *lib. 3.*
and nat bonde.
Vindico, care, to reuenge, to defende or delyuer a man from iniurie or damage.
Vindicta, vengeance. sometyme lybertie.
Vinditia, a rodde, whyche the lorde delyuered to his bondeman, whan he infraunchysed hym.
Vinea, a vyneyarde. It is also an ordynance of warre made of tymber and hardelles, vnder the whiche men went surely to the walles of a towne that was besieged.

Ee iiij Vinea

Vinealis, le, apt or pertaining to a vineyard.
Vinearius, a, um, idem.
Vineaticus, ca, cum, pertaynyng to vynes.
Vineolus, he that behaueth hym selfe wantonly or tenderly.
Vinetum, a vyneyarde.
Vinitor, he that ordreth the vyncyarde.
Vinolentus, drunke with wyne.
Vinosus, he that loueth to drynke wyne.
Vinosus, a, um, full of wyne.
Vinulus, a, um, delycate.
Vinum, wyne.
Vio, are, to go a iourneye.
Viola, a vyolette.
Violabilis, le, whiche is apte to be violated.
Violaceus, a, um, of violette colour.
Violaris, are, idem.
Violarius, he that dyeth vyolette colour.
Violenter, violentelye, parforce, maugre his hedde.
Violentia, vyolence.
Violentior, tius, more vyolente.
Violentissimus, ma, mum, moste vyolent.
Violentus, ta, tum, vyolent, forcible.
Violo, lare, to vyolate, to corrupt, to defile.
Vipera, a kynde of adders.
Viperinus, na, num, of an adder.
Vipiones, yonge cranes.
Vir, uiri, a man, it is also a husbande, it signifieth also one of a good courage.

No. Mar. Virago, a woman hauynge the courage of a manne.
Viratium, of moche strength.
Virbius, twyse a man, whiche name was giuen to Hippolitus, the sonne of Theseus after that Aesculapius had broughte hym eftesoones to lyfe.
Vireo, es, rere, & viresco, scere, to be greene, to be more lusty.
Viretum, a grene place.
Viretus, ta, tum, greene.

Plautus. Virga, a rodde or yarde.
Virgator, he that beateth with roddes.
Virgeus, a, um, of roddes.
Virginalis, le, & virginarius, a, um, of a virgin
Virgindemia, a gatherynge of roddes.
Virgineus, a, um, idem quod virginalis.
Virgo, virginis, a vyrgyn or mayden.
Virginitas, vyrginitie.
Virgulata, seu virgata vestis, a ray gowne.
Virgula, a lyttell rodde or yarde.
Virgultum, a place full of yonge roddes.
Virguncula, a yonge mayden.
Viriatus, a stronge manne.
Viriculae, lyttell strength.
Viriculum, a wymble or percer.
Viridans, that whiche is grene.
Viridarium, a grene place inclosed, wherin beastes or fowles are kepte.

Viridia, a groue or place sette with greene trees for pleasure.
Viridicatus, ta, tum, made grene.
Viridis, de, grene.
Virido, dare, to make grene.
Virilia, the membres of a man.
Virilis, le, of a man, also manlyke or valiant.
Virilis toga, was a garment of the Romans whiche they beganne to weare at the age of. xvi. yeres.
Virilitas, manlynesse.
Viriliter, manly.
Viripotens, tis, a mayden maryageable.
Viritaneus ager, a fielde dyuyded amonge the people.
Viritim, of euery man, also oone man with an nother, man by man.
Viriditas, & viuor, roris, greneneffe.
Viro, rare, to fortifye.
Virosa mulier, a womanne desyrous of the companye of manne.
Virosus, a, um, of ylle sauour or taste, sometyme stronge.
Virtus, tutis, vertue, strengthe, sommetyme power, also helpe, merite or deserte.
Virulentus, venymouse.
Virus, venyme, greuousenes of sauoure or taste, lyghtnesse in colour. Sometyme the humour of generation propreiy in beastis. Also naturall vertue or power.

Vis, power, strengthe, possibilitie, aboundance, vyolence, multitude. Liuius.
Viscatus, ta, tum, dressed with byrd lyme, also lymed or taken with byrde lyme.
Viscera plurali, bowelles.
Visceratio, a dystrybution of fleshe.
Visceratim, by the bowelles.
Visceror, rari, to distribute meate, whiche is boyled or rosted.
Viscidum, clammy, or cleuing to the fingers.
Viscosus, clammy or cleauynge.
Viscum, Myscelden or Myscelto, whyche communely groweth on crabbe trees, and wyld peare trees.
Viscus, sci, byrde lyme.
Viscus, sceris, all that is betwene the bones and the fleshe.
Visenda, thynges worthy to be sene.
Visibilis, le, that whiche may be sene.
Visitatio, vysitynge or visitation.
Visito, tare, to vysite, to see often.
Viso, sere, to go to see, also to see.
Visum, a dreame. Visum, for videre, to see.
Visiones, vysyons, fantasyes.
Visus, us, syght. Visa, dreames.
Vita, lyfe. Vita functus, deade.
Vitabundus, he that escheweth a thynge.
Vitalis, le, that lyueth.
Vitellus, the yolke of an egge.

Vitex,

V ante I.

Vitex, a kynde of wythy called ofyar.
Vitiarium, a place, wherin yong vines ar set.
Vitiata mulier, a womā rauished or deflored.
Vitiatio, a rauysshemente, a corruption, or defourmynge.
Viticula, a lyttell vyne.
Viticulus, the shote of a vyne.
Vitigineus, a, um, of a vyne.
Vitilia, thynges whiche maye be wounden lyke an ofyar.
Vitiligator, toris, a detracter or backebiter.
Vitiligo, ginis, a foulenesse of all the bodye, haiynge spottes of sondry colours.
Vitiligo, are, to backebyte or detracte a man or womanne.
Vitio, are, to corrupte or viciate, to defyle, to distroye, to defourme.
Vitiositas, vyce, corruption, an inconstaunte affection.
Vitio dare, to blame or reproue.
Vitio uertere, to dyspryfe, to lacke.
Vitiosi magistratus, offycers not ryght constitute or made.
Vitiosus, sa, sum, vitious, or full of errours.
Vitis, a vyne. Also a thynge, whyche a capytayne in warres dyd beare in his hand.
Vitis alba, an herbe, whiche runneth vp in hedges, and wyndeth aboute the settes, hauing a leafe like a vine leaf, but rougher and a redde berye. It is callyd also Brionia, and in englyshe
Vitis nigra, a lyke wiede, whiche commonly groweth amonge herbes, & byndeth them togither, hauinge a leafe in facyon lyke to ruy, and lytle tendrynges with knappes, and is called of some men
Vitisator, he that selleth vynes.
Vitisco, scere, to sprynge vnto a vyne.
Vitium, vyce, contrarye to vertue. Alsoo a faut or errour. also sycknes, an impedimēt.

Terent. in Hecyra. Vitium offerre virgini, to defloure a virgine.
Vito, tare, to eschewe, or beware.
Vitreus, a, um, of glasse.
Vitrinus, na, num, idem.
Vitrearius, a glassemaker, or a glasyer.
Vitreolum, an herbe growynge on walles, wherwith vesselle beinge scoured, becommeth wonderfull bryght.
Vitricus, a father in lawe, or steppefather.
Vitriolum, a dyminutiue of vitrum.
Vitrosus, a, um, which hath plentie of glasse.
Vitrum, glasse.
Vitta, a fyllette or heedbande.
Vitula, an heffar, or yonge cowe.
Vitulari, to reioyce.
Vitulatio, reioycynge.
Vitulinus, a, um, of a calfe.
Vitulinæ carnes, veale.
Vitulus, a calfe, not only of a cowe, but also

V ante I.

of an olyphant, and of great fysshes. It is also a fyshe callyd a seale.
Vituperium, a rebuke.
Vitupero, rare, to rebuke.
Vituperatio, a rebuke gyuen.
Vituperator, he that rebuketh or blameth an nother.
Vituperones, rebukers.
Viuacitas, & uiuatia, amonge olde wryters bodyly strength.
Viuacissimus, most liuely or strōg of nature.
Viuaciter, strongely.
Viuarium, a place, where wylde beastes, byrdes, or fysshes be kepte. It may be callyd as welle a ponde, as a parke, a counnyngar, a walke for byrdes.
Viuatior, more lyuely.
Viuatus, & viuidus, full of lyfe or naturalle strengthe.
Viuax, uacis, lyuely, stronge of nature.
Viuere diem, to lyue without any prouysion or stoore.
Viuerra, a ferette.
Viuidus, da, dum, lyuely, quycke.
Viuior, & viuissimus, olde wryters vsed for more lyuynge or moste lyuynge.
Viuiradix, icis, a yong vine set with the rote.
Viuitur. Quid agitur? T. Viuitur, How is the mattier? L. I lyue as well as I may.
Viuo, uixi, viuere, to liue, to haue a mery life.
Viuus, ua, uum, that whyche lyueth, alsoo quyck, natural, strong, vehement, or great.
Vix, vncthe, scantly, hardily. Vix dum, idem.
Vix tandem, in conclusyon.
Vix, for Non. Vix Priamus tanti, totaq̄ Troia fuit, Kynge Priamus and all Troye was not so moche worthe.

Ouidius epistola Penelopes.
Vix, with moche a doo. Si idem istuc imitamur, ita tamen uix viuimus, Althoughe we do the lyke, yet with moche a do we lyue.

¶V, ANTE L.

Vlcero, rare, to make a scabbe. also to exasperate or make grefe.
Vlcerariæ herbæ, herbes that make blysters.
Vlciscor, sceris, sci, to auenge.
Vlcus, ceris, a hydde myschiefe. It is alsoo corrupt matter gathered within the skyn, and couered with a scabbe.
Vlex, an herbe lyke to rosemarie, which draweth to ti golde.
Vliginosus, sa, sum, soked with longe abode of water.
Vligo, ginis, moysture of the erthe alwaye remaynynge.
Vlius, a name of Apollo.
Vllo, old wryters vsed for vltus fuero, I shal be re-

V ANTE M.

be reuenged.
Vllus, la, lum, any.
Vlmus, a tree callyd an elme.
Vlmeus, mea, eum, of elme.
Vlmarium, a groue of elmes.
Vlna, a fathom, also an elle.
Vlpicum, great garlyke.
Vls, of whome commeth vltra.
Vlterior, ulterius, further, more beyonde.

Plautus in milite.
Vltima platea, at the ende of the strete.

Terent. in Heautont.
Vltimis ædibus, on the back side of the hous.

Ver. æne. 8
Vltimus, ma, mum, laste. sometyme it signifieth fyrste.

Vltio, vengeance.

Terentius
Vltor, & vltrix, he or she that taketh vēgeāce.
Vltra, beyonde, more, moreouer, sometyme shrewdely or frowardely.
Vltro, willingly, without desyre or cohercion
Vltro citroq, hyther and thyther.
Vltroneus, a, um, wyllyng, with a fre wylle.
Vlubræ, a citie in Italye.
Vlula, a shryche oule.
Vlulatus, a barkyng.
Vlulo, lare, to howle as a dogge or a wolfe.
Vlysbona, a cite in Portugal, callid Lushbon
Vlysses, the moste eloquent and wise prince of the Grekes, which came against Troy

¶ V ANTE M.

Vmbella, a lyttel shadow. also a skrine to kepe away the light of the sonne.
Vmber, of the countrey of Umbria.
Vmbilicatim, in the facyon of a nauyll.
Vmbilicatus, ta, tū, made like a nauill.
Vmbilicus, the myddes of euery thyng. also the nauyll. also a lyttelle cerkle made in the gronnde, to knowe whyche waye the wynde standeth. Also it is a lyttell smothe stone, or pyppell stone, a bose, suche as is sette on the backe of a boke. Ad umbilicū adducere, to brynge to a poynt.
Vmbo, bonis, the bose of a buckler or shield
Vmbra, a shadowe. It was also that, whiche was callid a gost of a man being deed, whiche not only paynims but also christen men supposed dyd appere visibly vnto me.
Vmbraculum, a place, where men moughte be out of the sonne, or that whiche made shadowe.
Vmbraticus, ca, cum, lyke a shadowe.
Vmbraticus homo, a man lyuynge at ease, and out of all labour or busynesse.
Vmbraticæ artes, craftes exercysed in the shadow, as the more part of handy crafts.
Vmbratilis, le, that which is done in the shadowe, or as it were with ease, and without any sweate or payne.
Vmbratiles res, tryflyng thynges or trifles.

V ANTE N.

Vmbratilis pugna, exercyses of feates of warre out of batayle as in a house.
Vmbria, a parte of Italy.
Vmbrifer, fera, ferum, makynge shadowe, as a greatte wodde dothe.
Vmbrina, & vmbra, a fysshe, whiche by the description of Paulus Iouius, semeth to me to be an halybut, for the greattenesse and delycacie of the heed, and similitude to a sturgion.
Vmbro, brare, to shadowe.
Vmbrosus, a, um, hauynge moche shadowe.
Vmbro, bronis, a ryuer in Lumbardye, callyd also Lamber.

¶ QV ANTE N.

Vna, togyther. Vna cum Cicerone, togyther with Cicero.
Vnanims, & vnanimus, of one mynde and wylle. Vnanimus consensus, one hole consente.
Vnanimitas, tatis, concorde.
Vncia, an ounce. also an ynche.
Vnciarius, a, um, of an ounce.
Vnciatim, ynche by ynche.
Vncinatus, a, um, hoked or croked.
Vncinus, a litle club or bat crokid at the end.
Vnciola, an ynche.
Vnctio, an anoyntynge.
Vnctuarium, a place nigh to a stoufe or hote howse, where menne be annoynted after that they haue swette.
Vnctum, the leafe of a hogge, whyche is the fatte that lyeth by the backe & the rybbes, whyche husbandes vse to rolle vppe, and kepe for to make saulues, or els to frie meate, as fritowes and pancakes.
Vnctura, an annoyntynge.
Vnctus, ta, tum, annoynted or greased.
Vncus, a batte or croked clubbe. Also anye thynge croked at the ende.
Vncus, a, um, croked.
Vnda, water, properly a wawe.
Vndabundus, da, dum, makynge greatte or many wawes.
Vndans, wawyng or mouing like to wawes.
Vndatim, lyke to wawes of the see.
Vndeunde, of what place so euer it be, or frō whence so euer it commeth.
Vndecunq, idem.
Vnde, from whense, wherto, wherby, wherof, wherfore, what to do. Vndegentiū, idem
Vndecim, eleuen.
Vndecimus, ma, mum, the eleuenth.
Vndenus, na, num, idem.
Vndelibet, from whens thou wylte.
Vndeuigesimus, a, um, the one and twenteth.
Vndeuiginti, nynetene, lackynge one of. xx.

The

V ante N.

the lyke signification is, where Vnde is ioyned to any grete numbre.
Vndeuis, idem quod vndelibet.
Vndique, on euery syde.
Vndicola, he that dwelleth on the water.
Vndisonus, na, um, that maketh a noyse lyke to wawes whan they ryse and fall in the water, or doeth rore as the water doeth at a great floode.
Vndiuomus, a, um, that whiche casteth water out frome hym.
Vnedo, a kynde of wylde frute lyke apples, which is bitter, & hurteth bothe the heed, and the stomak.
Vndo, are, to ryse in wawes.
Vndosum mare, a troublouse see, and full of of wawes.
Vndulata vestis, Chamlet, or a garment wrought as it were with rynges.
Vndula, a lyttell wawe.
Vnguentum, & vngentum, a swete oynemēt, it is vsurped for euery oynement.
Vngues, muskyls.
Vngo, unxi, ungere, to enoynt.
Vnguen, nis, oynement, or any thinge that is fatty.
Vnguentarius, a maker of swete oynemētes.
Vnguentaria, the craft to make oynmentes.

Erasm. in chilia. Vngues arrodere, to gnawe on his nayles, a prouerbe applyed to them, which are in a study, how they maye alter suche thinges as they do repent theym of.

Vnguis, a nayle of the fyngars or toes. it is also a disease which at length couereth all the eye with flesh in the corner of the eye.
Vnguicula, a lytle soft nayle. A teneris vnguiculis, frome his tender youthe or infancye.
Vngula, a houfe of a hors or other beaste.
  Omnibus vngulis, with all myght & powar.
Vngulatus, he that hath foule great nayles.
Vngulum, of olde wryters was taken for a rynge.

Cato. Non. Mar. Vngularius, a great nayle and ragged.
Vngustus, a croked staffe, or suche as commonly men do cal a croke, wherwith they drawe to them any thynge.

Vnicalamum frumentum, wheate, whyche hath but one rede growing out of the rote.
Vnicallis, an herbe whyche hathe but oone stalke without any braunches.
Vnice, onely.
Vnicolor, oris, of one colour.
Vnicornis, Vnicornius, & vnicornium, a beest callyd an vnycorne.
Vnicuba, a woman whiche lyeth or companyeth but with one man.
Vnicus, ca, cum, one alone.
Vnigenitus, one chylde without moo.

V ante O.

Vniiuge uinee, vines in the whiche vpon the proppes being sette vp, sondry rayles are layde on the one syde.
Vnio, iui, ire, to ioyne togyther.
Vnio, onis, concorde, somtyme a perle.
Vnioculus, he that hath but one eye.
Vnipes, pedis, hauynge but one foote.
Vnitas, tatis, vnitie.
Vnitio, a ioynynge togyther.
Vnitus, ta, tum, ioyned togyther in one.
Vniuersalis, le, vnyuersall.
Vniuersipotens, he that hath power ouer al.
Vniuersipotentia, power ouer all.
Vniuersitas, vniuersitie or generaltie.
Vniuersus, a, um, vnyuersall, sometyme it signifieth all, or the hole.
Vniuira, a woman hauynge but one husbād.
Vniuocum, that whiche sygnifyeth but one thynge.
Vniuoce, of the same sygnifycation.
Vnose, olde writers vsed for simul, togither
Vnni, Hungariens.
Vnq̄, any tyme.
Vnus, na, num, one, also alone.
Vnus & alter, both, now one, now an other.
Vnusquilibet, Vnusquisq̄, Vna queq̄, Vnum quodq̄, eueryche.
Vnis ædibus, in the same house.   *Terent. in Eunucho.*
Vno animo, of one accorde.
Vnus quiuis, who so euer thou wylte.
Vni sex dies, syxe dayes contynuall.   *Plautus in trinummo*
Vno ictu, at one stroke.
Vno uerbo, at one worde.
Vnum, one thynge.
Vnus ex multis, Vnus ex omnibus, oone alone, onely.

¶ V ANTE O.

VOberca, a towne by Bilbo in Spain.
Vocabulum, the denomination of any thynge.
Vocalis, le, lowde, also that whiche hathe a voyce, also a vowell.
Vocalitas, a tune or sounde of a voyce.
Vocatio, a callynge.
Vocator, a caller.
Vociferatio, a cryenge out.
Vociferator, he that crieth out.
Vociferor, aris, ari, to crie out, to cry loude.
Vocifero, idem.
Vocito, to calle often.
Voco, care, to call, to byd, to aske.
Voconia, a kynde of peares.
Vocula, a lyttell voyce, somtyme obloquie.
Voculatio, an accent in speche.
Vola, the myddes of the hande or the fote.
  It is taken for the soole of the fote.
Volaticus, ca, cum, that which flieth or goth
                                                        away

V ante O.

awaye sodeynly, flittinge.
Volatilis, le, that which can flye.
Volatus, & volatura, a flight.
Volema, a great peare, a wardyn.
Volens, wyllynge.
Volenter, wyllyngly.
Volentia, will.
Volito, tare, to flye often.

Vide com. Volo, are, to flye, to runne or go quycklye, or fast.
Volo, uis, uolui, uelle, to will.
Volo tuam gratiam, I desyre your fauour.
Volo te, I wolde speke with the.
Volones, were bondemen at Rome, whiche in the warres of Cartage whan there lacked Romanes, offred them selfes to fyght for their masters, and bycause they dyd it willyngly withoute constraynt or called, therfore they were called Volones.
Volsella, an instrument to plucke heares frō the body or face.
Volua, for Vulua.
Volubilis, le, that which is easyly tourned.
Volucer, cri, swift, lyght
Volucra, a beast whyche eateth the tender vines.
Volucres, byrdes, foules.
Volucrior, more swyfte.
Volucris, cre, all thinge that doth flye.
Volucrum, the after byrthe in a woman.
Volumen, minis, a booke: sometyme part of a boke, called a volume.
Voluntas, tatis, will.
Voluntarius, a, um, voluntary, willynge.
Voluo, uere, to wrappe, to tourne.
Voluox, & Voluola, idem quod Conuoluolus, a lytle wurme with many legges, whiche eateth the leuys of vynes, and of other trees.
Volup, for Voluptas.
Volupe, delectable.
Volupia, & voluptia, goddesse of voluptie or delectation.
Voluptabilis, le, that which reioyceth.

Sal. in Ca. Voluptaria loca, placis of pleasure.
Voluptas, tatis, an inordinate reioycinge or delectation in thynges worldly, or carnall.
Voluptuarius, & voluptarius, he that is gyuen to carnall delectation.
Voluptuosus, a, um, voluptuouse, vnsatiable in carnall pleasure or delectation.
Volutabrū, a place where swyne do walow.
Volutabundus, walowynge, tournynge, tossynge in the mynde.
Volutatim, an aduerbe signifienge, eftsones tossinge in the mynde.
Voluto, tare, to tourne lyinge, to walow, to reuolue and tosse in the mynde.
Vomer, meris, the culter of a plowghe.

V ante O.

Vomica, a rotten impostume, wherout runneth matter.
Vomitus, vomite. Vomitio, idem.
Vomo, mui, mere, to vomyte or parbrake. *Vide com.*
Vopiscus, where two children are conceyued, and one of them is abort, he that cōmeth to perfyte byrth is called Vopiscus. it was also the name of one that wrate the lyues of Emperours. *Festus.*
Vopte, for Vosipsi.
Voraciter, lyke a glutton.
Vorago, ginis, a swolowe or gulfe.
Voro, rare, to swolowe downe meate ere it be chewyd. also to eate gredily.
Vorax, racis, a glutton.
Voracitas, gluttony.
Vorsura, for versura.
Vorsurā soluere, a prouerb applyed to them that so discharge them selues of one busynesse, that they entre into another more paynefull or dangerouse.
Vortex, for vertex.
Vortūnalia, a solemne feast to the god Vortumnus.
Vos, you.
Votiuus, ua, um, that whiche is vowed, also desyred.
Votiua verba, votiue preces, wordes and prayers, wherin we desyre somwhat.
Votum, a vowe, sometyme a desyre.
Votiuæ aures, eares whiche desyre to here.
Votitum, olde wrytars vsed for Vetitum.
Voto, & Votito, to make auowe.
Voti compos, he that hath that whiche he desyred.
Voueo, ui, uere, to vowe, or make auowe. *Vide com.*
Vox, uocis, a voyce.
Voce assa, with the voyce onely of a manne without any instrument of musyke.

¶ V, ANTE P.

Vpupa, a lapwynk or blacke plouer.

¶ V, ANTE R.

Vrania, one of the Musis, whiche is president of Astronomy.
Vragus, of olde writars was vsed for Orcus, dethe.
Vrbanatim, & vrbane, lyke a gentyl manne, courteysely, gratiousely.
Vrbanicani milites, souldyours of the citie.
Vrbanitas, courtesye, good maner, gentilnesse in speche, ciuilitye.
Vrbanus, a, um, ciuile, courtaise, gentyll in speche and gesture.
Vrbicula, a lytle citie.
Vrbicus, ca, cum, of the citie.
Vrbo, are, to cast a mere with a plough.
Vrbs, bis, a wallyd towne. also a citie.
Vrceolaris, an herbe whiche is called Pelitory of the wall.

Vrce-

V ante R

Vrceolus, a lytell water pitchar.
Vrceus, a pytcher pot, wherin water is caryed.
Vredo, dinis, the fault in corne or trees, whan they are blastyd. it signifieth also an yche and burnynge in the skynne.

Vergilius Georg. Vrgeo, ursi, urgere, to prouoke, to haste furth. sometyme to couer.
Vriculum, any thinge that is holow.
Vri, wilde beastis lyke oxen, called Bugles or buffes.

Lucanus Verg. Vrina, vryne or pisse.
Vrere, is also to byte as froste doeth the grasse.

Ter. in Eu. Vro hominem. Non malum hercle. G. vro hominem. P. vt falsus animi est. It is no harme. S. I haue gyuen hym a corsy. P. Se how falsharted he is.

Plautus in Most. Vrere, to tourment or vexe.
Vrito, tare, to burne sore or feruently.
Vropigium, is the lowest and narowest part of the chyne next to the fundement.
Vrsulus, & vrsellus, a lytle or yonge beare.
Vruat, Ennius vsed for Circundat.
Vruare, is also to drawe a furrowe with a plowgh aboute a place.
Vruum, a plowghe beame, or crooked part of a plowghe.
Vrinum, an adell egge.
Vrino, are, & Vrinor, ari, to dyue vnder the water.
Vrinator, toris, a dyuar.

Leo. Por. de Men. Vrna, a waterpot: it is propzely a vessell, which contayneth as moch water as doth way fourtye pounde waighte: and two of them do make Amphoram.
Vrnarium, a bourde wheron pottes where sette.
Vrnula, a lytle potte.
Vro, ussi, urere, to burne, to be turmented, or vexed.
Vror, reris, uri, to be bourned.
Vrsa, two figures of sterres, the one called Vrsa maior, and the other Vrsa minor.
Vrsus, a beare.
Vrsa, a shee beare.
Vrsinus, na, um, of a beare.
Vrtica, a nettyl. also a fisshe, which as Paulus Iouius writeth, is of the quantitie of a wallnutte, and the keuerynge of hym is betwene a shell and a hard skynne, and is somewhat redde, and the fysshe of hym is harde.

¶ V. ANTE S.

Vsia for essentia.
Vsitatio, an vsage.
Vsitor, taris, tari, to vse often.

V ante S

Vspiam, in any place, to some place, any where.
Vsquam, any where, in any wyse or maner.
Vsqʒ gentium, any where.
Vsqʒ, vntyll, well nygh, diligently, continuelly, so longe, allwaye.
Vsqʒ dum, vntyll.
Vsque adeo, as longe.
Vsque eo, in so moche.
Vsquequaqʒ, all aboute, euery where, allwaye.
Vsquequo, vntyll whan, or what.
Vstrigo, ginis, blast of corne.
Vstrina, the meltinge house, or place where metall is molten or het.
Vstulo, are, to burne or sere a thinge.
Vstus, ta, tum, bourned.
Vsucapio, & Vsucaptio, a possession by prescription of a long tyme.
Vsuarius, he that is in possessiō, the pernour of the profytes, the occupyar.
Vsura, the occupation.
Vsurarius, a, um, that which is occupyed.

Leo. Port. de Pond. Vsura semissium, where they gyue syxe for the yerely lone of one hundred, As if I borowe of one a hundred poundes, and paye to hym euery moneth ten shillynges, duryng the tyme of the lone: this yeldeth euery yere. vi. lb. for the hundred.
Vsurpo, pare, to vsurpe, to vse often and moche.
Vsus, us, vse, sometyme the occupation or exercise of a thinge, also profyte or frute.
Vsurpatio, an vsurpynge or vsurpation.
Vsus fructus, the vse of an other mannes goodes by the consent of the owner, the substance of the thinge being saued.
Vsuuenit, it happeneth ofte.

¶ V. ANTE T.

VT, as, that, as soone, howe, lyke as, wolde to god, how moche, all be it, sometyme for quippe & ita, lest not.

Cæs. in co. Vt satis commode supportari posset, uereri dicebant, They sayde, that they feared, that it mowght not be.

Plautus in Persa. Vt, as well as. Vt uales? R. vt queo, Howe farest thou? R. as well as I maye.

Vt, beholde howe. Vt sæpe summa ingenia in occulto latent, Beholde how that moste exellent wittes do lye hyd in a corner.
Vt, admit it, or set the case, or put the case.

Ci. in Phi. Legem illam appellare fas non est, & ut sit lex, non debemus illam Hircij legem putare, It is not conuenient, that we call it a lawe, and admit that it be a lawe, we shuld not yet suppose it to be Hircius lawe. Etenim ut circumspiciamus omnia, quæ populo gra=

lo grata, atq; iucunda sunt: nihil tam populare quàm pacem, quàm cōcordiam, quàm otium reperiemus, for put the case that we mought se perfitcly all thinges that were plesaunte and delectable vnto the people, we shoulde nothinge fynde, that they so moche desyre, as peace, as concorde, as vacacion from laboure.

Te. in Ad. Vt est dementia, Se the mans foly.

Vt istum dij deæq; perdant, I beseche god & all halowes send him a myschief.

Ci. in Bru. Vt, for postquàm. Nam vt illos de Republica libros edidisti, nihil à te sanè postea accepimus, for sense ye set forth your bookes of the weale publike, I neuer after receiued any thinge from you.

Pli. in epi. Vt in limine auditur, he was as well herde, as if he had bene within.

Plautus in pœnu. Vt, so that. Olent, salsa sunt, tangere vt non velis, They be so salte and stinkinge, that thou wilt with, that thou haddest not touched them.

Plautus in Curcu. Vt, se that. Operam vt det, See that he do his indeuour.

Ter. in He. Vt ad pauca redeam, To make a short tale.

Vt ne addam, To be short.

Vtcunq;, In what maner or facyon. Sed nostrum est intelligere, vtcunque, & vbicunque opus est obsequi. But it is oure part to knowe, in what facyon, and where soeuer we shall gyue oure attendaunce.

Vtcunq;, how so euer.

Liuius. Vtcunq; erit, how so euer it shall happen.

Vtenfile, necessary to be vsed.

Vter, tris, a botell.

Vter, teri, a wombe, a bealy.

Vterum gerere, to be great with childe.

Vter, tra, trum, which of the twoo.

Plin. Vter alteri dixerit nescio, which of them told it to the tother, I can not tell.

Cicer. pro Milo. Vter vtri insidias fecerit, which of them layd awayte for the tother.

Terentius in Phorm. Vterq; utriq; est cordi, They do lyke wel the one the other.

Vterq; alterum uerberauit, the tone beete the tother, eche dyd beate other.

Vterculus, a litle bealy.

Vterlibet, which ye will.

Vterque, bothe, the one and the other.

Vteruis, which of them thou wilt.

Vti, for vt.

Vtica, a citye in Affrike, where Cato dyd sle hym self, and therfore was afterward called Cato Vticensis.

Plautus in Trinūmo. Vtibilis, le, for vtilis, profytable.

Vtibilitas, for vtilitas, profyte.

Plautus in Mercator. Vti, sometyme sygnifyeth to haue. Et te vtar iniquiore, & mens me ordo irrideat, that I may haue the, the warse toward me, & that

Plautus in Aul.

my company maye mocke me. Mihi si vnq̃ filius erit, vt ille facili me vtetur patre, If euer I haue a sonne, he shal haue me a gentyll father. **Ter. in Eu.**

Vti amore, to loue.

Vti amicitia, to fauoure, or be in amytye. **Plaut. in Asi.**

Vti eadem disciplina, to be of the same lernynge.

Vti oculis, to see perfytely, or well. Maris caussa hercle hoc ego oculo vtor minime, In good fayth the se maketh that I se not well with this eye, or I se not a whit with this eye. **Plautus in Mili.**

Vti officio, to do the office or part.

Vtilis, le, profytable, conuenient

Vtilitas, profyte.

Vtiliter, profytably.

Vtique, lyke as, veryly.

Vti valitudine, to be in helth. **Plin.**

Vti foro, to take the market as it cometh, a prouerbe applyed to theym, which canne take the state of euery tyme and chaunce, as it commeth. also it may signifye, to apply him self to the facions and condicions present.

Vtor, teris, ti, to vse, to be conuersaunt with one, to occupye.

Vtere vt vis mea opera, Take my seruyce at youre commaundement. Da mihi operam amabo. M. tua est, vtere, atq; impera si quid uis, A good felowshyp lend me thy helpe. M. It is redye for the, haue here, commaunde what thou wilt. **Plautus in Per.** **Plautus in Aul.**

Vtpoté, bycause that he was, as.

Vt puta, for quemadmodum, as.

Vtquid, for quamobrem, for what cause, wherfore.

Vtraque, by both places, by the tone place and the tother.

Vtricularius, he that pypeth in a botell.

Vtriculus, the place in a woman wherin the childe lyeth.

Vtrinque, of the one part and the other, of thone and thother. **Plautus in Amphitri.**

Vtris, a skynne blowen full of wynde, also a ball filled onely with wynde.

Vtrobique, in the one place and the other, on thone syde and the other. **Plautus in Mili.**

Vtroque, to thone place and the other.

Vtroque versum, on both partes, on thone part and thother, on euery part.

Vtrum, whyther.

Vtut, how so euer it be, in what facyon. Hæc adeo mea culpa fateor fieri, non me hanc rē patri, vtut erat gesta, indicasse, I confesse, all this happened by my defaulte, that I shewed not to my father the mater, in what facyon it was done.

V.

¶ V ANTE V.

Vva, a grape, it is alsoo that, whyche is in the roufe of a mannes mouth, whyche sometyme wyll swelle, and is also callyd Vuula. It is also a swarme of bees hangynge rounde.
Vua passa, a greatte reason.
Vueus, a, um, of a grape.
Vueus succus, wyne.
Vuidus, da, dum, moyste.
Vulcanus, called Jupyters smythe. Also it is taken for fyre.
Vulcanius, a, um, of Vulcane.
Vulga, a skryppe or sachelle, sommetyme a womannes bealy.
Vulgaris, re, commune, moche vsed.
Non. Mar. Vulgaria, for vulgaris.
Vulgatus, ta, tū, commonly knowen or vsed.
Vulgo, abrode amonge all men.
Vulgo conceptus, whose father is not certayne.
Vide com. Vulgo, gare, to publyshe, to manyfeste, to make commune.
Vulgus, uulgi, the common people.
Vulnerarius, a surgeon.
Vulnerarius, a, um, belongynge to woūdes.
Vulnero, rare, to wounde.
Vulnus, a wounde, sometyme griefe.
Vulpes, a foxe.
Vulpecula, a cubbe or a yonge foxe.
Vulpinus, na, num, of a foxe, sometyme subtyll and crafty.
Vulpinor, naris, nari, to be wyly.
Vulsinus, a ryuer in Italye.
Vulsinienses, people dwellynge aboute the ryuer of Vulsinus.
Vultorij, certayne dyse.
Vultuosus, sa, sum, heuye, sorowfulle of countenaunce.
Vultuose, dysdaynfully, heuyly, with frownynge countenaunce, with gesture agreable vnto the matter.
Vultur, turis, & vulturius, a rauyn.
Vulturinus, na, num, of a rauyn.
Vulturnum, a towne in Campania.
Vulturnus, the northeaste wynde.
Vulta, Lucretius vsed for the plurell number of Vultus.
Vulticulus, a lyttell vysage.
Vultus, of olde wryters is taken for wylle, a Volendo.
Vultus, vultus, & vultum, countynaunce or chicre.
Vulua, the wombe or mother of anye female kynde. It is alsoo a meate vsyd of the Romaynes, made of the bealye of a sowe, eyther that hathe farowed, or is greatte with farowe.

¶ V ANTE X.

Vxor, vxoris, a wyfe.
Vxorius, he that doteth on his wyfe.
Vxorius, a, um, of the wyfe.

¶ X ANTE A.

Xantha, a nymphe.
Xanthij, a people in Asia whose citie beinge besieged of the captayne of Cirus, they broughte into the castelles theyr wyues, seruantes, and goodes, and puttynge therunto fyre, bourned all togyther, and afterwarde issuinge out of the citie, faught vntyll that they were all slayne.
Xanthicus, amonge the Jewes was the moneth of Apryll.
Xanthus, a, um, yelowe.
Xanthus, a riuer of Troy, callid also Scamāder, also a citie in Licia, also Hectors horse.
Xantippe, the wyfe of Socrates the phylosopher.

¶ X ANTE E.

Xenia, presētis sent by one to an other.
Xeniolum, a smalle present.
Xenodochium, an hospytall.
Xenocrates, a philosopher discipleto Plato.
Xenophon, a philosopher, whiche as wel in marcial actes, as in eloquence excellyd.
Probus. Xerampellinæ uestes, garmentes of a colour, whyche I suppose is callyd Murrey. Somme doo suppose it to be blacke *Calepinus* garmentes.
Xeria, drye playsters.
Xerophagia, eatynge of drye meates.
Xerophthalmia, whanne the eyes be soore without droppynge or swellynge.
Xerxes, a kynge of Persia.

¶ X ANTE Y.

Xyline uestes, garmentes of cotton.
Xyloaloes, a swete and precious wod callid Lignū aloes, our women hauing beades made therof callyd it Acellula.
Xylobalsamus, the wodde wherof baulme naturall commeth.
Xylophagus, a worme bredinge in old wode, whiche is white and great belyed, and hath a blacke heed.
Xilon, cotton.
Xiphis, certayne blasynge sterres, whiche haue beames lyke to a sworde.

Xisticus, he that exercyseth hym selfe in a place couered out of the sonne or rayne.
Xyphius, a fyshe named a sworde fyshe, whiche hath in his nose a bone, lyke to the scaberde of a sworde, suche one haue I sene.
Xystus, et Xystum, a place, wherin menne do exercyse wrastlynge and other like pastyme in wynter. It may be taken for a galerye or place to walke in out of the rayn.

Z ANTE A.

ZACANTHEI, people in the mountaynes callyd Pyrenei, by the riuer of Hiberus.
Zacharias, the name of a prophete. Also the father of sayncte Johan Baptiste.
Zacynthii, people of the yle of Zacynthus.
Zacynthos, an ylande in the see callyd Jonia, wherin is a cytie of the same name.
Zagrus, a mountayne, which diuideth Media from Babilonia.
Zancle, a citie in Grecia, an other in Sicile.
Zaphyrus, a fyshe of the kynd of gylt hedes but that he is somwhat blewe in colour.
Zathene, a stone lyke to aumber, now black, nowe yelowe.

Z ANTE E.

Zea, a kynde of wheate.
Zelo, are, & zelor, laris, for æmulari.
Zelor, zelaris, ari, to be angrye, or to haue zeale.
Zelotes, for æmulator, he that hathe enuye at one, or assayeth to folowe an nother in lyuynge.
Zelotypia, ialowsye.
Zelotypus, ialowse.
Zelus, sometyme enuy, somtyme loue, some tyme emulation.
Zenobia, a quene of Siria, which in greke and latyne was very well lerned, and was also valyant in armes.
Zephyrus, the weste wynde.
Zeros, a kynde of chrystall, whyche hathe spottes whyte and blacke.
Zeta, & zetecula, a place made in a chaumber, wherein was a bedde and three stoles, whyche with courtaynes was so diuided from the chaumber, that sometyme it was parte therof, sometyme it was separate from it, and it hadde three wyndowes or lowpes, by the whyche the sonne mought entre into it.
Zeugma, a fygure, wherby many sences ar ioyned togyther with one verbe, as, Neq̈ is es Catilina, ut te, aut pudor a turpitudine, aut metus a periculo, aut ratio a furore reuocarit, He thou arte suche a man Catilyne, as eyther shamefastnesse canne withdrawe from dishonestie, or feare from daunger, or reason from vengeable angre.
Zeusis, an excellent paynter, which so painted a boy carryeng grapes, that byrdes cam to the table and pecked on the grapes, wenynge that they had ben very grapes, whiche Zeusis beholdynge, was with hym self angrye, and sayd, If I had made the boye, aswel as I haue done the grapis, the birdis durst not haue come so nygh to the grapes.
Zeus, a fyshe taken about Calys in Spain, whiche is blacke, but he is very delicate.

Z ANTE I.

Zigena, a fyshe of the see.
Zigari, people, whyche we doo calle Egyptians, that wander about in euery royalme and be horrible theues.
Zigarum, the contray from whens the said people doo come.
Zizania, cockle, whiche groweth in corne.
Zinziber, gynger.

Z ANTE O.

ZOdiacus, a cerkle in heuen, wherein be the xii. sygnes.
Zographia, the pycture of beastes.
Zoilus, was a poete, whyche enuyed Homerus, and therfore the enuiers of welle lerned men are callyd Zoili.
Zœlicum, certayne flaxe, that commeth out of Spayne, whereof threde is made for nettes to take byrdes.
Zomos, gruelle.
Zona, a gyrdell.
Zonatim, in compasse aboute. Non. Mar.
Zopissa, pitche taken from shyppes, whiche being tempred with waxe and salte, is of more efficacie than other pytche.
Zopyron, an herbe, which some do suppose to be Pulyol mountayne.
Zopyrus, was a man, whiche by phisnomye knew euery mãs cõdicions. And whã in beholding Socrates he iudged him to be vnthrifty, & therfore was scorned of many mẽ, Socrates answered, Zopyrus is not deceiued, for in dede I had ben suche one as he saith, if I had not by philosophy subduid nature. Also Zopirus was a noble Persian, seruant to Darius, which whan the citie of Babylon rebellid agcinst king Dariº, & that he had made long warre, & coulde not subdue thẽ, vnwares to any mã, did cut of his owne nose, & wouded him self, & fled to Babylon,
sayeng

The Additions.   A ante B.

sayinge, the kynge had so diffygured hym, bycause that he perswaded hym to haue peace with the Babylonians, whiche they heryng, made him their chiefe capitayne. Than by lytell and lytle declaryng to them the strength of the kynge, and howe they mought not indure longe agaynste hym, at the laste he caused them to submit them selues to the kynge, & to receyue hym into the citie. wherfore Darius was wonte to saye, that he had leauer haue one Zopyrus, than twenty Babylons.

Zoroanda, a ryuer, whiche the great water of Tigris maketh on the one syde of the mountayne Taurus.

Zoroastes, the fyrste fynder of Magike.

Z ANTE V.

¶ Zura, bearies of whyte thorne.

¶ Zygia, a pype, wherin menne dyd playe at weddynges.

Zithus, drynke made with barley sodden. It maye be taken for ale or biere.

— Finis Dictionarii.

THE ADDICION OF
SYR THOMAS ELIOT KNIGHT
vnto his Dictionarye.

¶ A ANTE B.

Varro.

ABAGIO, gere, to fetche a compasse in speaking, & not to consist or abide in one oratiõ or sentẽce.

Abalienatio, alienation.

Abalienator, he that doth aliene or putte awaye a thinge, or altereth the possession therof, an alienour.

Abanec, a gyrdel, which priestes did weare, wrought with colours of scarlet & purple, in suche wise that there seemed to be in it floures and precious stones set in order.

Abania, is interpreted the father, vnto god acceptable, or gratifienge vnto god.

Abarceo, cui, cere, to prohybyte or put of.

Abauia, my great grandames mother.

Abbreuio, are, to abbreuiate or make shorte.

Abbatia, the dignitie of an abbotte. Some tyme the monasterie.

Cic. in Pisonem. & ad Att.

Abdicatio, a renoũcing of one whom I take for myn heire, a puttyng out of fauour.

Abdidit se domum, he kepte hym at home.

Abdere se ex conspectu heri, to kepe hym away that his maister see hym not.

Abdere se literis, to lyue vnknowen in continuall study. Abducere clauem, to take the kaye oute of the doore.

Abecedarius, he that setteth any thynge in order by letter.

Abedo, dere, to consume.

Aberuncare iram deorum, to withdrawe the vengeance of god with prayers.

Aberuncasso, sere, to tourne vppe.

Cicero.

Abhorreo ab urbe relinquenda, I haue noo mynde to forsake the cytie.

Abhorret ab illo mea sententia, myn opynion is contrary to his.

Abhorret a suspitione, it is contrarye to my supposalle.

Abhorret a charitate uulgi, he tendreth not, or passeth nothynge on the poore people.

Cicero de Amic.

Abhorret hilaritudo, thy myrthe is tourned into sadnesse.

Plautus in cistell.

Abhortatio, a contrary aduyse.

Abhortor, tari, to gyue contrary aduyse.

Abi in malam rem, go hens with a mischefe.

Abibitur, I or he wyl depart or go away.

Plautus in Mercator.

Abiectus, a vyle persone.

Abiegnus, na, num, of firre tree.

Abigena bos, was amonge the diuinours, callid Augures, the oxe, whiche was to be sacrifised, aboute whom the other beastes to be sacrifised, were sette.

Varro.

Abigere ex ædibus, to driue out of the dores

Abricio, cere, to poure oute. Sommetyme to gyue awaye.

Plautus in Asinar.

Abricior, ci, to be out of reputation.

Abijt hora, the tyme passed.

Abijt sol, the sonne is gone downe.

Abitus, tu, a departynge.

Terent. in Eunucho. Plautus.

Abyla, a mountain in the se ageinst Spain in affrica, callid one of the pillers of Hercules

Ab incunablis, from his infancy.

Ab ineunti ætate, from his chyldehode.

Abitio, a departure or going away, old writers toke it for deth, as we may call it, the decesse of one. Abiudicare a uita, to put to dethe. Abiudicabit nunq̃ ab suo triobolum, He wylle neuer be of the mynde to gyue thre halfe pens of his owne.

Plautus in Asina.

Ff ij   Abiu.

The additions. A ante B.

Abiuratio, a forswearynge, an abiuration.
Ablectæ ædes, nete faire & pleasant houses.
Abludo, lusi, ludere, to speake of a thynge couertly, that other shall not espie what the matter dothe meane.
Ablutio, a washynge.
Abluuium, a vnyuersall floudde, wherwith a countray is drowned.
Abneco, care, to strangle.
Abnepris, a daughter in the fourth discent.
Abnormis, out of rule.

Festus. Abolitus, ta, tum, rased oute, putte oute of remmbraunce.
Ab oloes, olde wryters vsed for ab illis.
Abominalis, le, abhomynable.
Abortor, & aborto, idem quod abortio.
Abraham, the name of a patriarche, significenge father of many nations.
Abradere de bonis, to polle or spoyle a man of his goodes.
Abripuit repente sese, he went away sodeinly
Abrogare fidem, to bring out of credence.
Abrogatio, the dissoluynge or repellynge of a lawe.
Abrupta loca, rockes & hylles here & there broken or dygged, so that one may vnethe go or crepe vp to them.

Plautus in Ruden. Abruptum, that whiche hath suche a fall or stepenesse downe, that no man maye passe by it, but onely fall downe.

Terent. in Adel. Abs te stat, it standeth vppon the, or it lyeth in the.
Abs quiuis homine, of euery man what soo euer he be.

Val. max. 6 Abscissus, a, um, broken, sharpe.
Abscissior iustitia, sharpe iustyce.
Absconsus, a, um, hydde.

Liuius. 2. Absoluere vno uerbo, to telle at a worde, to make an ende shortely.

Plautus in capt. in Amphitri. Absoluere suspitione, to discharge or putte of all suspition.
Absoluere, to depeche of busynesse.
Absolute, persytly.
Absolutio, a discharge, or depeche.
Absolutus, ta, tum, discharged, depeched.
Absonum fidei, not credible.
Absonus uoce, he þ hath an vntunable voice
Abstergeo, si, gere, to wype, to wipe awaye.
Absterrere, to feare awaye, or dryue awaye with feare.

Plautus in Mili. Abstinenter, with abstinence.

Plautus in Ruden. Abstinere incomoditate, to behaue him honestly. Abstinere manum, to hold his hand.

Sueton. in Clau. Abstineas me manum, take hede that thou stryke me not.

Pli. in epi. Abstinuit diu publico, it was long or he came abrode. Abstinere uerbis, to take heede, what he speaketh.
Abstinens alieni, he that medleth not with other mennes goodes.
Abstraxi me illinc, I gatte me thens.
Abstractum, taken by force.
Abstrudere colaphos, to buffet or giue blowes.
Abstrusus, a, um, hydde or shutte vp.
Abest mihi animus, I haue no courage.
Absit uerbo inuidia, a forme of speking whā one wolde not be suspected of arrogāce in some thynge that he wyll speake.
Absente nobis, whyle I was away.
Absento, tare, to kepe from a place, or cause to be absente.

Plaut. in Mostel.

Absumpti sumus, we are vndone.
Absumedo, dinis, dispence, waste of money or other lyke thynge.
Absumptio, a wastynge, waste.
Absurde, without purpose or reason, to no purpose. Absynthium marinū, wormesede.
Absynthium santonicum, maye seeme to be Lauander cotton.
Abundanter, abundantely.
Abunde est, it is ynoughe.
Abundans, a ryche manne.
Abundare ingenio, to haue a great wytte.
Abuerto, tere, to tourne from a place.
Abusq; mane ad vesperam, frome the mornynge to nyghte.
Ambustus, ta, tum, bourned vp.
Abusum, worne out.
Abusus, us, & abusio, abuse, yll vse.
Abutor, ti, to weare out.

Terentius in Prolog. Andri.

Abutitur operam, he loste his labour.
Abydeus, a man borne in the ile of Abydos.

¶ A ANTE C.

ACananthide, the olde name of the yle of Cypres.
Acanthus, is an herbe cōmonly callid Brankursyn. Loke afore in Acanthis.
Acapis, a ryuer in Asia.
Acarpos, vnfruytefull. Acasta, a nymphe.
Acar, & Acarus, a lyttell worme that bredeth in waxe.
Acatia, a thorne growynge in Egipt, wherof commeth a gumme, whyche is medycynable for many diseases.
Acatium, a bote.
Accede adiutare, come helpe me.

Plautus in Truculen.

Accedit huc, more ouer than that.
Accedere obuiam, to mete with one.
Accedere periculum, to take on hym the daungiere.

Plautus in Epidic.

Accedere alicui, to graunt to an other, to be of an other mans opinion.
Accelerare gradum, to go apace.
Acceleratio, haaste or spede.
Accento, tare, to synge often.
Accessio, an augmentacyon, increase, Also a commynge. Accessio morbi, the begynnynge of a syckenesse.

Accersio

The Additions. A ante C.

Accersio, sire, to sende or call for one.
Accersitus, ta, tum, callyd for.
Accersi iube filiam, commande thy daughter to be sent for, or callyd for?

Liuius. Accido, cidere, to extenuate or make feeble, to destroye.
Accisus, a, um, made feble, decayed.
Accidit, there happened, it is chaunced.
Acccinere, to synge to an instrument, or to synge a parte, as a treble to a tenoure, or a descant to a playne songe.
Accipenser, a fysshe hauynge the skales turned forewarde, contrary to other fysshes, which in the old time was of most estimation at the tables of kynges and princis.

Plautus in casina. Accipere auribus, to here.
Ci. Tyro. Accipere causam, to holde excused.
Accipere cladē, to haue great losse in bataile.
Accipere corde, to perceiue well. Pol haud satis meo corde accepi querelas tuas, in good faythe I do not well perceyue the cause of thy griefe.
Accipere conditionem, to take the offre.

Cicero de Amic. Accipere dolorē, to take thought, to be heuy
Accipere nomen, to take accounte.
Accipere potestatem, to haue leaue.
Accipere uulnus, to be wounded.
Acceptus, receyued, entertayned.
Acceptus, ta, tum, accepted, acceptable.
Accepti & expensi ratio, accompte of receites and expenses.
Accipiter humipeta, a sparhawke.
Accipiter hierax, an hawke callid a sakre.
Accipiter pecuniarum, a poller of people.
Accipitrarius, a faulconer.
Accliuitas, a raysynge vp of a hylle.
Accommodatus, ta, tum, applyed to a thyng besemyng, couenable.
Accommodus, da, dū, apt, mete, conuenient.
Accreduo, duis, duere, idem quod accredo.
Accubatio, a syttynge at the table.
Accubitores, they that sytte at the table.

Plautus in Trucu. Accumbere alicui, to syt by one at the table.
Accurare, to do a thynge dylygently.
Accurare prandium, to make redy the diner.
Accurata malitia, malyce prepensed.
Accuratum habere, to prepense.
Accusatio, an accusement.
Accusatorius liber, a bylle of complaynt.
Accusare, to blame.
Accusabilis, le, worthy to be blamed.
Accusator, an accuser, a rebuker.
Accusatrix, a woman rebuker.
Acedaria, saletts, or meate lyghtly spared.
Acri ingenio, quycke wytted.
Acer equus, a swyfte horse.
Acerrimi inimici, mortall enemies.
Acer morbus, a greuous syckenes.
Acres oculi, cleere eyes.

Acerrima uxor, a very shrewde wyfe.
Acere, a cytie by Naples.
Aceratum, mortar, or claye myxte with hey or strawe, wherwith walles are daubyd.
Acerbe, bitterly, vnripely, cruelly, vehemēt
Acero, rare, to myxte with chaffe. (ly.
Acernus, na, num, of the tree callyd Acer.
Acerra, a shyppe, wherein frankyncense is put. some do name it an aultar, which was sette before a deed corps, wheron incense was burned. Some call it a cuppe, wherin they dyd sacrifyce wyne.
Acerosus panis, browne bredde not ranged.
Acesinus, a great ryuer in Persia, whiche runneth into the ryuer of Indus, wherein do growe canes of suche greatnesse, that they doo make betwene euery knotte or ioynt therof, botes to rowe in.
Acesis, an herbe, which is yelow in colour.
Acestus, a great ryuer in India.
Acetabulum, a measure contayninge in it of water measure, two ounces.
Acetositas, aigrenesse or sowrenes.
Acetosus, a, um, eygre, sowre.
Acetum in pectore. Nunc experiar, sit ne acetum tibi cor acre in pectore, Nowe wylle I proue, yf thou haste any thynge that doth prycke the in the stomacke.
Aceum, a citie in Colchis, on the banke of the ryuer callyd Phasis.
Achantia, a fyshe, whiche some men do suppose to be thornebacke.
Achar, a citie in Siria, nowe callyd Nisibis.
Achateon, the mayne sayle of a shyppe.
Achelous, a ryuer in Grecia, so named of a kynge of that name.
Acheloeus, of that ryuer. sommetyme it is put for aqueus.
Achemenia, a countray in Persia.
Acherontinus, & Acherontius, of the ryuer of Acheron.
Acherusia, a fenne in the realme of Naples.
Achilleias, a kynde of barly, peraduenture that whiche is callyd beare corne.
Achilleon, some do suppose to be mylfoyle.
Achras, a wylde peare.
Achylus, without lyppes.
Aciale, harde yron.
Acidalia, a name of Venus, of a foūtayn in a citie of Bœotia, callyd orchomenæ.
Acidylus, a knotte in the gyrdell of Venus.
Aciem trahere, to sette in edge.
Acies animi, the capacitie of a mans wytte.
Acinaceus, a, um, full of kernels.
Aciritani, were a people in Spayne.
Acis, a ryuer in Sycil, which cometh from the mountayne of Aethna.
Aciria, an Ilande callyd also Melos in the see by Candye.

Ff iij   Acilon,

The additions.   A ante C.

Acilon, the bearye of holy.
Aclassis, a garmēt vnsowed frō the shulders
Acon, aconis, a fyshe, whiche after the description of Paulus Jouius, I suppose to be that, whiche at London is callid a shad.
Acopus, an herbe callyd also Anagyris, full of braunches, and hathe flowres lyke to colewortes, and hath an ylle sauoure, the sede therof is in longe coddes, harde and lyke in facion to kydneys.
Acorus, an herbe with longe leaues, lyke the blade of a sworde. I suppose it be that, whiche is callyd Gladwen or Bladen.
Acratismus, & acratisma, a breakefast.
Acris, a ryuer of Italye.
Acrodria, be all frutes, which haue an hard rynde or shale, as pomegranades, nuttes, chestyns, pistaces, and other lyke.
Acre, swyft, sowre, cruell, valiant, vehemēt, dyligent, circumspecte.
Acritas, sowrenesse, crueltie, dilygence.
Acriter, swiftly, cruelly, vchemētly, diligētly
Acrisius, kynge of Argiues, the father of Danaes, on whom Jupiter begate Perseº.
Acroama, a subtyle sentence, whiche requireth an exquysite study to perceyue.
Acroamata, were certayne lectures of Aristotle, whiche he radde to his scholers, wherin was the moste subtylle and counnynge parte of philosophie.
Acroceraunia, mountaynes of wonderfulle heyght, betwene Armenia and Hiberia.
Acrocomus, one hauynge longe heare.
Acrocorinthus, an high mountayne in Morea, betwene the two sees Aegeū z Ioniū.
Acropolis, a castell sette on a hylle.
Acte, an elder tree.
Action, the bearye of an elder.
Acteus, a, um, of Athenes.
Actia, orum, plays made ones in fiue yeres.
Actitatus, ta, tum, determyned by iugement.
Actitatio, a debatynge of a case in lawe, or pleedynge.
Actius, a noble poete that wrate tragedies.
Actiuus, actyue.
Actualis scientia, a science that declarethe thinges by their operation, of the which ar thre partes, morall, dispensatiue, and ciuile.
Acta ætas, age whan youth is paste.
Acta agere, to doo that whiche is all redye done, to lose laboure.
Actus, put in feare.
Actus, a braid in tillage, it is also a cartway.
Actuosus, alway in busynesse.
Actuosus ignis, fyre whiche alway burneth.
Seneca.   Aculeatus, ta, tum, any thyng that prycketh.
Acupedius, he that hath a quycke and apte foote to runne with.
Paul. Iouiº   Acus, a fishe, whiche is longe and somwhat grene, and hath a beke, as it were the byll of a crane, I suppose it is that, which som calle an hornebeke.
Acustici, they whiche do here all, and speke nothynge them selfes.
Acute, quyckely, subtilly.
Acuti oculi, cleere eyes.
Acuti cibi, sharpe meates.
Acutum ingenium, a subtyll or quycke wyt.
Acylon, an holye beary.
Acyphantes, a cytie in Thessaly, whiche is also callyd Pindus.

¶ A ANTE D.

A DAD, in the Syrian tounge, is the sonne. also it signifieth onely.
Ad me, with me. Commodum ad te dederam literas, de pluribus rebus, cum ad me bene mane, Dionysius fuit, I had scarsly sent my letters vnto the, whan Dionyse was with me erly in the mornynge.   *Cice. Attī. lib. 9.*
Ad breuissimū tempus, for a very short time.   *Pli. in pan.*
Ad id tempus, at that tyme.
Ad sapientiam huius, nimius nugator fuit, In regard of his wysedom he was but a fole.
Ad illam faciem, ita ut illa est, ut emerem sibi, mandauit mihi, He commaunded me to bie for hym one, whiche had suche an nother face as she hath.   *Plautus in Mercator.*
Ad cyathum stare, to awayte on the cuppe.   *Sueton. in Cesare.*
Ad manum seruus, he that is clerke to one, or wryteth for hym.   *Ci de oratore. 4.*
Ad pedes, a lakay.
Ad manus venire, to come to handestrokes, to cope togyther.
Ad meridiem, vntyll noone.
Ad multam noctem, late in the nyght.   *Terentius Cice. Atti.*
Ad tempus, in season, sometyme accordyng to the tyme. also for a tyme.
Ad dextram, on the ryght hande.
Ad hoc exemplum, nunq̄ amaui, I neuer loued of that facyon, or in that maner.   *Plautus in mercator.*
Ad hunc modum, this way or in this maner.
Ad extremum, fynally, in conclusyon.   *Plin.*
Ad postremum, idem.   *Plautus in Aulul.*
Ad summum, at the moste.   *Cicero.*
Ad uerbum, worde by worde.   *Plinius.*
Ad vnum, not one lefte.   *Cicero de Amic.*
Ad vnum idem sentiunt, they be all of oone opynyon.   *Plinius.*
Ad assem, to the vttermoste penye.   *Plautus in Ruden.*
Ad annos sedecim, syxtene yeres herafter.   *Plautus.*
Ad rauim poscere, to aske vntil one be hoorse   *Terentius in Phorm.*
Ad restim res redijt, It is come to the poynt that he wyl hange him selfe. it is a sentēce signifienge desperation.
Ad rem suam sapere, to be wyse for his own profytte.   *Plautus in Trucu.*

Ad-

The additions.   A ante D.

Cicero. Adæquo, are, to make or be equall.
Adaggero, rere, to gather and lay togither.
Adam, the fyrste manne, whyche sygnyfyeth redde.
Adamanteus, & Adamantinus, of a diamand, or as harde as a diamande.
Adamaster, a gyaunt, whiche was of an incredible greattenesse.
Adamiani, were certayne heretykes, whiche went naked aboute all their busynesse, sayenge that they dyd folowe the nakydnes of Adam beinge in Paradise, who beleuyd that there shulde haue ben no mariage, if no man had synned.
Adaperio, rire, to open a thynge.
Adapertilis, le, for apertum, open.
Adarca, a salte fome, whiche cometh of the ryndes of caanes or reedes grownyge in fennes.
Adasia, an olde ewe, which hath late eaned or hadde a lambe.
Adasso, olde wryters vsed for Adigo, to compelle.

Non. Mar. Adaucto, tare, to augment or increase.
Adaugeo, gere, idem.
Adauctus, ta, tum, augmented.
Adaxint, for adegerint, lette them compelle, or constrayne.
Adcensi, souldiors put in the place of them whiche are deed.
Addico, cere, to sette to sale.
Addicere animū, to gyue or apply his mynd.

Terent. in Eunucho. Addictus, bounden to one.
Addebat hoc, he sayde moreouer.
Addere animum, to gyue courage.
Addere gradum, to make hym go faster.

Vergilius. Additus, for an ennemie. Nec Teucris addita Iuno, usq̃ aberit, Neither Iuno ennemy to the Troyans shall lacke or be away.
Addo, dare, to gyue to one.
Addormisco, scere, to slepe.
Addubito, tare, to doubte.
Adducere habenas, to hold strait the bridel.
Adductus, ta, tum, brought, ledde, moued.
Adduplico, care, to double any thynge.
Adelphi, brethrene, it is also the name of a comedie in Terence.
Adeo res redijt, the matter is comme to that poynte.
Adeousq̃, vntyll that.
Adest ei animus, he hath a good courage.
Adest, he is at hande.
Adesse, to ayde or succour one.

Terent. in Andria. Adesdum, come hyther.
Adeor, the passyue of adeo.
Ader, a place by Bethlem, where angelles dydde synge at the byrthe of Christe, and Iacob kepte there his shepe.

Non. Mar. Adesus, a, um, consumed.

Ad exitam ætatem, for ad ultimam ætatem, at the vttermoste age.   **Festus.**
Adfabrum, well wrought.
Adhærescere, scere, idem quod adhereo.
Adhesus, a, um, cleaued to.
Adhibere animū, to take hede what is spokē
Adhibere aures, to harken, to gyue an eare.
Adhibere in consilium aliquem, to aske counsayle of oone.
Adhibere modum, to vse moderacyon or temperaunce.
Adhibere parsimoniam, to spare.
Adhibere sermonem, to deuyse or talke togyther.
Adhibere testes, to brynge forth wytnes.
Adhibere uim, to doo a thyng by vyolence, to inforce.
Adhinnio, to neye as a horse dothe after a mare. Cicero by a metaphore maketh it to sygnyfie to reioyce.   **Cic. in Pisonem.**
Adhuc locorum, for adhuc.   **Plautus in capt.**
Adiabene, a countray beyonde Armenia.
Adiantum, an herbe growinge about sprynges of water, hauynge smalle leaues lyke to Coriander. somme doo nowe take it for Maydenheare.
Adiaphoron, indifferente.
Adij te heri de filia, I came yesterday to talk with the for thy doughter.
Adijcere album calculum, to approue a thing   **Plin. epist.**
Adijcere animum, to set his mynde or loue on oone.
Adijcere oculum hæreditati. Plane uidebant adiectum esse oculum hæreditati, They saw playnely, that the other wente aboute to gette the inheritaunce.   **Ci. in Ver.**
Adimere animam, to kylle.
Adimere ius, to prohybyte.
Adimere uestem, to pulle of his garmente.   **Pli. de usuris illustr.**
Adimere suum alteri, to take an other mannes goodes from hym.
Adinuenio, to inuente a thynge.
Adinuentum, an inuention.
Adipisci senectutem, to come to age.   **Cicero de senectu.**
Adipisci, to ouertake one.
Adiposus, ryche.   **Plautus in Epidic.**
Adipson, a swete roote callyd lykorys.
Adipsos, a certayne date tree growynge in Egypte, the fruite wherof hath no stone. Plinius callyth it Myrobalanum.
Adire ad pactionem, to come to a poynt.
Adire discrimen, to put hym in daunger.
Adire hæreditatē, to take on me, the, or him, the inherytaunce.
Adire periculum, to take a daungerouse thynge on hym.
Aditiculus, a lyttell entrie.
Adiungere, to wynne or optayne. Errat lōge mea quidem sententia, qui imperium credat gra-   **Terent. in Andria.**

The additions. A ante D

grauius esse aut stabilius, ui quod sit, quàm id quod amicitia adiungitur, He is foule deceyued in myne opynion, that thinketh, that rule to be more ferme and stable, whiche is goten by vyolence, than that which is obtayned by frendship. *Plautus in Men.*

Adiurgium, debate.

Adiuratio, a coniuringe.

Adiurati, confederate or allied togither by othe.

Adiutor, an helper, Adiutrix.

Adiuuamen, helpe.

Adlino, nere, to enoynt, or rubbe a thinge with any thinge liquide.

Administer, a stuarde of householde.

Administro, rare, to do seruyce, to exployte, to fournyshe.

Administratio, exploytynge or doynge of a thinge, seruice.

Admirabilis, wonderfull.

Admirabundus, he that doeth wonder or maruayle at a thinge.

Admisceo, scui, cere, to myngle or mixte one thinge with another.

Admistio, onis, a menglynge or mixture.

Admiste, an aduerbe signifyenge, one menglyd with another.

Admistura, idem quod admistio.

Admittere uitam, to retayne lyfe, to lyue. *Salust.*

Admittere, to do. Quid tandem admisi in te? what haue I offended the? *Plautus in Men.*

Admittere noxiam, to pardon an offence. *Plautus in Pen.*

Admittere diem, to open the wyndowe, that the lyght maye come in. *Plin ep. 21*

Admittere equum, to lyte vp to horsebacke, or as we saye, to take his horse. *Cicero de finib. 2.*

Admittere, to put the male beste to the female for generacion. *Tit. Liu. 2. Valerius. 3*

Admittere sumptum, to do great coste. *Te. in Ad.*

Admodum, ye.

Adnato, rare, to swym to a place.

Adnecto, tere, to knyt to a thynge.

Adnexio, a knyttynge or fastning to a thing. *Festus.*

Adnicto, nixi, nictere, to wynke on one.

Adnitor, niteris, niti, to leane to a thinge, to beare or sustayne it.

Adnotatio, a titillinge, or short notinge of that, which we do reade or here.

Adnumero, rare, to adde to.

Adolabilis, without grief or sorowe.

Adolescens, tis, a yonge man, whiche is yet growynge.

Adolescentulus, a ladde.

Adonai, the name of god amonge the Iues, which signyfyeth, The Lorde of all creatures.

Adoperio, rire, to kouer or hyde.

Adoptatitius, he whome a manne ordayneth to be his heyre, and taketh vnto him in the stede of his sonne.

Adoptio, where a manne maketh one his heyre, and taketh hym for his sonne, beinge of his owne kynne or a straunger.

Ador, & Adoreum, a kynde of wheate, called also Far, which by the description semeth to be the wheate, whyche we calle ducke byll.

Adorno, nare, to apparayle, to prepare, to prayse.

Adquiro, quisiui, quirere, to geate, to conquere.

Adquo, for quousque, vntyll.

Adramelech, an ydolle of Syria, whome also the Samaritanes honoured.

Adrastia, a contraye not ferre from Troye, also the name of a citye there. It was also called a goddesse, which toke from manne both memory and wytte.

Adrastus, a kynge of Argyuei in Greece, who hadde two dawghters, of the which the one was maryed to Tideus, the other to Polynices, reade the historye of the syege of Thebes.

Adrepo, psi, pere, to reache at a thynge, to take it with vyolence.

Adscisco, scere, to ioyne or take to, as whan one ioyneth another with hym in auctoritty, or taketh one to ayde him in his office.

Adscriptitii, were men of warre, whyche were taken into an armye to supplye the places of them that were slayne, or otherwyse lacked.

Ascripti, were they that were appoynted to inhabyte townes or cityes, made by the Romanes, called Coloniæ.

Adscriptiui, idem quod Adscriptitii.

Adsitus domi facite, Se that ye be bothe at home.

Aduallas, a mountayne, frome the whyche the great ryuer called the Rene, runneth Northward.

Adubanus, the famouse ryuer called also Danubius and Hister.

Aduelitatio, a mutuall reprochinge, or contention in wordes.

Aduentus, tus, a commynge.

Aduerbialiter, lyke an aduerbe.

Aduersaria, a rcknynge booke of expensis, wryten fyrst afore the booke of accompte be made.

Aduersa ærumna, aduersyty, dammage. *Terentius in Phorm.*

Aduersa valetudo, syckenesse.

Aduersatus, ta, tum, agaynst or contrary.

Aduersis vulneribus, with woundes in the forepart. *Pli de uiris illustr.*

Aduerso flumine, agaynst the streme.

Aduersus, sa, sum, that whereof onely the fore parte is sene, as Auersus, wherof only the

The additions.   A *ante* E.

onely the hynderpart is sene.

Aduorso animo, agaynst my wyll, thy wyll, or his wyll: agaynst his hart.

Aduersum, agaynst. Quis eſt hic, qui aduersum mihi sit? who is he that commeth agaynst me, or marchyth towarde me?

Aduersum, for erga.

Aduertere, to perceyue.

Aduertere animum, to take hede, or herken.

Pli, in pan. Aduertere oculos, to perceyue, to see, to beholde.

Aduesperascit, the euenynge, or euentyde is commen, or it waxyth late, or it is nyght.

Aduigilo, uigilare, to watche, to take good heede.

Adulteror, rari, idem quod Adultero.

Adumbratus, a, um, fayned, countrefayted, portured.

Adumbratio, portrayture.

Adulator, toris, a flaterar.

Adulatrix, a woman that flatreth.

Aduocito, tare, to call for one often.

Aduocatus, he that defendeth an other mans cause.

Aduocatio, pleadynge.

Aduoluo, uere, to wrappe rounde togither.

Aduorsor, for Aduersor.

Aduorsem, olde wrytars vsed for Aduersarium.

Aduro, ussi, urere, to rost, to burne.

Adustio, rostinge, or burnynge.

Adustus, ta, tum, rostyd, or burned.

Adyticulum, a dyminutif of Adytum.

¶ A, ANTE E.

AEantion, a towne in the promontory or hill of Troye, called Sigeum.

Aeas, xantos, a ryuer of a contraye called Epyrus, whiche runneth oute of Macedonia, and falleth into the Se called Ionium.

Aeacus, was the sonne of Jupiter and Europa, whome Paynymes dyd suppose to be of suche iustice, that he was appoynted by Pluto, called godde of hell, to be one of the iuges there, with Minoes and Radamanthus, to discusse the transgressyons of menne beynge deed, and to assigne to theym punysshement accordinge to their merites.

Aedificatio, buyldynge.

Aedificator, a buyldar.

Aeditio, a publication of a thinge.

Aeger, ægra, um, sycke, sorowfull.

Aegerrime, very greuously.

Aedes, a chambre.

Aedilirius, a, um, pertayninge to Aediles.

Aedititinus, idem qui Aedituus.

Aedon, a Nightingale.

Aege, a citie in Cilicia, also an Ile in the Se called Aegeum.

Aegeon, a gyant called also Briareus, also it is one of the names of Neptunus.

Aegæa, a cytye in Macedonia, another in Mauritania.

Aegeria, a Nymphe or goddesse, with whō Numa Pompilius the seconde kynge of Romanes, fayned to haue familiar company and communicacion concernyng religion and worshyppynge of goddes, to the intent that he mought thereby withdrawe the people frome the appetyte of warres, wherewith they were inflamed.

Aegæum mare.

Aegeus, the father of Theseus.

Aegealus, was a countraye called also Achaia, in Grece.

Aegides, of Aegeus, patronymicum.

Aegylops, wylde otes.

Aegina, a citie ioynynge to Peloponeso or Morea, agaynste the countraye of Athenes, also an Ile frome Pireum. xii. myles.

Aeginenses, the people of Aegina the citie.

Aeginiræ, people of the Ile of Aegina.

Aegineticus, ca, cum, of Aegina.

Aegimuros, an Ile called also Capraria, beyonde Corse.

Aegiochus, a name of Jupiter.

Aegis, gidis, an haubergeon, whiche onely the goddis were paynted with.

Aegium, a towne in Peloponeso, now called Morea, where they fayned that Jupiter was noryshed with a gote.

Aegle, a Nymphe.

Aegloga, a communication of shepcherdes togither.

Aegocephalus, a byrde, which is withoute a splene.   *Aristot. de animali. 2.*

Aegocerus, idem quod Capricornus.

Aegonomus, a gote herde, or kepar of gotes.

Aegos, a ryuer in Thracia.

Aegre, with moche payne, or difficulty.

Aegrefero, tuli, ferre, to be sory.

Aegresco, sci, scere, to be sycke.

Aegrum, idem quod ægritudo, sorowe, displeasure.

Aegrius, more sorowfully, more displeasauntly.

Aegrio, I am sycke.

Aegritudo, dinis, grief of mynde, or sorow.

Aegrotare, to fayle, or be feble of courage.

Aegrotus, feble of courage.

Aegula, a kynde of brymstone, wherewith in some places they doo perfume wulle to make it whyte.

Aegylops, a fistula in the corner of the eye

by the

The additions.   A ante E.

by the nose of a manne, whiche rouuneth mattier.
Aegyptini, people of Ethiope, marchynge on Egypte.
Aegyptius, & Aegyptiacus, a, um, of Egypt.
Aegyptus, the countrey callyd Egypte.
Aegystus, he that slewe Agamemnon.
Aelius, the propre name of a Romayne.

Festus. Aelurus, a catte.
Aemidum, swollen.
Aemilius, the propre name of a Romayne.
Aemilia, a countray in Italy, callid also Flaminia, & Romandiola.
Aemulatio, enuye, or imitation.
Aemonia, a countray callyd also Thessalia.
Aeneas, a noble man of Troy, which with Anthenor betrayed the citie of Troy.
Aenobarbus, the name of a Romain, so callyd bycause he had a berde as red as brasse.
Aeolium mare, the see ioynynge to Asia.
Aeolus, callyd the kynge of wyndes.
Aequalitas, equalitie.
Aequatio, the equall diuision of a thyng, or where one thing is made equal to an other.
Aequidium, idem quod equinoctium.
Aequilanium, seu aequilaneum, the half deale of the hole.

Varro. Aequimentū, hyre of a horse, or other beest.
Aequipollentia, equalitie in estymation or valewe.
Aequipondium, of equall or lyke weight.
Aequiter, iustely.
Aequiualentia, equall value.
Aequiuocatio, makynge dyuers significations to one worde.
Aquiuocé, dyuersely sygnyfyenge in oone worde or terme.
Aequoreus, ea, um, of the see.
Aerius, a, um, of the ayre.

Cicero. *Plautus.* Aerarius, he that was put from his fredom of a cytesin, & payd tribute as a straunger.
Aera, ræ, dernel, whiche groweth in corne.
Aeratus, indetted.
Aerarii Tribuni, were treasourers, whiche payde to the souldiours their wages.
Aerarii præfectus, hygh Treasourer.
Aere meo. Multi. n. anni sunt, cum ille in aere meo est, It is longe time passed, that I accompted hym in the nūbre of my frendes, or for one of myne.
Acrificium, the crafte to make any thynge of brasse or copper.
Aero, rare, to dresse with copper or brasse.
Acromantia, diuynation or coniecture of thynges to come by the ayre.
Acrosus, a, um, that wherin brasse or copper is, or wherof it is made.
Aerumnalis, le, where in is greatte peyne or laboure.

Aerumnatus, brought to myserye.   *Plautus.*
Aerumnosus, a, um, myserable, full of peyne or trauayle.
Aerumnulæ, lytell croked staues, wherwith menne doo carye fardelles and trusses on theyr backes.
Aes circumforaneum, money layd in banke.
Aesculapius, the sonne of Apollo, callid god of medycine.
Aesopus, an auncient wryter of fables, also the name of a famous player in tragedies.
Aestimare litem, to taxe the damages and costes, that a man hath susteyned by wrong.
Aestus, doutfulnes, or flittyng of the minde.   *Pli. in epi.*
Aeta, an hylle in Thessalye.
Aetabula, chyldehode.
Aetalia, an Ile in the see by Scane.
Aetatem meam me viduam esse mauelim, quā   *Plautus.* istæc flagitia tua pati, quæ tu facis, I hadde leauer be a wydowe all my lyfe, than to indure this trouble that I haue with the.
Aetatem uelim seruire, Litanum modo ut cō-   *Plautus.* ueniam, I wolde do seruyce all the dayes of my lyfe, on the cōdicion that I mought mete with Litanus.
Aetas acta est mihi, my tyme is passed.   *Cicero.*
Aetas bona, the flowre of youthe.
Aetate adulta, of full age.
Aetate affecta, of olde age.
Aetate exacta, very aged, in extreme age.
Aetate confectus, idem.
Aetate integra, in the floure of youth.
Aetate prouecta, aged, or of great age.
Aetatem, an aduerbe, signifieth longe time. Iam dudū ætatem lites sunt inter eos, There hath bē variance betwene them long time.
Aeterne, euerlastyngely.
Aeterno, nare, to make perpetuall.
Aethereus, a, um, of the firmament. Anaxagoras putteth it for the element of fyre.
Aethiopia, a great countrey in Affrike, conteynynge many regyons, callyd Ethiope: wherin be founde people, beastes, and serpentes of meruaylous forme. It hathe on the west, the mountaynes callid Athlantes, on the easte it extendeth to the marches of Egypt: on the south it hath the see occean: on the northe parte, it is inclosed with the ryuer callyd Nilus.
Aethiopicus, ca, cum, of Ethiope.
Aethiopissa, a woman of Ethiope.
Aethiops, æthiopis, a man of Ethiope.
Aethon, one of the horses of Phebus.
Aethrusci, the olde Inhabytauntes of the countray in Italy, callid nowe Tuscana.
Aetiologia, a rehersynge of the cause.
Aetites, a precious stone, whiche hath the colour of an egles tayle that is whyte.
Aetius, the name of a famo[9] writer in phisik.
                                              Aetolia,

The additions.   A ante F.

Aetolia, a countraye in Grece.
Aeuitas, eternitye.

¶ A, ANTE F.

Sueton. in Vesp. — Affecta, almoste fynyshed, or nyghe at a poynt.
Affecta fides, credence almost lost.
Plautus — Affectus uirgis, beaten with roddes.
Affectus morbo, vexed with sycknesse.
Cice. — Affectum bellum, warres nyghe at a poynt.
Affecta æstas, Somer well nyghe passed.
Cice. — Affectio, affection, sometyme trouble of mynde.
Affector, taris, idem quod Affecto.
Varro. — Afferre auxilium, to helpe, to ayde.
Varr. de re rust. — Afferre dentes, to byte.
Afferre manus, to set violent handes on one.
Afferre uim alicui, to make assault on one.
Afferre molestiam, to do displeasure to one.
Afferre morbum, to make sycke.
Catullus. — Afferre pedem, to come. Abite, vnde malum, pedem attulistis, Goo hense, frome whense with a myschief ye came.
Affero ad te salutem, I come to salute you.
Afficere cura, to brynge in care.
Afficere lucro, to make one to wynne or gayne.
Plaut. — Afficere bonis nunciis, to brynge good tydynges. Vti bonis uos, uestrosque omnes nuntiis me afficere uultis, As ye will that I brynge to you and yours good tydinges.
Plaut. — Affecit præda atq; agro populares suos, He made his countray men ryche both of landes and goodes.
Cicero. — Afficere stipendio, to paye to hym his wages.
Affici, to be moued with affection.
Affinis negociis publicis, he that medleth with the affaires of a communalty.
Affinitas, tatis, affinity, aliance.
Affinis rei capitalis, gylty of a great offence, which deserueth deth.
Affinis sceleris, gylty of the trespace.
Affirmatiue, with an affirmaunce.
Afflatus, tus, a blast.
Plautus. — Affleo, affleui, flere, to wepe in the remembraunce of a thinge.
Salust. — Afflictus, stryken downe to the grounde.
Affligere, to throwe or beate downe to the grounde.
Plaut. — Affligam te ad terram scelus, si me uno digito attigeris, I will beate the downe to the grounde wretche, yf thou touchest me but with one fyngar.
Affluenter, abundantly.
Affluentia, abundance.
Affluens, tis, abundant.
Afformido, dare, to haue greate feare.

Affricus, ca, cum, of Affrike.

¶ A ANTE G.

Agar, the mayden of Sara, on whom Abraham begate Ismael.
Agaricum, a thynge lyke to a whyte mussheron growyng on the stem of a tree, and is called Agarike, which is medicinable in pourginge of fleame.
Agaso, sonis, a horse kepar, a muletour.
Agatho, the name of one of the sonnes of Priamus, also a boye, whom Plato louyd.
Agathyrsi, people by Scithia, whyche be ryche of golde, and yet be neyther couaytouse nor enuyouse, and their heares are blue.
Agathocles, was a kynge of Sicile.
Age dicat, let hym speke on, let hym speke hardyly.
Age, age ut lubet, well go to, do what ye wyll.
Age, & agite, go forth, furth on.
Agea, a way in a shyppe.
Agelastus, he that neuer lawghyd.
Agenor, the father of Europa, whome Iupiter rauyshed, & of Cadmus, who buylded the citye of Thebes.
Plautus. — Agere, to here, to perceyue. Vos agite spectatores, ye that beholde, heere, or take heede. Hoccine agis, an non? Perceyuest thou this matter or no? also to conclude.
Terentius. — Herus me relictis rebus, iussit Pamphilum hodie obseruare, ut quid ageret de nuptiis scirem, My master hath commaunded me, that layenge all thinges apart, I shoulde awayte vppon Pamphilus, to thintente I mought knowe, what he wolde conclude, touchinge the mariage.
Terentius — Agere, to go. Quo hinc te agis? whyther goest thou from hense? Sometyme it signifieth to come. Vnde agis te nunc Dorpales? from whense commest thou now, Dorpalus.
Plautus. — Agere. Pectus mihi agit nunc cubito: She hitteth me on the hart with her elbowe.
Agere ad præscriptum, to do that, that he was appoynted.
Agere ætatem, to lyue.
Plautus. — Agere ambages. Quid opus me multas agere ambages? what nedeth me to make many wordes? or to speke by circumlocution?
Agere animam, to dye.
Agere annum octingentesimū, to lyue eight hundred yeres.
Agere apologum, to tell hym a fable. *Plautus.*
Agere amicum, to do lyke a frende, or playe the part of a frende. *Pli. in ep.*

Age-

The additions. A ante G.

Plautus. Agere cum aliquo, to treate with one, or to speke. Cum mecum sæpe ageres, ut de amicitia scriberem: where often tymes thou dyddest intreate me, that I shulde wryte of frendshyppe. Illo præsente, mecum agito, si quid uoles: If thou wilt any thinge with me, speake it in the presence of that manne.

Agere iniuriarum, to sue one for trespase or wronges done.

Agere summo iure, to procede with rigour.

Agere suo iure, to execute his auctoritie.

Agere lege, to sue, to procede by the waye of Justice.

Plautus. Agere diris malis, to curse.

Agere mensuras fideliter, to measure thinges iustly.

Cicero. Agere nugas, to mocke, to tryfle.

Agere orationem, to pronounce an oration.

Agere uineas, to laye ordinaunce to a thing.

Actum de me est, I am vndone.

Agesilaus, a kynge of Lacedemony, which was lytle of stature, and haltyd on the one foote, but in vertue, wysedome, and prowesse he excelled all princes of his tyme, whose lyfe is wryten by Plutarche and Xenophon.

Plautus. Aggerre, to brynge to one. Namque ecastor, amor & melle & felle est foecundissimus, gustu dat dulce, amarum usque ad satietatem agerit, for in good fayth, loue hath abundance both of hony and galle, in taste it is pleasaunte, but it bryngeth with it bytternesse, so moch that it becometh lothesome.

Aggrauatio, a grief, a bourdon.

Aggrauesco, scere, to waxe more greuouse.

Aggredi, to assayle.

Ennius. Aggretus, idem quod Aggressus.

Agiliter, nymbly, quyuerly.

Cicero. Aginor, nari, to marchandyse vyle thinges, or of small value.

Agis rem actam, thou lesest thy labour.

Agit rem suam, he goeth aboute his owne busynesse.

Plautus. Agit hic perpetuum diem sol, The sone shyneth here all the daye longe.

Terentius Plautus. Agitare, to intreate well, to compell to go. Iam calcari quadrupedem agitabo aduersum cliuum: Howe will I with a spurre make my horse runne vppe the hill.

Plautus. Agitare conuiuium, to banket and make good chiere. Age ergo, hoc agitemus conuiuium, uino et sermone suaui, Therfore go to, lete vs banket, drynke talke and make goode chiere.

Plautus. Agitare custodiam, to take good hede in kepynge of one.

Plautus. Agitare diem, to passe forth the daye.

Agitare imperium, to gouerne. In pace vero, beneficiis magis quàm metu imperium agitabant: In the tyme of peace, they gouerned, more by gentylnesse, than by feare.

Agitare iustitiam, to exercise iustice.   Plí in epi.

Agitare letitiam, to make ioye.   Salust.

Agitare mente, to conceyue in the mynde, to thinke.

Agitare cum animo, to renolue in the mynd.   Salust.

Agitare præsidium, to be in garyson.   Salust.

Agitare uigilias, to kepe watche.

Agitare uitam, to lyue.

Agitatio, a meuynge or styrringe. alsoo exercise.

Agitator, a dryuer of a cart, or of beastis.

Agitedum, ite mecum, than forth, and come ye on with me.

Agitur mecum bene, I am in good condicion.   Val. Max. de Militia.

Agere bene, sometyme is of a lyke sygnyfication.

Agitur de capite, de fama, &c. whan the life or renomme is in daunger to be lost.

Agitur res capitis, the question or mater in debate, concernyth lyfe.   Terent.

Aglaia, one of them which are called Charites, gracia.

Agnascentia membra, membres whiche are superfluouse, as where one hath thre legges, or syxe fingars on one hande, and other lyke.   Plinius.

Agnitio, knowlege.

Agon, agonis, a contention in fourme of batayle, or a wrastlyng, also the place where it was exercysed.

Agonalia, certayne festiuall dayes kepte amonge the Romaynes.

Agonensis porta, a gate of Rome callyd also Colina.

Agones, were sometyme callyd hylles.

Agonia, sacrifice done on hylles.

Agonius, was named a god, whiche hadde preemynence ouer thynges to be done.

Agraria lex, a lawe made for the common disposition of landes, as be oure statutes of inclosures and decayenge of husbandry, but amonge the Romaynes they were suche lawes as dyd appoynte, howe moche lande a Senatour shuld haue, and not excede, and howe moche shulde be dyuided amonge the people.

Aggrigentinus, tina, num, of the towne of Agrigentum, whiche is in Sicile.

Agricolatio, tyllage or husbandry.

Agricultura, husbandry.

Agricultor, an husbandeman.

Agrippina, the name of the mother of Nero the Emperour. Also the dawghter of Octauyan.

Agrippina, Colonia, the citie of Coleyne.

Agylla, a citie in Thuscane.

A ante

The additions. A ante L.

¶A ANTE H.
¶Ah, a voyce of lamentyng or sorowyng.

¶A ANTE I.
Aiax, the name of .ii. noble mē of Grece — *Terentius*
Ain, for aisne, is it as thou sayst?
Ain uero, idem.
Aiutamini, for adiuuate. — *Non. Mar.*
Aizon, an herbe callyd Syngrene, it groweth on a tyled house.

¶A ANTE L.
Alabande, a citie in Grece, in the coūtrey of Ionia.
Alabandicus, ca, cum, of that citie.
Alabarches, he that hath the rule ouer salt: and amonge the Egyptians it was an honourable name.
Alabaster, & alabastrum, a kynde of marble callyd alabaster.
Alacriter, promptly, couragiously, gladly.
Alacre, idem.
Alania, a region of Scithia in Europa, whiche stretcheth vnto the greatte fennes of Meotis.
Alani, people callyd also Massagete.
Alaricus, a kynge of Gothes, whyche destroyed Rome.
Alarij equites, horsemen, whyche are in the wynges of a battayle.
Alauorsi, people in the vttermoste parte of the Northe.
Alba, the name of two cities in Italy.
Albana, a cite in Arabia. also a region in the east, wherein is also a citie callyd Albania.
Albanus, a riuer not farre from the citie of Rome. also the name of two cities, one in Macedonia, the other in Armenia.
Albanus, a, um, of Alban in Italy. albani patres, the Senatours of Alba.
Albegmina, parte of the inward of bestes, which was offred to Dis, callid god of hel.
Albenses, people of Alba.
Albesco, scere, to be white.
Albi calculi, whyte stones, with the whiche the people of Creta dyd note or mark the dayes, wherin they had good fortune: like as they marked yll dayes with blacke stones, callyd nigri calculi.
Albia, a ryuer, whyche passeth through the realme of Boemia.
Albicera, a kynde of olyue tree.
Albiceratę ficus, brode fygges, with a small stalke. Albidus, da, dum, somewhat white.
Albinga, a towne in Liguria.
Albinus, the name of an emperour.
Albion, the ancient name of England. also the name of one of the sonnes of Neptune.
Albis, a ryuer in Boemia, whyche cometh to the citie of Prage.

Albogalerus, a hatte, whyche the greatte priestis of Iupiter, callyd Flamines Dialis, dydde weare.
Albor, albugo, & albumen, the whyte of an egge. albugo, is alsoo a whyte spotte in a mannes eye.
Albosia, shieldes or targates.
Albula, the olde name of the ryuer of Tiber. also a water in the felde callyd Tiburtinus, which was medicinable for sore eien.
Album plumbum, tynne.
Albunia, a wodde and fountayne by the riuer callyd Aniene, in Italy.
Alburnus, a hyll in Lucania.
Alcea, a lyon.
Alce, a wylde beast in the woddes of Germany, in facion and skyn lyke to a gote, but greter, which haue no iointes in theyr legges, & therfore they do neuer ly, but only do leane to trees, whan they do rest thē, which the hunters knowyng, doo sawe the trees that they leane to, halfe a sonder, whereby they falle downe, and be taken.
Alces, a beast in France lyke a mule, but he hath his ouer lyppe so longe, that whā he fedeth, he goth backewarde, or els he can not bite of the grasse and herbes, whiche he shulde eate. The horsekynde of them haue hornes on their ouer browes.
Alceste, seu Alcestis, the wyfe of Admetus the kinge of the people callid Pherei, who being sicke, and hauing answere of the goddis, that he shuld escape dethe, if any of his kynne or frendes wold die for him willingly, whan all men and women refused it, only Alceste his wife consented therto, and wilyngly dyed.
Alceus, a famous poete.
Alchech, in the Araby tongue, is the beast, whiche is callid Linx, whiche is begotten betwene a lyon and a lybarde.
Alcibiades, a noble capitayne of the Athenienses, whiche in nobilitie, beautie, prowesse, actiuitie, & eloquēce, passed al other in his tyme, nat withstandynge his vyces were accompted equall vnto his vertues.
Alcides, idem quod Hercules.
Alcinous, the name of a kyng of a peple callid Pheaces, excellēt in Iustice, which had a fayre and magnifike palyce, with orchardes which bare most plentuously fruites twyse in the yere. Alcman, a famous poete. — *Homerus Odyss.*
Alcmena, the mother of Hercules.
Alcmenes, a cunnynge grauour.
Alcon, was a good archer of Creta, which beholdynge a dragon redy to deuoure his sonne, dydde shoote so craftily, that as the dragon was imbracynge of the chylde, the arowe passed vnto his harte, and hurte nat

G 2 his

The additions.   A ante L.

his son, so that the dragon immediatly died.
Alcyone, the name of .ii. ladies, wherof the one was wife to Ceisis, who seing the deed body of her husband cast on land, threw her selfe into the see, whom the poetes fained to be turnid into a bird of that name: the other was doughter of Euene, callid also Marpesia
Aleatoriū, a dice playing, or a dycyng hous. Suetonius calleth it aleatorium forum.
Alebria, thinges whiche do nourishe well.
Alec, is a sauce made of the liuers of fishes. Also a fyshe, callyd a hearyng.
Alecto, one of the furies of Hell.
Alectoria, a stone founde in a cockes gysar or mawe, of the greatenes of a beane, of the colour of chrustall.
Alemani, peple of Germany, callid Germais
Aléo, aleonis, a dysar, or dyseplayer.
Aletudo, fattenesse of the body.
Alexander, the name of a man, specially of a kyng of Macedony, which conquered al the east part of the world, and was in prowesse and wysedom incōparable: but being drowned in ouermoche felicitie, he felle into excedinge pride and crueltie, and was at the laste poysoned, and died in Babylon, excedynge lyttell the age of thirty yeres.
Alexandria, the name of a great citie in Egypt. also of dyuers other cities.
Alexandrinus, na, num, of Alexandria.
Algenses, fyshes callyd also purpurę.
Algidense, a kynde of radyshe, longe and clere through.
Algidus, a mountain .xii. myles from Rome.
Algida sylua, a wod at the fote of that moūtayne.   Algo, idem quod algeo.
Alguasen, an herbe like to a lyly.
Algus, uel algu, colde.

Plautus. Alia, a ryuer .xi. myles from Rome.
Alias res agis, thou thinkest on other matters. Vnde anulū istū nactus? dic mihi, ille alias res agere se simulare, Tel me where gattest thou this ryng? he made semblance as yf he thought on an other matter.
Alicarii, they that do sell alicam.
Alicariæ, common harlottes.
Alicastrum, a diminutiue of alica.
Alienatio, an alienation or alteration.
Alienator, he that altereth a thynge.

Terentius Alienior ætate, of nō age, not of cōpetēt age.
Alienus animus, Iam primum illum alieno animo a nobis esse, res ipsa indicat: The thing selfe declareth, that euen nowe he hath no fauour toward vs, that he is not my frend.
Alieno more mihi uiuendum est, I must lyue after an other mans facion.

Salust. Aliena consilii, vnmete for the counsell.
Alienum suis rationibus, vnprofytable for his purpose.

Alienatus, a, ū, put away, altered, estranged.
Alienos agimus, we become strāge vnto thē
Alimentarius, a, um, pertaining to liuinge or sustinance. Alimonia, idem quod alimentum.
Alimodi, idem quod aliusmodi, of an nother facion or maner.
Aliouersum, towarde an other place.
Aliptes, he that annoynteth a man.
Aliquis, aliquę, aliquod, some.
Alirei, Plautus vseth for alię rei.
Alisma, an herbe callyd also barba syluana, water plantayne.
Aliter ac, aliter atq̃, aliter quā, otherwise thā.
Alites, byrdes.
Aliubi, for alicubi, somewhere.
Aliuta, olde writers vsed for aliter.
Aliusmodi, i an other mañ, of an other faciō
Alligare aliquē furto, to apech one of felony
Alligare se furti, to charge him self of felony
Alligator, he that byndeth.
Alligatura, a bonde.
Allobrox, allobrogis, a man or womā of the countray in Fraunce, callyd Dolpheny.
Allocutio, a speakynge to one.
Allocutum ire, to commune with one.
Alloquium, communication, speche.
Aludor, idem quod alludo.
Alluuium, idem quod alluuies. Alluuio, idem.
Almities, quietenes, secretenes.
Almopia, parte of Macedonia.
Aloe, aloes, is vsed cōmonly for a iuyce of an herbe congeled lyke a gūme, wherof be two sortes, one is named Succotrina, which is like a lyuer, redde, bright, & bronkle: the other is callyd Caballina, and is sandy and grosse. The fyrste clenseth and confirmeth the stomake of a man, and therfore is mixt with purgatiue medicines, bicause they shal not anoy or hurt the stomake, the last is occupied about horses and other beastis.
Aloe lignum, or lignū aloes, is a swete & precious wod, which beinge receiued in medicine, comforteth the stomake, and all the inferior partis of a mā, & maketh swete breth.
Alogia, vnreasonable or beastly feding, and ingurgitation of meate and drinke.
Alopecus, he that hath a pylde heed, that is to say, the heares fallynge with scurfe.
Alosa, a fyshe callyd also Laccia, and Clupea, is that, whiche by the description of Paulus Iouius semeth to be a cheuyn.
Alphabetarii, they whiche do lerne first the order of letters.
Alphabetum, the order of letters, as a.b.c.
Alpheus, a riuer in Arcadia, also the name of a manne.
Alphos, a morphy or staining of the skinne.
Alpinus, a, ū, of the mountains of Alpes.
Alpus, pale, carefull, or studious.

Alsine

The additions. A ante L.

Alsine maior, an herbe callyd wodbynde.
Alsine minor, an herbe callyd the seconde mouse eare.
Alsiosus, a, um, colde of nature. also whiche are soone hurt or anoyed with colde.
Altanus, a wynd, which is on the depe sees.
Alte, on hygh.
Altellus, a surname of Romulus the founder of Rome.
Alter & vicesimus, one and twentie.
Alter quisq̃, any other.
Alteras, olde writers vsed for alias.
Altercatio, a contention in wordes, where one man purposeth, an nother replyeth.
Altercum, siue altercagenum, an herbe callyd also faba porcina.
Alterplex, plicis, old writers vsed for duplex (double).
Alterra, idē quod alterutra.
Altior, altius, hygher.
Altissimus, ma, mum, hyghest.
Altimetor, an Instrument wherwith highe thinges are mette.
Altinũ, an old citie by the riuage of Venice.
Altinates, people of Altinum.
Plautus. Altitudo, height, or depenes.
Altrouersum, on the other parte, or on the other syde.
Altum otium, longe reste, great leysure.
Aluini, they whiche haue frettyng in theyr bealyes with contynuall fluxe.
Alumnatus, nouryshed.
Alyba, a countraye not farre frome Abista, where as Homerus dothe write, were mines of syluer.
Alysius, the name of Bacchus.
Alysina, an herbe callyd water plantayne.

¶ A, ANTE M.

Amalthea, a woman, whiche with her syster callyd Melissa, nouryshed Jupiter with the milke of a gote. Also the name of a prophetesse.
Amantior, more louynge.
Amantissimus, moste louynge.
Amantissime, moste louyngely.
Solinus. Amanthes, people in Affrike, whiche haue suche plentie of precious stones, that they buylde therwith houses.
Amanus, a mountayne callyd also Taurus.
Amaracinum, an oyle made of maioram.
Iosephus. Amaramis, the father of Moyses.
Amarantus, an herbe, which groweth a fote in height, & hath leues like basile, and hath a floure facionid like an ere of wheat, of crimson colour, which neuer dieth: in frenche it is callid Passeuelure. some there be, whiche do suppose it to be callid in englysh Baldar.
Amarico, are, to make bitter, to make angry
Amaror, idem quod amaritudo.
Amarus, ra, rum, bytter, very angry.

Amariscus, an herbe callydde Mathis, or Dogge fenell.
Amarillis, the name of a shepeherde in the bucolicis of Vergile.
Amasenus, a ryuer in Italy.
Amasias, a kyng of Iewes: whiche signyfieth as moche as populum tollens.
Amasis, was a noble kynge of Egypt, whiche made a lawe, that euery yere, eche mā shulde make a rekeninge to the heed officer of his realme, of his life, & shew wherby he liued, or by what occupation he was susteined, and he that dyd not make suche accompt, shulde be put to deathe.
Amasso, idem quod amauero.
Amatio, a louynge.
Amastrum, uel Amastris, the principall citie of Paphlagonia.
Amath, the sonne of Chanaan.
Amathus, thūtis, a cite in Ciprº, dedicate to Venus. Amathuntius, a, um, of the sayd citie. *Iosephus.*
Amathusa, the yle of Ciprus.
Amaurosis, the dymnesse of the eyen.
Amazones, womē of Scithia, which wāne a great part of Asia: who slewe all the men chyldren, and kept the women chyldren, of whom they burned the right pappe, bicause it shulde not lette them to throwe their Iaselyne, or to shote.
Amazonicus, ca, cũ, pertaynyng to the Amazones. Amazonius, a, ū, idē qd Amazonicus.
Amazonicus, nici, a countraye callyd afterwarde Cesaria.
Ambarualis hostia, was a sacrifice made for the fieldes, with a sowe great with farowe.
Ambedo, ere, to eate or gnaw about a thing
Ambegni, were an oxe and a rāmme, where on euery side of them lambis were brought to be sacrificed. Ambesus, a, ū, eaten rounde.
Ambes, idem quod circumest.
Ambiani, seu Ambianenses, people in Frāce about Languedoke.
Ambidentes, shepe of two tethe, of somme callyd Hogges, of some theaues.
Ambiguitas, doubtfulnesse.
Ambitus, ta, tũm, enuyronned or compassed.
Ambitus, tus, inclosure, alsoo ambycion or desyre of promotion.
Ambra, a very swete thyng, whiche is fou̅d on the see, as mushcrons are on the erth, wherof is made very precious and cordial medicines.
Ambracia, a cite in the coūtray callid Epirº in Grece. Ambracienses, peple of Ambracia
Ambrices, tyles, which be layd ouerthwart betwene other tyles.
Ambrones, people in France.
Ambrosia, an herbe, whiche some men doo suppose to be Tansey.

Gg ij Ambu-

The additions. A ante M.

Ambubeia, the commune cykorye with the longe leafe, and the blewe floure, whyche wyll be closed at the goinge downe of the sonne, and opened at the rysynge.

Ambubeiæ, dronken drabbes, whiche wander about the stretes.

Ambulariuncula, a lyttell walke.

Ambustus, ta, tum, bourned.

Amecus, & ameca, olde writers vsed for amicus, & amica.

Amen, a worde of Hebrue, which after the interpretation of Aquila, significth fideliter, faythefully, after the lxx. interpretours, it signifieth fiat, be it.

Amentia, foly.

Amento, tare, to bynde a thonge aboute any thynge.

Amentior, tius, madder.

Amentissimus, a, um, maddest.

Ameria, an olde citie in Italy.

America, a countrey late founde in the east by Amercum Vesputium.

Amerinum, a citie in Italy.

Amethystus, a precious stone of vyolet colour, an ametyst.

Amethystinus, a, um, of an ametyst.

Amia, a fyshe lyke to a Tuny, but he hathe no scales, but a playne skynne, which shyneth lyke to syluer mixte with blue, and his tayle is in facyon lyke a newe moone.

Amica, a woman that is loued. also a concubyne.

Amicibor, for amiciam, I wyll clothe or put on a garment.

Amicior, ciri, to be cladde.

Amicissime, moste frendely.

Amice, frendely. Amiciter, idem.

Amicissimus, a, um, moste frendely.

Amicius, more frendely.

Amictorium, a lynnen rayle that womenne doo weare.

Amicula, a diminutiue of amica.

Amiculum, a short cloke.

Amiculatus, he that weareth a short cloke.

Plautus. Amicabilis, le, frendely.

Aminee vites, vynes growynge in a countrey by Salerne.

Amyson, a famous citie in the royalme of Pontus.

Amissio, the losse of a thynge.

Amissus, a, um, loste.

Amiternum, a towne in Campania, where Salust was borne.

Amites, perches, wheron haukes be sette.

Plautus. Amittere iusiurandum, to breake an othe, to lose credence. Quod si non dederit, atque hic dies præterierit, ego argentum, ille iusiurandum amiserit, If he doo not paye it, and this day do passe, I shall lose my mo

ney, but he shall lose his credence.

Amittere libidinem. Iam non possum, amisi Plautus. omnem libidinem, I may do no more, I am paste all pleasure.

Ammon, a surname of Iupyter, worshypped in Egypte.

Amnestia, forgetfulnes of thynges passed.

Ammoniacum, a certayne gumme.

Amnicus, ca, cum, of the broke.

Amo, are, to loue.

Amæne, merily, pleasantly.

Amomum, a spyce growynge in India, lyke to a wylde vyne, and is in colour somwhat yelowe or browne, & very soote in sauour.

Amorrhei, peple beyond Hierusalem, & had their name of Amorrhe[9] the son of Canaan.

Amores, wanton passetymes, or affections of lecherye.

Amosio, for annuo. Festus.

Amouere segnitiem, to caste away slouth.

Amouere crapulam, to perbreake when one Plautus. is dronke.

Ampendices, old writers vsid for appendices.

Ampelos agria, a wylde vyne.

Amphibea, beastes or byrdis, which do liue as well on the water, as on the lande.

Amphilogia, a forme in speakyng, where a sentence may be taken two sondry or contrary wayes.

Ampelusia, an yle callyd nowe Tinge.

Amphibolum, a doubtefull sentence.

Amphibrachus, a foote in meter, beynge of thre syllables, the fyrste and laste short, the mydell syllable longe, as Cupido.

Amphilochus, a phylosopher.

Amphesibene, a serpent, hauynge two heddes, wherof the one is before, the other behynde, where his tayle shulde be.

Amphimacrus, a foote in meter, hauing the fyrst syllable and the last longe, the mydell syllable shorte.

Amphimalla, garmentis rough on both sides

Amphitapetes, garmentes of Cotton on bothe sydes hearye.

Amphimerimon, a feuer cotidyane, whiche commeth of fleume.

Amphion, a man, whiche with naturall eloquence, brought rude and wilde people to a ciuile forme of lyuynge: and as some do suppose, founde first harmony.

Amphipolis, a citie nigh to Macedonia.

Amphiroe, a nimph or maide of the ryuers.

Amphitana, a precious stone, the brimme or edge wherof shineth lyke to golde.

Amphitheatrū, a round place made with seates or scaffoldis, where men beheld plays.

Amphitreatrales ludi, playes exercysed in those places. Amphirrite, the wyfe of Neptunus. it is also taken for the see.

Amphi

Amphitrio, trionis, the husband of Alcmena, mother of Hercules.
Amphitrionides, he that comith of the ligne of Amphitrio.
Amphictyones, the generalle or commune counsayle of all Grecia.
Ampiruo, are, is proprely where in dauncing like meuing or coutenāce that one maketh, he vnto whom it is made, shal do the semblable, it was first vsid of the priests callid Saly.
Amplant, olde writers vsid for amplificant, they enlarge.
Ample, amply, largely.

Non. Mar. Amplexa, for amplexare, imbrace or take to Amplexari, for amplecti. (you.
Amplexus, imbracynges.
Ampliatio, a deferrynge of iudgement.
Amplificatio, an augmentation.
Amplifico, care, to augment.
Amplior, larger, greatter.
Amplissimus, a, um, greattest, largest.
Amplissimus ordo, was vsed for the Senate of Rome.
Amplissimus magistratus, the highest office.
Ampliter, largely, abundantly, magnifikely.

Plautus. Ampliter occupatus, let with moch busines.
Ampliter testis, witnes of al the hole matter.

Cæsar. Amplius, more ouer, more largely.
Amplius horas quatuor fortissime pugnauerunt, They foughte mightily more than foure houres. Cœperunt amplius tria millia

Liuius. hominum, They toke prisoners thre thousande men and aboue.

Cicero. Ampliare, to deferre or delaye a thynge in iugement, to reprie.
Amplius pronuntiare, idem.
Ampron, a corde or chayne fastened to the yokes, wherby beastes do drawe a wayne.
Ampullarius, a bottell maker.
Amuleus, the gret vncle of Romulꝰ z Remꝰ
Amussitatus, tata, tum, made by lyne, welle proporcyoned.
Amycle, a citie in Lacedemonia, where Castor z Pollux were borne, also an other citie in Italy. Amycleus, a, um, of that citie.
Amylum, is wheate laide in water .iii. dayes, and euery day the water chaunged fyue times, and being soft, to poure out the water softly, that none other thing do passe, than to poure in a litle z rubbe the corne, and to skymme away the huskes and the branne, z strayn the residue, and being somwhat dried in a clothe, than to lay it on newe tyles, and set it in the sonne, and drye it.
Anagallis, an herbe, whiche hath a square stalk, z leues like to peritory of the wal, but moche lesse, the male hath red floures, the female blewe. some do suppose it to be our pympernell, some take it to be chykweede.

¶ A ANTE N.

ANabasius, he that rideth by post horsis. Hieronymus contra Rufinum.
Anabathrum, a pulpyt or other lyke place, whiche standeth on hygh, wher vnto a man must go vp by a ladder or griesee. Iuuenalis.
Anabula, a beaste in Æthiope, hauynge a heed like a camell, a necke like a hors, legges lyke an oxe, and is of colour a bryght redde, full of white spottes. Plinius.
Anacephaleosis, a shorte recapytulation or repetition of thynges before rehersed.
Anacharsis, a philosopher of a meruaylous wysedom, all be it that he was borne in the barbarous coūtrey of Scithia, whom Pliny supposeth to haue fyrst foūden the potters whele: And beinge in the tyme that Solon made lawes to the Athenienses, he sayde, that lawes were lyke to copwebbes, which tyed fast lyttell flyes, z the great flyes brake them, and went clene through them. In like wyse the poore z meane men are fast wouden in the penalties and dangers of lawes, but lordes and men in great auctoritie daily breake lawes, and are not corrected.
Anachorita, an hermite: the interpretation therof is, he that lyueth a parte, and oute of companye.
Anaclinterium, a mattresse.
Anadiplōsis, is a doublynge of a worde, as the last worde of the fyrst verse, is the fyrst word of the second verse: as, Certent & signis ululæ, sit Tytirus Orpheus, Orpheus in syluis inter delphinas Arion. Spartian in Ceio uio,
Anaglypha, & anaglypta, vessell or plate of golde or siluer chaced, as cuppis or bolles beaten with the hammer, z not ingraued.
Anaglyptes, he that worketh suche vessell.
Anagliptice, ye craft to chace or iboce plate.
Anagnostes, he that redeth to other men, as bible clerkes, or any other clerke, whiche redeth whyle an other writeth.
Anagoge, the high and subtylle vnderstandynge of scripture.
Analecta, fragmētis of meat, which fal vnder the table, z be afterward swept awaye.
Analesia, is a sicknes of the heed, which taketh away sensiblenes from the hole partis of the heed, z cometh of the weakenes of the stomak, or of to moch meat, or of to moche lechery, or drinking moche cold water, or to moche study, drinke, or of indigestion.
Analogia, conueniēcy or proporcion, whose propricie is to cōferre that which is doutfull, with that whiche is like to it, whiche is more certayne, to make it more playne.
Analogos, proporcionable.
Anapestus, a fote in meter of .iii. sillables, hauing .ii. the fyrst fete short, the laste longe.

Gg iii Anapis,

Anapis, a ryuer in Sicyle, tenne furlonge from the citie of Syracusis.

Anarchos, without a prynce, or without a begynnynge.

Anastrophe, a tournynge out of a commune order, as, Italiā contra, for contra Italiam.

Anaticula, a lyttell ducke.

Anatorius, a keper of duckes.

Anauros, a ryuer in Thessalia.

Anaxagoras, a famous philosopher, noble of bloode, but more noble in vertue & wisedome, whiche abandonynge all his possessyon, gaue hym all holly to the study of naturall philosophie: and whan one said vnto him, Haste thou no care for thy countreye, he aunswered, Yes verily, I haue excedīg care for my countrey, poyntynge vp to heuen with his fynger. Also whan he hadde ben longe out of his countray, and was eftsones returned, and behelde his possessions distroyed and wasted, he sayd, I had nat ben safe, except these thinges had be loste.

Anaxarchus, a philosopher, whiche fallyng in the indignation of a tyrant, callyd Nicoreon, kyng of Cipres, was by hym apprehēded, and put into a great morter of stone, where he was beaten or pounde with yron pestyls: whiche tourment he toke so paciently, that he doubled these wordes, worthy of remembraunce, Beate on, beate on Anaxarchus wynd bagge, for Anaxarchus thou beatest not. By the which wordes he accoūted his body but a bagge ful of wind.

Anaximander, a philosopher, which fyrste founde the description of the compasse of the see and land, and made first the sphere.

Ancesa, grauen vessell.

Anceps, cipitis, doutfull. sometyme it signifieth double. also cuttyng on bothe sydes.

Anchises, the father of Aeneas.

Anchorarius, a, um, pertayning to an anker.

Ancillula, a lytle or poore wenche seruant.

Anclabra, vessele whiche priestes vsed.

Anclare, seu antlare, to empty a vessell.

Ancona, a Cytie in Italye, vppon the see of Uenyce.

Anculi, & **Ancule**, goddis and goddessis of seruynge womenne.

Ancus, he that hath a croked elbow. it was also the name of a kynge of Romaynes.

Anchusa, an herbe, of whose rote commeth a redde iuyse, wherwith sanguyne colour is dyed.

Ancyra, the name of two cities, the one in Phrigia, the other in Galatia.

Andabate, certayne men that faughte with swordes wynkynge.

Andegauia, a countray in Fraunce, callyd Angiewe.

Andrachne, an herbe callyd purcelau.

Andrago, a woman hauyng a mans harte.

Andricus, an hylle in Cilicia.

Androdamas, a stone, which is like to siluer.

Androgeus, the sonne of Minoos, kyng of Crete, whiche by enuye was slayne of the Atheniensis. For the whyche many yeres after the sonnes of Athenienses were sent to Crete, to be delyuered to the monster callyd Minotaurus, whiche was afterward destroyd by Theseus. It was also the name of a noble Briton, whan Julius Cesar came hither into this realme of Brittayne.

Androgyne, people in Asia, beinge of both kyndes in one person, man and woman.

Androgynos, a man hauyng both membres of a man, and also of a woman.

Andromache, the wyfe of the valiāt Hector.

Andromede, the wyfe of Perses, whom he saued from a monster of the see.

Andron, a chaumber, wherinto men onely do come, and not women. Also a space betwene two houses, wherinto the rayn falleth. **Andronitis**, idem.

Androne, festis, wherunto only mē do com.

Andros, an ile betwene Grece and Asia, directly agaynst the citie of Ephesum.

Andruare, olde writers vsed for Recurre, to runne ageyne.

Ancillus, a lyttell rynge.

Anemone, wylde popie, with red floures.

Anethum, an herbe callyd dyll.

Anger, a certaine serpent, after whose stingynge hapneth intollerable peynes.

Angerona, was callid the goddesse of pleasure, callyd also Volupia.

Angile, people in Affrike, of whom the women, the fyrst nyght that they be wedded, do accompany with al men, which come to the wedding, but euer after they be chast.

Anglia, Englande.

Angaria, a constrayned seruyce.

Angarie, arum, some doo expounde it for a poste or a currour.

Anguimanus, an Olyphant.

Anguinus, na, num, of a serpent, or winding and crepynge lyke a serpent.

Angustitas, a strayte or strayte place.

Anhelator, he that fetcheth his wynde often, or bloweth moche, poursike.

Ania, a Romayne woman, whyche beynge fayre & yonge, after that her husband was deed, was counsailed to take an other, but she wold nat consent therto, For if said she, I shall hap to haue as good as I haue had, I wyll not be in feare to lose him: If I shall haue an yll husbande, what shall I nede, after a good man, to suffre a shrewe?

Anicetum, idem quod Anethum, dyll.

Ani=

The additions.   A ante N.

Anicula, a lyttell olde woman.
Animam adimere, uel extinguere, to kyll.
Animam debet, he oweth more than he is worthe, he oweth soo moche, that he hath not his lyfe but in lone.
Anima, somtime signifieth brethe. Dic amabo, an foetet anima uxori tuae? Telle me of good felosship, doth thy wiues breth stinke?
Plautus. Animam comprime, holde thy brethe.
Anima, sometyme signifieth wynde, sommetime water. Si situlam iamiam caepero, nunq̅ ædepol tu mihi diuino quid credas post hunc diem, ni ego illi puteo, si occepso, animam omnem intertraxero, If I take the buckette, neuer beleue me for a prophete after this day, if I drawe not cleane out, if I ones begynne, all the water of the welle.
Animitus, from the very soule or lyfe.
Animo male est, it greueth hym at the verye harte.
Animum eijcere, to putte awaye affection or fantasye.
Anio praesenti, with a bold spirite or corage
Animo obsequi, to take pleasure, to folowe appetyte or wylle.
Animo morem gerere, idem.
Animum explere, to accomplisshe wil or desire
Animum adiungere, to applye or set mynde to a thynge.
Animum aduertere, to take hede.
Animum appellere, to dispose or apply hym to do a thynge.
Animum adiicere ad uirginem, to sette his loue on the mayden.
Animum recipere, to take harte or courage.
Animus tibi pendet, thou standest in doubte what thou mayste do.
Animo bono esse, to be of good chere.
Animus impotens, an vnpacient courage.
Animo iniquo pati, to suffre vnpaciently.
Animos lactare, to drawe mens hartes with fayre promyses, to make fooles fayne, to brynge men in fooles paradyse.
Anime mi, my dere harte.
Animule, idem.
Plautus. Animi causa, for pleasure. Cur eam emit? T. Animi causa, wherfore dydde he bye hir? T. for his pleasure.
Plautus. Animatus, ta, tum, hauynge a fantasye or fauour to a thynge, or to be disposed. Ita animatus sui, itaq; nunc sum, ut ea te patera donem, I had suche a fantasy, and yet haue, that I wold gyue the cuppe to you. Amabo si quid animatus est facere, fac iam vt scis am, If he be disposed to do any thyng, let me knowe it.
Animaduerto, uertere, to take hede, to perceyue. Experrecta nutrix animaduertit dor-
Plautus. mientem, circumplicatum serpentis amplexu,

The nouryce awaked, and perceyued the childe beinge on slepe, wrapped all about in the wyndynge of the serpent. Dare operam *Terent.* & cū silentio animaduertite, Take you hede, and with sylence perceyue what I wylle saye to you. It is also to punysshe or correcte, Ea sunt animaduertēda peccata maxi- *Cicero.* me, quæ difficillime precauentur, Those offences ought to be moste sharpely corrected, whiche mooste hardlye are eschewed. Hac re animaduersa, Caesar iubet signa con- *Caesar.* uerti, After that that matter was punysshed, Cesar commaunded to aduaunce the standerdes.
Animaduersio, punysshement, correction.
Animaduersi, they whyche are punysshed or corrected.
Animaduersor, he that punyssheth.
Anio, anienis, a ryuer in Italye in the felde callyd Tiburtinum.
Anisum, an herbe callyd Anyse, wherof commeth anyse seede.
Annarius, a, um, aged. Aniculatis, &c, idem.
Annibal, the moste valyant capitayne of the Carthaginestes, a mā most expert in marcial prowesse, who at .xxv. yeres of age subdued Spayne, percyd the mountaynes, callyd Alpes, where afore neuer was passage, destroyed all Italy, and slewe the more parte of the nobylitie of Rome, and kept warres with the Romaynes .xxx. yeres.
Anniuersalis, the compasse of the yere.
Anniuersarius, a, um, that euery yere returneth at one tyme.
Annonarius, & annotinus, a, um, pertaynyng to vytrayle.
Anodina, thynges, whyche do putte away payne or grefe.
Anomalum, vnequall, dyuers, rough.
Anonymum, without a name.
Anonium, an herbe callyd deade nettylle or archaungelle.
Anophytus, sprongen or growen vppon a thynge.
Ansatus, ta, tum, hauynge a handell.
Ansanctus, on euery parte holy.
Ansula, the diminutiue of ansa.
Ants, jambes. also postes of a doore.
Anxeus, was a gyant in Libia, whiche was xl. cubites longe, as it appered by his sepulchre founde by Sertorius in a cite callyd Tigena.
Antandros, a citie in Phrigia.
Antarcticus, the fyfthe cerkle in heauen, callyd the southepole.
Antariū bellū, bataile before a cite or towne.
Anteambulo, lonis, a lackey or other seruāt that gothe afore his mayster.
Antefixa, thynges caste in mouldes, and set
ouer

over doores.

Antelapides, stones sette at bothe the sydes of a doore for strength.

Antelucani ue̅ti, wyndes that do blowe from the water, or from some creeke.

Anteluco, an aduerbe, before day.

Anteluculo, an houre afore sonne.

Antenor, a prince of the Troianes, whiche betrayed the citie of Troy: he fyrst inhabited the countray of Uenice.

Ante oculos, before his eyes: but it signifieth further than Coram oculis.

Antermini, the inhabitantes of the marchis or frontiers of a contray.

Anteros, loue mutually sette betwene two persones.

Antesum, antefui, anteesse, to excel an other in any thynge.

Anteurbanus, a, um, nyghe to the citie: as Anteurbanum predium, a manour nygh to the citie.

Antexpectatus, ta, tum, come before that he was loked for.

Anthedon, a kynde of medlars, which hath leues lyke an almonde tree, the fruite lasse then the common medlar, but moche pleasaunter, and wyll be longar kepte.

Anthemis, an herbe called chamomyll.

Anthrax, cis, a stone called a carbuncle, whiche shyneth in the nighte: it is also an aposteme or swelling callid a carbucle or botch.

Anthracides, a stone, in the which there semeth to be sparkes as it were of fyre.

Anthracinus, na, um, blacke as a cole.

Anthraceus, a colyar.

Anthracia, a burnynge cole.

☞ Anthropophagi, people in Asia, which eate men.

Anthropomorphite, were heretikes, which of a folyshe symplicitie affirmed, that god had membres lyke a man.

Antibacchius, a foote in metre, hauynge the firste syllable and the laste shorte, and the myddell syllable longe.

Anticthones, people dwellyng in the vttermost part of the world, directly agaynst vs.

Anticyra, an Ile in Asia, where the herbe called Elleborus groweth, which purgeth melancoly, and there it may be taken without any daunger: wherof grewe this prouerbe spoken to men in theyr melancholy, Nauiga ad anticyras: Go sayle to Anticyra.

Antidora, gifte for gift, one for another.

Antigerio, olde wryters vsed for very shortly, forthwith, or the thynge were done.

Antimetabole, a fygure in speache, where wordes are repeted to a contrary sente̅ce: as, Non vt edam viuo, sed vt viuam edo. I lyue not to eate, but I eate to lyue.

Antiochia, a great citie in Siria, another at the riuage of Persia.

Antiochus, the name of dyuers kynges of Siria.

Antiperistasis is that thinge, wherby where heate commeth colde is expelled, where colde is, heate is expelled: by this, well water in the wynter time is warme, for as moche as the hygh partes of the ayre beinge colde, the heate withdraweth him to the lowest partes. like wise in the body of man the spirite is kepte in more feruente by the outwarde colde, by the ioynt conscent & tolleratio̅ of al partes of the body.

Antipater, was a philosopher, borne in the citie of Tirus, of the sect of Stoici, whiche from the tyme of his byrthe, vntyl his deathe, had alway a feuer, and not withstandyng he lyued vntil he was olde.

Antipathia, a naturall dyfference or repugnancy of thynges.

Antipelargesis, one good torne for another.

Antiphrasis, a worde or sentence hauynge a contrary meanynge: as, Parce, the mynisters of deathe be so called, bycause they spare no man.

Antipodes, people whiche doo inhabite the part of the world, in respect of the roundenes therof, vnderneth vs, that it seemeth that theyr feete be agaynst our feete.

Antiqui homines, men of the olde facion.

Antiquus hospes, myne host of longe tyme.

Antiqua ratio, the maner of tyme passed. *Vergilius.*

Antiqua terra, a noble countray. Terra antiqua, potens armis, et vbere glebe, A noble countray puissaunt in warres, and of a fertile soyle.

Antiquatio, an abolicion of a lawe.

Antiquum obtinere, to kepe the olde facion.

Antistitor, he that stadeth before them that do worke and controlleth them.

Antithesis, a fygure, where one letter is set for a nother: as olli, for illi.

Antitheton, a fygure, wherby one contrary is ioyned with a nother.

Frigida pugnabant calidis, humentia siccis, Mollia cu̅ duris, sine po̅dere habentia po̅dus. *Ouidius in Metamor.*
Colde thynges contended with them that were hote, moyst thynges with dry, hard thynges with softe, lyghte thynges with heuy kept not one note.

Antium, a citie in the parte of Italy called Latium.

Antlia, a pumpe or lyke thynge to drawe vp water. *Martialis.*

Antæci, people whiche dwel in the contrary Zone or gyrdell, to Anticthones.

Antrum, a denne vnder the erthe.

Anubis, was a god of the Egiptians, which they

The additions.   A ante P.

they honoured for Mercurius.
Anxur, a citie, called also Tarrasina.
Anygrus, a ryuer in Thessalia.

¶A, ANTE O.

Aonia, the countray called Thracia.
Aonius, a, um, of that countray.
Aornos, a place, wherunto no birde maye come.

¶A, ANTE P.

Plautus. Apage, fy, fy. Apage, haud nos deces at fugitiuos imitari: Fy, fy, it wyll not beseme vs to play the michers.
Apage te, gette the hens.
Apage a me, haue away from me.
Apalæstris, he that can neither wrastell nor do any other maistrie.
Apamia, the name of oone citie in the lasse Asia, an nother in Parthia.
Aparine, an herbe that growethe in corne feldes, whiche is rough, and cleaueth to the garmentes of them, which passe by it, and hath a white floure, the siede lyke to a nauyll: I suppose that it be goose grasse or clyuers.
Apadies, were phylosophers, whiche of a frowarde and stubborne nature, held opinion that a wyse man had none affections or passions.
Apedes, a byrde, whose fete be so lytle, that they seeme to haue none. I suppose they be martlettes.
Apelles, the moste excellente paynter that euer was.
Apello, lere, pulsum, to amoue or putte of from a thynge.
Appenninus, the part of the mountaynes of Alpes, whiche begynne at Geane.
Aperté, openly, playnly, euidently, without dissimulation or colour.
Apertus, ta, tum, open, playne, euident, discouered, without colour or cloke.
Apesus, suntis, a mountayne in Grece.
Apexabo, bone, a pudding callid a bludding
Aphæresis, a figure, wherby a letter or syllable is taken from a worde: as Pone meü, for depone merum, mi, for mihi, tun, for tu ne.
Aphilos, he that hath no frende.
Aphracta, a lyttell barke or brygantine.
Aphrodisia, days dedicate to Uenus, or venerial pastymes.
Aphronitrum, the fome of saltepeter, callid of the Arabiens, Baurach.
Apiculus, the diminutiue of Apex.
Apinus, a tree, wherof commeth pitche.
Apina, a tryfle.

Apiria, infynitenesse.
Apis, callyd also Serapis, & Osyris, whome the Egyptias honored for their chief god.
Aplanes, the parte of heuen, whiche neuer moueth.
Apluda, wheaten branne.
Aplustre, et aplustria, orum, the taklynge of a shyppe.
Apocalypsis, sios, a reuelation.
Apocleti, counsaylors of the priuie councel.
Apocope, a fygure, by the whiche a letter or sillable is take away, as peculi, for peculij.
Apocopi, men beinge gelded.
Apocroti, men that be harde and myserable in lyuynge.
Apocryphus, a, um, hydde, not knowen.
Apocryphi libri, bokes, the authors wherof be vnknowen.
Apocynon, a lyttell bone in the left syde of a frogge, wherwith it is supposed, thinges may be done, whiche were not expedient to be openly knowen.
Apodixis, an euydence, demonstration.
Apodyterium, the place by a bayne, where they whyche wyll be bayned, do putte of theyr clothes.
Apogei, wyndes that doo aryse out of the grounde.
Apogeum, an habytation vnder the groud.
Apolactizo, are, to strike with the heles, also to despise or set at nought.
Apollinaris, an herbe callyd henbane.
Apollinares ludi, playes made in the honor of Apollo.
Apollo, linis, whom the gentyles honored for god, referrynge to hym the inuencion of musyke, of poetrie, and of phisike: It is sometyme taken for the sonne.
Apollonia, the name of a cite in Epiro, now callid Valonia, an other in Creta, an other in Siria, also an ile by Thracia.
Apolloniate, people of Apollonia.
Aponus, a broke of hotte water by Padua.
Apoplecticus, he that is take with the palsy.
Aposiopesis, where somewhat is lefte out, specially in speakyng, and left to the coniecture of them that be herers.
Apostasia, rebellyon or forsakyng of a mans profession or allegiance.
Apostata, a rebelle or rennagate.
Apostrophe, a conuersion in speakyng from one to an nother.
Apotelesma, a pronostication or declaratiö of the signyfications of sterres at a mans natiuitie, or the beginnyng of any thynge, what therof shall happen.
Apotheosis, a dedycation or consecration, proprely of men into goddes.
Apozema, a decoction of dyuers herbes and spyces.

Appa-

The additions.   A ante R.

Apparere questioni, to serue processe as sergeantes and baylyffes done.
Apparo, are, to apparayle or trymme, to be redy to do a thinge, to prepare or ordeine.
Apellare Cæsarē, to apele to the Emperour.
Appendicula, a diminutiue of Appendix.
Appia uia, the name of a high way at Rome
Appiana poma, a kynde of appulles as gret as quinces, and hauyng as great a sauour as they.
Applicat primum ad Chrisidis patrem se: He fyrste made repayre to Chrisis father.
Apronia, an herbe called also Vitis nigra, a blacke vine, whiche runneth vp, and wyndeth about trees and stalkes of herbes, & hath a leafe lyke an yuy, but greatter, and beareth beryes in clusters, whiche at the begynnynge are greene, and blacke whan they be rype, also the rote is blacke without, and within is yelowe lyke boxe.
Approbo, aui, are, to approue or allowe.
Appropinquo, are, to approche, to drawe nyghe to.
Appropinquatio, an approchynge or drawinge nyghe to.
Appropero, aui, are, to make hast to come.
Aprurius, et Aprugnus, a, um, of a bore.
Aprunum, uel Aprugnum callum, the brawne of a bore.
Apsis, the fely of a carte wheele.
Apsorus, an Ile in the Uenecian See.
Aptera, a citie in the countray of Licia, and a towne in Crete.
Apud eum est primus, he is his pryncypall mynyon.

Terentius Apud me priores partes habet, he maye doo moste with me. Facio te apud illum deum, I wyll make hym to take the for a god.

Terentius Per eam te obsecramus ambe, si ius, si fas est, uti aduersa eius per te tecta, tacitaque apud omnes sint, we bothe desyre you on her behalfe, if it may be by any meanes possible, that by you, polycy her mysfortune maye be keuered, and from al men kept secrete.

Terentius Apud aliquem mentiri, to make a lye to one.
Apud nos imperium tuum est, we remembre your commaundement.

Salust. Apud animum meum statuo, I determyne in my mynde.

Apud forum, In the market, apud ædes, In the house. apud horcum, in hell.
Apud quem, in whose presence.

Cic. in off. Apud maiores nostros, In the tyme of our forefathers.

Terent. Apud se non est, he is out of his wytte, or he is not in his ryght mynde. Vix sum apud me, ita animus cōmotus est metu, spe, gaudio, mirando hoc tantō tam repentino bono: I am well nyghe out of my wytte, my mynde is so vexed with feare, hope and ioye, with this good chaunce, whiche is so wonderfull, so great, and so sodaynely hapned.
Apud te sis, thynke what thou haste to doo, remembre thy selfe.
Apud ignem, by the fyre. apud aquam, apud quem, by whome. apud eum, by hym.   *Salust.*
Apud te exemplum experiendi habes, non eges foris: ye haue the experience at home, ye neede not to seeke for it abrode.   *Plautus.*
Apulia, a countraye in Italy, marchynge on the see called Hadriaticum.
Apus, odis, a byrde lyke a swallowe, but he hath larger winges, and is most commonly about the see costes where alway he eyther flyeth or houereth in the ayre, & bredeth in a rocke.
Apyrena, swete pomegranates.
Apyrotus, a stone that no fyre may damage, or deface.

¶A ANTE Q.

Aquelicium, rayne water vsed in medicine.
Aquaintercus, cutis, water which runneth betwene the skynne and the fleshe, the dropesy.
Aquarioli, boyes whiche do attende vppon common harlottes.
Aquarius, one of the xii. sygnes.
Aquarius, a, um, partaynynge to water, as aquarius sulcus, a forow, by the which water is drayned.
Aquifolia, a wylde medlar, or a tree lyke a wylde medlar.   *Vide Theophrastū.*
Aquilegium, a gourde of water, which cometh of rayne.
Aquileia, a citie in Italye, in the countreye wherof the people are called Carni.
Aquula, a lyttell water.

¶A ANTE R.

Arabarches, a lorde of Arabia.
Arabia, a great countrey ioynyng to Iudea and Siria, Araby.
Arabs, arabis, a man or woman of Araby.
Arachne, the name of a woman, whiche first inuented spynnyng of lynnen, and making of nettes, it is also taken for lynnen yarne, or the woufe.
Arachnæus, a lyttell beaste, whiche gothe a softe pace.
Arachnion, fyne threde.
Arachosia, a countrey in Asia.
Aracis ficus, fygges brode and whyte, whiche do growe on a lyttell stalke.
Aracynthus, a mountayne in Grece, in the countray callyd Aetolia.

Ara=

The additions. A ante R.

Araneolus, a yonge or lyttell spyder.
Araris, et arar, a ryuer in Fraunce, whiche runneth out of the countray of Languedocke by Burbone and Burgoyn, into the ryuer of Rone.
Ararus, a ryuer of Scithia, whiche runneth thronghe the realme of Armeny.
Arath, a countraye in Armeny wonderfull fertyle.
Aratro, aui, ari, to ploughe eftsones lande that is sowen, to make the grounde fatte.
Araxis, a ryuer in Armeny, where it is supposed, that the arch of Noy abode, whan the flodde ceased.
Arbea, a citie in Judea, where Adam and other thre patriarches were buryed.
Arboses, olde writers vsed for Arbos.
Arcadia, a countray in Greece, in the parte called Peloponesus, nowe Morea.
Arcadicus, ca, cum, of Arcadia.
Arcas, cadis, one of the sonnes of Jupiter. it is also a man or woman of Arcadia.
Arcatus, ta, tum, bent lyke a bowe.
Arcesilaus, a philosopher, which affirmid by Sophemes, that he nor none other knewe any thynge.
Arcessere, to purchace or gette a thynge.
Archarius, a treasorer, or coferer.
Archidamus, a noble man of Sparta, who being demanded howe moch money wold serue to the warre of Peloponesus, answered, sayinge, that warre sought for no certaynty.
Archigenes, the name of a famous phisition. it is also he that wold be taken for the wisest of his kynne.
Archigramateus, a chauncellour or chyefe secretary.
Archimedes, was a geometrician of Siracusis, in Sicile, whiche inuented a sphere of glasse, in the whiche all the mocions of heuen were playnely perceyued. he made also a dooue of woode, whiche conteyned suche an equall poyse, that it wolde hange in the ayre.
Archytas, a noble philosopher of the citie of Tarentum in Italy, whiche was of the sect of Pythagoras, and was a great frend vnto Plato.
Archon, was the chief dignitie in Athenes.
Archimimus, the mayster or chyefe of the players.
Architectonice, ces, idem quod architectura.
Archontici, certayn heritikes, whiche affirmed that the vniuersal state of thinges was not made by god, but by princis, and they also denied the resurrection of the body.
Arcirna, a lyttell carte, a whelebarowe.
Arconicum, a thynge called Arcenyke.

Arctophylax, a certayne fygure of sterres, folowynge Charles wayne.
Arctos, a fygure of sterres callyd Charles wayne. also Vrsa maior.
Arctous, & arcticus, ca, cum, of the northe.
Arcturus, a sterre whiche is at the tayle of that, whiche is callyd arctos, or vrsa maior.
Arcuor, ari, to be made bent like a bowe, or to be vaulted. Arcatus, ta, tum, idem. — *Liuius. Plinius. Ouidius in Metamor. 12.*
Ardeates, people of the citie of Ardea.
Ardeola, an hernesewe.
Ardére cupiditate, to couete ardently.
Ardére iracundia, to be inflamid with anger.
Ardére maximo flagitio, to haue done, or to be infamed of a myscheuous dede. — *Plautus.*
Ardére, to shine. Tyrioqʒ ardebat murice læna, His mantell dydde shyne of fyne purple of Tyre.
Ardens, burnyng, ardent, feruent in doinge.
Ardum, olde writers vsid for arduum.
Arelate, a citie in France, callid Orleance.
Arenarius, a, u, ptaining to a fighting place.
Areopagitæ, were Judges, whiche sate in a place by Athenes, and iudged causes of murder, and weighty thynges concerning the comune weale.
Areopagus, Marces towne, where the said iudges dyd sytte in iudgement.
Areopolis, a cite in Araby, callid also Moab.
Areopolitæ, the inhabitātes of Areopolis.
Arete, in latine virtus, in englishe vertue. It was also the name of the wife of Alcinous kyng of Phæacis, of whom Homere writeth in Odyssea.
Arethyssa & Arethusa, a ryuer in the greate Armenye.
Arethusa, the companion of Diana. it is also the name of a fountayne in Sicile, and of dyuers other.
Aretium, a citie in Tuscana.
Aretinus, a, um, of that citie.
Arferis, wyne or water offred to the infernall goddes, or rather deuyls.
Argentarius cōmeatus, prouisyon of money.
Argentaria cura, care for moneye. — *Plautus.*
Argētariæ illecebræ, thinges getting money
Argentaria inopia, lacke of money.
Argentaria, a banke of exchaunge.
Argentum uiuum, quycke syluer.
Argestes, the westerne wynde.
Argeus, a, um, of the citie of Argos.
Argiæ plurali, a citie in Laconia.
Argiletum, the sepulchre of Argus. it is also a place, where potters clay is dygged. it was also a strete in Rome, where the boke sellers dwelled.
Argiletanę, boke sellars dwelling in the said strete callyd argiletum.
Argimyssę, thre lytle iles in Asia, by the iles of — *Stra. li. 13.*

of Mitelene, and Lesbus.

Argis, at the citie of Argos.

Argo, the shyppe wherin Jason and his company sayled in to Colchos, to wynne the flyse of golde.

Argolicus, ca, cum, of Argos.

Argonautæ, were the noble men, which accompanyed Jason vnto Colchos.

Argos, singulari: Argi plurali, a citie not far from Athenes, a nother in Achaia. it is also a countray, part of Greece.

Plautus. Arguere, alique pecuniæ interuersæ, to accuse one for stealynge of money.

Arguta diuisio, a subtill diuision.

Argutū caput, a sharpe or pikyd hedde lyke a sugar lofe.

Argyranche, the syluer sykenesse.

Argyraspidæ, men bearyng shildes of syluer

Argyritis, the spume or fome of syluer.

Ariadne, a lady, the wife of Theseus, whom he forsoke, notwithstandyng that she hadde sauyd his life.

Aricia, a city in Italy.

Aricinum nemus, a woode by the sayd citye where Numa kynge of Romaynes fayned to speke with Aegeria the sayry.

Plautus. Aricinus lacus, a brooke by Aricia.

Aridus homo, a dry felowe, of whom no thynge maye be goten: some do call hym, *Plinius.* a pelt, or a pynchebeke.

Arimaspi, peple in the north part of Europa whiche haue but one eye, & that is in theyr forehed, which do fyght contynually with Gryphons.

Ariminū, a citye in Italy.

Arimphæi, people in the north part of Asia, whiche all though that they haue onely woodes for theyr dwellynge, and onely beryes for theyr sustynance, yet kepe they iustice and peace amonge them selues, and *Herodot⁹.* be temperate of maners.

Gellius.
Plinius. Arinca, a corne called Rye.

Arion, a famouse harper, whom the maryners wolde haue throwen into the see, for to haue his money: but he desyryng them to let hym play a songe on his harpe or he dyed, afterwarde lepte into the water, but a dolphyn receyuyng hym on his backe, & brought hym to lande alyue.

Aristathea, the malowe with the great lefe.

Aristarchus, a famouse grāmarien, whiche corrected the bookes of Homere, tryeng out what verses were his, and what verses were counterfayt. Therfore they vse to call hym Aristarchus, that is a sharpe correctour of other mennes workes.

Aristides, a noble man of Athenes, who for his playne and iust dealing, as well in deedes as in wordes, hadde the surname gyuen hym, Ryghtuous, or Juste: He that readeth this mannes lyfe, in the lyues of Plutarche, shall thinke hym before all other to be folowed by a counsaylour or gouernour vnder a prynce.

Aristippus, a philosopher, whiche fyrst dyd put the principall good thynge in the pleasaunt mocions of the mynde: the pryncipall yll thinge, in gryefe.

Aristocratia, the fourme of gouernaunce of a weale publike, where they do rule, which are of moste vertue.

Aristolochia, an herbe, wherof be two kyndes: one is called longe, the other round. The rounde hath leues in facyon like yuy, but somwhat rounder, wherin is a sharpe and soft odoure, the floure white lyke a lytle bonet vpon a redde knoppe, the rootes are rounde and many. The longe Aristolochia, hath lenger leues, small braunches, and a purple floure, which stynketh: and whan it spryngeth, it is of the facyon of a peare, the rote therof is long, and of the greatnesse of a mannes fyngar: bothe of them do beare beryes lyke to capers, within of box coloure, whiche are bytter and stynkynge.

Aristomenes, a man of Messene, whiche was called Iustissimus, moste iuste. This man, whan he was dead, was founden to haue his hart all heary.

Aristophanes, a famous poete, which wrate Comedies, wherin he taūted them, whom he dyd not fauoure: all be it he was very eloquent, and moch myrth is in his workes

Aristophorū, a disshe, wherin meate is borne to dyner.

Aristoteles, a philosopher, of whom Quintylyane writeth in this wyse: whatte saye you by Aristotle, whome I wote not, whither I maye iudge more excellent in knowlege of thinges, or in abundaunce of wrytynge, or in swetnesse of eloquence, or in sharpnesse of witte, or els in diuersyte of workes. Notwithstandynge he was lytle of personage, crooke backed, yll shapen, and stuttynge.

Aritudo, drythe, or dryenesse.

Arma coquinaria, vtensyles of the kechyn.

Armenia, a royalme in Asia, lyeng betwene the two great mountaynes, Taurus and Caucasus, and stretcheth from Cappadocia to the see called Caspium.

Armeniacum pomum, a pome citron, or a Citron, whiche is lyke an orenge, but that he is somwhat in length.

Armentarius, the keper of an armery: somtyme Esquiar de Esquyry.

Armille, an instrument of falshode or craft.

Armi

The additions.   A *ante* R.

Armilustrum, was a festiual day, in the whiche the Romaynes dyd sacrifice armed, and trumpettes dyd blowe bluddy soundes. also the place wherin suche sacrifyce was made.

Palladus. Columel. Armocea, a wylde radyshe.

Armoradum, the tendrels or yonge stalkes of wylde radyshe.

Iosephus. Armon, a ryuer that cometh from the hilles of Arabye, and dyuydeth Moabitide from Amonitide.

Arnoglossa, an herbe callid brode Plantain or waybred.

Aroma, atis, pleasant sauour, also spyce.

Aromatites, a precious stone, whiche hathe the sauour of Mirre.

Aromatorius, & aromatopola, he that selleth thynges hauynge swete sauour.

Aros, an herbe, callyd wake Robyn. It is callyd of some Serpentaria minor, bycause it hath leaues lyke to Dragons, but broder, and hauynge blacke spottes, it groweth moche about hedges.

Arpinum, an auncient towne in Italye, famous and noble by the byrthe of Plautus, Tulli, and Marius.

Arpinas, a man or woman of Arpinum.

Arquites, olde wryters vsed for an archer.

Arquus, arqui, the raynbowe.

Plaut Arrideo, ere, to smyle on one. also to lyke or seme pleasant. Aedes mihi arridebant, The house lyked me well.

Terentius. Arrige aures, lay to thyn eares, or gyue an eare to that whiche is spoken.

Salust. Arrexit animos, it aduanced their courage.

Arrectarii parietes, walles made with tymber and parget, to diuide chambers.

Plautus, Arripere se foras, to gette hym oute of the doores.

Arripere sermonē, to take hym at his word.

Arripere maledictum, to take hede of an yll reporte.

Cicero. Quare cum ista sis authoritate, non debes Marce arripere maledictum ex triuio, aut ex scurrarum aliquo conuitio, wherfore in as moche as ye are in this auctoritie, or of this estimation, ye ought nat Marc, to take hede of an yll worde spoken abrode, or of the rebuke of a raylynge knaue.

Sueton. de claris grā. Arripere conditionem, to take the offer.

Arrugia, a Coney.

Ars parasitica, the feate of flaterye.

Arsaces, was the general name of the kynges of Parthia.

Aristotel. Arsenothelea, a beaste, whiche is both male and female, as some do saye that a haare is one yere male, an other yere female.

Artaba, a measure of the Egyptians, contaynynge thre score and xii. Romayn mesures, called Sextarii.

Artaxata, a cytie in Armenye.

Artaxerxes, the name of dyuers kynges of Persia, of the whiche one of theym callyd Artaxerxes with the longe hande, vsed to say, that it was moche more kingly to giue, than to take.

Artemisia, was the name of a noble princesse whiche was wyfe to Mausolus, kynge of Caria, who was of a notable chastitie, & in loue towarde her husband so excelled, that whan he was deade, she caused his harte to be dryed in a vessell of golde, into pouder, and by lyttell and lyttell dranke it vppe syrenge, that their two hartes shulde neuer departe asonder, and that she thought, that there mought be made noo worthye sepulchre for it, but her owne body. But withstādynge, she made for his body suche a sepulchre, that for the excellent warkemanshyp that was in it, also the beautie, and costlynesse, it was taken for one of the meruayles of the worlde, and for the notable fame therof, all sumptuous and great sepulchres were afterwarde callydde Mausolea. She found also an herbe called Artemisia, Mugwort, or Motherwort in englyshe, of great vertue in womens diseases.

Artemisius, the moneth of Maye amonge the Macedonians. also a hyll in Arcadia.

Artemon, monis, a troukle, wherby ropes do runne. It may also be taken for any instrument, which hath troukles.

Artitus, well instructed in sciences.

Arthetica passio, callyd also Morbus articularis, the ioynt syckenesse, is thus diuided into Coxendix, callyd Sciatica, whyche is in the huckle bone, Podagra, the goute of the legges & fete, and Chiragra, the goute of the fyngers.   *Galenus, Plautus.*

Arthuntis, idem.

Articularius, he that hath the gout.

Articulare, articulately, as whan one dothe expresse euery syllable.

Arthritica, som do suppose it to be that herb and floure, whyche is callyd Prymerose.

Artocrea, maye be callyd a pasty or pye, with fleshe or fyshe baken.

Artolaganum, fyne cakebreade.   *Plautus,*

Artopta, a bakynge panne, wherein they baake tartes, or other thynges made of fyne paste. Some take it for a vessell to kucade in.

Artoptely, tartes or cakes baken in a panne.

Artopritius panis, browne breade, or breadde of course wheate.

Artotyritæ, people, whiche didde offer vnto god, bread and chese.

Aruales fratres, were supposed to be the foster brethrē of Romulus, to whom he gaue the dignitie of priesthode, to make sacrifice for growynge and increace of corne, and preseruation of the corne feldes.

Aruisium, an hyll on the see coste of the ile callyd Chium, where groweth the wynes callyd Aruisia vina.

Arunca, a towne in Italy.

Aruncus, the bearde of a gote.

¶ A ANTE S.

Asarum, an herbe, whose leaues are lyke vnto yuie, but they be lesse and rouder, and hath a good sauour, the floure is purple, lyke to the floure of henbane, but it sauoreth swetely, and groweth betwene the leaues by the roote, the stalke is edged, and somwhat roughe, the rootes ar smal, croked, & like to grasse, full of knottes: it is commonly callid Asarabaccha, som calle it wylde Spikenarde.

Asarotum, pauynge tile with pictures enelyd, which may not be swept with a besom, but the dust and other thing must be swept with a wynge and gathered vp.

Ascalon, a citie in Palestina.

Ascalonix, a kind of onyons called scalions.

Ascanius, the sonne of Eneas.

Ascitę, Arabians.

Asclepiades, the name of a famous phisitian. Alsoo of a philosopher, whiche beinge blynde, was demaunded in skorne, what his blyndnes dyd profit him, and he answered, that he had the more company by one boye that dyd leade hym.

Ascopera, a bagge of lether.

Ascra, a citie in Boeotia, where Hesiodus the poete was borne.

Ascriptus, ta, tum, inrollyd.

Ascripti milites, sowldiours, whose names are regystred or entred with other.

Ascriptiuus, idem quod ascriptius, he that is regystred with other.

Asellus, a lyttell or yong asse. also the name of a see fyshe, callyd an haddocke.

Asianus, a, um, of Asia.

Asiaticus, a surname gyuen to oone of the Scippyons, bycause that he subdewed the lasse Asia.

Asilus, a great flye, whiche byteth beastes, and is callyd a horse flye.

Asion, an owle, whiche hath fethers on euery syde of her heed lyke vnto eares.

Asiortum, a kynde of spyders, with whyte strakes, of whom if that one be stunge, his knees shall bowe and waxe faynt.

Asomatos, vnpalpable, or that cā not be felt

Asopus, a ryuer in Achaia.

Asotia, ryotte.

Asotus, ryottous.

Aspalathus, a thorne growynge in the easte partes of the worlde, the rynde wherof is somwhat redde, and within, the wodde is of a sadde purple, and smellith very swete, and therfore is vsed in parfumes.

Asparagus, an herbe callyd of cōmon apotycaries Sparagus, in englyshe Sperage.

Aspello, aspuli, aspellere, to dryue awaye from one. *Plautus.*

Asperum uinum, a roughe wyne.

Asper numus, money newe coyned.

Aspersus infamia, stayned with dishonour. *Cicero.*

Aspergere comitatem seueritate, to myxt famyliaritie and grauitie togyther.

Asphaltum, a water in Syria, wherein nothynge that hath lyfe may be drowned. It is callyd Mare mortuū, the dead see. It is supposed, that in that place stoode the cyties of Sodoma. It is also a certayn lyme myxte with brymstone, whiche being ones bette, may neuer be extincte.

Asphodelus, an herbe callyd daffadyll.

Aspidisca, a lyttell targate or shielde.

Aspilates, a stone lyke to syluer.

Assę, drye stones.

Assatura, rosted meate.

Assectator, a companyon.

Assentio, to perceyue. Sed assentio aperiri fores, quę absorbent quicquid uenit infra pessulos. But I perceyue the dores are opened, whiche deuouren all that commethe within the boltes. *Plaut.*

Assentatio, flatterye.

Assentatiuncula, a flatterynge tale.

Assequor, assequi, to render as moch to one as he hath deserued. Nullam partem uideas tuorum meritorum assecutus, It may nat be founde in me, that I haue rendred to you any thynge after youre merytes, or haue doone soo moche for you, as ye haue deserued. *Cicero*

Assequi nomen, to gette renoume. *Plinius.*

Asser, asseris, a pole.

Asserculi, & assiculi, lytel bourdes or lathes.

Asserere aliquem manu, to set one at libertie or to manumyse a bondman.

Asserere in seruitutem, to brynge in bondage or seruytude. *Plautus.*

Asserere ab iniuria, to defende from wronge or daunger.

Asserere se studijs, to leaue al other besynes, to applye study.

Assertor, toris, he that setteth one at libertie, or defendeth hym from bondage.

Assidela, a byshops seate or chaire, wherin he sytteth whan he ministreth.

Assidere literis, to be alwaye in studye of letters.

Assiduus scriptor, an author appued, whose sentence

The additions. A ante T.

sentence is holden for certayne and true.
Assiduitas, continuance in a thinge.
Cicero. Assidue, & assiduo, aduerbes, whiche do signifie continually.
Assignare famę, to applye hym selfe to get renoume.
Assimilo, are, to do a thynge lyke to an nother man, to immitate or folowe one.
Assimilis, le, lyke or semblable.
Assimiliter, al semblably.
Plautus. Assimulo, are, to fayne to do a thynge, and nat to doo it.
Assipondium, a pounde weight.
Assisia, one of y names of Pallas or Minerua
Assoleo, lere, to be wont or accustomed.
Assono, are, to sowne or make a sowne.
Assa uoce cantare, to synge without an Instrument.
Varro. Assuefactio, a bryngyng of one in custome.
Cato. Assuesco, scere, to vse of a custome.
Assumptio, a takynge.
Assur, a cytie in Judea, buylded by kynge Salomon.
Assus, a, um, tosted or rosted.
Assyria, a region in Asia, callyd now Syria, in englyshe Surrye, hauynge on the easte Indie, on the west the ryuer of Tigris, on the south Medi or Mede, on the northe the mounte of Caucasus.
Asta, departe nat, stande styll.
Astachus, a kynde of crabbes of the see.
Astare, to stande by, or to be present.
Astare in genua, to knele.
Astare aduocatus, to assyst or speake for one.
Plautus. Astaroth, an olde citie sometyme belonging to Og, kyng of Basan, in the which dwellyd gyantes, and afterwarde it came to the lotte of the tribe of Manasses, and is in the countray of Bethania. There be two castelles of that name nyne myles a sonder, betwene the citie of Adara and Abella.
Asterte, a goddesse of the Sirians, to whom Salomon to please his concubyne, raysed an Aultar.
Asterias, a kynde of herons, I suppose that it is an Egrette.
Asthma, matis, a sycknesse, where one maye not fetche his wynde but with moche difficultie, with weasynge of the breast: whiche hapneth by straytenesse of the pypes stopped with toughe fleume, or of somme impostume growen in the pypes.
Astomi, people of Indie, hauynge no mouthes, whiche lyuen by ayre and smelle of swete thynges.
Astręa, sygnyfieth Justyce.
Astringere fidem, to promyse.
Astringere se furti, to yelde or make him self gyltie of felonie.

Astroites, a stone lyke to a fyshes eie.
Astrologus, an astrologien, he that studieth the speculation of astronomie.
Astronomus, an astronomer.
Astruere dignitati alterius, to augment an other mans dignitie or honour. *Plinius.*
Astruitur his, is putte for more ouer, or furthermore. *Plinius in Epistolis.*
Astur, any thyng of Asturia, a cite in Spain.
Astur'equus, a spanysshe horse, callyd a genette. Asturcones, idem.
Astura, a towne and ryuer in Italy.
Asturia, a citie in Spayne.
Asuestinum, lynnen threede, whiche maye nat be burned.
Asymbolus, he that commeth to a bankette, without appoyntement, an vnboden geste.

¶ A ANTE T.

AT, yet, or at the least way. Si non propiquitatis, at ætatis suæ, si nõ hominis, at humanitatis rationem haberet, All though he had not consideration of kinred, yet shulde he haue had regarde to his age, and though he caryd not for the person, yet shulde he haue hadde respecte vnto good humanitie. *Cicero & Flacco.*
Atabulus, a feruent wynde, whyche whan it bloweth in the realme of Naples, pestylence immediately insueth.
Atalanta, a mayden, whiche was doughter to the kynge of Argiues, whiche kepynge perpetuall virginitie, haunted forestes and woodes, and dyd slee wylde beastes, & was the fyrste that wounded the greatte bore of Calidonia.
Attalus, a kynge in the lasse Asia, of meruailous rychesse, of whome all magnifyke and stately thynges, are callyd Attalica.
Attamen, but yet.
Atechna, thinges vnkunningly handled.
Ategia, a bouthe, or place made vppe with trees and boughes.
Ater panis, broune breadde.
Athacus, a byrde with foure legges, hauing the longest behynde.
Athanatos, immortall.
Athenæ, narum, the citie of Athenes.
Atheneum, a place at Rome, where all syences were radde.
Athenodorus, a phylosopher, whiche lefte with Octauian the Emperoure this lesson, whã he toke his leue of him: Noble prince, whã thou art attached with wrath, neither say nor do any thing, vntyl thou hast by thy selfe peruesed the .xxiiii. greke letters, and remembred the order of places where they stand, to thintent that the passion of yre, by withdrawyng the mind to an nother thing, mought languisshe and vanisshe away.

Hh ij   Athes

Atheromata, lyttell pouſſhes in the necke, and vnder the armes.

Atheos, he that doth not beleue that god is.

Atheſis, a ryuer in Italy that paſſeth by the cyties of Verona and Tridentum callyd Trente.

Athos, a hylle in Macedonia, of a wonderfulle heyght.

Athrax, a citie in Theſſalia.

Athracia ars, arte magike.

Atlanticę inſulę, the yles callyd nowe fortunatę, where fruite and herbes doo growe without labour.

Atlantides, the doughters of Atlas, alſoo certayne ſterres.

Atlas, Atlantis, the name of a kynge, whiche fyrſte taughte the courſe of ſterres, and therfore it was fayned of hym, that he ſuſteyned heuen on his ſholders. It is alſo the name of a hylle in Barbaria, highe and ſmall, that it perceth the cloudes.

Atlantes, Moores dwelling about that hyl.

Atocion, a medicyne, which maketh a woman to be barrayne.

Atocius, a certayne ſpyder which is heary.

Plautus in Pſeud. Terent. in And. Atq̃, than. Illi ſunt alio ingenio atq̃ tu, They be of an nother maner of wytte than thou art. Non Appollinis magis verum, atq̃ hoc reſponſum eſt, Appolloes aunſwere was neuer truer than this is.

Plautus in Caſina. Atq̃ adeo, and that more is. Eſurio hercle, atq̃ adeo nunc haud parum ſitio, I am hungrye, and that more is, I am a thyrſte not a lyttelle.

Atq̃ eccum, but lo where he is.

Atractilis, an herbe, hauing a longe ſtemme and rough, with long leaues growyng by the toppe, the reſidue without leaues, the toppe full of prickes, and a yelowe floure, women were wonte to make ſpyndelles of the ſtalkes therof.

Atricapilla, a byrde, with blacke fethers on the crowne of his heed.

Atrifer, a ruſhe that beareth a blacke ſede.

Atriolum, a lyttell ynner court.

Atriplex, an herbe callyd orache or arage.

Atritas, blackeneſſe.

Atrophia, an affecte or diſcraſye, wherin the body can nat be nouryſhed with any thing but conſumeth with leanneſſe.

Atrophus, he that hath that affecte.

Atropos, one of the fatall ladies, whyche is fayned to breake the threde of lyfe: it is ſomtyme put for neceſſitte of dethe.

Atra, is he that gothe ſo on the ſoles of his fete, that he ſwepeth the grounde, rather than walketh.

Attagen, & attagena, a byrd, whiche is found in Ionia, and is very delycate, and hathe fethers of ſondry colours, and beynge at large, is alwaye ſyngynge or chatteringe, whan he is taken, he maketh no noyſe, nor ſemeth to haue any voice. They ar deceiued that take hym for a woodcocke.

Attalica toga, a gowne of tynſette.

Attelanę fabulę, were comedies or enterludes, whiche onely were in ieſtes and mery ſcoffes, or bourdynges.

Attelę, a citie nygh to Naples.

Attentus, he that hereth diligętly, attentiue.

Attentus ad rem, carefull to get goodes.

Attero, triui, terere, to rubbe againſt a thing.

Saluſt. Atterere famam, Poſt ubi eorum famam atq̃ pudorem attriuerat, maiora alia imperabat, After that he hadde made theym conſume their good name and honeſtie, he ſet them in hande with other greatter attemptatis.

Attica, a countray in Grece, wherin ſtoode the famous citie of Athenes, the nourice of all ſcyences.

Atticę, an aduerbe, ſygnifyenge in the eloquence of ſpeche of Athenes.

Atticiſmus, the fourme of that ſpeche.

Atticiſſo, ſere, to ſpeake lyke an Athenienſe.

Attigo, idem quod attingo.

Attilus, a fyſſhe, whyche is in the ryuer of Po, very gret, and with longe reſt waxeth meruaylous fatte, which Franciſcus Philelphus ſuppoſed to be a ſturion, but that is denied by Iouius, which affirmeth that he is greatter than a ſturion, and vnlyke to hym in fourme, taſte, and price.

Plinius. Attingit me ſanguine, he is nigh of my blod.

Attingere ſenectam, to come to greate age.

Vergili, in Geor. Attingere partes naturę, to com to the knowlege of naturall cauſes.

Attingere ſtudia, to ſauour of letters.

Aningitur, it is nyght.

Attondeo, attondêre, to clyppe or ſheare a thynge nygh.

Plautus. Attondere arbores, to ſhrede trees.

Attondere auro, to rydde one of his money, to take all away from hym.

Attributus, ta, tum, attributed.

Attributa pecunia, moneye delyuered to be gyuen to an nother manne.

¶A ANTE V.

Auarus, coueytous of money.

Aucupare ſermonem alicuius, to harken or take hede what one ſayth.

Audiſn tu? Hereſt thou not?

Audire bene, to haue a good name.

Audire male, to haue an yll name.

Audiens dicto, redy to doo that he is commaunded, at commaundement, obedyent.

Audienciam facere, to commaunde or make ſylence

The additions. A ante V.

sylence, as they doo whiche are cryers in places of iustyce.

Auello, auulsi, auellere, to plucke awaye by vyolence.

Auellere se a meretrice, to withdrawe hym, or go away by force from an harlotte.

Auenaria, a kynde of grasshoppes, whiche appere nat vntyll the corne be rype.

Auentinus, an hylle at Rome.

Auerni, people in France, callid Auergnes.

Auernus, a lake in Campania, whyche was dedicate vnto Pluto kyng of Hell, where men supposed, that there was an entrie or passage to helle.

Auersus, a, um, straunge, vnacquaynted.

Vergilius. Auertere ab aliquo loco, to lette or prohybyte one to enter.

Aueruncus, god whiche putteth awaye all euylle.

Aufero, abstuli, auferre, to take away.

Terentius Aufer te hinc, gette the hense.

Aufer te domum, gette the home.

Plautus. Auferas iurgium, leaue thy chydynge.

Auferre litem, to gette by action or processe of the lawe. Maiore mulcta mulctat, quam *Plautus in Ruden.* litem auferunt, He maketh them to spende more than they may wynne by their sutte.

Aufer nugas, leaue these trifelynges, leaue your mockes.

Plautus in Cur. Auferre petitionem, to haue the thynge that he asketh. Tuo arbitratu, dum auferam abs te id quod peto, Euen as ye wyll, soo that I maye haue the thynge that I aske or demaunde.

Auferre pignora, to take a dystresse or gage.

Plautus in Asina. Auferre tacita, to make oone to confesse a thynge secrete. Suspendas potius me, quam tacita hæc auferas, Thou mayst rather hange me, thanne make me confesse that secrete.

Terentius in Andria. Auferre inultum, to goo quyte without punyshement. Ergo pretium ob stultitiam fero, sed inultū id nunq̄ auferet, I am well rewarded for my folyshenes, but yet he shall not go quyte away without punyshement.

Cic. Tusc. quest. 3. Auferri sibi, to be vexed in mynde, or frome hym selfe.

Ennius. Augifico, for augeo.

Augere auxilia, to make a newe hoste, after a discomfyte.

Auguratus, the dygnitie of theym, whiche were Augures, of whome was a colledge in Rome: as there be nowe of priestes in Cathedrall churches.

Augurium, dyuination or tellynge before of thinges, which shall happen, specially by the flyght or voyces of byrdes.

Cicero p L. Murena Auguror, ari, idem quod Auguro.

Auguror opinio̅e, I suppose in myn opinyon

Augusta Cæsaria, a cytie in Spayne, vppon the ryuer of Iberus.

Augusta emerita, a cytie in Portugall.

Augusta Vindelicorum, a goodly and beautyfulle citie in Germanye, nowe callydde Awsbourghe.

Augustalis, ale, the Emperours Palayce or Pauyllyon.

Augustus, a place consecrate, full of maiestie and honour, it is also a name of addicion gyuen to emperours.

Auiarius, & auiaria, he and she that hath the charge of the kepynge of pultrie or wildfoule. It may also be vsed for a pultar, whiche selleth pultrie.

Auiarium, the place where pultrie is kept, also busshes sette for byrdes to haunte and sytte in.

Auide, affectuously, couetously, ardantly, with great desyre.

Auidis moribus, of an excedynge couaytous appetite.

Auiditas, desyre of a thynge, couetyse, ardant affection.

Auidus cibi, hungrye. *Terent.*

Auilla, a lambe lately yeaned.

Auius, uia, uium, wherby there is no passage or waye. *Plaut. Vergil. Salust.*

Auius, he that gothe out of the way.

Aula, of old writers was vsid for olla, a pot.

Aulula, a lyttell potte, wherof cometh Aulularia, a comedye of Plautus, wherein is declared the couetous mynd of one, whiche hydde his money in a potte, thynkyng that noo man knewe hit but hym selfe, and yet was he deceyued of it.

Aulicotia, boyled meate.

Aulicus, a courtyar.

Aulicus, ca, cum, of the court, as aulicus apparatus, courtely apparayle, but most properly the apparayle of pryncis. *Sueton. in Nerone.*

Aulis, lidis, a lyttelle countraye or shyre in Boeotia in Grece. It was also a great cytie and hauen, where the princis of Grece assemblyd, and conspired togyther the distruction of Troy.

Aulon, the name of a Mountayne and citie in Calabria, where growethe excellente good wynes. Also of two other cyties, the oone in Macedonia, the other in Cilicia.

Aulę, shaulmes or waytes.

Auleticus, he that playeth best on a shalme or wayte.

Auocare animum, to withdrawe the mynde from a thynge.

Auocamentum, passetyme, recreation, that withdraweth the mynde from heuynesse or melancholy.

Hh iii   Aurata,

The additions. A ante X.

Aurata, a fysshe of the see, which I suppose to be a gylte heed, for he hath in his forheed a thinge congelate, which in the water shyneth lyke golde, and also hath a set of tethe lyke checke tethe, wherwith he hathe ben harde of fyshers in the night to crushe cockyls, and suche other lytell shell fyshes, wheron he fedeth.

Terentius in Andria. Aures arrigere, to lyfte vppe the eares, to here attentyuely.

Cicero in Salust. Cicero p G.Planco. Plautus in Trinūmo. Plautus in Mili. Trebonius Cicero. Cic. Volsi. Aures calent illius criminibus, myne eares glowe or burne to here of his mischeuous actes. Aures hebetes habet, he is dulle in herynge, or he lysteth nat to here.
Auribus accipere, to haue herde.
Auribus capere spolia, to harken & beare away our secrefies, or secrete counsayle.
Auribus dare, to flatter, to speake that whiche shall content a mans eare.
Auribus æquissimis alicuius uti, to be fauorably harde of one.

Apuleius. Auribus prouehi, to be caried by the eares, it is properly vsed, where we wyl declare, that beinge in iourney with one, we delyte so moch in his cōmunication, that we fele no labour or payne by going or riding. So may we say, auribus prouehimur, in hering of hym our paynes are relieued, or in herying him talke, our iorney semeth shorte, or is abbreuiate.
Auricularius, a, um, pertayning to the eares.
Auricularis confessio, cōfession made secretly, as priestis do here it.
Auricularis, re, idem.
Aurigo, a sicknes callid the yelow iaundise.
Aurilegus, he that hath stollen golde.
Auripigmentum.
Aurum coronarium, was golde gathered of the people, to make crownes, to sende to Emperours, after their vyctories.

Plaut. in Mercator. Auscultabitur, he wyll do as ye byd hym.
Auscultare alicui, to obeye one, or be at his commaundement.
Auscultare inter sese, to whyster oone in an nothers eare.
Ausim, sis, sit, is put for audeam, as, at.
Ausitis, the contray callid also Hus, where Iob dwellyd.
Ausonium, Italy. Ausones, were the anciēt kynges of Italy.
Ausum, & ausus, a presumptuous enterprise.

Plautus in Persa. Auspicium liquidū, a manifest signe or token.
Auspicia optima, tokens of good lucke.

Plautus in Aul. Auspicio malo, with ylle lucke, or in an ylle tyme. Ne ego edepol ueni huc auspicio malo: I camme hither in an ylle time, or, An vnhappy or vnlucky fortune broughte me hyther.
Auspico, are, to seke for a thing by diuinatiō.

Auspicatus, ta, tum, honourably enterprised.
Auspicato, happyly.
Austrum, the spoke of a whele.
Aut certe, or at the least. Quo enim uno uincebamur a victa Grætia, id aut illi ereptum est, aut certe nobis communicatum. That oone thyng, wherin we gaue place to Grece, whiche is vanquyshed by vs, eyther it is taken cleane away from them, or at the lest we be therin equall vnto them. *Quintilia.*
Autenticus, ca, cum, of auctoritie. *Ci.in Bru.*
Autochthones, people which beganne in the countray that they doo inhabyte, whyche name was gyuen to them of Athenes.
Autodidactus, he that lerneth without a master by his owne study.
Automata, thynges without lyfe, whyche seme to moue by them selfes: as it may apere in olde horologes, and ymages, whiche by vices do moue.
Autopyros, breade of cleane wheate without other mixture, sauing a lyttell leuen.
Author, the fyrste Inuenter or maker of a thyng. also a reporter of newes. also he that hath the custody of one within age. also he that doth sell or delyuer a thing on warrantise. also he whom a man foloweth in doing any thynge. *Ti.Liuius. Paulus ius recōsult9. Ci. in Ver. Plautus in Cur. Terentius in Prolog. Andri. Plautus in pœnu.*
Authoritas, authoritie, credence, puissance, opinion, iugement, the inioying of possessiō.
Authoritatem defungi, to deny to haue done any thynge, or to haue bene the cause that it was doone.
Authoritatem defugere, to refuse to do that whiche he is commanded. *Terent. in Eunucho.*
Authoritatem interponere, to commaunde a thynge to be done.
Authoramentum, wages, or hyre.
Authoro, rare, to bynde one by couenant to doo seruyce.
Authoratus, ta, tum, bounden by couenaunt.

¶A ANTE X.

AXis, an extree of a cart, somtyme the hole carte. Sometyme it is shyngle, wherewith howses are couered in the stede of tyle. *Iuuenalis*
Axilla, the armehole.
Axamenta, verses made by the priestes of Mars, called Salii, in quycke tauntynge of all men.
Axare, olde writers vsed for nominare, to name or aske.
Axioma, a sentence spoken and proued: as If Plato walketh, Plato moueth, if it be day, the son is aboue the erth. It is put by Tulli for that, which sophisters do call a proposition, whiche is a sentence trewe or false.

A, ante

The additions.

¶ A ANTE Z.

Azymus panis, vnleuened breadde.
Azanium, was a welle, the water wherof beinge dronke, caused menne to hate the sauour and taste of wyne.
Azotus, a citie in Siria.

¶ B ANTE A.

BAAL in the tongue of Siria, signifieth lorde, & is attrybute to Jupiter.
Babe, an interiection of wondrynge.
Babylon, a great citie in Caldey, and signyfyeth confusion or trāslation. where was a towre edyfied by Nembroth, whiche was in height fiue myles, and a hūdred thre score and tenne paces, afterward being enlarged by Semiramis, the wyfe of Ninus kyng of Assiria, it was so great, that it conteyned in compasse thre score myles, and the walles were in height thre hundred fete, and in thyckenes or bredthe thre score and fyftene fete, and hadde a hūdred gates of brasse, and there ranne through the middell therof the noble and moste famous riuer Euphrates, whyche is oone of the ryuers, wherof the sprynge or hedde is in Paradyse.
Babylonia, the countray where the citye of Babylon stode.
Babylonicus, ca, cum, and Babylonius, a, um, of Babylon.
Babylonica, are clothes wouen with sondry colours.
Baccalia, a kynde of bay trees or laurell, but it hath larger leues, and great plentye of beryes. It is also called Augusta.
Baccar, caris, & Baccharis, is an herbe hauynge a lefe in facyon and greatnesse betwene violet leues and the herbe, whiche is called Moleyn or longwort, the stalke square, and somwhat rough, whiche is in hayght a foote and a half, hauyng a floure lyke purple, myxte with whyte, the roote blacke, but that sauouryth lyke vnto Cinamome, some do call it Asdrabacca, some our ladies gloues.
Bacchari, to do a thynge lyke a madde man or vexed with spirites.
Bacchatim, lyke a madde man.
Baccaricum, a swete oyntment, made of the roote of Asdrabaccha.
Bacchius, a, um, of Bacchus.
Baccifera, a tree bearynge bearies.
Baccula, a lyttell bearye.

B ante A.

Bacillum, a lyttell staffe.
Bactra, trorum, a contray in Scithia, beyōd Assiria, it is also the name of a citie in that countraye.
Bactriani, people of that countray.
Bactrianum, a coūtray wherin were a thousande cities.
Badizare, to goo.
Bagous, in the Persian tounge signyfieth a geldyng, or a man gelded. *Plautus in Asina.*
Bagrada, a ryuer in Affrike by the citie callyd Utica, where Attilius Regulus, and the hoste of the Romans, slewe a serpent, whiche was in length one hundred & xx. fete.
Bahal, the ydoll of Tyre.
Balanites, a stone, whiche is a lyght grene, and hath a vayn in the myddell lyke a flame of fyre.
Balanitis, a kynde of rounde Chestens or cheste nuttes.
Balaustium, the floures of wylde pome granades.
Baleares, two Iles by Spayne, wherof the one is now called Maiorca, the other Minorca.
Ballistarium, the place where a great brake or slynge is layde.
Balneatorius, a, um, of a bathe.
Balneolum, a lytell bayne or bathe.
Balito, tare, to blete often.
Balsamum, baulme.
Bambia, a kynde of olyue tree.
Banausus, an artificer that worketh at ye fyre.
Banchus, called an haddok.
Baphia, a dyehouse.
Baptæ, men whiche hadde theyr visages paynted.
Baptes, a stoone greene, of the colour of a frogge.
Baptismus, & Baptismum, & Baptisma, matis, Baptym.
Barbula, a lyttell berde.
Barba iouis, an herbe called Singrene, and groweth on tyles.
Barba senis, is an herbe, which groweth amonge stones, the leaues wherof be lyke to long heares. It is also callyd Barba petrę, it hathe a yelowe floure, and the roote therof is bytter.
Barbatulus, he that hath a yonge berde.
Barbus, & barbo, a fyshe callyd a barbyll.
Barce, a citye in Libia, also an other citye called Ptolomais.
Bardesanes, was an excellent astronomer.
Bardiacus, a certeyne garment.
Baris, baridos, vel baridis, a bote in Egypt, wherin they caried ded bodies to burieng.
Bariona, idem quod filius columbę, the Culuers sonne. It was the surname of saynte Peter

The additions.   B ante D & E.

Peter the apostell.

Barnacida, a garmēt that childern did wear.

Martialis. Barrus, a toothe. Quid tibi vis mulier, nigris dignissima barris: what woldest thou haue woman, that arte worthy blacke tethe?

Basan, a countray beyond the ryuer of Jordane in Judea, which was diuyded to two of the Trybes: whyche may be interpreted moste fertile and fatte.

Martialis. Bascanda, a certayn vessel, whiche came out of Englande, whan it was callyd Britayn.

Basilea, a citie in Germanye.

Basilia, an Ile in the northe occean see.

Plaut. in capt. Basilicæ edictiones, the kynges ordynaunce or commaundementes.

Plautus in Trinūmo. Basilica facinora, actes or gestes of kynges.

Basilica nux, a wall nutte.

Plautus in Persa. Basilicè agere, to do a thinge royally.

Basilicus, a certayne chaunce at dyce.

Plautus in Curcu. Basilides, a certayne heretike, whiche affirmed to be. CCClxv. heuens.

Basilidiani, the folowers of Basilides.

Bassaris, ridis, a prieste of Bacchus.

Bat, is a worde that is spoken to one, whan we wyl haue hym spcke no more, as peace or huysht.

Batauia, a countraye in Germanye, callyd Hollande.

Batauus, an Hollander, or man of Hollande.

Batiochus, a lyttell potte, out of the whiche wyne is poured at the tablel

Batrachion, an herbe, whiche I do suppose is that whiche is cōmonly called goldknap, or crowefoote. It is also callyd of Democritus Chrisanthemon, for it hathe a flowre as yelowe as golde, and the leafe is somewhat lyke vnto parcily, but that it is moche greatter.

Battologia, idem quod multiloquium, moche talke or speche, clatterynge.

Iosephus. Batus, is a measure for lycour amonge the Hebrues, whiche conteyned lxii. measures of Athenes, callyd Sextarios, euery Sextarius contaynynge xviii. ounces, which amounteth to foure score and xiii. li. of englyshe galons.

B ANTE D, & E.

BDelium, is a tree growyng in Arabia & Scithia, also a gumme commynge of the same tree, lyke to waxe, but clere as gumme, within vnctuous or fatte, verye swete of sauour, whan it is rubbed or burned, and bytter in taste.

Bebrytia, a coūtray callid the gret Phrigia.

Bebrytius, a, um, & bebrix, bebricis, of the countray of great Phrigia.

Bebritium, seu Bebriacum, a towne in Italye betwene Cremona and Verona.

Beelphegor, a gapynge ydoll.

Beelsephon, lorde of the northe, an ydol set vp in the places of espiall.

Beelsebub, an ydoll callyd god of flyes.

Beemoth, the deuyll, and signifieth a beast.

Belbus, a beast callyd also Hiena.

Belge, people of Gallia, betwene the riuers of Ryne, Marne, and Seyn, and stretchith to the northwest see, in the whiche are now conteyned the countrays of Brabant, Flāders, Holland, Ghelder, part of Friseland, Gulyke, Hennow, Pycardy, part of Champayne, the great forest of Arden, the cities of Acon, Colayn, Triere, Rheines.

Belial, the deuyll, whiche is interpreted Apostata, without yoke.

Bellatula, lyttell swete harte. *Plautus.*

Belliatus, ta, tum, beautified. *Plautus in Ruden.*

Belle, welle.

Belle se habet, he dothe or fareth well.

Bellerophontes, seu Bellerophon, was the sonne of Glaucus kynge of Ephyra, who beinge a man of moche beautie and prowes was ardātly beloued of Stenobea, the wife of Pretus king of Ephyra, next after Glaucus, and whan she desyred him to committe adulterie with her, he fearynge the vengeance of Jupiter god of hospitalitie, and remembrynge the frendshyp shewed to hym by her husbande, refused her, and dyd put hyr away from him, whiche she disdaynyng, and beinge in a woode rage, accused hym to her husbande, that he had rauyshed her, but he like a sober man wolde nat than flee hym in his owne house, but delyueringe to him letters to his wyues father, sent hym into Licia, where he than reigned, who perceyvynge therby the mynde of Pretus, encouraged Bellerophon, to distroy the two mōsters callid Solymos and Chymera, and sent him therto that he mought be slayn vnder the colour of a valiaunt enterprise, but he acheuyng it nobly, returned with honor. *Note here the malyce of harlots.*

Bellica, was a pyllour in the temple of Bellona, callyd goddesse of battayle, where they vsed, whanne warres were proclaymed, to cast a Jauelyn.

Bellicrepa, a certayne fourme of daunsynge in harneyse.

Bellator equus, a horse of warre.

Bellatrix, tricis, a woman valyant in warres.

Belligero, rare, to make warre.

Bellona, callyd goddesse of battayle.

Bellis, seu bellium, the white dayspe, callyd of some the Margarite, in the northe it is callyd a Banwort. It is also a fyshe with a longe beake lyke a crane, whiche is callyd of some a kckehorne.

Bellouaci, people of Beauuosyne in France

Bellum

Cice, Atti. Bellum merum loquitur, he speaketh oonely of warre.
Belon, the name of a citie & riuer in Spaine.
Beluosus, a, um, full of monsters of the see.
Belluatus, ta, tum, paynted or kerued with great beastes.
Belluata tapetia, Tapistrye wroughte with great beastes.
Belus, the fyrste kynge of Assiria, father of Ninus, and it signifieth the sonne. it is also a ryuer in Syria, which hath sande of the nature of glasse, whiche it casteth vppe. also it torneth all other mettall that commeth into it, into glasse.
Bembina, a towne by the forest called Nemeus. Bembinatus, of that towne or woode.
Benacus, a great lake in Lumbardy.
Bene accipere aliquem, to entreate one well, or entertayne hym.
Bene acceptus, well entertayned.
Plautus. Bene agitur, the thynge is wel done.
Bene ambulato, god be with the.
Bene audire, to be well spoken of.
Bene conuenire inter eos, they agreed welle to gether.
Plinius. Bene cogitare de aliquo, to haue a good opinion of one.
Plautus in Pseud. Bene curare ætatem, to lyue pleasantly.
Bene hercle denuncias, thou tellyst me good tydynges.
Plautus in Trinum, Plaut Benedico, dixi, dicere, to prayse, to say well.
Benedicé, an aduerbe, signifieng in praysing or saying wel. Cum illiciebas me ad te blande et benedicé: whan thou dyddiste trayne me vnto the with plesant wordes and praisynge of me.
Benefacio, cere, to do well.
Benefactum, it is well done.
Benefacta, Benefytes, pleasures.
Beneficiū, a benefite, a plesure, or good torne.
Beneficentia, is not onelye lyberalitie in gyuing of money, or possessions, or other like thynges, but also in helpynge a man with counsayle, solicitation, or other labour.
Plautus in Rude. Bene ferre gratiam, to do pleasure to one.
Plautus in Epidic. Bene habere, to behaue me or hym well.
Bene hoc habet, this matter commeth well to passe.
Bene longus sermo, a very longe tale.
Bene magnus, very great.
Bene mane, very tymely.
Bene mereri, to do pleasure to one.
Bene multi, very many.
Bene nummatum marsupium, a purse wel stored with money.
Bene nummatus homo, a well monyed man.
Bene successit, it came well to passe.
Bene uale, farewell, adewe.
Bene ualere, to be in good helthe.

Bene uertāt dij, god turne it to good: I pray god brynge it well to passe.
Bene uiuere, to make good chere.
Beneuolens, beneuolent, he that loueth well an nother.
Benigna terra, a grounde that is fertile.
Benigné, an aduerbe, whiche signifieth curteysly, graciously, bounteously.
Benignitas, curteysie, lyberalitie, gentylnes.
Berecyntus, a mountayne and citie in Phrigia, where Cybele, callid the mother of the goddis was chiefely honoured.
Berecyntia, callid the mother of goddis.
Bersabe, a citie in Iudea, callyd also Puteus iuramenti, the pytte of the othe, where Abraham dwellid, whiche is the confynes of the lande of beheft.
Berillus, a stone whiche is verye clere, and somewhat inclynynge to a grene colour. it is not that, whiche we commonly do calle Berall, in drynkynge cuppes, but it is rather that, whiche we do call chriftall, whiche beinge wrought into squares, hathe in them a glymse of a lyght grene.
Beta, an herbe callyd Beetes.
Bethania, a towne two myles from Hierusalem, on the side of the mounte Oliuete.
Bethel, a citie in Samaria, where the people dwelled whiche were callyd Iebusei.
Bethleem, the citie of Dauyd the prophet, where he was borne and dyed, where alsoo our sauiour Christe Iesu was borne: there also dyed Rachel the wyfe of Iacob the patriarche. it was assigned to the tribe of Iuda, and was distant from Hierusalem. vi. miles, and was firste called Euphrata, and signifyeth in the hebrewe tongue, the howse of breadde.
Bethsaida, or Bethesda, was a great ponde in Hierusalem, wherin the priistis washed the shepe, whiche shuld be sacrifised, and may be interpreted the house of cattell. It was also the name of a towne, where Peter & Phylyp the apostels were borne.
Bethsamis, a citie in Galilee, where Christe dyd many myracles.
Bethsamite, people of Bethsamis.
Bethsura, & Bethsure, a stronge fortresse of the Iewes.
Beticatus, he that weareth a black or broune garment.
Beticus, ca, cum, blacke or browne.
Betica, a prouynce or countray in Spayne, callyd nowe Granado.
Betis, a ryuer in Spayne by Granado.
Betonica, an herbe callyd Betayne.
Betonica altilis siue coronaria, I suppose hit to be Gyllofers.
Betphage, a towne in Iudea, and may be interpre-

The additions. B ante D & E.

terpreted the house of a mouth, or a iawe.
Betula, a tree, called birche.

¶ B ANTE I.

Bixon, wheate whiche is hard to be beaten out of the huskes.
Bias antis, was one of the vii. wise men of Grece, and was gouernour of the citie called Priene, and was very rigorouse in iustice agaynst ill men, and defended his contray longe agaynste outwarde hostilitie: at the last the towne being taken, and the people fleinge aware, and carienge with them suche treasure as they had, he went quietly out of the towne, leuyng all his substance behynde hym: and whan he was demaunded, why that he onelye caryed nothynge with hym, he aunswered: I cary al with me that is myne owne, meanynge therby, that his wysedome and vertue were his propre goodes, al other thynges were the goodes of fortune, & by her appoynted to them that mought catche them, but wysedome & vertue were constante, and mought by no man be taken from hym.
Bibisia, bybbynge.
Biblio, blere, to make a sowne as a pot doth, whan drynke is drawen into it.
Bibliographus, a wryter of bokes.
Bibitur. Mature ueniunt, discumbitur, fit sermo inter cos, et inuitatio vt græco more biberetur, They come at the tyme appoynted, & there was among them talkynge and quaftynge, that euery man mought drynke after the Greekes facion.

Ci. in Ver. act. 3.

B ANTE. L.

Blandiloquentulus, a pleasant speaker.
Blandè, graciousely, amorousely, flateryngely.
Blanditer, idem.
Blandicia, flatery, pleasaunt motion, intysement by wordes.
Blapsigonia, losse of generation, proprelye in bees.
Blatio, tiui, tire, to speke or talke lyke a fole, or without any purpose or reson, to bable.
Blatero, ronis, a babbler, he that talketh to noo pourpose.
Blattaria, an herbe callyd Woleyn.
Blatteus, a, um, purple.
Blitteus, ea, eum, vnsauery.

Plautus in Trinumo.

moleyn

B ANTE O.

Boa, is also a sicknes, wherin the body is full of redde blysters.
Boalia, playes made for the helthe of oxen and kyne.
Boaria, an herbe callyd a clote or burre.
Boca, uel Bocas, a fyshe, whiche hathe his backe as it were paynted with sondrye colours, Iouius saythe and affirmeth, that he is taken in all costes in greate sculles, nat withstandynge I do nat yet fynde his name in englyshe.
Bœbis, a lake in Thessaly.
Bogud, a towne in Affrike, alsoo the name of a kynge.
Bolus, a throw or cast at dyse, also a draught with a net in waters, it is also a morsell.
Bombax, an aduerbe spokē of him, that setteth nought by that whiche is spoken, as one wolde say, whanne he is rebuked of a faute, And what than? or tushe, I care not for that.
Bomolochus, a common scoffar, or he that susteyneth all vyllanie for to gette money. It was also taken for a boye, that stode at the aulters end, to stele away the candels.
Bona caduca, the goodes of theym that be damned, goodes escheted.
Bona dea, was she that some callyd fatua, or fauna, of whom Uarro writeth, that in her lyfe neuer man did see her but her husbād, nor herde hir named.
Bonæ ædes, a substanciall house.
Bona dicere, to reporte well.
Bona fide dicere, to say truely and playnly.
Bona pars, the more parte.
Bona uerba quæso, say well I pray you.
Boni frugi, honest, of good condicions.
Bonaria, the calmenes of the see.
Boreæ, Iasper stones.
Borsyrites, a kynde of olyue, hauynge many boughes, white & spotted with sāguine.
Bosra, a citie of Idumea.
Botytillus, a lyttell cluster of grapes.

Plautus in pseudolo.

Terentius in Andria.

B, ANTE R.

Brachicatalecton, where oone syllable lacketh at the ende of a verse.
Brachicalecticum carmen, a verse lat kynge one syllable or mo.
Breuiculus, a lyttell shorte man.
Breuiter, shortly. Breuis, idem.
Bryonthalassion, or Marinum, a thinge growynge on the rockes, wheron the salte water beateth, somewhat lyke to mosse, and is called of the northern men slanke.
Bryonia, a wilde vine, hauynge redde berries, & the leaues more rough thā of a vine.
Britanica, an herbe lyke greatte sorelle, but blacker, thycker, and therwith mosye, the roote blacke and litell, and in tasting strat neth the tounge.

Bro=

Bromus, one of the names of Bacchus.
Bronchocela, a waxinge kernell.
Bronteus, the surname of Jupiter.
Brupeo, ere, old writers vsed for stupeo, stupere, to be abashed.

B ANTE V.

Bva, the word of yonge children whan they aske for drynke, with vs they vse to saye Bumme.
Bubula, Befe.
Bubonocele, where the bowell is braste by the share of a man toward his priuy membres.
Bucea, a thynne huske in a beane within the hulle.
Bucerum pæcus, an herde of rother beastes
Bucolicū carmen, a poeme made of herdmē.
Bulbine, nes, scalions.
Bullula, a lyttell water bell or bobill.
Buphonum, an herbe, wherof if catell eate, they do dye of a griefe in theyr throte.
Buphthalmon, an herbe, called also Cotula fetida, and is lyke to camomyll, but it grow with more vpright, maywede.
Buprestis, a fly lyke to a blacke bytel, but he hath lenger legges, whiche if a beast doth eate, he swelleth, and therwith dyeth.
Burbarus, a fyshe, whiche by the descriptiō of Paulus Iouius, semeth to be a Carp.
Burrum, a depe redde colour.
Busicon, a great figge.
Bustuarij, sworde players, whiche went before the ded corpsis whan they were borne to be burned.
Buteo, onis, a bussarde.
Buttubata, a trifle of no value.
Buxeus, a, um, of boxe.

C, ANTE A.

BY HIM SELFE, sygnyfyeth Caius, the propre name of a man, and therfore is ioyned with an other name, as C. Iul. Cæsar, Caius Iulius Cæsar.
Cl. signifieth Claudius.
Cabala, a tradicion of the Iewes, lefte amonge them by Moyses without writyng, but from the father to his sonne, and so cōtinually in their generation, wherein is included the vnderstandynge as welle of the secretes of nature, as the mysticalle sence, included in the wordes of holy scripture.
Cabus, a mesure of the hebrues, containing two sextarios and a half. vi. ounces, and. iii. drammes of Athenes measure, whyche amounteth to foure pounde, thre ounces, and thre drammes.
Cacaturio, to desyre to go to the stole.
Cachexia, a spyce of a consumption, which procedeth of an yll disposition of the body, and the body and vysage is therwith verye leane, and yll coloured.
Cacia, viciositie, or that whiche we cōmonly do calle, a faute in a thynge.
Cacoblepa, a lyttell beaste in Egypte in the bankes of the ryuer of Nilus, whiche hath suche venenosytie in his eien, that who that beholdeth them, dieth incontinent.
Cacoethe, a vyce or sore ingendred in oone frome his infancie, harde to be recouered or curyd.
Cacologia, ylle speche.
Cacologus, an yll speaker.
Cacophaton, is an yll fourme of speakyng, or where the wordes do not sowne wel and conueniently.
Cacozelus, an yll folower or imitatour.
Cacus, a gyaunte, whome Hercules slewe in Italye.
Cadiscus, a vesselle, wherinto are gathered scedules, billes, or lottes, where thynges ar done by a consent of many counsaylours, or of the people.
Cadmites, a stone, whiche hath lyttell blue sparkes aboute it.
Cadmus, the name of a kyng of Phenicia, whiche buylded Thebes: by whome some men do suppose, that dyuers of the Greke letters were founde.
Cadit animus, the courage faylethe, or is abated.
Cadere, to be slayne. *Plautus in Amphit.*
Caduceus, the rodde, whiche Mercurius dyd alway beare in token of peace.
Caduceator, ambassadour or heraulte at armes, sent to demaunde peace.
Caduca, thynges that wyll shortly peryshe or decaye, olde wryters vsed them for significations of that whiche shulde happen.
Caduca hereditas, an inheritaunce whiche is fallen in escheate, for lacke of heyres. *Ci. in phil.*
Caducus labor, labour loste.
Caducæ literæ, letters whiche wyl be shortly put out. *Plinius.*
Caduci tituli, honours and dignities, which endure but a lyttell while. *Pli. in pan.*
Caduci, they whiche are decessed. *Vergili. 7.*
Caducor, ceris, duci, to be ouerthrowen.
Cadulæ, the dryppyng of fleshe rosted.
Cadus, a vessell contayynge the same measure that Amphora dothe.
Cæa, an yle in the see called Aegeum. It is also called Coa, where sylke wormes were
fyrst

The additions. C ante A.

fyrst founde, the countrey of Hippocrates, the prynce of Phisitions.

Cēus uel Cous, a, um, of that Ile called Cēa or Coa.

Lucreti9. 2 Plautus in pseudolo. Cēcigeni, they whiche are borne blynde.

Cēca die, Eme die cēca hercle oliuum, id ne̅ dito oculata die: bye oyle oliue good chepe and sell it agayne dere, orels, bye oyle for dayes, and sell it againe for redy money.

Cēcus morbus, a siknesse that is hid, or may not be discerned.

Cēcihemorroides, emeraudes or piles, whiche are within the foundement, and do not appere.

Cēca uestigia, where one may not se his way that he rydeth or goeth.

Cēcum uallum, a trenche, which in tyme of warre is pyght priuily with sharpe stakes, which are hydde with brakes or busshes.

Cēcum intestinum, is a bowel, which cometh from the ryghte syde, at the poynt of the houkle bone, and goeth to the left syde in length, and is also called Monoculus.

Cēcitas, blyndnesse, not onely of the bodyly eyes, but also of the mynde.

Cēdes, murdre.

Cic. ad Q. fratrem. Vergil. Cēdere calcibus, to kycke.

Cēditur testibus, he is conuict by witnesse.

Cēdere, to sacrifice. Cēdunt binas de more bidentes: Accordyng to the custome they sacrificed two hoggrelles.

Cēlatus, ta, tum, grauen.

Celestis, te, et hoc celeste, of heuen or heuely.

Celibaris hasta, was the staffe of a Iauelyn, which had ben in the body of one of them, whiche were called gladiatores, and was slayn: with the which staffe the heade of a mayden newe maried was kempt and striken, sygnifieng, that lykewyse as the staffe was stycked faste in the body of hym that was slayne, so shulde she stycke fast, and be ioyned with hym that maried her.

Cælostomia, a vyce in speache, where one speketh inwardely, and maketh rather a sounde than a pronunciatio̅ of his wordes

Plinius. Cælum, the palate or roufe of the mouth.

Cēlipotens, all myghty god.

Cēneus, the surname of Jupiter.

Cēpi, I beganne.

Cēremoniæ, ceremonies.

Cēretē, a citie in Thuscana.

Cēris, a sore lyke an hony combe.

Cēroferarii, they whiche do beare candels in the churche before the crosse in procession, or do any lyke seruice in the churche

Cēroferarium, a candell stycke, wheruppon tapers are sette.

Cēroma, et Ceromatum, an ointment, wherwith wrastelers were annoynted, to make them the more delyuer and stronge.

Cēsim, edgelynge, or with the edge.

Cēsitium, a clene napkyn or handkerchefe.

Cēsura, a cutte, a garse, an incisyon, also in taylyng or caruynge in stone or tymber.

Cēsuratim, briefly, succinctly.

Cætera doctus, lerned in other thynges. **Cice. de na tura deoru̅**

Calamitæ, lyttell grene frogges.

Calasastri, boyes whyche doo synge with a shyll voyce.

Calatores, seruauntes whyche are alwaye callyd for.

Calcaria fornix, a lyme kylle.

Calcata, a house whiche is gargetted.

Calcearium, a showe.

Calceatus, tus, idem.

Calceatus, ta, tum, shodde.

Calceare, to show an horse or mule.

Chalcos, seu æreola, the xxxvi. parte of a Dramme. **Sueton. in Resp.**

Calculum album adijcere, to approue or allowe a thynge.

Calculum ponere, to yelde accompte. **Plinius in panegyr.**

Calculosus, a, um, grauelly, or stony.

Caldariæ, hote bathes.

Caldarium, a cauldron wherin water is het.

Calendæ, the fyrst day of euery moneth.

Cales, a towne in Fraunce.

Calim olde writers vsed for Clam, priuily.

Callaria, a cole whitynge, meane betwene a haddocke and a whytinge.

Callipolis, a citie in Thracia.

Calleo, lui, lēre, to perceyue, to knowe by longe experience.

Calliblephara, medicines to make heres to growe in the chekes or browes.

Calliblepharon, a medicine for the eies, specially whan the eie lyddes doo cleaue to gyther.

Calliscere, to waxe harde, proprelye in the skynne and floshe.

Callitrichum, an herbe called maiden heare.

Callum obducere, to harden, to make to indure labours or peynes.

Calones, shoes of wodde. Also scullyons and boyes, whiche do folowe an hooste to cary baggage, wodde, coles, or other like thynges.

Calophanta, a mocker.

Calorificus, ca, cum, that whiche heateth or maketh a thinge hotte.

Calotechnus, a good workeman.

Calpar, a tunne.

Caltha, an herb callid marigoldis or ruddis

Calthula, a garment of the colour of Marygoldes.

Caluaria, the hole heed of a man or beaste. It was also a comon place of buriall. some men do suppose, that it was the place where
Adam

The additions.   C ante A.

Adam the fyrste man was buried.
Caluaster, a man somwhat balde.
Caluor, ueris, ui, to be dysappoynted.
Calx, calcis, masculyne gender, the hele.
Calx, the feminyne gender, lyme made of stones burned, it is taken somtyme for the ende of a thynge.
Calydon, a citie in Grece.
Camarina, a stynking herbe, the ayre wherof prouoketh one to vomyte.
Cammarus, a fishe callid a creuyse, specially of the freshe water, a creuyse de caudoulx.
Camerinam mouere, is a prouerbe spoken to one, signifieng that he hurteth hym self, which proceded of a fenne so callid which being dried vp, there hapned a great pestilēce, wherfore the peple adioynyng, asked of Apollo, if they shuld make it drye for euer, who answered, Ne moueas camerinā, as he shoulde saye, styrre no myschyefe to thy selfe.
Camuri boues, oxen or kyne, with crooked hornes.
Canaan, the sonne of Cam, the son of Noe, of whome commeth Cananeus.
Canalitium aurum, golde dygged in pyttes.

Iosephus in antiqui. Canan, the countray callyd Arabye.
Canança, a part of Siria, now callid Iudea.
Cananitis regio, idem.
Canaria, an yle in the see callyd Atlanticū, nygh to the fortunate yles.
Canarius, a, um, pertaynynge to dogges.
Canatim, an Aduerbe, sygnyfyenge lyke a dogge.
Cancellarius, in the olde tyme was taken for a scrybe or notarye, nowe it is callydde a chauncellour.
Cancellatim, lattyse wyse.

Cicero de lege agraria. Cancelli, lyttell crabbes of the see.
Canere sibi, to speake for his owne profite.
Canere sibi & musis, to synge or wryte for his owne pleasure, and for theym that doo fauour hym, nothing caring for any other.
Canta, olde wryters vsed for cantata.
Cantito, tare, to synge often.

Plautus in Trinūmo. Cantare, to monysshe or exhorte. Hęc dies noctesq; tibi canto ut caueas, This I exhort the daye z nyght, that thou mayste beware.
Cantatio, a syngynge.
Cantator, a synger.
Capere rationem, to fynde the meane.
Rationem cœpi ut & amanti obsequerer, & patrem non offenderem, I founde the mean to please my louer, and not withstandyng I dyspleased not my father. also to knowe the cause why, Scio tibi esse hoc grauius multo, ac durius cui sit: uerum ego haud minus ęgrē patior id qui nescio, nec rationem capio, nisi quod tibi bene ex animo uolo, I knowe wel

Terent. in Heautont.

that to you, whom the thynge toucheth, hit is moche more displeasant and greuous: but yet it greuith me no lesse, I can not tel why, but onely bycause I loue you.
Capere rationem oculis, to iudge by syghte. Hi loci sunt atq; hę regiones, quę mihi ab hero sunt meo demonstratę, ut ego oculis rationem capio, These are the places z stretes, that my mayster shewed me, as farre as myn eyes can iudge, or as farre as I canne perceyue.

Plautus in Pseud.

Capere uoluptatem, to delyte.
Capere uersoriam, to chaunge a pourpose, to tourne saylle, to doo contrarye to that he intended.
Capere usuram corporis vxoris alterius, To commytte aduoultrie with an nother mannes wyfe.

Plautus in Amphitri.

Capidulum, a hoode.
Capillatia uela, be clothes of heare.
Capito, tonis, a see fyshe, greatter cōmonly than a Myllet is, whiche as I suppose, we do call a base.
Capitulo, lare, to diuide by chapiters.
Capnion, an herbe callyd Fumitorie, it is also callyd Capnos.

Plinius li. 26.

Capo, a fyshe callyd a Gurnarde.
Caprilis, le, of a gote.
Caprillus, la, lum, idem.
Caprotina, a surname of Iuno.
Capsis, for cape si vis, take it and thou wylt.
Captare impudicitię, to lye in awayt to take one in the acte of lecherie.
Captare cœnam, to get a supper of fre cost.

Martialls.

Captare sermonem, to harken priuyly what menne talke.
Captatio, a purchase.
Carba, a wynde that bloweth frome the Southe.
Carbunculatio, is a faut in vynes, whan the clusters of grapes are nat sufficiently couered with leaues, by the whyche occasyon, they be wythered and dried.
Carbunculus, is also a kynde of erthe, the whiche with the heate of the sonne, waxeth soo hotte, that it burneth the rotes of herbes and trees.
Carchedonius, a kynde of Carbuncle stones, whiche in the house seme of purple colour, abrode in the aire they ar fyrie, against the sonne they sende oute sparkles, and yf waxe be touched with them, it melteth.
Carcinus, a crabbe.
Carabus, a fysshe callyd a lopster, lyke to a Creuyse, but that he is greater, and is red whan he is alyue.
Chalchis, a fysshe of the see, of the kynde of Turbutte.
Charax, a Fysshe, callydde alsoo Dentix,

li   with

The additions.   C ante A.

with teethe standinge out of his lippes, & is a brode fysshe, and somewhat redde, with a chaungeable colour.
Cardomine, an herbe callyd water cressis.
Cardopos, an huche or coffar, wherin bread is layde, In the Northe countraye hit is callyd an arke.
Carduus, a thystell.
Caricus, ca, cum, of the countrey of Caria.
Carides, a fysshe callydde Pranes, lyke to shrympes.
Cariem trahere, to waxe rotten, or to be putrified or vinnewed.
Cariophillon, a spice callyd cloues.
Carnus, na, num, fatte.
Caros, excesse of meate or drynke. also an herbe and sede callyd carwayes.
Carpere iter, to take his iourney.
Carpocrates, an heretyke, whiche denyed that god made the worlde.
Carpophyllon, a tree, which hath leues like to laurell.
Carthallum, a baskette.
Caryopos, the iuyce of a nutte.
Carynus, na, num, of a nutte: as oleum carynum, the oyle of nuttes.
Carystę, & Carystos, an Ile in the see called Euboicum, wherin is plentie of marbyll of dyuers colours.
Carysteus, a, um, of that yle.
Casabundus, da, dum, fallynge often.
Caseale, a stable.
Casner, in the Oske tunge is an olde man.
Casito, tare, to falle often.
Cassinum, an olde market place.
Cassiterus, tynne.
Cassiterides, certayne yles, wherein tynne is dygged.
Cassutha, a wede that windeth about hempe or lynne, callyd Doddar.
Catabasis, the sonne sette.
Catachresis, a fygure, wherby the proprietie of a worde is abused: as, Facies simillima lauro, where facies oonely belongeth to a man, and not to a tree, although it doth signifye there a similitude or fygure.
Cathysta, a garment close all aboute.
Catacrysis, a condemnation.
Catagrapha, ymages lokyng diuers wayes, and in dyuers fourmes.
Catalepsis, occupation or deprehencion.
Catalexis, a fynysshynge of a thynge.
Catalyma, refection, also an ynne.
Catamidio, are, to sette one vp with a paper on his heed to be mocked or rebuked for some offence, as they vse to doo with men periured, or with forgers of euidences.
Catapultarium pilum, a bolte.
Catatyposis, a fygure, where one thynge is described by an nother.
Cato, wyse. Also the name of a noble Senatour of Rome.
Catoblepas, a beaste full of poyson, callyd a Basylyske.
Catillo, are, to eate lyke a glutton.
Catorthoma, the ryght exercise of vertue.
Catulinus, na, num, of a catte.
Caudece, lytell coffers of wyckers, or a iūket, wherin eles are taken in ryuers.   Plautus in Rude.
Caudeus, a, um, of the stemme of a tree.
Caudex, is a dulle brayned felowe, a dulle hedde.
Caudicalis, ale, pertaynynge to the stemme of a tree.
Caudicariæ naues, shyppes made of thicke plankes.
Cauere alicui, to gyue counsaylle to oone in matters of lawe, or concernynge contractes.
Cauere, with accusatiue case, sygnifyeth to byd to beware.
Cauere sibi ab aliquo, to take a quytaunce or other discharge for the payment of money or delyueraunce of any thynge. At uero, inquam, tibi ego Brute non soluā, nisi prius a te cauero, amplius eo nomine neminem, cuius petitio sit, petiturum, Truely (sayde I) Brutus I wyll not pay the, excepte I haue fyrst a quyttance of the, that thou shalte nat eftesones demaunde it of hym, of whome thou moughtest aske it.   Cf. in Bru.
Cauere capite, to be bounde body for body.
Cauere, to prouyde. Quid isti caueam? B. Vt reuehat domum, whatte shall I prouyde for hym? B. one to brynge hym home.   Plinius li. 34. plautus in Bacch.
Caueri, to be taken hede of.
Caueares hostię, & caug, were partes of the beastes nexte to the tayle, to be sacryfysed for the byshoppes.
Cauillatio, a cauillation, a subtyl forged tale
Cauillor, lari, to speake in mockage.
Caulias, the iuyce of colewortes myxt with bran, and being tossed togider, was brought into the fourme of a paste.
Causam accipere, to take the matter in hād. also to take an excuse.
Causam capere, to take an occasion.
Causam dicere, to aunswere vnto that, whiche is layde to his charge.
Caussam dicere, to saye contrarye, to deny. Hoc si secus reperies, nullam causam dico, quin mihi & parentum, et libertatis apud te deliquio fiet, If thou doest fynde hit other wyse, I wylle not saye contrarye, but that it is at thy pleasure, that I shall lose both my parentes and lybertie.   Plautus in capt.
Caussam dicere ex uinculis, to aunswere in warde, or beinge a prisoner.

Caussam

The additions. C ante E.

Terent. in Heauto.	Causa mea, for my sake. Syro ignoscas uolo, quę mea causa fecit, I wyll that ye forgyue Syrus all that he hath done, for my sake.
Liuius.	Caussas nectere, to fayne matters.
	Caussam orare, to pleade.
	Caussam quęrere, to seke an occasyon.
Cice. Atti.	Caussam sustinere, to beare the blame.

¶ C ANTE E.

Sueton. de claris grā.	Cedere creditoribus, is properly where one not being able to pay his dettes, leaueth all his goodes or landes to his credytours.
Plautus in pseudolo.	Cedere ex transuerso, to go sydelynge lyke a Crabbe.
Plautus in capt.	Cedere ad factum, to come to effecte.
Colu. 12.	Cedere pro, to be in the stede of an other thynge. Nam pro pulmentario cedit sicuti ficus, For it is in steede of the meate, lyke as fygges be.
Pli. epi. 50	Cedentes capilli, heares hāgyng down right
	Cedrelate, tes, a great Cedre tree.
	Cedrium, certayne kynde of pytche founde in Siria.
	Cedrinus, na, num, of a cedre tree.
Cic. de Se.	Cedunt dies, the dayes passe awaye.
	Celatus, ta, tum, hydde.
	Celebratus, brata, bratum, moche spoken of, or haunted.
	Celebris locus, a place moche haunted and knowen.
Accius. Sisenna.	Celeranter, for celeriter, hastily or quyckly.
	Celeratim. idem.
	Celeres, olde wryters vsed for Equites, horsemenne.
Plautus in Merca.	Celeris copia. Date di quęso coueniundi mihi eius celerem copiam, God graunt that I may very shortly mete with hym.
Varro.	Censere, to be angrye. Ne uobis censeam, si ad me referretis, Lest I wolde be angrye, if ye tolde me.
Plautus in Stico.	Censere, to speake or tell. G. Quid grauare? censeas. Telle me, what is that, that greueth the?
Plinius. 8.	Censeri, to be had in estymation, or to be set by, also to be meruayled at.
	Censio, onis, a price, aduyse, or opinion.
	Censoria nota, the rebuke or checke of the maister of maners.
	Censoria animaduersio, was a punyshement of them, whiche were of yll maners.
	Censorius, a, um, pertaynyng to them, whiche had ouersyghte of the maners of the people, whyche were callyd Censores.
	Centaurium, an herbe, wherof there be two kyndes: The great, whyche apotycaries doo call Reuponticum: And the lasse, whiche is callyd Centorye, Alsoo felterrę, & Febrifugia.

	Centenariae coenae, were suppers on the whiche by a lawe callid Licinia, was bestowid but one hundred of the brasyn coyne callyd Asses.
	Centesimae ursurae, were gaines of the hundred peny value of euery thynge, for euery moneth lone.
	Centesimus, ma, mum, the hundred, as Centesima pars, the hundred parte.
	Centralis, le, that which is sette in the very myddes of a thynge.
	Centurupe, a feld in Sicile, wherof is Centurupinum crocum.
	Cephalocrustes, a worme, whyche is in the leaues of a peache tree.
	Cepa, pę, & cepe indeclinabile, an oynion.
	Cepas edere, to eate onions, was a prouerbe spoken of them, whiche do seme to wepe, or doo wepe often.
	Cephenes, vnprofytable bees, which make no honye, but onely with the multitude of them, do kepe warme the yonge bees.
	Cera, wexe, also wexed tables.
	Ceramion, the same mesure that amphora is
	Cerea pruna, wheate plummes.
	Cereus, a, um, softe, also fatte.	Horatius.
	Cerinum, a garment of the colour of wax.	Actius.
	Cerium, a soore lyke an hony combe.
	Ceritus, madde.
	Cerinthe, an herbe hauing the taste of waxe and hony togither.
	Cerinthus, the meate of bees, whyche is founde in hony combes, seperate from the honye, whiche is in taste bytter and is also moyste.
	Cernere, to deuyse togyther, or talke oone with an nother. Verecundari neminem apud mensam decet, nam ibi de diuinis atque humanis cernitur, Noo manne oughte to be abasshed at the table, for there men doo deuise or talke of matters concernyng as well god as manne.	Plautus in Trinamo.
	Cernere, to syfte or range floure of corne.	Plinio. 18.
	Cerno animo, I doo foresee or consyder before.
	Cernulus, he that is busye to fynde faute in an nother man.	Hier. con. Ruffinum.
	Cernus, nus, nui, a certayne showe.
	Ceroma, oyle myrt with wex, also the place where wrastlers were annoynted.	Cic. in ca.
	Certatio, debate, stryfe, study, prouocacion.
	Certo, tare, to stryue or contende.
	Certi, certayne other.	Cicero. Salust.
	Certi homines, sure men and faithfull.
	Certę opes, ryches that is permanent.
	Certum habere, to knowe surely.
	Ceua, a lyttelle cowe that gyuethe moche mylke.	Ci. ad Att.

li ij   Certo.

Certo, without doubte.
Ceruchus, a cabyn in the hyghest parte of a shyppe.
Cessare, to be ydelle.
Cestus, a gyrdell, wherwith the housbande dydde gyrde his wyfe, whiche was sette with lyttell studdes.
Ceu, as it were.

C ANTE H.

Hære, for salue.
Chalasis, the knotte wherwith womens garmentes were knytte about they neckes.
Chalastricum nitrum, saltepeter, whiche is very pure, and lyke to salte.
Chalcantum, a kynde of ynke lyke to brasse.
Chameleuce, ces, an herbe growynge by riuers, hauynge leaues lyke a poplar, but moche greatter. *(Plinius, 24.)*
Chamemirsyne, is a busshe or tree, whiche hath sharpe pryckes in the leaues, & redde bearies cloustred, I suppose it to be that, whiche is callyd holy or holme.
Chamitterę, & chamitteridę, lyttell ymages, made folowynge a greatter ymage.
Chaniscus, the hyndermost part of a shyp, by the whiche the anker hangeth.
Chanona, a tarte or marchepayne, or other lyke delycate thynge.
Chaonides, wolfes that do slee hartes.
Charchesia, a cuppe longe and smalle in the myddell, and full of handels.
Charisma, matis, a grace or speciall benefite.
Charistium, a grene marble.
Charmesinum, a kynde of sylke, which deluteth the beholders. I thinke it be crimsin.
Charopus, amyable, pleasant, or hauynge a good grace.
Chartula, a lyttell leafe of paper.
Chelonalopices, I suppose to be the byrdes whiche we do call Barnakles.
Chenotrophia, a house or place where waterfoule are kepte.
Cheospes, a kynge of Egypt, whyche made the great steple at Memphis, wheron were so many men workynge, that the same king spent only in parcely, oynyons, and garlike, a thousande and thre score talentes, whych if it were the greate talent, it amounted of oure moneye, to CCL.thousande fyue hundred and fyfty poundes.
Chirogylius, an hedgehogge. *(Leuit. 11.)*
Chironomus, a daunser of a moriske.
Choa, a certayn measure. also vessel, wherin was put lycour, whiche was offred to idols.
Chœnix, a mesure conteining xxvii.ounces, which is one Sextarius of Athenes, & a half

Chomer, idem quod Chorus.
Chorocitharista, he that ledethe a daunce, and playeth hym selfe on an instrument.
Chors, tis, a place inclosed, wherin cattelle is kepte, a barton callyd in some place.
Chortales aues, pultrie fedynge abrode in a barton or court of husbandry.
Chorus, siue chomer, a measure of the Hebrues, whiche contayneth tenne tymes as moch as Batus, or Ephi, and amounteth to as moche as one and fourtye measures of Athenes, callyd Medimni, whiche in all maketh two thousand, nyne hundred. xii. pounde of measure, euery pounde being xii.ounces.
Chorus, a measure of grayn, salt, and other lyke thynges, whiche conteyneth as moch as tenne of the measures callyd Medimni Attici, where in euerye Medimnus be. lxxii. Sextarii Attici, Rede in Sextarius. so that hit contayneth of our galons
Chreston, an herbe callyd also cykorie.
Chrysoberillus, a chrystal stone, wherin the colour of golde shyneth.
Chrysoprassus, a stone grene as a leke, hauynge speckes of golde.
Chus, seu choa, a measure contaynyng nine poundes of measure, whiche is
Chytracus, a tryuet or cradel, wheron pottes are sette to boyle meate.

¶ C ANTE I.

Ibum subducere, to take meate away frome one.
Cibum facere, to make redye meate. *(plautus in Truculen.)*
Mane aliquid fiet cibi, There shall be some meate made redy betyme.
Cibi repositi, meate set vp to be kept. *(Quintilia. Ci.tus.q.I Varro.)*
Cibarius panis, raged bred or crybbil bread.
Cibarium uinum, smalle wyne.
Cibatus, tus, tui, vyttayles.
Cicatrico, care, to strike one so that a marke alway remayneth.
Cicatrizo, idem, also to heale a wounde, soo that onely a seame or scarre may appere.
Ciceronianus, he that coueyteth to folowe Cicero in eloquence.
Cicerbita, an herbe callyd Southistell.
Cichorea, & cichoreu, an herb callyd cikory
Cicum, a thynne skynne, whyche is within a Pomegranate.
Cicur, euery beaste or byrde, whyche ones beynge wylde, is made tame.
Cicuro, rare, to make tame.
Ciere, to trouble or make hym angry. Quid negotii est, Pistoclerum Lydus quod herum tam ciet? what is the mattier that Lydus thus troubleth or angreth his maister? *(Plautus.)*

Ciere,

The additions.

Festus. Ciere, is somtyme to name.
Cinabulum, a cradelle.
Cinara, an herbe, whiche some men do suppose to be an artochoke.
Cinifactum, brought into ashes, as thynges whiche are bourned.
Circania, a byrde, whiche in his flyght fetcheth a compasse.
Cirsion, an herbe, which we do cal buglosse.
Circulo, are, to compasse aboute, or to make a cerkle or compasse aboute a thyng.
Circumcidaneus, a, um, cutte rounde about.
Circūcisitum mustum, wine, which after that the grapes are pressed, is taken out of the same grapes, being cut and newe pressed.

Sueton. de claris rhetoribus. Ser. Sul. ad Ciceronē. Circumcise agere, to make an oration by pecis, without comming to the purpose.
Circumcirca, all aboute.
Circumcurso, are, to run hither and thither.
Circundo, dare, to enuyronne or compasse aboute.

Paulus de re iudicata Vlp. de iudiciis. Circunduco, duxi, ducere, to lead one about. It is also to abolysshe or put asyde an acte. Quod si is qui edictum peremptorium impetrauit, absit die cognitionis, tunc circūducendum erit edictum peremptorium. And yf that he that hath optayned the peremptorie decree, be absent the daye whan the matter shuld be determined, than the peremptorie decree is to be dyssolued or abolyshed.

Plautus in Pseud. Circūducere, is sommetyme to deceyue by cautelles.
Plautus ibidem. Circumducere aliquem argento, to get ones money by falsehode.
Plautus in Capt. Circumductus, ta, tum, ledde about.
Circumductio, deceyte.
Circumferre se, to go braggynge about the streetes.

Vergilius. Circumflecto, tere, to turne hither & thyder.
Circumfundo, dere, to caste water or other lycour aboute.

Vergili. Circumfusus, a, um, gathered about, as people whan they desyre to se a thyng. somtime wrapped about lyke an adder or serpent.

Plin. de ussris illusstr. Circumlino, to annoynte aboute.
Circummissus, a, um, sente aboute.
Circummunio, ire, to enuyron strongely, to fortifie with walles or men.

Cicero Circumpedes, lackayes awaytynge at their maisters styrop. also fote men of princis.
plautus. Circumspecto, are, to beholde about.
Circumspectatrix, a woman that beholdeth aboute, or watcheth.
Circumsto, stare, to stande aboute.
Plautus. Circumtego, texi, tegere, to couer al aboute.
Circumuerto, tere, to tourne aboute.
Cirri, be thinges lyke heares about oysters.
Cirratus, he that hath his heares brayded.

Cis paucos dies, within fewe dayes. **Plautus.**
Cis vndiq, in all places aboute.
Cisium, aut cissium, a cart with two wheles.
Cispello, puli, pellere, to kepe out oone that **Plautus in Amphit.** he come nat into the house.
Citta, a pye.
Ciuiliter, lyke a citesyn. Also courtesly, or with good maner.

¶ C ANTE L.

Clauola, seu clabula, a bough or stocke, **Varro.** wherinto a graffe is sette.
Clā me, clā te, I or thou not knowing.
Clam alter alterum, the oone knowyth not of the other.
Clam omnes, no man knowynge or witting. **Plautus in**
Clara pugna, a battayle worthy memorie. **Pseud.**
Claritudo, idē qd claritas, also brute, renome.
Classici, they which in a towne were moste ryche and substanciall.
Classici authores, writers of most estimatiō. **Vergilius.**
Classiarius, a man of warre on the see.
Claudere, to turne about. Claudite nymphę Dictee, nymphę nemorum, iam claudite saltus, Tourne aboute ye goddesses of Dictea, ladyes of the forestes tourne youre daunse aboute.
Clementia æstatis, the tēperatnes of somer. **Plautus in**
Clementer uolo, I am well content. **Stich.**
Clementer tractare, to entreate gentylly or swetely.
Cliduchus, he that beareth a mace.
Clingo, gere, olde writers vsed for cingere to gyrde.
Cliuia, al thīgis hard to be brought to passe. **Festus**
Cloacare, to defyle or pollute.

C ANTE O.

Coaccedo, cedere, to be added to the principall somme.
Coaduno, nare, to assemble.
Coccinatus, he that wereth a scarlet gowne.
Coctona, quynces.
Codicarij naues, shyppes or barges made of thycke plankes.
Codicilli, epistels, sometyme it is taken for **Suetonius** letter patentes of a prince.
Coeli, the part of Siria, that ioyneth to Arabie.
Coenatus, he that hath souped.
Coenatiuncula, a lyttell drinkyng house.
Coenare alienū, to sup at an other māns cost. **Plautus in**
Coenabis hodie magnum malum, thou shalte **persa.** haue thy supper soone in shrewde rest.
Coire in foedera, to make alyance.
Coire societatem, to be famyliar.
Coepio, piui, pere, to begynne. **Plautus,**
Coeptus, ta, tum, begunne. **Cato.**
Coepta, torum, thinges or matters begunne.
Coepto, tare, to begynne.
Coepulonus, a banketter or reueller.

Coer—

The additions.

                        C ante O.

Coercere ignes, to stynte the fyre, whyche burneth a house or other lyke thynge.

Plautus su Mili. Cogitat curas, he thynketh on his matters.

Plautus. Cogitaté, aduysedly. Cogitatum, idem.

Cogere oues, to putte vp the shepe into a stable or folde.

Cogere in ordinem, to sette in order.

Cohæreo, cohęsi, hęrere, to be ioyned, or to cleaue to a thynge, also to come to passe.

Nuptię non cohęrent, The mariage come nat to passe. also to agree togyther.

Cohęres, he that is iointelye heyre with an nother.

Cohibere, to retayne or kepe to hym selfe.

Cic. de Se. Cohibete intra limen, kepe you within the doores.

Plautus in Milite. Cohibere filium, to kepe vnder his sonne.

Plautus in Mercator. Cohibere se, to moderate hym selfe.

Cohibitus, ta, tum, lette, refrayned.

Ter. in He. Cohors, is also a company of seruantes aboute a noble man.

Colina, for culina, a kytchen.

Collabefactari testula, to be banysshed out of the citie by lottes of shelles, as it was vsid in Athenes. Se after Ostracismus.

Collacteus, he that sucketh of the same brest and at the same tyme.

Collatitius, a, um, that whyche is gathered and brought togyther.

Collaudo, are, to prayse with other.

Collegium, a company of them, which haue equall authoritie. also a companye of men whiche be of one mysterie or crafte.

Collibet, & collubet, collibuit, collibitum est, collibére, to lyke, to please. Vtcunq̃ animo collibitum est meo, Euen as it pleaseth me, or lyketh me.

Plautus in Amph. Colligere uestem, to tucke vp his garment.

Colloco, care, to sette in a place.

Plaut. in Aulul. Collocare se in arborem, to klim vp on a tree

Plautus in Amph. Colocare aliquem in soporem, to stryke one in suche wyse that he is amased, and lieth as he were on slepe, or to speake hit more shortly, to laye one aslepe with a stroke.

Plautus in Merca. Colloces te in otium, drawe the to ease.

Collocatus, ta, tum, put or set in some place.

Collocupleto, tare, to enryche.

Colloqui aliquem, to speake to one.

Colloqui alicui, to deuyse or talke with one.

Colloquor, queris, qui, to talke with one, or to talke togyther.

Colluuiaris porcus, an hogge that walloweth in the myre, and there hath meate giuen hym.

Colludo, dere, to play with one, or togither.

Collusor, oris, a playfelowe.

Plautus in Capt. Collus, idem quod collum.

Collybus, money receyued by exchaunge, or in banke, as menne do whiche goo into straunge countrays, delyuering money of this realme, to receyue as moche of another coyne, where he commeth.

Collybistes, & collybiste, he that deliuereth money by exchaunge, a banker.

Collyra, a lofe of breadde, or a bunne.

Colere se, to apparayle hym selfe. *Plautus.*

Colere officium, to do his duetie or indeuor.

Colere pietatem, to haue his parentes in reuerence. *Plautus in Ruden.*

Colere uitam, to lyue.

Coloratus, ta, tum, coloured.

Columbulus, a pygeon.

Columnæ Herculis, are two mountaynes in the see, where menne do entre out of the myddell see into the occean, the one is in Europa by Spayne, the other in Affrica.

Colunus, na, num, of hasyll.

Colutea, the tree callyd Sene, wherof the leaues and coddes are ministred in medicines, to pourge melancoly.

Comedim, olde writers vsed for comedam.

Comest, for comedit, he eateth.

Comessabundus, ouercharged with meate and drynke. *Q. Curti.*

Comessans, idem quod comessor.

Comesse for comedere, to eate.

Commessatio, ryottous bankettynge.

Comessator, a ryottour.

Commemini, I remembred. *Plautus in milite.*

Commeminere, to remember.

Commentariensis, was callyd a gayler.

Commereri culpam, to do an offence. *Pla. in aul.*

Commigro, grare, to go frome one place to dwelle in an nother.

Comminuo, to cutte in smalle pieces.

Commisceo, scui, scere, to myxe togither.

Commiseresco, scere, to haue compassion. *Terentius in Hecyra.*

Commissio, a conferrynge togyther by exercise, as two lerned mens wyttes togyther, or other lyke thynge.

Commissa, confyscations.

Commissus, a, um, commytted to the keping of oone.

Commissum bellum, open warre. *Ti. Liuius.*

Commodare loquelam, to speake. *Plautus in Ruden.*

Commodare operam, to helpe.

Commodare capillum, to kembe his heed, or decke his busshe. *Plautus in Mostel.*

Commodatarius, he that hathe borowed any thynge.

Commodé, well, or to the purpose.

Commodé uerba facere, to speake thynges to the purpose.

Commodé cadere, to happē or succede well or to the purpose.

Commoditas hominis, the facilitie or curteysie of one, the whiche agreeth to any requeste. *Terent. in Adelphis.*

Com-

The additions. C ante O.

Terent. in Eunucho.	Commodum id non est, it maye not be easily done.
Plautus in Asin.	Commoda statura homo, a man of good stature, nor to great nor to lyttell.
Plautus in Mostel.	Commoda et faceta mulier, a pleasaunte and mery woman.
	Commodus capillus, a bushe well decked or kempte.
Idem in Pseud.	Commodus homo, a tractable or reasonable man.
	Commodū obsonare, to vse moderate fare.
	Commodum discesseras heri, cum Trebatius uenit: Ye were scantely departed from me yesterday, whan Trebatius came to me.
Plautus in Pseud. Terentius in Andria.	Commonere aliquem officium suum, to aduertise one what he ought to do.
	Commonere aliquem, to remembre one of a thynge.
	Commonstro, to shewe a thyng that is hyd.
	Commorior, riri, to dye with one.
Plautus in Amphit.	Commoror, rari, to abyde with one: also to dwell in a place for a tyme: also to tary one that is goinge. Male facis, properantem qui me cōmorare, sol abit: Thou doest naught to tary me, sens I go in hast, and the sonne is nowe sette.
Plautus in Amphitri.	Commorari, to cause one to tary. An te auspitium commoratum est? an tempestas continet, qui non abisti ad legiones ita vt dudum dixeras? Did the token shewed by the byrdes, cause the to tary? or elles the wether kepe the backe, that thou wentest not vnto the army as thou saydest a whyle a go that thou woldestest?
	Commossem, for commouissem.
Donatus.	Commotus, ta, tū, meued, troubled, afraid, angrye: also quicke.
	Communes dies, were vnlucky dayes to go about any thynge, suche as we do call dysmoll dayes or crosse dayes.
	Communiter, in commune.
	Commutabilis, le, that whiche may be changed easyly.
	Commutatus, ta, tum, chaunged.
	Commutatio, an exchaunge, one thynge for a nother.
	Compareo, rui, rere, to apiere, to be seen.
Plautus in Amphit.	Comparebunt quę imperas, You shall see all thynges done, that ye do commaunde.
Plautus in Trinūmo. Cicero.	Comparet ratio argenti, it doth appere how the money is spent.
	Comparare se, to dysose hym selfe to any thynge.
Plautus in Bacch.	Comparare, to fynde the meane or deuyse. Nunc hoc tibi curandū est Chrysale. C. Quid uis curem? M. Vt ad senem etiam alteram facias viam, compara, fabricare, singe quod lubet, Howe Chrysalus thou must take good hede. C. what wylt thou that I shulde do?

	M. Deuyse yet to goo an nother waye to warke, ymagyne, contryue euen as thou thynkest beste.
Plautus in capt.	Compacto rem agere, to conspire a matter, or to do a thynge by one accorde.
	Comparare, to gete or purchace.
	Comparare conuiuium, to prepare a banket.
Plautus	Comparare malum, to purchace an yl turne or a myschiefe.
Terentius in phorm.	Comparatus, ta, tum, ordeyned or receyued in an vsage. Quam inique comparatum est, hi qui minus habent, ut semper aliquid addāt ditioribus? what an yll vse is this, that they, whiche haue but a lyttell, shall gyue more to them that be ryche?
Ci. de ami. cicero de amicitia	Quando quidem ita ratio comparata est vitæ naturęq; nostræ, vt alia ætas oriatur ex alia, Sens the fourme of our lyfe is so ordeyned by nature, that of oone age commeth an nother.
	Compedio, diui, dire, to gyue or fettar one.
Varro.	Compelluceo, luxi, lucere, to shyne veraye bryghte.
	Compellucidus, da, dum, very bright.
	Compendifaceo, facere, to make brie for be shorte in speakynge.
	Comperendinatus, ta, tum, adiorned.
	Comperendinati rei, they whose iudgement is deferred vntyll an nother tyme.
Plautus in Bacch.	Compesce in illum iniuste dicere, leane to say ylle of hym.
	Competitor, he that sueth for that which an other man sueth for.
plautus in Men.	Cōpingere in oculos, to thrust it in his eies.
	Compita, are places where many wayes do mete, or where two stretes do crosse.
	Complaceo, cui, cere, to please or lyke well.
plautus in amph. Cato. plautus. Terentius	Complacitum est, it lyketh or contenteth.
	Complano, are, to make playne.
	Complures, complura, & compluria, many.
	Complusculi, scula, idem.
	Compluuius lacus, a dyche, whereinto water falleth out of dyuers gutters.
	Componere lites, to agree menne togither, whiche are at variance.
plautus in Truculen.	Compos culpæ, he that hath don an offence.
	Compos patriæ, he that is come home into his countraye.
	Compos prædæ, he that hathe gotten the praye that he loked for.
plautus in Rude.	Compotio, tiui, tire, to gette one the thynge that he desyred.
	Compoto, taui, tare, to drynke with an nother man.
	Compotrix, she that drinketh with an other.
	Compotatio, a bankette.
	Comprecor, cari, to desyre or praye.
Cicero	Compræhendo, hendere, to take holde on a thyng, to comprehende or contayne. Also to fauour and defende.

Com-

The additions.   C ante O.

Comprimere animā, to hold in a mans bieth.
Comprimere manus, to holde his handes that he stryke not.
Plautus in Casina
plautus in Truculen.
Comprimere se, to cease or refrayne to doe a thynge.
Comprime, let be, peace.
Comprimere alique, to beate or torment one
Plautus in Ruden.
Comptum, a certayne offerynge of lycour, whiche was made with meale.
Cōcaleo, lui, ere, to be het, to be made warme
Concalfacio, feci, facere, to inflame, to be stered or prouoked.
Concameratio, a warke made lyke to a vault with arches.
Concalleo, lui, lere, to be made harde as a mannes handes with moche workynge, or his feete with moche goynge.
Concastigo, gare, to chastise with an other.
Plautus
Concede hinc, go hense a lyttell.
Concedere fato, to dye.
Concelebro, brare, to celebrate with other.
plautus in casina.
Concelebrare plateā hymenęo, to make ioye abrode with syngynge and daunsyng in the honour of mariage.
Concento, tare, to agree in one tune.
Festus.
Conceptiuę ferię, holy dayes kept at a tyme certayne yerely.
Columel.
Conceptus, ta, tum, conceyued, purposed. sometyme gathered: as, Ne cum a uertice torrens imbribus conceptus affluxerit, fundamenta conuellat: Leste whan the streme gathered by the showers of rayne, shall runne vnto it, it shall pull vp the foundatiō of that whiche is buylded.
Conchyta, he that seeketh for the shell fysshes, out of the which commeth purple: we maye take hym for a fysher of oysters and muskelles.
Concinnatitius, a, um, compendiouselye and aptly gathered to gether.
Ci. in Ver. act. 4.
Conciliare pecuniā, to gather moneye of the people.
Concinnitudo, an aptnesse, a conueniencye.
Plautus in capt.
Concinnare, to make. Vt illi mastigię cerebrū excutiam, qui me insanum verbis concinnat suis, I wyll surely brayne this knaue, that with his wordes maketh me out of my wyt.
Concinnare lutum, to make morter.
Plautus in Trinum.
Concinnare se leuem suis, to put his freendes to no coste. Nunquā erit alienis grauis, qui suis se concinnat leuem: He shall neuer be greuouse to other, whiche wyl not be burdenous vnto his frendes.
plautus in Men.
Concinnare struices patinarias, to make sondry bankettynge dishes.
Ibidem.
Concinnare vestem, to amende a garment.
Plaut. in Sticho.
Concinnare viam, to make rome that a man maye passe.
Plautus in Amph.
Concinnare vxorem lachrymantem, to make his wyfe to weepe. Lachrymantem ex abitu concinnas tu tuam vxorem, By youre departynge hense, ye make youre wyfe to weepe.
Concinnatus, concinnata, tum, apparailled, trymmed.
Concinne, properly, honestly, trymly.   **Terent. in Heautont.**
Concire, to moue or stere. Disperij, scelestus, quantus turbas, concini insciens: I am vndone wretche that I am, what a busynesse haue I made vnwares?
Concire lites, to moue debate.
Concionem habere, to make an oration or sermon to the people.   **Plautus in Pęnulo.**
Concipere oculis, to see or beholde.
Concipere fędus, to make a league.
Concipere metum, to be aferde.
Concipere scelus, to imagin to do an yl dede
Conclamo, mare, to cry to one. Vbi abijt cōclamo, heus quid agis tu? in tegulis? whan he was gone, I cried vnto hym, Howe serra, what doest thou amonge the tyles? Also to make a cry or proclamation. Vis conclamari auctionem fore quidem? wylt thou haue it proclaymed that there shalbe porte sale.   **Plautus in Milite.**
Plautus in Menech.
Conclamata vasa, proclamation made to trusse, to gather bagge and baggage, as is vsed in the raysynge of a syege, or remouynge of a campe in batrayte.
Conclamito, tare, to make many cries.   **Festus.**
Conclauia, many chaumbers or places vnder oone kaye.
Conclauium, idem quod conclaue.
Concoquere odia, to suffre dyspleasures or malyce.
Concredo, didi, dere, to delyuer or committe a thynge vppon truste.
Concorditer, by assent, or agrement.
Concresco, creui, crescere, to grow togither.
Concretus, creta, tum, ioyned or congelyd to gyther, as a thynge that is lyquide, to be made harde.
Concubinatus, hooredome, fornication.
Conculco, care, to treade vnder the foote.
Concuro, rare, to care for a thynge.   **Plautus in Bacch.**
Concurro, rere, to rounne with an nother, sometyme to accorde.
Concursus, sus, a runnynge of people togyther to one place.
Condecoro, rare, to honour a thynge in makynge it more commendable.
Condignus, na, num, worthy, and accordyng as it is estemed.
Condigne, worthyly, honestly.
Condisco, scere, to lerne.
Condiscipulus, a scholefelowe.
Conditura, saulse or pyckelle made with spyces.
Condolet caput, my heed aketh.   **Plautus.**

Condo=

The additions. C ante O.

Condono, are, to gyue, to forgyue a det or duety, to pardone.
Condormio, ire, to flepe with other.
Condormifco, fcere, to flepe a lytell, to nap.

Plautus in Afin. Conduci non poſſum, I cannot be made to beleue: no man can make me beleue.
Conductus, ta, tum, to be fette to hyre.
Conductor, he that hyreth a thynge.
Condus, a ſtewarde of houſholde, or he that kepeth the ſtore of houſholde.
Conduplico, care, to paye the douule of a thynge.
Conduplicatio, doublynge.

plautus in Rude. Conferre, to deuyſe, to talke togyther.
Conferre amorem, to loue.
Cōferre animū alio, to ſet his mind els wher
Conferre capita, to aſſemble for counſaile, to lay theyr heades to gether.

Plautus. Confer gradum, come forthe.
Conferre in pauca, to conclude ſhortly.
Conferre manus, to aſſayle eche other.

Pli, in pan. Conferre tempus in aleam, to ſpend the time in playenge at the dyce.

Terent. in Eunucho. Plautus in Bacch. Conferre uerba ad rem, to do as he ſayth.
Conferre ſe in pedes, to runne away, to take his legges.
Confert, it is profytable.

Cæſ, in cō. Confertus, ta, tum, full. alſoo in a flocke, or multitude, in a buſhment. Vt nunquam conferti, ſed rari, magniſque interuallis prælia-rentur, That they mought fyght, not a multitude togyther, but a fewe at oones, and a greate diſtaunce on ſonder.

Ti, Liuius. Turba conferta-iter clauſit, The people gathered in a buſh-ment, ſtopped the waye.

Ceſar. Qua parte hoſtium acies confertiſſima uiſa eſt, erupit, He brake out on that ſyde, where the hoſte of the enmyes ſemed to be moſte thycke of people.
Confertim, in a buſhement.

Plautus in Mercator. plautus in perſa. Conficere penſum, to ſpynne out her threde, it is tranſlatid into this ſentence, To haue done or broughte to an ende that thynge, whiche he was commanded or appointed.

plautus in Men. Conficere prandium, to haue dyned. Pallium ad phrigionem fert confecto prandio, whan dyner was done, or whan he had dyned, he caried hir mantell to the brouderar.

Terentius in Andria. Ci pro L. Flacco. Conficere ſolicitudines alicui, to bryng one into heuynes, or to make him ſorowfull.
Conficientiſſimus literarum, he that putteth all thynge in wrytynge.
Confidentia, truſt, hope, certayn aſſurance, alſo madde hardyneſſe.
Confidentiloquus, he that ſpeaketh boldly, without feare.

Plautus. Configo, fixi, figere, to ſtycke or thruſte in to a thynge.
Confingo, finxi, fingere, to fayne a thynge to be trewe.

Confingere dolum, to fynde a meane to de-ceyue one.
Confirmo, are, to confyrme, or aſſure a thing to be as it is ſpoken.

Cl, Tyro. Confirmare ſe, to make hym ſelf ſtronge af-ter his ſickneſſe.
Confirmare animum, to take courage.
Confirmitas, aſſuridneſſe.
Cōflagro, are, to be on a fyre, to be inflamid

Donatus. Conflictatio, is where as one thyng beateth agaynſte a nother.
Confluuium et confluxus, a metynge to ge-ther of many ſtreames.
Confluus, a, ū, that which floweth togeder.
Confœduſti, olde writers called them whi-che were ioyned in leage, confederates.
Confodio, dere, to dygge.

Terentius. in And. Confore, to be brought to paſſe.
Conformo, are, to brynge to a facyon or fy-gure, to make apt or lyke to a thynge.
Confringo, fregi, fringere, to breke or bruiſe.

Plautus in Ciſtell. Confringere teſſeram, to be out of fauour, or no more welcome to one.
Confringere rem, to ſpende awaye all his ſubſtaunce.

Ibidem. Confragoſus, a, um, roughe, as a grounde whiche is nat playne, alſo harde to be vn-derſtande, rude in language.
Confugere ad aliquid, to reſorte for ſuccour or excuſe.

Liuius, 6. Confundere, to trouble all, alſo to myxe out of order.
Confutatio, a diſprouynge of that whyche is ſpoken.
Congelatur, it is froſen or congelyd.
Congemino, nare, to double.
Congeminatio, a doublynge.
Congermino, are, to grow ioyntly togither.

Plautus in Moſtel. Congerro, ronis, a mery companion, he that kepeth company only in paſtyme and me-ry deuyſynge.
Congeſtitius, a, um, caſte vp in a heape.
Conglacio, aui, are, to be froſen.
Conglobatim, in a rounde fourme lyke to a bottome of threde.
Conglutino, nare, to ioyne togyther, as it were glewyd.
Congræcor, cari, to eate and drynke exce-dyngly, after the commune worde, to make good chere.
Congreſſus, us, is alſo company with other.
Congruens, accordynge, lyke.
Coniicere in ſaginam, to put to fattynge, to go where he may fyll his bealy.
Coniugata, be thoſe wordes, whiche beinge of one kynde, be diriued one of an other, as of Iuſtitia, iuſtus, & iuſtum, wherof an ar-gument may be made in this wyſe, If Iu-ſtice is to be chiefely honoured and loued
of

of men, a iuste man is to be had in estimation and reuerence amonge men.
Coniugatio, a ioynynge to gether.
Coniunctura, idem.
Coniunctus, ta, tum, ioyned.
Coniunctim, to gether.
Connato, tare, to swymme to gether.
Connecto, nexui, nectere, to binde together.
Conniuentia, a sufferaunce of a thynge, or a sayinge not to se or espye.
Connatio, a swymmynge to gether.
Conquassatio, a bruysinge together.
Conqueror, queri, to complayne.
Conquiesco, eui, escere, to cesse, to leaue of.
Conquiro, quisiui, quirere, to seke all about.
Conquisitor, a sercher, also an officer, which is sent to attache a man for a great offence.

Festus. Conregione, old writers vsed for e regione, on the other syde, or agaynst a thyng.
Conscindo, scidi, scindere, to cut with other.
Conscindere sibilis, to whystell oone oute of a place.

Ci. ad At. Conscindere, is also to scorne or rebuke one pryuyly.
Conscio, sciui, scire, to knowe with other.
Conscium facere aliquem, to make one priuie to a matter.

Columell. Conciscere, to drawe to. Diligens pastor stabulū cotidie conuerrit, nec patitur stercus humorem consciscere, A dilygent shepherde euery day sweepeth his stable, and letteth nat the dunge drawe moysture vnto it.
Conscribello, are, to write togyther.
Conscribere, is also to inrolle or register.

Ci. ad att. Cic. ad Q. fratrem. Consecro, are, to putte in remembraunce by wrytynge.
Consecrare memoriā nominis, to putte his name in perpetuall remembrance.
Consensus, consent.

Cicer. off. Consepio, piui, ire, to inclose with an hedge.
Conseruo, are, to kepe, to preserue, to gather goodes.
Conseruus, & conserua, a felowe or companyon in seruyce.

Cicero. Consignifico, care, to shewe by tokens.
Consigno, nare, to seale and close vp, as letters, also to sygnifie or declare, propreley by letters.

Cic. Acad. Consignatus, ta, tum, sygnified, testified.
Consilium est ita facere, I haue purposed so to doo.
Consimilis, le, in all thynges like.
Consolatio, comfort in aduersitie.
Consolabilis, he that may be comforted.
Consomnio, are, to dreame.

Cic. off. 3. Consortio, cionis, felowshyppe.
Cospergo, spersi, spergere, to scatter or sperkyll about aboundantly.
Conspectus, tus, a beholdyng or syght.

Conspirare, to wynde rounde like an adder.
Conspondio, di, dere, to promyse mutually.
Consponsi, they whiche haue mutually promysed one to the other.
Consponsor, sors, he that bindeth him selfe by promyse, to hym that hathe made lyke promyse.
Conspuo, ere, to spette on one.
Consputo, to spette often on one.
Constabilio, liui, lire, to make sure.
Constituere, to be aduised or determined to do a thynge.
Constituere in diem tertium, to determyne to do a thing thre dayes nexte folowyng.
Constituere disceptationē, to make his plee formall, or to foresee that which shall come in contencion.

Constituere iudiciū, after our maner of speakynge is to demourre in lawe, or dwelle in lawe, to remytte a thynge to the better opinyon of the iudges. *Cicero in parti. ora.*

Constituere maiestatem, to confyrme or aduance the reuerence dewe to the supreme authoritie. *Salust.*

Constituere quæstionem, to decree, that vppon strayt examination, execution be done.
Constituere statum causę, is whan the iudge dothe determyne, where hit be a matter in lawe, or a matter in dede, which is in controuersye.
Constituere vadimonium, to put in pledges.

Constet modus, lette there be a measure. *pli. in epi.*
Constat ratio, there is a reasonable cause.
Constat hoc mihi tecum, we be both agreed.
Constrepo, pui, ere, to make a noyse togider.
Constringo, strinxi, gere, to bynde faste, to wringe harde.
Consuetudo, conuersation.
Consuetus, ta, tum, accustomed.

Consumo, sumpsi, sumere, sometyme signifyeth to fynyshe or make vp, or to brynge to a poynt, also to spende, as Consumere diē in apparando, to spende all the daye in preparynge. *Terentius in And.*

Consumere fidem, to lose credence. *Salust.*
Consumere operam, to employ labour. *Terentius in Heau.*
Consumere orationem, to telle a longe tale without a conclusyon. *Salustius in Iugurt.*

Consurgo, surrexi, gere, to aryse to gyther with other.

Contabesco, scere, to waste away, or relent, lyke salt put in water. *Plautus in Mercator.*

Contechnor, nari, to inuente somme thynge to deceyue. *Plautus in pseudolo.*

Contego, texi, regere, to hyde a faute that it be nat espied. *Terentius in Hecyra.*

Contemptim, dysdaynefully.
Contemptus, ta, tū, contemned, nat estemed.
Contero, triui, terere, to weare out with occupieng

The additions.

Plautus in Cistell.	cupienge, also to make warre.	Conuentus, ta, tum, accorded.
	Conteris tu tua me oratione mulier: Thou makest me very woman with thy talkynge	Conuenta pax, peace, accorded.
Plautus in Bacch.	Conterere ætatem, to spende his lyfe.	Conuenticulum, a lyttell assembly.
Te. in Hec.	Conterere diē, to spend the day vnprofitably	Conuerro, rere, to swepe to gether into one place. also to rubbe.
	Conterere operam, to lose laboure.	Conuersē, klenly.
	Conterere questum, to spende al that he hath goten or wonne.	Conuexus, a, um, imbosed rounde and holowe within.
	Contestatus, ta, tum, proued by wytnesse.	Conuexitas, the imbosynge or roundnesse of the backeside of that whiche is holowe.
	Contexo, ere, to ioyne to gether.	Conuiciū dicere, to speke to a mans rebuke.
	Contexere dolos, to fynde crafty meanes.	Conuicium facere, to do a thynge to a mans rebuke.
	Cōticesco, cere, to kepe sylence with other.	Conuiuam abducere, to brynge one to a dyner or banket.
	Continere se domi, to abyde at home.	Conuiuiones, companyons at drynkynge or bankettynge.
Plautus in Amph.	Continebat me tempestas, The foule weder letted me.	Conuoco, care, to calle to gether, or to assemble many to gether.
	Continenti biduo, two dayes continuall.	Conuola, lare, to fly to gether.
	Contignus, a, um, that whiche toucheth or is next to a thynge.	Conuoluolus, an herbe called withwynde.
Plautus in Aulul. Vergil. Geor. Ver. æn. 2.	Contollam gradum, I wyl go nerre.	Copen, olde wryters vsed for Copiosum, plenteouse.
	Contorqueo, torsi, torquere, to plucke vppe and drawe with hym.	Cophinus, a basket.
	Contorquere telum, to shoote an arrowe or darte, and therwith to hit or perce a thing	Copio, are, to gather moche to gether.
	Contortuplico, are, to wrappe or wynde a thynge, that with great payne it maye be vnwounde.	Copiola, some plenty.
		Copia, is also ayde.
Plaut. in persa.	Contortuplicata nomina, names soo dyffuse, that they may vneth be pronounced.	Copiam dare, to gyue power, or lycence, also to gyue occasion.	Terent. in Heautont.
Ci. tusc. q.	Contra, on the other parte.	Copia est. Nam apud patrem tua amica tecum sine metu ut sit, copia est, For thou mayste nowe brynge to passe, that thy wench may be with thy father without any drede.	Ibidem.
Ouidius in Metamor.	Contrahere animum, to take thought.	
Pli. in epi.	Contrahere tempus, to abrege the tyme.	
Cicer. off.	Contrahere valitudinem, to gette sickenesse.	
Ti. Liuius.	Contrahere, to make couenant.	
Cic. Tusc. questio.	Contrahere bona, to geate goodes.	Copia est, I may or mought. Ego in eum incidi infelix locum, ut neque eius sit amittendi, nec retinendi copia: I am vnhapily come to that poynte, that I maye neyther leaue her, nor kepe hir.	Terentius in phorm.
	Contractio animi, stonyinge of the minde.	
	Contractus, ta, tum, gotten.	
	Contractus, tus, contracte, bargayne.	
	Cōtrasto, stare, to be agaīst one, to repugne.	Copia uix fuit eum adeundi, with great difficultie or peyn mought I come vnto him.
Plautus in Sticho	Contrunco, care, to mynishe.	Copia cuntandi non est tibi, Thou haste noo leysure to tarye.	Plautus in Epidic.
Cicero in clodium.	Contueor, eri, to defende, to see.	Copia est tibi magis, thou mayst more easily.	Plautus in Capt.
	Contumaciter, dissobediently.	Copia nulla est tibi in illo, He canne nothyng helpe the.	plautus in Epidico.
Plautus in Stich.	Contundere facta alicuius, to putte a nother mannes actes out of estimation or remembraunce.		
		Copiam efficere alicui, to fynde the meanes that one may come in.	Plautus in Milite.
Plautus in Asin.	Contuor, eri, to see.	Copiam facere argenti, to lende one money.	pli. in epi.
Ci. ad At.	Conturbo, are, to trouble. also to spende in wast. conturbare fortunas, to spende al his goodes in waste.	Copiam facere, to communicate any thinge with an nother.	
	Conuador, dari, to compell oone to fynde suertyes.	Copi, for copioso.	
Plin. 11.	Conueho, uexi, uehere, to cary or bryng frō many places vnto one place.	Copiose, abundantly.	
		Coquito, tare, to boyle often.	
Cice. Atti.	Conuector, toris, a maryner that conueyeth ouer many.	Corbito, tare, to caste into a baskette.	
Plautus in Amphitri. plautus in Curcu. plautus in Amphit.	Conuello, uulsi, uellere, to shake, or pull out of his place: also to take from one by robery	Cordapsus, a syckenes that is nowe called Illiacus, whiche is a peyne in the guttes.	Plautus in Casina.
	Conuenit, I am content. also it is conuenyent or meete.	Cordate, wysely.	
		Cordilla, the yonge frie of the fysshe callyd Tunye.	plautus in penulo.
	Conueniens, conuenient.		

Cor-

The additions. C ante R.

Vitruuius. Corgo, olde wryters vsed for Profecto.
Coria, coriorum, are in buyldynge certayne settyng or layeng of thynges in one order, or in height, or in thycknes.
Coriandrum, an herbe and seede callydde Colyander.
Coriarium, of lether.
Corinthiacus, ca, cum, that whiche is of the citie of Corinthus.
Corporatura, corpulencie, quantitie of the bodye.
Corpore uiciati, they whiche do lacke some membre at theyr natiuitie.
Corrector, an amender of fautes.
Te. in Hec. Corripere sese ad alique, to go to one hastily
Plautus in mercat. Corripere se repente, to go his way sodeinly
Corriuales, they whyche do loue togyther one womanne.
Corroboro, are, to make stronge or bygge, to harden.
Cornuda, an herbe callyd wylde Sperage.
Salustius in Iugurt. Corrumpere rem familiarem, to waste his substaunce.
Ibidem. Corrumpere igni, to burne vp.
Corrumpere oportunitates, to lose oportunitie or occasyon.
Corruptor, a distroyer, a waster, a corrupter of thynges.
Corruo, rui, ruere, to falle downe togyther.
Cors, cortis, idem quod chors, a court, whiche serueth for pultrie, to fede at large.
Corus, a southwest wynde.
Corymbifer, an yuy tree.
Cosmitto, for committo.
Cotyle, a measure contaynynge nyne ounces, as well at Rome, as in Grece.
Cotyla hyppoiatrica, that is to saye, whiche was vsed in medicines for horses and cattel contayned. xii. ounces.
Cotyla georgica, that is to saye, which was vsed in thynges concernynge styllage, conteynyd. xiii. ounces and a halfe. sometyme it is vsurped for Sextarius.

¶ C ANTE R.

Cracentes, for graciles.
Crambe, a kynde of colewortes.
Cramben repetitiam, is callyd of Iuuenalis a Declamation to be often herde, with moche tediousnes to the herers.
Crapulam exhalare, to vomyte whanne one is drunke.
Crapulam edormiscere, to sleape out drunkennes vntyll he be freshe ageyne.
Crasis, a greke worde, sygnyfieth complection, temperature, or myxture of naturall humours.
Crassamen, thyckenesse.

Crassę compedes, weyghty gyues. *Plautus in pseudolo.*
Crasso, are, to make fatte.
Crater, is also the bason of a water cundite, wherinto the water runneth out of pypes or cockes.
Creator, the fyrste maker of a thinge.
Creber, bra, brum, is also standyng, or being thycke togyther, as trees.
Crebritas, & crebritudo, oftennesse, or thiknes in beinge or growyng togither.
Credere verba alicui, to telle to oone his counsaylle.
Creditur tibi, I truste the. *Plautus in Sticho*
Creditur male, it is ylle lente. *plautus in Curcu.*
Creduis, uel creduas, for credas. *Plautus. Columel. 6. cap. 25.*
Cremasteres, the synewes, wherby the stones of a man or beaste doo hange.
Cremo, are, to bourne.
Crepa, of olde wryters is vsed for Capra, a Goote.
Crepare, to be broke, also to speke or prech. *Vergill. Horatius.*
Crepidatus, he that weareth slyppers.
Crepidula, a lyttell slyppar.
Crepitare dentibus, to crashe with the teth. *Plautus in Ruden. plautus in Amphit.*
Crepitat mihi uenter, my bealy courleth.
Crepuit foris, the doore craked.
Crispus, he that hath a curlyd heare.
Crista, a kreste, or any thynge growyng on the heade of a foule or beaste, as a cockes combe, or the fethers on the heade of a byrde, callyd a coppe.
Crociatus, ta, tum, coloured lyke saffron.
Crocito, tare, to croke like a rauen or crow.
Crocitus, the noyse that a rauen or crowe maketh, callyd krokynge.
Crocitatio, idem.
Crocomagma, matis, the duste or refuse of Saffron.
Cronia, the feastes of Saturne.
Cruciabilitas, & cruciatus, turment, affliction.
Cruci dare aliquem, to hange one. *Plautus in Milite.*
Crucifigo, fixi, gere, to crucyfie.
Crucio, are, to tourment.
Cruda poma, fruites that are not rype.
Crusculum, a lyttell or small legge.
Crustum, is also a morcel of bread or meate. *Vergill.*
Crux, sygnifieth all maner of tourment.

C ANTE V.

Cucurbitula, a lyttell gourde or cuppe, wherwith bloode is drawen out of a man, whan he is scarified.
Cucuma, a vessell of brasse or tynne, facioned lyke a Cucumer, wherwith bathes were fylled and emptied.
Cudetur in me faba, all the blaame shall be layde to me.
Cuiusmodi, what, what facion, what maner.

Cius-

The additions. C ante V.

Plautus in Menech. Cuiusmodi homines erunt? what maner of men shall they be?
Cicer. pro cluen. Cuiusmodicunq̄ mater sit? what so euer a mother she be?
Cicer. pro Roscio. Cuiusq̄modi. Vereor enim cuiusq̄ modi es Rosci, ne ita hunc uidear voluisse seruare, ut tibi omnino non pepercerim, I feare me that in what so euer state thou arte in Ros. lest it shall be thought, that I wolde so excuse or defende hym, forasmoche as I haue nat at all spared the.
Salust. in catelin. Cuiuscunq̄ modi genus hominum, of all maner of sortes of men.
Culcitrula, a lyttell fether bedde.
Festus. Culcitula, a lyttell staffe.
Culeus, amonge the Romaynes was the greattest measure, and receyueth twenty of the measures callyd Amphora, whyche amounteth to two thousand, eight hundred, foure pounde of measure, euery pound beinge twelue ounces. It was also a sacke of lether, wherinto they, whiche hadde slayne their fathers or mothers were sowen, and with them were also put alyue, a Cocke, a Serpent, and an Ape, and throwen al togither in to the riuer of Tyber. And this was the punyshment of paricides or murderers of their parentes.
Plautus in Capt. Culpa carere, nat to offende.
Culpam commereri, to committe an offence.
Culpam in alterum conferre, to lay the blame to an nother.
Culpito, tare, to blame often.
Culpo, pare, to blame.
Cululus, a lyttell chalyce or cuppe of erth, whiche the byshops vsed in sacrifice.
plautus in pēnulo. Cum, all be it. Nam cum sedulo munditer nos habemus, uix ægre amatorculos inuenimus, All though we do appoynt vs neuer so kleanly, yet vneth fynde we any louers.
Cum dicto, forthewith, as soone as it was spoken.
Terentius in Hecyra. Cum maxume, to moche.
Cumulatus, ta, tum, augmented.
Cumulate, abundantly.
Vergilius. Cunabula, is also taken for the begynnyng of thynges.
Cunctanter, flowely, softe and fayre.
Cunctatio, & contatio, taryenge.
Cunctus, ta, tum, all togther.
Cunilago, a kynde of sauerye.
Cupiens, he that desyreth a thynge.
Cupiens tui est, he loueth the hartyly.
Cupienter, with great desyre.
Cupitus, ta, tum, desyred.
Cupressus, a Cypresse tree.
Cupressinus, na, num, of cypres tree.
Curiata comitia, were assemblyes of people in places of iudgement, for matters in varyaunce.
Curio, is also a curate, or he that hathe the spirituall charge in a paryshe.
Liuius.
Curionatus, the offyce of a curate.
Curionium, the money that is giuen to a curate for doinge his offyce.
Curmundula, peares very delycate, hauing so thynne parynges, that men dydde eate them vnparyd.
Curare, to care for a thynge, to take heede, or be dilygent aboute a thyng. Cura ut valeas, Looke to thy helthe. Curasti probé, Thou haste done euery thynge well.
Terent. in Andria.
Curare ædes, to take hede to the house, that nothynge be loste.
Plautus. Terent. in Heauto.
Curare aliena, to meddell with other mennes busynesse.
Curare amicos, to entertayne frendes or acquayntaunce.
Plautus in Sticho
Curare fidem, to kepe promyse.
Plautus in Trinūmo.
Curare munus suum, to do his offyce.
Curabo illi pecuniam, I wylle prouyde that he shall haue money.
Curabitur, it shall be prouyded.
Curatus, ta, tum, done with dilygence.
Curatus, in good poynt or state.
Curatio, charge. Curatio mea est, It is myn offyce or charge.
Plautus in pœnu.
Currens, he that runneth.
Currentem incitare, to exhorte or sette forwarde hym that of his owne courage is well disposed to a thynge.
Cursim, with al spede, very spedyly.
Cursura, a course.
Cuticula, a thynne skynne.
Curiones, they whyche in sellynge make many prices er they come to a poynte.
Cuturnium, a vessell, out of the whiche wine was poured in sacrifices.
Festus.

¶ C. ANTE Y.

Cyanus, a blewe flowre growynge amonge corne, callyd a bluebottell.
Cyathisso, are, to syppe or to quafte, all out, or halues.
Cyathus, the xii. parte of the mesure callyd Sextarius, whyche was supposed to be as moche as commonlye a temperate man dyd drynke at one draught. Rede more after in Sextario.
Cyborium, a kind of appuls of Alexandria.
Cydarum, a bote.
Cynodontes, are dogges tethe, whiche doo growe in the latter age.
Cyperus Babylonicus, Galyngale.
Cypsili, byrdes callyd swalowes.
Cyrnij, people of the Ile of Cors.
Cysthus, a kynde of yuye.
Cytinus, the floure of a gardē pomegranate.

Kk D ante

The additions. D ante E.

D ANTE A.

DAGNADES, were lyttell byrdes, whyche in Egypte men vsed to make faste to garlandis whan they went to drinkynge.

Damascœna, prunes.

Damnas dare, to pay damages. Damnum facere, to suffre damage, to haue losse. — *Vlpian. L. aquilia. Cic. Epist. libr.17.ad Volumnium Cic. in L. pisonem.*

Damnatus, condemned.

Damnatior, more worthy deathe.

Danista, an vserer.

Danisticus, ca, cum, pertaynynge to vsery.

Dapsilis lectus, an excellent good bedde. — *Plautus in Trucu.*

Daphnoides, an herbe callid Lorell or Laury, whiche cuseth a vehemente purgation.

Dapsilia dicta, wordes frankely spoken.

Dascia, thyckenes of brethe.

Daucus, yelowe carette, wherof the rootes sodden in brothe are pleasant and holsom.

D ANTE E.

DE nocte abijt, he went away at night. — *Plautus in Rude. Cicero. Plautus.*

De nocte uigilare, to wake i the night.

De die, to day. Ergo ne una orationis pars de die dabitur mihi, Than shal nat I be suffred to speake one lyttell worde to day.

De die uiuere, euerye daye, or from daye to daye, to lyue. — *Ci. in phil.*

De meo, of my good, de tuo, of thy good. — *Plautus in persa.*

De mea sententia, by my counsayle.

De illis verbis caue tibi, beware howe thou spekest suche wordes. — *Plautus in Bacch.*

De imperio decertatur, they fyghte for the empire, or chiefe rule. — *Plautus in Menech. Cicero.*

De manu in manum, from hande to hande. — *Cicero.*

De filia te adij, I comme to speake with you for your doughter. — *Terentius in Hecyra.*

De meo exemplo ædificet, lette hym buylde accordynge to my platte. — *Plautus in Mostel.*

De istac te amo, I loue the for her sake. — *Terent. in Eunucho.*

De compacto, by agrement.

De industria, of purpose. — *Plautus in Capt.*

De integro, eftesoones from the beginning. — *Terent. in Heauto.*

De improuiso, at auenture, vnsought for, or vnlooked for. — *Plautus in Trucu.*

De more, as it hath ben accustomed.

De nihilo nihil est irasci, It is folye to be angry for nothynge. — *plautus in Epidico.*

De præfacili exores, Thou shalte lyghtely opteyne.

De proximo senex, the olde man that dwelleth hereby. — *plautus.*

De repente, sodaynly. De subito, idem.

Deambulatio, a walkynge forth, or abrode, out of the house.

Debilito, tare, to make feble or weake. — *Festus. Non. Mar.*

Deblatero, terare, to speake foolysshely, to babble rebukefully.

Decaluo, to make very balde. — *Ci. ad At.*

Decaphorus, a lytter borne by tenne men. — *Plinius.*

Decedere, to gyue place to an other.

Decedere itinere, to tourne out of the waye for some purpose. — *Plautus Ci. in Ver.*

Decedere uia, to go out of the way.

Decedere de suo more, to chaunge his custome. — *Ti. Liuius.*

Decedere instituto suo, to do otherwise than he was wonte. — *Ci. in Ver. Liuius.*

Decedere officio, to do agaynste his duetie to do no more his duetie. — *Terent. in Adelph. Cic. Att.I.*

Decedet nihil de summa, there shall be nothynge minyshed.

Decedere, to dye.

Decedi, to haue place or way gruen. Hęc enim ipsa sunt honorabilia, quę uidentur leuia atq communia, salutari, appeti, decedi, assurgi, deduci, reduci, For those thynges ar honourable, whiche seme to be of small effecte and commune, to be awayted on, to be sued vnto, to haue the way giuen, to be rysen vnto, to be brought to the court, and brought agayne home. — *Cicero de senectute.*

Decem, the number of tenne.

Decemuiri, where tenne men be in one authoritie. Suche were at Rome soone after that they ceassed to haue kynges, and they had authoritie to gather lawes, and also to make lawes: At the laste they conspired to haue a perpetuall authoritie, and fynallye were therfore deposed for euer.

Decemuiratus, the dignitie or offyce of Decemuiri. — *Colu.li.4.*

Decenus, na, num, a dosen.

Decies, tenne tymes.

Decennalis, le, of tenne yeres.

Decennium, the space of tenne yeres.

Decenter, comelye, seemely, or as hit is conuenyent. — *Terent. in Hecyra.*

Decermina, thynges pulled away, in makinge thynges cleane.

Decernere, to purpose. — *Plautus in Mostel.*

Decernere questionem, to ordeyne that an examination be made.

Decernere, to fyght in battayle.

Decet me hęc vestis, this garmente becommeth me well. — *Pli. in epi. 105. Terent. in Heautont. Plautus in Bacch.*

Decidit ab archetypo, he dyd nat folowe his fyrste example.

Decidere de spe, he loste all his hope.

Decidit fructus, he loste all the profite that shulde come of it.

Deciduus, a, um, that whiche falleth, as Decidua folia, leaues that do fall.

Decies

The additions. D ante E.

Decies sestertium, was vsed of the Romains for a thousande Sestertia, whych amounteth of our money to syxe thousande, fyue hundred, foure score and seuen pounde, & tenne shyllynges.

Plinius. Varro. Decliuis, ue, that whiche is redy to fall.
Decliuis ætate, fallen in age.
Decollare, to fayle.
Decolorus, a, u, lackyng colour, or yl colorid
Decoloratus, ta, rum, idem.
Decoxit domino suo fœtura, the increase of cattayle came to lyttell aduauntage vnto his mayster.
Decore, honestly.
Decortico, care, to barke a tree.
Decoses, thredebare garmentes, or garmentes worne to the vttermoste.
Decumbo, bere, to lye downe.
Decures, olde writers vsed for decuriones.
Decuriatio, making of knightes or captains
Ti. Liuius. de bell. macedonico lib. 10. Decurrere, to iuste.
Decussis, ten hole partes, also peces equally cutte, more ouer the diuisions of tymber sawen in equall partes.
Decussatim, in euen porcions cutte.
Dedecet, it is not honest or conuenient.
Dedecoro, rare, to dishonest.
Dedecus, dedecoris, dyshonestie.
Dedignatio, dysdayne.
Deditus, ta, tum, gyuen, rendred.
Dedita opera, for a pourpose, by his owne consente.
Deducere riuos, to tourne the ryuer.
Deducere vocem, to speake smalle.
Deducere, to abate of a somme.
Defæcatus, ta, tum, fyned or cleane from the lyes or dregges, as wyne, whyche is nat troublyd.
Defatigo, gare, to make oone weerye, or to satygate.
Defatigatio, weerynesse.
Deferre aliquem furti, to appeache oone of felonye.
Cicero de lege agraria. Deferunt de me apud uos, They reporte of me falsely vnto you.
Priscianus Defetiscor, sci, I am weery.
Defessus sum, idem.
Defectus, a, u, that which lacketh any thing.
Defectio, rebellio, departing from one captayn to go to an other, also lacke or defaut.
Plautus in persa. Pli. in pan. Cicer. off. Defigere aliquem colaphis, to gyue oone a cuffe on the eare, or to beate one with the handes. Definite, shortly, or at few wordis.
Definitum est, It is concluded.
Deflectere ex itinere, to turne out of the way.
Deflexit de via consuetudo, The custome is chaunged or tourned.
Plautus in Epidic. Defleo, eui, ere, to wayle or lamēt, to be sory.
Defloccatus, worne for age, som tyme passed the floure of youthe.
Defore, to lacke in tyme to come.
Defunctus iam sum, I haue nowe doone my duetie. *Terent. in Eunucho.*
Defuncta morbis corpora, bodies recouered from syckenes or diseases. *Liuius.*
Defunctus fato, escaped his destenye. *Ibidem.*
Defungi in hac re, to be cut of this busynes, to be discharged of this matter. *Terent. in phorm.*
Defungi regis imperio, to doo the kynges commaundement.
Defunctus, ta, tum, deed.
Defunctorie, remyssely, lyghtely, withoute studye, or dyligence. *Vlpian.*
Degero, degessi, degerere, to cary away. *Plautus in Aulular.*
Degerere laborem alicui, to ease one of his labour. Degrumor, ari, to lay a thing by line.
Dehortor, tari, to discourage, to exhorte to the contrarye.
Deijcere de gradu, to bryng out of a constant or temperate mynd, also it signifieth, to depriue of dignitie. *Cic. de off. Ci. ad At. lib. 16. Cicer. pro cecina. Ci. de sen.*
Deijcere, to disease or putte out a man of his possession.
Deiectus, & deiectio, a castynge out of possessiou, or a disseison.
Deiungo, xi, gere, to vnioyne.
Deiuro, to sweare depely.
Delabor, lapsus sum, labi, to falle downe of a hygh place. Also to be consumid and come to nought.
Delacero, rare, to teare in pieces.
Delachrimo, idem quod delachrimor.
Delauo, uare, to washe myghtily.
Delectamentum, pastyme, solace.
Delibatio, tastynge, or the takynge of assay. It is also sacrifyce of meate or drynke.
Delibatorium, a place apt for suche sacrifice.
Delibare, is also to hurte.
Delibutus periuriis, stayned or defyled with periurie. *Columell. Gellius. Saluit.*
Delicate, wantonly.
Delicia, the tymber, whiche maketh the end of a house aboue, callyd a Gable. *Festus.*
Deliciares teguæ, the tiles at the gables end
Delici porci, yonge suckynge pygges.
Delingo, linxi, lingere, to lycke of. *Varro. 2.*
Delirans, dotynge.
Deliratio, dotage, foly. *Cicero*
Deliramentum, idem.
Delius, a, um, of the Ile callyd Delus.
Delius natator, was one perfytte in swymmyng, which became a prouerbe, that whā a thynge was spoken, or written, harde to be vnderstande, and reqnyred a cunnynge expositour, than wolde they say, Delio natatore eget, It requyreth a cunnynge or subtyll expositour.
Deludificor, cari, to begyle.

Kk ij De

The additions. D ante E.

Delutamentum, clayenge.

Terentius in ph orm. Plautus in Menech. Demensum, a certayne portion of meat and drynke allowed by the moneth to the seruantes. It is also a measure contaynynge foure Romayne busshelles.

Demeter, the name of Ceres.

Demigro, grare, to goo from one house, to dwelle in an nother.

Vergilius. Georg. 2. Deminuo, nuere, to mynyshe, or make lasse.

Demittere, to drygge.

Cice. pro Murena. Demissi homines, men fallen from rychesse to pouertie.

Demere soleas alicui, to pull of ones shoes.

Demere vngues, to pare ones nayles.

Plautus in Aulul. Demogorgon, was an enchaunter, whiche was supposed to be of suche excellencye, that he had authoritie ouer all yll spirites, whiche made men aferde.

Demoliri culpam, to dyscharge hym of the faute or blame.

Plautus in Bacch. Demolio, idem quod demolior.

Demoueo, uere, to remoue.

Demuto, tare, to change his maner or facion

Tonstall9. Cassius hemina animalium, 2, Denarius, in weight is the seuenth parte of an ounce: In coyne hit was as moche in poyse and valuation, as our olde sterlynge grote, of the whiche there wente seuen to the ounce.

Denascor, denasci, to ceasse to be, to dye.

Denominatio, the namynge of a thyng.

Dens, is also euery thynge, wherwith an other thynge may be holden faste.

Dentatus, he that hath great tethe, stronge tethe, or many tethe.

Dentifrangibilum, a thynge wherwith tethe are broken.

Denumero, rare, to paye money.

Denunciatio, menassynge.

Cesar. Cicer. pro Flacco. Denunciatio testimonij, an instuction to apere

Deoro, rare, among our lawyers, is to perpleade, or to conclude in pleadynge.

Deorsum uersum, downe ryght.

Terent. in Adelphis. Depaciscor, sci, to make couenant, to agree vpon certayne couenantes.

Depaupero, rare, to impouerysshe, or make poore. Depectus, kempte.

Dependere opera, to take pein about a thing

Depingo, xi, gere, to paynt a thynge to the quycke, also to reporte.

Deprecatio, whan we confesse that we haue offended.

Deprecator, he that sueth or intreatethe for another man, that he shuld nat be punished.

Depressus, a, um, lowe.

plautus in penulo. Terentius Depropero, rare, to make moche haste.

Depugnatus, ta, tum, well fought.

Deputare rationes, to reken, or make accopt

Derado, si, dere, to shaue of, or barke of.

Deriduculum, a skorne or mocke.

Deripere aliquem capillo, to pull one downe by the heare of the heed. *Plautus in Menech.*

Derogito, to make instant desyre, to praye hartyle. *Plautus in Asina.*

Des, a poyse of eyght ounces.

Descendere in sese, to humble hym selfe. *Persius*

Descensus, sus, a goynge downe.

Descensio, idem.

Deseco, care, to cutte.

Desedeo, dere, to sytte downe.

Desertor, he that leaueth his countrey, and gothe to his ennemyes.

Deseruire studijs, to apply lernyng or study. *Plinius in Epistolis.*

Desideo, sedi, desidere, to sytte stylle, to abyde in a place. *Plautus. Terentius*

Desido, sedi, sidere, idem.

Designare, to chese a thynge, and appoynte it for some purpose.

Desistere litibus, to leaue suite. *Terent. in in phormi.*

Despectio, a lokynge downewarde.

Despicor, cari, to despise or disprayse.

Despicatus, tus, disprayse. *plautus in Milite.*

Despoliare digitos, to pulle the rynges of from ones fyngers.

Despondere prouinciam, to gyue charge or rule of a countrey. *Cicero de prouinc. consu.*

Desponso, are, to affiance a woman.

Destinare, is also to sende. *Iuuenalis.*

De subito, sodaynely.

Desudasco, scere, to labour vntyll he sweat.

Desuefactus, out of custome, or vse.

Desydero, rare, to desyre.

Desyderati, men deed, propicly in battayle.

Desyderium, desyre, also speciall loue. *Cicero*

Desyderatio, idem.

Detrecto, tare, to refuse to do a thynge, or nat to doo it.

Detrudere, to sette forthe one by force.

Detrudere regno, to putte oone oute of his royaulme.

Deturbare aliquem aedibus, to thruste oone out of the house.

Deuerbium, the laste ende of a worde.

Deuersus, tourned downewarde.

Deuoro, rare, to deuoure. *Plautus in Asina.*

Deuorare dicta, to take good heede vnto wordes. Deuorare libros, to reade bokes with ardent desyre.

Deuorare molestiam paucorum dieru, to indure peyne or displesure for a lytel while. *Ci, in phil.*

Deuorare nomen alicuius, to forgete a mans name. Deuorare orationem, to here a taale without takynge any hede of it. *Plautus in Trinumo. Ci, in Bru.*

Deunx, deuncis, xi. tymes the measure callid Cyathus, whiche was as moch as a temperate man vsed to drynke at xi. draughtes.

Dextans, x. tymes the mesure callid Ciathus

Dextera uel dextra, the ryght hande. sometyme on the right syde.

Dextram

The additions. D ante I.

Dextram dextrę cōmittere, to promyse faith and trouthe in hande. — *Laur. Val.*
Dextimus, olde writers vsed for dexter.
Dextero, rare, to leade in the ryght hande.

D ANTE I.

Diabathra, showes that the grekes vsid
Diaulus, a measure of grounde contaynyng two furlong, euery furlong beinge of .Lxxv. fete.
Diacodion, a syrope made of the heedes of poppe and water.
Dibapha, purple twyse dyed.
Dicam impingere, to bryng an action against one, or to laye agaynst ones charge. — *Terentius in phorm.*
Dicam scribere alicui, to enter an action agaynste one. — *Plautus in Aulul.*
Dichas, a measure of two palmes, or .viii. fyngers. — *Terentius in phormi. Ci. in Ver.*
Dicare operam suam, to offre his seruyce.
Dicere nummos, to promyse money.
Dicere ex animo, to speke as a man thinketh. — *Salusti. in histo.*
Dicere ex tempore, to make an oration without study. also to speake vnaduysedly.
Dicere, is also to call a thynge by a name.
Dicasis, for dicas. — *Plautus in curgul.*
Dice, for dic. — *Ibidem.*
Dictamen, a thyng writen by an other mans instruction.
Dictare rationem, to yelde accompte. — *Plautus in Amph.*
Dictatum, a mynute gyuen by one to an nother, to write a letter by.
Dictito, to tell a thynge ofte.
Didragma, a coyne, whiche was of the value of .viii. of the money callyd Sestercii, whiche of oure moneye is two olde sterlynge grotes.
Didymus, is in latyne Geminus, in englishe, one man double as moche as an other.
Diffarreatio, a certayne sacrifyce, whyche was betwene a man and his wife.
Differitas, olde wryters vsed for Differentia, dyfference.
Differre sitim, to endure thyrste.
Differre vadimonium, to gyue to one a longer day of apparaunce. — *pls. in epl.*
Differre famam alicui, to sprede ones name abroode.
Differri, to be soo vexed in mynde, that a man wotteth nat what to doo.
Difficultas, difficultie. — *Plautus in Cistell.*
Difficulter, with great peyne or labour.
Difficul, for difficile.
Difflo, are, to blowe downe.
Digestio, dygestion, dystribution. — *Plautus in Mili. Iouius.*
Digiti, ar muskyls, or a like kind of shel fishe.
Digitum tollere, to fauour a matter.
Digitus, is also a mesure, being of the bredth of foure cornes of wheate layde togyther.

Digitulus, a lyttell fynger.
Digladiatio, a fyght, a stryfe, a debate.
Dignatio, greate estimation, sometyme fauour, or familyarytie with noble men.
Digressus, a departynge.
Diligenter, dylygently, aduysedly.
Dilucide, cuydently.
Dimissorię literę, letters myssiue.
Dimixos, a lampe with two lyghtes.
Dinumero, rare, to paye money.
Diobolaris, a common and vyle harlot.
Diomedes, a noble captayne of the Grekes at the syege of Troye.
Dipsacus, a wylde tasyll.
Dirimere litem, to make an ende of a matter in varyaunce or suite. — *Cicero*
Dirimere actionem, to delaye a matter.
Dirimere societatem, to breake felowshyp.
Diripere oppidum, to sacke a towne. — *Plinius.*
Diruo, rui, ruere, to breke down to the groūd
Dirutus, ta, tum, broken down to the ground dystroyed.
Discalceo, ceare, to pull of ones shoes.
Discalceatus, vnshodde.
Discedere in diuersa, to be of sondry opiniōs
Discernere armis, to fyght in battayle.
Discupio, to desyre very moche.
Discursus, runnynge hyther and thyther. — *plautus in pęnulo.*
Discutere, to dissolue humours gathered into an impostume.
Discussoria medicamēta, medicins which do dissolue or breke thinges congelid or tough.
Disiunctio, a separation.
Disiunctus, ta, tum, separate.
Dispar, vnlyke, vnmete.
Disparo, rare, to seuer.
Disparatum, is that whych is separate from any thynge by layenge to his contrary.
Dispartior, tiri, to diuyde, or be dyuided.
Dispeream, I praye god that I dye: it is a worde vsed in the steede of an othe, in the affirmance or denyenge of a matter.
Disperij, I am vndone.
Displiceo, cēre, to displease. — *plautus in cistell.*
Displicina, she that hath displeased.
Dispolio, idem quod despolio.
Dispoliabulum, a despoyle, a place where all myschiefe or robberye is done. — *plautus in Bacch.*
Dispudet, I am ashamed, or he is asshamed of that, whiche is done.
Dissoluere, to pay that whiche is owed.
Dissoluere aliquem, to despatche one frome longe taryenge. — *Terent. in phorm. Plautus in Mercator.*
Dissuadere, to turne one frō doing of a thing
Dissuo, cre, to vndoo a thynge.
Distędet, I am wery of a thynge.
Distinctio, distinction, separation.
Distincte, distinctly in order, as it may welle be vnderstande and perceyued.

Distor-

The additions. D ante O.

Terent. in Eunucho.
Plin. de uiris illustr.
Plautus in Trucu.
Plautus in Bacch.

Distorqueo, si, quere, to sette awrie. Ah illud uide, os ut sibi carnifex distorsit, O, loke how the hangeman setteth his mouthe awrye.
Distractus, ta, tum, pullyd on sunder.
Distractio, a pullynge away or a sunder.
Districte, straytely.
Distrunco, care, to cutte in two pieces.
Diuidia, busynes, trouble, variance.

¶ D, ANTE O.

Plautus in capt.
Idē in Aul.
In amphit.

Dare in ruborem, to make ashamed.
Dare insidias, to deceyue one.
Dare iusiurandum, to take an othe.
Do lego, I gyue by testament or laste wyll.
Dare malum alicui, to do one a shrewd turne
Dare manus, to yelde hym self vanquished.
Dare mancipio, to delyuer on warrantise.

Plautus in persa.

Suo periculo is emat, qui eam mercabitur, mancipio neq promittet, neq quisq dabit, He that wyll haue her, let hym bye her at his owne peryll: for no man shall promyse or delyuer her on warrantise.
Dare mutuum, to lende.
Dare vitio, to dispraise.

Plautus in in trinum.
in pseudo.

Danunt, idem quod dant, they gyue.
Datu meo, of my gyfte.
Datarius, a, um, that whiche is to gyue.
Datatim ludere, to tosse frome one to an nother, as men playe at tenys.
Doctor, he that teacheth other.
Doccus, a tymber piece.
Dodrans, is also ix. of the measures, callyd Cyathi, also ix. inches in length or bredth.
Dogmatistes, he that foloweth an nother mans doctrine.
Dolenter, sorowfully.
Dolium, a vessel for wyne, som call it a tūne, and conteyneth xxx. of the olde measures callyd Amphoras.
Doloro, aui, are, to cause one to haue sorow or peyne.
Domi, at home.
Domo, from home.
Domum, to the howse, or home, sometyme at home.

Cicero de diuinatiōe Tibullus.

Domuitio, a departynge home.
Domitus, ta, tum, made tame, subdewed, or vanquysshed.
Domator, idem quod domitor.
Dominus, is also an owner.
Domina, the lady or maistresse.
Dominatus, tus, domynation, or authorytie ouer other, maystershyp.
Domus, is sometyme a temple or churche. also a familye or kynrede, alsoo a mannes countrey, also a neste of byrdes.
Donaticæ coronæ, garlandes that in the olde tyme were worne in playes.

Dormire in vtramuis aurem, is a prouerbe whiche sygnifyeth to be without any maner of care. It may be englished, To slepe soundly on bothe sydes.
Dormisco, scere, to begynne to slepe.
Dormitator, a sleaper.
Dormitorium, that whiche pertaynethe to sleape.
Dorophorus, he that caryeth a present.
Dorsum in mari, a heape of sande gathered in the see, which watermen do cal a shelpe.
Dorsus, idem.
Dotes animi, the gyftes of grace.
Dotes corporis, the gyftes of nature.
Doxa, in greke, sygnifyeth opinion, somme tyme glorye.

Terent. in Heauto.
Plautus in curcu.
in Trinum.
Vergilius. Seruius.

¶ D ANTE R.

Drachma, the coyne, which is in value v. q. ob. halfe farthyng, somwhat lesse, after fyfty of them to fyue crownes of the sonne.
Dracena, the female dragon.
Draguntea, an herbe callid dragons.
Dragma auri, a coyne whiche in value was as moche as one ounce & a halfe of siluer.

D ANTE. V.

Dvbenus, old writers vsed for dominꝰ
Dubitatim, doubtfully.
Ducere animo, to thynke.
Ducere bellum, to make warre.
Ducere spiritum, to drawe breath, to lyue.
Ducere vultum, to lowre.
Ducere, is also to suppose. Hanc esse in te sapientiam existimant, ut omnia tua in te posita esse ducas, Then thynke that wysedom to be in you, that ye thinke all that whiche is your owne, to be in youre selfe and not in fortune.
Ducere honori, to repute it honourable.
Ducere minoris, to sette lesse by it.
Ducere officij, he supposid it to be his dutie.
Ducere probro, to dyspraise.
Ducere mortuum, to be deed. Meos ne ego ante oculos illam patiar, alios amplexarier? mortuum hercle me duco satius, Shal I suffer hym to imbrace her before myn eyes? by god I had rather be deade.
Ductare, to take to wyfe, also to esteme.
Ductare restim, to leade the daunce.
Ducatus, the gouernance or condute of mē
Ductus, ta, tum, ledde.
Ductus, tus, tui, a coundyte, whereby water dothe rounne.
Ductor, toris, a guyde.
Duellator, a warryour.
Duel=

Vergilius.
Ci. ad qui.
Ci. de ami.
Salustius in Iugurt. Ibidem.
Plautus in Asin.
Plaut. in persa.
Terent. in Adelphis.
Plautus in Capt.

The additions.　　D　ante V.

Duellica ars, the feate or science of armes.
Duicensus, he that is sette with an other to pay money for a taxe or subsidie.
Duidens, a shepe of two tethe.
Dulceo, cere, to be swete.
Dulcidulus, a, um, a lyttell swete.
Dulcesco, scere, to be made swete.

Plautus in Mercator.

Dum, as longe as. Vsque ne valuisti? C. perpetuo recte dum puidem illic fui: Dyddeste thou well all that while? C. ye alway well, as longe as I was there.
Dumosus, a, um, full of brembles.
Duodeuiginti, eyghtene.
Duodecim, twelue.
Duodecimus, a, um, the twelf.
Duonum, olde wryters vsed for bonum.
Dupliciter, two wayes.
Duricoria, thynges which haue harde skins
Duricors, dis, harde harted.
Duratus, ta, tum, hardned.
Duro ingenio, dull wytted.
Duré, cruelly.
Duriter, with moche payne.
Duricies, rudenesse, rygour.

D, ANTE Y.

¶ Dynastea, a rule or gouernaunce.

E FOR THE MORE parte signifieth of.
E re nata, consyderynge the matter.
E re nata melius fieri haud potuit, quam factum est: Considerínge the matter, or as the matter chaunced, it coulde not haue bene better done than it was.
E regione, on the other parte, on the other syde agaynste.

¶ E ANTE B.

Ci. ad Att.
Idē planc.
Columell.

E Beati, they whiche from great prosperitie are fallen into mysery.
Ebeo, are, to brynge out of prosperitie.
Ebibo, bibere, to drynke all out.
Eboracum, a citie in England, called Yorke.
Eblandior, iri, to gette a thynge by flatery: also to lyke.
Eblanditus, ta, tum, goten by flatery.

Laberius.
pla. in aul.

Ebriolus, la, lum, a lyttel drunke, or a lyttle persone drunke.
Ebriulo, are, to make drunke.
Ebriatus, drunke.
Ebullo, are, to boble out, or braste out.
Ebulus, an herbe called walworte, which is lyke to yonge elder tree.

¶ E ANTE C.

E Castor, an othe of the paynymes.
Ecce me, lo here I am.
Eccere, some vsed it for an othe, as it were, by Ceres: some onelye for Ecce, lo nowe, or se nowe.
Eccillum, for ecce illum, see hym.
Eccistam, for ecce istam, se her.
Echnephias, a storme, where a cloude is broken and falleth.
Echi, lyttel narowe valeys or dales betwene two hylles.
Econtra, contrary wyse.
Ectrapeli, they which abhorre the common facion or olde vsages.
Ectypum, that whiche is made accordynge to a paterne.

Plautus in mercator.

Plautus.
Terentius.

Columel.

Ci. in phil.

E, ANTE D.

E Dem, signifieth pleasure, dilectation.
Edētatꝰ, he that hath his teth takē out.
Edicto, tare, to declare or pronounce often tymes.
Edictio, idem quod edictum.
Edor, ederis, edi, to be eaten.
Edo, edis, edidi, edere, to execute or doo a thynge, or to cause a thynge to be done.
Edere annos, to tell what age a man is of.
Edere cedes, to make great slaughter.
Edere clamorem, to cry out.
Edere exemplum, to shewe an exaumple.
Edere fœtus, to brynge forth fruite.
Edere iudicium, to reherce the iugement.
Edere librum, to publyshe a boke.
Edere ludos, & spectacula, to cause playes and pageantes to be shewed to the people
Edere nomen, to tell his name to be written or regestrid.
Edere oracula, to gyue answeres, as the diuell dyd in the ydolles of paynymes.
Edere prelium, & bellum, to make warre.
Edere rationem, to yelde accompte.
Edere risus, to lawghe.
Edere scelus, to commyt a myscheuouse act.
Edere scriptum, to shewe by wrytynge.
Edere spiritum, to dye.
Edere stragem, to make a greate slawghter of men.
Edititius iudex, a iudge whom the one parte hath chosen.
Edoceo, cui, cere, to instructe or informe one of a thynge.
Edormisco, scere, to slepe soundely.
Edormiscere crapulam, to slepe vntyll he be sober agayne.
Educere, sometyme sygnifyeth educare.
Eduro, rare, to make very harde.

Plautus in Epidic.

Cicero

Cicer. pro planco.

Plautus.
Te. in Ad.

E. ante

The additions. E ante F.

E ANTE F.

Effascino, nare, to bewytche any thing, as wytches doo, whyche dysfygure chyldren, and distroye grayne and other thynges with sorcery.

Effata, were certayne prayers, whiche the diuinours vsed to make at the end of their diuination or telling the successe of thingis

Effectum dare, to brynge to passe.

Efferre sese, to prayse hym selfe. *Terent. in Adelphis. Cicer. hortensio.*

Efferre manum, to lyfte vp his hande.

Efferre aliquem laudibus, to extolle oone with prayses.

Efferre, to deuulgate, or to telle abrode.

Efferre, to aduaunce or promote.

Effero, rare, to make woode as a beaste.

Efferueo, ere, to boyle moche.

Efferuesco, scere, to begyn to boyle or sethe. *Cicero de oratore.*

Efferuescentia uerba, hotte angry wordes.

Effexis, for effeceris.

Efficere argentum alicui, to gette money for a man by some meane or deuyse. *Plautus in Casina.*

Efficientia, idem quod effectus.

Effigio, are, to counterfayte ones ymage in payntynge or keruynge.

Effilo, lare, to sowe.

Effilatum, that whiche is sowed or stitched on a garment, as a garde or purfle.

Effio, fieri, to be doone. *Plautus in persa.*

Effligo, flixi, fligere, to tourment. *Plaut. in Asin.*

Efflare animam, to dye.

Efflauit animam spes, I haue noo maner of hope or truste. *Plautus in persa.*

Effluet, it shall oute, I wylle nat keepe it, all men shall knowe it. *Plautus in Trucu.*

Effluxit, it is quyte gone. *Ci. de sen. Terent. in Eunucho. Cice. tusc.*

Effœtus, ta, tum, hatched, as a byrde that is come out of the egge.

Effœtum corpus, a weake body.

Effreno, nare, to vnbrydell.

Effringo, effregi, gere, to breake to pieces.

Effractus fame, made feble for lack of meate

Effugit memoria, to be forgotten.

Effugere nuptias, not to be maried.

Effusè, effusius, effusissime, abundantly, more vehemently, excedyngly. *Plautus in Bacch. Terent. in Andria. Pli. in epi. & in pane.*

E ANTE G.

Egens est consilij, he lacketh counsayle

Egeria, was an ydol, to whom women with chyld dyd offer, supposyng that therby they shulde trauayle easily.

Egerit aquam fons, the fountayne powsheth out water.

Egestio, onis, distribution abrode, it is also the puttynge forthe of ordure or dunge.

Ego, I.

Egomet, I my selfe.

Ego ne, who I.

E ANTE H, & I.

Hem, is a worde spoken, whan a man is moued with some thynge, which is newly hapned. *Terent. in Eunucho.*

Eheu, alasse.

Eho tu, howe serra, whan one calleth a man to hym, forgettynge his name.

Eiectus, ta, tum, caste oute.

Eiecto, tare, to throwe oute.

Eiulatio, a brayenge out with lamentation.

Eiurare, to renounce.

Eiuratio, renouncynge.

E ANTE L.

Elangueo, ere, to be sycke.

Elanguesco, scere, to waxe feble.

Elauare se bonis, to be cleane wasshed frome all his goodes, to spende all, and leaue nothynge. *Plautus in Asina.*

Elapsus, a, um, escaped.

Elapsa est spes, hope is loste.

Elleborus albus, an herbe callid Lyngwort, the roote wherof is callyd nesyng pouder.

Elleborus niger, an herbe callid beares fote

Elix, licis, a furrow made for water to passe. *Colu. li. 2.*

Ellobia, thynges whyche were hanged at the eares of women.

Ellum, for ecce illum, see where he is. *Donatus.*

Elops, a fyshe callyd also Accipenser. *Vergilius.*

Eluceo, cere, to shyne.

E ANTE M.

Emaciatus, ta, tum, made leane.

Emancipatus, ta, tum, alyened.

Emancipati, are also they, whyche are out of theyr fathers rule, or they, whyche are made subiectes to an nother. *Festus. Cic. in catelius.*

Embata, a shyppe callyd a barque

Embolium, the argument or fyrst entree into a playe or interlude.

Embolismus, the adding of a day in the yere

Emeritum stipendium, the laste wages that a man taketh in warres.

Emeriti senes, olde men excused frome labour by age.

Emico, care, to shyne forthe.

Emicare, to daunce or leape.

Emigro, grare, to goo frome oone place, to dwell in an nother. *Plautus in Aulular. Vergilius.*

Emmanuel, is interpreted, God is with vs.

Emoueo, uere, to put away.

Empyrium cœlum, the heuen, which is next aboue all the seuen spheeres, and signifieth the fyry heuen.

Emutio, tire, to humme or make anye other sowne lyke a man that is dumme.

E ante

The additions.   E ante V.

¶ E ANTE N

Enarro, rare, to telle a thyng at length.
Enato, tare, to swymme out.
Encaustes, he that fourmeth or facyoneth a thynge with fyre.
Encaustice, makyng of images with the fire.
Enimuero, forsothe.
Enixa, a woman late delyuered of chylde.
Sueton. in othone. Enotesco, scere, to come to knowledge.
Enterocela, a disease whan the bowelles be fallen into a mans codde.
Enucleate, clerely.

¶ E, ANTE O.

Sueton. de claris grā. Eo serius, neuer the lesse.
Eo loci, in that state.
Eo inficias, I denye.
Eo obuiam, I goo to mete with one.

E, ANTE P.

Epacta, thynges added to.
Ephesus, a citie in Grece.
Ephialtes, is that disease, which is callyd the mare in slepynge.
Ephimeron, the great wylde Lylly.
Ephod, a stole, whiche a prieste weareth about his necke, whan he is at masse.
Epicœnum, of bothe kyndes.
Epicia, callyd æquum & bonum, equytie, which is iustyce without rigour of the law.
Epimytheon, the declaration of a fable.
Epiphora, a syckenes of the eyes, callid the droppynge of the eies.
Epiroticus, ca, cum, of the countray callyd Epirus.
Eporhedicæ, good breakers of horses.
Epulæ, larum, a banket made to many psons.
Epha, seu Ephi, a mesure of the Hebrues or Iewes, contayning lxxii. times the measure callyd Sextarius Atticus. Rede more after in Sextarius.

E, ANTE Q.

Equiceruus, a beaste in the oryente, hauynge hornes, and a longe mane to the shulders, and a bearde vnder his chyn, and fete rounde lyke a hors, and is as great as an harte.
Equisetum, an herbe callyd horsetayle.

¶ E ANTE R.

Plautus in Epidico. Eradico, care, to pluck vp by the rotis.
Eradicare aures alterius, to pulle oone harde by the eares.
Erasus, a, um, rased or scraped out.
Erogatio, distribution of thynges to other men, a lyberall gyuynge.

Erogito, tare, to desyre hartily.
Eros, loue.
Erotema, tis, a demaunde.
Erotematicus, he that often demaundeth.
Errare de verbis alicuius, to mysvnderstande the wordes that one speaketh.
Erratio, a goinge out of the way.   *Terent. in Adelph.*
Erratum, an errour.
Erumpo, rupi, erumpere, to braste out, some tyme to leape forthe.
Erumpet in neruum istæc fortitudo, is a prouerbe, whiche is dyuersely expounde, for it may signifie, This courage of thyne maye brynge the to a halter, or to sytte by the heles, or it may sygnify, This great strength or courage of thine wyl come vnto nothing. whyche prouerbe is taken of archers, whiche oftentymes whan they put forth moste strength: they breake the strynge of their bowe, and the arowe falleth downe at their fete, wherby the shotte is loste, and cometh to nothynge.   *Terent. in phorm. Donatus. Erasmus in Adag.*
Eruptio, is whan an host issueth hastily out of a campe or fortresse, and falleth on their ennemies.
Eruum, the grene peason.
Eryngion, an herbe lyke a thystel, the rote whereof beinge condite or conserued in hony with cynamome and cloues, comforteth nature, and styrreth courage, and is of some men callyd Yringus.

E ANTE S.

Esalon, is a byrde, which breaketh crowes egges, and her byrdes be distroyd by the wolfe, and lykewyse she kylleth the wolfes whelpis, if she may com by them
Esau, the son of Isaac, & brother of Iacob.
Essedarius, a charyot man.
Estrix, a woman rauenour or deuourer.
Esurio, onis, an hungrye felowe.   *Plautus in persa. Varro.*
Esurigo, ginis, hunger.

¶ E, ANTE T.

Etenim, for, also, semblably, surely.
Etiamne, is it so? is that ynoughe?   *Plaut. in Asin.*
Etiaminum, vntyll than, vntyll that time.   *Terent. in Eunucho.*
Etiamnunc, vntyll nowe.   *Plautus in Amphit.*
Etiamsi, although. Etsi, idem.   *Cicero de amicitia.*

E ANTE V.

Evangelia, liorum, pluraliter, were sacrifices and solemne prayers made after good tydynges.
Euanno, are, to van corne or other like thing
Euceria, oportunitie.   *Ci. de fini.*
Eudoxia, good renoume or good fame.   *Cic. ibidē.*
Euenit ex sententia, it camme to passe as I thou

The additions. E ante X.

thou, or he wolde haue it.
Euenit præter sententiam, aut præter spem, It happened otherwyse, than I, thou, or he thought, or trusted.
Euerriculum, a fyshynge nette callid a drag.
Euersus, a, um, destroyed.
Euersio, destruction.

Plautus in Menech. Euhœ, a noyse, whyche they doo make that are in great heuynes and waylyng.
Euidenter, clerely.
Euiresco, scere, to become grene.

Plautus in Cistel. Euolo, lare, to flee away. also to escape, It signifieth sometyme to take away by stelth.

Terent. in Eunucho. Euoluo, uere, to tourne hyther and thither.
Euoluere se turba, to wynde hym selfe oute of trouble.
Euomo, mui, mere, to vomyte, to caste out.
Euomere iram, to wreake anger.
Euomere uirus, to spytte out his poyson.
Eupatorium, an herbe callyd agrimonye
Euphrasia, an herbe callyd eybright.
Eutrapelia, gentylnesse, good maners.
Eutrapelus, gentyll and pleasant.
Euxinus Pontus, a parte of the see, whiche diuideth Europa from Asia.

E ANTE X.

Terent. in Adelph. EX aduersum, euen agaynst it, on the other syde.
Ex æquo & bono facere, to doo iustely or indifferently.
Ex animo, of good wyll, of a good courage

Cic. Epist. Ex dignitate nostra, accordyng to our astate or dygnitie.
Exacuo, cuere, to make very sharpe, to sterc.
Exæquo, quare, to make egall.

Ti. Liuius. Plautus in Trucu. Exæuio, uire, to waxe gentyll or mylde.
Exagoge, they whyche carie anye thynge out of the house.

Plin. Exagoga, rente, reuenues.
Exalburno, nare, to take out the fatte iuyce that is in some wodde.
Exaluminati, orient perles.
Examen, is also examination or triall.
Examina infantium, a companye or sorte of chylderne.

Plautus in Truculen. Cic. Tusc. Cicero de amicitia. Examo, mare, to loue well.
Exanclo, is also to vanquyshe.
Exardeo, si, dere, to be vehemently inflamid.
Exardesco, scere, to waxe hotte, or to be vehement.

Plautus in Mili. Plautus in Capt. Exarco, rere, to be drye.
Exaugeo, gere, to increase moche.
Exauspicaui ex vinculis, I haue had yll lucke sens I came out of prison.
Excalceo, ceaui, are, to pull of hosen or shoes
Excalfacio, cere, to make very hotte.

Terent. in Andria. Excessit ex ephebis, he passed boyes age.

Excedere pueris, idem.
Excedere officium, to do more than duetie.
Excellens, excellent, surmountynge.
Excelsitas animi, the valyantnes or heighte of courage.
Excidere formula, to lose his action.
Excidit numero ciuium, he is not of the nũber of citeiyns.
Excidit animo, it is out of my mynde.
Excido, cidi, cidere, to distroy. also to cut out of a quarrye of stone.
Excipere, to take vnwares or sodaynly.
Excipere furem, to receyue a felone, as an accessarye.
Excogito, tare, to fynd or inuent by thinking.
Excogitatio, inuention.
Excoquo, quere, to boyle a thynge vntylle it be drye.
Excrucio, are, to tourment.
Excruciabilis, le, worthy to be tourmented.
Excubo, bare, to kepe watche.
Exculco, care, to treade out, or wryng out.
Exculpo, psi, pere, to graue or intayle ymages, also to get any thing by hering of one.
Exculpere oculum, to thruste out ones eie.
Excurio, are, to put out of company.
Excuro, rare, to dresse a thynge curiously.
Excuratus nictus, meate curiously dressed.
Excuratus homo, a galyarde felowe.
Excurro, rere, to runne out of a place.
Excursus, sus, where one passeth his boudes
Excursor, a currour.
Excusabilis, le, that whiche may be excused.
Excusatius, more excused.
Excutere aliquẽ, to robbe one, to shake oone out of his clothes.
Excutiunt cerebrum tua dicta, thy wordes do trouble my brayne.
Excutere iugum, to shake of the yoke.
Excutere lachrymas alicui, to make the teares come out of ones eyes.
Excutere uomitum, to make one to spue.
Excussi grandine, beaten with hayle stones.
Excutere, is also to chese. Iuuentutem ex tota Asia excussimus, we haue chosen oute all the yonge men that are in Asia.
Exector, idem quod execro.
Exegeticon, idem quod expositiuũ, uel enarratiuum, by the whyche oone expoundeth or declareth a thynge.
Exit in fabulam, it is made a tale.
Exequi mortem, to dye.
Exequi sermonem, to speake.
Exercere ætatem, to lyue.
Exercere Bacchanal, to be drunke.
Exercitatus, exercysed.
Exerere uincula, to stryke of his gyues, or to take out of prison.
Exfodio, dere, to drygge out.

Cice. pro Archia. Plinius in Epistolis.

Sueton. in Claud.

Plinius in Aulul.

plautus in cistell.

Terentius in phormi. Varro. Plautus in Pseud. Plautus in Casina Plautus in Mostel.

Plinius.

pli. in epi. Ci. in phil.

Plautus in pseudolo. plautus in Trinum. plautus in Milite.

Exgure

The additions. E ante X.

Exgurgito, tare, to take or caste out of the chanell or streame.
Exheredatus, disinherited.
Exheresimus dies, the daye whiche maketh the leape yere.
Exhaurire labores, to spende labour.
Exhebenum, a stone wherwith goldsmyths do polyshe golde
Exhibere rationes, to make accompt.
Exhibere spectaculum, to make commune playes or triumph.
Exhillaro, rare, to comforte or reioyce.
Exigere ætatem, to lyue. *Plautus. Pli. in epi.*
Exigere tempus, to passe forth the tyme. *plautus in Mercator.*
Exigi matrimonio, to be deuorced. *plin. de viris illust.*
Exigere supplicium ab aliquo, to punish one. *Ci. in Ver.*
Exigere nomina, to compell menne to paye their dettes. *Cic. in oratore.*
Exacta ætate, at the last ende of age.
Exacto mense, the moneth passed.
Exiguus, a, um, lyttell.
Exilica causa, a matter agaynst them, whych were in exile.
Exigué, an Aduerbe, whiche signifieth verye lyttell.
Exilis, le, sclender, smalle. *Columel.*
Eximie, excellently.
Eximius, a, um, excellent.
Eximere ex reis, to acquite one of an offence *Ci. in Ver. Cicero de oratore.*
Eximere ex ærariis, where one hath his Quietus est in the escheker, or other like place, to discharge one vpon his account. *Tit. Li. 8.*
Eximere noxæ, to release one of a trespasse committed.
Eximere actionē, to barre one of his action.
Exinde, idem quod exin, afterwarde, from thenseforthe. *Vlpia. titulo Ex quibus causis.*
Exloquor, qui, to speake as it is, to speke all. *Plautus in milite.*
Exobsecro, crare, to make great desyre.
Exoculatus, whose eyes be put out.
Exoculo, lare, to put out ones eies.
Exoculasso, sere, idem. *Plautus in Ruden.*
Exodia, were also wanton toyes myxte with verses in a comedy or interlude.
Exonero, rare, to discharge or vnburdeyn.
Exopto, tare, to desyre feruently, or wysshe. *Plautus in Epidico.*
Exorbeo, bui, bere, to sucke vp. *Ci. in phi.*
Exorbo, bare, to make oone that he canne nat see. *Plautus in Bacch.*
Exorare ueniam, to aske pardon.
Exorabilis, he that is easye to be intreated in a matter.
Expalleo, lui, lere, to be pale. *pli. in epi.*
Expallio, aui, are, to rob one of his garmētes. *Plautus in casin.*
Expectatus, ta, tum, desyred. *Donatus. Terent. in Adelphis.*
Expectati parentes, were yll parentes, and worthye to be hated, as who saythe, their death were dayly to be desyred. *Donatus.*
Expectatio, desyre of thynges certayn and loked for.

Expedire se cura, to discharge hym of care. *Terentius in phor.*
Expedire rationes, to dispatche matters.
Expedi, telle on quyckely. *Terentius in Eunuch. Idē in pho. pli. in epi.*
Expedire rem, to declare the matter plainly.
Expeditum erat, it was expedient.
Expedibo, for expediam.
Expeditus, dispatched. *Plautus in Truculen.*
Expendere scelus, to be punyshed iustly for his offence.
Expendere, is also to examyn and to cōsider *Vergilius. æneid. 2.*
Expensum, uel expensam, hath also an other propre signification. Mentio facta est de legione ea, quā expensam tulit C. Cæsari Pompeius. Mention was made of the legyon, whiche Pompeye reckened to be atte the charge of Cesar. Creditores suæ negligentię expensum ferre debent, The creditours ought to beare the losse, whiche is hapned by their neglygence. *Cælꝰ Ci. Sceuola, quę in fraude. L. pu pillus. Cicero*
Experge te, awake.
Expergere facias, idem.
Expergitus, wakened by an nother. *Festus.*
Expetunt multa iniqua, many vnhappy thinges chaunceth. *Plautus in Amphitri. plautus in pęnulo.*
Expetit tuam ętatem illud facere, thyne age requyreth to do it.
Expetere, is also to pourchace. Mirum quin tuum ius meo periculo expetam, It is meruayle but that I shall pourchase thy ryghte with my great danger. It is also to redoūde or tourne. Nam deum non par uidetur facere, delictum suū, suamq̃ culpam expetere in mortalem ut finat. It is nat syttynge for god to doo, that his offence and faute, shoulde redounde to a mortall person. *Plautus in Ruden. Plautus in Amphit.*
Expetendus, da, dum, worthy to be desyred.
Expetesso, sere, to demaunde. *Plaut. in persa.*
Expetisso, sere, to desyre vehemently. *Plautus in Trinūmo. Asconius. Ci. in Ver. Cicero in pisonem.*
Expilator, a robber, which leaueth nothing behynde hym.
Expiare scelera. Tua scelera dis immortales in nostros milites expiauerunt, God hathe punyshed oure menne of armes for thyne offences.
Expiamentum, satisfaction.
Explanto tare, to pull vp that whiche is set. *Columell. Sueton. in Tito. Te. in Hec.*
Explendesco, scere, to appere clerely.
Exple animum curis, put all care oute of thy mynde.
Explicare, is also to telle or shewe a thynge playnely. *Plautus in Epidic. Cicero in pisonem. pli. in epi. Cic. de senectute. Idem de amicitia. Plinius in Epistolis.*
Explica æstum meum, put me out of this fantasy or doubte.
Exploratū est mihi, I know surely, I am sure
Exploratum habeo, idem.
Exporto, tare, to beare or carie out.
Expresse dicere, to speake properly and to the poynte.

Expro

The additions.   F ante A.

	Exprobratio, a reproche.
Terent. in Andri.	Exprompta memoria, a redy wytte.
Terent. in Eunucho.	Expuere miseriam ex animo, to put myserye clene out from the mynde, to forget misery.
Plautus in milite.	Expurgo, are, to make all cleane.
	Expurgare se, to declare hym selfe innocent of that whiche is layde vnto hym.
	Expurgationem habere, idem.
Columell. planc. Cic.	Exputare, is also to cut cleane awaye: also to coniecte.
Plautus in curcu.	Exputresco, scere, to rotte.
	Exquisitus, ta, tum, exquysyte, moche serched for.
	Exquisito opus est, it must be loked for.
	Exquisite et exquisitim, exquisitely, with moche study and diligence.
Plautus in Bacch. pli. in pan. Plautus in Bacch.	Extendere, is also to continue, to prolonge.
	Extentare uires, to thrust out strength in doinge a thynge.
	Extergeo, tersi, tergere, to wype cleane.
	Extergo, idem.
	Exterus, tera, terum, that whyche is not of this countrey or place.
	Extimeo, mere, to haue great feare.
	Extirpo pare, to plucke vp by the rootes.
	Extollere, is also to lyfte vp.
Plautus in Mostel.	Extollere liberos, to brynge vp chyldren: also to prolonge: also to magnify.
	Extortus, constrayned by tourmentes.
Plautus in pænulo.	Extra precium, aboue any pryce.
Plautus & Cicero	Extra, excepte.
Ci. Treba.	Extra iocum, in erneste.
Sueton. in Claud.	Extraneᵘ heres, he that is not the very heire
Cæsar.	Extraho, traxi, trahere, to drawe out.
Ti. Liuius.	Extrahere diem, to put of a matter from day to day.
Paulus iu reco̅. ad exhiben.	Extrahere certamen, to deferre battayle.
	Extrahere iudicium, to deferre iugement.
plautus in pænulo.	Exuerre, the swepynges of a house.
	Exuerto, tere, to preuente.
	Ex uinculis causam dicere, to plede in warde.
	Exungo, xi, gere, to anoynte.
Plautus.	Exungulo, are, to cut of ones nayles.
	Exuere, is also to depryue.
Vergilius.	Exue mentem, put away that mynde.
	Exurgo, gere, to aryse vp.

F ANTE A.

plautus in Milite. Plautus in capt.	FACETE, meryly. Facere aucupiu̅ auribus, to herken as a spye. Facere carnificina̅, to execute the offyce of an hangeman, in hanging, behedynge, or quarterynge of men.
Cic. Cato.	Facere castra, to set a campe.

Facere certiorem, to ascertayne, or aduertise one by letters or messager.	
Facere compendiu̅, to make short, to abrege.	Plautus.
Facere compote̅, to gyue to one, that thyng, whiche he desyreth.	
Facere coniecturam, to coniecte or deeme.	
Facere contumeliam, to do displeasure.	Plautus in Asina.
Facere copiam argenti, to lende money.	Terent. in phorm.
Facere copiam alicuius, to let hym take his pleasure of one.	
Facere delitias, to speake for pleasure, or in mockage.	Plautus in pænulo.
Fac esse, admyt that it be soo, or put the case it be soo.	Cicero in philip.
Facere fidem, to make one to beleue.	Plautus in pænulo.
Facere frugem, to brynge gaynes.	
Facere funus, to minister funeralles.	Cicer. pro cluen.
Facere gradum, to walke or go a iournay.	
Facere gratiam, to gyue thanke.	Plautus in curcul.
Facere gratum, to do pleasure to one, or to wynne a mans fauour.	Terentius in Eunuch.
Facere grauidam, to geate with chylde.	
Facere iacturam, to haue a great losse.	Plautus in Amphitri.
Facere inditium, to tell or to gyue warnynge of a thynge that he knoweth.	
Facere ingenium suum, to do accordynge to his wyt or nature.	Plautus in Mercator.
Facere insidias, to lye in a wayte to do harme to oone.	plautus in pænulo.
Facere ludos, to mocke or skorne.	Terentius in phorm.
Facere magni, to esteme moche.	
Facere nequiter, to do shrewdely.	
Facere ocium, to gyue to one leysure.	Plaut. in Mili.
Facere palam, to tell a thynge abrode.	
Facere periculum, to proue, to assaye.	
Facere pluris, to set more by.	
Facere propitium, to make hym thyne or his good lorde or mayster.	
Facere questum, to gayne.	
Facere reducem, to brynge one agayne.	Plautus in capt.
Facere re̅, to get profite or gayne by a thing.	Terent. in Adelphis.
Facere reum, to accuse or sue one in a criminall cause.	
Facere risum, to laughe.	Quintilia.
Facere scelus, to do a myscheuous deede.	
Facere sementem, to sowe grayne.	Cicero de oratore.
Facere stipe̅dia, to be in wages in the warres	
Facere superbum, to sle one.	plin. de uiris illustr.
Facere technam, to playe a craftye pageant.	
Facere transacta omnia, to brynge all thynges to a poynte.	Plautus in Amphit. Non. Mar.
Facere turbas, to make busynesse.	Plautus in Bacch.
Facere uadimonium, to lay in gage or suerte.	
Facere uerba aut uerbum, to speake.	Terent. in And.
Facere uindemia̅, to gather grapes to make wyne.	Plautus in Epidico.
Facere uitium, to fall in decaye.	Ci. in Top
Facere uoluptatem, to satisfye myn thyn or his pleasure or appetite. also to delyte with pleasure.	plautus in Trucu.

The additions. F ante E.

pleasure.

Fagineus, et Faginus, a, um, of beche. — Vergili. 9.

Falarica, were waypons, which were throwen out of toures.

Falce, falsely.

Falcimonia, deceyptes. — Plautus in Bacch.

Falsus, a, um, false.

Famam dissipare, to sowe a brute or noyse in the people,

Famigero, to diuulgate or publishe a thyng. — Varro.

Fatrago, ginis, dyuers grayne & pulse corne myngled for prouander, called in Cambryge shyre, bolymonge. it is sometyme vsed for a myxture of any other thynge.

Fatuus, a, um, vnsaucry, without any maner of taste. — Iuuenalis.

Fauoniana, peares whiche are redde.

F, ANTE E.

Felicones, men whiche are necessary for no thynge.

Feriæ esuriales, fastynge dayes. — plautus in capt.

Ferinus, ferina, ferinu, pertaynyng to wylde beastes.

Ferre conditionem, to proffer, to put to the choyse, to offer a condition.

Ferre gradum, to go forthe. — Plautus in mercat.

Ferre grauiter, to take a thinge greuously.

Fer manum, gyue me thy hande.

Fer me, supporte me, helpe me. — Plautus in Truculen. Terent. in Heauto.

Ferre moleste, to take a thyng displesantly.

Ferre osculum, to kysse.

Ferre sententiam, to shewe his opinion.

Ferre suppetias, to succour.

Festra, a lyttell wycket.

F, ANTE I.

Fictus, ta, tum, made to the similitude of a thynge.

Fidem deserere, to breake promyse. — Ci. in phil. Cicero de senectute. Terent. in And. Te. in Hec.

Finge animo, suppose or put the case.

Fit, it happeneth.

Firmare fidem, to perfourme promyse, also to accorde to a thynge.

Firme, stedfastly.

Firmiter, idem.

ANTE L.

Flagrare inopia, to be in great pouertie.

Flamasca, a tree burned with lightning

Flamearius, a dyer of yelowes.

Flameum, a veyle or typpette of yelowe, whyche women dydde weare, whan they were newe maryed.

Flammigena, commen of fyre.

Flegmen, is where with moche goynge the — Festus. bloudde issueth out of the toes.

Flexipes, pedis, he that hathe crooked fete.

Flustrum, the fulle tyde in the see, or other water, whyche ebbeth and flowyth.

F ANTE O.

Foenusculum, a bottell of hey.

Forago, a skayne of yerne.

Formastata, a meane beaultie or stature.

Fors, Fortune.

Fors suat, god sende the good fortune, god speede the well. — Terent. in Hecyra. Donatus.

Fors fortuna, good chaunce.

Forsitan, & forsan, peraduenture.

Fors, is sometyme vsed for Forsitan, peraduenture.

Forte fortuna, by good aduenture.

Forresco, scere, to waxe or be stronge. — Neuius.

Fortiter, puyssantly, valyantly.

Fortunæ, goodes, good fortune, aduancemente.

Forensia, Judges robes, or the habytes the whyche are worne in the places of Judgemente. — Sueton. in Augusto.

Fouere in pectore, to thynke pryuyly. — Plautus in Bacch.

F ANTE R.

Fracecre, to be resolued, putryfyed, or rotten.

Fraces, lyes of oyle.

Frænos inijcere alicui, to lette oone of his pleasure, to brydell hym that wolde nat be rulyd.

Fractæ res, thynges spent or loste.

Fracti bello, werye of warres.

Fractus, ta, tum, broken.

Fragilis, le, frayle, broukle.

Fragilitas, fraytltie or brouklenes.

Fratricida, he that hath slayne his brother.

Fratrueles, brothers chylderne, cousyne germaynes.

Frequentissimæ ædes, a house moche hanted with people.

Frequens adest, he commeth often.

Frontem explicare, to loke meryly. — Terentius Plinius.

Frontem exporgere, idem.

Frontem contrahere, to loke sowerly.

Fronte exporrecta, with a merye countenaunce.

Frugaliter, temperately, soberly, withoute excesse or ryotte. — Plautus in Epidico. Cato. Terent. in Heautont. Plautus in Bacch. Plautus in Amph

Fruiscor, sci, for fruor.

Frui ingenio suo, to doo as he wyll.

Frustra es, Thou arte deceyued or abused.

Frustra habere aliquem, to abuse or deceyue oone.

Ll Frustrari

The additions. H ante E.

Columel.	Frustrari expensas, to loose his costes and charges.
	Frustratio, abusynge or deceyuynge of one

F, ANTE V.

Fvat, for fit.

Plautus in Amphitri. Cicero. — Fugere, is also to exchue. Fugit te ratio, thou vnderstandeste not the matter.
Fugit me, I haue forgoten it.
Fugiens uinum, wyne that hath loste his verdure.
Fugientes litere, blynde letters.
Fugitiuus, a, um, fugitiue, not abydynge.
Fugitiuarius, a, um, that gladly and quickely runneth awaye.

Plautus in Trinsimo. Plautus in Trinum. — Fulcimentum, a botreulx, or that wherwith a thynge is sustayned.
Fulguritasunt, stryken with lyghtnynge.
Fulguritum, striken or blasted with lyghtenynge.

plautus. Martialis. — Fullonica, fullars crafte.
Fumos uedere, is the practise of them, whiche beinge nygh about a prynce, or in his fauour, do beare men in hande, that they speake for them to the prynce, where they speake neuer a worde: and cause menne therby to lyue in fooles paradyse.

Lampridius in vita Al.

Plautus in Bacch. — Funditus me perdidisti, thou hast vtterly vndone me.
Funditus perii, I am vtterly vndone.
Fundere exercitum, to dyscomfite an armye.
Fundus, is somtyme taken for a foundation, also for the chiefe authour of a thynge.
Fungi officio suo, to do his deuour.
Funginus, a, um, of a mousheron.

Plautus in Asina. — Funus facere, to cause one to dye.
Futio, tis, tere, to poure out, or runne out.
Futis, a vessel, wherwith water was poured in to a lauer, to brynge water into a parlour or soupynge chamber.

G, ANTE A.

GABA, a towne in Galile
Gabalum, a towne in Fraunce, nyghe to Narbona, where there was made very good chese.
Gabaon, a cytie in the holy lande nyghe to Rama, where Salomon doing sacrifice, spake with god.
Gabaonite, men of that towne.
Gabba, a citie in Siria.
Gabriel, signifyeth the puissaunce or myght of god.

Galatia, a countrey in the lasse Asia.
Galgulus, a byrde, whom if one do beholde that hath the yelowe iaundise, furthwith the man becommeth hole, and the byrde hath the syckenesse.

Plinius — Galilea, is a countray, whiche marcheth on Siria, Arabia, and Egypt.

Pau. Iouius — Gallaria, a lampurne.
Gallus, a, um, of Fraunce.

Columell. — Gangaride, people betwene Assiria & Inde.
Gangilium, a sickenesse in the hed of a beast, wherwith the hed becometh ful of water.
Ganzæ, geese.
Garuna, a ryuer in Fraunce, called Gyrond.
Gastrimergia, gloteny.

G, ANTE E.

Gebuseus, the son of Canaan, of whom the olde inhabitauntes of Hierusalem were called Gebusei.
Gedeon, the name of a iudge in Israell.
Gedrosia, a countray in Asia.
Gemellariæ, an instrumente, by the whiche oyle runneth out of the presse.
Gemmosus, sa, um, that whiche is all of preciouse stones.

Vergilius. — Gemit cymba, the bote cracketh beynge ouercharged.

Colum. 3. — Generositas, an aptnes to ingendre, to bring forthe. somtyme it signifyeth nobilitie.
Genezareth, a great mere or ponde in the lande of promission, and it is alsoo called Mare Tiberiadis.
Genocha, a beaste lasse than a foxe, in color a darke yelowe, full of blacke spottes: I suppose it to be a blacke Ienet, the furre wherof is in Englande estemed aboue all other furres.
Genselia, whiche is compacte of many families or kynredes.
Geodesia, is a science of thinges concerning sensible greatnesse and fygure.
Gergonia, a towne in Guyen, standynge on an hyghe hyll.

Pli. in pan. — Gerere bellum, to make warre.

Terent. in Adelph. Cicero de amicitia. Plautus in penulo. Plautus i.. Amphit. — Gerere honores, to be in honour or autorite.
Gerere morem, to obeye.
Gerere negotium, to do his busynesse.
Gerere præturam, to be in the authirotye of a iudge.
Gerere pudorem, to be shamefaste.
Gerere rempublicam, to mynistre the publyke weale.
Gerontocomion, an hospitall, wherin olde men are kept, an almesehouse.
Gesta, thynges whiche haue benne doone, actes.
Gethy, people, whiche some suppose to be those

The additions. H *ante* A.

those, whiche are in Norway and Gothia: some say that they be more in the northeste in Scithia parteynynge to Europa.

G, ANTE I.

Gibbosus, idem quod Gibber.
Githago, cokyll growynge amonge corne whiche is rype.
Giruli, fysshes whiche I suppose to be menowes.

G ANTE L.

Glomus, mi, et glomus glomeris, a botome of thede.
Glucidatum, swete and delectable.

G ANTE N.

Gnafalium, an herbe, which is also called Chamezelon, whose leaues are so white & soft, that it semeth to be floxe
Gnafos, a tesyll, whiche towkars do vse in rowynge of clothes.
Gnarauit, et Gnarauisse, for Narrauit et Narrauisse. *Liuius.*
Gnariter, for gnare, wyttily.
Gnauus, quicke, actiue, apt to euery thing.
Gnauiter, dyligently, lustily, valiantly.
Gnitur, et Gnixus, old wryters vsed for Gignitur, et Nixus.
Gnoro, for Noro.
Gnosco, for Nosco.
Gnossos, a citie in Creta or Candy.
Gnosius, a, um, of that citie.

G ANTE O.

Gomor, is a measure of the hebrues, and is the tenth part of Ephi, wherfore it conteyneth .vii. times the measure called Sextarium. iii. ounces, an halfe ounce, ii. scruples, on halfe obolus, halfe one siliqua, and the tenthe part of Siliqua
Gobio, idem quod Gobius, a gogeon.
Gorgonius, a, um, partryning to Gorgones
Gotthia, a countray beyond Norway, wherof the people are called Gotthi, whyche destroyed the Empire of Rome, with the more parte of Europa.

G ANTE R.

Gradus, a griece wherby a man goeth vpwarde. Also a degree. *Liuius.*
Gradu mouere, to cause one to steppe backe.
Gradu dimoueri, to be put out of estimation or authoritie. *Ci. Tus. 2. Ci. de off. 1*
Gradu deiici, to be putte from a constaunte purpose.

Gradus, honour.
Graeca salix, red wyllowe. *Ci. in philipp. 2.*
Grecisco, are, to folowe the grekes.
Graecia, the countray called Greece.
Graecus, a greke.
Grandiusculus, a, um, a lyttell greatter.
Gratiam habere, to thanke.
Gratiam inire, to get thanke.
Gramma, idem quod scriptulum, uel scrupulū, a scruple, the .xxiiii. parte of an ounce.
Gratiam referre, to require one with a good tourne or an yll.
Gratia tui, for thy sake.
Gratus, a thankefull man.
Gratitudo, dinis, kyndenesse.
Grate, kyndely.
Grauastellus, an auncient father. *Plautus.*
Grauis nuntius, heuy tydynges. *Vergilius.*
Graue pretium, an hyghe pryce.
Grauedinosus, a, um, heuy or vnlusty, disposed to do no thynge.
Grauicors, cordis, he that hath a gret hart.
Grauiloquus, he that speaketh grauely and seriousely.
Gremium, is the space betwene the twoo thighes, specially of a woman.
Gruina, herbe roberte.

G, ANTE V.

Guesselli, beastes lyke to myse, which haue their dunge as swete as muske
Guberno, nare, to gouerne. *Plinius in Epistolis.*
Gubernator, a mayster of a shyp. also a gouernour of a countray. *Ci. in phi.*
Gubernacula nauis, the Instrumentes, wherby the shyp is ruled.

H, ANTE A.

Habet eum arcte, he kepeth hym short or from lybertie. *Plautus in Mercator.*
Habere contionem, to preache, to declare a thynge to the people.
Habere rationē cū terra, to labour the erthe.
Habitus, ta, tum, had.
Habraham, is interpreted father of manye dyuerse people.
Hadria, beinge the masculyne gendre, is taken for the gulf of Venice, or the see ther. beynge the femynine gendre, it is a towne by Ferrare.
Hadrianus, a noble emperoure, whiche in al sciences was excellntly lerned.
Hadriaticum mare, the see, which is betwen the northe parte of Italy and Illiria, or Slauony.

Ll.ii. Hac,

Terent. in Eunucho. Idē in Ad.   Hac, hense. somtyme by this place.
Hac non successit, it came not well to passe this way.
Hebudes, are Iles beyonde Scotlande two dayes saylynge, wherof be fyue.
Herba, an herbe.
Herbaceus, a, um, that is of herbes.
Herbarius, he that knoweth herbes, & their vertues.
Herbarius, a, um, of herbes.
Herbesco, scere, to be an herbe.
Herbidus, et Herbosus, a, um, hauynge many herbes.
Hagiographa, holy scripture.
Hagiographus, a wryter of holy scripture.
Hallux, the greatte toe, whyche lyeth ouer the nexte toe.
Halyetus, a faulcon.
Hanus barbatus, a lyttell pot with a greate bely, wherin wyne and water were wonte to be brought to the table.

Terent. in Eunucho.   Haud inuito, wyllyngly.
Vergili.   Haud nihil, some thynge.
Vergilius.   Hausit cœlum, he sawe heuen.
Cicer. pro M. Cælio.   Hausit corda pauor, feare made theyr courages faynt.
Augustinꝰ.   Haurire dolorē, to endure heuines or sorow
Hauritorium, any thynge wherby water is drawen out of a welle.

H ANTE E.

Heana, a foundation.
Hebetesco seu hebetasco, scere, belongeth proprely to the eyes, to be dulle in syght.
Hebrei, Iewes.
Hecatontarchus, the Capytayne of a hundred menne.
Hecta, vel heta, a tryfle.
Hemina, is a measure, whiche is halfe asmoche as Sextarius, that is to say, conteyneth x. ounces, and is also callyd Dextans, in the pounde of measure.
Vid. Cæsa.   Hedui, people in Fraunce, nowe callydde Burgonyons.
Helciarius, he that draweth a bote agaynste the streame.
Helicon, a mountayne in Bœotia.
Heliopolis, a citie in Egypte.
Helleborum edere, is a prouerbe spoken to men, whyche are very melancholye, or be wylde brayned.
Heluella, smalle herbes or wortes.
Helxine, an herbe called pelitory.
Hemionitis, siue hemonion, an herbe whyche we commonly call hartes tunge.
Hemicadia, vesselles callyd a tierce, halfe a hogges heed.
Heo, an interiection, howe.
Heptaphillon, an herbe called tormentill.

Hercle, a worde vsed to ornate a sentence by affyrmation.
Here, for heri, yesterday.
Herinarius, an hedgehogge.
Hermathena, was two ymages to gether of Mercury and Mynerua.
Heros, herois, an halfe god, or he whiche for the loue of vertue susteyneth great labours and peryl.
Hera, the lady, the maystree, the dame.
Herilis, le, perteinyng to the lord or master.
Hexaplum, vel hexapla, an example.
Hexasticum, syxe verses together.
Hexapeda, a measure called a fathom.

H ANTE I.

Hibiscus, wylde malowes.
Hic, Tu si hic sis, aliter sentias, if thou were I, or as I am, thou woldeste thynke other wise.   *Terent. in And.*
Hieratica, fyne paper.
Hin, a measure of the Hebrues, which conteyneth xii. tymes the measure callyd Sextarius, rede more in Sextarius.
Hinnus, hinna, & hinnulus, hinnula, a mule engendred betwene an asse and a mare.
Hinc, an aduerbe sygnyfienge from thense.   *Terent. in Adelph.*
Hinc illinc venit, he commeth I knowe not frome whens.   *Idē in Eun.*
Hinc loci mei, from my countray, or towne that I cam fro.   *Idē in and.*
Hinc, for that cause. Hinc illę lachrimę, For that cause were the teares, or that was the matter wherfore he wepte.
Hiant flores, the floures doo spreade.   *Vergili. 6.*
Hiare, to wonder or meruayle.
Hippagogius, an instrumente, wherewith stones are polyshed.
Hipparchus, captayne of the horsemen.
Hippei, cometes or blasyng sterres, hauing manes lyke horses.
Hippiades, images of womē on horsback, as the womē of Amazon were alway paynted.
Hippias, was a philosopher in Gretia, whiche aduauntid hym selfe to knowe al sciences and artes: for in eloquence he was excellent, meruaylouse in poetry, also in musyke, and made the instrumentes, whereon he played, and al the garmentes that he did weare, and the rynge on his fynger, which was wonderfully well grauen, and wrought his gyrdell with nedell worke incomparably, and in philosophy dysputed with al mē.
Hippobotos, a feder of horses.
Hippolapathum, an herbe, whiche some doo suppose to be pacience.
Hypericon, an herb callid saint Johns wort.
Hydropiper, semeth to be the herbe whiche the potecaries do cōmonly cal Eupatory.
Histria,

The additions.   I ante A.

H ANTE O.

Hodiernus, na, um, of this day.
Homonymon, where manye thynges haue one name, but dyuers in effect: As a man, which is alyue, or paynted, deuided by this addicion, a very man, a paynted man.

Cicero. Honorificētissime, in a very honorable forme or maner, very honorably.

Honorem prefari, is where one shal speke of any thynge, that is not honest, than to say, Sauynge your reuerence.

Hora, is somtime take for a day: also for time
Hordeaceus, a, um, of barly.

Plinius. Hordearij, they whiche do lyue with eating barley.

Horiola, a lyttell fyshers bote.
Horno, an aduerbe sygnifienge this yere.
Horrent agri, the fyldes are vnpleasaunt and vnfrutefull.
Horti pensiles, gardeynes made on the toppes of houses, or vpon pylars.
Hortensis, se, perteynynge to a gardeyne, or of a gardayne.
Hospitium, a house alwaye redy to receyue frendes. Sometyme a lodgynge. also an hospytall. somtyme frendeshyppe shewed in hospitalitye.

H, ANTE Y.

Hyades, the seuen sterres.
Hydragogus, he that bryngeth water to a place by furrowes or trenches.
Hydrargyrū, a certayne thynge, wherwith syluer is gilt in the stede of quicke syluer.
Hypenium ouum, an egge whiche hath neyther whyte nor yelke.
Hypotheca, a pledge. also a doctryne.
Hypothesis, an argument, matter, or cause, wherupō one shuld argue, dispute, or speke.
Hycca, a greate fysshe, whiche Hermolaus Barbarus taketh for a Sturgeon.

I, ANTE A.

Pli. in epi.
Cicero de amicitia.

Quintil. 9. Cicer. pro Roscio. Cicero.

I A, was the yonger sonne of Atlas, and sounethe as moche as a voyse.
Iacet grauiter, he lyethe sycke.
Iacens animus, a desperate mynde.
Iacet oratio, the oration is without any grace or spirite.
Iacent pretia, they are of a lowe pryce.
Iacent, they are without vertue, courage, or estimation.

Iacēre, to extende out or be of length.
Iacio, ieci, iacere, to caste or throwe.
Iacere fundamentū, to set or lay a foundation.
Iacob, a patriarch, sonne of Isaac.
Iam, is also incontinent or forthwith.
Iam ne imus? shall we not go nowe?   *Terent. in Eunucho.*
Iatros, a phisition.

I, ANTE B.
¶Ibidem, there, or in the same place.

I, ANTE D.

ID curat scilicet, he careth moch therfore, whiche is spoken as who sayth, he careth nothynge for it.   *Ter, in An.*
Id locorum, for Id.
Id temporis, at that tyme, or suche a tyme.   *plau. in ca. & in pænu. Ci. de orator. & pro Milone.*
Id temporis est: The tyme is suche.
Idaspes, a ryuer runnynge by Parthia and Inde: and at the laste falleth into the gret ryuer called Indus: in this ryuer is found moche golde and precious stones.
Idem, also signifyeth lyke or sembable.
Idipsum, the same thynge, or one thynge.   *Plautus in Epidico. Ter. in an.*
Idomeneus, the sonne of Deucaliō and king of Crete.

I, ANTE E.
¶Iessen, a towne, where Ioseph met his father Iacob, and brought hym into Egypt.

I, ANTE G.

IGnarius lapis, a fyre stone, or flynte, out of the whiche fyre is beaten.
Ignauia, is also lacke of courage.   *Affranius.*
Ignauit, he made him a foole.
Ignauiter, with a fals harte, or cowardly.

I, ANTE L.

ILlabor, beris, labi, to throw hym selfe into a thynge. Mediecq minans illabitur urbi: And thretnynge theym, he threwe hym selfe into the citie.   *Vergili.*
Illaboratus, ta, tum, that whiche is made or done without labour.
Illac, on that syde.
Illiusmodi, of that sorte.
Illepidus, without dilectation or grace.
Illiberalis, vngentyll, withoute kyndenesse or courtesy.
Illiberale facinus, an vncurteyse pageaunt.   *Te. in Ad.*
Illinc, from that place.
Illiteratus, vnlerned.
Illo, to the place.   *plautus in capt.*
Illotis manibus rem aggredi, to go aboute a great thynge without reuerence, or dishonestly

Ll iii   nestly

The additions. I ante M.

nestely to treate a thynge of greate estymation.

Gellius. Illotis pedibus, fere idem, also without shame
Macrobi. Illuc, in that place or there.
Illutibilis, that whiche can not be wasshed awaye.

I, ANTE M.

Imaginosus, sa, um, full of images.
Immemor, forgetfull, he that dothe not remembre.
Plautus in Immemorabilis, le, vnworthy remembrance.
Capt. Immensus, a, um, of suche greatenesse, that it can not be measured.
Suetonius Immerens, he that hath not deserued.
Plautus in Immerito meo, without my deserte.
Asina. Immerito, an aduerbe, without deseruinge.
Immergo, mersi, gere, to drowne, or to plõge a thynge in the water.
Cicer. pro Immersit se in alicuius consuetudinem, he
cluen. brought hym selfe into deepe acquaintance with one.
Plautus in Immersit se in ganeum, he is goten into a ta-
Menech. uerne: or he hath thraste hym selfe in to a tauerne or ale house.
Plautus in Immigro, to go to dwell in a place.
Mostel. Immigraui in ingenium meũ, I came to mine owne rule, or to be ruled by min owne wit.
Imminere, signifyeth also, to be nygh. Mors propter incertos casus quotidie imminet, Dethe, by vncertayne chaunces, is euery daye nyghe.
Cicero in Imminent in fortunas nostras, they be at hand
philip. and redy to robbe vs of our goodes.
Ouidius Imminet exitio alterius, he is redy to sle one.
Ci. in Ver. Imminens, that whiche is at hande.
Act. 4 Imminens ingenium, a runnynge wytte.
Imminuere caput alteri, to breke ones hed.
Plautus in Imminuere pudicitiam virginis, to defloure a
Mostel. mayden.
Imminuere maiestatem, to commyt treason.
Immisceo, scui, scere, to mengle to gether.
Immisericorditer, without pitie.
Terent. in Immitis, te, cruell, without pitie.
Adelphis. Immitia poma, apples whyche are not yet
Plinius rype.
Immobilis, le, vnmoueable.
Plautus in Immodestus, ta, tum, without temperaunce.
pœnu. Immodeste, out of measure: also to moche.
Immodicus, ca, cum, great or moche.
Martialis. Immodici, many.
Immodice, to moche.
Immola, a citie in Italy, whiche was sometyme called Forum Cornelii.
Immortalitas, a perpetuall lyfe.
Immortalis, le, vnmortall, that lyueth euer.
Immoror, rari, to abyde or contynue in a thynge.

Immustulus, a lyttell byrde, I suppose it be a wrenne.
Immuto, tare, to chaunge one thynge for a nother. *Plautus in Epidico. Ibidem.*
Immutabilis, le, vnchaungeable.
Impancro, crare, to inuade, or go into a place
Impar, not equall, not sufficient.
Imparens, disobedient.
Imparatus, vnredy, vnpuruayed. *Festus. Plautus in Amphitri.*
Impatibilis, le, that whiche can not suffre or susteyne.
Impauidus, he that feareth not.
Impendent mala, myschiefe is nyghe. *Cic. planc.*
Imperium exequi, to do that is commanded.
Imperare cupiditatibus, to rule desyres or appetytes.
Impertio, tiui, tire, et Impertior, tiris, perti, to partycipate with one, to giue parte of that whiche he hath.
Impertire salute, to salute. *Terent. in Eunucho.*
Impertitur, parte is gyuen. *Festus.*
Impesco, scere, to putte a beaste in to a good pasture to feede.
Impigre, diligently, without slouthe.
Impio, are, to defile, to stayne him selfe with a dishonest or foule dede, specially agaynst god or his parentes.
Implere, somtyme signifyeth to accomplishe or put in execution. *Sueton. plinius. Columell. Non. Mar. plautus in Epidic.*
Impluo, ere, to rayne in.
Implutus, wet in the rayne.
Impluiatus, ta, tum, coloured as it were wet in the rayne.
Imponere legem, to set a lawe on a thynge.
Imponere alicui, to deceyue one.
Importuosus, a, um, without porte or hauen.
Improbus alię rei, good for non other thing. *plautus in Milite. Ibidem. Moste.*
Improba merx, ill marchaundise.
Improbi postes, rotten postes, or decayed, or feble.
Improbe, an aduerbe signifyenge il, nawghtly, vnhappely.
Improlis, vel Improlus, he whiche is not yet a cytezen.
Improuidus, he that prouydethe not for the tyme commynge.
Improuidus, da, dum, that whiche commeth sodaynely and vnloked for.
Improuisus, a, um, idem.
Improuise, vnthought on, or vnloked for.
Imprudens harum rerum, not knowynge of those matters.
Imprudentia, lacke of foresyght, that it was not thought on.
Imprudenter, vnwysely, vnaduysedly.
Imputare, is also to reken one thynge with a nother, or to accompte one somme with a nother. *Vlp. Caius*

I, ante

The additions.   I ante N.

I, ANTE N.

Ci. in Ver.	IN annum, for a yere.
Cicero de amicitia.	In bonis, amonge good men.
Terent. in Andri.	In cœnam, for supper.
	In conspectum aspice, loke before the.
Plautus in persa.	In diem uiuere, to lyue without carynge for to morowe.
Quintilia.	In numerato habere, redy, or at hande.
Plautus in Asin.	In partem, for thy parte. Age sis, tu in partem nunc iam hunc delude, atque amplexare hanc: Goo to nowe for thy parte, deceyue hym hardely, and take her vnto the.
Cicero.	In pedem, for euery foote. Is se ternis nummis in pedem tecum transegisse dicebat: He sayde, that he bargayned with the for thre pence a fote, or for euery fote.
Cicer. pro lege Ma.	In potestatem esse, vnder the rule, or at the pleasure of one.
	In presentia, at this present tyme.
	In primis, aboue all other thynges.
	In procliui, that maye be lyghtely or easyly done.
	In promptu est, it is easy to knowe, it is apparaunte.
Plautus in pseud.	Inanis accedit, he commeth withoute bryngynge any thynge with hym.
Festus.	Inciens, a woman nygh her tyme to trauaile of chylde.
	Inclareo, uel inclaresco, ere, to be knowen of all men.
	Inconsulte, without counsaile, or vnaduisedly
	Incontinens, he that is not chaste, or kepeth hym not to one woman.
	Incoquo, xi, coquere, to seethe or boyle in a thynge.
Festus.	Incoctus, ta, tum, vnboyled or rawe.
	Incocte mulieres, women whiche do trymme theyr heares to moche.
	Incoctile, a brasyn or copper vessell, tynned within.
Cic act. 4. in Verrem	In consilio adesse, to be of counsayle in a mater in lawe. Me quoque Petilius, vt sibi consilio adessem, rogauit: Petilius alsoo desyred me, that I wolde be of counsayle.
Plautus in cistell.	Incordio, aui, are, to put into a mans harte, to perswade hym.
	Incubo, bonis, they that set al theyr study on treasure.
Plautus in Aulular. Ibidem.	Incumbere, to be inclyned to some thynge.
	Incumbere gladium, to thrust hym selfe on a sworde.
	Indecens, vnsyttynge, vnconuenient.
	Indecoris, re, idem quod Indecor.
	Indecore, an aduerbe, syghnifyeng vnhonestly, vnconueniently.
	Indico, dixi, dicere, to denounce properlye warre.
	Indicere consilium, to call or commaunde a counsayle.

	Indicere iustitium, to commaunde a vacation, or as we do say, to kepe no terme.
	Indicere pecuniam populo, to sette a taxe or subsydie on the people.
	Induere postes pice, to laye on pytche on the postes.	Plautus in mostel.
	Induere personam alterius, to speake in the name or stede of a nother man.	Quintilia.
	Induere personam iudicis, to represente a iudge.
	Industrie, wyttyly.
	Inire rationem, to fynde the meane.
	Inire, to leape, as a horse lepeth a mare.
	Ineunte ætate, in youthe.
	Ineunte uere, at the begynnyng of the spring of the yere.
	Inexhaustus, a, um, neuer ceasynge.
	Inferre crimen alicui, to laye to ones charge.
	Inferre sermonem, to talke.
	Infectus, infected, stayned, dyed.
	Infectum reddere, to vndoo that whiche is doone.
	Infecta pace, without any peace made.
	Infector, a dyar of colours.
	Infit, he sayde, he beganne.
	Inflecto, tere, to bowe or plye.
	Influo, xi, ere, to runne into a thynge, as water or other lycour dothe.
	Infuco, care, to coloure a thynge, intending deceipte.
	Infuscare uinum merum, to slaye wyne with water.	Plautus in cistell.
	Ingeniculus, a fygure amonge the sterres, called nowe Hercules.
	Ingenua facta, noble actes.
	Ingens animus, a great courage.	Plautus in milite.
	Ingerere dicta in aliquem, to chyde with one, to say ill of one.	Plautus in Asina.
	Ingerere malum, to do displeasure.
	Ingerere pugnos, to strike with the fyste.
	Ingratijs, maulgre one.	Plautus in Amphit. & in curcu.
	Ingratus, ta, tum, vnthankfull, dyspleasaunt, constrayned, or agaynste a mannes wyl. also vnkynde, and not remembrynge frendshyppe, or beneuolence.	Terentius in Eunuch.
	Inguinium, a citie in Liguria, aunciente and ryche.
	Inhabilis, le, vnapt.	Plinius in Epistolis.
	Inhabito, tare, to dwell in a place.	Plautus in Sticho
	Inhibere imperium, to haue charge or rule.	Ci. in phil.
	Inhibere supplicia alicui, to execute turmentes on one, or to put one to dethe.
	Inhibere nauem, to caste ancre, or to staye a shyppe, which is vnder sayle, that she saile not a full course.	Terent. in Eunucho.
	Inhonestus, ta, tum, dishoneste.
	Inhoneste, dishonestly.
	Inhonoratus, ta, tum, lackynge honour.

Ll iiij   Inhos-

The additions. I ante T.

Inhospes, he that wyl lodge no man.
Inhospita tecta, houses where no man maye lodge.
Inhospitalis, le, vnapte for lodgynge.
Cicer. pro Roscio. Inhumo, are, to put into the grounde.
Inijcere manus in aliquem, to apprehende or attache one.
Terentius in phormi. Inijcere scrupulum alicui, to put one in a fantasye.
Sueton. Inijcere studium alicui, to cause one to study.
Iniquo animo ferre, to be myscontented or sorowfull.
Iniqué, myscheuousely, or vniustly.
Plautus in Truculen. Cicero de senectute. Iniuria tua, throughe thy defaulte.
Iniussu imperatoris, without the emperours commaundement.
Iniusta, ta, tum, vniuste. also excedynge iuste measure.
Iniusté, vniustely.
Innascor, sci, to be ingendred in one.
Innatus, ta, tum, ingendred.
Innocens, vnharmefull, innocent.
Innocentia, integritie, true intente.
Pli. in epi. Paulus. Inoffensus, vnhurte.
Inofficiosum testamentum, where the father by testament gyueth away from his sonne his landes or goodes without cause.
Cicer. pro domo sua. Inops ab amicis, dyspouruayed of frendes.
Inops amicorum, idem.
Inopia, pouertie, lacke of thynges necessary
Inopinatus, vnthought on or vnloked for.
plin. in epi. 291. Plautus in Aulul. Salusti. in In quantum, in as moche, or for as moche.
Inquam, I sayde.
Insanitas, madnesse.
Insaciabilis, le, vnsaciable.
Inscendo, dere, to go vp, or to clyme.
Terent. in Heauto. Cicer. pro P. Sylla. Tit. Li. 4. Insciens, vnwyttinge. also not thynkynge on that he doeth.
Inscientia, ignoraunce.
Instaurare bellum, to make warre eftsones.
Institor, may also be called a factour whiche byeth and selleth for a nother man.
Institoria actio, an action brought by the master agaynste his factour, or by the factour agaynste his master.
plautus in Epidic. Instituere astutiam, to finde a craft to deceiue oone.
Terent. in phorm. In integrum restituere, to restore a thynge to as good poynte as it was in.
Cicero in philip Integrum est, hit is at his pleasure or in his power.
Integré, truely, and diligently.
Cicero de oratore. In integro esse. Sed quoniam hęc iam neque in integro esse possunt: But for as moche as there is no remedy, or that these thynges maye not be holpen, or maye not be in as good poynte as they were.
Cic. de Se= nectute. Intemperans, he that doth euery thyng without order or measure.

Intendere formulam, to brynge an action agaynste one.
Suetonius in Vitell. Sueton. in Tyberio. Cic. ad Q. fratrem. Terent. in Eunucho.
Inter coenam, for In coena.
Inter nos amamus, we loue togyther oone an nother.
Inter uias, by the waye rydynge or goinge.
Intercessor, he that letteth a matter, that it may nat goo forwarde.
Interpellatio, a lette in a mans busynesse.
Interpellator, he that letteth oone that he may nat speake or doo a thynge.
Intrarius amicus, a speciall frende.
plautus.
Intybum, seu Intybus, is the generalle name to all kyndes of Cichorye or Succhorye, as commune Succhorie, Scariole, Endiue, and Dendelyon.

I, ANTE S.

Ischiros, idem quod fortis, stronge.
Isatis, Ode, wherewith clothes are dyed blewe.

I, ANTE T.

Ita me deus amet, Soo god loue me, or helpe me.
Plautus. Terentius
Ita ut sit, as it happeneth. Dum rus eo, cœpi egomet mecum inter uias, ita ut sit, ubi quid in animo est molestiæ, aliam rem ex alia cogitare, whanne I wente downe into the countraye, by the waye rydynge, as it happeneth oftentimes, whan any displeasure commeth to my mynde, I bethought me of one thynge and other.
Terent. in Eunucho.
Ita ut erat, as it was in dede.
Ita ne? but is it so? or is it as thou sayste?
Also it sygnyfieth a note of dysdayne. Ita ne contemnor abs te? Settyst thou soo lytelle by me?
Terent. in Andria.
Itaq, wherfore than.
Itáque, and soo.
Item, euen as, also, in lyke maner.
Iter facere, to goo a iourney.

I, ANTE V.

Iucundé, merilye, gladdely, pleasauntly, dylectably.
Iucunditas, dilectation, pleasure.
Iudicio perfundere, to bryng one to the point to be condempned.
Cicer. pro Sex. Rosc.
Iurare in uerba alterius, to doo fealtie, or to be sworne a subiecte.
Iurare in lege alterius, to sweare to kepe the lawes or ordinances of an nother.
plin. de viris illustr.
Ius bonum dicis, thy request is reasonable.
Ius dicis, thou speakest reason.
Iure, with good cause.
Plautus in Stico. Plautus in Epidico.
Iure uel iniuria, by right or wronge.

Iusta

The additions.

Terent. in Andri.
Plautus in Capt.
Ter. in Ad.

Iusta seruitus, seruyce without rygour.
Iusti honores, honours due.
Iuuat mihi, It dothe me good, it is a pleasure to me.

L ANTE A.

LABIO, is a fysshe, whiche I suppose to be that that is callyd Cod, with the great lyppes. it was alsoo the Surname of a Romayne.
Labrum, a lyppe. also the brymme of a ryuer. also a wasshynge basyn.
Laccia, a fysshe callyd a cheuyn.

Plautus in Sticho
Plautus in Asin.
Priscianus Festus.

Lacerare diem, to lose the day, to spende the tyme aboute nought.
Lachrimula, a lyttell teare.
Lacio, lacui, & lexi, lacere, to brynge into a snare, or to wynde one in to deceyue him.
Lamia, is alsoo an herbe callyd a blynde or deade nettyll.
Lagopus, an herbe, whyche I suppose to be Auyns.
Latheris, an herbe callyd Spurge.

L, ANTE E.

Lechia, a fysshe, whiche some haue taken to be Tunye, for the symylitude of them.
Legere, to chese.
Lege agere, to sewe in the lawe, also to doo execution.
Lens palustris, duckes meate, whyche is in standynge waters.
Leo, a shelle fysshe callyd a lopstar.
Lepide, pleasantly, pratyly.
Lepista, a lyttell potte or vyole.
Lepta, is the smalleste poyse that maye be, wherof there ar. lxxxiiii. in one scruple, in a dramme. CCliii.
Leucophlegmantia, a spyce of the dropsye, where the face and membres are whyte, and swollen great.
Leuare aliquem onere, to discharge oone of his burdeyne.
Leuare laborem, to mynysshe his labour.
Leuare morbum, to put out of payne.
Leuia uina, smalle wynes.
Leuita, a deacon.
Leuiter, lyghtly.

L, ANTE I.

Lia, oone of the wyues of Iacob the patriarche.
Libella, the diminutife of Libra, it was also a smalle coyne, and of them were two sortes, one was worthe the tenthe part of Sestertius, the other the tenthe parte of Denarius.
Libelliones, caryers of letters.
Libere, frankly, liberally, without constraint.
Libere uiuere, to lyue at pleasure.
Liberalis forma, a good fauour.
Liberale ingenium, a free courage.
Libertus, a bondman manumised.
Libra, a pounde weight, wherof were dyuers, one was the Romayne pounde, whiche contayned. xii. ounces, or foure score z xvi. drammes, an nother was belonging to exchaungers or bankers, and was but of viii. ounces, an other was callid Mina, wher of rede more in Mina.
Lichen, an herbe called Lyuerwort.
Limaria, the fysshe callid Tuny, whan it doth nat excede one foote in length.
Lingulaca, a fysshe callyd a sole.
Litem contestari, I suppose dothe sygnifie as moche as that whiche our lawyers doo saye, to enterpleade whan oone, whiche is nat partie to the action, cometh in, or is callyd in to pleade with the other, to thintent to saue his title or interest, whiche is supposed that he hath with them.

L ANTE O.

Locus obiurgandi, occasion to chyde.
Locare filiam, to bestowe his dowghter in mariage.
Locusta, a fysshe callid a creuyse.
Locutor, he that speaketh moche.
Log, is the same measure of the Hebrues, that Sextarius atticus, is amonge the Grekes. Rede more in Sextarius.

Terent. in And.

Gellius.

L ANTE V.

Lucigena, ingendred of lyght.
Lucto, idem quod luctor.
Ludos reddere, & ludos facere, to mock
Ludia, a mery wenche full of sporte.
Luminibus obstruere, to stoppe vp the lyght, to lette that the lyghte maye nat come in to a house.
Lumina preferre, to inspyre.
Lumminosus, a, um, full of lyght.
Lumbrici, lytell fysshes taken in small riuers whyche are lyke to lampurnes, but they be moche lasse, and somewhat yelowe, and are callyd in Wyltshire prides.
Lupus, is a fysshe, whiche some men take for a pyke.
Lupus salictarius, hoppes, wherwith biere is made.

Terentius
Martialis.
Cicer. pro domo sua.

Cic. anteq fret in exilium.

L ANTE Y.

Lydius lapis, a prouerbe spoken of an exact iugement, or that whiche is exactly tried.
Lysi

The additions.   M ante A.

Lysimachia, a cytie in Ponto, whiche felle downe with an erthquake.

M, ANTE A.

MACER, seu Macir, a spyce callyd Maces.

M ANTE E.

¶ Medica, an herbe, whyche I suppose to be clouer grasse with purple rounde floures.
Melandria, the leane partes of the fishe callyd Tuny.
Melanurus, a kynde of perches, callydde Ruffes.
Melita, an yle lyenge betweene Sycile and Affryke, whiche is nowe callydde Malta, where at this tyme the companye of the knyghtes hospytilers do inhabite, as they dyd at the Rhodes.
Merula, a fyshe callyd Merlyng or whiting.
Minutum, idem quod lepta.
Mygala, a felde mouse with a longe snoute, callyd a shrewe.

O ANTE C.

Ocymum, an herbe callyd Basyll.
Oculata, a perche fyshe.
Olus atrum, an herbe callid Alisāder.
Orchynus, a great Tuny fyshe.
Orphus, a fyshe lyke to a Gurnarde.
Orcha, a great fyshe of the see, whiche deuoureth men and beastes hole, of the whiche fyshe we do see great bones hanged vp in the kynges houses. It is also a great pytcher, whiche serueth for wyne or oyle.

P, ANTE A.

PAGRI, fyshes, which I suppose are dacis.
Paliurus, some do suppose it to be a fryse, or a whyn.
Partheniū, is supposed of some well lerned men to be tansye, whiche opinion I thynke to be beste.

P, ANTE E.

Pectines, shell fyshes callyd Scalopes.
Pectunculi, cockylles.
Perca, a fyshe callyd a perche.
Perficaria, an herbe, whyche is supposed to be Arsmerte.
Pertica, a measure conteynyng xvi. fete, and is callyd a perche or a pole, or a rodde, it is sometyme but x. fete, and in wodde land xviii. fete.

Petasites, a clote, the leaues whereof are layde on butter.

P ANTE H.

Phellandrion, an herbe callid Filipēdula
Philago, Cudworte.
Phisides, fyshes lyke tenches, but that they are greener.
Physiter, a greate fyshe, whyche spoutethe out of his mouth great goulfes of water.
Phœnix, waybenet or bent.
Phocena, a fyshe callyd Porpuse, or lyke vnto it.

P ANTE O.

Polygonon, knotte grasse.
Pompilus, a kynde of great Tuny.   Iouius.
Populus alba, an aspe tree.
Porca, in mesure was reckned halfe a rounde   Columel.
lande, or the viii. parte of an acre.
Pseudonardus, lauander.
Psitta, a fyshe callyd turbutte.
Pugillus, as moche as the holownes of the hande may conteyne.
Pychis, a cubyte.
Pygmei, people, whyche are but a Cubyte in lengthe.

R ANTE A.

RAIA, a fyshe callyd skeate.
Ranunculus, an herbe callyd crowfote or goldeknappe.
Rhombus, a Fysshe callyd a Turbutte.
Ricinum, an herbe callydde Palma Christi.

R ANTE V.

Rubea maior, an herbe callyd madder.
Rubea minor, an herbe callid cliuers.
Rumex, dockes, sometyme it is taken for Sorell.
Ruscum, kneholme or hethbrushe.

S, ANTE A.

SABINA, an herbe callyd Sauyne.
Sampsuchus, an herbe callyd Maioram gentyll.
Satureia, an herbe callydde Sauerye.

S ANTE C.

¶ Scarus, is a fyshe, whyche I suppose is in Deuonshyre callyd a Bekar.
Scilla, some do call it a sturgion.

S ANTE E.

¶ SEDVM maius, houseleke or syngrene
Sedum minus, an herbe callid stonecroppe.
Selis

The additions. S ante E.

Selibra Romana, the Romayne half pound comprehended asmoch as our hole poūd.
Sæpia, a fyshe hauyng but one bone, wherin goldesmythes do make mouldes, and is callyd a cuttyll.
Seris, an herb callid white endiue & scariole
Sextula gemina, is the thyrde parte of an ounce, callyd also Duella.
⸿ Siclus, amonge the hebrewes was halfe an ounce.
Siliquastrum, an herbe which some do suppose to be coste mary.
Smilax, lacis, frenche peasyn.
⸿ Solanum, an herbe, whych some do suppose to be nyghtshade or morell.
Solanum soporiferum, an herbe, whyche I suppose to be Dwale.
Solonos uesicaria, Alkakengi.
Sonchus, an herbe callyd Southistell.
Sportula, the stipende giuen to tayly awaiters, for them and theyr company, amonge the noble Romayns, amounted to. ii. poyse grotes, and a halfe grote, or .x. pence of the olde coynage.
Stater argenteus, was a coyne of halfe an ounce weight, and was also callid Siclus & Tetradragmon.
Striatus, ta, tum, imbowid or made with ridges and furrowes, or lyke vnto it.
⸿ Symphitum, an herbe callyd Comfrye.
Sysimbrium, horsemynte as I suppose.
Sysymbrium cardanine, water cresses.
Tithimallus, a kynde of spurge. Some take it for wertwort.
Tussilago, an herbe callyd coltisfote.
Typhonicus uentus, a whyrle wynde, which pluckcth vp trees by the rootes.
Vettonica, an herbe callyd Bittayne.
Vettonica coronaria, Gyllofers.
Vmbelicus veneris, an herbe callydde Penygrasse.
Verbena, an herbe callyd Veruen.
Vitia, a pulse callyd a vetche.
Vlua, a flagge.
Xestes, idem quod Sextarius.
Finis Dictionarij.

TO THE HONEST AND
gentylle readers.

TO THE MORE playne declaration of these tables folowynge, briefely compiled out of the bokes of Georgius Agricola, and Robertus Senalis, whiche wrate last and most exactly of poises & measures, It shal be expedient to the reder to haue in remembrance these thynges folowynge.

FYRST whan he redeth in any boke of poyses, coynes, and measures, to consyder whither they be of Rome, Grece, or of the Hebrues, and than to seke the columnes, ouer the which those countreys ar written, & there shal he fynd that which he seketh for.

Also to remember the valuation of all our coyns, as they be rated at this present time, and accompt .xii.d. to a shylling .xi. grotes & ii.d. to an oūce .xx.s. to a pound .xiii.s.iiii.d. to a marke .xii. ounces to a pounde, as well of measure as of poyse.

Moreouer that euery ounce or ynch measure quadrate as a dye, is diuyded into the same minutes or porciōs, that an oūce poise is, and .xii. ounces in measure, concernynge vesselles, is not callydde there a footte, but a pounde measure.

Also that the vessellcs or receptories are first counted by measure, bicause that therin it is more certain than poise, as a poise oūce of honye is not in quantitie lyke to a poyse ounce of wyne or oyle. Wherfore Vncia red in old authors without addicion of pondus, is to be taken for the measure ounce, as ye shall fynde more aboundantly in the bokes of the sayde Agricola and Senalis.

Item in the redyng the mesures of greke, yf ye fynde them not here declared, ye must alway remember, that the englishe pynte is xxiiii. ounce measures, the pynte of Rome callyd Sextarius, is .xx. ounce mesures, the greke pynte callyd also Sextarius, and the hebrue pynte callid Log, is but .xviii. ounce mesures, & accordyng to that rate, ye muste make calculation in conferryng togyther all other measures.

And this I trust shall at this tyme suffise, for the vnderstanding of this matter, wher by the reders, as well of olde hystories, orations of Tulli, as also ancient phisitions, & the bokes of holy scripture callyd the Bible, shall apprehende more vnderstandinge, with singular dilectatiō and plesure. For the whiche I shall require them to giue praises to god, of whom it hath chiefely proceded, and thankes to our most excellent soueraynn lorde, by whose most gracious comfort and ayde, I haue perfourmed it, and to pray to god to gyue me grace and tyme, to accomplyshe suche warkes, as I haue purposed for the cōmoditie honour and weale of this my naturall countrey.

POISES.

The computation of Georgius Agricola.

¶ Romayne poyse.

Scriptulum, the .xxiiii. parte of an ounce.
Victoriatus, the .xiiii. part of an ounce.
Denarius, the seuenth part of an ounce.
Sextula, the syxte parte of an ounce.
Sicilicus, the fourthe part of an ounce.
Duella, the thyrde part of an ounce.
Semuncia, halfe an ounce.
Vncia, an ounce, the .xii. part of a pounde troy.
Sescuncia, an ounce and halfe.
Sextans, two ounces, or the syxt part of any thynge, hauyng poyse or measure.
Quadrans, a quarterne of a pounde, or thre ounces, or the .iii. parte.
Triens, foure ounces, or the fourthe parte.
Quincunx, fyue ounces, or the fyfte parte.
Semissis, halfe a pounde or halfe any thynge.
Septunx, seuen ounces or the seuenth parte.
Bes, viii. ounces, or the eight parte.
Dodrans, nyne ounces, or the nynthe parte.
Dextans, ten ounces, or the tenthe parte.
Deunx, xi. ounces, or the leuenth parte.
Libra, Pondo, seu As, twelue ounces.
As, is sommetyme taken for the hole of that whyche is diuided in partes.

Greke poyse.

Granum, the .iiii. part of Siliqua, the .CCCCC. xvi. parte of an ounce measure or poyse.
Siliqua, the thyrde parte of obolus, the .CxIiii. part of an ounce poyse and measure.
Obolus, the halfe of Scriptulum, or Scrupulus, the .xxxii. part of an ounce.
Scriptulum, the third part of Drachma, the .xxiiii. parte of an ounce.
Drachma, the .viii. part of an ounce, whiche practysers in phisyke haue estemed to the weighte of. lx. barley cornes taken oute of the myddell of the eare, the .viii. parte of an ounce poyse and measure.
Vncia, an ounce, the .xii. part of a poūd poyse and mesure.
Mina Attica, twelue ounces and halfe.
Mina medica, xvi. ounces.
Mina Alexandrina, xx. oūces.
Talentū atticū minus, conteyneth. lx. Minas atticas, whiche of our Troy weight amoūteth to. lxii. poundes and half a pounde.
Talentum atticum maius, conteyneth. lxxx. Minas, whiche is of troy weyghte. lxxxiii. li. and foure ounces.

Hebrue poyse.

Siclus, in poyse is halfe an ounce or foure drāmes.
Mina hebraica, cōteineth two poundis and a half, troy, or. lx. Siclos.
Talentum hebraicum, conteineth. C. Minas, that amoūteth to. CCL. poundes troy.
Talentum Syrum, contayneth Minas Atticas. xv. that is. xv. poundes. vii. ounces ꝫ a half.

ℭ The olde Englysshe poyse standerde.

Foure graynes of wheat poyseth the .iiii. parte of a penye, so. viii. graynes oughte to waye a farthynge xxxii. graynes a penye.
Peny and farthynge maketh the .xvi. parte of an ounce.
Foure Royalles maketh an ounce of golde.
Xii. ounces maketh a pounde of troy weight.

Romayne coyne.

AS, before the tyme of Augustus the emperour, was rated to the

COINE.

Romayne coyne.

tenth parte of Denarius, and afterwarde to the. xvi. parte of Denarius.
Sextans, the .vi. part of As.
Quadrans, the fourthe parte.
Semissis, halfe As.
Sestertius, the fourthe part of Denarius, contayneth .iii. Asses.
Victoriatus, the halfe of Denarius.
Denarius, whereof. vii. made one ounce, was by estimatiō of our moneye. vi. d. ob. and the .vii. parte of a halfpenye, after. xi. grotes and. ii. d. to an ounce.
Tressis. iiii. Asses.
Senarius. vi. Asses.
Decussis. x. Asses.
Solidus, was dyuersly taken, sometyme for a brasyn coyn, contayning. xii. small coynes. Somtyme for Drachma, in siluer, as primi Esdrę octauo ca. &. 2. eiusdem .7. et Paralipo. xxix. Some were the value of Drachma, as in the tyme of Alexander the emperour. Also Solidus aureus, was in the tyme of the same emperoure. ii. drammes of golde. After in the tyme of Justinian. vi. of them made an oūce, whyche was the iuste poyse and value of our royals.
Centussis, x. denarij, of oure money. v. s. vi. d. ob. half farthyng, halfe halfe farthynge.
Mille æris, a hūdred Cētusses, which is of our money xxvii. li. xvi. s. vi. d. q̄.
XX. Sestertij, ar. v. Denarij, of our money. ii. s. vii. d. ob. half farthinge, and the. xxiiii. part of a farthynge.
XL. Sestertij. v. s. iii. d. ferthig ꝫ the. xii. parte of a farthing.
Lxxx. Sestertij. x. s. vi. d. ob. and the. vi. parte of a farthyng.
Centum sestertij, xiii. s. ii. d. halfe farthyng, the. vi. parte of a farthyng, and the. xxiiii. parte of a farthynge.
CC. Sestertii. xxvi. s. iiii. d. q̄. the thyrde parte, and the. xii. part of a farthynge.
CCCC.

The cōputation of Robertus Senalis, bysshop of Abrent

COINE.

Greke coyne.

CCCC. Sestertij, lii. ʃ. viii. ð. ob. a half farthing, a quarter and the .vi. part of a farthing.
DCCC. Sestertij, v. li. v. s. v. ð. a farthing, half farthing, and the third part of a farthinge.
M. Sestertij, vi. li. xi. s. ix. ð. ob. or there aboute.
Sestertium, is euen as moch.

¶ Greke coyne.

Aereolum, seu Chalchus the .xxxvi. parte of drachma, by estimatiõ the poyse of .ii. barly cornes.
Semiobolus, the .xii. parte of Drachma. [marginal note: 48 areola cʒ ʒ ʒalʒob]
Obolus, the .vi. part of drac.
Drachma argenteum, a coyne whereof .viii. made an ounce, which is of our money after the rate of this present tyme v. pens halfpeny farthing, an ounce conteininge .xi. grotes and .ii. pence.
Didrachma. ii. drachmas, of our money. xi. ð. ob.
Stater, seu, Tetradrachmũ. iiii. drachmę, of our mony. xxii. ð
Decẽ drachmę, iiii. s. ix. ð. ob.
XX. drachmę, ix. s. vii. ð.
XXX. drach. xiiii. s. iiii. ð. ob.
XL. drach. xix. s. ii. ð.
L. drach. xxiii. s. xi. ð. ob.
LX. drach. xxviii. s. ix. ð
LXX. drach. xxxiii. s. vi. ð. ob.
LXXX. drach. xxxviii. s. iiii. ð.
LXXXX. drach. xliii. s. i. ð. ob
Centum drach. xlvii. s. xi. ð.
Drachma auri, is in value .xii. drach. argenti, v. s. ix. ð.
Mina, or Mna attica Solonis, a hundred drachmę, of our money. xlvii. s. xi. ð.
Mina uętus, xxxv. s. xi. ð. q̃. lxxv. drach.
X. Minę seu Mnę atticę, uel cõmunes, xxiii. li. xix. s. ii. ð.
XX. minę, xlvii. li. xviii. s. iiii. ð
XXX. minę, lxxi. li. xvii. s. vi. ð
Xl. minę, lxxxxv. li. xvi. s. viii. ð
L. Minę, Cxix. li. xv. s. x. ð.
LX. Minę, Cxliii. li. xv. s.
Lxx. Minę, Clxvii. li. xiiii. s. ii. ð
LXXX. Minę, Clxxxi. li. xiii. s. iiii. ð.

[marginal note: 96 sʒalʒob]

COINE.

Hebrue coyne.

LXXXX. Minæ, CCxv. li. xii. s. vi. ð.
Centum Minæ, CCxxxv. li. xi. s. viii. ð.
Talentum atticum minus aut cõmune, cõtayneth .lx. Minas, whyche is of oure moneye Cxliii. li. xv. s.
Talentum atticum maius, conteyneth .lxxx. Minas, of oure money. Clxxxxi. li. xiii. s. iiii. ð
V. Talenta minora, DCCxviii. li. xv. s.
X. Talenta, MCCCCxxxvii. li. x. s.
XX. Talenta, MMDCCC. lxxv. li.
XXX. Talẽta, MMMMCCC. xii. li. x. s.
Xl. Talẽ. MMMMDCCL. li.
L. Talẽ. vii. M. Clxxxvii. li. x. s.
LX. Talen. viii. M. DCxxv. li.
LXX. Talen. x. M. lxii. li. x. s.
LXXX. Talenta. xi. M. D. li.
LXXXX. Talenta, xii. M. D. CCCCxxxvii. li. x. s.
Centum Talenta. xiiii. M. li. CCClxxv li.
Mille Talenta, Clviii. thousãd and fyfty pounde.
In the accomptynge of Talẽtum atticum maius, adde to euery Talentum minus, xlvii. li. xviii. s. iiii. ð.

Hebrue coyne.

Siclus argenteus, was in value. iiii drachmas, of our money. xxii. ð.
V. Sicli. ix. s. vii. ð.
X. Sicli. xix. s. ii. ð.
XX. Sicli, xxxviii. s. iiii. ð.
XXX. Sic. lvii. s. vi. ð.
XL. Sicli. iii. li. xvi. s. viii. ð.
L. Sicli. iiii. li. xv. s. x. ð.
LX. Sicli. v. li. xv. s.
LXX. Sicli. vi. li. xiii. s. ii. ð.
LXXX. Sicli. vii. li. xiii. s. iiii. ð
Lxxxx. Sicli, viii. li. xii. s. vi. ð.
Centum Sicli. ix. li. xi. s. viii. ð.
Mille Sicli, Cv. li. viii. s. iiii. ð.
Mna Hebraica, to. lx. Sicli, of our money. v. li. xv. s.
Talentum Hebraicũ sanctuarij, contayneth a hundred Mnas hebraicas, of oure money. D. lxxv. li.

MEASVRES.

Rom. ⁊ Greke measure.

Talentum uulgare, containeth halfe soo moche. CClxxxvii. li. x. s.
V. Talẽta uulgaria, MCCCC. xxxvii. li. x. s.
X. Talent. MMDCCCllxxv. li.
XX. Talenta, v. M. DCCl. li.
XL. Talen. xi. M. CCCCC. li.
Lxxx. Talenta. xxiii. M. li.
Centum Talenta. xxviii. M. DCCl. li.

¶ Measure in length or breadthe. Romayne and Greke.

Granum, is the fourthe part of digitus a finger.
Digitus, a finger brede is the length of foure grains iiii. digiti maketh .iii. ynches.
Pollex, seu Vncia, callydde an ynche is the iuste lengthe of thre barly graynes, or foure whete cornes, and a quarter, taken out of the myddelle of the eare. of this one is vncia linearis, or an ynche by lyne: an other quadrata, or square, that is to say an ynch in lẽgth ⁊ brede: an other cubica, or in .iiii. quarters lyke a dyse, euery quarter beinge an ynch.
Palmus minor, cõtaineth .iiii. fyngers or .iii. ynches.
Palmus maior, cõtayneth the handbrede. iiii. fyngers, ⁊ the thumbe in depenes.
Palmus duplex seu dichas, conteyneth. viii. fyngers.
Spithame seu Dodrans, a span whiche is the space betwene the thumbe and the lytle finger stretched forth, ⁊ conteineth. ix. inches, or .xii. fingers
Pes, a fote, cõteineth .iiii. palmes, xii. inchis, or .xv. fingers which measure is made with a span and the length of halfe the myddell fynger, or with the two fistes closed, and the two thumbes extended metyng togither, but these measures are nat so certayne as the ynche before reherfed, by reason that all mens handes are nat like greate. And

Exod. 25.

MEASVRE OF VESSELL.

Hebrue measures.

therefore as I haue proued, the foote which is made by the sayd ynche, to be the fote which Budeus supposeth to be brought by the Romayns into Fraunce, as Glareanus saith, but the Romayn foote, wherof Portius makith mencion, is shorter than that fote one inche, and the .vi. part of a fynger. And the fote of the squire vsed by our Carpentars is shorter than the Romayne foote of Budeus one ynche, soo that it conteyneth xv. fyngers, wherby apereth the diuersitie of fote mesure, notwithstäding the said first fote is the true fote, and therby all other mesures shall be compted most perfitely.

Palmipes, containeth a fote & a palme, or .v. palmes.

Cubitus, conteyneth one fote and halfe.

Gressus, a steppe, conteineth two fote and a halfe.

Passus, a pase, contein. v. fote.

Orgia, a fathome, it is proprely .vi. fete.

Pertica, a perche, amonge the Romans conteineth .x. fete.

Plethrum, conteyneth a hundred fete.

Stadium, a furlonge, conteyneth .Cxxv. pacis.

Diaulus, conteinith .ii. furlõg.

Milliare, seu Milliarium, a mile conteineth .viii. furlong, or a thousande pacis.

Dolichos, contcineth xii. furlonges, or .MCCCCC. pacis.

Parasanga, xxx. furlonges.

Schœnos. lx. furlonges.

Stathmos, Statio, seu Mansio, one days iourney conteineth xxviii. myles.

Porca, Cxx. fete in length, and xxx. in bredth.

Actus, Cxx. fete square.

Iugerum Romanũ. in lengthe CCxl. fete, in bredth Cxx. fete

Hebrue measures.

Zereth, a palme.
Cubitus sanctuarij, conteineth .vi. palmes,

Romayne measure.

Gomor, as moche as a man maye receyue betweene his two armes.

Calamus sanctuarij, coteinith x. fete and a halfe.

Calamus vulgaris, conteineth ix. fete, of our measure three yerdes.

Chœmis, coteineth .iiii. miles

Castra, seu Stationes, conteine euery of them .ix. myles.

Iuger, seu Iugerum, as moche land as a yoke of oxen coude falowe in a day.

Decem iugera, as moche land as ten yoke of oxen moughte falowe in a daye.

Measure in vessell or thinges to receyue.

Romayne measure.

Ligula, siue Cochlear, the iiii. part of Cyathus, and receyueth .iii. drachmas and one Scriptulũ, of the inch measure.

Cyathus, wherof one maketh acetabulum, and is of mesure one ynche & a half, a dramme, and a scriple, and receyueth of oyle one ounce and halfe, of wyne one ounce .v. drachmas and one scriple, of hony two ounces di.

Acetabulũ, the halfe of Quartarius, is two inches and half of mesure, receiueth of oyle ii. ounces and .ii. drachmas, of wyne .ii. ounces and a halfe, of hony .iii. ounces di. and .ii. drachmas.

Quartarins, the halfe of Hemina, is .v. inches of measure receiueth of oyle .iiii. ouncis and di. of wyne fyue ounces, of hony .vii. ounces di.

Hemina, the half of Sextarius is .x. inches of measure, and receiueth of oyle .ix. ounces, of wyne ten ounces, of hony xv. ounces.

Sextarius Romanus, is xx. inches of measure callyd Cubica, and receyueth in poise of oyle .xviii. ounces, of wine xx. ounces, of hony xxx. oun-

Greke meas. in vessell.

ces, & is the .vi. part of Congius, in our measure it is lesse than a pynte by foure ynches of measure.

Modius, is of grayn and salt, and conteineth .xvi. Sextarios and of our measure a galon & pottell and a quarte, sauynge iiii. ynche measures.

Congius, hath .vi. Sextarios, Cxx. ynches, in mesure callid Cubica, and receiueth of oile in poyse .ix. poundes of wine x. li. of hony .xv. poundes: of our measure it is .v. pintes, or a potttell and a pynte.

Vrna, coteineth .iiii. Congios and receiueth of oyle. xxxvi. poundes: of wyne. xl. poundes: of hony .lx. poundes. It is of our measure. ii. galons and a pottell.

Amphora, seu quadrantal, conteineth .xlviii. Sextarios, is a foote square in measure, calyd cubica, or lyke a dyse, and coteineth of oyle. lxxii. pound of wyne .lxxx. pounde, of hony. Cxx. pound weight. It is of our measure. v. galons.

Culeus, conteyneth .xx. Amphoras, It is of our measure a hundred galons, a pype sauynge .xxvi. galons.

Greke measure.

Cochlearium Atticũ, seu medicum, is of ynche mesure a dramme, halfe a scriple .ii. graynes, and two fiue partes of a grayne, and receiueth in poyse a dramme and .ii. scriples of oyle, and of wyne as moche in poyse as in measure.

Chema, hath .ii. Cochlearia, is in mesure .ii. drames one scriple .iiii. graynes, and .iiii. fyue partes of a grayn, and receiueth in poise double as moch as Cochlearium.

Mystrum medicum, hath e. ii. Cochlearia, and a halfe, one Cheme and a quarter, and is in measure .iiii. drammes, and recciueth in poyse of wine or
pure

MEASVRE OF VESSELL.

Greke meaf. in vessell.

pure water, as moche as in measure.

Cochlearium ueterinariū, belongyng to cattell, is in measure a quarter of an ynche, & receyueth in poise of wyne a dramme.ii.scriples, one obolū, one graine and a thirde part of a grayn, of honye.ii. drames.ii.scriples.vii.grains and very lytle more.

Myſtrū ueterinariū, belonging to catel, is in meſure halfe an ynche, and receiueth in poiſe of oile.iii.drames and a scriple, of wine.iii.drames.ii.scriples.ii.graynes and. ii. third partes of a grayne, of honye v.drammes, an half.iii.grains and.v.ſixte partis.

Myſtrum Georgicū, or of huſbandry is in meaſure halfe an ynche and half a dramme and receyueth in poyſe of wyne half an ounce and half a scriple, of hony halfe an ounce & two drammes, a quarter of a dram and half a scriple.

Concha, is double as moche as Myſtrum.

Cyathus medicus, is double as moche as Concha, in meaſure an inche and a halfe, and receyueth in poyſe of wyne, one oūce.iii.drames, and.iiii. Siliquas, of hony.ii. ounces & ii.scriples, of oyle one ounce and.ii.drammes.

Cyathus georgicus, or of huſbandry is in meſure.ii.inches and a quarter, and receyueth in poyſe of wine. ii. ounces & ii.scriples, of hony.iii.ounces one dramme and. ii. scriples, of oyle one ounce and seuen drammes.

Cyathus Veterinarius, pertaining to cattel, is in meſure.ii. ynches, & receyueth in poyſe of wyne one ounce, an halfe, a drāme.ii.scriples.ii.siliquas ii.grains.ii.third partes of a grayne, of oyle one ounce, a halfe, one dramme, & a scriple of hony.ii.ounces, a halfe, a quarter, oone obolū.iii.grayngs and a thyrd part.

Greke meaf. in vessell.

Oxybaphum medicum, is in meaſure.ii.ynches a quarter, receiueth in poyſe of wine.ii. ouncis and.ii.scriples, of oile one oūce a half. iii.drammes.

Oxybaphum Georgicum, or of huſbandrye, is in meaſure iii.inches a quarter, & a dram receiueth in poiſe of wine.iii. ounces and a dramme, of oile ii.ounces, a halfe, a quarter, a half, a dramme, of hony.iiii. ounces a halfe, a quarter, and half a dramme.

Oxybaphum ueterinariū, pertaynyng to cattell, is in meaſure.vi.inches, and receiueth in poyſe of wine. v. ounces & a half, one scriple.ii.siliquas: of oyle. v. ounces, of honye viii.ounces, a quarter and.ii. Scriples.

Quartarius, is double Oxybaphum.

Cotyle Medica, is dowble Quartarius, and is in meaſure ix.ynches, and receyueth in poyſe of wyne. viii. ounces a quartern and.ii.Scriples, of oyle.vii.ounces and a halfe, of our meaſure it lacketh. iii. inche meſures of half a pynt. Galenº saith, that there were dyuers opinions of Cotyle, for somme affirmed it to conteyne.xii. ounce meſures and some sayd.xvi.

Cotyle georgica, is in meſure xiii. ynches and a halfe, and receiueth in poiſe of wyne, a pounde and half an ounce. of oyle.xi. ounces, of honye a pounde a halfe, and.vi.drammes, of our meaſure a pynte and one ounce meſure.

Cotyle ueterinaria, pertaining to cattel is in meaſure.xii.inches, and receiueth of wyne xi.ounces.ii.scriples, one obolum and one ſiliqua, of oile x.ounces, of hony one pound iiii.ounces a halfe one dram, and one ſcriple. It is of oure meaſure iuſte half a pynte.

Sextarius atticus, is.xviii. meſure ounces, and conteyneth in poyſe of oyle. xv. ounces,

Greke meaf. in vessell.

of wyne a pounde.iii. onnces v.drammes and a Scriple, of hony.ii.pound and one oūce. It is of our meaſure a pynte sauynge a quarterne or ſyxe ounces.

Chus attica, or medica, receyueth. vi. Sextarios atticos, and is in meaſure.ix. pounde in poyſe of oyle. vii. pounde & a halfe, of wyne.viii. pound iii.ounces, a halfe & iii. drammes: of hony.xii.pounde and a halfe. It is of our meaſure a pottell and halfe a pynte.

Chus Georgica, or of huſbandry is in meaſure. xiii. pound and di, and receiueth in poiſe of oile.xi.pounde.iii.ounces. of wyne.xii. pounde and di, of hony.xviii.pounde and.ix. ounces, and is of our meſure vi.pyntes, a halfe, and a quarter or.xviii.ounces.

Chus veterinaria, is in meſure xii.pounde, and receyueth in poyſe of wyne. xi. pound one ounce.ii.drammes and.ii.scriples, of oyle.viii.pounde, of hony.xvi.pounde, a half, one ounce a halfe, and a dramme. It is of our meaſure a pottell and a quarte.

Metretes attica, contayneth xii.Choas atticas, & is in meaſure. Cviii.pounde, in poyſe of wyne. £. pounde, of oyle lxxxx.pounde, of honye. Cl. pounde. It is of our meaſure ſyxe galons a pottelle and a quarte.

Metretes georgica, is in meaſure lyke to attica.

Chœnix, conteyneth.iii. Cotylas, and is in meaſure.xxvii. ynches. It is in our meaſure a pynte and thre ynches.

Medimnus atticus, conteineth xlvii.Chœnices. It is of our meaſure. vi.galons a pottelle and a quarte.

Medimnus georgicus, is a hūdred.lxii.meſure. It is of our meaſure. x. galons and oone pynte, or a buſhel a pecke and one pynte.

Sextarius Medimni, the ſyxte parte

MEASVRE OF VESSELL.

Hebrue measures.

parte of Medimnus. Artaba, fyue Modios, of our measure, a bushell, a pottell, a pynte, and .iiii. ynche measures.

Hebrue measures.

Log, is the hebrue Sextarius, and is equall to Sextatius atticus, and conteynyth in measure. xviii. ynchis.

Hebrue measures.

Satum, contayneth .xxiiii. Logim, and is in measure .xxxvi. pounde, receiueth in poyse of wyne .xxxiii. pound, and foure ounces, of oyle .xxx. li. of hony: l. pound. It is of our measure .ii. galons and a quarte. Hin, is halfe Satum, is in measure .xviii. fete, receyueth in poyse of wyne .xvi. li. of and ii. ounces. of oyle .xv. li. of hony .xxv. li. of our mesure a galon and a pynte.

Hebrue measures.

Batus, conteyneth .iii. Satz, whiche is of our measure .vi. galons a piottell and a quart. Ephi, seu Epha, a measure of drye thynges, as corne & salt, and is equall with Batus. Gomor, the tenth part of Ephi, & lacketh of our pynt. ii. ounces, and almoste half one ounce.
Chorus hebraica, contayneth x. Ephim, whyche is of oure mesure .vii. bushell & a halfe.

FINIS.

THIS AT THIS TYME shall be sufficient for the declaration of poisis and mesures. And he that desireth a more ample and exquisite triall of them, let him diligently rede the bokes of Georgius Agricola, and Robertus Senalis, who writinge last of all other in that kind of matter, haue found dyuers thinges, which were nat before of other remēbred, as it dayly hapneth in all kyndes of wriring. I knowe well that Budeus, Alceatus, and Portius are men of excellent lernynge, and their bokes to be made with an exact study & diligence: But Agricola beinge a great phisition, and therfore more accustomed to rede the warkes of Galenus, than the other, whyche in their profession be lawyers: semblablye the warkes of other, whiche wrate of the diseases of cattel, and remedies for them, moreouer attaynyng the bokes of Cleopatras, a noble and great lerned woman, whiche also wrote of measures, specially pertaininge to husbandry: no meruail though that he more perfitly hath determined that thing, which among the other was in contencion. Semblably Senalis an honorable bysshop, folowing Agricola, and approuyng his diligēce by makynge true conference betwene hym and the other, and more ouer beinge welle lerned in the hebrue tunge, and consequētly in holy scripture, trieng out studiousely the poyses and mesures to the hebrues pertaining, hath happily brought vnto lyght that whiche the other hath remembred, or elles nat vnderstandyng substancially the hebrue tounge, they purposely omitted. For these causes I haue preferred the computation of these two before any other, exhortynge nat withstanding al them that do vnderstād latine, that they do not therfore neglect the others bookes, but to imbrace and reade them studiously, as in whom they shall fynd meruailous knowlege, which elsꝑchaunce they shal lacke. And as concerning my calculation, whiche I haue done with moche study and incredible labour for the profit of other, if I haue therin any thyng fayled, as I trust that I haue not (although the diuision in breking of numbers callid fractions, is a thinge subtyll and meruailous harde to obserue alway truly) I hartily pray al gentyll reders, fyndyng it by an exquisite tryall to correct it without indignation: and lykewyse all the resydewe of the dictionarye preceding, and frendely communicate with me their labours, for the which I wyll giue vnto them moste harty thankes, not leauing vnremembred, god gyuing to me lyfe, their honest labours, being beneficiall vnto theyr countrey.

Tho. Berthelet. regius impressor excudebat.
ANNO. M. D. XXXVIII.